Selected works of Jawaharlal Nehru

Personal

31. 8. 62

Dear Renu,

I feel I must tell you how distressed and deeply pained I was this morning at the extraordinary display we had [?] in the Lok Sabha. Any person may lose his temper occasionally though even that is regrettable. But persisted rowdyism and defiance and even insult of the Chair is something we had not experienced in the way of the last dozen years or more. The members of the Socialist Party have a way of behaving in a deplorable manner. That is unfortunate but perhaps they do not know anything better. What surprised and pained me was the behaviour of the Communist members of the Lok Sabha who gave their support to the Socialist misbehaviour. I only think this can only lead to a breakdown of our System.

Yours Sincerely
Jawaharlal Nehru

NEHRU TO RENU CHAKRAVARTTY ON THE BEHAVIOUR OF
SOCIALISTS IN THE LOK SABHA, 31 AUGUST 1962. (SEE ITEM 11).

Selected works of Jawaharlal Nehru

SECOND SERIES
Volume Seventy Eight (20 July – 30 September 1962)

Editor

MADHAVAN K. PALAT

Jawaharlal Nehru Memorial Fund
New Delhi

Enquiries regarding copyright
to be addressed to the publishers

PUBLISHED BY
Jawaharlal Nehru Memorial Fund
Teen Murti House, New Delhi 110 011

ISBN : 0-19-949477-0
ISBN : 978-0-19-949477-4

DISTRIBUTED BY
Oxford University Press
YMCA Library Building, Jai Singh Road, New Delhi 110 001
Mumbai Kolkata Chennai
Oxford New York Toronto
Melbourne Tokyo Hong Kong

PRINTED AT
Aditya Arts,
I-66, Jadunath Enclave,
Sector 29, Faridabad-121008

CONTENTS

No.	Item	Date	Page

I. GENERAL

(b) Industry and Labour

(c) Agriculture

(g) Language Controversy

IV. EXTERNAL AFFAIRS
(a) General

(b) Disarmament

(k) China

FOREWORD

Jawaharlal Nehru is one of the key figures of the twentieth century. He symbolised some of the major forces which have transformed our age.

When Jawaharlal Nehru was young, history was still the privilege of the West; the rest of the world lay in deliberate darkness. The impression given was that the vast continents of Asia and Africa existed merely to sustain their masters in Europe and North America. Jawaharlal Nehru's own education in Britain could be interpreted, in a sense, as an attempt to secure for him a place within the pale. His letters of the time are evidence of his sensitivity, his interest in science and international affairs as well as of his pride in India and Asia. But his personality was veiled by his shyness and a facade of nonchalance, and perhaps outwardly there was not much to distinguish him from the ordinary run of men. Gradually there emerged the warm and universal being who became intensely involved with the problems of the poor and the oppressed in all lands. In doing so, Jawaharlal Nehru gave articulation and leadership to millions of people in his own country and in Asia and Africa.

That imperialism was a curse which should be lifted from the brows of men, that poverty was incompatible with civilisation, that nationalism should be poised on a sense of international community and that it was not sufficient to brood on these things when action was urgent and compelling—these were the principles which inspired and gave vitality to Jawaharlal Nehru's activities in the years of India's struggle for freedom and made him not only an intense nationalist but one of the leaders of humanism.

No particular ideological doctrine could claim Jawaharlal Nehru for its own. Long days in jail were spent in reading widely. He drew much from the thought of the East and West and from the philosophies of the past and the present. Never religious in the formal sense, yet he had a deep love for the culture and tradition of his own land. Never a rigid Marxist, yet he was deeply influenced by that theory and was particularly impressed by what he saw in the Soviet Union on his first visit in 1927. However, he realised that the world was too complex, and man had too many facets, to be encompassed by any single or total explanation. He himself was a socialist with an abhorrence of regimentation and a democrat who was anxious to reconcile his faith in civil liberty with the necessity of mitigating economic and social wretchedness. His struggles, both within himself and with the outside world, to adjust such seeming contradictions are what make his life and work significant and fascinating.

As a leader of free India, Jawaharlal Nehru recognised that his country could neither stay out of the world nor divest itself of its own interests in world affairs. But to the extent that it was possible, Jawaharlal Nehru sought to speak objectively and to be a voice of sanity in the shrill phases of the 'cold war'. Whether his influence helped on certain occasions to maintain peace is for the future historian to assess. What we do know is that for a long stretch of time he commanded an international audience reaching far beyond governments, that he spoke for ordinary, sensitive, thinking men and women around the globe and that his was a constituency which extended far beyond India.

So the story of Jawaharlal Nehru is that of a man who evolved, who grew in storm and stress till he became the representative of much that was noble in his time. It is the story of a generous and gracious human being who summed up in himself the resurgence of the 'third world' as well as the humanism which transcends dogmas and is adapted to the contemporary context. His achievement, by its very nature and setting, was much greater than that of a Prime Minister. And it is with the conviction that the life of this man is of importance not only to scholars but to all, in India and elsewhere, who are interested in the valour and compassion of the human spirit that the Jawaharlal Nehru Memorial Fund has decided to publish a series of volumes consisting of all that is significant in what Jawaharlal Nehru spoke and wrote. There is, as is to be expected in the speeches and writings of a man so engrossed in affairs and gifted with expression, much that is ephemeral; this will be omitted. The official letters and memoranda will also not find place here. But it is planned to include everything else and the whole corpus should help to remind us of the quality and endeavour of one who was not only a leader of men and a lover of mankind, but a completely integrated human being.

Indira Gandhi

New Delhi
18 January 1972

Chairman
Jawaharlal Nehru Memorial Fund

EDITORIAL NOTE

While the Chinese threat is building up to the invasion in October, Nehru was preoccupied with numerous other important matters also. There was a major influx of Santhals and others from East Pakistan, leading to bitter exchanges with Pakistan. While the State of Nagaland was finally formed, Assam sought to decide unilaterally the royalty that the ONGC would have to pay for prospecting, and it required Nehru's determined mediation to sort out the problem. Trouble was brewing on the language front, with Hindi enthusiasts strenuously objecting to English continuing as an official language after 1965; with it there is some interesting correspondence on the quality of Hindi in the All India Radio broadcasts. Nehru attended the Commonwealth Prime Ministers' Conference, where he had to assess the possible impact of Britain entering the European Common Market. Finally, there is correspondence on Nehru's personal and household expenses, with Ram Manohar Lohia making extreme charges and Nehru rebutting them very effectively.

Some of the speeches have been transcribed; hence the paragraphing, punctuation, and other such details have been inserted. Words and expressions which were inaudible or unintelligible have been shown by an ellipsis between square brackets thus: [...]. When no text or recording of a speech was available, a newspaper report has been used as a substitute. Such a newspaper report, once selected for publication, has been reproduced faithfully; other information has been added only by way of annotation. Most items here are from Nehru's office copies. In personal letters, and even in official letters composed in personal style to personal friends, the salutation and concluding portions were written by hand; such details are not recorded in the office copy. Therefore these have either been inserted in Nehru's customary style for such persons or his full name has been used, but the editorial intervention is indicated by square brackets. Information on persons may always be traced through the index if it is not available in the footnote. References to the *Selected Works* appear as SWJN/FS/10/..., to be understood as *Selected Works of Jawaharlal Nehru*, First Series, Volume 10. In the case of the Second Series, it would be SWJN/SS/.... The part and page numbers follow the volume number.

Documents, which have been referred to as items, are numbered sequentially throughout the volume; footnote numbering however is continuous only within a section, not between sections. Maps of the boundary between India and China have been reproduced from official documents and are placed at the end of the volume.

Nehru's speeches or texts in Hindi have been published in Hindi and a translation into English has been appended in each case for those who might need or want one.

A large part of Nehru's archives is housed in the Nehru Memorial Museum and Library and is known as the JN Collection. This has been the chief source for items here, and has been made available by Shrimati Sonia Gandhi, the Chairperson of the Jawaharlal Nehru Memorial Fund. Unless otherwise stated, all items are from this collection. The Nehru Memorial Museum and Library has been immensely helpful in so many ways, and it is a pleasure to record our thanks to it. The Cabinet Secretariat, the secretariats of the President and Prime Minister, various ministries of the Government of India, All India Radio, the Press Information Bureau, and the National Archives of India, all have permitted us to use material in their possession. We are grateful to *The Hindu*, the *National Herald, Shankar's Weekly*, and in particular to the late R.K. Laxman for permission to reproduce reports and cartoons.

Finally, it gives me great pleasure to thank those who contributed to preparing this volume for publication, most of all Amrit Tandon and Fareena Ikhlas Faridi. The Hindi texts have been edited by Mohammed Khalid Ansari, and the translation from the Hindi was done by Chandra Chari.

Madhavan K. Palat

LIST OF ILLUSTRATIONS

1. To Nath Pai: No Need for Emergency Session of Parliament[1]

July 24, 1962

My dear Nath Pai,
I have received the letter dated today signed jointly by you, Mukut Behari Lal[2] and Farid Ansari.[3]

As you know, Parliament is meeting on the 6th of August, that is, twelve days from now. I do not know how long it takes for an emergency session of Parliament to meet. I take it, even that will take a week or more. I do not think it is worthwhile convening such a session when especially the normal session is going to meet soon.

[THROUGH THE LOOKING-GLASS]

(From *The Times of India*, 29 July 1962, p. 1)

Apart from this practical consideration, I do not think it is necessary for an emergency session to be convened at this stage. It is true that I have stated that the situation in Ladakh is serious.[4] So it is and it has been so for some time and

1. Letter to PSP, Lok Sabha MP; address: 18 Windsor Place, New Delhi. NMML, Nath Pai Papers. Also available in the JN Collection.
2. Mukut Behari Lal Bhargava, Congress, Lok Sabha MP.
3. Faridul Haq Ansari, PSP, Rajya Sabha MP. For the joint letter, see appendix 9.
4. Nehru, while entering his office on 21 July, was asked questions by presspersons on the two recent incidents of the Chinese opening fire on Indian soldiers in Ladakh. He described the developments as a "serious situation" and said "the country had to be wide awake to the situation there." *National Herald*, 24 July 1962. For Nehru's clarification on this comment at the CPP meeting on 5 August 1962, see item 23.

is likely to continue to be so. I do not think, however, that any major crisis is going to take place in the near future. The situation is certainly unsatisfactory and we should be vigilant in every way. But to show anything in the nature of panic would be quite undesirable and might even help in making the situation worse than it is.

It is right, as you say, to demonstrate national unity in the hour of danger. Fortunately, on this issue there is national unity in the country and I have no doubt that if necessity arose, that unity will show itself in many ways.[5]

Yours sincerely,
[Jawaharlal Nehru]

2. To A.B. Vajpayee: Emergency Session of Parliament[6]

July 25, 1962

Dear Vajpayeeji,

I have your letter of today's date. As I am leaving Delhi, I am replying to it briefly.

The situation in Ladakh is no doubt serious, but that does not mean that it is likely to develop on dangerous lines in the near future. I did not say that India's position in Ladakh was sounder or stronger than that of China. What I said was that it was a greatly improved position from what it was. It is indeed due to our increasing strength there that has worried the Chinese and made them take some aggressive action.[7]

Undoubtedly we should be wide awake, but for the present the question is essentially one of military tactics and our army is completely alive to the position and is taking such steps as are within our power.

I do not think it will help my taking the extraordinary step of convening an emergency session of Parliament a few days before it is going to be held. The earliest it could be held would be perhaps four or five days earlier. That is not worthwhile and I think it is not desirable.

---

5. See also item 2.
6. Letter to Jan Sangh, Rajya Sabha MP; address: 30 Dr Rajendra Prasad Road, New Delhi.
7. Vajpayee's letter has not been traced. *The Hindu* of 26 July 1962, however, reported him as having written to Nehru that the "people's disconcertment" "had been particularly intense because of the two statements made by Mr Nehru recently. In one of these statements the Prime Minister had stated that China was desirous of a peaceful settlement and in the other that India's position in Ladakh was 'sounder than that of China.'"

But I shall gladly meet the party leaders to discuss the situation with them. I am afraid I am leaving early tomorrow morning and returning on the 30th forenoon. On my return I shall try to arrange a meeting of party leaders.[8]

I do not think there is anything wrong in the Defence Minister leaving the country for five days. We discussed it fully and I was clearly of opinion that he should represent Government at the last stages of the Laos Conference in which we have been engaged and have played an important part.[9] We have issued clear instructions as to what should be done in Ladakh in view of any possible developments and the matter is now in charge of our Defence Chiefs.[10]

Yours sincerely,
[Jawaharlal Nehru]

3. For the Cabinet: Leak[11]

Note to be sent to the Members of the Cabinet and others who were present at the Cabinet Meeting on 1st August, 1962

Yesterday, at the Cabinet Meeting, brief statements were made about the frontier situation in Ladakh. I made a brief statement and the Defence Minister[12] also gave some facts. This morning's newspapers contain a fairly detailed account of what was said. This is not wholly a correct account though much of it is true.

Whether this account is true or not, it is deplorable that something happening in the Cabinet should immediately reach the press in some form or other, usually distorted form. I am much distressed at this and I should like the cooperation of the Members of the Cabinet to prevent this kind of thing. This is a wholly bad practice and even casual remarks are apt to be misinterpreted. I

8. The meeting with the party leaders of the Opposition in Parliament was held on 3 August 1962. The MPs who attended were: H.K. Mahatab and S.M. Ghosh, Congress; M.N. Govindan Nair and Renu Chakravartty, CPI; S.N. Dwivedi, Ganga Sharan Sinha and Nath Pai, PSP; U.M. Trivedi and A.B. Vajpayee, Jan Sangh; B.C. Seth, Hindu Mahasabha; R.S. Yadav, Socialist; P.K. Deo, Swatantra; and Frank Anthony, Nominated. Defence Minister V.K. Krishna Menon was also present. The *National Herald*, 4 August 1962, p. 1.
9. An international conference on Laos that had been in session in Geneva from 16 May 1961 concluded on 23 July 1962 with the signing of an International Agreement on the Neutrality of Laos.
10. See also item 1.
11. Note, 2 August 1962.
12. V.K. Krishna Menon.

shall be glad to know if any Member of the Cabinet made such casual remarks to a press correspondent or someone who subsequently spoke to a press correspondent. Press correspondents sometime go to see Members of Cabinet or even wait for them, after a Cabinet Meeting and manage to get something out of them. We must put an end to this kind of thing as it is basically bad for Cabinet proceedings to be talked about to others.

. I shall be grateful if you will kindly let me know if you spoke, directly or indirectly, to any press correspondent, after the Cabinet Meeting yesterday.[13]

4. For S.S. Khera: Leak from the Cabinet[14]

This morning's papers contain a fairly full account of what we said in the Cabinet meeting yesterday about the Ladakh situation etc. It is not wholly a correct account though much of it is true. It is very unfortunate that immediately after a Cabinet meeting there should be these accounts in the press. Even if these accounts do not do much harm, the practice is deplorable.

2.   You would remember, on the last occasion, when the Defence Committee met there was some such report in the press immediately after. We enquired into it and some facts came out. You need not pursue that particular matter anymore, but I do think something should be done about this new leakage.

3.   I am enclosing a brief note[15] that I should like you to send under a confidential cover to all the Members of the Cabinet and others who were present at the Cabinet meeting.

5. To Mehr Chand Khanna: Rajghat Memorial[16]

August 8, 1962

My dear Mehr Chand,
Your letter of the 7th August about the Memorial at Rajghat. I do not quite understand what you mean by Phase II. We have definitely given up the idea of having the monument.

---

13. T.T. Krishnamachari, Minister without Portfolio, wrote to Nehru on 13 August 1962: "I have not discussed the subject mentioned therein with any person." See also item 4.
14. Note, 2 August 1962, for the Cabinet Secretary.
15. Item 3.
16. Letter to the Minister of Works, Housing and Supply.

I agree to the new committee you propose and to Bhagwan Sahay[17] being the Chairman of the Committee.

I shall try to come to Rajghat to see the Memorial.[18]

Yours sincerely,
[Jawaharlal Nehru]

6. To Margaret Butcher: Not Retiring[19]

August 11, 1962

Dear Miss Butcher,

Thank you for your little letter. I have no intention of retiring in the foreseeable future. I am keeping well and hope to continue my work.

Thank you for your good wishes.

Yours sincerely,
[Jawaharlal Nehru]

7. In New Delhi: Press Conference[20]

Jawaharlal Nehru: I fixed the day for this press conference today expecting that the discussion in the Lok Sabha would be over yesterday.[21] Well it isn't. One result of it is, apart from my being rather in a hurry this morning, that questions on the frontier are banned, [Laughter] because it will be discourteous to the Lok Sabha. Of course, whatever I said yesterday is open to you.

Correspondent: You can postpone the Press Conference for tomorrow.

Jawaharlal Nehru: Tomorrow I have to go to the Red Fort,[22] you forget that.

---

17. The Chief Commissioner of Delhi.
18. Nehru visited the Rajghat samadhi, the memorial of Mahatma Gandhi in Delhi, on 31 August 1962. See item 12.
19. Letter; address: Chestnut Lodge, 500 West Montgomery Avenue, Rockville, Maryland.
20. 14 August 1962, at Vigyan Bhavan, New Delhi. PIB, checked against AIR Tapes, TS No. 8442, NM No. 1664-1665 in the NMML. At the beginning of answers to questions, "Prime Minister" in the PIB version has been replaced with "Jawaharlal Nehru".
21. For Nehru's speech, see item 404.
22. For the Independence Day function.

Correspondent: Both the reports will simultaneously appear tomorrow.

Jawaharlal Nehru: I have had one say there. I concisely put forward what our entire policy was. So you can ask me other questions.

[MIG]

Question: What is the latest position about the MIG?[23]

[RUSSIA DOES NOT COME CHEAP]

You Said It

By LAXMAN

"MIG is economical!"—I don't see any advantage in it—the expenditure on delegations going abroad to find it out must be pretty high!

(From *The Times of India*, 16 August 1962, p. 1)

23. The MIG military fighter aircraft produced in the USSR.

Jawaharlal Nehru: I cannot tell you exactly. I do not know. There is a team there which has not come back, except one member of it—the scientist has come back who will presumably go back again—I am not sure.[24]

[India's Progress]

Question: On the eve of the Fifteenth Anniversary of your Independence, could you tell us what you think is the most striking thing that has happened in India in that period?

Jawaharlal Nehru: It is rather difficult to pick out one thing. I think that in spite of all our industrial progress, which is striking indeed, e.g., the big plants and factories, the change that is coming over the rural people—which is very fundamental—seems to me the most hopeful sign. Of course, it is not all over the place. There are all kinds of people. It is difficult to pull up 300 million people, but the thing is working.

Secondly, I think the spread of education in India, much criticized as it is in various ways, is a fairly remarkable feature and it has spread, especially to the rural people and to people whose forefathers and others had never been inside a school. Now they are coming to schools and colleges. It is having a revolutionary effect. It will continue to have that, in effect, whether it is in industry or agriculture or education or health. Health is remarkable, because we have reached an expectation of life age which is approaching 50. Now, that figure itself, considering it was about 32 sometime before Independence, is a remarkable growth. It doesn't show that medicine is being given to a large number of people. It shows that they are, broadly speaking, better fed than they were, although many people may not be. But still, broadly speaking, it does show that. For food is the first thing in regard to health. All these indicate a certain pulling up in various directions, a certain impact of modern conditions on a country which, by and large, was in a rut, pulling it out. Of course, the rut is still there. It is very easy to spot it, but the process of coming out of it is getting more and more obvious.

---

24. S. Bhagavantam, Director of the Indian Institute of Science, Bangalore, and honorary Scientific Adviser to the Defence Minister, led the Indian technical team to Moscow for the evaluation of the MIG-21 supersonic jet aircraft. He had come to Delhi for consultations. *The Times of India*, 17 August 1962.

See SWJN/SS/77/item 1, section MIG; paragraphs 14 and 15 in item 3; and items 370, 373, 382, 431-432.

Question: At the recent conference of Community Development, you expressed dissatisfaction about the progress of the community development programme.[25] Will you kindly elaborate your remarks?

Jawaharlal Nehru: You expect me to remember all I have said in the past? I must have said it in some particular context. I do not remember the context.

Question: In the context of this subject what are you disappointed with? What is it that has failed in your targets?

Jawaharlal Nehru: To continue this question, what I really stressed was that the community development programme had, I felt, become rather officialised, and lost its *élan* to some extent; particularly, as is my habit, I spoke against too many jeeps about. Of course, the jeep is not a bad thing, it is a very good thing, but this jeep mentality is a bad thing as it is too far removed from conditions in our villages.

[Power Breakdown in Delhi]

Question: What are the steps you are taking so that we do not get this power crisis again in Delhi?[26]

Jawaharlal Nehru: Well, in regard to this power crisis, it is very unfortunate, because it inconvenienced large numbers and industry has suffered. I think many of the criticisms, especially of the Government, are unjustified. Of course, I cannot say anything much. There is a Committee of Enquiry sitting there and I hope they will sift the evidence and give their verdict on whoever it is. If the Government is at fault, they will not, I hope, hesitate to do so; but the fact is that certain equipment, transformers, generators, whatever they are, failed. Now, that may be due to the failure of the engineers in charge or the person in charge.

The Government comes into the picture really to do something to help in it. The Government does not go down to examine it every day. This time, the moment this occurred, I think it was in a day or two, I received a report from the Minister of Irrigation and Power[27] about it and his suggestions—what should be done, and that a Committee of Enquiry should be appointed immediately—to which I agreed.

25. Item 309.
26. On 26 July one of the two transformers supplying power from the Bhakra-Nangal system to Delhi, failed. See section Politics, subsection Delhi.
27. Hafiz Mohammed Ibrahim.

The very next day, he said that the Punjab Government, though completely willing to have the Committee, any Committee, in fact the Committee he wanted to appoint, they were prepared for that, but on the constitutional plane they object to the Union Government appointing the Committee. They said they would appoint the same Committee, but they would do it, which they did. We agreed to that because they said this is Bhakra and the sub-station at Rohtak was under their charge. But apart from these constitutional questions, it is very unfortunate that such things should happen and I should imagine that the fault lay on the technical side, those responsible for it, whoever they may be.

[Bandung Conference]

Question: Sir, what is your view of the proposed second Bandung Conference.[28]

Jawaharlal Nehru: It has been talked about for two, three or four years. It hasn't taken shape yet to my knowledge.

Question: Is it necessary soon after the Belgrade Conference[29] to have this Bandung Conference?

Jawaharlal Nehru: I do not know. It was talked about before the Belgrade Conference and then the Belgrade Conference took place and most people thought that it was not necessary in the immediate future. That is the opinion of many participants.

[Economic Development and Inequality]

Question: Sir, you have mentioned the progress which India has made during the last fifteen years but at the same time there is clear evidence of increasing economic inequalities which is creating discontent in large areas in this country, as is evident in the agitation against the indirect taxation going on in several States. Are any steps being taken to counter this?

Jawaharlal Nehru: You know perhaps that a very high level expert Committee has been considering this matter for some time now—for a long time. It was not that we specially referred this matter to them—a committee under the

---

28. The first one, 18-24 April 1955. See SWJN/SS/28/pp. 97-158.
29. The Belgrade Conference of non-aligned nations, 1-6 September 1961. See SWJN/SS/71/section External Affairs, subsection Non-Aligned Conference at Belgrade.

chairmanship of Professor Mahalanobis and other economists and others. They found it, they told me, a much more intricate problem and would take some time to collect all kind of facts and figures, etc.[30] So we had better wait for that, but to some extent there is always a tendency for this kind of thing to happen. In a developing economy, certain persons engaged in their development profit a little more. But by and large, I doubt whether that is so, and you may point out a handful of persons who have profited, but, generally speaking, that would not be the case.

[Jawaharlal Nehru's Health]

Question: Whilst going up, I saw you bounce on the dais as usual. How is your health?

Jawaharlal Nehru: My health according to me is extraordinarily good. According to doctors it is also very good. So I do not know.

[Bokaro Steel Plant]

Question: We have been told many a time that the Government was determined to set up the fourth steel plant at Bokaro. There are reports that the project has since been shelved or abandoned. Could you kindly throw some light on it?

Jawaharlal Nehru: Bokaro steel plant project cannot be shelved or abandoned. That is an absolute impossibility. It is our mainstay for the future. But unfortunately, it has been delayed because of various enquiries and things. At the present moment, I believe there are some people from the United States inquiring into it. I am very sorry that it has been delayed, because we attach great importance to it. Bokaro is a place where we cannot only have a steel plant—a good steel plant—but a plant which can be expanded almost indefinitely. By indefinitely I do not mean indefinitely, but suppose we have it for a million tons, it can go up to 10 million tons—conditions there are such. Therefore, it is a particularly happy place to have it and as we must have more steel and pig iron we are bound to take it up.

---

30. The Committee on Distribution of Income and Levels of Living, appointed by the Planning Commission on 13 October 1960 under the chairmanship of P.C. Mahalanobis, member, Planning Commission. It reported in two stages: Part I on Distribution of Income and Wealth and Concentration of Economic Power in 1964, Part II on Changes in Levels of Living in 1969.

[Rise in Prices]

Question: Why is it that this agitation against high prices is being tackled only as a law and order problem and not as an economic problem?

Jawaharlal Nehru: It is not the agitation against high prices that has to be tackled, but the way that agitation may be conducted may induce State Government or other Governments to do so.

Question: Is it an economic problem?

Jawaharlal Nehru: It is an economic problem, but it has to be dealt with.

Question: Is it not a political problem rather than an economic problem?

Jawaharlal Nehru: Yes, it is a political problem, and ...

New Taxes in Bihar, Punjab, Uttar Pradesh

Question: About the new taxes to be imposed in Bihar, can they be justified or can you throw some light?

Jawaharlal Nehru: I can't talk to you about a particular tax in a particular State, but broadly speaking, it has become essential to raise revenues for the Five Year Plan which, mind you, these revenues that are raised go back—most of them—to the village panchayats, this Panchayati Raj business.

Question: But, Sir, in Punjab the Chief Minister[31] has said that these taxes are meant for the welfare of a particular community, that is, Harijans?

Jawaharlal Nehru: What in Punjab is being done is rather special to the Punjab. That is so. They have done it for Harijans and for the welfare of the backward classes. But the other things, they will go back. Take the UP ones. As I understand, it will go to the panchayat samitis for the fulfilment of their constructive work.

[Maharashtra – Mysore border]

Question: Would you enlighten us on the Maharashtra – Mysore border?

31. Partap Singh Kairon.

Jawaharlal Nehru: No, I won't [Laughter] because I really don't know where it stands now except that I have a vague idea that it is gradually moving towards a solution. But I cannot say much more.

[Commonwealth Prime Ministers' Conference]

Question: Do you think, Sir, that the coming Conference of the Commonwealth Prime Ministers[32] will be of any value, since Britain will not be in a position by that time to tell you what are the terms she has been able to secure for the Commonwealth countries?[33]

Jawaharlal Nehru: Well, suppose they had told us, what then? After all, each country has to decide for itself. The Conference is a forum where discussion takes place, views are expressed and influence each other. If they had settled something and presented something which has already been decided upon, there would be less room for discussion.

[Kashmir]

Question: There was a statement by a Pakistan Minister that some mediation is going on on the Kashmir issue. Could you kindly enlighten us?

Jawaharlal Nehru: Some statement by Pakistan Minister?

[Medical Treatment in London]

Question: Sir, have you any plan for medical treatment when you go for the Commonwealth Prime Ministers' Conference next month?

Prime Minister: I have no plans for medical treatment. But whenever I go to London—for the last seven or eight years—I have always visited my doctor there and I propose to visit him again.[34]

---

32. Held in London, 10-19 September 1962.
33. The UK was seeking to join the European Common Market at this time. For discussions at the Commonwealth Prime Ministers' Conference on the possible impact of Britain's membership of the ECM on the other Commonwealth countries, see section External Affairs, subsection UK.
34. For health bulletin on Nehru, 20 September 1962, see item 325, fn 37.

[Meeting Chou En-lai]

Question: Is there any possibility of your meeting Premier Chou En-Lai in the near future?

Jawaharlal Nehru: Who? Premier Chou En-lai? I am not aware of it. If there was a possibility, I would welcome it but I do not see any possibility. I do not believe in this. Some members in the Lok Sabha, etc., whose idea of untouchability has expanded very much, because I invited the Chinese Ambassador to my room, when he was going away, to lunch.[35] Some newspapers objected to it.[36] I am sorry, my ideas are completely different.

[Talks and Negotiations on Border]

Question: Have we now drawn a distinction between negotiations on the border question and talks to ease the tension? This arises out of yesterday's statement and not as a fresh question.[37]

READY FOR "TALKS"

(From *The Times of India*, 17 August 1962, p. 1)

35. Nehru invited Pan Tzu-li, the Chinese Ambassador, to lunch on 13 July 1962. According to a PTI report in *The Tribune* of 14 July 1962, "Asked whether it was customary for the Prime Minister to give such farewell lunches to retiring diplomatic representatives, an External Affairs Ministry spokesman said: 'It is not uncustomary.'" See also SWJN/SS/77/item 402.
36. See also item 405.
37. Nehru made a distinction between talks and negotiations in his speech in the Lok Sabha on 13 August 1962, see item 404. He returned to the topic on 14 August 1962, when the debate was resumed, see item 405.

Jawaharlal Nehru: Where is the distinction? First of all, there is a distinction between—you are going back to a subject I would not talk about—between negotiations, and secondly, between talks. Talks may take place anywhere—people meet just to explore, to probe, and here even the subject is limited. The subject of talks—it should be about how to create a climate for more worthwhile talks.

[Pakistan]

Question: Recently, in a speech in Calcutta, you have suggested the idea of a ministerial level conference between India and Pakistan. Could you say something more about it?

Jawaharlal Nehru: I really don't know where the matter stands now. I said it will be a very good thing to discuss matters on a ministerial level or some other level. I had said so. But just recently, as you know, the Chief Secretaries have met there. I do not know at what stage any proposal to have a ministerial level conference has reached.

[Reddy as Governor of Punjab]

Question: As Mr Reddy is going as Governor, do you think of having any reshuffle in your Cabinet, Sir?

Jawaharlal Nehru: Inevitably, some changes will have to be made.[38]

[Soviet Defence Support]

Question: There are current rumours that the Soviet Union has offered to intervene or come to your assistance in the event of an attack from Pakistan or China. Is it a fact?

Jawaharlal Nehru: In the attack on Pakistan?

Question: From Pakistan or China.

---

38. K.C. Reddy, Minister for Commerce and Industry, was recommended for appointment as Governor of Punjab but eventually Pattom A. Thanu Pillai was appointed Governor of Punjab and Reddy held the same portfolio until 19 July 1963.

Jawaharlal Nehru: No. There has been no such offer or suggestion nor did one expect it. This kind of thing is not done.

[Language Question]

Question: Have you seen the report of the Indian Languages Conference held in Delhi and their resolutions?[39] Do you have any comments to offer?

Jawaharlal Nehru: I have not read the report of the Languages Conference [Convention] except that there is something against English, I suppose. Wasn't that? Well, I think that I don't agree with that. I believe in the development of the Indian languages, in the development of Hindi. But I think, apart from other reasons, for their very development, English is necessary. By English, I mean essentially foreign languages. English is a foreign language which is better known than others. Therefore, it is necessary, because it will strengthen our languages, the ideas; even the words will be strengthened. There is this slight risk about English being continued as an associate language tends to delay a little its substitution by Hindi. Well, that risk is worth taking because the foundation will be more firmly laid.

Apart from everything, you will remember that some years ago, two or three years—I forget when—Pandit Govind Ballabh Pant was Home Minister; he gave an assurance and I gave an assurance, and in the Presidential Order

---

39. A two-day All-India Languages Convention was held on 11-12 August 1962. As reported by *The Times of India* on 13 August 1962, the convention in a resolution demanded the use of regional languages in government work; and said that "for inter-State communication and Central Government purposes the provisions of the Constitution should be respected." It also "strongly opposed the move to make English an associate official language of the country and demanded that it should cease to be the official language after 1965." See also appendix 39.

that assurance was repeated and Parliament was informed of it, and presumably agreed to it, that we would have English as an associate language.[40]

The assurance was welcomed in many places, especially in the South. We thought that that was enough. But now we thought it better to embody it in an Act.[41] Apart from other reasons, we cannot go back on the pledge we have given. But, I think, from the point of view purely of the development of our own languages, it is very necessary for our minds to be open to foreign languages, foreign literatures, foreign ideas, etc.

We have a tendency in India—I suppose, other countries may have it too, but in India especially—of going back into our shell. The shell is wide enough and big enough admittedly, but it is a shell all the same, and it is necessary to come out of it.

Question: English may be all right for administration or university teaching, but how is it your policy is affecting even the school stage of teaching? People are going back to English even in schools.

Jawaharlal Nehru: We do want English in schools, not as a medium but as a subject, as a compulsory subject.

40. In his speech in the Lok Sabha on 4 September 1959, Nehru had commended the report of the Committee of Parliament on Official Language, see SWJN/SS/52/item 46. The Committee, chaired by Govind Ballabh Pant, was constituted to examine the recommendations of the first Official Language Commission. The President's Order of 27 April 1960 was based on the Parliamentary Committee's report; its general approach was that:

    (i) "English should be the principal official language and Hindi the subsidiary official language till 1965. After 1965, when Hindi becomes the principal official language of the Union, English should continue as the subsidiary official language;"

    (ii) "No restriction should be imposed for the present on the use of English for any of the purposes of the Union and provision should be made in terms of clause (3) of Article 343 for the continued use of English even after 1965 for purposes to be specified by Parliament by law for as long as may be necessary."

        The President's Order also said that the use of an Indian language for the purposes of the Union had become a matter of practical necessity, "but there need be no rigid date-line for the change-over. It should be a natural transition over a period of time effected smoothly and with the minimum of inconvenience."

41. *The Times of India* of 2 August 1962 reported that the GOI had decided to introduce in Parliament, during the session beginning 6 August, a Bill for the continuance of English as an official language after 26 January 1965. The period of fifteen years from the date of commencement of the Constitution, provided under Article 343 of the Constitution for the use of English, was to end on that date. See also item 290.

[HINDI, A FOREIGN LANGUAGE]

Babu ji . . .

**"None of your guides is interested in me after
I told them I can speak Hindi!"**

(From *The Times of India*, 18 September 1962, p. 3)

Question: Now, even basic education is being abandoned. They want to replace it by English.

Jawaharlal Nehru: Are you talking of English as a medium of education or English as a subject?

Question: English is coming back as a medium of education even in schools.

Jawaharlal Nehru: Well, that I do not recommend, but as a subject. The medium should be the regional language or Hindi. But English should be a compulsory subject. That is the decision which has been arrived at.

Question: Do you favour a switch-over to the regional languages, because that seems to be the main reason which gives rise to apprehension in non-Hindi areas—the switching over of medium of instruction at the university stage from English to the regional languages, which confers obvious advantages to the Hindi speaking areas? Do you have any proposal to say that medium of instruction at the university stage should be English throughout India?

Jawaharlal Nehru: Well, when I said the medium should be in the regional language, I was referring more to school education.

In regard to universities, the question is more doubtful. There is a great deal of difference of opinion. It may well be that, shall I say, there should be a dual medium in universities, that is, some subjects may be taught in the regional language and some in English. Technical, scientific and other subjects may well be taught in English. But the main idea is, the difficulty of having regional mediums, that universities will be cut off from each other. That will be very unfortunate. Therefore, the process has to be a slow one—it may be a gradual one. It is quite easy, for instance, to teach, let us say, history in a regional language. It may be a little more difficult to teach technology in it. It can be done. But also, you will remember that we have recommended that technical terms should approximate to the international terminology.

Question: Do you attach any significance to the DMK success in the Tiruchengode constituency after all that has happened in Madras?[42]

Jawaharlal Nehru: Well, some significance, I suppose, has to be attached. But we needn't worry too much about it.

---

42. In the by-election for the Tiruchengode Lok Sabha seat, S. Kandappan, DMK, defeated T.R. Sengoda Gounder, the Congress candidate, by a narrow margin in a straight contest. The seat had been vacated by P. Subbarayan, Congress, when he became Governor of Maharashtra in April 1962. See also item 29.

Question: The Education Minister[43] has been saying that he wants universities to switch over to the regional medium by the end of the Third Plan. Recently, he even showed statistics to show that the majority of the Indian universities were switching over to regional languages, contrary to what you say. What do you think of this?

Jawaharlal Nehru: You do not expect me to enter into any controversy with my colleague here. [Laughter].

Question: Should English continue as the official language of the Centre or the States. Apart from this medium issue, what do you think about the continuation of English as the official language? Does the granting of the associate status tend to make it indefinitely the official language?

Jawaharlal Nehru: I have just said that we came to this decision some years ago and announced it that English should continue as an associate language even though Hindi may be as a principal professional language. As an associate it will continue, and I added that on my part I would not take it away till I was asked to take it away by the non-Hindi speaking areas.

Question: Coming back again to the language problem, what has been the correct position about the implementation of the three language formula in UP, because there seems some confusion. Firstly, whether the formula should be implemented at all or not; secondly, what should be the third language, because the UP Government, we hear, is eager to have a South Indian language as the third language, whereas you, in a letter to late Mr Hifzur Rahman, had said that even Urdu could be permitted as a third language?

Jawaharlal Nehru: No question of my writing, that is, Urdu is one of the modern languages given in the Schedule.[44] So, obviously, a person who wants to take can take it as the third language. But the difficulty that UP is having is different. They want to introduce Sanskrit as one of the languages.

For my part, I do not mind. I like, if possible, almost everybody learning Sanskrit. It is a magnificent language. Not that I know it very well, but still. [Laughter]. And it is the base of most of our languages. That is, they would

43. K.L. Shrimali.
44. For Nehru's letter of 1 July 1962 to Hifzur Rahman, then Congress, Lok Sabha MP from Amroha, UP, see SWJN/SS/77/item 300.

like us to take Hindi; of course, another language for those who want to. Of course, you cannot force down Sanskrit. It does not come in accordance with the formula—the formula applied to modern languages, not classical. For my part, I have no objection. Those who want to take Sanskrit can take it. But Urdu can certainly be taken by those who want to take it as one of the languages. That is admitted by the UP Government and everybody.

[Nagaland]

Question: Have you seen the Assam Chief Minister's criticism and other MLAs' criticism about your Nagaland Bill. He has called it a disintegrating factor.[45]

Jawaharlal Nehru: I saw briefly some press reports of it.

[Kailas Nath Katju's Defeat in Madhya Pradesh]

Question: How do you react to Dr Katju's defeat in Madhya Pradesh? Dr Katju is out of the Cabinet. How do you react to it?[46]

Jawaharlal Nehru: How I react to it?

Question: How do you like Madhya Pradesh without Dr Katju?

Jawaharlal Nehru: They all get on. Every place gets on without … Some of us consider ourselves rather essential but we come and go and others take our places.

[Zones in lieu of Linguistic States]

Question: There was a suggestion by the Kerala Governor[47] that the country should be split up into zones so that the havoc caused by the formation of linguistic provinces could be removed.

---

45. On 7 August 1962, the Assam Legislative Assembly opposed the move. According to *The Statesman* of 8 August 1962, p. 9, B.P. Chaliha, Chief Minister of Assam, moving a resolution on the State of Nagaland Bill in the Assam Assembly on 6 August, stated that the Bill was "not 'conducive' to the objective, among others, of a co-ordinated development and greater political stability of the Eastern region of India." For the Assam Assembly resolution, see item 147, fn 466.
46. K.N. Katju, the Chief Minister of Madhya Pradesh from January 1957, lost to a Jan Sangh candidate in the State Assembly elections in February 1962.
47. V.V. Giri.

Jawaharlal Nehru: The idea is to create another havoc in order to remove the effects of the previous havoc. [Laughter].

[India-China Relations]

Question: There is an impression in the mind of the people that it is not India but China that has isolated us. This is because the US has not supported us. Britain has not said anything, except on the legal point. Russia has not said anything in support of it. What is the correct position? Who has in fact isolated us?

Jawaharlal Nehru: I do not know, talking in terms of isolation, but I should think that politically we are much better off than we were two or three years ago, on that subject, I mean. You saw the reason that the US Ambassador gave. It is a very good reason.[48]

Question: How is it that Burma and Nepal seem to be more pro-China today than they were two or three year ago?

Jawaharlal Nehru: That has nothing to do with—I do not know if you are quite correct but even if it was correct, it has nothing to do with our troubles with China.

Question: On some of our great achievements during the last fifteen years, could you kindly tell us whether on the political scene, whether India as a whole achieved a better position?

---

48. J.K. Galbraith, the US Ambassador, in a public speech at the Constitution Club in New Delhi on 8 August 1962, contrasted the current "sympathetic" US policy towards India in the matter of India-China relations with "a policy of reticence" adopted by the US Government in 1959, when Chinese hostility had become "more manifest" in the wake of the Dalai Lama's flight to India. He revealed that the US policy then was based on the advice of two former US Ambassadors to India, Chester Bowles and John Sherman Cooper, who "thought that proclamations of American support to India, however reassuring these might be at the moment, would persuade the Chinese that the cold war had spread to these distant plateaus. The Chinese might be led to think that we were somehow involved with you against them. And you, in turn, might wonder if it were our design to involve you in some larger argument." Talking about recent times, he said that he had "had informal discussions [with the GOI] affirming our sympathy for India, our hope for a fair settlement and our desire to do nothing that might prejudice such a settlement." *The Times of India*, 9 August 1962.

Jawaharlal Nehru: Politically, you mean vis-à-vis the other countries or what?

Question: Compared to the fifteen years' achievement, whether it has improved politically?

Jawaharlal Nehru: It has obviously improved. It may not have improved as much as we wanted to but it has obviously improved and that fact will be further impressed upon you if you look around other countries.

Question: The prospects of war and peace.

Jawaharlal Nehru: I think even in the balance, the prospects of peace are better than those of war.

Question: Since all questions on China have not been banned, can I put a question? And that is, if the alternatives before you are armed conflict with China or peaceful settlement by ceding Indian territory, what would you prefer?

Jawaharlal Nehru: This is a very leading question. [Laughter].

Question: It has been mentioned in Parliament also that we are getting isolated politically and also in other fields, but would you consider calling a conference of non-communist countries in South East Asia, friendly to us, to consider how to contain the Chinese expansionism?

Jawaharlal Nehru: I should like to see a list of those countries and how much strength they have to contain anything including themselves. [Laughter].

Question: Could you say something on this question of our differences with China? Is it our policy to explain our stand on the border issue or differences to friendly countries and solicit their support, or just explain the position and leave it at that?

Jawaharlal Nehru: Where do you draw a line, even if at all you explain it? You expect understanding from them?

Question: In spite of the fact that Burma is one country which has been consistently friendly to us, an official publication, a fortnight ago, said that the Chip Chap region has always been a part of Sinkiang. What is it due to? Is it due to ignorance on their part or indifference on our part?

Jawaharlal Nehru: I cannot explain on their behalf but we seem to think, and some people think, that whatever we stand for must automatically be accepted by all others. It does not naturally follow.

Question: Some of the countries which do not have a common border with China at least may join us?

Jawaharlal Nehru: In what?

Question: In what way, in what method, can we try to stop this Chinese expansionism?

Question: I put to you this question, which I put at a Press Association dinner—I think, in 1959, three years ago—and you were not able to give an answer at that time. Perhaps you could now today and I will repeat that question. What is it precisely that so suddenly made China so antagonistic to us after the time of Panchsheel,[49] after the time of Hindi-Chini bhai-bhai? Was it our giving refuge to Dalai Lama and the Tibetan refugees or something deeper? That is a mystery.

Jawaharlal Nehru: I cannot answer that question. I suppose, it is some belief or fear complex originally that Tibet might be used against China by the British people, coming from the British times, that Tibet might be used and India as an inheritor or a successor state might follow British policy, so a feeling of apprehension lest this might happen, which was wholly, of course, without foundation. We couldn't do it; we did not want to do it. And then there was rebellion in Tibet which, by some queer feat of imagination, they thought had been organized and encouraged from India and then came the flight of the Dalai Lama and others. You see, they start with a certain basic presumption and everything seems to fit into that, although it had no real foundation. But that is not exactly an answer to you but only some factors to be considered. But what the real answer might be, I do not know.

Question: Could it be, Sir, that if you see the Chinese map, all the Chinese frontiers except India and Burma—Nepal I am leaving out—are more or less with communist powers. Could it be China wanted India to follow a policy which would be pro-Chinese and on that account they have done it?

49. On Panchsheel, see SWJN/SS/26/pp. 410-412.

Jawaharlal Nehru: How, if they wanted to do that, how are they succeeding in that? It is just the reverse.

Question: They might not succeed.

Jawaharlal Nehru: I do not think so. They can easily see that it is having the reverse effect.

Question: Could we not have avoided all this trouble if we supported Tibet independence.

Jawaharlal Nehru: Where do we support it? By a statement at a press conference? How do we do it or what do we do?

Question: As Pandit Jawaharlal Nehru, the historian, wrote in his book in 1934, in the *Glimpses of World History*, that Tibet became independent after the fall of the Manchu dynasty, on that basis we could have supported.

Jawaharlal Nehru: What, may I ask, I do not remember exactly what I wrote, but it functioned for certain number of years as an independent state. But internationally, it was not considered so and no country had recognized its independence. But this is neither here nor there. But how could we help Tibet by declaring that?

Question: They wanted to be independent and they wanted friendly countries to support their move.

Jawaharlal Nehru: How do we support it except, as you said, morally, by stating it. How else do we support it?

Question: By not saying that Tibet has been part of China through the ages.

Jawaharlal Nehru: I am not saying that it has not been part of China. We stated that it was under Chinese suzerainty. That, I think, was the fact. That is, I think all these things are rather vague and historical evidence showed that. But apart from that, whatever we stated, what difference does it make to Tibet?

Question: As the Russians supported Outer Mongolia to become an independent state, we should have done something like that for Tibet also. Outer Mongolia was a part of China recently. Outer Mongolia has become a state today. Tibet has been much more independent than Outer Mongolia.

Jawaharlal Nehru: Outer Mongolia had a rebellion at the time of the Revolution in Russia some years ago, and the Soviet people, I believe—I am not quite certain—gave it some help, established a government.

Question: We gave up our rights in Tibet, whatever rights the British had, because they were the legacies of the British. The biggest legacy of British imperialism in Tibet was the recognition of Chinese suzerainty over Tibet. If we give up one legacy, why cannot we give up the other legacy?

Jawaharlal Nehru: I cannot quite understand this, that is, we should not have accepted, as the British did, the Chinese suzerainty. Well, normally, we accept things as they are and our reading of history showed that there were broad patches when sometimes Tibet functioned independently, sometimes as a part of China and sometimes under the suzerainty of China broadly.

[European Common Market and Commonwealth]

Question: Sir, what are the prospects of Commonwealth after Britain joins the European Common Market and, politically, Western Europe?

Jawaharlal Nehru: I imagine that it will be a weaker association than it has been.

Question: That is all? [Laughter]

Jawaharlal Nehru: Naturally, the political integration of United Kingdom into the European scheme will lessen the significance of the wider association even with the parts of the Commonwealth—I mean, the so-called White Dominions; even they would become looser.

Question: Are there any consultations between India, Pakistan and Ceylon with a view to the three premiers putting up a common front at the coming Prime Ministers' Conference, by the Prime Ministers of these countries?

Jawaharlal Nehru: There have been consultations between their representatives whenever they go to these places. In fact, everything that we had put forward has been stated for India, Pakistan and Ceylon because we stand more or less on the same footing. So, it has been a common approach.

Question: Are there any plans to visit the Sundarbans in the near future?

Jawaharlal Nehru: I did say to some delegations that came that I would like to go there next November. Somebody asked me ...

25

Question: Where?

Jawaharlal Nehru: Sundarbans! [Laughter].

Ghana and Nigeria: I intend to go there for a few days on my way back from England.

Question: How about Bonn and Paris?

Jawaharlal Nehru: No, not Bonn. I may go for a day or two to Paris on way to Nigeria.

Question: What about your going to Goa?

Jawaharlal Nehru: I shall go to Goa after I come back and after the rains are fully over.

[Admitting Minor Children to Matinée Film Shows]

Question: Sir, I wish to draw your attention to a letter regarding the admission of children below the age of 18 years to matinée cinema shows. I understand the Public Relations Committee of the Delhi Administration is planning to reverse its original decision banning the entry of children of 18 years' age to matinée shows. Now the pressure seems to have been exercised by the Delhi Pradesh Congress President.[50] Therefore, we wish to know, because you are very much interested in the children (below 18 years of age) of Delhi and of India as well. What will be your reaction if this decision is reversed?

Jawaharlal Nehru: I know nothing about it.

Question: It was previously brought to your notice, when this original decision was taken, that children below the age of 18 years should not be allowed entry to the matinée shows because they were not attending classes. Therefore, this decision was taken and the same is being reversed without any reference to higher authority.

Jawaharlal Nehru: I do not know. Prima facie it was a good decision—the previous one.

50. Brij Mohan.

[Meeting Ayub Khan]

Question: At the time of the Commonwealth Conferences, is there any possibility of direct talks with Mr Ayub Khan[51] about Kashmir?

Jawaharlal Nehru: There is no present proposal of direct talks, or any meeting to have direct talks.

[China]

Question: In the July 26 note, why have you not said about Chinese withdrawal from Indian territory? Is it an oversight or deliberately ignored?[52]

Jawaharlal Nehru: If you will see in the last note, considerable stress was laid on the creating of a proper climate on the border, etc. etc. In the previous notes that has been said so often.

[Panchayati Raj and New Man]

Question: About Panchayati Raj institutions there were two views. One view is that it is a means to an end, the end being increased food production. And the other view is that it is an end in itself because it links Gram Sabha to Lok Sabha. What is your personal view on this subject?

Jawaharlal Nehru: The aim is creating better human beings. That is the main aim. And that is helped by Panchayati Raj, making them more self-reliant. Of course, one of the aims is greater production, agricultural production. But ultimately it is better men and women.

Question: If the second view is accepted, something is diverted from food production which is probably the most important need today.

Jawaharlal Nehru: It is very odd that if the view is accepted, that we produce better men and women, we divert them for food production. I don't understand that at all.

51. The President of Pakistan.
52. On 6 August 1962, Nehru had read out a portion of the Indian note of 26 July 1962 to the Government of China, see item 401. For the complete note, see *Notes, Memoranda and Letters exchanged between the Governments of India and China, July-October 1962. White Paper No. VII* (Government of India, Ministry of External Affairs), pp. 3-4.

Question: May I, at this stage, refer to the answer that you gave at a Press Conference held four years ago? You said that the "New Man" will be created by the end of the Third Five Year Plan. Do you still subscribe to this view? You said that the "New Man" will be created, will be born, the "New Man" will be ready.

Jawaharlal Nehru: I don't remember what I said and how, but "New Man" is being constantly created. [Laughter]. I don't exactly mean it in that way. What I mean is that changes don't come about by some sudden type of thunder. Changes creep in in a society. We are modernizing ourselves. As I just said, we are modernizing our agriculture. Gradually, changes creep in and affect people's thinking, ways of living, methods of production, etc. You cannot say, from now on it is a "New Man" and before that it was an "Old Man".[53]

[Resignation of Manikyalal Verma]

Question: Mr Manikyalal Verma,[54] the Congress leader, has sent a letter of resignation to you so that it is delivered to the Speaker of the Lok Sabha. Have you accepted his resignation or have you passed the letter back to him?

Jawaharlal Nehru: I believe I have received a letter. I have not read it fully. [Laughter].

[China]

Question: Going back to the July 26th note to China, can we take it for granted that the words "appropriate climate" means that they should get back or march to the international frontier? The last misunderstanding was caused because our note omitted that condition.

53. Reference to creation of the "New Man" by the end of the Third Five Year Plan has not been traced in Nehru's press conferences of four years before. However, in a speech in Los Angeles on 13 November 1961, while speaking of India's planned economic development, Nehru referred to Mahatma Gandhi's mission to make a "new man" in India. He said: "But always we have told our people, as Mr Gandhi said, that the principal burden was being carried by them, and unless they carried that burden, even the good that they may get from others will not produce the results that are necessary. Because he was always thinking in terms of making a new man in India and not merely getting something from outside and taking advantage of it." See SWJN/SS/72/ item 254, here pp. 593-594.
54. Lok Sabha MP from Chittorgarh, Rajasthan; former Prime Minister of United State of Rajasthan, 1948-1949, and an influential Congress leader of Udaipur region.

Jawaharlal Nehru: Whatever it means, it is not an appropriate question at the present moment.

[Public Image]

Question: Fifteen years ago nobody could dare to criticize you. There were fights in the railway trains whenever somebody criticized you. It was not the case ten years ago. People have started criticizing you. Is it because of the spread of education or lack of political understanding or what?

Jawaharlal Nehru: I should say merely that some people are rather tired of me considerably. [Laughter].

Question: No, Sir. They still love you. [Laughter]. Everybody loves you. You are the only leader in the country. Even then, people have started criticizing you.

Question: There are many people in the villages who are saying: What has Pandit Nehru, our Prime Minister, done to keep these 79 swarms of locust away from us?[55]

Jawaharlal Nehru: Well, I am afraid we better adjourn now. [Laughter]. Thank you.

8. In Delhi: Independence Day Address[56]

भाइयो और बहिनो और बच्चो,
आपमें जित्ते यहाँ बच्चे बैठे हैं उनको तो कोई याद भी नहीं होगी उस ज़माने की, जब हिन्दुस्तान में आज़ादी नहीं थी। जो आपमें जवान हैं वो शायद बच्चे हों उस वक़्त, बहुत याद न हो। पन्द्रह बरस हो गये जबकि क़ौम ने, हमारे देश ने करवट ली और एक नया युग शुरु किया। पन्द्रह बरस हुए और आज उसका जन्म दिन है, सालगिरह है और हम उसको मनाने को यहाँ आये हैं, इस लाल क़िले पर जो कि पहली निशानी थी आज़ादी आने की, यहाँ झण्डा फहराना। तो इस, यह पन्द्रह बरस तो आपको मुबारिक हों, हम सभों को। लेकिन इस पन्द्रह बरस में क्या हुआ, क्या-क्या हमने किया और क्या-क्या हमने नहीं

55. There were frequent reports of locust invasions in various parts of northern India during July-August 1962.
56. Speech, 15 August 1962, from the Red Fort. NMML, AIR Tapes, TS No. 8439-8440, NM No. 1662.

29

किया जो करना चाहिए था? हज़ार दिक़्क़तें पेश आई हैं, आप जानते हैं, और बहुत काफी दिक़्क़तें अब भी हैं हमारे मुल्क के सामने। बहुत कुछ हमने किया, और बहुत कुछ यक़ीनन आप लोग और हम मिलके करेंगे। क्योंकि कोई हम आज़ाद हुए तो कोई महज़ एक ऊपर की कार्यवाही नहीं थी, यह एक बलबला था जो कि क़ौम में, करोड़ों आदमियों में उठा था और जिसने यह नतीज़ा हासिल किया था। वो चीज़ अपना काम पूरा करके रहेगी और उस काम को पूरा करने के माने हैं कि मुल्क में जित्ते लोग हैं वो ख़ुशहाल हों, वो एक ऐसी समाज में रहें जिसमें बराबरी है, ऊँच-नीच बहुत कम है, जो कि समाजवादी समाज है और जात-पात का भी जिसमें फेर नहीं गिना जाता, ऐसी समाज हम चाहते हैं। इसको बनाने की कोशिश है लेकिन उस कोशिश के शुरू में भी काफी दिक़्क़तें हैं, हुई हैं और हैं। उनका सामना करना है। सामना हमने बहुत बातों का किया। याद है आपको इसी दिल्ली शहर में आज़ादी के बाद जो मुसीबत आई थी, जो कि हौलनाक बातें हुई थीं, उसका भी सामना हमने किया और उसको भी क़ाबू में लाये। तो उसके बाद और क्या होगा जो हमें हिलाए या हममें घबराहट पैदा करे।

आजकल भी आप देखें मुल्क के पचासों सवाल हैं। बहुत कुछ हमें तकलीफ़ें भी होती हैं और हमारी सरहदों पर भी हमें होशियार रहना है, क्योंकि लोग ऐसे मौजूद हैं सरहदों पर जो कि बुरी आँखों से देखते हैं हमारे मुल्क की तरफ और हमलावर होते हैं। इसके लिए कोई क़ौम भी, ज़िन्दादिल क़ौम जागती रहती है, तैयार रहती है उसका सामना करने को, रोकने को। आप जानते हैं कि हमारा उसूल शुरू से क्या रहा है? शांति का, अमन का, अपने मुल्क में, बाहर के मुल्कों के साथ। हमने सब मुल्कों से दोस्ती की कोशिश की और कामयाब भी उसमें बहुत दर्जे हुए, लेकिन फिर भी एक बदक़िस्मती है कि हमारी सरहदों पर हमारे जो भाई रहते हैं वो लोग इस निगाह से, ग़लत निगाह से हमारे तरफ देखें और कभी-कभी लड़ाई का चर्चा करें। हमें फिर भी कोई घबराना नहीं चाहिए, हाथ-पैर हमारे नहीं फूलने चाहिये, लेकिन होशियार रहना चाहिए, तैयार रहना चाहिए, तगड़े रहना चाहिए। इसी तरह से हम सामना कर सकते हैं हर मुसीबत का।

मुल्क के अन्दर हमारी ताक़त कैसे बढ़ती है? ताक़त के लिए, मुल्क को बचाने को फ़ौज है और और चीज़ें भी हैं, लेकिन आख़िर में एक क़ौम बचाती है आजकल के मुल्कों को। एक क़ौम काम करके, मेहनत करके, एक क़ौम जिसमें एकता हो, एक क़ौम जो मेहनती हो, वो मुल्क की ताक़त बढ़ाती है, चाहे वो खेत में काम करता है या कारख़ाने में या दुकानों में। सब अपना-अपना फ़र्ज़ ईमानदारी से अदा करें, मेहनत से, ताकि मुल्क की ताक़त बढ़े और एकता हो। तब कोई भी दुनिया में उसके ऊपर हमला नहीं कर सकता है। हमारी कहानी रही है कि आपस की फूट की, जिससे बाहर वालों ने फ़ायदा उठाया, अब तो वो नहीं होनी चाहिए। छोटी-छोटी बातें होती हैं बहस की, ख़ैर, बहस हो, ठीक है बहस में तो कोई हर्ज नहीं, लेकिन हमेशा हमें याद रखना है कि मुल्क के साथ ग़द्दारी करनी है आपस में फूट करना, मुल्क को कमज़ोर करना है, और यह जो आज़ादी इत्ती मुश्किल से आई थी इसको ख़तरे में डालना है।

तो मैं चाहता हूँ आज के दिन ख़ासतौर से आपको ज़रा याद दिलाऊँ उस ज़माने की पन्द्रह बरस पहले और उसके भी पहले जबकि आज़ादी की जंग हमारे मुल्क में होती थी, जबकि हमारे पास हमारे बड़े नेता महात्मा गांधीजी थे और हमें क़दम-ब-क़दम ले जाते थे, हम ठोकर खाते थे, लड़खड़ाते थे, गिरते थे, लेकिन फिर भी उनको देखकर हिम्मत आती थी और खड़े हो जाते थे। और इस तरह से उस ज़माने के लोगों को उन्होंने तैयार किया, इस तरह से उन्होंने एक मज़बूत क़ौम को तैयार किया जिसमें एकता थी, जिसमें किसी क़दर सब लोगों में सिपाहीपना था और उन्होंने सामना किया बड़े साम्राज्य का और आख़िर में शांति से कामयाब हुए। ज़माना याद करने की बात है हमें, क्योंकि उससे कुछ अपने दिलों को बढ़ाना है, कैसी मुसीबतों का सामना हमने किया था।

आजकल के ज़माने में छोटी सी भी तकलीफ़ हमें बड़ी तकलीफ़ मालूम होती है। तकलीफ़ तो ज़ाहिर है नहीं होनी चाहिए, हमें हटाना चाहिए उसे, लेकिन नये हिन्दुस्तान के बनाने के लिए आप और हम बना नहीं सकते उसे बग़ैर बोझे उठाये, बोझे बढ़ाये और उनको, उन बोझों को उठाके आगे बढ़ें। ख़ाली हम एक रंजीदा हों और शिकायत करें, तो यह तो नहीं हो सकता। आजकल तो छोटी बातें हैं। अगर फ़र्ज़ कीजिये इत्तेफ़ाक़ से कोई असली ख़तरा हिन्दुस्तान की आज़ादी पे हुआ, हमारी सरहदों पे, और जगह तब कित्ती तकलीफ़ उठानी पड़ेगी आपको, याद कीजिये। मैं आशा करता हूँ कि ऐसा नहीं होगा, लेकिन उसके बचाव के लिए भी आज से तैयार होना है, यह नहीं कि हम इस वक़्त ग़फ़लत में पड़ें और उस वक़्त सब लोग दिखायें कि हम भी बड़े बहादुर हैं, पहलवान हैं। इसलिए हमें इन छोटी बातों को छोड़ना है, बड़ी बातों को देखना है और एक क़ौम को बनाना है जिसमें पक्कीतौर से एकता है। हमारा हिन्दुस्तान बहुत लोगों, बहुत मज़हबों का है, बहुत तरह के लोगों का है, हिन्दू हैं, मुसलमान हैं, ईसाई हैं, सिक्ख हैं, बौद्ध हैं, पारसी हैं, वग़ैरह। सब बराबर के हैं हमारे मुल्क में, याद रखिये। और जो आदमी इसके ख़िलाफ़ आवाज़ उठाता है वो हिन्दुस्तान को धोखा देता है और हिन्दुस्तान की राष्ट्रीयता को कमज़ोर करता है। हम एक राष्ट्र में हैं और जो कोई राष्ट्र में रहता है वो भारत माता का प्यारा लड़का या लड़की है और सब हमारे भाई हैं और बहिन हैं और एक बड़ी बिरादरी है। [तालियाँ]। तो इस तरह से हमें देखना है एक फ़िरक़ापरस्ती से देखना, हमारा फ़िरक़ा, हमारी सम्प्रदाय, और सब अलग हैं, जातिभेद की तरफ जाना, उससे कमज़ोरी होती है।

आजकल का ज़माना क्या है ज़रा आप देखिये। शायद आप में से बाज़ लोगों ने रात को देखा हो कि कैसे आजकल आसमान पर दो नये सितारे घूम रहे हैं। दो आदमी, सितारे मैंने कहा, लेकिन दो आदमी दुनिया से अलग होके सैंकड़ों मील दुनिया का घेरा कर रहे हैं जो रूस से निकले हैं।[57] उसके पहले अमरीका से ऐसे निकले थे। तो कैसी दुनिया है जहाँ ऐसी बातें होती हैं? सारी दुनिया बदल रही है, इंसान बदल रहा है, नई-नई ताक़तें आती हैं और अगर हम उनको नहीं समझें, और हम नहीं उनको इस्तेमाल करें अपनी भलाई के

---

57. Two Soviet cosmonauts, orbiting the earth in separate spaceships, spoke to each other and held three-way talks with their ground station. See also items 370-371.

लिए और दुनिया की भलाई के लिए तब हम पिछड़ जायेंगे, रह जायेंगे। ख़ाली हम ऐंठते रह जायें और लम्बी-लम्बी बातें करें, दुनिया आगे बढ़ जायेगी। इसलिए हमें समझना है कि हम एक बदलती हुई दुनिया में, बदलते हुए हिन्दुस्तान में रहते हैं और अगर हम तेज़ी से नहीं बदलते उसी के साथ तो हम पीछे रह जायेंगे, हमें बदलना है। हमें विज्ञान को बढ़ाना है, हमें अपनी मेहनत करके इस मुल्क में नये तरीके निकालने हैं, कारख़ाने बनाने हैं, ख़ासकर हमारी खेती की तरक्की करनी है क्योंकि वो जड़ है हिन्दुस्तान की, यहाँ के किसान उसकी पीठ हैं, जड़ हैं, जो कुछ कहिये। लेकिन जभी है, जभी तक वो ठीक हैं, जब तक आज की दुनिया को समझते हैं और आजकल की दुनिया के तरीकों को लेते हैं, आजकल के औज़ारों को इस्तेमाल करते हैं और आजकल के हल चलाते हैं और यह नहीं कि हज़ार बरस पुराने के औज़ार चला रहे हैं। दुनिया बदल गई और खेती एक हज़ार बरस पुरानी रही, इसमें हम पिछड़ जाते हैं। हमें बदलना है, यह सब बदल रहे हैं।

हमारे यहाँ पंचायती राज है और तरह-तरह की बातें इतिहास में हो रही हैं जो कि हमारे करोड़ों आदमियों को जो कि गाँव में रहते हैं हल्के-हल्के बदल रहे हैं। सबमें बड़ी बात यह है। यह नहीं कि आपने एक बड़ी इमारत देखी या बड़ा कारख़ाना देखा, बल्कि यह कि हिन्दुस्तान के किसान किस तरह से बदल रहे हैं हल्के-हल्के। पढ़ाई से, स्कूल पहुँचे, वहाँ गाँव-गाँव में उनके बच्चे पढ़ रहे हैं। एक दिन आने वाला है बहुत जल्दी जबकि कोई बच्चा हिन्दुस्तान में नहीं रहे जिसको पढ़ने-लिखने का मौक़ा नहीं मिला है।

हमारा स्वास्थ पहले, आज़ादी के ज़रा ही पहले, बत्तीस बरस की उम्र हमारी औसत समझी जाती थी, अब क़रीब पचास की हो गई है बावजूद इत्ती आबादी के बढ़ने के। क्या माने हैं इसके? इसके माने नहीं हैं कि सब लोग पचास के होते हैं या पचास के ज्यादा कोई नहीं होता लेकिन औसत यह है। इसके माने यह हैं कि मुल्क भर को देखते हुए बावजूद आबादी बढ़ने के लोगों की सेहत ज्यादा अच्छी है। क्यों सेहत अच्छी है? इसलिए कि उन्हें खाना अच्छा मिलता है पहले के मुक़ाबले में। पहले तो फ़ाक़ेमस्ती थी, अब नहीं होती, बाज़ की होती हो मैं नहीं कह सकता, लेकिन आमतौर से नहीं होती। सेहत अच्छी है, सबमें बड़ी बात सेहत में, खाना मिलना। सबमें जरूरी बात है एक क़ौम के लिए खाना उसको मिले, कपड़े मिलें, घर रहने को मिले, उसके स्वास्थ्य का प्रबंध हो और उसके पढ़ाई का हो और उसके काम का हो और यह सब बातें हों। यह हमारा ध्येय है, मक़सद है। तो छोटी-छोटी बातों में हम फंसे रहते हैं, रोज़मर्रा की दिक्क़तों में, लेकिन हमेश हमें यह याद रखना है और यह याद रखना है कि पुराने, कि आज़ादी के पहले जो लोग थे गांधीजी के नीचे और गांधीजी के नेतृत्व में, क्या-क्या उन्होंने किया, कुछ उससे हम सबक़ सीखें, कुछ जान आये हममें और उसी रास्ते पर हम चलें। क्योंकि मेरा ख़्याल है जिस रास्ते पर महात्मा जी ने हमें चलाया था, जिसमें, हम लोग कमज़ोर थे, दुर्बल थे फिर भी हममें कुछ हिम्मत भर दी थी, हमें भी कुछ सिपाही बनाया था, उसी रास्ते पर हमें चलना है। सिपाही ख़ाली वर्दी पहन के फ़ौजी लोग नहीं होते हैं, सिपाही हरेक आदमी होता है जो एक काम को उठाये, सिपाही की तरह से करे और हमें सारे हिन्दुस्तान को, बच्चों-बच्चों को, और बड़ों को उधर दिखाना है। और याद रखिये, हमारी फ़ौज को देखिये, उस फ़ौज में हर

धर्म के आदमी हैं, हर मज़हब के आदमी हैं, फ़ौज में फ़र्क़ नहीं है, सब बराबर के हैं, सभों को बराबर के अधिकार हैं। इस तरह से हमें अपने मुल्क को बनाना है।

आज का दिन यों भी शुभ दिन है, आज़ादी का दिन है, लेकिन आज और एक तरह से शुभ दिन है, आज रक्षा बंधन है और हम एक-दूसरे को राखी बांधते हैं। राखी किस चीज़ की निशानी है? [तालियाँ]। राखी एक वफ़ादारी की निशानी है, एक-दूसरे की हिफ़ाज़त करना, रक्षा करना, भाई बहिन की करे, औरों की करे। आज आप राखी समझिये अपने दिल में बांधिये भारत माता को [तालियाँ] और उसके साथ, उसके साथ फिर से अपनी प्रतिज्ञा दोहरायें, अपनी इक़रार दोहराइये कि आप भारत की सेवा करेंगे, भारत की रक्षा करेंगे चाहे जो कुछ भी हो। और उस रक्षा करने के माने हैं यह नहीं कि अलग-अलग आप कोई बहादुरी दिखायें, वो भी हो सकता है वक़्त पर, लेकिन उसके माने हैं कि हम आपस में हम लोग मिलके रहेंगे, हम नाजायज़ फ़ायदा एक-दूसरे का नहीं उठायेंगे, हम एक-दूसरे की मदद करेंगे, सहयोग करेंगे, सहकार करेंगे, और इस तरह से एक क़ौम बनायेंगे जिसको कोई हिला भी न सके। तो आज के दिन, आज़ादी के दिन और आज़ादी के दिवस और रक्षा बंधन के दिन हम और आप इस समय यहाँ मिलकर इस पवित्र भूमि में जहाँ के पहले बार पन्द्रह अगस्त को, पन्द्रह बरस हुए हमने झण्डा यह फ़हराया था, एक निशानी आज़ादी की।[58] हम फिर इस बात की प्रतिज्ञा करें, इक़रार करें कि हम चाहे जो कुछ हो, कोई ऐसी बात नहीं करेंगे जिससे भारत के माथे पर धब्बा लगे, कोई बात भी हो जो कि भारत को नुकसान करे, और उसकी सेवा करेंगे।

भारत की सेवा करने के माने क्या हैं? भारत एक कोई तस्वीर नहीं है। हमारे दिल में तस्वीर तो है। भारत की सेवा करना, भारत के रहने वालों की सेवा करना, भारत में जो सब रहते हैं वही भारत की सेवा है और कोई अलग कोई जंगल में बैठके उसकी सेवा तो होगी नहीं, जनता की सेवा है, जनता को उभारना है। बहुत दिन से दबी हुई जनता उभर रही है, उसको मदद करना है, इस तरह से हमें बढ़ाना है। तो इसका हम इक़रार करें और इक़रार करके याद रखें इसको और सच्चे दिल से इस काम को करने की कोशिश करें, चाहे जो कुछ हमारा पेशा हो या काम हो। सभों का काम जो कुछ हो, एक थोड़ा सा अलग भी काम है वो भारत की सेवा का और भारत की सेवा के माने हैं अपने पड़ोसियों की सेवा का, अपने मुल्क वालों की और सभों को एक समझना, चाहे वो कोई मज़हब हो, कोई धर्म हो। अगर हिन्दुस्तानी हैं तो हमारे भाई हैं, यों तो हमारे बाहर के भाई भी हो सकते हैं, लेकिन ख़ास यह हमारी बिरादरी है। तो यह मैं चाहता हूँ आप करें और छोटे झगड़ों में न पड़ें, छोटी बहसों में न पड़ें। अलग-अलग राय होती है, वो ठीक है राय होनी चाहिए अलग-अलग। ज़िंदा क़ौम है हम, कोई हम सभों के दिमाग़ नहीं बांध देते हैं कि

58. Probably Nehru is using the words "15th August" here as a metaphor for Independence Day. In fact, the Independence Day function at the Red Fort in 1947 was held on 16 August. For Nehru's speech on the occasion, see SWJN/SS/4/pp. 2-3. On 15 August 1947, the official function took place at Princess Park near India Gate in New Delhi. *The Statesman*, 18 August 1947.

एक ही तरह से सोचें, एक ही तरह से करें, लेकिन बाज़ बातों में अलग राय की गुंजायश नहीं है। हिन्दुस्तान की ख़िदमत में अलग राय की गुंजायश नहीं है, हिन्दुस्तान की रक्षा में, हिफ़ाज़त में अलग-अलग राय की गुंजायश नहीं है, वो हरेक का फ़र्ज़ है चाहे जो कुछ हो। तो इसका हम पक्का इरादा आज कर लें और रोज़ कुछ याद रखें तो हमारे थोड़े से काम से, थोड़ी-थोड़ी सेवा से एक पहाड़ हो जायेगी, पहाड़ बनेंगे जो कि भारत को बढ़ायेंगे और हिफ़ाज़त करेंगे।

जयहिन्द!

अब मेरे साथ आप तीन बार जयहिन्द कहिये।

जयहिन्द! जयहिन्द! जयहिन्द!

[Translation begins

Brothers, Sisters, and Children,

The children seated here would have no recollection of the time when India was not free. The youth of today must have been small children then. Fifteen years have gone by since a new age started in our country. Today is the anniversary of our independence and we are assembled here at the Red Fort to celebrate it. The hoisting of the tricolour at the Red Fort was the first symbol of the arrival of independence. So I congratulate all of you, rather all of us, for these fifteen years.

This is a good opportunity to take stock of our achievements and failures in the last fifteen years. As you are aware, we have had to face great hardships and difficulties during these years, and even now we are beset with problems. In spite of all that, we have managed to achieve a great deal and I am sure we will continue to do so with the cooperation of the people.

Independence was not brought about merely through some changes at the top. It was the result of a great upheaval among millions of people in India which shook the nation to its core. The process started during the freedom struggle will not be over until it reaches its logical conclusion. That means raising the standard of living of India's millions and bringing about equality and equal opportunities for everyone. Our goal is to reduce the disparity between the haves and the have-nots and establish a socialist pattern of society. We want to get rid of the caste system. We have had to face tremendous difficulties in our efforts to bring this about. Do you remember the terrible events which shook the nation in the aftermath of Partition? Anyhow, we faced them and brought the situation under control.

Even now, there are great problems before us and some of them are quite troublesome. For instance, we must be vigilant on our borders because there are forces with evil intention operating there. A nation which wants to hold on to its independence must remain vigilant and watchful. You are aware that our foreign policy has been based right from the start on principles of peace and non-violence. We have tried to maintain friendly relations with all the countries and have succeeded to a very large extent. But unfortunately our neighbours are always hostile and often talk of war. We must not panic but remain vigilant and strong enough to face any eventuality. That is the only way to face a problem.

[PROGRESS BEYOND INDEPENDENCE]

You Said It

By LAXMAN

The country has made impressive progress in many spheres! For instance . . . for instance . . . well, as I said, it has made impressive progress.

(From *The Times of India*, 17 August 1962, p. 1)

35

How can we become strong as a nation? It is necessary to have strong army. But ultimately it is on the people that the defence of a nation depends, on their hard work, unity and determination. Everyone in the country must do his duty honestly, work hard in his own chosen profession, and foster unity. Then no power in the world can conquer them. India's story has always been one of disunity and internecine feuds. We tend to argue about petty things. Not that there is any harm in debates or arguments. But we must always bear in mind that disunity is traitorous to the country. It weakens the nation and endangers our hard-won freedom.

So I want to remind you on this day particularly about the events which led to our getting independence and the struggle for freedom which we waged under the leadership of Mahatma Gandhi. He led us step by step, and though we often stumbled and fell, we derived courage from him. This is how he moulded the people in those days and organized the nation into a strong and united force, imbued the people with a national spirit and discipline. He challenged the might of a great empire by peaceful, non-violent methods and ultimately succeeded in winning freedom for India. We must bear all this in mind because it infuses spirit and courage into us and prepares us to face difficulties.

Nowadays even small hardships seem unbearable to us. It is obvious that nobody must have to bear hardships. But we cannot build the edifice of a new India without shouldering some burden. We must not have grudges and keep complaining. The problems we are facing are small ones. For instance, suppose if some real danger threatened our freedom on our borders, what hardships we would have to put up with. I hope that it will not happen. But we are prepared to face any danger. We must not fritter away our energies in petty matters. We must rise above them and look ahead to larger issues and build a strong nation based on unity. There are people belonging to various religions in India, Hindus, Muslims, Christians, Sikhs, Buddhists, Parsis, etc. But you must remember that everyone is equal and the man who raises his voice against this principle betrays India and weakens Indian nationalism. All of us are citizens of one country and every one of us is a beloved son or daughter of India. All of us belong to one large family [Applause]. Communalism and the caste system weaken the country.

We are living in a new age. Some of you might have observed two new stars in the firmament at night. I am using the words stars, but actually they are two men from the Soviet Union who are orbiting our planet, hundreds of miles away from earth.[59] Earlier the Americans did such a thing. We are living in a revolutionary world where everything is changing rapidly. New forces

59. See fn 57 in this section.

are making their appearance and unless we understand them and utilize them to our own advantage, we will become backward while the world goes ahead. Therefore, we must realize how essential it is to change and progress in order to fit in with the modern world. We must advance in the field of science, work hard and adopt new techniques of production. We must industrialize the country and improve agricultural production. Agriculture is the backbone of the country. But it is essential to adopt new techniques befitting the modern world. We must not stick to outdated ploughs and tools when the world has advanced so much. We must change with the changing times.

We have adopted the Panchayati Raj system and all kinds of revolutionary changes are taking place which are transforming the rural areas. The important thing is not the huge buildings and new factories which are coming up everywhere but the way the Indian farmer is gradually changing. Education is spreading and a time will soon come when there will not be a single child in the country who does not have the opportunity of going to school.

Before independence, the average life expectancy in India was thirty-two years. Now it has risen to fifty in spite of the rapid increase in population. What does that imply? It does not mean that everyone lives only up to fifty. That is the average. It means that in spite of the increasing population, the health of the people is improving because they are better fed than before. Generally speaking, people do not starve any more except perhaps in rare cases. The health of the nation is improving. It is extremely important for the people to have enough to eat, clothes to wear, houses to live in, health care, education facilities and the means of earning a livelihood. It is our goal to provide these.

We are often engrossed in our petty day-to-day difficulties and problems. But we must always remember the lessons that we learnt under Gandhiji's leadership during the freedom struggle. Gandhiji infused a new spark of life in us and we followed the path that he showed us. Though we were weak and cowardly, by following the path shown by him we developed some courage. He made us into soldiers and we have to continue on the path shown by him. Merely wearing the military uniform does not make one a soldier. Those who take up a task and discharge it faithfully are soldiers. We have to show this path to the entire country, including the children. Look at our Army. There are people of all religions in it and there is no distinction of caste or religion. Everyone is equal and everyone has equal rights. We have to build our country in this way.

Today, the anniversary of our independence, is an auspicious day. But it is auspicious for another reason too. Today is Raksha Bandhan. What does this festival stand for? [Applause]. The rakhi is the symbol of loyalty. Brothers pledge to protect their sisters on this day. I want you to mentally tie a rakhi on Bharat Mata today. [Applause]. You must renew your pledge once again to serve

India and protect her no matter what happens. That does not mean that each one must pull in different directions. It implies that we must maintain unity and discipline, not take undue advantage of one another, cooperate with and help one another, and in this way build a strong nation which nobody can touch. So on the occasion of this anniversary of our independence and Raksha Bandhan, when all of us are assembled here at this sacred place, where we had unfurled the tricolor for the first time on 15th August fifteen years ago as a symbol of our freedom,[60] let us pledge once again that no matter what happens, we will not do anything to stain India's honour or cause harm to her but always to serve her.

What does serving the country mean? India is not a mere image but we have an image of India in our hearts. Service to India is service of her people. We cannot sit by ourselves in some isolated spot and hope to serve India. We must serve the people of India, particularly the downtrodden sections of society and help them to achieve a better standard of living. We must pledge to do this and try to work honestly and with sincerity to fulfill our pledge, no matter which profession we are in. Apart from whatever we do in our day-to-day living, we must remember that it is our duty also to serve the people of India, our neighbours and friends, irrespective of their religion and castes. All Indians are our brothers no matter which religion they follow. We are part of a large family. I want you to do this and not get bogged down in petty problems and arguments. Everyone is entitled to different opinions and there must be no restriction on free thinking. But there is no room for differences of opinion when it comes to serving the country or protecting and defending her freedom. This is the duty of every single citizen of India. Therefore, we must make a firm determination today and do our mite to serve the country. Every little bit will add up to a great deal and we will be able to build the edifice of a new India and maintain her freedom.

Jai Hind!

Please say Jai Hind three times.

Jai Hind! Jai Hind! Jai Hind!

Translation ends]

---

60. See fn 58 in this section.

9. To Ramgopal Goenka: No Celebration of Birthday[61]

August 18, 1962

Dear Ramgopalji,

Your letter of 11th August. I do not like my birthday being celebrated. I have, therefore, even requested people in Delhi not to celebrate it as my birthday. They celebrate it as Children's Day. It so happens that 14th November has been fixed as Children's Day.

If I do not celebrate my birthday here in Delhi, obviously I cannot go about to other States to celebrate it.

Yours sincerely,
[Jawaharlal Nehru]

10. To Hukam Singh: Misconduct in Lok Sabha[62]

August 31, 1962

My dear Mr Speaker,

The unhappy and distressing events that happened in the Lok Sabha today have caused me deep pain.[63] What took place was not only an insult to the Chair but, as you were pleased to say, to the House. Any democratic procedure requires some discipline, some restraint and some propriety. All these were lacking today in the Lok Sabha. During the fourteen or fifteen years that I have been functioning in Parliament, I do not remember of any such occurrence and what troubles me greatly is that such occurrences might happen again.

All of us in the Lok Sabha must bear their share of responsibility to some extent for what took place. As leader of the House, I should like to express my deep regret to you for this distressing occurrence and to express the hope that every member will realise the consequences of such behaviour in future and behave with propriety and a measure of discipline.[64]

Yours sincerely,
Jawaharlal Nehru

---

61. Letter to the General Secretary of the National Children's Day Festival Committee, 4 Jagmohan Mullick Lane, Calcutta-7.
62. Letter to the Speaker.
63. Ram Sewak Yadav, Socialist Party MP from Barabanki-SC, UP, and leader of the Socialist group in the Lok Sabha, defied the Speaker by insisting on a discussion on his motion on floods in UP, Bihar and Assam. He was suspended for a week.
64. For Nehru's observations at the CPP on 7 September 1962, see item 38.

11. To Renu Chakravartty: Socialist Bad Behaviour in Lok Sabha[65]

Personal

31.8.62

Dear Renu,

I feel I must tell you how distressed and deeply pained I was this morning at the extraordinary display we had today in the Lok Sabha.[66] Any person may lose his temper occasionally though even that is regrettable. But persistent rowdyism and defiance and even insult of the Chair is something we had not experienced in this way for the last dozen years or more. The members of the Socialist Party have a way of behaving in a deplorable manner. That is unfortunate but perhaps they do not know anything better. What surprised and pained me was the behaviour of the Communist members of the Lok Sabha who gave their support to the Socialist misbehaviour.[67] Surely this can only lead to a breakdown of our system.

Yours sincerely,
Jawaharlal Nehru

12. To S. Radhakrishnan: Inscription on Mahatma Gandhi's Samadhi[68]

September 2, 1962

My dear Mr President,

I have just seen your letter of the 2nd September about Gandhiji's samadhi.[69] I entirely agree with you that the words "He Ram"[70] should be put on the Samadhi.

---

65. Handwritten letter to the deputy leader of the Communist group in the Lok Sabha. NMML, Renu Chakravartty Papers, Miscellaneous Collection, Accession No. 1968. Reproduced in *Mainstream*, 29 May 2004, p. 18.
66. See item 10.
67. During discussion in the Lok Sabha on 31 August 1962, on the motion of suspension of Ram Sewak Yadav, Socialist MP, from the House, Renu Chakravartty had said: "This is a particular issue which has moved the people in the country and hon. Members of this House, deeply. But at such a moment, it is not necessary to raise this question of decorum. We know that we have to keep decorum. We know that we should respect each other." *Lok Sabha Debates*, Third Series, Volume VII, 1962, 22 to 31 August 1962, col. 5307.
68. Letter to the President.
69. The memorial of Mahatma Gandhi at Rajghat in Delhi.
70. Gandhi's last words, spelt in English often as "Hey Ram" also.

So far as I know, nobody has suggested that they should not be there. Two days ago I went to the samadhi and the only question that arose was where we should put these words. Thin steel plates giving these words have to be put in there so that there might be some permanency about them.

Some people suggested that they should be put on the top of the side of the samadhi. Some others were of the opinion that they should be at the top. On the whole, it was thought that it would be better on the side, and the top should be a smooth marble surface. Of course, on the sides also there is some kind of marble. I myself was slightly in favour of the side, but if you prefer it, they will certainly be put at the top. Anyhow, they are going to be there.

Thank you for sending me the book by Gollancz.[71] I am returning it.

[Jawaharlal Nehru]

13. To Chief Ministers[72]

September 3, 1962

My dear Chief Minister,

In another four days, I am leaving India to attend the London meeting of the Commonwealth Prime Ministers. After that meeting I hope to go for about two days to Paris to meet President de Gaulle. From there I go to Nigeria and Ghana. On my return journey I shall spend a few hours at Cairo. I hope to be back in Delhi on October 1st.

2. I have travelled about a good deal, but I have not been to South America at all, and in Africa I have only been to Egypt and the Sudan. Both these vast areas of South America and Africa are changing fast and are likely to play an ever increasing part in world affairs. Indeed, Africa is already attracting a great deal of attention. It is a vital continent, and now that it is awake, it is bound to go ahead, even though it may have many difficulties. I am glad, therefore, that I am going to Ghana and Nigeria, two of the important newly independent countries in West Africa. I hope, sometime in the not distant future, to visit the North African countries, and East Africa.

3. Usually I look forward to a visit abroad. It brings about a change in scene for me and refreshes me. But on this occasion I do not feel at all happy at leaving India and her many problems. These problems fill my mind and I

71. It is not clear whether this is Victor Gollancz the author or publisher.
72. Letter to all Chief Ministers and to the Prime Minister of Jammu and Kashmir State. PMS, File No. 25 (30)/62-PM, Sr. No. 3-A.

confess they distress me. We seem to be passing through a peculiarly difficult phase. In the life of a human being the 15th and 16th years are supposed to be rather critical as they bring about many biological and psychical developments. We are now in our sixteenth year of Independence, and I wonder if some such process of change bringing about a new social structure is now taking place in India leading to various crises. The country is being industrialised, and many social developments are taking place. Modern mechanical civilization is gradually creeping in and coming into conflict with the old agricultural order. The machine requires definite organisational work and it often imposes its own will. Our youth, passing through this phase, find great difficulty in adapting themselves to it. Often they take up a negative attitude towards patterns of behaviour transmitted by their elders. There is a rejection of old moral patterns and standards some times and emphasis on their being different. In Western countries especially, there is a desire for eccentricity and a cynicism and a negative attitude to work. There is in the West a great deal of juvenile delinquency and alcoholism. All this leads to many individuals becoming socially useless and sometimes even harmful.

4. In India we have not gone that far. But the beginnings of this deterioration are visible. This often leads to our youth turning to communal and disruptive organisations and our education helps very little in preparing the young people to take part in collective life and to perform useful functions for society.

5. It is not much good blaming our young people. They react to the environment and to changing patterns of behaviour. But it does become important for our educational system to lay stress on certain intellectual and moral features, and more specially to prepare them for the collective life which we hope to build up in India.

6. We live in a world today which has lost its old permanence. The atomic age is made up [of] whirling atomic particles of vast energies which can be released for good and evil, and the possibility of destruction on a wide scale. Scientists and technicians create modern machinery and new sources of energy. But the use of all this is decided upon by people who are hardly capable of understanding them. In the old days, people grew up with a picture of nature in which the world was built with solid materials and there was an element of permanence in our lives. That is no longer there. The tragedy of every generation, especially during a period of rapid change, is the discovery of the divergence between the ideals and actual picture of the world. The change in the developed countries is great. In India it is likely to be even greater because we have to cover the track of centuries. This will inevitably bring about changes in the individuals and a sense of tension and often of frustration.

7.   We are supposed to be a people with an ideological and philosophical and even metaphysical background. With the coming of a technical civilization and the forms of social life accompanying it, there is inevitably [a] lack of harmony. Possibly, after the present transitional phase and the development of new techniques, a new base of civilization and new forms of collective life will be established which will lead to a new ideology and philosophy of life. In the old days, economic theories were often a rationalisation of dominant interests. Even metaphysics and religion were sometimes exploited to this end. The growth of the sciences and technology may lead to a new science of sociology, that is if we survive the atomic and the hydrogen bombs. The amazingly swift diffusion of technology and its advance gives little time to mankind in order to adjust itself to the new conditions of life.

8.   It is the degree of maturity of society's productive resources that determines the general character of social, political and intellectual life. We aim at socialism, but socialism in a backward underdeveloped country becomes inevitably backward and underdeveloped socialism.

9.   In our planning, we are beginning to realise more and more that five years is too brief a period to keep in view. Even in regard to industrial progress that is too short a time. But if we consider the long-term interests of a nation, then we have to keep in mind always the kind of society we are building up and the patterns of behaviour that we wish to encourage. Education and health may not bring immediate profit in terms of cost, and yet from the long-term and national point of view, they are essential.

10. It amazes me that some people in this age of swift transition should still cling to ideas which have no relevance today; should be attracted to communalism and provincialism; and should be powerfully influenced by caste. That itself shows how backward we are and the great distance we have to cover. It is distressing that elections should turn on caste and communal aspects. The chief value of election propaganda is to lay stress on our basic objectives and our programmes to reach them. I think that our people generally in the mass are sound and have a good deal of commonsense. Even in the general elections, it was my experience, and it may have been yours also, that when the approach is on that level, they were greatly interested and reacted favourably. But, unfortunately, this was seldom done, and narrow slogans and appeals took the place of reasoned arguments and a peep into the future that we were building up. Many of our Opposition parties especially, and sometimes even the Congress, approached the electorate in a narrow way, imaging that they would gain advantage thereby. It is possible that occasionally they gained some advantage. But, even if they did so, it was only for a very short time. They laid no foundations of the future.

11. I am repeating some platitudes. Yet platitudes often embody truths and have to be remembered. The strength of the Congress and its mass appeal has been due to the fact that we have in the past spoken to our people frankly and fully about the ideals that moved us. Those ideals seeped down to the people and found an echo in their minds and hearts. That strength was also due to an appreciation by the general public of the moral fibre of Congressmen as a whole. I fear that appreciation is sadly lacking today and, without it, our message cannot go far or carry conviction. We have, therefore, to pull ourselves up in our personal lives as well as in our organisations and, of course, in our governmental activity. This conviction is growing upon me more and more. It is right that we should think clearly and put our policy and programme before the public. But, even more so, it is necessary for us to create the impression of a certain unselfish service of the nation.

12. Coming to our broad policies and programmes, I find that we take some of our resolutions about socialism for granted and say little about them. As a matter of fact, this requires constant reiteration not only to others, but to ourselves also, so that we may not slip away from the straight and narrow path. We have adopted socialism not only because it seemed to us a right goal, but also because the compulsion of events in India forces us in that direction. There is no other way of progress and certainly no other way of mass betterment. But we need not think of this socialism as some rigid doctrinaire theory, but rather as a broad objective and pattern of society which should be adapted to a country's backgrounds and needs. Above all, we should always keep in mind that any real advance must have a moral and spiritual foundation in the broadest sense of those terms.

13. I have no doubt that we have made marked progress in the last fifteen years in India. The mere continuation of an orderly democratic structure of Government and society is commendable. But, even in the industrial and agricultural fields, we have gone ahead though not as much as we had hoped. This very progress has not only created new problems for us to solve, but has also aroused our people to demand more and more. Our Plans are meant to ensure this continuing progress and to fulfil, in so far as we can, the legitimate demands of our people. It may be that we have erred from time to time. I have no doubt that we have. But the general progress made is, I believe, in the right direction in spite of the many pulls to the contrary. But the time has come when we should, far from being complacent, be critical of what we have done and what we should do. While we want industrial and agricultural progress, there is always a tendency for the more favoured people to profit by these and not so much those who are down and out. That is, I suppose, to some extent,

inevitable. Yet we must check that and pay greater attention to those who lack the basic necessities of life.

14. We had in the Lok Sabha a Bill for acquisition of land recently. This aimed rightly but it gave rise to a furore in Parliament because it was felt that this might be to the advantage of favoured individuals and at the cost of our poor agriculturists. That urge which Parliament exhibited was all to the good, and we should always have that urge. Finally, the Bill was passed with many amendments which improved it greatly and ensured, to a large extent, the welfare of the agriculturists.[73] Apart from this, I think it should always be borne in mind that any industrial progress that we make, should not spoil the good agricultural land that we possess. This is bad from the point of view of food production as well as the peasantry. This might even be kept in mind in the planning of growing cities, though sometimes it is a little difficult to do so. Delhi, for instance, is a rapidly growing city and we are planning on a large scale for this future growth.[74] It threatens to swallow up some of the best agricultural land that we possess. I hope this will be avoided.[75]

15. One question that worries almost every householder today is the question of prices. Wholesale prices have gone up a little, though not very much; but retail prices often tend to shoot up. We have repeatedly said that we must control prices, and we are trying our utmost to do so. It may be possible to control wholesale prices. But it is exceedingly difficult to do so in regard to retail prices. Some method of controlled distribution may have to be devised, though it is exceedingly difficult to control the innumerable retailers. Cooperatives can certainly bring about a great change. We are making fairly good progress in the establishment of cooperatives in the rural areas. But, in regard to consumer cooperatives, not much has been done. Yet it should not be difficult to build up these consumer cooperatives.

16. The growth in the public sector, which is so important from our larger point of view, will affect wholesale prices. The private sector, although it is a necessary part of our Plan, has no such social outlook, and its main objective is rapid profit. If our public sector gradually controls our basic industries, it can exercise a strong influence on the private sector and prevent it from going astray.

17. It must be remembered that we run our public sector industries so as to make profits which will help in our Plans for investment. The old idea that a

73. The Land Acquisition (Amendment) Act of 12 September 1962.
74. Delhi's 20-year Master Plan, with an outlay of Rs 732 crores, approved on 1 September 1962.
75. See item 116.

45

public sector industry must be on a no-profit and no-loss basis is quite absurd. The Public Sector is not only good in itself, but it should be considered as a nucleus and starting point of the development of a socialist economy. It should gradually lessen and remove the existing concentrations of private economic power. If it becomes subservient to these concentrations of economic power, then it has lost its function.

18. Foreign exchange difficulties encompass us, and a great part of this foreign exchange is required for spares and accessories and maintenance of our existing industries, especially in the private sector. Why should not these spares and accessories be made in India? I think that we have the capacity to make almost everything. We should aim, therefore, at making these ourselves so as to reduce the need for foreign exchange. Meanwhile, of course, we have inevitably to cut down our imports. There has been a tendency to increase our private sector industries regardless of the future burden in the shape of foreign exchange that they might cast upon us.

19. There have been some amendments of our Constitution which, though relatively small, have a historic significance. The 288-year old French rule over Pondicherry has ended in law and this former French enclave has become fully a part of India.[76] So have Goa and the other Portuguese territories. The freedom of India is complete. We have no claims on other territories except insofar as there are some territories which have been occupied by other Powers.

20. I regret to say that our relations with Pakistan have worsened. There are constant incidents on our eastern border with Pakistan and those in authority in Pakistan talk constantly in terms of violence and war.[77] We have often repeated that we mean no ill for Pakistan. It is our conviction that India and Pakistan should be friendly nations cooperating [with] each other. We shall hold to that objective even though we have to take steps to protect our territory from attack and invasion.

21. A much more serious threat comes to us from China. Much has been said about this in Parliament and I shall not repeat it here. But the situation continues to be serious and the notes we get from the Chinese Government become progressively more strident and abusive. What this indicates it is difficult to say. But it seems to me obvious that we have to be on the alert and guard our country. At the same time, we have to be prepared for a long term of tension and possibly petty conflicts. That is presuming that there is no major conflict.[78]

76. See items 155 and 159.
77. See Ayub Khan's speech in Lahore on 15 August 1962, *Dawn*, 16 August 1962.
78. See section External Affairs, subsection on China.

22. An additional autonomous State of India is coming into existence with the amendment of our Constitution in regard to Nagaland.[79] This area has caused us many headaches, and I fear that our troubles are not over yet. But the step that we have taken is a right step and I feel that it will help us greatly in normalising that area and in convincing the people who live in Nagaland that they can live in freedom and dignity in the larger family of India.

23. We have decided to give a large measure of autonomy to all our Union territories. The present Bill that has been introduced in the Lok Sabha does not include two areas—the Andaman Islands and Delhi. These areas are at opposite

[POWER TO THE PEOPLE]

Babu ji . . .

**"Let there be another power crisis.
Then you people will also clamour for a
democratic set-up in the Capital!"**

(From *The Times of India*, 3 September 1962, p. 3)

---

79. The State of Nagaland Act of 4 September 1962. See also items 147 and 150.

poles. The Andaman Islands have to be dealt with separately because of its backwardness and other like reasons. Delhi, on the other hand, is an advanced area which will require special treatment. [80]

24. I am not writing to you about the rest of the world, troubled as it is. One of the saddest developments is the internal conflict in Algeria whose brave people sacrificed so greatly for their freedom.

25. There is one thing to which I should like to draw your special attention, that is, the question of exports. It is obvious that this is of the highest importance to us. Today we are exporting about 5½ per cent of our gross national product. If we raise this percentage to 6, we can achieve the target we have set for ourselves. I have no doubt that we can increase our exports adequately. We are trying to do our best to this end, and I should like your cooperation in this matter by removing the hurdles and bottlenecks of administrative procedures and particularly in simplifying sales tax on exports. I hope you will give thought to this matter and get it examined by your experts. If we do not succeed in increasing our exports to the minimum figure aimed at, our whole Plan will be in jeopardy.

26. Just when we are struggling with this export question comes a new blow from the European Common Market and the probability of the United Kingdom joining it. We are trying our best to maintain our exports to the United Kingdom and to increase them in the area of the European Common Market. But the outlook is not a very happy one.

Yours sincerely,
Jawaharlal Nehru

80. Nehru told a seven-member delegation of the Delhi Pradesh Congress Committee, which met him on 1 September 1962 to present the case for "an effective and popular set-up" in Delhi, that "there was no question of ignoring the aspirations of the people of Delhi for the grant of responsible government;" that the status of Delhi needed special attention of the Union Government, but those who wanted a change in the existing set-up "should think dispassionately without mixing up the question with the set-up in other Union Territories." Nehru, however, "did not seem sure what could be the most effective and suitable set-up for Delhi." *The Times of India*, 2 September 1962. See also item 118.

14. To Prabodh Chandra: Understand Context[81]

September 4, 1962

My dear Prabodh Chandra,

Your letter of September 2nd. Thank you for it. You will not expect me, I hope, to answer you in the somewhat metaphysical language that you have used.

I forget where I said that people were getting sick of me. It must have been a casual remark and then too, it probably was qualified by my saying that "some" people were getting sick of me because I was carrying on. I have got rather fed up recently by constant reference to my being ill. It almost showed that those who referred to it so often, want me to be ill and out of the picture. It was because of this that I might have said something like it. It had no other meaning.

There is no point in my giving assurances to people. Obviously I am functioning and working, and I propose to go on doing so so long as any strength is left to me. Naturally I get somewhat depressed occasionally. But even that becomes a reason for working and not for escaping from work.

So please do not worry about my casual statements.

Yours sincerely,
[Jawaharlal Nehru]

15. Arrangements during Nehru's Absence[82]

Note for Arrangements during Prime Minister's absence.

Both the Finance Minister[83] and I are leaving tonight and going abroad. I shall not return till the 1st October. The Finance Minister will probably return later. The Defence Minister[84] will also be going out of India within a week or so.

During my absence, Cabinet meetings should be held whenever necessary. The senior Minister present will preside over them. I presume that Shri Jagjivan Ram[85] will do so if he is present.

---

81. Letter to the Speaker of the Punjab Vidhan Sabha (Legislative Assembly), Chandigarh.
82. Note, 7 September 1962, for S.S. Khera, the Cabinet Secretary, and MEA Secretaries. MHA, File No. 14/51/62-Pub. I, p. 1/n.
83. Morarji Desai.
84. V.K. Krishna Menon.
85. The Minister of Transport and Communications.

I should like External Affairs Ministry to keep me informed by cable whenever necessary of important developments. They should keep in touch with the Home Minister, Shri Lal Bahadur Shastri. In regard to any important matter that may arise, they should consult the Home Minister and Shri T.T. Krishnamachari, Minister without Portfolio. I understand that normally both of them will be in Delhi, but in any event one of them will remain in Delhi.

16. In New Delhi: With Presspersons[86]

Question: We would like five minutes. You might care to say a few words, just to set the tone for the Conference.[87]

Question: Prominent leaders in Europe are already saying that the Economic Community will be a political alliance.

Jawaharlal Nehru: ECM, you mean? Well, the Treaty of Rome[88] says so; not now but at a later stage.

Question: The dangers of such a political alliance ... also threatened, they are democratic ... totalitarian.

Jawaharlal Nehru: There is the NATO alliance already.

Question: Sir, I wonder if you would care succinctly to say two or three lines for our quotation purposes as to what do we aim at this Conference, ECM and otherwise.

Question: Whether this would mean ...

Jawaharlal Nehru: We aim? We aim at protecting our interests, our economic interests, obviously, what more?

Question: If you can spell that out a little more, Sir.

---

86. Talk, 7 September 1962, at Palam Airport, before departure for London. NMML, AIR Tapes, TS No. 8436, NM No. 1662.
87. The Commonwealth Prime Ministers' Conference.
88. The treaty of 1957 establishing the EEC. See also item 322.

Jawaharlal Nehru: We are immediately concerned with our exports, that any arrangement there should not affect our exports, it should encourage them.

Question: The position of neutral countries in Europe, like Sweden, Switzerland, Austria …

Jawaharlal Nehru: I do not know. They will do what economically they consider profitable to them.

Question: Do you think, Sir, that the response of the Western countries to our complaints has been encouraging.

Jawaharlal Nehru: Which complaints?

Question: I mean complaints about trade representations, about trade problems?

Jawaharlal Nehru: They are all hard bargainers. [Laughter].

Question: Some of the British commentators have said that in the greater interest of the Commonwealth, that it will mark the beginning of the end of the Commonwealth; the ECM, the Common Market will mark the beginning of the end of the Commonwealth. What is your view on that?

Jawaharlal Nehru: Not exactly. I have said, I think it will weaken it; it will not form the end of it. Of course if other political alliances take place … that is the next step.

Question: The question of African Association is rather important and since you are going to Nigeria and Ghana, and also in London, are you likely to have any talks with African leaders, particularly as to what they intend to do about this?

Jawaharlal Nehru: I suppose I will have talks with them. They will be there. I will be meeting them frequently.

Question: I take it, Sir, that disarmament also is an important subject for the Conference.

Jawaharlal Nehru: It is the most important subject today but whether it will be discussed much, I do not know.

Question: Sir, do you feel that Britain is trying for greater safeguards for the White Commonwealth than for the other partners of the Commonwealth?

Jawaharlal Nehru: I do not know.

Question: Is there any other subject, Sir, you might be talking about with anyone, in Paris, take it up with General de Gaulle?[89]

Jawaharlal Nehru: No special subject, general subjects.

Question: Awfully sorry, Sir, to come from international to something very small and remote. Have you had a telephonic talk with C.B. Gupta[90] about this hoo-ha in UP about the land revenue?[91]

Jawaharlal Nehru: There is no hoo-ha in UP.

Question: There is, Sir. The Finance Minister is wanting to ...

Jawaharlal Nehru: Well, I do not know. There is something in *The Statesman* today.[92] That is all I can say. [Laughter].

Question: But did he come here, Sir?

Jawaharlal Nehru: No, he did not come. I spoke to him on the telephone and wanted to know why he did not come. His plane did not function properly or something.

Question: Are they postponing the Bill, Sir? Do you know anything about it?

A correspondent: It has to be announced in the Lok Sabha.

---

89. Charles de Gaulle, the French President.
90. The Chief Minister of UP.
91. There was much dissension within the UP Congress Legislature Party over the Land Holdings Tax Bill introduced in the State Assembly on 4 September. The Bill provided for a tax of 2½% on the capitalized value of land holdings with certain remissions. *The Statesman*, 10 August and 7 September 1962. See also Section Politics, subsection UP. See also items 191-194.
92. *The Statesman* reported that Kamlapati Tripathi, the Finance Minister of UP, had threatened resignation and C.B. Gupta had been summoned to Delhi to meet Nehru.

Question: Are you allowing, Sir, Mr Sukhadia to reconstitute his cabinet?

Jawaharlal Nehru: Who am I to allow or not allow? Who am I to allow or disallow? [93]

Question: Before you depart we are asking this question because of the difficulty of MIGs, because we do not want to debate in your absence. [Laughter].

Jawaharlal Nehru: That is a dead secret.

Question: Thank you very much, Sir. Bon voyage.

---

93. Mohanlal Sukhadia, the Chief Minister of Rajasthan, see item 178.

II. POLITICS

(a) Indian National Congress

17. To Raghunath Singh: David Munzni Wants to Join Congress[1]

July 24, 1962

My dear Raghunath Singh,

I had a visit this morning from Shri David Munzni, MP, from Bihar who until now has been a member of the Swatantra Party. He desires to join the Congress. I told him that he had better see you and then we shall consider his proposal in our Executive Committee. He should formally write on this subject. Probably we shall send his proposal to the Bihar Pradesh Congress Committee and the AICC before coming to any decision ourselves. We do not want to hustle in these matters as we are not desirous of pulling away members of other parties into the Congress. Also even if we agreed to take him, we shall do so on a provisional basis for some months and then finalise his membership later if all goes well.

He told me something about an attempt that is being made to have a joint party of the Opposition which the Swatantra Party and the Jan Sangh will join. Apparently, the lead has been taken by Bishan Chander Seth[2] of the Hindu Mahasabha. I enclose a brief note prepared by my office after my PPS[3] had met Shri David Munzni.

Yours sincerely,
[Jawaharlal Nehru]

---

1. Letter to the Secretary of the CPP.
2. Lok Sabha MP.
3. Kesho Ram.

18. To Purshotam Das: Hafiz Mohammed Ibrahim Festschrift[4]

July 24, 1962

Dear Shri Purshotam Das,
Your letter or the 24th July.

I think that Hafiz Mohammed Ibrahim[5] certainly deserves all our good wishes and felicitations on the occasion of his entering his 75th year. I am sorry, however, that I cannot agree to be a signatory to the appeal as I have expressed myself against the publication of these abhinandan granths.[6]

Yours sincerely,
[Jawaharlal Nehru]

19. For the *Congress Sandesh*[7]

I send my good wishes to the Kannada weekly *Congress Sandesh*. I wish it success in its work of spreading Congress ideas and programmes. It is necessary that people, and especially Congressmen, should not only have enthusiasm for the work they have to do but they should understand the ideas underlying it. If they understand this, they can explain it to others.

4. Letter to the President of the Organising Committee of the Hafiz Mohammed Ibrahim Abhinandan Granth Citizens' Committee, C-27 Nizamuddin West, Mathura Road, New Delhi.
5. Rajya Sabha MP and Union Minister of Power and Irrigation.
6. Felicitation volumes.
7. Message, 27 July 1962, for the journal's Independence Day number. Sent from Anand Bhavan, Allahabad. PMO, File No. 9/2/62-PMP, Vol. V, Sr. No. 42-A. Also available in the JN Collection.

20. To Prithvi Singh Azad: Meeting[8]

30 जुलाई, 1962

प्रिय पृथ्वी सिंह जी,

आपका 25 जुलाई का ख़त मुझे इलाहाबाद में मिला। मैं 30 तारीख़ को दिल्ली वापस आऊंगा। इसके बाद अगर दिल्ली आयें तो मुझ से मिलें।[9]

आपका
जवाहरलाल नेहरु

[Translation begins

30 July 1962

My dear Prithvi Singhji,

I received your letter of the 25th July in Allahabad. I shall return to Delhi on the 30th. If you come to Delhi after that, you can meet me.[10]

Yours sincerely,
Jawaharlal Nehru

Translation ends]

21. To Jagpat Dube: Remove Cause for Complaint[11]

July 30, 1962

Dear Jagpat,

I have received a letter in which certain complaints are made about you. Indeed, I have received two letters of this kind. One is from the Sabhapati of the Mandal Congress Committee, Purkhas, District Allahabad, and the other is from the Sabhapati of the Gram Sabha of Gaon Banthari. One of these is enclosed.

I can hardly believe that the complaint made is correct. In any event, any such impression created is bad, and you should try to remove it.

Yours sincerely,
Jawaharlal Nehru

8. Letter to an MLC in Punjab and a former Punjab Minister. Sent from Anand Bhavan, Allahabad. NMML, Prithvi Singh Azad Papers.
9. For an earlier reference, see SWJN/SS/73/item 39.
10. See fn 9 in this section.
11. Letter to political agent; address: Anand Bhavan, Allahabad. NMML, JN Papers – Jagpat Dube.

22. For the Youth Congress Day[12]

I send my good wishes on the occasion of the Youth Congress Day. Young men and women must feel that they are living in stirring times, both from the point of view of our country and of the world. All of us have many problems to face. This is natural in a period of great change and advance. We must develop the spirit of facing problems bravely and solving them.

The Congress had indicated its broad policies both in the world and in India. They are not based on sentimental desires but on clear thinking. I hope that young people understand this thinking behind our external policy as well as our internal policy. Internally we wish to work for a secular State where everyone has equal opportunity of progress, all religions are respected and none is specially favoured by the State at the expense of others. In the modern world, progress depends on scientific and technological advance and of course always on the hard work put in. We aim at a socialist structure of society.

I hope that young people will think all these matters out and discuss them among themselves and above all realise that the great adventure of living in the world today is before them and they must face it boldly.

23. At the CPP[13]

जवाहरलाल नेहरु: सबमें पहले, हमारे एक अज़ीज़ मैम्बर मौलवी हिफ़्ज़ुर रहमान का देहान्त हो गया है, अभी दो-तीन रोज़ हुए,[14] तो उसके लिए हम कुछ देर खड़े हो जायें, शोक का इज़हार करें।

राज्य सभा के एक सदस्य हैं श्री सुधीर घोष, उन्होंने कुछ दिन हुए दरख़्वास्त दी थी मैम्बरी की। वो एक स्वतंत्र मैम्बर हैं, इंडिपेन्डेंट। पहले शायद वो प्रजा सोशलिस्ट पार्टी में थे, बहुत दिन हुए, लेकिन शायद इलेक्शन के बाद से स्वतंत्र हैं। इलेक्शन तो उनका

12. Message, 2 August 1962, forwarded to Brij Mohan, President of Youth Congress and of the Delhi Pradesh Congress Committee. PMO, File No. 9/2/62-PMP, Vol. V, Sr. No. 54-A. Also available in the JN Collection.
13. Participation in meeting, 5 August 1962. NMML, AICC speeches, Tape No. 63 (ii).
14. Hifzur Rahman, Lok Sabha MP from Amroha, UP, died on 2 August 1962. Nehru paid his tributes to the "brave soldier and brave leader of the country" at a public meeting organized by the Jamiat ul-Ulema-i-Hind at the Parade Grounds. He had been secretary of the organization. See *National Herald*, 6 August 1962, p. 4. The public meeting seems to have been organized after this CPP meeting, for at the end of this sitting Nehru says: "Some of you may wish to go to the function arranged for Hifzur Rahman. It is being held in front of the mosque where Maulana Azad is buried. I think it is called Urdu Park …"

नहीं हुआ राज्य सभा में लेकिन उसके बाद स्वतंत्र हैं। तो पहले तो हमने उनसे कहा था कि कुछ दिन और ठहर जायें, क्योंकि अच्छा नहीं लगता और पार्टियों से लोगों को लेना। हालांकि वो पार्टी में नहीं थे किसी में, इस वक़्त। फिर हमने ए.आई.सी.सी. को और प्रदेश कमेटी को लिखा था, उन सभों ने मंज़ूर कर लिया तो एक्ज़ीक्यूटिव काउंसिल ने आज उनको मंज़ूर कर लिया है। आपकी सूचना के लिए आपको बताया।[15]

एक हमारा दस्तूर सा हो गया है कि पहले सभा में, हमारी मीटिंग पार्टी की, मैं कुछ आपसे कहूँ, चाहे वजह हो चाहे नहीं। समझा जाता है कि कुछ अरसा हुआ मिले को,[16] उसके बाद वाक़ियात हुए हैं, उसकी निस्बत मैं कुछ न कुछ कहूँ। तो कुछ ... अच्छा नहीं लगता बैठके, बड़ी सभा और बात होती है कुछ। तो इस ज़माने में ख़ास बातें, क्या हुई हैं ख़ास बातें, एं, ख़ास बातें क्या हुई हैं? हाँ, वो तो मुझे याद है और अलावा उसके क्या बातें हुई हैं। मैं चाइना, लद्दाख़ का दो-चार शब्द मैं कहूँगा, कुछ कल थोड़ा सा कहूँगा। असल में जो कुछ हुआ है उसके हमारे, जो पत्र-व्यवहार होता है, ख़तो-किताबत, वो सब छपता गया है। तो आपको अच्छी तरह से मालूम है, और ज़रा सख़्त होता है दोनों तरफ से, उनकी तरफ से शायद ज्यादा सख़्त होता है। अब वो कल मैं लोकसभा की मेज़ पे रखूँगा, आप सभों को मिल जायेगा।[17] एक पत्र है जो उसमें नहीं है, लेकिन मैं शायद उसे रखूँ, पिछला हमने भेजा है, हफ्ता भर हुआ। मुख़्तसर, उचित नहीं है कि लोकसभा के फौरन पहले। क्या आपको मिला है बाँटने को? हाँ वहाँ मिले थे, ठीक है। ये एक छोटा सा पैम्फ़्लेट है जिसमें वाक़ियात दिये हैं बहुत मुख़्तसर, सन् सैंतालीस से जब हम स्वतंत्र हुए, आज तक, चीन और हमारे रिश्ते में कोई ख़ास बात इसमें नहीं है, जमा कर दिया है सब सामने है। और एक नक़्शा है, बाद में, मुझे ठीक मालूम नहीं कि हमारे पास काफी है कि नहीं सभों को देने को, लेकिन कुछ तो है ही। ये मैं वहाँ लाइब्रेरी में कुछ रखवा दूँगा। राज्यसभा का क्यों हो, औरों का क्यों न हो, अच्छा, शायद हो जाये। वो, ... क्या रानीगंज, प्लानिंग एण्ड फ़ॉरेन असिस्टेंस, हाँ इत्ता में, इत्ता कह लूँ।

अक्सर मैं कोई बात कहता हूँ चलते-चलते वो दूसरे रोज़ एक हेडलाइन हो जाती है अख़बारों की। मैं एक रोज़ लिफ़्ट पे चढ़ने वाला था, एक अख़बार वाला खड़ा था, कहने लगा, क्या हाल है लद्दाख़ का। मैंने कहा सीरियस है, जागे रहना चाहिए। अब बस हेडलाइंस आ गई कि सीरियस है हाल।[18] सीरियस तो है ही, था, है और रहेगा सीरियस, उसमें तो कोई शक नहीं, लेकिन सीरियस के माने ये नहीं है कि कल वहाँ कोई एक क्राइसिस आ गयी है और भी बड़ी, यों तो है ही सीरियस। हमारी ज़मीन पे क़ब्ज़ा किये बैठे हैं, फ़ौजें

15. The website of the Rajya Sabha, accessed on 2 July 2018, mentions Sudhir Ghosh as Congress Member of the Rajya Sabha, from 3 April 1960 to 2 April 1966. See also SWJN/SS/77/item 25 and appendices 29 (a) and 29 (b).
16. On 2 July 1962, see SWJN/SS/77/item 34.
17. Nehru placed *White Paper No. 6* before the Lok Sabha on 6 August 1962. See item 401.
18. See item 1, fn 4.

एक-दूसरे का सामना करती हैं तो सीरियस है, है ही, लेकिन इस माने में मैंने सीरियस नहीं कहा था उस वक़्त कि मैं समझता था कुछ नयी बात हो जायेगी। अब वही हालत है कि हल्के-हल्के हमने अपनी ताक़त बढ़ायी है। ये सही नहीं है, बाज़ लोग कहते हैं कि हमने ताक़त, मैं कहूँ कि बढ़ा ली है हमने कि चीन से बहुत बढ़ गयी है ताक़त, लेकिन हमारी जित्ती पहले थी उससे बढ़ गयी है और बहुत सारे हमारे चेक पोस्ट्स बन गये हैं जिसको बग़ैर हटाये, बग़ैर उनका मुक़ाबला किये कोई आगे नहीं बढ़ सकता ज़्यादा, कहीं इधर-उधर थोड़ा सा हो जाए वो और बात है। ये बात हुई है, लेकिन अभी तक मामला बड़ा मुश्किल है, कठिन है, उनकी फ़ौजें हैं, उनके पीछे मैदान है जिसमें लॉरीज़, बसेज़ चल रही हैं, सामान ढोके ला सकती हैं। हमें हज़ार पहाड़ पार करके वहाँ पहुँचना पड़ता है, या हवाई जहाज़ से पहुँचें। ये है।

अब मेरा ख़्याल है, उसको मैं कोई सबूत नहीं दे सकता, न मुझे ख़ुद पक्का इत्मीनान है कि बात बढ़के कोई बड़ी लड़ाई के पैमाने पे नहीं होगी, कम से कम बिलफ़ेल नज़र नहीं आती है। क्योंकि हम अपनी तरफ से लड़ाई शुरू नहीं करेंगे जिसका नतीजा बहुत दूर तक जाये, और मालूम नहीं कब ख़त्म हो, क्या हो, और मालूम होता है कि वो भी कुछ ज़्यादा लड़ाई के शौकीन नहीं हैं इस मामले में। लेकिन इसकी बात नहीं है कि हम कोई इस बात से राज़ी हो जायें या समझौता करें कि वो क़ाबिज़ रहें हमारी ज़मीन पर। वो कहते हैं कि उनकी ज़मीन है, हम कहते हैं हमारी है, कुछ वाक़ियात हैं उनको भी रोकते हैं, उनके मुल्क की हालत क्या है, दिक़्क़तें पेश हैं। कुछ हमारे मुक़ाबले से वो बदनाम काफ़ी हो गये हैं एशिया में, और और जगह भी, यानी ऐसे मुल्कों में जिनकी उन्होंने बहुत कोशिश की दोस्ती लेने की। तो ये हालत है।

ज़ाहिर है हमें अपनी ताक़त बढ़ानी चाहिए वहाँ और उससे भी ज़्यादा मुल्क में। मुल्क में ताक़त बढ़ाने के माने हो जाते हैं प्लानिंग वग़ैरह का बढ़ाना। इसपे काफ़ी विचार हो रहा है, हुआ है, आप भी जानते हैं। किसी क़दर आसान हैं बड़े-बड़े कारख़ाने खड़े कर देने। आसान नहीं है, पैसे की ज़रूरत है, सामान की, वग़ैरह, लेकिन है। लेकिन रोज़ बरोज़ ज़्यादा हमारा ध्यान जाता है खेती वग़ैरह पर, एग्रीकल्चर पर, क्योंकि उसमें कमी हो तब सारी हमारा इंडस्ट्रियल इमारत जो हम खड़ी करें वो कमज़ोर पड़ जाती है, बाक़ी भी। और हम तरक़्क़ी कर रहे हैं, कोई शक नहीं इसमें, और मुझे पूरा इत्मीनान है, जैसे कि हमारे मिनिस्टर एस.के. पाटिल[19] ने कहा है कि तीसरे प्लान के अंत तक हम काफ़ी पैदा करेंगे खाने-पीने का सामान।[20] लेकिन फिर भी मुझे इसकी फ़िक्र होती है कि जित्ती तरक़्क़ी मैं चाहता हूँ नहीं होती। जित्ती हो सकती है वो होती है यानी इस माने में कि हम नहर खोदते हैं, नहर बनायी कहीं, पानी ले गये, अब वो नहर गाँव में नहीं जाती, वो नहर का पानी गया और बह जाता है, क्यों? पुराने ज़माने में दस्तूर था कि गाँव के चैनल्स थे वो गाँव वाले खोदते थे, अब कहाँ हज़ारों-लाखों चैनल्स सरकार के लोगों की तरफ से खोदे जायें। अब

19. Minister for Food and Agriculture.
20. The Third Five Year Plan covered the period 1961-1966.

वो कुछ इत्ते, ऐसी आदत उन्हें हो गई कि हर बात सरकार की तरफ से हो, और पानी बह जाता है, पानी नहीं लेते, पानी नहीं लेते, उससे इरीगेशन नहीं होता, इरीगेशन नहीं होता, बढ़ता नहीं। ये दिक़्क़तें हैं यानी गाँव वालों को ख़ुद ज़िम्मेदार होना चाहिए अपना काम करने के लिए, चैनल्स वग़ैरह खोदने के लिए, लेकिन मुझे पूरी उम्मीद है फिर भी ये बढ़ेगा।

प्लानिंग का मैं आपसे और क्या कहूँ? क्योंकि प्लानिंग तो आमतौर से लोगों के ख़्याल में होता है कि कारख़ाना बन जाये या कोई और नयी बात कहीं हो, किस प्रान्त में हो वग़ैरह, वो तो नतीजा है प्लानिंग का। प्लानिंग तो ख़ाली ये नहीं है कि बस चीज़ें बना दें हम। प्लानिंग का अगर पूरीतौर से समझें तो वो एक इमारत है जिसके बहुत मंज़िल हैं और अगर आप ऊपर की मंज़िल बनाइये बग़ैर नीचे की, वो रहेगी नहीं, वो गिर जायेगी, बुनियाद उसकी डालनी होती है मज़बूत, उसके ऊपर हल्के-हल्के बनता है। तो बुनियाद तो हमने मज़बूत डाल दी और बन भी रहा है। मैं चाहता हूँ कि इस दौरान में कुछ, आप लोगों में कुछ काग़ज़ात, कुछ जो और लोगों ने लिखे हैं इस पर, जिससे कुछ आप समझें हमारी प्लानिंग का नक्शा वग़ैरह, तो वो बाँटें मैम्बरान में। जहाँ तक बन पड़ेगा मैं उसको, मैं कुछ लिखवा रहा हूँ, तैयार होने पे बाँटूंगा। एक और काग़ज़ मैं आपको बाँटने वाला हूँ, एक स्पीच भी है जो प्रोफ़ेसर महालानोबिस ने वियना में दी थी, उसमें उन्होंने कुछ दिखाया है, एक साइंटिस्ट की तरह से इस सवाल को देखा है, क्या जरूरत है उसमें साइंस के ज़रिये और टेक्नोलोजी वग़ैरह की। वह भी, शायद आपको उसमें दिलचस्पी हो।[21]

एक बात मैं कहना चाहता हूँ, कुछ ख़ासकर दिनकर जी[22] को देखके मुझे याद आ गयी कि शिकायत है कुछ हिन्दी की। अब मैं कोई, मैं इसमें कोई ख़ास राय नहीं दे सकता तो क्योंकि मैं बहुत कम ए.आई.आर. को सुना करता हूँ क्योंकि मुझे वक़्त ही नहीं मिलता। मुझे पता नहीं, पहले कहते तो क्या आप कहते। मैंने एक शिकायत जरूर की थी कि जो सवाल के जवाबों में लोकसभा में हिन्दी का प्रयोग होता था वो अक्सर मुझे बहुत कठिन और ऐसी जो समझ में न आये, शब्द होते थे। मैंने कहा था उसको ज़रा सादा करना, क्योंकि मेरी राय ये है अलावा इसके कि हिन्दी को हम तेज़ी से बढ़ाना चाहते हैं आम लोगों में जो बहुत पढ़े-लिखे नहीं हैं। तो उसको सादा करके कर सकते हैं, सादी भाषा हो। अब, हाँ, साहित्य में वो लिखी जाये वो कैसी हो, वो दूसरी बात है, लेकिन ऐसे आम सहज भाषा हो ये मैंने कहा था।

और मुझे मालूम नहीं, क्या शिकायतें आती हैं क्योंकि उसमें उर्दू, फ़ारसी लफ़्ज़ ज्यादा आ गये हैं, शब्द, मुझे तो पता नहीं। जब मैंने कुछ सुना ये तो मैंने लिखा कि मैंने शिकायत सुनी है, आप इसपे विचार कर लें और अगर एक तरफ से कठिन थी, दूसरी तरफ से कठिन कर दी जाये तो मुनासिब नहीं है। और ये बात एक ऐसी है कोई बहुत बहस की नहीं बल्कि आपस में मश्वरा करके, सलाह करके हो सकता है किसी से ग़लती हो। अब

---

21. For the speeches by P.C. Mahalanobis, Member, Planning Commission, and Statistical Adviser to the Cabinet, GOI, at an international conference in Vienna in July 1962, see appendices 16-17.
22. Ramdhari Sinha Dinkar, Rajya Sabha MP from Bihar.

दिनकर जी हैं वो ख़ुद जाके अपनी सलाह दें, उनकी सलाह का असर होगा उन पर, या और लोग ऐसे हैं। इस तरह से हम उसको निकाल लें, हल्के-हल्के बन रही है, ढल रही है ऐसे कामों की भाषा। उसमें कोई गोपाल रेड्डी जी[23] ख़ुद कुछ बंगला भी जानते हैं और कुछ हिन्दी भी जानते हैं क्योंकि शांतिनिकेतन में पढ़े हुए हैं। उनके साथ लाला शामनाथ जी[24] हैं वो उर्दू ज्यादा जानते हैं। हो सकता है उनपे कुछ असर हो उर्दू की तरफ, लेकिन कोई किसी को ज़िद तो नहीं है किसी तरफ जाने की, सब अपने कोशिश करते हैं। तो उनको सलाह दी जाये, मश्वरा किया जाये, आप उसपे सलाह करके जो बात ग़लत हो हटा दी जाये, जो सही हो रखी जाये।[25]

तो अब इस सेशन में थोड़े ही दिन हैं, मालूम नहीं कब तक है। कब तक रखा है तुमने? सात तारीख़ तक रखा है, शायद सात के एक-दो दिन पहले मुझे चला जाना पड़े लंदन।

सत्यनारायण सिन्हा:[26] यों तो हमने इक्तीस तक रखा है, उम्मीद है कि चार-पाँच तक ख़त्म हो जायेगा, कुछ बढ़ जाये तो बढ़ जाये।

जवाहरलाल नेहरु: मैं छः को जाऊँगा शायद। इसमें, अलावा और बिल्स के, एक बहुत दिन से जिसका हम इंतज़ार कर रहे थे वो भी आपके सामने आयेगा, वो पांडिचेरी के बारे में। ...
आइये दिनकर जी।
क्या खाने-पीने का मेरे लिए कुछ नहीं रखा?

रामधारी सिंह दिनकर: पूज्यवर पंडितजी, भाइयों और बहनों, रेडियो के बारे में मैं प्रश्न उठाना चाहता था।...

जवाहरलाल नेहरु: जैसा कि आप चाहते हैं कि इस मसले पर बहस हो, क्योंकि बुनियादी तौर से इसपे कोई दो राय नहीं हैं। कहीं नाराज़गी हो जाती है किसी ख़ास शब्द पर कि ये आया था, ग़लत आया था, सही आया, लेकिन जो हमारी है, जिस ढंग से हम देखना चाहते हैं उसमें कोई दो राय नहीं है। यानी कि ऐसी जगह जैसे ए.आई.आर. है वहाँ सरल भाषा हो। अब बहस की बात है, सरल भाषा के मायने नहीं हैं कि एक कठिन शब्द निकाल के दूसरा कठिन शब्द रख दिया या ये माने नहीं हैं जैसे दिनकर जी ने कहा कि एक भाषा की एक जीनियस होती है, उसके ख़िलाफ़ ठूँस दिया, वो तो गड़बड़ हो जाता है। तो अगर आप चाहें तो हम एक प्रस्ताव कर दें कि हमारी राय में भाषा ए.आई.आर. की, और कहीं की जहाँ तक हो सके सरल होनी चाहिए और इस बारे में उनको सलाह दे

23. B. Gopala Reddy, Minister for Information and Broadcasting.
24. Deputy Minister for Information and Broadcasting.
25. On the simple Hindi question, see items 285, 287-288 and appendices 14 and 18.
26. Minister for Parliamentary Affairs.

दें, मिनिस्टर को, कि वो एक सलाह लेने के लिए अपनी एक कमेटी बना लें और उनसे सलाह-मश्विरा करके अमल करें।

एक सदस्यः कमेटी का अभी नाम तय कर दें।

जवाहरलाल नेहरुः नहीं कमेटी का नाम, हम उन्हें सलाह बता देंगे, उन्हीं को बनाने दीजिए। यहाँ से हम कमेटी बनाते हैं तो उनकी कमेटी नहीं होती है। एक बात मैं आपसे कहूँ कि असल में मामूली बोलचाल के शब्द मैं समझता हूँ अधिक से अधिक पाँच हज़ार होंगे। पाँच हज़ार से, बहुत लोग जानते भी नहीं पाँच हज़ार से ज़्यादा शायद। एं, हाँ। अगर उनको निकाल दें आप, ख़ासतौर से जो टेक्नीकल शब्द कहलाते हैं, बड़ी-बड़ी डिक्शनरीज़ निकली हैं टेक्नीकल शब्दों की, कोश निकले हैं मोटे-मोटे, उनको निकाल दीजिए। तो और मैंने एजूकेशन मिनिस्ट्री से कहा कि पाँच हज़ार शब्दों का एक कोश तैयार करें, उसमें चाहे दो शब्द लिख दें किसी एक के, जल, पानी वग़ैरह, ये और बात है, जो आम हों, सरल शब्द जहाँ तक हों, वो निकालें। अब वो पाँच हज़ार, हम पक्की तौर से सिक्का लगा दें हरेक को जानने चाहिये। उसके बाद जो पर निकाल के उड़ा चाहता है और तरफ़ वो उड़े, यानी पाँच हज़ार जानने चाहिये उसे। उन्होंने कहा कि पंजहज़ारी[27] ... तो उन्होंने कहा है कि इस साल के आख़ीर तक शायद तैयार हो जाये। तो ... उनसे कह दिया वो ख़ुद बनायें, ज़्यादा अच्छा है, वो उनकी होगी बजाय इसके कि सौंपे उनको कोई कमेटी। बनी है? मैं तो समझता हूँ नहीं है ... उनको बनाने दीजिए। हाँ, हाँ आप जाके प्राईवेटली सलाह देने के लिए उन्हें बता दें वो और बात है। ...

तो, अगर आप मंज़ूर करें तो जलसा, अब, क्योंकि छः बजे मीटिंग है उनकी, हिफ़्ज़ुर रहमान साहब के सिलसिले में, वहाँ शायद कुछ लोग जाना चाहें, वो जहाँ मौलाना आज़ाद[28] का वो है, दफ़न हुए वो जहाँ, उसी के आस-पास मस्जिद के सामने, उर्दू पार्क कहलाता है शायद। ...

एक सदस्यः सेठ अचलसिंह जी[29] को आज धन्यवाद है, उन्होंने दालमोठ और पेठा आगरे का खिलाया, लेकिन तादाद उसकी कम थी थोड़ा। ...

[Translation begins

Jawaharlal Nehru: Firstly, one of our dear colleagues and Member, Maulvi Hifzur Rahman, passed away two to three days ago.[30] Let us stand up as a mark of respect.

27. Raghbir Singh Panjhazari, Rajya Sabha MP from Punjab.
28. Abul Kalam Azad.
29. Lok Sabha MP from Agra, UP.
30. See fn 14 in this section.

Sudhir Ghosh, Independent member of the Rajya Sabha has applied to be enrolled as a Member. I think he was in the Praja Socialist Party a long time back. But after the election he is Independent. I had asked him to wait for some time because it is not a good thing to take in people who had belonged to other parties though he does not belong to any Party just now. Then we wrote to the AICC and the PCC who accepted his application. So today the Executive Council has also approved. I am telling you this for your information.[31]

It has become a tradition for me to say something at our first meeting, whether there is reason or not. It is felt that I should say something about the events that may have occurred in the interval since we had met earlier.[32] So, what are the important things that have happened in this period? [...] Apart from that, what else has happened? I will say a few words about Ladakh and China tomorrow. Actually, whatever exchanges there have been, letters etc., have been published, so you are well aware of them. There have been strong words on both sides, perhaps more from their side. I will place these documents on the table of the House tomorrow and you will get it.[33] I may place one more which has not been printed the one that we have sent them last week. It is not proper to show it just before the Lok Sabha meets. What? You have got it? Oh, you got it there? Alright. This is a small pamphlet which traces the relations between China and India from 1947 when we became independent till today. It does not contain anything special. All the facts have been put together and a map is appended. I don't know if there are enough copies for everyone but some are available. I will have them placed in the Library. Why should Rajya Sabha have it and not the others? Yes, perhaps, what about Raniganj? Planning and foreign assistance. Yes, let me say this much.

Often I find that even a casual remark of mine hits the headlines of newspapers the next day. One day I was about to go up in the lift when a newspaper man who was standing there asked me, "What is the situation in Ladakh?" I said, "It is serious. We should be alert." Next day there were headlines saying the situation is serious.[34] Obviously it is serious and it will remain so. There is no doubt about that. But that does not mean that there is going to be a big crisis tomorrow. They are in possession of our territories and the troops are poised there facing one another and so the situation is serious. But I did not use the word serious to mean that I thought some fresh crisis was imminent. The same thing happened when I said we have increased our

31. See fn 15 in this section.
32. See fn 16 in this section.
33. See fn 17 in this section.
34. See fn 18 in this section.

[GETTING IT RIGHT]
You Said It
By LAXMAN

The situation was not dangerous though serious! It's a lot better now—it's not serious, though pretty dangerous!

(From *The Times of India*, 18 August 1962, p. 1)

strength there. That does not mean that it is more than that of the Chinese; our strength has increased in comparison with the earlier position and we have established many new check posts. No one can advance without first facing them. There may be some advance, that is a different matter. But the matter is very complicated. They have the plains behind them, where the movement of troops, lorries, buses and equipment can take place easily. We have to cross the mountainous terrain to reach there, or we go by planes. This is the position. I cannot produce any evidence but I am fully convinced that the matter will not escalate into a full-scale war. At least it does not look like it just now because we will not start a war which may carry on for a long time and have far reaching results and it does not seem as if they are very keen on fighting over this issue. But that does not mean that we will concede our territory to them. They claim that it is theirs and we say it is ours. But they are restrained by internal factors and some other difficulties. By having a confrontation with us they have acquired to some extent a bad reputation in Asia and elsewhere, in those countries which they tried very hard to befriend.

So this is the situation. It is obvious that we should increase our strength at the borders but, more important, in the whole country which means paying more attention to planning, etc. This matter is being given a great deal of thought, as you know. In a sense it is an easy matter to put up big factories, though, of course, we need money and material, etc. But increasingly our attention is turned towards agriculture because if there is shortfall in that area, our entire industrial structure will be weakened. We are no doubt making progress. I am fully convinced, as our Minister, Mr S.K. Patil,[35] pointed out, that by the end of the Third Plan[36] we would have made a great advance in food production. But I feel worried that the production does not increase as much as I want. Whatever is possible is being done. For instance, we build canals but the water does not reach the villages. It flows away and is wasted. Why? In the olden days, it was a tradition that the villagers would dig channels for irrigation. Now, it is not possible for the government to build hundreds of thousands of channels. The villagers have got into the bad habit of expecting the government to do everything. So the water is allowed to flow away and they do not utilize it for irrigation and the production does not increase. These are the difficulties. The villagers should shoulder the responsibility themselves and build channels, etc. But I have full hopes that the production will increase.

What more can I tell you about planning? People often think that planning merely means putting up a factory here, something else there, which state gets

35. See fn 19 in this section.
36. See fn 20 in this section.

what, etc. That is only a result of planning. Planning does not mean merely putting up things. If you want to understand the meaning of planning fully, it is like a structure which has many storeys and if you make the top storey without first making the first, it cannot stand, it will fall down. You have to lay a firm foundation and then build gradually on it. So now we have laid the foundation and are trying to build on it. I would like to have some literature on this subject distributed among the Members to help you understand the map of planning. I am trying to have something written on the subject and as soon as it is ready, I will have it distributed. I am also going to give you the speech made by Professor Mahalanobis in Vienna in which he has tried to look at the matter from the scientist's point of view, to analyse what we require for the scientific and technological development of the country. You may find this interesting.[37]

I want to say one more thing. I was reminded of it particularly by seeing Mr Dinkar[38] here. There is some complaint about Hindi. I cannot give any special opinion on this because I seldom listen to the AIR as I don't have the time. I don't know what you would have said if you had spoken before me. I have certainly made one complaint and that is that the Hindi used in the answers given to the Lok Sabha questions is very tough and full of difficult, incomprehensible words. I have suggested that the language should be simplified because if we want to propagate Hindi among the common people rapidly, we can do so only by simplifying it. What high-brow intellectuals write in the name of literature is a different matter. But the language commonly spoken should be simple. That is what I had suggested.

Then, there is a complaint that the Urdu and Persian words which have been incorporated into Hindi make it more difficult. I don't know how far it is so but I wrote back that if it is true, something should be done about it because it is not correct to simplify it one way and introduce other difficult words. This is not a matter for debate but something that should be tackled after mutual consultations. Shri Dinkar himself should be asked to give advice because that will carry weight with his colleagues and friends. This is how we can deal with the language problem. Mr Gopala Reddy[39] knows Bengali and Hindi because he has studied at Santiniketan. Lala Sham Nath[40] is more familiar with Urdu so there may be a bias towards Urdu. But there are no fixed rules in this. Everyone has to make an effort to rectify the faults that may creep into the language and keep whatever is right.[41]

37. See fn 21 in this section.
38. See fn 22 in this section.
39. See fn 23 in this section.
40. See fn 24 in this section.
41. See fn 25 in this section.

So this Session is only for a few days. I don't know when it will end. How long is the Session? [...]. So it is till the 7th [of September]. I may have to leave for London a day or two before the 7th.

Satya Narayan Sinha:[42] It was planned to close on the 31st [of August]. Now it is likely to be over by the 4th or 5th [of September]. It may extend slightly.

Jawaharlal Nehru: Perhaps I will leave on the 6th. Apart from other Bills, a long awaited Bill about Pondicherry will come up soon. [...]
Please come, Dinkarji.
What, you have not left anything for me to eat?

Ramdhari Sinha Dinkar: Respected Panditji, brothers and sisters, I wanted to ask a question about [All India] Radio. [...]

Jawaharlal Nehru: Basically, there can be no two opinions about this. There may be some differences of opinion about a particular word or two, but there can be no differences in our basic view point—for instance, that the language used by AIR should be simple. Similarly, it is not open to debate that simplifying does not mean substituting one difficult word by another, or, as Shri Dinkar pointed out, to force words into it which are against the genius of the language. So if you wish, we can pass a resolution that in our opinion the language used by AIR and elsewhere should, as far as possible, be simple and it can be suggested to the Minister that he can form a committee to advise him in the matter. [...]. What is he saying?

From the floor: He is saying that the members of the committee should be named now.

Jawaharlal Nehru: No, we will give our suggestion to him; let him form the committee. If we do so, it will not function as his committee. I would like to tell you that in actual practice, I don't think there would be more than 5,000 words used in language commonly spoken. Most people may not know even that many words. Eh? Yes, if you take away what are called technical words, which fill huge dictionaries. So I have suggested to the Education Ministry to prepare a dictionary of 5,000 simple, commonly used words, and, if they wish, they can also provide one simple synonym for each word. Once approved,

42. See fn 26 in this section.

everyone would be expected to understand them. After that, those who wish to be high flown can do so. But everyone must know those 5,000 words. They said Panjhazari[43] [...]. So they said that the dictionary may be ready by the end of this year ... We have told him to do it himself because that would be better than entrusting it to a committee. Is there a committee? ... I don't think so. Let him do it. Yes, yes, you can go and advise him privately, that is different.

So, if you agree, let us go. Some of you may wish to go to the function arranged for Hifzur Rahman. It is being held in front of the mosque where Maulana Azad[44] is buried. I think it is called Urdu Park ...

From the floor: Thanks to Seth Achal Singhji[45] who offered us dalmoth and petha from Agra. But the quantity was rather small. [...]

Translation ends]

24. To Joginder Nath Joshi: No Job for You[46]

August 8, 1962

Dear Shri Joshi,

I have your letter of the 7th August. I do not quite know how I can help you. I can offer you no post connected with Government, and I do not suppose you desire one. Any post connected with the Congress organisation would be decided upon by the Congress President or the AICC.

Please do not talk about "Save Nehru". Nehru does not require to be saved and it does not help anyone to talk in this way.[47]

Yours sincerely,
[Jawaharlal Nehru]

---

43. See fn 27 in this section.
44. See fn 28 in this section.
45. See fn 29 in this section.
46. Letter; address: Goraya, District Jullundur.
47. See also item 28.

25. To Mahavir Tyagi: Revamping the Congress[48]

August 8, 1962

My dear Mahavir,

Your letter of the 8th August.[49]

I entirely agree with your analysis of the situation. Many things that are done by Congressmen and by Congress Committees distress me greatly.

But your proposal to limit members of the Congress to certain categories does not appeal to me. The four-anna membership may not be good and might be changed. But limiting the membership largely to old people will make it lose significance and vitality. I think we have to find some other way.

As you have written to the Congress President,[50] he will no doubt consider your suggestions with his colleagues.

Yours affectionately,
Jawaharlal Nehru

26. To Arun Gandhi: Phoenix Settlement Trust[51]

August 10, 1962

My dear Arun,

Your letter of August 10.

I am glad to learn of the new arrangements which have been made for the Phoenix Settlement Trust. I am particularly glad that you have got well known Africans to join it.

As for the Gandhi Nidhi contributing anything to the Trust, I rather doubt if they can or will do so. They have very little left which is not allotted. However, you have written to them, and they will, no doubt, consider your letter.

I am afraid I cannot be a patron of the committee you suggest.

Yours affectionately,
[Jawaharlal Nehru]

---

48. Letter to Congress MP; address: 16 Dr Rajendra Prasad Road, New Delhi. NMML, Mahavir Tyagi Papers. Also available in the JN Collection.
49. Appendix 27.
50. D. Sanjivayya.
51. Letter to a grandson of Mahatma Gandhi, c/o *The Times of India*, Bombay. Arun Gandhi was at this time Information Officer, *The Times of India*, Bombay.

27. To N.M. Anwar: Tyagi's Resignation from CPP[52]

August 11, 1962

My dear Anwar,

I have your letter of the 9th August. I think that Shri Mahavir Tyagi's resignation from the Executive Committee for the reason that he gave, was perfectly correct and right.[53] At the same time, I feel that what you have written is also appropriate.[54]

But, in the circumstances, I do not think it will be right for Tyagiji to stand again for this election. It would have a bad effect and Tyagiji himself will, as he himself says, become rather an object of ridicule for a gesture. I showed your letter to Tyagiji. This is his opinion.

In the circumstances, I think his resignation should stand and he should not put himself up for election again. A Muslim member of our Party should stand for election. That would be in the interests both of the Party and of the larger causes we espouse.

Yours sincerely,
Jawaharlal Nehru

28. To Joginder Nath Joshi: Observing 2 October[55]

August 18, 1962

Dear Shri Joshi,

I have your letter of the 16th August.

I doubt very much if the appeal of an individual will result in a big scale response all over India. If much is to be done, the lead has to be taken by responsible organisations.

---

52. Letter to Congress MP; address: 43 Western Court, New Delhi.
53. *The Times of India* reported on 6 August 1962 that the CPP had at its meeting the previous day accepted the resignation of Mahavir Tyagi from the Executive Committee. Tyagi, a member of the executive for the last 15 years, "mentioned the absence of adequate representation of minorities on the executive as the principal reason for his resignation." Nehru suggested at the meeting that Tyagi "should be one of the permanent invitees to the meetings of the executive."
54. N.M. Anwar's letter has not been traced.
55. Letter; address: Goraya, District Jullundur.

October 2 is already observed as a special day all over India. I believe some organisations have already suggested that this should be a day of dedication. It has also been suggested that it should be a day against nuclear arms.[56]

Yours sincerely,
[Jawaharlal Nehru]

29. To K. Kamaraj: Tiruchengode Elections and Rise of DMK[57]

August 18, 1962

My dear Kamaraj,

The recent by-election at Tiruchengode has come as a mild shock to many of us.[58] The by-election need not be very important. But this does show a certain tendency which is objectionable. Some people tell me that the Congress candidate was not a good choice. Also that he did not work hard enough. But the fact remains that the DMK is slowly increasing its strength.

Soon the DMK people who have been put in jail will be coming out after their term is over. They will take advantage and pose as martyrs for their cause.[59] The question now is what policy we should adopt to meet this situation. Obviously we cannot allow it to drift, and some effective measures will have to be taken. What these should be will depend largely on your advice and the advice of your colleagues. I hope you will give thought to this matter and perhaps, sometime later, come to Delhi for a talk with us.

Yours sincerely,
[Jawaharlal Nehru]

---

56. See also item 24.
57. Letter to the Chief Minister of Madras State.
58. See item 7, fn 42.
59. A large number of DMK volunteers, including P. Sivasankaran, Lok Sabha MP, were arrested for violent protests in Madras on 19 July 1962 over the price rise. Sivasankaran was sentenced on 28 August 1962 to three months' imprisonment.

30. To Ganesha Singh Pakhtoon: No Offence to Majithia[60]

August 18, 1962

Dear Ganesha Singhji,

Your letter of the 17th August. Sardar Surjit Singh Majithia is a fine man and I have affection and respect for him. There is no question of our doing anything which should hurt him. But it is often necessary to change Ministers. Otherwise the same old Ministers must continue indefinitely. That involves no discourtesy.[61]

Yours sincerely,
[Jawaharlal Nehru]

31. To Virendra: Party Camp at Nangal[62]

August 25, 1962

Dear Virendra,

Your letter of August 24.

I was glad and pleased to learn of the proposal to hold a Camp of Ministers and Members of the Congress Party at Nangal. This is, indeed, a good idea. Most of us are so busy with our day to day problems that we seldom sit down to discuss the basic issues before us. The Camp you are having will help in such consideration provided it does not lose itself in minor matters.

I send my good wishes to the Camp.

Yours sincerely,
[Jawaharlal Nehru]

---

60. Letter to a freedom fighter; address: 2 Doctor's Lane, New Delhi.
61. S.S. Majithia, Deputy Minister for Defence, August 1952 to April 1962, was dropped from the Union Cabinet after the General Elections.
62. Letter to Punjab MLC, and editor of *Daily Pratap*, Jullundur.

32. To D. Sanjivayya: Complaint against Communists infiltrating Congress[63]

August 26, 1962

My dear Sanjivayya,

I enclose a letter I have received, as there is a reference to you in it.[64]

I do not know anything about Balraj Sahni[65] or about the meeting which was held by the Bombay Suburban District Congress Committee.

Yours sincerely,
Jawaharlal Nehru

33. For the Indian Youth Congress[66]

I send my good wishes to the Fifth All India Convention of the Indian Youth Congress to be held at Tirupathi. The youth of India may have some difficulties to face and sometimes even some frustrations may come in their way. But they should realise that they are living at a time when their own country and the world are changing fast. I am sure that India will be very different in another decade or two. To help in this building up of our dear country and serving our vast population is a mighty task which should enthuse our young men and women. Let them feel proud of being alive at this time of our country's history and let them take full part in the great adventure that lies before all of us. Thus they will make their lives worthwhile.

63. Letter to the Congress President. NMML, AICC Papers, File, OD-23 (D).
64. Appendix 46.
65. 1913-1973; film and stage actor, began his career with the Indian People's Theatre Association (IPTA) in Bombay.
66. Message, 30 August 1962, forwarded to Brij Mohan, President of Youth Congress and of the Delhi Pradesh Congress Committee, c/o the AICC, 7 Jantar Mantar Road, New Delhi.

34. To Mahavir Tyagi: Criticism Valid but Extreme[67]

September 1, 1962

My dear Mahavir,

Your letter of the 31st August.[68]

Some of the criticisms you have made are justified, but not quite, nor to the extent as you have made them. It is true that we are passing through a difficult period, and the rise in prices is a bad sign. The actual wholesale rise is not much. But some retailers put up prices exorbitantly. While this matter has to be considered fully and is being so considered, it is very difficult to deal with a vast number of retailers. The only real method is to have cooperative stores. I do not know why these are not started.

I do not agree with your criticism of the present Minister of Railways.[69] I think he is a competent and capable person. Nor do I think that the Ministry of Defence is being neglected. I have been in intimate touch with it and I feel that it has made considerable progress.

Yours affectionately,
Jawaharlal Nehru

35. To Raghunath Singh: CPP Executive Committee[70]

September 2, 1962

My dear Raghunath Singh,

Your letter of September 2nd. I suggested a meeting of the Executive Committee not for the linking of the sugarcane prices but for the other Bill which is coming up tomorrow.[71] Shri S.K. Patil[72] wanted a whip to be issued about it. I thought that if a whip has to be issued, this should be decided at a meeting of the Executive Committee.

Yours sincerely,
[Jawaharlal Nehru]

---

67. Letter to Congress MP; address: 16 Dr Rajendra Prasad Road, New Delhi. NMML, Mahavir Tyagi Papers. Also available in the JN Collection.
68. See appendix 56.
69. Swaran Singh.
70. Letter to the Secretary of the CPP.
71. The Land Acquisition (Amendment) Bill.
72. Minister of Food and Agriculture.

36. To Raghunath Singh: Executive and General Body of CPP[73]

September 3, 1962

My dear Raghunath Singh,

Your letter of September 3rd. I am afraid it is very difficult for me to go out to dinner. I am heavily occupied during the last few days here before I go abroad. If I go about to dinner, it takes too much time. Also, I eat very simple food and am prohibited from taking anything that is rich. So you must forgive me.

As for the General Body meeting, the only possible day is the 7th September. I shall be going that evening. But I can attend the meeting for some time. I do not think we shall be able to discuss all the matters you have mentioned in your letter.

The Executive Committee meeting can be held on the 7th September morning at about 10 or 10.15.

Yours sincerely,
[Jawaharlal Nehru]

37. In New Delhi: To the Conveners of Women's Sections in PCCs and DCCs[74]

सभानेत्री जी[75] और बहनो,

मैं यहाँ कोई ख़ास भाषण देने नहीं हाज़िर हुआ हूँ लेकिन आपकी कांफ्रेंस को अपनी शुभकामनाएँ देने। मैं तो अक्सर इधर-उधर बोला करता हूँ। जरूरत यह है कि आप जहाँ-जहाँ से आयी हैं अपने काम के निस्बत बातें करें, ख़ाली लम्बे-लम्बे स्पीचें देने से नहीं काम चलेगा। क्या दिक्क़तें हैं आपको, क्या आपकी राय में बात हमें करनी चाहिए, यह सब देखना है।

तो मैं ज्यादा नहीं कहूँगा, लेकिन मैं समझता हूँ कि हमारी बहनें जो कांग्रेस में काम करती हैं उनके ऊपर एक ख़ास ज़िम्मेदारी है। यह अफ़सोस की बात है कि अक्सर जगह कांग्रेस में दलबंदी, बड़ी ग़लत बात है, खेंचातानी है। कांग्रेस के मेम्बर बनाये जाते हैं, शिकायतें हमारे पास आती हैं, नकली बनाने वाले हैं। इस क़िस्म की बातें होती जायेंगी

73. Letter to Lok Sabha MP and Secretary of the CPP.
74. Speech, 3 September 1962, at Constitution Club, inaugurating the all-India convention of the conveners of women's sections in Pradesh and District Congress Committees. NMML, AIR Tapes, TS No. 11349, NM No. 1968.
75. Indira Gandhi.

तो वो कोई बेजान संस्था हो जाती है, उसमें जान नहीं रहती। तो मैं आपसे पहले तो कहूँगा कि आप इन बातों में न पड़ें, आप कांग्रेस की कमेटियों वग़ैरह में दलबंदी में न पड़ें, अलग रहें, अपना काम करें, क्योंकि जहाँ तक मैं जानता हूँ उसकी पूरी कोशिश होगी, हमारे कांग्रेस के अध्यक्ष[76] बैठे हैं यहाँ, वो भी पूरी कोशिश कर रहे हैं कि इन बातों को ख़त्म कर दिया जाये, क्योंकि हमारे सामने बड़े-बड़े काम हैं। जो आदमी दलबंदी में पड़ता है वो हमारे काम की हैसियत को कुछ समझता नहीं है। हम देश को, देश की समाज को बदलना चाहते हैं, देश को बढ़ाना चाहते हैं। जैसे हम स्वराज लाये, एक क्रांतिकारी बात हुई, वैसी ही समाज में क्रांति लाना चाहते हैं। बड़ी बातें हैं, इसको कोई एक छोटे दिल के आदमी नहीं ला सकते या बैठकर खेंचातानी करके — तुम इस दल में हो, उसमें हो, जो यह करता है वह छोटा आदमी होता है, वह बड़ा काम नहीं कर सकता है और जो छोटे आदमी होते हैं तो संस्था भी छोटी हो जाती है — तो यह बहुत ग़लत बात है। यह ज्यादा अच्छा है कि हमारे आदमी, थोड़े आदमी हों संस्था में, लेकिन पक्के हों और मज़बूती से काम करें, बजाय इसके कि ओहदे के लालची हों। तो पहली बात तो मैं आपसे यह कहना चाहता हूँ।

दूसरी बात, आजकल हमारे समाने बड़े-बड़े सवाल हैं। सारे सवालों का तो आपसे चर्चा नहीं करूँगा लेकिन आज़ादी के बाद सबमें बड़ा सवाल हमारा आर्थिक हुआ, सामाजिक हुआ, लोगों की तरक्की हो, देश की तरक्की हो, देश में अधिक धन पैदा हो और उस धन का बंटवारा काफी ठीक तौर से हो, ये सवाल हैं। इसीलिए ये पंचवर्षीय योजना वग़ैरह बने और उनका अच्छा असर हुआ है। जित्ता हम चाहते थे, जित्ती दूर तक ले जाना, उत्ता नहीं हुआ क्योंकि कोई जादू तो है नहीं। जित्ता देश मेहनत करता है उत्ता ही उसको मिलता है, नीति कुछ भी हो उसके पीछे मेहनत और एकता की जरूरत है। तो ये सवाल हैं।

अब उसमें कठिनाइयाँ पड़ती हैं। ये कठिनाइयाँ और ये सवाल एक बढ़ते हुए देश के होते हैं, जो बढ़ता है उसके नये सवाल उठते हैं। आजकल आपमें से अक्सर शिकायत करें कि चीज़ों के दाम बढ़ते हैं, बढ़ गये हैं। बात सही है और इस पर काफी ध्यान देना चाहिए आपको, हमको और उसकी रोकथाम करनी चाहिए। अब चीज़ों के दाम बढ़ते हैं, कुछ रोकथाम कोशिश करने से हो सकती है, क्या कहते हैं उसे "होलसेल क़ीमतों", "थोक", लेकिन ये काफी मुश्किल है कि लाखों करोड़ों जो छोटे-छोटे दुकानदार हैं उनको एक इस मामले में क़ाबू में लाया जाये। अगर क़ाबू में लाने की कोशिश हो तो फिर और दिक़्क़तें पेश आ जाती हैं। जो लोग क़ाबू में लाते हैं वही बेक़ाबू हो जाते हैं। तो दिक़्क़त है।

लेकिन एक बात मैं आपसे कहूँगा कि हमें कोशिश पूरी करनी चाहिए। एक बात जो हर जगह जो कामयाब हुई है वो कोऑपरेटिव स्टोर्स हों, सहकारी स्टोर्स हों जिसमें चाहे छोटे हों, चाहे बड़े हों। दिल्ली शहर में छोटे भी हो सकते हैं और हैं और बड़े भी हो सकते हैं जिसमें हरेक आदमी जाये। उसमें कोई गुंजाइश नहीं रहती दाम के बढ़ाने घटाने के, क्योंकि उसमें यह सवाल नहीं होता कि उसके मालिक को फ़ायदा हो जायेगा, वो फ़ायदा

76. D. Sanjivayya.

76

बंट जाता है सब उसके। तो मैं आपसे कहूँ कि इधर आप ख़ासतौर से ध्यान दें, सारे देश में कोऑपरेटिव स्टोर्स की तरफ, ऐसे बने कन्न्यूमर्स स्टोर्स, हर चीज़ मिले। और मुल्कों में बड़े-बड़े हैं, यहाँ क्यों नहीं बढ़े, मेरी समझ में नहीं आता। हम बड़ी कोशिश कर रहे हैं गाँव में, देहात में सहकारी संघ बनाने की। बहुत अच्छी बात है और अच्छा बढ़ रहा है लेकिन शहरों में विशेषकर कोई इसकी ख़ास कोशिश नहीं हुई। हालांकि शहरों में आसान होना चाहिए, कोई दिक्क़त नहीं, ज़रा भी कुछ लोग तवज्जो दें और मुझे हैरत होती है, आश्चर्य होता है कि इधर ध्यान नहीं दिया जाता, सीधी सी बात है जिसका फौरन आपको लाभ होता है। और अगर काफी ऐसे स्टोर्स हों तो उसका असर मामूली दुकानदारों पर पड़ जाता है, फिर वो नहीं बढ़ा सकते हैं। दूसरी जगह एक चीज़ अच्छी, सस्ती मिलती है तो वो नहीं ज्यादा बढ़ा सकते। इसके माने नहीं हैं कि हम छोटे दुकानदारों को निकाल दें, लेकिन उन पर एक दबाव पड़े एक जिससे वो, जिसकी वजह से वो बढ़ा नहीं सकें दाम। क्योंकि अक्सर थोक की क़ीमत बहुत ज्यादा नहीं होती, कुछ बढ़ी ज़रा हो, लेकिन दुकानदारों के पास जब आती है मालूम नहीं लोगों को बेचने के लिए तो बहुत बढ़ा देते हैं। एक आने, फ़र्ज़ कीजिए एक आना किसी चीज़ का टैक्स बढ़ा, उसकी क़ीमत वो छः आने बढ़ा देंगे, फ़ायदा उठायेंगे। इन बातों को रोकने के लिए कुछ उपाय हो सकते हैं, पेचीदा हैं तो उस पर तो विचार होगा, लेकिन सबमें सीधा जो है, वो जो मैंने आपसे कहा कोऑपरेटिव स्टोर्स, सहकारी स्टोर्स हों, जो कि कोई भी बना सकता है, दस-बीस-पचास आदमी या हज़ार आदमी और बड़े शहरों में बड़े भी हो सकते हैं, छोटे भी हो सकते हैं। तो इधर आप जरूर ध्यान दीजिए, एक ठोस चीज़ है, ख़ासकर औरतें कर सकती हैं, हम भी कर सकते हैं और करें, लेकिन औरतों को ख़ास उधर ध्यान देना चाहिए क्योंकि उनको परेशानी है क़ीमतें बढ़ने की वजह से।

और आजकल आप देखें एक बहुत सारे सवाल हैं। एक सवाल जिसकी तरफ ख़ास ध्यान कांग्रेस ने और देश ने दिया है उसको नेशनल इन्टीग्रेशन कहते हैं यानी एकता का सवाल। अलग-अलग यानी जो हमारे मुल्क में दो ताक़तें हैं, एक ज़बरदस्त ताक़त है जो मुल्क को बांधती है, एक करती है, दूसरी ताक़तें हैं जो उसको टुकड़े-टुकड़े किया चाहती हैं जैसे साम्प्रदायिक ताक़तें, कम्यूनल ताक़तें, वो उसको कमज़ोर करती हैं, अलग-अलग खेंचती हैं। साम्प्रदायिकता है, प्रान्तीयता है, भाषा के ऊपर झगड़ने का है, ये सब बातें अलग-अलग करती हैं जिससे हमारे देश की तरक्की का, देश के तबाह होने का ख़तरा है। तो उसका मुक़ाबला हमें पूरा करना है ज़ोरों से। ये देश है हमारा, बहुत बड़ा देश है, अनेकता इसमें बहुत है, अच्छी बात है अनेकता, अनेकता में कोई ख़राबी नहीं है, कोई फ़र्क़ नहीं कि हम सब एकसे हों। एकसे कपड़े पहनें, एकसे खाना खायें, कोई बात नहीं, बड़े देश में फ़र्क़ होते हैं, लेकिन उस फ़र्क़ के पीछे एकता होनी चाहिए जो सभी को बांधती है, एक विचार होना चाहिए, हम सब एक बड़े परिवार में हैं और कोई ख़तरा है तो मिलकर उसका सामना करें। आपस में जो कुछ बहस है वो करें, लेकिन ख़तरे का सामना करें। इस ढंग से हमें इन बातों को देखना है और इसका मुक़ाबला करना है।

और मुझे अफ़सोस है कि हमारे कांग्रेस में भी ऐसी चीज़ें आ जाती हैं। चुनाव होते हैं तो कहीं-कहीं, हर जगह तो मैं नहीं जानता, अक्सर जगह जाति के ऊपर होते हैं, कास्ट के ऊपर होते हैं। यह बात तो बिल्कुल ग़लत है। देश में होना इसका ख़राबी है और कांग्रेस में आना उससे भी ज्यादा ख़राबी है। हम कांग्रेस को ख़राब कर रहे हैं, तबाह कर रहे हैं और हमारी इत्ती ऊँची संस्था को, जिसने देश में गांधीजी के नीचे रहकर उनसे सबक़ सीखकर बहुत कुछ काम किया देश को उठाने का, स्वराज हासिल किया, उसको हम गिराते हैं और एक दुर्बल कमज़ोर चीज़ कर देते हैं, जो जातिभेद में पड़े और और-और बातों में पड़े, साम्प्रदायिकता में। इसका मुक़ाबला करना है।

हमें याद रखना है कि हमारे देश में एक, एक बात आती है, धर्म। अक्सर धर्म हैं, अधिकतर हिन्दू धर्म है, हम उसका आदर करें, लेकिन और धर्म हैं, बड़े-बड़े धर्म हैं दुनिया के, इस्लाम है, ईसाई धर्म है, क्रिस्चीऐनिटी है, बौद्ध धर्म तो हमारे देश का है और जैन हैं, सिक्ख हैं, सब हमारे देश के धर्म हैं और सभी का हमें आदर करना है। यह कोई नई बात नहीं है, यह हमारे देश का तरीका रहा बहुत पुराना। उन्होंने, सम्राट अशोक ने दो हज़ार वर्ष से ऊपर पत्थरों में खोदकर यहाँ छोड़ दिया कि हरेक आदमी को दूसरे के धर्म का आदर करना। जो आदमी दूसरे के धर्म का आदर करता है उसके धर्म का और लोग आदर करते हैं, मोटी बात है, और यह हमारे देश की ख़ास संस्कृति रही है। लेकिन अब देश के नाम पर, धर्म के नाम पर लोग लड़ते हैं, लोग अनादर करते हैं, लोग कहते हैं कि जो लोग हमारे धर्म के नहीं हैं वे इस देश के नहीं हैं। ये कहाँ की बात है? वो तो महामूर्खता है। हमेशा मूर्खता थी और आजकल तो अधिक तौर से मूर्खता हो गयी है, जब दुनिया, एक हवाई जहाज़ हमें — चार-पाँच रोज़ में मैं जा रहा हूँ भारत के बाहर, वहाँ जा रहा हूँ इंग्लैंड, वहाँ एक प्रधानमंत्रियों की कांफ्रेंस है, सम्मेलन में, उसके बाद एक और जगह जाकर फिर वापिस आऊँगा। और मैं यहाँ से जाऊँगा, यहाँ से बारह बजे रात को और सुबह सवेरे ही नौ-दस बजे वहाँ पहुँच जाऊँगा मैं लंदन, जाने कितने मुल्कों को पार करके। आजकल इस तरह से सफ़र करते हैं और आप अख़बारों में, समाचार पत्रों में पढ़ते होंगे कि, ख़ासकर रूस और अमरीका में कैसे, उनको कहना हवाई जहाज़ तो ठीक नहीं है, एक बम के गोले से होते हैं जिसमें आदमी बैठकर भेज दिये जाते हैं बड़ी दूर, दुनिया के चारों तरफ घूमते हैं, सैंकड़ों मील बाहर दुनिया के, नयी-नयी बातें होती हैं, थोड़े दिन में चाँद पर आदमी जायेंगे, और जगह जायेंगे।

ये सारी दुनिया बदल रही है। अगर हम उसी के साथ ख़ुद बदलें नहीं और कुछ समझें नहीं क्या हो रहा है, हम एक मेंढक की तरह से कुएँ में पड़े हैं, कुएँ में पड़े रहें और समझें सारी दुनिया वह कुआँ है, वो, वो मूर्खता है, इससे काम नहीं चलेगा। तो हमें ज़रा आजकल की हालत समझनी है अपने देश की और दुनिया की और उसे बदलना है। क्या बात है कि और देश, अंग्रेज़ों का देश, जर्मनी, रूस का देश, फ्रांस है, अमरीका है, ये क्यों धनी देश हो गये, विचार करें, क्यों हम ग़रीब हो गये? माना कि इसमें अंग्रेज़ी राज में हम दबाये गये, हमें मौक़ा नहीं मिला, लेकिन वो काफी वजह नहीं है। हम ख़ुद ग़रीब और दुर्बल हो गये थे इसलिए अंग्रेज़ी राज आया। और इसलिए कि और दुनिया आँखें खोलकर

बढ़ रही थी आगे, नयी-नयी कलें निकालती थी, नयी-नयी मशीनें निकालती थी, नये-नये तरीके खेती करने के, नये-नये तरह के हल, ये सब निकलते आये, नयी-नयी शक्तियाँ, उससे वो धन पैदा करते गये, ज़मीन से निकाला, कारख़ाने से निकाला, वो उनको मिला और हम वहीं रहे समझकर कि हम तो बड़े लायक़ हैं, पहुँचे हुए हैं। हमने कुछ कोशिश नहीं की, दुनिया आगे बढ़ गई हम पीछे रहे।

और अब जो पंचवर्षीय योजना वग़ैरह है, उसमें आप देखते हैं हम कारख़ाने बनाते हैं, हम खेती में कुछ फ़र्क़ करते है, ये सब बातें तो हैं। लेकिन सबके पीछे बात यह है आदमियों को बनाना, आदमियों को, औरतों को बनाना, उनको ज़रा बदलना, उनकी ज़रा आँखें खोल देना आजकल की दुनिया की तरफ, और उनमें एक जिज्ञासा हो सीखने की क्या है ये, आगे बढ़ें वो और काम करें। असल में आदमी के बदलने से सब चीज़ें बदलती हैं, ख़ाली एक मकान खड़ा कर देने से, कारख़ाने खड़ा कर देने से तो कुछ ख़ास नहीं होता। तो यह बड़ा काम है, चालीस-पैंतालीस करोड़ आदमियों को बदलना है हमें और इसमें सबमें ज्यादा आप मदद कर सकती हैं। आप तो हर तरह की मदद कर सकती हैं, शिक्षा में माँए मदद कर सकती हैं, और बातों में।

ख़ैर, ये तो लम्बी-चौड़ी बातें हैं लेकिन मैं चाहता हूँ आप जानें इस समय जो हम जीवित हैं, ज़िन्दा हैं वो कैसा समय है? वो समय है क्रांति का, दुनिया में क्रांति हो रही है, दुनिया बदल रही है, हमारा देश बदल रहा है। ऐसे मौक़े पर जो लोग समझे हुए होते हैं क्या हो रहा है दुनिया को, देश को, और ठीक रास्ते पर चलते हैं, उनका असर होता है, और ख़ाली गुलशोर मचाने से, नारे उठाने से और समझने से इन बातों से तो कुछ होता नहीं। हमारा ध्येय क्या है? आपने सुना होगा, समाजवाद हमारा ध्येय है कि हम अपनी समाज को ऐसा बनायें, कुछ समाजवाद के सिद्धांतों पर चलें, उसके माने क्या हैं? उसके माने ये हैं कि हरेक पुरुष को, स्त्री को, बच्चे को बराबर का मौक़ा मिले। सब लोग एकसे तो नहीं होते, फ़र्क़ होता है लोगों में, कोई लम्बे हों, कोई छोटे हों, कोई अक़्लमंद हों, कोई मूर्ख हों, लेकिन सभी को बराबर का मौक़ा मिलना चाहिए। पुराने ज़माने में यह नहीं था, अब भी नहीं है। अब कुछ हल्के-हल्के हो रहा है। हम नहीं चाहते कि हमारी क्रांति में, सामाजिक क्रांति में बहुत या थोड़ी हिंसा हो, हमारा ये दस्तूर नहीं, हालांकि अफ़सोस की बात यह है कभी-कभी झगड़े होते हैं, जातिभेद के झगड़े होते हैं, अफ़सोस की बात है, लेकिन हमारा दस्तूर यह नहीं है, हमारे राज्य की नीति नहीं है। तो हम लाते हैं सब, समाजवाद यहाँ लाना चाहते हैं शांति के तरीकों से, सहयोग से।

ज़ाहिर है समाजवाद लाने में कुछ लोगों की, उसमें जो आजकल थोड़े से लोग हैं शायद उनकी कुछ हानि हो, वो लाभ उठाते हैं आजकल के समाज से, लेकिन अधिकतर लोगों का लाभ होगा और आख़िर में सभी का लाभ होगा। तो उसको हमें याद रखना चाहिए, हमें समझना चाहिए कि समाजवाद क्या चीज़ है। समाजवाद के माने ख़ाली नहीं हैं कि सब बराबर हो जायें, बराबर हम सभी को नहीं कर सकते, लम्बों को छोटे, सिर काटकर हम बराबर नहीं कर सकते। बराबरी के माने हैं कि हम काफी देश में धन पैदा करें और उसका बंटवारा ठीक तौर से कमोबेश हो। धन कैसे पैदा होता है? धन कोई

79

सरकारी ख़ज़ाने से तो नहीं आता, सरकारी ख़ज़ाने में तो लोग देते हैं, कर देते हैं, टैक्स देते हैं, लगान देते हैं, तब जमा होता है। धन तो पैदा होता है कोई चीज़ पैदा करने से, ज़मीन में किसान के पैदा करने से धन पैदा होता है, कारख़ाने में कुछ बनाने से पैदा होता है, कारीगर बनाये वो धन होता है, जित्ता अधिक कोई देश पैदा करता है उत्ता ही धन होता है। अमरीका बहुत धनी है इसलिए कि कारख़ानों की वजह से वह बहुत कमाता है, बहुत पैदा करता है, इसलिए धनी है। हमें भी करना है और इसीलिए पंचवर्षीय योजना है। हमें, अपने किसानों को विशेषकर अधिक पैदा करना है। कैसे अधिक पैदा करना है? ज्यादा समझें, अच्छी कलें हों उनके पास, अच्छे हल हों, अच्छी खाद दें, अच्छे बीज बनें, कोई इसमें जादू नहीं है, हम अपने खेती से जो पैदा होता है उसका दुगुना-चौगुना पैदा करें। तो इस तरह से समाजवाद आयेगा। ग़रीब मुल्क में समाजवाद नहीं होता है, गरीबों के समाजवाद के कोई माने नहीं। समाजवाद हो सकता है जब कुछ आमदनी हो, उसका बंटवारा हो, ख़ाली पेट का समाजवाद क्या, वो तो फ़ाक़ेमस्ती है।

तो ये सब हैं, पेचीदा बातें हैं, मैं आपसे इसके बारे में कुछ कहूँगा नहीं इस वक़्त, लेकिन यह याद रखिये कि हमारा ये ध्येय समाजवाद है। उसका एक, मैं आपको एक बता दूँ, मैं, उसके माने सब लोगों को बराबर का मौक़ा मिले तरक्की का, फिर उसकी जित्ती शक्ति हो बढ़े, सब लोगों को, पुरुष और स्त्री को एवं बच्चों को, काफ़ी बड़ी बात है करना। हम, पढ़ाई बहुत हमारी बढ़ रही है बच्चों की फिर भी अभी बहुत बाक़ी है। ख़ैर, शायद तीन-चार बरस में सब लोग स्कूल जायें, सब छोटे बच्चे थोड़े दिन के लिए, फिर हमें उसको बढ़ाना होगा उम्र में ताकि पूरा मौक़ा उन्हें मिले। इस वक़्त आप जानते हैं इसमें कोई शक नहीं है कि जो ख़ुशहाल लोग हैं ज़रा अमीर लोग हैं, उनके बच्चों की कहीं ज्यादा अच्छी देखभाल होती है बनिस्बत ग़रीबों के। यह बात ठीक नहीं है, सभी को मौक़ा मिलना चाहिए, फिर जितनी उनमें लियाक़त है करें। तो यह हमें करना है। इसको समझकर आप जाइये।

कोई बातें होती हैं, फ़र्ज़ कीजिये कोई चुनाव होता है, इलेक्शन होता है। इलेक्शन तो एक मौक़ा है हमारे लिए, वहाँ हम अपने सिद्धान्तों को बतायें, हम समाजवाद का समझायें, क्या करना है, लोगों को बतायें। ख़ाली हुल्लड़बाज़ी और गुलशोर, नारे उठाना और जाति का चर्चा करना यह ठीक नहीं है। अक्सर मैं देखता हूँ चुनाव वग़ैरह में जाके, इन बातों में लोग पड़ जाते हैं और असली बातें भूल जाते हैं। चुनाव में हारें या जीतें वो और बात है लेकिन चुनाव का मौक़ा है जब हम सब अपने सिद्धान्तों को समझायें, साम्प्रदायिकता का विरोध करें, जातिभेद का विरोध करें और समाजवाद को समझायें और एकता बढ़ाने की कोशिश करें, तो उससे फ़ायदा होगा। और मैंने देखा है जहाँ इस ढंग का प्रचार होता है उसका असर होता है और जहाँ ख़ाली छोटे दिमाग़, छोटे ढंग पर जाते हैं, छोटी बातें कहते हैं वो तो हमारे ख़िलाफ़ में वो भी कहता है। तो उमसें कुछ हम अलग नहीं हो जाते, हम इसी नीचे क़द के हो जाते हैं और कोई हममें फ़र्क़ नहीं। क्या हममें फ़र्क़ था? गांधीजी के ज़माने में फ़र्क़ था हर चीज़ का, जो सब लोग देखते थे, कुछ हमारी इज़्ज़त हर जगह होती थी और क्योंकि कांग्रेस वाले गिने जाते थे सच्चे लोग जो कि मेहनत करते हैं, काम

करते हैं, त्याग करते हैं, ईमानदार हैं, वो बात अब पूरीतौर से नहीं रही। अब हमें उस बात को लाना है फिर से और ज़ाहिर है शायद उस तरह का जोश एकदम से न पैदा हो सके सारे देश में, लेकिन फिर भी हमारे काम से हमारी तरफ लोग झुकेंगे, काम से झुकते हैं, चालबाज़ी से नहीं झुकते हैं और ईमानदारी से काम हो।

अब ये बातें जो कांग्रेस में ग़लत आ गयी हैं इसका बड़ा चर्चा आजकल होता है — नकली मेम्बर बनाना, बोगस मेम्बर बनाना। यह तो जो करते हैं वो बजाय कांग्रेस की सेवा करने के कांग्रेस में एक ख़ंजर भौंक देते हैं, वो मारते हैं और बड़ी हानि पहुँचाते हैं, आप समझ लें। जो आदमी यह बात करता है वो कांग्रेस का दुश्मन है, चाहे वो कुछ भी समझे कि मैं एक ईमानदारी से करता हूँ, वो कांग्रेस की दुश्मनी का काम करता है और कांग्रेस की हत्या करता है। बोगस मेम्बर बनाना और इस तरह से चालबाज़ी करना और जातिभेद में पड़ना, ज़ातपात पे ज़ोर देना, उसको हटाना है, हर सूरत से हटाना है, लड़कर हटाना है, नहीं तो देश की सेवा क्या करेंगे? अपनी, अपनी संस्था को शुद्ध नहीं रखे देश की सेवा क्या करेंगे?

यही चंद बातें मैं आपसे कहना चाहता हूँ। फिर मैं आपको दोहरा दूँ कि ज़रा आप लोग समझें, आप लोग यहाँ आये हैं, एक दो-तीन रोज़ कांफ्रेंस करेंगे, प्रस्ताव करेंगे, अच्छा है। लेकिन मैं कुछ चाहूँ कि आप लोग मुल्क के अलग-अलग जगह जो कुछ कहिए, केन्द्र कहिए, कैम्प कहिए, जो कुछ हो, वहाँ आप बैठकर कुछ सिखाने का तरीका निकालें कि आजकल के देश के सवाल क्या हैं, कांग्रेस के क्या सवाल हैं, दुनिया में क्या सवाल हैं बड़े-बड़े। तो आप देखिये हमारे सामने बड़े ख़तरे हैं, हमारी सरहद पर, सीमा पर हमले हैं, चीनी हमला है, पाकिस्तान से धमकी दी जाती है अक्सर। हम तो चाहते हैं दोस्ती से रहें और मुल्कों की, तो इसके माने नहीं हैं कि हमारे ऊपर लोग हमले किया करें। ये सब बातें हैं, इनको समझना चाहिए, तब देश का नक्शा कुछ सामने आता है और तब आप ठीकतौर से देश की सेवा कर सकेंगे, कीजिए।

और आख़िर में फिर से मैं आपको याद दिलाऊँगा कि सहकारी स्टोर्स, सहकारी संघ के स्टोर्स, ये मेरी राय में बहुत जरूरी हैं जो क़ीमतें बढ़ती हैं उनको क़ाबू में लाने के लिए।

जयहिन्द!

[Translation begins

Madam Chairman[77] and Sisters,
I am not here to give any special speech but only to give my good wishes to your conference. I often speak here and there. What is important is that you should all speak here about your work in the places that each one of you has come from. Nothing will be achieved by making long speeches. You should consider the difficulties you face and what in your opinion we should be doing.

---

77. See fn 75 in this section.

I will not say much. But I think that the women who work in the Congress have a special responsibility to shoulder. It is a matter of regret that in many places there is factionalism within the Congress; that is very wrong. There is constant pulling in different directions. We get complaints that members being enrolled into the Congress are bogus. If such things continue to happen, the institution will become lifeless. It will lose its energy. So first of all, I would like to tell you that you should stay away from such things and not encourage factionalism, keep aloof from such things and do your work. As far as I know, every effort will be made and the President of our Congress Party[78] who is sitting here is also trying his best to put an end to such tendencies because there are major challenges ahead of us. Those who indulge in factionalism fail to understand the importance of our work. We want to transform the country, society, and take it forward just as we brought Independence which was a revolutionary event. We wish to usher in a social revolution. These are major things. We cannot have narrow-minded people who pull in different directions or indulge in factionalism while handling the great tasks at hand. Having such people in the organization lowers its status. All this is very wrong. It would be far better that there are fewer members but those should be of calibre who are sincere and work hard instead of being greedy for positions. This is the first thing I wish to talk to you about.

Secondly, there are major tasks ahead of us. I will not talk about all of them but after Independence, the issues before us have been economic and social. The challenge before us is that the country should develop, more wealth should be produced and that wealth should be distributed equitably. So we have made Five Year Plans which are yielding good results. We have not gone as far ahead as we wished to for there is no magic wand after all. A country can get only as much as the people work. Whatever policy we may adopt, it has to be backed up by hard work and unity. So these are the issue before us.

Often difficulties crop up. But these difficulties are those that any developing nation faces. As it grows and develops, new issues crop up. Nowadays there are complaints about inflation. We must pay attention to this and together all of us should try to control rising prices. Inflation can be controlled by trying to keep wholesale prices down. But it is extremely difficult to control the hundreds and thousands of small shopkeepers in this matter. If we try to control them other difficulties crop up. Those who are supposed to control them are the ones who become out of control themselves. But I will say one thing, that is, we should make all attempts to do this.

78. See fn 76 in this section.

However, one thing that has succeeded everywhere is cooperative stores which cater to all classes of people. They can be set up in Delhi and in other places too, big and small. There is no possibility of increasing or lowering prices by them because it is not a question of more profit for owners. The profit is distributed equally among all stakeholders. So I would like you to pay special attention to setting up cooperative stores all over the country. All goods of daily necessity should be available there. Cooperatives have succeeded very well in other countries. I cannot understand why they are not developing in India. We are trying very hard to set up cooperative societies in the rural areas and it is a good thing that they are developing well. But there has been no special effort to do this in the cities, though if people were to pay attention it should be easier in the cities. Therefore, I am surprised that no attention is being paid to this. This is something straightforward which is directly beneficial. And if there are enough number of such stores then it has an impact on ordinary shopkeepers also. Then they cannot inflate the prices. After all, if the same thing is available cheaper in another place they cannot sell at higher prices. That does not mean eliminating the ordinary shopkeepers but it would put pressure on them, something which can prevent them from inflating prices; because often the wholesale rates are low but by the time the goods reach the shopkeepers, they hike up the prices. Imagine, for instance, that the tax is enhanced by one anna; they will raise the price by six annas to make a profit. There are ways of preventing this, but they are complicated and we will consider them. But the most straightforward is, as I mentioned, cooperative stores which can be set up by a few or many, ten, twenty or a thousand people. They can be set up in big cities as well as in the small ones. So you should definitely pay attention to this; it is something worthwhile which women can particularly do successfully. We can also do it and will do so, but women should pay special attention to this as they are affected by rising prices.

There are many issues before us. One issue which the Congress and the nation have paid special attention to is that of national integration, of unity. In India we have two forces, one, a tremendous force which binds the nation together, and the other, the force of fissiparous tendencies which can tear the country apart, the communal forces, for instance, that pull in different directions and weaken the country. Communalism, regionalism, linguistic divisions, all these are divisive forces which can bring the country's progress to naught and could ruin it. We have to combat these forces with all our might. Ours is a very large country. There is much diversity which is not bad in itself, diversity is good. There is no need for everyone to be alike, to wear the same clothes or eat the same food. There is bound to be diversity in a very large country. But behind that diversity should be unity which will keep everyone together. The feeling of belonging to one large family ought to prevail and the desire to face all dangers together. We can argue among ourselves but we should present a united front to any danger that threatens us. We have to look at these things in a particular way and face the challenges.

I am sorry to say that these fissiparous tendencies are visible in the Congress too. During elections in some places, I don't know if it happens everywhere, seats are often contested on the basis of caste. This is absolutely wrong. The caste system is pernicious in itself and for it to prevail in the Congress is even worse. We are bringing ruin upon a Party which has learnt under the tutelage of Gandhiji and worked for the uplift of the nation and acquired independence for it. And now we are making it a weak Party filled with casteism and communalism. We must combat this.

We must bear in mind that in our country, religion has played an important role. The majority religion is Hinduism, but there are other great religions, like Islam and Christianity; Buddhism is from India itself; then there are Jains, Sikhs; we must respect all religions. Tolerance is nothing new in India. Two thousand years ago, Emperor Ashoka had it engraved on stone that all religions should be respected and that those who treat other religions with respect beget respect for their own. This is pretty obvious and it has been the hall-mark of our culture. But now we fight in the name of religion, denigrate other religions, and say that those who do not belong to our religion are not Indian. This is the height of stupidity. It has always been a stupid thing to do but it is even more so in the present situation, when you can roam the world in a few days because of aero planes. I am going today to England where there is a Conference of Prime Ministers. After attending that, I will visit some other places and return. I will leave at midnight and will be in London by 9 or 10 in the morning flying over many countries. This is how people travel today. You may have also read in newspapers how, especially in the Soviet Union and the United States, people are being sent to outer space, not in aero planes but in some kind of missiles. All kinds of new inventions are taking place. Soon man will land on the moon and to other planets.

So the world is changing very rapidly and if we do not change with it, or do not grasp what is happening but continue to live like frogs in a well, that would be the height of stupidity. We must understand the present and change along with the rest of the world. Why is it that countries like England, the Soviet Union, France and the United States are all extremely wealthy? Just think about it, why have we become so poor? Agreed that we were exploited during British rule, and that we did not get opportunities, but that is not adequate reason for our poverty. We became poor and weak and so British rule was established. But it is because we became complacent, we thought we knew everything, while the rest of the world went ahead—new machines were invented, new methods of agriculture and new implements were adopted. With new sources of production, they began to produce vast wealth from the land, from industries, etc., and we lagged behind. We did not think we had to learn anything and so we made no effort.

Now, you will find that under the Five Year Plans we are setting up factories, new industries and increasing productivity from land. All this is going on. But behind all this is the need to mould and develop the human beings, men and women, to change their attitudes, to make them open their eyes a little to the outside world to see what is happening, to kindle their curiosity to learn new things. It is only then that they will progress and achieve something. As a matter of fact, everything changes when human beings change. It is no great achievement to build houses and factories, etc. The important thing is to change the attitudes of the forty to forty-five crores of people. And it is you who can help the most in doing this. You can help in every field. Mothers can help, educating the children and in other ways.

Well, anyhow, these are all long term plans. But I want you to understand the times that we live in today. These are revolutionary times. There is a revolution going on in the world; it is changing very rapidly and so is our country. In these times it is the people whose minds are attuned to what is going on in the world who can guide the nation on the right path and make an impact. Nothing can be achieved by merely making a noise, shouting slogans, etc. You must have heard what our goal is. Our goal is socialism, to build a socialistic pattern of society. We wish to adopt the principles of socialism. What does that mean? It means that every man, woman and child must get equal opportunity. Everybody is not exactly like one another, of course. There are differences in height, weight, intelligence, etc. But everyone must get equal opportunities. This was not so in the olden days and even now, it is not the case. We want to bring it about gradually. We do not want that there should be any violence in our social revolution because that is not our practice, though it is painful to see that there are feuds over caste differences. But in general it has not been our practice and it is not our state policy. So we want to usher in socialism by peaceful means, through cooperation.

It is obvious that in ushering in socialism, it is possible that a certain class of people may have to suffer losses, the class which has been exploiting society till now. But it will benefit the majority of people. And ultimately it will be beneficial for everyone. We must bear that in mind. We must understand what socialism means. Socialism does not mean merely that everyone is regarded as equal. We cannot make everyone equal physically, by cutting off the heads of the tall ones. Equality means that we should produce a great deal of wealth and ensure, as far as possible, equitable distribution of that wealth. How is wealth produced? Wealth is not to be found in the government treasury. Money comes into the treasury when people pay taxes. Wealth is generated through increasing productivity. What the farmer produces from land constitutes wealth. Goods produced in factories constitute wealth. Whatever an artisan produces is wealth. The more a country produces, the greater is the wealth generated. The United States is a very rich country because the production from its factories is enormous. We too must produce more wealth. That is why we have the Five Year Plans. Farmers especially must increase productivity from land. How can they do so? They should adopt new methods of agriculture, get new implements and tools, better ploughs, good seeds and fertilizers, etc. There is no magic trick in all this. We need to increase productivity from land, double or quadruple it. This is how we can usher in socialism. A poor country cannot have socialism. Poor people's socialism has no meaning. Socialism can be ushered in only when there is some wealth which can be equitably distributed. What meaning can the socialism of poverty have?

So these are all complex matters. I will not go into everything just now. But please remember that our goal is socialism, which means that everybody gets equal opportunities for progress. Then each individual can progress to the best of his or her ability. Every man, woman and child must get equal opportunity. This is a very big challenge. Education is spreading but much remains to be done. We hope that within three to four years every single child will be able to attend school at least for a few years. That will have to be taken further so that they get better opportunities. There is no doubt about it that at the moment, in the countries which are well off, the children are much better looked after than the children in poor countries. This is not right. Everybody should get equal opportunities so that each one can progress to the best of one's ability. We have to do this and I want you to understand this well.

Well, things happen. For instance, take elections. Elections are an opportunity for us to express the principles that we follow. We must explain about socialism and what needs to be done. Mere slogan-mongering and agitations or raising the issue of caste is not right. I find that people often get into these things during elections, forgetting the things that really matter. Winning and losing in elections is a different matter. But elections give an opportunity to explain our policies and principles to the people. We must oppose communalism and casteism and should talk about socialism and make an effort to promote unity among the people. That would be more useful. I have found that whenever such election propaganda is done, it makes an impact. And wherever the issues raised are petty, it betrays a narrow mentality and speaks against us in any case. Our stature is reduced by such tactics and there is no difference left between us and other parties. How were we different? During the days of Gandhiji we were different in every way and everyone could see that. We were held in respect everywhere because Congressmen were perceived as being sincere, honest and hardworking people, who made sacrifices. Now, all that is no longer completely true of us. We must try to bring that ethos back. It is obvious that we may not be able to create the same level of passion in the entire country like it was then. But people will lean towards the Congress when they see how we serve the country, not by manoeuvrings. playing games. We must work hard and honestly.

Nowadays there is a great deal of criticism about the functioning of the Congress, like enrolling bogus members, etc. Those who indulge in such tactics, instead of serving the Congress, are actually stabbing the Congress in the back. Please understand that they do great harm. Those who indulge in such activities are actually enemies of the Congress, whatever their motives might be. Even if they think they are doing something honest, they are killing the Congress ethos. To enrol bogus members to play underhand tricks, indulging in casteism, etc., is wrong. We must eradicate casteism by every possible means. If we cannot keep our Party pure, how can we serve the country?

These are some of the things that I wanted to share with you. Let me repeat, and I want you to understand, that you are here in this Conference for two to three days and will pass resolutions, etc., which is a good thing. But I would like that at the various Party centres or camps, or whatever you call them, in the country, you should evolve methods to make the people aware about the issues which face the Congress Party, the country and the world. As you can see, there are dangers all around us, on our borders. There is the attack by China. Pakistan often issues threats. We want to maintain peace and amity with all nations but that does not mean that we will tolerate any aggression on our soil. So you need to understand all this in order to get a clear picture of where the country stands and to be able to serve the country well.

Finally, I will remind you once again that cooperative societies are in my opinion extremely essential in order to curb inflation.

Jai Hind!

Translation ends]

38. In New Delhi: At the CPP[79]

जवाहरलाल नेहरुः हालांकि राज्यसभा अभी चल रही है और सुना है कि घंटे-डेढ़ घंटे और चलेगी ज़रा, ख़ैर, मामूली बात है राज्यसभा के लिए लेकिन ... तो हम किसलिए मिले हैं मेरी समझ में नहीं आता।

एक सदस्यः आपको विदा करने के लिए।

जवाहरलाल नेहरुः विदा करने को ... ये तो आपकी कृपा है, इनायत है।

एक सदस्यः फॉर हैप्पी एण्ड सेफ रिटर्न।

जवाहरलाल नेहरुः कोई ख़ास बात कहिये तो मैं आपसे कहूँ, कोई मज़मून बताइये। क्या? मैसेज आप ख़ुद दे दें। बात ये है कि हमारे सामने अक्सर मुश्किल और पेचीदा सवाल हैं। जब ऐसे सवाल होते हैं तो उनका सामना ज्यादा चुस्ती से करना होता है, ढीले तो हो नहीं जाना होता। अब पिछले पाँच-सात दिन में महावीर त्यागीजी के कई ख़त मेरे पास आये।[80] बहुत अहम बातों पर उन्होंने अपनी राय दी और अक्सर राय से उनकी मुझे इत्तिफ़ाक़ भी है और कुछ उस तरफ़ ध्यान भी दे रहे हैं, कोशिश भी कर रहे हैं प्लानिंग कमीशन भी और कुछ गवर्नमेंट भी। मामला पेचीदा है। तो हमने अक्सर बातों पे महज़ ये तय किया है कि उसपे ज्यादा ग़ौर करेंगे, प्लानिंग कमीशन वग़ैरा इस महीने में ताकि वो पक जायें फ़ैसले के लिए अक्टूबर में, हम सब यहाँ हों।

अब आप लोग जायेंगे अपने-अपने घर या कांस्टीट्यूएंसी, तो कुछ ये ज़रूरी मालूम होता है कि आप ज़रा अपने कांस्टीट्यूएंसी के लोगों से और औरों से मिलें, कुछ उनको समझायें क्या सवाल हैं, कैसे हम कोशिश कर रहे हैं क्योंकि आजकल काफ़ी हमारे जो ख़िलाफ़ लोग हैं वो गुलशोर मचाते हैं। अफ़सोस की तो ये बात है गुलशोर बाहर मचायें, मचायें, पार्लियामेंट के अन्दर मचाने लगे हैं जो कि सारे, जिसके माने ये हैं कि वो इस

---

79. Participation in meeting, 7 September 1962. NMML, AICC speeches, Tape No. M-64/C (i).
80. Only one recent letter, dated 31 August 1962, from Mahavir Tyagi is included in this volume, see appendix 56. Probably Nehru was not referring here to Mahavir Tyagi's earlier letter of 8 August 1962, see appendix 27.

Nehru might be referring to two other letters also from Mahavir Tyagi, both dated 18 August 1962, addressed to the Secretary, CPP, which are not published here but available in the NMML, Mahavir Tyagi Papers. These contain notices of resolutions, one of which suggested the need for legislation to deal with "the spectacle of the growing concentration of wealth amongst the fortunate few in the country;" the other recommended the need "to take steps to nationalise General Insurance business at an early date."

तरीके को नामंज़ूर करते हैं जैसे काम होता है पार्लियामेंट में, उसको तोड़ देना चाहते हैं। अब दो-चार आदमी तोड़ेंगे नहीं, लेकिन हमें आगाह हो जाना चाहिए, होशियार हो जाना चाहिए इन बातों से और हमें ख़ाली कांग्रेस को नहीं बल्कि जो भी यहाँ पार्टीज़ हैं जो कि डेमोक्रेटिक काम को मानते हैं क्योंकि ये तरीका तो है ही नहीं। ये एक पहला सवाल हमारी पार्लियामेंट के हो गया है, ये जो जानबूझ के, डेलिबरेटली किया जाता है, इसकी ताईद न की जाये। और बल्कि राय का इज़हार हो हम सभों की तरफ से, सब पार्टीज़ की तरफ से कि ये नामुनासिब है, ग़लत है, हम इसको बर्दाश्त नहीं करेंगे, क्योंकि मोटी बात है कि दस-पाँच आदमी भी गुल काफ़ी मचा सकते हैं और सैंकड़ों आदमियों के काम को रोक दे सकते हैं। और स्पीकर या चेयरमैन पर बड़ा बोझा पड़ जाता है क्योंकि सब बातों में एक, डेमोक्रेसी के पीछे एक लिहाज़ है, एक बरदाश्त है। अब लिहाज़ कोई न करे और बरदाश्त न करे और उसको तोड़ने की कोशिश करे तब डेमोक्रेसी आसानी से चल नहीं सकती, ये ग़ौरतलब सवाल है। मुझे मालूम नहीं आइन्दा बढ़ेगा कि घटेगा कि क्या हो ये तरीका, लेकिन ये बहुत ज़रूरी बात हम सभों के लिए हो गयी। आपको याद होगा पहले दिन, कोई सात-आठ दिन हुए जब एक कुछ हुल्लड़ मचा था लोकसभा में और एक मेम्बर साहब[81] सस्पेंड हुए थे हफ़्ते भर के लिए। मुझे बहुत रंज हुआ था और मैंने एक ख़त स्पीकर को लिखा था माफ़ी का अपनी तरफ से। मुझे आपने इज़्ज़त बख़्शी, लीडर ऑफ़ दा हाउस बनाया कि हाउस में ऐसी बात हो तो किसी क़दर उसका इल्ज़ाम, बोझा मेरे ऊपर पड़ता था। तो मैंने, मैंने उनसे माफ़ी मांगी थी, उनसे।[82] और ये बात है, याद रखनी है हमें और क्योंकि ये किसी पार्टी की बात नहीं है, ये हरेक की बात है कि अगर वो चाहते हैं पार्लियामेंटरी सिस्टम चले या न चले। चलेगा वो तो और जैसे कि स्पीकर ने कहा था उस रोज़ अगर यहाँ लोकसभा या राज्यसभा में ये बातें हुईं थोड़ी भी तो उसकी दस गुनी ज्यादा स्टेट असेम्बलीज़ में होंगी। हमें तो एक मिसाल देनी है औरों को ये डेकोरस बिहेवियर की, ठीक काम करने की। सब देखते हैं, वहाँ तो कुछ ज्यादा होता है, उनको संभालना है और पहले अपने को संभालना है।[83]

और ख़ैर, उसके अलावा मैं आपसे क्या कहूँ? सवाल हैं, प्राइसेज़ के सवाल हैं, बहुत ज़रूरी सवाल हैं जिसका हरेक पे असर होना है, चाहे प्राइसेज़ इत्ती ज्यादा न बढ़ी हों लेकिन थोड़ा सा भी बढ़ने में असर होता है। और उस तरफ उसका जाना एक ख़तरनाक बात है, रोकथाम कैसे हो। मुझे उम्मीद है कि मेरे आने के बाद अक्टूबर में इस मसले पर, ग़ौर तो ख़ैर हो ही रहा है लेकिन कुछ फ़ैसले भी हों। और क्या कहूँ? एं। बस।

---

81. Ram Sewak Yadav, leader of the Socialist group.
82. For Nehru's letter to Hukam Singh, Speaker of the Lok Sabha, see item 10.
83. Nehru told the Executive Committee of the CPP on 7 September 1962 that if a considerable number of members defied the Chair and broke the rules in legislatures, "nobody could stop it." He said, "The main remedy is to isolate such persons." PTI report in *The Hindu*, 8 September 1962, p. 6.

एक सदस्यः ये तीन आदमी पार्टी में शामिल हुए हैं।

जवाहरलाल नेहरुः वो तो हम पहले ही कर चुके हैं। ... तीन आदमी हमारी पार्टी में लिये गये हैं, एक्ज़ीक्यूटिव कमेटी ने मंज़ूर कर लिया था — डेविड मुंज़िनी बिहार के और दो गोआ के, डॉ कोलेको और डॉ गैतौंडे। और हमारे चीफ व्हिप साहब ने तीन व्हिप मुक़र्रर किये हैं — डिप्टी ...

कोई साहब मेरी हिन्दी नहीं समझे हैं? सब समझ गये?

[Translation begins

Jawaharlal Nehru: The Rajya Sabha is still sitting and I believe it will continue to do so for another hour and a half. Anyhow, it is unusual for the Rajya Sabha but ... I don't understand why we have met.

From the floor: To bid you goodbye.

Jawaharlal Nehru: Farewell? This is really very kind of you.

From the floor: For happy and safe return.

Jawaharlal Nehru: If you want me to speak about something in particular, I shall do so. What? You can send the message yourself. The thing is that when we have complicated problems before us, we have to deal with them promptly. In the last few days I have received a number of letters from Mahavir Tyagi.[84] He has given his views about many important matters and I agree with many of them. The Planning Commission and the Government are considering these things carefully. The matter is complicated. So we have decided in most cases to let the Planning Commission consider it more carefully so that in this one month they might be ripe for decision by October when all of us will be here.

[Decorum]

Now you will be going home to your constituencies. You should meet people in your constituencies and explain to them about the problems facing us and our efforts to solve them because these days many people are against us and often raise a hue and cry. The sad thing is that they have started doing this in the Parliament which proves that they do not accept the functioning of Parliament and want to create disturbances. The working of Parliament cannot

84. See fn 80 in this section.

be brought to a standstill by a handful of people but we have to be careful and take this as a warning—not only the Congress but other parties too which believe in a democratic way of functioning. So this is a very important question before Parliament, not to tolerate this kind of deliberate hooliganism and rowdy behaviour. We should express our displeasure on behalf of all the parties and show that we will not tolerate that ten or fifteen men should stop hundreds of people from doing their work by their rowdy behaviour. It also imposes a great strain on the Speaker on Chairman. Democracy implies a certain tolerance and respect for others. When that is not there and an attempt is made to destroy, democracy cannot function easily. We have to bear this in mind. I do not know whether this trend will continue or disappear but it has become very important to all of us. You may remember that about seven to eight days ago when this kind of rowdy behaviour first took place in the Lok Sabha and one member was suspended.[85] I was very upset and I wrote to the Speaker apologising on his behalf because I have been given the honour of being the Leader of the House and the responsibility for the behaviour of members rests with me. So I apologized to him.[86] This is not a matter for any one party; whether we make the parliamentary system work or not depends on all of us. As the Speaker said the other day, if these things happen in the Lok Sabha or Rajya Sabha, they will take place on a much larger scale in the State Assemblies. We should set an example of decorous behaviour, of being able to work well, to others. All eyes are upon us to see how we behave. So we should control ourselves.[87]

[Prices]

Apart from this, the question of prices is very important because it affects everyone. The prices may not have risen very much but even if it rises a little, the effect is felt. The fact that there is a tendency in that direction can be dangerous. How is it to be controlled? After I come back in October, the matter will of course be considered but I hope that we will be able to take some decisions too.

What more should I say? Eh?

From the floor: Three new members have joined the Party.

85. See fn 81 in this section.
86. See fn 82 in this section.
87. See fn 83 in this section.

[Foreign Tour]

Jawaharlal Nehru: We have already dealt with that. No, no. The executive committee has approved of three names to be enrolled in the Party, David Munzni from Bihar and two from Goa, Dr A. Colaco and Dr Gaitonde. Our Chief Whip has appointed three deputy whips. [...]

Is there anybody who has not followed my Hindi? Has everybody understood?

Translation ends]

Has everybody understood what I said in Hindi? ... Did not do so? Do you want me to repeat something? Well, I won't repeat that.

You know I am going away tonight or perhaps [...] Has everybody understood? Tomorrow, perhaps tomorrow, meaning I am going after midnight, so it becomes tomorrow. I am going to London straight off and I shall stay there about twelve days, I think, for the Commonwealth Prime Ministers' Conference, which is considered to be rather an important one this year. I shall come to that later. Then I am going for two days to Paris, principally to see President de Gaulle. After that I am going to Nigeria and Ghana. There is no immediate occasion for me to go there but for some years past I have been worried at the fact that I have not been to Africa at all, except to Egypt and Sudan, and all these things happening in Africa, new countries becoming independent.

Now, Africa can be divided up into three or four parts: North, West, East and Central Africa. I am leaving out South Africa. Now, in Central Africa there is the Congo and other countries which are in a state of turmoil, but East Africa, West Africa and North Africa all very much deserve our friendly relations, deserve a visit from me, because they are friendly countries, all of them. They have repeatedly invited me, not me personally but as the representative of India; and Africa today is a very vital continent, to some extent a troublesome one too. After centuries, it is waking up, and having woken up, the people of Africa have so much vitality and energy in them; may go wrong or right, but they have energy and vitality which is the great thing, and so they are likely to change the face of Africa with some rapidity.

And we in a sense are far from Africa. In a sense we are near East Africa, it is just across the Indian Ocean, and there are many Indians there too. We have always adopted the policy that Indians who go there owe a great deal to the country they work in. We are not satisfied with the idea that the Indians go there to exploit those places for their personal advantage. Naturally they work for their advantage but they should work for the advantage of the country they are working in and be loyal to it and help in the attempt to gain their freedom, political or economic. So I thought on this occasion that I might try to visit part of Africa, say West Africa, and therefore I am going to Nigeria and Ghana.

I confess that usually when I go abroad, out of India, I like the change, it is a relief to me from the daily work here, although it may be somewhat of a strain there, but a different kind of a strain. On this occasion I did not have the same urge to go. I wanted to remain here because my mind is full of the problems we have to face here and I did not wish to function in an escapist way. But I thought I had to go to the Commonwealth Conference, it is an important meeting; and then I added a week to it to visit Nigeria and Ghana. On my way back from Ghana I expect to spend a few hours in Cairo, just a few hours. I get there at about eleven and I leave at eleven at night for India.

[UK and the ECM]

Now, in the Commonwealth Conference many problems will come up, but in the main this question of England joining the European Common Market comes up. Well, if England wants to join, where do we come into the picture? We cannot come in the way, we do not want to come in the way of their decision—they are an independent country—just as we would object to their coming in the way of any action that we took. But their joining the European Common Market has certain direct results which we have to shoulder. That is, our exports to England which are duty free will be largely affected because in the European Common Market, if they join, we have to pay a duty and so it affects us greatly, this question of export, which is so important. That will be affected. Now, you have heard our Finance Minister[88] talking about this, so I need not say much.

One or two aspects I would like to bring to your mind. The first of course is that we did not want anything to happen which will affect our exports and that will hurt us, our planning and everything, and therefore we are trying to get—we are not coming in the way of England joining or not, it is up to them to decide—but we are trying to get as good terms as possible ... and if our trade with England suffers, it has a consequence, whether we wish it or not. Automatically their trade in India suffers, so they have to consider that aspect too. We have tried, not only through England but by direct approaches to the European Common Market countries, to deal directly with them. We had appointed an Ambassador[89] specially to the European Common Market people—one of our able men—and his work has resulted in impressing these European Common Market countries with the value of their close association

88. Morarji Desai.
89. K.B. Lall.

with us in regard to exports, etc., because ultimately they balance, tend to balance if we can export, we can buy things from them. At the present moment, our relations with Western Germany are not in that sense to our advantage, we take much more from them than we give them. This cannot continue for long. Sometime or other we shall have to stop getting things from them; we cannot pay for them by our exports.

Apart from this there is a wider consideration. As India is developing industrially and otherwise, it is offering, it is going to offer, one of the biggest markets in the world. It is a tremendous market of 450 million people or thereabouts. Even a slight advance in our purchasing value, per capita purchasing value, makes a vast difference to the total amount that we can spend. We naturally want to develop our own industries and will develop them, but as we develop them, oddly enough our demands in other countries increase. You cannot remain cut off from the world in trade and commerce. So that it is to the advantage of all these advanced countries in the West to cultivate us, cultivate trade with us, even from the point of view of their own personal gain in the future. So it is not merely a question of personal gain offered by an ever growing market in India. So it is not merely a question of our asking them for favours but having something that is valuable which we can give them and they realize it. I do not know what the result of all this would be. Anyhow we shall try to do our best.

In England itself there is, I do not know, the Government in the UK is more or less committed to join the European Common Market. But there is a fairly strong sentiment there in favour of their not joining it, may be a minority but it is a strong sentiment and I do not know what the ultimate result will be; that is for them to decide. There is one of the aspects of it which applies not only to the possible losses caused to us by our exports being limited, by England joining the European Common Market, but also the question of the aid which we get from friendly foreign countries. Naturally we want aid at this present stage of our development and therefore we try for it, we hope to get it and we are grateful to the countries who give it even though it is mostly in the shape of loans and credits and anything else.

[Foreign Aid and Self-Sufficiency]

There is one aspect: that we are getting into a mentality in India of living in hope of aid all the time, and therefore perhaps not relying on our own efforts as much as we ought to. That is a dangerous thing. As I said we want aid but even if we get aid it is our own efforts that pull us out; aid may come whatever it may be, 20 per cent, but 80 per cent remains with us and then we have to pay that apart from the aid. Anyhow the burden has to be shouldered by us in India.

But it is a dangerous thing I feel, this mentality imagining that aid will come and will do the job. That is particularly relevant, if India, private industry, big industry I am talking about, get tied up with somebody in America, somebody in Japan, somebody in Germany and build up their concerns with that. I just wanted to warn you about the dangers inherent on relying too much on others, although we welcome aid.

We are passing through a difficult phase in our development in many ways. Economically of course, on the social side too, because gradually basic changes are taking place among our people, the widespread schools, boys and girls going there in our rural areas, in villages, have a powerful effect on moulding them, different from what they were. Their fathers, parents did not go, their grandfathers did not go; that is, a revolutionary change is being brought about among our people. On the whole, slow as it has been in our agriculture, it is gradually taking to better techniques, better ploughs, better implements and thereby not only doing the job better but changing their minds. One of our Chief Ministers, Mr [Biju] Patnaik of Orissa, being himself a very successful businessman and a public man, he has evolved a scheme to have a small factory in every block for producing something which can be used in the rural areas, but his main purpose is to introduce, to change the minds of people, to change the average peasant and make him do some work with a machine so that he may get accustomed to that machine, the basic things about industrialization. I think it is an excellent idea. I do not know how soon he will be able to do it, but he is a man of great ability and great enthusiasm and great capacities to do things. So I am looking forward to the countryside, the rural areas of Orissa changing perhaps more rapidly, although they are more backward now, more rapidly than many other areas of India, by the introduction of this system of small factories, in every little group of villages.

[Education and Human Resources]

So we are after—apart from the things we do, put up hydro-electric works and factories and the like—we are ultimately after changing the quality of human beings in India, taking them out of the routine of thought and action and the kind of work they do, they have done for hundreds of years, and bring them up to the industrial and scientific age to some extent. That is a vital thing. Once you have got the men, money does not matter very much. I shall remind you of something which you must have in mind, how very rapidly after the last war Germany, Soviet Russia and Japan built themselves up. It is amazing: they were destroyed during the War, and yet within ten years of the war ending they were as prosperous as they were. Why? Because they have the trained men and the mentality and the hard work, Germans built themselves up and

95

Germany is more prosperous than it has ever been in the past. And prosperity means strength. It is a strong nation. In some ways it carries more weight—although it was defeated a few years back—than it did previously. Japan also made remarkable recovery and Russia also, all due to trained personnel. All the money in the world could not have changed them, but trained people can take advantage of opportunities and therefore it is very important to have trained people and a background of education.

In Russia one good thing they did right from the days of their Revolution was to build up their educational system. They pay great attention to it and in some ways it may be said it is difficult to compare, but it may be said, it is an extraordinarily good educational system, and the result is they have vast numbers of scientists, engineers and those scientists and engineers are also given training in literary subject, humanities, etc. They do not merely become scientists and it is due to this educational effort that their science has increased and their industry has increased. Therefore, the importance of a base of education, on top of it of large numbers. Everything follows. If there is a little delay because of lack of money that is made good, but you cannot make good if you have not got the base.

[Socialism]

You talk of socialism and once or twice I have addressed you on socialism. There is no such thing as socialism for a poor country, it has no meaning. It means just a poverty-stricken lot; they may share between themselves but it does not mean anything. Socialism can only come, it only came in the world, with the growth of technology and industry. Then socialism came, because there was something to be socialistic about. You cannot be socialistic about poverty; if we build socialism we have to build up wealth.

Of course, it is perfectly true that in building up wealth we must not encourage tendencies, urges, which come in the way of socialism. There is something like that happening today and Members know, have protested against it, this growth of monopoly, etc., that certainly comes in the way of socialism. Not the growth of industry but the growth of monopoly; not even the growth of private industry, it is spread out but monopoly may come and we have to be careful about that. Unfortunately, the group of very able individuals whom we appointed have not produced their report. I understand that they are likely to produce their report, or the first part of their report, may be in a month or so, and they told me how complicated the question was. It is not very easy just to say, name half a dozen names, they control so many concerns; that is so, but we have to go deeper down, how they do it and how we can prevent this group from monopoly.

There are many other subjects which we have to consider from time to time, from the point of view of nationalization. It is no good nationalizing every factory and all that, but a time will come when we have to consider. Mr Tyagi proposed today nationalizing some branches of State Insurance or Banking or something like that. These are the basic things; a factory or two being nationalized or not does not make much difference. It should be nationalized if it supplies essential needs for us and occupies a prestigious position. So all these big problems come before us.

You must remember that once you are out of the woods and have built up an industrial and advanced agricultural system the progress becomes rapid. The progress of Japan since the war is phenomenal. Fast, fast, fast, speeding faster than it was before the war, because they have got the background, the training and all that. So also all the big countries, Germany, England, America, they create every year so much that even though they are wasteful, even then they have much to be left over.

We cannot afford to do that now, but once this industrial machine gets going and, above all, once our agriculture is put on a modern footing, then we shall advance fast. Agriculture is and remains and will continue to remain the most important foundation of our economy and of our growth and the one thing that is rather distressing is, that the growth in agriculture is not as good as we like it to be. You will presently see, I suppose, the new statistics about incomes, etc. They have been depressed by agriculture, otherwise we are progressive. The per capita income has gone up a little but not as much as we hoped. Then again this year we had these floods and other things on a big scale, they again tend to depress the total food production and therefore the per capital income. I have often told you that the per capita income in India depends far more on agriculture than industry, because so many people are involved in it. Industry of course makes a difference, it is important, but if we increase the agricultural growth by whatever percentage, even a small percentage per capita you may put it, it becomes an enormous figure, as so many people are taking part. Therefore, agriculture is the base of all, and we have to rely on mother earth, more than anything else, but mother earth being treated properly and scientifically being served so that it may yield the best return.

It is really extraordinary if you think of it, the rapidity of scientific growth today, all these are symbols of it, cosmonauts going round the earth and all that, they are just symbols of vast power coming into the hands of humanity and unfortunately humanity being unfit to use it properly. That is a misfortune and I do not know how long it will take for humanity to catch up to the power it possesses, and use it in a good way.

Going back to our own country, on the one side we see this great growth of science; on the other we see at the same time people spending vast sums on armaments, on nuclear bombs, nuclear tests, which is quite illogical. Everybody has recognized it, that the nuclear war will destroy humanity. Why then go on doing something which will lead to a nuclear war? It shows how lacking in good sense people are, how fear is a more powerful thing than logic or sense.

[National Integration]

Coming to our own country we talk of emotional national integration. It is a patent thing, without it we cannot be strong, yet we quarrel about the littlest thing. Two states quarrel for months and years about something common between them, may be water, may be hydro-electric works, may be some villages this way or that way, and not realizing that by doing so they are injuring both, because the growth of that area stops for that time. In this connection I should like to say how happy I was to learn, was it yesterday or day before, of an old standing quarrel between Orissa and Andhra Pradesh being settled by the two Chief Ministers, and they were quarrelling about it whether they should be here or there but fortunately both the Chief Ministers are young, they are not tied down by old age as some of us are, and so they sat for two, three days continuously and came to an agreement. And I will tell you, Mr Patnaik of course is a host in himself, how Mr Sanjiva Reddy worked, the clever man, he did not talk, he did talk of course, he called in all the opposition leaders and put them before Patnaik: you talk to them. He got the opposition people to agree to this settlement and naturally after that everybody agreed to work. That was a sign of statesmanship, how to do it.[90]

But really it is very sad, all this business of communal trends in India— communalism, provincialism, casteism, linguism. All these are disruptive things which have their value in their own places no doubt, a language has, but linguism, quarrel between languages has not got. Take the question, a relatively minor question, which excites some people, this AIR language. You will remember that we set a suggestion on behalf of our party to them that they should evolve a simple language, and a language which was in accordance with the genius of Hindi. That was really very good direction. And no doubt I think we appointed an advisory committee or something and I hope they will help. It really does not matter, people seem to get afraid if a few Urdu words [are] coming to Hindi or a few Hindi words going to Urdu. Nothing to get excited about; it enriches the language. The language which can easily adapt

90. See items 210-211.

foreign words to its own use, is the language which has the future. A language which sticks to old phraseology and cannot extend, it does not grow. It simply remains stuck, it may be a very beautiful language; it is the language which adapts words from other languages that grows and if it is a strong language it adapts it in its own way. Vast number of Hindi words, what is called Urdu, is roughly 80 per cent Hindi and 20 per cent Persian, Arabic and foreign words.

[PURE HINDI]

"I don't like the way these non-Hindi members deliver Hindi speeches in Parliament. Are they not strengthening the cause of AIR Hindi?"

(From *The Times of India*, 4 September 1962, p. 3)

Urdu has one advantage over Hindi. Urdu is more, it finds it more easy to adapt a foreign word than Hindi; it absorbs it immediately. There are so many. You take the word, the simple word, take *pubji* [sic – *subzi*?]. It is not a Urdu word, it is almost a Hindi word too but it comes in, and so many other words. That is also in Persian. They have adopted hundreds and thousands of words from Western languages with slight differences. Academy, they made it Akademi, a slight change to fit in with the genius of a language. So why should we be afraid, I do not understand it.

Here, I can understand, educationists and others deciding that this language should be used in AIR or for a question to Parliament, etc. There are some, one or two questions answered by my colleague, Mr Dinesh Singh,[91] who was reading out an answer and I saw a blank look on Mr Tyagi's face, he did not understand it at all, neither did I, so very *shudh*,[92] but nobody, very few persons understood it. It is one thing for us to say this is a better word, let us use it, let us not be afraid of other words coming in, it shows vitality and strength of a language to absorb the words.

Here yesterday some of you may have gone, I went to an old Delhi custom, *Phool Walon Ki Sair*. It is a fair beyond Mehrauli, about 15 to 16 miles from here beyond the Qutub. It is an old fair, started at the beginning of the nineteenth century, 160 years ago by the then Mughal emperor. He was not much of an emperor, because the British had come in round about then but still he was there. It was started then by some lady in keeping a promise she had made—her son I think had been imprisoned by somebody or other in Allahabad and he had lain there—*minnat ki thi* [Translation: "prayed for wish fulfillment."] I do not know what the English word for *minnat*[93] is. She made the promise that if her son is released she will do something, this fair, and she ran this fair. It became very popular there, and they are trying to revive it. They had it eight or nine years ago, then they did not continue it; this time they revived it again. And I think they will go on reviving it.

It is a good thing; it had a touch of old Delhi about it. Old Delhi, that composite culture that old Delhi has developed into, it is getting changed now because of a large number of outsiders who have come as a result of Partition and all that; that does not matter. But it has, apart from other things, old things,

---

91. Deputy Minister in the Ministry of External Affairs.
92. Pure.
93. A prayer.

they had cock fights, *titaron ki larai, murgon ki larai*,[94] not that I am very keen on that, but still people enjoyed that. They had swimming festivals, and things, and wrestling, *kushti*,[95] and all that. And finally they had recitations and songs of all old Delhi poets. Delhi used to be an old centre of Urdu poetry specially, some Hindi too, chiefly Urdu, Ghalib[96] and Josh[97] and others, recitations and singing too. It had more of a touch, as I said, of old Delhi than a new [Delhi] but it was very pleasant and people enjoyed it.

And so we have to keep in touch with the old and build up the new and the combination of the two is likely to be good; you give up either, it is not good. So also in languages, you have to take whatever you can from another language and build one language up with the help of another. Well, I am gossiping now. I think I better stop.

[Floods]

What shall I say about floods?

As a matter of fact, well, I cannot answer the question, how much money will be available or not, but I think we are thinking more in terms of money. Then we get a wrong idea of the problem. Our problem is something more than money can solve, all the money in the world cannot wholly solve it. That is one remark. Remember, our problem is, especially in North India, Assam, Bengal, Bihar, UP, Punjab, all those [areas] adjoining the Himalayas, you have got the highest mountain in the world and sub-mountain tracks, you get not only heavy rain but you get vast quantities of waters from the mountains, snow is melting and all that and they come down suddenly like mountain rivers Now, how are you going to deal with that? By putting up a wall? All the dams in the world cannot stop that. That is the main thing. You seem to have put up enough dams and you are protected. Dams are only helpful in protecting a city, may be a particular area, a city or something; for the rest dams are harmful because dams impede the flow of water, you cannot stop, at present at least. The rains are coming down; if they come down, they come down. You may in future be able to control the rain, I do not know, it is a possibility, divert them. So rains will come down. If this vast quantity of water comes down it must flow, you cannot stop it by dams, any number of dams; you can divert it near a city, it is possible, like a good river might be protected or some other place, you can canalise it to some extent, but the only real thing is to let it flow away as rapidly

94. Cock fighting.
95. Wrestling.
96. Mirza Asadullah Khan Ghalib.
97. Josh Malihabadi.

as possible. Even if it comes down it can flow within a day or two. And one of the things which is giving us trouble are the old embankments of railways that were built a hundred years ago, seventy years ago. Nobody thought of floods then. They prevent the flow of water, canals prevent the flow.

Therefore it is not a question of money. Of course, some money will help and for important matters money will be given, will be found somehow, but you must realise that it is a much deeper problem than can be solved by money. I do not know if we are getting more rains than we are used to. What has happened— of course, in Assam you are perfectly right, deforestation, and in Assam, of course, everything was upset by the great earthquake, it has raised the level of the Brahmaputra and now people say that to dredge the Brahmaputra, it is a terrific job, dredging a huge river all the way; you see it is. And meanwhile another thing has happened, population has grown so much that they now live on the low lying areas. Previously the villages, etc., were high lying; they go in low lying areas, the water comes in there. All these things are mixed up and you cannot easily solve it by mere grant of money, you cannot even spend that money. But I am quite sure that first of all we have to make a long term plan and having made that long term plan, we should proceed along it, every year some part of it and, what is most urgent, should be taken up immediately whatever the cost, because the loss caused by floods is very great.

So, thank you, I wish you well during your vacation.

From the floor: On behalf of the Party I convey you our best wishes and wish you the best of the luck and we always pray for your success wherever you are and your good wishes also are assumed.

Jawaharlal Nehru: Success is in India, not outside. Happy Returns. Ram Subhag is going to Kuala Lumpur.[98]

98. To attend the International Rice Commission session and Food and Agriculture Organization conference.

(b) Congress Socialist Forum

39. To Gulzarilal Nanda: Another Socialist Forum a Nuisance[99]

August 2, 1962

My dear Gulzarilal,

You have asked me to send you a message for the Socialist Forum which you have started.[100] I would gladly do so but I am not quite sure what to say. I had an idea that Forum was essentially meant for studying the various aspects of socialism in order to give an intellectual background to people's thinking. I find, however, that it is something more than that. In fact, the name itself refers to socialist action. What this action is I do not know.

I am afraid that there is a possibility of this group becoming sectarian and needlessly raising conflicts within the Congress. Something of this kind has happened in Ahmedabad. If it is meant to be a mass organisation for some action this kind of conflict is going to arise. What is the relation of this Forum to the Congress Socialist Forum which was started a year or two ago? Have you discussed this with them? It would be rather unfortunate if we have two or three parallel lines of action which do not meet.[101]

Yours sincerely,
Jawaharlal Nehru

99. Letter to the Minister for Planning, Labour and Employment. PMO, File No. 17(502)/62-66-PMS, Sr. No. 7-A. Also available in the JN Collection.
100. The inaugural meeting of the Congress Forum for Socialist Action, 18 Congress MPs attending, was held in New Delhi on 25 May 1962. According to the scheme of the Forum formulated at its meeting held on 23 June 1962, "The purpose of the Forum is to engage as many members of the Congress as possible in: (1) study and discussion regarding issues and problems connected with labour, planning and socialist action; (2) activities intended to strengthen the Congress, and to promote planned development of the country and the establishment of a socialist society in India." *Congress Forum*, Vol. 1, No. 1, 15 August 1962, pp. 14 and 17.
101. See C.B. Gupta's objections to such a Forum in UP, appendix 20, and Nehru's disquiet, items 40-41. See also Nehru's guarded message, item 42.

40. To Gulzarilal Nanda: Congress Socialist Forum in UP Divisive[102]

August 6, 1962

My dear Gulzarilal,

I enclose a letter I had from Chandra Bhanu Gupta, Chief Minister of UP.[103] He refers in this to the formation of a Congress Socialist Forum under the leadership of Mohanlal Gautam in the UP. From what he writes it does appear that this initiative of Mohanlal Gautam is not on the lines you had suggested for the Congress Socialist Forum and is rather meant to encourage the formation of a certain group consisting not only of Congress but non-Congressmen also. I do not know how far this has been encouraged by you, but it is an unfortunate development.[104]

Yours sincerely,
Jawaharlal Nehru

41. To C.B. Gupta: Congress Socialist Forum in UP[105]

August 6, 1962

My dear Chandra Bhanu,

Your letter of August 3, about the formation of the Congress Socialist Forum under Mohanlal Gautam's leadership.[106] It would appear from what you have written that this is not in line with what Gulzarilal Nanda had suggested, and is

102. Letter to the Minister for Planning, Labour and Employment and Deputy Chairman, Planning Commission. PMO, File No. 17(502)/62-66-PMS, Sr. No. 10-A. Also available in the JN Collection.
103. Appendix 20.
104. See previous letter to Nanda, item 39, and letter to C.B. Gupta, item 41. See also a guarded message, item 42.
105. Letter to the Chief Minister of UP. PMO, File No. 17(502)/62-66-PMS, Sr. No. 9-A. Also available in the JN Collection and in NMML, AICC Papers, Box 10, File No. CD- 30-D/1962.
106. Gautam was a member of the Executive Committee of the UPCC and former Cooperation Minister in UP; he had been recently appointed Chairman of the Rajasthan Police Commission. A convention of the UP Socialist Planning Forum, attended by about 250 Congressmen from the State, was inaugurated by him in Lucknow on 30 July 1962. For C.B. Gupta's letter, see appendix 20.

likely to result in the encouragement of a particular group. I am sending your letter to Gulzarilal Nanda.[107]

Yours sincerely,
Jawaharlal Nehru

42. For the Congress Socialist Forum[108]

The Congress Socialist Forum is meant to spread socialistic idea and outlook among our people. More especially it is meant to help the study of various aspects of socialism in order to give an intellectual background to our people's thinking. This is welcome because there is a great deal of vagueness in our thinking.

I hope, however, that the Congress Socialist Forum will not develop a sectarian viewpoint and encourage the formation of groups within the Congress. That would be unfortunate. We do not wish to build up a group or a sect believing in socialism and utilising this for Congress power politics. That, I know, is not the object of the sponsors of the Congress Socialist Forum. I hope this will be kept in view and encouragement will be given chiefly to study circles and discussion on the best way to build up a socialist structure of society in India. This requires a thought out approach and not merely a sentimental urge.[109]

43. To D. Sanjivayya: Mohanlal Gautam's Conduct Undesirable[110]

September 1, 1962

My dear Sanjivayya,

You will remember that at the last meeting of the Working Committee, C.B. Gupta, Chief Minister of UP, drew our attention to the activities of Mohanlal

107. See also Nehru's letters to Gulzarilal Nanda, items 39-40, and a guarded message, item 42.
108. Message, 10 August 1962, forwarded to Gulzarilal Nanda, Minister for Planning, Labour and Employment. PMO, File No. 17(502)/62-66-PMS, Sr No. 14-A. Also available in NMML, AICC Papers, File No. OD-54/1963, Box 26, and in the JN Collection.

The message was published in *Congress Forum*, a journal of the Congress Forum for Socialist Action, Vol. 1, No. 1, 15 August 1962.
109. See also items 39-41.
110. Letter to the Congress President. NMML, AICC Papers, Box 10, File No. OD-30-D/1962. Also available in the JN Collection.

Gautam.[111] It was, I believe, agreed that you would write to Gautam. I do not know if you have done so.

I have today received a letter from C.B. Gupta, which I enclose.[112] From this it appears that Gautam is acting in a manner which is wholly undesirable, and he should be pulled up.[113]

Yours sincerely,
Jawaharlal Nehru

44. To Mohanlal Gautam: Groups within Party Deplorable[114]

September 1, 1962

My dear Gautam,

For some time past I have noticed your efforts to form some kind of a group which is supposed to be socialistic. This group apparently includes both Congressmen and non-Congressmen. The matter came up before the Working Committee of the Congress and such attempts at group formations were not welcomed. In fact, they were disapproved, and it was suggested that the President[115] might write to you on the subject.

I now find that you are carrying on a campaign against the taxation proposals of the UP Government. It seems to me that this is a completely wrong approach and a breach of discipline.

Shri Gulzarilal Nanda[116] has also started an organisation for furthering socialist ideas.[117] This is of an entirely different kind, and many of us approve of

---

111. Member of the UPCC Executive Committee and former Minister for Cooperation in UP.
112. Appendix 52.
113. See correspondence on Congress Socialist Forum, items 40-41; appendices 20 and 24.
114. Letter to member of the UPCC Executive Committee and former Minister for Cooperation in UP. PMO, File No. 17(502)/62-66-PMS, Sr. No. 16-A. Also available in the JN Collection.
115. D. Sanjivayya.
116. Minister for Planning, Labour and Employment and Deputy Chairman, Planning Commission.
117. The Congress Forum for Socialist Action.

it. Its chief purpose is to promote study circles for clarifying ideas on socialism and it is confined to Congressmen.

I am surprised at the way you appear to be functioning in this matter.[118]

Yours sincerely,
Jawaharlal Nehru

(c) Subhas Chandra Bose

45. To Suresh C. Bose: No Letter from Subhas Chandra Bose[119]

July 23, 1962

Dear Suresh Babu,

Your letter of the 19th July. I have received no letter from Netaji Subhas Chandra Bose, nor have I received any letter concerning him on the lines you have mentioned. I do not know about the secret report to which you refer either.

Yours sincerely,
[Jawaharlal Nehru]

46. To Suresh C. Bose: Subhas Chandra Bose is Dead[120]

August 12, 1962

Dear Shri Bose,

I have your letter of the 8th August. I wrote to you that all the circumstantial evidence made me believe that Netaji Subhas Chandra Bose had died.[121] Much of this evidence was given in the report made by the committee appointed for this

---

118. See related correspondence in section Politics, subsection Congress Socialist Forum.
119. Letter to elder brother of Subhas Chandra Bose; address: Garia, PO Garia, District 24 Parganas, West Bengal.
120. Letter to elder brother of Subhas Chandra Bose; address: Garia, PO Garia, District 24 Parganas, West Bengal.
121. See SWJN/SS/77/item 97.

purpose, which visited Japan. You will find the date, place and circumstances mentioned in that committee's report.[122]

Apart from that report, the length of time that has elapsed is itself confirmatory of the fact of his death.[123]

Yours sincerely,
[Jawaharlal Nehru]

47. To Rina Bose: Observing Subhas Chandra Bose's Birthday[124]

August 20, 1962

Dear Mrs Bose,

I have your card of August 15th. I certainly hope that Netaji's birthday will be suitably observed on the 23rd January. But it is not possible for me to visit Calcutta at that time. That is a heavy time for me because of various engagements and especially the coming of the Republic Day. Several eminent visitors will also be coming here then from abroad.

I do not think I should become President of your Committee in these circumstances.

Yours sincerely
[Jawaharlal Nehru]

122. Suresh Chandra Bose was a member of the Netaji Enquiry Committee set up by the GOI in April 1956, with Shah Nawaz Khan as chairman and S.N. Maitra as the other member, to enquire into the circumstances leading to Subhas Chandra Bose's alleged death as a result of an aircraft accident in August 1945. The majority report signed by Shah Nawaz Khan and S.N. Maitra stated categorically that Subhas Chandra Bose met with his death in the air crash.

According to Sugata Bose, *His Majesty's Opponent. Subhas Chandra Bose and India's Struggle Against Empire* (New Delhi: Allen Lane, 2011), p. 317, all "the three members of the Committee signed a draft of principal findings" on 2 July 1956 saying that "the plane carrying Netaji did crash." However, after putting his signature to this draft, Suresh Chandra Bose "changed his mind and wrote a rambling dissent claiming that the crash had not occurred and that his brother was alive."

123. See also item 45.
124. Letter; address: 12 Brindaban Bysack Street, Calcutta-5.

48. To Haridas Mitra: Location of Subhas Chandra Bose's Statue[125]

August 24, 1962

Dear Haridasji,

Your letter of the 6th August. Netaji's statue should certainly be put up at some appropriate place. But I am afraid the front of the Delhi Red Fort has been reserved for a large composition denoting freedom-fighters of India. This is being done by an eminent sculptor. This was decided on the centenary of the Indian War of Independence, 1857.

At Imphal, or rather near it, whatever is constructed should have the goodwill and agreement of the Manipuris. This applies even more to Rangoon and Singapore.

Yours sincerely,
[Jawaharlal Nehru]

125. Letter to the son-in-law of Suresh Chandra Bose, the elder brother of Subhas Chandra Bose; address: 14 Asha Biswas Road, Calcutta 25.

Haridas Mitra was associated with the Indian National Army (INA); sentenced to death and later, following Mahatma Gandhi's intervention, given a life sentence; Deputy Speaker of the West Bengal Assembly, 1967-68 and 1972-77. Gopalkrishna Gandhi (ed.), *A Frank Friendship. Gandhi and Bengal: A Descriptive Chronology* (Calcutta: Seagull Books, 2007), p. 363.

49. To Atul Sen: Secret Protocol on Subhas Chandra Bose[126]

August 31, 1962

Dear Professor Sen,

Your letter of August 28th.[127]

I have never heard of any secret protocol about Netaji Subhas Chandra Bose. Certainly the Government of India have not bound themselves to any such thing. Even if any country asks the Government of India to hand him over, it is not going to be agreed to.

Yours sincerely,
[Jawaharlal Nehru]

50. To Kalyan Bose: About Subhas Chandra Bose[128]

14th September, 1962

Dear Kalyan Bose,

I have your letter of the 11th September. I am sorry to learn that you are still unwell. I hope that you will get over your indisposition.

---

126. Letter to a former associate of Subhas Chandra Bose; address: 18/22/4A Dover Lane, Calcutta-29.
127. Atul Sen's letter to Nehru has not been traced in the NMML. However, it has been cited by Deepu Madhavan in an article entitled "These Are The 5 Top Mysteries That The Recently Unveiled #Netaji Files Are Trying To Unravel" published in Indiatimes. com, updated 24 January 2016:
  "I take the liberty of addressing these few lines to you in the matter of the widely prevalent belief that Netaji Subhas Chandra Bose is not dead. Mine is not mere belief but actual knowledge that Netaji is alive and is engaged in spiritual practice somewhere in India. Not the sadhu of Shoulmari, Cooch Behar, in West Bengal about whom some Calcutta politicians are making a fuss. I deliberately make the location a little vague because from the talks I had with him for months together not very long ago, I could understand that he is yet regarded as Enemy No.1 of the Allied Powers, and that there is a secret protocol that binds the government of India to deliver him to Allied 'justice' if found alive." Link https://www.indiatimes.com/news/india/these-are-the-5-top-mysteries-that-the-recently-unveiled-netajifiles-are-trying-to-unravel-249788.html accessed on 22 May 2018.
128. Letter; address: 53 Pont Street, London SW1. Sent from London.

110

I do not exactly remember when I first met Netaji Subhas Bose. I met him, I think, in the early days of the non-cooperation movement. It could not have been in London or Cambridge because I did not come to England at all during those years. In fact, I did not visit England between 1912 and 1926.

I am going away tomorrow out of London for the weekend. On my return I shall be here for two or three days for the Commonwealth Prime Ministers' Conference and then leave. Those days are very fully occupied and I doubt if it will be possible for me to find any time for meeting you. Also, as you are not quite well, I would not like to give you the trouble to come here.

Yours sincerely,
[Jawaharlal Nehru]

(d) Social Groups

51. To P.C. Sen: Santhal Exodus from East Pakistan[129]

July 29, 1962

My dear Prafulla Sen,

Your letter of July 23 has reached me here in Calcutta. Today, at a meeting of your Cabinet Members we discussed this question of the exodus of Santhals and others from East Pakistan.

It would be desirable, as you suggest, to have a ministerial level meeting with Pakistan. On my return to Delhi I shall find out if this can be done.[130]

Yours sincerely,
[Jawaharlal Nehru]

129. Letter to the Chief Minister of West Bengal. Sent from Raj Bhavan, Calcutta.
130. See noting on this subject, item 52.

52. Santhal Influx from East Pakistan[131]

[Letter, 23 July 1962, from P.C. Sen, Chief Minister of West Bengal, begins]

My dear Panditjee,

As you already know, more than 9,000 Santhals and Hindus have crossed over from East Pakistan into West Bengal during the last three months. The exodus still continues and we get reports daily from our border districts of the arrival of families from across the border. A certain number of Muslims have also crossed the border from West Bengal into East Pakistan. The East Pakistan Government have given this number as more than 5,000, but our enquiries show that about 1,000 Muslims have gone across from Malda, and a very small number from Jalpaiguri. This steady and continuous flow of people from East Pakistan has naturally created a good deal of tension and strong feeling in West Bengal, particularly in our border districts where, as you know, there are large settlements of Hindus who came over from East Pakistan at different times since 1947. If the flow continues, this tension is likely to worsen. The whole situation is most disquieting, and may suddenly lead to an outburst against the minority community in West Bengal. We have taken the utmost precautions to prevent any such thing happening and so far with success, but much anger and bitterness have been generated by the happenings in East Pakistan.

2. The root cause of Hindus coming over from East Pakistan is apparent from statements made by these refugees when they were interrogated by our officers. They have said that for some time past they have been living in a state of terror, members of their families have been murdered or beaten up, local goondas have been helping themselves to their properties with impunity, their women have been molested, and all this has happened without any effective interference from the local Police or Magistracy. Obviously, in some areas of East Pakistan, the Government have completely failed to ensure security and protection of the minority community. Until and unless this state of affairs is radically altered, not only is there no chance of any of the evacuees agreeing to go back but the exodus is likely to continue with its dangerous potentialities.

3. I would, therefore, suggest for your consideration whether it is not worthwhile having some sort of a meeting with Pakistan at Ministerial level. A meeting between the Chief Secretaries of West Bengal and East Pakistan will be held on the 1st August. I feel, however, that nothing much is likely to be achieved at Chief Secretaries' level. Each side will produce long lists of refugees who have come over from the other side, and there will be mutual allegations

131. Noting. MEA, File No. 8(21)/62 – P. IV, Part IV, p. 18/Note.

and recriminations, but I have serious doubts as to whether anything lasting and effective is likely to be achieved. It is for this reason that I am writing to you to consider the question of having a high level conference with the Central Government of Pakistan at which something more positive and effective for the protection of minorities might be worked out. I hope you will kindly think over this matter.

With kind regards,

Yours sincerely,
Prafulla Chandra Sen

[Letter, 23 July 1962, from P.C. Sen, Chief Minister of West Bengal, ends. MEA, File No. 8(21)/62 – P. IV, Part IV, pp. 19-20/Corr.]

[Note, 29 July 1962, from Nehru for Y.D. Gundevia, the Commonwealth Secretary at the MEA, begins]

I enclose a letter from the Chief Minister of West Bengal.[132] I think it would be worthwhile to suggest a meeting with Pakistan at the ministerial level. Probably a Minister each of East Bengal and West Bengal could meet and consider the problem. You might discuss this matter with me on my return to Delhi.

J. Nehru
29.7.62
Raj Bhavan, Allahabad[133]

CS

[Note, 29 July 1962, from Nehru for Y.D. Gundevia, the Commonwealth Secretary, MEA, ends]

[Note, 30 July 1962, from Y.D. Gundevia for M.J. Desai, the Foreign Secretary, begins]

Would FS also please see?

Y.D. Gundevia
30/7/62

[Note, 30 July 1962, from Y.D. Gundevia for M.J. Desai, ends]

132. See Nehru's reply to P.C. Sen, item 51.
133. Nehru was in Calcutta on 29 July. "Allahabad" must be a typographical error.

[Note, 30 July 1962, from M.J. Desai for Y.D. Gundevia, begins]

Seen, thanks.

2. I am not sure that West Bengal would welcome a meeting with East Pakistan at Minister level. What the Chief Minister wants is a Minister level meeting between the two Central Governments. Perhaps latter could be arranged, the West Bengal Minister nominated assisting the Union Minister concerned.

M.J. Desai
30.7.62

CS

[Note, 30 July 1962, from M.J. Desai for Y.D. Gundevia, ends]

[Note, 2 August 1962, by Y.D. Gundevia, begins]

I have briefly spoken to the PM on 30.9.62 [sic].[134] We may await developments particularly at the Chief Secys' [Secretaries'] Conference.

Y.D. Gundevia
2.8.62

[Note, 2 August 1962, by Y.D. Gundevia, ends]

134. Should be 30.7.62.

53. To N.C. Chatterjee: Minorities in East Pakistan[135]

August 2, 1962

Dear Shri Chatterjee,

Thank you for your letter of the 1st August. I received the memorandum to which you refer, in Calcutta and I read it. We are all anxious to help the minorities in East Pakistan. But sometimes it so happens that the very steps we might take add to their burdens.[136]

Acharya Vinoba Bhave is for the present not making an extensive tour of East Pakistan. He intends to pass through a corner of East Pakistan between Assam and West Bengal.[137] As usual, he will walk from village to village. Later, I hope it may be possible for him to have a more extended tour of East Pakistan.

Yours sincerely,
[Jawaharlal Nehru]

54. To Lal Bahadur Shastri: Malerkotla's Nephew[138]

August 7, 1962

My dear Lal Bahadur,

I wrote to you on July 12[139] about a letter from the Nawab of Malerkotla who wanted his nephew to come to India from Pakistan. I do not know if you have come to any decision about it.

The Defence Minister has sent me the attached letter.[140]

---

135. Letter to a former President of the All India Hindu Mahasabha; 7B Pusa Road, New Delhi.
136. Expressing concern over the exodus of minorities from East Pakistan to West Bengal, Nehru said in Calcutta on 29 July "that while all possible assistance to the incoming refugees should be given, migration should not be encouraged;" and that "No Indian national should leave India because of his religious belief." *National Herald*, 30 July 1962.
137. Sarvodaya leader Vinoba Bhave intended to pass through East Pakistan en route to West Bengal to enable him to take a shortcut. See SWJN/SS/77/item 48. See also SWJN/SS/76/item 468.
138. Letter to the Home Minister. MHA, File No. 10/40/62-F. III, p. 11/c.
139. SWJN/SS/77/item 73.
140. Appendix 26.

It is for you to decide, but I still do not see any danger in his coming here on a visa for a relatively short time.[141]

Yours affectionately,
Jawaharlal Nehru

141. See the following:

D.S. Dang (not identified) to Fateh Singh, Joint Secretary, MHA.

24 August, 1962

Dear Shri Fateh Singh,
Kindly refer to your D.O. letter No. 10/40/62-F. III, without date, to Shri E.N. Mangat Rai, [Chief Secretary, Punjab] regarding the request of the Nawab of Malerkotla for the grant of permanent resettlement facilities in India to his brother and some other members of his family.

2.   The Punjab Government have no objection to the grant of permanent resettlement facilities in India to Shri Kazim Ali Khan whom H.H. the Nawab of Malerkotla wishes to adopt as his son.

3.   As regards the other relatives, this Government is of the view that they should not be granted these facilities.

With regards,

Yours sincerely,
D.S. Dang

MHA, File No. 10/40/62-F. III, p.14/c.
and V. Viswanathan, Home Secretary, to Ifthikhar Ali Khan, Nawab of Malerkotla.

21. 9. 1962

My dear Nawab Saheb
I am writing this with reference to your letter dated the 1st July, 1962, to the Prime Minister, regarding your nephew Sahibzada Kazim Ali Khan.

2.   We have issued instructions to the Indian High Commission, Karachi, to grant to Shri Kazim Ali Khan a visa valid for one year's stay in India. You may kindly advise him to contact the Indian High Commission in the matter.

Yours sincerely,
V. Viswanathan

MHA, File No. 10/40/62-F. III, p. 16/c.
For earlier correspondence, see SWJN/SS/77/items 65-66.

55. In the Lok Sabha: Tibetan Students in Denmark for Studies[142]

Will the Prime Minister be pleased to state:[143]

(a) whether it is a fact that 20 Tibetan students have been sent to Denmark to study agriculture;

(b) if so, who is bearing the expenses for their study; and

(c) how long they will be in Denmark and on their return how their experiences will be utilised?

The Deputy Minister in the Ministry of External Affairs (Dinesh Singh):

(a) Yes, Sir.

(b) Their travelling expenses were borne by the American Emergency Committee for Tibetan Relief and their maintenance and training expenses are being met by the Danish Committee for Tibetan Assistance.

(c) Their training period is 3 to 4 years. On their return, their experiences can usefully be utilised in the agricultural settlements set up in India for permanent rehabilitation of Tibetan refugees.

P. Kunhan: What is the reason for selecting only Tibetan students?

Speaker:[144] Why only Tibetan students were selected?

Jawaharlal Nehru: Because the fund is meant for Tibetan students only.

Renu Chakravartty: Is it a fact that there is a whole department in the Ministry of Education at the Centre dealing with these Tibetan students—as a separate entity?

Jawaharlal Nehru: I do not know how the Education Ministry deals with it. The External Affairs Ministry is broadly in charge. But, so far as education is concerned, they have asked the Education Ministry to look after it. So far

---

142. Oral answers, 9 August 1962. *Lok Sabha Debates*, Third Series, Vol. 6, 6 to 18 August 1962, cols 841-843.
143. Question by P. Kunhan and Renu Chakravartty, both CPI.
144. Hukam Singh.

as I know there is no special department. Somebody has to deal with it; and, probably, some official is there in charge.

Hem Barua:[145] May I know whether citizenship rights have been granted to the Tibetan refugees or they are treated as foreign nationals? If so, how can Government expect that the experience of these Tibetan students who have gone abroad and who will come back will be utilised for the benefit of the country?

Jawaharlal Nehru: I am sorry I have not quite understood the hon. Member's question. This problem of Tibetan refugees has arisen and we are more particularly interested in their education, in the education of the younger people. Various agencies abroad have helped in this and have even taken away some people; we have agreed to that. There is, for instance, a children's village in Switzerland and about 20-30 Tibetan children with some of their parents have gone there.

Speaker: His question was this. Would they be Indian citizens or foreigners? If they are foreigners, how would they be absorbed in agricultural pursuits in India?

Jawaharlal Nehru: I cannot say what they will be in future. At the present moment, they are not Indian nationals, whatever they might be.

Hem Barua: My question was not properly understood. May I submit that these are foreign nationals and the Deputy Minister said that when they come back their experience might be utilised for our country. I asked how it can be binding on them since they are foreign nationals.

Speaker: Nobody has said that it would be binding upon them. Next question.

145. PSP.

56. To Syed Mahmud: Indo-Arab Society[146]

August 18, 1962

My dear Mahmud,

Your letter of the 18th August. I think you might fix your meeting of the Indo-Arab Society[147] on Saturday, the 1st September, at 5.30 P.M.[148]

Yours affectionately,
Jawahar

57. To T.A. Pai: Holidays for Important Festivals[149]

August 18, 1962

Dear Shri Pai,

Your letter of August 17th. I agree with you that the really important festivals of Hindus, Muslims and Christians should be declared as holidays. There is a difficulty, however, that we have too many holidays, far more than any other country that I know of.

Good Friday is recognised as a holiday in many places in India.

Yours sincerely,
[Jawaharlal Nehru]

58. To S.A. Sohoni: Meeting Golwalkar[150]

August 20, 1962

Dear Shri Sohoni,

I have your letter of the 16th August. I am glad to know of the success of your daughter in her studies in the United States.

---

146. Letter to Congress, Rajya Sabha MP and President of the Indo-Arab Society; address: 20 Tughlak Crescent, New Delhi. NMML, Dr Syed Mahmud Papers.
147. The General Body Meeting of the Society.
148. For Nehru's speech at a symposium on "What India Owes to Arabs and What Arabs Owe to India," held in New Delhi on 1 September 1962 under the auspices of the Indo-Arab Society, see item 382.
149. Letter to the President of the South Kanara District Congress Committee, Udupi.
150. Letter to Advocate, Supreme Court, Jathar Peth, Akola, Maharashtra.

You refer to the death of the mother of Shri Golwalkar.[151] I am sorry to learn of this. But as I did not know the lady at all and my contacts with Shri Golwalkar have been very limited, I think it will be out of place for me to write to him a special letter of condolence.

I am afraid that my views about India and her future and our problems here are basically different from those of Shri Golwalkar and those of the RSS. If Shri Golwalkar wishes to see me, I shall of course agree to it. But I do not know if it will be worth while for me to trouble him to see me.

Yours sincerely,
[Jawaharlal Nehru]

59. To Valerian Cardinal Gracias: International Eucharistic Congress[152]

August 28, 1962

My dear Cardinal,
Thank you for your letter of the 28th August.

I am sure that the Bombay Government will give such help as is possible for the International Eucharistic Congress which is to be held in 1964. I shall mention the matter to the Chief Minister.[153]

With all good wishes,

Yours sincerely,
[Jawaharlal Nehru]

60. To Y.B. Chavan: International Eucharistic Congress[154]

August 28, 1962

My dear Chavan,
Cardinal Gracias has written to me about the International Eucharistic Congress which is going to be held in Bombay in 1964. He tells me that he has informed

---

151. M.S. Golwalkar, head of the Rashtriya Swayamsevak Sangh (RSS), 1940-1973.
152. Letter to the Archbishop of Bombay.
153. See item 60.
154. Letter to the Chief Minister of Maharashtra.

you of it and that you have promised him every cooperation. We should help him in so far as is possible for this Congress.[155]

Yours sincerely,
[Jawaharlal Nehru]

(e) Expulsion of Muslims from Northeast

61. Deporting Pakistanis[156]

I agree with your approach to this question. Broadly, that has been my approach too. Perhaps, I did not make myself quite clear to Shri Patnaik,[157] and this led to a slight misunderstanding. What I told him was:

(1) that deportation should not take place for some months. I did not mean it should start automatically after a period. But we should watch the situation.

(2) that meanwhile, enquiries regarding nationality should continue. Further, when the enquiries are completed, notices should be issued to persons definitely found to be Pakistani nationals, and they should be asked to quit after a month or so. This itself would result probably, as you say, in many of these Pakistani nationals leaving.

(3) That when we start any deportations again would depend on the circumstances then prevailing. We shall decide at that time. In any event, large numbers of Pakistanis should not be deported in a bunch. I did suggest that small batches might be sent.

I did not suggest that eight or ten batches every month should go. I said that a number of batches might be sent like this in a month.

2. I had also suggested that some kind of a notice might be sent informing Pakistan authorities to the effect that, after a careful enquiry, we had found a number of Pakistani nationals who had entered India illegally. We have given them notice to quit. It need not be stated when and where they will be asked to leave India.

3. But what you have suggested appears to me the better way to proceed. You can inform the Chief Commissioner of Tripura accordingly.[158]

155. See item 59.
156. Note, 8 August 1962, for Y.D. Gundevia, the Commonwealth Secretary at the MEA.
157. N.M. Patnaik, Chief Commissioner of Tripura, met Nehru on 6 August 1962.
158. See also items 62-64.

62. In the Lok Sabha: Hindus in Noakhali[159]

Will the Prime Minister be pleased to state:[160]

(a) whether the attention of Government has been drawn to press reports published in Calcutta giving news of the incidents directed against Hindu minorities at Chowmohani Bazar in the District of Noakhali in East Pakistan; and

(b) whether any enquiries have been made by Government from the Deputy High Commissioner of India at Dacca[161] as to the veracity of these press reports?

The Deputy Minister in the Ministry of External Affairs (Dinesh Singh):

(a) Yes, Sir.

(b) Reports from our Deputy High Commissioner in Dacca have confirmed these incidents.

Tridib Kumar Chaudhuri: May I know if the attention of the Government has been further drawn to the fact that these incidents are said to have occurred as a measure of reprisal by certain Pakistani seamen coming from Noakhali who have been discharged from the docks and marine service in Calcutta. Is there any truth in that report?

Dinesh Singh: No, Sir. I do not know. I do not think there is any truth in what the hon. Member said.

Tridib Kumar Chaudhuri: May I ask if the attention of the Government has been drawn to the press reports to which the question refers? The same press reports refer to the reports of alleged reprisals. Have the Government received any specific report from the Deputy High Commissioner at Dacca about this thing?

---

159. Oral answers, 9 August 1962. *Lok Sabha Debates*, Third Series, Vol. 6, 6 to 18 August 1962, cols 837-840.

160. Question by Tridib Kumar Chaudhuri, Revolutionary Socialist Party.

161. S.K. Chowdhry.

Jawaharlal Nehru: We have no information on this subject, we have not heard about it, and it is not mentioned in any report that we have received.

S.M. Banerjee:[162] As these incidents are taking place not only in Noakhali but in many places in East Pakistan, I would like to know whether the Prime Minister will have a meeting with the President of Pakistan[163] to discuss this matter once and for all.

Speaker:[164] But the question is specific.

S.M. Banerjee: I would like to know whether the Prime Minister is likely to have a talk with the President of Pakistan only on this issue.

Jawaharlal Nehru: I have not quite clearly understood. Something about my meeting the President of Pakistan?

Speaker: And having a talk on this issue.

Jawaharlal Nehru: There is no proposal at present of my meeting the President.

D.C. Sharma:[165] The Foreign Minister of Pakistan[166] shouts about any small incident that takes place in India affecting the Muslim minority. How is it that when such incidents take place in Pakistan affecting the Hindu Minority, our Ministry of External Affairs keeps silent?

Jawaharlal Nehru: I do not quite understand what the hon. Member means. Our Missions keep silent?

D.C. Sharma: Even when a small incident affecting the minorities in India takes place, the Foreign Minister of Pakistan shouts about it in the Assembly[167] and everywhere. How is it that when such incidents take place in Pakistan affecting our minorities, our Ministry of External Affairs does not take any notice of them?

162. Independent.
163. Ayub Khan.
164. Hukam Singh.
165. Congress.
166. Muhammad Ali.
167. National Assembly of Pakistan.

Jawaharlal Nehru: I do not know what the hon. Member expects us to do. I hope any hon. Member of this hon. House does not shout unreasonably.

Mahavir Tyagi:[168] It is a question of publicity. The hon. Prime Minister must realise that his publicity is lacking. It is not a question of shouting.

Renu Chakravartty: May I know whether, when the Chief Secretaries of West Bengal and East Pakistan met recently in Dacca, this particular matter of the Chowmohani Bazar riots was gone into and the steps have been evolved to deal with this entire matter of incidents in the two countries?

Jawaharlal Nehru: I have not seen the report of the meeting. But, presumably, some reference was made to it because of their talks.

Tridib Kumar Chaudhuri: In regard to these incidents and similar other incidents which occurred in Pakistan last month and the month before, may I know whether, apart from the Chief Secretaries' Conference, any exchanges have taken place between our Government and the Government of Pakistan and whether any specific policy mutually agreed upon has been reached.

Dinesh Singh: Our Deputy High Commissioner in East Pakistan handed over a note to the Government and our High Commissioner[169] in his talks with the President of Pakistan on the 8th July referred to these matters.

Tridib Kumar Chaudhuri: What is the outcome? Apart from the reference, what has been the outcome; whether any protection ...

Speaker: If there had been some outcome that would have been conveyed just now. Probably, there was no outcome.

Jawaharlal Nehru: Usually there is an agreement. There is no difference that protection should be given. On either side, they refer to some incidents happening on the other side and our people draw pointed attention to what has happened on that side. It is agreed that every attempt should be made to give protection. The details have already been worked out previously on this kind

168. Congress.
169. Rajeshwar Dayal.

of things. Broadly, the general policy is agreed upon. Whether it is given effect to or not is a different matter.[170]

63. Eviction of Muslims from Assam and Tripura[171]

I enclose a telegram I have received from Noakhali.[172] I was under the impression that no Muslims are being evicted from either Assam or Tripura at present. I think we should go slow in this matter.[173]

I am sending a copy of this telegram to the Home Minister.[174]

64. Meeting with Ayub Khan[175]

Last evening I met President Ayub Khan at a Reception, and had a short talk with him. He referred to the expulsion of illegal immigrants from Tripura and Assam and expressed his gratitude to me for having intervened in this matter.

He further said that whether these people were illegal immigrants or not their expulsion created a difficult situation for them in Pakistan and people there were excited over the matter. This again had its reactions in India. Thus, however justified we might be in expelling them, this led to a chain of events with much more undesirable consequences. He hoped therefore that this would not be done.

I told him that we had told our people to slow down this process. In fact, after the first expulsion of some groups numbering about 3,000 or so from Tripura, we had stopped further steps of this kind at least for a period. But about 5,000 other illegal immigrants had themselves left Tripura for Pakistan probably because they feared that some action might be taken against them.

170. See also items 61 and 63-64.
171. Note, 27 August 1962, for Y.D. Gundevia, the Commonwealth Secretary at the MEA. MEA, File No. P. I/108/62, Vol. II, p. 5/Note.
172. Telegram from Mahendrakumar Saha, Satiranjan Saha, Jyotilal Saha and Kalimohan Bhowmik, sent on 25 August 1962: "Kindly stop eviction of Muslim minorities from Tripura and Assam in the name of humanity. Displaced persons pouring in Pakistan by hundreds daily creating problems."
173. See also items 61-62 and 64.
174. Lal Bahadur Shastri.
175. Note, 12 September 1962, for Y.D. Gundevia, the Commonwealth Secretary, MEA, sent from 9 Kensington Palace Gardens, London. MHA, File No. 1/76/62-F. III, p. 26. Also available in the JN Collection.

I did not give any particular assurance or undertaking to President Ayub Khan. But I do feel that we should proceed very cautiously in this matter and for the present at least we should stop this business. There is no doubt that this leads to consequences on both sides of the border and creates further difficulties.

I think that the most that should be done at present should be to send notices to proved illegal immigrants and ask them to leave. Further steps might not be taken at present. I suppose the notice itself will have some effect.

We can consider this matter further on my return.[176]

65. To Lal Bahadur Shastri: Expelling Muslims from Northeast[177]

12th September, 1962

My dear Lal Bahadur,

I am sending you a copy of a note I am sending to our Commonwealth Secretary.[178] I think that we should proceed very cautiously in this matter and for the present avoid expelling people. If any go of their own accord that is good enough. I would suggest that instructions be sent to both Tripura and Assam to this effect.

Yours affectionately,
[Jawaharlal Nehru]

(f) Laws and Administration

66. For the Madras High Court[179]

I send my good wishes to the Madras High Court on the occasion of its completing one hundred years of its existence. During these years the Madras High Court has had a succession of very eminent judges who have enhanced not only the reputation of the court but of the judiciary in India. I remember in my early days as a practising lawyer, I used to read with admiration some of the judgments of the Madras High Court.

---

176. See also items 61-63.
177. Letter to the Home Minister. Sent from London.
178. For Nehru's note to Y.D. Gundevia, Commonwealth Secretary, MEA, see item 64.
179. Message, 22 July 1962.

The independence and ability of our judiciary is one of the stout pillars on which our democratic structure stands. To this the Madras High Court has contributed greatly. I hope that this high record will be maintained in the future as it has been in the past.

67. To Asok K. Chanda: Rajya Sabha or a Job[180]

July 23, 1962

My dear Asok,

Your letter of July 23. You are quite right in saying that you were encouraged by various senior colleagues of ours to stand for election to Parliament. I myself would have welcomed you. But, as you say, various developments took place which came in the way. I do not think these developments had anything to do with any opposition to you. The matter did not come up before me as I was not on the Selection Committees. But I have a vague recollection that the question came up before the Selection Committee as to whether you should be nominated as a candidate or your sister-in-law. They thought that the sister-in-law, for various reasons, should be given preference.

If you can be selected for election to the Rajya Sabha, I shall be glad, but I do not know if any elections will take place in the near future from Assam. It will be difficult to ask the President to nominate you to the Rajya Sabha.

I cannot think of any other deliberative or executive organisation which you might have in mind.

Yours sincerely,
[Jawaharlal Nehru]

180. Letter to former Comptroller and Auditor General of India; address: 46 Friends Colony, New Delhi 14.

68. To A.N. Khosla: Construction Projects and Committee[181]

July 31, 1962

My dear Khosla,

Your letter of the 26th July.[182] I do not think it will be advisable to appoint Karnail Singh[183] as Chairman of the Committee you mention.[184]

Yours sincerely,
Jawaharlal Nehru

69. To S.P. Singha: No Holidays to Honour Anybody[185]

August 2, 1962

Dear Shri Singha,

Your letter of the 31st July. I do not approve of any addition to the holidays, nor do I think it is desirable to honour the memory of any person by declaring a new holiday. As it is, we have more holidays in India than, perhaps, in any country in the world. I should imagine, that on a day, when we think of great men we should work all the harder.

Yours sincerely,
[Jawaharlal Nehru]

---

181. Letter to Member of the Planning Commission. PMO, File No. 17(514)/62-66-PMS, Sr. No. 1-A.
182. Appendix 13.
183. Chairman of the Railway Board from April 1960, was due for retirement on 16 August 1962.
184. See also item 70.
185. Letter; address: Mahabir Singh Quarters, M.E. School Road, Jugsalai, Jamshedpur-2.

70. To Gulzarilal Nanda: Not Karnail Singh for Construction Committee[186]

August 2, 1962

My dear Gulzarilal,

A.N. Khosla[187] wrote to me a few days ago suggesting the formation of a Committee for the reduction of construction costs.[188] With this proposal I am in full agreement.

But he suggested that Karnail Singh should be Chairman of this Committee. I did not think this was desirable for a variety of reasons, and I have written to Khosla about it.[189]

Yours sincerely,
Jawaharlal Nehru

71. To H.C. Mathur: Retirement Age of Judges[190]

August 3, 1962

My dear Mathur,

I have received a copy of your letter dated 3rd August addressed to the Secretary of the Congress Parliamentary Party.[191] This relates to the age of retirement of High Court Judges.

I believe there is a proposal to raise this age limit somewhat. If you like, this may be mentioned in the Party Executive. But this is hardly a matter of policy. I might mention that in the United States of America, judges are appointed for life and there is no mandatory age of retirement. They may however retire after ten years of service at the age of seventy. In England, the age of retirement has only recently been fixed for judges at seventy-five. Previously there was no such age limit.

It is usually considered that High Court and Supreme Court Judges in all countries do not have that kind of strenuous work which wears officers out. It was for this reason that they have been given a much longer period in other

---

186. Letter to the Deputy Chairman of the Planning Commission. PMO, File No. 17(514)/62-66-PMS, Sr. No. 4-A.
187. Member, Planning Commission.
188. Appendix 13.
189. Item 68.
190. Letter to Congress, Lok Sabha MP; address: 216 North Avenue, New Delhi.
191. Raghunath Singh.

countries. As a matter of fact, there is considerable shortage of suitable persons for these posts.[192]

Yours sincerely,
J. Nehru

72. To S. Radhakrishnan: Appointment of Governors[193]

August 4, 1962

My dear Mr President,

When I saw you last at Hyderabad,[194] I mentioned to you the vacancies that are going to occur in the post of Governor and suggested some names for them. The Andhra Pradesh Governor, Shri Bhimsen Sachar, is retiring at the end of this month. Shri N.V. Gadgil has expressed his desire to resign from the Governorship of the Punjab.

The Home Minister[195] and I have considered this matter carefully. We feel that in Andhra Pradesh it will be desirable for us to transfer General Shrinagesh from Assam for the remainder of his term, that is, a little over two years. The Chief Minister of Andhra Pradesh[196] has agreed to this and General Shrinagesh has also expressed his willingness.

In the vacancy created in Assam by the transfer of General Shringesh, we suggest that Shri Vishnu Sahay, Member of the Planning Commission, be appointed. Assam is a difficult and complicated State and the Government has to deal also with Nagaland and NEFA. There are also the difficult problems created by the demand for a new State in the Hill districts of Assam. We feel that Shri Vishnu Sahay, who has already spent some months as Governor

---

192. The CPP Executive Committee on 10 August 1962 approved a proposal for the extension of the retirement age of High Court judges from 60 years to 62. *The Times of India* reported on 11 August 1962 that while some members "expressed the fear that such an extension might have repercussions on other services," the consensus was in favour of the proposal. "Mr Nehru pointed out that, as in the case of technical personnel and specialists, the experience of High Court judges also deserved to be utilised over as long a period as possible for the good of the country." See also item 86.
193. Letter to the President. MHA, File No. 19/51/62-Public-I, pp. 1-2. Also available in President's Secretariat, File No. 1(8)/62, pp. 1-2.
194. Nehru was in Hyderabad, 18-20 July 1962.
195. Lal Bahadur Shastri.
196. N. Sanjiva Reddy.

in Assam,[197] will be able to deal with these problems effectively. The Chief Minister of Assam[198] is agreeable to the appointment of Shri Vishnu Sahay.

[THE LIFT-OFF]

(From *Shankar's Weekly*, 30 September 1962, p.12)

For the Punjab, we recommend Shri K.C. Reddy, now a Minister of the Central Government. The Chief Minister of the Punjab[199] has agreed to this appointment, and Shri K.C. Reddy is willing to go there.

These appointments can take effect on a suitable date early in September. But Shri N.V. Gadgil would like the changeover to take place about September 15th or a little later.

197. From 12 November 1960 to 13 January 1961.
198. B.P. Chaliha.
199. Partap Singh Kairon.

We, therefore, recommend for your consideration that:

(1)   General Shrinagesh should be transferred to Andhra Pradesh as Governor for the remainder of his term,

(2)   Shri Vishnu Sahay be appointed as Governor in Assam on the transfer of General Shrinagesh, and

(3)   Shri K.C. Reddy be appointed as Governor of the Punjab on a date to be fixed later as convenient to the two persons concerned.[200]

I trust that these recommendations will meet with your approval.

Yours sincerely,
Jawaharlal Nehru

73. For Police Conference[201]

My good wishes to the All India Police Duty Meet on the occasion of its 10th Conference. Our Police have a difficult task to perform. This can only be done if the Police are not only efficient, but feel at one with the people whom they serve. This feeling of oneness will enable them to serve them much better. Also, it is important that they should do their work with integrity and gain a reputation for this among the people.

74. To S. Radhakrishnan: Governor of Orissa[202]

August 6, 1962

My dear Mr President,

I have already written to you about certain recommendations for the post of Governor. I am sorry I forgot to mention one case which I have already discussed with you. This was about the Governorship of Orissa.

---

200. Eventually Pattom A. Thanu Pillai, the Chief Minister of Kerala, was appointed Governor of Punjab. K.C. Reddy continued as Minister of Commerce and Industry until 19 July 1963.

201. Message, 5 August 1962, forwarded to B.B. Banerji, Inspector General of Police, Delhi.

202. Letter to the President. MHA, File No. 19/44/62-Public-I, p. 7/c. Also available in the JN Collection.

The Home Minister[203] and I recommend that on the conclusion of Shri Sukthankar's term there as Governor, Shri A.N. Khosla, at present Member of the Planning Commission, be appointed Governor of Orissa.

The Chief Minister of Orissa[204] is particularly desirous of having Shri Khosla there as Governor as he thinks Shri Khosla's presence will be very helpful in his developmental work in Orissa. Shri Khosla has gladly agreed to this suggestion. I recommend, therefore, for your favourable consideration that Shri A.N. Khosla be appointed as Governor of Orissa to succeed Shri Sukthankar.

Yours sincerely,
Jawaharlal Nehru

75. To Bhimsen Sachar: Not Governor of Punjab[205]

August 6, 1962

My dear Sachar,
Your letter of the 2nd August.

I fully appreciate what you have written, even though it is unusual. I am afraid, however, that it will not be possible. I have already recommended to the President to appoint my colleague here in the Union Cabinet, K.C. Reddy, to be Governor of the Punjab in succession to Gadgil.[206] It would be very odd indeed to withdraw my recommendation which was made after reference to the parties concerned.

Apart from this, it would be a breach of our normal practice to appoint a person as Governor from the State concerned.[207] Our rule is not to do so, and we have followed this rule consistently except on one occasion when for some time Dr Mookerjee[208] was Governor of Bengal.

I can quite understand your desire to be helpful in the Punjab, and I believe you can be helpful. But in view of what I have said above, I am sorry we cannot make any change in the arrangements already made.

Yours sincerely,
[Jawaharlal Nehru]

203. Lal Bahadur Shastri.
204. Bijoyanand (Biju) Patnaik.
205. Letter to the Governor of Andhra Pradesh.
206. N.V. Gadgil. See item 72.
207. Bhimsen Sachar was a former Chief Minister of Punjab.
208. H.C. Mookerjee, Governor of West Bengal, 1951-1956.

76. To T.T. Krishnamachari: Reorganizing Economic Ministries[209]

August 8, 1962

My dear T.T.,

I have sent your three notes to the Cabinet Secretary, S.S. Khera. I enclose a copy of a note I have sent him.[210]

As I mentioned to you, the note on the reorganisation of the Economic Ministries should be considered by a committee consisting of Morarji Desai,[211] Gulzarilal Nanda,[212] Lal Bahadur Shastri[213] and, of course, you, with Khera as Secretary.

The other two notes might be considered by Gulzarilal Nanda and Vishnu Sahay.[214]

I think that Khera might deal with all these notes as Secretary. Perhaps you might send for him and have a talk with him explaining how you would like him to function.

Yours sincerely,
[Jawaharlal Nehru]

77. Reorganizing Ministries[215]

Shri T.T. Krishnamachari, Minister without Portfolio, has been good enough to send me three notes on the subject of reorganisation. One of these notes deals with important changes in the present organisation of our Ministries. The other notes also contain important suggestions.

2. All of these have to be considered carefully before we can come to any decisions. I am enclosing the three notes he has sent me.

3. One of these dealing with reorganisation of Ministries and Departments specially requires careful consideration. I suggest that a Cabinet Committee consisting of the Finance Minister Shri Morarji Desai, the Minister of Labour

209. Letter to the Minister without Portfolio.
210. Item 77.
211. The Finance Minister.
212. The Minister of Labour and Planning.
213. The Home Minister.
214. A former Cabinet Secretary, Vishnu Sahay was a Member of the Planning Commission and Governor-designate of Assam.
215. Note, 8 August 1962, for S.S. Khera, the Cabinet Secretary.

134

and Planning, Shri Gulzarilal Nanda, the Home Minister Shri Lal Bahadur Shastri and Shri T.T. Krishnamachari himself should consider this note or such other note on the subject as Shri T.T. Krishnamachari might prepare. You might function as the Secretary of this Committee.

4. I suggest that you should discuss this matter with Shri T.T. Krishnamachari and take his directions as to what note you should send to the other members of the Committee. It is possible that he may revise his old note for this purpose.

5. The second note which he has sent me deals with the Planning Commission. This also requires careful consideration with Shri Gulzarilal Nanda and Shri Vishnu Sahay.

6. The third note deals with Public Sector projects and suggests an Inspectorate. This is a preliminary note and Shri T.T. Krshnamachari has said that he would draw up more detailed proposals. This matter will also have to be considered with Shri Gulzarilal Nanda, the Deputy Chairman of the Planning Commission. Possibly Shri T.T. Krishnamachari might desire to prepare a fuller note for consideration.[216]

78. In the Rajya Sabha: Non-Officials as Ambassadors[217]

Will the Prime Minister be pleased to state:[218]

(a) the number of non-officials appointed as Indian Ambassadors or High Commissioners in foreign countries during the last five years ending 30th June, 1962; and

(b) the number of officials appointed to these posts during the same period?

The Deputy Minister in the Ministry of External Affairs (Dinesh Singh):

(a) Nineteen.

(b) Twenty-three.

M.P. Bhargava: May I know whether it is the opinion of the Government that officials can interpret better the foreign policy of the Government of India than non-officials?

---

216. See item 76.
217. Oral Answers, 8 August 1962. *Rajya Sabha Debates*, Vol. 40, Nos. 1-8, 6 to 16 August 1962, cols 587-89.
218. Question by M.P. Bhargava, Congress.

Jawaharlal Nehru: It depends upon individuals, Sir. Some non-officials can interpret it better than officials; some officials can interpret it better than non-officials.

> M.P. Bhargava: May I know whether it is due to the non-availability of suitable non-official candidates that very few non-officials have been appointed as ambassadors as against quite a number of officials?

Jawaharlal Nehru: The whole Foreign Service of the country is created and kept up for that purpose. Normally, the Foreign Service supplies the diplomatic personnel in every country and it is only with exceptions that non-officials are appointed. And the tendency in most countries where non-officials used to be appointed has been that they are appointed much less now than they were previously. We have appointed more non-officials than most countries have done.

> Arjun Arora:[219] May I know when the last non-official was appointed?

Dinesh Singh: A few months ago.

> N. Sri Rama Reddy:[220] I would like to know whether the policy of the Government of India is that qualifications being equal with regard to officials and non-officials, preference would be given to non-officials instead of to officials?

Jawaharlal Nehru: Qualifications? They are not university qualifications. The qualifications are the training and knowledge of foreign languages which is not very often found in non-officials. The officials have to learn them, two or three foreign languages, and that is very important. Apart from that, a so called official in the diplomatic service, after he has passed a very difficult examination, has to go through a period of training for three years and then he is appointed as an apprentice. This is a continuation of his training, and all the time he is learning foreign languages, so that he is trained for this type of work. Non-officials may have higher university qualifications but they have not that background of experience and training.

> A.D. Mani:[221] Is there any fixed quota, mental or written quota, for the appointment of non-officials as ambassadors? I am told that the quota is full now and that there will not be any more appointment of non-officials.

219. Congress.
220. Congress.
221. Independent.

Jawaharlal Nehru: There is no quota but originally when we started the Diplomatic Service, naturally there were not many trained people available for it. Now it has grown, it is an established service and, therefore, it occupies most of the posts. In special cases, non-officials are sent. As such there is no quota. We consider people on their merits. From the answer to this question it will be seen that the number of non-officials appointed in the last five years was 19 and of officials 23. There is a very larger number of non-officials.

79. To Morarji Desai: Discretionary Grant for Vice-President[222]

August 9, 1962

My dear Morarji,

I saw the Vice-President[223] today. He mentioned to me casually that as Governor of Bihar, he had some discretionary grant at his disposal which he used for helping deserving causes and students. Now he does not have any such thing, and indeed his salary is much less than what he got as Governor.

I suggest that you might give him a discretionary grant of rupees twenty-five thousand for the year.

Yours sincerely
[Jawaharlal Nehru]

80. To C. Rajagopalachari: President's Pension[224]

August 9, 1962

My dear Rajaji,

Your letter of the 7th August about the recent amendment to the President's Pension Act.[225] When I received your previous letter on the subject, I got in touch with Lal Bahadur.[226] I have asked him again today and he tells me that

---

222. Letter to the Finance Minister.
223. Zakir Husain; he was the Governor of Bihar, 6 July 1957 – 11 May 1962.
224. Letter to leader of the Swatantra Party; address: 60, Bazlullah Road, Madras-17.
225. Rajagopalachari's letter has not been traced. The matter related to revision of the President's Emoluments And Pension Act, 1951. For previous reference, see SWJN/SS/77/item 87.
226. Lal Bahadur Shastri, the Home Minister.

he is having certain simple rules framed under the Act. He hopes to send these to you in a day or two. I trust that these will meet your wishes in the matter.[227]

Yours affectionately,
[Jawaharlal Nehru]

81. For S.S. Khera: Include Petrochemical Industries in Mines and Fuel Ministry[228]

I enclose a letter from the Minister of Mines & Fuel.[229] I am broadly of opinion that the Petro-Chemical Industries should be placed under his Ministry. The division of these industries broadly comes in the way of their integrated development. I think, therefore, that it would be better to accept his suggestion and postpone any decision till the consultant's report is available.

You are acquainted with these matters and I should like your opinion.

82. To Gulzarilal Nanda: Using Surendra Singh in Planning Commission[230]

August 13, 1962

My dear Gulzarilal,

Raja Surendra Singh of Nalagarh[231] came to see me today. He was finding himself at a rather loose end. He has done good work in agriculture, and I think we should utilise him fully. Would it not be advisable to make him an Adviser in Agriculture in the Planning Commission? It is far better to have a so-called non-official than officials always to do this work.

---

227. Changes in rules were announced on 1 October 1962 through two notifications: The President's Pension Rules, 1962, and the President's Pension (Maintenance of Secretarial Staff and Medical Attendance) Rules, 1962.
228. Note, 13 August 1962, for the Cabinet Secretary. PMO, File No. 17(481)/61-68-PMS, Sr. No. 4-A.
229. K.D. Malaviya.
230. Letter to the Deputy Chairman of the Planning Commission. PMO, File No. 17(189)/60-65-PMS, Sr. No. 37-A.
231. 1922-1971; former ruler of Nalagarh state in Punjab; Adviser, Ministry of Food and Agriculture, 1958-1962; Adviser, Colonization, Ministry of Home Affairs, for some time in 1962; Member, Programme Administration, and Ex-Officio Additional Secretary, Planning Commission, 1962-1966.

I believe he is a member of the Evaluation Committee. That does not give him enough scope. He has just come back from the Andamans.

Yours sincerely,
Jawaharlal Nehru

83. To Jagjivan Ram: Extension for P.C. Lall at IAC[232]

August 14, 1962

My dear Jagjivan Ram,

A few days ago, Air Vice Marshal Lall came to see me and to bid good-bye to me.[233] I was sorry to learn from him that he was leaving his present job and indeed Government service. I have a high opinion of him both for his competence and as a man. So far as I know, he has done very well in the IAC.

I gathered from him that an extension of a year or two was offered to him, but he felt that it would not be enough and he would be left high and dry after that period. I think he is a man we should not lose. We should be prepared to give him a longer period of extension. It is not necessary that he should remain in the IAC all the time. We could use him for some other public sector industrial enterprise. But, for the moment, he might continue in the IAC.

I hope you will give thought to this matter.

I might mention that I discussed this with several of our colleagues, and they all had a very high opinion of Air Vice Marshal Lall.

Yours sincerely,
Jawaharlal Nehru

---

232. Letter to the Minister of Transport and Communications. PMO, File No. 35(11)/56-70-PMS, Sr. No. 111-A. Also available in the JN Collection.

233. Air Vice Marshal P.C. Lall was deputed to the Ministry of Civil Aviation as General Manager of the Indian Airlines Corporation (IAC) in 1957. At the end of his tenure with the IAC on 30 September 1962, he resigned from the Indian Air Force, but was reinstated in December 1962 as Air Officer Maintenance. He was Chief of Air Staff, 16 July 1969 to 15 January 1973. Website http://www.bharat-rakshak.com accessed on 9 April 2018.

84. To Lal Bahadur Shastri: Muzaffar Ali Jobless and Penniless[234]

August 14, 1962

My dear Lal Bahadur,

I enclose a copy of a letter from Anis Ahmad Abbasi, Editor of the daily *Haqiqat*, Lucknow. His nephew, Muzaffar Ali, saw me today. He was in a very frustrated condition and said he could get no job or work. He had come here with great difficulty and did not have enough money to go back. I gave him some money and told him that his qualifications were not very good, but I would see if it was possible to find some work for him

Will you give some thought to this matter?

Yours affectionately,
[Jawaharlal Nehru]

85. To P.C. Sen: Exchanging Judges between States[235]

August 14, 1962

My dear Chief Minister,

Perhaps you know that it was decided at the Chief Ministers' conference held last year and also, I think, by the National Integration Conference, that it would be highly desirable for High Court Judges to be exchanged between various States.[236] This was one of the suggestions for promoting national integration. To some extent, we have been giving effect to this, but I gather that the West Bengal Government does not like the idea of having any Judge from outside West Bengal.

The Chief Justice of India[237] has drawn my attention to this matter and I am writing to you to request you to give further consideration to it and to agree to a suitable Judge from outside West Bengal to be appointed, when occasion arises, to the Calcutta High Court.

Yours sincerely,
J. Nehru

---

234. Letter to the Home Minister.
235. Letter to the Chief Minister of West Bengal.
236. See the report of the National Integration Council meeting, 3 June 1962, in SWJN/ SS/77/item 7.
237. B.P. Sinha.

86. To Lal Bahadur Shastri: Judges' Benefits and Appointments[238]

August 14, 1962

My dear Lal Bahadur,

Chief Justice Sinha[239] came to see me this evening and talked about various matters for nearly an hour.

First he referred to the age limit of High Court Judges and their pensionary benefits. He urged strongly that the age limit should be raised to 65 and not, as suggested, to 62. Also, they should have more adequate pension. Together with that, they should be prevented from practising or accepting any office afterwards. At present, he said, they were hankering after some jobs afterwards and this came in the way of their independence.

I told him that even our proposal to have the age limit raised to 62 was discussed in the Executive Committee of our Party in Parliament and some persons objected to it. However, at the end, the majority agreed to 62. He again impressed on me that 62 was not enough.[240]

He also referred to the reluctance of some High Courts to exchange Judges from elsewhere. This was especially so in Calcutta.

One of the difficulties was that an outside Judge did not find it easy to get proper accommodation and he had to pay very heavily for a house. Therefore, houses should be provided by the State. Apparently you were thinking of giving an allowance of ten percent, that is, Rs 350/-, a month. That, he said, would not be enough in Calcutta, Bombay or Madras. Elsewhere it might do.

Then he complained of some State Governments, namely UP & Punjab, holding up the appointment of Judges because they did not like the persons recommended by the Chief Justice. This resulted in vacancies for a long period of time and work suffering. The Chief Minister should not hold these up. Even if they disagreed, they should send their disagreement. I think that he is quite right in saying this.

He then referred to Jafar Imam's[241] case which is very unfortunate. After a long absence from the Court because of serious illness, he now insists on attending, although physically he is hardly capable of doing so and mentally he is not alert. Apparently, all the efforts of our Chief Justice to make him take

---

238. Letter to the Home Minister.
239. B.P. Sinha, Chief Justice of India.
240. See also item 71.
241. A Judge of the Supreme Court from 1955, and former Chief Justice of the Patna High Court.

more rest have failed, chiefly because of Jafar Imam's wife who insists that he should go to court. This was becoming a laughing matter and the Chief Justice suggested that something should be done about this. He thought that some kind of a certificate of fitness might be asked for by the Home Ministry in such cases. I think something of this kind should be done. You can have the matter looked into. It is absurd for a person who is physically hardly capable of walking and is not at all well, to be made to sit in court.[242]

He then spoke about the case for criminal libel which Sikri, Advocate General of the Punjab, has instituted against the ex-Chief Justice Khosla. He said this was very unfortunate and would have a bad effect on the reputation of the Judiciary. We should try our best, he added, to have this matter settled out of court. According to the Chief Justice, the article which Khosla wrote was pretty bad and Sikri had a good case.[243]

You will be seeing the Chief Justice one of these days and so I have told you what he said to me.

I am writing letters to the Chief Ministers of UP, Punjab and Bengal, copies of which I enclose.

Yours affectionately,
[Jawaharlal Nehru]

242. Justice Imam resigned in January 1964 at Nehru's instance after the All India Institute of Medical Sciences found him unfit for service. See M.C. Setalvad, *My Life. Law and Other Things* (Bombay: N.M. Tripathi Private Ltd, 1971), p. 508.

243. A complaint filed by Sarv Mittra Sikri, the Advocate-General of Punjab, against G.D. Khosla, a former Chief Justice of the Punjab High Court, had come up before a local magistrate in Chandigarh on 11 August 1962. Khosla was alleged to have made defamatory references to Sikri and his wife, using disguised names for them, in a story entitled "The Snake—A Fable for Grown-ups" published in *The Sunday Tribune Magazine* of 29 April 1962. For the story, see appendix 1.

M.C. Setalvad, the Attorney-General of India, 1950-1963, wrote in his memoirs that eventually, at the suggestion of Chief Justice B.P. Sinha and P.B. Gajendragadkar, a Judge of the Supreme Court, he persuaded Sikri to withdraw his criminal complaint after a public apology by Khosla. Setalvad, ibid, pp. 508-509.

Khushwant Singh, the writer, also refers to this incident in a brief memoir in *The Tribune*, Saturday, 25 June 2011, in the following words: "He [G.D. Khosla] wrote a short story, which he showed to me, before he sent it to *The Tribune*. He did not tell me it was a concealed diatribe against Justice Sikri and his wife. Sikri filed a complaint of criminal libel against him. He fled India and stayed abroad as long as he could, hoping the matter would be forgotten. Sikri pursued him till he made an abject apology."

Neither Setalvad nor Khushwant Singh have clarified what form the apology took.

87. To Kishen Pattnayak: Rebutting Lohia's Charges on Expenses[244]

August 15, 1962

Dear Shri Pattnayak,

I have received your letter of the 14th August with its enclosure. I have read the note you have sent. This is the first time I have read anything of this kind. Dr Lohia's analysis of my expenditure is very extraordinary and is full of statements which are not true.[245] I am very reluctant to enter into these personal controversies. There are certain normal canons of decency which Dr Lohia does not observe.

For your information, however, I am stating some facts.

All Ministers of Government are given a salary plus a house. The gardens attached to the houses are looked after by the Public Works Department. The value of the furnished house is, however, included in the calculations for income-tax.

In regard to my case, the house in which I live is treated as part of the President's Estate and is looked after by it. An arrangement was made many years ago when I first came here that I should be charged for expenses in the house in regard to food etc. on actual basis. I am, therefore, presented with a bill every month of the actual cost incurred. I live in this house almost like a hotel. I pay for my personal guests and the Government pays for State guests who stay here.[246] Most of the servants here come from the Rashtrapati Bhavan staff.

There is a certain aircraft kept for the President's use. Some Ministers, including the Prime Minister, are according to our rules entitled to use it. This aircraft has anyhow to do certain hours of flying. Instead of flying for practice, it carries the President and the Prime Minister. No charge is made for this except when it is used for some other than official purpose.

---

244. Letter to Socialist Party, Lok Sabha MP; address: 30 North Avenue, New Delhi.
     This is the first of three letters written to Kishan Pattnayak in reply to Pattnayak's letters on Nehru's personal expenses. For Nehru's two other letters, see items 90 and 96. Pattnayak's letters and the Hindi translations of Nehru's replies are available in Rammanohar Lohia, *Pradhanmantri Mr Nehru Par Pratidin Pachchis Hazar Rupay* (Darbhanga: Kautilya Prakashan, 1963), pp. 148-163.
245. Pattnayak had sent copy of a statement issued on 13 August 1962 by Rammanohar Lohia, Socialist Party leader; it is published in Rammanohar Lohia, ibid, pp.122-128. Lohia had lost to Nehru in the Lok Sabha election from Phulpur in February 1962.
246. See Nehru's earlier observations about his house being unsuitable, SWJN/SS/38/pp. 273-286.

My house in Allahabad[247] has been substantially repaired. This was not done by Government but by private contractors to whom I paid the full cost. As for the rent of my house, it is fixed by the Municipality. In Allahabad, houses, however big, cannot fetch much rent. I do not think there is any house there which fetches a rent of Rs 2,000/- a month, or even half of that. Anyhow, that is a matter for the Municipality to fix. I forget now how much they have fixed now. I do not know if my house has earned on land values. Land values in Allahabad are not heavy.

The so-called cinema house on the premises of my Delhi house is a little hall which was made for the children of the neighbourhood. As a matter of fact, it has never been used as such and it has been converted into residential accommodation for members of the staff.

There is some reference to the up-keep, high living and schooling and the like of my dependents. I presume this refers to my daughter[248] and two grandchildren.[249] They certainly live in my house except when the children are at school. My daughter is not my dependent and she pays herself for the schooling of her children. Certainly their food etc. in my house is paid for by me. For the rest, my daughter pays for it. I do not understand where the question of favours come[s] in. One of my grandchildren has recently passed an examination for Cambridge, and he will be going there in two or three months. No public or Government favour has been shown to him in this matter.[250]

I do not know what security arrangements cost. When I go out, my car is preceded by a motor-cyclist outrider.

As for airfields and circuit houses, none so far as I know, has been built for me. But occasionally, where these have been on the programme of the Government, their repairs have been expedited. I do not know what is called pomp in regard to me. I am not aware of any, and I dislike it exceedingly.

The Prime Minister's National Relief Fund is certainly used at my discretion. But full accounts of it are sent to all the Trustees and have been laid before Parliament. Almost entirely the money has been sent to Governors and Chief Ministers for the relief of distress on occasions of natural calamity. I do not understand the reference to "large sums being drawn for a relation." I am not aware of any such payment, nor have any relations of mine been paid

---

247. Anand Bhavan.
248. Indira Gandhi.
249. Rajiv Gandhi and Sanjay Gandhi.
250. Rajiv Gandhi was admitted to Cambridge without a testimonial from Nehru, see SWJN/SS/70/item 426.

anything out of a public fund. Nor has any part of this fund been used for political purposes.

As for royalties on my books, I receive them from India, from England, from the USA, from the Soviet Union and from a number of other foreign countries. I do not understand the reference to a publishing company in England financed directly or indirectly by one of our Ministers. My English publishers have been issuing my books for a quarter of a century.

I have rather hastily given you some information in regard to the various statements made by Dr Lohia about me.

Yours sincerely,
[Jawaharlal Nehru]

88. For the Sea Cadet Corps of Bombay[251]

I am glad to know that the Sea Cadet Corps of Bombay continues to make good progress. Ever since I saw the boys of this Corps for the first time, I have been much impressed by them. Whenever they participate in the Republic Day parade, it is a pleasure to see their fine and smart bearing. I wish them well.

89. To Lal Bahadur Shastri: Private Member's Act Amendment[252]

August 16, 1962

My dear Lal Bahadur,
Shri S.M. Siddiah, MP,[253] has written to me (and sent a copy of that letter to you) in regard to Private Members Bill to amend Sections N and 4 of the Act of 1955.[254] It seems to me that the lacunae he has pointed out in the present Act are unfortunate and do deserve some attempt to fill them up. How this is to be done is not clear to me.

---

251. Message, 15 August 1962, forwarded to Captain G.S. Ahuja, Captain Superintendant of the Sea Cadet Corps, Bombay.
252. Letter to the Home Minister.
253. Congress, Lok Sabha MP from Chamarajanagar-SC (Mysore).
254. Thirteen Acts were passed in 1955; it is not clear which Private Member's Bill is referred to.

You have apparently consulted the Law Minister.[255] What do you propose doing now?

Yours affectionately,
[Jawaharlal Nehru]

90. To Kishen Pattnayak: Official and Personal Expenses[256]

August 18, 1962

Dear Shri Pattnayak

Your letter of the 17th August. As you rightly say, I did not wish that my letter to you should be published. I dislike such publicity. I have not got over my surprise at Dr Lohia making various charges against me which, on the face of them, were extraordinary, without any reference to me which I would have expected, from an old colleague.[257]

Ever since I became Prime Minister I have taken strong exception to security arrangements. As a result of my continuous efforts, they have been toned down greatly and I do not think they are fantastically high as you suggest. As for decoration and pomp, I am not aware of any insofar as they concern me on behalf of Government.

Yours sincerely,
[Jawaharlal Nehru]

91. To Niharendu Dutt-Mazumdar: *Judiciary in Peril*[258]

August 24, 1962

My dear Dutt-Mazumdar,

I have your letter of August 14th and the booklet *Judiciary in Peril.*[259]

I do not see in what way the particular matter you refer to leads to the judiciary being in peril. Independence of the judiciary is not affected thereby.

255. A.K. Sen.
256. Letter to Socialist Party, Lok Sabha MP; address: 30 North Avenue, New Delhi.
257. See items 87 and 96.
258. Letter to a former Minister of the West Bengal Government; address: 101-A Ballygunge Place, Calcutta 19.
259. (Calcutta: N. Dutt-Mazumdar, 1962).

All I can say is that I went into this matter when it was referred to me, rather carefully with the Home Minister[260] and it seemed to me that his decision was a correct one. As you know, it was supported by the Chief Justice of India.

I am however, sending your letter and the booklet to the Home Minister.

Yours sincerely,
Jawaharlal Nehru

92. To K. Kamaraj: Smuggling from Ceylon[261]

August 24, 1962

My dear Kamaraj,

I have received a letter from Ceylon in which it is stated that there is a great deal of smuggling going on from Ceylon to the southern coast of India.[262] Mechanised boats apparently come from Ceylon to a place called Kolladam or Kolroon near Chidambaram. It is further stated that the Customs staff at Chidambaram is paid a monthly bribe to pass these things.

I have referred this matter to the Finance Ministry. But I am writing to you because it is stated that the leader of this gang of smugglers is one Mariappa Vandayar who is said to be a prominent Congressman of the place.

It is also stated that some Communists send papers through this route.

Yours sincerely,
Jawaharlal Nehru

93. To S. Ramachandra Iyer: Madras High Court Souvenir Volume[263]

August 25, 1962

My dear Chief Justice,

Thank you for your letter of the 18th August and the Souvenir volume of the Centenary Celebrations of the Madras High Court. The Souvenir is attractive

---

260. Lal Bahadur Shastri.
261. Letter to the Chief Minister of Madras State.
262. Appendix 37.
263. Letter to the Chief Justice of the Madras High Court.

147

and well prepared. I am very glad that the Centenary Celebrations passed off so happily.[264]

Yours sincerely,
Jawaharlal Nehru

94. To S. Radhakrishnan: Tarlok Singh for Planning Commission[265]

August 29, 1962

My dear Mr President,

My colleague, Shri Gulzarilal Nanda, Minister of Planning and Deputy Chairman of the Planning Commission, has recommended to me that Shri Tarlok Singh, at present Additional Secretary to the Planning Commission, be appointed a Member of the Planning Commission. This will necessitate his resigning from the Indian Civil Service, of which he has been a member for many years. I am wholly agreeable to this proposal.

The arrangement will come into effect after Shri Tarlok Singh's resignation from his present service.

Shri Tarlok Singh has been connected with the Planning Commission ever since its inception and has functioned during all this period as Additional Secretary under the Cabinet Secretary who has been the Secretary of the Planning Commission. Shri Tarlok Singh has done very good work in the Planning Commission and is thoroughly acquainted with all the aspects of work in the Commission.

I trust you approve of this recommendation.

Yours sincerely,
Jawaharlal Nehru

264. The centenary celebrations were inaugurated by the President on 6 August 1962. For Nehru's message on the centenary, see item 66.
265. Letter to the President. PMO, File No. 17(189)/60-65-PMS, Sr. No. 38-A. Also available in the JN Collection.

95. To Morarji Desai: Jogendra Singh Director of Indian Refineries[266]

August 31, 1962

My dear Morarji,

Your letter of the 31st August about the proposed appointment of Sardar Jogendra Singh as a Resident Director of the Indian Refineries Ltd. Jogendra Singh is, I think, a competent man and is especially good at developing contacts. I should imagine that he is a good Director of the Indian Refineries. The only question that arises is of his having a rent-free house and daily allowance. It is difficult to get houses here. If the Indian Refineries Limited wishes to pay him some small allowance, it is up to them to decide to do so. I doubt, however, if it will be possible to find a rent-free house for him.

Yours sincerely,
[Jawaharlal Nehru]

96. To Kishen Pattnayak: No Patience to Debate Expenses with You[267]

September 5, 1962

Dear Shri Pattnayak,

I have received your letter of September 3rd. I am afraid I have neither the time nor the patience to enter into a long correspondence with you. It seems to me that the charge that the expenses made on me amount to Rs25,000/- per day, is absurd and ludicrous, and apparently it can only be made by some underlying malice.[268]

Yours sincerely
[Jawaharlal Nehru]

266. Letter to the Finance Minister.
267. Letter to Socialist Party, Lok Sabha MP; address: 30 North Avenue, New Delhi.
268. See earlier letters to Kishen Pattnayak, items 87 and 90.

149

97. To T.T. Krishnamachari: Objections to Opening Offices in different Cities[269]

September 7, 1962

My dear TT,

Mehr Chand Khanna[270] came to me today about a proposal to spread out his Chief Engineers in various parts of the country. On the face of it, this appears to be a proper proposal. I got a deputation, however, from a large number of clerks who strongly objected to being sent to Calcutta or elsewhere where their office was being shifted.

Mehr Chand Khanna suggested that you might look into this matter and advise him. I hope you will kindly do so.

Yours affectionately,
Jawaharlal Nehru

98. To K.L. Shrimali: No PS for Sri Prakasa on UNESCO Visit[271]

25th September, 1962

My dear Shrimali,

I have received your letter of September 21st.[272] I agree with you that we would not be justified in incurring additional expenditure of a Private Secretary

---

269. Letter to Minister without Portfolio. NMML, T.T. Krishnamachari Papers, File 1962, Auto.

270. Minister of Works, Housing and Supply.

271. Letter to the Minister of Education. PMO, File No. 42(7)/56-71-PMS, Vol. I, Sr. No. 70-A. Also available in the JN Collection.

272. The letter was as follows: "My dear Prime Minister, You would kindly recall that some time back you had suggested to me that Shri Sri Prakasaji [former Governor of Maharashtra] might be included in our delegation to the forthcoming General Conference of UNESCO to be held in Paris during November-December, 1962. When Shri Sri Prakasaji came to see me a few days ago, I enquired from him if he would be willing to serve as a delegate to the UNESCO General Conference. Shri Sri Prkasaji said that in view of his age and the present state of health, it would be essential for him to be accompanied by a Private Secretary whose expenses he expects the Government to bear. Apart from the additional expenditure in foreign exchange involved, such a proposal would set up an embarrassing precedent. Under the circumstances, perhaps, we should not trouble Shri Sri Prakasaji. I shall be grateful to have your instructions in the matter. With respects, Yours sincerely, K.L. Shrimali." PMO, File No. 42(7)/56-71-PMS, Vol. I, Sr. No. 68-A.

accompanying Sri Prakasaji to UNESCO. I would have liked Sri Prakasaji to go to UNESCO very much, but in the circumstances I fear we cannot agree to his suggestion. As you say, this would be a precedent which, it is better, we should not set.

Yours sincerely
Jawaharlal Nehru

(g) Teja Singh Swatantra

99. To C.B. Gupta[273]

August 13, 1962

My dear Chandra Bhanu,
I enclose a memorandum[274] which was given to me this morning by a deputation from the Punjab. I knew many of the members of this deputation as well known fighters for Indian independence. The memorandum is really addressed to you, and you may have got it directly.

It is for you to decide what to do in this matter. My own inclination is that if Sardar Partap Singh Kairon[275] is agreeable, you might perhaps withdraw the cases against Sardar Teja Singh Swatantra.[276]

Yours sincerely,
[Jawaharlal Nehru]

273. Letter to the Chief Minister of Uttar Pradesh.
274. Appendix 29.
275. Chief Minister of Punjab; see similar letter written to him, item 100.
        A similar letter (not published here, but available in the NMML) was addressed to Lal Bahadur Shastri, the Home Minister.
276. Freedom fighter wanted in dacoity case, see appendix 29.

100. To Partap Singh Kairon[277]

August 13, 1962

My dear Partap Singh,

I enclose a copy of a memorandum[278] addressed to the Chief Minister of UP about Teja Singh Swatantra. This was given to me by a deputation which came to see me this morning.

This is a matter to be decided by the UP Government. Personally I feel that it might be advisable to withdraw the cases against Teja Singh Swatantra. But your advice in this connection is important. Could you please let me or the Chief Minister of UP know what this advice is?[279]

Yours sincerely,
[Jawaharlal Nehru]

101. To Lal Bahadur Shastri[280]

12th September 1962

My dear Lal Bahadur,

Some weeks ago a deputation of some leading Sikhs came to me asking me to intervene and get the case against Teja Singh Swatantra withdrawn. They said that he had suffered enough during the last few years as an absconder. He was an old man and not in good health. Others in his position who had been tried in court had been acquitted. It would be a good gesture for the UP Government to withdraw the case against him and this would be greatly appreciated in the Punjab.

Thereupon I wrote to the Chief Minister of the Punjab asking what his views were.[281] He wrote back strongly recommending that the case against Teja Singh Swatantra should be withdrawn after all that had happened. I sent the Chief Minister's letter to C.B. Gupta. He has sent me a reply which I enclose in original.

---

277. Letter to the Chief Minister of Punjab.
278. Appendix 29.
279. See similar letter to C.B. Gupta, Chief Minister of Uttar Pradesh, item 99.
       A similar letter (not published here, but available in the NMML) was addressed to Lal Bahadur Shastri, the Home Minister.
280. Letter to the Home Minister. Sent from London.
281. Item 100.

I also enclose a copy of the reply I am sending to Gupta. In view of the circumstances I am inclined to think that it would be desirable now to withdraw the case against Teja Singh Swatatntra. I have, however, written to C.B. Gupta to consult you in the matter.[282]

Yours affectionately,
[Jawaharlal Nehru]

102. To C.B. Gupta[283]

12th September 1962

My dear Chandra Bhanu,
Your letter of the 6th September about Teja Singh Swatantra has reached me here in London.

It is difficult for me to give a final opinion on the subject. I am rather inclined to agree with the Chief Minister of the Punjab.[284] Teja Singh Swatantra has led a hunted life for eleven years or so, as you say, and the charge against him is of conspiracy and not actually of dacoity. There is some chance at least that he might be acquitted like some other persons who were sent up for trial on a charge of conspiracy. There can be little doubt that his discharge or withdrawal of the case against him would be much appreciated by people in the Punjab. Also, that he is, I think, incapable of misbehaving in this way in the future.[285]

I would suggest your consulting the Home Minister, Lal Bahadur Shastri, and also, if you like, write to the Chief Minister of the Punjab.

Yours sincerely,
[Jawaharlal Nehru]

---

282. See item 102.
283. Letter to the Chief Minister of Uttar Pradesh. Sent from London.
284. Partap Singh Kairon.
285. See also items 99-100 and appendix 29.

(h) Andhra Pradesh

103. To N. Sanjiva Reddy: Shrinagesh as New Governor[286]

July 25, 1962

My dear Sanjiva Reddy,

As you know, your present Governor, Shri Bhimsen Sachar, would be completing his term of office soon. We have been giving thought to his successor. We feel that General Shrinagesh, who is at present the Governor of Assam and was previously a Chief of the Army Staff, would be suitable for Andhra. He will go there for the remaining part of his term i.e. about two years or a little more. I think he will be good for Andhra and I hope you are agreeable to this proposal. [287]

Yours sincerely,
[Jawaharlal Nehru]

104. To S.M. Shrinagesh: To Andhra Pradesh as Governor[288]

July 25, 1962

My dear Shrinagesh,

We are considering various Governors' appointments. In this connection it has struck us that a change at some places would be advisable. We would like you to go from Assam as our Governor of Andhra Pradesh where the present Governor[289] is retiring.

Andhra Pradesh is one of our bigger and more important States and I hope you will agree to this suggestion. I am writing to Sanjiva Reddy about it.[290] Your term in Assam will not be over for another two years or a little more.

---

286. Letter to the Chief Minister of Andhra Pradesh.
287. S.M. Shrinagesh was the Governor of Assam from 14 October 1959 to 12 November 1960 and, after a break, again from 13 January 1961 to 7 September 1962. He served as the Governor of Andhra Pradesh from 8 September 1962 until 4 May 1964.
288. Letter to the Governor of Assam.
289. Bhim Sen Sachar.
290. See item 103.

You might, therefore, go to Andhra Pradesh, to begin with, for the remaining part of your term.

Yours sincerely,
[Jawaharlal Nehru]

105. To N. Sanjiva Reddy: Offensive Speech by Minister[291]

August 20, 1962

My dear Sanjiva Reddy,
I enclose a letter from Tenneti Viswanatham[292] and a press cutting which he has sent me. I must say that the speech of one of your Ministers is not at all happy, more especially his talk of "spilling blood" is peculiarly unfortunate.

Yours sincerely,
[Jawaharlal Nehru]

106. To Tenneti Viswanatham: Offensive Speech by Minister[293]

August 20, 1962

My dear Viswanatham,
I have your letter of the 18th August with its enclosure. I agree with you that it is not right to say or do anything which comes in the way of healthy democratic standards. I am referring your letter and the press cutting to the Chief Minister of Andhra Pradesh.[294]

Yours sincerely,
[Jawaharlal Nehru]

291. Letter to the Chief Minister of Andhra Pradesh.
292. MLA, Andhra Pradesh.
293. Letter to MLA, Andhra Pradesh; address: Maharanipeta P.O., Visakhapatnam-2.
294. N. Sanjiva Reddy.

(i) Bhutan

107. To P.K. Deo: Relations with Bhutan[295]

August 21, 1962

Dear Shri Deo,

Your letter of the 20th August.[296]

Bhutan is an independent country in treaty relations with India. According to our Treaty, we do not interfere at all in its internal affairs, but in regard to the external affairs we are to guide its policy. We have, in fact, been encouraging Bhutan to play some part in international contacts. Thus we have recommended that it should become a member of the Colombo Plan.

Our relationship is a sound one and we have had no trouble but undoubtedly it is a little delicate. We do not wish to say anything which would lead Bhutan to think that it is not independent. At the same time, we do not also wish to say anything which would lessen the relationships according to the terms of the Treaty.

I do not think that the news item in the *Indian Express*, to which you refer, can be correct.[297] Shri Dorji, the Prime Minister of Bhutan, was interested in enquiring about certain matters which might be helpful to Bhutan. We have not got the details of this. When he comes back to India he will no doubt keep us informed.

I would add that our relations with the Bhutan Government and the people are the happiest. I hope you will share this letter with the co-signatories of your letter.[298]

Yours sincerely,

[Jawaharlal Nehru]

295. Letter to Swatantra Party, Lok Sabha MP; address: 29 Feroz Shah Road, New Delhi.
296. P.K. Deo's letter has not been traced.
297. According to a report in the *Indian Express* of 16 August 1962, Jigme Dorji, the Bhutanese Prime Minister, had been in London for the past two months "to get his country accepted as a separate state in the international field." He also reportedly demanded that Bhutan be made a member of the Colombo Plan with the idea of getting "aid for Bhutan directly from the Colombo Plan countries and not through India." The report said "it is presumed that his demand has been accepted."
298. See also item 413.

(j) Bihar

108. To Binodanand Jha: Funds for Flood Relief[299]

August 22, 1962

My dear Binodnandandji,

I see that Bihar is again suffering from floods and a large number of people must be greatly distressed by this. I am sending you a cheque for Rs 50,000/- from the PM's National Relief Fund for special relief.

Yours sincerely
Jawaharlal Nehru

109. To Hafiz Mohammed Ibrahim: Floods in East UP and Bihar[300]

September 1, 1962

My dear Hafizji,

Thank you for your letter of August 30, with which you have sent me a note on flood control in Assam.

You must have read in the papers of the rather disgraceful episode that occurred in the Lok Sabha and which resulted in a Socialist Member being suspended for a week.[301] He was trying to get an immediate discussion on the flood situation especially in Bihar and Eastern UP.

After this incident, the question of having a discussion on the flood situation again arose, and the Speaker fixed Tuesday, the 4th September for it. I hope that you will get a statement prepared for the occasion, chiefly dealing with the floods in Bihar and Eastern UP where you have recently been. The discussion is likely to last for two or three hours.

Yours sincerely,
Jawaharlal Nehru

---

299. Letter to the Chief Minister of Bihar. PMO, File No. 7(247)/61-64-PMS, Sr. No. 72-A.
300. Letter to the Minister of Irrigation and Power. PMO, File No. 7(261)/62-66-PMS, Sr. No. 24-A. Also available in the JN Collection.
301. See item 10.

110. To Hafiz Mohammed Ibrahim: Power Failure in Delhi[302]

July 30, 1962

My dear Hafizji,

Thank you for your letter of the 30th July.[303] I learnt of the position in Calcutta when I was there yesterday. I am glad that some progress has been made there.

As for Delhi, all our foreign diplomats are complaining. I do not know what more can be done apart from the steps you have taken. It would be desirable to set up a committee in consultation with the Punjab Government.

Yours sincerely,
Jawaharlal Nehru

111. In the Lok Sabha: Power Failure in Delhi[304]

Speaker:[305] I have received notices of adjournment motion by Shri Frank Anthony,[306] Shri Surendranath Dwivedy,[307] Shri Nambiar,[308] Dr L.M. Singhvi,[309] Shri Yashpal Singh,[310] Shri Bishanchander Seth,[311] Shri S.M. Banerjee[312] and Shri H.N. Mukherjee[313] and also three calling attention notices by Shri Bagri,[314] Shri Ram Ratan Gupta[315] and Shri P.C. Borooah,[316]

---

302. Letter to the Minister of Irrigation and Power. PMO, File No. 7(258)/62-66-PMS, Sr. No. 2-A.
303. Appendix 15.
304. Adjournment motion, 10 August 1962. *Lok Sabha Debates*, Third Series, Vol. 6, 6 to 18 August 1962, cols 1177-1182.
305. Hukam Singh.
306. Nominated.
307. PSP.
308. K. Ananda Nambiar, CPI.
309. Independent.
310. Independent.
311. Hindu Mahasabha.
312. Independent.
313. CPI.
314. Mani Ram Bagri, Socialist Party.
315. Congress.
316. Congress.

all relating to the power shortage and the reply given by the hon. Irrigation and Power Minister yesterday.[317] I will call upon Shri Frank Anthony to explain how this adjournment motion is admissible.

Nath Pai (Rajapur): There has been a further breakdown and we are submitted to further torture.

S.M. Banerjee (Kanpur): It has come in today's papers ...

Speaker: That is different.

Frank Anthony (Nominated – Anglo-Indians): Sir, my adjournment motion reads as follows:

> "The failure of the Central Government to exercise its authority over the Union Territory of Delhi as avowed by the statement of the Minister of Irrigation and Power yesterday that ..."

I have sought to translate it into English —

> "So far as the constitutional and legal responsibility is concerned, that is not mine. I have no authority whatsoever. I cannot intervene."
>
> Apart from the question of responsibility, I submit that this is a matter of extreme importance to the House to know what the constitutional and legal position is and whether with regard to a Union Territory, it can lie in the mouth of the Minister or the Government to say, "We have no authority and we cannot intervene." I will just place the law before the House within two minutes, because I feel this is a matter which must be decided ...

Speaker: The question boils down to this that we should determine whether the Central Government has the authority or not. The position, according to Shri Frank Anthony, is that by the Constitution and other laws, the Centre has the authority, but it is disowning it. The question is whether that could be a subject matter of an adjournment motion. I will certainly take that up afterwards, but firstly, the Minister says that it is not his responsibility. If I accept the statement of the Minister and [sic] the Centre has no

317. Hafiz Mohammed Ibrahim; for his statement in the Lok Sabha on 9 August 1962, see *Lok Sabha Debates*, Third Series, Vol. 6, 6 to 18 August 1962, cols 1035-1046.

responsibility whatsoever, then, of course, no adjournment motion can come in. Unless the Central Government has some responsibility, how can there be an adjournment motion on the failure on the part of Government?

Frank Anthony: I shall explain, Sir. Under article 239—I do not want to read it—the President is charged with administering Union Territories. That cannot be denied. Under the Corporation Act, there is specific power given to the Centre to direct the management and control of the electricity undertaking,[318] and any decision by the Centre is final. When the Minister was asked about this chaos after this breakdown, he says "I have no proper [sic] except – मोहब्बत, जो कुछ हो सकता है मोहब्बत से ही हो सकता है । [Translation: We can get something done only if we approach someone in an amiable manner.] This thing is continuing. The Constitution charges the President ...

Speaker: According to Shri Frank Anthony, the statement of the Minister is not correct.

Frank Anthony: It is palpably wrong.

Renu Chakravartty (Barrackpore): This is a question of the refusal of the Minister to take responsibility.

Speaker: Should I accept the statement of the Minister so far as those proceedings are concerned? If that is wrong, there are other methods.

Frank Anthony: Unless you want us to bring a no-confidence motion, I thought this would be a better way.

Speaker: I will just now call upon the Government to say whether they own that responsibility or not.

Jawaharlal Nehru: Mr Speaker, Sir, I was not here yesterday when this debate took place. I do not know exactly what he said, except this quotation of a sentence. It depends upon the context and all that. But, apart from that, I certainly do not take the position that the Centre has no responsibility.

318. The Delhi Electric Supply Undertaking.

Surendranath Dwivedy (Kendrapara): So far as the point raised by Shri Anthony is concerned, there is no ambiguity.

Frank Anthony: The more important thing is the question of responsibility.

Jawaharlal Nehru: The Centre is responsible, and it is true that that responsibility is shared as many things are. Even the Government of India is somewhat shared by various ministries. The Home Ministry, as generally responsible for the governance of the Central territories, is responsible. Specialised subjects are dealt with by special ministries—like health, irrigation and power, etc., under the general superintendence of the Home Ministry. That is true. So, in that sense, the statement made by the Minister of Irrigation and Power is not quite correct. But, of course, I do not know what preceded it and followed it. I do not deny the responsibility of the Central Government.

Speaker: But, if I may be permitted to say, the Minister said that it was only by private arrangement between Pandit Pant, the previous Home Minister,[319] and himself that he had agreed to answer these questions; otherwise there was no responsibility at all.

Jawaharlal Nehru: That is true. I understand, when Pandit Pant was Home Minister, questions, etc., on these matters dealing with Delhi were referred to him and he asked the various ministries to deal with specialised subjects although Pandit Pant continued to exercise his own authority as Home Minister in regard to the centrally administered territories. That statement is true. But that is a matter of division of responsibility between the ministries. The Central Government is certainly responsible; some part of it may be dealt with by this ministry and some by that.

Speaker: The difficulty has arisen because all the points that were raised yesterday were not answered at all, and protection or, rather, shelter was taken that this is not the responsibility of the Central Government. Therefore, hon. Members felt dissatisfied that no explanation had been given.

Frank Anthony: More important than that, Sir, was the claim of the Minister that he had no authority to intervene. That was the dangerous position.

319. Govind Ballabh Pant, Union Home Minister, 10 January 1955 – 7 March 1961.

Jawaharlal Nehru: It may be said that the executive authority to intervene would lie with the Home Ministry.

Surendranath Dwivedy: Then the Home Minister[320] should have participated in the debate.

H.N. Mukerjee (Calcutta Central): In that case, Sir, the Home Minister should have been here. A certain default has taken place for which some amends have got to be made.

Jawaharlal Nehru: I am trying to explain the limits of authority and competence. I should imagine—I am not dealing with this particular question because I do not know all the facts—that, broadly speaking, the Central Government is responsible, whatever may be the allocation of work between the various departments or ministries of the Central Government. And, as regards execution, I presume, I speak subject to correction, that an order or directive in regard to execution should come from the Home Ministry. Of course, advice can be given and is usually followed. That is a different matter. But, electric power and such like things being specialised subjects would be dealt with by the Irrigation and Power Ministry. If it cannot deal with it, then the Home Ministry might perhaps issue a directive.

I do not know, Sir, if I have made the position much clearer, but I certainly admit the responsibility of the Government of India. Take the case of a power failure in a State like Bengal, Maharashtra or any other State. Well, to some extent, if it is a Central undertaking, the responsibility would be with the Centre. If it is a State undertaking the responsibility would be entirely of the State. Even if it is a Central undertaking it may be that the State might have got something to do with it. This subject of power is rather spread out and it is difficult to draw hard and fast lines. So far as Delhi is concerned, as it is a Union territory, the Central Government is responsible as a whole and, on behalf of the Central Government, the Home Minister is broadly responsible for the governance of Delhi. Then, in Delhi itself, there is the Corporation of Delhi which may have something to do with it, which is more or less an autonomous body, though I am not saying that the Corporation has much to do with it. Then, with regard to specialised subjects like irrigation and power and health the Ministries concerned have normally to deal with them and probably no definite order has to be passed by the Home Ministry.

320. Lal Bahadur Shastri.

[Exchanges on procedure omitted.]

Speaker: It cannot be admitted on the ground that it has already been dealt with. But I was talking of the other adjournment motion that has been tabled. I should know the reaction of the Government to it. Are they prepared to answer it just now or do they want time till the afternoon or tomorrow morning so that I can hold over this adjournment motion?

Hem Barua:[321] After the hon. Prime Minister's statement—he said categorically that it is the responsibility of the Central Government ...

Speaker: Hon. Member should realise that that was also qualified so far as I could follow it.

Surendranath Dwivedy: No, Sir.

Hem Barua: It was not qualified. The hon. Prime Minister has a peculiar way of balancing sentences ... (Interruption).

Speaker: Order, order.

Jawaharlal Nehru: What I ventured to say was on the constitutional issue. I regret to say that I am not wholly acquainted with the detailed facts. The hon. Minister of Irrigation and Power referred to the Punjab—I have just now got a copy of it—and to this matter pertaining to the Punjab and Delhi. Actually, if something happens to electricity supplied by the Punjab; if some unfortunate occurrence happens in the Punjab, to some extent it is not the direct responsibility of the Central Government—ultimately it may be. Something has happened. An accident has happened. I said that so far as Delhi is concerned, it is the Government of India's responsibility. They may put forward, as an explanation, that something happened in the Punjab for which Punjab was responsible. But their responsibility remains. I do not deny that ... (Interruption).

Speaker: Hon. Members should allow me to make myself clear. The hon. Minister said:

मैं अर्ज़ करूं कि जो वह फरमाते हैं वह कहीं नहीं लिखा है। लेकिन लिखा न होने के बावजूद हम इंटरवीन करते हैं, वह एक अलग बात है। मैं तो इस वक्त यह

321. PSP.

163

अर्ज कर रहा हूं कि जहां तक कांस्टीट्यूशन और लीगल ज़िम्मेदारी का सवाल है, वह मेरी नहीं है। मुझको कोई अख़्तियार नहीं है। मैं उसके अन्दर दखल नहीं दे सकता।
[Translation: May I say that what the hon. Member says is not mentioned anywhere. That we intervene in spite of that is a different thing. What I am trying to say is that as far as the constitutional and legal responsibility is concerned that is not mine. It is not within my powers to intervene.]

Brahm Prakash (Outer Delhi):[322] The transformer which has failed belongs to the Punjab Government.

Surendranath Dwivedy: That is a different thing altogether. That has nothing to do with this.

Brahm Prakash: I want to say that Delhi ... (Interruption).

Speaker: Order, order. I might remind the hon. Member, Shri Brahm Prakash, that this position had been explained yesterday, namely, that the transformer belongs to the Punjab Government; the cables and the wires are all of the Punjab Government; everything belongs to the Punjab Government and they brought it; they fixed it up here; it is their property; the failure is there and they have to run it ... (Interruption). I should be allowed to finish what I am saying. That has already been dealt with and the hon. Minister of Irrigation made it very clear.

Jawaharlal Nehru: That is the difficulty. It is one thing to have responsibility in theory and in law which I admit; but in practice it may be divided up. Now, they have fixed it. It may not be directly the fault of this Ministry. That has happened. Subsequently what happens will be more in the charge of the Ministry.

Hem Barua: He said about the legal and constitutional position.

Speaker: He should have the patience to listen.

Jawaharlal Nehru: Constitutionally I admit the responsibility of the Government of India subject to explanations etc. which we may make. It is an explanation that the Punjab Government did it; the Punjab Government is at fault or the Corporation of Delhi did something, whatever it may be. That is a different matter.

322. Congress.

Frank Anthony rose –

Priya Gupta (Katihar):[323] On a point of order, Sir. The question here is only whether the Central Government can intervene or not. The hon. Prime Minister is bringing in other factors, that is, the liability of the Punjab Government etc. Here the point is whether the Central Government can as well ask the Punjab Government to do it or not. The position boils down to that, namely, whether the Central Government can take action or not. That is my point of order.

Jawaharlal Nehru: Intervention may be in many things. We always intervene in the sense of advice on this and that.

Priya Gupta: On this particular issue.

Speaker: Order, order. He has said that in the point of order also.

Jawaharlal Nehru: I doubt very much, subject to what the Law Minister[324] might say, if we can issue a directive to the Punjab Government in regard to some such thing. We can and they do accept our advice. They have tried their best. If a breakdown occurs in something under their charge, I do not quite see how we can issue directive constitutionally. Otherwise, we intervene, of course.

Speaker: Would the Law Minister enlighten us?

A.K. Sen: As the Prime Minister has already said, it is a matter in which the field is covered by so many concurrent authorities exercising jurisdiction in different ways; the Punjab Government, the Delhi Administration, the Irrigation and Power Ministry, the Delhi Electricity Supply Corporation and the Delhi Corporation itself. It will be extremely precarious for me to try to make an answer off hand to say who particularly has the principal responsibility in this matter. Having not studied the matter with that care that it deserves, I would not venture an answer offhand.

Speaker: Can he help me in the afternoon or tomorrow morning?

323. PSP.
324. A.K. Sen.

A.K. Sen: In the afternoon, certainly, I can tell you. As the Prime Minister stated, the constitutional responsibility of answering to this Parliament on a matter concerning ...

Speaker: He should say he is going to express his opinion or if he wants time, I can give him time till Monday morning. This question must be thrashed once for all and we should know the position.

A.K. Sen: That is exactly why ...

Speaker: Till Monday morning I will keep this pending. I will hear him.

S.M. Banerjee: On Monday we are having the International affairs debate.

A.K. Sen: We can take it at 4 o'clock.

Speaker: At four o'clock, all right.

[Exchanges on procedure omitted.]

Jawaharlal Nehru: May I say a few words before the hon. Home Minister makes his statement? I am giving really a factual information on this subject and I am not dealing with the Constitution or the law. I am sorry the Minister of Irrigation and Power has not been able to come here because he did not know that this is taking place; he went to Chandigarh last night or this morning and he could not suddenly be transported here; otherwise he would obviously be here. But very soon after this failure took place, he wrote to me that he wanted immediately to appoint a committee to enquire into it. I replied to him that certainly he should do so and take urgent steps in the matter.[325] He had even mentioned certain names, etc. The very next day, he wrote to me that when he was at the point of appointing a committee the Punjab Government came in the way and said that they had no objection to the appointment of a committee but they objected to his appointing it because he would then come in the way of their authority. And so he said "I have agreed to it, the appointment of a committee by them, making one or two changes in it; otherwise, the same names were there".

So, the impression in his mind was that because this was confirmed, ... he could not take action; the Punjab Government came in the way. It is not a legal point that I am saying. Normally, ever since the late G.B. Pant was the Home

325. See item 110.

Minister, he had rightly told him that it was up to him to answer questions but the rest of the matters would be dealt with by the Home Minister—matters in regard to Delhi. So, this impression was created in his mind. It is not a legal or constitutional thing.

Apart from that, the question of exercising any authority arises only when one's advice is not accepted. Then directions can be sent. What I mean to say is, all the time he was much exercised about this failure naturally and he was consulting various people, various authorities, and as the Home Minister will presently say, I suppose, various steps were being taken.

I merely wished to state before the House how the impression arose in his mind, because—it is both—of the late Home Minister's written directions to him and very lately when he tried to take action the Punjab Government came in the way and said they would take action and he had no authority in which they were concerned.[326]

112. Power Failure in Delhi[327]

The attached memorandum was given to me this afternoon by Shri Ram Charan Agarwal and two other members of the Delhi Municipal Corporation.

I have asked the Defence Ministry to give all the help they can in this matter to supply any generators that they have. The Defence Minister[328] has promised to do so, although their generators are rather small.

I think that an appeal should be made by the Chief Commissioner for the non-use of air-conditioners for the next few days. Foreign Embassies might be exempted from this appeal. The appeal will surely have some effect.[329]

326. The Speaker finally did not allow the adjournment motion. See also items 112–113 and appendix 31.
327. Note, 10 August 1962, for Lal Bahadur Shastri, the Home Minister, and others. PMO, File No. 7(258)/62-66-PMS, Sr. No. 9-A. Also available in the JN Collection.
328. V.K. Krishna Menon.
329. An appeal was issued by Bhagwan Sahay, Chief Commissioner of Delhi, on 10 August, and published in newspapers the next day.

113. To D.N. Tiwary: Hafiz Ibrahim on Delhi Power Failure[330]

August 11, 1962

Dear Tiwaryji,

I have your letter of August, 10.[331]

I am much troubled about Hafizji.[332] He is a fine man and one of integrity and ability. Unfortunately, he is a little deaf and cannot always follow what has happened. Hence he is not able to answer questions quickly.

I can understand Members of Parliament and others being much exercised over the power failure.[333] We shall certainly take all steps we can to put it right and punish those who are guilty. But I do not think it is quite fair to blame Hafizji for this failure. From the very first day it occurred, he has been doing his best and he has been writing to me frequently to tell me what he is doing.

Yours sincerely,
Jawaharlal Nehru

114. To Hafiz Mohammed Ibrahim: Reply to No Confidence Motion[334]

August 12, 1962

My dear Hafizji,

I have just received your letter of the 12th August enclosing the statement which you wish to make in reply to the No Confidence motion. This No Confidence motion is in the whole government and, as such, I shall answer it first and you can then read your statement.

I do not know when this No Confidence motion will be taken up. The mover suggests tomorrow, but I presume the Speaker[335] will fix some definite date for it, possibly day after tomorrow. Anyhow we shall await the Speaker's directions

---

330. Letter to Congress MP; address: 9 Windsor Place, New Delhi. PMO, File No. 7(258)/62-66-PMS, Sr. No. 11-A. Also available in the JN Collection.
331. Appendix 31.
332. Hafiz Mohammed Ibrahim, Minister of Irrigation and Power.
333. See debate in Parliament, item 111.
334. Letter to the Minister of Irrigation and Power. PMO, File No. 7(258)/62-66-PMS, Sr. No. 15-A. Also available in the JN Collection.
335. Hukam Singh.

in the matter. Tomorrow has been fixed for the debate on the frontier question and I doubt if any matter will be led to interfere with that debate.

Yours sincerely
Jawaharlal Nehru

115. To Hafiz Mohammed Ibrahim: Power Failure not your fault[336]

August 26, 1962

My dear Hafizji,

Thank you for your letter of today's date. It is very good of you to write to me at some length.

May I assure you that I have the highest regard for you not only for your integrity, but also for your ability? I have been happy to have you as my colleague here in the Government and in the Congress. It would pain me for you to do anything which affects our close contacts.

As for the power failure, I am sure that it was certainly not your fault or that of your Ministry. It was the fault of the transformer in the Punjab. As for Delhi, it was the fault of the Electric Supply Undertaking here.[337] I think that the engineers or others in charge of that have not functioned efficiently at all. I hope this matter will be thoroughly enquired into by the committee that has been set up.

I was disturbed by what people were saying in Parliament including many of the Congress, who told me at the same time that they had a high regard for you. Probably it was, as you say, the result of a newspaper campaign. Most of the newspapers in Delhi, as you must know, are continually attacking many of us in Government whenever they have any chance to do so, and sometimes with hardly a pretext.[338]

In the course of the next few days, that is before I leave for my tour abroad, I should like to meet you and have a talk with you.

Yours sincerely,
[Jawaharlal Nehru]

336. Letter to the Minister of Irrigation and Power.
337. The Delhi Electric Supply Undertaking.
338. See other items in section Politics, subsection Delhi.

116. Land Acquisition in Ghaziabad[339]

A large number of peasants from roundabout Ghaziabad came to Parliament House in Delhi today.[340] I met them in the evening. They were much disturbed and distressed at the prospect of having their land acquired for the Delhi Master Plan.

2.   It appears that originally the UP Government had decided to acquire 35,000 acres. Later, they had released 29,000 acres out of this and intended to acquire 6,000 acres only for various schemes which had to be undertaken under the Master Plan. Further that this acquisition was to be done in the course of five years.

3.   It was explained to them that various businessmen in Delhi and elsewhere were acquiring the land or would try to acquire it in order to speculate and profiteer. Further that it was inevitable that land near a great city would gradually be acquired for the extension of that city and its industries.

4.   They acknowledge this, but still they were very distressed. They said that this land was very good for agricultural purposes and had three good harvests a year. It would not only mean their being pushed out, but our losing food production to a considerable extent. In any event, being given compensation was not enough. They wanted alternative land as they could do nothing else but cultivate. They further said that near this land, there was bad land about a mile and a half away and if this could be acquired, it would do no harm to anybody or to food production.

5.   I confess that I agree with them to a great extent. I realise, however, that it may become inevitable to acquire some land near Delhi because of the Master Plan. But if this land is really very good land, and there is "banjar" land nearby, would it not be possible to vary the Plan and acquire the "banjar" land and leave the good land for agricultural purposes? It is not a bad thing to have some agricultural land even in the middle of built-in areas.

6.   Secondly, an attempt should be made to give them some alternative land.

7.   I should like this to be examined so that whatever is possible, could be done to accommodate these peasants and to save good agricultural land.[341]

---

339. Note, 28 August 1962. It is not mentioned to whom this note is addressed.
340. A PTI report published in newspapers the next day gave the number of "peasants from the Meerut and Bulandshahr districts of UP" who marched to Parliament House as "about one thousand." The procession was led by Kanhaiya Lal Balmiki and Mrs Kamala Chaudhri, Congress MPs from UP. *National Herald*, 29 August 1962.
341. See item 188.

117. To Brij Mohan: Delhi is Special[342]

August 31, 1962

My dear Brij Mohan,

Your letter of August 31st. I do not quite understand how you expected Delhi to be put on a level with other Union territories. Whatever may be done to Delhi has to be especially considered as Delhi stands on a very special footing. Among other things, there is the important consideration of the Corporation. How will the Corporation fit in with any other development?

It should be remembered that Delhi is not differentiated against. It is more important and more politically conscious and otherwise developed than the other Union territories. Hence the special consideration which must be given to Delhi. It overlaps with the Union Government. It has to deal with all kinds of foreign missions and so on. The matter should be considered fully and independently.[343]

Yours sincerely,
[Jawaharlal Nehru]

118. In the Lok Sabha: Bill for Union Territories[344]

Jawaharlal Nehru: Yes. But, Sir, I wish to say just a few words about the question of Delhi. Delhi is obviously, both because it is a capital and it is a great city of India, a very important part of India. It is absurd for anyone to think that Delhi is excluded because the people of Delhi are not advanced enough. That is ridiculous. We are all people of Delhi, all who are sitting here. The real difficulty is not as to what should be done to Delhi. That has to be carefully considered. But it cannot be easily put in here in this Bill, because the problems that face Delhi are different from the problems that face all the other Union Territories. Therefore, I may mention some of the problems. I do not know how the hon.

---

342. Letter to the President of the Delhi Pradesh Congress Committee.
343. See also items 118 and 160.
344. Intervention in debate on proposed amendments to the Constitution Fourteenth Amendment Bill, 4 September 1962. *Lok Sabha Debates*, Vol. 8, Third Series, 3 to 7 September 1962, cols 5941-42.

   The Bill sought to create Legislatures and Councils of Ministers in the Union territories of Himachal Pradesh, Manipur, Tripura, Goa, Daman and Diu and Pondicherry, and to confer necessary legislative power on Parliament to enact laws for this purpose.

Member opposite said that the Home Minister[345] said something or the other. Anyhow, I do not understand the statement that it may go out of control of somebody. Where will it go, I do not know. There is no meaning in it.[346]

First of all, Delhi has got a corporation and whatever other amendments we may put to the Constitution in regard to Delhi must fit in with the Constitution. It may be, the Constitution has to be changed too, more powers or less powers, whatever it may be. We cannot deal with it, apart from that. It becomes two overlapping things.

Secondly, Delhi being the capital with such a large number of foreign legations, embassies, etc. it has to be considered in that context. None of these is the final reason, but all these matters have to be considered. None of the questions arises in regard to the other Union Territories. Therefore, merely to push in Delhi there has no meaning. It confuses that issue.

I can concede all the arguments which the hon. Members have advanced independently of Delhi, but not for Delhi as part of this. We have to consider Delhi separately. Frankly, if I may say so, I have not been satisfied with the present arrangement in Delhi. There are many things which are not satisfactory and I think it requires a change, may be a radical change. Some of the things which hon. Members opposite have suggested have to be considered separately; but they cannot be pushed in here. We cannot put Delhi on the same level as the other Union Territories. Therefore, I submit that this amendment should not be pressed. Whatever may be said about Delhi, that may be considered separately.[347]

---

345. Lal Bahadur Shastri.
346. Indrajit Gupta, CPI, who moved an amendment to include Delhi within the ambit of the Bill, said that, as far as he could understand from the statement of the Home Minister, the whole impression sought to be given by him "was that if some form of popular rule is established in Delhi there will be some sort of difficulty or there may arise some difficulty in controlling or keeping over the federal capital." *Lok Sabha Debates*, ibid, col. 5937.
347. For Nehru's views on the need for a reconsideration of the constitutional status of Delhi, see item 160.

(l) Goa

119. In the Lok Sabha: Indians in Portuguese Colonies[348]

Will the Prime Minister be pleased to state whether the Government of India have taken any step against the Portuguese Government's decree cancelling the residence permits of Indians in the Portuguese overseas territories and liquidating their assets?[349].

The Deputy Minister in the Ministry of External Affairs (Dinesh Singh): The Government of India have asked the Government of Portugal through the United Arab Republic Embassy in Lisbon to rescind their Decree No. 44416 of 25th June, 1962 and to extend the necessary facilities to Indian nationals to wind up their affairs and repatriate their assets in accordance with the terms of Agreement reached on the subject between the two Governments. In addition, at the request of the Government of India, the Government of the United Arab Republic have sent Mr Wagih Safwat, a First Secretary of the UAR Embassy in Lisbon, to Mozambique with a view to ensuring that the Indian nationals who have to leave these Portuguese territories get the benefit of the terms of the Agreement. A reply from the Government of Portugal is still awaited in the matter.

मणिराम बागड़ी:[350] स्पीकर साहब, हिन्दुस्तानी में तर्जुमा हो जाये तो अच्छा है ताकि पूरक प्रश्न पूछे जा सकें।

अध्यक्ष:[351] मैंने आपसे एक-दो बार कहा है आप कोशिश करें किसी दूसरे से मतलब जानने की ...

मणिराम बागड़ी: कोई अंग्रेज़ी वाला मेरे पड़ोस में नहीं, अगर सवाल हिन्दी में पूछा जाता है तो उस का जवाब अंग्रेज़ी में दिया जाता है। ऐसा क्यों किया जाता है? बना तो रहे हैं हम हिन्दी को सगी भाषा लेकिन उसके बारे में ...

---

348. 6 August 1962. *Lok Sabha Debates*, Third Series, Vol. 6, 6 to 18 August 1962, cols 31-37.
349. Question by Bishwanath Roy, Congress, and 25 other MPs: 15 Congress, four CPI, two PSP, one each from Socialist Party and Swatantra Party, and two Independents.
350. Mani Ram Bagri, Socialist Party.
351. Hukam Singh.

अध्यक्षः माननीय सदस्य बैठ जायें। इसका उनको इतिहास मालूम है, सारा काम पहले अंग्रेज़ी में हो रहा था और अब आहिस्ता-आहिस्ता हम हिन्दी की तरफ जा रहे हैं। इस वास्ते उन्हें उस पुराने इस्तेमाल के मुताबिक ऐसा करना पड़ता है। लेकिन इससे यह मतलब नहीं है कि हम तेज़ी से हिन्दी की तरफ बढ़ना नहीं चाहते। मगर जब कभी भी कुछ होता है आप इसको साथ लाते हैं। हमारी कोशिश रहती है कि आहिस्ता-आहिस्ता सब कुछ हिन्दी में हो मगर इसमें कुछ वक़्त लगेगा। आप कुछ पूछना चाहें तो दूसरे साथी के पास बैठकर पूछ लें। मैं कोशिश यह करूँगा कि अगर आपको तकलीफ़ हो और आप बतलायें तो आपको सवाल बतला दिया जाये।

मणिराम बागड़ीः क्या मंत्री महोदय इसका तर्जुमा हिन्दी में नहीं कर सकते?

अध्यक्षः हिन्दी तर्जुमा तो बहुत से मंत्री महोदय कर सकेंगे, यह मैं मानता हूँ, लेकिन यह भी तो देखना है कि इसमें कितना वक़्त ख़र्च होता है अगर हम एक सवाल का दोनों ज़बानों में तर्जुमा किया जाये। कुछ कष्ट हमें भी उठाना चाहिए इस बात को जल्दी लाने में, और कुछ मैं भी कोशिश करूँगा कि हमारे मंत्री महोदय जब कोई बयान दिया करें तो हिन्दी में भी समझा दिया करें। माननीय सदस्य भी इस में कुछ यत्न करें और समझ लिया करें ताकि दोनों मिलकर चल सकें। थोड़ा सा आपका ताव्वुन भी इस में चाहिए। इस समय मंत्री महोदय हिन्दी में बतला देंगे।

दिनेश सिंहः भारत सरकार ने पुर्तगाल सरकार से कहा है कि जो उन्होंने अपनी नई डिक्री पास की है, जिसका नम्बर है 44416, उसे वे रद्द कर दें। यू.ए.आर. सरकार ने, जो हमारे इस मामले में पुर्तगाल सरकार से बातचीत कर रही है, अपने फ़र्स्ट सेक्रेटरी को मोज़ाम्बिक़ भेजा है, जहाँ पर कि ज्यादातर हिन्दुस्तानी हैं, जो वहाँ से भेजे जा रहे हैं यह देखने के लिए कि जो एग्रीमेंट पहले हुआ था हमसे और पुर्तगाल से, वह पूरा किया जाये और उनको दिक्क़त न हो।

[Translation begins

Mani Ram Bagri:[352] Hon. Speaker, Sir, it would be good if the speech is translated into Hindustani so that supplementary questions may be asked.

Speaker:[353] I have told you a couple of times to try and get the gist from someone else.

---

352. See fn 350 in this section.
353. See fn 351 in this section.

Mani Ram Bagri: None of my neighbours speak English. If a question is asked in Hindi, the reply is given in English. Why is that so? On the one hand, we are trying to have Hindi as our very own language but ...

Speaker: The Hon. Member may kindly sit down. He is aware of the entire history. All the work was being carried out in English earlier and now slowly we are moving towards Hindi. That is why we have to carry on as we did in the past. But that does not mean that we do not wish to promulgate Hindi as quickly as possible. You bring up this matter whenever something happens. Our effort is to gradually conduct all work in Hindi but it will take time. If you wish to ask a question, you can ask another member to help you. I will try to see that if you have some difficulty then the question may be explained.

Mani Ram Bagri: Could the hon. Minister not interpret it into Hindi?

Speaker: I believe the Hindi interpretation can be done by several hon. Ministers. But one also has to take into consideration the time spent on interpreting each question. However, we should take some pains to bring about this change early. I shall also try to see that when hon. Ministers give statements they should explain them in Hindi also. Hon Members can also cooperate in this by making efforts to understand the statements made. Now the hon. Minister will explain in Hindi.

Dinesh Singh: The Indian Government has told the Portuguese Government that they should annul the new decree, Decree No. 44416, that they have issued. The UAR Government which is interceding on our behalf in this matter has sent their First Secretary to Mozambique where there are a large number of Indians and who are being repatriated to ensure that the earlier Agreement between India and Portugal is being adhered to and they face no difficulties.

Translation ends]

Bishwanath Roy: May I know whether the Government of India have got any idea about the value of the property of the Indian nationals, which is being liquidated in the Portuguese colonies?

Dinesh Singh: No, we do not have full information.

Shree Narayan Das:[354] May I know the number of persons who are going to be affected by this decree?

Dinesh Singh: The number of persons is 2,239 approximately.

म.ला. द्विवेदी:[355] मैं जानना चाहता हूँ कि मोज़ाम्बिक़ से जिन भारतीयों को भगाया जा रहा है उनकी जायदादों को वापस दिलाने के लिए क्या भारत सरकार कोई कार्यवाही कर रही है।

दिनेश सिंहः मैंने अभी अर्ज़ किया कि इस सम्बन्ध में हमने यू.ए.आर. सरकार से कहा है कि वे इस मामले को पुर्तगाल सरकार से उठायें।

[Translation begins

M.L. Dwivedi:[356] I wish to know if the Indian Government is taking any action to see that the Indian nationals who are being repatriated from Mozambique may get their property back.

Dinesh Singh: As I just explained, we have asked the UAR Government to take up this matter with the Portuguese Government.

Translation ends]

Joachim Alva:[357] Despite the integration, are there still any financial obligations or commitments on the side of India towards Portugal, which can be set off against the losses suffered in Mozambique?

Jawaharlal Nehru: I cannot answer precisely; I am not aware of them; I am not definite about it.

Hari Vishnu Kamath:[358] Have government realised at least now how wrong it was to repatriate Portuguese personnel from Goa without making it conditional upon the safe and honourable repatriation of Indians from Portuguese colonies?

354. Congress.
355. Congress.
356. See fn 355 in this section.
357. Congress.
358. PSP.

Speaker: This question need not be answered.

Jawaharlal Nehru: No, Sir. We hold that our action was perfectly correct.

Hari Vishnu Kamath: Why should it not be answered?

Speaker: It does not ask for any information.

प्रकाशवीर शास्त्री:[359] अभी पीछे मोज़ाम्बिक़ से कुछ इस प्रकार के भारतीय आये हैं जिन्होंने मोज़ाम्बिक़ के कैम्प में रहने वाले भारतीयों की दर्दनाक स्थिति का चित्रण किया है और यह भी कहा है कि पाशविक ढंग से रखने के कारण बहुतों की मृत्यु भी हो गई है। मैं जानना चाहता हूँ कि क्या सरकार सही स्थिति को जानने का यत्न करेगी और उसके निराकरण का भी कुछ प्रयत्न करेगी?

दिनेश सिंहः जी हाँ, मोज़ाम्बिक़ से कुछ लोग भी अभी आये हैं। एक्सटर्नल अफ़ेअर्स मिनिस्ट्री ने एक अफ़सर को बम्बई भेजा था जिसने उनसे बातें की हैं। उसने अपनी रिपोर्ट अभी दी है। उसके ऊपर विचार किया जा रहा है।

[Translation begins

Prakashvir Shastri:[360] Recently some such Indian nationals have returned from Mozambique who have described the pitiable condition of the Indians who are in camps in Mozambique, and have also said that due to the inhuman conditions prevailing in the camps, many people have even died. I want to know whether the Government will try to find out what the true situation is and also try to rectify it?

Dinesh Singh: Yes, some Indians have just arrived. The External Affairs Ministry sent an official to Bombay who has talked to them. He has just sent in his report and it is being deliberated upon.

Translation ends]

P.C. Borooah: May I know whether it is a fact that most of the Indians who have been dislodged from Portuguese territories have come to India penniless, and most of them have never seen India before and know none

359. Independent.
360. See fn 359 in this section.

of the Indian languages, and if so, in what manner Government are going to establish them in India or give assistance to them?

Dinesh Singh: I mentioned just now that we have sent an officer to Bombay to discuss this matter with the refugees who have come. The matter is under examination. We shall make every effort to see that there is no hardship suffered by these people.

P.K. Deo:[361] From the statement of the first group of Indians who came to Bombay lately, we find that recently six Indians died in the Portuguese prison camp. At the same time, we have come to know that about 30,000 Indians are facing expulsion from Portuguese colonies. May I know what steps are being taken to receive these 30,000 Indians and rehabilitate them?

Jawaharlal Nehru: This has been explained in answer to various questions.

Hem Barua:[362] Is it not a fact that we entered into an agreement with Portugal that the Indian nationals in Portuguese colonies would be allowed to come to this country at their convenience after liquidating their assets? The Deputy Minister has said that a protest has been made against the decree only. What action do Government propose to take against this breach of the agreements?

Dinesh Singh: This decree is a breach of the agreement, against which we have protested.

H.N. Mukerjee:[363] While obviously Portugal is not a particularly decent member of the international community, may I know if Government is still trying to think out some steps under which before the international forums this kind of refusal to accept the canons of international intercourse can be punished, or at least some sort of judgment of the world conscience made upon it? Can we not use the international forums for which we pay so much these days?

Jawaharlal Nehru: This is a matter for consideration.

361. Swatantra Party.
362. PSP.
363. CPI.

Hari Vishnu Kamath: We could not hear.

Speaker: The Prime Minister said that it would be considered.

Hari Vishnu Kamath: Not just now!

Ram Ratan Gupta:[364] Have Government made any assessment of the assets left behind by the Portuguese in India and have they any scheme to recompense the losses suffered by Indians in Portuguese colonies?

Jawaharlal Nehru: No, Sir.

120. To D. Sanjivayya: Goa Ad-hoc Committee and Azad Gomantak Dal[365]

August 13, 1962

My dear Sanjivayya,

You have formed an ad-hoc Committee for Goa and, I understand, it is doing well.

The question has arisen as to whether representatives of the Azad Gomantak Dal should be taken into this committee. I gather that the Lt. Governor[366] suggested that some of the members of this group, including Shri Lawande,[367] might be co-opted to the ad-hoc Committee. I am rather doubtful about this being done at this stage.

You must know that the Azad Gomantak Dal was definitely a party of violence. I do not blame them for this, but the fact remains that they carried on a policy that was not in line with ours. If we put their representatives on the ad-hoc Committee now, there is bound to be tension and a pulling in different directions, and the Committee will not be able to work adequately.

If Lawande and his group wish to become ordinary members of the Congress, this of course can certainly be agreed to. But, as I have said above, to make them members also of the ad-hoc Committee will create difficulties.

Yours sincerely,
Jawaharlal Nehru

364. Congress.
365. Letter to the Congress President. NMML, AICC Papers, Box 4, File No. OD-22/ 1962.
366. T. Sivasankar, Lieutenant-Governor of Goa, Daman and Diu.
367. Vishwanath Lawande, one of the founders of Azad Gomantak Dal, a revolutionary group which adopted the strategy of direct action to fight the Portuguese.

121. In the Rajya Sabha: Anti-Indian Activities in Goa[368]

Will the Prime Minister be pleased to state:[369]

(a) The number of persons against whom complaints have been received by Government in regard to their indulging in anti-Indian activities such as destroying of Government properties or instigating other persons to indulge in such activities since Goa came under Indian possession;

(b) what action was taken against such persons; and

(c) what steps were taken to inculcate faith in the Government of India, in some of the people of Goa area by removing the pro-Portuguese feelings from their minds?

The Deputy Minister in the Ministry of External Affairs (Dinesh Singh): (a) to (c). No specific complaints have been received against any individuals in respect of their indulging in anti-Indian activities. The Union Territory is, however, facing certain problems of rehabilitation and there are matters relating to trade, employment, development etc., which need to be dealt with quickly and effectively. The Government are giving their full attention to these problems.

विमल कुमार मन्नालालजी चोरड़ियाः क्या श्रीमन्, यह बतलाने की कृपा करेंगे कि गोवा में भारत का कब्जा होने के पश्चात जो बम विस्फोट की कार्यवाहियां हुई थीं उसके बारे में किसकी जांच पड़ताल की और किसके खिलाफ शिकायत पाई गई, या क्या हुआ?

दिनेश सिंहः उनकी जांच पड़ताल हो रही है। काफियों की जांच पड़ताल हो भी गई है। जिनकी अभी तक जांच हो गई है उससे यह पता चला है कि यह किसी के किये हुए काम नहीं थे बल्कि जो पुर्तगीज़ के छोड़े हुए पुराने बम वग़ैरह थे वही वहां फटे हैं।

विमल कुमार मन्नालालजी चोरड़ियाः मेरे प्रश्न के भाग (ग) का उत्तर स्पष्ट नहीं हुआ जो इस प्रकार हैः गोआ क्षेत्र के कुछ निवासियों के मन से पुर्तगालियों के प्रति अनुकूल

---

368. Oral answers, 21 August 1962. *Rajya Sabha Debates*, Vol. 40, Nos. 9-16, 17 to 29 August 1962, cols 2475-2478.

369. Question by V.M. Chordia, Jan Sangh.

भावना हटाकर भारत सरकार के प्रति निष्ठा उत्पन्न करने के लिये क्या कदम उठाये गये? क्या इसका जवाब देने की कृपा करेंगे?

दिनेश सिंहः इसकी जरूरत नहीं है क्योंकि गोवा के जो निवासी हैं उनका दिल भारत की ही तरफ है।

[Translation begins

Vimal Kumar Mannalalji Chordia: Sir, will you please explain what investigation has been done and against whom has evidence been found in the matter of the bomb explosions which took place in Goa after it became part of India?

Dinesh Singh: Investigation is going on. Much of it is complete. From what has been learnt from interrogating people so far it seems that this is not the work of any individual but some bombs left behind by the Portugese have exploded.

Vimal Kumar Mannalalji Chordia: The reply to part (c) of my question is not yet clear. Could you please answer my question about what steps are being taken to remove the favourable feeling of some people in Goa towards the Portuguese and to create commitment to the Indian Government.

Dinesh Singh: There is no need for any steps because the hearts of the Goanese people are with India.

Translation ends]

Bhupesh Gupta:[370] May I know, Sir, if the Government is aware of any activities directed against the new authorities established there now. He said no complaint has been received against an individual, but is he aware of such activities going on in that part of the country?

Dinesh Singh: Matters in connection with any activities that may go on about any individual, that we have not covered in this question?

Bhupesh Gupta: That is not the point. My question was: Is he aware of any such activities directed against the authorities there going on? If so,

370. CPI.

181

is there any presumption that some people must be responsible for such activities? And if this presumption is there, what steps did the Government take in order to find out the people?

Jawaharlal Nehru: I suppose the hon. Member refers to some kind of an organised activity. As far as an individual says something, well, action against him depends on what he says and how he says it. There is no organised activity as such. There were, as my colleague has said, a number of bomb explosions. The enquiry into them is not yet quite complete, but it is clear that they were the bombs the Portuguese had left with the intention of blowing up some place, but they had to leave rather in a hurry. So these bombs later exploded. The report has not yet been finalised.

Bhupesh Gupta: It seems that these bombs that are exploding there are not likely to be time bombs, as far as we can make out, that they are left by the Portuguese and that they seem to be exploded by some people there. And is it not a fact, Sir, that there were many henchmen of the Portuguese there and that some of them are trying to get into the key positions in the administration? Is the Prime Minister aware of such things?

Dinesh Singh: Most of them as I mentioned, exploded by accident, some one running over them or touching them.

N.C. Kasliwal:[371] It appears from press reports that the Cardinal of the Portuguese Church had decided to stay in Goa after Goa's liberation but that he is going away now. So, may I know, Sir, whether he is going away out of his own volition, or Government have asked him to leave the country?

Dinesh Singh: I think the hon. Member is referring to the Portuguese Patriarch in Goa. I believe a new patriarch is coming to replace him.[372]

---

371. Congress.
372. José Vieira Alvernaz was, from 1953, Coadjutor Archbishop of Goa and Daman and Patriarch of East Indies, whose headquarters was Goa. On 25 November 1961, the Lisbon-based Bishop José Pedro da Silva was appointed Coadjutor Bishop of Goa and Daman with the right of succession as Patriarch. However, the appointment did not take effect and Alvernaz continued as Patriarch and Archbishop until 1975. Website www.catholic-hierarchy.org accessed on 20 June 1962.

122. Panchayats in Goa, Daman and Diu[373]

[Note, 27 August 1962, from V.C. Trivedi, Joint Secretary, MEA, for M.J. Desai, the FS, begins]

It is proposed that a Regulation be promulgated by the President in respect of establishment of Panchayats in Goa, Daman and Diu. I submit herewith a draft summary for the Cabinet for approval.

2.   A draft of the Regulation is also placed below.

V.C. Trivedi
27.8.1962

FS

[Note, 27 August 1962, from V.C. Trivedi for M.J. Desai, ends]

[Note, 27 August 1962, from M.J. Desai for Nehru, begins]

PM need see only the draft summary for the Cabinet.

2.   One draft regulation proposed deals only with Panchayats. We may have to follow this up with similar regulation for municipalities a little later. All these will cease to be operative after we bring in regular legislation on the pattern of class (c) states after the necessary constitutional amendments approved by Cabinet last week have gone through.

M.J. Desai
27.8.62

PM

[Note, 27 August 1962, from M.J. Desai for Nehru, ends]

[Note, 28 August 1962, from Nehru for M.J. Desai, begins]

I agree with the Summary.[374] I have not read the draft Regulation. It seems to me to be exceedingly long. I do not know if it is necessary to have these very detailed provisions.

J. Nehru
27.8.1962

FS

[Note, 27 August 1962, from Nehru for M.J. Desai, ends]

373. Noting, MHA, (MEA, File No. 6(19)/62-GOA), pp. 1-2/n).
374. The Summary for the Cabinet is available in MHA, (MEA, File No. 6(19)/62-GOA).

[Note, 28 August 1962, from M.J. Desai probably for V.C. Trivedi, begins]

Please issue the summary and check the draft regulation before finalising it.

2. It has to be comprehensive and detailed, there is no other way.

M.J. Desai
28.8.62

[Note, 27 August 1962, from M.J. Desai, ends]

(m) Gujarat

123. To Rasiklal Parikh: Charges against Colleagues[375]

August 27, 1962

My dear Rasiklalbhai,

I have your letter of the 24th August with its enclosures. I have read all these papers. As you have written already fully to the Congress President[376] and to Shri Sadiq Ali,[377] there is nothing more that I can do in the matter.

Dr Jivraj Mehta,[378] when he was here a short while ago, gave me some information about the kind of charges that had been made. I was surprised to learn about some of them.

I hope this matter will be cleared up soon.

Yours sincerely,
[Jawaharlal Nehru]

375. Letter to the Minister for Home and Industries, Gujarat.
376. D. Sanjivayya.
377. General Secretary, AICC.
378. The Chief Minister of Gujarat.

(n) Jammu and Kashmir

124. To Prem Nath Bazaz: Status of Kashmir[379]

July 26, 1962

Dear Prem Nathji,

I have your letter of July 18 which I have read with interest and care.[380] It is a little difficult for me to send you a full answer as it would mean writing out at considerable length.

But I can assure you that I am very largely in agreement with you about civil liberties and freedom of expression. I may, however, point out to you that even in the most advanced countries in the world, where a State is in peril, such as in war time, freedom of expression is limited. In the United States of America in many ways, even now, freedom of activity and expression is limited insofar as Communists are concerned. In fact, in a democracy there is grave danger of such limitations. In India at present there is a strong demand for action to be taken against communalists and communal organisations, also against the DMK in the South. I have resisted it but I realise that occasions may arise when some such action may have to be taken. Much depends on the growth of liberal ideas in the country and the general atmosphere that prevails. Repeatedly we have seen liberal ideas being suppressed because they were considered dangerous for the State; but my inclination is towards giving the largest measure of freedom.

You wrote to me about the accession of the State being not complete. I do not quite understand this. It is complete. It is true, however, that a measure of autonomy is given to the Jammu & Kashmir Assembly in regard to a few matters unlike the other States. This does not limit the accession in any way. It is the result of historical circumstances. As a matter of fact, during the last few years, much advance has been made in this matter. The Supreme Court, Elections, the Auditor-General etc. function in the State as in other States. The whole trend, therefore, is to bring the Jammu & Kashmir State nearer to the rest of India. What remains are relatively unimportant matters and gradually they are lessening.

While accession is complete, it is true that Pakistan is there to create trouble which it continues to do in a variety of ways. There is hardly a day when intruders from Pakistan do not indulge in some bomb outrage or other.

---

379. Letter to a former associate of Shaikh Abdullah and founder of the Kashmir Cultural Society; address: F/8 Hauz Khas Enclave, New Delhi 16. Sent from Anand Bhavan, Allahabad.
380. Appendix 4.

The speeches delivered from Pakistan go on referring to Jehad and war. All this does create a certain abnormal atmosphere.

The real problem of Kashmir is whether it continues as a secular state as the rest of India or not. This affects the whole of India because secularism in India also has not got such firm foundation as I would like it to have. Anything happening in Kashmir will undoubtedly affect the rest of India with its vast Muslim population.

I hope you do not mind my sending your letter to me to Bakhshi Ghulam Mohammed.[381]

Yours sincerely,
[Jawaharlal Nehru]

125. To Prem Nath Bazaz: State of Kashmir[382]

August 7, 1962

Dear Shri Bazaz,

I have your letter of August 4. I am afraid it is difficult to write at length to you in regard to the various points you have raised. I agree with you that much can be done in Kashmir to improve the situation. I think gradually something has been done. It is true that political liberty does not exist there in the same measure as in the rest of India. At the same time, there is much more of it than there used to be.

At the present moment, there are continuous threats from the Pakistan side of war of some kind or other.

If you have no objection to it, I am sending your letter to Bakhshi Ghulam Mohammed.

Yours sincerely,
[Jawaharlal Nehru]

---

381. Prime Minister of Jammu and Kashmir.
382. Letter to a former associate of Shaikh Abdullah; address: F/8 Hauz Khas Enclave, New Delhi-16.

126. To Prem Nath Bazaz: Don't Publish Correspondence[383]

August 10, 1962

Dear Prem Nathji,
I have your letter of August 10. I do not think it will be desirable to publish the correspondence you have had with me. That was a personal correspondence so far as I am concerned, and to publish it will not be appropriate. It would make it appear that your letters to me were meant really for propaganda.

Yours sincerely,
[Jawaharlal Nehru]

127. To Bakhshi Ghulam Mohammed: Shaikh Abdullah Case and Kashmir[384]

21st August, 1962

My dear Bakhshi,
Thank you for your letter you sent through Pathak. My own first reaction was against our side bringing any fresh charge against Shaikh Sahib.[385] But then Pathak explained to me, as he must have done to you, that this was more a question of procedure than really bringing a charge. It was a difficult matter to decide.

If we are to proceed with this case, then we should do it as thoroughly as possible. If not, then it is another matter. However, I shall see you when you come here.[386]

Prem Nath Dogra and company came to see me the other day and talked to me about Kashmir not having a special status etc.[387] I told them that it was not desirable to make any change at present. Gradually these changes take place.

---

383. Letter to a former associate of Shaikh Abdullah; address: Gashagur, F-8, Hauz Khas Enclave, New Delhi 16.
384. Letter to the Prime Minister of Jammu and Kashmir.
385. Shaikh Abdullah, former Prime Minister of Jammu and Kashmir State, was being tried in the court of the Additional Sessions Judge in Jammu for the Kashmir Conspiracy Case. G.S. Pathak, Congress, Rajya Sabha MP, was the chief prosecution counsel in the case.
386. See appendix 49.
387. A delegation of the Jammu and Kashmir Praja Parishad led by its President Prem Nath Dogra met Nehru on 18 August 1962.

As a matter of fact, very little was left of the special status. It was largely a question of sentiment, but sentiment sometimes is important.

As I have been sending you letters from Prem Nath Bazaz, I enclose yet another one from him.[388]

Yours sincerely
[Jawaharlal Nehru]

128. To Prem Nath Bazaz: Kashmir Status[389]

21st August, 1962

Dear Prem Nathji,

I have your letter of August 18th. It is true that I had a small deputation the other day led by Shri Prem Nath Dogra. I explained to him that what he said was not advisable. As a matter of fact, much has been done in spite of the Article in the Constitution[390] which is supposed to give a special status to Kashmir and gradually what little remains will also go. The question is more a sentimental one than anything else. Sentiment is sometimes important, but we have to weigh both sides and I think that no change should be made in this matter at present.[391]

Yours sincerely,
[Jawaharlal Nehru]

129. To E. Pauline Quingly: Shaikh Abdullah and Kashmir[392]

September 19, 1962

Dear Mrs Quingly,

Thank you for your letter of the 17th September.

I am sorry that Shaikh Abdullah is being tried in Kashmir. I should like however to say that I was not aware of any evidence to the fact that the 1953

---

388. See items 124-126.
389. Letter to a former associate of Shaikh Abdullah; address: F/8 Hauz Khas Enclave, New Delhi.
390. Article 370.
391. See item 127 and other items in this subsection.
392. Letter; address: Alancote, Limpsfield, Surrey. Sent from 9 Kensington Palace Gardens, London W8.

coup d'état was conspired in London. Indeed, I have never heard of this before. Indeed, it may surprise you to learn that I was not even aware of this coup d'état till it had occurred. I knew that the situation was a serious one in Kashmir and something might happen. But the actual happening took place without my knowledge till afterwards.[393]

At the present moment Kashmir is an autonomous part of India. The Government may not be an ideal one, but it is entirely elected by the Kashmiris themselves and undoubtedly it has helped in the development of Kashmir during the last few years. The country's resources have increased greatly and have been used to finance this development together with large sums given by the Government of India. I do not know what foreign loans you refer to.

We have had three general elections in Kashmir excepting the part which is occupied by Pakistan and they have been conducted with some success. Therefore, to say that Kashmir is considered as a conquered territory is far from correct. The difficulties that have arisen in Kashmir are partly due to pulling in different directions in Kashmir itself.

I greatly regret Shaikh Abdullah's continued trial and imprisonment. In spite of my differences with him in many ways I had and still have regard for him. I can only hope that this chapter will end satisfactorily soon.

Yours sincerely,
[Jawaharlal Nehru]

(o) Madhya Pradesh

130. Paper Mill in Hoshangabad[394]

[Note, 6 August 1962, by Nehru for Kesho Ram, his PPS, begins]

Please see the attached letter from Rajkumari Amrit Kaur.[395] I do not know who is in charge of this paper mill that is being erected in Hoshangabad. It may be

---

393. For previous references to Nehru's statements and observations on developments at the time, see SWJN/SS/23/section on Kashmir.
394. Noting. The file name reads: "Representation from the Friends Rural Centre, Hoshangabad, Madhya Pradesh, against the proposed acquisition of their land by Govt for the establishment of a new paper mill." PMO, File No. 17(515)/62-64-PMS, Minute No. 2.
395. Chairman of the Indian Red Cross and former Health Minister. See appendix 22.

the Commerce & Industry Ministry. Please refer to them or, if necessary, write to the Madhya Pradesh Government.

Here is some good work which has been done in this area, for how long I do not know. I have known it for more than thirty years. They have achieved results and merely to dispossess them for some inadequate reason does not seem to me enough. Surely some land can be found elsewhere instead of removing a well-established industry which has been doing such good work.

You can find out who is in charge of this matter and I shall write to the Minister of C&I[396] myself. Meanwhile, you can enquire from the District Magistrate of Hoshangabad how far this matter has proceeded and tell him that we are giving thought to it.

Jawaharlal Nehru
6.8.1962

PPS

[Note, 6 August 1962, by Nehru for Kesho Ram, his PPS, ends]

[Note, 9 August 1962, by Kesho Ram for Nehru, begins]

As desired by PM, I wrote to the Ministry concerned regarding this matter. We have now been informed that the Ministry of Finance have reviewed the position and have decided to give up the land belonging to the Friends' Rural Centre which they were going to acquire for their Security Paper Mill Project at Hoshangabad.

2.   I am informing Rajkumari Amrit Kaur of this.

K. Ram
9.8.1962

PM

[Note, 9 August 1962, by Kesho Ram for Nehru, ends]

---

396. K.C. Reddy, Minister of Commerce and Industry.

(p) Madras State

131. In Honour of K. Kamaraj[397]

Shri Kamaraj has risen to eminence not only in Madras State but in India by his continuous service of the people. Few persons have a greater right to be called a servant of the people than Shri Kamaraj. It has been my privilege to know him as a friend and a comrade for many years, and my regard for him has grown the more I knew him.

As Chief Minister of Madras, he has presided over a government which has been a model of efficiency and good administration. I hope he will be spared for many long years to serve the people of India.

132. To K. Kamaraj: Nuclear Power Station in Madras[398]

September 28, 1962

My dear Kamaraj,

Your letter of the 21st September has reached me here in Rome. In this you suggest that necessary steps should be initiated in regard to starting a nuclear power station in Madras. As you know, two nuclear power stations have been decided upon already. The first is at Tarapore in Maharashtra and the second in Rajasthan. It is intended to have a third nuclear station in the South, probably in Madras.

Even the two nuclear stations which have been decided upon will probably take at least four or five years to function. A third station will naturally take longer. However, we shall keep what you have written in mind.

Yours sincerely
Jawaharlal Nehru

397. Message, 7 August 1962, on the occasion of the birthday celebrations of the Chief Minister of Madras State. PMO, File No. 9/2/62-PMP, Vol. V, Sr. No. 92-A. Also available in the JN Collection.
398. Letter to the Chief Minister of Madras. Sent from Rome.

(q) Maharashtra

133. To P. Subbarayan: Plans to Meet[399]

8th August, 1962

My dear Subbarayan,

I am sorry to learn from your letter of August 6th that you have been ill. I hope you have quite recovered by now.

I do not think I shall be stopping in Bombay on my way to London. I shall probably go in a through plane from Delhi. It was for this reason that I have fixed another day to go to Bombay for Munshi's[400] Engineering College and I think I shall stick to this engagement.[401] I hope to reach there on Sunday the 19th August forenoon and will return in the morning of the 20th.

I am feeling quite fit now.

Yours affectionately,
[Jawaharlal Nehru]

(r) Mysore State

134. To Vijaya Lakshmi Pandit: Mysore Governorship and other Matters[402]

September 2, 1962

[Nan dear,]

I received your letter about three days ago. I wanted to reply to it immediately, but as you had already made a decision and communicated it to Nijalingappa,[403] there was no immediate hurry. Lately there has been a multitude of things happening which have distressed me. Usually I like going abroad, but on this occasion I must confess I do not at all like leaving India. So much is happening that distresses me greatly. I suppose one must get used to this and face every contingency.

---

399. Letter to the Governor of Maharashtra.
400. K.M. Munshi, Chairman of the Bharatiya Vidya Bhavan.
401. For Nehru's inaugural speech at the Sardar Patel Engineering College in Bombay on 19 August 1962, see item 250.
402. Letter to sister; address: 8-E Mafatlal Park, Bhulabhai Desai Road, Bombay-26.
403. Chief Minister of Mysore State.

192

I was pleasantly surprised to learn of your decision about Mysore. The impression I had gathered was that you were not likely to accept this. But, on the whole, I think you have done right. You need not stay in Mysore for very long. That is entirely up to you. But going there for a year or so would be a new experience and, I think, a worthwhile one.[404]

I am glad that you are going to Heidelberg. After the previous incident when you were unable to go there, it is desirable that you should make up for it. You can certainly also go to Bonn and, if you like, to Essen also. It does not much matter if you go to one or two other places in Germany, if you feel like it.

Indu and I will be leaving on the 7th night. We shall not pass through Bombay. I shall go direct to London. After the Conference there, I shall go for two days to Paris and then to Nigeria and Ghana. I expect to return to Delhi on the 1st of October.

[Jawaharlal Nehru]

135. To S. Radhakrishnan: Vijaya Lakshmi Pandit Governor of Mysore[405]

September 4, 1962

My dear Mr President,

I have received a letter from the Chief Minister of Mysore State, Shri Nijalingappa, informing me that Vijaya Lakshmi Pandit[406] has agreed to be appointed as Governor of Mysore. She has added that she will not be free to go there till about the middle of November.[407] I have also received a letter from her to the same effect,[408] and I understand she has written to you directly also.

I presume that you agree with this appointment as you had yourself urged her to accept.

I am writing to the Home Minister on the subject so that he can process this at a suitable time.[409] There is no immediate hurry to do so.

Yours sincerely,
[J. Nehru]

404. See appendix 55; items 135-136.
405. Letter to the President. MHA, File No. 19/61/62-Pub. I., p. 2/c. Also available in the JN Collection.
406. Nehru's sister.
407. Appendix 55.
408. See item 134.
409. Item 136.

136. To Lal Bahadur Shastri: Vijaya Lakshmi Pandit Governor of Mysore State[410]

September 4, 1962

My dear Lal Bahadur,

I enclose a letter from Nijalingappa about the Governorship of Mysore. Vijaya Lakshmi also wrote to me on the subject and expressed her willingness to go there, though she did this somewhat reluctantly.[411]

I think you should now process this at the suitable time. There is no hurry yet because she is not prepared to go there till the middle of November.

I am writing to the President, copy enclosed.[412]

Yours affectionately,
Jawaharlal

(s) **Northeast**

137. To K.D. Malaviya: Assam Pettifogging on Oil Royalty[413]

July 23, 1962

My dear Keshava,

Your letter of July 22nd reached me just before Chaliha,[414] Chief Minister of Assam, came to see me. I spoke to him rather strongly on the attitude of the Assam Government in regard to this business of oil exploration etc. I pointed out that if they were not cooperative, then it was absurd for us to spend time, energy and money over the development of Assam. Assam was a place crying out for development and raising difficulties about petty matters would come in the way of that development.

He did not seem to know very much as to what had happened about the prospecting licence of O&NGC. He said that he would immediately enquire.

---

410. Letter to the Home Minister. MHA, File No. 19/61/62-Pub. I, p. 1/c.
411. Item 134.
412. Item 135.
413. Letter to the Minister of Mines and Fuel. PMO, File No. 17(490)/62-70-PMS, Sr. No. 33-A. Also available in the JN Collection.
414. B.P. Chaliha.

As I think I told you, he had previously written a letter to me a few days ago about our proposal to refer the controversy about royalties to Morarjibhai.[415] He had said that it would be better to refer the question of principle involved to the Supreme Court[416] but that for the present Morarjibhai should advise. I had made clear to him that whatever the decision of Morarjibhai was going to be, we did not want the Assam Government's Five Year Plan to suffer in any way and, therefore, we might make good any possible loss that might occur because of that decision.

In view of his desire to have the question of principle referred to the Supreme Court for their advice, I agree to this. I propose to tell Morarjibhai about this and to ask him to go into the matter for some temporary decision.

I have made it clear to Chaliha that whatever happens, there should be no obstruction and delay in exploration, prospecting or any other matter. Whatever is decided about royalties will apply retrospectively, if necessary. That is to say, for the present, licences etc. should be issued and the Assam Government's attitude should be fully cooperative. He agreed to this.

The Assam Government's attitude is most unfortunate and irritating. But we should not get excited about it. It is the attitude of the man who is afraid of losing what little he has and who does not look to the future. I hardly think it is necessary to amend the Constitution, as suggested by you. However, we can consider this, if necessary.[417]

Yours affectionately,
Jawaharlal Nehru

138. To Morarji Desai: Assam Oil Royalty[418]

July 23, 1962

My dear Morarji,

You will remember our controversy with the Assam Government about the royalties to be paid by them on oil. They asked that this matter might be referred to the Supreme Court for their advice. When I mentioned this in the Cabinet, it

---

415. Morarji Desai, the Finance Minister. Appendix 3. See also SWJN/SS/77/item 185.
416. See also SWJN/SS/77/item 184.
417. See also item 138 and earlier correspondence on this subject in SWJN/SS/77/section Politics, subsection Northeast.
418. Letter to the Finance Minister. PMO, File No. 17(490)/62-70-PMS, Sr. No. 34-A. Also available in the JN Collection.

was suggested that instead of the Supreme Court, you might be asked to look into it and advise and your advice will be accepted.

I wrote accordingly to Chaliha[419] and in his answer he did not wholly agree with our suggestion.[420] He said that this was a matter of principle and it would be better if that principle was decided by the Supreme Court, but pending that advice he would be glad to have your arbitration in the matter.

Since he is very anxious for this matter to be referred to the Supreme Court, I think we should agree to it. He is really afraid of criticism in his own party and the rest of Assam. He is here at present and you can have a talk with him on the subject. I had made it clear to him that if by virtue of your decision there was any reduction in his resources of the Five Year Plan, this would be made good by us.

I am afraid the Assam Government is acting very narrowly and does not realise that they are injuring their own cause and that of the development of Assam greatly by their obstructions and delays. I spoke rather strongly to Chaliha about this matter. Recently they have refused an application for prospecting and exploration of oil from our Oil & Natural Gas Commission. This seems to me very wrong and, as I told Chaliha, rather scandalous. Whatever the decision on royalties might be, it will be applied even retrospectively. But this refusal of allowing the Government of India to prospect is really amazing. I have told Chaliha that nothing should be done to delay or obstruct our work. Any matters in dispute could be considered and the decisions will be given effect to.[421]

I might mention that there are all kinds of undesirable developments taking place in some of the Hill Districts of Assam. Some of them are likely to give us trouble and then the Chinese frontier situation is pretty serious.

Yours sincerely,
[Jawaharlal Nehru]

419. B.P. Chaliha, the Chief Minister of Assam. See SWJN/SS/77/items 184-185.
420. Appendix 3.
421. See item 137.

139. To K.D. Malaviya: Assam Oil Royalty[422]

July 25, 1962

My dear Keshava,

Your letter of the 24th July.[423] What I wrote to you was what Chaliha had told me. I think that is the correct position. This morning he met Finance Minister Morarjibhai[424] who tried to induce him to accept his arbitration for the entire matter. Chaliha appeared to be convinced but he said that as this was a Cabinet decision, he would have to refer it to the Cabinet.[425]

It will do us no good to quarrel with any State or to create an impression that we cannot get on with them.

Yours affectionately,
[Jawaharlal Nehru]

140. To B.P. Chaliha: Oil Royalty Arbitration[426]

August 17, 1962

My dear Chaliha,

I have received your letter of August 14th.[427] Since you have left the matter to me and asked me to appoint any forum that I might decide upon, I am asking Shri Morarji Desai[428] to consider this question fully and report to me. You can send any papers in connection with this matter either to me or directly to Shri Morarji Desai.

Your two colleagues, Shri Fakhruddin Ahmed[429] and Shri Tripathi,[430] should get in touch with Shri Morarji Desai and fix a suitable time to meet him.

422. Letter to the Minister of Mines and Fuel. PMO, File No. 17(490)/62-70-PMS, Sr. No. 37-A.
423. Appendix 11.
424. Morarji Desai.
425. See appendix 12.
426. Letter to the Chief Minister of Assam. PMO, File No. 17(490)/62-70-PMS, Sr. No. 43-A. Also available in the JN Collection.
427. Appendix 35.
428. Union Finance Minister.
429. Fakhruddin Ali Ahmed, Minister of Law and Finance in Assam.
430. K.P. Tripathy, Minister of Industries, Assam.

I note that you have issued directions that petroleum exploration licences be issued to the parties concerned.[431]

Yours sincerely,
Jawaharlal Nehru

141. To K.D. Malaviya: Assam Oil Royalty Arbitration[432]

August 17, 1962

My dear Keshava,

I enclose a copy of a letter I have received from B.P. Chaliha, Chief Minister of Assam; also my answer to him. You will notice that I have asked his colleagues, Fakhr-ud-din Ahmed and Tripathi, to get in touch with our Finance Minister[433] and fix a suitable time for them to put their case before him. You will kindly arrange also to place any papers or other material before the Finance Minister.

Yours affectionately,
Jawaharlal Nehru

142. To B.P. Chaliha: Army Expels Tribals[434]

17th August, 1962

My dear Chief Minister,

I enclose copy of a letter I have received from Shri G.G. Swell, MP,[435] about the evacuation of tribal land in the Khasi Hills for field artillery practice.[436] Shri Swell came to see me about it too and said that the evacuation is to be done for a full year. I cannot understand this business at all. I do not know who is responsible for this. I am writing to the Defence Ministry here,[437] just as I am writing to you. I should be glad if you would look into this matter immediately

---

431. See also other correspondence on this subject in this section.
432. Letter to the Minister of Mines and Fuel. NMML, K.D. Malaviya Papers. Also available in the JN Collection.
433. Morarji Desai.
434. Letter to Chief Minister of Assam.
435. Lok Sabha MP of the All Party Hill Leaders' Conference, from Autonomous Districts-ST, Assam.
436. Appendix 38.
437. See item 143.

because this kind of thing creates needless discontent and harassment to the people concerned.

Yours sincerely,
[Jawaharlal Nehru]

143. For V.K. Krishna Menon: Army Expelling Tribals[438]

I enclose a copy of a letter I have received from Shri G.G. Swell, MP.[439] He came to me about this matter also today.

2. I do not understand this. I suppose the field artillery practice is connected with some defence exercises. I am told the place is not far from Shillong and there is much consternation about the orders that have been issued.

3. I am sending a copy of these papers to the Assam Chief Minister also.[440] I should like you to look into this matter because it does seem to me very hard for thousands of people to be moved away from their homes and villages and told that this is to be done for a whole year. I do not understand this at all.

144. To B.P. Chaliha: Funds for Flood Relief[441]

August 22, 1962

My dear Chaliha,

When I met you last, you said that you would let me know if you required more money from my National Relief Fund for flood relief work. You have not written to me about it. But from the accounts in the press, it is clear that distress from the floods must be very great. I am therefore sending you a cheque for Rs 50,000/-. I shall gladly send you some more money when you write for it.[442]

Yours sincerely,
Jawaharlal Nehru

---

438. Note, 17 August 1962, for the Defence Minister.
439. Appendix 38.
440. Item 142.
441. Letter to the Chief Minister of Assam. PMO, File No. 7(261)/62-66-PMS, Sr. No. 2-B. Also available in the JN Collection.
442. See also item 146.

145. In the Lok Sabha: Situation in Nagaland[443]

Will the Prime Minister be pleased to state:[444]

(a)   whether Shri Shilu Ao, Chief Executive Councillor, Nagaland had met the Prime Minister in June last; and

(b)   what is his assessment of the situation and suggestions for further improvement?

The Parliamentary Secretary to the Minister of External Affairs (S.C. Jamir):

(a)   Yes.

(b)   Shri Shilu Ao's assessment was that the morale of the hostiles was low and central direction of their activities had been non-existent for some time. The small bands into which the hostiles had been split up were short of men, money and equipment. Shri Shilu Ao's broad view with regard to the future course of action which agreed with ours, was that the present pace of development work should be maintained and, if necessary, increased and that the degree of pressure exerted by the Security Forces against the hostiles should continue.

Harish Chandra Mathur: May I know what administrative deficiencies in particular, in respect of the strength of staff and personnel were referred to by him and what is the nature of these deficiencies and Government's reaction to it?

S.C. Jamir: Actually, he came here to attend the Community Development Conference, and he had some administrative matters regarding the organization of the Nagaland Secretariat as well as the formation of directorates for various departments. These matters were discussed and analysed.

Harish Chandra Mathur: May I know to what extent the position of the rebel Nagas has been weakened and what positive actions are being taken by way of development and national integration?

443. Oral answers, 22 August 1962. *Lok Sabha Debates*, Third Series, Vol. 7, 20 to 31 August 1962, 2nd Session, cols 3327-30.
444. Question by Harish Chandra Mathur and D.C. Sharma, both Congress.

S.C. Jamir: The Security Forces are giving continuous pressure on the hostiles and that has reduced hostile activities. The positive action is that not only they defeat the hostiles but they apprehend and arrest those people who are helping the hostiles. In fact, the Security regulations enable the Nagaland Government to apprehend and arrest those persons who are indulging in this kind of activity.

Harish Chandra Mathur: I am afraid the hon. Parliamentary Secretary did not answer my question about national integration and also the extent to which the rebel position has been weakened.

Jawaharlal Nehru: There are two Bills introduced which aim at that—the two Nagaland Bills.

D.C. Sharma: May I know if the latest move of Phizo[445] going to Pakistan and going abroad to USA to extend his activities has had any repercussions in Nagaland?

S.C. Jamir: Definitely, there are some repercussions on the hostiles, not on the masses, because people, as a whole, know that independence is not possible and it is out of question. Moreover, Phizo, as I have stated, is a British citizen; and so he cannot take up the Naga case anywhere.

Hem Barua:[446] May I know if it is a fact that the astonishing revelation made by a London News Magazine called *Topic* that Government has, in its possession, certain documents to show that big business interests in Calcutta, jointly owned by British and Indians, were helping the Naga hostiles through finances? If so, may I know whether that matter was discussed between Shri Shilu Ao and our Prime Minister?

S.C. Jamir: Except the administrative matters no such discussion was held with Shri Shilu Ao.

Jaipal Singh:[447] Since, in the two Bills which the Prime Minister has presented to us—or rather introduced in the House—no particular mention is made about a Public Service Commission for this would-be State of

445. A.Z. Phizo, the Naga rebel leader.
446. PSP.
447. Jharkhand Party.

Nagaland, may I know whether in the talks last June there was any specific mention made of personnel for this new State being, as far as possible, of local people? Was there any specific demand or even suggestion towards that?

Jawaharlal Nehru: What was the suggestion about, as far as possible, local people?

Jaipal Singh: Whether any indication was given in the talks, last June, that for some time, for some years at least, the Secretariat, the services and so forth, should as far as possible be of Nagas only?

Jawaharlal Nehru: It is presumed that it will be in charge of the Naga leaders there and it is up to them. And, I suppose they require some specialized knowledge, fully, of the Naga people.

146. To Liladhar Kotoki: Funds for Flood Relief in Assam[448]

August 26, 1962

Dear Liladharji,

I have received your letter of the 25th August which has been signed by a number of Members of Parliament from Assam. I agree with you that the reports from Assam about the flood situation are deeply distressing. The Ministry of Irrigation & Power have sent some senior engineers immediately there to help.

The question of protecting Assam from floods is, as you say, an old one and a great deal of thought has been given to it. No doubt, more thought should be given and such steps as are possible for us should be taken. But you will appreciate that these extraordinary floods are difficult to deal with, whether they occur in Assam or Bihar or UP or elsewhere. Bunds and embankments can only protect a town. They cannot protect wide areas. Sometimes, by interfering with the natural drainage, they create new problems. However, every attention should be given to this matter.

I had previously sent seventy-five thousand rupees to the Chief Minister[449] for immediate relief work. I have sent a further fifty thousand rupees for this

448. Letter to Congress, Lok Sabha MP from Assam; address: 50 South Avenue, New Delhi. PMO, File No. 7(261)/62-66-PMS, Sr. No. 15-A. Also available in the JN Collection.
449. B.P. Chaliha.

purpose.[450] These grants are from the Prime Minister's National Relief Fund. So far as governmental help is concerned, this will, of course, be given to the best of our ability.

You will kindly share this letter with the other signatories of your letter.

Yours sincerely,
Jawaharlal Nehru

147. In the Lok Sabha: Nagaland Bills[451]

Jawaharlal Nehru: Sir, I have followed with great interest the preliminary canter of some hon. Members of the Opposition.[452] I confess that I was impressed by the volume of sound but not by the sense. Because, as you have been pleased to say, these two Bills[453] are wholly and absolutely interdependent. Now, if the hon. Member Shri Hari [Vishnu] Kamath's[454] views are to prevail, it becomes impossible for us to deal with the question or give effect to our agreement with the Naga Convention[455] in regard to the Bill. It will be an extraordinary position if an argument is raised on the basis of some rule—I do not think the argument is correct—that we cannot move at all in the direction we want to: that is presuming that this House wants to go that way, but it cannot.

450. See item 144.
451. Motions, 28 August 1962. *Lok Sabha Debates*, Third Series, Vol. 7, 20 to 31 August 1962, 2nd Session, cols 4498-4507, 4594-4603 and 4622-4625.
452. Nehru's speech was preceded by discussion on another motion moved by Nehru earlier the same day: "That the proviso to Rule 66 of the Rules of Procedure and Conduct of Business in Lok Sabha in its application to the motions for taking into consideration and passing of the Constitution (Thirteenth Amendment) Bill, 1962, and the State of Nagaland Bill, 1962, be suspended."

Nehru stated that "Under the proviso to this Rule, if a Bill be dependent on another Bill, such Bill cannot be taken into consideration and passed until the enactment of the other Bill. This proviso may, however, be suspended under Rule 388 of the Rules of Procedure."

Eventually the motion was adopted and the rule suspended.
453. The Constitution (Thirteenth Amendment) Bill and the State of Nagaland Bill.
454. PSP.
455. For the agreement arrived at in July 1960 with the leaders of the Naga People's Convention, see SWJN/SS/61/appendix 2 (b).

Hem Barua (Gauhati):[456] We have closed that chapter. Why does he make reference to that?

Hari Vishnu Kamath (Hoshangabad): It is irrelevant.

Speaker:[457] Order, order.

Jawaharlal Nehru: I am glad that the hon. Member realises that he is irrelevant.

Hari Vishnu Kamath: Along with you. We share the honours.

Jawaharlal Nehru: You cannot.

It is immaterial to me how at the time of voting, you, Sir, are pleased to get the voting done, whether on the one Bill first or on the other. But the two have to be considered at the consideration stage together, so that hon. Members may be able to deal with, and see, the whole picture and criticise it or try to amend it. Afterwards, we shall naturally take them separately. Now, I beg to move, therefore:

"That the Bill further to amend the Constitution of India be taken into consideration."

Shall I stop now or move the second motion too at the same time?

Speaker: He may move both the motions formally and then make a common speech on both.

Jawaharlal Nehru: I also beg to move:

"That the Bill to provide for the formation of the State of Nagaland and for matters connected therewith, be taken into consideration."

Hari Vishnu Kamath: On a point of order. Leave has not been granted to move the second Bill, namely the State of Nagaland Bill.

Speaker: What leave?

456. PSP.
457. Hukam Singh.

204

Hari Vishnu Kamath: I believe that the motion was made only for the first Bill. Leave must be granted first for the motion on the second Bill.

The Minister of Law (A.K. Sen): That is only at the stage of introduction.

Hari Vishnu Kamath: We cannot consider the Bill unless it is introduced and the next motion is made.

A.K. Sen: There is no necessity for leave for consideration.

Speaker: I do not quite follow. To what leave is the hon. Member referring?

Hari Vishnu Kamath: The motion must be made first, and then only he can speak on the Bill.

U.M. Trivedi (Mandsaur):[458] He says that the motion has not been moved.

Speaker: That is what he has done just now.

Hari Vishnu Kamath: We did not hear.

Speaker: He has just moved the two motions, one after the other, that the two Bills be taken into consideration.

Jawaharlal Nehru: Almost exactly two years ago, I made a statement in this House in regard to Nagaland and in regard to a certain agreement that had been arrived at with the leaders of Nagaland, of the Naga Convention party there, so that what we are doing today is in continuation of that agreement that we came to. It is not an entirely new thing. An agreement was arrived at and it has been acted upon during these two years to the extent it could be, without having an amendment of the Constitution etc.

We would have had this earlier but for the fact that the situation in Nagaland was not normal and has not been normal, as the House very well knows, and we wanted it to approach normality before we took this step. I do not pretend to say that it is absolutely normal, but, undoubtedly, it is much better now than it has been. And the Provisional Council of Nagaland that was formed as a result of that agreement has been functioning, on the whole, with success.

---

458. Jan Sangh.

And as they desired that further steps should be taken now, we thought that the time had come for us to implement that agreement of two years ago fully.

In effect, therefore, this House had accepted the basic point that these Bills raise, that is, of Nagaland with certain powers etc., apart from details which are given in the Bills; this House has accepted it, and we have acted upon that for all this period.

Now, I am happy to be able to move this amendment because it is in continuation of the policy that we have followed in regard to Nagaland throughout. We have never relied on using military forces merely to deal with the situation there, although, unhappily, we had to use them because of the activities of certain hostile elements there. We have always made a political approach, the approach to make these people friends and citizens of India. It was in continuation of that that we had these Conventions there which produced ultimately, two and a half years ago or thereabouts, a sixteen-point memorandum which the Nagas themselves brought before us and placed before us, that is, the Naga leaders of that Convention. We accepted it then not fully but we accepted it almost entirely except for some minor changes which we could not give effect to; and the matter was one of agreement between the Government representatives and the members of the Naga People's Convention. I submit that this matter, the basic matter, has been accepted—not in the form of a law—but it was placed before the House and it agreed that in the circumstances that should be done. Now, I am coming forward with detailed provisions to give effect to that agreement arrived at and broadly accepted by this House.

I do not propose to go into the history of what happened in the Naga Hills, because this matter has been before us in various forms, and many questions are asked from time to time. After the transfer of power in 1947, the Naga Hills district and the Tuensang district were incorporated in the North-East Frontier Agency, and they were included in the Sixth Schedule of the Constitution.

Later, some people organised armed resistance, and not only armed resistance, but there was a succession of murders, forcible exactions, arson etc. With great reluctance, we had to take measures, that is military measures or police measures, to deal with the situation. May I say here that our military and police forces and the Assam Rifles have had an exceedingly difficult time there, not difficult in the military sense, but difficult in the sense that they had always to be held back by us so that innocent people might not suffer? It was very difficult. It was not organised armies that we were dealing with but snipers and others. Occasionally, some innocent people did suffer. We are sorry for that. We even took steps to punish those who are guilty, although they might have been innocently guilty, that is, our forces. And yet, in spite of all this, in spite of all the care that we have taken, the kind of propaganda that has been made by Mr Phizo and some of his lieutenants has been quite extraordinary and quite outrageous in its character.

I cannot guarantee, naturally, that in several years of operations, things have not been done by any individual member of the police or the Army, which are undesirable. We are trying to stop that, and our policy has been that these should not happen, but under the extreme stress and strain of this place, something may have happened; wherever we have found out, we have taken steps against them. But I do wish to pay a tribute to the general behaviour of our Army and the Assam Rifles in these Hills in the face of exceedingly difficult circumstances; it is not regular fighting, but picking them off from behind, from bushes, ambushes and the rest.

So, this thing increased. The terrain was very difficult, and there was a frontier also, the frontier with Burma. Later, the hostile Nagas used to retreat on the other side of the frontier where we could not follow them; we could not go into the Burmese territory against the wishes of the Burmese or without their permission, and so, they found shelter there and came back when they could.

Now, this went on for some time when this Convention, to which I have referred, was held. The people of Nagaland became exceedingly weary of the suffering they had to undergo and all the exactions that were made from them by the hostile elements, and they gathered together in a big convention. I think that was the first Convention.

Hem Barua: On the 26th August.

Jawaharlal Nehru: It was in 1957.

Renu Chakravartty (Barrackpore):[459] 22nd August.

Jawaharlal Nehru: I have not got the exact date; it does not matter. But the first demand they made on us was that the Naga Hills area and the Tuensang Division should be made into a separate unit under the External Affairs Ministry. We acceded to that demand, so that although in theory and constitutionally these areas were still parts of the Assam State, in effect they were separate, made into a separate unit under the External Affairs Ministry, that is, under the Government of India. This has continued since then.

Now, I wish to draw special attention to this fact that this has remained a separate unit, because now that it is proposed to form the State of Nagaland, it is largely renaming the area plus some powers given to it, Assembly etc. But

459. CPI.

the unit has been separate for several years. It is not creating a separate unit. It has been separate by the decision of Parliament and it has functioned as such. So that all that these present Bills intend doing is to rename it—in fact, even the naming part has been practically done—and to give it certain autonomy. The separation from Assam took place some years ago.

It was in December 1957 that this was separated and this was accompanied by the general amnesty, for the release of convicts and undertrials responsible for offences against the State. A second Convention of the Naga people was held in May 1958. They went to the extent of appointing a liaison committee to contact and win over the misguided Nagas in support of the Convention's policy of securing the maximum autonomy for the areas inhabited by the Nagas in order that they can share the responsibilities of the government of Nagaland.

This effort, however, did not meet with success. Then a third Convention was held at Mokokchung in October 1958 and this prepared the 16-point memorandum for the consideration of the Government. Their main demand was for the constitution of a separate State within the Indian Union to be known as Nagaland. Then a delegation came under the leadership of Dr Imkongliba Ao, President of the Convention, and met me, two years ago, in July 1960. That resulted in this agreement, and subsequently the matter being placed before Parliament. A Council was formed and during the last two years it has been functioning as a preliminary to the changeover; progressively, the Governor, although in law he had authority, has acted in accordance with the wishes of the Council of the Nagas.

The House may remember the tragedy when that great leader of the Naga, Dr Imkongliba Ao, was shot down by some of the hostiles.[460] That itself indicates the kind of people the hostiles are—shooting down one of their own great leaders who himself had at one time supported them earlier but had subsequently found that this would lead to no results, and had worked for an agreement and for peace and harmony there.

In the agreement that was arrived at, there was a transitional period, as desired by the Naga leaders themselves, during which an Interim Body consisting of 45 members chosen from the tribes of Nagaland and a Council of not more than 5 members from the Interim Body were to be constituted, to assist and advise the Governor in the administration of Nagaland. These interim arrangements were brought into force and had been functioning satisfactorily. Elections to the village, range and tribal councils had been held and the

---

460. Imkongliba Ao, Chairman of the Interim Council of Nagaland, was assassinated on 22 August 1961, see SWJN/SS/71/items 108-109.

administration of Nagaland has increasingly become the responsibility of the representatives of the Naga people themselves.

Apart from the desirability of this change on the merits, it is something to which we are completely committed. I would submit that even this Parliament is committed to it, apart from the minor points of it, and any hesitation in giving effect to it will not have good results; it will show that we give our word and cannot keep it, which is not a good thing for a government and certainly not for Parliament.

The State of Nagaland Bill we are considering has certain special provisions. One is that for the time being the Governor will have special powers in regard to law and order and finance, but as soon as the situation is normal, that will not be so. That can be declared by the President. I may add that all those special clauses have been made by the Naga leaders. As for finances, the actual income of Nagaland is very little at present. It could be more, but it is little. The Government of India has been spending a large sum of money in welfare schemes, and we thought that the Governor should have special powers to see that the finances were not misused.

These are the two temporary powers that he is given. As soon as the situation improves, the Ministry which will be in existence in Nagaland will be in charge completely.

But there is one part of this State of Nagaland, which is the Tuensang Division or District. That has been treated separately, not because we wanted to treat it separately but because the Tuensang representatives wanted it to be treated separately and the Naga representatives who had come to that Convention agreed with that. This area is somewhat more backward than the other two districts of Nagaland. Therefore, it has been decided that this area will have a Regional Council, and the Governor will play a little greater part in that area for the first ten years, the period being shortened if need arises.

I should like to stress that this proviso about the Tuensang district is not of our seeking. We agreed to it because the representatives of Tuensang and the representatives of the Nagas put it forward, and we thought it was a proper provision to make for the future, because conditions are different, and they were a little afraid, that is the people of Tuensang, that their interests might not be properly looked after otherwise.

It is proposed that the Governor of Nagaland will also be the Governor of Assam, or the other way about, the Governor of Assam will be the Governor of Nagaland; that is, he will be there not as Governor of Assam, but as Governor of Nagaland.

Also, it is too cumbersome a procedure to have another High Court. The High Court of Assam will continue to function for Nagaland.

I do not wish to go into further details of this. Naturally, in forming a State with all kinds of special provisions, the Bills are rather lengthy. For instance, we do not wish to interfere with their tribal customs, tribal ways of justice, and therefore, we have left these tribal laws in tact, and their tribal councils will deal with them; and an exception has been made about that, as well as about transfer of land.

Thus, by these Bills, we do an important part, that is add to the number of autonomous States of the Indian Union. The State is a small one, and the State, for the time being, will have certain restrictions on its autonomy in regard to law and order and finance, and certain special provisions in regard to the Tuensang District. Otherwise, it will be a full State of the Union, and in course of time, I hope as the situation returns to normality, it will have all the other powers of the States of the Indian Union.

I think that considering the background that we have had, and the trouble we have had in this area, it is a happy consummation that we solve it not purely by military means, but by this political and friendly approach, making them equal partners in this Union of India to all the other States and to ourselves. I beg to move.

[Speeches by various MPs on the two motions omitted.]

Jawaharlal Nehru: Mr Speaker, Sir, the House has on the whole welcomed these Bills. Some hon. Members have pointed out some defects in them and have suggested some amendments. I shall deal with them a little later. But on the whole every hon. Member who has spoken, except one or perhaps two, has welcomed the whole idea underlying these Bills. I am happy about that.

Before I deal with these Bills I should like to say a few words about what our fundamental approach should be. That approach has been, not from today but from the day of independence and even before that, that we shall build up a united India with the goodwill of the Indian people, preserving the variety of India in its unity. That has been the approach and not the approach, fundamentally, of the hon. Member opposite, Shri Trivedi, who believes in everything which divides India although he talks about the unity of India. I was amazed at the crudity of his approach and his expressions in the House today which, if given effect to, would split India into a thousand fragments. He calls himself a nationalist and yet his nationalism is confined to the frog-in-the-well policy where he believes that he is a nationalist and everybody else is not a nationalist; the Muslims are not nationalists; the Christians are not nationalists.

Everybody who is not a Hindu is not a nationalist. Apparently that will be the next stage.[461]

U.M. Trivedi: That is not what I have said. I never meant that.

Jawaharlal Nehru: That is what he said about Muslims to my ears. But I am very glad that he does not believe in that.

So, I take it that Shri Trivedi believes that India consists of Hindus, Muslims, Christians, Buddhists and atheists and that everybody who lives in India is a full-fledged nationalist. Let us understand that.

U.M. Trivedi: Everybody who believes in India and believes himself to be an Indian has got a right to live in this country. That is what I believe in.

Buta Singh (Moga):[462] Please do not forget or try to neglect the Sikhs.

Jawaharlal Nehru: The hon. Member has now defined his creed. Everybody who lives in India and believes himself to be an Indian has a right to live in it. That right, of course, he has in law in spite of Shri Trivedi. But the point is whether he is in any way in his opinion any the less nationalist than he is. I think personally—and I speak with great respect—that he is not a nationalist—I mean Shri Trivedi—because nationalism is something which includes everybody in India.

461. Blaming Christian missionaries for creating a feeling of separate nationhood among the Nagas, U.M. Trivedi said that "the creation of Nagaland is being resented by the whole of Assam only on this ground that this territory is being created as a sort of shelter for these Christian missionaries who have converted hundreds of thousands of these people."

He further said that in India religion was "treated synonymous with culture," and Muslims, whether they lived in Kerala, Tamilnad, Andhra Pradesh or Gujarat, claimed Urdu to be their mother tongue, "whether they understood one word of Urdu or did not understand, and created trouble for us." When Ansar Harvani and Raghunath Singh, both Congress, tried to correct the Jan Sangh Member on his remarks about the Muslims' mother tongue, he used some unparliamentary words, which were expunged as ordered by the Chair. Nehru, who was among the Members who protested Trivedi's sweeping remarks questioning the loyalty of Muslims, had observed: "The hon. Member talks of the unity of India and is making charges all over, and false charges, I say." See *Lok Sabha Debates*, Third Series, Vol. 7, 20 to 31 August 1962, 2nd Session, cols 4543-4545.

462. Akali Dal.

U.M. Trivedi: To make that statement that I am not a nationalist is going too far.

Jawaharlal Nehru: I said so with all respect. Nationalism cannot be confined to a religion, however great that religion may be. Nationalism is something to the nation and everything pertaining to that nation comes within its scope. The hon. Member and some others, perhaps very few in this House fortunately, and some outside believe in that and talk in terms of nationalism as if that was their private preserve and everybody who did not fall in line with them is outside that domain. That is the mind which, I can very well understand, does not appreciate this Bill. It talks about disruption. The hon. Member who spoke last[463] went on talking about disruption because a State was being created. I do not understand that. I am not quite sure if his idea was that India should be one unitary whole and the creation of a State is disruption. He did not say that but I think this was the trend of his argument. I do not understand that. That is fundamentally opposed to our approach which is that the great variety of India should be contained within our unity. India has grown great in the past and has lived thousands of years. If India or the great men of India in the past had followed the policy suggested by the hon. Member opposite, India's greatness would not have risen to the heights that it did. Indian culture spread all over Asia. Indians went abroad. Others came here, and they were absorbed here. Their ideas were absorbed; their religions were absorbed, so that India is a country of many religions which are all Indian in a sense because they have been here for hundreds and hundreds of years. India is not a one-religion country or a one-language country. These are the varieties that have come together to make this great Indian nation. And what makes an individual or a community or a nation great is its wideness of vision, its receptiveness, not its exclusiveness, not untouchability. Unfortunately, exclusiveness came to India and made a very great people narrow-minded and small and led to their fall.

Well, I hope that we aim in a different way, in a different direction. We are not exclusive. And I hope that a time will come, as it is rapidly coming, when even nationalism is not enough. When people are going to the stars and to the moon and all that, nationalism, that is, the concept of national boundaries etc., is getting rapidly out of date. However, that is not for the present. And, therefore, our whole approach has to be to welcome all people who live in India as of one family, whatever religion they may belong to, and whatever customs they may have, and work in co-operation with all.

463. Ram Chandra Bade of the Jan Sangh.

This Bill, as I stated, is a right Bill. I am talking on the merits of the two Bills. But, apart from that, it is the product of an agreement, an agreement not only based on the original sixteen-point memorandum which came two years ago, which Mr Imkongliba Ao brought here with his colleagues. But even after this Bill was drafted, it was largely by agreement with their representatives, that is, the Naga leaders, who came here and had seen it, so that many of the criticisms made in regard to some provisions in it are rather beside the point.

For instance, some of the criticisms made were about the Governor's powers. First of all, we should realise that so far as this Bill goes, it establishes a full-fledged State. It is not a restricted State. It is a full-fledged State with certain temporary restrictions. The temporary restrictions are, first, in regard to the law and order situation, secondly in regard to certain finances, and thirdly in regard to the Tuensang district. These are the three where there are temporary restrictions. For the rest, it is a full-fledged State.

Now, in regard to the first restriction in regard to the law and order situation, hon. Members will realise, as our Naga friends realise, that the situation still in Nagaland is one which is not quite normal. It has to be dealt with abnormally. We hope that it is much more normal than it was, but it has to be dealt with abnormally. Therefore, it is desirable for the Governor to shoulder that burden partially; of course, partly, the Ministry there will shoulder the burden, but it is not right to leave it to them entirely; it is a heavy burden. In regard to that, it is stated here that as soon as the conditions return to normal, the Governor will report to the President to put an end to these special provisions, so that it is a temporary provision which is necessitated by the conditions of today.

As for finances, we have rather an odd position here. These finances mean, apart from small sums, the moneys given by the Central Government by way of subvention. Of course, subventions are given to other States too, but a great part of their expenditure comes from their own revenues. But, here a small part only comes from their own revenues. Since large sums are going, it was thought that the representatives of the Central Government, or call them what you will, should be partly responsible for the disposal of these funds, which mostly goes, of course, for developmental works. It requires some experience and some judgment as to how to do it. They can raise their own revenues. All revenues will, of course, be spent with their concurrence. The final decision in a matter of this kind will temporarily be the Governor's.

As for the Tuensang district, whatever has been put down is word for word what was suggested by the representatives of the Tuensang district and agreed to generally by the Naga leaders. For various reasons, into which I need not go, the Tuensang district people require it. They wanted it. We agreed to it. It did not strike us to have special provisions for them, but when they wanted it and when the Naga leaders agreed to it, we had no choice in the matter.

So far as the Governor is concerned, he is not some Grand Moghul sitting there and doing things. The Governor is the servant not only of the Central Government, not only of the President but of this Parliament. He has always to function under strict limitations and whatever he does comes up here and before Government.

Ram Chandra Bade: If there is a difference of opinion, the Governor's opinion will prevail. That is the provision here.

Jawaharlal Nehru: Shrimati Renu Chakravartty asked: why not a separate High Court?; why not a separate Governor? Well, why a separate High Court? I ask. Here is the High Court of Assam which, I am glad to say of all High Courts in India, has no arrears of work.

Hari Vishnu Kamath: Because it is very efficient.

Hem Barua: That shows how smart we are.

Jawaharlal Nehru: To create another High Court there for a relatively small area, with not enough work, with very little work, is hardly worthwhile. Of course, it is open to the High Court, specially it is always open to the Chief Justice, to have a Bench there or do anything of that kind. That is a different matter. But it would not be worthwhile from any point of view to increase the number of High Courts for such small areas.

As for a separate Governor, there is nothing in these draft Bills which prevents that. At the present moment, I think it is desirable to have the same Governor. I do not say it is likely that it will continue to be desirable. But I say that there is nothing to prevent that.

There is another thing. The Governor of Assam has a special responsibility in regard to NEFA. The North-East Frontier Agency used to include the Tuensang region that was separated two or three years ago by Parliament. Conditions are different in the two places. Nevertheless, he has a special responsibility. That is why, if I may say so, we have to take very special care about whom we send as Governor to Assam. He has, of course, the same functions as Governors have elsewhere plus something plus NEFA ...

Hem Barua: The Governor of Assam is the most heavily worked Governor in India.

Jawaharlal Nehru: Yes, he has heavy work and great responsibilities. We have had a very eminent Governor[464] who has done very well and we are sending very soon a very experienced public servant there,[465] because he has to face difficult problems. Therefore, it is purely from the point of view of practicality that it is desirable to have the same person as Governor of Nagaland. Of course, he is Governor of Nagaland, because he is separately Governor of Nagaland, but there would be no point in appointing a Governor there who, the chances are, would not be so experienced.

Renu Chakravartty: What would be his seat of office? Will it be Shillong or Mokokchung in Nagaland? When you are giving him such large administrative functions—not only political functions, but also administrative functions—would it not be better that you have a separate Governor?

Hari Vishnu Kamath: By rotation. He will function in both places by rotation.

Jawaharlal Nehru: He will go to both places.

Some hon. Members thought that by creating this Nagaland the financial burden would be very great, Rs 4 crores, but they did not seem to realise that those figures, that that burden is more now. The fact is that the area that is going to be called Nagaland has been separate, a separate entity all along; nothing is being separated. It was separated some time back, some years back, it has been functioning like that. Now that separate entity is being given a certain name. The separation does not take place now. It took place years ago, but it is given some autonomy, and the amount, what has been spent on that separate entity thus far, is likely to be spent in future. The separation again does not add to the expenditure, at least I do not suppose it will add very much.

Then, some one asked me about NEFA and Manipur and Tripura. NEFA stands on an entirely separate footing, and so far as we are concerned, we have, at the present moment, no particular intention of changing the administration there. It is not very easy to apply some general rules everywhere regardless of conditions. So far as Manipur and Tripura are concerned, presumably fairly soon, my colleague the Home Minister would put forward suggestions or proposals for the Union Territories, and those proposals are based on giving them large measure of autonomy.

---

464. S.M. Shrinagesh.
465. Vishnu Sahay.

I really do not know why I should take the time of the House when the House is so agreeable to these Bills, but I would like to say that something has been said about Assam, about the Assam Assembly resolution.[466] It is perfectly true that the Assam Assembly viewed this question with some distaste, and the resolution they passed was presumably passed with some reluctance, but we must recognise first of all that this was not a new thing for the Assam Assembly. This very Bill which has come up today was envisaged more than two years ago, they knew it, we knew it, it is not a surprise to them.

Secondly, whatever they may have had in their hearts, this area was separated from Assam some years ago completely. They had nothing to do with it in the last two or three years. It is only recognising a fact, and recognising another fact which I am prepared perfectly to admit, as we should admit whenever there is some failure on our own part. What happened in this Naga territory, and the troubles we have had and the Naga people have had, have distressed us exceedingly, distressed us for a variety of reasons, because firstly any such problem distresses one, and secondly, that we should have to use the military and our police force to deal with people is always distressing. But what I was going to say was this, that in some measure at least, the fault was ours and that of the Assam Government—I am including both the Central Government and the Assam Government. It may be our fault because we did not pay enough attention to begin with. We were busy after independence with our own innumerable problems, and perhaps if we had dealt with it, and if the Assam Government which was directly in charge had dealt with it, somewhat differently, the consequences might have been different. That may be. I am not

466. P.C. Borooah, Congress MP, read out the Assam Assembly resolution on the State of Nagaland Bill, in the Lok Sabha on 28 August 1962, "because," he said, "the wording and the construction [of it] will go a long way in explaining the mind of the people of Assam." The resolution was:

"This Assembly is of the opinion that in the interest of national solidarity and also with a view to bringing about a co-ordinated development and greater political stability of the eastern region of India, there should be an integrated political and administrative set-up of the various units within this area and that nothing should be done which may have an effect of weakening this unity.

This Assembly further considers that in such an integrated set-up, special arrangements could be made to meet the needs of different regions of the area.

This Assembly is of the view that the provisions of the State of Nagaland Bill, 1962, are not conducive to the aforesaid objectives.

This Assembly, however, notes that the Government of India is committed to the setting up of Nagaland as a separate State within the Union of India." *Lok Sabha Debates*, Third Series, Vol. 7, 20 to 31 August 1962, 2nd Session, cols 4535-4536. See also item 7, fn 45.

blaming anybody, because I am including ourselves. There it is, but a certain situation having arisen, we have to find a way out of it. There is no use getting annoyed at everything that happens. And, I do think that the way out which we have found is a good way on the merits and it is a good way about all because I think it is satisfactory to a great majority of the Naga people. And, what is more, it will, I earnestly hope, bring about not only superficial changes but changes of heart among the people so that there may be cooperation between all of us.

It is interesting to see, talking about the Assembly, that the two Members—as far as I can see only two from Assam spoke—have supported these Bills heartily and fully.[467] And, the speech which I am sure all hon. Members must have listened to with great interest here, was the speech from my young colleague, the representative from the Nagaland itself.[468] He spoke with fire, young as he is and with greater authority because he comes from that place, and knows the place and he knows the people and he is one of the people. Therefore, I venture to say that these Bills should be formally approved and passed as they are.

[Exchanges on procedure omitted.]

Speaker: Would the hon. Prime Minister like to say anything on the other objections raised?

Jawaharlal Nehru: The first point is about the Governor being the same for Assam and Nagaland. The Constitution says:

"There shall be a Governor for each State:

Provided nothing in this article shall prevent the appointment of the same person as Governor for two or more States."

The amendment that the hon. Member proposes is a limitation on the power given by the Constitution.[469] I personally think it is desirable in present circumstances for the same Governor to be there for both. That is on the

467. In fact, three from Assam spoke: Hem Barua, PSP, and Dharanidhor Basumatari, Congress, readily supported the Bill; P.C. Borooah supported it "with sorrow and pain."
468. S.C. Jamir, from Naga Hills-Tuensang Area, Parliamentary Secretary to the Minister of External Affairs.
469. An amendment moved by Renu Chakravartty proposed that the Governor of Nagaland "shall be a separate incumbent from that of the Governor of Assam."

merits. Apart from that, it will constitute a limitation on the power given by the Constitution. That will not be proper at all.

Speaker: Whenever desired, a separate Governor can be appointed.

M.S. Aney:[470] These are territories which are outside the legislative jurisdiction of Parliament. For them, the powers are different from those territories which are within the jurisdiction of this Parliament. (Interruption).

Speaker: Order, order. Let the Prime Minister reply to the arguments.

Jawaharlal Nehru: As regards Shri Kamath's suggestion to change the name "Nagaland" into "Naga Lok" or "Naga Pradesh", I might inform him that this matter was gone into repeatedly two years ago. Frankly, we would have preferred some such name as Naga Pradesh. But our Naga friends were so insistent on the name "Nagaland". They attached so much importance to it and we did not think it worthwhile not to agree with them and so we accepted it. It does not make any change, whatever name is given. I do not think the name "Nagaland" indicates that it is some foreign country and so on.[471]

Hari Vishnu Kamath: It sounds so.

Jawaharlal Nehru: I do not think so.

Hari Vishnu Kamath: Sound does count.

Jawaharlal Nehru: Then there are some amendments suggested by Shri Hem Barua. As I listened to him, I did not think it possible to accept them ...

Speaker: The point made was that the powers given to the Governor should be the same as other Governors and these special powers should not be given.

Jawaharlal Nehru: That is the whole basis of the scheme. It is not a trivial thing.

---

470. Independent.
471. In fact, it was U.M. Trivedi who suggested that the new State might be called "Nagapradesh" or "Nagalok," etc. He said, "England, Switzerland, Ireland are all 'lands'. In India, however, there is one land only, and that is India. To have the term 'Nagaland', therefore, is a misnomer." *Lok Sabha Debates*, Third Series, Vol. 7, 20 to 31 August 1962, 2nd Session, col. 4537.

As I have explained, the Governor has special temporary powers so far as law and order and finance are concerned. As for Tuensang, the arrangement arrived at is by agreement with the parties. At their suggestion, we have given some more powers. How can I change that basic thing, that part of the agreement? I submit that those powers should remain as they are considering the circumstances we have to deal with.

Hari Vishnu Kamath: What about the other amendments? Will the President's Order be laid on the Table? Does he object to that?

Jawaharlal Nehru: I do not object. But that does not mean that every petty order, which is not important, should be laid here. Every important thing will, of course, be laid here.

Hari Vishnu Kamath: Without a provision, how can it be laid? There is no guarantee.

Jawaharlal Nehru: Not that.

Hari Vishnu Kamath: The President will not pass "petty" orders. Will he?

Jawaharlal Nehru: I am referring to day-to-day orders on different aspects of administration. How can we say that every little order will be laid on the Table?

Mahavir Tyagi:[472] I also want a clarification. Will these orders be submitted forthwith to the President for his consent?

Jawaharlal Nehru: Which order?

Mahavir Tyagi: Because it says that the regulations made under clause (b) of sub-para (1) of this paragraph shall be submitted forthwith to the President and until assented to by him, shall have no effect. This is in the schedule. Will that also affect this new power being given?

Speaker: So far as the hill areas are concerned, the Governor was given those powers. Perhaps he is reading from that.

472. Congress.

148. To Jairamdas Daulatram: Nagaland Bill[473]

August 28, 1962

My dear Jairamdas,

Your letter of the 28th August. I am afraid it is too late to make any important changes in the Nagaland Bill. There may be some risks, whatever we may do. We have to face them. As a matter of fact, we have ourselves said that Phizo's people, instead of committing violent and subversive acts, should come out and stand for election.

Yours sincerely,
[Jawaharlal Nehru]

149. To Bakhshi Ghulam Mohammed: Funds for Assam Flood Relief[474]

August 29, 1962

My dear Bakhshi,

Thank you for your letter of the 25th August sending me a cheque for Rupees fifty thousand for the Prime Minister's National Relief Fund for flood relief work in Assam State. I am sure the Assam Government and people will much appreciate this. I shall send the amount to the Chief Minister[475] there.

Yours sincerely,
[Jawaharlal Nehru]

150. In the Rajya Sabha: Nagaland Bills[476]

Chairman:[477] For the sake of convenience and economy of time both the motions regarding the Constitution (Thirteenth Amendment) Bill, 1962, and

---

473. Letter to Nominated, Rajya Sabha MP and a former Governor of Assam; address: 14 Tughlak Road, New Delhi.
474. Letter to the Prime Minister of Jammu and Kashmir.
475. B.P. Chaliha.
476. Motions, 3 September 1962. *Rajya Sabha Debates*, Vol. 40, Nos. 17-23, 30 August to 7 September 1962, pp. 4657-60, 4707-17.
477. Zakir Husain.

the State of Nagaland Bill, 1962, may be considered together and moved by the Prime Minister.

Jawaharlal Nehru: I am grateful, Sir, for suggesting that these two motions should be taken up together. I shall move them one after the other; of course, in the consideration at the second reading stage they may be taken up separately clause by clause. But they are wholly interdependent, and it is difficult clearly to consider one without keeping in mind the other.

Sir, I beg to move:

"That the Bill further to amend the Constitution of India, as passed by the Lok Sabha, be taken into consideration."

Sir, I also beg to move:

"That the Bill to provide for the formation of the State of Nagaland and for matters connected therewith, as passed by the Lok Sabha, be taken into consideration."

This House is aware of the history behind these two Bills. About two years ago or thereabout this matter was considered together with the representatives of the Naga People's Convention, and ultimately a certain settlement was arrived at about the formation of the State of Nagaland.[478] It was, I admit, somewhat unusual for a relatively small area to be formed into a State. There is nothing against it, and the peculiar circumstances prevailing there—I am not referring to the disorder and the law and order difficulties that we have had although they are very much before us—the special circumstances of the place induced us to agree to the proposal that they should be made a State. But although we agreed to that, there were certain difficulties in the way; first, the law and order position, and secondly, the financial position of the State was not a very happy one. It depended very largely on subventions made by the Central Government. Mostly subventions are for development of the area. It was, therefore, decided in agreement with the representatives of the Naga People's Convention that there would be for a certain period certain powers reserved to the Governor, certain powers relating to the law and order position and to financial position. These are only till such time as the Governor thinks that they are necessary. The Governor of course functions as a representative,

478. See item 147, fn 455.

as an agent of the Central Government, and he will be in constant touch with us. Now, as a matter of fact, although Nagaland was not declared to be a State of the Union, it has been a separate entity for some years. Constitutionally, I suppose, it has continued to be part of Assam, but some two or three years back it was formally separated and constituted into a separate entity under the Union Government, and Tuensang Division which was a part of NEFA, North East Frontier Agency, but which is inhabited by Nagas was attached to this Naga area. Now Tuensang is somewhat different from the rest of Nagaland because, I do not wish to use the word, but in some way it is a little more backward, and the Tuensang people's representatives themselves were a little anxious that they should not be put completely on the same level as the rest of Nagas, and they wanted a period when they should be both joined on to this of course as a State but where they would have a Regional Council and the Governor would have certain additional powers in regard to the Tuensang Division.

The whole point is that these two Bills resulted from the agreement arrived at with the representatives of the Convention of Naga leaders as well as Tuensang leaders, and I submit, Sir, that having accepted that and created a separate entity and later accepted the idea of a State, you must abide by the agreement arrived at. Making changes here and there would probably not fit in with the scheme and would not fit in with the agreement arrived at. For instance, the reserve powers of the Governor both in regard to the Tuensang Division and generally in regard to Nagaland were specially agreed to by the representatives of the Convention who met us, and indeed they originally passed their resolution in a convention and subsequently came to discuss details with us and we agreed to them. So, I would beg of the House to consider these as a whole and not amend them so as to take away any essential part of them which was agreed to.

Some hon. Members perhaps do not like the name of the State to be Nagaland. Frankly the Naga leaders were anxious to have that name, and we thought that it was best to please them in this matter when they attach so much importance to it. There was no particular reason against it and so we agreed, and I hope this House will agree.

Having decided on creating a State of Nagaland, which is a full State of the Indian Union, I should like to say, subject for a temporary period to some reserve powers in the hands of the Governor, it becomes necessary to amend the Constitution, and the first Bill that I have moved before the House is, therefore, the Constitution (Amendment) Bill. The second deals with details about the State of Nagaland. I submit, Sir, that these Bills should be accepted by this House and adopted. I would like to say that the law and order conditions in Nagaland, though very much better now than they were, are still not wholly satisfactory. Only about two or three days ago a member of the Interim Council of Nagaland, Mr Phom, was murdered,[479] and that itself is evidence of the abnormal conditions that prevail there and the necessity of some reserve powers to be given in the hands of the Governor. But even so, even before these Bills are passed, although in theory the Governor had all powers, our instructions to the Governor were, when they were carried out, to consult the Interim Council on all the measures to be taken and to act as far as possible in accordance with their advice. He has done that. Now, of course, with the passage of these Bills, the Governor would all the more accept the advice of the Government of Nagaland that may be formed under these Acts. But it is desirable, in view of these law and order difficulties, for the Governor to have authority to deal with any emergency situation that might arise. As the House knows the matter is being dealt with to some extent, in parts of Nagaland by the Assam Rifles and by some of our Army people. It is easier for the Governor to deal with it than for any other State authority.

I submit therefore, Sir, that these two Bills—the Constitution (Thirteenth Amendment) Bill, 1962 as well as the State of Nagaland Bill, 1962—be taken up for consideration.

The questions were proposed.

[Speeches by various MPs on the two motions omitted.]

Jawaharlal Nehru: Madam,[480] I would like to express my gratitude to all the members of the House who have spoken and welcomed this measure. In particular, may I express the feeling which I have had and which, I am sure, every Member of this House will share, of gratitude to the last speaker Shri Jairamdas Daulatram,[481] for the fine, eloquent and wise speech that he has delivered? And he delivered it out of his knowledge, not merely from a theoretical approach, because he was himself concerned with Nagaland and Tuensang Division, and as Governor of Assam, it was his special responsibility to deal with the NEFA area and other territories. What he said was so much to the point and so relevant to the conditions there that there is little that I can add.

I would, however, like to explain one or two points. Prof. Ruthnaswamy[482] said that this Bill was not artistically drafted. Perhaps, he is right. But we were not writing on a clean slate. We had to incorporate in it an agreement arrived

---

479. See item 151.
480. Violet Alva, Deputy Chairman.
481. Nominated, Rajya Sabha MP; was the Governor of Assam, 1950-1956.
482. M. Ruthnaswamy, Swatantra Party.

at with the representatives of the Naga People's Convention, and that perhaps to some extent, came in the way of artistry. Also we were not writing a full constitution for the State, but rather putting in this agreement that we had, and that introduced some special features which otherwise would not have been there. If the agreement had not been there and only a new State had been created, the Bill would have been a very small one, not a whole complete introduction of a State. All that the Constitution contains. Their charter is not this Bill. Their charter is the Constitution of India plus this Bill. So it is true and may be that if we had the advantage of some of the hon. Members of this House we might have improved the language here and there. For instance, Mr Mani[483] has suggested an amendment which, prima facie, appears to be a better form of words. Yet I dare not accept it because it is a form of words and it is not of vital consequence, and I would rather adhere to what the agreement lays down than change it. Apart from that, Mr Mani objected to the phrase "internal disturbance" and said something about it. I would like to remind him that in our Constitution in articles 352 and 355 these words occur repeatedly. For instance, article 352 says:

"If the President is satisfied that a grave emergency exists whereby the security of India or of any part of the territory thereof is threatened, whether by war or external aggression or internal disturbance, he may, by Proclamation, make a declaration to that effect."

Again in article 355 it is stated:

"It shall be the duty of the Union to protect every State against external aggression and internal disturbance."

So, it is not a new phrase that is used here. I would submit that though the words of Mr Mani's amendment read better, nevertheless, because of the fact that this represents more the agreement, it should be there. Also, frankly, I should not like that this Bill should be delayed and go back to the Lok Sabha again.

Now, many of our hon. Members will have in mind the history of the past ten or twelve years in regard to this area. I do not wish to go into it. Mr Jairamdas Daulatram referred to an incident where the killing of the postal runner led to retribution and revenge on a big scale. It may interest the House to know that this incident had nothing to do with our forces, it was one tribe against another, and yet this is one of the major charges that Mr Phizo brings

483. A.D. Mani, Independent.

against our forces. He is collecting all these charges and says that we sacked and killed sixty persons to which reference was made. It was the early days when this thing happened. Since then, much has happened.

Now, from the very first stage, I cannot say the first stage but from the earliest period, the then Governor of Assam, Sir Akbar Hydari,[484] dealt with the Nagas and came to some kind of agreement with them, the ten-point agreement, I think, it is called. I confessed frankly to him that we were so wholly occupied with our troubles here—it was immediately after independence and we had the vast migration and other troubles—that although I was the Prime Minister I had not considered the ten-point agreement. Later on, when the Constitution was being drafted, the Sixth Schedule was introduced specially for these tribal areas in Assam, Nagaland, etc., and although we all took part in it, perhaps if we had the knowledge that we possess today, we might have worded it differently. The question of amending the Sixth Schedule has been with us for the last several years not merely because of Nagaland but because of the hill areas, the hill districts and the autonomous districts. Even then, according to the Sixth Schedule, these hill areas including Nagaland were given a considerable measure of autonomy for their districts. Our first approach, therefore, was to give them autonomy, maybe less or more, but to give them autonomy. Subsequently, we repeatedly discussed the matter in the early days with Mr Phizo himself and then with others representing the Nagas, hostile or not, and always we made it clear to them that we want to give them the fullest autonomy within the Indian Union. It is true that I told them that I was not prepared to discuss any secession from the Indian Union but short of that I was prepared to discuss anything with them.

So, this is not a new development of policy or a change in our outlook that has induced us to bring this Bill but rather certain developing circumstances. We could not by ourselves enact anything like this unless they were willing to have this and unless we agreed with them. This process took a number of years. They held then their first convention and then a year or two later the second convention was held which was largely attended by the representatives of the various tribes of Nagaland and in the third convention in another year they passed and formulated this paper of sixteen heads of agreement. It was only then that the matter became ripe enough for us to consider. We did not want to produce a constitution for them and thrust it on them. We wanted it to come from them so that they may have a feeling of getting what they wanted, not that they had to accept whatever was given to them.

484. From May 1947 to December 1948.

These areas were troubled areas, and as the House knows, constantly there were attacks, there were ambushes and people were killed. Large numbers of people have been killed in these areas While we had to deal with them in the normal manner, maintain normal law and order with the help of the police or the military we had always in view the fact that we had to win over the Nagas and make them feel that they were one with us. When they talked of independence to me, I asked them, "What do you mean by talking about independence? You are independent just as much as I am and you have as much freedom and authority as any other person in India." Now, to get this idea accepted by them was a problem. It was, as Mr Jairamdas Daulatram said, a question of some emotional integration. You cannot do that unless you realise completely that all the steps we are taking, army steps, military steps, were essential, were necessary, They were essential, they were necessary and we could not do without them but some other process had to be adopted. We tried to start it although it was difficult in the circumstances. You cannot have two rather contradictory processes, that is, a military process fighting people and a conciliatory process. They somehow conflict and yet they were carried out during all these years, except for the early two years or so when it was difficult to have any developmental work there, to have any schools, even the old schools ceased to function because of the terroristic tactics of the hostiles, yet, within the last two or three years, we have started developmental works. I am sorry I have not got the figures but hundreds of schools were started, a number of high schools, some colleges, technical institutes, etc., were started and in the field of agriculture too much was done. All this was done partly because the people required it and partly, and deliberately, to make them feel that they can live a free and happy life.

So that this then is the developmental policy that has been pursued right from the beginning. Sometimes circumstances made it difficult for us to go ahead in this direction as much as we wanted but I am happy that at present although we are not wholly out of the wood, I admit, yet I feel we are very near the edge of it and the situation is much better even though, as I said, a young man, a member of the Naga Council, was shot dead only two or three days ago. It shows how the people are functioning. The members of the Naga Council and other Naga leaders are cooperating. Our officers and others are constantly facing danger and even death. I am happy that this stage has been reached and these two Bills will soon, I hope, be the law of the land and will establish the new State in the brotherhood of the States in India and I am sure that they will have this idea of emotional integration and feeling that they are part of India and that they can live freely as independent citizens governing their own State as they wish and they will be partners in the larger adventure that we are undertaking in India. This idea will grow there.

Now, Madam, although the State is just like any other State—it has to be realised that it is a full State—certain powers are reserved temporarily for the Governor. It is not permanent. As soon as he thinks or feels that the situation so necessitates, he will give up his power and the State will have full autonomy and powers.

Shri Dahyabhai[485] wanted to know whether the Chief Minister will be called the Prime Minister or the Chief Minister. He will be called the Chief Minister, of course, like any other place. Well, in regard to the powers of the Governor, apart from the fact that this is part of the terms of the agreement, I would like to assure the House that it was not as if we laid great stress on these powers. They were agreed to without much discussion and as for fixing the powers of the Governor in regard to the Tuensang district, pressure came from them, not from us. Actually, pressure came from the Tuensang representatives who, I believe, were a little nervous at being put under the new Government of Nagaland to begin, with. As Shri Jairamdas Daulatram said, the people of Nagaland minus Tuensang are educationally and otherwise more advanced. And these Tuensang people wanted, if I may use the word, some protection and it was their proposal, their insistence that the Governor as representing the Government of India should have these powers for ten years or so. At the same time they wanted to join. They have got a Regional Council. The House will observe that it has been laid down that one of their number will be among the Ministers of Nagaland Government. So, while they become part and parcel of this Nagaland State they want some kind of a slightly separate existence for ten years. And we agreed and must say that the Nagaland people also agreed. This was not a disputed point. This was an agreed point so that broadly speaking all the powers that are given to the Governor were parts of the agreement, of course, broadly speaking. But what I meant was they did not give rise to much argument and I think we should keep them. All these things depend very greatly on the persons who exercise them. The Governor, of course, is the representative of the Government of India, of the President; whatever he does he refers to the Government of India, that is, the External Affairs Ministry, but apart from that the personality does count, and we have taken trouble therefore to choose for the Governors of Assam rather specially. A distinguished Member of this house, Mr Jairamdas Daulatram, was there as Governor. The Governor there has a double function or triple function. Not only is he the Governor but he is the direct representative of the Government of India for the North East Frontier Agency and used to be for Nagaland also.

---

485. Dahyabhai V. Patel, Swatantra Party.

There was Mr Fazl Ali[486] who became very popular and indeed I understand that the people are putting up a memorial to him in Nagaland in the shape of a college called after his name. Then there was General Shrinagesh who was peculiarly suited to the place because unfortunately in the last few years there have been these military operations there and we thought a military person of note would be able to understand them and coordinate civil activities with the military. And now within a few days we are sending one of our most experienced officers, Shri Vishnu Sahay. So, what I wanted to put before the house was that the Governors we send there are even more specially selected than Governors elsewhere where they have to be only purely constitutional Governors.

I think Mr Ruthnaswamy laid great stress on a separate Governor for Nagaland. Well, to begin with we have this; it is open under the Act, there is nothing to prevent separate Governors being appointed when considered necessary, but at the present moment we did think and we do think that one Governor is more desirable. It is not so much a question of more money being paid although there is no reason why we should waste money; it is not that question. The question is, the Governor of Assam even under the present circumstances has special responsibilities for NEFA; they are special responsibilities and much the same I should say for Tuensang and because of that we thought that one man dealing with these areas with relatively common problems would be desirable. And some of our friends in Assam are regretful about Nagaland becoming a separate State. Although they accept it they are naturally rather sorry although I might remind the House that separation really came in effect some years ago when it became a separate entity. It is only constitutionally it has come now. So, although it is a separate State we thought it would be a good thing if one or two links were left. One link was the common Governor. Another link was the High Court. They do not interfere with the internal freedom of the State and we thought it would be a good thing to have these two links because after all they are neighbours and they have to carry on in a friendly way.

Then Mr Nafisul Hasan[487] said something about clause 27 of the Nagaland Bill. He seemed to think that there is some difficulty about this. There is nothing extraordinary about this. This has been repeated in many other places. If you see article 3 of the Constitution it says that Parliament may by law form a new State by separation of territory from any State, increase the area of any State, diminish the area of any State, etc. It did not require, therefore, a constitutional amendment if only this had to be done. Articles 2, 3 and 4 refer to this being

486. Saiyid Fazl Ali, Governor of Assam, 1956-1959.
487. Congress.

done by law. Now clause 27 of the Bill refers in particular to certain adaptation of a law for a particular area, the substance remaining the same. Sometimes very minor things come in the way and if you apply the law as it is in its rigidity, it may not fit in with the Tuensang district. It is obvious conditions are very different. But it is not construed entirely differently but accepting the substance minor matters may be there. It is a very desirable provision which has been given I believe in other Acts too. My colleague here reminds me that in the recent Act passed about Nagar Haveli this particular phrase occurs.

Mr Dahyabhai Patel said something about the name, Nagaland. Frankly I would have preferred—not that I have any objection to Nagaland—Naga Pradesh. We did suggest that but they have strong sentimental attachment to Nagaland. They have been calling it this way for some years past and sometimes, as hon. Members will realise, sentiment is a strong thing and we did not think that we should by-pass or come in the way of that sentiment. Well, it did not make any difference and so we accepted Nagaland.

Mr Dahyabhai also referred to the question of land in Nagaland and he referred to Kashmir too. May I remind him that the rule in Kashmir that no non-Kashmiri can possess land is a very old one, I should think at least 100 years old? It is from the 19th century; the old Maharajas introduced it. The original reason for its introduction was rather a wise one. They did not want crowds of Britishers to come in, occupy land and settle down there, because the climate of Kashmir was peculiarly suited to them and peculiarly pleasant. They did not just want it. At some time about a hundred years ago, there was actually a rule that at one single time not more than three Britishers could remain in Kashmir, only a fiat of the then Maharaja. Gradually, those rules were relaxed, but this rule continued. At that time chiefly Britishers went there. Very few Indians went there. Some Indians went from Lahore or other places of North India. Then, came the further reason that monied Indians go there and buy up the land there—it is a poor country and the people are poor—and thereby deprive the people living there of their land. I think it is a very healthy provision and I do not see why even now it should be changed. I cannot buy land there. I may by origin be a Kashmiri, but I do not come within the definition. Otherwise, a large number of people, rich people, who have no particular alignment with Kashmir, if I may say so, historically, culturally or otherwise—only for the climate may go there—buy up large quantities of land, thereby depriving the other people, who are possessing it, of land later on. Now, here in our Constitution, in regard to hill areas, Nagaland and the other hill districts of Assam, there is already a provision in the Sixth Schedule of the Constitution preventing land being alienated to any outsider. It is a very good provision too, because otherwise the people of those areas, who feel passionately about their land, would gradually be dispossessed of it. Difficult situations would arise. So, I think some reference has been made even here that land in Nagaland will only vest in the new State. No outsiders will be able to go there. Clause 24 says:

> "All property and assets situated in, or used for, or in connection with the administration of, the Naga Hills-Tuensang Area and vested in the Union immediately before the appointed day (other than any property or assets so vested for purposes of the Union) shall, as from that day, vest in the State of Nagaland."

Anyhow, it is for the people of Nagaland to make their rules about their land.

I have nothing further to say in the matter. I entirely agree with Mr Jairamdas Daulatram that we should pass these Bills unanimously and I regret I cannot accept the amendments that have been proposed.

A.D. Mani: On a point of clarification. I should like to ask the Prime Minister one or two points for clarification. At page 2 of the Bill, proposed article 371A (1) (a) (iii) says:

> "administration of civil and criminal justice involving decisions according to Naga customary law."

> Does this mean that in so far as those decisions conflict with the Indian Penal Code, the Civil Procedure Code and the Criminal Procedure Code, these Codes will have to be set aside?
> The second point I should like to ask is whether the right of the Supreme Court to hear appeals against decisions according to the customary law of the Nagas is admitted in this Bill or has been denied in this Bill.

A.K. Sen:[488] The whole scheme of the Bill is that no law of the Central Government will have automatic application to the new State. They will apply only if they are so applied by the new Legislature of the new State of Nagaland. That is the whole scheme.

---

488. Law Minister.

151. In the Lok Sabha: Assassination of Pauting Phom in Nagaland[489]

P.C. Borooah: (Sibsagar):[490] Under rule 197, I call the attention of the Prime Minister to the following matter of urgent public importance and I request that he may make a statement thereon:

> "The reported shooting of Mr Pauting Phom, a Member of the Interim Body of Nagaland on the 29th August, 1962."

Jawaharlal Nehru: It is my sad and painful duty to report to the House the loss of another valuable Naga leader, Shri Pauting Phom, a Member of the Interim Body of Nagaland, at the hands of an assassin on the 29th of August. Pauting belonged to the Phom tribe which is a small tribe of about 16,000 people, living in the Tuensang District. On the night of the 29th August, he was sitting in his kitchen in Longtang village with his bodyguard when some unknown assailant fired a couple of shots from outside his house and injured him. On hearing the shots, a detachment of the Security Forces commanded by an officer immediately rushed to the spot. Pauting was evacuated to the Civil Hospital. Despite all medical help, he succumbed to the injury at 0345 hrs on the 30th August. The Security Forces combed the surrounding area but could not find any trace of the assailant. The Sector Commander from Tuensang has proceeded to the spot for personal investigations.

I would like to add that every effort is being made to give protection from attacks from the hostile elements to the leading political fugures in Nagaland.

Shri Pauting Phom originally belonged to the so called Naga National Council. When this body chose the path of violence and bloodshed and went underground, he was courageous enough to come overground and take part in the deliberations of the Naga Peoples' Convention. He was a member of the negotiating body which came to Delhi in July 1960 to discuss the 16-Point Agreement which only yesterday culminated in Parliament giving its approval to the constitution of a separate State of Nagaland. I feel sad indeed that Pauting is not alive to see the fulfilment of the cherished dream of the Naga people to have a separate State of their own but I have no doubt that his brave example will inspire others to revert to paths of peace and constructive activity and his sacrifice, as the sacrifice of many other Nagas, will not have been in vain.

---

489. Adjournment motion, 4 September 1962. *Lok Sabha Debates*, Vol. 8, Third Series, September 3 to 7, 1962, cols 5799-5800.
490. Congress.

We have conveyed the condolences of the Government of India to the leaders in Nagaland and to the bereaved family. I would like to convey the heartfelt sympathies of this House to the Government and people of Nagaland and to the family of Shri Pauting Phom.

152. To G.G. Swell: Meeting for Clarifications[491]

September 7, 1962

Dear Shri Swell,

I have received your letter of the 7th September. As you perhaps know, I am leaving Delhi on a tour abroad tonight. I shall not return till early in October.

I am always glad to meet our colleagues if they wish to see me. But there is little point in meeting me merely to present rigid demands. If they really wish to seek any elucidation from me of what we have suggested, I shall gladly meet them after I return from abroad.

Yours sincerely,
Jawaharlal Nehru

153. David Astor and the Naga Question[492]

Mr David Astor[493] came to see me the other day. He spoke about various matters. Among them was the Naga question. He was rather apologetic about it. I told him of the position and how it was up to the hostile Naga leaders to stop their violent activities. They were getting isolated more and more from the people. We have done our best and it was open to them to join in the election that would come. They were getting full autonomy except for some reservations for a brief period.

He appreciated all this but said that could we not issue an amnesty to these leaders and invite them to cooperate. I said we had issued an amnesty long ago generally and we have not withdrawn it. I am not sure how far it applies to all the Naga leaders. But generally those who come to us and surrender arms are treated as they were amnestied. We had no desire to be vengeful towards any

491. Letter to Lok Sabha MP of the All Party Hill Leaders' Conference, from Autonomous Districts-ST, Assam; address: 72 South Avenue, New Delhi. MHA, File No. 4/1/62-SR(R)-A, p. 63/c.
492. Note, 19 September 1962, from London, for M.J. Desai, the Foreign Secretary.
493. Editor of *The Observer.*

leaders. But in this matter we could not take any step without the consent and cooperation of the Interim Council of Nagaland.

I told him about the tribal rivalries and conflicts there and the danger to these leaders themselves from rival tribes etc., in Nagaland if they went back.

Mr Astor said that he was not at all speaking on behalf of Phizo[494] and others and he was not sure that they would even accept any offer of amnesty etc., from us. But he was anxious to get this matter settled peacefully. Otherwise there would be continuous trouble. I told him again that we had done our utmost and it was upto to the people of Nagaland to function now as they wanted to.

(t) Orissa

154. To Biju Patnaik: Konrad Adenauer's Visit[495]

September 21, 1962

My dear Biju,

Your letter of the 17th September has reached me here in Paris. Dr Adenauer[496] will probably visit India in November and may go to Rourkela. Please remember that he is 86 years old and cannot be made to rush about. If he is agreeable, he can certainly visit Bhubaneswar and Konark. But I doubt if he is interested in old temples and the like.

Yours sincerely,
[Jawaharlal Nehru]

(u) Pondicherry

155. On Status of Pondicherry[497]

PM met the Councillors from Pondicherry this morning. I had a preliminary meeting with them half an hour earlier. The Councillors expressed their thanks

---

494. A.Z. Phizo, the Naga rebel leader.
495. Letter to the Chief Minister of Orissa. Sent from Paris.
496. Konrad Adenauer, Chancellor of the Federal Republic of Germany, 1949-1963.
497. Note, 3 August 1962, by M.J. Desai, the Foreign Secretary, for the Joint Secretary (UN), MEA. MHA, File No. 3/362-SR(R)-A, pp. 5-6/c.

to the Government of India for the happy conclusion of the de jure transfer[498] and represented that in the new constitutional arrangements that will be made an advance should be made on the existing administrative and constitutional set up of Pondicherry—the pattern to be evolved being the same as of other states in the Indian Union. They also asked that arrangements for representation of Pondicherry through election to the Lok Sabha and the Rajya Sabha should be made.

2. PM asked what the population of Pondicherry was. The Councillors said that it was about 400,000 and that on population basis they may not be entitled to even one seat in Parliament. They, however, pressed for one seat in the Lok Sabha and one in the Rajya Sabha.

3. As regards the future administrative and constitutional pattern, PM told them that the paraphernalia of a full state's structure was very expensive and not suitable for Pondicherry. He agreed, however, to maximum autonomy being given to Pondicherry as a Union Territory, the administrative apparatus being kept to the minimum required. He said that there can be elected legislatures and elected councillors with full powers in the subjects in which the territory was autonomous. The Councillors went on urging the desirability of having a pattern similar to the other states for political reasons, keeping the administrative apparatus to the absolute minimum. PM said that so far as the next session of the Parliament is concerned they cannot deal with this complex question but would try to get a bill through to make Pondicherry part of India and provide the representation in Parliament. The other matters mentioned by the Councillors can be considered later. He, however, reiterated that the paraphernalia of a state on the pattern of other major states is not suitable for Pondicherry.

4. The Councillors asked for location of at least one public sector industrial project in Pondicherry so as to increase employment opportunities. PM said that the location of public sector industrial projects is decided by expert advice on the basis of availability of raw materials, transportation facilities, etc., and could not be a purely political decision. The request will, however, be borne in mind.

5. The Councillors raised the question of making facilities for a Cobalt Therapy Centre against cancer available to the Medical College in Pondicherry under the Colombo Plan Scheme of assistance. This proposal is now under

---

498. The de facto transfer of the French territories Pondicherry, Karaikal, Mahe and Yanam to India on 1 November 1954, was ratified by France only on 12 July 1962. By the Treaty of Cession between India and France on 16 August 1962, these territories became Indian. See also item 156.

consideration of the Ministry of Health and they requested that the matter should be expedited.

6.   The Councillors incidentally referred to Clause II of the 1955 Agreement regarding de facto transfer which referred to changes requiring the consent of the people, gave a copy of the speech by the French Commissioner in 1947[499] and requested that this be borne in mind in connection with the future administrative and constitutional set up of Pondicherry as the latter must be an improvement on what the French intended at the time. They also requested PM to visit Pondicherry on his way back from Ceylon during late autumn or winter this year.

7.   Please follow up para 5.

156.   Cession of Pondicherry[500]

[Note, 13 August 1962, by Nehru, begins][501]

I agree with the proposals made in A and B.[502] No particular statement need be made except some words of congratulation.

I think that 10 a.m. on the 16th August will be suitable. A photographer can be present. No other press people need come.

J. Nehru
13.8.62

[Note, 13 August 1962, by Nehru, ends]

---

499. Charles François Marie Baron, French Commissioner of Pondicherry, 20 August 1947 – May 1949.

500. Noting. MHA, (MEA, File No. 31(3)/Pond/62, pp. 23-24).

501. This note is apparently in response to the note by V.C. Trivedi, Joint Secretary, MEA, which is published after this. MHA, (MEA, File No. 31(3)/Pond/62, p. 24).

502. In V.C. Trivedi's note, the portion marked "A" is the following sentence: "I presume it is not our intention that there should be any statements of an important nature at this ceremony."

  The portion marked "B" is the following sentence: "He [Counsellor of the French Embassy] suggested that if convenient to the Prime Minister, the exchange might take place sometime on Thursday, the 16th of August. The French Ambassador proposes to leave for Paris on Saturday, the 18th of August."

  NB: "A" is in the third paragraph, whereas "B" is in the first paragraph.

[Note, 13 August 1962, by V.C. Trivedi, Joint Secretary, MEA, begins][503]

Subject: Exchange of the Instruments of Ratification of the Treaty of Cession with France in respect of the former French possessions.

The Counsellor of the French Embassy saw me this afternoon and said that the Instrument of Ratification of the Treaty of Cession in respect of Pondicherry, etc. will be received by the Embassy on the night of the 14th / 15th of August. It will, therefore, be possible to exchange the instruments on any day after that. He suggested that if convenient to the Prime Minister, the exchange might take place sometime on Thursday, the 16th of August. The French Ambassador[504] proposes to leave for Paris on Saturday, the 18th of August.

2.   The French Counsellor said that the procedure they proposed to adopt was to exchange the Instruments of Ratification signed by the Presidents of India and France and, at the same time, exchange procès-verbal indicating that the Instruments were exchanged between the Prime Minister of India and the French Ambassador on a certain date. We shall follow this procedure and have the necessary documents ready.

3.   The French Counsellor added that his Ambassador would be glad to accept whatever arrangements we made regarding the ceremonial aspect of the exchange. He would leave it to us to invite press people and photographers, etc. He inquired, however, whether the Prime Minister would like to make any important statement beyond, of course, the usual expression of gratification and congratulations. If the Prime Minister wished to make an important announcement, the ceremony would be delayed as the French Ambassador would then have to refer to the Government of France for their approval the text of his reply. I presume it is not our intention that there should be any statements of an important nature at this ceremony. If approved, I shall inform the French Counsellor accordingly and then work out arrangements in consultation with Protocol and XP[505] Divisions.

4.   The French Counsellor then referred to the understanding reached between the two Governments to the effect that after the ratification there would be discussions between representatives of India and France on certain minor issues arising out of the Treaty. The French Ambassador had received instructions to commence these discussions before his departure for Paris. The

503. This note is presumably for M.J. Desai, the Foreign Secretary. MHA, (MEA, File No. 31(3) Pond/62, p. 23).
504. Jean-Paul Garnier.
505. External Publicity.

French Ambassador appreciated that there was no point in troubling the Prime Minister on these minor matters. After the signature, however, he would like, for the sake of form, to mention that he had a few points to discuss. At that stage the Prime Minister might say that the Government of India were willing to discuss whatever points he wished to raise and that he should get in touch with the Foreign Secretary in that behalf. A preliminary meeting between the Ambassador and the Foreign Secretary could then be arranged for Friday, the 17th. Further discussions will take place subsequently.

    5.   FS may like to consult PM about the time and date for the exchange and for approval of the procedures suggested.

V.C. Trivedi
13.8.62

[Note, 13 August 1962, by V.C. Trivedi, ends]

157. Pondicherry Representation in Parliament[506]

[Note by M.J. Desai, the Foreign Secretary, 20 August 1962, begins]

I would submit that the request made by the Pondicherry Councillors to give Pondicherry representation both in the Lok Sabha and the Rajya Sabha may be accepted.

    This would involve amendment of the Fourth Schedule to the Constitution but it could be included in the Constitutional Amendment Bill which is being drafted to include Pondicherry, Mahe, Karaikal and Yanam, in the First Schedule under Union Territories.

M.J. Desai
20.8.1962

PM

[Note by M.J. Desai, the Foreign Secretary, 20 August 1962, ends]

[Note by Nehru, 20 August 1962, begins]

This question will have to be decided by the Cabinet. It may either come up together with the other papers relating to Pondicherry or be dealt with separately.

---

506. Noting, 20 August 1962. MHA, (MEA, File No. 31(10) POND/62. Vol. I, p. 5/c).

It is not clear to me in what manner Pondicherry will be represented in the Rajya Sabha. Perhaps the Assembly or Territorial Council that is framed there would elect a person. This would be in keeping with the procedure in the other States.[507]

J. Nehru
20.8.1962

[Note by Nehru, 20 August 1962, ends]

158. Engineers and Doctors in Pondicherry[508]

I understand that there are some very eminent engineers and doctors who have retired from holding the highest posts in India, in the Pondicherry Shri Aurobindo Ashram. I think the Pondicherry Government might well take advantage of their presence there. They will probably work free. I believe one such doctor is doing some work in the Medical College there.

2. The Pondicherry Councillors are not on good terms with the Ashram. I do not suggest that they should beg favours of the Ashram, but it does seem to me desirable to take advantage of eminent specialists who are there. You might draw the attention of our Chief Commissioner[509] there to this.

159. In the Lok Sabha: Pondicherry Bill[510]

Jawaharlal Nehru: So far as Pondicherry and all these small territories are concerned, we have declared any number of times that they will remain a separate entity and there will be no change in them so long as this is not demanded and approved by the people there themselves. Our treaty with the

507. For Nehru's speeches in Parliament on the Pondicherry Bill, see items 159-160.
508. Note, 29 August 1962, for M.J. Desai, the Foreign Secretary.
509. S.K. Datta.
510. Discussion on the Constitution (Fourteenth Amendment) Bill, 4 September 1962. *Lok Sabha Debates,* Vol. 8, Third Series, September 3-7, 1962, cols 5919-5922.

The Constitution (Fourteenth Amendment) Bill provided for the territories of Pondicherry, Karikal, Mahe and Yanam being specified in the Constitution as a Union territory called "Pondicherry". The Bill also sought to increase the number of representatives from the Union territories in the Lok Sabha from 20 to 25 to enable representation being given to Pondicherry in the House and also provided for representation of the territory in the Rajya Sabha. See also item 155.

French Government was based on this, and I have no doubt that apart from every other consideration, we have to keep our word to the French Government. That is quite adequate for me.

But I recognise that so far as Yanam and Mahe are concerned, there are considerations which would, presumably, lead us to attach them to their respective States. They are small areas of a district. But at this stage, when for the first time we are getting these old French territories formally and legally into the Union of India, I think we should stick to the old arrangement of the French. After that, it may well be that Yanam and Mahe are attached. Whether Pondicherry will be attached or not, is a different matter. That depends on the goodwill of the people. So far as I know, the people in Pondicherry, that is, a majority of them, want to keep it as a separate entity. But anyhow, at present we have to give effect to the agreement arrived at with the French Government.

H.N. Mukerjee (Calcutta Central):[511] I want a clarification. The Prime Minister seems to suggest that when France was compelled by force of circumstances to agree to the cession of these territories to India, there were certain conditions or presuppositions attached. I do not understand why the Prime Minister referred to the fact that certain understandings with the French Government have to be respected. It was an unconditional cession and that is why after having waited for so long, the country is waiting for the fulfilment of that cession. Now we are told that we have some understandings with the French Government which have to be respected. This is absolutely out of keeping with the entire spirit of what we are doing.

Jawaharlal Nehru: I do not understand what the hon. Member means. We have given specific, clear and repeated understandings to the Pondicherry people, to the French Government and to the whole of India that Pondicherry would be kept separate till such time as the people of Pondicherry desired a change. It was an understanding given to everybody. I do not think this is laid down in writing with the French Government, but it was a very clear understanding given to them and to the people of Pondicherry. I am quite certain that the great majority of the people of Pondicherry want to remain separate.

Renu Chakravartty:[512] Then how do Government propose to proceed? Does it mean that we are going to have a plebiscite on this whole question?

511. CPI.
512. CPI.

Jawaharlal Nehru: Surely there are many ways of finding that out later. At the present moment, I am giving my opinion that the great majority do not want to join Madras but want to remain as a separate entity. But regardless of what I may feel in the matter, at this first stage of its incorporation into the Indian Union, I think it is essential to keep it a separate entity. We have said to everybody concerned, including the French.

Renu Chakravartty: What will happen to the villages of Mahe and Yanam?

Speaker:[513] He has explained that.

Jawaharlal Nehru: In regard to the villages of Mahe and Yanam, there is good argument. But at the present moment, I should like to treat them as a whole, attached to Pondicherry. Later on, it may be feasible to separate them and to let them go to their respective States.

Mahavir Tyagi:[514] Even at this stage, when we are amending the Constitution and when these villages also become part of that Constitution, could we not make a provision? I am glad that the Prime Minister agrees that this word may not be kept for all time to come. When practical politics require it, something should be done in the case of these villages. Could we not at this stage make a provision whereby it may not be necessary to amend the Constitution for this purpose later on? Could we not have provision so that we may have the liberty of taking whatever step we want with regard to these small territories? If that is done, we shall not have to resort to another amendment of the Constitution for this purpose.

Lal Bahadur Shastri:[515] It would not be necessary. If any part of these Union Territories is merged with any other area, it should not require an amendment of the Constitution. Parliament can do it by ordinary legislation.

---

513. Hukam Singh.
514. Congress.
515. Home Minister.

160. In the Rajya Sabha: Pondicherry Bill[516]

Jawaharlal Nehru: I am grateful to you for giving me this opportunity to intervene in this discussion. I am not the last speaker. The hon. Member opposite will no doubt have his chance. I am grateful to you because this is the only time I have. I am rather pressed for time today as I am going away this evening.

This little Constitution (Amendment) Bill, small as it is, has a certain historic significance because it puts an end to all colonial regimes constitutionally in India. Of course, Pondicherry and the other French establishments have been factually within India but now after six years of waiting they will become part of the Union of India; so also Goa.

Now, there are two matters especially that I should like to speak about. There are two amendments that have been proposed; one is about Pondicherry and the other French establishments, whether they should remain as a separate entity or be merged into the adjoining State, and the other is about Delhi. As for the first, hon. Members have been reminded, I suppose many times, of the undertaking and the assurance we gave to the French Government at that time, not only to the French Government but to the people of Pondicherry. I myself have given it at public meetings, at private assemblies in Pondicherry and diplomatically and otherwise to the French Government. One may say that such an assurance is not legally binding but it is more than legally binding; it is morally binding. And apart from that, for my part I think it is desirable for Pondicherry to be a separate entity. But it is not for me to determine that. As we have said in our assurance to the French Government, it is for the people of that area to decide in future what they would like to do, whether they would like to merge in the adjoining States or remain as a separate entity. The question rests not with us. That is perfectly clear. We cannot go behind that undertaking and I feel that the hon. Member who moved this amendment has done so regardless of the wishes of the majority of the people of Pondicherry.

P. Ramamurti:[517] We said we were prepared for the referendum.

Jawaharlal Nehru: I am expressing my own analysis of the situation. I have no doubt about it and I have been in touch with Pondicherry all these years. I have

---

516. Intervention during discussion on the Constitution Fourteenth Amendment Bill, 7 September 1962. *Rajya Sabha Debates*, Vol. 40, Nos. 17-23, 30 August to 7 September 1962, cols 5648-55.

On the Constitution (Fourteenth Amendment) Bill, see item 159.

517. CPI.

been there repeatedly and the one thing we have always stressed is that they should remain a separate entity. Whether they do so in future or not remains to be seen. As I said, I think it is a desirable thing. Some hon. Members may not attach importance to it but I think it is desirable for Pondicherry which has been for several hundreds of years a part of the French empire and, therefore, has imbibed a great deal of French culture. You may say, language etc. It is a beautiful language. It is a good thing that we should have a centre for French language in India. That does not mean any disrespect of the language of the great majority of the people there. It is Tamil; of course that will have its full place but it is desirable to have a centre for French language and culture there. So speaking for myself I think it is a desirable thing apart from our undertakings. There are some smaller enclaves like Yanam and Mahe. It is not very logical to keep them under the same Administration as Pondicherry and Karikal and I think there is something in that argument. At the present moment, I would beg of the House to consider that we had better give effect to our assurance and agreement as a whole and keep them with Pondicherry and Karikal rather than separate them although administratively it might have been a little easier to deal with them in their respective States.

Now, coming to Delhi, I feel rather strongly in regard to Delhi because with all respect to the hon. Member who has moved the amendment, I have Delhi in my blood. I am a Delhi man to some extent. The hon. Member knows Delhi as the capital and the seat of this Government. But I attach a great deal of importance to Delhi. Delhi evokes images in me of 5,000 years and more, of a succession of kings, governments, empires falling and rising, great things happening, mixed cultures evolving and all that. Good and bad comes up to my mind. I rather doubt if the same images are evoked in the hon. Member's mind. Delhi as the capital is important enough and for any one to imagine that we wish to differentiate against Delhi is completely wrong, because we attach so great an importance to Delhi, to the improvement of Delhi, to the old historical background of Delhi, that we hesitate to do anything at the present moment which would prevent us from going in, what we might consider to be, the right direction. My point is, to include Delhi in this Bill casually just like any other place, Manipur, Tripura, Pondicherry or Goa, is not paying regard to the special questions that are tied up with Delhi. I said in the other House the other day that I am not satisfied with the present arrangements for Delhi.[518] I know to some extent from personal experience and a great deal from what I have been told that it has developed into a very complicated and complex system of Government here with the result that responsibility hardly attaches

518. See item 118.

to anybody. There is the Central Government of course with its numerous Ministries separately dealing with Delhi, Works Ministry, Health Ministry, Education Ministry and so on. There is the Chief Commissioner of Delhi; there is the Corporation of Delhi. There are numerous foreign embassies in Delhi and I could go on enumerating. There is the Master Plan Committee for Delhi. There is the Delhi Electric Supply Undertaking and other specialised agencies which in their own sphere are practically free to act as they choose of course subject to some control. But they are autonomous really. The other day we had some trouble in Delhi about the power supply question which caused a good deal of distress to many people.[519] Well, it is not for me now to say who is responsible for that but primarily obviously the Electric Supply Department which was dealing with it. The Electric Supply Department is partly controlled by the Corporation. Many members of the Corporation say that under the existing circumstances they have no power at all, no real power. The Chief Commissioner exercises it. I am not criticising anybody but as we have grown up it has become a place where it is very difficult to fix responsibility. The Central Government is there but the Central Government obviously cannot come into the picture at every stage. The Chief Commissioner is there and he is, if I may say so, one of our best administrators[520] and we specially chose him and we have kept him there although he is due for promotion elsewhere. We have kept him there because we feel he is probably the best man we could find and he is popular but again his powers are limited. It is extraordinary that everybody's powers are limited by somebody else and the result is unfortunate. Neither the Corporation can function with the satisfaction that it is doing things that it wants to do, nor the Chief Commissioner nor the many other special undertakings, nor the Master Plan Committee. I have had some experience in this matter because for some years past I have been interested in the slums of Delhi and I have repeatedly called people together representing various organisations and consulted them. In theory everybody was agreeable, but in practice not much was done. Something has been done, I admit, and done not only by the Government and its apparatus, but also by private organisations. I admit that. But still the progress has been slow and every time we have come up against this lack of responsibility and everybody having the power to obstruct somebody else doing something. So, it is a very complicated thing. Then, there are the foreign Embassies which have to be treated specially. It is difficult to put them just as Himachal Pradesh or Tripura or some other Territory. You have to devise some method, and it has to be devised, I admit, which will simplify this administration, give it as much

---

519. See section Politics, subsection Delhi.
520. Bhagwan Sahay.

of popular backing as possible and so that work can go on in Delhi adequately. That is, I think, the main reason and an adequate reason why Delhi cannot be included in this Bill, whatever the views of hon. Members may be about Delhi. I have indicated rather negatively what my views are, that is, it cannot be treated in the same kind of way as various other Union territories, but that it should be treated rather specially. That as great a popular backing as possible should be given to any apparatus in Delhi is obvious to me. That is the main point I would like to raise.

About Pondicherry, Mahe and Yanam, in the present Bill no change can be made. At least I would not wish any change to be made, because to some extent it would be going against the undertaking we gave. That is enough for me. It is not good for a country like India or for any country, especially for us to go back on everything that we have said repeatedly.

Of one thing I have to remind this House. Many of us have been very impatient about the delay in the change in Pondicherry, that is, the delay in the de jure transfer, after the de facto transfer had taken place. It was rather a frustrating experience, but the change has come about now and even though it has taken some years it has come about and it has come about in friendship and peace, peacefully and in a friendly way with France. It was worthwhile waiting a few years to get that done in a friendly way with a great country.

And finally about Delhi I would submit that Delhi cannot, whatever the views may be of any hon. Member, be included in this Bill, to be tacked on as "a place". It is not a place. It is "the place" of India and has to be considered with its history stretching back, with all kinds of backgrounds that past history has left us. It is true that Delhi has changed considerably since independence and that huge migrations have taken place and displaced persons have come. They are welcome here and Delhi is their home. But the fact remains that in spite of all that, Delhi still remains Delhi of old. Five thousand years of history attaches to it and we cannot be casual about it. We have to think hard, consult the people of Delhi and others connected with Delhi as to what to do. It is a difficult matter and I cannot quite frankly suggest anything. I have no clear idea in my own head, except that all these matters should be considered separately and we should not do it in a hurry and casually put it in this Bill. Thank you.

Bhupesh Gupta:[521] I would like to know from the Prime Minister why he has only told us negatively what is in his mind that something is wrong with the Delhi Administration. From his speech here and from his earlier speech in the other place, we did not get any indication of the lines along

521. CPI.

which his mind is working. Do we take it that when the matter is under consideration, he has also in mind the proposal for creating an Assembly and a responsible Government for Delhi?

Jawaharlal Nehru: May I say that if we had it clearly in our mind, we would have put it in the Bill? That is what I have just said.

Niren Ghosh (West Bengal):[522] May I ask the Prime Minister this? He says that French culture should be preserved. If Pondicherry is merged in Tamil Nad, why cannot there be a clause in the Bill safeguarding French culture? It is quite possible. This is one point. Another point is as regards Delhi. London is the seat of Government in the UK, but responsible government has not been denied to it and history is associated there too. How do you make a special point of difference? That is what I want to know.

Jawaharlal Nehru: I regret I cannot reply. I have failed to understand what he said.

Niren Ghosh: I said that the Prime Minister said that French culture should be preserved in Pondicherry. If Pondicherry is merged in Tamil Nad, why cannot there be a clause in the Bill, especially safeguarding French culture there? It is quite possible to do that. This is one point.

Jawaharlal Nehru: I will repeat what I said, because I think that the great majority of people in Pondicherry do not want that. I do not want to force it. Certainly it is no good contradicting me, because I can contradict hon. Members opposite. I cannot go about on this issue taking a plebiscite or referendum, because the other fact is there. I have given an assurance to the French Government and I am going to stick to it. I think it will be unfair for us and not befitting our honour not to do that.

P. Ramamurti: With regard to the undertaking to the French Government, unless they desire it, we do not want a change. I agree. But how is the Government going to find out their desire? Do you want an agitation or something like that? Obviously not. There must be some method by which the desire of the people should be ascertained.

Jawaharlal Nehru: There are many ways of finding out the desire of the people.

522. CPI.

Anyhow, at this moment, the first step of bringing them into the Union of India, that cannot be done. Afterwards we can consider that question separately.

(v) Punjab

161. To Lal Bahadur Shastri: Transfer of Judge in Passport Fraud Case[523]

August 2, 1962

My dear Lal Bahadur,

You know that the passport scandal case in the Punjab has attracted a great deal of notice.[524] Some of the persons involved are men of money and influence. Among those who were arrested and let out on bail, thirteen jumped their bail and went abroad. Six of them were in England and I think three were arrested in Hong Kong.

What has surprised me very much is that the judge who was trying this case in Jullundur has suddenly been transferred when he was almost finishing the case. Another judge has been appointed in his place. The reputation of this other judge is none too good.

I have written to Partap Singh Kairon[525] and Darbara Singh[526] about these cases and all about this transfer of the judge. I am writing to you just to keep you informed.

One of the big men involved in these cases is Man Mohan Singh Joul. He is a man both of money and influence.

Yours affectionately,
[Jawaharlal Nehru]

---

523. Letter to the Home Minister.
524. For previous references, see SWJN/SS/49/items 110, 117 and 120-121.
525. The Chief Minister of Punjab.
526. Minister in Punjab.

162. To Partap Singh Kairon: Transfer of Judge in Passport Fraud Case[527]

August 2, 1962

My dear Partap Singh,

As you know, the passport scandal cases have attracted a great deal of attention in the country and indeed in other countries also. We are very anxious that these cases should be dealt with strictly and as rapidly as possible. Some persons involved in them are not only men of money but are men of some influence and, I am told, that they are trying their best to get out of them.

I do not know all the facts but I understand that the judge who is trying them at Jullundur has been transferred when the case was nearly completed. This is surprising and naturally one is led to consider why such a transfer has been made at this stage. I shall be grateful to you if you will please look into this matter yourself and see that nothing improper is done and the cases are proceeded with as quickly as possible. Among those who were arrested and let out on bail, thirteen jumped their bail and left the country. I think nine of these were subsequently arrested in England or in other places like Hong Kong. We are dealing with a very unscrupulous gang who made a great deal of money and they deserve no consideration whatever.

Yours sincerely,
[Jawaharlal Nehru]

163. To Darbara Singh: Transfer of Judge in Passport Fraud Case[528]

August 2, 1962

My dear Darbara Singh,

There was one matter which I would have wished to speak to you about this morning but I forgot to do so. We are much concerned about the cases in what is called the Passport Scandal. This has attracted attention not only in India but in other countries and the way these people made large sums of money by forging passports is scandalous. These cases have been going on for some time

---

527. Letter to the Chief Minister of Punjab.
528. Letter to Minister, Punjab Government.

and repeatedly enquiries are made about them. Indeed, only today I asked my PPS[529] to make further enquiries in the matter.

One of them has come to my notice and has surprised me greatly, that is, that the judge trying these cases has been transferred to another place and some other judge has been appointed. This is very odd, more especially in such a case. I am writing to Sardar Partap Singh Kairon on this subject but I thought I might also draw your attention to this case so that every step should be taken to expedite proper disposal of it.[530]

Yours sincerely,
[Jawaharlal Nehru]

164. To Buta Singh: Explaining Why No Invitation[531]

August 5, 1962

Dear Shri Buta Singh,
I have your letter of the 4th August. This refers to certain developments in the Punjab. I am not in a position to say anything about the Punjabi University recently established in Patiala. That is a matter for the university authorities there.

But you have referred to the meeting of political groups and parties which I held on August 3.[532] The list of such leaders was provided to me and invitations were issued to all of them. I gather that the Akali leaders having attached themselves to the Swatantra Party in Parliament were taken to be members of that Party. I would have gladly invited you if I had known that you were a separate party functioning in Parliament.

Yours sincerely,
[Jawaharlal Nehru]

529. Kesho Ram.
530. See item 161.
531. Letter to Akali Dal, Lok Sabha MP; address: 128 South Avenue, New Delhi.
532. See item 2, fn 8.

165. To Partap Singh Kairon: Hindi in Punjab[533]

August 6, 1962

My dear Partap Singh,

Swami Rameshwaranand, MP, and another Member of Parliament came to see me today about Hindi in the Punjab.[534] They showed me a printed pamphlet which you had circulated some three years ago when the Hindi agitation was going on. They complained that the assurances given then were not being fulfilled.[535] I cannot go through the Hindi pamphlet or even the long letter which they gave me today and which I enclose.

But two matters, I think, deserve notice.

(1) Whatever the language of an area, we have laid it down that primary education should be in the mother tongue, and that normally this should be decided by the parents. That is, if the mother tongue is of minority, some special provision should be made for primary education in the early stages in it.

(2) Any application or petition can be given in Hindi even in the Punjabi area, and in Punjabi even in the Hindi area. Indeed, I would go so far as to say that any petition can be given in any of the recognised languages of India.

I hope you will consider this matter.

The Swami was especially upset by some recent legislation in the Punjab probably called The Language Act, which is to be applied from the 2nd October. I have not seen this Act and can say nothing about it.

Yours sincerely,
[Jawaharlal Nehru]

---

533. Letter to the Chief Minister of Punjab.
534. Rameshwaranand, Jan Sangh, Lok Sabha MP, and President of the Punjab Hindi Raksha Samiti, was accompanied by Prakashvir Shastri, Independent, Lok Sabha MP.
535. The delegation told Nehru that the Punjab Government had violated the assurances given by him "with regard to the right of the parents to select the language for their children at the primary stage and adoption of Hindi at all stages in the administration." Nehru was also told that the State Government "had decided to enforce Punjabi in the Gurmukhi script at the district level in the administration and schools with effect from October 2." *The Times of India*, 7 August 1962.

166. To Ranbir Singh: Foreign Exchange for Beas Project[536]

August 8, 1962

My dear Ranbir Singh,

Your letter of the 6th August.[537] I am sending it to our Finance Ministry and to the Ministry of Irrigation & Power. I do not know anything about the past history and to what extent the World Bank had undertaken to provide foreign exchange assistance. But our Finance Ministry will know this and will, no doubt, take steps to help you as far as possible.[538]

I am afraid it is exceedingly difficult and hardly possible for us to provide two crores of foreign exchange from our normal sources. We are at present very badly placed for foreign exchange and the situation is almost critical.

Yours sincerely,
Jawaharlal Nehru

167. To Morarji Desai: Foreign Exchange for Beas Project[539]

August 8, 1962

My dear Morarji,

I enclose a copy of a letter from Chaudhuri Ranbir Singh, Minister, Punjab. He refers to some undertaking that the World Bank gave to provide foreign exchange assistance for the Beas Project. I do not remember much about this. I have a vague recollection that at the time of the Canal Waters Treaty, some such assurance was made. I do not know how far this was followed up. I suppose your Ministry knows about it. Whatever is possible for us we should do to help this project.[540]

Yours sincerely,
Jawaharlal Nehru

536. Letter to the Minister of Irrigation and Power, Punjab. PMO, File No. 17(372)/59-69-PMS, Sr No. 28-A. Also available in the JN Collection.
537. Appendix 25.
538. See letter to Finance Minister, item 167; see also appendix 36.
539. Letter to the Finance Minister, File No. 17(372)/59-69-PMS, Sr. No. 29-A. Also available in the JN Collection.
540. For Morarji Desai's reply, see appendix 36. For other correspondence on this subject, see item 166 and appendix 25.
    Nehru informed Hafiz Mohammed Ibrahim also on 8 August 1962. See PMO, File No. 17(372)/59-69-PMS, Sr. No. 30-A.

168. To Partap Singh Kairon: Languages and Scripts[541]

August 20, 1962

My dear Partap Singh,

I am sending you a copy of a letter I have received from an MP, Prakash Vir Shastri. I wrote to you sometime ago[542] about an interview which I had with Swami Rameshwaranand and others. That letter must have reached you and I am sure you must have given consideration to it.

What I am particularly anxious about is that no application or the like matter in Hindi or Gurmukhi should be refused in any part of the Punjab. Indeed, as I said, if the application is in Urdu or English or any other Indian language, it should not be refused, much less in Hindi or Gurmukhi.

Yours sincerely,
[Jawaharlal Nehru]

169. To Ramnarayan Chaudhari: Model Villages and Blocks[543]

अगस्त 26, 1962

प्रिय रामनारायणजी,

आपका 23 अगस्त का पत्र मिला। आपकी योजना एक गांव को, एक ब्लाक को और एक ज़िले को एक नमूना बनाने की, अच्छी मालूम होती है। लेकिन आपके नोट को देखकर यह ज़ाहिर होता है कि आप चाहतें हैं कि पंजाब गवर्नमेंट इन मकामों पर काम करे।

अलावा इसके मेरी ठीक समझ में नहीं आया कि जो पंचायत समितियां हैं और जिनकी ज़िम्मेदारी है इन कामों को करने की, वह इस योजना में कहां आती हैं।

आपने लिखा है कि सरदार प्रताप सिंह कैरों[544] से आप इस बारे में मशवरा कर रहे हैं और उन्होंने सहयोग देने का वचन दिया है। अगर वह सहायता देंगे तो बहुत कुछ आपका काम अवश्य हो जायेगा।

आपका
जवाहरलाल नेहरु

---

541. Letter to the Chief Minister of Punjab.
542. Item 165.
543. Letter to the founder of Akhil Bharatiya Gram Sahyog Samaj; address: Lakshmanbagh, Faridabad, District Gurgaon. Earlier he was associated with the Bharat Sevak Samaj.
544. The Chief Minister of Punjab.

[Translation begins

26 August 1962

Dear Ramnarayanji,

I received your letter of 23 August. Your scheme for one village, one block and one district to be made into a model seems good. But from your note it appears that you want that the Punjab Government should work on this scheme.

Apart from this, I cannot understand very clearly how the panchayat samitis, whose responsibility it is to implement such projects, come into this plan.

You have written that you are consulting Sardar Partap Singh Kairon[545] about this matter and that he has promised to cooperate. If he cooperates, then I am sure your work will certainly get done to a large extent.

Yours sincerely,
Jawaharlal Nehru

Translation ends]

170. To N.D. Kapur: Death of Bakshi Tek Chand[546]

August 30, 1962

Dear Shri Kapur,

I have your letter of the 30th August. I am sorry I am unable to attend the public meeting on the 1st September but I would like to convey my deep sorrow at the death of Bakshi Tek Chand.[547] I came in contact with him during the Martial Law days in the Punjab and since then we have been friends and I admired him. It is a great loss to us that he has passed away.

Yours sincerely,
[Jawaharlal Nehru]

---

545. See fn 544 in this section.
546. Letter to the General Secretary of the Arya Kendriya Sabha Delhi, 15 Hanuman Road, New Delhi.
547. Lawyer and former judge of the Punjab High Court, he was associated with several educational and charitable organizations in Punjab. He died on 28 August.

171. To Buta Singh: Office of National Sample Survey[548]

September 4, 1962

Dear Shri Buta Singh,

Please refer to your letter of 16th August 1962 offering certain suggestions regarding the Punjab Block of the National Sample Survey. The headquarters of the field staff have been fixed with reference to easy and economic access to the villages which the Investigators and Inspectors are required to visit. As regards the Block Office, for the reasons stated in your letter, it is proposed to transfer part of the supervisory staff from Delhi to some suitable place in Punjab.

Yours sincerely,
[Jawaharlal Nehru]

172. To Partap Singh Kairon: Accept Le Corbusier's Opinion[549]

September 4, 1962

My dear Partap Singh,

I sent you the other day a telegram from Le Corbusier, about the transfer of some Secretary. I have now received a letter from him.[550] This is in French. He says in this that this is an SOS appeal from him about Prabhawalkar[551] whom he describes as an Indian of high capacity. He says that merely for an administrative question to endanger the fate of Chandigarh would be very sad. He hopes earnestly that this will not be done.

Le Corbusier has sent me a copy of the letter from Prabhawalkar. I enclose this. In such matters, as far as is possible, one should abide by the opinion of these experts.

Yours sincerely,
Jawaharlal Nehru

---

548. Letter to Akali Dal, Lok Sabha MP; address: 128 South Avenue, New Delhi.
549. Letter to the Chief Minister of Punjab. PMO, File No. 7(118)/56-66-PMS, (Vol. I), Sr. No. 125-A.
550. See item 174. Le Corbusier was Architectural Adviser to the Government of Punjab, Capital Project.
551. A.R. Prabhawalkar, a town planner on Le Corbusier's team for the Punjab Capital Project; appointed the first principal of the Chandigarh College of Architecture, 1961.

173. To Partap Singh Kairon: Decision for Himachal Pradesh[552]

19th September, 1962

My dear Partap Singh,

I have received your letter of September 11th here in London. In this letter you express your deep disappointment at the decision arrived at by the Government of India in regard to Himachal Pradesh.[553]

You can, of course, see me or our Home Minister[554] at any suitable and convenient time in Delhi.

But I fear there is no chance of our changing our decision about Himachal Pradesh in the present context. That was taken after full consideration of all the facts. There is no doubt that the people of Himachal Pradesh were anxious to have a separate existence and it was not possible to impose any merger upon them.

I do not see, however, why it should not be possible to have common working in matters of mutual concern between the two States. This can easily be worked out. Indeed, this is necessary between any two adjoining States, more so between Punjab and Himachal Pradesh.

We cannot ignore the human element in such matters and proceed on some logical geographical basis. The other day, I think, you made a suggestion for the merger of Jammu & Kashmir as well as some other States with the Punjab.[555] I was surprised to read it and it has, as I expected, raised a good deal of apprehension and opposition in Kashmir.

I hope to return to Delhi on the 1st of October.

Yours sincerely,
[Jawaharlal Nehru]

---

552. Letter to the Chief Minister of Punjab. Sent from London.
553. The Constitution (Fourteenth Amendment) Act, 1962, gave Parliament the authority to create by law Legislatures and Councils of Ministers for five Union territories including Himachal Pradesh.
554. Lal Bahadur Shastri.
555. Talking to presspersons in Chandigarh on 4 September 1962, Kairon suggested the merger of Rajasthan, Jammu and Kashmir, Himachal Pradesh and Punjab into a single administrative unit. He said that his proposal would, if implemented, serve as "a good psychological counter to the demand for Punjabi suba;" would be economically sound; serve as "a strong fortress against possible foreign aggression;" and "counter the trends unleashed by the British policy to divide and sub-divide the people on the basis of religion and caste." *The Hindustan Times*, 5 September 1962.

174. To Partap Singh Kairon: Indulging Le Corbusier[556]

September 28, 1962

My dear Partap Singh,

You will remember my forwarding to you a telegram which I received in Delhi from Le Corbusier.[557] He was much agitated at the prospect of B.B. Vohra being transferred by the Punjab Government from his work in the Chandigarh project to some other department.[558]

Le Corbusier came to see me in Paris a few days ago and spoke to me about this matter again. He was much distressed over it and said that the training and experience of Vohra in this project will be lost if he is transferred and a new man can hardly be expected to gain that experience and training and enthusiasm for it. The whole project must be looked at from the point of view of the original inception by Corbusier and it is difficult for a new man to grasp all this.

I do not remember having had an answer from you to my letter then. I think there is much in what Corbusier said and it would be a pity for an experienced man who knows his job to be transferred to some other department. Service considerations are usually considered in these matters, but it is more important to think of the work in hand. I hope therefore that you will consider this aspect. Corbusier has been connected with the Chandigarh project from its inception and it will be unfortunate to go against his particular wishes in such a matter.

You know that the French Government has presented some kind of a door for the new Assembly building in Chandigarh. Corbusier suggested, and I agree with him, that the Punjab Government might invite Monsieur André Malraux, who is a senior member of the French Government and the Minister of Arts and Culture, to come and present this door himself. I think this will be desirable. As a matter of fact, apart from this presentation of this door, I have invited Malraux to India if he can come. I hope therefore that you will send a

556. Letter to the Chief Minister of Punjab. PMO, File No. 7(118)/56-66-PMS, (Vol. I), Sr. No. 126-A. Also available in the JN Collection. Sent from Rome.

557. Architectural Adviser to the Government of Punjab, Capital Project.

558. B.B. Vohra was Secretary, Buildings and Roads, PWD, Punjab. According to E.N. Mangat Rai, then Chief Secretary, Punjab: "On 20 June 1962, after a cabinet meeting Kairon asked his Ministers and me to stay on and announced that he was not satisfied with this officer's performance in regard to the sale of a house by auction to K.S. Malhotra, and the lease by tender of a hotel site at Chandigarh. He had decided that B.B. Vohra should be censured and transferred forthwith." *Commitment My Style. Career in the Indian Civil Service* (Delhi: Vikas, 1973), p. 216. See also item 172.

letter of invitation to Monsieur André Malraux for the purpose. This may be sent through our External Affairs Ministry.

Yours sincerely,
Jawaharlal Nehru

(w) Rajasthan

175. To Kumbha Ram Arya: Resign from Executive Bodies[559]

August 12, 1962

Dear Kumbha Ramji,

Indiraji[560] has sent on to me your letter addressed to me of the 9th August.[561]

I have given careful consideration to this matter and have discussed it with Indiraji also. Shri Khandubhai Desai's Report[562] did not deal with individual charges but dealt rather with the political situation in Rajasthan. A high level seven-man committee[563] also considered the question from the political point of view and the good of the Congress organisation in Rajasthan. Their decision was that you should be asked to resign from the Membership of the Executive Committee of the Rajasthan Pradesh Congress Committee and membership of the Election Committee of the Rajasthan Pradesh Congress Committee, which were executive bodies. They did not ask you to resign from the Membership of the AICC or the Membership of the Rajya Sabha, which are deliberative bodies.

After giving careful consideration to this matter, I think that the decision of the seven-man committee should be honoured by you, that is to say, that you should resign from the Executive Committee of the Rajasthan Pradesh Congress Committee as well as the Election Committee of the Rajasthan

---

559. Letter to Congress, Rajya Sabha MP; address: 16-B Ferozeshah Road, New Delhi. NMML, AICC Papers, Box No. 13, File No. OD 41(c).
560. Indira Gandhi, member of the CWC and of the Party's Disciplinary Action Committee.
561. Not reproduced here, but available in the NMML.
562. A seven-man subcommittee of the CWC, appointed to consider steps required to be taken to deal with the question of indiscipline that had arisen in connection with the 1962 General Election, had asked Khandubhai Desai to enquire into the major cases of indiscipline in Rajasthan. His report was considered by the subcommittee.
563. The seven-member subcommittee consisted of: Lal Bahadur Shastri, Indira Gandhi, C. Subramaniam, S.K. Patil, Gulzarilal Nanda, Sadiq Ali and U.N. Dhebar.

Pradesh Congress Committee. You need not resign from the Membership of the AICC and the Rajya Sabha.

[SOBBING CHEERFULLY]

You Said It

By LAXMAN

You may say he has accepted the decision of the High Command Cheerfully

(From *The Times of India*, 14 August 1962, p. 1)

I hope that you will carry out their decision in these matters and thus help in the proper organisation of the Congress in Rajasthan and remove any idea of group functioning there. As you have said that you are prepared to abide by my decision, I am sending your two resignations from these two bodies to the Congress President, who will take necessary action. I am returning to you your resignations from the Rajya Sabha and the AICC.

Yours sincerely,
Jawaharlal Nehru

176. To D. Sanjivayya: Kumbha Ram Arya's Resignations[564]

August 12, 1962

My dear Sanjivayya,

I enclose the letter which Shri Kumbha Ram Arya wrote to Indiraji and me together with the resignation which he tendered from various bodies. I also enclose my letter to him which is in accordance with the decision of the seven-man committee as confirmed by the Working Committee today.[565]

Kumbha Ramji had also sent me his resignation from the Rajya Sabha and the AICC. I am returning these to him.

One of the letters of resignation is from the membership of the Rajasthan Pradesh Congress Committee. This, as far as I can see, is not quite accurate. It should be resignation from the Executive Committee of the Rajasthan PCC.

Yours sincerely,
Jawaharlal Nehru

177. To Jainarain Vyas: No Disciplinary Action Yet[566]

August 18, 1962

My dear Jainarainji,

I have received your letter, without date. I am forwarding it to the Congress President[567] who will no doubt consider what you have written.

---

564. Letter to the Congress President. NMML, AICC Papers, F. No. O.D. 41(C), Box No. 13. Also available in the JN Collection.
565. Item 175.
566. Letter to Congress, Rajya Sabha MP and a former Chief Minister of Rajasthan; address: 83 South Avenue, New Delhi. NMML, AICC Papers, Box 13, File No. OD-41(c) – Rajasthan/1962.
567. D. Sanjivayya.

So far as I know, no final decision was taken about you by the Disciplinary Committee of the Congress.[568]

Yours sincerely,
Jawaharlal Nehru

178. To Mohanlal Sukhadia: Controlling Factionalism[569]

August 30, 1962

My deer Sukhadia,

I sent you a brief reply to your last letter in which you asked me about your seeking a vote of confidence.[570] I understand you are doing this on the 4th September. That is right.

But the more I think of it, the more I feel that it will not be good for you to change about your present Ministry. Those who were opposed to you have promised to support you and cooperate with you. It is well to take them at their word, and thus endeavour to put an end to the group spirit.

Yours sincerely,
[Jawaharlal Nehru]

568. The CWC had on 12 August 1962 considered the following recommendation of the seven-man subcommittee dealing with indiscipline: "Shri Jainarayan Vyas has admitted that he opposed certain Congress candidates [during the General Election]. Whatever may be the motive, there is no doubt that such indiscipline cannot be tolerated. Shri Vyas, on his own admission has been guilty of indiscipline and is, therefore, suspended from primary membership of the Congress for one year and is debarred from holding any elective post in the organisation for 2 years." According to the minutes of the CWC proceedings, "Some members of the Committee objected to the mild punishment recommended against Shri Jainarayan Vyas. No final decision was, however, recorded." *Congress Bulletin*, No. 7, 8, 9 & 10, July-October 1962, p. 136. For previous references to Vyas, see SWJN/SS/73/items 43 and 51; and SWJN/SS/74/item 73, here pp. 195 and 213.

569. Letter to the Chief Minister of Rajasthan.

570. Nehru wrote to Sukhadia on 28 August: "Of course you have the right to reconstitute the Ministry, but my advice to you would be not to upset the Ministry too much. I should not like you to create the impression that you are working on group lines."

179. To Mohanlal Sukhadia: Rana Pratap Sagar Atomic Power Plant[571]

September 1, 1962

My dear Sukhadia,

Your letter of August 30 about the Atomic Power Plant at Rana Pratap Sagar. However we might expedite this, it will take a number of years. We have to go about it carefully without taking the slightest risk. It is a good thing, however, that we have decided about it and work will begin in the near future.[572]

Yours sincerely,
[Jawaharlal Nehru]

(x) Uttar Pradesh

180. In Jamunipur: Inauguration of the Nehru Gram Bharati[573]

राज्यपाल जी,[574] बहनो और भाइयो,

कुछ बरस हुए मैं यहाँ जमुनीपुर आया था, जो यहाँ विद्यालय था अब इण्टर कॉलेज हो गया[575] उसको देखने, हल्के-हल्के ये बढ़ा है, सोलह वर्ष हो गये, सोलह-सत्रह वर्ष हो गये इसको। तो बहुत तेज़ी से नहीं बढ़ा, काफी कठिनाइयाँ उसके सामने आईं, लेकिन जो लोग उसको चलाते थे उन्होंने उस बोझे को उठाया और किसी तरह से उसको संभालते गये, चलाते गये और अब वो ज़रा बड़ा भी हो गया है, इण्टर कॉलेज हो गया है। अब इस शताब्दी के स्मारक के सिलसिले में ग्राम भारती की योजना बनी यहाँ पंडित मोतीलाल के स्मारक में।

अब मैं क्या कहूँ मेरे पिताजी के स्मारक के बारे में। मुझे ख़ुशी होती है, लेकिन विशेषकर मुझे ख़ुशी इस बात की है कि यह काम जो हो रहा है ये इलाहाबाद के किसानों

571. Letter to the Chief Minister of Rajasthan.
572. The GOI announced on 20 August 1962 their decision to locate a nuclear power station, the second in the country, at Rana Pratap Sagar near Kota in Rajasthan. See also item 303. For previous reference, see SWJN/SS/74/item 130.
573. Speech, 26 July 1962, near Durbasa Ashram on the northern bank of the Ganges, at Jamunipur Kakra, 26 miles from Allahabad. NMML, AIR Tapes, TS No. 8441, NM No. 1663, 1786. Nehru Gram Bharati, a rural polytechnic institute, was named after Motilal Nehru. See report of 26 July 1962 in the *National Herald* of 27 July 1962, p. 1.
574. Biswanath Das, the Governor of Uttar Pradesh.
575. Motilal Nehru Inter College.

के भलाई के लिए हो रहा है, हमारे ज़िले के रहने वालों के लिए है। ये नहीं कि इलाहाबाद शहर में एक बड़ा सा मकान बन जाता, बड़ा हॉल बन जाता, बनते, ऐसे अक्सर स्मारक होते हैं। मुझे विशेष ख़ुशी इस बात की है कि यहाँ इलाहाबाद के ज़िले के देहात में एक ऐसी चीज़ बन रही है जिससे आपके बाल-बच्चों को बहुत फ़ायदा होगा और आपको फ़ायदा होगा। ख़ाली विद्यालय ये नहीं बन रहा है, मैंने सुना कि ये बन रही है पोलिटेकनिक। अब पोलिटेकनिक क्या होती है? विद्यालय में तो किताब पढ़ना-लिखना सिखाया जाता है, वो तो सभों को सीखना चाहिए। पोलिटेकनिक में नये-नये काम करने सिखाए जाते हैं, नये-नये औज़ार चलाने।

आजकल की दुनिया क्या है? आप देखें आजकल की दुनिया नये-नये औज़ारों की है, नये-नये मशीन की है, नये-नये हल हैं, नये-नये खेती के लिए सामान हैं। ये देश हैं और दुनिया के, अंग्रेज़ों का देश है, अमरीका का देश है, रूस का देश है, वो बहुत आगे बढ़ गये हैं, बहुत धनी हो गये हैं। कैसे हो गये हैं, कैसे हो गये? क्योंकि उन्होंने अधिक ज़मीन से और कारख़ाने से पैदा किया। धन कोई टपकता तो है नहीं ऊपर से, धन तो जो पैदा करे आदमी अपने परिश्रम से, किसान हो, कारीगर हो, मज़दूर, हो, वो धन होता है। तो वहाँ लोगों ने बहुत पैदा किया अपनी ज़मीन से, हमसे बहुत अधिक। एक एकड़ ज़मीन में जित्ता वो पैदा करते हैं बहुत ज्यादा हमसे और कारख़ानों में बहुत पैदा करते हैं। कैसे पैदा करते हैं वो? यह नहीं कि परिश्रम करते हैं, परिश्रम की बात नहीं। इसलिए कि वो नये-नये औज़ार लगाते हैं, अच्छा हल चलाते हैं ज़मीन पर। कहीं-कहीं तो वो हल होते हैं आपने सुना होगा ट्रैक्टर, मोटर के हल। वो तो, ख़ैर, उसको बिलफ़ेल छोड़ दीजिए, कहीं-कहीं हमारे यहाँ भी चलने लगे हैं, बड़े-बड़े ज़मीन पर चल सकते हैं। लेकिन उसके अलावा अच्छे हल मामूली जो आप चला सकें, आपके बैल खींच सकें, वो अच्छे होते हैं। होता क्या है? उससे काफी गहरा खोद सकते हैं और उससे जो आपके खेत से पैदा होये तो बहुत अधिक होता है। तो आप भी जानते हैं, आपको मैं क्या बताऊँ? आजकल की दुनिया नये-नये औज़ार की है, नये-नये सामान की है, जिससे अधिक पैदा होता है। आप अधिकतर किसान यहाँ बैठे हैं, अब हमारा देश का सबमें पहला सवाल है कि कैसे यहाँ की ज़मीन से, भूमि की सेवा ठीक हो तब देती है। परिश्रम आप इत्ता करते हैं और अक्सर फिर भी पैदा अधिक नहीं करते। अब पैदा करने के तरीके हैं जिसमें खाद अच्छी डालें, फ़र्टिलाइज़र डालें। अब आप सीख गये हैं, उससे बढ़ जाता है, लेकिन सबमें बड़ी बात ये है कि जो औज़ार आपके हों, जो हल हों, जो और सामान हो खेत में चलाने का वो अच्छे हों, नये तरीके के हों। और इसके माने नहीं कि बड़ी महंगी चीज़ें आप खरीदें, मोटर ख़रीदें, मोटर-वोटर तो ख़ैर जाने कब हो यहाँ, लेकिन पचास-साठ-सत्तर रुपए में बड़ा अच्छा हल मिल जाता है जिससे आपकी आमदनी दुगुनी हो जाये, डेढ़ गुनी, आपका लाभ हो, देश का लाभ हो।

मैं फिर आपसे कहता हूँ सबमें पहला सवाल देश के सामने इस वक़्त, बहुत सारे सवाल हैं, लेकिन पहला सवाल है यहाँ की खेती से आमदनी बढ़े, जिससे किसान का लाभ हो और देश का लाभ हो। और भी बहुत सवाल हैं, हम कारख़ाने सब जगह बनाना चाहते

261

हैं जिसमें लोगों को काम मिले और जिससे देश का धन बढ़े, जित्ता पैदा होता है वो देश का धन होता है, लोगों का धन होता है। तो पोलिटेकनिक जो यहाँ बनाने की आशा रखते हैं लोग, वहाँ हाथ का काम, ये नये-नये औज़ार, नई-नई चीज़ें सिखाई जाती हैं, सिखाई जायेंगी। किसानों के लिए भी और और काम के लिए भी। आप अपने ग्रामों में छोटे कारख़ाने शुरू करें, छोटा-छोटा काम करें और बड़ा भी करें, लेकिन छोटा काम अवश्य करें। ये बात अगर हमारे सब गाँवों में हो तब इत्ती जल्दी हमारी तरक्की हो, उन्नति हो कि दिल ख़ुश हो जाये। इस समय तो हम उससे दूर हैं और इस समय तो हमारे स्कूल, विद्यालय भी अभी सब जगह नहीं बने हैं।

हम तो चाहते हैं कि इन तीन-चार वर्ष में जो आने वाले हैं कोई बच्चा हमारा न हो, कोई बच्चा, लड़का या लड़की, जो विद्यालय में नहीं जाये। जरूर जाये, क्योंकि उसके बग़ैर हमारी उन्नति नहीं होती, तरक्की नहीं होती। और इसलिए नहीं जैसे पहले लोग समझते थे कि विद्यालय में पढ़के सरकारी नौकरी करें। विद्यालय में पढ़के अपना काम करें, किसान किसानी करे, बढ़ई बढ़ईगीरी करे, लोहार लोहारी करे, जो कुछ करे, करे, लेकिन अच्छी तरह से करे, अधिक कमाये। तो इसलिए हम चाहते हैं कि सब बच्चे स्कूल जायें। हम तो चाहें कि बड़े भी जायें लेकिन अब बच्चों का प्रबंध करना कठिन हो गया और उसको हम बढ़ाते जाना चाहते हैं। अभी तो चार-पाँच बरस स्कूल में रहें, फिर अधिक बढ़ा देंगे और वहाँ से पढ़के निकलें, फिर जो उनमें तेज़ बच्चे हों उनको अधिक पढ़ायें, नये-नये काम करने के तरीके सिखायें, खेती का सिखायें, जो दुनिया में और बातें होती हैं उसे हम सीखें, नई-नई बातें कुछ हम भी सिखा सकते हैं, कुछ सीख सकते हैं, तो सीखें। और इस तरह से वो आके अपने खेत पे काम करें, औरों को सिखायें अपने गाँव में, तो हमारी बड़ी उन्नति हो, हमारा बड़ा पैदावार बढ़ जाये और उससे आप लोगों को फ़ायदा हो और देश को फ़ायदा हो और उसी के साथ अगर वहाँ छोटे-मोटे कारख़ाने बनें तब और भी लाभ हो। बहुत बेकारी, बेकार लोगों को काम मिले और गाँव ख़ुशहाल हो जायें। ये आप याद रखें मोटी बात है।

क्यों है कि हमारा देश ग़रीब है इत्ता? क्यों है कि अंग्रेज़ों का देश अमीर है? अंग्रेज़ों को देश हमेशा अमीर नहीं था, ये पिछले सौ-दो सौ बरस की बात है कि हमसे बहुत बढ़ गया। इसलिए कि अंग्रेज़ों के और यूरोप के देशों में उन्होंने विज्ञान की सेवा की। विज्ञान की सेवा की। विज्ञान क्या है? विज्ञान है, खोज है, विद्या की खोज है और इस तरह से क्या-क्या बातें प्रकृति में हैं। हमारी ये प्रकृति है सुंदर चीज़ है, इसमें क्या-क्या शक्तियाँ हैं उसको ढूँढना और उसको काम में लाना। आप रेल पे चढ़ते हैं, क्या चीज़ रेल है? कौन जादू है उसमें? इंजन खींच ले जाता है, इंजन को कौन चलाता है? गरम पानी की भाप चलाती है, कोई बड़ी बात नहीं है, सब जानते हैं आप, हमारी बहनें जानती हैं कि पानी को गरम करो तो भाप निकलती है और बड़े ज़ोर से निकलती है। अब एक आदमी ने उसको सोचा कोई डेढ़ सौ बरस हुए, दो सौ बरस हुए कि भाप में बड़ी शक्ति है पानी की, भाप को अगर पकड़ लें तो उससे काम करायें, तो उसने भाप को पकड़ा और ट्यूब बना के उसमें से भाप से एक पहिया चलाया उसके ज़ोर से, वेग से। जब पहिया चलाया तो

काम निकल गया, पहिये के ऊपर गाड़ी रख दी, गाड़ी चलने लगी, इंजन हो गया, खींचने लगा। अब इसमें कोई जादू तो नहीं है रेल के चलने में, आप सब कोई चला सकते हैं, देख सकते हैं, ख़ाली पानी को गरम करके भाप निकल के पहिया घुमाते हैं और पहिये पर गाड़ी चलती है। लेकिन इस छोटी सी बात को समझ कर दुनिया में कित्ती ऊँच-नीच हुआ, बड़े-बड़े देश भर में गाड़ियाँ, रेलगाड़ियाँ चलने लगीं, जहाँ पहले आप सफर करें, यात्रा करते थे, कितने दिनों लगें, बरसों लग जाते थे बड़ी यात्रा में, अब आप जल्दी से पहुँच जाते हैं। यहाँ से आप कलकत्ते जायें, बम्बई जायें, दिल्ली जायें, एक-दो दिन में पहुँच जाते हैं रेल पर। तो ये क्या कोई नई बात नहीं है, ख़ाली नई बात विज्ञान की तलाश में लोगों ने सीखी, एक प्रकृति की शक्ति की, भाप की, फिर और ऐसी-ऐसी बातें निकलीं, फिर बिजली निकली।

बिजली क्या चीज़ है? वो भी कोई जादू नहीं है, सब लोग बहुत दिनों से देखा करते थे, कड़कती थी बिजली आसमान पर और कभी-कभी गिर जाती थी, हानि होती थी और लोग उससे डरें और लोग उसकी पूजा करें, लेकिन बजाय पूजा करने के लोगों ने उसको समझने की कोशिश की कि क्या चीज़ है, हल्के-हल्के समझे। आपको आश्चर्य होगा कि कैसे उन्होंने समझने की कोशिश की थी। एक बड़े विद्वान थे, उन्होंने पतंग उड़ा के समझने की कोशिश की कि क्या चीज़ है बिजली बादल में। पतंग बादल में उड़ाई और उसमें तार लगा दिया देखने को कि तार से उतरती है कि नहीं। वो तार से उतरी, जैसे अब हम भेजते हैं तार से। फिर उन्होंने देखा कि अगर हम कुछ चीज़ों को रगड़ते हैं, ख़ास चीज़ें, तो बिजली पैदा होती है और बिजली भी एक शक्ति, एक प्रकृति की शक्ति। अब वह शक्ति क़ाबू में कर लो तो उससे लाभ होता है, उससे काम करा सकते हो, कित्ता काम बिजली से होता है। बिजली से आपने देखी ही है, रोशनी होती है, पंखा चलता है, मैं बोल रहा हूँ ये बिजली से आवाज़ मेरी फैलती है। लेकिन यह तो छोटे काम हैं। असली काम तो बड़े-बड़े कारख़ाने चलते हैं बिजली से। किसान लोग और देशों में बिजली से बहुत काम लेते हैं। इस तरह से, क्योंकि बिजली तो आपके हाथ में एक शक्ति आ जाती है, उस शक्ति से जो-जो काम करो। तो ये हुआ। अब नई-नई शक्तियाँ निकलीं, अब मैं आज आया हूँ दिल्ली से यहाँ। कैसे आया इलाहाबाद? मैं हवाई जहाज़ से आया, वो भी एक नई चीज़ निकली। अब रेलगाड़ी हल्के चलने लगी उसके मुक़ाबले में, और नई-नई चीज़ें निकलती आती हैं।

तो हमारा देश कुछ पिछड़ गया नई चीज़ें सीखने में, और देश बढ़ गये। तो इससे और देशों को धन मिला, अमीर हो गये, और देशों की शक्ति बढ़ गई, उनके हाथ में शक्ति आ गई न, प्रकृति की, वो बढ़ गई और उन्होंने हमारे देश पर, हमारे पड़ोसी देशों पर एशिया के, अपनी हुकूमत जमा ली, जैसे अंग्रेज़ों ने जमाई थी। इसलिए कि उन्होंने नई दुनिया को समझा, नई दुनिया को स्थापित किया, नये-नये प्रकृति की शक्तियों को समझे। तो इन सब बातों को हमें सीखना है, नहीं तो हम पिछड़ जायेंगे। पिछड़े हैं ही, और बढ़ना है। इसलिए जब हमें स्वराज्य मिला तो पहला काम हमने ये किया कि बड़े-बड़े हमने, क्या कहते हैं उसे, बड़े-बड़े पढ़ाने की जगह बनाई, जहाँ कि हम नया विज्ञान सिखायें।

263

नया विज्ञान सिखायें नहीं, विज्ञान की आज़माइश करें, देखें क्या होता है, क्योंकि वो चीज़ किताब पढ़ने से नहीं आती, वो करके आती है। बड़े-बड़े हैं ऐसे, सारे देश भर में फैले हैं और तब हम वैज्ञानिक लोगों को, अपने नौजवानों को बना रहे हैं अच्छा।

अब एक नई शक्ति आई है, महाशक्ति, जिसको आपने सुना हो, जिससे एटम बम्ब बना। बहुत भयानक चीज़ है एटम बम्ब, लेकिन उसके पीछे एक महाशक्ति है, जिससे लाभ हो सकता है, बहुत बड़ा लाभ हो सकता है। शक्ति को आप अच्छा काम करें, बुरा काम करें औज़ार का, आपके पास एक चक्कू हो, चक्कू, बड़ा अच्छा काम करते हैं उससे, दूसरा आदमी चक्कू से किसी का गला काट दे वो बुरा काम हो गया। तो चक्कू तो नहीं बुरा हुआ, वो तो उस शक्ति को ठीक से काम में लाना हुआ। अब एटम बम्ब फेंका, बड़े-बड़े नगर तबाह हो गये। ये हमने सुना पन्द्रह बरस हुए, हुआ था ये, सोलह-सत्रह बरस हुए, दो बड़े नगर जापान के एटम बम्ब ने पूरे उड़ा दिए, हवा हो गये, ख़ाक हो गये। तो बुरा काम है, लेकिन वो जो शक्ति है अणुशक्ति, बड़ी शक्ति है, उसको क़ाबू में लाके उससे अच्छा काम करायें तो बड़े-बड़े काम हमारे हो जायें। तो उसको भी, हमें उसका भी अध्ययन करना है।

तो हमें अब इस नई दुनिया में जाना है, पुरानी दुनिया में तो हम हैं ही और पुरानी दुनिया में जो अच्छी बातें हैं उसको हमें रखना है अपनी, हमारे देश की बातें हैं, उसको हम भूल कैसे जायें, लेकिन नई दुनिया को भी समझना है, नहीं तो हम पिछड़े रहेंगे। नई दुनिया को समझने के माने हैं हमारे सब बच्चे विद्यालय में जायें, स्कूल में जायें और बढ़ के पोलिटेक्नीक में जायें या ऐसी और संस्थाएँ हैं, ऐसे कॉलेज हैं उसमें जायें, जहाँ पढ़ने-लिखने के अलावा हम काम करना सीखें, नये-नये काम। इसलिए ये बहुत आवश्यक है और इसलिए मुझे ख़ुशी है कि यहाँ ये ग्राम भारती जो बन रहा है यहाँ पोलिटेक्नीक होगा। मैं आशा करता हूँ कि अच्छा पोलिटेक्नीक हो और आपके लड़के-लड़कियाँ यहाँ आके उससे सीखेंगे और फिर वो वहाँ से सीख के निकलेंगे। वो कहीं दूर जाके नौकरी की जरूरत नहीं है उनको, वे यहीं इलाहाबाद के ज़िले में पचासों नये काम कर सकेंगे जिससे यहाँ के रहने वाले किसानों को और लोगों का बड़ा लाभ होगा। इसी तरह से देश की तरक्की होती है।

अगर हम पुरानी बातें ख़ाली करें, कुछ नई सीखें नहीं तो हम आगे नहीं बढ़ते। अगर हम अपनी आँखें बन्द कर लें और नई बातें जो हो रही हैं उसको नहीं देखते तो हमारा क़सूर है। हमने बहुत दिन अपनी आँखें बन्द कीं, अब खोलकर सीखना है और इसके लिए पढ़ना है और विशेषकर नये-नये काम सीखने हैं। नये काम में नये तरीके खेती करने के भी हैं। नये काम के माने, खेती आप अच्छी तरह से जानते हैं, लेकिन आपको बहुत नये तरीके नहीं मालूम हैं। अब थोड़े दिनों से आपके पास फ़र्टिलाइज़र आता है, वो एक क़िस्म की खाद निकली, उससे कित्ता लाभ होता है। अब आप समझ गये हैं, अब आपको जरूरत है फ़र्टिलाइज़र की। हम बड़े-बड़े कारख़ाने बना रहे हैं, सारे देश भर में, जिससे फ़र्टिलाइज़र बने, पैदा हो, आप तक पहुँचे, फिर आपका उत्पादन बढ़े।

ये सब होता जाता है लेकिन इसके पीछे आदमी होने चाहिये सीखे हुए। इसलिए हमें, विशेषकर हमारी इच्छा है सब बच्चे स्कूल में जायें, तैयार हों भारत की सेवा करने को,

अपने परिवार की सेवा करने, अपनी सेवा करने, अपने ग्राम की सेवा करने। इस तरह से हो। बड़े-बड़े काम सारे भारत में हो रहे हैं। शुरु-शुरु में वो बड़े काम का बहुत फल नहीं दिखता जैसे आप कोई मकान की जड़ लगायें, बुनियाद डालें, नींव डालें, वो तो ज़मीन के नीचे होती है, दिखता नहीं है लेकिन उसी के ऊपर बड़ा मकान बनता है। तो हम तो चाहते हैं मकान बनाना वहाँ, वो ऐसा कि हिन्दुस्तान के सब किसान, सब जनता बयालीस करोड़ उठें, ख़ाली थोड़े से आदमी की नौकरी देने का प्रश्न नहीं है, उठें और ख़ुशहाल हों, और तरक्की करें और हमारा देश भी दुनिया में एक अव्वल देश हो। तो ये हम करना चाहते हैं। चूँकि बड़ा काम है, उसमें बड़ा परिश्रम की ज़रूरत है, मेहनत की और आप सब लोगों के सहयोग की। तो चाहता हूँ कि आप सब इन बातों को समझें। ये ख़ाली बात ऊपर से कुछ करने की नहीं। नौकरी दे दी, लगान बढ़ा दिया, घटा दिया। वो सब इस जिसकी आवश्यकता हो वो हो, लेकिन असल बात यह है यही कि हम भारत को एक नया देश बनायें। पुराना तो है, पुराने देश को नया रूप दें और नये रूप देने के माने हैं।

भारत क्या है? भारत ख़ाली कोई पहाड़, नदियाँ और खेत तो नहीं है, भारत तो भारत के आदमी हैं, भारत के बयालीस करोड़ आदमी हैं पुरुष-स्त्री-बच्चे, वही भारत हैं। तो उन पुरुष-स्त्री-बच्चों को सीखना और उसमें एक आवश्यक बात है कि वो लोग पहले सीखें कि हमारा देश है, हम सब लोग जो इस देश में रहते हैं हम एक हैं, चाहे हमारा धर्म जाति कोई हो, हम एक हैं। हम भारतीय हैं, हम हिन्दुस्तानी हैं, चाहे हिन्दू हों, चाहे मुसलमान हों, चाहे पारसी हों, चाहे ईसाई हों, चाहे बौद्ध हों, चाहे जैन हों, चाहे कोई हों, चाहे कोई जाति हो, अपना, अपने धर्म पे लोग रहें, उसकी सेवा करें। लेकिन एक सबमें बड़ा धर्म है अपने देश की सेवा करना, उसमें सब लोग एक बड़े परिवार के होते हैं, सारे भारत के बयालीस करोड़ आदमी। आप वहाँ रहते हैं इलाहाबाद के ज़िले में, लेकिन आपको सारे ख़ाली आपका गाँव नहीं है ये, लेकिन आपका सारा देश है। हिमालय पहाड़ से लेके, जो हमारी रक्षा करते हैं उत्तर में, दक्खिन में कन्याकुमारी, रामेश्वर तक, वो सब हमारा, आपका है, जैसे औरों का भी है। तो ये विचार कीजिये आप क्योंकि जो हमारे जो लोग समझदार नहीं हैं, छोटे दिमाग़ के, छोटे मन के हैं, वो आपस में लड़ाई पैदा करते हैं, ये हमारा ये तुम्हारा। लेकिन असल में यह भारत सबका है और हम सब लोगों को मिलकर इसमें काम करने से सभों की तरक्की होती है। भारत में स्वराज्य मिला, किसी एक जाति को तो नहीं मिला, एक धर्म वालों को तो नहीं मिला, एक ज़िले को तो नहीं मिला, सारे भारत को मिला, जिसमें हिन्दू, मुसलमान, ईसाई सबको बराबर का हिस्सा है, सब जातियों को।

तो इस ढंग की बड़ी भारी बात है कि हम भारत की एकता को मज़बूत करें क्योंकि बहुत दिन से हमारा यही जो बीमारी रही, हम दुर्बल हो रहे, वो इसलिए कि हम आपस में लड़ते बहुत हैं। मूर्खता की बात है, कभी धर्म के नाम से, कभी जाति के नाम से। यह नहीं समझते कि अब दुनिया में ऊँच-नीच बहुत नहीं रहेगी, हल्के-हल्के हटती है, न पैसे की, न जाति की, सभों को बराबर का अधिकार होगा, जो-जो परिश्रम करे उसको लाभ अधिक हो, जो अक़्लमन्द हो, बुद्धि का लाभ हो उसे वो और बात है। तो ये बात तो बुनियादी है, इन बातों को आप याद रखें।

आपके यहाँ और सारे उत्तर प्रदेश में और सारे देश ही में पंचायती राज्य शुरु हुआ है, ये एक बड़ी भारी चीज़ है। मुझे मालूम नहीं यहाँ किस ढंग से हो रहा है, शुरु हुआ कि नहीं, अगर हुआ है तो अभी शुरु हुआ है, जमा न हो लेकिन वो जम जायेगा। ये बड़ी अच्छी बात है क्योंकि इसमें अधिकार पंचायतों को जनता के हाथ में दिया जाता है। ये बड़े-बड़े जो अफ़सरी राज्य था पहले अंग्रेज़ी ज़माने में और उसके बाद भी, अब वो अफ़सर तो रहेंगे क्योंकि अफ़सर बग़ैर काम कैसे चले, वो सीखे हुए आदमी होते हैं, अच्छा सिखायें, लेकिन हुकूमत करने का अधिकार उनका बहुत कम हो जाता है। पंचायतों को अधिकार हम देते हैं ताकि सारी जनता की ज़िम्मेदारी हो, वो सीखे। अधिकार लेने से आदमी बढ़ता है हमेशा, अगर अपने ऊपर भरोसा न हो तो कैसे बढ़े।

तो ये पंचायती राज्य बहुत बड़ी चीज़ है और उसी के साथ-साथ सहकारी संघ, कोऑपरेटिव जिसे कहते हैं अंग्रेज़ी में, सहकारी लोग मिल के काम करें। किसान, आप लोग छोटी हैसियत के लोग हैं, पैसा अधिक पास नहीं, जो आप खेत में पैदा करें उसके बेचने में कठिनाई हो और लोग बनिये, साहूकार आपका लाभ उठायें आपके अनजानपने से, ये बातें ठीक नहीं हैं। इसीलिए सहकारी संघ ठीक होता है जिसमें आप लोग एक-दूसरे की सहायता करें, एक-दूसरे से सहकारी संघ के द्वारा आप चीज़ खरीदें, आप चीज़ बेचें, आपका बीच में कोई हिस्सेदार नहीं होगा, आपका ही होगा माल। और इस तरह से बहुत काम आप बड़े-बड़े, आपको नये हल लेने हैं, आप सहकारी संघ द्वारा ख़रीद सकते हैं, उसमें सस्ता पड़ेगा, नये बीज अच्छे मिलें आपको और दस बातें। तो सहकारी संघ हम चाहते हैं हर गाँव में हो, बल्कि हम तो एक और बात भी चाहते हैं कि सहकारी संघ का काम खेती से भी बढ़ जाये लेकिन वह पीछे आये। जब आप समझ जायें, उसको स्वीकार करें तब आये, लेकिन बहुत बातें तो आप अब भी कर सकते हैं। ये सब बातें हैं।

देश बदल रहा है, देश नया हो रहा है। मुझे तो अच्छा नहीं लगता, मैं आपके पास आता हूँ और अब भी देखता हूँ, हमारे बच्चों को देखता हूँ, सुन्दर बच्चे होते हैं, उनकी देखभाल ठीक नहीं है, कपड़े ठीक नहीं हैं, मालूम नहीं उनको खाना ठीक मिलता है कि नहीं, घर रहने को ठीक है कि नहीं, स्कूल ठीक है कि नहीं। स्कूल तो बढ़ते जाते हैं, और बढ़ेंगे, लेकिन और तेज़ी से हमें तरक्की करनी चाहिए और होगी, लेकिन कोई हुक्म से नहीं होती, वो तो आप लोगों की सहायता से होगी, और उसके पीछे सीखना है, और परिश्रम करना है। सीखने के लिए जो यहाँ ग्राम भारती में बनेगा वह भी एक बड़ी चीज़ है आपके इस इलाक़े को सिखाने के लिए और नई दुनिया को एक आप झांक सकें, देखें और सीखें, उसमें ले जायें। इसीलिए ये अच्छा है और मुझे खुशी है कि ये स्मारक बनायें, तो ऐसा बने जिससे आप सब लोगों का लाभ हो।

आपको धन्यवाद।

जयहिन्द!

[Translation begins

Governor,[576] Sisters and Brothers,
I had come here a few years ago to visit the school in Jamunipur which has now become an inter college.[577] It has grown very slowly, for more than sixteen years have passed since then. It has not grown rapidly because there have been numerous obstacles in the way. But the people who have been running it have had to shoulder great burdens which they have somehow continued to do. Now it has been expanded into an inter college. A memorial to Pandit Motilal Nehru has been started in his centenary year in the form of Gram Bharati.

What am I to say about a memorial in my father's honour? I am naturally happy about it but what makes me happier still is the fact that it is being done to benefit the farmers of Allahabad and its other residents. Memorials are often built in the form of a big hall or some other building in big cities. I am happy that this memorial is in the rural area of Allahabad district and it will benefit the people directly. I am told that it will not be only a school but a polytechnic as well.

Now, what is a polytechnic? In schools, children are taught to read and write but in a polytechnic, the students are trained in new ways of working. If you look around, you will find that the world today belongs to machines. And all kinds of new implements and machines have been invented in the world. The countries of the West like England, United States and the Soviet Union have advanced very far and become extremely rich and powerful by taking advantage of the modern inventions. They have increased production enormously from land and industries. After all, wealth cannot drop from anywhere outside. It has to be produced by the hard work and effort of the people.

The people in the West have increased production enormously. They produce far more than we do from an acre of land and from their industries. Apart from the hard work that they put in, they use good implements and machines. They have mechanized farming. You may have heard of tractors which are of course being used in some places in our country also. But tractors can be used only in large farms. For the smaller land holdings, better ploughs can be used which will dig deeper and increase production. All of you are aware of all this. What can I tell you?

The world today belongs to new machines and inventions. Most of the people present here are farmers. Now the most urgent priority in India is to increase agricultural production. But that requires proper care and service to

576. See fn 574 in this section.
577. See fn 575 in this section.

the land. The farmers work extremely hard and yet fail to produce very much. It is essential to use better ploughs, fertilizers, etc., which you are gradually learning about. The most important thing is to use good implements and tools of agriculture. That does not mean that you should go in for expensive equipment like tractors, etc. You can get a good plough for sixty or seventy rupees which will immediately enable you to double the production. You as well as the country will benefit by that.

I would like to repeat that the most important problem before the country today is that agricultural production must increase so that the farmer as well as the country might become better off. We want to industrialize the country so that unemployment may decrease and the wealth of the country may increase. Whatever is produced in the country constitutes the wealth of the nation. The polytechnic that you are hoping to build here will train people in new types of work which will enable the villages to set up small industries. The farmers can also take advantage of this. If this happens in all the villages, the country will progress very fast. We are still very far from that goal because we do not even have schools everywhere yet.

We want that within the next three or four years, there may not be a single child in India who does not attend school. They must attend. Because we cannot progress without education. Education is no longer to equip people for government jobs but must help them to do their own chosen task better whether it is farming or carpentry or something else. Everyone must try to become better at their chosen task. So we want that all children must go to school. We want the adults also to be educated. But it is difficult even to make arrangements for the children. We want to extend the school-going age so that the bright ones can go in for higher education. We must encourage them to learn modern methods of working. We can teach them ourselves and also encourage them to learn from other countries. After completing their education, they should go back to their villages and teach others. This is how there can be progress. Production will increase and if small industries can come up side by side the country will benefit even more. Unemployment will become less and the people in the rural areas will become better-off. This is something for you to remember.

Why is our country so poor? Why are the countries of the West so wealthy? They were not always so. It is only during the last couple of hundred years that they have advanced so much because they took advantage of the latest scientific methods. What is science? It is the search for the truths hidden in nature. There are all kinds of sources of power hidden in nature which must be taken advantage of. You travel by train. How does it move? Does it do so by magic? It is pulled by an engine which is propelled by steam. It is no great matter. Everyone knows that boiling water produces steam. But a couple of hundred years ago, an intelligent man thought out how it could be utilized as a source of power. He tried to pass steam through a tube and succeeded in rotating a wheel with it. So the railway engine came to be invented. There is no great magic in it. All of you can see for yourselves what a great source of power steam can be. But a small thing like this has revolutionized the entire means of transport of the world. Now we can travel long distances in a day when it used to take months earlier. You can travel to Bombay, Calcutta or Delhi in a day by train. So there is nothing complicated about it. It was a question of discovering something which was already there and harnessing it to our needs.

Then came electricity. What is electricity? There is no magic in that too. People have always seen lightning in the sky which would sometimes strike. So people used to be afraid of it and worshipped it. Then one day an individual became curious about this phenomenon and tried to understand it by flying a kite with wires attached to it to see what happened. There was a flow of current through the wires. Then he discovered that friction produces electricity and so gradually, this hidden source of energy came to light, and now it is being used in so many different ways. It produces light and there are millions of small things it can be used for. But the real use of electricity is in industries. In other countries, electricity is being used in agriculture also. It is a source of power which can be used in various ways. Today I came to Allahabad from Delhi by plane which is another modern invention. Now train seems slow in comparison.

India has lagged behind in taking advantage of these new inventions. Other countries have become wealthy and powerful by harnessing these hidden sources of power. So they conquered Asia and began to rule over us. They built up vast empires by understanding the modern world. We must also learn all these things for otherwise we will become backward. Therefore the first thing we did after getting freedom was to establish science institutes and laboratories all over the country to train our young boys and girls to be scientists.

Now, yet another source of energy has made its appearance. Atomic energy has been used to make the atom bomb but it is also a great source of power which can be used for the good of mankind. After all, power can be used for good as well as bad purposes. A knife can be put to good use or to cut someone's throat. The fault is not of the knife. It is a question of what use it is put to. The atom bomb can raze whole cities to the ground. You may have heard that fifteen or sixteen years ago two big cities in Japan were turned into ruins by the atom bomb. That is bad. But if atomic energy is harnessed to good use, we can achieve great things. We have to do research in this area.

We have to keep in step with the modern times and get out of the old rut. We must hold on to the good things of the past and at the same time understand the modern world for otherwise we will become backward. We must educate

269

our children and enable them to go in for higher education, to colleges and polytechnics, etc., where they can learn new ways of working apart from reading and writing. Therefore, I am happy that there will be a polytechnic in this Gram Bharati which is to come up here. I hope that it will be a good one where your children will be trained. Then they will not have to go far to look for jobs. There will be hundreds of new avenues of employment open to them right here in Allahabad district which will benefit everyone. This is the only way for a country to progress.

If we continue to remain in an old rut and refuse to learn anything new, we cannot progress. It is a crime to close our eyes to the new developments all around us. We have closed our eyes to them for a long time and must now learn to keep them open and learn new things. We must learn new techniques of production, particularly in agriculture. You have been getting fertilizers which are very good for the soil. Now you have begun to understand the need for fertilizers. We are setting up huge fertilizer factories all over the country so that all of you may get as much as you need.

All this is going on. But the most important requirement is of trained human beings. We want that all our children must go to school and be educated and trained to serve the country, their families, themselves and their villages well. Big things are happening all over the country. You cannot get results right at the beginning just as the foundations of an edifice are not visible to the eye. We want to build an edifice where the entire population of forty-two crores in India can become well off and prosperous so that India is one of the leading countries in the world. It is a gigantic task which requires hard work, effort and the cooperation of the people. I want all of you to understand these things, for nothing can be achieved by doing a few jobs here and there and decreasing some revenues or something. What really counts is to build a new India by transforming the old one.

What is India? India is not merely mountains, rivers or land. India is her people, forty-two crores of men, women and children. They must all be educated and trained and above all understand that all of us are the citizens of one country. We are one, irrespective of our religion. We are Indians, whether we are Hindus, Muslims, Parsis, Christians, Buddhists, Jains or something else. Each one must adhere to his religious beliefs but the one great religion for all of us is service to the country. We are all part of a large family of Indians. You live in the district of Allahabad but the whole of India is your heritage, from the Himalayas to Kanyakumari and Rameshwaram in the south. It is the small, narrow-minded, foolish people who make distinctions and create problems. India belongs to all of us and every one of us must work for its progress. After all, freedom came to all of us, not to any particular religious sect or caste or a district. The whole of India became free and people belonging to all religions are equal shareholders in that.

Therefore, it is essential that we should be united because an ancient vice of ours has been disunity and the tendency to fight among ourselves. It is absolutely foolish. We fight in the name of religion, caste or something else forgetting that the days of such distinctions are now going. There will be greater equality among the people and those who are capable of hard work and are intelligent will go far. This is a fundamental thing which everyone must remember.

It is a great thing that Panchayati Raj has been established in your area, in Uttar Pradesh, in fact, in the whole country. I do not know how it is going on here or whether it has even been started. Even if it has, it may not yet have had time to put down roots but it will gradually do so. Through the panchayats, people will be able to hold the reins of power. There will be officials too who are good, trained people. But they will not hold the reins of power. It is the panchayats who will have the powers so that the people may learn to shoulder responsibilities. That is the only way to grow and acquire self-confidence.

Therefore, the Panchayati Raj system is a great thing; and hand in hand with it goes the system of sahakari sangh, which is called the cooperative system in English. The small farmer who is constantly losing out to the middleman can benefit a great deal by joining a cooperative society. It can help the members in buying and selling and the profits do not go into the pockets of middlemen. It can also help farmers in buying new implements, good seeds and fertilizers, etc. Therefore, we want that there should be a cooperative society in every village. In fact, we would like to go a step further and have cooperative farming. But that can come later when the people have understood and accepted the principle of cooperation. But a great deal can be done right now.

The country is changing very rapidly. But I do not like when I come here and see, even now, that our beautiful young children are not well looked after. They are not properly clothed or well fed. I am not sure whether they have proper houses to live in or schools for them. Schools are being opened. But we must progress faster. It cannot be done by orders from above. The people must cooperate and work hard. Training is an essential part of it and the Gram Bharati which will come up in this area will be a big centre for it. It will give you a glimpse of the new world and enable you to learn something. I am happy that a memorial like this is being built which will benefit everyone.

Thank you.

Jai Hind!

Translation ends]

181. In Allahabad: Public Meeting[578]

भाइयो और बहनो,

मैं बहुत परेशान हूँ कि आप लोग इत्ती तकलीफ़ में पानी में यहाँ आये और पानी में खड़े हैं। मैं तो उससे बचा हुआ हूँ, यहाँ साये में हूँ। मेरा तो ख़्याल था कि आजकल के मौसम में बड़ी सभा करनी उचित नहीं है, बारिश हो, लेकिन फिर भी हमारे दोस्तों ने कर दी। तो मुझे तो उसमें कुछ तकलीफ़ नहीं है लेकिन आप लोगों की तकलीफ़ देखकर परेशानी होती है, पानी में खड़े हैं।

मैं यहाँ पहली बार इस चुनाव के बाद आया हूँ इलाहाबाद। मेरा इरादा था फौरन आने का चुनाव के बाद, आप लोगों से मिलने का, कुछ देहात में घूमने का, और कुछ आप लोगों का धन्यवाद देने का, शुक्रिया, आपने या ज़िले वालों ने मुझे चुना। मुझे हर वक़्त यह ख़्याल होता है कि वो क्या-क्या आशाएँ रखकर चुनते हैं और कहाँ तक उनकी आशाएँ पूरी होती हैं। क्योंकि जो काम हमारे पास हैं, हमारे ऊपर हैं वो बहुत बड़ा है और कोई जादू से तो हल हो नहीं सकता था। फिर भी मेरा ख़्याल है, पिछले दस-बारह वर्ष में हमने काफी तरक्की की है और एक मज़बूत बुनियाद डाली है जिस पर एक नया भारत बन सके।

नया भारत बनने के माने क्या हैं? बहुत माने हैं, हमारी खेती अच्छी हो, हमारे कारख़ाने बनें, हमारे यहाँ स्कूल हरेक के लिए हों, कॉलेज हों काफी, पढ़ाई अच्छी हो, अस्पताल हों, सड़के हों। यह सब बातें तो ऊपर की हैं । लेकिन असल बात यह है कि नये आदमी बनें, नई औरतें बनें, जो नई दुनिया को समझें, जो कि असल में हिन्दुस्तानी हों, हम तो किसी की नकल नहीं किया चाहते, हाँ हम औरों से सीखना चाहते हैं, लेकिन अगर हमारी हिन्दुस्तानियत निकल जाये तो हम एक नकली लोग रह जायें। तो हमें हिन्दुस्तानियत तो रखनी है, हज़ारों बरस की है हमारी, लेकिन उसी के साथ हमें और दुनिया से सीखना है क्योंकि और दुनिया हमसे बढ़ गई है आगे, नई दुनिया विज्ञान की, साइंस की हुई है, मशीन की। बड़ी-बड़ी बातें होती हैं आप जानते हैं, लोग चाँद पर जाने की कोशिश कर रहे हैं और पहुँच भी जायेंगे और कहाँ-कहाँ तारों पर। अलग-अलग मुल्कों का होना यह भी कुछ एक किसी क़दर पुराने वक़्त की बात हो गई है जबकि आप एक जेट हवाई जहाज़ पर बैठकर चंद घंटों में कई मुल्कों के ऊपर से उड़ सकते हैं। तो सरहद वग़ैरह यह सब बातें कुछ पुरानी सी हो गई हैं, एक नई दुनिया इस कोशिश में है कि पैदा हो। हो कि न हो यह मुनहस्सर इस बात पर है कि कोई दुनिया में लड़ाई होकर आजकल की इस दुनिया को तबाह नहीं कर दे, क्योंकि दुनिया को साइंस से, और बातों से ताक़त इतनी आ गई है कि अब हरेक इंसान को ख़ुशहाल कर दे, थोड़ा वक़्त लगे लेकिन कर दे। अब पुराना ज़माना नहीं रहा जबकि देश की दौलत कम थी, पैदा कम होता था, उसका, काफी नहीं

---

578. Speech, 27 July 1962, at the K.P. College, Allahabad. NMML, AIR Tapes, TS No. 10368-10369, NM No. 1837-1838.

थी कि सभी को पहुँचे, तो कुछ थोड़े से अमीर हो जाते थे, बाज, ज्यादातर ग़रीब। अब यह हालत है कि हम दुनियाभर के आदमी ख़ुशहाल रह सकते हैं, इत्ती शक्ति है, प्रकृति की शक्तियों को पकड़कर उससे लाभ उठा सकते हैं। लेकिन इसके लिए ज़रा समय लगता है और आदमियों को सिखाना पड़ता है, कर सकें जो। उनके मन ज़रा बदलें, ख़ाली पुराने गढ़ों में न पड़े रहें। यह बड़ा काम है। सबमें बड़ा काम, बड़ी बात तो इसमें है शिक्षा। शिक्षा महज़ यह नहीं कि आप कोई इम्तहान पास कर लें। तो भी अच्छी है, लेकिन असल में हमारे मन पर और दुनिया का असर हो, उसको हम समझें, उसको यहाँ लायें।

आजकल हमारे यहाँ जो अच्छे-अच्छे वैज्ञानिक लोग हैं, साईंटिस्ट हैं, काफी अच्छे हैं हमारे नौजवान लड़के-लड़कियाँ दोनों, बहुत होनहार हैं, उन सबसे हमें बहुत उम्मीद है, अब बढ़ते जाते हैं, इंजीनियर अच्छे हैं, वो भी बढ़ते जाते हैं, वो बदलेंगे इस मुल्क को। तो मैं तो चाहूँ आपको ये पूरी कहानी सुनाऊँ कि क्या हो रहा है मुल्क में, क्या बदल रहा है मुल्क, क्या हम चाहते हैं बदले। मुश्किल यह है कि हमारा ध्यान आपस के झगड़ों में पड़ा रहा है, छोटी बातों में, परेशानियों में, उससे हम पूरी ताक़त नहीं लगा सकते देश के बढ़ाने में और आजकल ख़ासकर ख़तरे हैं हमारे देश के सामने। हमें अफ़सोस है कि हमारा रिश्ता पाकिस्तान से अब तक अच्छा नहीं हुआ और वहाँ से धमकियाँ होती हैं और लड़ाई का चर्चा और जेहाद वग़ैरह का। हालांकि हम चाहते हैं उनसे समझौता करना और उनसे दोस्ती करना। हाँ, दोस्ती करने के माने नहीं हैं कि हम कोई अपनी जरूरी बात को जिसमें हम अहमियत देते हैं छोड़ दें, वो तो नहीं है, ऐसी तो दोस्ती नहीं होती। लेकिन हम चाहते हैं कि पाकिस्तान और हिन्दुस्तान मिलजुल कर रहें, एक-दूसरे का फ़ायदा हो। एक दिन आयेगा जब यह होगा। और हमें इस बात को याद रखना है कि कोई ऐसी बात नहीं करनी जिससे झगड़ा-फ़साद बढ़े।

इधर और भी एक ख़तरनाक बात हो रही है हमारे सरहदों पर, तिब्बत और चीन की सरहद पर। चीन ने हमारे ज़मीन पर लद्दाख़ का क़ब्ज़ा किया है। पहाड़ी ज़मीन है, बड़े-बड़े ऊँचे पहाड़, बर्फ़िस्तान हैं, वहाँ लोग कोई रहते नहीं हैं लेकिन हमारी ज़मीन है, उनको कौन सा हक़ है उस पर क़ब्ज़ा करने का। यह बड़ी भारी बात हमारे सामने हो गई है, ख़तरे की बात और उसी के साथ हम उसको समझें तो हमें जोश दिलाने की बात और एक तरह से तेज़ी से हम आगे बढ़ें, अपनी ताक़त बढ़ायें। हम नहीं चाहते कि चीन से हिन्दुस्तान की लड़ाई हो, दोनों बड़े मुल्क हैं, अगर लड़ाई हो तो न हम जीतें उसमें, न वो जीतें, तबाही आये दोनों तरफ। बड़े मुल्क हैं, बहुत बड़े दोनों मुल्क हैं। तो वो एक अहम मसला है।

अब उसमें क्या हमें करना है? मैंने आपसे कहा हम नहीं लड़ाई किया चाहते, लेकिन कोई हम पर हमला करेगा, हमला करना चाहे तो हम उससे अलग तो नहीं हो सकते, हमने हिफ़ाज़त करनी है अपनी ज़मीन की। मेरा ख़्याल अब भी है कि हम इस मसले को हल कर सकते हैं, शांति से हल कर सकते हैं, लेकिन एक ही तरह से कर सकते हैं कि हम तगड़े रहें, मज़बूत रहें, जागते रहें हम, यह नहीं कि ख़ामोशी से हम इन बातों को हो जाने दें। और दो-ढाई बरस से हमारे ऊपर यह ख़तरा है, काफी बड़ा ख़तरा है और बिलफ़ेल

273

तो बेशुमार ख़तोकिताबत हुई हैं, हम बयान उनको देते हैं सख़्त चुस्त, वो अपना देते हैं और भी सख़्ती, इससे तो कोई हल होता नहीं है। लेकिन इस ज़माने में, पिछले दो बरस में हमने कोशिश की अपनी ताक़त बढ़ाने को उस मुक़ाम पर। यों तो हमारी ताक़त एक माने में काफ़ी है, लेकिन उस जगह, उन पहाड़ी इलाक़ों में हममें एक कमी थी कि हमारा वहाँ पहुँचना दुश्वार था, सड़कें नहीं थी, महीनों लगें लोगों के जाने में। लोग जायें वहाँ उनके खाने को कुछ नहीं है, वहाँ कोई दरख़्त नहीं होता इतने ऊँचे पहाड़ों पर, कोई चीज़ नहीं मिलती, न लकड़ी, न खाना, कोई चीज़ किसी क़िस्म की नहीं, सब ले जाना पड़े, और कैसे? हवाई जहाज़ से तो दिक़्क़त है, चीनियों को आसानी है क्योंकि दूसरी तरफ मैदान है, मैदान से वो मोटर लारी से वो ले आ सकते हैं, यह आसानी है उनको। तो हमें सड़कें बनानी जरूरी हो गई। हमने पिछले डेढ़-दो बरस में काफ़ी सड़कें पहाड़ों में बनाई हैं, उससे हमारी जगह ज्यादा मज़बूत हुई, लेकिन जित्ती हम बनाना चाहते हैं उत्ती सब नहीं बनी हैं, और बना रहे हैं तेज़ी से। ख़ाली बना भी सकते हैं साल में पाँच-छः महीने, सर्दियों में तो वहाँ किसी का भी रहना दुश्वार होता है, गर्मियों में भी मुश्किल है, सर्दियों में तो बिल्कुल नामुमकिन क़रीब-क़रीब हो जाता है, जब तक कि ख़ास एहतियात न हो। ये बड़े-बड़े सवाल हैं।

तो इस चीन और हिन्दुस्तान के मामले में मैं चाहता हूँ आप इसको मोटी तौर से समझ लें, तफ़्सील में। क्या हम करें, क्या शायद वो करें, मैं कह नहीं सकता, लेकिन मोटी बात यह है कि हमें अपने मुल्क की हिफ़ाज़त करनी है, रक्षा करनी है। जो हममें और उनमें झगड़ा हो रहा है, बहस है उसको हम हल किया चाहते हैं शांति से, लेकिन उसी के साथ हमें तैयार रहना है उसका मुक़ाबला करने के लिए। एक माने में कहा जा सकता है कि जित्ते हम ज्यादा तैयार होंगे, हो गये हैं, हमारे बहुत अड्डे हैं फ़ौज के वहाँ, उत्ता ही कुछ पिछले चन्द महीनों में, दो-तीन महीनों में चीनियों को कुछ फ़िक्र ज्यादा हुई कि हम ज्यादा ताक़तवर होते जाते हैं और उससे कुछ अन्देशा हुआ कि वो भी आगे बढ़ने की कोशिश करेंगे। एक जगह गोली भी चल गई है। हमारी राय में उन्होंने चलाई, वो कहते हैं हमारे लोगों ने चलाई है, उससे हमारे दो आदमी जख़्मी हो गये ज्यादा नहीं। उससे अन्देशा था कि कहीं और बढ़ न जाये यह बात, बढ़ जायेगी तो फिर बहुत बड़ी चीज़ हो जायेगी, हम तो नहीं चाहते बढ़े। मेरा ख़्याल यह है, हालांकि मैं कह नहीं सकता कि उनकी भी ख़ास इच्छा नहीं है कि बड़ी लड़ाई हो, रोकथाम वे करते हैं, क्योंकि कहीं-कहीं जहाँ वो हमला कर सकते थे उन्होंने नहीं किया। ख़ैर, ये पेचीदा बातें हैं। इन सब बातों के माने यह हैं कि हमें होशियार रहना है, हमें तैयार रहना है, हमें आपस के झगड़ों को मिटाना है, कम करना है, क्योंकि फ़ौज तो हमारी हिफ़ाज़त करेगी ही, हमारे हवाई जहाज़ हिफ़ाज़त करेंगे, लेकिन फिर भी असल में एक मुल्क की एकता और इत्तिहाद और मुल्क के काम और मेहनत से मुल्क की हिफ़ाज़त होती है।

फ़ौज क्या है? फ़ौज कैसे लड़ती है? उसके पीछे हज़ारों लाखों आदमी काम करते हैं उसको सामान देने के लिए, उसको खिलाने को, उसको हथियार देने को, तब उसकी ताक़त होती है, यानी मुल्क में जो काम होता है उससे मुल्क की ताक़त, फ़ौज की ताक़त होती

है। पुराने ज़माने गुज़र गये कि जब लड़ाइयाँ होती थी, थोड़ी सी फ़ौज गई तलवार लेकर लड़ने, लूटमार किया, अब बहुत इंतज़ाम की जरूरत है। इसलिए बहुत काफ़ी जरूरी बात है कि हम आपस की छोटी बातों को छोड़कर बड़ी बातों को सोचें और बड़ी बातों में यह जरूरी है कि मुल्क तेज़ी से मज़बूत हो, तरक्की करे।

एक माने में हमारी पंचवर्षीय योजना है। पंचवर्षीय योजना में बहुत सारी बातें उसमें करनी हैं लेकिन उसके माने आख़िर में यही हैं कि मुल्क एक ख़ुशहाल हो और मज़बूत हो। ख़ुशहाल और मज़बूती की ताक़त निकलती है जो फ़ौज में जाती है, हवाई जहाज़ों में और जगह। अगर फ़ाक़ेमस्त मुल्क है तो ख़ाली फ़ौज उसकी रक्षा नहीं कर सकती, यह तो एक छोटी-मोटी बातें कर सकती है उसमें। फ़ौज के पीछे ताक़त होनी चाहिए एक मुल्क की और बहुत दलबन्दी न हो, हमारे यहाँ दलबन्दी की आदत है, मुझे अफ़सोस होता है। इलेक्शन होते हैं लोग झगड़ा करते हैं उसमें, ग़लत बातें कहते हैं, झूठ बातें कहते हैं। मेरे इलेक्शन में मैंने जो पर्चे देखे, मुझे बहुत हैरत हुई। एक पर्चा बहुत निकाला गया, बहुत अर्से से कहा जाता है कि मेरे ऊपर पच्चीस हज़ार रुपये रोज़ ख़र्च होते हैं। मेरे सर-पैर कोई समझ में नहीं आया कि कहाँ चले जाते हैं पच्चीस हज़ार, कौन ख़र्चता है, कैसे होते हैं, मुझे जो तनख़्वाह मिलती है उसको टैक्स निकालकर मुझे सौलह सौ रुपये मिलते हैं महीने में, रोज़ नहीं। और मेरी कुछ आमदनी है, कुछ किताबें लिखी हैं उसकी रॉयल्टी की। ज़ाहिर है मुझे कोई फ़िक्र नहीं, कुछ कम हो तो कम ख़र्च कर दिया जाये, लेकिन इस क़िस्म की ग़लत बातें, झूठ बातें, अब मैं कहाँ किस-किस को समझाता फिरूँ कि पच्चीस हज़ार रुपये कहाँ से आते हैं। शायद पच्चीस हज़ार रुपयों में, फ़ौज के दाम हों, पुलिस का ख़र्चा हो, जाने क्या-क्या हो।[579]

अब मैं नहीं जानता क्या है, वो तो ख़ैर छोटी बात है। मैंने और बातें सुनी, अजीब-अजीब बातें, ग़लत बातें जो कही जाती हैं, मेरे निस्बत नहीं लेकिन और मुझे इस बात का ख़ास रंज हुआ कि हमारे यहाँ पंचायती राज हो रहा है। पंचायती राज को मैं बहुत अहमियत देता हूँ क्योंकि वो इंसान को बनायेगा, इंसान को तगड़ा करेगा, हमारे किसान जो सबमें बेचारे ग़रीब लोग हैं उनको मज़बूत करेगा, उनको सिखायेगा कैसे काम करें। अच्छा काम करें क्योंकि हमारे किसान बहुत अच्छा काम करते हैं लेकिन उन्हें फ़ायदा काफ़ी नहीं होता, क्योंकि आजकल की दुनिया के तरीक़ों को सीखे नहीं हैं वो लोग — हल ज्यादा अच्छा करें, गहरा खोदे, उससे ज्यादा पैदा होगा, फ़र्टिलाइज़र डालें, खाद डालें, बीज अच्छे चुनकर डालें, उसका इंतज़ाम होता है, लेकिन असल में किसान ही कर सकता है। मैंने अभी एक जगह मैं कुछ बोल रहा था, मैं बता रहा था उन्हें कुछ जापान का। जापान में जो ज़मींदारी वग़ैरह थी वो सब बन्द कर दी गई, आज नहीं दस-बारह बरस हुए और शायद ज्यादा से ज्यादा ज़मीन एक के पास पंद्रह एकड़ रह सकती है। यहाँ शायद मुझे ठीक याद नहीं, बीस एकड़ रखी है, हालांकि आम लोगों के पास तो एक एकड़, दो एकड़, तीन एकड़ से

---

579. See also Nehru's letters to Kishen Pattnayak on this matter, in the subsection Administration in this section.

275

ज्यादा नहीं है। आमतौर से लोगों के पास वहाँ पाँच-छः एकड़ से ज्यादा नहीं है। पाँच-छः एकड़ में वो इत्ता कमाते हैं कि ख़ुशहाल हैं, उनके यहाँ रेडियो, उनके यहाँ टेलीविज़न, क्या-क्या किसानों के यहाँ रखा है, मैं तो हैरान हुआ देखके, क्यों? क्योंकि नये तरीके वो इस्तेमाल करते हैं और मेहनत करते हैं, बड़े मेहनती हैं और मिलकर रहते हैं। तो जापान ने अपने को बढ़ाया एक तो यों ही एक पुराने ज़माने से नये ज़माने में ले आया, पिछले सदी से लेकर और इस पुरानी बड़ी लड़ाई में हारकर तबाह हो गया था, कैसे उसने दस-बारह बरस में अपने को खड़ा कर लिया, यह एक आश्चर्य की बात है। और ख़ामख़्वाह के लिए इनकी क़दर होती है, क़दर होने के क़ाबिल बात है, क्यों? उन्होंने अच्छी बुनियाद डाली, पढ़ाई की डाली, सब मिलकर यहाँ अच्छी पढ़ाई होती है, स्कूल में सब जाते हैं, पढ़ते हैं अच्छा, फिर कॉलेज वग़ैरह, फिर इंजीनियरिंग वग़ैरह काफी सिखाते हैं, कारख़ाने बहुत बने हैं, लेकिन सबमें ज्यादा खेती अच्छी करते हैं वो और खेती से पैदा करते हैं। आख़िर जो दौलत हमारे पास है वह कोई आसमान से तो आती नहीं है, न कोई बहुत ज्यादा बाहर से आती है, कुछ बाहर से मदद करने को आती है, कुछ हम क़र्ज़ा लेते हैं और मुल्कों से। हम उनके शुक्रगुज़ार हैं कि क़र्ज़ा हमें देते हैं, ठीक है लेकिन आख़िर में तो हमें बोझा उठाना है, बयालीस करोड़ आदमियों को कौन उठाये, कौन बाहर वाला, किसी की ताक़त है उठाये। वो एक ही तरह से कि हम उनको तैयार करें, खेती सबसे अव्वल बात, खेती अच्छी करें और कारख़ाने बनायें। बड़े-बड़े का तो आप नाम सुनते हैं, हम चाहते हैं छोटे-छोटे गाँव में हों, बिजली आये।

अब मुश्किल यह है इन सब बातों में कि जित्ता हम करें, जो-जो करें उसमें रुपया लगता है और ग़रीब मुल्क की निशानी है कि उसके पास रुपया नहीं है, नहीं तो ग़रीब क्यों हो। इसलिए हम एक पेंच में पड़ जाते हैं, एक चक्कर में कि कैसे हम, कहाँ से हम रुपया लायें उसमें लगाने के लिए, ताकि हमारी आमदनी ज्यादा हो, ताकि लोग ख़ुशहाल हों। अगर हम यह करें जैसे कुछ लोग यहाँ कहते हैं कि लगान माफ कर दो, लगान माफ कर दो जिनके पास बहुत कम ज़मीन है, पाँच एकड़ से कम है उनका माफ कर दो। पाँच एकड़ से कम का हम माफ कर दें तो कुछ थोड़ा सा उनको साल-दो साल आराम हो जाये, लेकिन फिर बाद में क्या हो, तकलीफ़ें बढ़ें क्योंकि मुल्क की तरक्की बिल्कुल बन्द हो जाये। मुश्किल यह है कि हमारी आमदनी जो लगान से है काफी बड़ी है, उसी से हम मुल्क की तरक्की का काम करते हैं, उसी से हम स्कूल चलायें। अब हमारा इरादा है कि लगान की आमदनी को हम पंचायतों को दे दें अधिकतर, उससे वो सड़कें बनायें, स्कूल बनायें, अस्पताल बनायें, उन्हीं पर ख़र्चें, अपने ऊपर ख़र्चें, लेकिन बग़ैर इसके किये, पढ़ाई के और छोटे-छोटे कारख़ाने खोलने के और सहकारी संघ बनाने के, हम आगे नहीं बढ़ते, वहीं के वहीं ग़रीब, फ़ाक़ेमस्त रहते हैं क़ौम। तो कोशिश करनी है हमें, पूरी कोशिश करनी है, किसी तरह अपना पेट ज़रा कसकर भी हम रुपया निकालें इन बातों में ख़र्चने को जिससे हमें फ़ायदा होता है, गाँव वालों का फ़ायदा होता है, ये पेंच हैं। अगर हमें बाहर से रुपया मिले तो कुछ बोझा हम पर कम होता है चाहे क़र्ज़ा ही क्यों न मिले। हालांकि क़र्ज़े को अदा करने का बड़ा बोझा हो जाता है और हमने बड़े क़र्ज़े लिये हैं, लेकिन फिर

276

भी मुल्क तरक़्क़ी करेगा, हम अदा करेंगे, लेकिन कितना ही क़र्ज़ा मिले, आख़िर में बोझा अपने ऊपर पड़ता है, इत्ता बड़ा मुल्क किसी और के सहारे नहीं ठहर सकता, न हमारी शान के माफ़िक़ है उसको करना। तो ये करना है।

अब हम क़रीब-क़रीब इस बारह बरस के काम के बाद एक चौराहे पर पहुँचे हैं पेचीदा, किस तरफ हम जायें। एक तरफ तो इसलिए कि इस काम को देखकर कि मुश्किल है कि घबरा जायें, हम वहीं के वहीं अटक जायें या ग़लत रास्ते पर जायें, जिससे हो सकता है कि कुछ हमें फ़ायदा बिलफेल हो जाये, कुछ आराम मिल जाये, अच्छी बात है, लेकिन उसी के साथ आइन्दा तरक़्क़ी हमारी रुक जाती है। किसी मुल्क ने तरक़्क़ी नहीं की बग़ैर रुपया जमा किये और उसको इन्वेस्ट किये, लगाने के लिए बड़े कामों में जिससे आइन्दा तरक़्क़ी हो। एक अमीर आदमी अमीर कैसे हो जाता है? उसके पास रुपया ज्यादा होता है, रुपया बचता है, वो लगाता है और कामों में, उससे और बड़ी आमदनी होती है। उसी तरह से एक देश भी कैसे बढ़ता है? वो रुपया बचाकर वो लगाये और कामों में जिससे उसकी आमदनी हो, लोग ख़ुशहाल हों। हर मुल्क को करना पड़ा है।

अब कुछ दिन हुए, एक डेढ़ सौ वर्ष हुए, एक बड़ा इंक़लाब दुनिया में हुआ था। वो इंक़लाब इंडस्ट्रियल रेवोल्यूशन कहलाता है यानी कारोबार की एक क्रांति, नये तरीके निकलने काम करने के, खेती करने के, कारख़ाने बनाने के, मशीन चलाने के और उसमें समझदार लोगों ने प्रकृति, फ़ितरत की बातें सीखीं। उन्होंने सीखा, स्टीम इंजिन बनाया। कैसे बनाया, क्या उसमें ख़ूबी है? पानी की भाप से इंजिन चलता है, उससे रेलगाड़ी चलती है, उससे बड़ी-बड़ी मशीन चलती हैं, बिजली उन्होंने देखी। बिजली भी एक चीज़ है, मामूली चीज़ है, हरेक आदमी जानता है, लेकिन बिजली को पैदा करके और पकड़कर उन्होंने उससे बड़े-बड़े कारख़ाने चलाये, ये सब नई बातें सीखीं, पिछले सौ बरस में और हज़ार बातें सीखीं आप जानते हैं। अब इन्हीं ताक़तों से एटम की ताक़त आई, बहुत बड़ी है, उसको बुरा इस्तेमाल करें तो मुल्क क्या सारी दुनिया तबाह हो जाये, अच्छा करें तो दुनिया उठ जाये। हम अजीब मौक़े पर पैदा हुए हैं जब एक करवट ले रही है दुनिया। या तो करवट लेने में अपने को तबाह कर देगी, लड़ाई-झगड़ा करके या ख़ुशहाल सारी दुनिया हो जायेगी, ये हाल है। और तेज़ी से होगी, हालांकि कित्ती ही तेज़ी से हो, एक-दो बरस में तो नहीं होती। मेरा ख़्याल यह है कि हमारे दस-बारह बरस गुज़रे, हमने अच्छी बुनियाद डाली और एक और दस बरस में हम इस करवट को ले जायेंगे। उसके बाद सारी दुनिया ख़ुशहाल नहीं होगी, लेकिन हम ख़ुशहाली के रास्ते पर तेज़ी से चलेंगे, हमारे हाथ में बागडोर होगी, हमारे हाथ में दौलत पैदा होगी काफी जिसको हम लगा सकें।

दस बरस मैंने कहा। दस बरस या पाँच भी, हमें ज़रा मुश्किलें उठानी हैं इसमें कोई शक नहीं, क्योंकि इस करवट लेने में ज़रा दिक़्क़तें होती हैं क़ौम की, और क़ौम को सीखना पड़ता है, क़ौम को दिमाग़ अपना बदलना पड़ता है, पुराने गढ़ों से निकालकर, क्योंकि आदमी की मेहनत से ही देश बढ़ता है, जैसे आदमी हो वैसा देश हो, आदमी या औरत। कोई जादू तो है नहीं कि उससे हो जाये, न कोई तारों की तरफ देखकर हम इसको कर

सकते हैं, तारों की तरफ आजकल लोग देख रहे हैं कि वहाँ पहुँचेंगे हम हवाई जहाज़ पर या किसी न किसी तरह से। ये हालत है दुनिया की।

तो ये बड़े-बड़े सवाल हमारे सामने हैं और इसीलिए हम पंचवर्षीय योजना बनाते हैं, यह नहीं ख़ाली कि हम कहीं सड़क बना दें, कहीं अस्पताल, कहीं स्कूल, कहीं कुछ और चीज़ें। सब जरूरी हैं और बनती हैं वो, बननी चाहियें, लेकिन असल बात यह है किसी तरह से हम हिन्दुस्तान की गाड़ी को चलायें जिससे एक दिमाग़ नया बने, हिन्दुस्तान का, किसानों का, औरों का। बन रहा है। हमने पंचायती राज उनको दिया, उनके ऊपर ज़िम्मेदारी हुई, बड़ी ज़िम्मेदारी चलाने की, अधिकार उनका हुआ। बहुत कुछ अधिकार जो बड़े अफ़सर हैं उनका कम हुआ, किसानों का हो गया, पंचों का, बड़ी भारी बात है। मुमकिन है ग़लती करें, कर रहे हैं ग़लतियाँ, लेकिन फिर भी वो ज़िम्मेदारी को लेकर, वो बढ़ते हैं। ज़िम्मेदारी से आदमी बढ़ता है, अपने ऊपर भरोसा होने लगता है, ख़ाली दरख़्वास्तें नहीं देता औरों को जाकर। अब मेरे पास पंच आयें, मुझसे कहें कि यह करा दो, वो करा दो, मेरा जवाब सीधा होता है कि तुम्हें अधिकार है तुम करो जाकर। सब बातें नहीं कर सकते लेकिन बहुत बातें कर सकते हैं। इसलिए अब मैं किसी पंचायतों में जाता हूँ अक्सर राजस्थान में, और जगह, तो वहाँ पंच जमा होते हैं, उनकी बातें दूसरे तरह की होती हैं, शिकायतें नहीं होती। हालांकि शिकायत करने की बहुत बातें हैं, बल्कि वो सोचते हैं कि हम क्या करें, कैसे हम अपनी तरक्की करें, इसपे सलाह लेते हैं। इसी से आप देख सकते हैं उनके दिमाग़ कैसे बदल रहे हैं।

हमारे नौजवान हैं, उनको सोचना चाहिए, आजकल काफी दिक्कतें उनके सामने हैं लेकिन सोचना चाहिए कि किस ज़माने में वो पैदा हुए हैं, आजकल रहते हैं, आजकल पढ़ते हैं, आजकल सीखते हैं, अब ज़माना बदल रहा है, अब ज़माना हज़ार रास्ते खोल रहा है उनके बढ़ने के लिए। अब चाहे दिक्कतें हों, जिते ज्यादा वो सीखेंगे, उते ही ज्यादा आगे जायेंगे, मुल्क को ले जायेंगे। कहा जाता है कि मुल्क में कोई तख़्त ख़ाली नहीं रहता, कोई न कोई उस पर बैठ ही जाता है अगर ख़ाली हो जाये तो। तो एक तख़्त नहीं, हिन्दुस्तान में हज़ार तख़्त ख़ाली होने वाले हैं, होते जाते हैं और हज़ार रास्ते निकल रहे हैं। हाँ, जरा शुरु में पहुँचने में दिक्कतें हैं, परेशानियाँ हैं, कठिनाई है। तो उस कठिनाई को हम दूर नहीं कर सकते हाय-हाय करके। मेहनत करके और अपने को सिखाना है। मैं तो चाहता हूँ आप लोग कुछ हमारी पंचवर्षीय योजना को पढ़ें, सीखें, देखें क्या नक्शा है। यह तो आसान बात है, बतायें आपको क्या-क्या करना है और मुल्क को क्या करना है। लेकिन उसका बताना और प्लान बनाना एक बात है और करना दूसरी बात है, काफी कठिन बात है। क्योंकि उसमें सीखना है, पढ़ना है, परिश्रम उठाना है, जरा पेटी ज्यादा कसनी है, तकलीफ़ें उठानी हैं, फिर हम उस पार पहुँचते हैं।

यह ज़माना हमारा है। मेरा ख़्याल है और मुझे यक़ीन है कि जब इस ज़माने में हल्के-हल्के निकलेंगे और इन दस बरस बाद काफी तौर से हम आगे बढ़ जायेंगे, और बढ़ने की कूवत हममें होगी। ये बात मैं चाहता हूँ आप समझें, पढ़के समझें उसको या आपस में बहस करके और समझकर फिर राय क़ायम करें। क्योंकि आपमें राय क़ायम करने का

278

मादूदा होना चाहिए, यह नहीं जो मैंने कहा मेरी बात मान ली, आपको फ़ैसला करना है। मैं आज का हूँ, कल का हूँ, परसों का हूँ, अभी से लोग परेशान हो गये कि मैं बहुत दिन से प्रधानमंत्री हूँ। हमेशा तो ख़ैर मैं नहीं रहूँगा, आप में से कोई न कोई होगा प्रधानमंत्री। मैंने कहा था कहीं, मालूम नहीं कहाँ, कि हिन्दुस्तान का एक-एक बच्चा, लड़का और लड़की को रास्ता साफ है अगर वो तेज़ हो काफी, मेहनत करे, काम करे, सीखे प्रधानमंत्री, राष्ट्रपति होने का, आप सभी को रास्ता साफ है। अगर आप तैयार हों उस मेहनत करने को, परिश्रम करने को, त्याग करने को और आप वहाँ पहुँचें। ख़ैर, प्रधानमंत्री तो हिन्दुस्तान का एक होगा, लेकिन हज़ारों जगह ख़ाली हैं। हमारी फ़ौज है, एक ज़माना था सारे अंग्रेज़ अफ़सर थे, अब हज़ारों हिन्दुस्तानी अफ़सर हैं ऊँचे से ऊँचे। हमारी फॉरिन सर्विस है, दूत भेजते हैं, राजदूत हम और जगह, इसमें हज़ारों आदमी हैं अच्छे से अच्छे चुने हुए, लड़के और लड़कियाँ हैं, जाते हैं, उनके साथ और हैं, जाते हैं काम करने। हमारे यहाँ तिजारत बढ़ रही है, इंजीनियर कित्ते बढ़ रहे हैं, पाँच-छः बरस में हमने एक मर्दुमशुमारी की थी, एक इंजीनियर की गिनती, उस वक़्त एक लाख थे। अब मेरा ख़्याल है कि कोई सवा लाख या डेढ़ लाख हो गये हैं, फिर भी कम पड़ रहे हैं क्योंकि काम इत्ता हो रहा है। मुश्किल यह है कि हमारी तालीम का सिलसिला जो है, बाज़ अच्छा है, कुछ न कुछ सीखते ही हैं लेकिन नया हिन्दुस्तान जो बन रहा है उसमें एकदम से चस्पा नहीं होता। इंजीनियर बन रहे हैं, साइंटिस्ट बन रहे हैं वग़ैरह, ख़ाली तालीम में डिग्री ले लेने से काफी नहीं होता। डिग्री लेने में आपको मुमकिन है नौकरी मिल जाये लेकिन मैं तो चाहता हूँ आप ख़ुद, आपमें मादूदा हो काम करने का, चलाने का। चाहे आप, चाहे आप इंजीनियरिंग डिग्री हो, चाहे साइंटिस्ट हो, ख़ुद करें। आप देख सकते हैं जहाँ यह है मादूदा वहाँ तेज़ी से तरक्की हो रही है।

पंजाब को आप लें, पंजाब में, जैसे सब सूबों में अच्छाई है, ख़राबी है, लेकिन पंजाब के लोगों में, चाहे वो हिन्दू हों या सिक्ख हों या मुसलमान हों, काश्त बहुत अच्छी करते हैं, बहुत मेहनती हैं और हाथ-पैर चला सकते हैं, अच्छे मैकेनिक्स हैं, मशीन को समझते हैं, सारे हिन्दुस्तान में जहाँ जाइये वहाँ टैक्सी पंजाबी चलाते हैं, सिक्ख चलाते हैं। कहीं भी हम बड़ा कारख़ाना खोलें वहाँ इंजीनियर पंजाब से आते हैं। क्या बात है और असल बात यह है पंजाब में ख़ास पिछले ज़माने में, पिछले दस-बाहर बरस में एक हज़ारों कारख़ाने छोटे-छोटे खुले हैं, बड़े नहीं हैं जिनका आप पढ़ते हैं और सरकार की तरफ से नहीं, ख़ुद लोगों ने खोले हैं क्योंकि उनमें मादूदा था। पंजाब के लोग आये कुछ उत्तर प्रदेश में उधर ग़ाज़ियाबाद वग़ैरह की तरफ, ग़ाज़ियाबाद को जगा दिया उन्होंने, पचासों छोटे-छोटे कारख़ाने हैं, ख़ुशहाल हो गई जगह। यह तो इंसान में मादूदा होना चाहिए। हम लोगों में भी मादूदा है, ख़ाली एक तो मौक़ा देना चाहिए सीखने का और दूसरे एक मेहनत करने का और उस पर हावी होने का मादूदा होना चाहिए।

रूस एक ख़ुशहाल मुल्क हो गया है। ज़रा आप रूस की तारीख़ देखें, इंक़लाब के बाद बीस बरस तक कित्ती तकलीफ़ उन्होंने उठाई हैं, कित्ती फ़ाक़ेमस्ती की, मुसीबतें झेलीं, लेकिन वो करते गये और ख़ुशहाल हो गये, एक नई समाज बनाई, अच्छी समाज बनाई। अब हम बिल्कुल उस तरीके से नहीं चलते लेकिन बहुत कुछ हमें चलना है, यह बात

279

आप याद रखिये। रूस और अमरीका इस वक़्त दुनिया के मैदान में दो पहलवान खड़े हैं एक-दूसरे का मुक़ाबला करने। अगर बदक़िस्मती से उनमें लड़ाई हुई तो दोनों में इतनी ताक़त है कि महज़ अपने को नहीं तबाह करेंगे, दुनिया को तबाह कर देंगे, कोई बचेगा नहीं, लेकिन दोनों में यह भी ताक़त है अपने देश को ख़ुशहाल करते जायें। लेकिन एक बात मैं आपको बताऊँ दोनों में मिलती हुई क्या बात है, वो लड़ने को बहुत तैयार हैं, लेकिन दोनों में आजकल के ज़माने की समझ है। आजकल के ज़माने में यह मशीन का ज़माना है, विद्या का ज़माना है, साइंस का ज़माना है, दोनों समझते हैं, दोनों उसकी पूजा करते हैं और दोनों ने इसीलिए तरक्की पाई है इसमें कि उन्होंने इसकी तरक्की की है। यह कम्युनिज़्म और साम्यवाद वग़ैरह ये अलग चीज़ है, पूँजीवाद वग़ैरह वो अलग चीज़ है, उस पर बहस करें वग़ैरह, जो चाहें, लेकिन कोई भी बात आप करें उसके पीछे ये आजकल की बात है साइंस की और टेक्नोलोजी की और मशीन की, इससे मुल्क बढ़े हैं।

जो कुछ हमने तरक्की की है इस पिछले ज़माने में वो यही है। हमने साइंस में काफी तरक्की की है, हमारे लेबोरेट्रीज़ सब जगह फैले हैं, अच्छे लोग सीख रहे हैं, अच्छी-अच्छी बातें निकाल रहे हैं और हमारे बड़े कारख़ाने बन रहे हैं। और पावर की जरूरत है, शक्ति की। शक्ति कहाँ की है आजकल? शक्ति होती है कोयला जलाने से, पानी गरम करने से शक्ति होती है। दूसरी शक्ति है बिजली की, बड़ी भारी शक्ति है। बिजली कैसे पैदा होती है? बिजली पैदा होती है रगड़ से बाज़ चीज़ों की। रगड़ कैसे हो? पहिये चलाये जाते हैं, बड़े-बड़े, आप सुनते हैं नदियों की योजनाएँ हैं, क्या हैं वो? बड़ी नदी को पकड़कर उससे पानी गिराते हैं ज़ोर से और गिरते हुए पानी से पहिये चलाते हैं, पहिये ज़ोर से चलते हैं, बड़े-बड़े पहिये, और उनकी रगड़ लगती है, रगड़ से बिजली पैदा होती है बहुत, हज़ारों किलोवाट, लाखों, और बिजली की तार से हम ले जाते हैं, उससे काम लेते हैं। बिजली तो एक बड़ी भारी सेवक है आपकी सबकी, सब शक्तियों की सेवक है। जैसे पुराने ज़माने में कहा जाता है अलिफ़-लैला के बड़े-बड़े जिन्न होते थे, उन जिन्नों से बड़े जिन्न तो आजकल की प्रकृति की शक्तियाँ हैं, जो हमारे पास हैं। तो उसको पैदा करना है और उसको समझना है, कर रहे हैं हम, और करना है, इस दुनिया को समझना है लोगों को, किसान को समझना है। मेरा मतलब नहीं किसान कोई बड़ा वैज्ञानिक हो जाये, बड़ा इंजीनियर हो, हालांकि किसानों के बच्चे होंगे वैज्ञानिक भी, इंजीनियर भी, मौक़ा मिलेगा उन्हें, लेकिन उनको भी कुछ समझना है दुनिया क्या चीज़ है। ख़ाली एक पुराने गढ़े में रहकर काम नहीं चलता।

यह बात मैं चाहता हूँ आप समझें जो आप पढ़ते हैं, नौजवान हैं उनको मौक़ा मिलता है, सीखें, नया दिमाग़ बनायें और लोगों को भी कुछ न कुछ मौक़ा मिलता ही है नई दुनिया में, कुछ न कुछ तो बदलते ही जाते हैं। यह है दुनिया। और दुनिया इस तेज़ी से बदल रही है कि जैसे मैंने आपसे कहा अब आप देखिये यह स्पेस में सैंकड़ों मील दुनिया से लोग जाने लगे हैं। लोग कहते हैं कि वो जायेंगे, चाँद तक जायेंगे, तारों तक जायेंगे, कभी न कभी जायेंगे जरूर, बढ़ते जाते हैं। यह बातें हैं। अभी कुछ दिन हुए आपने पढ़ा होगा अमरीका में एक सैटेलाइट निकला, एक चीज़ जो दुनिया के चारों तरफ घूमता है, उसके

ज़रिये से उन्होंने टेलीविज़न बहुत जगह कराये।[580] ये क्या-क्या बातें हैं, क्या-क्या हो रहा है, तरक्की हो रही है, हम भी कर सकते हैं, हमारे अच्छे साइंटिस्ट हैं, करेंगे, तरक्की कर रहे हैं, लेकिन मैं हवा चाहता हूँ विज्ञान की फैले।

मैं आपसे पंचायतों का कह रहा था। हमने बड़ी बात की पंचायतों को अधिकार दिया। बहुत लोग कहते थे भई वो ख़राब करेंगे ये, जो मुझे भरोसा है अपने लोगों पर, लेकिन एक बात से रंज हुआ कि पंचायतों में चुनाव होते हैं तो वो लड़ाई बहुत लड़ने लगते हैं और यहाँ तक कि कभी-कभी मारपीट हुई, कभी-कभी क़त्ल तक हो गये जो चुने गये। यह बात तो बुरी बात है। इस तरह से मुल्क कहाँ बढ़े अगर एक-दूसरे को हम क़त्ल करें, मारपीट करें अगर वो चुना गया हम नहीं चुने गये। कभी-कभी हमारे और जगह भी, और चुनावों में भी बहुत बहस होती है—जम्हूरियत है, प्रजातंत्र है, चुनाव से हम चलाना चाहते हैं, क्योंकि अच्छी चीज़ है वो। हम नहीं चाहते बादशाह हो, नवाब हो वग़ैरह। मुल्क में हम नहीं चाहते कि अफ़सरी राज हो, बड़े-बड़े अफ़सर हों। अफ़सर बहुत जरूरी चीज़ है, क्योंकि अफ़सर सीखे हुए होते हैं, ट्रेन्ड होते हैं, वो सलाह दे सकते हैं, काम कर सकते हैं हुकूमत के इंतज़ाम में, और कामों में भी। लेकिन मैं तो चाहता हूँ कि हमारे यहाँ एक-एक किसान, एक-एक लड़का, एक-एक लड़की, इन बातों को समझें, जानें और कर सकें। अपने हल्के में करें, गाँव में करें, तहसील में करें, ज़िले में करें, सूबे में करें, फिर हिन्दुस्तान भर में करें, लेकिन कुछ न कुछ ऐसे फैले, उनमें मादूदा हो। यह नहीं कि एक तरफ अफ़सर हों हाकिम और दूसरी तरफ जिन पर हुकूमत करते हैं वो हाथ फैलाये बैठे हैं, यह नहीं। एक नक़्शे को आप लाइये, कैसे हमें करना है और उसके लिए हमें तैयार होना है, औरों को तैयार करना है, इज़्ज़त करनी है हमें एक-एक किसान की, उसके काम की, यह नहीं कि हम एक दफ़्तरी काम करते हैं इसलिए हम ऊँचे हैं। किसान के बग़ैर दुनिया नहीं चल सकती है और किसान भी, एक दिन आयेगा जब वो बहुत कुछ मशीन से काम करेगा।

तो इस तरह की दुनिया हम चाहते हैं। इस तरह की दुनिया बन रही है। जिन देशों ने इसमें तरक्की की है वो आगे काफी बढ़ गये हैं, ख़ुशहाल हुए हैं, और मज़बूत हुए हैं। ख़ाली एक कमी उनमें है, वो लड़ाकू बहुत हैं और डर रहता है जाने कब लड़ जायें, भिड़ जायें, अपने को तबाह करें, औरों को तबाह करें। इसीलिए विनोबा जी ने कहा है, आपने सुना होगा, कि आजकल के ज़माने में बजाय पुराने ढंग के मज़हब और पुराने ढंग की सियासत, राजनीति के, आजकल का ज़माना साइंस का ज़माना है, बुद्धि का ज़माना है। दो

---

580. Telstar 1, a communication satellite launched on 10 July 1962, relayed through space the first television pictures, telephone calls, and telegraph images.

चीज़ों की जरूरत है, साइंस की और स्पिरिचुऐलिटी की।[581] स्पिरिचुऐलिटी के माने बताने कठिन हैं, आध्यात्मिक विद्या जो कुछ कहिये। जो मज़हब की नहीं ऊपरी बातें ख़ाली, टीका लगा लेना, पूजा करना, पूजा करना अच्छा है अगर दिल से कोई करे। कोई नमाज़ पढ़े, पूजा करे, एक दिल की बात है, लेकिन स्पिरिचुऐलिटी एक अन्दर की चीज़ है, जो सब मज़हबों में एक है। वो इसलिए उन्होंने ज़ोर दिया कि अगर साइंस बढ़ती जाती है, इंसान की ताक़त बढ़ती जाती है बग़ैर उसकी रोकथाम किये, बग़ैर उसमें स्पिरिचुऐलिटी, शराफ़त हो, तो वो तबाह कर देगी दुनिया को, और इस वक़्त दुनिया को यह चुनना है कि वह तबाह होगी या बढ़कर बहुत ऊँची हो जायेगी।

ये दोनों बातें हमें सीखनी हैं और हमें बरदाश्त करनी है, पड़ोसी की बरदाश्त, दूसरे आदमी की बरदाश्त। चुनाव में लड़ते हैं, और भी लड़ते हैं। हरेक आदमी को हम अधिकार देना चाहते हैं, जैसे चाहे रहे, जो उसका धर्म-मज़हब हो रहे। कोई हम अपन धर्म को ज़बरदस्ती उस पर करें, वो ग़लत बात है। कोई भी बात, चाहे हम सियासत में ज़बरदस्ती करें, धर्म के मामले में, ग़लत बात है। अपने-अपने उसूलों पर चलें, लेकिन उसूल हों बरदाश्त करने के, सहन करने के औरों के, उनके साथ मदद करने के।

इसीलिए हमने कहा है कि सबमें अच्छी समाज होती है कोऑपरेटिव समाज, सहकारी समाज, जिसमें एक-दूसरे की मदद से, चाहे गाँव में हो, चाहे किसी पेशे में हो, मिलकर काम करते हैं। यह बहुत आवश्यक है। हमारे उत्तर प्रदेश में काफी बढ़ा है कोऑपरेटिव्स, सहकारी संघ काफी बढ़े हैं। कल मैं लखनऊ जा रहा हूँ, एक ऐसे लोगों की सभा है[582] और मुझे मालूम नहीं कितने, बहुत सारे करोड़ों के पर्चे देंगे, पैसे नहीं मुझे देंगे, लेकिन करोड़ों सहकारी संघ ने जो यहाँ हमारे प्रदेश में जमा किया है, उसके काग़ज़ देंगे, बतायेंगे। क्योंकि सहकारी संघ एक बुनियादी तौर से अच्छी चीज़ है और उससे फ़ायदा भी बहुत होता है, मिलजुल कर काम करने से ताक़त बढ़ जाती है। किसान मिलजुल कर करें, उनकी ताक़त बढ़े। बनिये, साहूकार वग़ैरह, ज़मींदार, वो सब अलग हो जायें, ख़ुद करें, ख़ुद ख़रीदारी करें, ख़ुद काश्त करें मिलकर, ख़ुद जो कुछ करना है करें मिलकर। एक-दूसरे की ताक़त से बढ़ती है, उनकी आमदनी होती है, बीच में फ़ायदा उठाने वाले नहीं होते, वो शक्ति बढ़ती है, अपने ऊपर भरोसा बढ़ता है। लेकिन ये सहकारी संघ हम तो चाहते हैं सारे देश में हों। देश के तरीके हों चाहे कारख़ाने बने वो भी सहकारी संघ के बने, और बने हैं बाज़-बाज़

---

581. Nehru in his speeches during the previous two years has often referred to this statement of Vinoba Bhave which was first published in *The Tribune* of 1 April 1960, p. 4. Vinoba Bhave had told the newspaper's staff representative in an interview: "The times have changed. It is the age of science—not of politics. With the birth of nuclear power the world has entered a new era. Politics and religion are on the exit; science and spirituality are marching in." The date of the interview is not mentioned in the report. Shriman Narayan had provided the newspaper source of Vinoba's words to Nehru at the latter's request, see Shriman Narayan (ed.), *Letters from Gandhi Nehru Vinoba* (Bombay: Asia Publishing House, 1968), pp. 105-106.
582. Item 308.

बड़े अच्छे और बड़े लाभ से काम कर रहे हैं। छोटे कारख़ाने हों, बड़े हों, ग्रामोद्योग हों और आख़िर में जो हमारी पार्लियामेंट है वो क्या है, वह एक बड़ी पंचायत है देश की। इस तरह से पंचायती राज हो सहकारी संघ के साथ, नीचे से ऊपर तक, सभों का लाभ हो और सभी के लाभ के लिए काम हो, ख़ाली थोड़े आदमियों के लाभ के लिए नहीं, इससे सभी की हैसियत अच्छी होगी। वो ज़माना गया कि कुछ लोग बड़े ज़मींदार हों, बड़े पैसे वाले हों, और लोग ग़रीब रह सकें। वो चल नहीं सकता ज़माना, कुछ दिन और चल जाये, कुछ लोग जो बहुत लायक़ या तेज़ हैं वो कुछ ज्यादा कमा लें ये और बात है लेकिन आमतौर से बहुत फ़र्क़ नहीं होना चाहिए, ऐसी समाज हम चाहते हैं। ऐसी समाज के लिए हम पंचवर्षीय योजना बना रहे हैं और काम तो उसमें बहुत करने हैं। और मैं चाहता हूँ आप समझें इन बातों को, पढ़ें इसके बारे में जो कुछ हो, हम छोटे-छोटे पर्चे, पेम्फ्लेट निकालते हैं उनको देखें, आपस में बहस करें, बात करें, हमें आप बतायें आप क्या समझते हैं, कुछ ग़लती हमसे हो हम उसे सही करें। यह तो नहीं है कि सारी अक़्ल ऊपर से टपकेगी, हम तो चाहते हैं गाँव वाले सोचें और सहायता करें हमारी, शहर वाले सोचें और इस तरह से बने, मिलजुल कर रहें।

हमारा देश, याद रखिये आप एक बहुत, इस देश में बहुत तरह के लोग रहते हैं, बहुत तरह की आबादी है, बहुत तरह के मौसम हैं। जहाँ मैंने आपसे कहा आजकल चीन का मुक़ाबला है, कहाँ वह मुक़ाम 16, 17, 18 हज़ार फ़ीट ऊँचा ज़मीन से, समुद्र से, जहाँ कि बेहद सर्दी रहती है, सर्दियों में तो कोई रह भी नहीं सकता और वहाँ कोई दरख़्त वग़ैरह कोई चीज़ ज़मीन से नहीं निकल सकता, सर्दी के और ऊँचाई के मारे। वो भी हमारा देश है, सारे हिमालय पहाड़ आपका, हमारा। यहाँ की आप गर्मी बरदाश्त करते हैं, कुछ सर्दी होती है मध्यम, दक्खिन में जाइये वहाँ गर्मी अधिक होती है, अलग-अलग मौसम हैं, अलग-अलग तरह से कपड़े पहनते हैं लोग, अलग-अलग खाना खाते हैं, मौसम पर है न। तो यह अनेकता बहुत है हमारे देश में और अनेकता इसको ख़ूबसूरत बनाती है। एक जैसे सब लोग हों तो क्या उसमें ख़ूबी है? और अनेक धर्म हैं हमारे देश में, अनेक भाषाएँ हैं, ज्यादातर भाषाएँ उन सबकी जड़ एक है, संस्कृत है, कुछ दक्षिण में भाषाएँ हैं, उनकी संस्कृत जड़ नहीं है लेकिन संस्कृत से बहुत शब्द उन्होंने लिए हैं। तो भाषाओं में बहुत अन्तर नहीं है, ये आप याद रखिये। और भाषा अगर अलग-अलग है इत्ते बड़े देश में तो कौन सा उसमें अपराध की बात है, क्यों हम ज़बरदस्ती करें? हम चाहते हैं कि हिन्दी भाषा सारे देश की भाषा हो जाये। इसके माने नहीं हैं कि और भाषाओं को हम दबायें। और भाषाएँ अपनी जगह रहें, कित्ती सुन्दर भाषाएँ हैं, बंगला है, गुजराती है, मराठी है, तामिल है, तेलुगू है, बड़ी सुन्दर भाषाएँ हैं। हिन्दी से कम नहीं हैं, हिन्दी से ऊँची हैं बाज़ बातों में। लेकिन सबमें अधिक लोग हिन्दी बोलते हैं इसलिए हमने हिन्दी को चुना और हिन्दी भी अच्छी भाषा है हमारी कि उसको हम बढ़ायें और बजाय अंग्रेज़ी के हम हिन्दी को ऐसी भाषा कर दें जिसमें आपस का काम अलग-अलग प्रान्तों में हो। इसमें भी हम नहीं चाहते ज़बरदस्ती कोई हो, क्योंकि ज़बरदस्ती से लोग रूठ जाते हैं, ख़िलाफ़ हो जाते हैं, जैसे कुछ लोग अनजानपने में तामिल देश में, मद्रास में झगड़ा करते हैं। हम नहीं ज़बरदस्ती करते,

लेकिन आपको आश्चर्य होगा कि मद्रास में झगड़ालू बहुत लोग हैं, लेकिन इतने लोग हिन्दी सीख रहे हैं स्कूलों में, और जगह, ख़ुद अपनी ख़ुशी से, ज़बरदस्ती से नहीं, क्योंकि वो सीखेंगे। बड़े तेज़ लोग हैं मद्रासी, बड़े दिमाग़ होते हैं उनके, और आपसे और मुझसे कहीं ज्यादा अच्छी हिन्दी बोलने लगेंगे वो थोड़े दिन में।

तो ये अनेक मज़हब हैं, अधिकतर हिन्दू यहाँ हैं, उसके बाद मुसलमान हैं, ईसाई हैं, पारसी हैं, सिक्ख हैं, तरह-तरह के लोग हैं। बहुत सारे धर्म तो ऐसे हैं जो कि भारत में पैदा हुए, बौद्ध धर्म, सिक्ख धर्म, और बहुत ऐसे हैं कि बाहर से आये हैं। बाहर से इस्लाम आया, पारसी लोग बाहर से आये, यहूदी लोग आये, लेकिन आज नहीं आये, डेढ़ हज़ार वर्ष पहले आये, एक ज़माना हुआ, खप गये, हिन्दुस्तानी हैं, वो कोई दूसरे देश के नहीं रहे, दूसरे देश से धर्म उनका आया, बहुत हैं। ईसाई धर्म आया यहाँ दो हज़ार वर्ष हुए, जब विलायत नहीं गया तब आया दक्षिण में। वो भी हमारा धर्म हो गया, हमें उसकी इज़्ज़त करनी है। इस्लाम की, उसकी। और ज़ाहिर है कि हिन्दुस्तान में सबमें अधिक जो धर्म है उसका असर उसकी अधिकता से ही है, उसने जो अपनी विचारधाराएँ देश में फैलाई हैं वो हैं उसकी, वो तो रहेगी, कोई उसको दबा थोड़े ही सकता है। लेकिन अगर हम किसी को दबाने की कोशिश करें समझ के कि ख़ाली हिन्दुस्तान में हिन्दू रहें या कोई मुसलमान समझे सारे हिन्दुस्तान को हम मुसलमान बनायें ये तो मिथ्या है, ग़लत बात है। न ईसाई बनेगा, न मुसलमान सब हो जायेंगे, न हिन्दू ज़बरदस्ती सबको आप कर लेंगे, सब अपने-अपने धर्म पर रहें और बड़े धर्म को सब माने, अपने देश के धर्म को। यही आजकल दुनिया का दस्तूर है। दुनिया में कहीं धर्म पर राजनीति नहीं चलती है, यह हमारे देश में ही, कुछ पिछड़ा हुआ था इसलिए इन साम्प्रदायिक संस्थाओं में राजनीति आयी, मुस्लिम लीग बनी। मुस्लिम लीग बनी बिल्कुल जिसके सामने कोई कार्यक्रम या प्रोग्राम नहीं था सिवाय उकसाने का लोगों को धर्म के नाम पर, डराने का उन्हें कि हिन्दू तुम्हें खा जायेंगे, दबायेंगे। हिन्दुओं में बनी संस्थाएँ साम्प्रदायिक, उन्होंने यही किया, इससे और बढ़ा लोगों का डर।

और पाकिस्तान हिन्दुस्तान में सबसे बड़ा फ़र्क़ क्या है? हम एक लोग हैं, एक बोली बोलते हैं क़रीब-क़रीब। और फ़र्क़ क्या है? फ़र्क़ यह है कि हमने यह निश्चय किया कि हिन्दुस्तान को हम, वो कहते हैं, सेक्यूलर बनायेंगे। सेक्यूलर के क्या माने? यानी हिन्दुस्तान में किसी एक धर्म को हम सरकारी धर्म नहीं बनायेंगे, हम सब धर्मों की इज़्ज़त करेंगे जैसे कि, आज की बात नहीं है, सम्राट अशोक ने लिखा है दो हजार वर्ष से ऊपर हुए। इसीलिए हिन्दुस्तान की दुनिया में इत्ती क़दर हुई थी। हम सब धर्मों की, सब विचारों की इज़्ज़त करेंगे, लेकिन सरकार किसी की तरफ नहीं झुकेगा, यह हमने कहा। यह आजकल सब देशों में यही बात है, एशिया में और यूरोप में, इधर लोग या तो जा रहे हैं या पहुँच गये। अंग्रेज़ हैं, अंग्रेज़ों में ज़ाब्ते से जो वहाँ की क्वीन है वो वहाँ के जो धर्म हैं, वहाँ चर्च ऑफ़ इंग्लैंड उसकी सबसे बड़ी क्या कहूँ धर्मात्मा हैं या अफ़सर है, लेकिन यह तो नाम के लिए बात है। असल में पिछले सौ वर्ष की लड़ाई के बाद इंग्लैंड में जो फ़र्क़ थे धर्मों में, राजनीति में, वो मिटा दिये गये। बड़ी मुश्किल से मिटे हैं, बड़ी लड़ाई हुई। अभी एक मेरा ख़्याल है सौ बरस हुए वहाँ रोमन कैथोलिक लोगों को कोई ओहदा नहीं मिल सकता

था, हालांकि ईसाई थे, ज़रा वो ईसाई धर्म दूसरा था, यहूदी तो बेचारे कहीं भी नहीं थे। अब बातें मिट गईं, अब राजनीति सभी को बराबर के तरह से देखती है, इस तरह से देश बढ़ता है, तरक्की होती है और धर्म पर अपने-अपने रहें, कोई उसमें अटकाव नहीं।

तो भारत सेक्यूलर देश है इस माने में और यही एक आजकल की निशानी है देश की, आजकल की साइंस की, दुनिया की निशानी है। पाकिस्तान में बदक़िस्मती से ये बात नहीं है और अब तक वो पुराना सिलसिला कुछ न कुछ चलता है, हालांकि वाक़ियात की मजबूरी से उनको भी बदलना पड़ रहा है। यही बहस है सेक्यूलर होना, न होना। कश्मीर का आप सुनते हैं, कश्मीर का सबसे बड़ा सवाल यही है कि कश्मीर एक सेक्यूलर देश में रहे और सेक्यूलर बातें वहाँ हों या वो भी अलग हो जाये, पुराने तरीकों पर चले। और कश्मीर हमारे लिए ख़ास है, इसलिए मैं उसमें नहीं जाता, कश्मीर तो हमारा है, हमसे मिल गया है, हिन्दुस्तान का हिस्सा है। मैं आपको एक बुनियादी बात बताता हूँ कि कश्मीर की अहमियत क्या है? यह है अहमियत कि कश्मीर जहाँ कि कसरत से मुसलमान होते हैं वो हिन्दुस्तान का एक सूबा है, आज़ाद सूबा है, यह है अहमियत, उसको भी आज़ादी है और और लोगों को भी।

अगर इस बुनियाद पर हम चलते जो पाकिस्तान कहते हैं कि कश्मीर में मुसलमान ज्यादा हैं इसलिए पाकिस्तान में हो जाये, तो इसके तो माने हैं कि जो मुसलमान हिन्दुस्तान में हैं उनकी कोई ख़ास इज़्ज़त नहीं है, वो पाकिस्तान की तरफ देखते हैं, हिन्दुस्तान गड़बड़ा जाये, हर गाँव में मुसलमान हैं, हर सूबे में हैं, उनकी क्या हैसियत हो, आप सोचो। तो सब बिगड़ जाता है, असल बुनियादी बात यह है हम एक सेक्यूलर देश हैं जो कि मज़हब की, सेक्यूलर के माने ये नहीं हैं कि मज़हब की इज़्ज़त न करें। हम मज़हब की, धर्मों की इज़्ज़त करते हैं, उनको मौक़ा देते हैं, लेकिन सरकार हमारी, हमारी गवर्नमेंट मज़हबी नहीं है यानी मज़हब की तरफ किसी के झुकती है, यह बराबर का देखती है। ये सवाल है। हम साइंस की तरफ देखते हैं, हम टेक्नोलोजी की तरफ देखते हैं और उसी से मुल्क बढ़ेगा।

अब फिर से बारिश होने लगी, मैं नहीं चाहता आपको ज्यादा तकलीफ़ हो। आशा है कि मैं कुछ दो-तीन महीने के बाद फिर यहाँ मेरा आना हो ज्यादा इत्मीनान से, क्योंकि मैं आपको समझाना चाहता हूँ कि आप समझें।

एक बात मैं आपसे कह दूँ कि आप मुझे देख रहे हैं, सुन रहे हैं, लोगों ने ख़बरें उड़ाई हैं कि मैं अज़हद बीमार हूँ। मैं तो नहीं अपने को बीमार देखता हूँ, न समझता हूँ और अब आप जो राय क़ायम करें ठीक है। जब तक काम की ताक़त है काम किया जाता है, जब नहीं रहती नहीं किया जाता है। फिर चाहे उस आदमी को आप वेस्ट पेपर बास्केट में फेंक दें, जरूरत नहीं रही उसकी, लेकिन जब तक है तब तक इंसान की वक़्त है। बहुत-बहुत आपका शुक्रिया।

आप इस तकलीफ़ में खड़े हुए हैं, मुसीबत में, पानी में और मैं आशा करता हूँ कि इलाहाबाद के शहर में, इलाहाबाद के ज़िले में, हमारा ज़िला कुछ पिछड़ा सा रहा है, हमारे सूबे में बाज़ ज़िले बहुत पिछड़े हैं, इधर के, और पूरब की तरफ जाइये, गोरखपुर, देवरिया, आज़मगढ़, बलिया, ग़ाज़ीपुर, बहुत पिछड़े हुए हैं, मुझे दुख होता है सोचकर। उनको उठाना

285

है। इलाहाबाद उत्ता नहीं पिछड़ा है, लेकिन उत्ती तरक्की भी नहीं इसने की। उधर मेरठ की तरफ जाइये, वहाँ किसानों को देखिये तो ख़ुशहाल हैं, अच्छे हैं, पंजाब के किसानों से मिलते हैं, मेरठ, मुज़फ़्फ़रनगर वगैरह।

तो इलाहाबाद को हमें उठाना है, इलाहाबाद शहर को हमें उठाना है। यहाँ अक्सर बहस होती है, कोई दफ़्तर उठ गया यहाँ से।[583] दफ़्तर को कोई उठने की जरूरत नहीं है, न उठना चाहिए, लेकिन एकाध दफ़्तर रहे न रहे, उससे इलाहाबाद नहीं बढ़ता, वो बढ़ता है और बातों से। ज़ाहिर है मुझे मुहब्बत है इलाहाबाद से, यहाँ पैदा हुआ, यहाँ बढ़ा, अब बाहर रहता हूँ ज्यादातर। और ख़्वाहिश है इलाहाबाद तरक्की करे, इलाहाबाद का ज़िला तरक्की करे जहाँ मैं इत्ता फिरा हूँ पुराने ज़माने में।

बस फिर से आपको धन्यवाद, शुक्रिया।

जयहिन्द।

मेरे साथ आप कहिये तो जयहिन्द तीन बार।

जयहिन्द! जयहिन्द! जयहिन्द!

[Translation begins

Brothers and Sisters,

I am perturbed that you have had to stand in this rain. I am under cover. I was not in favour of a meeting in such bad weather but my friends have arranged it. I have no problem but I feel bad to see you getting wet.

I have come to Allahabad for the first time after the elections. I had wanted to come immediately after the elections, to tour the countryside and thank all of you in the district who have elected me. I am constantly aware of the hopes with which you have done so and wonder how far we are able to fulfil them. There are hundreds of tasks waiting to be done and nothing is done by magic. Yet I think there has been great progress in the last ten to twelve years and we have been able to lay the firm foundations on which we can build a new India.

What does a new India mean? It has many meanings. It means improving our agriculture, industrializing the country, spreading education, building roads and hospitals, etc. But the real thing is to make new men and women of the people, by training them to grasp the realities of the modern times—people who would be true Indians for we do not want to copy anyone. Yes, we would certainly like to learn from others. But if we lose our Indianness, we will become mere copies of others. Therefore, we have to retain our Indian heritage of

---

583. Referring apparently to the proposal to shift an Officers' Training School from Allahabad. See SWJN/SS/77/items 220-221.

thousands of years and at the same time learn from the outside world because there has been a great advance in science and technology and machines. Great things are happening as you must be aware. People are trying to reach the Moon and the stars and will succeed eventually. Even nationalistic boundaries are becoming somewhat outdated at a time when it is possible to go from one country to another in a few hours by a jet plane. There is an effort to build a new world and we will succeed provided there is no outbreak of a great war which will destroy the whole world. Mankind has acquired, through science, the ability and the strength to make the whole world prosperous and a better place to live in. It is possible even if it takes time. Go near the time when the wealth of nations was limited and while a handful of men were rich, the majority of the population was poor. Now we have the resources to make everyone in the world prosperous and well off. It is possible to harness the natural sources of energy and utilize them to advantage. But all this takes time and people need to be trained, their thinking has to be changed so that they can get out of the old mental ruts. This is a great task and the most important thing is education. By that I do not mean mere book learning but a progressive thinking and a grasp of the modern times and scientific and technological advance, etc.

We have good scientists and engineers, young men and women, and we have great hopes from them. They will transform the country. I would like to tell you in detail what is happening all over the country, the changes that are taking place, and what we hope to achieve. The difficulty is that most of the people are engrossed in their petty problems and quarrels, and so it is impossible to pit our entire strength into the tasks of development. Dangers threaten the country today. I regret to say that our relations with Pakistan have not been cordial and there are constant threats of war and whatnot, though we want to come to an agreement with them and maintain friendly relations. But that does not mean that we can give up what we consider important principles. There can be no friendship in such circumstances. But we want that there should be cordial relations between India and Pakistan, for both will benefit and I am sure a day will come when this will happen. We must take care not to do anything which will worsen the situation.

There is a more dangerous development on our borders with Tibet and China. China has captured some of our mountain territory in the Ladakh. It is in high mountainous terrain, covered with snow, and an uninhabited area. But they have no right to capture our territory. This is a great danger that threatens us today. It makes it even more imperative that we should quickly reach a position of strength. We do not want that there should be war between China and India. Both are great countries and there is no question of winning or losing, there will be only ruin to both. So this is an important issue.

What is our duty in such circumstances? I said that we do not wish to attack. But if the other side forces the issue, we cannot keep quiet. It is our duty to protect our territory. I feel even now that we can solve this problem peacefully. But that is possible only by being strong and vigilant. We cannot silently acquiesce in what is happening. This danger has been looming over us for the last two and a half years and there has been a great deal of correspondence on both sides on the subject; statements are issued and counter arguments presented. But the problem remains unsolved. We have tried in the last two years to make our position in that area stronger. In a sense, we are pretty strong militarily but we were not fully equipped to reach the difficult mountain terrain for there were no roads. It took months for people to go there. There are no trees on the high mountain, and no fuel or food of any sort is available there. Things can be taken there by air, but it is not feasible. It is easy for the Chinese to transport things because there are plains on their side. They can transport everything by lorries.

Therefore it became essential for us to build roads, and in the last two years, we have built many mountain roads which have made our position stronger, but the work is not progressing as quickly as we want, though everyone is doing their best. It is possible to work only for five to six months in the year because nobody can survive those winters on the mountains unless special precautions are taken.

I want you to understand the broad facts of our dispute with China. I will not go into the steps that both sides are likely to take. I cannot say what steps we may take or perhaps what they might do. But the broad fact is that we have to defend our country. We want to peacefully solve the dispute that has arisen between our two countries. But at the same time we have to be prepared for combat.

In a sense, the greater our preparedness—and we are in fact more prepared, we have now many military posts there—the more the Chinese have become concerned, during the last few months, that we are getting stronger. This gave rise to the possibility that they also might try to move forward. There has been firing in one place. Both sides accuse one another of starting it. Anyhow, two soldiers on our side were wounded, though not seriously. Therefore, we feel that there is a possibility of escalation of the matter. We will not like that to happen. I would say, though I cannot be sure, that even the Chinese have no particular desire for a war on a big scale. They have shown restraint and not attacked even in areas where they could have easily done so. Well, these are complicated issues. But it means that we have to be prepared and vigilant, forget our petty squabbles and foster unity in the country. The armed forces are no doubt there to protect us. But we need unity and effort and hard work for the defence of the nation.

Behind the armed forces, there are millions of people at work, to supply them with food and arms and ammunition, etc. Therefore, the strength of the armed forces depends on the strength of the nation. Gone are the days when wars were fought by small units armed with swords. Now a great deal of preparation is necessary. Therefore, it is extremely important that we should leave aside our petty problems and concentrate on the larger issues, one of which is the need to progress as fast as we can.

For instance, the Five Year Plans ultimately aim at making the country strong and prosperous, which will be reflected in the strength of the armed forces. The armed forces cannot defend a poverty-stricken country. The entire strength of the nation has to be ranged behind the armed forces. There should be no factionalism in the country. I am sorry to say that this is a terrible vice in India. People tell lies, make false accusations and do all kinds of things during elections. I was amazed to see some of the election pamphlets. One of them said that for a long time now Rs 25,000 per day are spent on my personal expenses. It is absurd. I get sixteen hundred rupees a month after tax deductions as salary and I have some income from my royalties on books. I have nothing to worry about. How can I counteract such patently false accusations? May be the figure of Rs 25,000 includes expenditure on my security, and what not.[584]

Anyhow, that is a minor matter. I have heard even stranger things, wrong statements, not only about me, but about the various projects which we are taking up. I was pained to hear criticism against the Panchayati Raj which we are establishing in the country. I attach great importance to it because it will make the people, particularly the poor farmers, strong, and will train them to do their tasks better. Our farmers are extremely hardworking, but they are unable to reap the full benefits because they have not learnt the modern techniques of agriculture. Production can improve miraculously by the use of better ploughs which dig deep, fertilizers, good seeds, etc. Arrangements are being made to supply all this but ultimately everything depends on the farmers. I was speaking at a meeting recently and mentioned the progress which Japan has made. The zamindari system has been abolished there more than fifteen years ago and now the largest landholding permitted to each farmer is, I think, fifteen or twenty acres as far as I can remember, though the ordinary farmer does not own more than two or three acres or a little more. But even with such small holdings, they are able to earn so much that they are extremely well off. They own television and radio and what not. I was amazed to see this. It is possible because they are extremely hardworking and have adopted new and modern techniques of agriculture. This is how Japan has emerged out of the past into the modern times.

584. See fn 579 in this section.

Even after its crushing defeat in the Second World War and the terrible ruin it brought in its wake, Japan is once again on its feet within ten years. It is truly amazing. They are respected for this and justifiably so. They have laid strong foundations by the spread of education. Every child in Japan goes to school. A great many students go in for engineering. They are a highly industrialized society and yet they are very good at agriculture too. After all, the wealth of a nation does not drop from heaven, nor does it come from outside. We get a little by way of foreign aid or loans from other countries for which we are very grateful to them. But ultimately it is we who have to carry the burden of forty-two crores of human beings. Who else can do it for us? We can discharge our responsibility in only one way and that is by increasing production in the country from land and industries. The larger plants are well known. We want that there should be small industries and supply of electricity in all the villages.

The difficulty is that all this requires money and that is in short supply in a poor country, otherwise it would not be poor. So we are caught up in a vicious circle of how to get the capital to invest in tasks of development to increase the national wealth. Now, are we to do this or abolish land revenue, as some people demand we should, at least on the small landholdings? That may give them some relief for a year or two. But their problems will multiply after that because the progress of the nation will come to a standstill. The problem is that our income from land revenue is pretty high and it is that which we invest in the tasks of development. It is our intention, now, to give the land revenue to the panchayats, at least a large part of it, so that they can build schools and hospitals and roads with it for themselves. But we cannot progress without education, industrialization and cooperatives, etc., and we will stay where we are. Therefore, we must make a genuine effort, even if it means tightening our belts a little to get the money for these essential tasks which will benefit the people. This is the dilemma. With foreign aid, even in the form of loans, the burden on the masses can be reduced, though the repayment of the loan becomes a greater liability. However, India will undoubtedly progress and the loans will be repaid. But ultimately the brunt of the burden is bound to fall on the people, for a nation of this size cannot be supported by aid from outside and nor is it in keeping with our dignity to be in such a situation.

Now, after nearly twelve years of great effort, we have reached the crossroads and have to decide which road to take. On the one hand, we could give up in panic at the magnitude of the tasks before us; that will amount to taking the wrong road which may give us some momentary relief but will call a halt to future progress. No country has ever progressed without accumulating a surplus which can be invested in development. A rich man becomes rich by investing the surplus capital in other tasks, which increases his income. The same thing applies to a nation too.

A great revolution, the industrial revolution, took place in the world about 150 years ago. New modes of production, new techniques, new machines appeared and the intelligent ones took advantage of them. Then came the steam engine with the discovery of steam as a source of energy. Now steam is used to run railways and big machines. Electricity is also an ordinary, everyday thing which everyone has seen. But, by harnessing it, Man has acquired a great source of power. So, as you know, thousands of new discoveries have been made during the last hundred years. The latest and most significant is the discovery of atomic energy. Used unwisely, it could destroy the whole world but if it is put to good use it can transform the whole world. We have been born in extraordinary times, when the world is taking a new turn. Either it will bring destruction upon mankind or the whole world will become prosperous very rapidly, though it cannot be done within a year or two. I think that in the last ten or twelve years we have laid solid foundations for the future, and in the next ten years we would have taken a great leap forward. After that we will hold the key to our future prosperity in our hands. We will have enough capital to invest in essential tasks of development.

I mentioned ten years. But whether it is ten or five, we will have to undergo some hardships. There is no doubt about it, because the process of transition is a difficult one for any nation. It has to change its thinking and get out of its mental rut, because it is by the effort of human beings that a nation grows. A nation is what its men and women are. There is no magic formula for progress and nor can we learn its mysteries by gazing at the stars, though sights of some are certainly trained towards the heavenly bodies we shall definitely reach there by aircraft or some other mode of travel.

These are the crucial questions which we are facing today and the Five Year Plans are aimed at solving them. They do not mean merely putting up roads, hospitals, schools or something else here and there. All those are necessary and should be built, but the most important thing is to change the people's thinking in India. So we established the Panchayati Raj for the farmers to become self-reliant. They were given the responsibilities and powers hitherto shouldered by the officials. It was a big step. It is possible that the village panchayats may make mistakes but they will learn from their mistakes and experience. Responsibility makes an individual grow and have confidence in himself instead of running to the officials with applications. Now if any villager or a panch comes to me with some request, I tell them that they have all the powers and so they should solve their own problems. They cannot do everything but they enjoy pretty wide powers. Now when I visit the panchayats, particularly in Rajasthan, and talk to them, their tone is entirely different. They do not come with complaints though there is a good deal to complain about; instead they come out with schemes for improvement and progress of the villages. They seek advice on this. You can judge from this how their thinking is changing.

Our youth must learn to understand the times that they are living in today. They are living in rapidly changing times and a thousand new avenues are opening before them, in spite of all their problems. The more well trained they are, the farther they can go and take the country with them. It is often found that there are never any vacancies anywhere in the country or they are filled the moment they occur. But soon there will be thousands of vacancies in India and a thousand new avenues are opening. It is true that there will be problems and difficulties in the beginning. But we cannot remove them by moaning about them. We must work hard and train ourselves. I would like you to read the Five Year Plan document and try to understand a little about what we are trying to do. It is easy to tell everyone what needs to be done. But it is one thing to plan and quite another to implement it. It is extremely difficult because it involves education, training, hard work and tightening one's belts and bearing hardships. Only then can we leap across to the other side.

This is the situation today. I am convinced that when we gradually overcome this situation we should be able to make great progress in the next ten years for we would have acquired greater ability to do so. I want you to understand this. You should read, digest, argue about it and then form your own views. I want you to develop the ability to think for yourselves and not to take anything I say as gospel. It is for you to decide. I am here for a short while and already people are fed up that I should have been the Prime Minister for such a long time. Well, I shall not always be there. Somebody else will become the Prime Minister. As I said somewhere else, every boy and girl will find the path open before them if they have the ability and intelligence to become the Prime Minister, or the President. Any one of you can aspire to those offices if you are prepared to work hard and make sacrifices. Anyhow, there can be only one Prime Minister but there are thousands of other posts waiting to be filled. There are the armed forces. There was a time when all the officers were British. Now there are thousands of Indian officers. Then we have the Foreign Service and we select ambassadors from it and send them abroad. Brilliant young boys and girls are working in our embassies all over the world. Trade is increasing; the number of engineers is increasing. Five or six years ago, when we did a census of engineers, they numbered one lakh. Now the number must have increased to 125,000 to 150,000. Even so, we are short of engineers because so many new projects are being taken up. The problem is that our educational system is such that though the students are learning something, they do not fit in with the new India that we are building. Engineers and scientists are being trained, but a degree or book learning is not enough though they may get you a job. I want that you should have the ability to do original work and stand on your own feet. You will find that wherever this is the case, there is rapid progress.

Take the Punjab, for instance, which has its share of the good and the bad. But the people of the Punjab, Hindus, Muslims and Sikhs, are extremely hard working and good with their hands. They make good machines because they understand machines. You will find Punjabi or Sikh taxi drivers all over the country. Wherever we open an industry, most of the engineers are from the Punjab. Why is this so? The fact is that thousands of new industries, small industries, have mushroomed all over the Punjab in the last ten to twelve years. They are not the huge, famous ones that you read about. Nor have they been set up by the government. These are all private ventures, for the Punjabis have tremendous initiative. They have transformed parts of Uttar Pradesh, Ghaziabad, etc., by setting up hundreds of small units which have brought prosperity to the area. So human beings must show initiative. All of us have the ability and given the opportunity to be trained and by working hard, we can go very far.

We must develop habits of prudence. The Soviet Union is now an extremely prosperous country. If you read the history of Russia, you will find that they had to undergo tremendous hardships after the Revolution. For twenty years they faced starvation and underwent great trials and tribulations. But they persevered and ultimately overcame their difficulties and have created a new society. Now, our methods are slightly different but we could learn a great deal from them.

Today the Soviet Union and the United States are two great stalwarts in the world, standing opposed to each other. If by some misfortune there is a war between the two, both are so very powerful that they will not only destroy themselves, but the whole world too. Nobody can survive. But both powers have the capacity, also, to make their countries prosperous and wealthy. I will tell you one point of similarity between the two. They are both poised for war. But both the super powers have grasped the fundamentals of the modern world which belongs to the machine and science and they worship them; consequently they have both advanced. Communism and capitalism are two completely different ideologies. But no matter which you choose, science and technology and machines are the bulwark upon which the foundations have to be built.

Our progress in the last few years has been in these fields. We have established huge science laboratories all over the country in which our intelligent young boys and girls are being trained and are doing research. We are setting up huge industries for which we need power, electricity and steam, etc. Electricity is produced by friction. The huge river valley projects that you hear about involve building dams to harness the waters to turn the turbines to

293

produce electricity. Millions of kilowatts of electricity are produced which is transmitted through wires. Electricity is a great servant of mankind as are all sources of power. In the stories of *Alif-Laila* of the olden times one reads about the jinn in the lamp and what not. Electricity and other sources of power available today are greater than the jinn of those stories. We need to produce power, which we are doing. Our farmers must understand the modern world. I do not mean that all our farmers must become scientists or engineers though their children may do so in future. But everyone in the country must grasp the trends in the modern world and not remain in old ruts.

I want that our youth should prepare themselves fully well for the future. Their thinking must fit in with the modern times. The world is changing rapidly and, as I pointed out, Man is going out into space and trying to reach the Moon and the stars. He is bound to succeed one day soon. You must have heard recently about the satellite launched by the United States which has been orbiting around the earth. They have been able to take televised photographs and what not.[585] This is the pace of progress in the world today. We can also emulate their example for we have very good scientists in India. But I want the scientific temper to spread in the country.

I was telling you about the panchayats. Giving greater autonomy to them was a big step. There were many people who had doubts about this. But I have great faith in our people. However, I am unhappy about the fact that there are too many tensions and quarrels during panchayat elections, so much so that there has been violence and bloodshed; even an elected representative is murdered, which is very bad. How can a nation progress in this manner? Elections generate too much tension everywhere but we have to hold them under a democracy. We do not want kings and nawabs and officials to rule, though a trained bureaucracy is a great asset. It can guide and advise and handle administrative matters with competence. But I want that every single man, woman, boy and girl should become capable of handling all these matters, at least, in their own areas, in their own village, tehsil, district or province, and then in the whole country. They must not be totally dependent on bureaucrats, and sit waiting for them to do everything for them. You must have a mental picture of where your duties lie and then prepare yourselves for it. We must develop a respect for all forms of labour, not merely of file-pushing at a desk. The world cannot do without farmers for instance and soon a day will come when most of the agricultural work will become mechanized.

This is the kind of world that we want to build, and the countries which have advanced in the field of science and technology have progressed very far.

585. See fn 580 in this section.

The only weakness among them is that they are great warmongers and live in constant fear of others attacking them. They are on a path which will lead to ruin for themselves and others. You must have heard what Vinobaji has said, that this is the age of science and spirituality as against the old system of politics and religion.[586] It is difficult to define spirituality for it is not mere religious rituals. Spirituality is an inner strength which is recognized by all religions. Therefore, he has stressed the need for spirituality in the modern times when man is becoming increasingly powerful with the aid of science.

There are two things which we must learn. One is tolerance; tolerance of neighbours and other human beings. It is absurd to quarrel over elections. We want everyone to enjoy equal rights no matter what his religion is. It is wrong to force one's religion or politics down other people's throats. Each individual must be free to follow his own principles, but they should include tolerance of other people's way of life.

This is why we have said that the best form of society is a cooperative society in which everyone helps one another in their tasks. This is essential. The number of cooperative has increased considerably in Uttar Pradesh. Tomorrow I shall be going to Lucknow to attend a meeting of cooperatives where I shall be given the latest figures of the money collected by the cooperative societies in the State.[587] Cooperatives are fundamentally very beneficial and increase the strength of the people, whether they are farmers, businessmen or something else. Working together has great advantages: the middleman's profit is eliminated, self-reliance increases; it is for all these reasons that we want that cooperatives should be established all over the country. A few large ones have been established and are doing good work. There must be small, medium and big industries established through the cooperatives. After all, the Parliament is the biggest panchayat in the country. We want a panchayat and a cooperative society everywhere, so that people from top to bottom may benefit. We do not want it only for a handful of people. We want to improve the standard of living of everyone in the country. Gone are the days when a handful of zamindars and others were rich while the rest of the people remained poor. It cannot work like that anymore, and except for the natural differences arising out of the mental and physical make-up of individuals, generally speaking there should not be too great a disparity among the people. It is for this that we are implementing the Five Year Plans and I want you to read the small pamphlets that we are putting out about them, and try to understand what we are planning to do. You must discuss it among yourselves and point out the mistakes which we can then

586. See fn 581 in this section.
587. See fn 582 in this section.

rectify. We want everyone in the country to participate in planning, whether they live in the rural areas or in the urban.

You must remember that India is a vast country, with a large population, with different climates and ways of life. At the point where we are in conflict with China, our territory lies at a height of 16,000 to 17,000 feet above sea level. It is bitterly cold there and uninhabited during the winter. Not even a blade of grass can grow there during the winter. This bitterly cold Himalayan region belongs to us, as also the areas in the middle which have a more temperate climate; in the South, there is excessive heat. So there are different kinds of climate. People wear different types of clothes and eat different kinds of food, depending on the climate. So, there is great diversity in India which makes her a beautiful country. Sameness induces a kind of dull monotony. There are different religions in India, and different languages, most of which have their roots in Sanskrit. Only the languages of the South do not have their roots in Sanskrit but even they have borrowed a great deal from its vocabulary. So, there are similarities between the various languages of India. In any case having a number of languages in a large country like India is no crime. Why would we force them to become uniform? We want Hindi to become the national language of India. But that does not mean we want to suppress the other languages. They must all flourish, for all of them, Bangla, Gujarati, Marathi, Tamil, Telegu, etc., are great languages and in no way inferior to Hindi; in fact, in certain respects they are superior to Hindi. We selected Hindi only because the majority of the people in India speak the language and we wanted to substitute it for English for official work. Even here, we have no desire to compel anyone because that puts the backs of people up. We do not use coercion. However, some people in Tamilnad quarrel over the language issue without knowing the full facts. You will be surprised to know that many people in Madras are quarrelsome. But so many people there are learning Hindi, in schools and elsewhere, and doing so voluntarily, not by force. And they will learn the language because they are intelligent—the people of Madras State are quite brainy—and soon they will be speaking it better than you and me.

Then there are different religions in India. The majority of the people are Hindus, but there are a large number of Muslims, Christians, Sikhs, Parsis and others. Many of these religions, like Buddhism and Sikhism, are indigenous to India and others have come from outside. For instance, Islam, Christianity, Zoroastrianism, etc., came from outside to the shores of India more than 1,500 years ago. They came and were absorbed in the soil and have become Indian in character. They are no longer foreign religions. Christianity came to India two thousand years ago, long before it reached Europe, and was adopted here. We must respect all these religions. It is obvious that Hinduism will continue to be the most powerful religion in the country and its impact is unquestioned. Nobody can suppress it. But if we make an attempt to suppress the other religions in order to uphold Hinduism, or if the Muslims want to proselytize the whole of India, there will be neither Hindus nor Muslims nor Christians left in the country. Everyone should be free to follow his own religion and at the same time respect the other religions. It is only because India was backward that communal organizations like the Muslim League came into being. It had no other programme except to unite people in the name of religion and to tell the Muslims that the Hindus will suppress them and swallow them up. The same thing was done by the Hindu communal organizations, with the result that fear in both the communities increased.

What is the difference between India and Pakistan? The people in both the countries are the same, speak the same languages, etc. The only difference is that in India we have decided to be a secular state, meaning that we do not recognize any religion as the official religion of the state. We hold all religions in respect as has been the tradition in India from time immemorial. Emperor Ashoka inscribed this message on rocks and stones over two thousand years ago. India has always been famous in the world for her religious tolerance and lack of bigotry. The government will respect all religions but will not single out any particular religion for a special status, this we have stated. This is the situation in most countries of Asia and Europe and others are gradually following suit. In England, the Queen there is officially the head of the Church of England, but only nominally. The differences between the church and state in England were resolved with great difficulty after a struggle of a hundred years. I think until about a hundred years back, the Roman Catholics, who are also Christians though slightly different from the others, could not get any position there; and Jews did not figure anywhere. Things are now different. In politics everyone in England is equal now. This is how a nation progresses. Everyone should follow their own religion. There is no difficulty in that.

So, India is a secular country in this sense. This is the true sign of a modern nation, in accordance with the spirit of modern science. Unfortunately, this is not so in Pakistan and the old situation still exists there, though they are also beginning to change due to the compulsion of events. There is a debate there whether or not to become secular. The entire dispute about Kashmir hinges on whether Kashmir should remain with a secular country or merge with a non-secular one. Kashmir is very special as far as India is concerned and is a part of the country. I will not go into the details. But the fundamental importance of Kashmir lies in the fact that even though it is a predominantly Muslim state, it is a part of India, and it has got autonomy. If we were to accept the premise that because the majority of the population in Kashmir is Muslim, it should merge with Pakistan, it would imply that the Muslims in India do not deserve much respect or that they look to Pakistan; this would shake India's stability to its foundations. There are Muslims in every village in India. You can imagine what impact such an attitude would have on them. The basic fact is that we are a secular nation which believes in respect for all religions. But the government does not have a religious bias. We believe in science and technology which are important for the country's progress.

It is raining again and I do not want you to suffer. I think I will be able to come here again within the next two to three months. I would like to clarify one point. Rumours have been spread that I am extremely ill. Now you can see me and hear me and can judge for yourselves. I do not consider myself ill. So long as my strength permits, I will continue to work and after that you are free to throw me into the waste paper basket.

Thank you very much. You are getting wet in the rain. I hope that Allahabad will progress. Many of the districts in Uttar Pradesh, like Gorakhpur, Deoria, Azamgarh, Ballia, Ghazipur, etc., are very backward, which perturbs me. We must try to do something about it. Even Allahabad has not progressed as it should have. In Meerut and Muzaffarnagar, the farmers are extremely well off and are like the farmers of Punjab.

So, we have to develop Allahabad, we have to develop Allahabad city. There is often a great uproar here whenever some institution is shifted from here.[588] I think there is no need to shift any institution from here. It should not happen, though the development of Allahabad is not affected whether some office stays here or not. Its progress depends on other factors. It is obvious that I have a special fondness for Allahabad for I was born and brought up here. Now I live outside most of the time. But it is my desire that Allahabad, the area where I have roamed so much in the past, should progress rapidly.

I thank you once again.

Jai Hind!

Please say Jai Hind with me thrice.

Jai Hind! Jai Hind! Jai Hind!

Translation ends]

---

588. See fn 583 in this section.

298

182. To Swaran Singh: Izaat's Folly at Daraganj in Allahabad[589]

July 27, 1962

My dear Swaran Singh,

For some years past, there has been an agitation in Allahabad for a bridge across Ganga not far off from the Sangam. There is a bridge there near Daraganj, but very foolishly it was made only for the railway crossing. There is no road etc. in it. This was called Izaat's bridge and is usually known as Izaat's folly. This has caused great inconvenience to people many of whom have to cross the river daily as they work in Allahabad or Naini. In winter time there is a pontoon bridge on which much money is spent every year. During the Magh Mela in January and February, a number of pontoon bridges have to be made for the pilgrims. Sometimes the bridge collapses and there is tragedy.

I think that this bridge is very necessary but I fear it will not be possible to include this in the Third Plan. A temporary alternative is suggested which might help. This is the use of Izaat bridge for carriages and motors also by making a road over the railway track. Of course, this road can only be used when the railway trains are not passing. There is not much traffic of railways on this bridge. It is a metre gauge line.

I should imagine that it should not be difficult to make the suggested change. Arrangements will be made for the stoppage of the road traffic when the train passes over the bridge. Will you kindly have this matter enquired into from this point of view?

589. Letter to the Minister for Railways. Sent from Anand Bhavan, Allahabad. PMO, File No. 7(183)/59-64-PMS, Sr. No. 14-A. Also available in the JN Collection.

I might add that at my suggestion a narrow foot-path was added to this bridge some two or three years ago.[590] That is helpful but not enough.[591]

Yours sincerely,
Jawaharlal Nehru

183. To Seth D. Howard: Developing Eastern Districts of UP[592]

July 27, 1962

Dear Shri Howard,

The Home Minister, Shri Lal Bahadur Shastri, has forwarded to me your letter to him of 13th July with some enclosures. I am returning these enclosures to you.

I entirely agree with you that the conditions existing in the Eastern Districts of Uttar Pradesh are deplorable. I do not know how far conversion of Balrampur Division into a full-fledged district will help in this matter. Anyhow, that is something for the State Government to decide.

So far as the question of separation of judiciary from the executive is concerned, we are committed to it and it is being done all over India.

---

590. For previous references to Izaat's bridge, see SWJN/SS/49/items 2 and 47-48.
591. Extract from reply of 3 September 1962 from Swaran Singh to Nehru:

"Providing a temporary roadway decking across the bridge is not an insuperable task, but apart from the high initial and recurring cost of the proposal, its utility for the road users will be severely restricted and limited in scope, even during non-Mela periods. The bridge will have to be closed to road traffic during the Mela period, as the number of train paths required during this period will be as many as 40 in 24 hours and it will not be possible to keep the railway bridge open for road traffic.

A separate road bridge across the Ganga near about this site would obviously be the only satisfactory and permanent solution of the problem. I understand that the Transport Ministry wrote to UP Governments 4/5 years ago suggesting that they should undertake construction of a road bridge at this site but UP Government apparently have not been able to make any headway presumably on account of the paucity of funds. If you feel that it would be worthwhile our undertaking construction of a temporary roadway across the railway bridge, I shall sound the UP Government as they will have to accept the debit of initial cost and recurring expenditure." PMO, File No. 7(183)/59-64-PMS, Sr. No. 19-A.
592. Letter to a journalist and press correspondent, Balrampur, UP. Sent from Anand Bhavan, Allahabad.

I have drawn the attention of the Planning Commission specially to the Eastern Districts of UP and a good deal of thought is being given to this area.[593]

Yours sincerely,
[Jawaharlal Nehru]

184. To C.B. Gupta: Land Tax should exclude Groves[594]

July 27, 1962

My dear Chandra Bhanu,

As was to be expected I have received numerous complaints in Allahabad District about your new taxes, more specially about the increase in land revenue.[595] Not knowing enough about this subject, I could only talk generally.

But one thing surprised me. This was the complaint, repeated with great vehemence, that groves were being taxed in spite of the assurance that they will not be taxed.

Last year, when I came to Allahabad District, I heard these complaints often enough, when one of your Ministers who was with me stoutly denied this and gave the assurance that the groves would not be taxed. Yet again, this year the same complaints have been raised. People have told me that they are prepared to bring proof in support of their contention.

I do not know what the facts are but I presume that your policy is not to tax groves, but in practice many of these groves have been included in the taxable area. Something should be done to remove this complaint which appears to be fully justified. I wonder if you could take some steps to this end and appoint some competent authority to look into this matter and rectify any mistake that might have been committed in regard to groves. I think this is necessary. Apart from this, it will help Government to lessen the tension about the new taxes.

Yours sincerely,
[Jawaharlal Nehru]

593. See SWJN/SS/74/item 81 and the several items on poverty in east Uttar Pradesh in SWJN/SS/77/section Politics, subsection UP.
594. Letter to the Chief Minister of Uttar Pradesh. Sent from Anand Bhavan, Allahabad.
595. See item 16, fn 91.

185. To C.B. Gupta: Roads in Uttar Pradesh[596]

August 9, 1962

My dear Chandra Bhanu,

In January this year, I wrote to you about the necessity of a pucca road in Allahabad District round about Phulpur.[597] It seemed to me extraordinary that the headquarters of Community Blocks should not be properly connected by road. In fact, it is more important to have a road than Block building. The road I suggested seemed to me quite essential to connect various important parts of the District.

In reply, it was stated that your Government was short of funds for road making. I understand that subsequently a reference was made to the Ministry of Transport at the Centre, and they promised to give a grant equal to 50 per cent of the cost of the proposed work subject to a maximum of Rs 17 lakhs. I hope that you will accept this grant and proceed with the building of this road. Perhaps you cannot finish it within a year, but half of it might be made and subsequently the other half can be covered.

I had also suggested that new methods of road making were less costly. To this you had replied that the cheaper method known as "Mehra method" had not been found suitable. I had not mentioned any particular method. But Dr A.N. Khosla, who is a Member of the Planning Commission, had pointed out a method which was much cheaper and very effective.[598] The matter has been referred to him again, and on hearing from him I shall let you know.

But I do hope you will begin with this road in Phulpur.

Yours sincerely,
Jawaharlal Nehru

186. For V.K. Krishna Menon: Cantonment Land for Allahabad Corporation[599]

It seems to me that the request of Corporation of Allahabad for much of the Cantonment land round about the city is justified. It is impossible for the city

596. Letter to the Chief Minister of UP. File No. 17(519)/62-66-PMS, Sr. No. 31-A. Also available in the JN Collection.
597. See SWJN/SS/74/item 134. See also SWJN/SS/74/item 133 and SWJN/SS/75/item 154.
598. See appendix 13.
599. Note, 15 August 1962, for the Defence Minister.

to grow unless this land, which is of no present use to Defence, is given to the Corporation. The growth of Allahabad is limited by two rivers. Thus, it is only the third side which affords opportunities for growth of a growing city.

The requirements of the Defence Establishment are important, but these cannot override the requirements of the civil population of the city.

I gather that an equal area of land can be made available to Defence outside the city limits. That should suffice.

I am told that compensation at a heavy rate has been asked for by Defence, which would involve the Corporation finding Rs 1 crore or so. This is obviously unrealistic and totally beyond the capacity of the Corporation.

187. To C.B. Gupta: Tevatia Cooperative Farming Society[600]

August 29, 1962

My dear Chandra Bhanu,

I quote below from a letter I have received from the Editor of Sevagram:

> "I spoke to you about the Tevatia Cooperative Farming Society in village Banooi in Bulandshahr district (Uttar Pradesh). The Society got a raw deal from the consolidation authorities. It has been sanctioned power for a tube-well, but the supply has not been made even after 10 months, despite several representations made by the Society. This manner of official attitude kills the farmers' enthusiasm for cooperative farming. I do hope you would kindly ask the authorities concerned to look into the matter."

I hope you will kindly look into this matter.

Yours sincerely,
[Jawaharlal Nehru]

---

600. Letter to the Chief Minister of Uttar Pradesh.

188. To C.B. Gupta: Land Acquisition in Ghaziabad[601]

August 30, 1962

My dear Chandra Bhanu,

I wrote to you the other day[602] about a large number of farmers from Ghaziabad coming to see me. They were greatly excited at the idea that their lands would be taken away from them because of our Master Plan. I suggested to you that as far as possible good agricultural land should not be touched.

During the last few days we have had the Land Acquisition (Amendment) Bill before the Lok Sabha.[603] It created quite a furore in Parliament, and it was only after a number of changes were made in it and concessions agreed to that it was ultimately passed today. The Minister of Food & Agriculture[604] also made a strong statement to the effect that good agricultural land would be protected and would not be confiscated in this way unless some very extraordinary and overwhelming reasons compelled one to do it.

This Bill brought to my mind the case of the Ghaziabad farmers (and I think there were some Bulandshahr people too). Their land is first-rate, and as good as any one can find anywhere. It would be a great pity, and I think quite wrong, if this land was taken for extension work. I hope, therefore, that it will be possible not to do so and to leave this land for agricultural purposes. The Plan should be varied somewhat to do this.

I am writing to the Planning Authority here also about it.[605]

Yours sincerely,
[Jawaharlal Nehru]

189. To C.B. Gupta: Zaidi to replace Hifzur Rahman[606]

August 30, 1962

My dear Chandra Bhanu,

I had a deputation from the Jamiat-ul-Ulema today. They spoke about various matters to me. Among them was the vacancy caused by Maulana Hifzur

601. Letter to the Chief Minister of Uttar Pradesh.
602. Nehru's letter to C.B. Gupta, probably of 28 August 1962, has not been traced.
603. See item 230.
604. S.K. Patil.
605. See item 116. It is not clear whether the reference is to the Master Plan Committee for Delhi.
606. Letter to the Chief Minister of Uttar Pradesh.

Rahman's death.[607] They were very anxious that some Muslim should be put up for this vacancy. They mentioned one or two names. One of these names was that of Col. Zaidi, who is ceasing to be the Vice-Chancellor of Aligarh University. I pass this on to you for your consideration.

I think it will be better to have a Muslim there and Zaidi is likely to be a good candidate.[608]

Yours sincerely,
[Jawaharlal Nehru]

190. To C.B. Gupta: Candidate for Amroha[609]

September 3, 1962

My dear Chandra Bhanu,

I wrote to you the other day about the vacancy at Amroha caused by Maulana Hifzur Rahman's death. I understand that Kripalaniji[610] is going to contest it and that he is getting large-scale assistance from the Swatantra Party and the Jan Sangh.

This is not a personal matter. Kripalaniji represents opposition to our entire policy. We have therefore to put up our own candidate and he must be a strong candidate.

I had previously suggested to you that a Muslim might be put up and the name of Zaidi was mentioned.[611] I am told that Zaidi will not have much chance. He will be bitterly opposed by the Jan Sangh people because of his alleged treatment of Hindu students at Aligarh.[612] I do not think that he was to blame at all. I am merely mentioning this as a factor which may count in the election.

Another name mentioned was Ram Saran's. He is a good man, but I rather doubt if he has much chance there. I am merely mentioning these factors to you

607. Congress, Lok Sabha MP from Amroha, UP, died on 2 August 1962.
608. See also item 190.
609. Letter to the Chief Minister of UP.
610. J.B. Kripalani, PSP leader, who stood as an Independent from Bombay City North for the Lok Sabha, had lost to V.K. Krishna Menon, Congress, in the General Elections in February 1962.
611. See item 189. B.H. Zaidi was the Vice-Chancellor of Aligarh Muslim University from 7 October 1956 to 6 November 1962.
612. The reference is apparently to the incidents described in SWJN/SS/72/subsection Aligarh.

for your consideration. But it does seem important to me that the person we put up should be a strong candidate and should represent our policies firmly.[613]

Yours sincerely,
[Jawaharlal Nehru]

191. To C.B. Gupta: New Land Taxes[614]

September 3, 1962

My dear Chandra Bhanu,

I had your letter about Gautam.[615] I have written a brief letter to him disapproving of his activities.[616]

But quite apart from Gautam and his activities, I am a little worried about the wider effect of your proposals of taxation to earn revenue.[617] I don't exactly know what these proposals are and probably they are justifiable. But I have little doubt that they will create a furore among the peasantry in the UP and the Jan Sangh and the Swatantra Party will take every advantage of it. You are the best judge of the situation and you will do as you think best. But I wanted to put to you what many people told me.

The average peasant in the UP has probably got two to three acres of land and nothing will excite him more than this kind of addition to land revenue.

Yours sincerely,
Jawaharlal Nehru

613. See also item 195.
614. Letter to the Chief Minister of UP. PMO, File No. 31(124)/62-63-PMS, Sr. No. 3-A. Also available in the JN Collection.
615. Member of the Executive Committee of the UPCC and former Cooperation Minister in UP. For C.B. Gupta's letter, see appendix 52.
616. Item 44.
617. Under the Land Holding Tax Bill which the UP Government proposed to introduce in the State Assembly, all landholdings of more than one acre in the State were to be taxed. See item 16, fn 91.

192. To Gulzarilal Nanda: Land Taxes[618]

September 6, 1962

My dear Gulzarilal,

I enclose a letter from Mahavir Tyagi.

I confess I feel worried about this land taxation legislation. I have no doubt that it will cause great harm to the Congress. But, apart from that, I rather doubt if a uniform legislation for all peasants is the right thing. Most of the peasants hold uneconomic holdings. Also, with all these tremendous floods, the peasantry in large parts of the UP and Bihar must be in a bad way.

Dhebarbhai[619] came to see me today and mentioned his own concern about this taxation which will fall equally on all, whether they can pay it or not.[620]

Yours sincerely,
Jawaharlal Nehru

193. In the Lok Sabha: UP Land Revenue Bill[621]

S.M. Banerjee:[622] Sir, under rule 197, I beg to call the attention of the hon. Prime Minister to the following matter of urgent public importance and I request that he may make a statement thereon:

"Serious situation arising out of the suggestion of the Planning Commission to increase the land revenue in UP."

[Omitted: exchanges on procedure]

Jawaharlal Nehru: Mr Speaker,[623] Sir, this refers to Uttar Pradesh. The question affects in varying degrees various States. Some have, I believe, gone ahead and passed some legislation; others are in the process of doing so. But it is a

618. Letter to the Minister for Planning and Deputy Chairman of the Planning Commission. PMO, File No. 31(124)/62-63-PMS, Sr. No. 5-A. Also available in the JN Collection.
619. U.N. Dhebar, former Congress President and member, Central Parliamentary Board of Congress Party.
620. See also item 191.
621. Adjournment motion, 7 September 1962. *Lok Sabha Debates*, Vol. 8, Third Series, 3 to 7 September, 1962, cols 6885-6886.
622. Independent.
623. Hukam Singh.

matter which requires deep consideration. Normally, the Central Government does not interfere in this matter; nor am I aware—I do not know how far the Planning Commission, except for a general suggestion, went into it. But, I think, in view of the interest and anxiety of many hon. Members in this House, it would be right if we ask the Planning Commission to consider this matter fully and give us their advice.

    S.M. Banerjee: Since this Bill is likely to be passed, may I know whether the hon. Prime Minister will kindly see that this Bill is deferred till he actually comes back from abroad? Till the Planning Commission considers the whole thing will it be deferred? It should not be passed. I will request the hon. Prime Minister to give this assurance. He is going away tomorrow. It is only a question of one month.

Jawaharlal Nehru: I cannot give any assurance on this point because I do not know where each State may be. How can I bind down a State Government in a matter which is in their discretion. But, as I have said, we have, in fact, asked the Planning Commission to go into this matter. They will go into it thoroughly as a result of which it may happen that there is delay in considering that measure there.

    S.M. Bajerjee: It may be postponed till you come back.

Jawaharlal Nehru: I cannot ask the State Government that.[624]

194. To C.B. Gupta: The Land Revenue Question[625]

September 7, 1962

My dear Chandra Bhanu,

As I told you on the telephone, the question of enhancement of land revenue came up before the Lok Sabha today in a Motion for Adjournment. The Speaker did not allow such a motion but said he would call it a Calling Attention Notice so that Government may say something.

    The matter came up this afternoon and I was asked to make some statement. I told the House that I was naturally not competent to commit the UP Government

---

624. See also item 194.
625. Letter to the Chief Minister of Uttar Pradesh. PMO, File No. 31(124)/62-63-PMS, Sr. No. 7-B.

as it was entirely in their domain. But as the Planning Commission had been mentioned, I was prepared to draw the attention of the Planning Commission to this matter so that they may give such advice as they thought fit.[626]

I still think that it will be advisable for you to come here for a day and have full a talk with Gulzarilal Nanda[627] and some other members of the Planning Commission as well as Lal Bahadur.[628] I have spoken to Nandaji about this also and they are considering it in all its aspects.[629] After all this you will be able to proceed with strength.

There is no immediate hurry for this bill to be taken up by your Assembly and you may take your time over it.

This morning this matter came up before the Executive Committee of the Congress Parliamentary Party. There too various arguments were advanced. Ultimately at my suggestion the matter was referred to the Planning Commission.

I am sure that after your talks with Nandaji, Lal Bahadur, etc., some of the differences that have arisen will be removed. The main consideration is that peasants having uneconomic holdings should not have another burden cast upon them. The public reaction has also to be kept in mind.

Yours sincerely,
Jawaharlal Nehru

195. To C.B. Gupta: Defeating J.B. Kripalani in Amroha[630]

September 7, 1962

My dear Chandra Bhanu,
I have just spoken to you about the Amroha seat.[631] Subsequently I spoke to Govind Sahai.[632] Previously I had discussed this with Ajit Prasad Jain.[633]

I am quite clear that this seat has to be contested stoutly and every effort should be made to win it. This is not a personal matter but a national matter and if we do not contest it fully, it will affect our national position and do

---

626. See items 16 and 193.
627. Minister for Planning and Deputy Chairman, Planning Commission.
628. Lal Bahadur Shastri, the Home Minister.
629. See item 192.
630. Letter to the Chief Minister of Uttar Pradesh.
631. See item 190.
632. Minister of Jails, Relief and Rehabilitation and Youth Welfare in UP.
633. President, UPCC.

harm to our Party as a whole. Apart from this, although we have affection for Kripalaniji[634] he has come to represent opposition to Congress policies in every field, both national and international. After we have lost two seats of Parliament in the South, it would be very harmful if we show any weakness about this seat.

The question then arises as to who should stand. As far as I can make out, the best candidate from every point of view would be the son of Maulana Hussain Ahmed Madni of Deoband. There is no doubt that he will carry solidly Muslim votes and I am sure he will get some Hindu votes too. After all, Hifzur Rehman won from that seat easily although he was lying ill. The man I suggest will be a stronger candidate than Hifzur Rehman was. I am told that he is otherwise a progressive young man also and is popular. His standing will upset the calculations of our opponents.

The opponents are Kripalaniji and perhaps Lohia.[635] Some Muslim members of the Republican Party may also want to support Kripalaniji, but that will not carry any weight if the candidate I suggest is put up.

That is the opinion of Ajit Prasad Jain and Govind Sahai as well as others. I am, therefore, suggesting his name for your consideration. You can discuss this matter with Govind Sahai who will be returning to Lucknow.[636]

Yours sincerely,
Jawaharlal Nehru

(y) West Bengal

196. To P.C. Sen: Calcutta Programme[637]

July 23, 1962

My dear Prafulla Sen,
Your letter of the 20th July. The programme you have given will suit me, but I am now thinking of reaching Calcutta a little earlier, that is, in the evening of the 28th. This will give me a little more time in Calcutta, that is, the whole of the 29th.

---

634. J.B. Kripalani, PSP leader.
635. Rammanohar Lohia, Socialist Party leader.
636. Eventually Hafiz Mohammed Ibrahim, the Minister of Irrigation and Power, who had been re-elected to the Rajya Sabha in April 1962, was put up as the Congress candidate. In the by-election held in May 1963, he lost to J.B. Kripalani.
637. Letter to the Chief Minister of West Bengal.

I shall be going from Lucknow, and as I am finishing my Lucknow programme by about 5 p.m. on the 28th, I can start from the airport there at 5.30 p.m. This will make me reach Dum Dum at about 7.45 p.m., subject to the weather being not too bad.

If you think it is appropriate, I shall go straight from the Dum Dum airport to Dr B.C. Roy's residence.[638] Or I can go there early next morning, whichever you prefer. The rest of the programme can be as you have suggested or may be varied somewhat giving more time to the Congress meeting.[639]

Yours sincerely,
[Jawaharlal Nehru]

197. To Brohmachari Bholanath: Sundarbans[640]

July 29, 1962

Dear Brohmachariji,

I have your letter of the 28th. I would have gladly met your deputation but I fear it is difficult for me to find the time today because of other engagements. I have, however, fully in mind the case of the Sundarban area and I have talked about it to the Chief Minister, Shri Prafulla Chandra Sen.

Yours sincerely,
Jawaharlal Nehru

198. To P.C. Sen: Jains in Purulia[641]

August 4, 1962

My dear Prafulla Sen,

I have received some complaints from Jains about an unfortunate incident that appears to have happened in Purulia on the 8th of July. There is much

---

638. Located at Nirmal Chandra Street in Central Calcutta. B.C. Roy, the previous Chief Minister of West Bengal, died on 1 July 1962.
639. On 29 July 1962, Nehru addressed a meeting of Congress legislators and members of the West Bengal PCC at Congress Bhawan.
640. Letter to the General Secretary of the Sundarban Proja Mangal Samity, 92 Collin Street, Calcutta-16. Sent from Raj Bhavan, Calcutta. PMO, File No. 7(181)/59-66-PM, Volume II, Sr. No. 107-A
641. Letter to the Chief Minister of West Bengal.

consternation among Jains over this incident. I enclose a Hindi press cutting which gives some facts about it.[642] I hope you will kindly enquire into this matter.

Yours sincerely,

[Jawaharlal Nehru]

(z) Bidhan Chandra Roy

199. B.C. Roy[643]

Dr Bidhan Chandra Roy shone in the many activities in which he was engaged. As a physician he was at the top; as a statesman and administrator, he was also most outstanding; and so also in the many other activities he was connected with. He was, of course, a man of great ability, but what made him loved and what gave him his high position was his humanity. Perhaps his training as a physician brought out specially these human traits so that he considered persons as human beings to be helped. Of all the many virtues and qualities that he possessed, I think this was one which gave him a pre-eminent position.

200. For B.C. Roy Memorial[644]

Dr B.C. Roy is no more and we mourn for his passing away but everywhere in Calcutta one sees the impress of his hand and his work. He died, as a great man should, engaged till the end in activities for the public good. India, as a whole and not only West Bengal, while grieving for his loss, should rejoice also that this man of vision blessed us with his work and his example and passed away leaving a breath of his greatness behind.

---

642. The Hindi press cutting has not been traced. According to the *Amrita Bazar Patrika* of 10 July 1962, p. 6, the police resorted to a lathi charge and fired several rounds of teargas to disperse a violent crowd in Purulia on 8 July. The trouble started when the public protested against the cremation of a Jain sadhu inside the market area by the sadhu's disciples.

643. Message, 25 July 1962, for the Dr B.C. Roy Memorial Number of the *Bengal Medical Journal*. Forwarded to Debesh Mukherjee, Honorary State Secretary, Indian Medical Association, 67 Dharamtala Street, Calcutta 13. PMO, File No. 9/2/62-PMP, Vol. V, Sr. No. 40-A. Also available in the JN Collection.

644. Note, 29 July 1962, addressee not indicated. From Raj Bhavan, Calcutta. NMML, AICC Papers, Box No. 368, File No. G-1(A), 1962. Also available in the JN Collection.

It is fitting that we should build a memorial to him after his own heart. A Memorial Committee has been formed in Calcutta. The object of this Committee is to build a modern children's hospital properly equipped and with a children's hobby centre, a gymnasium and a library. The hospital will be situated in the centre of the city of Calcutta but surrounded by several parks.

Already over Rs 22 lakhs have been collected, chiefly from West Bengal, but it is necessary and highly desirable that the whole of India should participate in this beneficent scheme which would have been so much to Dr Roy's liking. I trust, therefore, that people all over India will contribute handsomely to this memorial. His real memorial is the good work he did for Bengal and for the city of Calcutta which he loved and served in numerous capacities, but it is desirable that we who remain should set up a particular memorial for him and that it should be a worthy one.

201. To S.K. Nag Chowdhury: Memorial Fund for B.C. Roy[645]

29th July 1962

Dear Dr Nag Chowdhury,

I have received your letter of the 20th July. I have come here to Calcutta in order to pay my tribute to Dr Bidhan Chandra Roy.

Your suggestion to raise a memorial fund for Dr Roy has already been acted upon. Such a fund was started a little while ago with the particular purpose of having a children's hospital in Calcutta, a purpose which was dear to Dr Roy. Already, within a few days a sum of Rs 22 lakhs has been collected for this purpose. Thus far the appeal was largely limited to West Bengal but it is proposed to extend it to the whole of India now. Shri Atulya Ghosh, President, West Bengal Pradesh Congress Committee, is the Treasurer of this fund.[646] I am sending your letter to him.

With all good wishes,

Yours sincerely,
[Jawaharlal Nehru]

---

645. Letter to a medical doctor; address: c/o K.R. Bose, British Embassy, Baghdad, Iraq. Sent from Raj Bhavan, Calcutta.
646. He was also General Secretary of the Dr B.C. Roy Memorial Committee, West Bengal.

313

202. To Y.B. Chavan: B.C. Roy Memorial[647]

5th September, 1962

My dear Chavan,

I am writing to you as Chairman of the Central Advisory Board of the Dr B.C. Roy Memorial Committee. It has been decided to collect rupees sixty lakhs for a 200-bed Children's Hospital and a Children's Park with Library and Hobby Centre in Calcutta. Nearly rupees thirty-five lakhs have already been collected by the Bengal Committee.

Dr B.C. Roy, as you well know, was a great and remarkable man. It is right that we honour him by a suitable memorial. A Children's Hospital would have been after his own heart, and it is fit and proper that the memorial should have an all-India character.

I hope that we shall have your goodwill and assistance in this work. May I suggest that you might form a small Committee of Maharashtra State, with yourself as Chairman of it.

I might add that all payments to the Memorial Fund have been exempted from income-tax.

For any further details, communications may be addressed to Shri Atulya Ghosh, Secretary, Memorial Committee, 58-B, Chowringhee Road, Calcutta 20.

Yours sincerely
Jawaharlal Nehru

203. B.C. Roy Memorial Fund[648]

I am glad to know that a Women's Coordinating Council consisting of 28 major women's organisations in West Bengal has been formed to raise funds for the Dr B.C. Roy Memorial Committee. It is particularly suitable that women should collect funds for a memorial which will benefit children most. I am very glad that the form of the memorial for Dr B.C. Roy is a hospital for children.

I send my good wished to the Women's Coordinating Council and wish them success.

---

647. Letter to the Chief Minister of Maharashtra. Similar letters were sent to the Chief Ministers of, Andhra Pradesh, Bihar, Gujarat, Madras, Mysore, Orissa, Punjab, Rajasthan and UP, and to Bharat Ram, industrialist.
648. Message, 7 September 1962, forwarded to Renuka Ray, Congress, Lok Sabha MP from Malda, West Bengal; address: 187 South Avenue, New Delhi.

III. DEVELOPMENT

(a) Economy

204. To Morarji Desai: I.G. Patel for World Bank Report[1]

25th July, 1962

My dear Morarji,

Your letter of the 25th July in which you suggest that I.G. Patel should be sent to Washington for the World Bank Report.[2] I agree with you that in the circumstances it is desirable to send him to Washington. Reference of this need not be made to the Cabinet.

Yours sincerely,
[Jawaharlal Nehru]

1. Letter to the Finance Minister. PMO, File No. 17(411)60-66-PMS, Sr. No. 29-A.
2. Morarji Desai wrote in his letter that while the statements made in the draft report of the World Bank Mission, which visited India in March-April 1962, were by and large factually correct, "the general critical tenor [of the report] is going to make it very difficult for us to negotiate future aid, unless we succeed in getting the other side of the picture also presented in the report." He, therefore, proposed to send I.G. Patel, Chief Economic Adviser in the Ministry of Finance and Economic Adviser, Planning Commission, to Washington "so that he may have detailed discussions with the Bank staff on the report with a view to securing whatever modifications are possible." He sought Nehru's approval to Patel's deputation without a reference being made to the Cabinet, as "we are treating the draft economic report as a top secret document in order to avoid leakage to Press, since the consequences of such leakage would be very embarrassing and unfortunate." PMO, File No. 17(411)/60-66-PMS, Sr. No. 28-A.

    Forwarding a summary of the World Bank Mission's report to Nehru on 20 July, T.T. Krishnamachari, Minister without Portfolio, had written: "The report itself is generally unfriendly which, I am told, is a departure from the previous reports. However, while some of our weaknesses are highlighted, it cannot be said that it is factually altogether incorrect." PMO, File No. 17(411)/60-66-PMS, Sr. No. 27-A.

205. To Raghunath Singh: Circulate P.C. Mahalanobis's Vienna Speeches[3]

August 16, 1962

My dear Raghunath Singh,

Some time ago, I had received a report from Prof. Mahalanobis of speeches he had delivered recently in Vienna at a conference there.[4] These were entitled: "The Social Transformation for National Development" and "The Scientific Base of Economic Development".[5]

It struck me that these speeches, though very concise, still dealt with the problems in a helpful way and it would be a good thing if the Members of our Party could see them. I have, therefore, got from Prof. Mahalanobis about 500 copies of these speeches. I am sending these to you and I suggest you send them to our members.

Yours sincerely,
[Jawaharlal Nehru]

206. To T.T. Krishnamachari: Cabinet Paper[6]

29th August, 1962

My dear T.T.,

Your letter of the 28th with the note attached. I agree with you that we must give urgent consideration to the matters you have referred to. Also, that we should have a Cabinet decision on your note and any other paper that the Planning Commission may produce.

I suggest that you send your note to the Cabinet Secretary[7] and ask him to include it in the agenda of the next meeting of the Cabinet. You may tell him that I have agreed that this should be done.

---

3. Letter to the Secretary of the CPP.
4. P.C. Mahalanobis, Member, Planning Commission, and Statistical Adviser to the Cabinet, GOI, attended the Conference for International Economic Cooperation and Partnership held in Salzburg-Vienna in July 1962.
5. See appendices 16-17.
6. Letter to the Minister without Portfolio. NMML, T.T. Krishnamachari Papers, File 1962, Auto. Also available in the JN Collection.
7. S.S. Khera.

I think you should inform Gulzarilal Nanda[8] of this so that he may also prepare any paper he wishes for this discussion.[9]

Yours affectionately,
Jawaharlal Nehru

207. To S.K. Patil: Price Policy[10]

September 5, 1962

My dear SK,

Your letter of September 5.[11] As for the point you have raised regarding price policy, we dealt with it in Cabinet today and in effect postponed further consideration till my return from abroad. Meanwhile, the matter will be considered by your Ministry and by the Planning Commission. The States will also have to be consulted.[12]

As for the second matter, if you like to postpone this till I come back, you can do so. Or else, you can even ask for a meeting of the Executive Committee[13] when I am not here.

Yours sincerely,
[Jawaharlal Nehru]

208. To Morarji Desai: IDA Capital[14]

September 5, 1962

My dear Morarji,

I have your letter of September 5 with which you have sent me a letter from Bijju[15] dated August 27. Also his letter of August 28.

8. Minister of Planning and Deputy Chairman of the Planning Commission.
9. The subject discussed was probably rising prices, see items 207 and 209.
10. Letter to the Minister of Food and Agriculture. NMML, S.K. Patil Papers. Also available in the JN Collection.
11. Appendix 59.
12. See also item 209.
13. Of the CPP.
14. Letter to the Finance Minister.
15. B.K. Nehru, Ambassador to the USA.

As for his proposal that the matter of the increase of IDA's[16] capital should be raised at the Commonwealth Prime Ministers' Conference in London, I have no objection to this. Indeed, it would be right to increase IDA's capital. If this matter is raised at the Commonwealth Conference, we should certainly support it. But I would much prefer that someone else raises it and we support it. If this is not possible, then I have no objection to this being raised on our behalf.

Bijju's letter of August 27—his first point about our Ambassadors making speeches etc. in certain Western countries. We can certainly supply material to our Ambassadors and they can occasionally take advantage of it. But it is not usual, outside the United States, for the Ambassadors to make propagandist speeches. But certainly they should be kept fully informed and asked to put forward our view whenever an opportunity offers itself.

His second point. I do not mind if "the three wise men" come here again.[17]

His third point. I do not mind some writers, columnists etc. being invited to come here. But too many of them from various countries roaming about India more or less at the same time would be a nuisance.

His fourth point. I do not mind some legislators being invited from the United States.

I am returning Bijju's two letters.

Yours sincerely,
[Jawaharlal Nehru]

209. To Gulzarilal Nanda: Rising Prices[18]

September 6, 1962

My dear Gulzarilal,

Yesterday's discussion in the Cabinet about how to deal with rising prices was interesting in so far as it went. But, of course, it did not go very far, and the matter has been referred back to the Planning Commission for further inquiry and consideration. It seems to me that this subject is of very high

---

16. The International Development Association, an affiliate of the World Bank.
17. Three prominent bankers of the industrially developed countries, Herman Abs, Chairman, Deutsche Bank of Frankfurt, Oliver Franks, Chairman, Lloyds Bank, London, and Allan Sproul, former Chairman, Federal Reserve Bank of New York, had, at the instance of Eugene Black, World Bank President, visited India and Pakistan, January-March 1960, as independent individuals to assess the aid requirements of these countries.
18. Letter to the Minister of Planning and Deputy Chairman of the Planning Commission. Copied to T.T. Krishnamachari, Minister without Portfolio.

importance affecting vast numbers of people. This requires, therefore, our urgent consideration and effective steps taken. I do hope that during September this will be done. There may well be some difference of opinion, but that should not prevent us from doing what we consider right. The difference of opinion can only be resolved ultimately by the Cabinet who can consider all sides of the question. I hope, however, that all that can be done to collect this material and make definite suggestions, will be done in the course of the next three or four weeks.[19]

[PLANNING AT HOME]

Babu ji . . .

"Dont't stand there expecting the Planning Commission to bring down prices. Bargain with that fellow."

(From *The Times of India*, 2 September 1962, p. 3)

19. Item 206 may be related to this subject.

I gather that the latest national income statistics do not make good reading and the per capita income has not gone up at all. We have, therefore, to address ourselves to our problems with a sense of urgency.[20]

Yours sincerely,
Jawaharlal Nehru

210. To Biju Patnaik: Solution of Sileru Waters Dispute[21]

September 6, 1962

My dear Biju,

I am very happy to learn that you and Sanjiva Reddy have solved your inter-State dispute about the Sileru waters.[22] I congratulate you upon this happy decision which has been pending for long.[23]

Yours sincerely,
Jawaharlal Nehru

211. To N. Sanjiva Reddy: Solution of Sileru Waters Dispute[24]

September 6, 1962

My dear Sanjiva Reddy,

Thank you for your letter of the 4th September. I want to congratulate you and

---

20. See also item 207.
21. Letter to the Chief Minister of Orissa. PMO, File No. 17(446)/61-70-PMS, Sr. No. 19-A.
22. Biju Patnaik and N. Sanjiva Reddy, the Chief Minister of Andhra Pradesh, signed an agreement in Hyderabad on 4 September on the construction of a hydel and irrigation project on the river Sileru, resolving a five-year old dispute on the location of the dam.
23. See also item 211.
24. Letter to the Chief Minister of Andhra Pradesh. PMO, File No. 17(446)/61-70-PMS, Sr. No. 18-A.

Biju Patnaik for the agreement arrived at. I wish all our State problems could be solved in this happy way.[25]

Yours sincerely,
Jawaharlal Nehru

(b) Industry and Labour

212. To Shriyans Prasad Jain: Industrial Policy[26]

July 21, 1962

Dear Shri Shriyans Prasad Jain,

I have your letter of the 20th July, which I have read with care.[27] I am not going to answer it at any length at present. The points you have raised are very much before us.

You can certainly see some of my colleagues in the Government of India. As for meeting me, I shall be glad to meet you, but I fear I cannot do so for the next fortnight or so.

Yours sincerely,
[Jawaharlal Nehru]

---

25. Extract from letter of 4 September 1962 from N. Sanjiva Reddy to Nehru: "When we were at Delhi in August myself and Biju Patnaik had agreed that the Inter-State dispute between Andhra and Orissa about the Sileru waters should be referred to the Prime Minister of India for arbitration, since the public agitation in both the States was whipped up to such an extent, we felt that it will be difficult for us to take any decision on merits. Orissa proposed Bellamela site for the construction of the dam while Andhra proposed Guntawada, eight miles downstream on the same river. Yesterday Sri Biju Patnaik came here [Hyderabad] and we discussed the matter again and resolved that we should come to some agreement before the next evening without resorting to arbitration. We are very happy that our discussions of last night and this morning have yielded good results and we signed the agreement at 2.00 p.m. today. I am also happy that the Leaders of the Opposition parties in my Assembly (Communists, Swatantra, Independent parties) agreed to my conceding to Orissa's Bellamela site for the construction of the dam. While conceding this to Orissa, we have secured some concessions for our diversion schemes lower down. By this method of give and take, we have resolved a dispute which has been pending since long." PMO, File No. 17(446)/61-70-PMS, Sr. No. 17-A. See also item 210.
26. Letter to the President of the Federation of Indian Chambers of Commerce and Industry, Federation House, New Delhi.
27. Appendix 6.

213. For C.P. Sadasivaiah[28]

When I was in Bangalore recently, Shri S.K. Dey, Union Minister for Panchayati Raj and Community Development, told me about Shri C.P. Sadasivaiah of the Shiva Industries in Tumkur, Mysore State. He spoke very highly of the enterprise of Shri Sadasivaiah and suggested that I should meet him and, if possible, visit his industrial establishment. Unfortunately, when I went to Tumkur, I could not meet him. Later he came to see me at Bangalore and brought a number of his improved agricultural implements. I was much impressed by these implements and even more so by Shri Sadasivaiah who had started from very small beginnings and by his enterprise and hard work built up this industry which does good service to farmers. I wish him further success.

214. For M.P. Gandhi: Problems are the Price of Progress[29]

I hope that many people will read and profit by this *Annual* in which some of our major industries are described. Our progress on many fronts produces new problems. Indeed, problems are the price and the resultant of progress. To solve these problems, knowledge and understanding of what is being done in India and what should be done are necessary.

We are trying to build up a planned economy of India. We have made considerable progress in planning. We have not wholly succeeded in implementing what we planned. Difficulties arise, shortage of coal and power, and transport not keeping up to the mark. We have to solve these difficulties and not merely complain of what has been done and has not been done. Often the difficulties are due to the very pace of our progress in some directions; sometimes the difficulties impede that progress.

Whatever the difficulties, they will have to be overcome. India is well on the march to industrialisation and nothing can really change that forward course. The test for everything that we do must necessarily be the good of India as a whole and her people. It is a long journey, but it is a worthwhile one and we are determined to reach our goal.

28. Message, 23 July 1962. PMO, File No. 9/2/62-PMP, Vol. V, Sr. No. 62-A. Also available in the JN Collection.
29. Foreword to *Major Industries of India: Annual 1962*, 24 July 1962. Sent to Professor M.P. Gandhi, Bombay 1.

215. For the Indian Labour Conference[30]

I send my good wishes on the occasion of the twentieth anniversary of the Indian Labour Conference.[31] It is of the utmost importance that industrial relations should be good and that labour should be treated with all fairness. The whole Five Year Plan ultimately depends on the results of the labour of industrial workers as well as agricultural workers. Unless labour is given a fair deal and is satisfied, it will be difficult to expect it to play its full part in this great enterprise which we have undertaken.

216. President's Award for Public Sector Undertakings[32]

The idea of giving Presidential Awards to the Public Sector Industrial Undertakings is a good one. This acknowledges merit where merit is due and draws the attention of the public to the excellent work being done by some of these undertakings. The public should realise this and commend this work.

217. To Manubhai M. Shah: Exporting Diamonds to Import Synthetic Stones Absurd[33]

August 9, 1962

My dear Manubhai,

A few days ago, the *Times of India* had a news item from Jaipur. This said that Government had decided to permit the import of synthetic stones against the

---

30. Message, 3 August 1962, forwarded to Gulzarilal Nanda, Minister of Labour. PMO, File No. 26(2)/57-65-PMS, Sr. No. 23-A. Published in the *National Herald*, 8 August 1962, p. 1.
31. The twentieth session of the Indian Labour Conference was held in New Delhi, 7-9 August 1962, under the chairmanship of Gulzarilal Nanda.
32. Message, 7 August 1962, forwarded to N. Kanungo, Minister of Industry. PMO, File No. 17(388)/60-64-PMS, Sr. No. 11-A.
33. Letter to the Minister of State for International Trade.

SELECTED WORKS OF JAWAHARLAL NEHRU

export of diamonds, jewellery and precious stones. Also that glass beads and artificial pearls are being imported.³⁴

I do not understand why we should encourage such imports when we are so short of foreign exchange. To pay for synthetic stones with diamonds etc. hardly seems wise to me.

Yours sincerely,
[Jawaharlal Nehru]

218. To Manubhai M. Shah: British India Corporation³⁵

August 12, 1962

My dear Manubhai,

What is happening to the British India Corporation of Kanpur? I have heard vaguely that some suggestions have been made that our shares in this should be disposed of to private parties. I think this will be very unfortunate and undesirable. The British India Corporation deals with imported items many of which are necessary for Defence purposes. If these go into private hands, there will be profiteering and will affect our Defence. I think we should try gradually to get full control of this Corporation.³⁶

Yours sincerely,
[Jawaharlal Nehru]

---

34. According to *The Times of India* of 6 August, Manubhai Shah announced at a jewellers' meeting in Jaipur the previous day that "Government had decided to permit the import of synthetic stones, except white and red, and platinum solders against the export of diamonds, jewellery and precious stones," and that "glass beads and artificial pearls could now be imported to the extent of the one-third f.o.b. [free on board] value of the exported imitation jewellery." He also said that "export promotion was a national obligation which they should try to discharge."
35. Letter to the Minister of State for International Trade.
36. See also item 229.

324

219. To V.K. Krishna Menon: Meeting to discuss Aircraft Manufacture[37]

August 15, 1962

My dear Krishna,

Will you come to my room in Parliament House at 4 p.m. tomorrow, 16th August? Please bring Dr Bhagavantam[38] with you. I am asking Morarji Desai,[39] T.T. Krishnamachari[40] and Lal Bahadur Shastri[41] also.

I met Bhagavantam today. I had a talk with Morarji Desai this evening and showed him the note you had sent me. He said that as regards the manufacture of the aircraft in India, no figures were given. He should have liked to be given some idea of how much the building and machinery etc. would cost.

He also raised the question of utility of HF-24 when you propose to get more suitable aircraft.

I should like to see you for a few minutes before you come at 4 p.m. tomorrow. I am rather busy in the morning with questions, and after. Perhaps you could come at about 1 o'clock to my room in Parliament House, or a little before 4 p.m.

[Jawaharlal Nehru]

220. Artistry of Handlooms[42]

India is set on her course of industrialisation and I have little doubt that she will progressively be an industrialised country, but I do hope that this process will not put an end to the handlooms of India. I have seldom seen anything more beautiful than the handloom fabrics which we have in our country. It is craftsmanship and artistry of the highest order. As a thing of beauty and something which keeps alive our great tradition of craftsmanship, I hope every effort will be made to protect and encourage these hand-woven fabrics.

---

37. Letter to the Defence Minister.
38. Suri Bhagavantam, Scientific Adviser to the Ministry of Defence.
39. Finance Minister.
40. Minister without Portfolio.
41. Home Minister.
42. Message, 16 August 1962, forwarded to Mulk Raj Anand, Marg Publications, 34-38 Bank Street, Bombay-1. PMO, File No. 9/2/62-PMP, Vol. V, Sr. No. 106-A. Also available in the JN Collection.

221. For the Geep Workers' Union of Allahabad[43]

I have seen the Annual Magazine of the Geep Workers' Union of Allahabad. Looking through it I have gathered some impression of the work of this Union and of the excellent relations that exist between employers and employees.

It is a good idea to have a trilingual magazine in Hindi, Urdu and English. The general outlook suggested to workers in this Magazine is excellent. This is to spread patriotism and cooperation and to help in national development so as to bring about a socialist pattern of society. This does not mean merely some legislation, but to raise the standards of our people and their working capacity. It is only through hard work that we can make good.

222. To Morarji Desai: Businessmen's Power Supply Problems[44]

August 24, 1962

My dear Morarji,
I had a visit from a deputation from the [Federation of] Indian Chambers of Commerce & Industry. They discussed with me various matters about shortage of coal and transport etc. They also talked about difficulties experienced in putting up electric power plants, and Naval Tata[45] gave me a note on this subject.[46] I enclose a copy of this. I have sent a copy to the Planning Commission.

Yours sincerely,
[Jawaharlal Nehru]

223. To K.C. Reddy: Kerala Titanium Factory[47]

August 25, 1962

My dear Reddy,
You have probably received a letter from A.K. Gopalan[48] about the proposal of the Kerala Government to denationalise the Titanium Factory and hand it

43. Message, 22 August 1962.
44. Letter to the Finance Minister.
45. An industrialist of the Tata group; chairman of the Tata electric companies.
46. Appendix 45.
47. Letter to the Minister of Commerce and Industry. PMO, File No. 17(517)/62-66-PMS, Sr. No. 3-A. Also available in the JN Collection.
48. CPI, Lok Sabha MP from Kasaragod, Kerala.

over to the Tatas. I do not know much about this. But, on general grounds, this seems to me a very undesirable proposal and opposed to our basic policies. A.K. Gopalan wrote to me about it[49] and sent me a copy of a memorandum addressed to the Minister for Commerce & Industry.

I have written to the Chief Minister of Kerala.[50] I enclose a copy of my letter to him.[51]

Yours sincerely,
Jawaharlal Nehru

224. To Pattom A. Thanu Pillai: Kerala Titanium Factory[52]

August 25, 1962

My dear Thanu Pillai,

I have received a letter from A.K. Gopalan, in which he says that the Kerala Government has resolved to denationalise the Titanium Factory and hand it over to private owners. I do not know how far this is true. But any such decision would seem to me to be against our basic policies. Titanium is a very important new metal and it is very desirable to keep it under State control. It is required for Defence purposes. Also, so far as I know, this Titanium Factory has been doing very well and earning a considerable profit. I understand it is going to be expanded.[53]

Yours sincerely,
Jawaharlal Nehru

---

49. Appendix 40.
50. Pattom A. Thanu Pillai.
51. Item 224; K.C. Reddy's reply, appendix 53.
    Reply, 8 October 1962, from R. Sankar, the Chief Minister of Kerala, appendix 68. R. Sankar, who was earlier the Deputy Chief Minister of Kerala, had become the Chief Minister on 26 September following the resignation of Pattom A. Thanu Pillai, who was appointed Governor of Punjab.
52. Letter to the Chief Minister of Kerala. PMO, File No. 17(517)/62-66-PMS, Sr. No. 2-A. Also available in the JN Collection.
53. For reply, 8 October 1962, from R. Sankar, the Chief Minister of Kerala, see appendix 68. See also item 223 and appendix 53.

225. To Swaran Singh: Pathankot – Jammu Railway to Exploit Minerals[54]

August 27, 1962

My dear Swaran Singh,

About a year or two ago we considered the question of extending the railway line from Pathankot via Jammu to some places beyond. It was then decided that a survey should be made of this area.

I believe a survey was made, though I do not know if this has been completed yet. Since then many valuable mineral deposits have been found in Central Jammu Province of the Jammu & Kashmir State. There is gypsum, bauxite and good quality coal. Indeed, there is a very valuable mineral belt.

The necessity for exploiting these minerals is arising now or will arise soon. The question of the railway has thus assumed even greater importance than previously.[55]

I should be glad to know what progress has been made in this survey or any other preliminaries.

Yours sincerely,
Jawaharlal Nehru

226. To T.N. Singh: Minerals in Jammu[56]

August 27, 1962

My dear TN,

I should like you to meet Shri D.P. Dhar, Minister of the Government of Jammu & Kashmir. He is here in Delhi now and will be here for another two or perhaps three days. He is specially in charge of mineral development in Jammu & Kashmir, and a Corporation has been formed for this purpose. There is apparently a rich mineral belt in Jammu Province. This contains coal, gypsum, bauxite, etc.[57]

---

54. Letter to the Minister of Railways. PMO, File No. 17(371)/59-66-PMS, Sr. No. 51-A. Also available in the JN Collection.
55. See item 226.
56. Letter to Member, Planning Commission. PMO, File No. 17(371)/59-66-PMS, Sr. No. 52-A. Also available in the JN Collection.
57. See also item 225; appendix 54.

I hope you will be able to get in touch with D.P. Dhar and fix up some time. You can do so through my office, if you have any difficulty otherwise.

Yours sincerely,
Jawaharlal Nehru

227. To C. Subramaniam: Expanding Steel Capacity[58]

August 29, 1962

My dear Subramaniam,

Your letter of the 28th August containing a proposal of the Indian Iron & Steel Company to expand their ingot steel capacity and later their finished steel capacity.[59] The proposal seems to be an attractive one.

I see from your note that the Planning Commission has already considered Phase I of this proposal and that you now intend preparing a note for the Cabinet which will be forwarded to the Planning Commission for their comments. I agree to this.

Yours sincerely,
Jawaharlal Nehru

228. To Gulzarilal Nanda: Dharma Teja and Cochin Shipyard[60]

August 31, 1962

My dear Gulzarilal,

Dharma Teja[61] came to see me today and spoke to me, among other things, about the Cochin Shipyard Project. He gave me a letter which I am sending you.

---

58. Letter to the Minister of Steel and Heavy Industries. PMO, File No. 17(518)/62-65-PMS, Sr. No. 2-A. Also available in the JN Collection.
59. Appendix 50.
60. Letter to the Minister of Planning and Deputy Chairman of the Planning Commission. PMO, File No. 17(79)/56-66-PMS, Sr. No. 24-A.
61. J. Dharma Teja, businessman and one of the Directors of Jayanti Shipping Corporation. For previous references, see SWJN/SS/64/items 114-115, SWJN/SS/70/items 244 and 251, SWJN/SS/73/item 202, SWJN/SS/74/item 192, SWJN/SS/75/items 179-180, and SWJN/SS/76/item 326.

As he says in his letter, he has spoken about this to our Transport & Communications Minister, Jagjivan Ram, also Raj Bahadur.[62] I am unable to express any opinion about this project. But I would suggest that it deserves examination.

Yours sincerely,
Jawaharlal Nehru

229. To K.C. Reddy: Taking Over British India Corporation[63]

September 2, 1962

My dear Reddy, ·

I wrote to you some time ago about the British India Corporation of Kanpur.[64] I think it is important that this Corporation should not go into private hands. I understand that Government own a part of their shares and the LIC also owns some shares. It should, therefore, not be difficult to gain control of the organisation and make it a public sector one.

The BIC control many industries. It may be that some of these industries are not of great interest to Government. But some of them are definitely of importance from the defence point of view.

Our Army people require large quantities of cotton and wool textile materials, also special protective clothing and equipment, tented shelters, waterproof covers, camouflage nets, and so on. Some of these are being made in our ordnance factories. But the basic textile materials have still to be purchased from private industry. As these have to be made to special specifications, Defence Science goes into the matter and draws up specifications etc. Private industry does not like to make particular types of qualities. Thus, both the private industry and the Defence Ministry have to face difficulties. There are considerable gaps between the qualities and the delivery time taken, and so on. Then there is trouble when the fabrics are not produced conforming to the specifications laid down.

---

62. Minister of State for Shipping.
63. Letter to the Minister of Commerce and Industry.
64. The letter to K.C. Reddy has not been traced. For an earlier letter of Nehru on this subject, addressed to Manubhai Shah, Minister of State for International Trade, see item 218.

I have mentioned some of these difficulties. Many of these things come from the BIC. It is, therefore, important and desirable to control the BIC and gradually to bring it into the public sector. This should not be difficult as we own a good number of shares already.

Yours sincerely,
[Jawaharlal Nehru]

(c) Agriculture

230. To A.P. Jain: Land Acquisition Amendment Bill[65]

August 22, 1962

My dear Ajit,
Your letter of August 22nd about the Land Acquisition Amendment Bill.[66] I am forwarding it to the Minister for Food & Agriculture.[67]

As you are yourself a member of the Committee dealing with this matter with the Minister, you will no doubt explain your suggestions to him.

Yours sincerely,
Jawaharlal Nehru

231. To Digambar Singh: Land Acquisition Amendment Bill[68]

अगस्त 25, 1962

प्रिय दिगम्बर सिंह जी,
आपका 25 अगस्त का पत्र मिला।[69] जिस बिल का आपने चर्चा किया है उसमें अब निश्चय हुआ है कि कई संशोधन हों। इसके बाद मैं नहीं समझता कि कोई बड़ा असन्तोष रह जायेगा। सिलेक्ट कमेटी की अब आवश्यकता नहीं है क्योंकि बहुत लोगों से इस बारे में सलाह की गई है।

65. Letter to Congress, Lok Sabha MP and President, UPCC; address: 5 Rafi Marg, New Delhi. NMML, A.P. Jain Papers.
66. Appendix 43.
67. S.K. Patil.
68. Letter to Congress, Lok Sabha MP; address: 4 North Avenue, New Delhi.
69. Appendix 47.

हमारी पंचवर्षीय योजना का काम कुछ जगह रुक गया है। इस लिये इस बिल के लाने की आवश्यकता हुई थी।

यह इरादा है कि बाद में इस पूरे सवाल पर ग़ौर किया जाये और एक नया बिल लाया जाये।

आपका
जवाहरलाल नेहरु

[Translation begins

25 August 1962

My dear Digambar Singhji,

I received your letter of August 25.[70] It has now been decided that there should be several amendments to the Bill about which you have written. Once that is done I do not think there will be any cause for dissatisfaction. There is no need now to set up a Select Committee because many people have been consulted in the matter.

Work on the Five Year Plan has come to a halt in some places. Hence it had become necessary to bring in this Bill.

Now it is proposed to take up the entire issue for consideration and bring in a new Bill.

Yours sincerely,
Jawaharlal Nehru

Translation ends]

232. To Ram Subhag Singh: Indian Council of Agricultural Education Conference[71]

September 5, 1962

My dear Ram Subhag,

You wrote to me on the 7th August about the Indian Council of Agricultural Education holding its Annual Conference on the 10th to the 12th October, and asked me to inaugurate it. I replied to you that I shall try to do so.

---

70. See fn 69 in this section.
71. Letter to the Minister of State for Food and Agriculture.

At that time I had not noticed that this Annual Conference was going to be held at Ranchi. I am afraid it is very difficult for me to go to Ranchi on that date. I am sorry, therefore, that I shall not be able to attend the Conference.

Yours sincerely
[Jawaharlal Nehru]

(d) Health

233. To P.V. Benjamin: Appreciation of Good Work[72]

July 20, 1962

Dear Dr Benjamin,
I have your letter of the 19th July.[73] Thank you for it. I should like to express my appreciation of the fine work you have done as Tuberculosis Adviser to the Government of India. I send you my good wishes.[74]

Yours sincerely,
J. Nehru

234. For the Niloufer Hospital[75]

I send my good wishes on the occasion of the opening of the Out-patient Department of the Niloufer Hospital for Children. I am especially interested in any work done for the benefit of children and the Niloufer Hospital is particularly noted for this type of work. I wish it success in bringing a measure of happiness to suffering children.[76]

---

72. Letter to the Tuberculosis Adviser to the GOI. PMO, File No. 28(81)/61-71-PMS, Sr. No. 16-A.
73. Appendix 5.
74. For previous references to P.V. Benjamin, see SWJN/SS/44/items 257-258, SWJN/SS/64/item 150 and SWJN/SS/69/item 260.
75. Message, 20 July 1962. PMO, File No. 9/2/62-PMP, Vol. V, Sr. No. 32-A.
76. According to the letter of 17 July 1962 from Harish Chandra, the Superintendent of the Niloufer Hospital in Hyderabad, it was a pediatric hospital and the out-patient department was to be inaugurated by Sushila Nayar, the Health Minister, with N. Sanjiva Reddy, Chief Minister of Andhra Pradesh, presiding. He also noted that Nehru had stayed on the premises in 1953, before it had become a hospital, for the Nanal Nagar Congress Session. PMO, File No. 9/2/62-PMP, Vol. V, Sr. No. 31-A.

235. For the Kitchen Garden Competition Committee[77]

I send my good wishes to the Kitchen Garden Competition Committee of the All India Women's Central Food Council. I am sure that much can be done in our kitchen gardens by producing vegetables and fruits. It would also be desirable to induce people to eat more vegetables from the point of view of a balanced diet. This can even be done in many of our villages.

236. To Sushila Nayar: Sanitary Privies[78]

August 10, 1962

My dear Sushila,

I am sending you a letter from Shri Saila Kumar Mukherjee.[79] Perhaps, you have heard from him directly.

This scheme is obviously desirable. Equally obviously, it will mean an expenditure of a vast sum of money. However, it would be a good thing to give a start to it. You might consult the Planning Commission about it.[80]

Yours sincerely,
Jawaharlal Nehru

237. In New Delhi: To the Red Cross[81]

मुझे हुक्म मिला है कि मैं अपने अमृत वचन अंग्रेजी में कहूं। मालूम नहीं मंजूर है कि नहीं, लेकिन खैर हुक्म की तामील करनी है।[82]

---

77. Message, 2 August 1962, forwarded to Mrs J.N. Sahni, Vice-Chairman of the Kitchen Garden Competition Committee of the All India Women's Central Food Council. PMO, File No. 9/2/62-PMP, Vol. V, Sr. No. 52-A.
78. Letter to the Minister of Health. PMO, File No. 28(96)/62-71-PMS, Sr. No. 1-A.
79. Minister, West Bengal Government. He proposed a scheme for conversion of service privies into sanitary septic privies in urban areas.
80. Nehru wrote in the same vein to Saila Kumar Mukherjee, on 10 August 1962, see PMO, File No. 28 (96)/62-71-PMS, Sr. No. 2-A. For Sushila Nayar's reply, see appendix 33.
81. Speech, 14 August 1962, inaugurating the Delhi Red Cross Bhavan in Golf Links. NMML, AIR Tapes, TS No. 11271, NM No. 1959.
82. It is not clear whose remarks was Nehru referring to. The transcript of the tape recording does not mention who else spoke before Nehru. However, newspapers of 15 August 1962 do report that Bhagwan Sahay, the Chief Commissioner of Delhi, and Rajan Nehru, Chairman of the Delhi Red Cross, were in attendance at the function.

[Translation: I have been asked to say some good words in English. I don't know whether it is acceptable to you. But, well, I must oblige.[83]]

Friends,

I am happy to be here for this Red Cross function, chiefly to pay my tribute to the work of the Red Cross, not only in Delhi or in India, but everywhere. In this world full of conflicts the Red Cross is a symbol of service and cooperation and absence of conflict. Even where there is conflict, the Red Cross goes in with its soothing message; and so the Red Cross organization deserves our help and cooperation in every way. I am glad that in India it is functioning well under the leadership of Rajkumari,[84] and now I am glad that I have come here for the Delhi branch, to lay the foundation stone of its home here.

I have often come in contact with this work and have always appreciated it. In Delhi especially, whenever any disaster or something like that occurs, the Red Cross is there to help, which is right, and it should. Therefore, I am glad of this opportunity to come here today to say a few words, praising the work of the Red Cross, and express the hope that they will receive in every way help and encouragement.

Thank you.

238. For the Synthetic Drugs Plant at Hyderabad[85]

I am glad that all preliminaries in respect of three of the four Drugs Projects, which we are setting up with Soviet collaboration, have been settled and actual construction work taken up. The help and cooperation which the State Governments have offered so generously will enable the Indian Drugs and Pharmaceuticals Limited to speed up the work and complete each Project within the Third Plan period. The synthetic drugs and the vitamins which are going to be produced at the Hyderabad Plant will go a long way in meeting our country's requirements of them. Such of the valuable foreign exchange which we are now spending on such preparations will be saved and we may even earn some by exporting a portion of our products. I look forward to the day which

---

83. See fn 82 in this section.
84. Amrit Kaur, former Health Minister, was Chairman of the Indian Red Cross.
85. Message, 8 September 1962, for the foundation-stone laying ceremony of the Administration Block of the Synthetic Drugs Plant on 9 September 1962. PMO, File No. 17(48)/56-66-PMS, Volume II, Sr. No. 135-A. Nehru was already en route to London, hence this message may have been prepared on 7 September before departure.

should come fairly soon, when we shall produce in the public as well as private sector all the medicines we need for our people.

As far as Andhra Pradesh is concerned, the Synthetic Drugs Plant at Hyderabad provides another affective link in the chain of industries which are being set up there, making it industrially as important as it is agriculturally.

239. For the Surgical Instruments Plant at Madras[86]

Some days ago, I spoke of the Synthetic Drugs Plant, which we are setting up at Hyderabad.[87] It is a matter of satisfaction that the Surgical Instruments Plant at Madras is coming up simultaneously and that efforts are being made to complete it before the target date. At present we are very short of good quality surgical instruments of even comparatively simple type. The Madras Plant will produce annually two and a half million pieces of surgical instruments of 180 types, which are used in general surgery, ophthalmology, gynaecology, etc. This Plant will mean a great relief to our hospitals, and specially to rural dispensaries, which, at present, are greatly handicapped for want of surgical instruments. I have no doubt that the Madras Plant will provide a good base for the manufacture of complicated surgical instruments of all types, for which we must quickly develop the necessary know-how and facilities. We are grateful to the Government of the USSR for the credit and assistance they are providing to us for the setting of three Drugs Plants and one Surgical Instruments Plant in the Public Sector.

240. To Zena Daysh: Nutrition Standards[88]

September 24, 1962

Dear Mrs Daysh,

Your letter of the 19th September has caught me up at Lagos in Nigeria. Thank you for it.

---

86. Message, 8 September 1962, for the foundation-stone laying ceremony of the Administration Block of the Surgical Instruments Plant on 15 September 1962. PMO, File No. 17(48)/56-66-PMS, Volume II, Sr. No. 134-A. For the date of this item, see item 238, fn 85.
87. See item 238.
88. Letter to environmentalist and Convener of the Committee on Nutrition in the Commonwealth, 63 Cromwell Road, London SW7. Sent from Lagos House, Lagos, Nigeria.

It is indeed important to raise nutritional standards. Mr Walter Nash[89] spoke to me about it and I agreed with the general principles. He did not put any definite scheme to me, but I suppose we discussed such matters when you were in India. We shall gladly consider with every sympathy proposals to that end.

Yours sincerely,
[Jawaharlal Nehru]

(e) Education

241. To K.L. Shrimali: Opposition to Tyabji as AMU Vice-Chancellor[90]

July 22, 1962

My dear Shrimali,

A.M. Khwaja[91] came to see me this afternoon. Among other things, he spoke to me about the Vice-Chancellorship of Aligarh Muslim University. He said he had heard that we are pressing Badruddin Tyabji[92] to become the Vice-Chancellor.[93] Personally he had nothing against Tyabji. In fact, at the meeting of the Executive Committee he had functioned well and supported Khwaja in some matters in opposition to the Vice-Chancellor's[94] proposals. But he objected to an ICS man and non-educationist becoming the Vice-Chancellor. This would mean more governmental interference, etc.

I told him that I entirely disagreed with him. Whether Tyabji became Vice-Chancellor or not, I did not know. That would depend largely on him, and he was pulled in different directions. But he was a competent, efficient, able and independent man, and to object to him on account of his being in the ICS seemed to me to be without reason.

Subsequently it came out later casually that one of the reasons he objected to him was that he was a Shia.

89. Former Prime Minister of New Zealand.
90. Letter to the Minister of Education.
91. Chancellor of Jamia Millia Islamia; member of the Executive Council of Aligarh Muslim University (AMU) for many years.
92. B.F.H.B. Tyabji, then Special Secretary in the MEA.
93. See SWJN/SS/77/items 306-307.
94. B.H. Zaidi was the Vice-Chancellor, 7 October 1956 – 6 November 1962.

The real reason, of course, is that he wants the present pro-Vice-Chancellor[95] to become the Vice-Chancellor or, in the alternative, the ex-Madras Judge, Bashir Ahmed.[96]

He then told me something about the activities of the Academic Council etc. of the Aligarh University. I did not understand him at all. He said that he had first proposed to move for a writ in the courts against some decision, but Tyabji had dissuaded him from doing so. He now gave me a long letter addressed to the President,[97] which I have not read carefully. I enclose this. I do not know if he wants me to send it to the President or this was only for my information. Anyhow, you can read it and deal with it as you think best.[98]

Yours sincerely,
[Jawaharlal Nehru]

242. To Balbhadra Prasad: Students' Agitation[99]

July 27, 1962

My dear Vice Chancellor,

You were good enough to send through the ADM a note to me about the students' agitation for seats for admission to various classes. I am grateful to you for this as it gave me some information which I could use when a deputation of the students came to see me.

These students gave me a representation which I enclose for your information. This mentions a number of matters, apart from the question of

---

95. Yusuf Husain Khan.
96. Basheer Ahmed Sayeed.
97. S. Radhakrishnan.
98. See further, item 253.
99. Letter to the Vice-Chancellor of Allahabad University. Sent from Anand Bhavan, Allahabad.

admission. I hope you will be good enough to consider them as I think they require some attention.[100]

Yours sincerely,
[Jawaharlal Nehru]

243. To K.L. Shrimali: B.F.H.B. Tyabji Vice-Chancellor of AMU[101]

2nd August, 1962

My dear Shrimali,

Badr-ud-Din Tyabji[102] came to see me this morning. He asked me again what I thought about his going to Aligarh as Vice-Chancellor. I told him that while I liked his work here, in the balance, I thought that his presence in Aligarh as Vice-Chancellor was desirable. It would bring a breath of fresh air and would improve the atmosphere there. He agreed to this and is going to see you about it.

He is rather anxious to avoid any controversy about it.[103] I do not know what the procedure is about choosing the Vice-Chancellor. I suppose the Executive Council makes some recommendation.

Tyabji while agreeable to going to Aligarh is anxious not to tie himself

100. The *National Herald* reported on 28 July 1962 that a deputation of the Allahabad University Students' Union, which met Nehru the previous day, drew his attention "to the lack of hostel facilities for the university students and urged him to intervene in the matter of reduction of seats in various departments of the university by the vice-chancellor for 'technical reasons'. Pandit Nehru is reported to have told the deputationists that he had received a letter from the vice-chancellor explaining the reasons for reducing the number of seats in various faculties. He is further reported to have expressed his regret over the fall in the standard of education and expressed the hope that the students and the teachers would try to maintain higher standard of university education."

Nehru also said "that every student should have an easy access to the books he needed. 'Books form the backbone of education and a good library is the true university'." He also "expressed the hope that the citizens would help the university union library in various ways—either gift of suitable books or by financial contribution or otherwise."

101. Letter to the Minister of Education.

102. B.F.H.B. Tyabji, Special Secretary at the MEA from January 1961.

103. On objections to Tyabji, see item 241. See also other items in section Development, subsection Education in this volume and in vol. 77.

up for too long. He suggested a year. It seems to me that two years is the least period. Anyhow, you can discuss this matter with him.[104]

Yours sincerely,
[Jawaharlal Nehru]

244. For Indian Students in Boston[105]

I send my good wishes to Indian students on the occasion of our Independence Day, August 15th. Indians who go abroad for study have a special responsibility when they come back to India. They have had opportunities which most other people do not have in India. They owe a debt to the people of India which they can discharge by service of the people here.

India is facing difficult problems. They are problems of growth. There can be no doubt that this growth is taking place in innumerable directions. But the problems we have to face are vast and they require all our labour and dedication.[106]

---

104. See further item 253.
105. Message, 6 August 1962, for students of the Greater Boston Area, forwarded to Lakshmi Chander Mehta, 105 Peterborough Street, Boston 15, Mass., USA. PMO, File No. 9/2/62-PMP, Vol. V, Sr. No. 89-A.
106. Letter, 6 August 1962, to Lakshmi Chander Mehta:

"Dear Shri Mehta,

I have received your letter of July 31st. I am afraid I am heavily occupied and shall not be able to find time to give an adequate message. So I do not think your wife should take the trouble to come to Delhi to record a message.

I am enclosing a brief message for Indian Students in the Greater Boston Area.

Yours sincerely,
J. Nehru"

PMO, File No. 9/2/62-PMP, Vol. V, Sr. No. 90-A.

Letter, 31 July 1962, from L.C. Mehta:

"Dear Mr Prime Minster,

We have a fairly large sized community of Indian students and residents in the Greater Boston Area. It would be a great pleasure to make them all hear your message when we meet to celebrate the Independence day on August 15, 1962.

If your honor accedes to this request, my wife would come flying to Delhi to tape record your message on or about 11th August, 1962 and mail it to me by Air the same day.

... [Section omitted in copy available in the NMML]

Very sincerely yours,
L.C. Mehta"

PMO, File No. 9/2/62-PMP, Vol. V, Sr. No. 88-A.

245. To C.B. Gupta: Three Language Formula[107]

August 8, 1962

My dear Gupta,

Your letter of August 7 about the three language formula.

I have no doubt that when this matter was considered, the regional languages referred to were the living regional languages in India and not classical languages like Sanskrit. This was not clearly stated, but it is obvious that this was the meaning of the formula. Also that among the other regional languages, Urdu was a language which could be included.

As for the third language, it was to be English or any other modern European language. Normally this is going to be English, but in special cases some people may learn French, German, Russian, Chinese or Spanish, etc. I do not think Sindhi or Tibetan or even Nepali could be included in the third category. The whole idea was that a language should be learned as a compulsory subject which keeps us in touch with modern scientific and technological thinking.

I appreciate your difficulty about Sanskrit and, for my part, I would have no objection to Sanskrit being one of the subjects taught even among the Indian languages. One advantage of teaching Sanskrit would be to give a base for the learning and understanding of many modern Indian languages.

That is my view. But I gather you have written to the Education Minister,[108] and he will no doubt send you his views.

Yours sincerely
[Jawaharlal Nehru]

246. For the University of Jodhpur[109]

I send my good wishes to the newly established University of Jodhpur which will be inaugurated by our President. Universities are growing up in many parts of India. This is a good sign. But the quality of these Universities is more important than the number of them. A country ultimately progresses by the quality of its trained personnel. I trust that the University of Jodhpur will maintain high standards of quality.

---

107. Letter to the Chief Minister of Uttar Pradesh.
108. K.L. Shrimali.
109. Message, 8 August 1962. PMO, File No. 9/2/62-PMP, Vol. V, Sr. No. 81-A. Also available in the JN Collection.

247. For the Orissa University of Agriculture and Technology[110]

I send my good wishes to the University of Agriculture and Technology which is going to be opened soon at Bhubaneswar. This type of University laying stress on agricultural technology is particularly welcome, even more so than an average university which goes in for literary courses. Practical courses involving the use of one's own hands in the fields and farms and giving technical knowledge will help in creating a new type of men who will get out of the old ruts and employ modern techniques.[111]

248. To Balbhadra Prasad: Handling Students[112]

August 11, 1962

My dear Vice-Chancellor,

Thank you for your letter of August 6th. I am grateful to you for having paid attention to the various matters I had referred to you.[113]

I can quite understand the difficulties you have to face in finding accommodation. I think non-resident student common rooms with some amenities attached are very desirable. They are easier to make than residential buildings. Such common rooms should have not only good reading accommodation, but bath rooms and cafeteria.

I am sorry the Student's Union is creating trouble. I was greatly surprised to learn some time ago that the Senate Hall was used for a badminton tournament. While we should do everything that is possible and desirable for the students, it is not right to be bullied by them.

Yours sincerely,
[Jawaharlal Nehru]

---

110. Message, 9 August 1962. PMO, File No. 9/2/62-PMP, Vol. V, Sr. No. 86-A. Also available in the JN Collection.
111. The University was inaugurated by J.K. Galbraith, the US Ambassador to India, on 24 August 1962.
112. Letter to the Vice-Chancellor of Allahabad University.
113. See item 242.

249. To S.R. Ranganathan: Documentation Research[114]

August 16, 1962

Dear Prof. Ranganathan,

Your letter of the 13th August has just reached me.

I am glad to learn of the inauguration of the Documentation Research & Training Centre at Bangalore.[115] As you say, India has made considerable advances in the technique of documentation. It is right, therefore, that we should have such a Research & Training Centre and invite people from abroad to it also. I wish you all success.

Yours sincerely,
[Jawaharlal Nehru]

250. In Bombay: At the Sardar Patel Engineering College[116]

Shri Munshi,[117] Chief Minister[118] and Friends,

I accepted this invitation to come here gladly and I am happy to be here for a variety of reasons. One, to be quite frank with you, is that I like coming to Bombay because apart from being a great cosmopolitan city there is a certain friendliness about Bombay, an atmosphere of friendliness which surrounds one and which warms one's heart and cheers one up. Then again, the fact that this engineering college is named after Sardar Patel was a particular joy to me to be associated with it in any way, because I think it is fitting that the City of Bombay should have this working memorial, not merely some immobile statue or something but a working, progressive memorial of a man who himself was a tremendous worker and who, in the course of his life, as is well known, did a great deal for building up modern India. So that was an adequate reason.

Then, I have admired for some years past the good work done in various fields by the Bhratiya Vidya Bhavan. It is a little difficult for me to remember

---

114. Letter to the librarian and the founder and head of the Documentation Research and Training Centre, Bangalore; address: 307/3 4th Main Road, Bangalore-3.
115. Established as a division of the Indian Statistical Institute, inaugurated on 18 August 1962.
116. Speech, 19 August 1962, inaugurating this College. NMML, AIR Tapes, TS No. 13778, NM No. 2639.
117. K.M. Munshi, Chairman of the Bharatiya Vidya Bhavan.
118. Y.B. Chavan, the Chief Minister of Maharashtra.

all the fields that it is working in but some are obvious, as the one which brings out books, the Bhavan Library, which has succeeded in doing something which I consider very important in India, that is, bringing out worthwhile classical or other books at a cheap price. I think it is essential for us to do that, for our people, publishers and others to interest themselves in the publication of cheap and good books, which means, of course, that they must have a large circulation otherwise they will be an uneconomic proposition. But you cannot have a large circulation unless the books are cheap. It is no good, an author or a publisher trying to make money out of a small edition at a big price. You know, that all over, in every country it is at present the paperback editions of books which are very popular and they have increased the habit of reading tremendously. I remember, in my early youth, the first time Everyman's Library[119] came out in England. That was not a paperback edition and it was not so cheap but still it was relatively cheap. That was the first attempt at good books, classical books, but not cheap, the stories he[120] brought out and made it within the reach of the people. That was a great innovation. Later, of course, other series came out, the Penguins and the Pelicans, and now the paperback is firmly established in every country. And the Bhavan's Library, I do not know if it is an initiator of these paperback editions here. Anyhow, it is one of those who have followed this practice early and I am very glad to learn of the success it has achieved because it is a remarkable success, considering the conditions in India, to have sold these books, a million of these books having been sold.

I think that the future of books in India, as indeed of newspapers, journals, etc., is tremendous, provided it is dealt with in an understanding and scientific way which, I fear, most people do not. They are beginning to do it now, I believe, publishers and others, because the public in India is vast. Even though the public is divided up into various linguistic regions, still it is vast and I have no doubt that both newspapers and books, if properly issued in easily understandable language and relatively cheap form, will have a vast circulation.

You must remember that we have in India—I do not know the exact figures—but probably fewer books are sold here than in any literate country. It is extraordinary. Fewer newspapers are read here than in most other countries. It is surprising. I am not thinking so much of the English newspapers or English books, but books in the regional languages which have a vast field and my complaint has been—this relates to Hindi chiefly which I know—that they are often written in a way which does not attract, which is often not understood

119. A series of reprints of classics conceived by the London publisher Joseph Malaby Dent; the series began in 1906.
120. Probably referring to J.M. Dent.

344

even. Sometimes the writer pretends to be erudite, thinking that learning consists in putting words which nobody understands. That is not learning, that is not good literature or good writing. We have yet to learn that good writing and good literature means simple literature, simple writing. So that, the field here is vast for almost everything, whatever you think of, in India, whether it is education, whether it is books or newspapers, or whether it is just the potentialities of the Indian market as it grows, the whole thing is tremendous. But coming to books, I do think, I do want people to read more, to possess books more. I do not know how many people here are fond of gradually building up their libraries, not spending much, perhaps as much as they would spend on a visit to the cinema once a week or once a month or whatever it is. And this will be, a book will be, of more abiding interest than a visit to the cinema. Not that I am against the cinema at all, I hasten to say this lest I be criticized afterwards, except that, unfortunately, I seldom visit it myself, purely for lack of time, no other reason.

So, I wish people would develop the habit of building up gradually, book by book, libraries of their own. Of course, they should utilize public libraries and there should be many public libraries. But, nevertheless, the personal ownership of books with your own individuality stamped upon them is a good thing. It distinguishes a person; you can find out, know much about, a person by looking around his room and seeing what kind of books he has got. I find that it is a greater indicator of a person than almost anything. So I hope this habit of building up libraries will grow private libraries and this can only grow in a big way if books are available in a fairly cheap form. The Bhavan's Library does that and the others also, many others are coming out.

I am connected with the Sahitya Akademi. The Sahitya Akademi has brought out quite a large number of books—I forget how many—but, I should think, about a hundred or a hundred and fifty and, of course, it particularly tries to serve the interests of all the languages of India and translations in them from English and from each other; so that it tries to bring the knowledge of various languages, all the languages of India, to various parts of India, publishes dictionaries and all that. I recommend those books to your notice because in these days of linguistic fanaticism we have to get out of it and the way to get out of it is not to run down any language but run it in and acquire it and get to know something of it. It is quite extraordinary how people seem to think it is degrading to learn a language which is not their own, here. They do not think that it is an accomplishment to know more languages, as indeed it is, and especially our languages which are intimately connected. So, the Sahitya Akademi is publishing many classical works, translations from English, French, Russian, German, Spanish, etc., in our languages, not in Hindi only but in other languages too. Unfortunately, like all governmental or semi-governmental institutions, it does things in a heavy way and most people do not seem to know much about it. It surprises me because it is doing excellent work in this linguistic field, literary field, because I do feel languages grow, not by living in isolation but by contact with other languages.

I am quite sure that, naturally, in India great languages have grown and will grow and will grow more, and are growing; but in doing so they will grow more, the more they are connected with each other and with foreign languages. If their contact with foreign languages and notably English—because English is the best known foreign language in India—is reduced, then, apart from English serving us or not, the growth of our languages would be somewhat impeded; because English is a window, like other foreign languages, to the whole world which is not represented at present in India but which is growing, the world of modern ideas, of science, technology, etc. It is all very well to say, "Get them translated." They do. We should get them, the main books, translated, but they come out by the hundred thousand. It is physically impossible. I do not know how many hundred thousand articles appear in the periodicals every year; you cannot keep pace with them. Knowledge is growing so tremendously fast that it is very difficult to keep pace with it.

Apart from the language question, you do not have the time to read all those articles. If you go to any big laboratory which is supposed to keep pace, what have they got to do? Take the [National] Chemical Laboratory in Pune and the [National] Physical Laboratory in Delhi. They get large numbers of periodicals in all the languages of the world, scientific periodicals, technological. They have to open a special department to translate those books. They cannot translate all of them, but they can make summaries of articles in foreign periodicals. They are all in their languages, so that their scientists may read them, and those that are important, they translate all of them. Therefore, it becomes exceedingly important for us to keep in touch with the thought of the world. The world is changing rapidly, and I tell you that we see this extraordinary phenomenon of these cosmonauts circling round the earth and greeting each other and greeting everybody with whom they are flying, it is really as much a miracle as anything can be.[121] And yet, that is a step only. All these distinctions which separate us seem to vanish before such an idea. The world becomes one.

Well, then, the third major reason why I came was to—I do not know what is the right word—am I inaugurating this Engineering College or what am I doing? The answer is not quite clear. It is something to do with the Engineering College, which is functioning already, and the building for it is being put up. It is not complete yet, so it is in an intermediate stage that I have come here.

121. For the Soviet cosmonauts' flight in space, see items 370-371.

Anyhow, I have come here because, important as I think all education is in India, of the utmost importance, mass education, good education, primary, secondary, university, I do think that education in engineering and technical subjects is of the highest importance. Naturally, it follows, you cannot jump to engineering before going through primary and the secondary stage.

All our progress in India, I should say I am, for the moment, leaving out the aspects which are very important, to which reference has been made by previous speakers, the aspects, or shall I say, which inculcate ideals, spirituality, etc., are very important, character, etc., but for the moment I am leaving that out. India requires two things or perhaps three: machines and trained men who can make the machines and work them, and I might add the third thing, power. Essentially, it is the trained men. The trained men, after all, can make machines, if not quickly, if not as quickly as we would like, they will ultimately make them. Trained men are the most essential thing. They will produce the power, they will produce everything because we have the natural resources for these things. Trained men are the most important thing, trained in modern sciences, in modern technology, engineering etc. You can almost measure the advance of a nation by one single fact: how many such trained personnel has that nation got? And you can say without knowing much else, where it is surely in the normal economic or industrial field.

Industries, if I may say so with all respect, are not particularly dependent on the men of money. I have a distant respect for money, it is very distant though, I must say, because it is not a fundamental thing in anything in life and it is often a harmful thing. We want money to do things; that is a different matter. But here, I say so, here in the City of Bombay where money is perhaps a greater god than anything, that the worship of money can be overdone. In fact, the less there is the worship of it, the better. Certainly it is useful too. It may have. But the real thing is the trained person, trained in character, trained in using his hands and his mind, trained in modern science, trained in technology. And all your industries which may suffer for lack of money, but lack of money normally does not kill any industry which has competent men in charge, competent engineers, competent men who can look after the machine, who can make them. Many people seem to think that money is the root of everything because they can buy everything with money, including the competent engineer. That is partly true, but not fundamentally true. It does depend a great deal on to what you give first place and to what you give the second, third, fourth places. If you give money and the moneyed man the first place it is all wrong, fundamentally wrong.

In India, as you know, from the most ancient times the first place was given to the learned man. In what countries of the world, I wonder, would a man like Gandhiji have had that tremendous position and place as he had in India?

It is peculiar to India that they value and admire and respect and revere men like Gandhiji or Vinoba Bhave who, from all normal standards, are faddists. They do not care for the good things of life that money brings and wander about aimlessly from village to village. Now, putting this in modern terms, it means that we want trained people in sciences and engineering and technology. They make the world work, not the man with money; he is only a tool who can be dispensed with but he cannot get on without the man with this trained experience. And, therefore, it is very important today for India to produce more and more trained engineers, scientists, etc.

Look at the havoc that was caused by the last great World War for various countries, notably Germany, Russia and Japan. These three, I suppose, suffered most. Others too, Poland and other countries suffered greatly. Yet it is quite amazing how soon they have rebuilt themselves, whether they are capitalist countries or communist countries, Germany and Russia and Japan; and within a period of ten or twelve years they are as prosperous and flourishing and even more so than they were before. They rebuilt themselves. Why? Well, because they have the men, trained men. Production of trained men takes time. You cannot do it by magic. It is not like producing politicians out of a hat. You can produce them out of hats here. But a trained engineer takes time, a trained doctor takes time. It is no good saying that we want so many and you get a large number of candidates for the job. Because Germany, Russia, although entirely different in their political ideologies, and Japan, they have the trained men. In spite of the great losses in wartime, they had, by and large, the machinery too. All they had to do was to put the machines and the men to work together and they produced the results in ten or twelve years' time, amazing results.

If you have the trained men and machines, ultimately the men produce the machines, and all the troubles of my colleague, the Finance Minister, would go. He thinks in terms of money all the time; naturally, he has to look after it and produce it. I think in terms of human beings a little more, trained human beings. They can produce, they can rebuild a shattered country, as you have seen. Money could not have rebuilt it. And training takes time, good training. I think we can put up a steel and iron plant, iron and steel plant with the help of people from other countries. We have put them up in five years or so, five or six years. But the man who will run that iron and steel plant requires—I do not know how much—ten or fifteen years training before he reaches that stage, training and experience to undertake that big job, as we are trying to do in our Five Year Plans.

First of all, may I say, it is quite wrong to confine our thinking to a Five Year Plan. Obviously, we have to think not only of the Third Plan in which we are living but the Fourth Plan and even the Fifth now. We have to have a perspective of where we are going. And suppose we have to build a steel plant in the Fourth Plan, we have to lay the foundations of it in our thinking, in our plans now, not wait till the end of the third year. And, what is more, we have to lay the foundations of training for those who will run our plants here and now, so that they may be ready ten years later to take charge of all our plants and machinery that will, no doubt, grow up by then. It is basic, therefore, that we should train our men. In fact, planning, if you come to our Planning Commission and go to the Perspective Planning Division of it, you will find fascinating charts all over: how many engineers we require five years hence, ten years hence, how many engineers of different varieties, each category mentioned, how many of every kind of person you will require. Because it is not putting up a plant; that is nothing; any moderately intelligent person who has money can put it up, and he can get others to put it up, but it is the thing of trained men running it, and you have to train them for what they will have to do five years, ten years later, train them today. Therefore, it is of the highest importance that this training should be given and specialized training for the kind of person, the kind of person we want today, we shall want tomorrow, in the next Plan, the Plan after. Apart from the importance to the nation, I have found this planning business fascinating; to see how logically one step leads to another. Of course, we may not succeed in them, in the first step or the second or the third, that is our failure because we have to deal not with iron and brick and mortar for our ingredients for the building of a nation, but human beings, and human beings are not like bricks or stone, they are different. You can expect a great deal, wonderful things from human beings and they may not come up to the mark, they may not work hard enough. But it is ability and work, combination of those two that produces results.

People seem to think, many people in India, that neither ability nor hard work is necessary, only a little shouting will do the trick. Well, that obviously has not done it anywhere and will not do it here, and if it does it, another bit of shouting will spoil what you have done. That is not the way. It is only hard work, intelligently directed, that will produce results. Our Five Year Plans have produced results to the extent that hard work has gone behind them, not some trickery, not some jugglery, financial or otherwise, and had work properly directed. Take the major sector of our national economy, agriculture. However much we may progress in the industrial field, and progress we will, there is no doubt about it, we have set certain forces in motion which must produce certain results, that is pure logic. It may be that owing to some failure or some mistake on our part, the result may be delayed by a year or two years, but they must produce it inevitably, and India will inevitably be industrialized, it is on the path to it, and build up a technical, technological, scientific civilization based,

I earnestly hope, on a spiritual foundation, but, nevertheless, a scientific and technological civilization. That is so.

But ultimately that too depends upon the progress of our agriculture. Our agriculture, simply because, first of all, agriculture is always important in every country but more so in India where a vast number of our people live on agriculture and work on agriculture, and it is the primitiveness of our agriculture that keeps us back. If we have trained, somewhat trained, people connected with our agriculture; if our peasants, who are very good but who have, by and large, been using primitive methods, primitive tools, primitive ploughs, primitive everything, if they took to new tools—I am not talking about wonderful, new, expensive machines from America or Russia but just a good plough, and it is a good thing, not very expensive—if they began thinking in terms of new tools, as they are beginning to do today—and I think in Maharashtra especially there is a wide awakening among the peasantry—that would be the greatest revolution in India, and all our agriculture colleges can help in that, not by the students who pass through aiming at becoming professors elsewhere, but going and digging and working with mother earth with their hands and not too much sitting at a desk.

So, I welcome this Sardar Patel Engineering College as another place where builders of India, future India, will be trained and go out, and I am particularly glad that it is associated with the name of Sardar Patel. I should like to congratulate Mr Munshi and his colleagues on the way the various activities the Bhavan is concerned with have developed, and now, more especially about this college which is taking shape. [Applause].

251. To Premlila V. Thackersey: Inauguration Rituals[122]

August 20, 1962

Dear Shrimati Premlila Thackersey,

I have your two letters dated 14th August. In one of these you invite me to inaugurate the Sevika Sammelan at Kasturbagram, Indore, some time in November. In the other, you wish me to perform the opening ceremony of the new building of the University at Bombay from the 7th to 10th February.

I am afraid it is very difficult for me to send you a definite answer at this stage. I am likely to be heavily occupied in November with Parliament which will be meeting here then. Also the second week of February is a time when

---

122. Letter to the Vice-Chancellor of Shreemati Nathibai Damodar Thackersey Women's University, Bombay.

our Budget Session of Parliament is held and it may be equally difficult for me to leave Delhi then. In any event, I cannot commit myself to any date now. If it is possible for me later to accept your kind invitations, I shall gladly do so.

Yours sincerely,
[Jawaharlal Nehru]

252. For the National Institute of Education[123]

The National Institute of Education, the foundation-stone of which is to be laid by the President, is a very desirable approach to the question of raising standards.[124] Also, it will be a good thing if educators from the various States come to a common Institution and live and work together for a period. I send my good wishes to it.

253. To K.L. Shrimali: Tyabji for AMU[125]

August 21, 1962

My dear Shrimali,

I enclose a message for your National Institute of Education.[126]

I have your letter of the 21st August about the Vice-Chancellorship of the Aligarh Muslim University. I have already agreed to Badr-ud-Din Tyabji's name for this post.[127] I am glad you have advised the Visitor[128] accordingly.

Yours sincerely,
[Jawaharlal Nehru]

123. Message, 21 August 1962, forwarded to K.L. Shrimali, the Minister of Education.
124. The Institute was established as part of the National Council of Educational Research and Training. Its foundation stone was laid by S. Radhakrishnan on 30 August.
125. Letter to the Minister of Education.
126. See item 252.
127. Badruddin Tyabji was Special Secretary at the MEA. See items 241, 243 and 254.
128. S. Radhakrishnan, in his capacity as the President of India.

254. To K.A. Hamied: AMU Vice-Chancellor[129]

August 23, 1962

My dear Hamied,

Your letter of the 21st August.

I agree with you that Colonel Zaidi[130] has done good work at Aligarh. Unfortunately, he has not had much cooperation from the members of the staff there. I fear that in the circumstances it will be difficult for him to continue there.

We have given much thought to the Aligarh University and its next Vice-Chancellor. I agree with you that Badruddin Tyabji is a good and appropriate choice. I would be reluctant to lose him even for a time in the External Affairs Ministry, but because we attach so much importance to Aligarh, I advised him to accept the Vice-Chancellorship if it was offered to him. He has agreed. I hope, therefore, that he will be able to go there.[131]

Yours sincerely,
[Jawaharlal Nehru]

255. To A.K. Roy: Chairing Visva-Bharati Society[132]

August 27, 1962

Dear Shri Roy,

I have received your letter of August 25th.[133] I am afraid it is not possible for me to be present at Santiniketan for the meeting of the Parishad of Visva-Bharati Society.

I did not know that it was necessary for me to nominate a person to preside over a meeting in my absence. Normally, the Vice-Chancellor should do it. Anyhow if it is considered necessary, you may consider this a letter of authority for the Vice-Chancellor of Visva-Bharati to preside over this meeting.

Yours sincerely,
Jawaharlal Nehru

---

129. Letter to Member of the Executive Council of Aligarh Muslim University; address: 289 Bellasis Road, Byculla, Bombay 8.
130. B.H. Zaidi, the retiring Vice-Chancellor of AMU.
131. For earlier correspondence on this subject, see items 241, 243 and 253.
132. Letter to the Assistant General Secretary, Visva-Bharati Society, 5 Dwarkanath Tagore Lane, Calcutta-7. PMO, File No. 40 (107)/59-69-PMS, Sr. No. 55-A. Also available in the JN Collection.
133. Appendix 48.

256. Teachers' Day[134]

I am glad to know that September 5th, which is our President's[135] birth anniversary, is going to be celebrated as Teachers' Day throughout India. This will, I have no doubt, help in bringing before the public generally the importance of the teaching profession and the vital role it plays in nation-building.

I wish this observation of Teachers' Day all success.[136]

257. To A.P. Jain: Kunwar Singh Negi's Education[137]

1st September, 1962

My dear Ajit,

I spoke to you on the telephone about Chandra Singh Garhwali.[138] I now enclose a letter to me from his son-in-law Kanwar Singh Negi.[139] I should like to give this young man an opportunity of further studies in an agricultural institute. Whatever his expenses might be I shall make myself responsible for paying them.[140]

Yours sincerely,
Jawaharlal Nehru

134. Message, 27 August 1962, forwarded to Ramgopal Goenka, General Secretary, National Children's Day Festival Committee, 4 Jagmohan Mullick Lane, Calcutta-7.
135. S. Radhakrishnan.
136. On 30 August 1962, Nehru sent another message to the Director of Education, Kerala, Trivandrum: "It was a happy thought to have a National Teachers' Day celebration. It was particularly appropriate that this should be on the 5th September which is the birthday of our President who is the great teacher of all of us.

I send you my good wishes on this celebration, I hope it will make people generally realise the high importance of the teaching profession and what we owe to them."
137. Letter to the President of the UPCC; address: 5 Rafi Marg, New Delhi. NMML, A.P. Jain Papers.
138. Belonged to the Garhwal Rifles and was court-martialled for defying the British Captain's orders to fire on Pathans in Peshawar in April 1930; following his release in 1941 after eleven years' imprisonment, he participated in the Quit India movement; was later associated with the CPI.
139. According to Kunwar Singh Negi's letter of 28 August 1962, he was the son of Trilok Singh, a captain in the INA who was defended by Nehru at the Red Fort trials. But he says he was still a bachelor, though Nehru says he was the son-in-law of Chandra Singh Garhwali. Copy of Negi's letter available in NMML, A.P. Jain Papers.
140. For A.P. Jain's reply, see appendix 57.

258. To P.E. Dustoor: Central Institute of English at Hyderabad[141]

14th September, 1962

Dear Dr Dustoor,

Your letter of September 6 has been forwarded to me in London. The letter refers to some ceremony connected with the Central Institute of English at Hyderabad[142] and you invite me to attend it. But I have been unable to find out from the papers you have sent me on what date this foundation stone ceremony is going to take place.

I certainly sympathise with the object you have in view, that is, teaching English well and you have my good wishes for it. But it is difficult for me to say definitely at this stage that I shall be able to come to Hyderabad for this purpose, more especially when I do not know the date. I suggest you might write to me after my return to India early in October.

Yours sincerely,
[Jawaharlal Nehru]

(f) Culture

259. To Nitya Narayan Banerjee: Universality of *Gita* and Narrowness Today[143]

July 21, 1962

Dear Shri Banerjee,

I have received today your letter without date. I thank you for it. I have read it with much interest. You will forgive me if I do not answer it at any length.

I might mention that I have read many of the books you have mentioned in your letter. I have been particularly fascinated by Swami Vivekananda's speeches and writings.

---

141. Letter to the Chairman of the Board of Governors, Central Institute of English, Bide-a-Wee, Kodaikanal. Sent from London.
142. Set up in 1958; renamed in 1972 as the Central Institute of English and Foreign Languages; renamed again in 2006 as the English and Foreign Languages University.
143. Letter to an author and journalist, who was with the Congress until 1944, later joined the Hindu Mahasabha; address: Hindusthan House, 67 Ekdaliya Road, Calcutta 19. PMO, File No. 2(285)/58-64-PMS, Volume I, Sr. No. 42-A.

You refer to our President, Dr Radhakrishnan. I admire him greatly and have learnt much from him. As for the Upanishads and the *Gita*, I have found much solace in them.

But I do not find that high spirituality of the *Gita* and the Upanishads in modern Hindu life in India. I find instead, something very narrow-minded. The breadth of universality which occurs in the *Gita* and the Upanishads is missing among the great majority of Hindus as well as others in India.

I believe in spirituality, but I find that religion as practised is something very narrow and separatist.

I have indicated in a few lines my broad views on the subjects you have referred to. I realise that these subjects are vast and cannot be dealt with so briefly. But I do not presume to say much about matters which require a much deeper knowledge and understanding than perhaps I possess. I can only indicate some of my reactions.

Yours sincerely,
[Jawaharlal Nehru]

260. To Mira Behn: Films on Mahatma Gandhi[144]

July 22, 1962

My dear Mira,

I have your letter of the 17th July. I am glad that your monthly allowance has been fixed now at Rs 500 by the Nidhi.[145]

As for the film of Bapu's life, none of us has yet seen the film that was produced recently. We have asked the producers to show it to us here. Then we can take a decision.[146]

---

144. Letter to British-born disciple of Mahatma Gandhi; address: Sittendorferstrasse 41, Gaaden bei Modling, N.O., Austria.

   Formerly Madeleine Slade before being nicknamed Mira Behn by Mahatma Gandhi upon her arrival in India in 1925; she returned to Britain in 1959 and shifted to Austria in 1960.

145. Gandhi Smarak Nidhi.

146. The film *Nine Hours to Rama*, produced and directed by Mark Robson, was in fact based on the life of Nathuram Godse, Mahatma Gandhi's assassin. It was released in the West in 1963, but banned in India. A novel of the same name written in 1962 by Stanley Wolpert, on which the film was based, was banned in India in September 1962. For a previous reference to the film, see SWJN/SS/75/item 211.

As for the American films, I know nothing about them.
I hope you are keeping well.

Yours affectionately,
[Jawaharlal Nehru]

261. To V.V. Mirashi: Declining Indian History Congress Invitation[147]

July 23, 1962

Dear Prof. Mirashi,
I have received your letter or the 21st July. Thank you for it.

It is good of your Executive Committee to invite me to preside over the next session of the Indian History Congress.[148] I am afraid, I cannot accept this kind invitation. It is not my practice to accept such engagements even though they might not lead to my giving much time to them. I have to concentrate on my present responsibilities which are heavy enough. I hope you will appreciate my difficulty.

Yours sincerely,
[Jawaharlal Nehru]

262. To T. Amrutharao: Gandhi Mission Anniversary[149]

July 26, 1962

Dear Shri Amrutharao,
I have your letter of the 16th July. You have my good wishes on the occasion of the celebration of the first anniversary of the Gandhi Mission in early August. I think that it is more necessary than ever to teach the ideals and principles which Mahatma Gandhi placed before the country. They may have to be adapted to

---

147. Letter to Professor of Ancient History and Culture, Nagpur University, Nagpur, and President of the Indian History Congress.
148. The twenty-fifth session, held at Poona, 1963.
149. Letter to a Gandhian; address: Gandhi Nilayam, Red Tank Road, Guntur-1. Sent from Anand Bhavan, Allahabad.

modern conditions but the basic ideals remain. I hope you will carry on the good work.

Yours sincerely,
[Jawaharlal Nehru]

263. To Prakashvir Shastri: Contribution to Book on Dayanand Saraswati [150]

जुलाई 31 1962

प्रिय प्रकाशवीर जी,

मैं आपको स्वामी दयानन्द सरस्वती की किताब के लिए कुछ थोडा सा लिखकर भेजता हूं।[151] माफ कीजियेगा उसके भेजने में देरी हुई।

आपका
जवाहरलाल नेहरु

[Translation begins

31 July 1962

My dear Prakashvirji,
I have written a few lines which I am sending for the book on Swami Dayanand Saraswati.[152] Please excuse me for the delay in sending it.

Yours sincerely,
Jawaharlal Nehru

Translation ends]

---

150. Letter to Independent, Lok Sabha MP.
151. See item 264.
152. See fn 151 in this section.

264. Swami Dayanand Saraswati[153]

उन्नीसवीं सदी में अंग्रेजी राज भारत में मज़बूती से जम गया। खाली राजनैतिक तरीके से नहीं जमा, लेकिन आर्थिक और सांस्कृतिक बातों में भी उसका बड़ा असर हुआ, और भारत के अंग्रेजी पढ़े-लिखे लोगों की हर तरह से मानसिक भावनायें उखड़ने लगीं। अपने देश की बातों की कदर कम होने लगी और योरप की बातों की तरफ अधिक देखने लगे।

इसी ज़माने में एक दूसरी हवा भारत में पैदा हुई। कुछ पश्चिम के विचार भी यहां आए विशेषकर राजनीति में, और कुछ साहित्य और संस्कृति में भी। लेकिन उसी के साथ भारत कुछ अपनी पुरानी संस्कृति का भी सोचने लगा, और राष्ट्रीयता की भावना फिर से जागृत हुई। अपने देश की संस्कृति पर अधिक विचार होने लगा और इसमें कुछ अभिमान भी हुआ।

इस ज़मानें में कई महापुरुष भारत में पैदा हुये जिन्होंने इस नई भावना को बढ़ाया। राजा राम मोहन राय एक बड़े विद्वान थे जो संस्कृत, अरबी, अंग्रेजी और कई और भाषाओं को अच्छी तरह जानते थे। उन पर पश्चिमी विचारों का असर पड़ा, और उन्होंने हिन्दू धर्म में जो कुछ पिछले जमाने में कमजोरियां आ गई थीं उनको हटाने की कोशिश की। श्री रामकृष्ण परमहंस का भी बड़ा असर हुआ। वह ज्यादा धर्म और सेवा की तरफ ध्यान देते थे। उनके बड़े चेले स्वामी विवेकानन्द ने हमारी राष्ट्रीयता पर बहुत ज़ोर दिया और भारत के धर्म और संस्कृति का कुछ प्रचार अन्य देशों में भी किया।

इसी उन्नीसवीं सदी में एक महापुरुष स्वामी दयानन्द सरस्वती ने भी जन्म पाया। उन्होने भी हिन्दू धर्म की कुछ नई खराबियों को निकालने की कोशिश की और प्राचीन धर्म को वापिस लाने की। उनका और जो संस्था उन्होंने शुरू की, आर्य समाज का असर देश पर बहुत बड़ा पड़ा। विशेषकर मध्यम श्रेणी के लोगों पर उनका असर पड़ा। आर्य समाज ने शिक्षा की ओर खास ध्यान दिया, और उतर भारत में विशेषकर उनकी वजह से शिक्षा की बहुत उन्नति हुई। हिन्दू धर्म को उन्होंने कुछ राष्ट्रीय ढंग दिया। और बाद में आर्य समाज ने राष्ट्रीय आंदोलन में काफी भाग लिया।

यह सब पुनर्जागृति की जो निशानियां भारत में उन्नीसवीं सदी में हुई उन में प्रायः स्वामी दयानन्द सरस्वती का और आर्य समाज का सब से बड़ा असर हुआ, विशेषकर उतर भारत में, और आम जनता को उन्होंने जगाया। हालांकि यह जागृति अधिकतर धार्मिक और सांस्कृतिक थी इसका नतीजा राजनीति की तरफ भी हुआ, और भारत में राजनैतिक आंदोलन की शुरुआत हुई। इंडियन नैशनल कांग्रेस भी पैदा हुई और हल्के-हल्के बढ़ी।

---

153. Essay, 31 July 1962, sent to Prakashvir Shastri, Independent, Lok Sabha MP. See item 263.

इन सब बातों में, भारत के फिर से जागने और उठने में, और नये भारत के बनाने में, स्वामी दयानन्द सरस्वती का एक बड़ा हाथ है, और यह उचित है कि हम उनको अपनी श्रद्धांजली पेश करें।

नई दिल्ली,
31 जुलाई, 1962

[Translation begins

British rule had been firmly established in India by the nineteenth century. It took roots not only politically but it had a great impact in the economic and cultural spheres also, and the English educated elite began to lose their emotional moorings in every way. They began to respect their heritage less and looked to Europe more and more.

In this period, another wind was blowing through India. Western ideas began to gain dominance in politics, and to some extent in literature and culture too. But at the same time India began to look towards its ancient heritage and a spirit of nationalism began to awaken. India began to look to her culture and take pride in it.

Many great men during this period began to give a fillip to a spirit of nationalism. One of them was Raja Ram Mohan Roy, a great scholar who knew Sanskrit, Arabic, English and many other languages. He was influenced by western ideas and he began to make efforts to reform Hinduism and rid it of some weaknesses which had crept in. Shri Ramakrishna Paramahamsa also had great influence. He was engaged in religion and social services. His chief disciple, Swami Vivekananda, laid great stress on nationalism and spread the message of Indian religion and culture in other countries also.

It was in the nineteenth century that another great man Swami Dayanand Saraswati was born. He too made great efforts to reform Hindu religion and bring its ancient glory back. He founded an organization, the Arya Samaj, which had a great impact on the country, especially on the people of the middle classes. Arya Samaj laid special emphasis on education, and in North India in particular, there was great progress in education. He gave a nationalist hue to Hinduism and later the Arya Samaj played a major role in the national movement.

Swami Dayanand Saraswati and Arya Samaj made a great impact on the new awakening which took place in the nineteenth century, especially in North India. They awakened the masses. Though this awakening was mostly in the religious and cultural spheres, it had an influence in the political sphere also and the political movement for independence began in India. The Indian National Congress was founded and gradually grew in strength.

It is fitting that we should pay tribute to Swami Dayanand Saraswati who played a major role in awakening India and in building a new India.

New Delhi,
31 July 1962

Translation ends]

265. To Krishna Kripalani: Japanese Translations of Tagore[154]

August 7, 1962

My dear Krishna,

I am sending you the Japanese translation of Tagore's *Gitanjali* and *Crescent Moon*. Apparently this was done out of some royalty money which I had donated for the publication of Tagore's books in Japan.[155] You may keep the book in your library.

Yours sincerely,
Jawaharlal Nehru

---

154. Letter to the Secretary of the Sahitya Akademi. NMML, JN Supplementary Papers, Box No. 105.
155. Mrs Tomi W. Kora had on 3 April 1962 sent Nehru the first copy of a combined volume of *Gitanjali* and *Crescent Moon*, "translated into current Japanese verses," as a "humble tribute at the Tagore Centenary."

On 12 July 1952, Tomi Kora had met Nehru in New Delhi. Later the same day she was informed by M.O. Mathai, then Special Assistant of Nehru, "The Prime Minister hereby accords permission for the publication of a Japanese translation of his books: *Discovery of India* and *Visit to America*." He further wrote that "the Prime Minister would like to use the royalty accruing to him out of the Japanese translations of his books for some beneficent purpose for the children of Japan. The Prime Minister would like to have any proposals in regard to this matter which you might like to make." On 14 April 1954, Tomi Kora wrote to Nehru asking to allow her "a few months more" to think of some appropriate proposal. In February 1960, she suggested that the royalties from Nehru's books could be used to publish two famous books of Tagore's, *Gitanjali* and *Crescent Moon*, retranslated into Japanese. Nehru agreed, see SWJN/SS/57/items 244-245.

266. To Biswanath Das: Don't Rename Deer Park at Sarnath[156]

August 9, 1962

My dear Biswanathji,
I have received the enclosed cutting about the renaming of the Deer Park at Sarnath.[157] I would welcome your name to be associated with public places, but I feel it was unwise to rename the famous Deer Park of Sarnath. That place is full of history and is associated closely with the Buddha as a Deer Park. I hope that something can be done about this.

Yours sincerely,
[Jawaharlal Nehru]

267. To B.V. Keskar: Sindhi Books for National Book Trust[158]

August 12, 1962

My dear Balkrishna,
I enclose a letter from Jairamdas Daulatram[159] about Sindhi. I think it should be included within the scope of the activities of the Trust just as we have included it in the Sahitya Akademi. How many books you publish in Sindhi is another matter.

Yours sincerely,
[Jawaharlal Nehru]

---

156. Letter to the Governor of Uttar Pradesh.
157. The name "Mrigadava" of Deer Park at Sarnath was changed to "Bishwanath Nikunj" or Bishwanath Park after the name of the UP Governor, on 27 July 1962. On 1 August, the Mahabodhi Society protested and demanded immediate restoration of the original name. The *National Herald*, 5 August 1962, p. 7.
158. Letter to the Chairman of the National Book Trust, 14 Tughlak Road, New Delhi.
159. A Gandhian leader from Sind, former Union Minister, former Governor of Bihar and of Assam, and Nominated, Rajya Sabha MP, 1959-1976.

268. To Mehr Chand Khanna: Lodging for Prabhakar Machwe[160]

August 16, 1962

My dear Mehr Chand,

Your letter of the 16th August about Dr Prabhakar Machwe.[161]

It is for you to decide what premises should be requisitioned or not. But I do think that people like Dr Machwe should be treated as Government servants in the matter of accommodation. The Sahitya Akademi is not a private organisation. It is entirely supported by Government money and Government rules apply to it. There are not many such organisations. There may be two or three like the other academies, and so this should not create any special aggravation of the accommodation problem.

Yours sincerely,
Jawaharlal Nehru

269. To Indra Narain Sinha: Honouring Mohammad Nooh Narvi[162]

August 18, 1962

Dear Indra Narainji,

I have your letter of the 16th August.

It is right that we should honour the Allahabad poet Shri Mohammad Nooh Narvi.[163] I am afraid, however, that it is not possible for me to go to Allahabad for some months. I am going abroad early next month and returning in the beginning of October. Later, I am going to Ceylon. Then there is the session of Parliament.

If, however, I happen to be in Allahabad when you do honour to Shri Mohammad Nooh Narvi, I shall be glad to associate myself with it.

Yours sincerely,
[Jawaharlal Nehru]

---

160. Letter to the Minister of Works, Housing, and Supply. PMO, File No. 40(7)/59-63-PMS, Vol. I, Sr. No. 185-A. Also available in the JN Collection.
161. 1917-1991; writer in Marathi, Hindi and English; joined the Sahitya Akademi in 1954, as Assistant Secretary; later was Secretary.
162. Letter to the President of the Anjuman Safina-e-Adab, 41 Chak (Zero Road), Allahabad.
163. 1879-1962; a disciple of Dagh Dehlvi.

270. To Joseph John: Hanging Gardens Safe[164]

August 19, 1962

Dear Shri John,

I received your letter of August 16th in Delhi. I gathered from it that the trees in the Hanging Gardens[165] were being cut down. I went there this evening. I could not see much of the gardens owing to the big crowd there. On enquiry, however, I found that no trees were actually cut down there. Some branches of trees were cut down as they went over some private land and also because of telegraph wires etc.

As for the buildings, I was told that one building was going to be put up, but the garden authorities are acquiring all the other land to prevent any further constructions which might impede the view. Apart from one block of buildings which, I take it, will not obstruct the view much, I hope there will be no further encroachments of this kind.

Yours sincerely,
[Jawaharlal Nehru]

271. To Ragho Raj Singh: Naming Buildings after Persons[166]

August 20, 1962

Dear Principal Ragho Raj Singh,

I have your letter of the 18th August. I do not like the idea of my name or indeed any names of persons being given to public buildings so long as the person concerned is alive. It is a bad practice though very rarely it might be justified. I would, therefore, suggest to you not to attach my name to this building but to give it a non-personal name.

I send you my good wishes.

Yours sincerely,
[Jawaharlal Nehru]

---

164. Letter to the Honorary General Secretary, "Friends of the Trees", Bombay 4. Sent from Raj Bhavan, Bombay.
165. Terraced gardens located on the western side of Malabar Hill in Bombay, laid out in 1881.
166. Letter to the Principal of Rajkumar College, Raipur.

272. For Humayun Kabir: Hindi in Cambridge[167]

Of the two courses you suggest I would prefer giving some scholarships. To have a Chair for Hindi at Cambridge would be a good thing, chiefly for prestige reasons and partly to encourage the learning of Hindi. But, I suppose, there would be just a very few students to take it up, perhaps two or three or four. I suppose we will have to find a teacher of Hindi here. There are not too many about who will know both Hindi well and English well. One person I know is Bachchan[168] who is now working in the External Affairs Ministry. He has got a doctorate of Oxford and is a Hindi poet of note.

2. The real difficulty is exchange now and for us to spend a tidy little sum for prestige reasons at present seems difficult.

3. I really do not know what I can suggest at present in view of our difficulties.

273. To Morarji Desai: Supporting Nandalal Bose's Grandson's Education[169]

21st August, 1962

My dear Morarji,

I enclose a letter I have got from Nandalal Bose.[170] Perhaps you know him. He is famous for his paintings and he was a close colleague of Rabindranath Tagore. He is now very old and in the late eighties, I imagine, if not more. He is feeble and is practically confined to his house.

I would normally have gladly recommended helping his grandson to go for architecture or something. We have neglected it and we should encourage it. The only difficulty is about foreign exchange. It is possible that after his grandson goes there, he might get a scholarship, but he cannot get that while he is here.

Yours sincerely,
[Jawaharlal Nehru]

---

167. Note, 21 August 1962, for the Minister of Scientific Research and Cultural Affairs.
168. Harivansh Rai Bachchan.
169. Letter to the Finance Minister.
170. 1882-1966.

274. To T.M. Advani: Promoting Sindhi[171]

August 21, 1962

Dear Professor Advani,

I have your letter of the 20th. We are trying to encourage Sindhi, both in the Sahitya Akademi and the National Book Trust. It is a difficult matter to change the Constitution and include Sindhi in the Eighth Schedule, but we are doing everything else to encourage it.

You can see me on the 29th August at 5.30 p.m. in my room in Parliament House.

Yours sincerely,
[Jawaharlal Nehru]

275. In the Lok Sabha: Serving of Indian Gin in Receptions[172]

Will the Prime Minister be pleased to state:[173]

(a) whether a news has appeared in the *Indian Express* dated the 23rd July 1962 (Vijayawada Edition) that a Central Government circular has lately been issued to serve Indian "Gin" along with fruit-juice before meals as modes of entertainment at receptions; and

(b) If so, whether such a circular has been issued by Government.

Jawaharlal Nehru:

(a) Yes, Sir.

(b) Government of India issued a circular in June, 1962 stating that Indian gin, diluted in the form of a light aperitif, could also be served at more informal entertainments financed out of the Hospitality Grant of the Government of India. This Grant is intended for the entertainment of foreign visitors only.

---

171. Letter to the Principal of the Jai Hind College, Bombay-1.
172. Written answers, 22 August 1962. *Lok Sabha Debates*, Third Series, Vol. 7, 20 to 31 August 1962, 2nd Session, col. 3419.
173. Question by P.K. Deo, Swatantra Party.

276. To Atulananda Chakrabarti: Contribution to Book[174]

August 23, 1962

Dear Atulanandaji,

Your letter of the 13th August.[175] I wish you success in your venture. But it is almost physically not possible for me to write an article for you. I am overburdened with work and can do no writing of that kind. This would not be routine writing but carefully thought out and I can find no time for that.[176]

Yours sincerely,
Jawaharlal Nehru

277. To K.M. Munshi: Inviting Eisenhower to Bharatiya Vidya Bhavan[177]

August 24, 1962

My dear Munshi,

Your letter of August 22nd.[178]

We have no objection to your inviting Mr Dwight Eisenhower as your Chief Guest for the Silver Jubilee of the Bharatiya Vidya Bhavan.

---

174. Letter to an author and founder of India Mission, who worked for Hindu-Muslim unity and national integration. NMML, Diwan Chaman Lall Papers, enclosure to Atulananda Chakrabarti's letter, 12 January 1963, to Chaman Lall.
175. Chakrabarti's letter has not been traced; in reply to another letter from him, Nehru had written on 14 July 1962:
    "Your idea of having an international symposium on India Since 1947 is an interesting one, and to some extent it appeals to me. But the subject is a vast one and has innumerable facets. I rather doubt if all these aspects can be dealt with in one symposium ... It is thus not clear to me what the ultimate shape of this might be and how it can help here." Only extracts available in NMML, Diwan Chaman Lall Papers.
176. S.P. Khanna, PS, wrote to Chakrabarti on 24 December 1962: "The Prime Minister has received your letter dated the 21st December, 1962, regarding your book *India Since 1947*. He has asked me to say in reply that, when the book is published, Government hope to take a large number of copies of it for their Missions abroad." NMML, Diwan Chaman Lall Papers.
    India Since 1947 (An International Symposium), edited by Atulananda Chakrabarti, was published in 1967. Publisher not known.
177. Letter to the Chairman of the Bharatiya Vidya Bhavan; address: Chaupatty Road, Bombay 7. PMO, File No. 40(240)/62-63-PMS, Sr. No. 2-A.
178. Appendix 44.

Mr Eisenhower is, of course, a famous man. But I should have thought that some person eminent in literature or arts would be more suitable for you. However, you can decide as you feel about it.

Yours sincerely,
Jawaharlal Nehru

278. To Arthur Geddes: Foreword to Tagore's Fourteen Songs[179]

August 27, 1962

Dear Dr Geddes,
I am sorry for the delay in answering your latter of the 19th June (posted on the 6th July). I am gladly sending you a short foreword for the *Fourteen Songs*.[180] I think that it is a happy idea of yours to ask for a note of introduction from some literary representative of East Bengal.

Yours sincerely,
[Jawaharlal Nehru]

279. For Arthur Geddes's Translation of Tagore[181]

I am glad to learn that Dr Arthur Geddes[182] is publishing some of the very old songs of Rabindranath Tagore in English containing some of his melodies. He had previously, many years ago, published some of Tagore's melodies, which met with the poet's approval. I feel sure that the new publication of *Fourteen Songs* will be equally welcomed in India and abroad.

Tagore was a remarkable and full-sided personality and the appreciation of his writings and of him as a man has continued to grow all over the world. In India, he is known as Gurudev, the great teacher, and his best memorial is the

---

179. Letter to Scottish geographer, and English translator of Rabindranath Tagore's songs; address: Social Science Research Centre, 39 George Square, Edinburgh-6.
    Arthur Geddes, 1895-1968, spent some years in India in the early 1920s; assisted the rural reconstruction projects at Sriniketan in Bengal and the town-planning work of his father Patrick Geddes in other parts of India.
180. See item 279.
181. Foreword, written on 27 August 1962, to *Fourteen Songs*.
182. Scottish geographer.

University he founded at Santiniketan. One of his songs has become the National Anthem of India ever since independence. In Bengal he is particularly known and loved because of his songs which have gone down to the villages. The partition of India and Bengal has not affected, in any way, the great appreciation of his writings, and especially his songs, in both parts of Bengal. To us in India, he is looked upon as one of the Rishis or Seers of old who carried on the ancient tradition in modern times. His influence over successive generations has been very great, even though it has not had the glamour and publicity attached to the successful politician; yet his influence was much deeper and will continue when the politician's name is hardly remembered.

Tagore and Gandhi overlapped for many years and were the outstanding representatives of India. They were different in many ways and sometimes criticised each other's views and activities, but, yet they were drawn to each other and each of them had great regard and affection for the other. It was fascinating to see these two men of great stature, representing different aspects of India, and both of them even though appreciating and understanding many modern trends yet representing fundamentally the old spirit of India.

Tagore was essentially a singer and it is perhaps easier to understand him through his songs than through his other writings. I welcome, therefore, this publication by Dr Geddes and hope this will make the spirit of Tagore better known in Western countries.

280. To H.J. Bhabha: Hanging Gardens[183]

August 30, 1962

My dear Homi,

I have just received your letter of the 29th August. I do not know what I can do about it. But I am writing to Chief Minister Chavan and, in fact, sending your letter to him.[184]

Yours affectionately,
Jawaharlal Nehru

---

183. Letter to the Secretary, Department of Atomic Energy. PMO, File No. 28/99/62-64-PMS, Sr. No. 2-A.
184. See item 281.

281. To Y.B. Chavan: Hanging Gardens[185]

August 30, 1962

My dear Chavan,

You will remember that when I came to Bombay, I visited the Hanging Gardens.[186] The information given to me was that no tree had been cut there. I also gathered that not much in the way of buildings would be put up on the slope leading to the sea. Perhaps, I misunderstood.

Anyhow, I have received a letter from Homi Bhabha, which I enclose. I have read this with some distress. To allow all these trees to be cut down and a huge building to be put up for private purposes, and thus spoil the outlook for the thousands who go to the Hanging Gardens, is most unfortunate.[187] I hope you will kindly try to save this place.

Yours sincerely,
Jawaharlal Nehru

282. To Joseph John: Hanging Gardens[188]

August 31, 1962

Dear Shri John,

Your letter of August 29th. I am sorry to learn of the destruction of trees etc. I have written to the Chief Minister about it.[189] I hope he will be able to help you.[190]

Yours sincerely,
Jawaharlal Nehru

---

185. Letter to the Chief Minister of Maharashtra. PMO, File No. 28/99/62-64-PMS, Sr. No. 1-A. Also available in the JN Collection.
186. On 19 August 1962. See item 270.
187. For Nehru's reply to Homi Bhabha, see item 280.
188. Letter to the Honorary General Secretary, Friends of the Trees, 182 Girgaum Road, Galwadi Naka, Bombay-4. PMO, File No. 28/99/62-64-PMS, Sr. No. 4-A.
189. See item 281.
190. On 31 August 1962, Nehru wrote to S.K. Patil, the Minister of Food and Agriculture, as follows: "An organisation of which you are the President, is much troubled, and rightly so, about the destruction of trees roundabout the Hanging Gardens in Bombay. I share their distress. I have written to the Chief Minister about it. Perhaps, you could induce the Mayor to stop this kind of thing. I enclose the letter I have received." PMO, File No. 28/99/62-64-PMS, Sr. No. 5-A. Also available in the JN Collection.

283. To Philip W. Groves: Modernity and Tradition[191]

September 1, 1962

Dear Dr Groves,

I have your letter of August 29.

Your project appears to be an attractive one. To some extent we are also aiming at some kind of a synthesis of modern science and technology with our own basic cultural traditions.

Your group will be welcome in India. I do not know what arrangements you have made in Madras for the working of your group there. I hope that you have got in touch with the Madras Government.

With all good wishes,

Yours sincerely,
[Jawaharlal Nehru]

284. To D. Sanjivayya: MRA is Political[192]

September 6, 1962

My dear Sanjivayya,

I enclose a letter I have received.[193] You must have received it also.

I confess I do not like Congressmen getting mixed up with the MRA.[194] The MRA pretends to deal with moral matters, but is very political in its outlook and opposed to our policies and indeed to the Congress as a whole.

Yours sincerely,
[Jawaharlal Nehru]

---

191. Letter; address: Flat I, 139 Ocean Beach Road, Manly, NSW, Australia.
192. Letter to the Congress President.
193. It was dated 5 September 1962, and from Paul P. Mani, Puthenveetil, Chottanikara, Ernakulam.
194. Moral Re-Armament movement, founded in 1938 by the American churchman Frank Buchman, 1878-1961.

(g) Language Controversy

285. To B. Gopala Reddy[195]

26th July 1962

My dear Gopala Reddy,

You will have noticed that a fairly widespread agitation is being organised among Hindi enthusiasts against what they call the new policy adopted by the AIR. I do not exactly know what this new policy is as I do not usually listen to broadcasts in Hindi. I myself felt that a variation in the old policy was necessary as the Hindi used was too difficult and stilted.

But this changeover should not be so sudden as to create too much opposition. It should be gradual and an effort should be made to consult Hindi lovers so as to carry them, as far as possible, with us. To ignore them would be wrong and would create trouble.

I had a letter from Mama Warerkar,[196] a well-known Maharashtrian playwright. He complained of the new policy.[197] As an instance he gave me, he said that instead of Pradhan Mantri[198] the word "Wazir-i-Azam"[199] was being used. If this was so, I think the change was wrong. Pradhan Mantri is very well known and is commonly used. "Wazir-i-Azam" is not so well known.

I would advise you to meet some of the Hindi enthusiasts who are MPs and have a talk with them and consult them. Tell them what you propose to have is a simple language which is bound to be largely Hindi. It should not be stilted and difficult. Such a consultation would lessen the opposition.

Yours sincerely,
[Jawaharlal Nehru]

---

195. Letter to the Minister of Information and Broadcasting. Sent from Anand Bhavan, Allahabad. PMO, File No. 43(117)/58-63-PMS, Sr. No. 29-A.
196. B.V. Warerkar, 1883-1964, Marathi writer and Nominated, Rajya Sabha MP.
197. See SWJN/SS/77/item 243 and other items in the same section.
198. Hindi term for Prime Minister.
199. Urdu term for Prime Minister.

286. To Bishan Chander Seth[200]

26-7-1962

प्रिय बिशन चन्द्र जी,

आपका 23 जुलाई का पत्र मुझे मिला।[201] बाज़ बातों में मैं आपसे सहमत हूँ। हमें भारत में आत्मगौरव और आत्मविश्वास पैदा करना है। लेकिन, इसके साथ हमें अपनी राष्ट्रीयता को बढ़ाना है और इसमें सब तरह के लोग जो भारत में रहते हैं शामिल हैं। आजकल की दुनिया में यही विचार फैले हुये हैं। हिन्दू दुनिया बहुत बड़ी है और शुरु में इसका बड़ा असर और देशों में हुआ। फिर इसका सम्बन्ध और देशों से छूट गया जिससे हमारे हिन्दू समाज को हानि हुई और हिन्दू समाज कुछ बंदी सा हुआ। आज इस हिन्दू समाज में हम नहीं रह सकते। अगर हम अपनी उन्नति चाहते हैं तो आत्मस्तर रखते हुए हमें सारी दुनिया को किसी क़दर अपनाना है और विशेषकर भारत की जनता और जो सब लोग भारत में रहते हैं।

जहाँ तक भाषा का सवाल है, हिन्दी ने काफी उन्नति की है, लेकिन हिन्दी के द्वारा ही सब दुनिया के विचारों से पूरा सम्बन्ध नहीं रख सकते। कुछ अनुवाद करके किताबें पढ़ सकते हैं, लेकिन वह काफी नहीं है। इसके अलावा आप जानते हैं कि दक्षिण में, विशेषकर मद्रास में कितना विरोध हिन्दी का हो रहा है। हालांकि आश्चर्य की बात यह है कि हिन्दी वहाँ काफी लोग सीख रहे हैं। मुझे कोई संदेह नहीं कि हिन्दी दक्षिण में बढ़ेगी, लेकिन अगर उन लोगों को विवश किया गया तो नहीं बढ़ेगी।

मैं आपसे सहमत हूँ कि तेज़ी से उन्नति होनी चाहिये, लेकिन इस उन्नति में हमारी दुनिया के विचारों की हानि हो, वह हमारे लिये हानिकारक होगा।

मुझे इसमें कोई कठिनाई नज़र नहीं आती, दोनों बातें साथ-साथ चल सकती हैं, राष्ट्रीयता भी देशभर की मज़बूत हो और हिन्दी की भी उन्नति हो।

आपका
जवाहरलाल नेहरु

[Translation begins

26 July 1962

My dear Bishan Chanderji,
I received your letter of 23 July.[202] I agree that we have to inculcate pride and self-confidence in India. But alongwith that we have to strengthen our

---

200. Letter to Lok Sabha MP of the Hindu Mahasabha. Sent from Anand Bhavan, Allahabad.
201. Appendix 8.
202. See fn 201 in this section.

nationalism which includes people of diverse hues who live here. The world of today is imbued with these ideas. The world of Hindus is very large and in ancient times it had a great impact on other countries. Then we lost touch with the outside world which did Hindu society great harm. It became stagnant. We cannot live in this Hindu society today. If we wish to progress then the people of India especially, and all those who live in India, have to adapt themselves to the world outside, while maintaining their self-respect.

As far as the question of language is concerned, Hindi has progressed a great deal. But we cannot keep in touch with the world of new ideas only through Hindi. Apart from this, as you know, in the South, especially in Madras, there is great opposition to Hindi, though the amazing thing is that the people there are learning Hindi in large numbers. I have no doubt about it that Hindi will spread in the South. But it will not spread if they are forced.

I agree with you that there should be rapid progress but if in the process we lose touch with the world of ideas, it will definitely harm us.

Nationalism should be strengthened in the country and Hindi should also progress. I see no difficulty in both these things happening simultaneously.

Yours sincerely,
Jawaharlal Nehru

Translation ends]

287. To Braj Narayan Brajesh[203]

अगस्त 2, 1962

प्रिय ब्रजेशजी,

आपका 26 जुलाई का पत्र मिला।[204] यह बात निश्चय है कि हिन्दी की उन्नति हमें पूरी तौर से करनी चाहिये ताकि वह देश की राष्ट्र-भाषा हो जाये। लेकिन आप जानते हैं इसमें क्या कठिनाई है, विशेषकर मद्रास से और कुछ बंगाल से। मद्रास में बड़े आन्दोलन इसके विरोध में हुए हैं। फिर भी बहुत लोग मद्रास में हिन्दी सीख रहे हैं। मुझे कोई संदेह नहीं कि हिन्दी बढ़ती जायेगी। लेकिन अगर हम ज़बरदस्ती करेंगे तो उसका उलटा असर

---

203. Letter to a former MP and the Organising Secretary, All India Hindu Mahasabha; address: Hindu Mahasabha Bhavan, Mandir Marg, New Delhi. PMO, File No. 52(12)/57-63-PMS, Vol. I, Sr. No. 78-A.
204. Appendix 14.

होगा और देश की एकता को भी हानि होगी । इसलिए ज़रा हलके चलना हिन्दी के लिए लाभदायक होगा ।

हमारे केन्द्र के दफ़्तरों में बहुत सारे मद्रास के और ऐसे प्रान्तों के लोग हैं जहां हिन्दी नहीं बोली जाती । उनके लिए पूरी तरह से हिन्दी का सीख लेना अब कठिन है । कुछ समझने तो लगे हैं । इसलिए कुछ वर्ष हुए निश्चय किया था, और उसकी घोषणा भी की थी, कि अंग्रेज़ी भी कुछ दिन हिन्दी के साथ-साथ चलेगी । इसका वचन हमने मद्रास वगैरह को दिया और उससे कुछ वहां शान्ति हुई । अब हम इसको तोड़ दें तो इसका बहुत बुरा असर होगा । मेरी राय में हिन्दी बहुत तेज़ी से बढ़ रही है देश में और बढ़ेगी । लेकिन अगर हम इसके नाम पर बाज़ प्रान्तों से लड़ाई लड़ें तो हिन्दी की बहुत हानि होगी ।

कोई भी भाषा अगर जनता के लिए हो तो उसको सरल होना चाहिए । कैसी भाषा वह हो यह मिल जुल कर निश्चय हो सकता है, और हलके-हलके अपने आप बन जायेगी ।[205]

आपका
जवाहरलाल नेहरु

[Translation begins[206]

August 2, 1962

Dear Brajeshji,

Received your letter of July 26.[207] It is certain that we have to work towards the progress of Hindi in every possible way so that it becomes the national language. But you know what the difficulty is, especially from Madras and somewhat from Bengal. There have been very big agitations against this in Madras. Even then lots of people are learning Hindi in Madras. I have no doubt about it that Hindi will grow. But if we force the people, it will have the opposite effect and it will also harm the country's unity. Therefore, to go slow will be beneficial for Hindi.

In the Central Government offices there are a large number of people from Madras and other provinces where Hindi is not spoken. It is difficult for them to learn Hindi totally. They have started to understand a little. That is why it was decided a few years ago, and it was announced also that English too would continue along with Hindi. We have made this promise to Madras and other states and that quietened things down. Now if we were to break it, it will have a very bad impact. In my view, Hindi is growing very fast and will continue to

---

205. See also items 285 and 288, and items in SWJN/SS/77/section Development, subsection Media
206. This translation is from the PMO file and not translated for the SWJN.
207. See fn 204 in this section.

do so in the country. But if we quarrel with some of the provinces in the name of Hindi, it will cause great harm to Hindi.

Any language meant for the masses ought to be simple. How the language should be moulded may be decided by mutual consensus and it will gradually grow on its own.[208]

Yours,
Jawaharlal Nehru

Translation ends]

288. To Prakashvir Shastri[209]

अगस्त 2, 1962

प्रिय प्रकाशवीर जी,

आपका 2 अगस्त का पत्र मिला ।[210]

मुझे खेद है कि हिन्दी के बारे में एक बहस शुरु हो गई है। मैंने अक्सर यह कहा है कि हिन्दी जहाँ तक हो सके सरल हो और आम लोगों की समझ में आये। कभी-कभी लोक-सभा में प्रश्नों के उत्तर में ऐसी हिन्दी बोली जाती थी जो बहुत कठिन थी और सबों की समझ में नहीं आती थी। आकाशवाणी की हिन्दी तो मैंने बहुत कम सुनी है और अब भी मुझे मालूम नहीं कि कैसी होती है। लेकिन हर सूरत से हमें इस बात को आपस में सलाह करके निश्चय करना चाहिए। कोई झगड़े फसाद की आवश्यकता नहीं है।

अंग्रेजी के बारे में निश्चय जो हुआ है वह नई बात नहीं है। यह तो बहुत बहस के बाद श्री गोविन्द बल्लभ पंत[211] के ज़माने में निश्चय हुआ था और कई बार लोक-सभा में इसका चर्चा भी हुआ था। आप जानते हैं कि मद्रास की तरफ और थोड़ा सा बंगाल में भी क्या गुल-शोर मचा है। मैं नहीं समझता कि इससे हिन्दी को कुछ हानि होगी। हिन्दी तो बढ़ रही है और बढ़ती जायेगी। बाज़ प्रान्तों में हिन्दी प्रान्त की भाषा समझी जाती है इस बात में ज़रा भी ज़बरदस्ती करने से उलटा असर हो सकता है।[212]

आपका
जवाहरलाल नेहरु

208. See fn 205 in this section.
209. Letter to Independent, Lok Sabha MP; address: 146 North Avenue, New Delhi. PMO, File No. 52(12)/57-63-PMS, Vol. I, Sr. No. 80 A.
210. Appendix 18.
211. Union Home Minister, 1955-1961.
212. See also items 285 and 287, and items in SWJN/SS/77/section Development, subsection Media.

[Translation begins][213]

August 2, 1962

Dear Prakashvirji

I received your letter of 2 August.[214] I regret that a controversy over Hindi has started. I have often said that as far as possible Hindi should be as simple as possible and must be understood by the masses. Sometimes such difficult Hindi used to be spoken in answer to questions in the Lok Sabha that many could not understand it. I have heard the All India Radio Hindi very seldom and even now I do not know quite how it is. However, in any event, we should decide this by mutual consensus. There is no need for quarrels and acrimonious debate.

The decision regarding English is nothing new. This was decided after much debate in the time of Shri Govind Ballabh Pant[215] and it has been discussed in the Lok Sabha also many times. As you know there was a hue and cry in Madras and somewhat in Bengal too. I do not think that it will harm Hindi in any way. Hindi is growing and will continue to do so. Hindi is regarded as the mother tongue in five States in India. Any attempt to force the issue will only have an opposite effect.[216]

Yours,
Jawaharlal Nehru

[Translation ends]

289. To Bishan Chander Seth[217]

अगस्त 18, 1962

प्रिय बिशन चन्द्रजी,

आपका 11 अगस्त का पत्र मिला।[218] आप मुझे माफ करेंगे अगर मैं उसका लम्बा जवाब न दूँ। मेरे पास बिलकुल समय नहीं लम्बे खत लिखने का।

---

213. This translation is from the PMO file and not translated for the SWJN.
214. See fn 210 in this section.
215. See fn 211 in this section.
216. See fn 212 in this section.
217. Letter to Lok Sabha MP of the Hindu Mahasabha.
218. See appendix 32.

आपके विचारों से किसी कदर मैं सहमत हूँ। लेकिन फिर भी मुझे आपकी विचारधारा सही नहीं मालूम होती और आजकल की दुनिया के लिए ख़ासकर मौज़ू नहीं है। ज़ाहिर है कि हर हिन्दुस्तानी को जो हमारा नागरिक है इस देश को अपनी मातृभूमि समझना चाहिए।

लेकिन आपको याद होगा कि हमने अपने विधान में 14 भाषाओं का चर्चा किया है। वह सब हमारी राष्ट्र भाषायें है। हां, यह सही है कि हिन्दी को सारे देश के लिए भाषा निश्चय की है। मुझे आशा है कि हल्के-हल्के यह बात हो जायेगी। लेकिन ज़बरदस्ती करने से यह भी ज़ाहिर है कि उसका उल्टा असर बहुत जगह होगा।

आजकल की दुनिया को समझने के लिए कुछ आजकल के हालात भी समझने चाहिये। अगर उनको न समझें तो हमारी दुनिया की तस्वीर ग़लत होगी।

आपका
जवाहरलाल नेहरु

[Translation begins

18 August 1962

My dear Bishan Chanderji,
I received your letter of the 11th August.[219] You will forgive me if I do not give a long reply. I have absolutely no time to write a long letter.

I am in agreement with your ideas to some extent. And yet your line of thinking does not seem right to me and it is not relevant especially in this age. It is obvious that every Indian who is a citizen of this country should regard this land as his motherland.

But you may remember that we have mentioned fourteen languages in our Constitution. They are all our national languages. Yes, it is correct that Hindi has been decided upon to be the national language. I am hopeful that it will happen gradually. But it is also obvious that if it is done forcibly it will have an adverse impact.

To understand the modern world we need to be aware of the realities of the day. If we fail to do so, we cannot have the right picture of the world.

Yours sincerely,
Jawaharlal Nehru

Translation ends]

219. See fn 218 in this section.

290. To Raghu Vira[220]

21st August, 1962

Dear Dr Raghu Vira,

I have your letter of the 17th August.[221] We all agree that Hindi and other Indian languages should be encouraged in every way. I believe we are making good progress.

So far as English is concerned, I think that it has not come in the way of the progress of Hindi or other languages. A foreign language like that here being associated with our other languages will make them fuller in the modern sense of science and technology etc. as well as modern ideas. A language which is flexible and takes words from other languages is more virile than one which keeps to itself.

But, apart from all this, there can be no doubt that in Madras especially and in Bengal there is considerable feeling on this issue and active opposition to Hindi in many places. Any attempt to force it down will lead to strong reactions against Hindi. It is far better to allow Hindi to progress without compulsion, as it is doing now.

As for the Government, we have a large number of officers and others serving the Central Government who, though they have picked up a little Hindi, do not know it adequately to do all their work in it. The next generation will no doubt be better. But for the present if we compel them to do their work in Hindi they will be wholly unable to do so and an unfortunate situation will arise. It is not that any of them is opposed to Hindi, but their capacity to learn it adequately at their present age [sic] [is limited?]. Therefore, I think that we should proceed slowly but surely, making a firm foundation in Hindi and trying to remove the objections to it in some States.[222]

Yours sincerely,
Jawaharlal Nehru

220. Letter to former Rajya Sabha MP and Chairman of the Reception Committee of the All-India Languages Convention; address: J-22 Hauz Khas Enclave, New Delhi-16. PMO, File No. 52(12)/57-63-PMS, Vol. I, Sr. No. 82-A.
221. Appendix 39.
222. According to *The Times of India* of 24 September 1962, Lal Bahadur Shastri, the Home Minister, told the All-India Convention of the Youth Congress in Tirupati on 23 September that "with a view to allaying the fears of the people living in non-Hindi-speaking areas and to bring the different areas close to one another the Government would introduce a Bill in the next session of Parliament to provide for the continuance of English as an associate language beyond 1965." The Official Languages Act, providing for the continued use of English as an official language beyond 1965, was passed in 1963. See also item 7, fn 41.

(h) Media

291. To Gopal Singh: A Journal for National Integration[223]

26th July 1962

Dear Dr Gopal Singh,

Thank you for your letter of July 17. I am glad that you are bringing out a quarterly which will lay stress on national integration. I wish you success at it. Nothing is more important in India today than national integration and the feeling that the unity of India is above all national and party conflicts. Indeed, from the point of view of spirituality and religion, it is far better for politics to be kept out of the ambit of various religious and national bodies. Thus we shall purify our politics also.

So far as Sikhs and Hindus are concerned, it is patent that both of them can only prosper by mutual understanding and tolerance. If this does not take place both will suffer and specially the Punjab will suffer. The Punjab is an ideal place to show all this unity in some diversity.

I hope that your quarterly will succeed in the message it gives to our people.

Yours sincerely,
[Jawaharlal Nehru]

292. To B. Gopala Reddy: Foreign Exchange Cuts for Newspapers[224]

August 7, 1962

My dear Gopala Reddi,[225]

Shri R.R. Diwakar, President of the Indian & Eastern Newspaper Society, saw me this afternoon and gave me the enclosed letter and copies of resolutions passed by that Society.

The Newspaper Import (Control) Order which has been passed very recently, according to the Society, hits the newspapers very badly. He had given detailed reasons how this may even amount to a 33% cut. I realise that we have

223. Letter to writer and journalist and Nominated, Rajya Sabha MP; address: 62 South Avenue, New Delhi. Sent from Anand Bhavan, Allahabad.
224. Letter to the Minister of Information and Broadcasting. PMO, File No. 37(35)/56-63-PMS, Volume III, Sr. No. 170-A. Also available in the JN Collection.
225. Nehru used both spellings of Gopala Reddy's surname, Reddy and Reddi.

to be very strict about imports and thus save foreign exchange. But I should have thought that newspapers and books deserve some special consideration. The reading public in India is not very great. We have been trying to increase, and it would be unfortunate if very restrictive orders are passed which will cut down even the present reading public. With the coming of Panchayati Raj etc. we are trying to increase magazines, newspapers etc.

In any event, I think that there should be some consultation with the newspapermen when such orders are passed so that their difficulties may be fully realised. I suggest that even now a talk with the representatives of the Society will be desirable. This will give them the feeling that their case is not completely ignored.

I do not know how far your Ministry can deal with this matter or whether the Commerce & Industry Ministry is solely responsible. If you like, you can send this letter of mine with its enclosure to the Commerce & Industry Ministry.[226]

Yours sincerely,
Jawaharlal Nehru

293. To R.R. Diwakar: Newsprint Import Cut[227]

August 8, 1962

My dear Diwakar,

I have addressed the Ministries concerned on the question of import of newsprint. I understand that you will be meeting the Finance Minister,[228] the Minister for Information & Broadcasting[229] and the Minister for International Trade.[230] You will no doubt have a full talk with them.

It has been pointed out to me that there has been a very big increase in the last few years in the amount of newsprint imported. It was to this high amount of 1961-62 that the cut was applied.

---

226. See item 293.
227. Letter to the Président of the Indian & Eastern Newspaper Society; letter addressed to him as Chairman of the Gandhi Smarak Nidhi, Rajghat, Delhi. PMO, File No. 37(35)/56-63-PMS, Volume III, Sr. No. 173-A. Also available in the JN Collection.
228. Morarji Desai.
229. B. Gopala Reddy.
230. Manubhai Shah.

I might mention that much as we dislike restricting newsprint, the situation in regard to foreign exchange is really very difficult, and there is no way out except to have restrictions all round.[231]

Yours sincerely,
Jawaharlal Nehru

294. To R.K. Karanjia: Cooperative Press[232]

August 26, 1962

My dear Karanjia,

Your letter of August 25th. I doubt very much if it will be appropriate for me to associate myself in any way with the new paper you might be bringing out. Normally I do not do so. But the idea of a cooperative press is certainly a good one.[233]

I shall be leaving Delhi in about ten days' time. These are heavily occupied days for me, and it will be difficult to find time for an interview. But you can certainly send me a note of your visit abroad.

Yours sincerely,
Jawaharlal Nehru

295. To Y.B. Chavan: Controlling Attacks by Press[234]

August 29, 1962

My dear Chavan,

You wrote to me long ago, on the 8th January 1962, on the question of scurrilous attacks in the Press and our inability to deal with them. As suggested by you, I

---

231. An import trade control notice issued by the GOI on 24 September 1962 announced reduction in "the cuts imposed recently on the newsprint quotas of newspapers to a uniform rate of 2.5 per cent of the entitlement." The cuts earlier announced were: Five per cent in the case of papers consuming 100 to 1,000 tons of newsprint and 7.5 per cent in the case of those consuming more than 1,000 tons. The changes were made by the Government after discussions with the Indian and Eastern Newspaper Society and the Indian Language Newspapers Association. *The Times of India*, 25 September 1962. See also item 292.
232. Letter to the founder and editor of the weekly tabloid *Blitz*; address: Framroze Court, Marine Drive, Bombay 1.
233. See also item 296.
234. Letter to the Chief Minister of Maharashtra.

sent your letter to our Ministry of Law. The question was examined both by the Law Ministry and by the Home Ministry. The Law Commission independently did this also. Thereafter, the Attorney-General[235] was asked for advice. I understand that the Law Ministry has now asked the Home Ministry to undertake necessary legislation in accordance with the advice of the Attorney-General.

Yours sincerely,
[Jawaharlal Nehru]

296. To K.A. Abbas: Cooperative Press[236]

August 31, 1962

My dear Abbas,
I have your letter of the 30th August. Karanjia[237] wrote to me about this proposal to have a cooperatively owned printing press etc. I replied to him that it was a good idea to have such a cooperatively owned printing press, but I could not associate myself with any such venture.[238] I have deliberately kept away from such associations. I used to be associated with the *National Herald*, but I gave up all contact with it long ago.

I do not know what kind of advice I can give you in the matter.

Yours sincerely,
[Jawaharlal Nehru]

(i) Science

297. To G.B. Pant: Tokyo Symposium[239]

July 21, 1962

Dear Prof. Pant,
Your letter of July 17. I have not received any message from the Tokyo University, as mentioned by you.

---

235. M.C. Setalvad.
236. Letter to journalist, writer, filmmaker and a columnist of *Blitz*; address: Philomena Lodge, Church Road, Juhu, Bombay-54.
237. R.K. Karanjia, editor of *Blitz*.
238. See item 294.
239. Letter to Research Professor and In-Charge Rocketry, Birla Institute of Technology, Mesra, Ranchi.

I am glad you are going to the symposium to be held in Tokyo. You can convey my good wishes to the symposium and my hope that the experiments carried on by them will be in the interest of peace.

I do not think it is necessary for me to send a special message on this occasion.

Yours sincerely,
[Jawaharlal Nehru]

298. Science Research Committee[240]

[Note, 25 July 1962, by Humayun Kabir, Minister of Scientific Research and Cultural Affairs, begins]

I spoke to the Prime Minister about the need for enquiring into the work of the different National Laboratories and their relationship with one another. His personal interest in and support for science have led to an enormous expansion in facilities for research in almost every field of science and also to a considerable improvement in the conditions of work of scientists. Before independence, there were very few research organisations outside Universities, but today, CSIR alone has 28 laboratories and I understand the Defence Science Organisation over 40. Laboratories connected with various other Ministries have also increased greatly in number and range of activities.

While some duplication in programme of research is desirable and perhaps also inevitable, it is a matter for consideration whether there is any justification for duplication of laboratories as a whole. Effective work cannot be done in any field of science unless there is a team with the minimum number of competent scientists. In a recent study, Prof. Blackett[241] has suggested that the minimum number for an effective scientific team is about twenty to twenty five, consisting of five or six senior scientists, ten or twelve research fellows and eight or ten technicians and scientific assistants. It is obvious that if these five or six senior scientists are distributed in two laboratories, there will be not only wastage of equipment but also wastage of scientific talent. We have found in many of the CSIR Laboratories that work suffers because an adequate number of scientists of requisite quality are not available. In this situation, duplication of laboratories may, instead of leading to advance of science, actually result in retrogression.

240. Noting. NMML, Humayun Kabir Papers, File No. 5/1958-62, Copy.
241. P.M.S. Blackett, British experimental physicist.

The British government appointed the Zuckerman Committee[242] "to inquire into the techniques employed by Government Departments and other bodies wholly financed by the Exchequer for the management and control of research and development carried out by them or on their behalf, and to make recommendations." The Prime Minister was kind enough to agree that a similar Committee may be appointed to undertake a study of the inter-relation of our National Laboratories with similar terms of reference, with special attention to division of responsibility between various Ministries and organisations and the size and content of research and development programmes. Such a survey would indicate the most effective use of scarce scientific manpower in the country and also the best utilisation of the limited financial and other resources.

I would suggest the following composition of the Committee:

1. Professor P.C. Mahalanobis[243] (Convenor)
2. Professor M.S. Thacker[244] (Planning Commission)
3. Dr D.S. Kothari, Chairman, University Grants Commission
4. Dr H.J. Bhabha, Department of Atomic Energy
5. Dr S. Bhagavantam, Scientific Adviser to the Ministry of Defence, and
6. The Director General of CSIR[245]

Humayun Kabir
25.7.1962

Prime Minister

[Note, 25 July 1962, by Humayun Kabir, Minister of Scientific Research
and Cultural Affairs, ends]

[Note, 27 July 1962, by Nehru, begins]

I think it would be desirable to have a Committee of the kind you mention but before we appoint this Committee, we should consult the two main departments concerned apart from the CSIR i.e. the Atomic Energy Department and the

---

242. Named after Solly Zuckerman, South Africa born scientist and adviser to the British Government; chaired the Committee on Management and Control of Research and Development, 1958-1961.
243. Member, Planning Commission, and Statistical Adviser to the Cabinet, GOI.
244. Member, Planning Commission, and Director General of CSIR until 1 August 1962.
245. S. Husain Zaheer, Director General of CSIR, from 1 September 1962 to 21 August 1966.

Defence Science Department of the Ministry of Defence. If they agree then we can appoint a Committee.

J. Nehru
27.7.62

[Note, 27 July 1962, by Nehru, ends]

299. Scientific Advisory Committee of the Cabinet[246]

[Note, 17 August 1962, by S.S. Khera, the Cabinet Secretary, for Nehru, begins]

Shri Vishnu Sahay, Chairman of the Scientific Advisory Committee of the Cabinet, will be leaving shortly to take up his new assignment as Governor of Assam; and a new Chairman is to be appointed in his place. Prime Minister will recall Dr Bhabha's[247] letter of April 18, 1962 and PM's own letter to Shri Vishnu Sahay of April 20 (papers placed below). The present composition of the Committee is given in Annexure 1.

The Cabinet Secretariat provides secretariat services for the Committee. The Cabinet Secretary as such need not be either ex-officio Chairman or ex-officio Member of the Committee, as Dr Bhabha has rightly pointed out in his letter of April 18.

PM may kindly consider as to who should be the Chairman of the Committee in place of Shri Vishnu Sahay. I would suggest the name of Dr Bhabha, or failing him, Dr D.S. Kothari.[248]

S.S. Khera
17.8.62

PM

[Note, 17 August 1962, by S.S. Khera, Cabinet Secretary, for Nehru, ends]

246. Noting. Cabinet Secretariat, Department of Science & Technology, File No. 84/2GF-60.
247. Homi Bhabha, Secretary, Department of Atomic Energy.
248. Chairman, UGC.

[Note, 17 August 1962, by Nehru for S.S. Khera, begins]

Dr Homi Bhabha should be the Chairman of the Committee. The Cabinet Secretary will continue to be a Member of the Committee.

J. Nehru
17.8.62

Cabinet Secretary

[Note, 17 August 1962, by Nehru for S.S. Khera, ends]

[Signed by S.S. Khera and forwarded to Homi Bhabha]

S.S. Khera
18.8.62

Dr Bhabha

[Note, 18 August 1962, by Homi Bhabha, for Nehru, begins]

In my view it is desirable that Shri S.S. Khera should be Chairman of the Committee. The Committee's recommendations impinge on many Ministries and Shri Khera will be in a better position to follow through the recommendations. I have consulted Shri Vishnu Sahay and Prof. Kothari who have seen the noting above and PM's minute. I have also consulted Prof. Mahalanobis[249] and some of the other members of the Committee, without however mentioning PM's minute. They are agreeable to my suggestion that Shri Khera should be the Chairman of the Committee. I, therefore, recommend that P.M. of the Committee.[250] I shall be willing to preside over meetings of the committee whenever Shri Khera is unable to attend. The present position that the Cabinet Secretary is neither ex-officio Chairman or Member of the Committee remains of course unaltered.

H.J. Bhabha
18.8.62

PM

[Note, 18 August 1962, by Homi Bhabha, for Nehru, ends]

---

249. P.C. Mahalanobis, Member, Planning Commission, and Statistical Adviser to the Cabinet, GOI.
250. In the copy available with the NMML this sentence is incomplete. The original is in the Cabinet Secretariat.

[Note, 20 August 1962, by Nehru, for S.S. Khera, begins]

In view of what Dr Bhabha has written, I am agreeable to Shri S.S. Khera being Chairman of the Committee in his personal capacity.

J. Nehru
20/8/62
Cabinet Secretary

[Note, 20 August 1962, by Nehru, for S.S. Khera, ends]

300. To Alladi Ramakrishnan: Congratulations to Physicists[251]

August 18, 1962

My dear Alladi Ramakrishnan,
I have received today, through the courtesy of Shri C. Subramaniam,[252] your letter of the 13th August with which a photograph was attached. I am very glad to know that two members of your Institute have been selected as participants in a seminar on Theoretical Physics in Italy. I hope you will convey my good wishes and congratulations to them. We shall look forward to the fine work they will do in the future.

Yours sincerely,
[Jawaharlal Nehru]

301. Information Flow to Department of Space[253]

[Note, 20 August 1962, from Homi Bhabha, Secretary, Department of Atomic Energy, for Nehru, begins]

DEPARTMENT OF ATOMIC ENERGY

When I saw the Prime Minster yesterday he mentioned to me a telegram which had been received from C.S. Jha[254] regarding our offer to act as "host

---

251. Letter to the Director of the Institute of Mathematical Sciences, Madras-4.
252. Minister of Steel and Heavy Industries.
253. Noting, 20 August 1962. MEA, File No. E(413)/DISARM/62, p. 5/Corr.
254. Permanent Representative to the UN until 29 July 1962; High Commissioner to Canada, 30 July 1962 to 4 January 1964.

country" for the International Sounding Rocket Launching Facility. C.S. Jha had asked, if I am not mistaken, whether we should circulate a request for aid to various countries in connection with this facility, and the Prime Minister wished to know my views. I told him that I had not seen the telegram and the Prime Minister asked me to get in touch with the Foreign Secretary[255] to get a copy of the telegram. Unfortunately, I had a meeting immediately after I left the Prime Minister with the Secretary, Department of Economic Affairs,[256] and I was not free till late in the evening. As the Department of Atomic Energy is the operative Ministry for the peaceful uses of space, it is clearly necessary that all exchanges of telegrams, letters, and notes on this subject that take place between Delhi and our Missions abroad should be sent to this Department. In the absence of such an arrangement it is clearly not possible for this Department to handle the peaceful uses of space in the same manner as it is handling the peaceful uses of atomic energy. The Prime Minister is requested to issue appropriate instructions.

H.J. Bhabha
20.8/62

Prime Minister

[Note, 20 August 1962, from Homi Bhabha, for Prime Minister, ends]

[Note, 20 August 1962, from Jawaharlal Nehru for R.K. Nehru, Secretary-General, MEA, begins]

I agree with Dr Bhabha. All such matters, that is those relating to the peaceful uses of space and space research, should be referred to the Department of Atomic Energy as they are broadly dealing with it and are competent to do so. External Affairs will of course consider any other aspects that may arise. Please arrange accordingly.

J. Nehru
20/8/62

[Note, 20 August 1962, for R.K. Nehru, Secretary-General, MEA, ends]

---

255. M.J. Desai.
256. L.K. Jha.

302. To I.C. Chopra: Regional Research Laboratory of Jammu[257]

August 24, 1962

Dear Dr Chopra,

Thank you for your letter of the 21st August and the Bulletin of the Regional Research Laboratory, Jammu. I have rather rapidly glanced through this Bulletin, even though I am a layman. I am glad you are issuing this and I am sure it will help considerably in our search for and utilisation of indigenous herbs for medicinal purposes.

Yours sincerely,
[Jawaharlal Nehru]

303. In the Rajya Sabha: The Atomic Energy Bill 1962[258]

Jawaharlal Nehru: Madam Deputy Chairman,[259] I beg to move:

"That the Bill to provide for the development, control and use of atomic energy for the welfare of the people of India and for other peaceful purposes and for matters connected therewith, as passed by the Lok Sabha, be taken into consideration."

Fourteen years ago the Atomic Energy Bill was passed by Parliament. That was the very beginning of our endeavours to promote work for atomic energy in India. We began from scratch. In these fourteen years we have advanced considerably and indeed we have made some mark in the atomic world in so far as the work and research work is concerned. Anyone who has been to the atomic energy plant at Trombay near Bombay will have some idea of the scope of its work, the extent of it, and will also probably be impressed by the ability that has gone to build all this up. Foreign scientists, physicists and atomic energy experts who have come here and visited it have spoken in very high terms of it. During these fourteen years much has happened, from the very early, small beginnings. Now, it is one of the most important establishments in India. I do

---

257. Letter to the Head of the Regional Research Laboratory, Canal Road, Jammu Tawi.
258. Motion, 30 August 1962. *Rajya Sabha Debates*, Vol. 40, Nos. 17-23, 30 August to 7 September 1962, cols 4395-4397, 4411-4425.
259. Violet Alva.

not remember the exact number of scientists employed there, but I think that among senior and junior scientists there are about 4,000 of them employed in the Trombay establishment.[260] It has a large number of experts and scientific workers and to some extent they are still growing. Of course, our work is growing. That work consists not only of what is done in Trombay but also what is done in Kerala, where the biggest deposits of monazite sand occur and other minerals, and a search all over India for various important minerals. Therefore, the scope of the work has grown greatly.

It was decided some time ago to have an atomic power station at Tarapore in Northern Maharashtra, and some progress has been made, and we shall probably start serious work there soon in a few months' time. At the same time, it has been decided to have another atomic power station in Rajasthan—I think it is Ranapratapsagar—which will give electric power may be to Rajasthan, of course, to Uttar Pradesh and to Punjab possibly. There is a third suggestion, which has not taken shape yet, of having an atomic plant in South India.

So, all these extensions, etc., have made the old Atomic Energy Act[261] out of date, and it is necessary therefore to, one could have told, improve it and make it more suitable to circumstances. One could have brought a large number of amendments to the old Act but that is a cumbrous procedure. It is far better to have a comprehensive new Act providing for all the needs of today. Among those needs is first of all to be able to control all the minerals used for atomic energy production, more especially uranium. Secondly, this Bill has stated something about patents. We do not recognise any patents, we will not recognise any patents referring to these minerals or anything connected with atomic energy. Thirdly—and very important—very effective safety measures have to be taken in dealing with the production of atomic energy anywhere. Those who have gone to Trombay may have some idea of the excessive caution that is used in storing this very dangerous material. So that is provided for. And fourthly, the penalties for non-observance and breach of any of these rules have been made more heavy. These are the main points of this new Bill. There is the rule-making power which is given to the Atomic Energy Commission also.

I will not take up the time of the House by going into the Bill in detail because it is a non-controversial measure, and it has largely been drafted, drafted originally, by the Department of Atomic Energy people themselves. It has been

260. Nehru is not very precise. On 28 August 1961, he informed the Rajya Sabha, "some of our brightest and ablest scientists are engaged in team work in Trombay and there are others elsewhere in India. Some 2,000 of them are there in Trombay engaged in this team work attempting to produce results." See SWJN/SS/71/item 2, here p. 22.
261. The Atomic Energy Act, 1948.

considered and vetted by all the other Ministries concerned and especially the Ministry of Law. So, I submit, Madam, that this Bill should be considered by this House and passed.

[Motion on debate follows. Speeches by various MPs omitted]

Jawaharlal Nehru: Madam, all the speakers who have spoken on this Bill have accepted it and more or less praised the work of the Atomic Energy Department. I am glad that they have done so because the record of our atomic energy work is a record which has brought praise from all the competent scientists in other countries. Dr Bhabha[262] has been referred to as a very eminent head of this establishment. He is very well known but I would like to say a word about the large number of very competent young scientists, some of them quite brilliant, who are working there and who have already made a name for themselves in international circles. One remarkable feature of this establishment is that out of the thousands of scientists who are working there, most of them are under thirty or in the thirties and they occupy very responsible positions and yet they have a right to be Heads of Departments and represent us often in international conferences and the like, so that the Atomic Energy Department is not only young in years and therefore it is, possibly because of that, a very vital and progressing Department and we can look forward to its further development with some confidence.

Regarding this question of using atomic energy for civil purposes, production of electric power, some hon. Members talked about a White Paper. I do not know what White Paper he was referring to but the Atomic Energy Department has issued annually and sometimes more than once a year, pamphlets on these subjects. Apart from that, Dr Bhabha has come here regularly and addressed Members of Parliament on this very subject of the use of atomic energy for civil purposes. There used to be, some time ago, some difference of opinion. Dr Bhabha has always maintained that it can be and should be used for civil purposes. Some people thought that it would be rather expensive. Even if it had been expensive, slightly expensive, it was worthwhile doing it for the purposes of research experience so that we may know exactly where we are and improve upon it.

But as a matter of fact it has become progressively recognised that it is not much more expensive. And the expense part depends so much, that is, the comparative expense part, on many factors. Where a thermal station is situated

262. Homi Bhabha, Secretary, Department of Atomic Energy, and Chairman, Atomic Energy Commission of India.

near a colliery, it is cheaper. That is, coal has not to be carried a long way. Hydro-electric works may be cheaper because power is obtained nearby. But there can be no doubt that atomic energy is competitive wherever coal is far off and no hydro-electric power is available. Therefore, if we have this in Rajasthan or in Tarapore in North Maharashtra on the borders of Gujarat, it is certainly cheap, and no other method can produce it at that cost. I am told—I cannot obviously guarantee the figures—by those who know that the figures that the hon. Member stated of 4.5 naye paise per kwt is a figure which our advisers think is reasonable and a correct figure. Apart from this, it is generally recognised now that the cost is likely to go down with improvements in processes, etc. It is going down and it is less now than it was some two or three years ago. So, it can be and is likely to be a major supplier of power in the future.

There was some talk about too much centralisation. If hon. Members will see the Atomic Energy Acts in other countries, they will find how much centralised they are. They have to be. It may be that in other countries they look upon this more as a measure useful for military purposes. We do not, and even in the long title of our Bill we have laid stress upon it that it is for peaceful purposes that we develop it.[263] But everywhere, whether it is for military purposes or for peaceful purposes, you cannot take any risks about it by allowing control to be spread out among other hands or anything of that sort. It is too dangerous. I remember an eminent scientist—not Indian—once saying to me only a few years ago that the day will come when you will be able to make atomic bombs in your back garden. Terrible prospect, that a scientist can make it in his back garden.[264] It was an exaggeration, of course, but it shows which way things are tending. It is essential that all those materials which go to the making of atomic energy should be under Central control. We cannot have various controls about it.

Mr Govindan Nair[265] was worried about other minerals that may occur in his area. He has proposed an amendment too. I may point out to him that it

---

263. The sub-title of The Atomic Energy Act, 1962, read: "An Act to provide for the development, control and use of atomic energy for the welfare of the people of India and for other peaceful purposes and for matters connected therewith."

264. Mark Oliphant, Australian nuclear scientist, had spoken about such a possibility at his meeting with Nehru in New Delhi in March 1955, which Nehru shared on 20 March 1955 with V.K. Krishna Menon, then Rajya Sabha MP, see SWJN/SS/28/p. 313. Reference to Oliphant's observation on this matter intermittently figured in Nehru's speeches and notings, see his address to the Commonwealth Parliamentary Conference in New Delhi on 10 December 1957, SWJN/SS/40/p. 536, and his note of 11 May 1958, in SWJN/SS/42/p. 260.

265. M.N. Govindan Nair, CPI.

is totally unnecessary, because the Atomic Energy Department is very much interested in working all the minerals that may occur in that particular area. They may allow others to work them, if they can be separated and if they are not interested; but surely they are not interested in allowing them not to be worked.

There are a multitude of amendments suggested by Shri Chordia.[266] I have looked through them and I would submit, Madam, that they are not necessary, and sometimes, they may be actually harmful, harmful in the sense—I will deal with them later—that they have legal implications. So, they are not desirable in that sense, or they are unnecessary. This Bill has been very carefully drafted and personally I would not dare to try to change the language of it, after it has gone through all this process of sifting, comparison with other Acts all over the world. We started with the Act of 1948. That was the basis and then we improved upon it and changed it and added to it. The subjects dealt with are so highly technical—although some matters in the Bill may not be technical—that I hesitate to touch any of its technical words or definitions or anything coming out of them, because it may have some implication of which I am not even aware. So, I regret I am not in a position to accept these amendments.

Gopikrishna Vijaivargia (Madhya Pradesh):[267] May I ask whether there is any necessity for the word "peaceful" in the title of the Bill?

Jawaharlal Nehru: We think it is very necessary. In fact, it was at one time thought that the word "peaceful" should occur in the body of the Bill, but if it does not occur there, it does not so much matter. But I think it is most important that it should be there in the title. It is our fundamental policy. Some people doubt it. Some people in other countries think that we say this to delude others or ourselves, and if necessity arises, we shall go in for using it for military or war purposes. Well, I do not think any necessity for that will arise, personally, and if it arises, well, if the world is coming to an end, I do not know what we will do or anybody else will do. That is a different matter. We want to lay particular stress, therefore, on peaceful purposes.

Bhupesh Gupta (West Bengal):[268] Anyway, we can amend it before any atomic destruction comes.

Jawaharlal Nehru: That is all, Madam. I beg to move.

266. V.M. Chordia, Jan Sangh.
267. Congress.
268. CPI.

Deputy Chairman: The question is:

"That the Bill to provide for the development, control and use of atomic energy for the welfare of the people of India and for other peaceful purposes and for matters connected therewith, as passed by the Lok Sabha, be taken into consideration."

The motion was adopted.

Deputy Chairman: We now take up the clause by clause consideration of the Bill.

Clauses 2 to 13 were added to the Bill.

Clause 13 – Innovation of certain contracts.

V.M. Chordia: Madam, I move:

"That at page 10, line 29, after the word 'person' the words 'or his authorised agent' be inserted."

विधान की धारा 13(2) में सेन्ट्रल गवर्नमेंट द्वारा उस आदमी को आब्जेक्शन देने के लिए और अपीयर होने के लिये जो प्राविधान है, उसके सम्बन्ध में मेरा यह निवेदन है कि यह मामला कोई ऐसा है नहीं कि जिसमें अगर उसके अथाराइज्ड एजेन्ट को आप अधिकृत कर देंगे तो उससे कोई नुकसान होगा। कई मामले ऐसे होते हैं कि उनकी फर्म के लोग काम करते हैं, कम्पनी के लोग काम करते हैं और ऐसी स्थिति में यदि हम यहां अथाराइज्ड एजेन्ट को भी अधिकार दे देंगे तो उसमें कोई विशेष होने की बात दिखती नहीं। इसलिये निवेदन है कि मेरा यह संशोधन स्वीकार किया जाये।

[Translation: The provision that under Article 13(2) of the Constitution, the person authorized to object or to appear is, I submit, not a matter in which there is any harm in giving the authorization to an authorized agent. There are many issues in which people of their firm work on their behalf. Under these circumstances, even if we empower the authorized agent, there could not be any harm. Hence my request is that my amendment may be accepted.]

The question was proposed.

394

जवाहरलाल नेहरूः यह तो मामूली कानून है कि अथाराइज्ड एजेन्ट नुमाइन्दगी कर सकता है ऐसे मौके पर। इसको लिखने की कोई जरूरत नहीं है यहां पर। मेरी राय में यह गैर जरूरी है। जो बात माननीय सदस्य चाहते हैं वह तो कैसे भी हो ही सकती है। मेरे पास समन आता है किसी मुकदमे में जाने का, तो मेरा वकील अपीयर हो सकता है उसमें।

[Translation: Jawaharlal Nehru: It is an accepted rule that an authorized agent can represent. There is no need to write it down. In my view, it is unnecessary. What the hon. Member wants is possible in the ordinary course. If I receive a summons to appear in some case, my lawyer can appear on my behalf.]

Deputy Chairman: The question is:

6. "That at page 10, line 29, after the word 'person' the words 'or his authorised agent' be inserted."

The motion was negatived.

Deputy Chairman: The question is:

"That clause 13 stand part of the Bill."

The motion was adopted.

Clause 13 was added to the Bill.

Clauses 14 to 20.

K. Santhanam (Madras):[269]   Madam Deputy Chairman, I want to make one or two remarks on these clauses. I have got one or two points to make. I want to speak on the clause.

Deputy Chairman: All right.

K. Santhanam: I have a suggestion to make. In clause 14 I think it is not enough merely to give a licence for the acquisition, production, etc. of atomic equipment. I think there should be a statutory Central Register which registers every kind of atomic equipment, whether it is in the hospitals, whether it is in the universities, which exists in this country. We found the

269. Congress.

other day that the Central Government had no register of big transformers and other equipment. This is the case with respect to almost all the other major equipment and I think registers for such equipment should be kept. In the case of atomic equipment, I think such a register is absolutely essential so that the safety of the country and the safety of the people can be protected.

On clause 20 I have got some doubts. This refers to patents. There are two classes of people involved, Indian citizens applying for patents and foreigners applying for patents in India. So far as an Indian citizen applying for patents is concerned, I am really surprised that while he cannot get a patent in India, under sub-clause (5) he can apply to a foreign government and get a patent. I think this is not a very wise provision. If his application has some meaning, the Government of India should take over the invention and pay him compensation; but he should not be allowed to apply to a foreign government and get a patent for atomic equipment which can be used against us and this country. So far as foreign governments are concerned, I am not sure that the Government wants to cut off all possibilities of even foreign collaboration in manufacturing atomic equipment in this country. I can understand their saying that no patent should be given except with the special permission of the Central Government. But by saying no patent should be given they are prohibiting foreign governments and foreign manufacturers of atomic equipment to come and manufacture it even for the Government of India, and even with their collaboration. I do not know if these points were considered but they may be kept in mind when making rules or for such action as may be necessary.

Jawaharlal Nehru: I do not quite understand what the hon. Member means when he says that we should keep a register of equipment. That I do not understand. There is no equipment—no small equipment—spread out all over India to manufacture atomic energy. Perhaps, he may be thinking of things like isotopes.

K. Santhanam: Small cyclotrons in the universities.

Jawaharlal Nehru: Cyclotrons cannot manufacture atomic energy. Reactors and much more complicated things are needed. Where do you draw the line between an ordinary equipment for the study of atomic physics which every college should have, I think, and the other equipment? An hon. Member pointed out the deficiency in the standards of our teaching. Well, I entirely agree with him. We have to improve the standards of our universities. Now, they may keep cyclotrons but what is the point in keeping a register of cyclotrons? Not that there are many; everybody knows that. At present I do not know how many there are—perhaps one or two—in India but that is a different matter. But what is the good of keeping a register of small equipment, I do not understand. Every university and college—they have not got it—should get it. But as far as isotopes are concerned, a register is kept. The Atomic Energy Department supplies them to hospitals and other places and for that a register is kept.

As for the invention business, I do not again understand the hon. Member. I might inform him that this is based on the recommendations of Mr Justice Rajagopala Iyengar who was appointed to examine and advise Government on the existing patent law—not atomic energy—and he has dealt with it at some length.[270] No question can arise, no possibility can arise, of any foreigner trying to produce atomic energy in India except with the permission, and under the supervision, of the Government. It is impossible; it cannot be done. We do not recognise any patent just as I do not think we should recognise patents in many things, apart from atomic energy. I think we should not recognise patents in drugs. I think this drug rackets is a bad thing and we should not recognise it. Some countries don't in fact. But in atomic energy we cannot recognise any patents. We are going to use all the information we have, or we can get, without paying royalty or we come to agreement with a foreign government or if necessary with a foreign firm. This is a matter to which we attach such considerable importance that we are not going to recognise any patents in atomic energy. It will produce all manner of confusions and restrictions on our work.

Deputy Chairman: The question is:

"That clauses 14 to 20 stand part of the Bill."

The motion was adopted.

Clauses 14 to 20 were added to the Bill.

Clause 21 – Principles relating to payment of compensation.

V.M. Chordia: Madam, I move:

7. "That at page 16, after line 31, the following be inserted, namely:-

270. A committee, chaired by Justice N. Rajagopala Ayyangar of the Madras High Court, was appointed in 1957 to examine the question of revision of the Patent Law; it reported in September 1959.

'(2A) Where the amount of compensation is not paid by the due date such amount shall be paid with interest thereon, at such rate as the Central Government may by order specify, from the date it becomes due till its payment;'."

यह संशोधन इसलिये प्रस्तुत किया गया है कि अभी तक सरकार के बहुत से कामों में यह देखा गया है कि सरकार अगर कोई भूमि अपने काम के लिये ले लेती है, एक्वायर कर लेती है तो उसका उपयोग तो वह उसी समय से करने लग जाती है मगर उसका मुआवजा वर्षों तक नहीं दिया जाता है। वैसे होना तो यह चाहिये कि जिस तरह से हम दूसरों पर प्रतिबन्ध लगाते हैं उसी तरह के स्वयं अपने कामों पर भी प्रतिबन्ध लगाना चाहिये। अगर सरकार किसी की भूमि को एक्वायर करना चाहती है तो उसका कम्पेन्सेशन भी तय कर देना चाहिये कि इतनी सीमा के अन्दर हम उसको पेमेन्ट कर देंगे। मगर इस बिल में इस तरह का कोई प्रोविज़न नहीं किया गया है। इस तरह के कई उदाहरण दिये जा सकते हैं कि सरकर काश्तकार से सड़क बनाने के लिये जमीन तो ले लेती है, सड़क भी बना लेती है मगर उसका मुआवजा आठ और नौ साल के बाद देती है। इस तरह से हम यह चाहते हैं कि जो कम्पेन्सेशन देना है वह आरबीट्रेटर के आधार पर देना चाहिये और उसके लिये कोई तारीख़ निश्चित कर दी जानी चाहिये कि इस समय तक कम्पेन्सेशन दे दिया जायेगा। यही हमारे संशोधन का आशय है और हम आशा करते हैं कि यह स्वीकार कर लिया जायेगा।

[Translation: This amendment has been presented because it has been seen in many official matters that if the Government acquires some land for official use, it starts using the land immediately after acquisition but compensation is not paid for years. Whereas what should be done is that just as we impose rules on others, we should also impose the same rules on ourselves. If the Government wishes to acquire someone's land, then the compensation should also be fixed and it should be laid down that the payment will be made within the time frame agreed upon. But no such provision has been made in this Bill. Any number of examples of this kind can be given where the Government has acquired land from the peasant to build a road, but the compensation is given eight or nine years later. Therefore we want that the compensation to be given should be decided upon by the arbitrator and a date must be fixed by when such compensation is paid. This is the purpose of our amendment and we hope that it will be accepted.]

The question was proposed.

Jawaharlal Nehru: I submit, Madam, that it is wholly unnecessary. Either it is agreed to and compensation is paid or there will be an award and the award will specify the conditions of payment even to the extent of saying that interest may be paid. Sometimes it is done, I am told. Anyhow, it would be wholly out of place here.

Deputy Chairman: The question is:

7.   "That at page 16, after line 31, the following be inserted, namely:-
    '(2A) Where the amount of compensation is not paid by the due date such amount shall be paid with interest thereon, at such rate as the Central Government may by order specify, from the date it becomes due till its payment;'."

The motion was adopted.

Deputy Chairman: The question is:

"That clause 21 stand part of the Bill."

The motion was adopted.

Clause 21 was added to the Bill.

Deputy Chairman: At five o'clock we have fixed the time for a "Half-an-hour discussion" but with the permission of the House I would like to finish this Bill and take up the other discussion later on.

Bhupesh Gupta: We are in agreement. We are waiving the rule now. Only because of the Prime Minister I am agreeable to suspending the rule to accommodate him. I want to make it absolutely clear and, therefore, I am in favour of your suggestion. But it should not be a precedent.

(No hon. Member dissented)

Deputy Chairman: The House has given its consent. There are no amendments to clauses 22 to 24.

Clauses 22 to 24 were added to the Bill.

Clause 25 – Offences by companies.

V.M. Chordia: Madam, I move:

8.   "That at pages 18 to 19, for lines 35 and 36 and 1 and 2, respectively, the following be substituted, namely:-

'Provided that any such person shall be liable to punishment if it is proved that the offence was committed with his knowledge or that he did not exercise all due diligence to prevent the commission of such offence'."

9.   "That at page 19, for lines 12 and 13, the following be substituted namely:-

'(a) "company" means a company as defined in the Companies Act, 1956'."

The questions were proposed.

विमलकुमार मन्नालालजी चोरड़ियाः अभी जो इसमें व्यवस्था है उसमें बर्डेन आफ प्रूफ उस आदमी पर है जिस पर यह आरोप लगाया जाये कि तुमने गुनाह किया है। किन्तु इस संशोधन के अनुसार जो उसको गिरफ्तार करने वाला है, जो उसको पकड़ने वाला है, उसको यह साबित करना होगा कि जिस पर आरोप लगाया गया है उसने वास्तव में गुनाह किया है। हमारे यहां कई कानून ऐसे हैं जैसे कोई चोरी करता है तो उस चोरी करने वाले को जो गिरफ्तार करता है उसको यह प्रमाणित करना पड़ता है कि उस आदमी ने चोरी की है, उसके पास यह चोरी का माल मिला है। मगर हम यहां पर उसका उल्टा व्यवधान कर रहे हैं कि बर्डेन आफ प्रूफ गुनाह करने वाले पर होगा। मेरे ख्याल से यह कोई ऐसी भयानक बात नहीं है जिसके लिये आप यह उल्टी व्यवस्था करने जा रहे हैं। इसलिये मैं आशा करता हूं कि इस संशोधन पर विचार किया जायेगा।

[Translation: Vimal Kumar Mannalalji Chordia: The provision which is there in the Bill at present is that the burden of proof is on the individual against whom a complaint is made, that he is guilty of crime. But according to this amendment the one who apprehends the culprit has to prove that he is in fact guilty. The burden of proof is with the one who apprehends, if someone is accused of theft, that the stolen goods were found on the culprit, etc. But here we are making provisions where the burden of proof will be on the culprit. In my opinion it will not be a terrible thing to bring in the amendment which I hope will be accepted.]

Jawaharlal Nehru: I regret I cannot accept them. I think they are wholly unnecessary.

Deputy Chairman: The question is:

8. "That at pages 18 and 19, for lines 35 and 36 and 1 and 2, respectively, the following be substituted, namely:-

'Provided that any such person shall be liable to punishment if it is proved that the offence was committed with his knowledge or that he did not exercise all due diligence to prevent the commission of such offence'."

The motion was negatived.

Deputy Chairman: The question is:

9. "That at page 19, for lines 12 and 13, the following be substituted, namely:-

'(a) "company" means a company as defined in the Companies Act, 1956'."

The motion was negatived.

Deputy Chairman: The question is:

"That clause 25 stand part of the Bill."

The motion was adopted.

Clause 25 was added to the Bill.

Clause 26 – Cognizance of offences.

V.M. Chordia: Madam, I move:

10. "That at page 19, line 16, after the word 'cognizable' the words 'and bailable' be inserted."

महोदया, अभी इसमें जो गुनाह बताया है वह कॉग्निज़ेबल ऑफेंस का बताया है। मगर निवेदन है कि इस ऑफेंस को बेलेबिल ऑफेंस बनाने में कोई खास कठिनाई नहीं आनी चाहिये। अभी इसके बारे में खास कहने की आवश्यकता मैं नहीं समझता। यह जरूर है कि अगर किसी आदमी ने गुनाह किया है और ऐसा हमारा शासन मानता है तो उसको जमानत पर रिहा करने में कोई आपत्ति हो नहीं सकती।

[Translation: Madam, it has been said that this is a cognizable offence. But I submit that there should be no special problem in making it a bailable offence. I do not have to go into the details. But I feel that if an individual has committed an offence and that is what the Government believes, there can be no objection to releasing him on bail.]

The question was proposed.

उपसभापतिः आपको सब अमेंडमेंट्स पर जवाब मिल गया है।

विमलकुमार मन्नालालजी चोरड़िया : अगर आप कहें तो मैं अपना कर्त्तव्य छोड़ दूं।

जवाहरलाल नेहरुः मैं इसे मंजूर नहीं कर सकता। यह मामूली कानून जैसा नहीं है। यों तो जो जज चाहे, कर सकता है इस मौके पर।

[Translation begins:

Deputy Chairman: You have got response to all your amendments.

Vimal Kumar Mannalalji Chordia: I will give up my duty if you say so.

Jawaharlal Nehru: I cannot accept this. This is not an ordinary law, though the Judge can rule in this matter as the Judge considers appropriate.

Translation ends]

Deputy Chairman: The question is:

10. "That at page 19, line 16, after the word 'cognizable' the words 'and bailable' be inserted."

The motion was adopted.

Deputy Chairman: The question is:

"That clause 26 stand part of the Bill."

The motion was adopted.

Clause 26 was added to the Bill.

Clauses 27 to 31 were added to the Bill.

Clause 32 – Repeal of Act 29 of 1948.

V.M. Chordia: Madam, I move.

11. "That at page 21, the existing clause 32 be re-numbered as sub-clause (1) of that clause and after the sub-clause as so re-numbered, the following be inserted, namely:-

'(2) Anything done or any action taken including the orders, notifications or rules made or issued in exercise of the powers conferred by or under the Atomic Energy Act, 1948, shall, in so far as it is not inconsistent with the provisions of this Act, be deemed to have been done or taken in the exercise of the powers conferred by or under this Act as if this Act was in force on the day on which such thing was done or action taken'."

महोदया, जितने हमारे कानून बनते हैं उनमें हम रिपील का प्राविजन रखते हैं और उसके साथ साथ सेविंग का क्लॉज़ रखते हैं। पहले कानून के अन्तर्गत जो हम नोटिफिकेशन इशु करते हैं या जो भी कार्यवाही की जाती है उसको प्रोटेक्ट करने के लिये हम दूसरे कानून में प्राविधान करते हैं। इस विधान में उस पुराने कानून को रिपील करने की व्यवस्था तो की गई है, किन्तु दुर्भाग्य से यह व्यवस्था नहीं की गई है कि उसके अन्तर्गत इशु किये गये नोटिफिकेशन उसके अन्तर्गत किये गये काम सारे इस कानून के तहत भी वेलिड होंगे। इसी आशय से मैंने यह संशोधन रखा है। यदि मेरा संशोधन मंजूर नहीं किया जाता है तो कल या परसों शासन को स्वयं यह संशोधन लाना पड़ेगा। इसलिए मैं आशा करता हूं कि मेरा संशोधन स्वीकार किया जायेगा।

[Translation: Madam, in all the laws that we promulgate, we always have a provision for repeal and along with it a saving clause. Under any earlier Act when a notification is issued, or whatever action is taken, a provision is made to protect it under the new Act. In this Bill, while provision has been made to repeal the old law, unfortunately no provision has been made to ensure that notifications issued under the old Act and all actions taken under it will still be valid under the new Act. That is why I have proposed this amendment. If my amendment is not accepted then the Government will have to bring in an amendment in the future. Therefore I hope that this amendment will be accepted.]

The question was proposed.

जवाहरलाल नेहरूः माननीय सदस्य को कुछ गलतफहमी है। यह कह देने से कि एटामिक एनर्जी एक्ट रिपील हो गया, इसके यह माने हो गये कि अब तक जो कार्यवाही हुई है वह सब रिपील हो गई। वह सब जारी है। जनरल क्लाज़ेज़ ऐक्ट की दफ़ा 24 में साफ है कि जो कुछ नोटिफिकेशन इशु हुए और कायदे कानून उसमें बने वे सब जारी रहेंगे। इसमें कोई गलतफहमी की जरूरत नहीं है।

[Translation: Jawaharlal Nehru: Hon. Member is under some misapprehension. In saying that the Atomic Energy Act has been repealed does not mean that all the actions taken so far under it have also been repealed. They will all be valid. Under Article 24 of the General Clauses Act it is clear that the notifications which have been issued and the rules and regulations made under it will continue to be valid. There is no room for any misunderstanding in this.]

Deputy Chairman: The question is:

11. "That at page 21, the existing clause 32 be re-numbered as sub-clause (1) of that clause and after the sub-clause as so re-numbered, the following be inserted, namely:-

'(2) Anything done or any action taken including the orders, notifications or rules made or issued in exercise of the powers conferred by or under the Atomic Energy Act, 1948, shall, in so far as it is not inconsistent with the provisions of this Act, be deemed to have been done or taken in the exercise of the powers conferred by or under this Act as if this Act was in force on the day on which such thing was done or action taken'."

The motion was negatived.

Deputy Chairman: The question is:

"That clause 32 stand part of the Bill."

The motion was adopted.

Clause 32 was added to the Bill.

Clause 1, the Enacting Formula and the Title were added to the Bill.

Jawaharlal Nehru: Madam, I move:

"That the Bill be passed."

The question was put and the motion was adopted.

304. To M.A. Jamal: Presenting Book on Physics[271]

September 5, 1962

Dear Mr Jamal,

I have your letter of September 1st. I am leaving for England in another two days' time and I shall be away for the whole of the month of September. Therefore, there is no point in your coming here to present your book to me till I come back.

I would suggest to you, however, to send a copy of your book to Prof. Humayun Kabir, Minister of Scientific Research & Cultural Affairs of the Union Government. He will have your book examined by competent persons and will, no doubt, report to me about the result of this examination.[272] Later, if you so wish it, you can present a copy of the book to me.

Yours sincerely,
Jawaharlal Nehru

305. To Humayun Kabir: Jamal's Book on Physics[273]

September 5, 1962

My dear Humayun,

I enclose a letter which I have received. In this the writer[274] talks about a book he has written about some new theory of his and wants to present the book to me. I am replying to him that the book should be sent to you so that you can have it examined by a competent physicist.[275] If there is any substance in that book, you might give him some facilities for research work.

Yours sincerely,
[Jawaharlal Nehru]

271. Letter; address: "Jamal Mansion", Amravati Camp, Maharashtra.
272. See item 305.
273. Letter to the Minister of Scientific Research and Cultural Affairs.
274. M.A. Jamal.
275. See item 304.

306. To M.S. Thacker: Inviting P.M.S. Blackett to India[276]

September 19, 1962

My dear Thacker,

I met Blackett[277] yesterday. I mentioned that we would very much like to have him in India for some time. He said that he would be prepared to spend two or three months there and advise us as to what we should do with the NPL etc., but he was too old now to undertake a job of reorganising on a big scale and implementing his own advice. Also he was too tied up with the disarmament problem which was taking up a lot of time.

I suggested to him at least to come to India, spend two or three months there and then decide about the future. He agreed to that. He is thinking of coming for the Science Congress early in January to Delhi. Perhaps you can discuss this matter a little more with him. Anyhow, invite him to come to India for two or three months and he and we can decide more about the future.[278]

Yours sincerely,
Jawaharlal Nehru

307. To S. Husain Zaheer: Inviting P.M.S. Blackett to India[279]

September 19, 1962

My dear Munne,

Your letter of the 12th September. I spoke to Professor Blackett as you suggested. His answer was not an acceptance of the Directorship of the National Physical Laboratory. But he was prepared to come for two or three months and advise us.

Ultimately I asked him to come for two or three months and then decide about the future.

I have written a letter to Professor Thacker, a copy of which I enclose.[280]

Yours affectionately,
[Jawaharlal Nehru]

---

276. Letter to the Secretary, Department of Science and Technology; address: Flat No. 4, 30 St James Place, London. Sent from 9 Kensington Palace Gardens, London W8.
277. P.M.S. Blackett, British experimental physicist.
278. See also item 307.
279. Letter to the Director General, CSIR. Sent from 9 Kensington Palace Gardens, London W8.
280. Item 306.

(j) Panchayats

308. In Lucknow: Panchayati Raj and Cooperation[281]

राज्यपाल जी,[282] मुख्यमंत्री जी[283] और भाइयो और बहनो,

आठ-नौ महीने से इसका चर्चा हो रहा है कि यह सम्मेलन हो और मैं उसमें आऊँ। मंगलाप्रसाद जी[284] ने बहुत कोशिश की मुझे यहाँ लाने की और मैं तैयार था लेकिन कुछ ऐसा इत्तिफ़ाक़ हुआ कि कोई न कोई काम आ गया और फिर चुनाव आ गया, जनरल इलेक्शन। ये उचित नहीं समझा कि उससे इसको जोड़ें। लोग समझें कि जनरल इलेक्शंस में हम यह भी एक प्रचार कर रहे हैं, एक पार्टी का, क्योंकि ये तो पार्टी एक अलग चीज़ है। तो आज आख़िर में जो यह हुआ और मैं आया तो मुझे बहुत ख़ुशी है। और यह देखकर कि पिछले दिसम्बर से और अब तक में नौ करोड़ से ऊपर जमा किये हैं। तो इसको मैं आपको बधाई देता हूँ। एक तो शुरू में बधाई दे देता हूँ ताकि बाद में और बातें कहूँ। [हंसी]।

एक तो ये कि ये जो सहकारिता है, कोऑपरेशन, आप तो ख़ुद ही कोऑपरेटर हैं तो मैं आपको क्या बताऊँ क्या चीज़ है, लेकिन फिर भी कुछ जुरत करूँगा, क्योंकि आख़िर में ये महज़ एक कुछ ख़रीदना-बेचना नहीं है, मार्केटिंग नहीं करनी है, ये एक बहुत बड़ी चीज़ है। आख़िर में तो एक ज़िन्दगी रहने का एक तरीक़ा है और शुरू हम करते हैं कुछ अपने ख़रीद-फ़रोख़्त से, और बातों से, बढ़ते-बढ़ते उसको हम और बहुत सारी सेवाओं में, सर्विसेज़ में करते हैं और बढ़के हम उसे अपने काम में मिल के करते हैं। और असल में बढ़के तो सारा हमारा जो स्टेट का, जो देश का एक विधान है वह भी एक सहकारिता संघ की तरह बन जाता है। शायद आप में से बाज़ लोगों को याद हो कि, याद नहीं मुझे, कोई बीस-पचीस बरस हुए कांग्रेस का विधान बना था तो उसमें लिखा गया था कि हमारा लक्ष्य है भारत में कोऑपरेटिव कॉमनवेल्थ बनाने का, आज़ाद हिन्दुस्तान में, वह अब तक है। उसमें एक लफ़्ज़, एक शब्द बढ़ा दिया गया है, "सोशलिस्ट कोऑपरेटिव कॉमनवेल्थ।" तो हमने लिख तो दिया था उस वक़्त और उसको हम पसन्द करते थे, उस विचार को, लेकिन मुझे शक है कि कितने लोग उस बात को पूरीतौर से समझते थे और जो कुछ थोड़ा बहुत समझते थे वह भी कोई साफ जवाब दे सकते थे कि नहीं। मुझसे पूछा गया बार-बार क्या चीज़ है कोऑपरेटिव कॉमनवेल्थ। तो मैं तो जवाब नहीं दे सका

281. Speech, 28 July 1962, Kesar Bagh Baradari. NMML, AIR Tapes, TS No. 8452, NM No. 1672.

    Nehru was addressing a convention of about 4,000 representatives of cooperative societies in Uttar Pradesh. See *National Herald*, 29 July 1962, p. 1.

282. Biswanath Das.

283. C.B. Gupta.

284. Former Minister of State for Cooperation in UP.

ठीक-ठीक। यह एक पेचीदा चीज़ थी, वह एक चीज़ अपने आप बढ़ेगी, बढ़े। जाने क्या रंग ले मैं कैसे उसका नक्शा पहले बता दूँ? हाँ, कुछ ऊपरी तौर से हम कह सकते थे। तो ये विचार कोऑपरेटिव्स का लम्बा है, बड़ा है, और आजकल की बहसें जो बहुत कुछ होती हैं, पूँजीवाद, साम्यवाद, समाजवाद कुछ सोलह आने किसी एक चीज़, पूरीतौर से नहीं जमता। हालांकि समाजवाद की तरफ है वह बहुत कुछ लेकिन फिर भी अपना ढंग रखता है और यानी इसमें कोई मुख़ालिफ़त का ढंग नहीं है कि लड़ाई हो रही है, एक वाद और दूसरे में, अपने ढंग का है। तो समाजवाद अधिकतर उधर झुकता है, लेकिन अपने तरह अपनी पोशाक पहनता है।

मैं समझता हूँ कि देश में इस विचार को, इस रहन-सहन को बढ़ना चाहिए, कोऑपरेटिव्स को। आपने अभी तक ज्यादातर देहात में किसानों में, ग्रामों में किया है, ठीक है, क्योंकि अधिकतर वही अधिकतर हिन्दुस्तान में हमारे, हमारे प्रदेश में, हिन्दुस्तान में है, उनमें करनी ही है लेकिन उनके करने में भी बढ़ाना है यानी उनके हर काम में। आप ज्यादातर, जहाँ तक मैं समझा हूँ, मार्केटिंग में झुके हैं। मार्केटिंग बहुत जरूरी चीज़ है इसमें कोई शक नहीं, लेकिन और जो सर्विसेज़ हैं, सेवाएँ हैं उनको भी उसमें शामिल करना है और फिर और बातों में भी। मैंने देखा कि आप सहकारी खेती भी यहाँ कुछ बढ़ी है, ज्यादा नहीं है, लेकिन कुछ बढ़ी है। मुझे ख़ुशी हुई। सहकारी खेती के मामले में काफी बहस हुई, काफी मुख़ालिफ़त हुई है। मेरे अब तक समझ में नहीं आया कि मुख़ालिफ़त कोई उसकी कैसे करे? इस माने में मैं समझता हूँ कि वो इसको उचित न समझें अपने लिए या किसी के लिए, लेकिन जो उचित समझते हैं, उनको रोकने के लिए, यह बात मेरे समझ में न आई।

कोई पचपन वर्ष हुए या कुछ ऐसे ही बावन-तिरपन बरस हुए हमारे महाकवि रबीन्द्रनाथ टैगोर ने पहला अपना भाषण दिया था, राष्ट्रीय कांफ्रेंस में, पॉलिटिकल कांफ्रेंस में बंगाल की, यानी कोई सन् पाँच-छः में दिया था, मुझे ठीक याद नहीं, जब वहाँ बड़ा आन्दोलन हो रहा था। और उनको तो बहुत मतलब नहीं था पॉलिटिकल आन्दोलन वग़ैरह से, लेकिन जब सब लोग हिल जाते थे तो उनकी, उनका मन भी हिलता था और उसमें शरीक होते थे। तो मुझे बहुत ख़ुशी हुई और आश्चर्य हुआ, मैं पढ़ रहा था कुछ रोज़ हुए उसमें, कि उन्होंने बहुत सफाई से इसी पर दिया था कि कोऑपरेटिव फ़ार्मिंग हो, बंगाल के लिए कहा था उन्होंने।[285] उसकी वजह बताई थी कि जहाँ इत्ती कसरत से लोग हैं और ज़मीन कम है, और एक-एक के पास थोड़ी ज़मीन है, वहाँ वह तरक्की नहीं कर सकता बग़ैर पूरीतौर से कोऑपरेशन किये। तो उस वक़्त यह बहस की बात नहीं थी लेकिन उनका यह कहना दूरंदेशी से पहले देखना और कहना इससे मुझे ख़ुशी हुई। अब जो हम कहते हैं पचास बरस बाद तो लोग एतराज़ करते हैं, कहते हैं इसमें नुकसान होगा, नहीं चलेगी, हो सकता

---

285. Nehru had referred to this speech of 1908, as he then said, in his address to the Jabalpur Agriculture College, see SWJN/SS/70/item 14, pp. 132-133.

है । लेकिन जब ये बात निश्चय है कि ख़ाली जब जो लोग ख़ुद स्वीकार करें ख़ुशी से वह इसको करें और उसमें भी यह है कि जब कोई निकलना चाहे तो निकलने का दरवाज़ा खुला रहे उसे, तब तो कोई गुंजाइश रहती ही नहीं किसी के उसमें एतराज़ करने की ।

उसूलन देखिये आप सिद्धान्त रूप से, थिओरी के हिसाब से, उसमें कोई शक नहीं कि आजकल की दुनिया में, मैं अक्सर कहता हूँ कि विज्ञान की है, साइंस की है, औज़ारों की है, टेक्नोलॉजी की है । अब ये औज़ार वग़ैरह छोटे-छोटे बहुत अच्छे बन रहे हैं, उसको हमें इस्तेमाल करना चाहिए । लेकिन कुछ बढ़ते जाते हैं यानी नाप-तोल में बढ़ते हैं । छोटा किसान नहीं आजकल के बड़े औज़ारों को ले सकता है, इस्तेमाल कर सकता है लेकिन मिलकर पाँच-दस-बीस-पचास आदमी कर सकते हैं, सभों को उससे फ़ायदा हो । तो कोई उसमें कोई शक नहीं है कि जो दुनिया का हाल है वह आपको ढकेलता है, यह तो और बात है कि बाज़ मुल्कों में जायें एक आदमी के पास एक जो कुछ चाहिए, मैं नहीं जानता जो कुछ चाहिए पचास-सौ एकड़ हो, सौ एकड़, दो सौ, चार सौ, पाँच सौ, हज़ार एकड़ हो, उसको तो, उसमें दम है आगे बढ़ने का, नया औज़ार लगाने का, नई टेक्नीक, नये विज्ञान के चीज़ों के सीखने का, ख़रचने को, लेकिन जिसके पास एक एकड़, दो एकड़, ढाई-तीन एकड़ हो उसके पास इत्ती ताक़त नहीं है, वो मिलजुल के ताक़त आ जाती है सभों की, ज़ाहिर सी बात है । लेकिन उसी के साथ हमने साफ कहा कि ये रज़ामन्दी से हो और रज़ामन्दी मेरा मतलब नहीं है कि कोई ज़ाब्ते की रज़ामन्दी आप करा लें क्योंकि ज़ाब्ते के कराने से वो चीज़ चलेगी नहीं । सारी कोऑपरेशन ऐसी चीज़ है कि लोग समझें उसको अच्छी तरह से, समझकर स्वीकार करें, तब वह चलती है । अगर कागज़ पर दिखाने के लिए आपने किसी तरह से उनके दस्तख़त करा दिये, बग़ैर उनके समझे, तो गाड़ी चलेगी नहीं, क्योंकि चलाना उनको है या उनको होना चाहिए ।

ये दूसरी बात है कि अभी तक, मैंने सुना है, कहाँ तक सही है मैं नहीं जानता, मैं उसमें ख़ुद नहीं गया हूँ, लेकिन मुझे रिपोर्ट मिली है कि आपके सहकारी संघ में सरकारी हाथ बहुत ज्यादा है, सरकारी अफ़सरों का हाथ । मुझे नहीं मालूम कित्ता है यानी ऑफ़िशियल । ऑफ़िशियल डाइरेक्शन इसका बहुत है और मैं इसके इन्तिहा दर्जे ख़िलाफ़ हूँ । मैं समझता हूँ कि कोऑपरेशन एक ही तरह है उसमें ऑफ़िशियल, सरकारी दख़ल कम से कम होना चाहिए, सलाह मशवरे का पूरीतौर से, लेकिन कोई हुकूमत चलाने का, कोई फैसले करने का सारा बोझा लोगों पर होना चाहिए अफ़सरों पर नहीं होना चाहिए, नहीं तो जो उसकी असली कोऑपरेशन की असली चीज़ है वह निकल जाती है उसमें से । अब असली चीज़ है, कोऑपरेशन से आप एक नई बात लोगों में पैदा करते हैं, उनको बढ़ने देते हैं, उनमें ज़िम्मेदारी आती है, उनमें फैसला करने की ताक़त आती है, ग़लती करने, अपनी ग़लती सीखते हैं, कोई और ग़लती करे, कोई और अच्छा काम करे तो उनपे असर नहीं होता, वो उससे बढ़ते नहीं है । तो ये जरूरी बात है, कोऑपरेशन की जड़ और बुनियाद है कि वह सरकारी चीज़ न हो, सरकार उसकी मदद करे, सरकार उसको सलाह दे, अपने लोगों को पेश करे, उनको इक्सपर्ट्स को बताये कि कैसे करो, लेकिन वो चीज़ नॉन ऑफ़िशियल हो । मैं इस पर ख़ास ज़ोर दे देता हूँ क्योंकि मैं उसे बहुत जरूरी समझता हूँ ।

409

दूसरे ये कि एक सहकारी संघ एक तरह से एक परिवार का सा होना चाहिए, जहाँ तक हो सके लोग एक-दूसरे को जानें, एक-दूसरे को भरोसा करें या न करें, जानें, और यह नहीं कि एक किसान एक बड़ी चीज़ में जा गया जिसका उसे पता ही नहीं कि क्या है। एक हज़ारों-लाखों आदमी उसमें हैं, वह खो जाता है और वह घबरा जाता है और मान लो वह हुकुम जो उसे दिया जाये यह और बात है लेकिन वह नहीं बढ़ता उससे। इसलिए बेहतर है कि प्राइमरी सोसाइटीज़ आपकी छोटी हों जिसमें एक-दूसरे को पहचानते हैं, जानते हैं और इसी पे क़दम-ब-क़दम बढ़ती जायें वह और बात है लेकिन प्राइमरी सोसाइटीज़ छोटी हों। इसी पर हमने ज़ोर दिया था, अब उसके एतराज़ हुए, कहा गया कि इसमें तो काफ़ी उनमें दम नहीं है, पैसा नहीं जमा कर सकते और क्या करें और रिज़र्व बैंक वाले कहते हैं कि हम कैसे रुपया दें छोटी सोसाइटीज़ को, हम नहीं, बड़ी सोसाइटीज़ को रुपया देंगे। हज़ार एतराज़ किये जो कि बहुत माक़ूल एतराज़ थे लेकिन जो जड़, जड़ की बात है, मूल बात है कोऑपरेटिव्ज़, उसको भूल जाते थे, वो यह कि आपस में एक-दूसरे को जानकर मिलकर काम करना है। अगर आप एक पचास हज़ार की कोऑपरेटिव बनाइये, पचास हज़ार आदमियों की, एक पचास गाँवों में, सौ गाँवों में फैले हुए हैं तब उससे कुछ फ़ायदा होगा। लेकिन वह चीज़ एक स्पिरिट आप नहीं पैदा करेंगे लोगों में जो एक-दूसरे को जान के करते हैं, कोई ख़राबी करें तो जान जायेंगे बहुत जल्दी।

तो यह एब बहुत आवश्यक बात है हमारे समझने की कि ऑफ़िशियल हिस्सा, सरकारी, यानी मैं कहता हूँ सरकारी हिस्सा तो हुई है उसमें और हो, लेकिन सरकारी डायरेक्शन, सरकारी बड़े ऑफ़िसर उसमें न हों, कोऑपरेटिव्ज़ में एक्स ऑफ़िशियो या कुछ ये बात नहीं होनी चाहिए और वाक़ई मदद करें हर तरह से, तो उनका काम है। कोऑपरेशन आख़िर में कामयाब होगा जबकि जो उसके ख़ास चलाने वाले लोग हैं वो एक तो उसकी हवा पहचान लें, स्पिरिट समझें उसकी, और दूसरे उसमें काम करने का तरीका सीख लें। महज़ उत्साह और जोश की बात नहीं है, वह तो होनी ही चाहिए लेकिन काम करने का तरीका। इसलिए आपके यहाँ भी हुआ ही होगा यह, कुछ ट्रेनिंग, कुछ सिखाना होता है ख़ास लोगों को जो आपके सैक्रेटरीज़, चेयरमैन वग़ैरह हों। बहुत पेचीदा बात नहीं है, कुछ न कुछ सिखाना है, तब ठीक चलती है।

हमारे देश में पहले यानी स्वतंत्रता आने के पहले सबमें अधिक सहकारी संघ शायद मद्रास में सफल हुए थे, बम्बई में हुए, महाराष्ट्र में, गुजरात में, इन जगह, मद्रास में जिसके माने हैं पुराने मद्रास में, आन्ध्र भी उसमें शामिल था। तो इसीलिए हुए कि वहाँ एक वो एक पॉपुलर चीज़ थी, सरकारी दख़ल कम था, और जगह नहीं चली ज्यादा, कुछ चले नाममात्र के लिए, उत्तर प्रदेश में मेरा ख़्याल है बहुत कम चले, और वे कम चले क्योंकि वह हवा ही नहीं पैदा हुई जिसमें वह चलें। हवा पैदा हो नहीं सकती थी, सरकारी ढंग चलाने के उससे। तो अब एक नये तौर से चलाये गये हैं। तो अब आप चल रहे हैं, ज़ाहिर है, मालूम होता है कि आपने एक जड़ पकड़ी है उत्तर प्रदेश में।

अभी जो शर्मा जी[286] ने कहा गाँव-गाँव में उसकी हवा फैली है, बन रही है, जरूरी चलेगी वह, अच्छी तरह चलेगी, लेकिन यह ख़्याल रहता है कि अगर कोई ख़राबी कहीं होती है तो उसका ज़हर और जगह फैलता है, लोग घबरा जाते हैं। इसलिए ख़ास एहतियात करनी है कि काम, काम अच्छा हो, काम की क्वालिटी अच्छी हो, उससे तेज़ी से फैलेगा। मुझे, मैं चाहता हूँ कि फैले, ज़ाहिर है जित्ता फैले उत्ता अच्छा है, लेकिन मुझे इस बात की ज़्यादा फ़िक्र है कि चाहे फैले हल्का लेकिन जहाँ है वहाँ मज़बूती से चले, सफाई से चले जिसका असर होगा तब फैल जायेगी अपने आप। तो यानी अब आप ऐसे मौक़े पर पहुँचे हैं, एक जड़ बुनियादी डाल के कि आप कोऑपरेशन की इमारत के और मंज़िलें बनायें, अच्छी ऊँची मंज़िलें। इसमें कोई शक नहीं है कि जित्ता आप बनायेंगे उत्ता ही आपको और और लोगों को जो उसमें हैं गाँव-गाँव में लाभ होगा, फ़ायदा होगा और एक चीज़ है जित्ता करो उत्ते ही फ़ायदा होता है यानी कोई, कोई यह नहीं है कि एक बोझा बढ़ता जाये। और जब फ़ायदा होता है तो और लोग उसमें दिलचस्पी लेते हैं, पैसा देते हैं, काम करते हैं। अपने आप इसके लाभ का फ़ायदा लोगों को होता है, उसके कामयाबी का।

तो वक़्त आ गया है अब आप ज़रा हाथ-पैर एक तो सबमें जो कि मैंने पहले कहा क्वालिटी की तरफ, अच्छे काम की तरफ ध्यान दें आप, दूसरे उसमें सरकारी ओहदेदार न हों, मददगार हों, ओहदेदार न हों यानी लोग समझें कि उनके ऊपर बोझा है काम करने का, फ़ैसला करने का। बात एक दूसरे ढंग, दूसरा पहलू है उसका, पंचायती राज का जैसे है कि हम चाहते हैं।

हम हिन्दुस्तान में बहुत काम करना चाहते हैं, लेकिन आख़िर में घूमघाम के होती है कि हिन्दुस्तान में इंसान को बढ़ाना चाहते हैं। इंसान को बढ़ाना चाहते हैं, एक अच्छा बनाना चहाते हैं पहले से और उसमें तो कोई बातें ज़ाब्ते से नहीं होती, वो तो एक, एक हल्के-हल्के सीखने से, ट्रेन्ड होने से, तजुर्बे से होता है। और पंचायती राज और सरकारी संघ, वो तजुर्बा आता है जिससे आदमी अपने ऊपर भरोसा करे, अपने पड़ोसी पर भरोसा करे, अपने संघ पर भरोसा करे और, बढ़ते-बढ़ते जाइये, अपने देश पे भरोसा करे। बढ़ती जाती है बात, विचार एक हो, इसलिए बहुत अच्छा है, क्योंकि वो मज़बूत, देश को मज़बूत करती है और देश को रास्ता दिखाती है चलने का, जिसमें वह सब मिलजुल के चलें। तो वो बात, उसके आप इमारतें, ऊपर की इमारतें खड़ी करने का समय आ गया है, एक बुनियाद आपने मज़बूत डाल दी है।

इन बातों को ख़्याल में रखें आप और मैं तो चाहता हूँ और मैं समझता हूँ कि मुनासिब है कि सहकारी खेती हो, लेकिन जैसे मैंने आपने कहा मैं नहीं चाहता कि उसमें ज़रा भी धोखेबाज़ी या ज़बरदस्ती हो। जो लोग बिल्कुल ख़ुशी से आते हैं आयें, न आयें न आयें, कुछ हरज नहीं है। आपके यहाँ जो हो रही है जहाँ-जहाँ उसकी कामयाबी देखके और लोग ख़ुद ही झुकेंगे उधर, हो जायेगा अपने आप अगर काम अच्छा हो। और अब आपके ज़्यादातर काम, अब ज़्यादातर आप खेती, खेती, एग्रीकल्चरल शायद सोसाइटीज़

286. Chaturbhuj Sharma, Minister of Cooperation in UP.

काम करती हैं, कुछ और कामों में भी बढ़ सकती हैं, कुछ उद्योग के, इंडस्ट्री के कामों में, काम बढ़ सकते हैं। वही, वही संघ, कोई दूसरे की जरूरत नहीं है क्योंकि गाँव की तरक्की अव्वल तो खेती से है लेकिन ख़ाली खेती से नहीं है, गाँव में कुछ न कुछ हमें छोटे-छोटे उद्योग-धंधे शुरू करने हैं। छोटे से मेरा मतलब ख़ाली वो नहीं है, ग्रामोद्योग, वो भी हैं ही, लेकिन उससे बड़े भी और अगर बिजली आ जाये तो छोटे-छोटे कारख़ाने तरह-तरह के। हमारी आशा तो है बिजली गाँव-गाँव में आयेगी। [तालियाँ]। हम चाहते हैं, हम चाहते हैं कि जल्दी से जल्दी आये लेकिन इतना ख़र्चा होता है बिजली के पैदा करने में कि हाथ कुछ रुक जाते हैं। आयेगी, सवाल यह है कि कित्ती जल्दी आये, कै बरस में आये, हर जगह पहुँचे। मेरा ख़्याल है प्लानिंग कमीशन से बातें वग़ैरह करने से मैंने देखा कि अब सारे प्लानिंग कमीशन के लोग बड़े उत्सुक हैं इस बात के। क्योंकि बिजली एक चीज़ है जो कि एक दम से दरवाज़ा तरक्की का खोल देती है गाँव का, ख़ाली इसलिए नहीं कि रोशनी आ जाती है, पंखा चलने लगता है वग़ैरह, वो तो हुई है, मोटी बात है, लेकिन एक शक्ति है, आ जाती है जिससे आप काम कर सकते हैं, जिससे आप छोटे-छोटे कारख़ाने, जिससे आप बहुत कुछ खेती का काम भी कर सकते हैं। और छोटे-छोटे कारख़ाने, जिस वक़्त हमारे गाँवों में छोटे-छोटे कारख़ाने खुलेंगे, जैसे कि खुल रहे हैं, पंजाब में अक्सर खुले हैं, उस वक़्त एक नई दुनिया किसानों के लिए और खेत में काम करने वाले के लिए खुल जायेगी और यह रोज़गार वग़ैरह भी मिलेगा। यह नहीं कि सब ज़मीन ही पे पड़े हैं, ज़मीन से निकलेंगे क्योंकि हमें, मुझे ठीक याद नहीं कि कित्ता, लेकिन हमारे ग़रीबी की एक निशानी है कि ज्यादातर लोग ज़मीन पर काम करते हैं, उसके शायद आधे भी हों, ज़मीन पर काम करने वाले काफी हैं। लेकिन बिचारों को काम नहीं मिलता तो क्या करें? तो हमें ज़मीन से लोगों को खींचना है और जगह। मेरा मतलब नहीं कि ज़मीन से शायद सब शहरों में आयें नौकरी ढूँढने के लिए, लेकिन ज़मीन के काम से वहीं गाँवों में रहके वहाँ छोटे-छोटे कारख़ाने हों, हाथ काम के वग़ैरह हों। इस तरह से गाँवों की आमदनी बढ़ेगी और लोगों को काम मिलेगा और बिजली आने से फौरन दरवाज़ा इसका खुल जाता है।

तो अब मैं आपसे क्या कहूँ सिवा इसके कि फिर से आपको बधाई दूँ, मुबारकबाद दूँ इस सहकारिता के तरक्की के ऊपर, यहाँ उत्तर प्रदेश में। मुझे ख़ुशी होती है। अक्सर मैं अपने प्रदेश में आकर टीका टिप्पणी किया करता हूँ। मुझे अच्छा नहीं लगता लेकिन अपने साथियों में कभी यह ख़्वाहिश होती है कि तेज़ी से बढ़ें। तो इस मामले में बग़ैर ज्यादा टीका किये मैं आपको मुबारकबाद दे सकता हूँ। कुछ बातें तो मैंने आपसे कह दीं, फिर भी कुछ बातें आपके सामने रख दीं, किस ढंग से मैं चाहता हूँ आप आगे बढ़ें। और कुछ न कुछ आप बढ़ेंगे उधर क्योंकि वही एक रास्ता है। और रास्तों में चलियेगा तो आपकी रफ़्तार हल्की हो जायेगी और आप बढ़ेंगे नहीं।

और आप देखें फिर मैं शुरु की बातों पर आता हूँ। कोऑपरेशन एक तरीका काम करने का है, माना, लेकिन उससे ज्यादा एक तरीका, क्या कहूँ, सोचने का है, एक तरीका मिलजुल कर काम करने का है। ये बड़ी भारी बात है यानी अगर लोग इसको सीख लें, अच्छी तरह से सीखें, तो सब काम इसी ढंग से हो या बहुत कुछ और वो हवा एक

412

कोऑपरेशन की हो जाती है जिसमें लड़ाई, दंगा, फ़साद, मुक़ाबला नहीं होता। पूँजीवाद एक ऐसी चीज़ है जिसने अपने वक़्त में फ़ायदा किया दुनिया को, उन मुल्कों में जहाँ थी, लेकिन कैसे फ़ायदा किया? देश का फ़ायदा किया बहुतों को कुचल के, बहुतों को दबा के। अब यह बात न हम चाहते हैं हमारे देश में हो, न हो सकती है। कोई आदमी कुचलने को तैयार नहीं है। यहाँ पुराने ज़माने में जो कुछ हो, वो हो नहीं सकती। और हम चाहते हैं समाजवाद—असल में समाजवाद में बहुत दर्जे ये कोऑपरेटिव की हवा आ जाती है लेकिन ये हवा कोऑपरेटिव की अगर ठीक फैले मुल्क में तो आपस में सब लोगों में एकता पैदा करती है क्योंकि मिलजुल कर करते हैं, एक-दूसरे के गले पर सवार होकर, उसको दबा कर उसकी पीठ पे नहीं चढ़ना चाहते हैं। हरेक फ़ायदा उठाता है, हरेक काम करता है, मेहनत करता है और उसमें शरीक होता है, उसमें फ़ायदा और नुकसान में। तो हवा हमें पैदा करनी है। और ख़ासकर हमारे बिचारे किसान हैं, ज़माना गुज़र गया उनको तकलीफ़ उठाते हुए, उनको भी फौरन कुछ फ़ायदा पहुँचेगा और उनकी पीठ ज़रा सीधी होगी और एक भरोसा होगा अपने ऊपर इससे और पंचायती राज से।

अगर ये दो चीज़ें कामयाब हों, पंचायती राज और सहकारिता, तब आपका स्वराज्य सोलह आने कामयाब हो गया। ऊपर की चीज़ें, ऊपर के उसके जो दर्जे हैं अपने आप कामयाब होंगे अगर नीचे मज़बूती है। ऊपर की ख़ाली संभालने से, नीचे का नहीं संभालने से, कोई फ़र्ज़ नहीं है कि सारा अच्छा हो, लेकिन नीचे अगर संभल जाता है तो ऊपर का फ़र्ज़ है संभल जाये।

फिर से मुझे ख़ुशी है आज यहाँ आने की और जैसे कि ढाई बरस हुए मैं आया था, ढाई बरस हुए, पौने तीन बरस हुए, और उस वक़्त मुझे कुछ सच बात यह है कि जब मैं आगरे के पास गया था इसमें तो मुझे कुछ शक थे कि कहाँ तक असली चीज़ है, कहाँ तक कागज़ी चीज़ है।[287] लेकिन हल्के-हल्के वह शकूक रफ़ा हुए मेरे, देखके यहाँ, काम का सुनकर, और आज — आज बहुत दर्जे बिल्कुल रफ़ा हो गये।

जयहिन्द!

[Translation begins

Governor,[288] Chief Minister,[289] Sisters and Brothers,
There has been talk for the last eight to nine months about this conference and that I should address it. Mangla Prasadji[290] has tried very hard to get me here and I was willing. But other things intervened including the general elections and I

287. Nehru went to Bichpuri village near Agra on 10 November 1959 to inaugurate the 10,016 service cooperatives set up in Uttar Pradesh, see SWJN/SS/54/item 3.
288. See fn 282 in this section.
289. See fn 283 in this section.
290. See fn 284 in this section.

did not think it proper to link this with elections. It may have given people the impression that it was part of our party propaganda. This is something beyond party politics. Anyhow, I am happy that I was able to come here finally, and also to note that over nine crores have been collected between last December and now. I congratulate you. I am doing that in the beginning so that I can say other things later. [Laughter].

What should I say about cooperation when you are yourselves cooperators? Yet I will be so bold as to say something because cooperation is not merely marketing. It is something far bigger than that. In the final analysis, it is a way of life. We begin by doing simple things like buying and selling and gradually expand it to include various other services. Ultimately the entire constitution of the state and nation becomes like a cooperative society. Perhaps some of you may remember that nearly twenty or twenty-five years ago, when the constitution of the Congress was drawn up it laid down as one of our goals the creation of the cooperative commonwealth of independent India. It is still part of our goal. One more word, socialist has been added to it Socialist Cooperative Commonwealth. We put it down in our constitution because we liked the idea. But I doubt whether many people understood its full implications. Even those who understood it a little could not give a clear answer to questions. I have been asked again and again what a cooperative commonwealth is but I have been unable to answer clearly. It is a complex movement and something which grows on its own momentum. Nobody knows what shape it will take ultimately. How can I tell you now? We can have a general idea. The idea of cooperatives has far reaching implications and does not fit in fully with any of the modern day isms like capitalism, socialism or communism, though it has socialist leanings. It has its own pattern. Often there is antagonism between different isms, but the idea of cooperatives is not antagonistic to any system. It leans mainly towards socialism but wears its own particular garb.

I feel that the idea of cooperatives as a way of life must take roots in the country. You have been trying to establish cooperatives mostly in the rural areas among farmers, which is proper because the bulk of our population lives in villages. But we must try to expand it in every walk of life. As far as I know cooperatives handle marketing and there is no doubt about it that marketing is extremely important. But they must include other services too. I have seen that there has been some progress in cooperative farming, not much but still there is some progress. There have been great debates about cooperative farming. There has been great opposition to it though I am unable to understand even now on what grounds people oppose it. I can understand their not wanting to join it themselves. But I cannot understand why they should stop others.

414

About fifty-five years ago our great poet, Rabindranath Tagore had given his first speech to the National Political Conference in Bengal—I do not remember if it was in 1905 or 1906—though he did not have very much to do with political movements. But his words used to move millions and they were inspired to join the movement. So I was very happy and a little surprised when I read recently that in that speech, he had laid great stress on cooperative farming in Bengal.[291] He had given his reasons for saying so. Most farmers have very small landholdings and cannot hope to progress very much without full cooperation. At that time, the issue was not open to question. But I was happy to note how farsighted he had been. Now fifty years later, there are people who are opposed to it and say it cannot work and that it will do harm. May be it will not work. But there is no ground for anyone to object when it is quite clear that the people who join a cooperative will do so only if they accept willingly and they will always have the option to leave.

If you look at it from the point of view of principle or theory, there is no doubt about it that this is the age of science and technology and machines, as I often point out. We must make use of modern tools and implements. But the average small farmer cannot afford the big machines. However, if five, ten, twenty or fifty farmers decide to form a cooperative, everybody stands to gain. There is no doubt about it that circumstances in the world today are pushing us in that direction. It is a different matter that in the affluent countries individual farmers own thousands of acres of land and can afford big machines and use new and scientific techniques of agriculture. But the farmer who has a couple of acres cannot afford very much. It is obvious that cooperation can make many things more accessible to them. But at the same time, we have said quite clearly that the people must be willing. I do not mean some formal agreement on paper. The whole point of cooperation is that the people must understand it properly and then accept it. If you get their signatures on paper somehow, cooperation will not work. It is the people who can make it work.

Secondly, I do not know how far it is true but I have heard that there is great government interference in the working of cooperative societies. I am absolutely opposed to official direction in cooperatives. I believe that cooperation can succeed only when there is minimum official interference in it. They can give advice and guide the people. But the entire burden of decision-making must rest with the people and not on officials. Otherwise the true purpose of cooperation is lost. Cooperation must foster a sense of responsibility and confidence in the people to take decisions. They may make mistakes but will learn from them. You cannot learn from the mistakes or achievements of others. Therefore, it

291. See fn 285 in this section.

is extremely important that the cooperative movement must not become a governmental effort. Government officials can advise and help the people, offer them experts and guide them. But the movement itself must be non-official. I lay special stress on this because I consider it extremely important.

Secondly, a cooperative society must be like one large family. As far as possible, the members must know one another well whether they trust each other or not. The organization a farmer joins should not be so large that he cannot even understand the basics of it. If there are hundreds of thousands of members in it, he gets frightened and feels lost. He may obey orders but does not grow in any way. It would be better if the primary societies are small in which everybody knows one another. It is a different thing that they gradually expand. But the primary societies must be small. We have laid great stress on this. The objection to that is that small societies do not have many resources. The Reserve Bank does not agree to give loans to small societies. All these objections are no doubt valid. But they fail to keep the fundamental principle of cooperatives in sight which is that it is only when people know one another well that they can work together. You may form a cooperative of fifty thousand people spread over fifty or hundred villages and it may do some good. But you will not be able to create the true spirit of cooperation which develops when people know one another. If somebody does a wrong it will be immediately found out.

So it is extremely important for us to understand that the role of officials in cooperatives must be minimal. It is the duty of officials to help and advise. But they must not occupy positions, ex-officio or otherwise, in the societies. A cooperative can ultimately succeed only when the people themselves run it, understand its true spirit and the proper method of working. Therefore, training becomes essential especially for the secretaries and chairmen of the cooperatives. It is not a complicated matter. But some training is essential. Then the cooperative runs well.

Before independence the largest number of successful cooperatives in India were to be found in Madras, that is the old Madras state which included Andhra too. There were also cooperatives in Bombay, that is Maharashtra and Gujarat. They were successful because they were popular and there was very little official interference. In other states, the cooperatives were there merely in name. I think they were least successful in Uttar Pradesh because the proper climate was not created. That was not possible because there was great official interference. Now a new method is being adopted and it seems that the movement is taking roots in this state.

Just now Sharmaji[292] mentioned that an atmosphere is being created in the villages and cooperatives will definitely succeed. But a possibility is there that report of any malfunctioning in a cooperative reaches elsewhere, and people there are scared. Therefore, we must take particular care to ensure that good work is done. Then it will catch on. I want it to spread. It is obvious that the more it spreads, the better it will be. But I am more concerned that, wherever they are established, the cooperatives must strike roots and work well, even if it takes time. Once that happens, they will automatically spread. You are at the cross-roads now. You can lay the foundations to build the edifice of cooperation. There is no doubt about it that the more you work the more the people in the rural areas will benefit. It will not become a burden. When there are obvious benefits, people begin to take an interest and help financially and in other ways. So the success of the movement will automatically make it beneficial to the people. The time has now come when everyone must work hard and pay more attention to the quality of work. Secondly, government officials must not hold any posts in the societies. The people must be made to realize that the burden of making decisions rests upon them.

Another aspect of this is the Panchayati Raj system. We want to do a great many things in India. But ultimately it comes round to the development of human beings. We want to build good human beings which can be done only by gradual training, education and experience. The Panchayati Raj and cooperative societies provide experience and teach self-reliance to the people who run them. They also inculcate mutual trust. So it is a very good thing because it strengthens the country and paves the way for harmony and cooperation among the people. The time has come to build the edifice now that the foundations have been laid.

I want you to remember these things. I think it is proper that there should be cooperative farming. But, as I said, I do not want any chicanery or coercion in the matter. Let the people join willingly and those who do not wish to join must be left alone. When they see how the movement is succeeding, they will automatically lean in that direction. The cooperative societies handle mostly agricultural work these days. They can expand to include industries and other things. The same societies can handle everything. For one thing, development in the villages does not depend on agriculture alone. We must start small industries in the rural areas. Once the villages are electrified, all kinds of small industries can be set up. We hope to supply electricity to every village very soon. [Applause]. We want to do it quickly. But it involves such enormous expenditure that we have to hold our hand. There is no doubt that every village will get electricity. The question is how many years it is likely to take. I have

292. See fn 286 in this section.

found that the people in the Planning Commission are very enthusiastic about it. Electricity opens the doors to progress almost instantly, not merely because it provides light, etc., but because it is a source of power which can be utilized for various purposes. It can be used for running small industries, for agriculture, etc. Once small industries are set up in the villages, as it is being done in the Punjab, they will open the doors to a new world of progress for our farmers and others in the rural areas. New avenues of employment will open up instead of everyone depending on land for their livelihood. I do not remember the exact figures but one of the signs of our poverty is that the majority of the people in the rural areas depend on land. But what are they to do when there is no other employment available? We must draw the people away from land. I do not mean that they must be encouraged to go to the cities in search of jobs. They must stay in the villages and get employment in small-scale industries, etc. In this way, income of the villages will increase and people will get jobs. Electricity opens up various doors of opportunity.

What should I say now except to congratulate you on the progress in cooperatives in Uttar Pradesh? I am happy to see the progress in Uttar Pradesh in this matter. I often criticize Uttar Pradesh when I come here, though I do not like to do so. I do so because I want my state to progress quickly. But in this matter, I can congratulate you instead of criticizing. I have told you about some of the things that you should bear in mind in order to progress. There is bound to be progress because that is the only way. If you do anything else, you will slow down and not go very far.

Now I am back to the things that I mentioned in the beginning. No doubt cooperation is a method of working. But more than that, it is a way of thinking, of working together in mutual cooperation. This is a big thing. If people learnt to do this well, a climate of cooperation will automatically be created and there will be no room for quarrels and disputes and competition. Capitalism did some good to various countries in its time. But in the process, it crushed others. Now we do not want to do that. It cannot be done in India. Nobody is prepared to crush others. It may have happened in the past. But it is no longer possible. We want to establish socialism in India which involves cooperation to a very large extent. Moreover, if the movement spreads properly, it fosters unity among the people too. They will learn not to pull down others or suppress them. Everyone is an equal shareholder in the work as well as the benefits, profit and loss. So we must create this atmosphere particularly among our poor farmers. They have been suppressed for centuries. Cooperation will bring them immediate relief and they will learn self-confidence.

If Panchayati Raj and cooperation succeed, we can take it that our freedom will be complete. Once the foundations are strong, everything else will succeed automatically. Therefore, we must pay attention to that first.

So I am happy to have come here. The fact is that when I visited some place near Agra more than two and a half years back, I had a doubt as to how far people meant business or whether it was merely a paper project.[293] But gradually my doubts have been dispelled by the reports I have been getting and today they have been laid to rest to a very great extent.

Jai Hind!

Translation ends]

309. In New Delhi: To Community Development and Panchayat Conference[294]

Shri S.K. Dey,[295] Friends and Comrades,

I have gladly come here to this conference of yours because I feel interested, greatly interested in the work you are doing in this Community Development, Panchayati Raj, Cooperation, etc. But I am not quite sure if I fit in into such a conference in the sense that most of you, who are engaged in the actual work at the ground level and above it in the States, fit in. You gain certain experience and you bring that experience to the common pool here. I have not got that experience. I can talk about some principles. I can perhaps sometimes, as suggested by Shri S.K. Dey, try to give a pet talk. But all that is rather beside the work of your conference, which is meant to deal with the actual problems that have arisen in your experience.

We have been reminded that it is just ten years since the Community Development movement started here. I remember very well with what great enthusiasm this movement started and how much we looked forward to that movement changing the whole background of the village. It did a lot, but it did not come up to expectations. Ultimately it became rather stale. I don't suppose it was anybody's fault. That was inevitable. Then it was given a new turn some few years ago by this talk of Panchayati Raj and we are at a stage now, I am at a stage, when I am full of enthusiasm for Panchayati Raj. And I do feel that it is something basic and something revolutionary in the context of India to establish this among the five hundred thousand or more villages of India, all over rural

293. See fn 287 in this section.
294. Speech, 3 August 1962, to the Annual Conference of State Ministers of Community Development and Panchayati Raj. NMML, AIR Tapes, TS No. 8435, NM No. 1661. Checked against the PIB version.
295. Minister of Community Development.

India. It excites my imagination to think of this vast democratic representative institution working right at the ground level, from the village upward.

Democracy is not merely a Parliament at the top or in the States, but something that affects every person, and something which claims everyone to take his proper place and indeed any place in the country if need arises. I have said and I meant it that all this Panchayati Raj talk of the things that we are doing are ultimately meant to train up every individual in India to be a potential Prime Minister of India. Everybody cannot be Prime Minister. I suppose a modicum of ability and other things is necessary. But I am sure that vast numbers of people can be trained up for that service.

Now, I have a peculiar background, if I may confess it to you. For over thirty years, I came in very close contact with the people of India, the masses of India and more particularly the peasantry of India. And I grew, not only to like them, and I was favoured by their affection, but also grew consciously and subconsciously to react to them, to feel what they were feeling, to realize that although I was very different from them, I could feel their pulse somewhat. Then I suddenly became Prime Minister of India, without any experience of the intermediate stages, what you might say, of administrative experience or any experience. So naturally, I brought a measure of enthusiasm, a measure of ability to the task and I grew to understand, to some extent, my responsibilities, etc.

But there was a big gap between the Prime Minister's work and the village experience, the big administrative gap, especially in the work for which States are responsible. I could understand it theoretically, but practically I have no experience. I have gradually gathered some knowledge and experience. But it is not adequate. And so I function quite adequately, I think, with a crowd, because I feel at home there; they understand me and I on the whole understand them in spite of our differences. But when you start discussing many problems at intermediate levels, I try to learn from men like Shri V.T. Krishnamachari,[296] who has great experience of these things. I try to learn, of course; I think I am a fairly good student still. But it is a slow process, learning from others, instead of from one's own experience. But my original experience, direct experience with the people, helps me to understand their reactions to things. I do not by any means idealise them or think that they are perfect. They are full of imperfections. There is no doubt about it. Yet in spite of all their faults and failings, I have not only liked them, but I have great confidence in them, as a whole. And it is that confidence in the future, confidence is one's country, not merely theoretical approaches, that has pulled me through. It is that confidence

296. Former Deputy Chairman of the Planning Commission.

that made me appreciate the Community Development movement and now the Panchayati Raj development of it.

Many people, I remember, when we talk of Panchayati Raj, we were rather doubtful about the capacity of our people to shoulder this burden. I didn't have any doubts; I was certain that they make certain mistakes and I know they had made mistakes.

In fact, it is sad to see that crime rate has increased, the murder rate has increased. A person is elected and a person not elected goes and murders the man who is elected. It is a terrible thing to see, it has happened. Nevertheless, we shall get over this and gradually develop this system of self-government at every stage. There is no half way house to it. Either you entrust it to them or you don't. Giving it partly, distrusting them, leaves you nowhere; they have no real responsibility and they do not develop properly. That is why, having given this authority and power to them, we should not dilute it by official interference. I am convinced of that. Let them make mistakes and let them suffer for them. The officials must only be advisers, must not be bosses, and not only the officials. Even this question, I believe, has been considered by you in various ways about MPs and MLAs being members of panchayat samitis and zila parishads. They should be members, they should be, but whether they are members with voting rights or not is another matter. Because the chances are that the MPs having greater experience and the MLAs being better-known personalities will probably boss over the zila parishad and the panchayat samiti. I want to avoid that. I want those people to feel that they are the bosses themselves, this kind of psychological atmosphere being created that they are masters of their household; they can decide, they can make mistakes and they will suffer for the mistakes. If somebody else interferes too much, whether it is an official or an MP there, then the responsibility is cast on him, the responsibility for a decision, as well as the consequences of the decision. Therefore, I wanted it to be fairly and squarely put on the panchayat samitis or zila parishads or wherever panchayat functions in whatever form.

Of course, I think, it is essential that our officials, who are experts at their job, who are supposed to be, should advise them, should help them in every way, but not as bosses. It is very important and that depends on doing things with the authority they may have, but in a special manner. They must behave not as superior persons doling out advice to inferiors, but as equals and even, if you like, a little humbly before the ordinary, ignorant peasants. Let him feel that he is responsible. It is important to make the people feel that they are responsible and have got to decide, and to unconsciously influence them, not consciously directing them. To a slight extent, that applies even to MPs and MLAs who

421

should fully participate and give their advice but must never lessen the sense of responsibility that the panchayat samiti has or should have.

Now, whether it is the Planning Commission or whether it is all this business of Community Development and Panchayati Raj, I find that we have made tremendous progress in planning. But our progress in implementing the Plan that we make is not tremendous at all. We still suffer from the theoretician's complex of writing down things on paper, thinking that they are done. Even the simplest things are not done, leave out the big things; and unless we develop that, the sense of doing things, not merely laying them down in a Plan, we will not make very great progress. I do not know, you know it better, but I do hear complaints of things being laid down, so many maternity centres to come up, but not one came up in that particular area although it was laid down beautifully in paper and provided for. And elsewhere too, I am quite sure, this kind of thing might happen. So how to ensure that what you decide is implemented is most important.

One thing I understand you have been considering at the Development Officers' Conference is child welfare. Now, it is patent that how you treat the child, what opportunities you give to the child, are vital for his growth. You take a boy or girl of seven and eight years and then you can train him or her. But it will be far easier if, as a child, he has had some interest taken in him and some opportunities given to him to grow properly. Child welfare is important, the difficulty is that there are so many important things we have to do and our resources are limited. We cannot spread out everywhere and do nothing at all, except on paper. But I am glad that the Planning Commission has, in the Third Plan, devoted some attention to child welfare and allotted a fair sum for that purpose. Now, many things, including child welfare, depends a little on money, but not so much on money.

Money is a much advertised thing, but I am sorry to confess I have no great respect for money. I require it occasionally, certainly, but I don't like it. One has to do with it. The country has to do with it. We have to ask for aid and we are thankful to the countries who give it, we have to raise taxes and all that; I admit that. But still I do believe that the human being is more important than any amount of money. A competent person interested and trained in child welfare can, without any money or almost next to nil, create a revolution in a village, so far as children are concerned. And I know some instances; government didn't do it. A competent woman went and sat in a village and the first thing she did was to gather the children, all of them there, and give them a bath. I am sure your development commissioner and others never think of giving a bath to children in the village. Child welfare to them consists putting up an office with the board and maybe a little museum for children, collecting them and lecturing them. A bath is more important than all the lectures that you give. This woman collected all the children and gave them a bath and saved them from some kind of ailment. Therefore, it is the spirit of some training that counts. Of course, a competent person is highly essential. For the rest, money will come; it does come but it is not important.

Whenever any kind of work is done, the government way is to think of a large number of functionaries and work out how much their pay will increase every month or every year and so on; and a chart is made—how much office space is required, how many vehicles are required, how many jeeps are required, all that is made before any work starts. I realize, of course, the usefulness of automobiles and jeeps and other things, but I think we can do without them. I have almost come to that conclusion. In my youth we went about by bicycle; the best of us sometimes went on a horse, sometimes even an elephant, but not in a jeep. I don't mean to say jeeps should not be used, but this hankering for jeeps everywhere increases the scale of expenditure and makes our human contacts less. On a bicycle, you can meet more people; maybe you go a lesser distance, but you are in harmony with the life of the villager which has risen to the bicycle stage. With the jeep, it is a case of the boss going round, giving some directions, and going away. With a bicycle you move more slowly. If you walk, better still; that only takes too much time. So all this business of putting up large-scale offices and large-scale apparatus and equipment for them, it is all helpful, but we must keep in tune with the level of the village in order to affect it, and the level of the village has not reached at that stage yet.

There are so many things you are doing and it is a little difficult to balance them, but I should think that there are some things which are more necessary than others. Take drinking water. That is a thing which one should make quite sure reaches everybody in the country, good drinking water in every village. That has been decided of course by the Planning Commission. How far it has been implemented I don't know; to some extent it is. But it is a good thing to concentrate on some things. Agriculture we lay great stress on and improvement is visible. It is coming up, it should be faster and every community development block or panchayat should realize that it is its first job because on that depends all its prosperity.

Agriculture includes cooperatives because without cooperatives, I am quite convinced, the village will not progress. We have talked about cooperative farming, and on the whole I find cooperative farms have developed fairly adequately, on a smaller scale of course, because we have not laid enough stress on them, and I don't want you to go about specially laying greater stress. Let us have service cooperatives, everywhere and wherever feasible, wherever people agree. If you suddenly have cooperative farming without training, etc., it will fail. But I am quite convinced of the importance of it. You must always consider the conditions in India and not decide theoretically that because something is good for Russia or America or England it is good for India. It does not follow. Russia and America are countries with vast tracts of land and relatively few men. Here we have too many men and women.

I remember reading last year—Tagore's centenary—some speeches by Rabindranath Tagore delivered as long ago as 1911, over fifty years ago. He strongly advocated cooperative farming in Bengal.[297] Because of the conditions in Bengal, the small holdings, etc., there was scope for it. It was not a political approach, it did not give rise to any controversy as it does not; it was a normal common sense approach. He suggested it, and I believe he adopted it on his own farm. Nevertheless, the first step is service cooperatives.

I have an impression that the cooperative movement is growing well in India, but fear seizes me that what I see on paper may not be there in effect. On paper it appears to be doing well. I think ten years have seen a lot of changes in our villages, tremendous changes. I have no doubt that the average villager is better off, but there are bad patches in every State. I am more acquainted with some bad patches in Uttar Pradesh. The south-eastern districts are bad, very bad; it is not the fault of the people, but there it is. I suggested to the Planning Commission and to the Community Development Ministry that these bad patches should be specially dealt with.[298] It is like a disease, it is infectious; it spreads unless it is dealt with properly.

In all our planning, we are laying great stress on industrial and agricultural development. There must be a level which every Indian can reach. In these bad patches, poverty stricken areas, you must raise them to a certain level, not the highest level but some level. At the present moment, some of them are woefully below that level. While we make big plans for agriculture and industry and all that, we must pay attention to the person who is down and out, too poor, and try to give them some amenities of life at any rate.

In spite of all the criticisms I have heard about the community development movement and the Panchayati Raj, I have always felt excited about this work, because it is a type of work to get excited about. I don't know how many people are affected by it, three hundred fifty million or three hundred million, all the rural people. It is an exciting thing to raise this vast number of human beings through cooperation. It is even more exciting to make them shoulder the burden themselves instead of doling out some help. The Panchayati Raj and

297. See fn 285 in this section.
298. See item 183; see also the several items on poverty in east UP in SWJN/SS/77/section Politics, subsection UP.

the cooperative movement is the way to make them shoulder the burden and in the process of doing that, growing themselves, understanding and growing, and probably solving many of the problems that trouble us today.

So I hope, now that you are entering the second decade of this movement, you will do so with a sense of excitement, full of energy, and by the time we reach the third decade, you will establish Panchayati Raj fully and satisfactorily all over India.

Thank you.

(k) Welfare

310. To K. Kelappan: Keep up the Good Work[299]

July 26, 1962

My dear Kelappan,

I have your letter of the 15th July. I do not know what the decision is or will be about the site for the Rural Institute; but I am glad of your decision to carry on the good work along the lines laid down by Gandhiji. Such good work always produces good results.

You can rest assured that I shall follow with interest the work that you are doing.[300]

Yours sincerely,
[Jawaharlal Nehru]

---

299. Letter to Gandhian activist; address: Sarvodayapuram Gandhi Smarak Kendram, P.O. Tavanur, via Kuttipuram, Kerala. Sent from Anand Bhavan, Allahabad.
300. See also SWJN/SS/74/item 118 and appendix 6.

311. To Brij Krishan Chandiwala: Attending Bharat Sevak Samaj Meeting[301]

अगस्त 4, 1962

प्रिय ब्रजकृष्ण,

तुम्हारा पत्र मिला ।[302] 12 अगस्त को कांग्रेस की वर्किंग कमेटी की मीटिंग दिन भर चलेगी । अगर हो सका तो मैं भारत सेवक समाज की मीटिंग में आ जाऊँगा, लेकिन ठीक नहीं कह सकता ।[303]

आपका
जवाहरलाल नेहरु

[Translation begins

4 August 1962

My dear Brij Krishan,

I have your letter.[304] The Congress Working Committee meeting will go on for the whole day on 12th August. I shall come to the Bharat Sevak Samaj meeting if it is possible, but I cannot say definitely.[305]

Yours sincerely,
Jawaharlal Nehru

Translation ends]

312. For the Bharat Sevak Samaj[306]

When the Bharat Sevak Samaj was started ten years ago, its objective appealed to me. But I was by no means clear as to how this will be attained. We now see

---

301. Letter to the convener of the Delhi Branch of the Bharat Sevak Samaj. NMML, B.K. Chandiwala Papers, Subject File No. 1.
302. Appendix 21.
303. For Nehru's speech at the meeting of the Bharat Sevak Samaj on 12 August 1962, see item 315.
304. See fn 302 in this section.
305. See fn 303 in this section.
306. Message, 5 August 1962, forwarded to Chakradhari Agarwal, the Editor of the *Bharat Sevak*, 17 Theatre Communications Buildings, Connaught Place, New Delhi-1. PMO, File No. 9/2/62-PMP, Vol. V, Sr. No. 66-A. Also available in the JN Collection.

a decade of work behind the Samaj which has spread to various parts of India. What appeals to me most in this record of work is the taking up of construction projects at various places and while executing them well and doing good to labour, resulting in considerable saving to Government.

In many ways the social work done by members of the Samaj is also satisfactory and deserves credit.

I hope the Samaj will continue this good work and make it even more widespread and effective.

313. To Sri Prakasa: Bhagwan Das Sewa Sadan[307]

8th August, 1962

My dear Prakasa,

I have received a letter from Dr Kumar Pal[308] and Dr W.S. Barlingay[309] on behalf of the "Dr Bhagwan Das Memorial Trust". They want me to attend the formal inauguration of the Bhagwan Das Seva Sadan and fix a suitable date for this purpose in September or October. It is stated that you will attend this function and also C.D. Deshmukh,[310] Kaka Kalelkar,[311] etc.

I am writing to ask you whether this is a bona fide institution and if it is desirable for me to attend it. Normally, I would have gladly gone to anything connected with Dr Bhagwan Das's name. But Lal Bahadur[312] tells me that Dr Kumar Pal is not a particularly desirable person. In fact, Lal Bahadur did not wish to be associated with this institution and resigned from it and he tells me

307. Letter to former Governor of Maharashtra and son of Dr Bhagavan Das; address: "Veerana", 9 Ballupur, Chakrata Road, Dehra Dun, UP.

Bhagwan Das, 1869-1958, also spelt as Bhagavan Das, was a scholar of Sanskrit, philosopher, theosophist, and freedom fighter; co-founder of the Kashi Vidyapith.
308. Honorary General Secretary, Dr Bhagwan Das Memorial Trust. He was a post graduate in philosophy from Banaras Hindu University, 1940; established, in 1955, the Yoga Health Centre in Delhi which in course of time was renamed the Yoga Institute for Psycho-Physical Therapy. Joseph S. Alter, *Yoga in Modern India. The Body between Science and Philosophy* (Princeton University Press, 2004), p.161.
309. Waman Sheodas Barlingay, 1904-1991; Minister in Madhya Pradesh, 1946-1952; Congress, Rajya Sabha MP from Bombay, 13 April 1952 to 2 April 1962.
310. Vice-Chancellor of the University of Delhi.
311. D.B. Kalelkar, a Gandhian, social reformer and Nominated Member, Rajya Sabha.
312. Lal Bahadur Shastri, Home Minister.

that you also had decided to resign. This has produced some doubt in my mind whether I should accept this engagement or not. I shall do as you advise me.[313]

Yours affectionately,
[Jawaharlal Nehru]

314. For the Visually and Hearing Challenged[314]

Among our many problems, we cannot forget the fate of physically handicapped persons, the blind and the deaf and dumb, and those who are orthopaedically handicapped. These unfortunate persons deserve our sympathy and help.

Fortunately, it has been found that even those who are physically handicapped can be suitable for certain posts if they are declared medically fit. To give them employment, a special Employment Exchange for the Physically Handicapped was started in Bombay some time ago. Two years ago a similar Employment Exchange was started in Delhi, and I understand that recently Madras has also opened an Employment Exchange for them.

I find that the Delhi Exchange has already found gainful employment for 124 of the physically handicapped persons. They are serving not only in Government offices but also in industrial and commercial concerns. Naturally they have to do particular jobs for which they are fitted. The Exchange has a follow-up programme to find out how these persons get on with their work with their employers.

I would appeal for the employment of these handicapped persons in posts for which they are found suitable.[315]

---

313. For subsequent correspondence, see items 317-318.
314. Message, 11 August 1962.
315. Circular, 5 December 1962, sent to all Ministries by A.V. Venkatasubba, Deputy Secretary, MHA:

"The undersigned is directed to enclose herewith a copy of Prime Minister's appeal dated the 11th August, 1962, regarding the employment of handicapped persons in posts where they are found suitable. In view of their appeal, the Ministry of Finance etc., are requested to kindly explore the possibilities of employing the physically handicapped persons either under them or in their attached and subordinate offices, if possible, on posts for which they are found suitable and they should send their requirements direct to the Special Employment Exchange for Physically Handicapped, 18, Gurdwara Rakabganj Road, New Delhi. A.V. Venkatasubba, Deputy Secretary to the Government of India."
PMO, File No. 9/2/62-PMP, Vol. 8, No. 23-A.

315. In New Delhi: To the Bharat Sevak Samaj[316]

नन्दा जी,[317] बहनो और भाइयो,

दस बरस हुए नन्दा जी ने मुझसे कहा था इस भारत सेवक समाज के शुरू करने का ख़्याल उन्हें आया है। ख़्याल तो अच्छा था, मुझे पसंद आया, लेकिन मैं झिझका कुछ कि अच्छी चीज़ें शुरू होती हैं, अच्छी संस्थाएँ और फिर वो कुछ फंस जाती हैं, ग़लत रास्ते पर चलने लगती हैं, झगड़े-फ़साद की जड़ हो जाती हैं। तो मैं झिझका था। फिर मैंने सोचा कि इस डर के मारे हम अच्छा काम न करें तो वो भी ग़लत है। उसको सम्भालने की कोशिश की जाये और ख़ासकर इसमें बात थी कि जो एक झगड़े की जड़ होती है राजनीति में, सियासत में पड़ना, चुनाव में पड़ना, वो इसमें बिल्कुल न हो और इसमें वही लोग लिये जायें जो ख़ुद कुछ काम करने को तैयार हैं, कुछ अपना वक़्त देने को। वो कुछ रुकावट थी।

आप जानते हैं, कांग्रेस को लीजिए। एक तो ज़माना था जब कांग्रेस में होना ख़तरे में होना था, ख़तरे में होना था, अंग्रेज़ी हुकूमत का मुक़ाबला करना था। तो एक रुकावट थी। हरेक आदमी उसमें नहीं आता था, बहुत आये, बहुत लोगों ने हिम्मत दिखाई, लेकिन उससे उनका फ़ायदा ख़ास नहीं होता था। तो रुकावट की वजह से वो एक ढंग से चली। फिर दूसरा समय आया जब हमारी आज़ादी आ गई, हम हुकूमत में हम लोग आये और चुनाव हुए और लोग चुने जाते हैं लोकसभा के लिए और सूबों में विधान सभाओं के लिए। तब एक दूसरा नज़ारा देखने में आया कि अज़हद लोगों को ख़्वाहिश कि हमें टिकट मिले, दूसरे को न मिले, और कुछ अच्छी हवा नहीं पैदा हुई। हम रोज़, जिनके हाथ में कुछ कांग्रेस की बागडोर थोड़ी बहुत है, इस बात पे विचार करते हैं, किस तरह से ये ख़राबियाँ और कमज़ोरियाँ जो आ जाती हैं संस्थाओं में, ख़ाली हिन्दुस्तान में नहीं, हर मुल्क में ये होती हैं, तो कैसे उनको दूर करना।

आज ही हमारी कांग्रेस की वर्किंग कमेटी की बैठक थी, वहाँ भी घंटों यही बातें हुई।[318] पेचीदा बात है कि एक तरफ़ से प्रजातंत्र हो, डेमोक्रेसी हो, और दूसरी तरफ़ से यह यह जो उसके साथ ख़राबियाँ आती हैं वो निकाल दी जायें, कोशिश होती है, कुछ न कुछ कामयाबी होती है। आख़िर में कामयाबी के माने यह नहीं हैं कि कुछ ऊपर के बड़े-बड़े नेता कुछ हुकुम चलायें, लोग मानें, बल्कि ये हैं कि लोग, आम लोग कुछ सिद्धान्तों को,

---

316. Speech, 12 August 1962, at a public meeting to mark the tenth anniversary of the Bharat Sevak Samaj (BSS). NMML, AIR Tapes, TS No. 8861-8863, NM No. 1708. The press reported it as the eleventh anniversary of the founding of the BSS. See the *National Herald* and *The Hindu*, both of 13 August 1962, p. 1.

The Bharat Sevak Samaj, conceived by the Planning Commission, was established in 1952. Nehru was its President.

317. Gulzarilal Nanda, Deputy Chairman of the Planning Commission and Chairman of the Bharat Sevak Samaj.

318. For the proceedings of the CWC meeting held on 12 August 1962, see *Congress Bulletin*, No. 7, 8, 9 & 10, July-October 1962, pp. 133-141.

उसूलों को समझ जायें और ख़ुद संभाल लें। क्योंकि ख़ासकर जब जम्हूरियत हो, प्रजातंत्र हो, तो जैसे उस देश के लोग होंगे वैसी ही उनकी हुकूमत होगी। देश ऊँचे दर्जे के हैं तो हुकूमत ऊँचे दर्जे की होगी। अगर देश के लोग रहने वाले अच्छे नहीं हैं, कमज़ोर हैं तो वो कमज़ोरी हुकूमत में भी आपको दिख जायेगी। ख़ैर, मैंने आपसे कहा कि जो दिक्क़तें हमारे सामने और हर मुल्क के सामने आती हैं, फिर भी मैं यह कहने का दावा रखता हूँ कि और मुल्कों के मुक़ाबले में, और आप देख सकते हैं दायें-बायें चारों तरफ जो मुल्क हैं हमारे हिन्दुस्तान के, बहुत दूर जाने की जरूरत नहीं है, उनके मुक़ाबले में फिर भी हमने अपनी डेमोक्रेसी को, प्रजातंत्र को बहुत दर्जे कामयाब बनाया। सोलह आने नहीं क्योंकि सोलह आने कामयाबी तो बहुत मुश्किल होती है, लेकिन फिर भी कामयाब है और दुनिया इसको पहचानती है।

ख़ैर, कोशिश हमेशा करनी है और ज्यादा अच्छा बनाने की। उस कोशिश के माने असल में यह हैं, ख़ाली यह नहीं कि आप अच्छे लोगों को गवर्नमेंट में रखें, बल्कि आम लोग अच्छे हों। आम लोगों के अच्छे होने के क्या माने हैं? आम लोगों को मौक़ा मिले अच्छे होने का, क्योंकि कोई पैदायशी अच्छा-बुरा नहीं होता है। तरह-तरह की बातें हैं वो उन्हें अच्छा करती हैं। बचपन में बच्चे को कोई खाना-पीना न मिले, सामान कुछ रहने का ठीक न मिले, मारा-मारा फिरे वो, कैसे बेचारे को मौक़ा कहाँ मिला? मैं गाँव में जाता हूँ, देखता हूँ ख़ूबसूरत, सुन्दर-सुन्दर बच्चे, उनकी देखभाल नहीं होती, मुझे बड़ा रंज होता है। तो किस तरह से हम मुल्क में ऐसी हालत पैदा करें जिसमें हरेक शख़्स को एक मौक़ा मिलता है। इससे ज्यादा आप नहीं कर सकते हैं, आप बेवकूफ़ को अक़्लमंद नहीं बना सकते हैं। अगर पैदाइशी बेवकूफ़ है और कुछ नहीं करना चाहता, तो वो बेवकूफ़ ही रहेगा वो, लेकिन उसको मौक़ा अक़्लमंद होने का देते हैं, मौक़ा देते हैं कि वो काम सीखें, मौक़ा देते हैं कि उसके ख़्यालात अच्छे हों, पढ़ाई-लिखाई वगैरह से। चुनांचे यह मौक़े हरेक का हक़ है, हरेक का हक़ है कि चन्द मामूली चीज़ें हरेक को मिलें और बचपन से मिलें, पैदाइश से मिलें तब बहुत सारे लोग, कुछ लोग नालायक हों और बात है, लेकिन बहुत सारे लोगों को मौक़ा मिलने से कसरत से लोग अच्छे हो जाते हैं और मुल्क को चलाते हैं। यह अच्छी जम्हूरियत है। ख़ाली कुछ लीडरों को चुनने की वजह से नहीं होता है।

तो हमने जो यहाँ डेमोक्रेसी क़ायम की, प्रजातंत्र, तो ख़ैर वोट देने का अधिकार सबको हो गया, चाहे कैसा ही आदमी हो, चाहे अक़्लमंद हो चाहे बेवकूफ़ हो सब बराबर हैं वोट देने में, वो एक चीज़ जरूरी थी। लेकिन उससे वो काफी नहीं थी, लोगों को और चीज़ें, जरूरी चीज़ें मिलनी चाहिये तब उम्मीद हो कि वो एक दर्जे तक पहुँच जायेंगे। अफ़सोस है कि इस वक़्त हमारे हिन्दुस्तान में, दिल्ली शहर में ख़ास नहीं, लेकिन गाँव वग़ैरह में अब तक वो दर्जा लोगों का बहुत नीचा है, बावजूद तरक्की के, बावजूद आगे बढ़ने के। आप जानते हैं कि एक ही बात की तरक्की दिखी है कि हमारी आबादी बहुत बढ़ रही है, बोझा बढ़ता है, लेकिन फिर भी हमारी स्वास्थ्य का इंतज़ाम देश में ऐसा हुआ है और स्वास्थय के इंतज़ाम के साथ खाना-पीना भी है कि जो पहले अभी आज़ादी के जरा पहले समझा जाता था कि आम उम्र किसी हिन्दुस्तानी बच्चे की जो पैदा हुआ है, कहा जाये उसकी

आम उम्र कितनी हो सकती है, आम हरेक तो बत्तीस बरस गिना जाता था। यों तो बहुत लोग बत्तीस से ज्यादा भी होते थे, लेकिन सब ऊँच-नीच बराबर करके, कोई बहुत छुटपन में पैदाइश के बाद पहले साल में मर जायें कुछ और बढ़े, तो आम बत्तीस निकलती थी। अब हिन्दुस्तान की आम उम्र करीब पचास की हो गई है, काफी बड़ा फ़र्क़ है बत्तीस में और पचास में, और बावजूद आबादी के इतने बढ़ने के। यह एक मोटा ग़ज़ है आपके नापने का कि हिन्दुस्तान में क्या हो रहा है, किस तरह की तरक्की हो रही है, क्यों हो रही है। वो क्यों उनकी उम्र बढ़ी, कोई दवाई खा खाके नहीं, लेकिन आमतौर से खाना ज़रा ज्यादा मिलने लगा, ज़रा अच्छा मिलने लगा, ज़रा कुछ रहन-सहन में उनको कुछ थोड़ा सा आराम मिला। ख़ैर, जो भी कुछ वजह हो यह वाक़िया है कि आम उम्र यही हिसाब लगा के गिनती करके क़रीब पचास बरस की हो गई है, और यह काफी बड़ी बात है।

तो यह तो एक बात मैंने बताई, लेकिन हम सब जानते हैं काफी ग़रीबी है, काफी बेरोज़गारी है, काफी मुसीबत है हर क़िस्म की। तो उसका कई इलाज हैं। एक तो बड़ा इलाज है जो हमारे पंचवर्षीय योजना में किया जाता है और बुनियादी है वो, यानी पंचवर्षीय योजना कोई ख़ाली कारख़ाने खड़े करने की चीज़ तो है नहीं, वो तो हर चीज़ में दख़ल देती है, पढ़ाई में, स्वास्थ्य में, कारख़ानों में, ख़ासकर खेती में, सबमें, कि हम ज्यादा मुल्क में पैदा करें सामान को, हर चीज़ के सामान को, किसान खेती में ज्यादा पैदा करें, वो देश की दौलत हो, उसकी दौलत हो, कारख़ाने बनें। कारख़ाने बनें तो कैसे बनें, छोटे-मोटे बनें, बड़े बनें? अगर बुनियादी कारख़ाने बनें तो उसका नतीजा होता है कि उसके बच्चे पैदा होते हैं छोटे कारख़ाने। कारख़ाने बनायें। हमें लोहे की जरूरत है। हमें एक चीज़ की जरूरत है जिसकी आजकल दिल्ली में कमी है, पावर की जरूरत है, बिजली की शक्ति की जरूरत है, जिससे कारख़ाने चलें, अलावा इसके कि और भी बातें उससे होती हैं। तो यह बहुत जरूरी हो जाता है कि बड़े पैमाने पर हम पावर पैदा करें, जैसे भाखड़ा-नांगल में, और जगह हुआ है, और लोहा पैदा करें, हर चीज़ में लोहा आता है, यहाँ तक कि किसान को भी लोहे की जरूरत है। हम बाहर से मंगा नहीं सकते। बाहर किसी चीज़ से मंगायें, उसके एवज़ में क्या दें? चुनांचे यह तो बुनियादी बातें हमें करनी हैं और हज़ारों कारख़ानें। और सबमें बड़ी बात खेती की, खेती की तरक्की हो, खेती में जितना हम पैदा करते हैं, समझदार लोग कहते हैं कि उसका हम चौगुना तक कर सकते हैं, यानी और ज़मीन लेके नहीं, जो ज़मीन है उसमें, हम कम पैदा कर सकते हैं। जापान को लीजिये, अमेरिका को लीजिये, रूस को लीजिये और मिस्र को लीजिये, वहाँ फ़ी एकड़ ज्यादा पैदा करते हैं। क्यों नहीं हम करें? और हम कर सकते हैं और अक्सर लोग कर रहे हैं। अगर आपकी औसत गेहूँ पैदा करने की दस मन है एक एकड़ में, तो बाज़ मुल्कों में तीस मन हो रही है एक एकड़ में। तीस मन हम न करें, बीस मन तो करें। हमारे सारे मसले हल हो जायें अगर हम दुगुना पैदा करें खेती से, गेहूँ वग़ैरह जो कुछ है, धान है, और ऐसा सामान भी जिससे जो हम और मुल्कों को भेजें, बेचें, उससे आमदनी हो।

यह बातें हैं, कैसे हों यह बातें? यह सब बातें होती हैं आजकल की नई दुनिया की नई बातें सीख के। तक़रीर करके मैं आपसे कहूँ करो या जादू से या माला जपने से नहीं

431

होती हैं। यह होती हैं समझ के, समझ के बात को, आजकल की दुनिया को, और मेहनत करके, मेहनत भी सही तरीके से करके। एक किसान बेचारा मेहनत करे, कितनी मेहनत करे, एक उसका हज़ार बरस पुराना हल है, वो एक मुश्किल से ज़मीन को ज़रा खुरच देता है, ज़मीन को ज्यादा गहरा जाता ही नहीं। क्या फ़ायदा उससे, उसका वो मुक़ाबला कैसे करे, उन लोगों का जो कि अच्छा हल चलाते हैं या ट्रैक्टर चलायें? ट्रैक्टर की कोई ख़ास जरूरत नहीं है, ट्रैक्टर भी चल सकता है जरूर लेकिन अच्छा हल हो, जो कि ज़रा गहरा खोदे, उसको दुगनी पैदावार हो। तो जरूरी हो गया कि किसान अच्छे हल चलायें और अच्छे हल चलाना सीखें। आप देख लें, हिन्दुस्तान में आप देखेंगे जहाँ-जहाँ किसान ज्यादातर अच्छे हल चलाते हैं वहाँ उनकी आमदनी ज्यादा है। पंजाब में आमतौर से अच्छे हल चलाते हैं, आमदनी ज्यादा है, दक्षिण में मद्रास की तरफ भी अच्छे चलाते हैं, आमदनी ज्यादा है। सबमें कम आमदनी किसान की है उत्तर प्रदेश में और बिहार में, जहाँ वो हज़ार बरस पुराने हल चलाते हैं। अब वो हज़ार बरस पुराने हल चलाने के माने हैं कि उनके सारे तरीके हज़ार बरस पुराने हैं। उनका क़सूर नहीं है, उनको मौक़ा नहीं मिला सीखने का। हमें उस गढ़े से उनको निकालना है, गढ़े से निकालना ताकि ज़रा उनका दिमाग़ जीता-जागता हो, नई बातें सीखें।

नई बातें भी बहुत पेचीदा नहीं हैं। क्योंकि आप जिस दुनिया में रहते हैं वो बिल्कुल बदल गई है, हम लोग न बदले हों, बहुत लोग हिन्दुस्तान में, लेकिन दुनिया बिल्कुल बदल गई है पिछले ज़माने में, सौ बरस में या कुछ और बदलती जाती है। आज के अख़बार में आप पढ़ें कि वो सोवियत रूस का एक आदमी फिर से एक, हवाई जहाज़ कहना तो ग़लत है, मालूम नहीं क्या कहते हैं उसे, वो दुनिया छोड़ के सैंकड़ों मील दूर गया है, और दुनिया के चारों तरफ घूम रहा है। एक घंटे में, एक घंटे से कुछ ज्यादा में, शायद सवा घंटे में वो एक दुनिया भर का चक्कर लगा लेता है और तीन दिन रहेगा और फिर कोशिश यह होगी कि वापस आ जाये वो।[319] आज़माइश हो रही है कैसे दुनिया के बाहर रह के लोग रह सकते हैं, अजीब बातें होती हैं वहाँ, दुनिया के बाहर कोई जाता है, आप एक चीज़ है, वज़न है हरेक का, हर चीज़ का। क्यों वज़न होता है आपका? क्योंकि एक खेंच है, आपकी हमारी दुनिया खेंचती है आपको, जैसे दुनिया को सूरज खेंचता है, उसके चारों तरफ घूमती है। तो जब आप काफी दुनिया के दूर हो जायें तो आपका वज़न नहीं रहता क्योंकि कुछ मुख़्तलिफ़ तारों और दुनिया के बीच में आके आप, वज़न ही नहीं रहता, फिर आप हवा में टंगे रहते हैं, कुछ कोई चीज़ तक उसका हाथ नहीं गिरे, आप ख़ुद नहीं गिरें, अजीब बात हो जाती है। तो इसका तजुर्बा हासिल करने के लिए वो इन लोगों को भेजते हैं। ख़तरा भरा है इसमें, ज़रा फ़र्क़ हो जाये, वो ख़तम हो जायें। और उसको सैंकड़ों मील दुनिया में चलाते हैं कैसे? यहाँ बैठे-बैठे चलाते हैं, यह अजीब बात है, ग़ौर करने की बात है। तो मैंने इसकी मिसाल दी, किस तरह से दुनिया बदल रही है, आपके उसूल सिद्धान्त न बदलें, लेकिन दुनिया बदलती है और जो आदमी, जो क़ौम बदलती हुई दुनिया को समझता नहीं

---

319. Vostok III. See item 370.

है वो पिछड़ जाता है, रह जाता है। हमारी मुसीबत यही रही है कि पिछले डेढ़ सौ बरस में दुनिया बहुत बदली, हमारे मुल्क में हम पिछड़ गये थे, हम नहीं बदले, हम कमज़ोर हो गये लड़ाई के मैदान में, हमारे पास हथियार नहीं रहे, नये-नये हथियार और हम पैदा करने के तरीके हमें नहीं रहे और यूरोप में ख़ासकर, फिर अमेरिका में दुनिया बदली।

अब वो ज़माना आया है कि वो दुनिया का बदलने का असर हमारे मुल्क पर है ज़ोरों से, और मुल्कों पर भी, हमें अपने मुल्क की फ़िक्र है और कोई ज़रिया नहीं हमें ख़ुशहाल होने का, क्योंकि ख़ुशहाल यूरोप हुआ है इसीलिए कि वो दुनिया बदली, उसके हाथों में नये-नये औज़ार आये, नये-नये हथियार आये, नये-नये तरीके आये पैदा करने के, दौलत पैदा करने के ज़मीन से, कारख़ानों से, क्योंकि दौलत पैदा ही करने से मिलती है। अगर हिन्दुस्तान ग़रीबी को दूर करेगा तो इसी तरह से कि हिन्दुस्तान की जनता अपनी मेहनत से दौलत ज्यादा पैदा करे, यह तो है नहीं कि सरकारी ख़ज़ाने में कोई दौलत है, वही आती है, आप ही लोग देते हैं, कुछ आ जाती है वहाँ। तो यह सवाल हो जाता है सब आपके प्लानिंग कमीशन वग़ैरह का। अब उसमें जरूरत हो जाती है बहुत बातों की। पहले तो यही कि आदमी, आदमियों को मौक़ा मिले, तगड़े हों, बच्चों से लेके पैदाइश से खाना-पीना ठीक मिले, कपड़ा मिले, घर रहने का मिले, कुछ स्वास्थ्य का, सेहत का इंतज़ाम हो और पढ़ाई हो। पढ़ाई निहायत जरूरी है, क्योंकि पढ़ाई आपको नई दुनिया की कुछ खिड़कियाँ खोलती है, जितने आप पढ़ें उतने ज्यादा खिड़कियाँ खुलेंगी और पढ़ाई आपको वो बातें सिखाती है करना, हाथ-पैर चलाना। ख़ाली किताबी पढ़ाई से मेरा मतलब नहीं है, पढ़ाई के माने हैं काम करना, सीखना, और दिमाग़ से भी और हाथ से भी। तो यह जरूरी है और फिर तरह-तरह के रास्ते खुलते हैं हमारे सामने और हम उधर बढ़ेंगे आगे।

तो इन सब बातों में तो लम्बा क़िस्सा है मैं कहाँ तक आपसे कहूँ, लेकिन मैं चाहता हूँ कि आप लोग ज़रा समझें कि किस दुनिया में आप हैं, कितनी जल्दी बदल रही है और बदलते-बदलते यह भी हो सकता है कि क़ाबू के बाहर हो जाये, लड़ाई हो और तबाही आये। वही ताक़त जो कि दुनिया को बदल रही है वो दुनिया को तबाह करने में लग जाये, यह हो सकता है। भयानक बात है लेकिन यह हो सकता है सारी दुनिया तबाह हो जाये। और नहीं तो दूसरा यह हो सकता है कि नई ताक़तों से हम दुनिया को एक बिल्कुल बदल दें, एक बहिश्त सा कर दें, कम से कम मामूली चीज़ों के लिहाज़ से। तो यह हमारे, हम लोगों के सामने दुनिया में यह एक चीज़ है चुनने की किस रास्ते पर हम चलें। हम चलें जिससे दुनिया को फ़ायदा होता है या दुनिया तबाह होती है? अगर इस तरह से मैं कहूँ तो आप सब कहेंगे कि साहब फ़ायदे के रास्ते पर चलो, लेकिन फ़ायदे के रास्ते पर चलने से मेहनत करनी पड़ती है, कुछ तकलीफ़ उठानी पड़ती है क्योंकि मेहनत से और तकलीफ़ से हम कामयाब हो सकते हैं। और ख़ासकर हमें खेती अच्छी करनी और कारखाने बनाना यह सब ठीक है, लेकिन असल बात यह है, बुनियादी बात है कि हमें, हमें आदमी अच्छे करने हैं, मर्द-औरतें, लड़के-लड़कियाँ, जो कि नई दुनिया को समझ सकें, जो कि काम कर सकें नये तरीकों से, पुराने तरीकों से, मेहनत कर सकें, आराम कर सकें, सब कुछ कर

सकें और आपस में मिल के करें, एक-दूसरे का गला न काटें, एक-दूसरे के कंधे पर सवार होके, दूसरे को गिराके बढ़ने की न कोशिश करें।

जिसको कोऑपरेशन कहते हैं, सहकारी संघ वगैरह, वो क्या है? वो भी एक दूसरे क़िस्म का एक समाज का संगठन है। आजकल के समाज का संगठन तो यही है कि आप दूसरे को धकेल के उसकी जगह हो जायें, उसके कंधे पर सवार होके ऊँचे हो जायें, वो चाहे दब जाये। यह तो कैपिटलिस्ट दुनिया है, साहूकारी दुनिया, पूँजीपति दुनिया यही है। उसने फ़ायदे किये दुनिया में जरूर, लेकिन उसका ज़माना ख़त्म हो गया है। अब हमें सहकारी दुनिया बनानी है जिसमें एक दूसरा मदद करे, जिसमें क़ौम बढ़े और ख़ुद भी बढ़े। सारे लोग बढ़ते हैं तो हम भी बढ़ते हैं। भारत को आज़ादी हुई तो सब लोग आज़ाद हुए। अलग-अलग आज़ाद कोई होने की कोशिश करता तो कहीं हो सकता था? भारत अगर ख़ुशहाल होगा तो सभी लोग होंगे। यह हो सकता है आजकल भी कुछ लोग ख़ुशहाल हो जाते हैं, अमीर हो जाते हैं, बाक़ी ग़रीब, लेकिन वो तरीका अच्छा नहीं है और वो उस तरीके से बहुत तरक्की नहीं हो सकती। तो ग़रज़ कि उस नतीजे पर हम पहुँचते हैं हर सूरत से कि एक तो मुल्क की तरक्की के लिए हमें आदमियों की तरक्की करनी चाहिए।

अब आदमियों की तरक्की के तो बहुत तरीके हैं, मैंने कहा पढ़ाई-लिखाई, वगैरह, वगैरह। लेकिन अलावा सरकारी काम के ख़ुद वे कुछ सीखें क्योंकि कहाँ तक सरकारी काम, सरकार पर तो बड़ा उस पर भरोसा करना भी ग़लत है, वो नहीं इतने बड़े क़ौम चवालीस करोड़ आदमियों को उठा सकते। इसीलिए हमने पंचायती राज बनाया कि यह बोझा एक-एक पंचायत पर गाँव की पड़े या पाँच-सात पंचायतें मिल के उठायें, सहकारी संघ हों वहाँ और इंतज़ाम करने की ताक़त उनमें हो। हम उन लोगों को मुंतज़िम बनाना चाहते हैं, इंतज़ाम करने को। मैंने कहीं कहा कि वो दिन, ऐसा दिन आये कि जब हिन्दुस्तान के क़रीब-क़रीब हरेक शख़्स को ऊँचे से ऊँचे ओहदे पर हो सकता है, प्रधानमंत्री हो, राष्ट्रपति हो, मर्द या औरत इस तरह से हो, तब हिन्दुस्तान चमके। तो सरकारी काम तो होता है लेकिन उसी के साथ हमें यह मादूदा हम सभों में होना चाहिए कुछ न कुछ ख़ुद मदद करने का, अपने काम में, अपने गाँव में, अपने शहर में, अपने मोहल्ले में और अगर हम करें तो, हालांकि हमारा काम बहुत नहीं है लेकिन लाखों करोड़ों आदमी करें तो बहुत हो जाता है।

अब मैं आपको एक दूसरे क़िस्म की मिसाल देता हूँ। हम बड़े-बड़े कारख़ाने बनाते हैं जो पैदा करते हैं लाखों-करोड़ों का लोहा और यह और वो, और सामान और कपड़ा लेकिन इस तरह से देखिये अगर फ़ी आदमी हिन्दुस्तान का अपनी जो पैदा करता है, अपनी मेहनत से, वो एक आना रोज़ ज्यादा पैदा करें, सिर्फ एक आना रोज़ ज्यादा करें, यानी चीज़ पैदा करें, तनख़ा बढ़ा देने का मैं नहीं कहता हूँ वो तो पैदा करना नहीं हुआ, एक आना रोज़ ज्यादा करें, तब आप हिसाब लगाइये कि चालीस करोड़ आने रोज़ हो जाते हैं। चालीस करोड़ आने रोज़ होते हैं तो कितने रुपये होते हैं? उसको महीने में लगाइये और साल में लगायें तो इतनी बड़ी रक़म हो जाती है कि सारा हमारा पंचवर्षीय योजना का ख़र्च उससे आ जाता है क़रीब-क़रीब। अब एक आना रोज़ तो बहुत ज्यादा नहीं मालूम होता है, अब उसमें आप बच्चों को छोड़ दीजिये, बूढ़ों को छोड़ दीजिये, फिर भी बहुत बचा रहता है। तो

आमतौर से हमें तरक्की करनी है, आमतौर से पैदावार बढ़ानी है, आमतौर से हमने माद्दा पैदा करना है कुछ करने का।

अब भारत सेवक समाज की बात जो मुझे पसंद आई वो काम की तरफ तवज्जो दिलाना। शुरु में भारत सेवक समाज ने दिल्ली में यहाँ की गंदी बस्तियों का काम कुछ उठाया और वो कुछ अच्छा किया, लेकिन हम दिक्कतों में पड़ जाते थे। जो अच्छा काम हो वहाँ, वो उसकी देखभाल न हो ठीकतौर से फिर ख़राब हो जाये, फिर वहीं के वहीं पहुँच जायें, वहाँ के रहने वाले कोशिश न करें। तब हमने सोचा कि जैसे कि हमने गाँवों में कम्युनिटी डेवलपमेंट स्कीम्ज़ जो हैं, विकास योजना, वहाँ कोशिश की है कि लोग अपने गाँव की देखभाल ख़ुद करें, वैसे हमें गंदी बस्ती में जो लोग रहते हैं उनमें महसूस करना चाहिए उन्हें कि वो देखभाल ख़ुद करें। हम मदद करें उनकी, उनको सिखा दें कैसे करें, लेकिन वो देखभाल करें, नहीं तो सब बिगड़ जायेगा, यानी सबमें सहयोग की जरूरत होती है और ख़ुद करने को कुछ न कुछ। एक और बात मैं आपको बताऊँ। नहरें बनती हैं, बड़ी-बड़ी नहरें बनती थीं, करोड़ों रुपया ख़र्च के, खेतों के लिए, अब हमने नहरें बना दीं, नहर के और छोटी नहरें बना दीं उससे ले जाने के लिए, लेकिन पुराने ज़माने में जब ज़मींदारी वग़ैरह थी तो यह काम था वहीं के लोगों का, पंचायतों का या किसानों का या ज़मींदार का जिसका, कि वो नहर का पानी एक-एक खेत में ले जायें और उसकी ज़रा सी नहर तो नहीं ज़रा सी नाली बनायें पानी ले जाने के लिए। अब यह एक हवा उड़ी कि अब तो सरकार करेगी हम क्यों करें? सरकार की तरफ से बड़ी नहरें बन गईं लेकिन और बड़ी नहर में पानी बहता है, उसका पानी उसमें खेतों में नहीं जाता क्योंकि छोटी नाली नहीं बनाई खेत के लिए जो पहले बन जाती थी। वो समझते थे अपनी ज़िम्मेदारी, अपनी बनाते थे, उनको फ़ायदा होता है, अब उन्होंने छोड़ दिया। चुनांचे पानी ज़ाया होके बह गया, और उनको फ़ायदा नहीं हुआ। यह तो निकम्मी बात है और यह नामुमकिन है कि गवर्नमेंट एक-एक खेत में नालियाँ बनाये। वो पचास हज़ार मील की नालियाँ बनें, कहाँ कितना ख़र्च हो बिल्कुल एक क़ाबू के बाहर बात है।

बात यह है कि हरेक शख़्स, हरेक गाँव, हरेक मोहल्ला एक अपनी ज़िम्मेदारी समझे, अपने हल्क़े में कुछ न कुछ करने की, अपने फ़ायदे के लिए, अपने पड़ोसियों के फ़ायदे के लिए, अपने ख़ासतौर से। अब वहाँ अगर सब लोग नहरें बना लें गाँव वाले जैसे अब बनाने लगे हैं, तब एकदम से उनको पानी मिलता है, उनको फ़ायदा होता है और जल्दी से हो जाता है, वो अपनी ज़रा सी बना ली गाँव में। और अब यहाँ से चलें हम दस हज़ार मील की नहर बनाने, एक बड़ा सीरा बनायें, बड़े इंजीनियर जा रहे हैं और यह और वो, और एक इस क़दर महंगा हो जाये, मुसीबत हो जाये, ख़र्चा उसका इतना हो कि कभी हमें वापिस ही नहीं मिले। इस तरह से हरेक आदमी कुछ न कुछ काम अपना करें। हरेक आदमी का फ़र्ज़ है ख़ासकर जो लोग हम में से किसी क़दर ख़ुशनसीब समझे जायें, जिनको मौक़ा मिला पढ़ाई से, पढ़ाई से कुछ अपने को अच्छा करने का, ख़ुशहाल करने का, वो उनको उनके ऊपर एक क़र्ज़ा है समाज का। समाज में आख़िर जो कुछ उन्होंने खाया-पिया, रहे, वो समाज का खाया, हरेक हम समाज का खाते हैं चाहे हमारे माँ-बाप अमीर हों या

435

ग़रीब हों। तो समाज से उन्होंने लेके, बड़े कोई चाहे बड़े इंजीनियर हो गये, बड़े डॉक्टर हो गये, उन्होंने समाज का रुपया और उनपे ख़र्च हुआ इसलिए बड़े डॉक्टर या इंजीनियर या बड़े कुछ और हुए। तो उनपे कुछ क़र्ज़ा है समाज का उसको देने का, और लोगों को मदद करने का। तो और लोगों को मदद, ख़ैर कुछ पैसे से कर सकते हैं, वो तो एक माने में अदना सी चीज़ है, पैसे की करनी चाहिए, लेकिन मेहनत से मदद करना वो ठीक है, समाज के लिए, हरेक का फ़र्ज़ है कुछ न कुछ समाज के लिए।

इसीलिए गांधीजी ने चर्खा चलाने का कहा था लोगों से। अब बड़े-बड़े अर्थशास्त्र के शास्त्री ने कहा क्या इस ज़माने में चर्खा चलाने से क्या फ़ायदा, यह और वो। लेकिन जो बात, उसमें दो बातें थी चर्खा चलाने से, एक तो वो हरेक को एक ज़रिया थोड़ा सा काम करने को देते थे, चाहे उस काम की आमदनी चार आने रोज़ हो। अव्वल तो यह भी आप सोच लें, मैंने अभी आपको मिसाल दी थी कि एक आना आप एक-एक आदमी ज्यादा पैदा करें रोज़ाना, तो सैंकड़ों करोड़ रुपया हो जाते हैं साल में। ख़ैर, तो कुछ न कुछ चर्खा चला के भी काम हो सकता है, लेकिन मेरा मतलब नहीं सब चर्खा चलायें। दूसरे उसमें जो मोटी बात यह थी कि हरेक आदमी समाज को कुछ देता था मेहनत करके, जो लोग बेचारे मेहनत करते हैं दिन-रात, वो तो करते ही हैं लेकिन हमारे पढ़े-लिखे लोग वग़ैरह, वो दफ़्तरी मेहनत करें लेकिन कुछ समाज के लिए भी उन्हें करना है। तो यह सिखाये, यह उसका उसूल था और तीसरा यह कि हम में बाज़ लोगों में जो ख़्याल कि जो हाथ-पैर चलाना कुछ नीच काम है यह तो बड़ी निकम्मी बात है, कोई मुल्क बढ़ा नहीं है ऐसा सोच के। अमेरिका इत्ता अमीर मुल्क है लेकिन हाथ-पैर चलाने वालों की, हाथ से काम करने वालों की बड़ी इज्ज़त है वहाँ और रूस में तो है ही, सब मुल्कों में है, यह यहाँ कुछ हमारे कास्ट सिस्टम और जातिभेद में कुछ लोग यह करें, कुछ लोग वो करें, अलग-अलग हो गया है जो कि बिल्कुल जनतंत्र और जम्हूरियत के ख़िलाफ़ बातें हैं। तो अच्छा है कुछ हाथ-पैर चलाना हर सूरत से।

तो भारत सेवक समाज ने यह सामने रखा कुछ हाथ-पैर चलाके काम करना, वो आपके और मेरे लिए मुफ़ीद है। कोई शक नहीं है, मेरे स्वास्थ्य के लिए मुफ़ीद है, मेरे दिमाग़ के लिए मुफ़ीद है। दिमाग़ ताज़ा हो जाता है हाथ-पैर चलाके कुछ देर, समाज के लिए मुफ़ीद है, आप समाज को कुछ क़र्ज़ा अदा करते हैं थोड़ा सा और उसमें अपनत हो जाती है और लोगों से, यह नहीं कि आप एक ऊँची कुर्सी पर रहते हैं, और लोग नीचे रहते हैं, और बातें निकलती हैं। वो हर सूरत से अच्छा है, लेकिन तीसरी बात यह है कि और कोई ज़रिया नहीं है इस मुल्क को बड़े पैमाने पे बनाने का, कित्ता ही हम बड़े-बड़े काम उठायें, हम कभी उत्ता नहीं कर सकते, थोड़े से आदमियों को, चुने हुए को लेके जित्ता कि सारी समाज कर सकती है।

अब पंचायती राज हमने किया, सहकारी संघ का कहा उनसे, और एक-एक गाँव वाले अपने गाँव की फ़िकर करें और गाँव में कुछ थोड़ा-थोड़ा काम करें तो हिन्दुस्तान के साढ़े पाँच लाख गाँव बदल जाते हैं और हम उन्हें एक सरकारी तौर से बदलना चाहें तो बड़ी मुश्किल है और ख़ूबी यह है कि उस बदलने में गाँव वाले ख़ुद बदल जाते हैं, यह बड़ी

भारी बात है। काम करने में आदमी ख़ुद सीखता है और कुछ उसका दिमाग़ भी बदलता है और कुछ नई दुनिया में आता है, जो काम-काजी दुनिया है, इसलिए बुनियादी तौर से मुझे भारत सेवक समाज का काम का तरीका पसंद है। अब ज़ाहिर है आप सुनेंगे, मैंने सुना है कि भारत सेवक समाज में यह ख़राबी, यह कमज़ोरी, यह ग़लती हुई, होगी, हैं और उसको हम हटाने की कोशिश करें लेकिन उसका उसूल अच्छा है। एक तो यह कि उसमें कोई राजनीति से मतलब नहीं, कोई राजनीतिक दल नहीं है, कोई उसमें टिकट नहीं मिलेगा खड़े होने का चुनाव वग़ैरह आये, कोई और फ़ायदा किसी को नहीं होगा आमदनी वग़ैरह का। फ़ायदा यह होगा कि उसके काम करने से उसको फ़ायदा होगा और वो समाज को काम करने से एक उसको उससे भी फ़ायदा होगा और एक क़र्ज़ा अदा करेगा समाज का।

एक और बात है, जिस मुल्क में लोग ख़ुद अपनी देखभाल कर सकते हैं, वो मुल्क तगड़ा है और सारी डेमोक्रेसी, प्रजातंत्र, जम्हूरियत के माने यह हैं कि आमतौर से लोग तगड़े हों और अपनी देखभाल करना जानें, यह नहीं कि बादशाह बैठा हुआ है, वो करे, वो कमज़ोर मुल्क होता है। बादशाह यहाँ बहुत रहे और आये, एक छोटी सी लड़ाई पानीपत में हार गये, सारा उनकी शहनशाहियत ख़तम हो गई, दूसरे बादशाह बनके बैठ गये। लेकिन अगर लोग सीखे हुए होते तो क्या मजाल थी कि एक लड़ाई हारते। एक-एक आदमी सिपाही होता, एक-एक लड़ता अपनी आज़ादी के लिए, नहीं आने देता, मुसीबत हो जाती, आख़िर में जो कुछ नतीजा हो, लेकिन तरीका दूसरा है। आजकल लड़ाइयाँ होती हैं, बड़ी लड़ाइयाँ, तो अंग्रेज़ी में उसे कहते हैं 'ऐ नेशन एट आर्म्स' यानी पूरी क़ौम, पूरे लोग सिपाही हो जाते हैं वहाँ के, सब फ़ौजी सिपाही नहीं जाते हैं, लेकिन उसके पीछे काम करते हैं लड़ाई का। और जैसा कि जब एक ख़तरा था जर्मन, क़रीब-क़रीब अंग्रेज़ों के मुल्क में पहुँच गये थे, पिछली बड़ी लड़ाई में, बिल्कुल फ्रांस के किनारे पहुँच गये फ़तह करते हुए, और वहाँ से बाईस मील तो इंग्लैंड है, सिर्फ़ समुन्दर। बाईस मील क्या चीज़ है? उस वक़्त वहाँ के जो वज़ीरेआज़म थे प्रधानमंत्री चर्चिल साहब उन्होंने लोगों से कहा था, एक हिम्मत वाले आदमी थे, उन्होंने कहा था कि वो आ जायेंगे तो हम उनसे एक-एक गली में, एक-एक सड़क पर, एक-एक मैदान में, समुन्दर के किनारे, समुन्दर में, हर जगह लड़ेंगे, हम नहीं हारेंगे, नहीं हम झुकेंगे। एक हिम्मत की बात थी, जिससे एक गिरी हुई, घबराई हुई क़ौम में जान आ गई, कहा कि हाँ हम लड़ेंगे। आख़िर में जर्मन वहाँ पहुँच नहीं सके, इत्तेफ़ाक़ है नहीं पहुँच सके, बिल्कुल इत्तेफ़ाक़ है, हो सकता है पहुँच जाते, एक बाल का फ़र्क़ था, लेकिन एक हिम्मत से इरादा किया। तो यह बातें वहीं हो सकती हैं जहाँ लोग अपनी देखभाल कर सकते हैं। सबमें, अगर सब लोग कुछ थोड़ी सी देखभाल करें, फ़र्ज़ कीजिये मैं नहीं कहता यह बात होगी लेकिन आज की दुनिया में कौन कहे क्या होगा क्या नहीं। फ़र्ज़ कीजिये एक बम्ब का गोला गिरे आपके ऊपर, मोहल्ले में दिल्ली के, तो आप क्या करेंगे, घबरा के भागें, जैसे पिछली लड़ाई में एकाध गोला कुछ गिर गया था आस-पास कलकत्ते के, कलकत्ते से भागे लोग, बहुत कुछ लोग भागे, ख़ासकर जो बाहरी और सूबों से गये थे कलकत्ते वो भागे। तो बेचारे नहीं इतने भागे, वो बाहर वाले भागे और एक भगदड़

मच गई, यह कौन सा तरीका है एक हिम्मत वाली क़ौम का, एक मुसीबत का सामना करने का तरीका है? अगर यहाँ बम्ब का गोला गिरे तो फिर हमें अपने दिमाग़ को तैयार करना है उसके लिए, मदद करनी है अलावा इसके कि हमारी फ़ौज करे। वो तो फ़ौज तो करे ही गी। फ़ौज मुक़ाबला करे, लेकिन फ़ौज काफी नहीं है, एक-एक आदमी को सम्भालना है, मदद करनी है एक-दूसरे की, मिलकर काम करना है और घबराना नहीं है, बड़ी बात यह है और इस तरह से हमें सिखाना है। काम करने से आदमी नहीं घबराता, यह बेकार लोग घबराया करते हैं, डर जाते हैं, कुछ करना नहीं, औरों पर भरोसा करने वाले। तो यह कुछ बातें तो बड़ी-बड़ी मैं आपसे कह रहा हूँ, लेकिन कुछ यह हवा पैदा करती हैं। भारत सेवक समाज काम करे अपने मोहल्ले में, अपने शहर में, गाँव में, कुछ न कुछ काम करके, उससे ताक़त होती है, मुल्क की ताक़त होती है, समाज की ताक़त होती है, अपनी ताक़त बढ़ती है और हमें तैयार करती है, कोई ख़ास मुसीबत आये उसका सामना करने, घबराने के लिए नहीं। यह बड़ी भारी बात है।

आजकल हमारे, आजकल क्या, कुछ ज़माने से एक ख़तरा है हमारी सरहदों पर, हम तो नहीं चाहते किसी से लड़ना, ख़ासकर पाकिस्तान से हम क्यों लड़ें, हमारे एक पुराने साथी, दोस्त, एक मुल्क के रहने वाले, उससे ज्यादा रंज की बात नहीं हो कि हम उससे लड़ाई लड़ें, हम उनको तबाह करें, हम वो करें, हार-जीत की दूसरी बात है लेकिन वो चीज़ ही एक निहायत ग़लत है। अब बदक़िस्मती हमारी है कि पाकिस्तान वाले समझते हैं कि हम उनको तबाह करना चाहते हैं, हम उनको नुकसान पहुँचाना चाहते हैं। हम नहीं चाहते हैं क्योंकि जितना आप नुकसान उनको करिये वो घूमके हमें नुकसान आता है। आप पड़ोसी को नुकसान कीजिये आपका भी नुकसान होगा। यह बात चलती नहीं और हर सूरत से वो ग़लत बात है और क्या कहूँ। अभी वहाँ के राष्ट्रपति जी ने, प्रेज़ीडेंट साहब ने मेरे निस्बत कहा कि मुझे बड़ी अदावत है, मैं उनको तबाह किया चाहता हूँ। अब मैं क्या कहूँ, किस ज़बान से कहूँ कि मैं नहीं चाहता लेकिन, हाँ, यह और बात है कि हम अपनी हिफ़ाज़त करना चाहें, हम किसी और को अपने दख़ल न देना चाहें, बेजा दख़ल, वो दूसरी बात है। हर मुल्क का फ़र्ज़ होता है, लेकिन हमारी कोई लड़ाई नहीं है, हम नहीं चाहते लड़ना।

दूसरा लीजिये, एक बड़ी सरहद पर, एक बड़ा सवाल हमारे सामने महीनों से, कोई दो एक बरस से ख़ास गर्म है, वो इधर चीन और तिब्बत की सरहद और वो काफी लद्दाख़ के पहाड़ों में, बर्फीले पहाड़ों में चीन की फ़ौजें आ गई हैं और जमी हुई हैं वहाँ, वो कहते हैं हमारी है ज़मीन, हम यहाँ हमेशा से हैं। हमारी राय में बिल्कुल ग़लत कहते हैं, हमारी है, हमारे नक़्शों में है और ज़माने से रही है। ख़ैर, मैं इस बहस में नहीं जाता, लेकिन आपको बताता हूँ कि ख़तरा है, ख़तरा है, वहाँ बहुत हिम्मत से, बहादुरी से हमारी फ़ौजें अपने अड्डे बनाये हैं और इतने ऊँचे हैं कहीं सोलह हज़ार फ़ीट के ऊपर, सोलह हज़ार फ़ीट पर आप में बहुत कम लोग हों जो कि शायद आसानी से सांस भी लें सकें, अलावा और तकलीफ़ों के, ऐसी-ऐसी जगह हों। तो वह बहुत हिम्मत से कर रहे हैं लेकिन हमेशा एक मुल्क की हिफ़ाज़त मुल्क की आम आबादी करती है, यह ख़्याल छोड़ देना चाहिए कि सिपाही करते हैं ख़ाली। सिपाही तो करते ही हैं और उनको पूरी मदद करनी चाहिए,

जो सामान उन्हें चाहिए हमें भेजना है, वो हमें बनाके भेजना है, लेकिन दूसरी बात यह है कि हमारे मुल्क में हमें शहरों में, गाँवों में एक हिम्मत होनी चाहिए अपनी देखभाल करने की, कोई मुसीबत आये तो हम देखभाल कर सकें, मामूली तरीके न हों। तो कुछ न कुछ कर सकें, यह नहीं कि हाथ-पैर फूल गये। असल कमज़ोरी की निशानी होती है हाथ-पैर फूल जाना किसी क़ौम का। वो एक दुर्बल क़ौम होती है। जिसकी हिम्मत हो वो हमेशा मुक़ाबला कर सकता है। मैंने कहीं कहा था कि हम लड़ाई लड़ें, हम नहीं चाहते, अगर लड़ाई लड़नी पड़े तो हम नये हथियारों से लड़ेंगे, अच्छे-अच्छे हथियार हमारे पास हैं ज़ाहिर है, लेकिन आख़िर में मुल्क की हिफ़ाज़त करने के लिए लाठी भी काम आयेगी, हम नहीं सिर झुकायेंगे। यह एक जज़्बा होना चाहिए लोगों में कि हम हर तरह से मुक़ाबला करेंगे, चाहे जो कुछ हमारे पास हो, अगर हमपे कोई हमला दुश्मन करे। यह सब बातों से क्या ताल्लुक़ भारत सेवक समाज का, जो कि शांति का काम करने की चीज़ है? ताल्लुक़ यह है कि वह जज़्बा पैदा करना अपनी देखभाल करने का, ख़ुद मेहनत करने का, कुछ काम करने का और उससे यह बातें निकलती हैं बड़ी-बड़ी दूर की बातें। आजकल, अब यह सही है कि आजकल की दुनिया ऐसी है जो बहुत सारे काम ऐसे हैं कि हम अलग कर नहीं सकते, बड़े पैमाने पे काम होते हैं।

आजकल आप लोग और दिल्ली के रहने वाले कुछ अर्से से बहुत तकलीफ़ में हैं, यह बिजली की कमी है, बिजली की, पावर की कमी से परेशान हैं। ख़ैर, वो अब ज़ाहिर है आप हरेक आदमी तो बिजली नहीं पैदा कर सकता, वो तो ख़ास मशीन से, ख़ास ढंग से होती है, कुछ भाखड़ा से होती है, कुछ और जैनरेटर से होती है, ट्रांसफ़ार्मर से होती है, मशीनों से होती है, आप नहीं कर सकते वो ठीक है। लेकिन फिर भी एक बात, एक-दो बातें आप सब लोग कर सकते हैं। एक तो यह जो हर बात में चस्पां होता है कि कोई मुसीबत भी आये हाथ-पैर नहीं फूलने चाहिये, अंग्रेज़ी में उसे कहते हैं अपनी नर्व को नहीं छोड़ना चाहिए, घबराना नहीं चाहिए, क्योंकि घबराया हुआ आदमी तो कुछ कर ही नहीं सकता, वो बेकार हो जाता है और सोचना चाहिए ठंडे दिल से क्या करना है हमें मुसीबत का सामना करने के लिए। अभी उन्होंने कल के परसों, चीफ़ कमिशनर साहब ने एक दरख़ास्त की है कि ख़ासकर यह जो बड़े मकानों के रहने वाले हैं और एयर-कंडीशनर वग़ैरह हैं उनसे कि वो आप ज़रा कुछ रोज़ उसका इस्तेमाल न कीजिये, ज़रा तकलीफ़ होगी लेकिन न करें, उससे बिजली बच जायेगी, औरों को देने को।[320] ठीक है यह। तो हमें मदद करनी चाहिए। जहाँ तक हम काम करें, करें। मेरा ख़्याल है बहुत कुछ वो एक चार-पाँच रोज़ में ठीक हो जायेगी। अब किसका क़सूर है यह बिजली का कम होना, उसकी एक जाँच कमेटी है। क़सूर हो उसको सज़ा दीजिये जरूर, ग़फ़लत हो, क़सूर हो, जो कुछ हो, क्योंकि यह तो काम इंजीनियर्स वग़ैरह का है या जो भी क़सूर हो, लेकिन सज़ा दीजिये उसे जरूर, जाँच करके। लेकिन हाथ-पैर फूलना, हाय-हाय करना, यह कोई शानदार बात

---

320. The appeal to the people of Delhi was issued by Bhagwan Sahay, the Chief
   Commissioner, on 10 August 1962, see item 112.

नहीं है, चाहे कुछ भी हो, और चाहे एक बड़ी लड़ाई का सामना हो, चाहे बम्ब गिरे, चाहे बिजली हटे या कुछ हो।

तो यह सब तो बड़ी-बड़ी बातें हैं, लेकिन छोटी बात, लेकिन बहुत जरूरी बात यह है कि हमें ख़ुद जहाँ तक हम समाज का काम कर सकें वो करना चाहिए, पड़ोसी का काम कर सकें, मोहल्ले का काम कर सकें क्योंकि उससे हमारी ताक़त बनती है, समाज की बनती है, हमारी बनती है। और भारत सेवक समाज का यही उसूल है, यह काम करने का और कराने का और उसमें कोई आपको इनाम नहीं मिलेगा, आमदनी का ज़रिया नहीं होगा लेकिन आपको इत्मीनान होगा कि आपने कुछ समाज का काम किया और उससे आपको भी कुछ फ़ायदा हुआ और औरों को भी फ़ायदा हुआ।

जयहिन्द!

[Translation begins

Nandaji,[321] Sisters and Brothers,

Ten years ago, when Nandaji mentioned his idea of starting the Bharat Sevak Samaj I liked it very much, and yet I hesitated a little because often institutions which start off with very good intentions go wrong after a while and become hotbeds of intrigues and quarrels. Then I thought that it would be wrong not to take up a good cause for fear of things going wrong. It was decided that the Bharat Sevak Samaj should have nothing to do with politics and elections and admit only those who are willing to give of their time voluntarily to do some constructive work.

Take the Congress, for instance. There was a time when it was dangerous to belong to the Congress which opposed the British Government. Everyone was not willing to risk joining it. Those who did so showed great courage. This obstacle gave it a certain complexion. Then came a time when India became free and elections were held to the Lok Sabha and the state legislatures. This brought to light a new spectacle of people's intense desire to be given the Congress ticket. This vitiated the atmosphere considerably. Some of us in the Congress are constantly aware of the need to rid the institutions of these weaknesses and evils and raise their standard. These things happen in all institutions, not only in India but everywhere. How to remedy these weaknesses?

There was a meeting of the Congress Working Committee today in which this issue was discussed for hours.[322] It is extremely complicated, on the one hand, to maintain democracy and, on the other, to get rid of some of the evils which inevitably creep up. An effort is made and with some success. But

321. See fn 317 in this section.
322. See fn 318 in this section.

ultimately, it is only when the people understand and abide by these principles that democracy can succeed, not by some leaders issuing fiats from above. A democratic government depends upon the people of the country for its standards. If the people are of high quality, the government will have high standards. If the people are weak, their weaknesses will be reflected in the government.

Anyhow, I am pointing out some of the difficulties which every country faces. Yet, of all the countries around us, we in India have made a success of democracy. It is not hundred per cent successful but that is very difficult. The world recognizes that we have succeeded. We must make constant efforts at improvement which means not only selecting good people to government posts but improving the quality of the common people. What does that imply? Nobody is born good or bad. Various factors mould their characters. So it is important that everyone should get an opportunity to improve themselves. Today millions of people are deprived of the basic necessities of life. When I go to the villages and see beautiful young children who are not looked after I feel very sad. Conditions have to be somehow created in the country in which every individual is ensured opportunity to improve himself. It is not possible to do more than that. No one can make a born fool intelligent, particularly if he is not willing to help himself. We can only provide an individual the opportunity to learn a useful profession and become skilled, to improve his ideas through education, etc. Everyone has the right to a few basic things from birth. If that is done, the general average goes up and the condition is created in which democracy can succeed. It is not enough to elect leaders.

Everyone in India has the right to vote which is essential. But that is not enough. People need other essential things. Only then there is some hope of their reaching a certain level. Unfortunately, even now, in the rural areas, the level of the people is very low, in spite of progress. The only field where there is progress is in the growth of population which increases the burden. The fact is that with improved healthcare facilities and availability of food, the average life expectancy has gone up from 32 to 50 which is big jump. This is a very good yardstick of the progress that has taken place in India. People are better-fed and enjoy a better standard of living. All these things have contributed to the increase in life expectancy.

However, all of us are aware of the tremendous problems of poverty and unemployment and hardship of every kind which plague the country. There are many remedies available. One of them is the Five Year Plan which does not mean just putting up an industry here and there. The plan impinges on every area of life like education, health, industries, agriculture, etc. What is urgently needed is to increase production by every possible means. We need big, medium and small industries. The basic industries lead to ancillary industries coming up.

441

We need steel and power which is in short supply. We must produce enormous amount of steel and power. Power is being produced in Bhakra-Nangal. Steel is essential in every walk of life. Even the farmer needs steel. We cannot keep importing it at an enormous cost.

These are some of the basic things that need to be done. But the most important thing is to improve agriculture and increase production from land. Experts feel that we can produce four times as much as we do now from the land already under cultivation. In Japan, the United States, the Soviet Union and Egypt, they produce far more from an acre of land. Many people in India are also doing this. The average yield per acre of wheat in India is ten maunds while in other countries it is thirty maunds. We can at least increase our production to twenty maunds per acre which will solve all our problems. We can export wheat and grain and other things if we increase production.

All these things are possible only by learning and adopting new techniques of production and science and technology. It cannot be done by making speeches or counting beads or through magic but by understanding the modern world and through hard work of the right kind. A farmer toils all day long but uses the ancient plough which barely scratches the surface and so his work is wasted. How can he compete with the farmers who use good ploughs or tractors? Tractors are not essential but he must have good ploughs which can double production. You will find that wherever farmers have used good ploughs, production has increased as in the Punjab and in Madras in the South. The lowest average yield is in Uttar Pradesh and Bihar where they use ancient ploughs which means that their methods of production are outdated. It is not their fault. They have not had the opportunity of learning. We must get them out of the rut so that their minds regain their vitality and become capable of absorbing new ideas. There is nothing very complex about modern ideas.

The world around us has changed completely though we have not changed very much in India. There has been a complete transformation in the last hundred years or so. Today's newspapers carry a report about a Russian-manned satellite orbiting the earth in space.[323] Within an hour or an hour and a quarter, it completes one orbit. He will remain in space for three days before coming back to earth. Experiments are being done to see if human beings can survive outside the earth. Here on earth, everything has weight because of the earth's gravitational pull. The earth orbits around the sun. But when you go into space, you become completely weightless because stars and planets come between us and the earth. You can remain suspended in space without falling. It is a strange phenomenon.

323. See fn 319 in this section.

So people are being sent into space at a grave risk for the slightest mistake can lead to disaster. The satellite is monitored from the earth. I am giving you an example to show how the world is changing. The basic principles however do not change. But those who fail to change with the changing times remain backward as India has been in the last 150 years while the world has changed rapidly. We became weak in many ways. Our weapons of war were outdated and so were methods of production.

The time has come when we are feeling the strong impact of change in India. We have no other way to become affluent because they have acquired new methods of production and of generating new wealth. India can get rid of poverty only if the people work hard and produce wealth in the country. It is not as if there is some hidden wealth in the treasury. It has to come from the people's efforts, from what they produce. This is where planning comes in. Planning is essential for providing the basic necessities of life for everyone like food, clothes, housing, healthcare and education, etc. Education is extremely important because it opens the windows to a new world and teaches new skills. I do not mean merely book learning but learning some useful profession as well, intellectual and manual. New avenues of work will open up and we will be able to progress.

This is a long story. But I want you to understand the world that we live in and the rapid changes which are taking place. It is possible that the changes may get out of control and lead to war and destruction, if the forces of change are used to destroy the world. It is a terrible thing, but it could happen. On the other hand, these forces can be used to transform the world into an earthly paradise. This is the choice that we face today. It is obvious what common sense would dictate. But it requires hard work and bearing hardships. We cannot succeed without that. It is particularly important to improve agricultural and industrial production. But even more important is to mould men and women into good human beings qualified and trained in new skills and techniques and capable of understanding the modern age. They must learn the importance of unity and cooperation.

What is cooperation, or a cooperative society? It is a kind of social organization. The modern social system is to push and scramble, uncaring about who gets hurt in the process. That is the world of capitalism. Capitalism has done some good to the world no doubt. But those days are over. We now need a world based on cooperation between individuals and between nations. We became free when India became free. Individuals could not have won freedom for themselves alone. Similarly, their prosperity depends on India's prosperity. Nowadays, a handful of people are rich while the majority is poor. But it is not a good thing for it cannot lead o progress. Therefore, we reach the conclusion that we need to improve the quality of human beings for India's progress. Now, there are various ways of doing so, including education and training, etc. But individuals must try to learn on their own instead of depending on government jobs. The government cannot uplift a large nation of 44 crores of people. That is why we have adopted the Panchayati Raj system so that the burden of running the country may fall on the village panchayats and cooperative societies. We want the people to be responsible for administering the areas they live in. As I remarked somewhere, we want that a time should soon come when almost every individual in India can aspire to the highest positions in the land, to be a Prime Minister or President. The government has, of course, to do its duty. But all of us must have the ability to stand on our own feet and to undertake the responsibility for the work in our street and city or village. An individual may not be able to do very much. But if millions of people do their bit, it can add up to a great deal.

Now, let me give you a different example. We are putting up huge industries to produce steel and other things. But if every individual in India were to produce just one anna worth of goods more every day, you can imagine what a huge amount it will add up to particularly if it is compounded over months and years. Almost our entire expenditure on the Five Year Plans could be met. I am not talking about raising the salary but of producing new wealth. An anna may not seem very much. And we can leave out the old and the very young children, even then it can add up to a great deal. Therefore, we have to aim at increasing production and creating the ability and skill to do so.

[DIGNITY OF LEISURE]

(From *Shankar's Weekly*, 19 August 1962, p.12)

What I like most about the Bharat Sevak Samaj is that it draws the people's attention towards constructive work. In the beginning, the Bharat Sevak Samaj had taken up the task of slum clearance and did a good job. But the problem is of maintenance and unless the people cooperate, things tend to slide back. So we have tried to see to it through the community development schemes that the people must look after their villages themselves. Similarly, we are trying to make the slum dwellers realize the need to keep their homes clean. We can help and train them. Otherwise everything will be ruined. Cooperation and self reliance are essential.

Let me tell you something else. We have built canals and dams at an investment of crores of rupees to provide water for irrigation. Now, small irrigation channels have to be built to allow the water to flow into the fields. In the olden days, under the zamindari system, it was the job of the panchayats or the zamindar who owned the land to construct these channels. Now somehow people seem to expect the government to do even this. So the water remains unutilized because the people are not willing to take on any responsibility at all. The water flows away and nobody benefits. This is absurd for it is impossible for the government to build fifty thousand miles of irrigation channels. How can we take on such enormous expenditure? It is out of the question.

Every individual must realize what he owes to his community and village and discharge his duty to everyone's benefit. If the people were to dig channels, immediately the fields will become green. It would be an easy task for them to take care of their own village. If we tried to do it, it would involve hiring engineers and what not and would be extremely costly. The returns would not be commensurate with the expenditure. It is the duty of every one of us, particularly those of us who can be regarded as fortunate in that we have got the opportunity of education and betterment to do something for the society. We owe a debt to society for whatever we consume. Every individual, rich or poor, consumes something. Those who get trained as doctors and engineers or in some other profession owe a greater debt to society because a great deal of money is spent on them. That debt has to be repaid by serving the people. They can do it by giving some money. But that is a very small thing. Every individual must give of his time and effort for the service of the community.

Gandhiji had advocated spinning for this reason. In those days, the great pundits of economics used to scoff at his idea. But spinning had two distinct advantages. One, it provided a means of some livelihood to everyone. As I said earlier, if every individual in the country produced even an anna's worth of goods every day, it can add up to hundreds of crores in a year. I do not mean that everyone must do spinning.

Secondly, it gave a chance to everyone to do some form of manual work. In our country, the poor toil endlessly, but the educated sit in offices pushing files. That is all right, but they too must do something for society. Thirdly, spinning helped remove the tendency to look down upon manual labour. It is absolutely wrong. No country has ever gone very far with this attitude. The United States is a very rich country but it has become so by respecting manual labour. It is the same in the Soviet Union. Somehow in India, due to the caste system and other factors, there has been a division of labour which is totally undemocratic. Some form of manual work is always good.

The Bharat Sevak Samaj provides an opportunity to the people to do this. There is no doubt about it that it is a good thing for the mind and body. Manual labour refreshes the mind. Our duty to society is also discharged at the same time. It also creates a sense of camaraderie among the people, instead of the gulf that divides the common masses from the white-collared workers and intellectuals. So manual labour is good from many points of view. Thirdly, there is no other way to build a new India and fulfill the great tasks that we have undertaken except through the cooperation of the entire society.

We have adopted the Panchayati Raj system and encouraged the people to form cooperative societies. Now it is up to the villagers to look after their areas. If every village does something towards its betterment, the rural areas will be transformed. It is difficult for the government to do it. The beauty of it is that in the process of changing their villages the people themselves will change. A human being learns when he does something constructive, his thinking changes and adapts itself to changing conditions. That is why I like the method of working adopted by the Bharat Sevak Samaj. It is obvious that there are certain weaknesses in the organization and mistakes are often made. We must make an effort to get rid of them. But its principles are good. For one thing, it has nothing to do with politics. None of the members is going to be given tickets or stand for elections. There is no question of any other gain or reward, monetary or otherwise. The people who work for it will benefit as human beings because they are doing something constructive and discharging debts in the process.

Moreover, a nation which is self-reliant becomes strong and the entire purpose of democracy lies in the masses becoming strong and powerful instead of waiting for someone at the top to do everything for them. That is a sign of a weak nation. There have been great emperors in India but entire empires have been lost in a single battle. There is the example of the battle of Panipat. If the people had been educated and trained, they would not have allowed freedom to slip away so easily. Every single man and woman would have fought for freedom.

446

Nowadays when a war is fought, an entire nation gets involved, which is called "A nation at arms." That does not mean that everyone fights at the front with weapons. They work behind the scenes. For instance, when a German invasion of England seemed imminent and the invading forces had conquered France in the Second World War, the British Prime Minister Churchill, who was a man of great personal courage, had declared that the people of Britain would fight the Germans on the streets and the fields, on the seashore as well as on the high seas, but will not give in. This was an act of courage which infused new spirit into the people whose morale was at low ebb. It is sheer chance that the Germans did not reach the English shores, though it could have happened at any time. The people of Britain showed great determination and courage.

So, as I was saying, a nation needs fear nothing if the people are self-reliant and capable of looking after themselves. Nobody knows what may happen in this world of ours today. Suppose, for instance, a bomb falls upon a street in Delhi. What will you do? Will you run away in panic as people did during the last war when a couple of bombs fell on Calcutta? It was not so much the people of Calcutta as the people from outside who were living in Calcutta; they behaved in this way and created a panic. This is no way for a brave nation to face crisis. If a bomb falls here, we must be mentally prepared to do everything we can to help. It is of course the duty of the armed forces to fight. But that is not enough. Every individual in the country has to help by cooperating and not panicking. It is not the hardworking who panic easily but the idle and the weak for they rely on others. What I am saying might seem like a tall order. But the Bharat Sevak Samaj can create the right atmosphere. People who participate in the Bharat Sevak Samaj can contribute greatly to the strength of the society and become strong themselves in the process. Such work prepares us to face any crisis that may arise without panicking.

For some time there is great threat on our borders. We do not want to go to war with anyone. Why should we fight especially with Pakistan? They are our neighbours, they are our old friends, we belonged to the same nation, and nothing can be worse than to go to war with them bringing ruin on both the countries. It does not matter who wins or loses. The idea is wrong. It is our misfortune that the people of Pakistan think that we want to ruin them. It is not true for if we do, we will ruin ourselves in the process. That is inevitable if we try to do harm to a neighbour. In any case, it is wrong no matter which way we look at it. The President of Pakistan has said recently that I have great enmity towards his country and would like to see it ruined. I do not know what to say to that. It is a different matter that we want to defend our country. But we do not wish to interfere with anyone else. Every country has a duty to defend itself. But we have no desire to go to war with anyone.

Then, for months or rather the last couple of years, our borders with China and Tibet, have been threatened. The Chinese troops are stationed on the icy mountains in the Ladakh area. The Chinese are claiming that area as theirs which is absolutely wrong. Those areas have been shown as our territory for a long time. Well, I shall not go into that now. But I want to tell you that there is danger. Our brave troops are manning the military posts at heights of sixteen thousand feet or more. Ordinary people would find it difficult even to breathe at that height. The people of India must realize where their duty lies in the defence of the country. Everyone must do his best to help the soldiers and to keep them supplied with everything that they need. Secondly, the villages and cities of India must have the courage and determination to defend themselves and to face any crisis unflinchingly and not get cold feet. That is a sign of weakness. Even a weak nation with courage can fight. As I said somewhere, though we do not like the idea of going to war, if we have to, we will fight with all the resources at our disposal. But ultimately, if necessary, we will use even sticks to fight for the defence of the nation and not give in. You may wonder how this concerns the Bharat Sevak Samaj which is a peaceful organization. It is concerned with creating a climate of self-reliance and hard work. Everything else stems from that. In the world that we live, we cannot do very much by pulling in different directions. Cooperation is extremely important.

The people of Delhi have had to put up with a great deal of trouble due to power shortage. It is obvious that individuals cannot produce electricity on their own. There is a special machinery and process for it. Power is generated from the Bhakra-Nangal. But you can help by doing one or two things. For one thing, the people must not lose their nerve or panic every time there is a crisis. A man who is afraid can do nothing. The Chief Commissioner has issued an appeal to people who own air-conditioners, etc., not to use them for a few days.[324] You may have to put up with difficulties. But it will conserve electricity. I think the situation will improve in a few days. A committee will go into the question of who is responsible for the fall in generation and the engineers who have slipped up will be punished. But at the moment we must not give into panic. It is not becoming, whether there is a major crisis or a small one. The important thing is to cultivate the habit of self-reliance and service to society. Cooperation contributes to the strength of the society. This is the principle on which the Bharat Sevak Samaj has been founded. There are no rewards or honours. But you will have the satisfaction of doing something constructive for society and will benefit in the process.

Jai Hind!

Translation ends]

324. See fn 320 in this section.

316. To Nargis Captain: Miscellaneous Welfare Matters[325]

August 15, 1962

Thank you for your letter of the 13th August. I am very fit now and I believe, quite well. So the doctors assure me.

I am glad to learn that the Mahatma Gandhi Memorial building is now ready and is an attractive building. If possible, I shall try to see it when I go to Bombay.

I have sent the copy of the letter from Mrs Nimbkar[326] to the Minister of Community Development[327] who, I think, is responsible in the matter. I do not myself know anything about this Evaluation Committee. If it is possible the Minister, S.K. Dey, will no doubt consider this matter with sympathy.

I hope Bul[328] is much better now. My love to you and Psyche.[329]

[Jawaharlal Nehru]

317. To Kumar Pal: Bhagwan Das Memorial[330]

August 17, 1962

Dear Dr Kumar Pal,

I am sorry for the delay in answering your letter of the 29th July.

I would gladly attend any ceremony connected with Dr Bhagwan Das. I think it is right and proper that we should honour his memory.

But the dates you suggest are not convenient to me. I am going abroad to Europe early in September and shall not return till early in October. On the 12th October I go to Ceylon for a few days. It is difficult for me even to suggest any

---

325. Letter to granddaughter of Dadabhai Naoroji and a friend of the Nehrus; address: 6 Salisbury Park, Poona-1. Salutation not available.
326. Probably Kamala Nimbkar (nee Elizabeth Lundy), an American who married an Indian businessman and settled in India; spent several years at Sabarmati Ashram; a pioneer in Occupational Therapy in India and Asia.
327. S.K. Dey, the Minister for Community Development, Panchayati Raj and Cooperation.
328. Khurshedben, a granddaughter of Dadabhai Naoroji.
329. Goshiben Captain, a granddaughter of Dadabhai Naoroji.
330. Letter to the Honorary General Secretary, Dr Bhagavan Das Memorial Trust, 2-F Lajpat Nagar, New Delhi.

other date in October because I am not sure of my programme then. If I am in Delhi when you have this ceremony of inauguration, I shall try to attend it.[331]

Yours sincerely,
[Jawaharlal Nehru]

318. To Sri Prakasa: Bhagwan Das Memorial[332]

August 17, 1962

My dear Prakasa,

Thank you for your letter of August 10. In view of what you have written I would, of course, like to be present at the inauguration ceremony of the Dr Bhagavan Das Memorial. But the dates Kumar Pal has suggested are very awkward for me. I am leaving early in September for Europe and then for Africa. I shall not return till early in October. I am going to Ceylon on the 12th October for a few days.

I have written to Kumar Pal that if I am here, I would gladly attend, but I cannot definitely say when I shall be in Delhi in October.[333]

Yours affectionately,
[Jawaharlal Nehru]

---

331. A function to observe the death anniversary of Bhagavan Das was held in Delhi on 16 September 1962. President S. Radhakrishnan and Sri Prakasa were among those who attended. *The Times of India*, 17 September 1962.

See item 313; NB: Nehru's citing Lal Bahadur Shastri's negative opinion of Kumar Pal. See also item 318.

332. Letter to former Governor of Maharashtra and son of Dr Bhagavan Das; address: "Veerana", 9 Ballupur, Chakrata Road, Dehra Doon.

333. See item 317; see also previous letter to Sri Prakasa, item 313.

IV. EXTERNAL AFFAIRS

(a) General

319. Revamping External Publicity[1]

I have read Shri Chagla's[2] letter. He suggests various additions to the staff here and elsewhere. Perhaps, to some extent, this is necessary.

2.   But what is even more necessary is, I think, a fresh outlook towards this whole question. We know how our publicity organisation is being continually criticised in Parliament and outside. Eminent Indians who go abroad, come back with many criticisms. Shrimati Indira Gandhi spoke to me the other day strongly on this subject. Dr V.K.R.V. Rao also spoke in the same strain.[3] The criticism is of many kinds. But it especially emphasizes that we are not amenable to any fresh ideas. We do not try to get the opinions of [sic] reactions of others. And so we move in the same circle and carry on with the same routines.

3.   I would suggest our doing something to remedy this lacuna and consult outsiders who are interested in this important work. We may not accept what they say, but this will have advantage: one is that we may get some fresh ideas and, secondly, they will realise what we are doing and our difficulties, and be less critical later.

4.   I agree with FS[4] that the External Publicity set-up should be under a senior and experienced officer.

---

1.   Note, 21 August 1962. MEA, File No. XPP/302(2)/7/62, p. 34/Note. Also available in the JN Collection.
2.   M.C. Chagla, High Commissioner to UK.
3.   V.K.R.V. Rao, Director, Institute of Economic Growth, Delhi, said at a public meeting in Nairobi on 29 July 1962 that Indian intellectuals were not taking as much interest in Africa as they had before India's independence. He also said that "he would try to get this rectified for he was convinced that India could assist emerging Africa in many ways." His impression was that "Africans were pro-Gandhi and pro-Nehru, but not 'pro-Indian'." *The Times of India*, 31 July 1962.
4.   M.J. Desai, the Foreign Secretary.

320. For the Pugwash Conference[5]

I congratulate the Pugwash Continuing Committee on arranging the tenth Session in their series of important conferences.[6] The capabilities of science in the modern world are so immense and far-reaching that scientists have a special responsibility in focussing the attention of the world community to the potentialities both of human betterment and of disaster inherent in the uses to which their achievements can be put. We all owe a debt of gratitude to the participants in the previous Pugwash Conferences who cut across political barriers to discuss freely and fully the opportunities and the dangers facing the world in our nuclear age. None of these problems is more important today than that of disarmament and peace and your past Conferences have done well in emphasising the urgent need for eliminating nuclear weapons and indeed the entire apparatus of modern war.[7] I am also glad that you are devoting your attention to the role of the scientist in other fields of national and international activity and particularly to the contribution he can make in helping underdeveloped nations to modernize and secure for themselves the benefits of scientific and technological progress.

I have supported your movement from the time the first conference was mooted[8] and I wish you success in continuing to provide the occasion for closer communication between scientists from all parts of the world.

321. To W.D. Tucker: Year of International Cooperation[9]

August 27, 1962

Dear Mrs Tucker,

I have your letter of August 21st.

As you have yourself mentioned, India was one of the sponsors of a proposal before the UN General Assembly for a United Nations Year of International

---

5. Message, 24 August 1962, forwarded to J. Rotblat, Secretary General, Pugwash Continuing Committee, 8 Asmara Road, London NW 2. MEA, File No. A(6) – Disarm/1962, pp. 20-21/C.
6. The tenth Pugwash Conference on Science and World Affairs was held in London, 3-7 September 1962.
7. The ninth Pugwash Conference, held in Cambridge, 25-30 August 1962, focussed on the "Problems of Disarmament and World Security." Vikram Sarabhai's report on the conference is available in MEA, File No. A (6) – Disarm/1962, pp. 31-44.
8. The first conference was held in July 1957.
9. Letter to the President, Voice of Women, Canada, 341 Bloor Street West, Toronto 5.

Cooperation. It was unfortunate that this could not be considered by the General Assembly last year. We still think that such a proposal is worth while and may well produce substantial benefits.

We have seen scientists from different countries cooperating with each other. In fact, the area of cooperation between countries even opposed to each other on political or ideological grounds, has increased. We shall welcome, therefore, if our proposal of last year is revived and given effect to.[10]

Yours sincerely,
[Jawaharlal Nehru]

322. In London: Meetings with Press[11]

No Plan to Discuss Kashmir with Ayub
ECM Will Weaken Commonwealth

London, September 8 – Prime Minister Nehru, answering questions on his arrival here today for the Commonwealth Prime Ministers' Conference, said that there was no plan to discuss Kashmir with President Ayub of Pakistan, during his stay here.

Asked whether he thought Britain's entry into the European Common Market would weaken the Commonwealth, Pandit Nehru replied: "I think so."

Questioned on what would be the specially important topics for the conference, besides the Common Market, Pandit Nehru said: "The major world topics are disarmament, peace and nuclear tests".

On his arrival, Pandit Nehru faced a battery of television cameras for a succession of short interviews.

On his way to London, Pandit Nehru made a brief stopover in Paris this morning.

Pandit Nehru, accompanied by Mrs Indira Gandhi, and the Union Finance Minister, Mr Morarji Desai, flew in from Geneva and was welcomed at the airport in Paris by the Indian Ambassador to France, Mr Ali Yavar Jung, and the French chief deputy of protocol, M. Emmanuel de Castéja.

Pandit Nehru had breakfast in the airport's banquet room, and picked a scarlet rose from the flowers on the table to wear in his buttonhole. He then boarded his Air-India plane and continued on to London.

---

10. The UN General Assembly designated 1965 as the International Co-operation Year.
11. Reproduced from the *National Herald*, 9 September 1962, p. 1.

Political Aspects

Asked for his views on the present stage of Britain's negotiations with the EEC, Pandit Nehru said the arrangements reached so far were not favourable to India. He hoped, however, that they would be made more favourable.

The agreements reached so far would definitely hurt India's trade with the UK and certainly would affect the expansion of trade unless some changes were made, he said.

Asked whether he thought Britain's entry into the Common Market would weaken the Commonwealth, Pandit Nehru replied: "I think so. It seems likely; to what extent, I cannot say, but it will be a weakening factor, more especially if it develops into some kind of a political union."

Pandit Nehru said possibly the political aspects of the EEC would come up not immediately, but some time later. "But I believe they will have some considerable effect on the Commonwealth—a weakening effect rather."

He pointed out that the Treaty of Rome envisaged the Common Market countries developing into a closer political union.[12] The result of that would be that each member would be bound, to some extent, by the decisions of the community as a whole. It would have to be a joint decision.

It was difficult to say what effect it would have on an organization like the Commonwealth. "It is clear that there is a possibility of conflict, and conflict in the sense of views," he added.

A correspondent referred to Pandit Nehru's own view that the Commonwealth had been a force for peace, and asked what effect Britain's entry into the Common Market and the latter becoming a close political union would have on the Commonwealth's role as a force for peace.

Pandit Nehru replied: "It all depends on how far the other is a force for peace or against peace. If it is just an expansion of the NATO alliance, then it seems to me it becomes a party to this world conflict".

No Favours

Pandit Nehru said that it was really for Britain to decide whether she wanted to join the Common Market or not and "we can only try to protect our interests as far as we can."

But, he added, India's increasing exports to the UK were not "a unilateral show". In the last several years, British trade with India had gone up very much.

---

12. See also item 16.

"It seems natural that if our exports are affected, it will have some effect on the other side too.

"We are not asking for any favours. But if (present trade) is beneficial to both parties and if it is affected, both sides will suffer".

He was asked whether the evolution of the EEC into a close political community would not be beneficial to the world, particularly because differences in Europe during the last sixty years had led to several wars.

Pandit Nehru said: "I do not think it will make any difference. It may be good for them (European countries) to come together, but the world of sixty years ago was different from the world of today. There are other nations, apart from Europe, which do count today."

Immigration Act

About the British Immigration Act restricting the entry of Commonwealth citizens in the UK, Pandit Nehru said that India had not liked it on principle.[13] The Government of India were not interested in Indians migrating to the UK, and they had themselves taken several steps to stop it. But on principle, the British legislation, the Government of India thought, was a bad thing.

Pandit Nehru said that his proposed official visit to Paris from September 20 to September 23 was "a purely friendly one". "There are no problems for India with France. We had one little problem—Pondicherry—for a number of years, but that has now been solved. We have no problems of any kind with France now," he said.

Pandit Nehru said that on his way back to India, he would visit Nigeria and Ghana also. He had been trying to go there for quite some time. Now that he had come so far, he thought he might as well take advantage of it and go to those two countries. – Reuter, AFP-PTI.

---

13. The Commonwealth Immigration Act 1962 made provisions to control the immigration into the UK of all Commonwealth citizens, except those who held UK passports. Under this Act those entering the UK to work would have to apply for a work permit.

323. In London: Meeting with Presspersons[14]

Brussels Pact. Misgivings of India
Concern about Exports
From K.S. Shelvankar

London, September 10 – Prime Minister Nehru met Indian journalists in London at his residence yesterday and spent over an hour with them, talking about a variety of subjects ranging from the situation in Nagaland to his coming visit to West Africa.

About the Commonwealth Conference itself, he had nothing new to say. He made it clear, as he has done before, that the decision whether or not to join the Common Market was entirely up to Britain, but the conference afforded the Prime Ministers an opportunity to express their opinion and point out what the consequences might be. Some remarks of the Finance Minister, Mr Morarji Desai, had given rise to a misunderstanding about India's attitude.

"It was tried to put aside India by saying that she was satisfied and that only Canada, Australia and New Zealand were the real problem," Mr Nehru commented. The misunderstanding had since been cleared up. India in fact had serious misgivings about the Brussels agreements regarding her exports. Also, Press reports circulating here that India supported Britain's entry into Common Market were "obviously incorrect," Mr Nehru said.

No Positive Decision Likely in London Talks

He added it was not customary at these conferences to pass a resolution, so it was unlikely that any positive decision would be recorded at the end of the discussions. In any case, the British were not putting forward any rigid formula at the conference. "The theory," Mr Nehru said, "is that the negotiations are still going on and it would be premature to adopt a hard and fast position at this stage."

The proposal that another conference should be convened before Britain took a final decision was something that Mr Nehru heard about only after coming here, and he was clearly not enthusiastic about it. "It is not easy for people to rush up to London every few months," he observed. It was open to others to suggest it, if they wished, but he for one was not going to ask for a second meeting.

Separation of Madras. DMK's Cry "Absurd"

14. Reproduced from *The Hindu*, 11 September 1962, p.1.

Questioned about developments in India, Mr Nehru said among other things:

On national integration: The movement is on the whole doing well, but the Press tended to publicise anything that went against it, as in the Punjab and Madras. In the Punjab, Akalis "have fallen out with each other", and in Madras, the cry for separation is "absurd" but "a mixed lot of people were voting for it."

[Anti-Nuclear Convention]

On Rajaji's[15] mission: The Government had granted facilities for delegations from the Gandhi Peace Foundation, one to Moscow and the other to Washington, London and possibly Paris. The Washington delegation includes Mr Diwakar,[16] Rajaji and Mr Shiva Rao.[17] The Moscow delegation consists of Mr G. Ramachandran[18] and Mr U.N. Dhebar.[19] The delegations will take a message to the Heads of Government on behalf of the "Anti-Nuclear Convention" recently held in Delhi.[20]

MIG Deal

On the MIG deal with Russia: The negotiations can no longer be considered to be at the exploratory stage, "they have gone a good deal further."[21]

[Nagas]

On Naga affairs: The Naga population in general is very much against the armed rebellion. That is perhaps why the rebels are "trying to do something outside India." One member of the Indian delegation to the UN Assembly this year is a Naga, one of the Prime Minister's Parliamentary Secretaries.[22]

15. C. Rajagopalachari, leader of the Swatantra Party.
16. R.R. Diwakar, Chairman of the Gandhi Peace Foundation.
17. B. Shiva Rao, former MP.
18. Secretary of the Gandhi Peace Foundation.
19. Former President of Congress Party.
20. See item 334, and SWJN/SS/77/items in section Anti-Nuclear Conference.
21. On MIGs, see SWJN/SS/77/items 373 and 381-382.
22. S.C. Jamir, Lok Sabha MP from Naga Hills-Tuensang Area, and Parliamentary Secretary to the Minister of External Affairs.

[Panchayati Raj]

The most hopeful thing about India today: Panchayati Raj, and development in the rural areas which are creating a new spirit of self-reliance. Also the spread of education, and the rise in the average expectation of life.

[China]

The border dispute with China: No reply had yet been received to the Indian note proposing preliminary talks.

Associate Status in ECM. "A New Form of Colonialism"

Reuter adds:

Mr Nehru said that associate membership of the Common Market for Commonwealth countries created "perspectives of a new form of colonialism."

Mr Nehru made it clear that the question of associate membership did not relate to India. As for the African countries, it was for them to decide whether to accept that status or not.

Mr Nehru said that since the Prime Ministers' Conference did not take any vote or pass formal resolutions, there was no question of the issue of associate membership being decided upon at the conference.

"Nevertheless," he added, "it is clear that the protection of the African countries' interests would be made difficult by associate membership. And they would continue to be exporters of raw materials to the manufacturing countries of Europe."

Mr Nehru said in reply to a question that so far he had not been approached by the African Premiers for support on the associateship issue.

Agreement on disarmament would depend very much on the establishment of some kind of a bridge between the US and USSR. "We want to help in some kind of understanding being reached, but we are not suggesting any rigid formula."

Jakarta Incidents

Referring to the recent anti-Indian incidents in Jakarta, Mr Nehru said the Indonesian Foreign Minister[23] and others had apologized profusely for it.[24]

---

23. Subandrio.
24. See item 438.

[Nepal]

Indo-Nepalese relations: India had made it clear that she did not want the country to be made a base for operations against the Nepal Government. But India, under her laws, could not prevent Nepalese in India from peacefully expressing their opinions. The Nepalese Government sometimes charged that incidents were staged from Indian soil. In three cases joint investigations were made and reports had been submitted by the respective officials of the two countries to the two Governments. India had suggested exchange of these reports but Nepal had not so far done so. When he had met King Mahendra last year and had been asked for advice he had told the King that India did not desire to interfere in Nepal's affairs, but the conditions could be improved only by being conciliatory. But recently action had been taken in the opposite direction in the matter of confiscation of properties of Nepalese leaders who had fled the country. They had also been sentenced to long terms of imprisonment.[25]

[Vinoba Bhave in East Pakistan]

Vinoba Bhave's visit to East Pakistan: It will do a lot of good. He had been received well by the people. But it will not influence very much the Governments. But as between the peoples of India and Pakistan there was no longer that bitterness and estrangement evident in the post-Partition period.

Visit to Nigeria and Ghana

Mr Nehru said in reply to a question that there was "no particular significance" attached to his visits to Nigeria and Ghana after the Premiers' conference.

Visit to France

Regarding his visit to Paris (September 20-22), Mr Nehru said that he had no particular problems to discuss with President de Gaulle. He would "discuss the Common Market casually" with the French President.

---

25. See items 429-430.

324. For the *O Estado de Sao Paulo*[26]

The Way of Understanding Nations: Nehru in Brazilian Paper

O Estado de Sao Paulo, a weekly,[27] in a recent issue, published an article by Prime Minister Nehru under the caption: "The way of the underdeveloped nations".

The following is a summary:

The fundamental fact of today is the outstanding rhythm of change in human life. I have seen many astonishing changes during my lifetime and I am sure that in the course of the next generation even greater changes will take place. If humanity is not overtaken and crushed by an atomic war ...

But though man has come to conquer external conditions, he has lost, at the same time, his moral strength and his self-control. He cannot conquer himself. This is the tragic paradox of this atomic age.

The fact that nuclear tests are still going on in spite of the danger they imply to the present generation and to the future; the fact that powerful weapons of destruction are still being produced even though they could exterminate the whole human race, makes the paradox obvious. On the one hand, there is this great and irresistible progress in science and technology with its various consequences; on the other, a certain mental exhaustion of civilization itself.

Communism and Violence

Communism offers a kind of faith and a kind of discipline. To a certain extent it fills the vacuum; to a certain extent it succeeds in giving a purpose to human life. But, in spite of its apparent success, it falls, partly because of its rigidity, but even more because it does not consider some essential needs of human nature. Communists point out the contradictions in the capitalist society and there is much truth in the analysis they make. But the control of individual freedom, the indifference towards the so-called moral and spiritual aspects of life, the unfortunate association with violence, all these show the growing contradictions within the rigid structure of communism itself.

I have the greatest admiration for many of the Soviet Union's conquests. There the children and the common people are valued, protected and cared for. Education and health there are perhaps the best in the world. However, individual freedom is limited. Unfortunately, communism has become too closely associated with the need for violence and so the ideal it put before the

26. Reproduced from the *National Herald*, 10 September 1962, p. 5.
27. Published from Sao Paulo, Brazil.

world is blemished. Here we can feel the powerful consequences of wrong methods.

Communism's principal plea is that the capitalist structure of society is based on violence and class struggle. I think this is essentially true. In spite of the fact that the capitalist system has undergone and is still going through a change caused by constant struggle against inequality. The question is how to free ourselves from this evil and create a society without classes with equal opportunities for all.

Can this be attained through violence, or are pacific methods effective? Communism has chosen violence; violent language, violent thoughts. Fascism had all these bad aspects of violence and extermination in their most brutal form without offering any acceptable idea.

All this goes directly against the way Gandhi showed us.

We have reached a stage where any violent imposition of any idea is hopelessly doomed to failure. In the present circumstances there will be no victory, all will be defeated.

What is Lacking

It is often said that in India there is a sense of frustration and depression and that at a time when enthusiasm and hard work are most necessary the old enthusiasm is found lacking. But this is not happening only in our country, in a certain sense it is happening in the whole world. Fighting for material prosperity, we have forgotten the spiritual element. Democracy and socialism are means to reach an end, they are not an end in themselves. We speak of the good society. If the individual is ignored and sacrificed for what is thought to be the good of society, is that goal worth fighting for?

The individual must not be sacrificed. As a matter of fact, true social progress will only come when the individual is given the chance to grow, provided that the word "individual" refers not to a selected group but the community as a whole. The important thing is to find out up to what point any political or social theory allows the individual to rise above his insignificant ego and to think in terms of welfare for all.

In a certain sense, every country, whether capitalist, socialist or economist, accepts the ideal of welfare for all. Democracy has, undoubtedly, lessened many of capitalism's evils. In industrially advanced countries there has been a continuous rising current of economic development. And this economic progress has reached—even though in different degrees—all classes.

As a rule, we can say that the forces of a capitalist society, if not controlled, tend to make various democratic procedures interfere with these normal currents. Therefore, capitalism itself has developed some socialist characteristics, although it maintains its most important features.

Socialism

Socialism of course wishes to deliberately interfere with normal processes in order to increase productive forces and mitigate inequalities. But what is socialism? Socialism is basically a way different from that of capitalism, even though the great distance between them tends now to be reduced ... Socialism is not only a way of life, but a particular scientific way for the solution of social and economic problems. If socialism is introduced in a backward and underdeveloped country, it does not all of a sudden make the country less backward. In fact, in this case we have a backward and poor socialism.

Socialism and Poverty

We must remember that merely the adoption of socialist or capitalist methods will not make poverty give way to wealth. Hard work, increasing a nation's productivity, followed by equitable distribution of its product, is the only way to prosperity. In an underdeveloped country the capitalist methods offer no opportunity. Only through planning and according to socialist patterns can rapid progress be made, even though it takes time.

Planning is essential, for if we do not plan we will waste our resources, which are limited. Planning does not mean a mere collection of projects or schemes, but an effort aiming at the progress of the community in all fronts. In India we have a choice to make; either pay attention only to production in chosen and favourable areas, forgetting temporarily the poor areas, or try to develop at the same time the backward areas, so as to lessen the inequalities among regions. A national plan does not have to be and, in fact, should not be rigid. It is not necessary for it to be based on any dogma. It must, instead, take into consideration existing facts.

Some of the problems India faces today are to a certain extent common with other countries, but there are many more which are unique, without any historical precedents. Therefore, western economics, although useful, has little to do with our present problems. The same thing is true of Marxist economics which, while explaining many things, is outmoded in others. We must think for ourselves, taking advantage of others' experiences, but trying to find, by ourselves, the right way for us.

Taking into consideration the economic aspects of our problems, we must always remember the basic need of peaceful means; and may be we can keep in view the ancient Vedic ideal of vital force, the fundamental basis of all that exists.

325. In London: Press Conference[28]

[Commonwealth]

Question: Sir, could you give us your comments now that the communiqué has been issued on the Prime Ministers' Conference?[29]

Jawaharlal Nehru: The communiqué represents our joint opinion, or perhaps bits represent the opinion of some people, other bits of it. As a whole we accept it. So far as we in India are concerned we were naturally anxious to protect our economy, more specially our exports which are very vital for our development schemes, and we hope that nothing will be done by way of this Common Market scheme to come in the way of our exports.

Question: Mr Prime Minister, could you tell us what you think will be the real value of the Commonwealth as it exists today?

Jawaharlal Nehru: The real value is its extreme flexibility which enables people from the four corners of the earth to gather together in a friendly way to discuss matters frankly and yet be able to come to some broad general conclusions. I think this type of association, the new type—new I mean since the Commonwealth developed so—is a very good type and far better than the associations which limit the way of each country and that is why the Commonwealth has succeeded in spite of differing opinions. It is an extraordinarily good thing that people from America, Europe, from Asia and Africa, Australia come together with their different problems, different outlooks and express them frankly and yet come to more or less common [conclusions] successfully. It is because of its flexibility that it carries on successfully. Rigid things tend to break up when there are vital differences. So I think the Commonwealth does play an important part not only within itself but in the world.

---

28. At India House, 20 September 1962. Transcript issued by the MEA, External Publicity Division, Press Relations Section. "Answer" has been replaced by "Jawaharlal Nehru" throughout the document as reproduced here. NAI, MHA, File No. NII/119(20)/63, pp. 34-44.

    This version of the press conference has been checked against the transcript of the tape version available in NMML, JN Master File. The MEA version contains questions as well as answers given by Nehru; the transcript of the tape version contains only answers.

29. The Commonwealth Prime Ministers' Conference was held, 10-19 September 1962.

Question: Do you think the Commonwealth has a future after Britain joins the political union of Europe?

Jawaharlal Nehru: That will depend very much on the nature of that union. It is very vague. Nobody knows, at least I do not know, what it is likely to be. It may possibly conflict in some ways with the Commonwealth ideas and it may not.

Question: (Unintelligible).

Jawaharlal Nehru: I suppose so, that is the whole purpose of that paragraph. It is not merely the expression of a pious wish, but that attempts will be made to give effect to what that paragraph contains.

[Commonwealth and the European Common Market]

Question: Mr Prime Minister, you have expressed some anxiety that Britain's entry in the Common Market would worsen the prospects of disarmament. Would you say it is possible that Britain's entry into Europe would, on the contrary, bring the Commonwealth spirit of flexibility you mentioned into Europe and strengthen those elements in Europe which ... (unintelligible) between East and West and disarmament?

Jawaharlal Nehru: I did not exactly say that, that it would come in the way of disarmament but what I said was in a kind of a friendly way that no steps should be taken that might possibly add to the tension of Europe. It is quite possible, as you say, that the association of Britain into the European Community may lead to easing the tensions but all that depends on how it is done.

Question: May I ask a two-part question? The first part is, would you say the Commonwealth Conference has weakened or strengthened the interest of the people of the Commonwealth, and secondly, do you believe that as a result Britain and India are closer together in the understanding of the problems of the Commonwealth?

Jawaharlal Nehru: I don't know. I should not say that it has weakened the Commonwealth. It has indicated some possibilities which might, if they took place in the future, weaken it. It has weakened it at this stage. As for the other part, I do not know what to answer. You said whether Britain and India were nearer, was that your question? Nearer what?

Question: Nearer understanding on the problems of the Commonwealth.

Jawaharlal Nehru: I would not like to distinguish between the members of the Commonwealth. They all have their understanding of it. May be each one stresses some aspect of it more than the other.

Question: Would you say that the relations between, for example, Canada and India are closer because they are both members of the Commonwealth than they would be if one or the other was not?

Jawaharlal Nehru: Well, I think they are. Naturally this is due to many causes. Probably due to being fairly close than if they had not been members of the Commonwealth. But the Commonwealth gives various opportunities of coming together, knowing each other, and having this personal equation counts. Right from the beginning, since we came into the Commonwealth nearly twelve to fourteen years ago, we have had the most excellent relations with the Canadian Prime Ministers, whoever they might be, Mr Mackenzie King,[30] Mr Saint Laurent,[31] Mr Diefenbaker,[32] all of them, and we found that in many ways we agreed. In spite of some different outlook there was a good deal of agreement. And so our relations have been very close. If they had not been in the Commonwealth, there would not have been so many chances of meeting together, of being, well, I hope, of being close.

[France]

Question: What could you expect from your visit to Paris?

Jawaharlal Nehru: My visit to Paris was decided upon rather long ago which has no relation to the Common Market controversy. When it was decided that I was coming to London, it was suggested to me that I might go to Paris on a short visit, to which I gladly agreed. One reason, though not a major one, for agreement was that we had finally solved so many problems between France and India, for instance, problems of the French enclaves, Pondicherry, etc. You will remember that some time ago, some years ago, Pondicherry, etc. were de facto handed over to India, but de jure this had not been done. We waited five or six years and now that has been completed. And I was happy that one of the problems between our two countries has been finally settled in a peaceful and friendly way. Also, we are glad at the outcome in Algeria, and so we are going to France without any so-called problems or issues between us but just to meet

30. William Lyon Mackenzie King, 1935-1948.
31. Louis Saint Laurent, 1948-1957.
32. John Diefenbaker, 1957-1963.

President de Gaulle, and apart from thanking him for these matters naturally we shall have talks on other matters too.

[Portrait]

Question: Do you like that painting of you on the wall?

Jawaharlal Nehru: It is very difficult to judge a painting of oneself. One has to be partial.

[Trade Conference Proposal]

Question: Could you please tell us your opinion about the proposal by the Canadian Prime Minister for a larger trading conference and whether you feel that such a conference could produce any effective results?

Jawaharlal Nehru: Ever since this question came before us we decided to cultivate direct contacts with the Six and we sent one of our ablest Ambassadors for the purpose and he has been accredited to the Six since then.[33] So we have been in close contact with them apart from the UK Government. And so, I take it, have been many other Commonwealth countries. Whether it will serve any useful purpose for all of them together to discuss the matter with the Six, I rather doubt.

[ECM and Neo-Colonialism]

Question: Would you consider the membership of West Germany in the Common Market as a guarantee against the European policy of neo-colonialism?

Jawaharlal Nehru: Well, I do not know. First, that is the firm European policy. Certainly some countries like ours were a little anxious that the Common Market arrangements might lead to some extent to the neo-colonial policy of encouraging economics to produce raw materials and not recognized goods and offering more or less cheap markets to industrial nations. Well, we are still a little afraid that might happen. I do not myself see what the membership of Germany—how that affects it this way or that way.

---

33. K.B. Lall. "The Six" refers to the six original members of the EEC when it was established in 1957: France, Federal Republic of Germany, the Netherlands, Belgium, Luxemburg and Italy.

[German Peace Treaty]

Question: President Nasser, President Sukarno and Marshal Tito are not prepared to join a peace treaty with East Germany. Could you tell us something about the Indian attitude?

Jawaharlal Nehru: First of all, I know nothing about the reports you mentioned about Marshal Tito, President Nasser and others. I do not know. But it seems to me that the sooner this German problem is dealt with in a realistic way the better it will be. I think all of us realize that they are two states—the Federal Government of Germany and the East German Government—and the fact that they don't recognize each other, look at each other, brings an element of unreality into the situation. Some time or the other there is bound to be a peace treaty. What the conditions or the terms of it will be I cannot obviously say. So far as we are concerned, we of course have an Ambassador in Bonn. We have no diplomatic relations as such with East Germany, though we have consular relations.[34]

[China]

Question: Sir, could you say something about the situation on China border? There has been a report in a British weekly that the Chinese Government has made efforts to make an alliance with Sikkim, Bhutan and also mentioned Nagaland as one of the possible members of this group?

Jawaharlal Nehru: I do not know what the Chinese may have in mind. Nor have I heard of any efforts on their part in connection with Sikkim and Bhutan. Sikkim and Bhutan are closely connected with India. Bhutan is an independent country, subject to certain treaty relations with us in regard to foreign affairs. Sikkim is more closely allied to us. I remember in some of our correspondence with the Chinese Government, they recognized our special relations with Sikkim and Bhutan. That of course does not prevent them from not recognizing it or dealing with it, as if they have not recognized these relations, in future. As for Nagaland, I do not know whom you mean by Nagaland. There is a Government in Nagaland. Nagaland is an autonomous state of the Indian Union and is functioning fairly well. I do not know how, with whom, the Chinese Government

---

34. In fact, consular relations with East Germany did not exist at this time. However, East Germany maintained a Trade Mission in India; but India did not reciprocate this.

    For reactions in German Press to Nehru's statement on the German question, see appendix 66.

is supposed to deal in Nagaland, certainly not with the Government there, nor the majority of the people.

[Pakistan]

Question: I would like to know whether there is any possibility of solution of the Kashmir problem of any sort between India and Pakistan during our life time.

Jawaharlal Nehru: I cannot talk about this, about life time. Naturally our desire is to have cooperative and friendly relations with Pakistan. That is natural. We are neighbours. We have a great deal of a common past, culturally. We speak the same language. My own language is the same as that of Pakistan. In fact, in some ways, linguistically and otherwise, I am nearer to Pakistan than, let us say, to South India, where I do not understand the language. We have large numbers of families, half of them living in Pakistan, half in India. So everything, and geography—everything points to close relations. Unfortunately, after Independence and Partition, and more especially after the awful things that happened immediately after Partition, the killings and tremendous migrations, that embittered the relations. Also there is a basic fact which comes in the way, that is, our national outlook, which is Indian. We want India to be a secular state where persons of every religion have an equal position. We don't want to consider it as consisting of different nationalities based on different religions. Pakistan apparently has a different outlook. I don't agree to that theory. We agreed geographically and took the consent of the people concerned.

Now, the conflict, I may say so, in regard to Kashmir arises principally from these different approaches. They say that because Kashmir has a majority of Muslim population there, it must necessarily go to Pakistan. We not only do not agree to that, but we think if we agree to it, it would be extremely harmful both to India and to Pakistan. We have 50 million Muslims in India. If we proceed on the religious basis of division what happens to those 50 million Muslims and what happens to the eight or nine million Hindus in Pakistan? They become something less than citizens, looking to another country, bearing allegiance to another country and that would break our nationalist movement. It is not a matter of territory but it is a matter of enormous consequence to us that this unity, religious and other, is maintained on a secular basis and every religion has to be given a full chance to develop. That is the real controversy and the real conflict of opinion between India and Pakistan shows itself in various ways.

So far as Kashmir is concerned, which is, as you might know, an autonomous state of the Indian Union and, as such, apart from some common matters which the Central Government deals with, it decides its own fate. We have adult franchise there as elsewhere. We had three major elections and the elected people formed a Government there, Assembly and the Government. I do feel that the old bitterness that had arisen between India and Pakistan immediately after Partition has died down completely, so far as the people are concerned. Politically it may be kept up but not with the people; it may be, some time, kept up by the Press. But the people, they come and go in their thousands from India to Pakistan and Pakistan to India and have friendly relations.

Question: Have you discussed this with President Khan?[35]

Jawaharlal Nehru: No. We referred to some matters, but we did not discuss. For instance, there is the question of waters in the eastern side of India and East Pakistan, which our engineers have been considering for some time and President Ayub Khan said that we might consider the matter at the ministerial level, but it is certainly a complicated matter. For two years we had been collecting facts about it, and we are quite willing to consider it at the ministerial or any level.

[Meeting Harold Macmillan]

Question: Mr Diefenbaker said last night that he expected to see Mr Macmillan[36] before the final entry of Britain into the Common Market. Would you say something about that?

Jawaharlal Nehru: He expected to see whom?

Question: Mr Macmillan.

Jawaharlal Nehru: No doubt, if he expected, he would have probably to see him.

[Health]

Question: Mr Prime Minister, we read with joy yesterday in one of the newspapers that you have been examined medically and found "A-1." Will you please confirm that?

---

35. Ayub Khan, the President of Pakistan.
36. The Prime Minister of UK.

Jawaharlal Nehru: Normally a person does not require examination to feel that way. But to satisfy the ignorant it is sometimes done.[37]

[Vietnam and Laos]

Question: Could you say something about the recent agreement on Laos and how it is functioning?

Jawaharlal Nehru: I think it is functioning fairly well except for one big drawback, that is, there is no money left with the Commissions to carry on, both the Vietnam Commission and the Laos Commission. They are very hard up. We certainly in India can't give them large sums of money. It is for the members of the Geneva Conference—it is they who are really liable and primarily the two co-Chairmen, that is, the UK and USSR.[38] We go on spending and informing them of the position. All the countries are liable to help, that is, France and a number of other countries. But the Laotian Agreement, as far as I know, has been working thus far satisfactorily.

[MIG Planes from USSR]

Question: Mr Prime Minister, would you say something about the possible purchase of MIG planes in Russia?

Jawaharlal Nehru: Well, there is not much to say except it is a commercial transaction and if it is to our advantage we will go into it. There is no political element in it.

[UK and ECM]

Question: Mr Prime Minister, apart from the political aspects of the proposed British relationship with the Commonwealth [sic][39] about which we understand India is not very lukewarm, from the purely economic aspect

---

37. A statement issued from India House, on 20 September 1962, said:
    "The Prime Minister, Pandit Jawaharlal Nehru, during his stay in London had a complete check-up by Lord Evans, Queen's physician, and also by a leading specialist in kidney disorders.
    Both these eminent physicians are of the opinion that the Prime Minister has made a complete recovery after his recent illness and is in a good state of health.
    He has been advised to lead a normal life."
    National Herald, 21 September 1962, p. 1.
38. The Geneva Conference on Indo-China, 1954.
39. Probably should read "Common Market."

if Britain were not to go into the Common Market, is it your opinion that Britain could continue to provide a bigger market for Indian exports as she does today?

Jawaharlal Nehru: Certainly, I don't see why it should not. Why should England, UK, not do that, unless you hint at England's incapacity to do it in the future? All we ask is—now we are asking—is that in case Britain goes into the Common Market, till such time as the trade agreement is arrived at between the European Community, including Britain, and us, the present trade relations between India and Britain should continue. Obviously, one of the vital things of our economy now are the exports. If our exports are certainly cut down it will have a very harmful result and upset our Third Five Year Plan.

Question: Sir, in view of your apprehensions regarding the terms of British entry into Europe have you any alternative plan?

Jawaharlal Nehru: Alternative plan?

Question: Yes. In case your requirements are not met, have you any alternative plan?

Jawaharlal Nehru: I have no alternatives.

Question: (Unintelligible).

Jawaharlal Nehru: I think so. It should be hard to define what that useful function was. I would say our meeting together itself is a good thing, discussing various matters. It did not deal with anything specifically, you see. It was rather general. Therefore, it is difficult to catch hold of any particular thing which you might say did good in that respect, but it did do good, I think.
[World Trade Conference Proposal]

Question: Mr Prime Minister, how do you feel about your proposal to convene a world trade conference to discuss the problem of trade discrimination between all the countries of the world?

Jawaharlal Nehru: That is not my proposal; that is the proposal of the ECOSOC, the Economic and Social Council of the United Nations, and that has been approved in the ECOSOC by the great powers, the UK, the USA and the USSR and other powers there. And now this proposal is coming up before the present session of the United Nations. We are all in favour of it. I think everything is so inter-connected today that we should think in terms of world trade rather than separate closed areas of markets.

[UK and ECM]

Question: May I refer to my previous question regarding the Common Market. I think the point of my question was that great many people in this country feel that in the event Britain fails to join the Common Market, however willing she may be to continue to buy from the Commonwealth people, her rate of expansion will slow down and she will not continue to be economically wealthy enough to continue the present rate of her imports from the Common Market.

Jawaharlal Nehru: That is a matter of opinion because, on the other hand, if their tariff duties, say, against India in Britain [go up], naturally India's exports to England will go down. Equally, naturally, India's imports from England will go down. Naturally, we can't pay for them. So the result is that England will suffer to some extent by not being able to export things to India and to other countries so affected. So balance the two and you can come to your own conclusions what the result will be. I am not an expert economist to be able to give any definite opinion on that subject.

[Congo]

Question: As a result of the Prime Ministers' discussions has the UN plan for Congo a better chance of success now?

Jawaharlal Nehru: I should think so, slightly better. Because everyone there agreed that the UN proposal in regard to the Congo should be supported. Even Sir Roy Welensky[40] agreed. What more do you want?

[UK and ECM]

Question: Have you formed any impression or have any information to suggest what is the British time-table for ECM entry—is it the aim to get in by Christmas as has been suggested by somebody?

Jawaharlal Nehru: No. I don't know what the time-table is. But anyhow, after probably fairly lengthy discussions, that is, presumably if they come to an agreement, then they will have to go to their Parliament—that is a lengthy

---

40. Prime Minister of the Federation of Rhodesia and Nyasaland.

process—and get it confirmed by Parliament. I do not know how long all this will take.

Question: Would you expect to attend the conference in which Britain, India, Pakistan and Ceylon will be represented before final British committal to the European Common Market?

Jawaharlal Nehru: I don't know that there is any such proposal to have such a conference. If such a conference is held, we shall have to consider this. As I said, we are dealing with the Commonwealth and the Six; as well as the British representative there, that is, Mr Heath,[41] who goes there directly all the time. All our countries, Pakistan, India and Ceylon at Brussels and in London have continuous consultations and information. At what time it may become necessary for us to meet together I don't know.

Question: (Unintelligible).

Jawaharlal Nehru: No. As I said this a little while ago, there was a fear in the minds of many people that it might add to tensions in the cold war attitudes. Nothing has happened at the conference this way or that way.

[Nepal]

Question: Sir, the Nepalese Ambassador in London[42] keeps on saying that India is not doing enough to stop the Nepalese, who are in India, attacking the Nepalese Government. Have you any comments? He said yesterday that your statement, which you have made recently, is not correct.

Jawaharlal Nehru: I cannot carry on an argument with the Nepalese Ambassador through a Press Conference. But our attitude to Nepal has been throughout of not wanting to interfere. I may tell you that in all these years we have been helping Nepal very considerably in her development and even now there are various major schemes of development in Nepal for which we are financially responsible as well as technically. They have not been affected. There has been internal trouble in Nepal. It is none of our creation if there is trouble there; we don't create it. The only difficulty is that a number of Nepalese ex-Ministers and prominent personalities came away to India when the King dissolved

41. Edward Heath, British negotiator with the EEC.
42. Kali Prasad Upadhyaya, Nepalese Ambassador to the UK, 1961-1965.

Parliament and arrested the Prime Minister and others.[43] Now, these people in India carry out some kind of propaganda for the re-establishment of some kind of parliamentary institutions. So long as there is peaceful propaganda we do not interfere because everybody has a right to carry and express their opinion peacefully. But we do object to India being made the base of any kind of operations against Nepal by these people. We have a long border with Nepal—I do not know how long it is—and there has been free entry, free communications through Nepal and India and there are no check-posts, nothing. It is very difficult to protect that long border. So our attitude is that we do not encourage but they say we have encouraged or acquiesced in gun-running from India to Nepal by these Nepalese; we have not consciously. We have, in fact, arrested some people trying to do so. But it is not very difficult in a long and unprotected border for individuals to come in and out. Essentially it is Nepal's internal matter in which India cannot very well take any steps.

[India – Common Market Trade]

Question: Sir, the economic relations between India and the Common Market countries have improved very much in the last few years even from the point of view of trade, point of view of foreign investments in India. This has been faster than between England and India itself. Do you think that this trade can improve the situation between India and the problem of the Common Market?

Jawaharlal Nehru: India's trade with the Common Market countries has improved not always to our advantage. What I mean is, take Germany; it is very adverse to us. I mean to say we buy much more than we sell to Germany, in that sense. We buy capital goods, of course. We don't import, we hardly import luxury articles or any such things, but we have been importing machinery and capital goods from Germany and we want to reduce that adverse gap. I might say that in discussions with the representatives of the Six at Brussels, when India's position was explained to them fully they, I believe, showed a great deal of appreciation of it, and I hope our trade will increase.

[Ghana Visit]

Question: Mr Prime Minister, your coming visit to Ghana, whether it is well-timed?

---

43. In December 1960, Mahendra dismissed the Nepali Congress government in Nepal; most of the party leaders were imprisoned.

Jawaharlal Nehru: Well-timed? I am sorry. I have been thinking of going to Ghana for the last three or four years. I have been invited there repeatedly and normally I can only visit these countries when I come to London for the Commonwealth Prime Ministers' Conference. It is difficult to make separate journeys. It is difficult to leave India as a rule, but there is just a gap period now that Parliament is not sitting. So when it was decided to have a conference here, I suggested, I thought I might go to Nigeria and Ghana. There was no other attempt to time it except my own convenience.

Thank you.

326. In Paris: To UNESCO[44]

Mr Director-General,[45] Excellencies, Distinguished delegates,
I am deeply grateful to you for having invited me to address this distinguished Assembly and for the kind words you have spoken about India and me.[46] You have quoted something I said about UNESCO many years ago. That represents our thoughts still and we attach the greatest value to the purposes and the work of UNESCO. It represents something which is of deeper importance than the political approaches to our problems.

You have also referred, Sir, to the great effort we are making in India through our Five Year Plans to raise the standard of our people and we are thankful to UNESCO who are helping us in this great task.

In the preamble of UNESCO it is said that "since wars begin in the minds of men it is in the minds of men that the defences of peace must be constructed." The main object of the United Nations and of UNESCO is to put an end to wars and to establish a peaceful world. Even in a peaceful world conflicts of opinion may take place as well as other tensions. But the question is whether those conflicts and tensions can be resolved in a peaceful manner without resulting in violent conflict.

If there is a way to resolve them peacefully, then why should we not try that method now to resolve the tensions and conflicts of the present day world?

---

44. Speech, 21 September 1962. PIB.
45. René Maheu.
46. According to a report in the *National Herald* of 22 September 1962, René Maheu said "the human and financial investment India was making to develop basic research, to train scientists and teachers and to apply the result of scientific research to promotion of human welfare, was an example to all countries." He also described Nehru as an "example, a guide, and an inspiration for all those who care, above everything, for the dignity of man."

The UNESCO Preamble rightly referred to the minds of men which give rise to wars and conflicts. It is then the minds and hearts of men that have to be approached for mutual understanding, knowledge and appreciation of each other and through the proper kind of education. That is essential. But we have seen that education by itself does not necessarily lead to a conversion of minds towards peaceful purposes. Something more is necessary, new standards, new values, and perhaps a kind of spiritual background and a feeling of commonness of mankind.

That commonness of humanity is already being brought about by technological progress, but the minds of men have not grasped it or kept pace with technological progress. So, we see that science and technology which have brought so many benefits to the world and gradually tend to go towards the formation of One World, are also used for the manufacture of terrible weapons of mass destruction. At the base of it all is fear and hatred.

How then can we get rid of this fear and hatred and use modern scientific progress in the cause of peace and tolerance?

The world is full of variety and that is good, for if there was a dead uniformity it would be a poor place to live in. But variety does not mean that we should interfere with others and try to impose our will upon them. We must recognize the right of other people to live their own life and be tolerant of differences and of those who do not agree with us.

The world is changing rapidly, but our minds often remain in the same ruts even though the old context has changed. There is the great conflict between the capitalist structure of society and the communist. Yet, every thinker knows that capitalism has changed its face in many ways and is continually changing. So also communism is developing into a new direction. In a sense it may be said that there is a certain lessening of the gap between them.

But even so, the old slogans continue to befog our minds and produce fear and hatred. How can we get out of these ruts of thought and look at the world without prejudice and fear?

During the terrible days of the last world war, my great leader, Mahatma Gandhi, said: Let us look at the world with clear eyes and not with bloodshot eyes. It is difficult to do so when we are full of passions and prejudice and even more difficult when fear oppresses us, for fear is a bad companion.

Strenuous efforts are being made to bring about disarmament all over the world and there is no greater need today than disarmament. If we succeed in that, these fears will undoubtedly lessen and enable us to think straight and more clearly. But disarmament itself will come when these fears are less. How then are we to get out of this vicious circle? Perhaps step by step we may advance towards our goal, each step creating conditions for the next step.

We in India do not pretend to know the answer to these questions and do not presume to tell others what they should do. But men of my generation in India have had a unique experience. We achieved freedom of a great and militarily weak country against a powerful empire by peaceful methods and without shedding blood. That was a unique example in human history and it was largely due to the leadership and example of Gandhi. Perhaps also to something deep in the spirit of India which fitted in with Gandhi's teaching. In the main that teaching was always to think of the means and not merely of the ends, for means fashion the ends. If the means are right, then the ends will also be right and will not have evil consequences trailing behind them.

We did not fully understand Gandhi; we could not do all that he told us and we failed him in many respects. But we have felt the warm glow of his presence and have had the joy of working under his leadership for a great cause through methods and means which seemed to us to be right. We were trained to cast out fear and hatred and not to wish ill to anyone. We did not come up to his expectations but still the change he brought among millions of his people was an amazing one.

We in India, as in many other countries of Asia and Africa, are trying to develop ourselves so as to put an end to our poverty and raise the standards of hundreds of millions of our people, ultimately aiming at the good life for all. This cannot be done, we think, without the help of science and modern techniques. The problem before us is whether in adopting the methods and techniques of science we might not create a society full of internal conflict and the urge for power which brings it into conflict with other groups. Can we succeed in bringing about a synthesis of modern science with something of the spiritual background which has ennobled life throughout the ages? Without science and modern technology we cannot better our lot or indeed even maintain our freedom, but without a spiritual background also the minds of men turn into wrong directions and conflicts occur resulting in great destruction and the degradation of men.

The UNESCO has set the right ideal before it to try to turn the minds of men and the way it is trying to do so is not the direct method of facing our many problems and conflicts but the indirect way of creating appreciation and understanding of art and culture. Presumably this is a surer method of dealing with these problems than the direct political method, though of course both methods have to be tried. In any event it is of the utmost importance that the purposes and objectives of the UNESCO should be remembered and we should always also remember that wars and conflicts begin in the minds of men and peace therefore has to be established there.

In the measure that UNESCO succeeds in this high endeavour will it help in the establishment of peace and rid humanity of the danger of war, and all the fears that encompass it.

I would again like to thank you, Mr Director-General, and the distinguished delegates of this great organization for the honour they have done to me by inviting me to address them. In a world which has many and ever-lengthening dark shadows, rays of light come out of this peaceful approach to men's minds. However great the darkness may be, the light remains and will ultimately pierce the gloom.

327. To René Maheu: On UNESCO Visit[47]

September 24, 1962

Dear Mr Director General,

I am happy to receive your letter of the 21st September. Thank you also for the albums and slides which you have sent me.

It was great pleasure to me to visit the headquarters of the great organisation of which you are the head and which, I think, is doing great good to the world. I hope I expressed adequately my appreciation of UNESCO when I had the privilege of addressing your members and delegates.[48]

Yours sincerely,
Jawaharlal Nehru

328. To Cyril Clemens: Article and Cartoon on Foreign Policy[49]

25th September, 1962

Dear Clemens,

Thank you for your letter of the 17th September which has reached me here at Lagos in Nigeria where I have come for a few days.

---

47. Letter to the Acting Director-General of UNESCO, Place de Fontenoy, Paris. Sent from Lagos House, Lagos, Nigeria. Also available in the JN Collection. PMO, File No. 42(7)/56-71-PMS, Vol. I, Sr. No. 69-A.
48. See item 326.
49. Letter to Editor-in-charge, *Mark Twain Journal*, Kirkwood 22, Missouri, USA. Sent from Lagos, Nigeria.

The article that you have sent me and the cartoon is, of course, completely wrong and based on some assumptions which are wholly untrue. To begin with, it is not true that I did not condemn the suppression of the people of Hungary by the Soviet Government.[50]

I do not think that our policy of being unallied with power blocs is wrong. The fact that the Chinese have misbehaved does not make our policy wrong. We shall take all possible steps to meet the Chinese aggression.

Yours sincerely,
[Jawaharlal Nehru]

329. In Cairo: Press Conference[51]

Question: ... of the *Daily Telegraph*, London. Mr Prime Minister, what would you say is the limit in the Indian-Chinese dispute which if exceeded India would fight China?

Jawaharlal Nehru: Well, there has been Chinese intrusion into Indian territory at various places, latest in the North East Frontier over the mountains and there have been a number of incidents. They have been relatively small incidents thus far where our patrols have come into conflict with their patrols.

Question: Noel Hudson, Reuters. Could you tell us, Sir, whether you discussed the possibility with President Nasser of holding the second Bandung Conference and if you did consider this matter, do you personally think that this is an appropriate time to convene such a meeting?

Jawaharlal Nehru: I did not discuss it at any length but it was mentioned in the course of our talk.[52] We in India had felt that it would be better to postpone it to a more favourable occasion.

---

50. For Nehru's views on the suppression by the USSR of the Hungarian uprising of October-November 1956, see sections on Hungary in SWJN/SS/35-36 and 39; see also SWJN/SS/68/item 357.
51. At Kubbeh Palace, 30 September 1962. NMML, AIR Tapes, TS No. 8430, NM No. 1658. This transcript has been checked against the text of the press conference released by the PIB on 20 October 1962.
52. Nehru had a two hour talk with Nasser in Cairo on the morning of 30 September 1962.

Question: *Daily Telegraph*. If the United Kingdom joins the Common Market without meeting India's requirements as laid down by Prime Minister Nehru at the recent Commonwealth Conference in London, would India leave the British Commonwealth?

Jawaharlal Nehru: That is a hypothetical question. As far as I can see, that will not be an occasion for our leaving it. It depends on other factors. But I have every hope that either through the British Government or directly in our dealing with the Six, our requirements will be met, our exports requirements, that is; because exports for us are highly important and vital and we shall suffer a great deal of harm if they are suddenly kept down.

Question: Mr Anker, Germany, (Duet). Mr Prime Minister, would India participate in new Bandung Conference if China is invited too.

Jawaharlal Nehru: I have just said in answer to another question that we do not think a Bandung conference at the present stage would be advisable, and it should be postponed. But our attendance on it would be governed not by China being invited or not; other factors will come in.

Question: Ba Wazir, correspondent of the Indonesian News Agency. Will you please explain for what reason do you consider this time not favourable for another Bandung conference?

Jawaharlal Nehru: It is rather difficult for me to go into all these questions at a press conference. But most of our countries have got difficult problems to face and even practically it is not easy for many of them, any important people from any country to attend it, to leave their countries.

Question: Rabat Hanifa of *Al Ahram* newspaper. What are the subjects that have been discussed between your Excellency and President Nasser?

Jawaharlal Nehru: We had no special subjects to discuss but as I had met him after a year or so it was a *tour d'horizon*. We discussed much that has happened in the past year. We have no problems with the United Arab Republic, between the United Arab Republic and India. So we discussed other peoples' problems. [Laughter].

Question: Could you give us some idea of your talks with the Yemeni Foreign Minister?[53]

53. Mohsen Ahmed el Eini.

Jawaharlal Nehru: He has just seen me for about ten minutes or less. I had learnt he desired to see me and I said he could. He told me about developments in Yemen and my reply to him was that it is for the people of Yemen to decide what they thought fit.[54] It is not for me to advise them. And so far as the question of possible recognition went, that naturally would have to be considered by us carefully before we came to a decision. We are not in touch with Yemen. We do not know much about it. We have to consider it fully before we could give any answer.[55]

> Question: Do you believe, Sir, that the continuous flow of arms from the United States and other countries to Israel would increase tension in the Middle East?

Jawaharlal Nehru: Are you asking me: do I think it will increase tension? Well, I suppose it will. Arms do increase tension wherever they go.

> Question: What other matters have been discussed between your Excellency and President Nasser besides the fact that there is no problem to discuss?

Jawaharlal Nehru: I have just answered it. It was a general survey of the world situation as it is. President Nasser was good enough to give me his views about events, especially in the Middle East and Africa and I told him something of what we were doing in India.

> Question: George McGraw of the Associated Press. In the present session of the United Nations General Assembly would India back a move to compel the erring members to abide by The Hague Court decision to pay the special and general assessments?

Jawaharlal Nehru: I cannot say in what form the matter will come up and what India's reaction to the particular resolution might be. I do not know. I do hope that all the members will agree to pay what is due from them but I do not know how one compels them without possibly creating greater conflicts. This matter should be more one of friendly approach. I do not want it to become another issue in the cold war.

54. A few days after the death of Ahmad bin Yahya Hamidaddin, the King of Yemen, on 19 September 1962, the country was plunged into civil war between the royalists and the republicans. Egypt supported the republicans.
55. The question by the Yemeni Foreign Minister and Nehru's answer to it are not included in the PIB release.

Question: Mr Prime Minister, I understand that the Indian government is going to place a ban on the sale and public consumption of alcoholic drinks. Is this true? And if it is, do you envisage bootlegging on the same scale as the bootlegging in America during the prohibition era?

Jawaharlal Nehru: Prohibition as policy, general policy, was adopted by us as soon as we became independent, in fact before independence. But it has been applied gradually in India in some cities, in some areas it has been applied, in others it was not. It may be extended, it is gradually being extended. As for bootlegging, in some cities there has been some bootlegging unfortunately.[56]

Question: Do you think that what happened during the Asian Games in Jakarta[57] has caused any change in the good relations between your country and Indonesia?

Jawaharlal Nehru: Well, our relations with Jakarta are more basic and fundamental and should not be affected by incidents of this kind. But it is true they caused a great deal of grief in India. The Government of India had nothing to do with those incidents there.

Question: Sir, you had seen the South African leaders...

Jawaharlal Nehru: Nobody is saying—we had asked—the name and the name of the paper and agency.

Question: Harish Chandola, *Indian Express*. You had seen the South African leaders in London. Do you think, Sir, that India is thinking of asking the UN for sanctions against South Africa because of the racial policy, in this session of the United Nations?

Jawaharlal Nehru: I did meet Indian and African leaders from South Africa; not the representatives of the government, but those who were opposed to the present government. They told me of conditions there. We did not discuss any special policy to be pursued in the United Nations.

Question: May I ask a personal question, Mr Prime Minister? I am [from the] *Daily Telegraph*. You look 20 years and you act 20 years younger than most men of your age. How do you manage it? Is there a secret behind it?

56. The question on prohibition and Nehru's answer to it are not included in the PIB release.
57. For the Jakarta incidents, see item 438.

Jawaharlal Nehru: I do not worry much. [Laughter]. Have you exhausted the questions?

Question: Rabat Hanifa of *Al Ahram*. Do you believe, Sir, that the European Common Market would have any adverse effect on the developing countries of Asia and Africa?

Jawaharlal Nehru: Well, it is because there is a possibility of that, we pointed out those possible adverse effects in these discussions in London. At the same time you might have seen that there are, in the communiqué issued by the conference, they have accepted the principle of helping the developing countries. I cannot say what will happen, I cannot say even on what terms ultimately these decisions will happen, I cannot say even on what terms ultimately these decisions will be made and what their effect will be.

Question: Is there any alternative to the European Common Market, by way of operation among the developing countries?

Jawaharlal Nehru: The question is whether the United Kingdom should join it or not, not India joining it. We are not joining it. And the alternative is for the United Kingdom to consider it, if at all. If you are referring to any other countries, any Asian countries or Asia-African countries forming a Common Market, that is always open to them. It is not an alternative to the United Kingdom joining it. That stands by itself. But in any event, we should always try to develop trade and commercial contacts between our countries in Asia and Africa. That stands by itself, whether anybody joins the Common Market or not, and I have no doubt these will develop.

Question: Mr Prime Minister, has the Yemeni Foreign Minister who is at present in Cairo contacted you to request that your government recognize the new Yemeni Republic and if he has not and if such a request is forthcoming, will the Indian Government view such request with sympathy?

Jawaharlal Nehru: I just said that he saw me for about six or seven minutes or ten minutes, just immediately before this Press Conference. He told me his version of what had happened in Yemen and asked for our sympathy. But he himself realized that we could not suddenly give him any answer. We had to consider it.

Question: He asked for sympathy alone or recognition as well?

Jawaharlal Nehru: Well, naturally, I think he mentioned the word recognition also, but he added that he realized that most countries would take their time over it.

Question: James Pectom, *Business Magazine*. Did you discuss any specific guarantee that the Common Market might give to India or Pakistan should Britain join the Common Market?

Jawaharlal Nehru: Discuss with whom?

Question: In London, at the …

Jawaharlal Nehru: It is not a question of guarantees. In this matter India, Pakistan and Ceylon have the same interests and we put forward our case. Broadly, it was this, that our exports to the United Kingdom market should not be affected, as they would be if a heavy duty is put on. They are duty free, many of them at present, and we urged that they should be exempted from duty at least for a fairly considerable period, at least till some kind of a trade arrangement is arrived at with the Six, between India, Pakistan and Ceylon and six countries of the European Community. And there were of course separate subjects, separate commodities which are affected. At present tea is the only major item which they have decided to exempt from any duty. There are several other things that affect us considerably. After all it is not enough for us merely to keep the existing conditions going but to increase our exports and this is to the interest of all countries, including the advanced industrial countries because firstly, it is only through exports that we can pay for imports. If exports go down imports will go down. Secondly, any progress in the level of living in these countries will be translated in greater consumption and a vast market. Imagine what a market there is in India if people can buy.[58]

Question: The Common Market countries are thinking of giving guarantees and concessions to African countries but they feel that the Indian and Pakistan industrial exports, such as textiles, can stay more or less on their own feet, and do not need these concessions. Do you have any comments to make on that?

---

58. This set of questions and answers on ECM guarantees to India or Pakistan on Britain joining the ECM is not included in the PIB version.

Jawaharlal Nehru: I do not know. I shall be very glad if they give guarantee to the African countries. I should like the African countries to progress. That is not the impression I gathered about India and Pakistan from them.

Question: News Agency of the German Democratic Republic. Please, Sir, what is your opinion about the present situation in Germany and especially in Berlin?

Jawaharlal Nehru: It is much too complicated for me to answer or even wholly to understand. It is one of the major points at issue today not only in Europe but in the world. I did say somewhere else, I do not know if I was wholly understood, I had said that the questions in Germany should be considered realistically and I suggested—I did not suggest that about recognition of one country by another—but I said that whether you recognize them or not one should deal with them as facts. I mean to say, Berlin, East Germany, there they are, there are constantly problems arising between them and I thought they must be dealt with directly whether you recognize them or not. In fact, they have been in the past dealt with under some cover or something or the other. I was not referring to recognition as such. That is a matter for the countries concerned to do.[59]

Question: If the question is not very vague, could we know your impressions about your present African tour?

Jawaharlal Nehru: African tour? Well, the African tour—I am excluding Egypt—consisted of my visit to Nigeria only. This was my first visit to any country in Africa south of the Sahara, and I attach a great deal to the new developments in Africa and wish them well. So I was interested to see and I have got some personal impressions. And one thing is obvious, that Africa today is bubbling all over with a certain vitality and I am sure that it will make progress and I am sure also that they will have many difficulties in their way, as all of us have.

Correspondent: Well, Sir, we know that you have other appointments. Thank you very much for giving us so much of your time.

Jawaharlal Nehru: Thank you. I might tell you one thing, not of international importance but it is very important for me. We have had terrible floods in India—I have just been reading reports from India—the biggest floods that we

59. The question and answer on the German situation is not included in the PIB version.

have had over a great part of India, vast numbers of villages have been washed away, food crops ruined in many areas, and so on, big disaster. So as soon as I go back that will be the first thing confronting me. One will have to deal with it. One can deal with it only in trying to help those who have suffered. Thank you.

Correspondent: Thank you very much.

(b) Disarmament

330. For the *Our Generation Against Nuclear War*[60]

I have read with pleasure some of the articles in *Our Generation Against Nuclear War*. I should like to congratulate those who are responsible for bringing out this quarterly.[61] Most people are, I suppose, fully against nuclear war. Some of them express themselves strongly about it. Having done that, there appears to be little more that a person can do. Events march on to some dreadful climax.

Yet I am convinced that the ever-widening circle of protests that the people make is not wasted and creates some effect even on the hardened people who control the destinies of different nations. But fear and hatred appear to be stronger forces than logic, common sense and tolerance. No statesman wants war because they realise that they cannot achieve any good from a war and yet the whole vicious circle goes on and the disarmament conferences are usually meant to put the other party in the wrong, and not to seek a real solution. In spite of this I do believe that public opinion in the world is creating a horror of nuclear war and it will be difficult to ignore this. I am even optimistic enough to think that the disarmament conference in Geneva[62] might yield some successful result, though I fear it will take some time.

Meanwhile we live on the brink, and as has often been pointed out, some unfortunate mistake may hurl us into the abyss. Therefore, it is necessary to carry on a crusade against a nuclear war. I like the quarterly journal *Our Generation Against Nuclear War* because it is conducted in this crusading spirit and I am

---

60. Message, 27 July 1962, sent from Anand Bhavan, Allahabad, to O.N. Khanna, c/o Systems Department, Esso Standard Eastern, Bombay-1. PMO, File No. 9/2/62-PMP, Vol. V, Sr. No. 47-A. Also available in the JN Collection.
61. See item 331.
62. The UN sponsored Eighteen-Nation Committee on Disarmament under the joint chairmanship of the US and the USSR.

sure it will impress the many people who read it and make them also join in this crusade.

Any major war will lead to nuclear war. It is dangerous to think that a major war can now be fought without the use of nuclear weapons. Any minor war, in the existing circumstances, may well lead to a major war. Thus the only result to aim at is to put an end to war itself. That involves to a large extent, a change in human mentality. I suppose that will come sometime or the other if, in the meantime, we are not going to be overwhelmed by war itself. But even before that spiritual change comes into man we can greatly reduce the possibility of war and especially nuclear war by disarmament. Such disarmament, if it is to be really effective, must be complete or almost so. Any big step towards disarmament will lessen the tensions that exist in the world and will create a much better atmosphere for the consideration of our major problems. War will solve no problems.

I wish all success to the crusade that is being carried on by the sponsors of *Our Generation Against Nuclear War*.

331. To O.N. Khanna: On *Our Generation Against Nuclear War*[63]

July 27, 1962

Dear Shri Khanna,

I have seen your letter of July 5 together with the copies of *Our Generation Against Nuclear War*. I have looked through these copies with some interest and I congratulate those who have brought them out and are thus carrying on a worthy crusade against nuclear war.

You ask me for an article. I am sorry I am unable to contribute it nor can I write something worthwhile as a suitable preface but I am writing a kind of a message which you can use if you like.[64] I am returning to you the two copies of the quarterly journal *Our Generation Against Nuclear War*.

Yours sincerely,
J. Nehru

---

63. Letter to O.N. Khanna, c/o Systems Department, Esso Standard Eastern, Bombay-1. Sent from Anand Bhavan, Allahabad. PMO, File No. 9/2/62-PMP, Vol. V, Sr. No. 48-A. Also available in the JN Collection.
64. Text of message, item 330.

332. To A.N. Bhat: Cartoons on Nuclear Weapons[65]

July 28, 1962

Dear Shri Bhat,

I have your letter of 23rd July. I am glad you have made effective cartoons on the subject of nuclear arms. I am afraid, I am not in a position to suggest what you can do with them in India. You might perhaps write to the Secretary of the Nuclear Committee[66] formed recently and find out what he can suggest. The Government of India is not carrying on any direct publicity in this matter.

I am returning to you Bertrand Russell's letter as well as his Secretary's note.

Yours sincerely,
[Jawaharlal Nehru]

333. To Arthur W. Erickson: World Bodies on Nuclear War[67]

August 5, 1962

Dear Mr Erickson,

Thank you for your letter of July 29th. I entirely agree with you that nuclear war, and indeed all war, must be avoided. I do not know if the World Court is in a position to issue injunctions of this kind. But the United Nations General Assembly can certainly express itself on those lines. I hope the next Assembly will take some such step.

Yours sincerely,
[Jawaharlal Nehru]

---

65. Letter to an artist; address: 3/34F Narayan Niwas, P.V. Road, Parel, Bombay-12. Sent from Raj Bhavan, Calcutta.
66. It is not clear which Nuclear Committee or Secretary Nehru is referring to. The Nuclear Committee probably relates to the Anti-Nuclear Conference in June 1962. See SWJN/ SS/77/section External Affairs, subsection Anti-Nuclear Conference.
67. Letter; address: 1860 Colonia Place, Camarillo, California, USA.

334. In the Rajya Sabha: Anti-Nuclear Arms Convention in Delhi[68]

Will the Prime Minister be pleased to state:[69]

(a) whether it is a fact that the Anti-Nuclear Arms Convention, which was held in Delhi in the month of June last, passed a resolution in regard to sending some eminent men to urge the big powers like the Union of Soviet Socialist Republics, United States of America, France and United Kingdom to stop the nuclear tests as well as the manufacture of atomic weapons; and

(b) if the answer to part (a) above be in the affirmative, whether any steps are being taken by Government to give effect to that resolution and if so, what?

Jawaharlal Nehru: (a) and (b) Yes, Sir, the final statement issued by the Anti-Nuclear Arms Convention, organised by the Gandhi Peace Foundation, in New Delhi last June, did contain such a suggestion, but it was supposed to be followed up by the organisers of the Convention. No action by the Government of India in this particular context was called for.[70]

335. To Rakusei Pen Friend Club: Nuclear Weapons Bad[71]

August 18, 1962

Dear friends,

I have received your letter. We in India think that nuclear weapons are thoroughly bad and should never be produced or used. We are against all testing of nuclear bombs. I hope that some agreement to stop these tests and to have complete disarmament will be arrived at.

Yours sincerely,
[Jawaharlal Nehru]

---

68. Written answers, 8 August 1962. *Rajya Sabha Debates*, Vol. 40, Nos. 1-8, 6 to 16 August 1962, cols 672-73.
69. Question by Nawab Singh Chauhan, Congress.
70. See items 336-338, and SWJN/SS/77/section External Affairs, subsection Anti-Nuclear Arms Convention.
71. Letter; address: 10 Komatsubara-Minami-Cho, Kitaku, Kyoto.

336. Anti-Nuclear Arms Convention Visits Abroad[72]

You will remember that at the Anti-Nuclear Arms Convention held about two months ago in Delhi, it was decided to send a deputation to the countries producing nuclear arms to convey to them the earnest request of our Convention to stop nuclear tests as well as the use and production of nuclear arms. Soon after the Convention, a committee was formed to take such action as might be feasible to give effect to the various resolutions of the Convention. This committee was, to begin with, rather against the sending of any deputation as suggested.[73]

Somewhat later the committee considered this matter afresh and felt that they should carry out the direction of the Convention in regard to the deputation. They decided to send two separate deputations, one to Washington, London and Paris, and the other to Moscow, the two deputations to go at about the same time. It was also then thought necessary to send the first delegation to Geneva where the Disarmament Committee was meeting. As the Geneva Disarmament Committee is going to adjourn for two months or so soon, this question does not arise now.[74]

Final arrangements as to who should go have not been made yet, but I understand that it is proposed to send a deputation consisting of Shri R.R. Diwakar,[75] President of the Convention, Shri Rajagopalachari[76] and Shri B. Shiva Rao[77] to Washington, London and Paris. It is not yet certain as to whether Shri Rajagopalachari will consent to go. This would probably be known in the course of the next two or three days.

The second deputation which will go to Moscow will probably consist of Shri U.N. Dhebar[78] and Shri Ramachandran, Secretary of the Gandhi Peace Foundation.

The deputation which will go to the USA and some other places will probably go direct to Washington first, spending a day en route in London for

---

72. Note, 25 August 1962, for R.K. Nehru, the Secretary-General, and M.J. Desai, the Foreign Secretary, at the MEA.
73. See item 334. See also SWJN/SS/77/section External Affairs, subsection Anti-Nuclear Arms Convention.
74. The Eighteen-Nation Disarmament Committee began its deliberations on 14 March 1962; it had 431 meetings until 26 August 1969, when it was reconstituted as the Conference of the Committee on Disarmament.
75. Chairman of the Gandhi Peace Foundation.
76. Leader of the Swatantra Party.
77. Journalist, author and former member of the Lok Sabha and the Rajya Sabha.
78. Former President of the Congress Party.

rest. From Washington it will go to New York where the deputation will meet the Secretary-General of the UN[79] as well as perhaps some leading representatives of the nuclear powers. Thereafter it will return to London and spend a few days there. They may also go to Paris before returning to India.

They want the time of visit to the USA to fit in with the meeting of the General Assembly of the UN. Thus, they will probably go to Washington etc. about the middle of September.

The deputation to Moscow will also go about the same time.

Both these deputations will get into touch with the respective Ambassadors here as soon as they finalise their programme.

We should inform our Ambassadors in Washington, Moscow and Paris and our High Commissioner in London about these visits and ask them to give every help to the members of these deputations in arranging interviews and in other ways.

Although the names have not been finalised, it is highly likely that the two deputations will go about the middle of September. I suggest that you might inform our Ambassadors and High Commissioner about this proposed visit. As soon as arrangements have been finalised, I shall let you know. Probably someone on behalf of the deputations will visit the External Affairs Ministry.[80]

In case Shri Rajagopalachari joins the deputation, I think he should be given a diplomatic passport.

337. Anti-Nuclear Arms Convention Delegations[81]

I have already spoken to you about the two delegations that the Gandhi Peace Foundation or the Anti-Nuclear Arms Convention, which was held under the sponsorship of the Gandhi Peace Foundation, are sending, one to the USSR and the other to the USA, UK and France.[82] I enclose a letter I have received from the Chairman of the Gandhi Peace Foundation[83] giving some particulars about these delegations. I hope you have written to our Ambassadors on this subject and asked them to give every assistance.

---

79. U Thant was the Acting Secretary-General; he was elected Secretary-General on 30 November 1962.
80. See items 337-338.
81. Note, 31 August 1962, to MEA officials.
82. See item 336.
83. R.R. Diwakar.

2.   The Gandhi Peace Foundation has already approached the Ambassadors and the High Commissioner concerned of these countries. Copies of their letters to them are enclosed.

3.   I have asked Shri Diwakar to remain in touch with the External Affairs Ministry and to give them all the necessary information.[84]

338.   To R.R. Diwakar: Anti-Nuclear Arms Convention Delegations[85]

August 31, 1962

My dear Diwakar,

I have your letter of 31st August with its enclosures. We shall give all the help we can to the two delegations that you are sending, one to Moscow and the other to the USA, UK and France. We have already sent letters to our Ambassadors concerned. We shall again write to convey to them such information as you may send us.[86]

I would suggest that some one on your behalf could visit the External Affairs Ministry and discuss the details of these visits.

I am sure that our Ambassadors will give every assistance to the delegations.

Yours sincerely,
[Jawaharlal Nehru]

339.   To C. Rajagopalachari: Against Nuclear Arms[87]

September 1, 1962

My dear Rajaji,

I have your telegram. I am glad that you have agreed to go in the delegation to Washington, London and France. Although we may differ in many matters, in regard to nuclear tests and indeed nuclear arms altogether, I believe we hold the same opinion. It will be a great thing if this infernal weapon is no longer produced. I think, however, that this by itself, although very important, will not finally put an end to the dangers that threaten the world. Only large-scale and

---

84.   See item 338.
85.   Letter to the Chairman of the Gandhi Peace Foundation.
86.   See items 336-337.
87.   Letter to leader of the Swatantra Party; address: 60 Bazullah Road, Madras 17. Copied to R.R. Diwakar, Chairman of the Gandhi Peace Foundation.

general disarmament will achieve that. But the fears and suspicions of countries are so great that they hesitate to take this step lest they might be weakened in meeting some crisis. I am sure that the general sentiment, and it is a growing one, is in favour not only of putting an end to nuclear tests but also to bring about disarmament. I have no doubt that this feeling is widely prevalent in the Soviet Union, in the United States of America and in the United Kingdom. I hope and believe that it will produce some effective result in the future. But the Great Powers have got into such a tangle that it will take some time, I fear, for them to get out of it.

Our general policy has been in regard to disarmament to encourage the two principal powers concerned, i.e. the USA and the USSR, to arrive at agreements. If they do so, I have little doubt that this will go through with others also.

Our representatives do not try to push themselves too much to the front in these discussions and abstain from putting forward any rigid proposals.

Your visit to these countries and your powerful advocacy for these causes which all of us hold in common will, I have no doubt, do good. I cannot say that this will solve a very difficult problem but it will help in creating a mentality which may lead to a solution.

We have instructed our Ambassadors in the countries concerned to give you every help and to arrange such interviews as you wish to have. I understand that you will be going to Washington first after a brief halt in London for rest. Our Ambassador in Washington is Brij Kumar Nehru. He has done very good work there and gets on well with the President and the administration generally.

In London, our High Commissioner is M.C. Chagla who will, I have no doubt, give you every kind of assistance. I am myself going to London for the Commonwealth Prime Ministers' Conference in just a week's time. I shall speak to Chagla more then about your visit.

I may pay a brief visit for a day or two to France also. Our Ambassador in Paris is Ali Yavar Jung who is a good man and will be helpful. Indeed, wherever you go, you will be welcomed by our Ambassadors and given every kind of assistance that is possible for them.

In the United Nations, our Permanent Representative is a senior Ambassador, B.N. Chakravarty. He will, I have no doubt, arrange interviews for you with the Acting Secretary-General[88] and others there.

I hope you will look after yourself during these long journeys and succeed in achieving your objective, if not wholly, to a substantial extent.

Yours affectionately,
Jawaharlal Nehru

88. U Thant.

340. To K.S. Vaitha: One World Idea Good but not Practical[89]

September 19, 1962

Dear Shri Vaitha,

I have your letter of the 15th September. I am afraid it may not be possible for me to accept your proposal to address a meeting in Madras on behalf of the World Association of World Federalists. I have every sympathy for the idea of one world. But I think that the approach made by various organisations that sponsor this idea is not very practicable. All that can be said for it is that it is good to do some propaganda in that behalf. The first problem before us is that of disarmament which will reduce the fears that corrupt the world.

Yours sincerely,
[Jawaharlal Nehru]

341. To John Grigg: Friendly Approach in Disarmament[90]

September 19, 1962

My dear Lord Altrincham,

Your letter of the 18th September.

I had said at the meeting that a friendly approach always creates a good impression on the other party. That, I think, is perfectly true. It may be, however, that the friendly approach may not go far enough to bring about any results. It may also be that it might be mistaken for weakness. Nevertheless, a friendly approach should always help. Or to put it negatively, an unfriendly approach will lead to wrong results.

There is no reason why a friendly approach should be from weakness. Nor have I suggested that the Western Powers should disarm unilaterally. Disarmament has to be on both sides so as not to give an advantage to any one side. Of course, the Russians will not disarm if the Chinese do not do so, nor will presumably other powers. Therefore, disarmament must include China. You are quite right in saying that India is not disbanding her armed forces because of various threats to her integrity. We are not pacifists and even though some

89. Letter to the Secretary of the World Association of World Federalists, 124 Rama Krishna Math Road, Madras 4. Sent from London.
90. Letter to the 2nd Baron Altrincham, 1924-2001, British journalist and politician; address: 32 Dartmouth Row, London, SE 10. Sent from London.

of us felt inclined that way, we could not in a democratic structure carry our people with us. There are some groups in India who talk about our disarming unilaterally, but I do not think they have much influence.

I do not think there is very much difference between the Russians misbehaving in Hungary and Mussolini being nasty to the Ethiopians. Both have to be condemned. Yet there is some little difference. Russia, at the time of the Hungarian tragedy, was afraid, I think, to the Suez affair leading to a world war and they did not want to lose any advantage in case of such a war. Hungary turning against them, in their opinion, would have been harmful to them in case of a war and possibly would have turned against them. Therefore, there was an element of self-defence in the action they took, although this action was bad. There was no such element in Mussolini attacking and bombing the Ethiopians.

In judging of Russian attitudes, we cannot attach too much importance to individuals, although individuals count and Khrushchev counts very much in Russia. I think however that it is to the advantage of the Soviet Union to have peace and I am convinced that there is an overwhelming desire for peace in the Soviet Union. If, in these circumstances, friendly approaches are made not through weakness, I feel that the reaction will be good. Khrushchev struck me as, in spite of his toughness, being rather emotional and very responsive to such approaches. But I entirely agree that no country can take obvious risks. Anyhow, risks have to be taken whatever steps we take or do not take. But an attempt should be made to minimise those risks.

Yours sincerely,
[Jawaharlal Nehru]

(c) USA

342. To Roy A. Lucier: Explaining National and World Views[91]

July 26, 1962

Dear Mr Lucier,

Thank you for your letter of 13th July which I have read with some interest. It is a little difficult for me in the course of a letter to deal fully with our world

---

91. Letter; address: 64 Kirkland Street, Cambridge 38, Massachusetts, USA. Sent from Anand Bhavan, Allahabad.

outlook as well as national outlook. These are, of course, the products of our past experience.

You will remember that my generation has been trained, apart from our past traditions, by Mr Gandhi and his great movements. We carried on our struggle against the British Empire more or less peacefully and succeeded in attaining freedom. Even in the course of our struggle we tried to maintain friendly relations with the British. That was Mr Gandhi's teaching and as a result of it, after independence, it was easy for us to be friendly with the British in spite of our past record of conflict.

That taught us to be firm in our policy and yet to be friendly with those who may oppose them [sic] and to try to win them over. That is our broad approach to all other countries though necessarily it varies somewhat in its content.

We are not Communists and dislike many things in Communism. We believe in a democratic structure of society; but we also believe in various social ideals embodied in the term "socialism". We do not accept socialism as some doctrinaire theory but as a practical approach to our own problems. Because the United States embodies many of the liberal democratic principles that we admire and adhere to we are attracted towards it and wish to learn much from it as we have learnt from the British. But we are convinced that at any time, and more specially in the present context of world affairs, the cold war outlook and approach are harmful. Indeed, today the cold war if persisted in for long must necessarily result in a hot war and that will lead to the use of nuclear weapons and the destruction of humanity. For this reason we feel that military alliances will not solve any problems today and they will lead to major conflict.

The sole object to achieve disarmament is to prevent the possibility of such a conflict. If disarmament is attained, as I earnestly hope it will be, I doubt even if the cold war will continue. For the present we feel that we must try to do everything to prevent the continuance of the cold war which may lead to disastrous consequences.

If we are opposed to military alliances, then naturally we cannot join them. We may have close relations with countries but not in the military sense.

You refer to the dangers we face from Communist China. We are fully aware of these dangers and have taken such steps to protect ourselves as are possible for us. Realising those things, I do not think it is at all easy for China to overcome us, though it may succeed in a minor way at the border for a time. That is a practical appreciation of the situation which fits in with our other approach. If we sought military aid from other countries to meet these dangers, it will not lessen the dangers but increase them and may well result in a world-wide conflict.

While we are not Communists and do not accept the communist viewpoint, we realise that the only way for the world to carry on is by some measure of peaceful co-existence and tolerance of people who do not agree with us; otherwise there is conflict, and conflict today, as I have said, will have the most disastrous consequences. Also, our knowledge of history tells us that revolutions toned down after a while. That has happened and is happening in the Soviet Union, though not so in China.

You refer to the Communist Party's newspapers and periodicals in India. It might interest you to know that most of these were started with British Government help in the course of the Second World War. At that time, the Communists were helping in the war-effort, after Russia joined the War, and the British were anxious to make the most of this. Many of us were imprisoned at the time.

I am convinced that the military approach will not solve the world's problems; though occasionally it may become inevitable to some extent. We have to deal with the minds of men and the circumstances in which they live. In a very prosperous and affluent country like the United States it may be a little difficult to understand the conditions in underdeveloped countries where poverty and unemployment are our constant companions. We have to fight them and yet keep true to our ideals. That is no easy task but I think we shall succeed.

Yours sincerely,
[Jawaharlal Nehru]

343. For B.K. Nehru: Soviet MIG Deal[92]

[Message from Nehru for M.J. Desai, the Foreign Secretary]

I think that you should send a telegram to Ambassador B.K. Nehru[93] in the following terms:

"Your telegram 534 of July 25. About three months ago, we intended sending a technical team to Soviet Union to evaluate MIGs more especially from the point of view of rapid manufacture in India. The advice given to us by our Defence experts was that it was essential to take steps for this manufacture and necessary to get a few complete planes in view of the

92. Message, sent on 27 July 1962 from Anand Bhavan, Allahabad.
93. Ambassador to USA.

497

situation vis-à-vis Pakistan and the constant threats that are made there against India and also the grave situation on our frontier with China. Our experts were strongly of opinion that we must take steps to meet any contingency that might arise.

Because of the protests made in US and UK, we decided to delay sending this team. We further decided to evaluate the British Lightnings[94] before we came to a decision. Thereupon we sent a technical team to England for this purpose, the idea being that immediately afterwards we would send a team to the Soviet Union for the same purpose. Our team which went to England, on return, gave an adverse report about the Lightnings and said that however suitable the Lightnings may be in England, their manufacture and use in India would not be at all suitable for us. Thereafter we decided to send the team to Moscow to evaluate the MIGs and report to us about the conditions of manufacture etc. That team will be going soon. We shall await their report before coming to a final decision. That is the position now.

The developments on our Tibetan frontier though they may not lead to an immediate and grave crisis, are a continuing threat and may at any time in future lead to such crisis. We cannot therefore delay much a decision on this subject.

We considered the question of delaying sending out the team till the aid question was over. But we felt that this would not be quite fair to those who are giving us aid and notably the United States. To have sent the team immediately after the decision of the aid question would have looked like playing a trick. We decided therefore to send the team, await their report and then take a decision.

We are grateful for the steps taken by President Kennedy and the US Government in connection with aid to India and we did not want to do anything to make him feel that we did not appreciate fully his efforts to this end. At the same time, we do not wish to act in a way which would appear to others as if we were playing a trick. That would not be fair to him.

The team we sent to England and which we are sending to Moscow is normally much more inclined to deal with Western countries as they have done in the past. But even they felt that British Lightnings would not only be much more expensive, but very difficult to manufacture in India and would take a very long time".[95]

94. The English Electric Lightning aircraft.
95. See SWJN/SS/77/item 377 and earlier items on the subject in the same volume.

2.   I think that the above telegram should be enough for the moment. We need not put out an official statement to this effect. But I may deal with it in one of my announcements in the course of the next few days.

344. American Bar Association Conference[96]

Please see the letter of Lord Shawcross to me.[97] I had sent this to the Law Minister[98] who has written to me at some length on the subject.[99]

Last year, when the question of our participating in a similar conference held in Tokyo arose, I expressed my opinion against such participation. I thought then that this was a conference with political motives and I did not wish to get entangled in it.[100]

From Lord Shawcross's letter it appears that the conference was not confined to those representing one political bloc only, but that even Russians and Yugoslavs attended it at its last session. Also, it appears that the conference is rather helpful in bringing different people together.

In the circumstances, I feel that our old objection does not hold. We might, therefore, agree to the conference being held in Delhi and to the participation of some of our people in it.[101] As a matter of fact, Lord Shawcross has not asked my permission to hold it in Delhi. It appears to be taken for granted.

The attendance is likely to be a large one, at least 1,000 delegates. With their wives and others, the number might well go up to 1,500 or even 2,000. The question of hotel accommodation may well create difficulties. However, we are not asked about it, and I do not see why we should trouble ourselves over it.

As far as I can see, no financial commitment on our part is necessary. Indeed, so many people coming from abroad will bring foreign exchange to us.

On the whole I think I shall reply to Lord Shawcross that I am prepared to inaugurate this conference in Delhi.

I should like your views on it.

---

96. Note, 2 August 1962, for R.K. Nehru and M.J. Desai, the Secretary General and Foreign Secretary respectively at the MEA. MEA, File No. UI/162-112/62, p. 1/note.
97. Hartley Shawcross, British barrister and Labour Member of the House of Lords. Appendix 10.
98. Asoke K. Sen.
99. Appendix 19.
100. The conference in Tokyo was held, 17-20 September 1961.
101. See item 345.

345. To Hartley Shawcross: American Bar Association Conference in Delhi[102]

August 3, 1962

Dear Lord Shawcross,

Thank you for your letter of the 24th July.[103] I have read it with much interest. When I first heard of the Conference "World Peace through Law", I was afraid that this might turn out to be an exercise in the cold war. Your letter has removed this misapprehension in my mind and it seems to me that the Conference may well serve a useful purpose in furthering the cause of world peace. I am glad that those invited to this Conference were from all countries regardless of their ideologies. In any event, it seems to me a good thing for representatives from the Communist as well as the other countries to meet together and exchange views. That in itself helps to create a better atmosphere.

You refer to an invitation which has been extended to me to make an inaugural address at the Conference. I do not remember having received any such invitation. But, treating your letter as an invitation, I gladly accept it.

We shall be glad to have the Conference in Delhi. But I have no idea of how many people it will attract. There is often some difficulty in finding adequate accommodation at that time of the year as a large number of tourists descend upon Delhi then. March is a fairly good time although it is not so cool then as it is a little earlier in the year.[104]

Yours sincerely,
Jawaharlal Nehru

346. To John F. Kennedy: Friendship[105]

August 5, 1962

My dear Mr President,

I have not written to you for a considerable time as I did not wish to take up your time needlessly. But now I feel I must write to you to express my gratitude to you for all the sympathy and goodwill you have shown to India, more particularly

---

102. Letter to British Barrister; address: St. Helen's Court, Great St. Helen's, London, E.C.3. MEA, File No. UI/162-112/62, p. 8/corr.
103. Appendix 10.
104. See also item 344, appendix 19.
105. Letter to the US President.

in regard to the aid to India for her development. You have not only given us generous aid from the United States, but have taken the trouble to induce other countries to do so also.

We appreciate very much the aid that is being given to us. But even more I am grateful for your friendly and sympathetic attitude. My colleagues here and I are particularly anxious to have the friendship of the United States in the great tasks that confront us. I believe that this friendship is good not only for our two countries, but also for the world. If I may say so, this has little to do with the aid you may give us. Even if circumstances arose which might make it difficult for you to help us in our development, we would still value your friendship and work for close relations between India and the United States. Your sympathy and appreciation of our task is much more valuable to us than material aid.

I say so because, during the last few months, newspapers in the United States and sometimes in India have referred to some differences of opinion between our two countries and drawn the conclusion that our relations were not so good as they ought to be. Differences of opinion might take place because our conditions and backgrounds are different, and it may be that sometimes we find it difficult to accept a policy which the United States pursues, just as you might find it difficult to accept some policy of ours. But at no time have I thought that this should affect the friendship of our two countries which we consider so important. I can assure you, therefore, that whatever might happen, our attitude will continue to be to encourage friendly relations between our two countries.

Mrs Kennedy was good enough to write to me some time ago in answer to a letter I had sent her.[106] I was happy to receive her letter. I hesitated to write again to her as that might cast a burden on her to reply to me again.

I earnestly hope that your efforts to secure peace on strong foundations and to bring about disarmament will meet with success.

Again thanking you,

Yours sincerely,
Jawaharlal Nehru

106. Nehru's letter to Jacqueline Kennedy has not been traced.

347. To Sudhir Ghosh: Hubert Humphrey Correspondence[107]

August 8, 1962

Dear Sudhir,

Thank you for your letter of the 8th August.[108] I am returning to you Senator Humphrey's[109] letter and the one you sent him.

Krishna Menon[110] knows a large number of Americans and gets on very well with them. Oddly enough, he got on very well with Cabot Lodge.[111] Unfortunately, he has not been able to hit it off with others.

Yours sincerely,
Jawaharlal Nehru

348. To J.K. Galbraith: Indian Independence and Anglo-Saxon Numerology[112]

August 16, 1962

My dear Ambassador,

Thank you for your good wishes on the Anniversary of Indian Independence. I did not know the particular point you mention about Anglo-Saxon numerology, but anything that is supposed to be auspicious is always welcome.

Yours sincerely,
[Jawaharlal Nehru]

---

107. Letter to former PSP member, later Independent Rajya Sabha MP, recently enrolled in Congress. See item 23. NMML, Sudhir Ghosh Papers. Also available in the JN Collection.
108. Appendix 28.
109. Hubert Humphrey, US Senator, Democratic Party.
110. V.K. Krishna Menon, Defence Minister; led the Indian delegation to the UN General Assembly for several years.
111. Henry Cabot Lodge, Republican Senator and US Ambassador to the United Nations, 1953-1960.
112. Letter to the US Ambassador.

349. To Hem Barua: US Action in the Security Council Understandable[113]

September 2, 1962

My dear Hem Barua,

I am sorry for the slight delay in answering your letter of the 28th August.

I saw the statement made by Professor Malasekhara, the Chief Ceylonese Delegate to the UN. [114] I think it is a more or less correct statement. But we need not take it very seriously. We knew that some such attempt was made by the US Delegates in the Security Council. The US was in a somewhat difficult position having given their word to Pakistan on the subject. They could not quite get out of it, although they did not like it.[115]

The US is particularly split up in a large number of authorities. There is the President,[116] of course, at the top. Then there are the military people and there is the UN Delegation under Adlai Stevenson. Often they pull in different directions. Sometimes they cannot get out of a previous commitment, usually made in Eisenhower's time.[117]

---

113. Letter to PSP, Lok Sabha MP; address: 59-B, South Avenue, New Delhi.
114. G.P. Malalasekera, Buddhist leader, professor and diplomat; High Commissioner of Ceylon to Canada at this time.
115. A Reuter despatch datelined New York, 25 August 1962, published in *The Statesman* the next day, said that in a leaked confidential report to his Government, Malalasekera had recorded on 7 July 1962 his observations, among other things, on the recent shift in US stance toward Pakistan. He wrote that US policy was "so firmly geared to strategic considerations that Pakistan was at last able to exert pressure, especially with the military overlords of the Pentagon, and contrary to higher political considerations of the Administration, by the threat of withdrawing herself from SEATO and CENTO." That the "acquisition of Kashmir by Pakistan would materially change the whole strategic situation at a time when the cold war is shifting from Berlin to Asia" was "evidently the bait that was dangled before the US militarists and they succumbed."

   Malalasekera described as "farce" the introduction of the Irish resolution of 22 June 1962 in the UN Security Council, which brought in the element of third party good offices in negotiations between India and Pakistan, and which was vetoed by the USSR (see item 383). He stated that the US did not bring the resolution herself, so as "to escape the responsibility in the eyes of India," but managed to find an unwilling small nation, Ireland, to do so, with Adlai Stevenson himself taking charge of the efforts to convince it.
116. John F. Kennedy.
117. January 1953 to January 1961.

I think that the President, as he has made clear on several occasions, certainly has friendly feelings towards us and means that. But sometime his delegates pull in another direction.

Yours sincerely,
[Jawaharlal Nehru]

(d) UK

350. To Louis Mountbatten: UK Programme[118]

July 23, 1962

[My dear Dickie,]
Thank you for your letter of the 20th July which has just reached me.

I shall gladly come to Broadlands.[119] Indeed that is an essential part of my visit to England. I have not made up my mind as to when I can go there. I might perhaps reach London two or three days before the Prime Ministers' meeting in order to have a fairly thorough medical check-up there. I am keeping fairly well, but many people make a fuss about my health and are insistent that I should have this check-up in London. If this is so, it would probably be difficult for me to go to Broadlands on the 8th September as you suggest. But the 15th should certainly suit me.

[Jawaharlal Nehru]

351. To T.N. Kaul: London Programme[120]

August 2, 1962

My dear Tikki,
I have your letter of the 27th July. As a result of that, we postponed a certain announcement that was being made about your going to Vienna. We shall consider your future posting further and keep what you have written in mind.

---

118. Letter to the UK Chief of the Defence Staff.
119. Mountbatten's home.
120. Letter to the Deputy High Commissioner in London.

There is some difficulty in bringing people to the Centre as vacancies do not occur soon enough. However, we shall look into this matter again.[121]

I hope to reach London probably on the 8th September.[122] I want to spend the second weekend in London at Broadlands. Indira[123] will probably accompany me to London though I am not quite certain yet.

I may have to go to Paris for a day or two after the Conference is over, and then I intend going to Ghana and Nigeria before returning to India.

I want to reach London a couple of days before the Conference. I want to utilise this time in having a medical check-up.[124]

Yours sincerely,
[Jawaharlal Nehru]

352. To Hukam Singh: Commonwealth Parliamentary Conference[125]

August 8, 1962

My dear Mr Speaker,

Thank you for your letter of August 6 about the Indian Parliamentary Delegation to the next Commonwealth Parliamentary Conference to be held in Nigeria.

In view of all the circumstances, I think we should participate in it though in small numbers, as small as possible. I was of opinion, as I had written to you previously, that the State branches need not send any delegates.[126] I feel, however, that West Bengal stands on a somewhat separate footing than others. They have actually sent their subscription. Yesterday, Shri Suniti Kumar Chatterji, Chairman of the West Bengal Legislative Council, came to see me and he appeared to be looking forward to being sent to Nigeria to this Conference. He is a good representative, specially to Africa, as he has written some good booklets on the new awakening in Africa.

---

121. T.N. Kaul remained in London until October 1962; he was appointed Ambassador to the USSR in November 1962.
122. For the Commonwealth Prime Ministers' Conference, in London, 10 to 19 September 1962.
123. Indira Gandhi.
124. For statement issued by the High Commission in London after Nehru's medical check-up, see item 325, fn 37.
125. Letter to the Speaker of the Lok Sabha.
126. See SWJN/SS/76/item 444.

I would therefore suggest that as an exceptional case he might be included from West Bengal and other States need not be represented.

I entirely agree with you that our delegation should be as small as possible. I am suggesting Shri Suniti Kumar Chatterji to be included more because of his personal competence than for any other reason. Indeed, I would even suggest your reducing the number from the Centre in order to include him.

Apart from other reasons, the question of foreign exchange is especially important for us at the present stage.

If you like I shall write to the Chief Ministers of the States affected, as suggested by you.[127]

Yours sincerely,
[Jawaharlal Nehru]

353. To Hukam Singh: Commonwealth Parliamentary Conference[128]

August 8, 1962

My dear Mr Speaker,

As suggested by you, I have addressed a letter to the Chief Ministers of Gujarat, Madras, Maharashtra, Mysore, Punjab, Rajasthan and UP. I have not sent this to West Bengal because I had myself suggested to you, if possible, to include a representative from there, who might be Dr Suniti Kumar Chatterji. If, however, you wish me to address West Bengal Chief Minister also, I shall do so.[129]

Yours sincerely,
[Jawaharlal Nehru]

127. Item 353.
128. Letter to the Speaker of the Lok Sabha.
129. See also item 352.

354. To Several Chief Ministers: Commonwealth Parliamentary Conference[130]

August 8, 1962

My dear Chief Minister,

The Speaker of the Lok Sabha, Sardar Hukam Singh, has kindly referred to me the question of sending an Indian Parliamentary Delegation to the next Commonwealth Parliamentary Conference to be held in Nigeria in October – November, 1962.[131] Perhaps you may remember that I wrote to you a letter on the 9th June 1962 on this subject.[132] In that letter, I suggested that it was perhaps not necessary to have State branches of the Commonwealth Parliamentary Association. It seemed to me that the main purpose of establishing these branches was to collect considerable sums of money as subscriptions.

At first it was suggested that we need not send any Delegation to this year's conference of the Commonwealth Parliamentary Association. Subsequently, however, it was felt that, as the next conference was being held in Nigeria, it would not be desirable not to be represented at it when it was held in an African country. It is proposed, therefore, to send a very small delegation to Nigeria, probably consisting of three persons. Our foreign exchange position is very difficult and we have to restrict any expenditure involving foreign exchange to the utmost. You will, I trust, appreciate that it will not be possible on this occasion to send representatives from the State branches. I hope you will be good enough to explain this to the Speaker of your Assembly, who, I presume, is the Chairman of the State branch.

Yours sincerely,
[Jawaharlal Nehru]

---

130. Letter to Chief Ministers of Gujarat, Madras, Maharashtra, Mysore, Punjab, and UP.
131. See items 352-353.
132. 1962 is a typographical error for the year mentioned here. The reference is to Nehru's letter of 9 June 1961, see SWJN/SS/69/item 3.

355. Foreign Tour Arrangements[133]

[Note, 27 July 1962, by S.P. Khanna, PS, for R.K. Nehru, Secretary-General, and B.F.H.B. Tyabji, Special Secretary, MEA, begins]

Reference Office Memorandum below from the Ministry of Home Affairs.[134]

2. The only papers which we have in the PM's Secretariat about the Commonwealth Prime Ministers' Conference and PM's proposed visit to Ghana and Nigeria are contained in the files below. The other papers are in the Ministry of External Affairs. SG and SS may kindly see and advise with regard to paragraph 1(2) of the Home Ministry's Office Memorandum.

S.P. Khanna
27.7.1962

SG
SS

[Note, 27 July 1962, by S.P. Khanna, PS, for R.K. Nehru, Secretary-General, and B.F.H.B. Tyabji, Special Secretary, MEA, ends]

---

133. Noting. MHA, File No. D-I/454 (10)/62, p. 1/note.
134. The MHA Office Memorandum of 24 July 1962 to J.S. Teja, the Deputy Chief of Protocol, MEA, was as follows:
   "Subject: Security arrangements to be made in connection with the visit to London by the Prime Minister in September 1962, to attend the Commonwealth Prime Ministers' conference.

   The question of making adequate security arrangements in connection with the ensuing visit to London by the Prime Minister to attend the Commonwealth Prime Ministers' Conference is at present under consideration in the Ministry of Home Affairs. The undersigned is to request that the following information may be furnished urgently:

   1)   Whether the Prime Minister would travel by an IAF aircraft or the aircraft of a scheduled air company; &
   2)   the detailed travel schedule with the dates and times of journeys, halts en route and numbers of flights.

   These details are necessary for reaching appropriate decisions regarding the security precautions in respect of the ensuing visit of the Prime Minister.

   This may please be treated as Immediate.

P. Sitapati
Under Secretary to The Govt. of India"
23/7/62

MHA File No. D-I/454 (10)/62, p. 1/corr.

[Note, 30 July 1962, by R.K. Nehru, Secretary-General at the MEA, for Jawaharlal Nehru, begins]

The Commonwealth PMs' Conference is scheduled to begin on Monday, 10th September and to last for about a week. There have been some reports in the newspapers that the Conference may be postponed as the negotiations in regard to Commonwealth agricultural products have run into difficulties. However, it does not seem to me likely that the Conference will be postponed.

2. If the Conference takes place on 10th September, presumably PM will leave, say, two days earlier. A suitable date might be late night on 7th September when the AII Boeing goes direct from Delhi to London via Beirut, Geneva and Paris. Arrival time will be 11.20 a.m. on 8th September.

3. It is too early to finalise the date, but I am mentioning it as a possibility for PM's consideration. As regards the return journey *via* Ghana and Nigeria, the dates and route can be settled later.

R.K. Nehru
30.7.62

PM

[Note, 30 July 1962, by R.K. Nehru, Secretary-General
at the MEA, for Jawaharlal Nehru, ends]

[Note, 9 August 1962, by Jawaharlal Nehru, for R.K. Nehru, begins]

I am sorry for the delay in returning these papers to you. I do not know why the Home Ministry is excited about security arrangements for me. Tell them not to worry. On no account do I want a security officer to accompany me.

2. I am thinking that perhaps it will be as well if I left Delhi on the 7th night and not on the 6th night as previously suggested. This will also not interfere with the Air India service.

J. Nehru
9.8.62

SG

[Note, 9 August 1962, by Jawaharlal Nehru, for R.K. Nehru, ends]

356. To P.C. Sen: Commonwealth Parliamentary Conference[135]

August 11, 1962

My dear Prafulla Sen,

A few days ago, I wrote a letter to some Chief Ministers of States which have branches of the Commonwealth Parliamentary Association.[136] I referred in this letter to the meeting of the Commonwealth Parliamentary Conference to be held in Nigeria in October – November 1962 and pointed out that it was very difficult to send a large delegation this year because, among other things, of the foreign exchange difficulty. I enclose a copy of this letter.

I did not write to you originally because I had in mind that West Bengal might be treated as an exception. It appears that it is the turn of West Bengal to be represented on the General Council (Executive Committee) of the Conference. Therefore, I thought, and our Speaker[137] was also of this opinion, that some representative from West Bengal might go with our small delegation. Perhaps, Shri Suniti Kumar Chatterji[138] could be included in this way, as he can go as a member of the General Council.

I might mention, however, that the chief reason for our sending a delegation this year is that the Conference is being held in Nigeria and we do not want it to appear that we have not participated because the Conference is being held in an African country. But, generally speaking, I do not attach much value to these Commonwealth Parliamentary Conferences and I do not think that it serves any useful purpose. In fact, I was not in favour of many state branches being formed which had to pay large subscriptions.

Yours sincerely,
[Jawaharlal Nehru]

357. In New Delhi: At the CPP[139]

Jawaharlal Nehru: Today we have met for a discussion on the European Common Market, and the Finance Minister[140] is good enough to agree to address

---

135. Letter to the Chief Minister of West Bengal.
136. Item 354. See also other correspondence in this section.
137. Hukam Singh.
138. Chairman of the West Bengal Legislative Council.
139. Participation in meeting, 20 August 1962. NMML, AICC Speeches, Tape M-64/c (i).
140. Morarji Desai.

the Party about it. Tyagiji's[141] Land Acquisition Bill is coming up tomorrow and quite a number of Members of the Party feel that it might perhaps, if you agree, it might be entrusted to a Select Committee and then take a decision on it ...

From the floor: Land acquisition so far has been divided into three categories: one for broad social objectives, such as land reforms ...

जवाहरलाल नेहरु: आप चाहें तो और बहस हो लेकिन मैं आपसे सजेस्ट ये करने वाला था कि यह एग्ज़ीक्यूटिव कमेटी के सामने रखा गया है, और राम सुभग जी[142] उनसे मिनिस्टर आफ फूड एन्ड एग्रीकल्चर[143] से खास कह दें कि आज उन्होंने सुना यहां क्या बाज़ हमारे मैम्बरान ने कहा। उनसे कह दीजिए कि इसपे बहुत गरमागरमी की राय है लोगों की। तो बेहतर है कि एग्ज़ीक्यूटिव कमेटी में आके बातचीत करें और आप चंद साहब ने जो स्टडी किया है वो एग्ज़ीक्यूटिव कमेटी में कल आ जायें

[Translation: If you want we can have more discussion. But this matter has been placed before the Executive Committee and I would suggest that Ram Subhagji[144] should specially convey the views expressed by some Members here today to the Minister of Food and Agriculture.[145] He may be told that Members are very much agitated over this matter and it is better that he should discuss this in the Executive Committee. And some of our Members here who have studied this matter should also attend the Executive Committee meeting.] ...

Morarji Desai: The question of the Common Market is a very important one for us and very vital too for our economy. All facts have been given in this matter through a memorandum ...

Jawaharlal Nehru: [This] sort of words makes us miss exactly what the point is. It is obvious that the ECM, EEC, is something which has happened. It is a kind of a historical development aided by various factors. Our Finance Minister has been referring to the economic consequences on India, which can harm us or hurt us somewhat, undoubtedly. Now, for us to expect that the British Government will be able to get much for us from the ECM is, I think, to expect too much. The British Government has been driven by facts towards

141. Mahavir Tyagi, MP.
142. Ram Subhag Singh, Secretary, Congress Party, and Minister of State for Food and Agriculture.
143. S.K. Patil.
144. See fn 142 in this section.
145. See fn 143 in this section.

the ECM. I do not yet know if they will finally decide to join it, because there are strong feelings in England against it too, although possibly the majority of the business people there and the government want to join it.

The Commonwealth, like Australia and Canada, are dead opposed to it. Now, apart from the economic consequences, you must remember that this is a movement towards further integration of western Europe leading even to political integration and building up a strong European community which can stand up on the one side to the Soviet Union, on the other to the United States of America and it represents a gradual change in the balances which we are used to in the world. It is difficult to go into the details of this but this political aspect of it is important which is bound to develop.

One odd thing has happened, Mr Menzies[146] pointed out. There is some truth in that: if one joins the European Common Market one loses to some extent one's freedom of action in one's own country, because a larger group determines it. You have your views in it, the country that joins has a view in determining it, but it is one voice out of ten, let us say, or eight, or six, seven, so that you lose to that extent your sovereign independence. Mr Menzies, the Prime Minister of Australia, has said that the Commonwealth is a union of independent countries. If Britain joins it [the ECM], it ceases to be wholly independent. Therefore, it loses one of the characteristics of a member of the Commonwealth. That may be perhaps exaggerating a little but there is some atom, some bit of truth in it. Most of the arguments that had been going on, whether for Australia or Canada or India, are based on the simple fact that we are afraid of losing what we have got and having barriers put there which will prevent our export, Australian export, Canadian, New Zealand. New Zealand sends—I do not know how much—80 percent of her goods to Great Britain, and they will lose. New Zealand, Canada and Australia are on a different footing from India because they are developed countries, not relatively underdeveloped like we are, and yet they deal with primary produce.

So far as we are concerned, the biggest thing in our favour is, because these people of the European Common Market or anywhere, often for the matter of that our own people, do not look upon this question in a sentimental way. They are hard and tough people bent on achieving their objective economically and politically. The point that I think affects them in regard to India is that India is going to be one of the biggest markets in the world. As our economic condition improves and people have more money to buy, more and more goods they hope can come in here from abroad, and as some Americans told me, the thought of this enormous market, it is a paradise for the seller. So they want, they have

146. Robert Menzies, Prime Minister of Australia, 1949-1966.

a certain good feeling for India conditioned by the fact that they expect much from India in the future as a market, and one may perhaps get some relatively good terms from them because of that balance of considerations.

Therefore, we cannot expect much from the UK arguing our case, although we want the UK to argue our case as far as possible as it can. Because it is the UK's business to join or not join, we are not joining the ECM. That is why a step that we took some time ago to put a special ambassador to the ECM

[DELEGATIONS ARE PERMANENT]

Babu ji . . .

**"Be optimistic, man. Whatever the Commonwealth
Prime Ministers decide about E.C.M.,
there is plenty of scope for sending out a
few more delegations to Europe!"**

(From *The Times of India*, 14 September 1962, p. 3)

in Brussels[147] was thought of in terms of direct dealings between us and the ECM, also through the UK, because we shall have to deal with these European Common Market countries whether we like that market or not, a bunch of countries, and we shall have to deal with them and we shall have to come to terms with them directly apart from what they may decide.

[One minute gap in tape] these developments, if we take them lightly, they will hit us, but it will also be an inducement for us, that is true. Everything has an inducement which bears down upon us. We are in a peculiar position compared to most of the underdeveloped countries. We are a developing country with the prospect within the foreseeable future of being largely industrialized and still, however much we may offer goods to our own people manufactured in India, still, because the market will become immense in India. if the capacity grows there will be room for other countries to come in too and indeed after all you cannot only sell, you have to buy and sell, and nor can you indeed buy only, because unless you sell you cannot pay for that.

These are some considerations I wanted you to consider. It is not a question of, it is natural, that we should try to get the best terms for India from these people without agreeing to anything which may injure us economically or politically, that is true. But the matter is not entirely in our hands. Then there is this political union that may come about in western Europe which will be a historical development of great importance and then there is this aspect of the associated countries of Africa being given a privileged position. Now, much can be said in regard to that. It may be some kind of economic dominance over them by the big European countries continuing, which is not a very desirable thing. So it is a major thing, a very big thing which has to be looked at from all these aspects and which may and indeed is likely to hit us somewhat—to what extent depends on the kind of terms we get and our own response to them here, what we do in India, how we increase our productivity and our ability to meet such a situation.

Well, that is all. Thank you.

147. Brussels, the site of the headquarters of the insitutions of the European Common Market. K.B. Lall, Ambassador to Belgium, was concurrently Ambassador to the ECM.

358. To Hukam Singh: S.K. Chatterji and the Commonwealth Parliamentary Conference[148]

August 24, 1962

My dear Mr Speaker,

I have received a letter from Shri Suniti Kumar Chatterji, Chairman of the Legislative Council of West Bengal. I quote a paragraph from his letter:

"Our Chief Minister, Shri Prafulla Chandra Sen, told me about your letter to him, in which you suggested that I might be included as a Member of the General Council of the Commonwealth Parliamentary Conference to be held in Nigeria in October-November, 1962. Shri Sen is wholly agreeable to this, but I do not know whether it would mean a membership of the delegation from the Calcutta Legislature or something else. In any case, if you could kindly ask the Officer-in-charge of the Conference matters to write to Shri P.C. Sen, proper arrangements might be made here during my absence, and as soon as I return, if necessary I might participate in it."

I do not know why this misunderstanding arose in his mind. Anyhow, I hope it will be cleared up. He has now, I believe, left for America to take part in the International Congress of Linguists.

I would suggest that you might have a letter sent to the Chief Minister of West Bengal about Shri S.K. Chatterji going to the Commonwealth Parliamentary Conference.[149]

Yours sincerely,
[Jawaharlal Nehru]

359. To Louis Mountbatten: London Plans[150]

27th August, 1962

[My dear Dickie,]

I have just received your letter of the 22nd August from Cliffoney. I hasten to reply to you that, as at present arranged, I shall not be able to come to

---

148. Letter to the Speaker of the Lok Sabha.
149. See other correspondence on this subject in this subsection.
150. Letter to the Chief of the Defence Staff, UK; address: Ministry of Defence, Storey's Gate, London, SW1.

Broadlands on the 8th September. I hope to come there on the next week-end. I shall be reaching London on the 8th and it would be difficult for me to get away immediately. I hope, therefore, to go to Broadlands on the 15th September.

I shall gladly come to Wilton Crescent for a meal. It is rather difficult for me to indicate the date now.

I would love to have a ride in "Hovercraft" if this can be managed. Probably, this might be arranged when I visit Broadlands on the 15th.

Indu[151] will be accompanying me to London. Nan[152] will not be coming then.

[Jawaharlal Nehru]

360. For the BBC: European Common Market[153]

Better Terms from ECM. Nehru Hopeful

London, Aug. 28 – Mr Nehru is still hopeful that India will get "much better terms" from the European Market countries than at present offered. He said so last night in an interview on the British Broadcasting Corporation's Television Service with Mr Ian Gilmour, Proprietor of the political weekly, *Spectator*.

Asked about Britain's negotiations to enter the Common Market, the Prime Minister said: "We are not at all satisfied and we still hope we shall get much better terms from those countries. All our planning and future economic position depend on the exports we send. Any limitation would make a great difference to us."

Mr Gilmour also asked Mr Nehru about India's proposed purchase of MIG aircraft from the Soviet Union, and about Mr Krishna Menon.[154]

Tribute to V.K.K. Menon

On the MIGs Mr Nehru said India looked at the transaction "purely from a commercial point of view in terms of manufacture rather than purchase".

"This has nothing to do with any military accord between the Soviet Union and us. It is a great advantage to us to be able to pay in our own goods. No foreign exchange is involved."

---

151. Indira Gandhi.
152. Vijaya Lakshmi Pandit, Nehru's sister and former High Commissioner to UK.
153. Report of interview, 27 August 1962. Reproduced from *The Hindu*, 29 August 1962, p.1.
154. The Defence Minister.

On Mr Menon, Mr Nehru commented: "He may occasionally say things which are not liked by others, but he has been remarkably successful in the things he has undertaken."

361. To Krishna Hutheesing: London Programme[155]

August 31, 1962

[Dear Betty,]

Your letter of the 30th August. I have received a telegram from Ajit[156] also inviting Indu,[157] Rajiv[158] and me to dinner in London. Rajiv is not going to London at that time. He will probably go after I have left London.

As for me, I would love to have a quiet dinner with Ajit and Amrita.[159] But it is going to be a difficult matter for me to find the time for it. In any event, I cannot do so from here. After I reach London and see my programme, we can consider this.

The Commonwealth Prime Ministers' Conference is a very exhausting affair, chiefly because of the many social engagements and a large number of other Prime Ministers one has to meet. The number of these Prime Ministers is growing. I have more or less decided to accept as few social engagements as possible. But I shall have to see the Prime Ministers or, perhaps, invite them to our Embassy[160] for meals. I am, therefore, unable to fix any time from here. You might inform Ajit to get in touch with me after I arrive there. I would have written myself, but I do not know his London address.

Rajiv is going to stay on here and, of course, Sanjay[161] will also be here. So it is not really necessary for you to trouble to come. Harsha[162] will not be lonely.

[Jawaharlal Nehru]

155. Letter to sister; address: Anand Bhuvan, 20 Carmichael Road, Bombay-26.
156. Younger son of Raja and Krishna Hutheesing.
157. Indu is Indira Gandhi.
158. Rajiv Gandhi.
159. Wife of Ajit Hutheesing.
160. The High Commission in London.
161. Sanjay Gandhi.
162. Elder son of Raja and Krishna Hutheesing.

362. In London: To the Commonwealth Prime Ministers' Conference[163]

Prime Minister,[164]
I am grateful to you and to Mr Heath[165] for the address you gave us yesterday. It appeared how hard he had bargained and tried to get good terms from the Six of the EEC.

We are grateful to him for all that. I must, however, confess that the ultimate picture that has emerged is hardly satisfactory. Each group of countries is somewhat differently affected. The Prime Ministers of Canada[166] and New Zealand[167] have stated their views as the present proposals affect the more developed countries. President Ayub,[168] whose country is faced with similar problems like ours, has stated his views. I largely agree with his general approach to the problem. I shall naturally deal with the problems facing developing countries like India. I should like to make some general remarks.

One is what you, Prime Minister, referred in your opening remarks to the world situation; the world conflict, two world wars and the need to prevent a collision between the two great Powers. You also referred to Europe's concern with the East-West conflict. We are all concerned with it. Every step we now take, therefore, must be judged from this point of view, namely, does it reduce tension between East and West; does it decrease the threat of war? We fear that the effect of the present proposals and UK's entry into the European Community might be the reverse and add to the tension between East and West. Some East European countries have claimed that the European Common Market will lead to an extension of the NATO alliance. That may not be wholly correct but it may well result in increase of tension between East and West. The chances of disarmament would grow less. That would be a terrible loss; for disarmament will lead to greater economic progress than creation or extension of economic communities. These are considerations that should be borne in mind in the context of the wider world situation.

Coming to the present proposals I should like to remind you, Prime Minister, and other Prime Ministers, that there is need for a new approach of developing

---

163. Speech, 11 September 1962, at the Commonwealth Prime Ministers' Conference. The Conference opened at Marlborough House in London on 10 September 1962.
164. Harold Macmillan, the British Prime Minister.
165. Edward Heath, Lord Privy Seal, 1960-1963, British negotiator to secure Britain's entry into the EEC.
166. John Diefenbaker.
167. Keith Holyoake.
168. Ayub Khan, the President of Pakistan.

a healthier relationship between developed and developing countries. The UN has declared the present decade as the Decade of Development. Declarations have been made in GATT to take immediate steps for programmes of action, to fix terminal dates to relax tariff and other barriers and expand exports of developing countries. Even some members of the Six in their agreements with us in 1959 had agreed to practical measures for an increase in our exports. For example, jute goods and cotton textiles in Germany. It was expected by us that as a result of growing realisation on their part that we could continue to import more and more from them only if we were able to export more and more to them, we would be able to work out trading arrangements to provide growing outlets for our products on the Continent.

This has been the general trend and approach to world developments. How far does this general approach fit in with the present proposals? I do not see they fit in. The present proposals are vague and the approach so far made is not satisfactory: Comprehensive trade agreements are a good idea but in the quest of what has been described as a balance of bargaining positions, the prospects of our being able to negotiate a really worthwhile agreement with the enlarged Community seem to us to have been seriously prejudiced.

Our developing countries are struggling hard to raise the standard of living of their people and the levels of our production. It is impossible for us to import machinery and capital goods necessary for our development plans unless we can increase the level of our exports. We are grateful for aid which is largely in the shape of loans and credits. It has to be paid back with interest; we can only pay them back through increasing our exports. There is no other way.

We are in the middle of the Third Five Year Plan. The existence of trade links is important. We are thinking of our Fourth and Fifth Five Year Plans in our perspective planning. We are naturally worried by the adverse effects on our plans. UK's entry into the EEC may well worsen the position not only in relation to our earnings of foreign exchange but in additional unemployment and have grave social consequences from the human point of view. All this does not fit in with an international approach or an approach of GATT as it is generally accepted.

The accession of UK to the EEC means some diminution of her sovereignty. We need not be afraid of that if it leads to a world order. But it does make a difference to the Commonwealth. Curious consequences flow from it, apart from its effect on outlets of trade, on flow of capital, it affects human beings, for even persons from the Community will have easier access. All this will weaken the concept of the Commonwealth. I do not see how the Commonwealth will survive unless a radical change is made in the present proposals.

Over the years economic relations inside the Commonwealth have developed in a manner so as to make it possible for countries like India to expand the export of our products to the British market and to increase imports from the United Kingdom. I was surprised to hear these economic relations described as characteristic of a period which was passing away. It is true that we did not like the Ottawa agreements because when they were concluded most of the gains accrued to the United Kingdom. It is only lately that duty free imports into the United Kingdom and preferential arrangements over the Commonwealth as a whole have helped us to build up a sizeable trade in our manufactures, a trade which has proved beneficial not only to ourselves but also to the United Kingdom. The provisions of these agreements now provide a good basis for evolving a constructive relationship between the developing and developed countries. How can these agreements be abandoned without adequate substitutes being found for them, perhaps over a wider field? It is the old concept, the colonial concept or something like that which seems to form the basis of the present proposals not wholly but to a large extent.[169]

We are grateful for the decision of a nil duty on tea and on a few other interesting articles, like cricket balls, bats and polo sticks. I hope the Prime Minister of Australia[170] will create interest in cricket on the Continent of Europe. These, however, are very small items of our export. Tea is, of course, a big item but it cannot be produced in most countries except in India, Ceylon and a few others.

The main object seems to be the controlling of industries and markets of industrial goods of developing countries. Reference has been made to our bargaining for trade agreements in the future, but our prospects have been greatly prejudiced. An esoteric value is attached to the Community's external tariff. We had every reason to expect that in evolving the level of this tariff for our products, due account would be taken of the volume of duty free imports from our countries into the United Kingdom and due attention would also be paid to the conditions in which countries in the process of development are able to market their industrial products. But the negotiators have already accepted the full tariff of the Community for our products and agreed on the steps by which this level will be reached. We have repeatedly urged that unless

169. Harold Macmillan had said that "the Ottawa Agreement had been entered into in 1932 at a time when most of the Commonwealth countries were producers of raw materials while Britain was one of the main industrial countries. Since the position had now changed and many other countries were becoming industrialized, therefore a change in the basis of the Ottawa Agreement was necessary." The *National Herald*, 13 September 1962, p. 4.
170. Robert Menzies.

status quo is maintained for our products in the United Kingdom during the transitional period, there will be little scope left for successfully negotiating practical measures for the expansion of our exports to the enlarged Community.

Textiles are important for us. Quantitative limitations do provide more than adequate safeguards for the Six. But where is the need for additional tariffs? They are not necessary. Only we will lose foreign exchange on it. The arrangements on jute goods are even more odd; while facilities are provided for increased imports from the Six into the United Kingdom, controls on our imports for which there is no justification even at present are proposed to be kept on till 1970.

High tariffs are rightly regarded as a barrier to trade expansion. To avoid the barrier erected by the Community, the United Kingdom is seeking to join the Market. But in the case of a developing country like India, whose need to develop exports is greater and whose difficulties in developing exports are manifold, it is proposed to erect a tariff where none existed before. The solution to the problem which concerns not only India but other developing countries in and outside the Commonwealth lies in extending duty free treatment to as wide a list of items as possible and to lower the tariffs on the rest. I do not see how else this problem can be solved.

There are a number of items like tobacco, East India kips, coir mats, hand knotted carpets, on which no decisions have yet been reached. A large number of our people are employed in concentrated areas on producing these items. Their exports are largely to the UK. There will be considerable unemployment if their future is not safeguarded.

We are terribly anxious to modernise our agriculture and develop our industries. This is a problem of urgent need and importance to us. Our economy will be badly hit and it will take us many, many years to come back even to the existing level if the present proposals are accepted. Even developed countries in affluent circumstances do realise that the poorer countries must grow and be provided wider markets. It is a short sighted policy to ignore the development needs of developing countries. If the UK joins the Common Market, then it will be on the other side of the barrier. It will become more difficult for India to expand her exports and our opportunities for the future will remain uncertain. I do not wish to go into details but I would submit the following:

(1) Any agreement made must help in the wider context of the world and not increase tension;

(2) It is essential, generally from the world point of view, to develop industrially other countries that are not developed today. This is even more important from the Commonwealth point of view.

(3) We must develop all countries industrially and not merely confine some countries to producing agricultural raw materials; otherwise we shall create fresh tension. It will create disturbance in the immediate present in the economies of developing countries;

(4) It will upset our Third Five Year Plan. We shall have to adjust and may have to change our whole trade patterns. We must not ignore this.

Other developing countries will have to face similar problems.

I can imagine that it may be good for UK to enter the Common Market. I am no judge of that, but it is not clear to me how any good can come if it causes harm to the Commonwealth.

The developing countries of Asia and Africa will face these problems. The sooner they develop the better it will be for world peace and world order. I would, therefore, submit that these proposals are considered further and changes made in the direction I have hinted. The proposals at present are not good even for the advanced countries of the Community. They tend to lead to a closed circle which may offer to those who are inside it some benefit now but will not be ultimately for their good.

363. In London: Commonwealth Prime Ministers' Conference[171]

European Economic Community

Mr Nehru said that he had to confess, however, that the picture which had emerged from the Brussels negotiations was hardly satisfactory. Each group of countries was differently affected by the proposals, and found himself largely in agreement with the general approach which President Ayub[172] had adopted in his statement during the morning session.

Mr Nehru said that the present proposals should be seen against the background of the world context. Mr Macmillan[173] had referred to the need to avoid a further conflict between world powers and it was true that the primary aim must be to avoid another world war. This meant that every step should be judged by whether it tended to increase or decrease world tension. The subject of their discussions, however, might add to the tensions which already existed, since the East European states already regarded the European Economic

171. Minutes, 11 September 1962.
172. Ayub Khan, the President of Pakistan.
173. Harold Macmillan, the British Prime Minister.

522

Community as an extension of NATO. If the result of the enlargement of the Community should be a growth in tension between East and West, the Eastern countries would feel bound to protect themselves against the Community and this would mean that the chances of disarmament would grow less. Any setback to the attempts to find a solution to the question of disarmament and to end nuclear tests would have far greater economic effects than the creation of new economic blocs. It was therefore necessary to be sure that any good which might derive from their creation would not be overshadowed by their consequences for ill. It was good that Western Europe should progress in its economic development but this should not have the appearance of being part of the cold war. The adhesion of Britain to the Treaty of Rome[174] would be bound to weaken the Commonwealth. If the ending of old feuds in Europe was achieved at the cost of greater enmity between the great world blocs the gain would not be great. Mr Nehru said that all of these general considerations should be borne in mind before coming to any final conclusion.

Turning to the proposals which had emerged from the Brussels negotiations, Mr Nehru reminded his colleagues of recent developments in the economic field affecting the underdeveloped countries. The United Nations General Assembly had designated the nineteen sixties as a "development decade" and member states had been urged to intensify their efforts to help the process of economic growth. Efforts were being made to the same end in the General Agreement on Tariffs and Trade whose members had been urged to fix terminal dates for the abolition of barriers to trade against the less developed countries. Even certain of the countries who were members of the European Economic Community had agreed to take practical measures to help underdeveloped countries and India herself had entered into bilateral arrangements with the Federal Republic of Germany. In this context India had made clear that she would only be able to import to the extent that she was able to export.

Mr Nehru could not see how the proposals which had emerged from the Brussels negotiations fitted into this background. The proposals were rather vague at present but they could be taken as an indication of what the final result was likely to be. It had been agreed that there should be a trade agreement between EEC and India but as Mr Heath[175] had hinted, the approach which had characterised the proposals now before the Meeting would also characterise the trade agreements. The developing countries were struggling hard to raise their standards. They were obliged to import machinery for this purpose but were unable to import unless they could obtain foreign exchange with their

174. See item 16, fn 88.
175. Edward Heath, British negotiator with the EEC.

exports. These countries received aid and he was grateful for the loans and credits which India had received from Britain, from the United States and from other countries, including some Commonwealth countries. But these loans could only be repaid out of the earnings of exports. It was therefore a matter of vital consequence to export. India was now in the middle of her third five year plan which had been drawn up on the basis of existing trade arrangements. The Indian Government was already giving thought to its fourth and fifth plans. All these would be completely upset by a major change in the pattern of trade. Mr Nehru said that he was naturally worried about this prospect since all India's hopes for development had been attached to the success of these plans. In place of these expectations even the present position might be worsened as a result of the proposals before the Meeting. A loss of foreign exchange and a reduction in the level of employment could bring about serious economic and social consequences. This did not fit in with the international approach agreed to by the United Nations and generally accepted.

Mr Nehru suggested that the pooling of sovereignty required by accession to the Treaty of Rome was not in itself a matter for concern since the pooling of sovereignty was a necessary stage in the development of a world order. But it had to be recognised that accession to the Community would inevitably entail some weakening of the concept of the Commonwealth. Joining the Community had consequences not only in political terms but on the pattern of trade and on the flow of capital; closer relationships would be bound to develop between members of the community than between members and third countries, whatever the previous relationship might have been. Mr Nehru suggested that radical changes would be required in the present proposals if the ideals and nature of the Commonwealth were to be preserved.

When the Ottawa agreements had been concluded trade within the Commonwealth had been based upon an exchange of British manufactures for raw materials and foodstuffs from the other countries. Now that the other countries were also producing manufactures, obstructions were to be put in their way. The concept of the Community still seemed to be that the developing countries should supply raw materials to be manufactured in the developed countries. India would for example be able to sell her raw jute but not her processed jute; and so it would be in other commodities. The Indian Government were grateful for the decision to adopt nil tariffs on tea and on such commodities as cricket balls and bats. These latter, however, were small items and tea could not be produced elsewhere than in the countries which at present exported it. The whole approach was based on the modern concept of helping developing countries to grow. It provided rather for the richer countries to grow still faster and to control the markets of the non-industrialised countries. It had been said that it would be possible for the Commonwealth countries themselves to bargain for better arrangements at a later stage but the respect seemed to him to have been seriously prejudiced by the arrangements so far drawn up. It seemed that some esoteric value was attached to the common tariff. The Indian Government had been led to expect that the level of the common tariff would take account of the amount of trade which at present entered Britain from the Commonwealth duty free but in the negotiations Britain had already accepted the final application of the full common external tariff and had agreed the steps by which it should be reached. Unless the status quo was maintained in the transitional period before trade agreements were concluded the bargaining position of the countries concerned would be prejudiced. It had been said that cotton textiles presented a delicate problem for Europe; it was delicate for India too. Quotas already provided and could continue to provide an absolute protection by Europe and there was therefore no need for tariffs. The same was true of jute; the present restrictions on jute imports had no justification, even now, although it was proposed that they should be kept until 1970. High tariffs were a barrier to trade and it was for this reason that Britain was seeking to join the Community. But the developing countries, whose difficulties were greater, would have to face barriers where there had been none before. Mr Nehru suggested that the proper solution was to abolish tariffs on as many commodities as possible and to lower them on the remainder.

The economic relationship of the Commonwealth countries which had existed till now had permitted countries like India to expand both their imports and their exports. Mr Nehru had been surprised to hear this relationship described as characteristic of a period that was passing away. It was true that there had been some dislike of the Ottawa Agreements when they were made. This was because they benefitted Britain more than the other countries. It was only lately that these agreements had allowed the underdeveloped countries to build up a trade in manufactures, a trade which had been helpful to Britain as well as to the exporting countries. How could these agreements be abandoned without provision being made for any substitute? India was anxious to modernise her economy, there being no other way to reduce unemployment and to raise the standard of living. If anything was done now which obstructed this development, India's recovery would be proportionately and substantially delayed. For this reason, the prospect of agreements to be negotiated in the future did not meet the crisis of the day. It was important, even from the point of view of the richer countries that they should help the developing countries in their capacity to buy and it was therefore short-sighted of them not to allow those countries to grow industrially. Aid was useful; but it could not help as much as trade. The present tariff of the European Community presented a barrier and if Britain joined, the opportunity for expansion would be uncertain and present exports would be hit.

For the reasons which he had outlined, Mr Nehru suggested that any arrangements which were now made should be such as would not tend to increase world tension. This would depend as much on the view which other countries—in Eastern Europe for example—took of these developments as on their real nature and objectives. The arrangements should also help the development of the underdeveloped countries, especially those of the Commonwealth. It could not be accepted that some countries should be developed while others supplied raw materials and primary produce. Proposals which took full account of these points would be helpful, but those which did not, would cause disturbance.

Summing up Mr Nehru said that he was concerned about the effects of the present proposals on India and her third Five-Year Plan. India would be able to adapt, but her whole trading pattern would have to change. He could imagine, but was by no means sure, that entry into the European Community would be good for Britain. He was not very clear, however, whether any advantage that accrued to Britain would not be balanced by harmful consequences. He was however certain that it would be better for world peace if the growth of the underdeveloped countries was not obstructed. He submitted that in the next stage of negotiation, the present proposals should be changed in the direction which he had tried to define. This would be for the good in the long run even of the advanced countries of the European Community. The building up of a closed circle cut off from the rest of the world would not ultimately be to their advantage.

Mr Goka[176] said that his President, Dr Nkrumah, was deeply sorry that he could not be present at the Meeting and had asked him to repeat what Dr Nkrumah has already written to Mr Macmillan; that his absence was not due to any doubt about the value of Commonwealth Prime Ministers' Meetings or about the importance of the main question before them on this occasion. Dr Nkrumah had also asked him to express a welcome on behalf of Ghana to the new members of the Commonwealth now represented for the first time: their membership would strengthen Commonwealth ties.

Britain's application to join the EEC raised vital political issues for the Commonwealth. Ghana was not opposed to Britain's entry into the EEC but she felt, upon the information available to her, that this development would do Ghana harm, and she must therefore consider its implications both to herself and for the Commonwealth. When Dr Nkrumah opened the Parliament of

176. Ghana was represented by F.K.D. Goka, its Finance Minister.

Ghana in July, 1961, he said that Ghana did not oppose any arrangements which the nations of Europe might want to make among themselves to free European trade, but that she did oppose any unification of Europe deliberately designed to cloak colonial exploitation in Africa. Ghana was therefore against any political measures concerted to discriminate against or otherwise operate to the disadvantage of African countries; and the EEC was bound to discriminate economically against African countries and to perpetuate the many artificial barriers which had been imposed upon Africa by European colonial powers.

These views had been conveyed to Mr Hare[177] when he visited Ghana in 1961, and had been repeated to the Commonwealth Finance Ministers in Accra not long afterwards. Dr Nkrumah and Ghana as a whole had not since modified them. Association with the EEC under the Treaty of Rome would prevent the full economic and political emancipation of the African countries and hamper the development of the unity of the continent. It had been suggested that African unity would be more readily attainable if all African countries were associated with the EEC but this was quite untrue and wholly disregarded African political sentiments. After long subjection to colonial rule the African countries were gaining independence one after another. Colonialism had tied them economically to metropolitan industrial powers and had restricted them to the role of primary producer, whereas history had shown that the development of nations was inevitably retarded if they failed economically to rise above that level. The new African States could not, therefore, enter into any relations outside Africa which appeared to renew this outworn colonial relationship, and which would be bound to impede Africa's development as a continental economy.

It had also been said that association with the EEC was open to African territories whether they were dependent or independent but he wanted to make it clear that, if Britain joined the EEC, Ghana would not seek association with it on any terms whatsoever.

Mr Macmillan had said that Britain was European and must play a leading part in Europe. This was as it should be but, as Dr Nkrumah had said, Africa was not an extension of Europe. In Ghana's view the emergent African countries must plan their futures in an African setting: although this would not exclude strong links with the rest of the world such links must not lead to discriminations between African countries. Those African States which were associated with the EEC might obtain some immediate advantage from this but would in the long-term pay heavily for it.

177. John H. Hare, the British Minister of Labour.

In Africa the economic future clearly lay in unity since only by unifying markets and pooling skills could the African countries achieve rapid industrialisation and economic development. Ghana therefore wanted a unified economic plan for Africa and was working, through the United Nations, for an African common market. The European powers should recognise that it was in their own interest that this endeavour should succeed. The two main principles of Ghana's foreign policy were positive non-alignment and African unity. She was not interested in association with the EEC, and if she were to obtain preferential treatment for her commodities in Europe, she would be discriminating against some of her friends both inside and outside Africa.

Because of Ghana's attitude to association with the EEC, and because Britain had apparently paid little regard to her declared views, Ghana wanted unambiguous replies to three questions. First, had Britain accepted the principle of association under the Treaty of Rome and if so, how did she reconcile this with Ghana's stated opposition to any such association? Second, had Britain accepted in principle that, if she joined the EEC, she would have to impose reverse preferences against any African countries which did not want to associate with the EEC? Third, had Britain accepted in principle that she would in her trade discriminate between those Commonwealth countries which had and had not accepted such association? Clear answers to these questions would greatly help consideration of the problem of British membership of the EEC both at the present Meeting and thereafter.

Mr Macmillan had said that Britain was not faced with a choice between Europe and the Commonwealth but Ghana did not share this optimism and felt that Britain could not join the EEC on the terms so far known without diverting her attention from the unique problems of an expanding Commonwealth whose membership was based upon belief in world peace and understanding between different races. The Commonwealth had so far withstood the tests to which it had been subjected and the question was whether it could survive Britain's entry into the European Community. Commonwealth values should not be sacrificed to new loyalties and Ghana would be greatly sorry if that came about.

Sir Milton Margai[178] expressed his own and his country's gratitude for the warm welcome which Sierra Leone had received on joining the Commonwealth, with its great past and future role in the field of human relations. She had joined with an open mind and would exercise independent judgment in all matters of common concern. There were genuine misgivings among the Commonwealth countries about Britain's application to join the EEC. When Sierra Leone sought membership of the Commonwealth she did so not as an automatic

178. The Prime Minister of Sierra Leone.

gesture, but fully believing in the value of its historic structure; and she thought that it behoved all members to be careful not to cause it damage by creating misunderstanding about its character, or about the extent of the differences of view which occurred in all families. Sierra Leone had always said that she did not want to influence Britain in the matter of joining the EEC since she assumed that every independent nation knew what was best for it and should be allowed to put its own interests first. But she also assumed that, in judging the merits of membership of the EEC, Britain would take full account of the views and interests of the other Commonwealth countries. Sierra Leone attached great importance to the development of the bonds uniting African countries, both economically and politically; and this must necessarily affect her attitude to the EEC and British membership of it.

The results so far of Mr Heath's hard and extensive labours in Brussels required careful study, but the balance of advantage was difficult to judge and he hoped that judgment would become easier when the Brussels negotiations had been concluded. Mr Macmillan had said that Britain's problem was how to reconcile the historic and living structure of the Commonwealth with the new and developing structure of Europe. The Commonwealth was an association of nations and, as he saw it, the core of this problem of reconciliation was to reach a solution which would strengthen Commonwealth cooperation so that the Commonwealth could grow in stature and authority. That was the task of this Meeting.

Mr Menzies[179] said that Mr Macmillan had given the Meeting a distinguished statement of the high political and historical reasons which had led Britain to apply for membership of the European Communities. Mr Heath had explained vividly and in great detail the stage reached in the negotiations so far. Perhaps he had ended on too optimistic a note by referring to very considerable safeguards for Commonwealth interests: as far as Australia was concerned the safeguards seemed a little sketchy. The problem with which they were confronted was of historical importance. He had attended many previous Commonwealth Meetings, but none in which the issues at stake had been graver or more significant. He thought it was right to feel a proper, though controlled, emotion in facing these issues and to pay particular regard to the economic considerations without getting them out of perspective.

The political issues deserved analysis. If Britain acceded to the Rome Treaty, this would, as far as he could see, be an irrevocable decision. There had been a good deal of comment about sovereignty. When a sovereign state limited its own autonomy, it was limiting sovereignty by exercising it and

179. Robert Menzies, the Prime Minister of Australia.

normally no problem was presented since most treaties had either a terminal date or provision for denunciation. It seemed that the Treaty of Rome was one of the rare exceptions and that it could only be dissolved in favour of one of the parties to it by the unanimous consent of the others.

He would like first to consider the position of Great Britain. He understood the deeply-felt reasons that had led to a decision which, if carried to a conclusion, would be revolutionary in its effect and would mark a new era in British history. They deserved close attention, although he must point out that they were not endorsed by everyone in the United Kingdom and therefore could not just be accepted by the rest of the Commonwealth in silence. He understood that the British Government considered that the balance of power theory was no longer tenable; that it had been falsified twice in this century by the two great wars; that if Britain were a member of the Community she would be able to play a greater part in removing possible causes of conflict; and that the influence of an outward-looking Britain was needed to counteract inward-looking tendencies in the Community.

These were matters for the judgment of Britain, and Australia did not even wish to appear to interfere in such political decisions. He could describe the arguments in favour of Britain's joining the Community as powerful, intelligible and well-understood. He was, however, entitled to point out some of the possible, or even probable, consequences of this step.

The Economic Community was closely planned and extensively controlled, there was to be free movement of labour and capital between members, social policies were to be harmonised, there were to be common institutions and far reaching administrative, judicial and financial implications: all this pointed to "an ever closer union among European people", as set out in the Treaty of Rome itself.

The Commonwealth had an obvious interest in the price that was to be paid for all this. If the United Kingdom were to confine itself to what he might call ad-hoc participation without supranational institutions, it seemed to him that sovereignty would not be significantly impaired. If, on the other hand, some sort of federation were to emerge, the nature of the Commonwealth would of necessity be drastically changed. He had some experience of federations, and it was clear that they necessarily involved the subordination of the sovereignty of their members. It was possible to envisage a confederation, where the central authority dealt with the member states and not with the people. The United States had in their early days examined both and had concluded that confederation was weak and shambling and that federation would lead, as it had led, to powerful unity. They had also come to the decision that the states comprising their federation were not sovereign and could not regain their sovereignty by seceding. Once federation was achieved, sovereignty had of necessity to be subordinated. Some looser arrangements had been thought of—more than ad hoc arrangements but less than federation. However, history showed that such arrangements either tended to develop into proper federation or to break apart completely. Britain could hardly enter the Community on the assumption that it would gradually break apart, and it was not possible to pretend that the nature of the Commonwealth as an association of sovereign independent states would not be greatly changed.

Mr Menzies said that he would like to enquire what the British Government were asking the other Commonwealth Prime Ministers to say or do. Perhaps he could make three propositions. He did not suppose that, with so many of the conditions still vague and undecided, the British Government expected Commonwealth Prime Ministers to endorse at this stage a decision to join— obviously the Commonwealth had to know first what they would be endorsing. On the other hand, realising the sense of historic purpose inspiring Great Britain, he would not wish to record an objection in principle. Whether Australia could approve the terms of Britain's entry was therefore a question which could not be answered in advance.

Mr Menzies said that on Britain's entry the Commonwealth as an association would sustain change—nominal or substantial. These changes might he accepted for purely practical reasons if individual members could he convinced that they would have genuine prospects of increasing their trade with an enlarged Community. But this did not seem to be in prospect and he would therefore like to ask what economic price the other members of the Commonwealth would be expected to pay if Britain decided to join the Community. In spite of all the negotiations Australia did not yet know the answer to this question. It was clear that Commonwealth preferences would disappear by 1970, and that the proposal for comparable outlets had not been acceptable to the Six. There had been some general talk about world-wide commodity agreements but nothing like a commitment. Price policies and reasonable price levels had been referred to—without specifying whether they would be reasonable from the point of view of European domestic producers or of outside exporters. Some commodities such as sugar, meat, metals and processed food covering indeed the bulk of Australia's trade had not yet been dealt with in the negotiations. He was not making criticisms and was well aware of what had been achieved in so limited a time: nevertheless, those were the facts. It seemed to him, therefore, that it might be necessary to hold further talks when the Brussels negotiations had been brought to a conclusion but these could perhaps he related to separate sectors of the negotiations.

Mr Menzies said that no unnecessary delay could be afforded in reaching a decision on Britain's relationship with Europe because of the damage that uncertainty did to the business confidence. On the other hand, it was obvious that every point in the negotiations had to be thoroughly discussed. So far he did not believe that the Six had moved at all in the direction of the Commonwealth. The Community did not seem prepared to offer adequate access to European markets or any certainty of proper prices. Commodity agreements provided a possible hopeful element and the United Kingdom, who had not always been keen on them, might play a decisive role if they were now to state their firm support and the principles on which they thought they should operate.

Great Britain had apparently decided that the economic losses entailed in joining the European Community would be outweighed by the economic gains. This could not have been an easy decision to reach and he hoped it was right. It was clear, however, that part of the initial price, and perhaps part of the final price, would have to be paid by the rest of the Commonwealth, and this was a compelling reason for them to do their utmost to influence the negotiations and to modify their results. He hoped that Australia had behaved constructively. They had their own great problems; the need for growth demanded a large volume of immigrants, the development of manufacturing industries and the continuous stimulation of agricultural production. There had been a great deal of expansion in Australia in the last ten years, but the terms of trade had moved against Australia in a phenomenal way. Between 1951 and 1961 Australian export prices had fallen by 42 per cent while import prices had risen by 6 per cent. This was not a process that could continue. Australia had to have a level of exports that would at least pay for imports.

Australia was not underdeveloped as regarded the standard of living of her people, but she was still underdeveloped as a country and had an enormous task before her. She needed increasing access to Western markets at prices that would enable her production to expand. Australia did not necessarily want to retain the old terms of trade. But faced with a loss of her preferential position and her right of duty free entry into the United Kingdom market she needed an assurance from the enlarged Community that policies would be adopted that would enable the Commonwealth to sell their products at fair prices and on fair competitive terms.

During the ten years 1951-1961 Australia had an adverse balance of trade with the United Kingdom of £504 million and an adverse invisible balance of £635 million, a total of £1,139 million. If the United Kingdom market was to be restricted, this balance would either deteriorate further or Australia would have to take special steps to improve it.

The argument had been advanced that the growth of the European Economic Community would be for the good for everyone, However, he must point out that in the years 1957-1961, when European industrial production rose by 30 per cent, imports from the sterling area (excluding the United Kingdom) rose by only 4 per cent. In years when Australian production was increasing, the increase was reflected in their imports. He hoped that the figures he quoted were not an indication that the European Community was proposing to promote its own agricultural production as well as its industrial production and to restrict imports.

In any circumstances Britain's entry into the Community would cause some damage to Australian interests. There had to be compensating factors, and of these there was as yet little sign. What Australia wanted was access to the European market on fair conditions and at fair prices so that she could continue her own development.

364. To the Borough of St Pancras[180]

Mr Mayor[181] and friends,
… More than nine years ago I was invited to come here and I responded to that which I see still [recording indistinct].[182] Today, I am grateful to you, Mr Mayor, for again inviting me here on an occasion which I consider an auspicious one. And I am grateful to the Borough of St Pancras for having given this thought and taking this action to put up a memorial to a person who, in spite of all that has happened and our own failures, still continues to inspire us and millions of people in India. I do not think there could have been a more grateful gesture on the part of the Borough of St Pancras. We were enthused by a person who is beloved so much in India and who represented India more than any other, in various high positions in India. Perhaps it is a good thing for his memorial to be here, in Tavistock Square, than in any official quarter of London.

As you know, Mr Mayor, he was a man of the people, with a vision of the people of India, and he always remained that, whatever else, however great his position might have become. It is a good thing that among the other things that

---

180. Speech, 19 September 1962, accepting a site for Mahatma Gandhi's statue from the St Pancras Borough Council, in Tavistock Square, London. NMML, AIR Tapes.
181. Mrs Grace F. Lee. See *The Tribune* (Ambala), 21 September 1962. Nehru addresses her, according to the transcript, as "Mr Mayor."
182. According to a report of Nehru's speech in the *National Herald*, 21 September 1962, p. 5: "Pandit Nehru recalled that nine years ago he had in the same square planted a sapling that was now flourishing."

we have in London and England, that is a special link with India in the shape of a memorial to Mahatma Gandhi here in this borough. I am happy therefore to be associated on this occasion and I am grateful to you and thank you, Mr Mayor, for having decided to put up this memorial of the greatest Indian of our times.

Thank you.

365. To Arthur J. Tarnowski: Travel in India[183]

September 19, 1962

Dear Count Tarnowski,

I have received your letter of the 10th September with its enclosures. I do not think there will be any difficulty about your tour across India. No restrictions for travel in India exist, except near some of our frontier areas where there is an "inner line", beyond which normally people are not allowed to go. In the list of places you have mentioned which you might visit there is no place which is beyond this inner line, except perhaps Badrinath.

I shall pass on your letter to our Tourist Department who will no doubt give you such help as may be necessary.

I am sorry I have not been able to find time to meet you. I have been heavily occupied here and I am going to return tomorrow morning from London.

Yours sincerely,
Jawaharlal Nehru

366. Meeting with Indian Workers Association Deputation[184]

I had a meeting with the deputation from the Indian Workers Association of Great Britain, who gave me a memorandum which I enclose. Also a note from the Deputy High Commissioner.[185]

---

183. Letter to a Polish émigré, 1930-2012, traveller and travel writer, and social activist inspired by Baba Amte; address: 35 Queensborough Terrace, London W2. Sent from London.
184. Note, 19 September 1962, from London, for Y.D. Gundevia, the Commonwealth Secretary, MEA. MEA, File No. Misc. 76/FSP-II/62, p. 7/note. Also available in the JN Collection.
185. The meeting took place on 18 September 1962. For the memorandum, see appendix 65, and for the note by the Deputy High Commissioner, T.N. Kaul, see appendix 64.

I think it is important and necessary for us to have more contacts with the Indian workers in the UK. There are over a hundred thousand of them.

I think that we should have some meeting place or social centre for them in London, Birmingham, etc. We may begin with London. As for expenditure involved, I think it would be possible for the Workers' organisations to raise funds for the purpose. But we must be prepared to have some officers paid by us to look after them and help them. There are many ways that this can be done and should not involve us in heavy expenditure. I have spoken to the High Commissioner[186] and the Deputy High Commissioner and asked them to explore this question.

I told the Deputation that came to see me that Indian workers here are rather unpopular because many of them do not know the language or the customs here and they keep in their small provincial groups. They often quarrel and drink and gamble. The Workers' Association should try to help them to get out of these habits and to utilise their time here in learning something worthwhile. We shall help them in this.

367. Lalitagauri Pant[187]

I met the other day the young Rani of Aundh[188] who has been here for some time. Her husband is a hopeless alcoholic addict. He came here for treatment which did him little good. He has gone back to India, but the Rani and her two children remain here. The two children are at school.

I was very much struck by this young woman. She is about 29 or so. Owing to the domestic difficulties she has had to face for many years she has matured and grown up. She knows a good deal about Indian history and the Indian classics and is very proud of India's past. She is attractive and very pleasant in her manners.

She suggested that she might be given some cultural post in our High Commission here. It struck me that she would be very useful in such a post especially in dealing with students here. Her influence would be all for the good and would give them a certain Indian background. She has also studied Indian classical music. She knows French very well.

186. M.C. Chagla.
187. Note, 19 September 1962, from London for Y.D. Gundevia, the Commonwealth Secretary, MEA.
188. Lalitagauri Pant.

I have suggested to the High Commissioner[189] to use her services for a while for some months and find out how she functions. After that we can decide more definitely about her. The High Commissioner told me that they were badly in need of some person to do this kind of social work with students and others.

I am writing to you in case a reference is made to our Ministry on this subject.

368. To Kensington Davison: Covent Garden Opera House[190]

September 19, 1962

Dear Mr Davison,

I have your letter of the 17th September. I entirely agree with you that the Covent Garden Opera House is a great national institution deserving of support. But I rather doubt if it would be quite appropriate for me to become a member of your organisation. I do not normally join organisations in other countries unless they are connected with India, even though the organisation might be [a] good one. Also much as I welcome your effort, I have not in any way been connected with the Opera House at Covent Garden, nor indeed specially with music. It would therefore be rather odd to join such an organisation. I hope you will appreciate my position.

With all good wishes to you,

Yours sincerely,

[Jawaharlal Nehru]

(e) USSR

369. Independence Day Message for Soviet Union[191]

Independence Day is a great day for us because that day saw the end of foreign rule in India and the culmination of our struggle for independence. Ever since

189. M.C. Chagla.
190. Letter to the Organisation Secretary of the Royal Opera House, Covent Garden, London WC2. Sent from 9 Kensington Palace Gardens, London W8.
191. Message, 11 August 1962, forwarded to V.N. Matyash, TASS correspondent, 155 Jor Bagh, New Delhi. PMO, File No. 9/2/62-PMP, Vol. V, Sr. No. 96-A. Also available in the JN Collection.

we gained independence, we have been engrossed in our attempts at economic progress and betterment of our people. The task before us is a very difficult one, but we are confident that we shall succeed.

While internal affairs and problems take up most of our time, we are naturally interested greatly in world peace and the freedom of colonial countries. We have followed a policy of non-alignment and endeavoured to be friendly to all nations. We are happy that our relations with the Soviet Union are friendly and cordial, and we are grateful to it for the help it has rendered us in our economic and industrial progress. We are glad that the cultural contacts between the two countries are growing.

370. For Soviet Space Scientists[192]

We live in an age of wonders and great advances through science. Another of these wonders is the new space ship "Vostok III"[193] which is now being piloted by the cosmonaut Major Andrian Nikolayev. Gradually our knowledge of the outer space becomes more and more. The question now is how this knowledge can be taken advantage of for the good of humanity. It seems to be absurd for people to talk of war on this earth when these great adventures are opening out to us.

I send my congratulations to the scientists of the Soviet Union who have made these space flights possible.

371. For Soviet Cosmonauts[194]

I think that this simultaneous flight of the two cosmonauts is a wonderful thing and indicates a great advance in space results.[195] It reflects great credit not only on the two cosmonauts but also on Soviet science which has made this possible. I trust that this great advance will further the cause of peace,

192. Message, 12 August 1962, forwarded to V.N. Matyash, TASS correspondent, 155 Jor Bagh, New Delhi-3.
193. Launched on 11 August 1962.
194. Message to Radio Moscow, 16 August 1962, reproduced from report in the *National Herald*, 18 August 1962, p. 5.
195. One day after the launch of the spaceship Vostok III, the USSR launched on 12 August 1962 another spaceship, Vostok IV, piloted by Pavel Romanovich Popovich. The two spaceships landed safely on 15 August 1962. See also item 8, fn 57.

because war becomes totally absurd in these circumstances. I congratulate the two cosmonauts.

(f) France

372. For *Le Monde*[196]

I am glad to know that *Le Monde* is issuing a social supplement devoted to India. *Le Monde* is a journal which we appreciate highly in India for its balanced views and I am sure that will help many people to have an insight into our problems and our efforts to solve them.

We are particularly anxious that there should be mutual understanding between France and India. We have not always agreed with what has happened in France, but we have a sentimental attachment to that great country for the part it has played in the enlargement to liberty and then the furtherance of culture. Now that the question of Pondicherry has been finally resolved,[197] there are no direct problems between India and France and I earnestly hope that Pondicherry will continue as a link between the two countries and a centre of the French language and culture.

We in India naturally take great interest in world problems because all of us are affected by them. In particular, we earnestly hope that peace will be preserved and put on a stable basis by an agreement of full disarmament. It seems to us clear that peace can only be preserved by tolerance and by recognition that each country should be free to follow its own internal course without interference from others. At the same time, the world is too closely knit together today for any country to lead an isolated existence. Inevitably

---

196. Message, 1 August 1962, sent to Jean-Paul Garnier, Ambassador of France. PMO, File No. 9/2/62-PMP, Vol. V, Sr. No. 49-A. Also available in the JN Collection.
   The covering letter of 1 August 1962 was as follows:

   My dear Ambassador,
   You will perhaps remember that I promised to send Monsieur Ariel of *Le Monde* a message for the special supplement on India which *Le Monde* is bringing out soon. I was asked to send this on to you. I shall be grateful if you will kindly forward it to Monsieur Ariel of *Le Monde*. I enclose two copies of this message.

   Yours sincerely,
   J. Nehru

   PMO, File No. 9/2/62-PMP, Vol. V, Sr. No. 50-A.
197. See section Politics, subsection Pondicherry.

we move towards some kind of a world order which will fit in with modern scientific development.

While we take deep interest in international problems, it is natural for us to concentrate our attention on the progress of India. We feel that that progress, comprising as it does over 440 million people, is of deep interest to the rest of the world. Our problems are vast. Apart from the numbers involved, we have to move from many mediaeval customs and practices to the modern age. Economic and social growth is therefore essential even for our survival as an independent and progressive nation. Behind that, however, is the legacy of Mahatma Gandhi which we cherish and which conditions our thinking. We may not agree to all that Gandhiji said because the world changes and conditions are different in a changing world, but his basic philosophy still governs our thinking. Economic and social changes, important as they are, must have some spiritual basis and we should move out of our narrow grooves and not only tolerate, but welcome the great variety of the world.

France should particularly welcome our ideal of a secular state. We do not pretend to have solved all the difficulties that come in the way, but that ideal is firmly established in our minds. Many of our problems will be understood better if we keep that in view. We dare not and will not accept anything which adds to our religious, communal or other disruptive tendencies. We hope to build a nation, strong in its past inheritance, but looking to the future, with a firm unity in the midst of our manifold variety.

We feel that in India, as she is circumstanced today, a socialistic approach is essential for our progress as well as for our unity. There are too many disparities in India and our social system in the past has encouraged these. Therefore, we aim at a removal or lessening of these disparities and a far greater measure of equality. We must put an end to the distressing poverty that prevails in India and give equal opportunities to all. That is a vast undertaking, but I believe that we are moving towards that and will ultimately achieve it.

We lay stress on big industries and small. But, at the back of our minds, the first problem is that of agriculture which employs the great majority of our population. The recent changes we have introduced in giving a large measure of authority and resources to our villages and their councils, are meant not only to improve agriculture and modernise it, but essentially to improve the quality of the human beings and take them out of the ruts in which they have lived. We want to make them self-reliant.

Our Five Year Plans attempt to cover various aspects of our life and economy. Behind the Five Year Plans is a longer perspective of fifteen or twenty years. We are grateful for the help we are receiving from foreign countries for the fulfilment of these Plans. We realise, however, that far the greatest burden will necessarily have to fall on our own people. It is faith in these people that moves us and gives us confidence for the future in spite of the great difficulties that face us. What we require, even more than material aid, are understanding and sympathy from others. We have no permanent enemies and even those countries like Pakistan and China, with whom our relations are not good today, we seek to convert. It must be remembered that there are too many close bonds, historical, geographical, cultural and linguistic, between India and Pakistan, for us to remain hostile to each other for long. Where aggression takes place or is threatened, we have naturally to defend ourselves, but even this is not caused by any basic hostility or enmity and we seek the friendship of all nations. Our internal problems are so great and absorb our attention so much that we cannot think of quarrelling with others.

In this rapidly changing world, we are convinced that the methods of cold war are very harmful. We have all to adapt ourselves to these changes in a spirit of mutual friendship. Gandhiji told us to look at the world with clear and friendly eyes and not with eyes that are blood shot. We may not always succeed because we have many failings. But that is the message which we always bear in mind.

373. In Paris: Reply to Welcome Address[198]

Mr Prime Minister,[199]
I am deeply grateful to you and to your government for your welcome. It is always a pleasure for me to come to this gracious and beautiful city. That pleasure is enhanced by the expectation of meeting and having talks with your distinguished President,[200] and you, Mr Prime Minister, and your other colleagues.

Fortunately, between France and India there are no problems at present. There are no issues. But we are all interested in world problems and the maintenance of peace and in developing friendly relations with each other. I entirely agree with you, Mr Prime Minister, that the talks we may have here will help to make us understand many things and will help the cause of peace and cooperation between our two countries. We are passing through, in India, a difficult phase, changing the face of old India and making it fit in with the modern age. We are industrializing our country and that means a great effort; and

198. Speech at the Orly Airport on arrival, 20 September 1962, NMML, AIR Tapes, TS No. 11637, NM No. 2122 (Cut I).
199. Georges Pompidou, the Prime Minister of France.
200. Charles de Gaulle.

540

in that effort, fortunately, we have the help of many friends in many countries. We are grateful to France for helping us in that process.

You referred, Mr Prime Minister, to the moral issues in the world. I entirely agree with you that in this changing and turbulent world, moral issues are important. We cannot live entirely on technology, although the machine and technology are very important. We have to have some moral standards to judge the modern world.

I thank you again, Mr Prime Minister, for your cordial welcome.

374. With Georges Pompidou[201]

Talks with the French Prime Minister

20 September 1962

1. M. Pompidou welcomed the Prime Minister and the opportunity to learn from him about Indian policies and problems and how the two countries could further collaborate with each other.

2. Prime Minister said our problem was chiefly domestic: how to raise the standards of living of the people and catch up with the age. Economically, our needs were two: modernisation of agriculture and industrialisation. Externally, both for its own sake and to enable us to fulfil our tasks at home within a short time, we wanted peace to be assured.

3. He would welcome India and France cooperating with each other. India had many reasons for being drawn towards France: its heritage of art and culture and its industrial and scientific techniques. The two countries, he felt, could cooperate to mutual advantage. M. Pompidou said France would be only too glad to do so and to lend its technical know-how.

4. M. Couve de Murville said the French Government was aware of the broad features of India's problems and plans. It was, both directly and through the Washington Consortium, trying to participate in assistance towards our Third Five Year Plan. Though modest, the contribution was all that France could make at present considering its prior obligations and commitments to Africa.

---

201. Record of talks of 20 September 1962 with the French Prime Minister, by Ali Yavar Jung, the Ambassador to France. MEA, File No. 101(66)-WI/62, pp. 1-9/Corr. Maurice Couve de Murville, the French Foreign Minister, also participated in the talks. See also appendix 69.

5. Prime Minister said he was grateful for the help and, above all, the goodwill shown. While aid was welcome, however, trade was even more valuable and lasting and he hoped that Indian development would be helped by the expansion of markets in Europe for Indian exports. The Common Market represented a historical development which was good in its own way; where we were concerned directly was that British entry into it would come in the way of our exports.

6. M. Couve de Murville said that, as he understood it, our principal concern was for Indian textiles. Prime Minister said there were some other commodities as well. M. Couve de Murville said that what France and the other Five had done for India and Pakistan, they would not do for Canada and Australia as they were developed countries; as far as textiles were concerned, more had not been conceded because of the fear that the same would have to be applied to Hongkong, and this they did not want to do. France was not interested in Hongkong, nor were the others.

7. Turning to international affairs, Prime Minister said that disarmament still remained the most urgent problem and need of the world and that he was sorry that France did not see its way to participate in the Geneva Conference.[202] France could have played a significant role in that conference. M. Couve de Murville explained the French point of view and the priority which France gave to nuclear disarmament and the destruction first of the vehicles of delivery. Later, the weapons would get dispersed and be hidden. The Prime Minister said that, if any such thesis had been suggested at Geneva, India would have supported it. M. Couve de Murville said that the principal countries concerned had not supported it. M. Pompidou added that he doubted if the Russians really meant to disarm. M. Couve de Murville said that the French feeling was that the disarmament question had got "blocked" and that the reason, in reality, was that there was lack of great leadership on both sides. Prime Minister said that the nuclear danger was undoubtedly the greatest and most imminent, and that it was all the more so because other countries might develop nuclear capability in the meantime. China, in particular, might succeed in developing atom bombs and this would contribute a new danger to the world. The Russians did not seem to like the idea of China becoming a nuclear Power; they were not helping China in that direction. M. Pompidou said that only meant a little more time, but the Chinese bomb would come. Prime Minister said that was why presumably the Americans were anxious to arrive at an agreement before such an eventuality. M. Couve de Murville said that, in any case, no agreement could be effective without China, and he could not see how China could refuse

202. The Eighteen-Nation Disarmament Committee, see item 330, fn 62.

as China would always be behind the Americans and the Russians and would thus favour nuclear disarmament.

8.　Prime Minister then asked about the present situation with regard to Berlin. M. Pompidou did not see any change; he said the Russians continued to blow hot and cold. He could not see why they raised the question at all; once raised, it was bound to become live. M. Couve de Murville said he thought the Russians did not anticipate so much difficulty and resistance from the Western side, and now it had become a question of prestige both vis-à-vis the West and vis-à-vis the other Communist countries, specially East Germany itself. But he did not think there was any danger of war. The Russians seemed, for the same reasons of prestige, to be creating situations in relation to Congo and Cuba, but there too, it was nothing grave. The threat about Cuba had been issued only after the American President had said there would be no intervention.[203]

9.　M. Pompidou asked the Prime Minister about the present situation vis-à-vis China. Prime Minister said it remained difficult; he did not anticipate a war, but "incidents" would continue unless agreement was reached. Prime Minister then briefly described the nature of both the north-eastern and the north-western frontiers and the history of the controversy (the old Chinese maps, the Chinese assertions regarding British imperialism, and the Chinese incursions and aggression). He then explained the Indian formula of withdrawal after which the question could be discussed. He said that India had now proposed a discussion on ways and means of lowering tensions on the frontier and between the two countries; this was necessary as a first step in view of all that had happened and was happening. M. Couve de Murville asked why the Chinese began such an action in spite of Indian support of China and the friendly relations between the two countries. Prime Minister said it was difficult for him to understand the real reason. It might have had something to do with Tibet as it happened soon after the Tibetan revolt. Some 30 or 40 thousand Tibetan refugees had come to India in the wake of the Dalai Lama and had sought refuge in India, and that might have annoyed the Chinese and also made them think that India had in some ways helped the revolt. There was no truth in this suspicion. M. Couve de Murville asked if the Chinese action was by way of reprisal. Prime Minister said it was possible and perhaps also reflected the Chinese concept of protection of the Tibetan frontier. M. Couve de Murville asked if we had any particular interest in Tibet. Prime Minister said there was a small trade interest; even Chinese trade passed through Calcutta. The cultural and religious interest was greater as the people are Buddhists and a number of Indian pilgrims went

---

203. See appendix 63 for note by M.J. Desai, the Foreign Secretary, on his meeting with the Ambassador of Cuba in New Delhi, on 6 September 1962.

every year to Tibet. There was no direct political interest as such; the British had it in regarding Tibet as a buffer against Tsarist Russia. Tibet was, of course, very backward, and the revolt started in that part of Tibet which was absorbed in China before where the Chinese tried to impose their doctrine and system and way of life on the Tibetans. M. Couve de Murville asked if it was now a question of prestige on either side or if strategic considerations were also involved. Prime Minister said that, as far as India was concerned, the fact remained that incursions and aggression had been committed which we could not accept or tolerate, nor could we accept the claims made for large chunks of Indian territory. He supposed that Chinese withdrawal would now be a matter of prestige for them, but the Indian formula of withdrawal provided some face-saving even though they would have to withdraw more than we. For this they were responsible as they had advanced far into territory claimed by India. M. Couve de Murville asked if the posts occupied by the Chinese had any strategic value for China. Prime Minister said that, on the north-western side, it had a certain military value as the old caravan route, which was developed recently by the Chinese into a military road, connected Tibet with Sinkiang.

10. Prime Minister then spoke briefly on the Indian position vis-à-vis developments in Indo-China. He said the International Commissions, in which India participated, were suffering from lack of promised funds. This needed being rectified urgently. M. Couve de Murville said that he knew that France was in default and that the question was being urgently examined. Prime Minister said that there were others also who were in default, including China. He said that the Laotian question was happily settled but that the position regarding Vietnam was still causing anxiety and instability. M. Couve de Murville agreed and said it was unfortunately so. Prime Minister referred to the report of the International Commission on Vietnam and said that it had blamed both the North and the South with the result that it had not pleased either side. M. Couve de Murville said that that was the best compliment that could he paid to the impartiality of the Commission. Prime Minister then referred to Cambodia and the request made by Prince Sihanouk to convene a Geneva type of conference to guarantee Cambodia's neutrality.[204] He said India had agreed in principle but had suggested that the two Co-Chairmen might first be sounded. M. Couve de Murville said that the French attitude was somewhat even in advance of the Indian in as much as France had accepted Prince Sihanouk's proposal. Since then, without withdrawing the proposal Prince Sihanouk had suggested the sending of UN Observers.

204. Item 437.

544

11. Prime Minister asked about the Congo and the position of France with regard to Mr Tshombe[205] and Katanga. M. Couve de Murville said that France had supported U Thant's[206] proposals and was in favour of a re-unification of the Congo but within a federal structure. Mr Tshombe had undoubtedly proved to be very difficult and unreliable, but he thought the problem would be settled satisfactorily. France was never, however, in favour of military action by the United Nations.

12. Prime Minister congratulated M. Pompidou and the Government for the way in which the Algerian question had been settled.[207] He wanted to know what was happening there now and what the French thought of it. M. Pompidou said that the GPRA[208] had not proved to be as effective after the settlement as it had shown itself to be during the negotiations and before. The result had been a tussle of power between the different leaders. France had remained strictly neutral in the struggle. Meanwhile, anarchy prevailed and advantage was taken by certain Algerian elements to provoke and commit acts of banditism and racism against French nationals. There had been some cruel revenges taken and acts of kidnapping had started again recently. It was possible some French elements were themselves responsible for a part of these in their attempts to attract French intervention or at least to create antagonism with the new leadership. He hoped that, as a result of the elections now proceeding, a strong government would emerge which would ensure the establishment of law and order. He also hoped that cooperation would be established between France and Algeria as in the case of Morocco and Tunisia.

13. Prime Minister said that, while a decision had been taken to preserve Pondicherry as a separate State and entity and not merged with any neighbouring State, India was keen on Pondicherry providing a window for looking at France. Even otherwise, Indo-French cultural and technical cooperation could be enlarged both in India and in France. He wanted to know if there were any problems which M. Pompidou or M. Couve de Murville would like to discuss with regard to Pondicherry. The latter replied that there were a few points of adjustment left which he was sure the forthcoming discussions in the mixed commission would satisfactorily settle.

---

205. Moïse Tshombe, President of Katanga.
206. The Acting Secretary-General of the UN.
207. Negotiations between the French Government and the Algerian National Liberation Front (FLN) commenced in Evian in May 1961; an agreement was reached in March 1962, when the French Government declared a cease-fire. Algeria gained independence after the referendum for self-determination on 1 July 1962.
208. *Gouvernement provisoire de la République Algérienne* (Provisional Government of the Algerian Republic) was the government-in-exile of the FLN, 1958-1962.

14. M. Pompidou concluded the talks and expressed to the Prime Minister his great satisfaction at his visit and the opportunity he had given for these talk. These, he was confident, would lead to greater understanding between the two governments and wider cooperation in all fields. He said that France was anxious to enlarge cooperation.

375. In Paris: To French Radio[209]

Jawaharlal Nehru: I think that the policy of nonalignment has been more and more appreciated recently even by the great powers who are members of military blocs. It helps to create an atmosphere when people can talk, when people can talk without getting too much excited, under tension. After all, it appears that there can be no military solution of the world's problems. That will mean destruction. There has to be a peaceful solution, and the nonaligned countries help in bringing about that approach which will lead to a peaceful solution.

Question: What are your views about the Communist bloc?

Jawaharlal Nehru: The policy of the Soviet Union and China? The Soviet Union has progressed greatly in the last many years and has become more normal. I do not think it is their ... expansion because they go on using the old slogans but the fact is they are not expansionists; they want peace above everything. In regard to China it is difficult to say. But they seem to be still in the full flood of revolutionary change and quite apart from communism they have often been expansionists in their history and they are today also somewhat expansionist, at present at our cost, of India.

Question: [in French]

Jawaharlal Nehru: ... more and more to improve world trade and ... it is good for the country. It may not be good for those who are outside. Therefore, I hope that it will develop into the first step towards organizing the world trade.

Question: [about development of industry]

Jawaharlal Nehru: That is a big question because ever since we became independent we have been eager to fight poverty and illiteracy in India and we have found that we have planned so as to use our resources to the best advantage

209. Interview, 22 September 1962. NMML, AIR Tapes, TS No. 11354, NM No. 1971. All questions have been translated from the French. In the transcript available in the NMML, JN Master File, only the subject matter of the questions is indicated, not the exact questions.

because our resources are limited. We have found that we must industrialize the country and modernize our agriculture, both, because India is an agricultural country, and thus increase our production greatly. That requires again large scale education, technical and general. We have paid much attention to this. At present about forty-six million people, boys and girls, are in schools. In another four years' time the number will increase to sixty-five million—increasing—and in technical education too we have made great progress, engineers and the rest. So we are tackling our problems on all fronts together and it becomes necessary to plan that so as not to waste our resources.

Question: [about Indo-French relations]

Jawaharlal Nehru: Well, to begin with, we have always had friendly relations with France. There were one or two problems which slightly came in our way, like Pondicherry, and we felt about Algeria too. Fortunately, all those problems are solved. So we have no problems left. And we feel attracted towards France. We have studied its history and have been inspired by many parts of that history. So we would like to have close relations with France. Also now in our national plan development, France with her high technology can help us also. So we would like to increase our technical, economic and cultural relations with France.

376. In Paris: Talk with Charles de Gaulle[210]

Prime Minister's own brief account of his talk with
General de Gaulle on 22 September 1962

I congratulated him on the settlement of the Algerian issue. Then I said there were no problems between France and India and that our relations could become much closer in the economic and cultural spheres.

---

210. Transcript of recording of Nehru's talk with seven American journalists at the Embassy of India, Paris, on 22 September 1962. MEA, File No. 101(66)-WI/62, p. 48/Corr.
    On 14 November 1962, Ali Yavar Jung, the Ambassador to France, wrote about the talk above, to R.K. Nehru, Secretary General, MEA:
    My dear Secretary General,
    I had promised to send you a transcript of the tape-recording of the Prime Minister's talk with 7 American journalists at the Indian Embassy on 22 September in which he referred briefly to his talks with General de Gaulle. The recording did not come off too well on account of disturbances but the enclosed is almost exactly as recorded. I am sending two copies of it.
                                                                    Yours sincerely,
                                                                    Ali Yavar Jung
    MEA, File No. 101(66)-WI/62, p. 46/Corr.

I said something about the Commonwealth Conference in London, that we had no objection to the Common Market. For us it was a question of how it affected our own interests. I told him how this could be mitigated and he seemed to think that the immediate effect of it on India could be looked into and postponed.

We discussed Indo-China, and the latest events in Cambodia where people were very excited over what they said was aggression on their frontiers by Thailand and Vietnam. We agreed that something should be done to give them some assurance so that their territorial integrity should be safe.

Then we talked about disarmament. He seemed to think that the idea of achieving something in disarmament soon was not feasible. He said that of course one could not destroy all nuclear arms immediately, but the problem of destruction of nuclear carriers should be dealt with first. The other Powers concerned should agree to this.

I told him something of our frontier trouble with China, and the possibilities latent in this frontier trouble. There was the possibility of China getting the atom bomb. I said I believed that China was certainly not producing an atom bomb at present. China was not nearly as developed in atomic energy as India. We were not thinking of producing an atom bomb, and we did not want to do it. (Some two years back the Head of the Russian Atomic Energy Delegation came to India. Some newspaper men asked him how China was doing, and he rather laughed at the idea and he said that India had made far greater progress in atomic energy). But the Chinese need some such thing for prestige reasons. I pointed out that it would be a very critical situation if they had it. It would, however, be some time before they could have it.[211]

377. In Paris: With Presspersons[212]

No special problems between India and France
Prime Minister Meets Press in Paris

Following are the main points of answers given by Prime Minister Nehru to questions from pressmen at a meeting held in his honour by the Diplomatic Press Association in Paris on September 22:

Replying to the welcome address by the President of the Association, Shri Nehru said: "It is perfectly true that we have no problems between India and

---

211. See also item 374 and appendices 69-70.
212. Interview, 22 September 1962. PIB.

France now and we are happy that the question of Pondicherry has been settled; we are also glad that the Algerian matter is over and we hope to develop closer economic and cultural relations with France."

Referring to India's role in the international sphere, Shri Nehru said: "It is difficult to say what role we will play in international organisations. Naturally we are interested in the maintenance of world peace, in the development of our own country as well as in the progress of other developing countries. Everything that helps in the general development of underdeveloped countries is welcome to us, and we help it. I do not quite know what other roles we can play. We were very anxious for colonial territories [to] be freed. That process has gone very far now. The only colonial empire left is that of Portugal. We hope that it will also be freed. As regards international politics, we are anxious that peace should be assured and free countries, developing countries, should be helped."

Referring to his talks with General de Gaulle, the Prime Minister said: "I can hardly talk about my conversation with President de Gaulle. They were very friendly and we touched many subjects. I don't think [it will be quite] proper for me to go into the details of our talks."

A correspondent asked: "You have taken great personal part in the settlement of recent conflicts and the conclusion of peace treaties. What do you think about the prospects of German peace treaty?"[213]

Shri Nehru replied: "You refer to the great part I have had—I do not know what part you are referring to. About Germany, naturally we tried very much for the solution of this problem. But we have tried to avoid pushing ourselves in other peoples' problems. If we can help, we help. Probably, I suppose, some time or the other there will have to be a formal peace. The peace treaty—in what form, I cannot say. There are at present two states; they do not recognise each other. It is for them to decide whether to recognise or not to recognise. But I should imagine that they deal with each other even if they do not recognise. They have, in fact, dealings in some ways. I really cannot indicate in what lines the German question should be settled. It is too complicated for me to interfere."[214]

---

213. Nehru's answer to this question is not mentioned in the PIB report. However, it is available in MEA, File No. 101(70)-WI/62, pp. 19-20, at the NAI. This is given here in a paragraph in bold immediately after the question.
214. For reactions in German Press to Nehru's statement on the German question, see appendix 66.

In reply to a question whether there were any political objectives for his official visit to France, Shri Nehru said: "I had no special political objects. I wished to thank General de Gaulle for the satisfactory and happy ending of the Pondicherry affair and also to have the opportunity to talk to him about various matters. We have no special problems between India and France to discuss."

About the Common Market, the Prime Minister said: "I believe that the British Government is anxious to join the European Community and the Common Market. But, as you know, the effects of that will be harmful to some of the members of the Commonwealth, whose exports would be affected. This has been pointed out to the British Government and they have said that they would try their best to look after the interests of the Commonwealth countries."

Question: Will the British acceptance of joining the Common Market stimulate trade between India and the Common Market countries of Europe?

Jawaharlal Nehru: The first result of that, that is, if the present proposals remain as they are, would be to injure India's trade with Britain. That is what we are concerned about. It has been suggested that India, Pakistan and Ceylon, which are in the same category, should have separate trade agreements with the Six. We are quite agreeable and we hope also that, independently of Britain joining the Six or not, our trade with the European Community will increase.

Question: What do you say about the fighting between India and China on the northern frontier?

Jawaharlal Nehru: Recent reports indicate that the Chinese have crossed our northeast border. They have not gone farther, few hundred yards or so, but they have crossed the border and there have been a number of petty conflicts between our military posts and patrols and their patrols. We think they have no business to be there.

An Indian correspondent asked whether Shri Nehru had conveyed any invitation to President de Gaulle.

The Prime Minister stated: "Yes, I have invited President de Gaulle and Madame de Gaulle to pay us a visit in India. He said that he would be very happy to come, but did not know when he will be free to come. But he would like to come."

Question: Do you take the latest Chinese intrusion, south of the McMahon Line, to mean the rejection of your Government's proposal to discuss the restoration of status quo in that area?

[HOLD ALL LINES]

Babu ji . . .

**"We have been thinking of holding the
price line, but now we have to hold
the McMahon line as well!"**

(From *The Times of India*, 15 September 1962, p. 3)

Answer: Well, it does not fit in with it. That's all.

About the situation in South Vietnam, Shri Nehru said: "The International Commission[215] presented a report some months ago. I think the report

215. The International Commission for Supervision and Control in Indo-China.

was objective and blamed all parties concerned with the result that the Commission is unpopular with everybody. It stated that North Vietnam committed incursions into South Vietnam territory and that was the breach of agreement. It said that South Vietnam also committed the breach of agreement. It is a different and serious situation. These countries of Indo-China, it was decided at the Geneva Conference of 1954, can only exist satisfactorily if they are neutral in their policies. Otherwise they become a place of great power conflicts. Cambodia has followed a neutral policy. It is complaining now of incursions into its territory, but it is neutral. The new Laos decision is also guaranteeing the neutrality of Laos, but in Vietnam the Geneva Agreement has not been followed. Hence the trouble has arisen."

Referring again to the Brussels negotiations, the Prime Minister said: "The United Kingdom has agreed to press for certain changes to avoid harmful consequences to some of the Commonwealth countries. It is not for me to say what changes will be made. But so far as India is concerned, I believe that some of the changes desired may perhaps take place. I find the French Government appreciates India's view point."

The last question referred to Pondicherry and France-Indian relations. The Prime Minister said: "There are many ways of cultural contacts and exchanges. Certainly, professors can go, students can be exchanged and I suppose there are other ways too. As regards Pondicherry we decided some time ago that we shall keep Pondicherry as a separate entity in India—not absorbed in any other big state in India—and keep it as a centre of French language and culture, as a window, I might say, of India towards France, and we hope to keep that window open apart from other contacts with France. I do think that in a sense there is some commonness, shall I say, of spirit, between the spirit of India and that of France and the greater the understanding of each other the better it will be for both countries."

378. For All India Radio: Visit to France[216]

Jawaharlal Nehru: My present visit to Paris has been a great experience and a pleasurable one. I have found friendship and sympathy everywhere and I believe that our relations with France, which are close, already, will become closer.

---

216. Message, 23 September 1962, to All India Radio, Paris, at airport before departure. NMML, AIR Tapes, TS No. 11354, NM No. 1971.

Question: What was the most memorable experience or moment of the two, three days that you were here?

Jawaharlal Nehru: Well, meeting people and talking to them, it was wonderful.

(g) Germany

379. Talk with Georg Ferdinand Duckwitz[217]

Yesterday the West German Ambassador came to see me. He began by saying that he hoped our Delegation to the UN will say some kindly words about West Germany. He gave me an Aide Mémoir which I enclose.[218]

I told him that we did not wish to say unkindly words about any country, least of all West Germany. As for the union of West and East Germany, this may be desirable, but short of war, this can only be brought about by peaceful negotiations. No peaceful negotiations are possible when there is tension and fear of war. As a matter of fact, there are two countries in existence—East Germany and West Germany. If their union is desired, then one must work for an ending of present tensions and a better atmosphere. For this it was necessary to come to an agreement about disarmament.

(h) Finland

380. To Alec Douglas-Home: Finland Peace Treaty[219]

September 19, 1962

My dear Lord Home,

I have received your letter of September 18th with the note attached to it. Although you have sent a full note, I should have liked to examine the actual treaty of peace with Finland. Also I feel that it would have been more appropriate for the Government of Finland to approach the co-signatories to the treaty directly.

---

217. Note, 7 September 1962, on talk with the German Ambassador. MEA, File No. 102(1)-WI/62, Vol. II, p. 1/note.
218. Appendix 62.
219. Letter to the Earl of Home, Secretary of State for Foreign Affairs, UK. Sent from 9 Kensington Palace Gardens, London W8.

However, as you wish me to let you have a reply before I leave London, and I am going away tomorrow morning, I am sending you this reply.

It strikes me that it is not merely a question of reinterpretation of the treaty of peace with Finland. There is an express provision in it which you quote, and I should have imagined that this requires an amendment of the treaty. But I gather from your letter that according to your legal advisers, this can be done by agreement between the co-signatories.

We have no objection to such an amendment being made as suggested, subject to the other signatories to the Treaty also agreeing to it. Also we agree with you that an assurance might be asked from the Finns that the weapons they acquire would in fact be used for purposes that are clearly defensive.

Yours sincerely,
Jawaharlal Nehru

(i) Middle East

381. Relations with Egypt[220]

I agree with the Deputy Minister. There can be no doubt that our relations with President Nasser[221] and with the UAR are and should continue to be close. We do not agree with every step that he has taken or his views in some matters. But, broadly speaking, we agree with him more often than with the other Arab countries. This does not mean that we should be any the less friendly to other Arab countries. We need not take part in their disputes with the UAR, nor need we go out of our way to express any difference we may have with the UAR unless it is a vital matter.

Indeed, it is not our policy to point out our differences with any country unless it becomes incumbent for us to do so. We should not act as judges in the affairs of other countries.

The fact is that the past few years have drawn us near to the UAR and to President Nasser and he has reacted with great friendliness to us. It would be unbecoming for us not to react in the same way.

---

220. Note, 4 August 1962, for Dinesh Singh, Deputy Minister of External Affairs, and B.F.H.B. Tyabji, Special Secretary at the MEA.
221. Gamal Abdel Nasser, the President of Egypt.

As far as I can see, there is no essential difference between the Special Secretary and our Ambassador in Cairo.[222] Perhaps there is a little difference in emphasis. I am inclined not to do anything which would be construed as being against the UAR. We should continue, as Deputy Minister has said, to maintain very friendly relations with the UAR.

382. In New Delhi: To Symposium on India and Arabs[223]

Mr Chairman, Excellencies and Friends,
I was grateful when Dr Mahmud[224] asked me to attend this meeting but after hearing the three addresses we have heard I am still more grateful to him and glad of this opportunity, because all the three addresses—and I am sure Dr [P.N.] Chopra's also must have been, but I have not heard it—have been illuminating in the sense that they either revive ideas in the mind or give new ideas to think about.[225] And so it has been very worthwhile for me to come here. I came here with the intention of listening and profiting by what I had heard, not so much to speak. And even now I do not propose to take up much of your time.

The past, with its various implications, political, cultural and the rest, of the relations between India and the Arab world, is a fascinating subject, which interests me greatly and should interest all of us, because we can learn much from it. We can learn, as we can see the dynamism of these countries in periods of their history, and surely in history I doubt if there is any period which exhibits such great dynamism as the Arabs showed soon after the Prophet Mohammed for about two hundred years. It is tremendous, it is amazing. Then later we see the slowing down of these movements and, you might say, the decline of those movements, which were even repeated in Indian history. And one wonders why this should happen. Why a sudden urge should come to a race and fill it with life, energy and dynamic quality which overflows almost and then quietens down, of course keeping the inheritance of that period of urge, but not losing somewhat the creative qualities which that period of urge showed. We see that, I suppose, in the histories of many countries. Certainly it is very evident both in the Arab world and in India.

222. Mohammad Azim Husain, Ambassador to UAR.
223. Speech, 1 September 1962, to the Symposium, "What India Owes to Arabs and What Arabs Owe to India", held at Vigyan Bhavan under auspices of the Indo-Arab Society, New Delhi. NMML, Jayaprakash Narayan Papers, File No. 693, checked against AIR Tapes, TS No. 11352, NM No. 1970.
224. Syed Mahmud, Rajya Sabha MP and President of the Indo-Arab Society.
225. The other speakers were: Tara Chand, historian; Maqbool Ahmed, lecturer at the Aligarh Muslim University; and Clovis Maksoud, the Arab League representative.

Long afterwards, after another long period elapsed, India and the Arab countries were under foreign control and domination, as a result of which we lost contact with each other largely. To some extent it continued of course, but that was all. Take India, for example. Our contacts were more with Western Europe than with our neighbours, with the Arab world or with any other country to the east or the west of us.

I remember, in the late twenties there was a congress in Brussels of the League against Imperialism, and many people were there from various countries of Asia and Africa—North Africa and Asia. And some of us met there and discussed how we can meet again and discuss matters, and we found that it was extraordinarily difficult for us to meet in our own countries because of foreign domination and of foreign obstruction. And such chances that we had of meeting were in Western Europe, London or Paris, Berlin or some such place. So, these barriers were created cutting us off though, of course, the memory of old contacts continued and were very vivid. And then came the independence of our countries bringing, apart from other things, the breaking down of those barriers and a desire to meet each other again and continue our own contacts afresh in this new age. Apart from the fact that there are political reasons, and very important political reasons, why we should meet together and cooperate, there are memories of the old times coming back powerfully and drawing us to each other. Although those memories by themselves, probably, would not be enough in the present age for why we should come together, those memories and contacts do form a strong basis for our coming together. We meet not as newcomers but as old friends; friends of ages past, and that is why in the present period our contacts have grown so rapidly. And our knowledge of each other is not entirely new. It is derived from old times. I liked a phrase which Mr Maksoud used. He said that coexistence is not good enough. I entirely agree with him. Coexistence is a passive thing. What we want is an "active co-discovery," as he said. In fact, what we want in all our countries is a certain vitality in our own lives and in our contacts with others. Co-discovery has an element of vitality and search.

All of us are confronted today, apart from our past, with the present—the present age of science and technology. Now, it seems obvious to me that none of our countries would be worth very much if it forgot its past. It is a rich past. It gives us depth, and gives us many things which we value in life. Therefore, we must hold to it. But equally it is important that we must understand the present. The present, not only because it is an age of science and technology, but because if we do not understand it, profit by it and learn from it and become creative in that respect, we do not make good in this world today. Indeed, and perhaps we do not. We are not strong enough even to maintain ourselves. That is generally recognized. But also there is a third aspect of the present and that is the social aspect to which Mr Maksoud referred. I think the most dominant urge of today is this social aspect, call it what you like, socialism or any variation of it. And I doubt if any country which ignores this can go very far today. Normally nationalist movements are so full of the idea of fighting and struggling against alien domination that the social aspect is somewhat submerged. Then, of course, it comes up slowly. But it is very interesting to see how in spite of that it is developed in the Arab countries and in India.

I know, naturally, more about India, and I venture to say that the nationalist movement of India became such a vast mass movement because even from its early days, certainly ever since Mahatma Gandhi came on the scene, it inevitably developed a social approach. It may not be, and I do not think, he was not a person giving out precise philosophies, he was much more interested in the work he did, in the immediate approach to a problem, but his whole approach was such that he roused up the masses of India, the peasantry of India. And because our national movement embraced a vast number of peasants, even the intellectuals in India, who probably for a very long time would not have developed the social aspect, individuals apart, were forced to develop it under the pressure from the peasantry who were part of that movement. And so this national movement in India, apart from the political objectives of independence from the fairly early days, had a social objective also, which brought it strength and which gave it a certain depth, and which carried us on. Naturally, the social objective could be only rather vague in those days.

We have to struggle with it now and we have to face very difficult problems. You will notice that in many of our countries, a process is happening, taking place, which is the reverse of the process which happened in the Western countries, that is to say, in England or in America or in Western Europe. Real political freedom which may be interpreted in terms, let us say, of adult franchise, did not come until quite lately. England is called a free country with parliamentary structure, but the whole parliamentary franchise was confined to a few people, relatively a few at the top. And all their industrial revolution took place hundred and fifty years ago when real power was in the hands of a few in England. It may be exercised through Parliament anyhow. The result was that they did not have those social pressures in those days, and they could, and they did, exploit the masses tremendously as Marx has shown in his books. And they built up a certain economic background and when later on they advanced politically, they brought the masses into the political sphere, and with that came the political consciousness of the masses. They were prepared to meet them because of the long process of economic stability which they had gained.

Now, we—and that applies to other countries too—we were and are economically underdeveloped and backward, if you like. We come into freedom, independence, not suddenly, it took a long time, but still the whole thing comes at once. And our whole struggle had given political consciousness to the people. They were expecting much from freedom. So, as soon as it comes they expect a great deal, and rightly so, not that they are wrongly expecting, but we have not the capacity to fulfil them. We have not the economic background. We have not developed economically. The result is this constant tension in the social sphere which every one of our countries, Arab countries, or our country, has to face.

Well, we have to face them, because we can no longer say about any country that the political freedom must be delayed till they have done something. As a matter of fact, apart from the extraordinary circumstances that happened in England, Western Europe and America, during the early period of the industrial revolution, they had an opportunity to develop their economic condition and could meet the demands of the political situation later. You cannot repeat that anywhere now. In fact, economic progress depends on political progress and the other way about too. In this matter, therefore, although conditions differ between Arab countries and other countries, there is much in common, essential, and we can learn a great deal from each other, and cooperate to a large extent. I think that at the present moment the area of cooperation may be limited, because we need the same things and therefore we are not complementary, let us say, to some extent. But this is bound to grow both in technical matters and in scientific matters, as in commercial and trade matters. And it is right that it should grow, partly regionally it is right that neighbouring countries should have close contacts, but otherwise too.

But apart from this that has bound all of us together, our worship of science and technology today, but apart from that, although that is inevitable, there is something else of deeper significance to which we attach value and which has governed our thinking, our philosophy, etc., and we cannot, and we must not let go. If you think of those values rather we come back to many of the thoughts which came to us from the Arab world or thoughts and philosophy that they took from us to the Arab world, and it is right that we should think of them in the modern context and not forget them in our search for pure scientific and technological progress, much as we value the latter. Because, after all, life is something more than handling machines, although machines are important today, and in that context we can learn much from our own contacts and from the new contacts that are growing and will no doubt go on increasing.

I thank you, Mr Chairman, and the Indo-Arab Society for this opportunity you have given us to listen to some learned discourses which will remain in our minds and make us think on new lines as well as revive old lines of thought.

(j) Africa

383. To Kwame Nkrumah: Kashmir Problem[226]

July 25, 1962

My dear President Nkrumah,

Thank you for your letter of July 12, 1962, relating to Kashmir, which was handed over to me by your High Commissioner.[227]

I can well understand your deep concern over relations between India and Pakistan and I share that concern. It is in this spirit that I have considered the proposal which you were good enough to make to resolve the Kashmir situation.

Our position was stated clearly in the recent debate on Kashmir in the Security Council. We went to the Security Council fourteen years ago with the request to resolve the situation created by Pakistan's aggression. Since then, various eminent people have been appointed by the Security Council to find a way out of the difficulties that faced us. They failed in this endeavour and we became convinced that third parties would not be able to give any effective help in resolving our differences. The only way to solve them was by direct talks between our two countries. This may not be an easy matter, but it seemed to us the only possible approach. It was for this reason that we persuaded your Government during the recent Security Council debates not to sponsor the Five Power draft resolution, which included a provision for third party mediation, and we were grateful for your appreciation of our point of view. The Irish resolution on which Ghana abstained, you will recall, also had indirect reference to mediation and arbitration, which we could not possibly accept.[228]

The recent Security Council discussions, I am sure you will agree, have not brought about a particularly healthy atmosphere. In other ways also this does not appear to be the best time even for direct negotiations, because there is, on the one hand, considerable tension on our northern frontiers aggravated by Pakistan's overtures to China on the demarcation of a portion of our border in Kashmir and, on the other, the rather serious communal incidents that have taken place in East Pakistan, deliberately whipped up by Pakistan authorities. I am hoping that in time a better atmosphere will prevail and we will then see

226. Letter to the President of the Republic of Ghana.
227. S.K. Anthong.
228. A draft resolution introduced by Ireland in the UN Security Council on 22 June 1962, which referred to the continued applicability of the UNCIP Resolutions and third party good offices in negotiations between India and Pakistan, was negatived by the USSR; Romania also voted against it. The UK and the USA were among the seven countries who voted in favour of the resolution; Ghana and UAR abstained.

whether we cannot make some progress in the matter of direct negotiations with Pakistan.

When I come to Ghana, after the Commonwealth Prime Ministers' Conference in September, I hope to be able to discuss all this with you in greater detail. In the meantime, may I trouble you to glance through a note on certain vital aspects of the Kashmir issue that has been very recently prepared by an outstanding Muslim, Mr B.F.H.B. Tyabji, who holds a high position in our External Affairs Ministry.[229]

Yours sincerely,
Jawaharlal Nehru

384. To Suresh Ram: World Peace Brigade in Africa[230]

26th July 1962

Dear Suresh Ram,

Thank you for your letter of the 19th July. I have read it with interest. Jayaprakashji[231] saw me after his return from East Africa and gave me an account of his activities there.[232] I have also read some of your articles appearing in the press. Africa is, no doubt, awakening rapidly and will produce many new problems for the world to solve. India should take a deep interest in these problems and try to help. I am glad that the World Peace Brigade is taking interest in Africa and that India is represented on it.

I am well now and hope to remain so.

Yours sincerely,
[Jawaharlal Nehru]

385. Africa Tour Programme[233]

It is rather difficult, even at this stage, to give any precise details about my tour in West Africa. Even the date of my leaving London after the Prime Ministers'

---

229. Special Secretary, MEA.
230. Letter to a peace activist; address: c/o World Peace Brigade, P.O. Box No. 822, Dar Es Salaam, Tanganyika. Sent from Anand Bhavan, Allahabad.
231. Jayaprakash Narayan, Sarvodaya leader.
232. See SWJN/SS/77/appendix 64 and Nehru's reply, item 418.
233. Note, 31 July 1962, for Y.D. Gundevia, the Commonwealth Secretary at the MEA.

Conference is uncertain.

2. I intend going to London probably a day or two earlier than the Conference, so as to give me time to consult some doctors etc.

3. As proposed, I shall go to Ghana and Nigeria. I do not think that I need go to Guinea at this stage. Ghana and Nigeria have repeatedly pressed me to go there. No such pressing invitation has come from Guinea and the President of Guinea[234] only came here on his way back from China for less than a day, I think. On no account can I go to Guinea for three days as I cannot afford that time. If I go for a day, this will be tiring and it may displease President Sékou Touré, because I will have spent more time in the neighbouring countries. I think, therefore, that the proposed visit to Guinea should be dropped.

4. We should not ask President Nkrumah[235] for his special plane from Lagos. There is no harm in my going by scheduled flights of air lines. If, however, later the President offers his special plane we might consider this then.

5. I have no present intention of stopping at Cairo on the way back.

6. There is a possibility however of my going to Paris from London for a couple of days before I go to Ghana and Nigeria. This possibility also makes it difficult to fix the exact dates for my visit to West Africa. Probably, these dates will have to be fixed finally in London after I arrive there.

386. For Uganda: Greetings of Independence[236]

The Independence of Uganda is an event of great significance and importance. To all those who have worked for independence from colonialism this is particularly welcome, and I send my greetings and good wishes on that occasion.

Independence, as we know well in our own country, brings tremendous new problems. I have no doubt that under the able leaders of Uganda these problems will be solved satisfactorily.

---

234. Ahmed Sékou Touré.
235. Kwame Nkrumah, the President of Ghana.
236. Message, 12 August 1962, forwarded to Peter W. Jambe, PO Box 1771, Kampala, Uganda. PMO, File No. 9/2/62-PMP, Vol. V, Sr. No. 100-A. Also available in the JN Collection.

387. For MEA Officials: Narain Singh's Account of Kenya Politics[237]

I enclose a letter sent to me by a journalist in Nairobi.[238] This letter contains obviously a one-sided appraisal of the Kenya situation. Yet it is worthwhile to know what this one-sided appraisal is. It indicates one thing at least, that our Commissioner should not enter into controversial politics in Kenya.[239]

It appears that a copy of this letter has been sent directly to Shri K.R.F. Khilnani, our Commissioner at Nairobi. You might write to him and ask him to give his views on what Shri Narain Singh's letter contains.

Later an answer will have to be sent to Shri Narain Singh.

388. To D.T. Arap Moi: Complaints about India Commissioner in Kenya[240]

August 17, 1962

Dear Mr Minister,

Your letter of August 8, 1962,[241] has rather distressed me. I cannot help feeling that it is based on a palpable misunderstanding of the role of our Commissioner in Kenya,[242] and of our policy which he is trying his best in rather difficult circumstances to carry out.

Nevertheless, I am encouraged by your reference to my own views in this matter, which you say are well known to you, and with which you are good enough to say that you agree. We have repeatedly been stressing that the Indian community in Africa should cooperate with the Africans in these territories, and identify themselves with their interests.

I am sorry indeed that you think that our Commissioner is not being helpful in this. There, I think, you do him injustice. We are in constant touch with him, and naturally follow each step that he takes in this, and in other matters,

---

237. Note, 15 August 1962, for R.K. Nehru, the Secretary-General, M.J. Desai, the Foreign Secretary, Y.D. Gundevia, the Commonwealth Secretary, and B.F.H.B. Tyabji, the Special Secretary, all at the MEA.
238. Narain Singh. See Appendix 34.
239. See item 388.
240. Letter to the Minister of Local Government, P.O. Box 30004, Nairobi, Kenya, and the All Union's Chairman, Kenya African Democratic Union, Private Bag, Kabarnet, Kenya.
241. Appendix 30.
242. K.R.F. Khilnani. See item 387, appendix 34.

with the greatest care and desire to be helpful. We were distressed that his recent attempt to promote inter-racial harmony in Kenya through forming an Indo-African Association has been so greatly misunderstood by members of your great party. It is possible that some mistake may have been made in the distribution of invitations for attendance at its inaugural meeting. These things do occasionally happen even in the best regulated organisations.

What is disturbing is that the bona fides of our Commissioner should continue to be questioned even after he has himself categorically stated that he had instructed that invitations should be issued to prominent members of your party. It may be that those invitations for one reason or the other did not actually reach the persons concerned. I regret this, but I would request you not to take an extreme view about it.

It stands to reason that no Indo-African Association could have been envisaged by our Commissioner, which did not extend its hand of friendship to one of the great African parties, which now shares the Government of Kenya.

I hope that you will be good enough to give an opportunity to our Commissioner to explain the matter to you personally and thereby dispel whatever misunderstandings you might have about this. I am asking him to seek an appointment with you for this purpose, and I hope that you will be good enough to grant it to him.

Thank you for your writing to me about this personally, as it has given me an occasion to exchange views with you directly.

With kind regards,

Yours sincerely
Jawaharlal Nehru

389. Supporting U Thant's Proposals on Congo[243]

[Note, 29 August 1962, by B.F.H.B. Tyabji, Special Secretary, MEA, for Dinesh Singh, Deputy Minister, MEA, and Nehru, begins]

The Prime Minister is aware that the UN Secretary-General, U Thant, has been making strenuous efforts for the past few months to break the deadlock in the Congo between Mr Adoula's[244] Central Government and Mr Tshombe's secessionist administration in Katanga.

---

243. Noting, 30 August 1962. MEA, File No. A II/101/13/62, Vol. V, pp. 86-87/Note.
244. Cyrille Adoula, the Prime Minister of Congo.

U Thant has held the view that the UN had no mandate under the present resolution to enforce a political settlement in the Congo by the use of force. He toyed with the idea of taking the matter up again in the Security Council, but thought better of it in the end.

In the meantime, the USA also realising that the situation in the Congo was deteriorating fast, encouraged him to exert his influence, supplemented with their own, on the various parties concerned and to produce some political formula which would be generally acceptable both to the Congo Central Government, and to the foreign powers primarily concerned, such as UK and Belgium, for a settlement which while essentially retaining the unity of the Congo, would yet give Mr Tshombe some substance of autonomy. With much difficulty, U Thant has now produced this formula which has been accepted by Mr Adoula, and also somewhat reluctantly by the British. The Americans are of course backing it.[245]

2.   These proposals were also submitted to the Congo Advisory Committee of which we are a member. There too they received general approval; though there were genuine doubts expressed of getting Mr Tshombe to play fair.

On the whole, they do not seem to be unsatisfactory from our point of view; though Mr Tshombe has been given more consideration than he deserves. As however Mr Adoula has accepted them, I do not see on what grounds we could reject them. The USA are anxious that we should openly back them. I would recommend our doing so. Perhaps, the best way of doing this would be either through a statement by the Prime Minister – something on the lines suggested by DS (Africa) in his note of 28.8.62 overleaf – in Parliament; or by our Permanent Representative in New York[246] on some suitable occasion.

B.F.H.B.Tyabji
29.8.62

DM/PM

[Note, 29 August 1962, by B.F.H.B. Tyabji, ends]

Signed by Dinesh Singh [Deputy Minister, MEA]
30/8

---

245. For US Government's statement on the UN Acting Secretary-General's proposals, see appendix 51.
246. B.N. Chakravarty.

[Note, 30 August 1962, by Nehru for B.F.H.B. Tyabji, Special Secretary, MEA, begins]

I do not think that a suitable opportunity will offer itself for me to make a statement in Parliament. But our Permanent Representative in New York can make our position clear whenever an occasion offers itself.

2.   I agree with you that although the Acting Secretary-General's proposals are not wholly satisfactory, we should accept them and do so openly. By not accepting them, we would be playing into the hands of Mr Tshombe.[247]

3.   Please therefore [inform] our Permanent Representative about this.

SS

[Note, 30 August 1962, by Nehru for B.F.H.B. Tyabji, ends]

390. To Jomo Kenyatta: Good Commissioners from India[248]

September 14, 1962

My dear Mr Kenyatta,

Thank you for your letter of September 3,[249] which has been forwarded to me to London where I am now attending the Commonwealth Prime Ministers' Conference.

I am naturally pleased at learning of your good opinion of the Indian Representatives that we have sent to East Africa. We have tried our best to send people there, who would help in promoting good relations between India and Africa, and between all the various parties and communities resident in Africa. It is unfortunate that sometimes these efforts are misunderstood, and political capital is made out of it. This cannot, however, be helped as in the rapidly changing political and social conditions of Africa there are bound to be disagreements and friction on the exact methods to be used even for the attainment of common objectives. You may rest assured that we follow all these developments with care, and try our best to steer clear of becoming partisans to narrow sectional interests or prejudices.

---

247. See also appendix 67.
248. Letter to the President of the Kenya African National Union, 1st Floor, Solar House, Nairobi, Kenya. Sent from London. MEA, File No. A-IV/103/21/62, p. 82/Corr.
249. Appendix 58.

I am very glad to hear that you appreciate this.
With kind regards and best wishes,[250]

Yours sincerely,
J. Nehru

391. For Cyrille Adoula: Support for United Congo[251]

I thank Your Excellency for your letter of 28th August which I received only a few days ago. We have always been convinced that a united Congo alone can ensure peace in Africa and we have tried our best to see that this objective is achieved. I would like to assure Your Excellency that we shall continue to support all measures to safeguard the territorial integrity, independence and unity of the Congo. I hope that the latest proposals made by the Acting Secretary General of the UN[252] will lead in this direction. Jawaharlal Nehru.[253]

392. For Y.D. Gundevia: Trade with Zanzibar[254]

I had a deputation the other day about the export of Zanzibar cloves. I have now received a letter which I enclose.

I told the deputation that any delegation that might come to India will be treated by us with all sympathy. Naturally I could not say what we could do in this matter without full consideration. We are ourselves in great difficulties about foreign exchange.

You might have this matter examined by our Commerce & Industry Ministry.[255]

250. For more on this subject, see items 387-388.
251. Telegram No. 3164, to Chargé d'Affaires, Embassy of India, Leopoldville, for the Prime Minister of Congo. Sent on 19 September 1962 from London to the MEA, New Delhi, and retransmitted by the MEA to the Embassy of India, Leopoldville, on 20 September 1962. MEA, File No. A-II/101/13/62, Vol. V, p. 666/Corr.
252. U Thant.
253. See also item 389.
254. Note, 19 September 1962, from London for the Commonwealth Secretary at the MEA.
255. For a previous reference to import of cloves from Zanzibar, see SWJN/SS/42/p. 703.

393. To M.J. Desai: Border Visits by Foreigners and Trip to Africa[256]

September 23, 1962

My dear M.J.,

I enclose a letter which was given to me by *The New York Times* Correspondent in Paris yesterday. I have already sent you a brief telegram informing you of this request.[257]

It seems to me obvious that at present we cannot allow any correspondents to go right up to the North East border. It is indeed physically difficult to take them there, apart from other factors. They have no place to stay there. They will actually stay with our soldiers. That too will be undesirable.

I suppose that our border outposts are still some distance away from roads and men have to march a good distance to reach these outposts. Then again we cannot possibly allow one correspondent to go. Nor can we give preference to foreign correspondents over Indian ones. I do not therefore see how this can be managed at all.

I told *The New York Times* correspondent that this was a matter entirely for our Military to decide and I further told him that if he wants to enquire more about it, he or some one of *The New York Times* should get in touch with you in Delhi. I do not think he should be encouraged.

Last night, as we were travelling to Lagos, we got a telephone message from Kakar[258] in Accra. He said that the Ghana Government, or rather the President, had decided to postpone our visit to Accra. Conditions in Accra were very disturbed and a state of emergency had been proclaimed.[259] In these circumstances President Nkrumah did not think it advisable that I should go

---

256. Letter to the Foreign Secretary. Sent from Lagos. MEA, File No. A-II/457/3/62, pp. 57-58/corr. Also available in the JN Collection.
257. Turner Catledge, Managing Editor of the newspaper, said in the letter: "We have the most urgent desire to send a *New York Times* staff correspondent into the North-East Frontier Agency in order to report on the situation there involving the troubles along the border with Tibet and the Chinese People's Republic. I am sure that you will appreciate the importance we give to accurate, first-hand reporting of a matter that is of such vital interest to your country and the world." He sought Nehru's personal intervention to obtain the authorizations necessary for their correspondent to enter the NEFA. MEA, File No. A-II/457/3/62, p. 59/corr.
258. J.C. Kakar, High Commissioner to Ghana, 1962-1966.
259. Kwame Nkrumah declared a state of emergency on the night of 22 September following a series of bomb explosions in Accra and Tema, 18-22 September 1962.

there now and wanted me to postpone the visit to some future date. Kakar naturally agreed.

I have now rearranged my programme somewhat. I have not finally fixed it yet, but our present intention is for me to spend an extra day in Lagos and then go to Rome where I shall spend one or two quiet days. From there, as previously planned, I shall go to Cairo for about 24 hours and then proceed to Delhi. According to this programme, I shall reach Delhi at the same time as previously arranged, that is, on the morning of the 1st October. As soon as all this is finalised, I shall send you a telegram.

It was surprising that the Peking Radio first announced some time today that I had given up my visit to Ghana. Reuter man came to ask us about it and we told him that at the suggestion of President of Ghana we had postponed our visit to some future occasion.

We have had a warm welcome in Lagos and there were large crowds on the streets for many miles from the Airport. Nigeria is still very much under British influence partly administratively and specially economically. People here are beginning to dislike this and they are trying to find out what they can do. In many ways they look to India. Haksar[260] thinks that we should encourage them in every way. There are quite a good number of Indians here in specialists' jobs. There are also a fair number of merchants. There is one suggestion I heard and that is they wanted our Navy people to come and help them to build their Navy. I do not know if this has been enquired into at our end.

Haksar specially wants us to encourage prominent Nigerians to visit India and see what is happening there. All those who have gone to India from Nigeria have come back very much impressed. Haksar suggests that we should deliberately encourage these visits not merely of prominent dignitaries, but also of others like professors or administrative personnel. We shall not of course pay their fare. But we will treat them as our guests in India. I think we might well do this. Nigeria is after all an important country in Africa and is bound to develop.

My visit to Paris was quite a successful one. I found a friendly atmosphere everywhere and an appreciation of India's difficulties. My talk with General De Gaulle was also a satisfactory one. He appeared to be agreeable to the Common Market Six accepting some of our proposals. But the main thing was that it appeared they attached importance to India and wanted to develop more contacts, economic, technical and cultural.[261]

Yours sincerely,
[Jawaharlal Nehru]

260. P.N. Haksar, High Commissioner to Nigeria.
261. See section External Affairs, subsection France in this volume.

394. In Nigeria: Radio and TV Interview[262]

Question: Mr Prime Minister, may I take this opportunity on behalf of the Nigerian people, press and Government to welcome you to Nigeria. Sir, in this conversation I shall try to get to know you and your country, to find how the Indian can best understand the Nigerian and vice-versa. Sir, the first thing that strikes me is the size of India, the diversity of its people. Would you say that this size and diversity has hindered or promoted India's struggle for freedom and later her efforts at nation building?

Jawaharlal Nehru: They have done both. India is a peculiar country with great variety and yet a basic, fundamental unity. That is to say, India was divided up many times politically into different kingdoms, but basically the cultural unity prevailed. And now that politically we have established the Union of India, there are fissiparous tendencies.

Question: Do you think it is possible to remove the greater part of this disunion in a large country?

Jawaharlal Nehru: Well, I should think so. For instance, even in our struggle for freedom, our leader, Mahatma Gandhi, built up a tremendously strong national movement which comprised the whole country, various religions in the country and everything. It could be done in opposition and similarly it can be done, I think, when we are trying to build up a new India. Naturally, there are pulls in different directions, different forces, but the real answer to your question is: In so far as we make economic progress we shall build up the unity of India.

Question: I had in mind particularly a new phrase which I have heard in connection with India, emotional integration.

Jawaharlal Nehru: Yes, I use it often.

Question: Yes, I do not know if...

---

262. 23 September 1962. NMML, AIR Tapes, TS No. 8601-8602, NM No. 1693.
     Nehru was interviewed by C.O.D. Ekwensi, Director of Nigeria's Federal Information Service. The *National Herald*, 25 September 1962.

Jawaharlal Nehru: That is, political unification—there is economic too, in that sense. But we want this emotional integration, people to feel as if they were members of a large family of the nation.

Question: Could you expand just slightly? Many of us are probably hearing of emotional integration perhaps for the first time and would like to get acquainted slightly more with it. What exactly are the principles of this? I understand it is …

Jawaharlal Nehru: Well, we have got, as I said, political union and we have other factors also keeping us together. Emotional integration means something felt by each person as one feels in a family, in a large family to some extent. It is, after all, a sense of nationality extended to the nation.

Question: One dominant note in your *Autobiography* has been your desire to develop the kind of world in which individuals are free. Another has been the nonviolent movement. A third, your love of peace. Would you kindly tell me, Sir, what you believe to be the most important of all your early influences? Was it a man, an idea or an ideal?

Jawaharlal Nehru: It is difficult to distinguish these. But, as you seem to have read my *Autobiography*, I have indicated some of these influences, apart from any individual, that ideas gradually took shape, ideas of freedom, ideas of India becoming independent and all that, not any special pacifist ideas. I could not exactly join together pacifism and gaining independence.

Question: I was thinking particularly of people like Rabindranath Tagore or Mahatma Gandhi or the Indian philosophers.

Jawaharlal Nehru: Of course, Mr Gandhi had a very powerful influence on me and not only the direct influence but what he created in India, the great movement of which I was a part, and living that part changed my life. Rabindranath Tagore had at first an intellectual influence on me, not that intense one that Gandhiji did, but Rabindranath's influence was rather pervasive, it grew, and I admired him greatly and he influenced me considerably.

Question: This I find to be very interesting, what I might call your spiritual approach to politics and nationalism as a whole. We live in this time in a material world. Do you think that the spiritual approach, the religious or spiritual approach to politics has a place in today's world?

Jawaharlal Nehru: I think at first I would not call it religious exactly, I would call it more a spiritual approach, spiritual, moral, etc. I think politics or anything, take modern science and technology, unless it has certain values—which can only be called by me as values pertaining to the spirit of man—it loses its foundations. Just like science goes to the atom bomb, there are some values which threaten the destruction of the world. There must be some other value which controls science, although science is a very good thing. I would say that a man in India now who most highly represents Gandhiji's doctrine is named Vinoba Bhave, who for the last eleven years has wandered about on foot in every village in India asking for land from those who have it, a bit of their land to give it to the landless. He has collected four million acres of land. It is a remarkable phenomenon. At the present moment he has just been to Pakistan, which is another country, with the goodwill of the Pakistan government, and made the same appeal and he had a great welcome there. He is an intensely religious man. He is not a politician, he does not dabble in politics. But the other day he said that politics and religion are out of date, he himself being very religious; what is now necessary are science and spirituality. He distinguished between the narrow religion; he took the higher side of religion which is spirituality, which is more or less a common factor of all great religions. I believe in that very much. Science, one must understand science in the world today and profit by it. One must control it by some measure of things of the spirit.

Question: When you came on the political scene, the world was standing virtually on the brink of war and you took a unique stand of settling international disputes by negotiation, concession, agreement and so on. This was rather almost, I like to use the strong word like revolutionary, in that it seemed not to be practical. Have you found now that with the passing of the years your stand was, do you feel in yourself, that your stand was justified, the non-violence and ...?

Jawaharlal Nehru: What did you say, when I came on the political scene?

Question: I mean when you took over the government.

Jawaharlal Nehru: Yes, when I took over the government, naturally we did not take a new stand, we carried on the stand we had previously taken, subject to some changes here and there. That was inevitable. We stood by it. We had repeated it so often so that our policy was largely governed by what we had been saying and resolving previously.

Question: The population of India is at least ten times that of Nigeria. When we think and plan for forty million people, you are thinking on planning for four hundred million people. That is why it is interesting to hear you refer to your early politics as that of the bourgeoisie. I would like to know, Sir, whether you feel that now you are nearer to understanding the problems of the common man?

Jawaharlal Nehru: Yes, I suppose so. Understanding can be an intellectual understanding, like a professor's. That understanding has come with my greater knowledge. But the greater understanding is an emotional understanding and that, as I have written in my *Autobiography*, came to me when I started in Gandhiji's movement, mixing with the peasantry, living with them. It came to me, the poverty of India came as a tremendous shock to me, of the peasantry, and not all the books that I have read and statistics that have come to me have not added to that emotional understanding, they have added to the detailed knowledge of the subject.

Question: I think you can give us a hint here. You mentioned poverty, the poverty of the country as a whole coming as a shock to you. This must be a shock to many leaders in what is collectively referred to as developing countries. Do you think there is something a leader can do to make the people have faith in him, as someone who can help them come out of this shocking poverty? I would like to take that further and say that, for instance, in India it is impossible to think of modern India without thinking of Pandit Nehru, even though India has been described as the largest democracy. The United States admits to being the second largest democracy, second to India. How has it happened that Pandit Nehru has managed to infuse, to become the symbol of India and at the same time to leave India free to think and act for herself? This I think is a great achievement because it cuts across the entire strata of the whole society, from the poorest right up to the richest.

Jawaharlal Nehru: Well, you refer to me, I think you give me a little bit too much credit. I am the outcome, as others are, of a change in India, of a revolutionary process in India, started, apart from objective factors, by Mahatma Gandhi, and it was that process which changed India. I was one of the many persons who functioned in it—not only changed India but changed many of us who functioned in it. And my present position in India is more due to my pre-independence activities than to my being Prime Minister. If I ceased to be Prime Minister I would be in no position of power but I would still be, I think, very popular with my people.

Question: That is a great thing. That is a great thing. I watched a film on your life and work about a week ago and I found that—I have asked you this before—I found that you bring a sort of dedication and devotion to your work which is very attractive, and that made me start thinking about here in Africa. For instance, we had our own indigenous religion and later on then there came Islam and Christianity and now there is independence and a tendency to reject what previously existed, whereas, on the contrary, India has managed to continue with things like yoga and Buddhism, and even the world now goes back to India to search for the conquest of mind over matter, and I do not know whether all this can help to contribute towards nation building. Do you think that the religious force is strong and essential towards the spiritual force and essential towards weaving the nation together?

Jawaharlal Nehru: Religion as a whole has had both these characteristics in the past. I am talking about religion, not spirituality. That is, it has been a cohesive force and a disrupting force, that is, it has come in conflict with other religions. But, as I have already told you, I think that any attempt to make a country progress and take advantage of science, etc., they are very important, we cannot do without science and technology, but unless there is some other motive force controlling the misapplication of these things there will be trouble. If there is much trouble on a big scale, great wars will destroy mankind, or on a smaller scale even a country. One has to combine various things.

India has been broadly a religious country, but also broadly a tolerant country. There have been far less—there had been trouble on a religious basis specially in the last twenty, thirty or fifty years which was partly encouraged by the British to weaken the national movement. But it has been remarkably tolerant compared to Europe which had seen repeated wars on religion. There have not been such wars in India, not at all. The principal ancient religion of India is Hinduism, after which Buddhism came. Islam came long, long ago. Christianity came to India before it went to Europe. There was no trouble, it came and established itself; there are millions of Christians in India. Islam came also about thirteen hundred years ago, soon after it came to Arabia and it also established itself peacefully when it came as a religion. When it subsequently came as a kind of a conquest, political conquest, then there was conflict, not the religious part but the political part. Even so, in India today there are fifty million Muslims, which is a large number. It is the third biggest Muslim country in the world. And generally speaking, people live together peacefully. As I said, lately, before independence and after, there has been trouble sometimes, petty troubles here and there. But basically people are not aggressive with their religion, trying to thrust it down.

Question: I like what you said about tolerance and I like to think that Nigeria is a very tolerant nation too.

Jawaharlal Nehru: I am glad.

Question: On many fields. I would like to talk of something slightly different, although I said at first that this was not going to be topic of our conversation, but I would like to ask you just one question about foreign policy. Every newly independent country has a sort of hazy foreign policy which becomes clearer as time goes on. In the case of India, it was nonalignment. Now, you set the pattern for nonalignment. But later on, now we are hearing things like positive neutrality. Some nonaligned countries talk about positive neutrality. Is there not a contradiction here?

Jawaharlal Nehru: Well, it is not for me to define positive neutrality. There is nothing wrong about the phrase. What lies behind that phrase may be different with different people. I do not think there is much difference except that the idea of nonalignment is not a negative-sitting-on-the-fence. That is the idea. There is a positive element in it. Nonalignment, as I have often said, is not neutrality—neutrality is fear of this and fear of that but consciously pursuing a policy which you consider right in the circumstances and at the same time not being pushed about by any power bloc—to some extent we are all pushed about, but I mean to say joining a power bloc means other people deciding my foreign policy, my action. That, I do not think is right.

Question: There has been a recent criticism of the nonaligned nations to the effect that the mere fact that they are all nonaligned and together means that they have created another bloc.

Jawaharlal Nehru: That is not correct because we have expressly said that we do not want to create a bloc. A bloc, formally, is some kind of an alliance for military purposes. We are not bound by any military arrangement. If you like, we have created a bloc of opinion. That is a different matter. Opinion does influence people.

Question: It seems to me that the power blocs which you mentioned a moment ago seem to be struggling for the possession of the soul of Africa or the soul of Asia. They seem to be struggling to possess something and especially of the newly independent countries. But these countries want to be free, to be able to think and act for themselves. Now, taking due regard of all problems, geographical, etc., how do you think—this is rather one of these large questions that I do not expect you to answer fully—but how do you think that say Africa and Asia can make their presence still more strongly felt in international affairs?

Jawaharlal Nehru: It is rather difficult to answer a general question like this affecting many countries. But broadly speaking, I am quite convinced that all these countries would make their position felt more and would be able to carry out their own policy if they are not tied up with military blocs. They can be friends with any country and every country, but the moment they are tied up, it not only comes in the way of what they might want to do occasionally but also a sense of dependence comes in. Other people decide, just like our policy before independence was decided not in India but in Whitehall, in London. It was declared in 1939 that India had joined the war. India had no intention of joining any war. You see, this kind of thing. We do not want to be dragged hither and thither. It is very important, apart from politics and economics. We want the aid of other countries but the moment a people think that they can progress only with aid, they become weak and flabby, expecting the aid to flow down and things to happen. No country can progress, however sane it may be, unless it stirs and works hard and depends upon itself.

> Question: I would like to jog your memory a little, if I may, Sir. You have had a very long and distinguished career, although you sounded rather modest. You said I was giving you more credit than you were due for, but I am only speaking with the voice of many Nigerians when I say most of what I have said. You have had a very distinguished career, and, well, you have been in the thick of the struggle, you have been in prison many times and so on and so forth because of your beliefs. Can you just look back up to the moment and perhaps try to tell me what you think has been your greatest triumph, if you were looking for triumph at all. I am not saying that you were—but is there a moment that you can look back upon and say at this moment I felt something more than at any other?

Jawaharlal Nehru: Well, I cannot at the moment, but undoubtedly the thing that has given me the greatest satisfaction and pride is the love of the Indian people because I am not merely a leader of the Indian people, I have received a tremendous deal of affection from them. There have been greater leaders than I am, but I doubt if anyone has received so much affection from the people of all groups and classes. That I think is a wonderful thing, to have that, and that has been, apart from my personal self, a cementing factor too in India. And that is due largely to the fact that I functioned before independence. It will be rather difficult for a person coming now to achieve the same dual character of pre-independence and after independence.

Question: I think in that you have answered more than my question and I am most grateful. I like to thank you, Sir, for granting us this interview.

Jawaharlal Nehru: May I say one thing? For many years past, at least since independence we have been thinking, Africa has been in our horizon. It is much more than on the horizon now and I see many difficulties in Africa, but I do think that we are entering on a phase when Africa will play a growing part in world affairs. And the one sensational fact about Africa, even from a distance, is the amazing vitality of this new Africa. It may go wrong, vitality leads you right or wrong, but it is the essential quality to have vitality. Not to have vitality, it does not matter how right or wrong you are, you do not do anything, if you have not got that vitality. Therefore, one hopes that that vitality will be turned towards constructive purposes and achieve great things.

Interviewer: Thank you, Sir.

Jawaharlal Nehru: Thank you.

395. In Lagos: To the Joint Session of the Federal Nigerian Parliament[263]

... [264] And so we learnt that we have to fashion our own path, learning from other countries as much as we could, but deciding for ourselves as to what was good.

Now, such as we are today, we have largely been conditioned by our struggle for independence. You were pleased to say, Sir, that that struggle was a peaceful

263. Speech, 24 September 1962. NMML, AIR Tapes, TS No. 8597-8598, NM No. 1690-1691.
    Nehru was the first foreign dignitary to address a joint session of the Nigerian Parliament since Nigeria's independence in October 1960.
264. Beginning of speech not available. The *National Herald* of 25 September 1962 reported Nehru as having told the Nigerian Parliament that it was "a great experience for him to visit Nigeria as he had long wished to visit resurgent Africa. It is a novel experience and fulfillment of a long-felt desire."

and nonviolent one.[265] That is perfectly true. But at the same time, it was a hard struggle and a long drawn-out struggle. The organization of India to which I have the honour to belong, the Indian National Congress, was founded as long ago as 1885. That is a long period. It grew gradually; from small beginnings, it became a great organization and from limited political ideas, it developed into an organization having social and economic ideas. It became a mass organization, covering every corner of the country.

Our country is a large country and a country with great variety. Yet, in spite of this variety it spread under the great leaders it had, notably Mahatma Gandhi. It spread all over the country and our leader, Mahatma Gandhi, brought new methods in the political domain and we who had the privilege to follow him, had unique experiences, unique not only in India, but in the rest of the world. And it is those experiences that conditioned us and the whole nation. It was an extraordinary experience to see this great man Gandhi by virtue not of power that he possessed, power of state, but by virtue of his, shall I say, some kind of inner power that he had, influence large masses of people and gradually discipline them, bring about the unity of the country and make them prepared for sacrifices in the attainment of their objective.

So, generation after generation, people laboured for the freedom of India, and often during that struggle we felt rather despondent because it took such a long time for us to realize our objective. But at the same time, we were always sure that we were on the right path and that we would gain our objective of freedom. As we struggled for national political freedom, gradually our minds included in that freedom other aspects such as economic freedom. It was not enough to have political freedom, unless we were economically free, social freedom, and so the scope of our struggle was enlarged and included social justice. When we had to deal with large masses of people, we had inevitably to place before them some objective, an ideal which benefited them. They were interested in political freedom but much more interested in having something for themselves, for their own betterment. So, social justice came into the picture

---

265. Dennis Osadebay, President of the Nigerian Senate, said "Nigerian nationalists were greatly indebted to Nehru, 'the chief lieutenant of Mahatma Gandhi' during the Indian independence struggle for it was from him that they (the nationalists) had borrowed the non-violent method through which Nigeria attained her independence." He added that the Nigerians also owed much to the Indian people, because they "took a leaf from India's experience" in their fight for freedom. The *National Herald*, 25 September 1962.

and gradually we developed ideas about agrarian reform as well as industrial organization.

Even in the days of our struggle and years before we have achieved independence, we gave thought to planning, we gave thought to agrarian reform and to industrial progress and economic advance. So we were partly conditioned even before independence in these matters. We had given thought to them, discussed them, differed from each other often enough and yet arrived at some general conclusions. This, but more especially, the kind of training that we had under Mr Gandhi which, as you perhaps know, meant hundreds of thousands of people spending long years in prison, conditioned our people and made them a little tougher than they were. And yet, there was this peculiar thing about this movement and this training under Gandhi, because he told us all the time not to bear ill-will even to our opponents, even to the British rulers of our country. I do not know that we who were humble folk could entirely absorb his lesson or act up to it, but it was an astounding and amazing thing that the millions of our people did absorb, to some extent, that lesson. And so we achieved our freedom, more or less without firing a shot. We achieved it not merely peacefully but at the same time by creating sanctions to achieve it, by unity and discipline of our people and by the capacity of sacrifice that they showed. We created sanctions which brought about freedom.

It is not quite correct to imagine that freedom came as a gift. It came because circumstances compelled the coming of it. [Applause]. It is true that in the last resort our struggle ended in a settlement with the British people, which did credit to both parties, and when the struggle was over and our country was fully independent, we had little animus left against the British people. We were friendly again and we developed friendly and cooperative relations, which continue, I am glad to say.

So, we became independent and immediately the problem before us was one of economic advance. India, like Nigeria, is a rich country, but the people of India are poor. The countries may be rich, but the people may be poor. We are, in India, we are rich in our resources, in the capacity of our people, but the fact is that it is one of the poorest countries in the world. Although small groups of people may be rich, the per capita income is very low. So we decided then, after independence, to struggle against this poverty of our people and to make them advance economically, socially.

You know, Sir, that the past of India is a long past. Historically speaking, we go back to about five thousand years, with gaps about which we don't know, but it is a tremendous past and there is much in that past of which we are very proud and which we wish to retain in full measure. There are also things, periods during this past history which have been not good from our point of view. And somehow, we had weakened and lost the strength, the ability that we possessed in more ancient days.

Now, the problem before us was how to recover after independence that strength and that capacity, which we had lost and so had fallen back in the race of nations, the race for life. The western world had gone ahead for various reasons; science and technology had given them strength. And we have to modernize ourselves, modernize our economy, our agriculture and thus to make ourselves fit in with the modern world and at the same time to keep our own great traditions of whatever was of value in them, to keep them alive and green.

We have to find a synthesis for these. But more particularly we thought of this problem of Indian poverty and, of course, we thought of it for many reasons, because this was the fundamental problem. We thought of it because, as representing in our organization the great masses of India, we were naturally impressed by their own feelings, by their own sufferings, the peasantry of India and others. We thought of it because our leader, Mahatma Gandhi, had himself made a representative, a living representative of the poorest people in India. He lived, he clad himself, he lived entirely for the people and as one of the people. It was a difficult example for us to follow and we did not wholly follow it but we were tremendously impressed by it. He told us that if you want to judge any problem, always think of the poorest in the country and see how it affects him. Will it benefit him or not? [Applause]. So we were conditioned.

Early in our period of independence, we started planning, national planning. As I have said, we had previously given much thought to it. We even had Planning Committees previously. Now we started it officially, always keeping in view, as far as we could, the interest of the masses of people. In India, the difference between the people, rich and poor, was very considerable. India was known to the western world largely as a country of maharajas and the like. On the other hand, India was the country of the poor peasant. Now, we wanted to remove these disparities as far as possible and to build up a society in which every person had an equal opportunity of progress. Doing that to four hundred million people was a tremendous matter. It was not only a question of building up and modernizing our agriculture, building up industries big and small, but, fundamentally, it was of training people, educating hundreds of millions to think on different lines, on modern lines. We undertook this task.

And we have Five Year Plans at the present moment; we have completed two Five Year Plans and we are in the second year of our Third Plan. It is difficult for me to judge or to express my opinion about these plans because I am rather partial to them. I am part of the plan myself. I think, however, that this planning has done much good to India. We have not succeeded all along the line, because it is a very difficult matter. We have failed occasionally, but on the whole we have made good progress and we have laid the foundations of a new economy. We are trying to modernize our agriculture, and in industry, we came to the conclusion that we can only solve our problems by industrializing the country. If we are to industrialize we felt we shall have to start the basic and heavy industries, out of which the smaller industries will grow. So we concentrated on heavy industries, knowing very well that we had to pay a heavy price for that because heavy industries mean great cost, not yielding a dividend for some time. And the country, as all countries have industrialized themselves, had to undergo a period of hardship. Because they build for tomorrow and not for today. Still we did that, although, of course, we cared for today also and did what we could for today. Now, this process will be going on, the building up of industry. Behind it all lay the educative process, education and other social measures, like health, and we laid particular stress on scientific advance, because the modern world is a world of science and technology. So we built large, many large scientific institutions and laboratories all over the country, we built many colleges of technology all over the country and engineering polytechnics, etc., because we felt it essential that we must pull out our people, out of the ruts of ancient habits, ancient methods of production, ancient thinking. That process is a tremendously long one and will take time. But I think, we have made a dent into these ruts of thought and once they change radically, the whole face of the country will be changed.

As you know very well, we believe in the democratic structure of government and of our society. Our Parliament functions democratically, but we have tried and that, if I may say so, is not a usual thing to try to plan, carry out great plans in a democratic way. We can only do whatever we do by convincing the masses of our people and getting their assent and approval of the plans that we make.

That is so, but we have carried this democratic process right down to the village, and we are building up now a structure at the village level of full democracy, giving them not only authority within a certain measure but resources to carry out the development plans themselves. Now, we have done this knowing very well that often those people may not know what to do, may quarrel because they have had no experience. Yet we had faith in our people and we realized that unless they were given this opportunity to do things and even make mistakes, they will never learn. We wanted them to become self-reliant. We did not want to continue the tradition of British times of some big officers bossing over them, because they attempt to do that even now, I shall admit. The officers are different. We have Indian officers instead of British officers now, but the old traditions continue and they are good officers but we did not wish to continue that tradition of bossdom. We wanted individuals to become self-reliant, self-respecting. So, we are introducing this system of democratization at the village level, and our old officers are there to help them, to advise them, but not to boss over them, not to order them about. The orders will come to them. It is a transition stage we are passing and we attach the greatest value to this stage, because, as I said, this should lead to a self-reliant community, indeed it would lead to better men and women.

In education, we are spreading it as fast as we can and at the present moment. I do not exactly know now, but the last figures I saw some year or two ago was about 45 or 46 million boys and girls at schools and colleges. [Applause]. They are growing, and according to our plans by the end of the present Third Five Year Plan period, that is, in about three or four years' time, there will be 65 million boys and girls at school and colleges. Of course, in spreading education this rapidly, to some extent we sacrificed quality for quantity. It is inevitable, although we attach great value to quality and we are trying to lay stress on that in every way we can. Then, apart from mass education, which seems to us essential to help in the process of not only modernization, but of industrialization, we are particularly laying stress on specialized technical, scientific and technical training by putting up a large number of institutes to that end. And I believe, in the scientific field, our young men and young women, if I may add, are doing remarkably good work. Now, this spread of education or spread of education in the villages, especially because the towns had it more or less, is producing revolutionary changes in the mentality of the new generation, more especially the girls going through the educational course, because girls, after all, have greater influence on their homes than the men folk here. And so the girls going through, women going through this educational course are creating, slowly and gradually, but, nevertheless, great changes in our society.

So all these things are happening and there is ferment in India at every level. Among our peasantry, more especially, we are trying to introduce modern methods after the land reforms that we have carried through. We are trying to introduce well irrigation first of all; of course, fertilizers, better methods of farming, scientific tools, good ploughs and other things, which is increasing our food production, in industry. It is easier to handle industry; we are making fairly good progress both in big industry and small industry.

In our planning as a whole, it is not merely a list of things to be done, that we list our priorities, but we try to take a picture of the whole, the entire picture of India as it is and as it should be. We look ahead. What should India be like 15 years or 20 years ahead? That is perspective planning, looking ahead; although we can only work today, but we must know where we are going to.

And something sometimes takes years to build up. Suppose we want to build up a steel plant; it takes six years, seven years to build, so that we cannot say it must be done in two or three years. Huge hydro-electric works. Above all, whatever, if we build a steel plant, we may make it in six years time, but the man who will run that steel plant requires fifteen years training. So, we have to start training our people not only for today but for the future that we are building, technical training, that scientific training. Therefore, perspective planning comes in and we have to look at this from the long-term point of view. We are doing that and as we progress, oddly enough our problems grow.

Now, new problems are a sign of progress, one should not be frightened with them. It is only a static society, which does not progress, that has the fewest problems. Once you start changing the structure of that society, whether economic or social or any other, problems multiply and bring difficulties, but that is in the nature of things and one must face them. Also, more especially, when you are changing a static society into a dynamic one, a rather traditional society into a modern society, big changes occur and big upsets occur. We are facing them and perhaps, I do not know, you may be facing them too. We have to face them bravely and stoutly because there is no other way of making good in the modern world except through modern science and technology, except by introducing an element of modernism in our societies. By that I don't mean that we should give up our traditional principles and traditions, our faiths, because science and technology teach us much which is quite essential for us to solve our problems today, but they do not necessarily teach us standards and values of life.

Thus today, probably the greatest problem of all today in the world is the question of peace and war. And next to that I would put the development of the less developed or developing countries. These are the two vital problems of the age. Now, if we cannot ensure peace in the world, all our plans of bettering ourselves in the world will go to pieces, will be reduced to dust and ashes, because war today is a terrible thing and it may well destroy civilization as we know it and humanity as it exists today. That is the most vital problem.

So we say, that while science and technology have brought great benefits to mankind they have also brought great dangers and we can only control those dangers by something other than science and technology, by raising, by attaching value to certain spiritual standards to control men and societies. Therefore, some combination of science on the one side and a measure of spirituality on the other seems necessary for this world to go ahead. If there is only science, with no restraining force of the spirit, it may well lead to final disaster for humanity by wars and the rest. [Applause]. On the other hand, without science, and science after all means modern knowledge, we do not make progress; we

582

will remain poor and become poorer still as countries, as individuals, much less can we progress in the realm of culture and other things. That is not good enough either. So that the two must go together. We venture to try to think on these lines in India. I don't mean to say that we succeed, and there are many approaches to these problems.

I have said that we have been planning in India and our experience of planning is very considerable now. We can plan rather well; the difficulty comes in implementing those plans. It is easy enough to make plans on books and papers but implementing them becomes difficult. Well, but in our planning it may interest you to know that we have drawn upon the advice of all kinds of people from all kinds of countries. We have invited expert planners, economists and others from, to mention a few of the countries, from England, from Ireland, from the United States of America, from France, from Germany, from Poland, from the Soviet Union, from Italy, from Japan and many other countries. We have not been afraid of discussing our plans with people of various views, communists, non-communists, capitalists, everybody. [Applause].

Inevitably, during the British domination of our country the kind of economy that was set up was what is called the colonial economy, a gradually changing economy but still basically a colonial economy. Which meant that India—and I take it this applies to other countries, perhaps to Nigeria also—should remain an agricultural country supplying raw materials to the others and industrialized goods should come from abroad. Now, that is the essence of a colonial economy. [Laughter]. We wanted to get out of it and part of our planning is an attempt to get out of it. We have largely got out of it by the growth of our industries. But even after independence it takes some time to get out of it, and one must be clear about it, because in that style of economy, rapid growth is very difficult. And such growth as occurs does more good to the dominating country than to the colonially governed country. Profits go out and much of the wealth of the country is drained out. Political independence is of course good in itself. But without economic independence and economic growth there is difficulty, we don't do good to our people and the people gradually become unhappy and the stability of the country is affected.

So economic growth is essential, that is admitted all round today. The United Nations passed a resolution about it, and we are now living through a period, according to the United Nations, the Development Decade, ten years of development, and every country recognizes that. And many countries, advanced countries, wealthy countries with affluent societies, have given a good deal of aid to other countries too. And we should be thankful for that. But far more important than aid is the creation of conditions of progress. That is to say, as often the two words are used, aid versus trade. Trade, which helps the development of a country, is more important than financial aid. What may happen is, you may get aid from a country, whatever it may be, say ten million pounds of aid comes. But the balance of trade is so fixed that you lose twenty million pounds over the balance of trade. [Applause]. So that, aid itself does not carry you very far unless it is accompanied by advantageous terms of trade. All these problems are more or less common—therefore I mention that—common between your country and mine.

I cannot, I do not know, in fact, all the details of your country's economy and other factors concerning Nigeria, but I imagine, because we have passed through, both of us, a colonial period and many of our problems may be similar and one can learn from each other and, therefore, I have ventured to place some of these observations before you.

One thing I should like to mention especially, that in the kind of structure we are building up in India, we attach the greatest value to the cooperative movement. We think that society in the future should essentially be based on the principle of cooperation, whether it is agricultural cooperatives or industrial cooperatives or others. [Applause]. One may look at that from the economic point of view, but even apart from that, we think the future can only be on a cooperative principle. The world is becoming too small, in a sense, and each country lives on the threshold of another country. We travel fast during this jet age, and space-age, all frontiers becoming less and less important, and we cannot live in this world for very long, without a measure of co-existence. If we are always trying to suppress somebody else or being suppressed, there is difficulty, there is trouble. There is trouble today, well, between, what might be called the capitalistic world and the communist world. Whatever our views may be about these matters, it seems essential that the countries should learn to live at peace with each other and not interfere with each other, because otherwise, if it comes to war, both will be destroyed. Therefore, the kind of world that we build up must be a cooperative world. Personally, I think that the old style capitalism of the past has changed and is very rapidly changing for the better, I think. In the same way, I think that the fury of communism is far less than it used to be and that is also changing and the gap between the two is lessening. It is not necessary for all the countries to be alike. There is a great variety in the world and it is good that there is variety because the world would be a dull place if it were all alike. [Laughter]. We should give perfect freedom to each country to develop according to its own genius, provided it does not interfere with other countries. That is the only principle I would lay down.

So, this too indicates that our approach to national and international problems should be more cooperative. In fact, even today, in spite of all these political difficulties and military and other blocs, there is a surprising amount of cooperation between nations. We lay stress on the conflicts and forget the cooperation. The world would not go on but for the cooperation between the nations. But applying that within a country, we do feel in India that the principle of cooperation should be extended, indeed to such an extent that the whole nation should become a kind of cooperative commonwealth.

Now, one thing more before I end. You know, Sir, that in international affairs we are said to be an unaligned or nonaligned country. That is to say, we have not aligned ourselves with any military blocs. We seek the friendship of all countries and we are glad that we have it. And we have succeeded in having it nearly with all countries, but we have definitely not thought it proper to tie ourselves up with military blocs. Now, that is not anything new in our thinking. It comes out of our old policy even previous to independence. We are conditioned that way, so that it was continuation of our old policy, that when we became independent we laid stress on nonalignment.

Nonalignment does not mean neutrality. Neutrality, the word "neutral" has no meaning. When there is war there are belligerents and neutrals. It almost means that if a person is neutral the other party is belligerent. The word now is used not quite correctly because we live in an atmosphere of war, mentally we are at war, that is, a cold war. And we think in terms of war and use terms of war. So the nonalignment is not neutrality. It is, first of all, an appreciation that the major problems of the world cannot be solved by war. War is bad. Therefore, military blocs also serve no useful purpose. Of course, every country has to defend itself. And every responsible government has to take steps for defence, where necessary. I do not doubt the approach, but the mental approach which is exhibited by forming military blocs is not helpful now. I am not talking about the distant past. And also, by belonging to a military bloc, a country, especially a weak country, loses its independence. Obviously, it cannot, it has to carry out the wishes of the group and the wishes of the group are determined by the strong nations of the group, not by the weak. So, in that measure it loses its freedom of action. Now, we don't wish to lose our freedom of action and, therefore, we were inevitably driven even before independence to think in terms of nonalignment and much more so after seeing the developments in the world.

I cannot say that every country in the world should follow the policy we have followed. Because there are many factors that have to be considered, geographical and other. But generally, I feel that if there were not a number of countries that were nonaligned the world would be in a worse state than it is. It would become two armed camps facing each other with nothing in between. Therefore, it is good even from the point of view of the military blocs for there to be nonaligned nations. And I am glad that, broadly speaking, the approach of this great country Nigeria is also one of nonalignment. [Applause].

I am afraid I have talked at some length to you, Sir, and to this Honourable House about various matters concerning my country chiefly. I have taken much of your time and you have been good enough to listen to me patiently. Because these problems fill my mind and we are constantly thinking of them. We have a hard task in India, and although we have achieved much, we have to achieve infinitely more before we are out of the wood. We shall work hard to that end. I have spoken about these because I felt here to be not only in a friendly atmosphere but also because I imagine that some of your problems may be similar to ours and possibly what we say, what we do in India might sometimes be helpful. You may consider it.

I thank you, Sir, and this Honourable House for the kindness they have shown me and I wish this House and this country and its people all good fortune in the future. [Applause].

396. In Lagos: Banquet Speech[266]

Mr Prime Minister, Excellencies, Ladies and Gentlemen,
I am deeply thankful to you, Sir, for what you have said[267] and for all the friendship and hospitality that you and your government and, if I may say so, the people of Lagos have shown us since our arrival. It is only two days since we arrived here and during these days I have been imbibing many impressions and there has been a feeling of excitement about this visit, excitement not only because it is my first visit to Nigeria but, in effect, my first visit to Africa, if we exclude Egypt and Sudan; the real Africa, if I may say so.

For many years past I have followed the events in Africa and even longer ago, when I had little to do with political affairs, I was interested in Africa. I read something of the history of the development of Africa, I read something of the terrible agony of Africa for centuries, and that moved me greatly. But I do not think there is any part of the earth's surface—although many parts have undergone disasters, terrible disasters—I do not think there is any part of the world which has quite suffered so much as Africa has for centuries. So it is

266. Response to the Toast proposed by Abubakar Tafawa Balewa, the Prime Minister of Nigeria, at Independence Hall, 24 September 1962. NMML, AIR Tapes, TS No. 11436, 8600, NM No. 2106, 1692.
267. Proposing a toast to Nehru as a "world statesman," Balewa said, "We admire the part you play in reducing tensions in the international sphere and if anyone achieved anything you have done it." He added, "You not only belong to India—you belong to the world. We have a lot of inspiration from you and the Indian people and will be always grateful to you." He also thanked Nehru for lending some Indian experts for Nigeria's public services. The *National Herald*, 26 September 1962, p. 4.

an exciting thing to see, the turn is so clear, and the great continent in essence is waking up and searching for—and I hope finding—a new life in freedom.

You said, Sir, that you were sorry that you were born in a period of many problems and difficulties. There is no doubt that the world faces many, many problems, and difficult ones. There is also no doubt that neither you nor I chose the time of our birth. [Laughter]. But I would say there is another aspect of this, which to some extent appeals to me, to be born and to live and work at a time of great events, great changes in the world. I think it is an exciting period to live in. Even in my life—a fairly long experience it has been—I have seen many changes in the world. In the last fifty years, or more, the world has changed mightily, changed because of scientific and technological developments, changed because of two mighty wars and now changing because of the developments in Asia and Africa, new nations coming out in freedom, old nations regaining their freedom. All this is very exciting. It is true that we live in the shadow of a possible war, we live in a kind of twilight period, and nobody quite knows whether that twilight will give place to the dark night of war or to the dawn of the new day. We hope for the latter. But it is a fearful thought that there is a possibility of the other thing happening, and happening at a time when so much hope has been roused in the world, when, looking at the scientific progress that has been made, it can be said with perfect assurance that there is enough food and the other good things of life for the entire population of the world if we use scientific and modern methods, just when we have it in our power to solve problems which have afflicted mankind for ages past, when we can abolish poverty and unhappiness and largely even diseases and illiteracy from the world, just then we should live in the shadow of a terrible disaster which might wipe out a good part of it. That is the first problem of the age.

If I may say so, the biggest problem, the next most exciting thing in the world today is the development of countries in Asia and Africa, which have found a new life and freedom and are trying their best to justify it. That, as I said, is a very exciting process. Even in my own country, beset as we are with problems—and they seem to grow—even as we solve one problem, two or three take its place. I suppose that is not a bad thing: it is a sign of growth to have problems; not to have them means a static, unprogressive condition; not to have them at all means death; only the dead have no problems, no further problems; the living have always problems, and the more life you get the more problems you have to face and to solve. In spite of these tremendous problems that we face in India, as you do in Nigeria, I feel a certain excitement and a certain joy in having to face them and try to solve them. But as I do think this age we live in is a very worthwhile age, in spite of its dangers and difficulties and problems. I have no doubt that if it survives the catastrophe, that is, if it avoids a war, it will change greatly. Modern science and technology, and other factors, will make it a better place for hundreds of millions to live in, and perhaps we shall be rid completely of the fear of war, etc. So there is something to live for, something to work and labour for, something to achieve, and only in the measure we respond to that call of the age, are we likely to succeed.

You referred, Mr Prime Minister, to many problems that you face, to certain common features in India and Nigeria. That is true. We are both federations, we are both nations with a great deal of diversity within our frontiers, and speaking for myself, for India, I would like to say that we do not disapprove of the diversity and we make no attempt to produce a certain uniformity, provided only that there is a basic unity in the nation. [Applause]. India has a curious history of both diversity and unity, there has been throughout the ages. Even when it was split up into many political kingdoms it possessed a certain cultural and other kinds of unity which held it together. Occasionally in the past it had seen political unity also, but mostly it was divided up into separate principalities. It is that feeling of cultural unity which has kept India together in mind and soul. That cultural unity is not something unchanging, because all kinds of currents have come to India from abroad, rivers of ideas, rivers of beliefs and other things have flowed into India and mixed in the ocean of humanity there, have affected them, have been affected themselves. The result is that we have evolved a certain composite culture in India, to which the latest addition has been brought by our fairly long association with England, part of which we dislike and part of which we like. So we have developed this composite culture, and no doubt it will develop still more now that the modern age is coming to India with a rush, industrialization and the like, science and technology, and that is adding and diversifying our culture.

So there is that feeling of unity from old, and this compositeness that has grown up with these fresh currents coming into India and there is also a feeling, which I may say, is rather typical of India from the long past, a feeling of live and let live, of tolerance. An ancient emperor of India, who practically ruled over all of India, including a certain part of Central Asia as it is today, Ashoka—he was an extraordinary man, a very great man. He left various monuments all over India and you find them even in the present day Afghanistan, which was part of his dominions; he left inscriptions on huge stone pillars, rocks and other places. You find them dotted all over, scores of them, and these inscriptions are very interesting. In one of them, a famous passage, he describes a certain war of his. He fought that war. Naturally, he was very much stronger than his opponent in that part of India, the south-eastern part of India. Then reports came to him in the moment of victory, of the horror of war, of the vast numbers killed and made prisoner and enslaved, and all this, the misery of it. He was so powerfully affected by these accounts that at the height of victory he stopped the war and he has inscribed this, described it in moving language on these pillars of stone, how, as he describes himself, his state of majesty was affected by these horrors created by war, and he decided to renounce war and to turn all his energy to the path of righteousness and peace.

The same emperor has another very interesting inscription—this was in the third century BC—in which, addressing his numerous subjects, he says that you must always honour people of another faith than yours, because if you honour them they will honour your faith and you will live peacefully together. Now, that is a lesson in tolerance. I do not mean to say that Indians, as individuals or as groups, are more tolerant always than others, but there is this, there is something in the culture and history of India which has continually taught them to be tolerant and to live at peace with others.

And therefore, all manner of things have survived in India in their separateness. There are many religions. India is a country of many religions but they have lived, by and large, at peace with each other and there are large numbers, followers of these religions in India. That is why when we became independent we followed that tradition and declared India to be a secular state. Now, some people imagine that means a non-religious state. That is utterly wrong. What is meant was, we did not wish to favour any religion by the state; we recognized all the religions existing in India, gave them the fullest freedom and respected them, but did not give one predominance by calling it a state religion, or anything like that. In fact, the modern ideal is that of the secular state in most countries. In Europe, you will remember, during the middle ages, the terrible wars that took place there, wars of religion. I do not think any real religious wars have taken place in India. There have been political wars of the conqueror and the conquered, and sometimes religion has been used for the purpose, exploited for the purpose. But the idea of a purely religious war is rather foreign to India's history. So there is a certain unity of culture in India which helps us very greatly, and there is this tremendous diversity of India, as there is bound to be in a big continental country where climates differ very much. There are the highest mountains in the world, the Himalayas, with sturdy mountain folk, going right into Central Asia, and there is the south of India, which is very beautiful and soft and which breeds a different type of people. Yet all of these have a connecting link, not merely a political link which has been created, previously by the British government and now by our Constitution, but something much deeper than that which has helped us to hold it together. And also in our struggle for independence which lasted for generations. I would beg of you to remember, that itself was a very unifying thing and we are all united, every part of India, men of all religions in it. And so we have strong foundations for unity, although it must be admitted, there are fissiparous tendencies and disruptive urges, and we have to face them. We talk, therefore, of unity, not in the political sense, which we have got, but rather in the emotional sense. Emotional integration we call it, that is, that people should feel that, not merely accept it, but feel that urge for unity.

For the rest, the great problems that we face, and that you face, are those of development. Because, when we became independent and even before it, probably the urge for independence was one to better their lot. Truly, independence by itself is certainly a powerful enough urge, but behind it was the urge to better one's lot and the feeling that independence would enable us to do so, and better the lot of the common people. Our leader, Mr Gandhi, always laid stress on that, and so when we became independent there was an expectation all over India for a sudden change for the better, in economic conditions. But as you said, Sir, it is difficult to change things overnight or indeed for a considerable period.

Now, something happened in India, and in many other countries. It was a process which was the reverse of the process that should have occurred in Western, in the countries of Western Europe in the past, and in the United States, and in more of the advanced countries now possessing an affluent society. They are in the last hundred or hundred and fifty years since the coming of the industrial revolution and aided by the position of colonies, anyhow, they increased their economic strength, and while politically their freedom was limited—in the sense I mean that if you consider the franchise as a measure of freedom of a people, even in England the franchise was very limited throughout the nineteenth century. It was a free country, yes, but the franchise was limited. In fact, it didn't get adult franchise till after the First World War. So they developed economically through the industrial revolution and through the position of colonies and built up reserve strength, so that as freedom advanced, internal freedom advanced. That resulted in demands being made as it does, as it is doing, no doubt, in Nigeria, it is doing in India. Because of their economic strength, they could meet the new demands that you have made upon them. They had built up economic strength before political freedom in that sense came to them in full measure.

Now, we have to face a reverse process, Political freedom comes to us in full measure before the economic strength is built up, the economic foundation. But at the same time, political freedom brings political demands, economic demands, all kinds of demands, which we are wholly unable to fulfill in a short time. And we have to go through a rather hard and lengthy process. However much we may try to hasten that, and we do try to hasten it, and we must hasten it if we are to avoid peril and disaster, even then it takes some time. It cannot be done by some magic. That is the basic problem of most of the developing countries today. Freedom has come without the economic background to sustain that freedom fully, and we have to hurry to fill this gap. That is why the need for development is so urgent in these countries. Not merely development in the national sense, although that is very necessary, but development, ultimately to be translated into the betterment of the people, in the rising standards of the people. Otherwise, social problems have to be faced, which cannot easily be answered; questions cannot be answered, unless there is this promise of better standards, etc.

I have mentioned one aspect of this problem which no doubt is before you, Mr Prime Minister. But this involves a certain speeding up of the process of development. We cannot wait for 150 years and go through the same process as America, or the western countries of Europe have gone through in 150 years. Apart from the fact that we all are dead and gone long before 150 years are over. But we just cannot, conditions in the world don't permit this, we have to proceed faster, much faster.

Apart from our own problems and urgent necessities, the world today as it is fashioned, which is largely, in spite of other differences being pointed out, the major difference of the world today is that there are a certain number of countries which are prosperous, which have affluent societies, and a much larger number which are very far from prosperous, and where people suffer even from lack of adequate food and other necessities of life. In the modern world, it was said, it has been said, that freedom and lack of freedom can't exist side by side without creating trouble. Similarly, too much affluence cannot exist side by side with too great poverty, whether inside a nation or among nations. It may last a little time; it will create social problems and other frictions and conflicts. Therefore, it is to the interest of all concerned including the prosperous nations, to help in the rapid development of the developing countries. It is to the interest, their personal interest too, because as the developing countries become richer, produce more, raise their standards of living, so world trade prospers; the richer countries also prosper because of that. Because we are becoming more and more one world.

You talked, Mr Prime Minister, about Africa pulling together. If I may say so respectfully, I entirely agree with you—that each country must look after itself and try to progress in cooperation, no doubt with other countries. But the fact is that in the world sense, we are inevitably being driven towards what might be called a world authority and a world state. How long it will take, I don't know. But the whole scientific and technological development of the world is putting an end to the frontiers and the like. In this jet age and space age, it is rather absurd to talk about frontiers although we are constantly talking about frontiers and their national states. But I have no doubt that the time may come, will come if we survive till then, when some kind of world authority will take shape, and we should welcome that. But meanwhile, we have to function as we are and try to meet the perils that confront us in the shape of possibilities of war, etc., and develop our own countries, both because development is necessary, essential, and also to protect ourselves from possible dangers.

You referred, Mr Prime Minister, to our association, Nigeria's and India's, in the Disarmament Committee conference in Geneva. That conference has not yielded very good results yet, though I have not lost hope of its leading to something worthwhile. But I am quite sure that the so-called neutral countries, eight of them I think there are, they have played an important and useful role there. I think, that is, if they had not been there probably this Committee, or conference, will have broken up long ago. But they have played this role, not so much at putting forward some magic formula—it is very difficult to do that. It is not a formality that is wanted, it is really a change in mind and heart; you can't do that by decree, or by compulsion, but nevertheless by their quiet and soothing behaviour, keeping the level of this conference to, if I may say so, a level of politeness; at least that is something. Because in the past, we have seen how it goes off in the wrong direction and then no reasonable talk is possible. And I do feel that there is that service we can perform, countries like yours and mine, and others in this world tangle today. After all, if there is to be peace, it will be a peace when the great and powerful countries agree. I regret to say your voice and mine and other small countries will not assure peace by itself. We can induce others to gradually move in that direction. Not because we are wiser, not that, but simply because we can do it in a calmer way, without the excitements of this cold war.

As I said, this stay of mine here has been full of excitement and the whole perspective of history comes up before me, not only in Africa but in the world. Over the last two hundred or three hundred years, the history of the world was largely dominated by the history of Europe. Previous to that, it was not so. But during these two or three hundred years, it has progressively dominated the history of the world. Now, that is no longer possible. In fact, no continent can dominate world history today. It would not be, I don't mean to say it will be a history of any other continent, but we have moved into the period when history has to be a world history. If there is a war, it becomes a world war. If there is peace, it affects the whole world; almost everything affects the whole world. I don't know how history is taught in your schools and colleges. But the kind, the way it was taught in my childhood was ludicrous in the extreme—history of England, history of India, learning the names of kings and queens and the like. Most distressful process, as if it makes the slightest difference to anybody.

592

But anyhow, an isolated history was taught of a country which has no meaning. It had some meaning in the old days when isolation was so great but later, in later stages of history, nowadays especially, it has no meaning. You couldn't understand history even in older times without knowing something that was happening in other countries. No country has ever existed in complete isolation. Anyhow, however it might be in the past, in the present age, there can be no such thing as isolated history of a country, or even of a continent. It has to be a world approach and world history. Thus we are marching towards a wider vision of the world as a whole.

I have ventured to say something about various matters, Mr Prime Minister, encouraged and egged on by what you said. I hope I have not presumed on you and your distinguished company. I would repeat that I am deeply grateful to you, and to the Federal Government of Nigeria, for the honour they have done me. And I hope that your efforts will lead not only to the wider domain of peace, lead to results, but in the development of Nigeria and the betterment of the people of Nigeria. May I request your Excellency, ladies and gentlemen, to drink to the health of the Governor-General, His Excellency the Governor-General of Nigeria,[268] and also to the Prime Minister of Nigeria. [Applause].

397. In Nigeria: To the Lagos Municipal Council[269]

It is rather painful now to move about in the streets of big cities like London and Paris and Rome because there are so many automobiles and motor cars that one moves with a pace less than the pace of walking. These are tremendous difficulties. Therefore, in a growing city one should think of the future rather than of the present and build very wide roads to provide for the future growth of communications. All these things are very fascinating, more specially if you are building for a living community. That is why I lay stress on keeping children in mind all the time.

Most of these big cities have very fine buildings but many of them also have very bad slums. I am not referring to Lagos, I do not know if there is any slum here. [Laughter]. But I know, in my own city, in Delhi, there are very fine buildings and there are very bad slums. It is extraordinarily difficult to get rid of these slums. However, we are trying and I hope we shall succeed. So the test of a city ultimately is not the palaces that it contains, but the slums it contains, and the real growth of the city is the removal of these slums and

268. Nnamdi Azikiwe.
269. Speech, 25 September 1962. NMML, AIR Tapes, TS No. 11639 (Cut II), NM No. 2133.

providing proper housing conditions for all.

I saw some of these works being done this morning at Lagos,[270] and I am happy to find that your Town Council is devoting attention to this important work of every municipality, because, as I said, governments at the top have undoubtedly great responsibility but they work rather at the top in the sphere of the nation's life, and municipalities have to work right down, coming down to the day to day activities, and pleasure of the people.

Therefore, I congratulate you, [inaudible] President and the Chairman of the Lagos Town Council,[271] and the members of this Council, on the important work that you do in beautifying and improving and providing adequate amenities for all the people living in Lagos. Lagos will grow.

398. To P.S. Jariwala: Nigeria Visit[272]

September 25, 1962

Dear Shri Jariwala,

I have received the letter signed by you and some other nationals of ours at present teaching at Hussey College, Warri. I am grateful for your good wishes. You were quite right in not coming to Lagos to see me when this would have come in the way of your work at the College.

I am very glad I came to Nigeria. The Government and people have been very friendly and hospitable. I have especially enjoyed meeting our many nationals here who are doing good work.

Jai Hind.

Yours sincerely,
[Jawaharlal Nehru]

270. Nehru drove through the heavily populated slum areas of Lagos "in a two-hour look-see tour." *The Hindu* of 27 September 1962, p. 5.
271. Adenji Adele was the King of Lagos and President of the local Town Council.
272. Letter; address: P.O. Box 161, Warri, Western Nigeria. Sent from Lagos, Nigeria.

(k) China

399. To UP Congress Members: Conflict with China Looming[273]

Nehru: India must be ready for any emergency
Worsening of Border Situation. Relationship with China in Dangerous Phase

Lucknow, Saturday, 28 July – Prime Minister Nehru said here today that though India did not want a war with China, the situation on the northern border had worsened of late, and he, therefore, would not entirely rule out the possibility of "suddenly, by some chance", an armed conflict breaking out between the two countries.

The Prime Minister, who was addressing a joint meeting of the members of the UP Congress Committee and of the Congress Legislature Party at Moti Mahal, said that he did not mean to imply by this that "there is bound to be a conflict between India and China: but if it comes, we should be ready to face it."

The Prime Minister, in his ninety-minute speech, dealt exhaustively with the relations of India with China and Pakistan, and the internal problems facing the country.

Referring to Pakistan, the Prime Minister said that it was a pity that relations between India and Pakistan were somewhat strained. "We wish that our relations should be friendly, and we should forge ahead in cooperation with each other", he remarked.

Referring to the situation on the northern border, the Prime Minister said that a threat from any country would be a matter of concern to India, and, more so, when such a threat came from a big country like China. The relationship between India and China had now entered a dangerous stage, he said.

Proceeding, the Prime Minister said that a war between two big countries like India and China would bring no benefit to any of the two nations. It would only bring death and devastation.

He added: "We have said it repeatedly that we do not want a war with China. China has also said the same thing repeatedly. A war between our two countries can only cause devastation. No one nation can conquer the other.

---

273. Report of speech, reproduced from the *National Herald*, 29 July 1962.

Difficult Terrain

"However, finding that we were weak in Ladakh, China occupied a portion of our land there. Actually, we were not weak. It was the terrain of that area which had created difficulties for us, and had placed us in a weaker position. It is an uninhabited, desolate area of cliffs, boulders and snow at great height, where it is difficult for an ordinary man even to breathe. They had the advantage of starting from a high plateau. It was easier for them to construct roads leading to Ladakh. For us it was an uphill task. There was no road in that area. We could not rush our forces there. The question of supplies was also difficult. We decided to construct roads, and during the last two years the work of road-building was done by the army, because it was much swifter in its work than the "go-slow" public works departments. The work of road-building in that area would be completed within one or one and a half years. With the construction of roads, the situation improved for us. It became easier for us to send supplies. We have also arranged for big transport planes. We have now become stronger in that area.

"During the last one year, the Chinese have not advanced in that area, except, may be, for some very minor advance. We have made good arrangements in that area to check the intruders. This, it seems, has not been liked by China, which has now alleged that we have intruded on their land. The recent correspondence was a reflection of it. The situation there is important. It, however, does not mean that there will be a war. But if it comes, we should be ready to face it. If anybody attacks us, we would fight back.

Need for Unity

"An essential prerequisite for meeting such a situation is complete national unity. We should, therefore, wipe out all traces of communalism from amongst us. A modern war is mainly a war of resources, and, therefore, it is necessary for us to develop our resources at a fast pace by implementing the Third Five Year Plan."

Turning to relations between India and Pakistan, the Prime Minister said that it was regrettable that the relations between the two countries were not good. He added: "We do not want to harm them. After all, the people of Pakistan are our brothers, who have taken a wrong path. When India was divided, we thought that even though we were separating, we would work together. But then there came the large-scale riots and murders. Then there came the question of Kashmir.

"Pakistan, however, looked the other way. Its formation itself was based on the ideology of the Muslim League. It was an ideology of dislike of India and the Hindus. This ideology was to some extent the outcome of the narrow-mindedness among a section of the Hindus themselves.

"The leaders of Pakistan had no idea what they wanted to do with the country that they had carved out. They had no constructive programme except to foster enmity with India. Apart from this, they became jealous of India when they saw her advancing at a fast speed. They themselves were incapable of doing anything to improve the condition of their country, dominated as they were by feudal elements and big bureaucracy. Therefore, in order to divert the attention of the masses of Pakistan from the internal, economic and social problems, they started raising the Kashmir issue in and out of season.

"Kashmir is a vital issue for us. It is the issue of secularism for India. It is a matter of honour for India that a Muslim majority state should be a part of her. Pakistan claims Kashmir because it is a Muslim majority state. We cannot accept this principle. If we accept this principle, then a number of problems would be created. We do not accept the principle of forming countries on the basis of religion. If this principle is accepted, then what would happen to the five crores of Muslims in India and about one crore of Hindus in East Pakistan.

"It was sad that the relations between India and Pakistan should be strained. We want the friendliest relations with Pakistan. So far as the people of Pakistan are concerned, they have no ill-will for the people of India, as the people of India have no ill-will for the people of Pakistan. It is the top leadership of Pakistan that is responsible for creating tensions. The Pakistan leaders raise the bogey of India to divert the attention of their own people from their own problems. But they cannot go on doing this for ever. The people of Pakistan are now themselves raising socialist and economic questions. Once these questions come to the forefront in Pakistan, this anti-Indian tirade of the Pakistani leaders would end by itself.

"We wish to have friendly relations with Pakistan, and we want that India and Pakistan should progress in cooperation with each other."

400. For the Embassy of China[274]

The Ministry of External Affairs presents its compliments to the Embassy of the People's Republic of China and has the honour to refer to two notes presented by the Chinese Government to Indian Chargé d'Affaires at Peking[275] on August 1, 1962.[276]

The Government of India in their note of 28th July[277] lodged a protest that a Chinese patrol had opened fire at 10.00 hours on 27th July, against an Indian patrol in the Chip Chap Valley area approximately in the region referred to in the Chinese note. The Chinese note presumably refers to the same incident. The allegation by Chinese authorities that an Indian patrol resorted to firing at a Chinese post is not only baseless, but appears to be an attempt to confuse issues and escape responsibility for the aggressive activity of the Chinese local forces against which a protest had been lodged in the Indian note of the 28th July.

The Government of India have satisfied themselves that no Indian military post has been established in any part of Chinese territory. It is the Chinese local forces, who have established Chinese military posts in Indian territory and caused serious tension by their continuing aggressive activities in the Ladakh region of India. The Government of India emphatically reject the Chinese allegation that Indian posts have been set up in areas that are nineteen and twenty kilometres respectively inside Chinese territory.

The Chinese allegation that on 27th July, a detachment of Indian troops fired at a Chinese post in Nyagzu north of Pangong Lake, is absolutely without any foundation. No Indian party was in that area on that date.

The Ministry of External Affairs avails itself of this opportunity to renew to the Embassy of the People's Republic of China, the assurances of its highest consideration.

---

274. Note, 5 August 1962, handed over to the Embassy of the People's Republic of China, New Delhi. GOI, MEA, Historical Division, *Sino-Indian Border Dispute*, Volume VI, Part III, (Chinese Incursions into Indian Territory), April 1962 – October 1962, p.4. This note is also available in *Notes, Memoranda and Letters exchanged between the Governments of India and China, July-October 1962. White Paper No. VII* (Government of India, Ministry of External Affairs), p. 19.

275. P.K. Banerjee.

276. *White Paper No. VII*, pp. 10-11.

277. *White Paper No. VII*, p. 7.

401. In the Lok Sabha: Ladakh Situation[278]

Jawaharlal Nehru: Mr Speaker,[279] Sir, on the 28th November, 1961, I placed *White Paper No. 5*[280] on the Table of the House.[281] This contained the further notes, memoranda and China. I am now placing on the Table of the House another *White Paper No. 6*,[282] which contains some ninety notes sent by us to China and some seventy-five notes sent letters exchanged between the Government of India and the Government of by China to us, since the 10th November, 1961. Many of these have already been published in the press. The Chinese Government sometimes publish their letters and notes to us even before they reach us. This led us to publish our replies to them earlier than was customary. Normally, according to diplomatic practice, publication takes place some time after receipt of the communication. We have drawn the Chinese Government's notice to this diplomatic practice and we hope, in future, this will be adhered to. Because of this we have not till now given publicity to our last note to the Government of China dated 26th July, 1962.[283] I am now, however, placing this note on the Table of the House. This is not included in the *White Paper No. 6*.

During the last session of Parliament, I referred to the measures taken by Government to stop further Chinese advances into Indian territory. These steps continue to be taken by our Government and a number of military posts have been established. It may be said that it is very difficult for Chinese forces to advance now because of the establishment of Indian posts at various points without an actual conflict between the two. It is in this context that the strong and almost abusive Chinese notes must be interpreted. We have in all our notes repeatedly pointed out to the Chinese authorities the dangers inherent in Chinese

278. Statement, 6 August 1962. *Lok Sabha Debates*, Third Series, Vol. 6, 6 to 18 August 1962, cols 120-124.
279. Hukam Singh.
280. *Notes, Memoranda and Letters exchanged between the Governments of India and China, November 1960-November 1961. White Paper No. V* (Government of India, Ministry of External Affairs).
281. For Nehru's statement while placing *White Paper No. V* on the Table of the House, see SWJN/SS/72/item 275.
282. *Notes, Memoranda and Letters exchanged between the Governments of India and China, November 1961-July 1962. White Paper No. VI* (Government of India, Ministry of External Affairs).
283. *Notes, Memoranda and Letters exchanged between the Governments of India and China, July-October 1962. White Paper No. VII* (Government of India, Ministry of External Affairs), pp. 3-4.

aggressive activities and our determination to defend our borders even though we will avoid doing anything to precipitate a clash.

In recent weeks Chinese troops in superior strength have sometimes come up close to our posts with a view to harassing and intimidating them. This has happened in the Galwan Valley. Our men exercised the utmost self-restraint and exhibited exemplary courage and patience in the face of grave provocations from the Chinese forces. The Chinese forces thereupon retired to some extent, but Indian and Chinese forces in this area continue to be in close proximity, though no untoward incident has occurred so far in this area.

In the lower reaches of the Chip Chap Valley, an Indian patrol, while performing routine duties, was ambushed by Chinese forces and attacked by rifle, machine gun and mortar fire. Our men had to return fire in self-defence. Two members of the Indian patrol were wounded, one slightly, in this incident. Another incident occurred in the Pangong area. Despite the provocation, our forces did not return the Chinese fire there.

A feature of Chinese propaganda in these incidents has been to allege that Indian troops have encircled Chinese forces and fired at them, while the Chinese are reported to have waved and shouted to our troops not to attack. We have found that these allegations are baseless and are merely attempts to cover up Chinese aggressive activity against our posts or patrols. As the House will notice from the correspondence contained in the *White Paper*, the Chinese notes display a characteristic ambivalence. The first part of the note generally contains baseless allegations, often in exaggerated and even abusive language, while the latter part refers to the Chinese desire to settle our border differences by peaceful negotiations.

The recent increase of tension in the Ladakh region has been the direct result of intensified Chinese military activity which is inconsistent with the Chinese professions of their desire to settle this question by peaceful negotiations. We in India are by our background and temperament peaceful by nature. We earnestly believe in settlement of differences by peaceful discussions and negotiations. The unwarranted Chinese aggression on our territory came, therefore, as a shock and surprise to us. Despite the Chinese aggressive behaviour and the inconsistency between their professions and practice, we still desire to settle our differences with China by peaceful discussions and negotiations. At the same time, we will not hesitate to meet any threat to our territorial integrity with firmness and, where necessary, by force.

In a note we sent to the Government of China on the 14th May, 1962,[284] we made concrete suggestions regarding mutual withdrawal to the boundaries

284. See *White Paper No. VI*, pp. 41-43.

claimed by the two sides in the Ladakh region with a view to creating the necessary atmosphere for settlement of the dispute by peaceful discussions and negotiations. The Chinese did not agree to it. Instead, the incidents during the last few months have created further tension. We have, in our recent note dated 26th July, 1962, again pointed out to the Chinese Government the necessity of avoiding incidents and reducing tension and of making an adequate response to the constructive suggestions made by us to create the necessary favourable climate for further talks and discussions of the boundary question. I quote the following paragraph from our note of July 26.

"Paragraph 8. The Government of India are prepared, as soon as the current tensions have eased and the appropriate climate is created, to enter into further discussions on the India-China boundary question on the basis of the report of the officials as contemplated during the meeting of Prime Minister Chou En-lai with the Prime Minister of India in 1960. The Government of India hope that the Government of China will give a positive response on the concrete suggestions made by the Government of India for relaxation of the current tensions and for creation of the right climate for negotiations."

To this note of ours we received a reply in the late afternoon yesterday.[285] This reply is rather disappointing as the Chinese Government continue to repeat the charges made by them and to maintain their position as stated previously. They go on to say in their final paragraph as follows:

"The Chinese Government approve of the suggestions put forth by the Indian Government in its note for further discussions on the Sino-Indian boundary question on the basis of the report of the officials of the two countries. There need not and should not be any preconditions for such discussions. As a matter of fact, if only the Indian side stop advancing into Chinese territory a relaxation of the border situation will be effected at once. Since neither the Chinese nor the Indian Government want war and since both Governments wish to settle the boundary question peacefully through negotiations further discussions on the Sino-Indian boundary question on the basis of the report of the officials of the two countries should not be put off any longer. The Chinese Government proposes that such discussions be held as soon as possible and that the level, date, place and other procedural matters for these discussions be immediately decided upon by consultation through diplomatic channels. The Chinese Government hopes that the Indian Government will give positive consideration to this proposal and kindly reply at an early date."

285. The note is dated 4 August 1962, see *White Paper No. VII*, pp. 17-18.

We are examining this note of the Chinese Government and we hope to send a reply to it at an early date. We shall keep the Parliament informed of developments.

402. To T.T. Krishnamachari: Meeting on Border Problem[286]

August 8, 1962

My dear T.T.,

This is to remind you to come to my house at 6 pm on the 11th August. We shall consider the frontier situation.

Yours affectionately,
Jawaharlal Nehru

403. Sikkim Maharajkumar's China Visits[287]

Please convey to the Lok Sabha Secretariat that to our knowledge the Maharajkumar of Sikkim[288] has not visited China even once during this year or previously so far as I know. He has, however, visited Hong Kong which is a British colony and is not under the control of the Chinese communist regime. I do not think there have been any contacts between him and the Chinese communist regime. Beyond this I can make no statement. We shall, however, get in touch with the Maharajkumar on his return to India and ask him what the facts are.

---

286. Letter to Minister without Portfolio. NMML, T.T. Krishnamachari Papers, File 1962, Auto.
287. Note, 10 August 1962, in response to the Calling Attention notice by U.M. Trivedi and Brij Raj Singh, both Jan Sangh, Lok Sabha MPs, regarding the reported visits of Sikkim Prince to China.
288. Palden Thondup Namgyal.

404. In the Lok Sabha: India-China Border – I[289]

Jawaharlal Nehru: Mr Speaker,[290] Sir, I beg to move:

"That the situation along the India China border, particularly in the Ladakh region, be taken into consideration."

A week ago, on the 6th of August, I placed a new *White Paper*, No. VI, on the Table of the House.[291] This contained the notes and correspondence between the Government of India and the Government of China since the previous *White Paper* was published. Similarly, I placed a letter which the Government of India had sent to the Government of China dated 26th July.[292] We received a telegram giving the purport of the reply from the Chinese Government, on the morning of the 6th August. In the statement I made then, I quoted some portions of the reply of the Chinese Government. Since then, we have placed the full text of the Chinese note in the library of Parliament and have also placed copies in the Parliament Office for the convenience of Members.

Since then, no major incident has happened on the frontier. According to our information, there were three instances of firing by Chinese troops from a distance. These occurred, on the 27th July in the Pangong lake area when two shots were apparently fired towards our forces; on the 29th July also in the Pangong lake area, three shots were fired; on the 4th August, north east of Daulat Beg Oldi, one shot was fired.

All these were from big distances and no damage was done. We have protested to the Chinese Government about the first two incidents.

The Chinese have protested to us as, according to them, the Indian troops fired in their direction on four occasions: on 27th July in Chip Chap river area, two shots were said to have been fired; on the 27 July also in the Nyagzu area, sixteen shots are reported to have been fired by our troops; on 31st July in the Galwan Valley area, one shot is said to have been fired; on 1st August, also in the Galwan Valley area, seven shots are alleged to have been fired by our troops.

According to our information, these allegations of firing by our patrols are not correct.

---

289. Motion, 13 August 1962. *Lok Sabha Debates*, Third Series, Vol. 6, 6 to18 August 1962, cols 1477-1481.
290. Hukam Singh.
291. Item 401.
292. *White Paper No. VII*, pp. 3-4.

For the rest, according to our information, some Chinese patrols have been moving about in the vicinity of the Galwan Valley area and have occasionally been observed digging in.

Otherwise, the situation remains the same. Our aircraft have been visiting our posts and giving them supplies. The Chinese have protested against our aircraft flying over what they call Chinese territory. They have given a long list of such flights. We have replied that it is absurd to allege that they were flying over their territory as they have all along been over Indian territory.

The situation, therefore, on the frontier remains serious as it has been in the past and is likely to continue in the future.

Since I made the statement in the Lok Sabha a week ago, there has apparently been some misunderstanding and misinterpretation of what I said. Some people, who ought to have known better, have had the temerity to suggest that we are going to take some action which would bring dishonour to India. I can only imagine that those who have said this are not very well acquainted with the training and background we have had in the past. That past training as well as our present mood lead us to seek peaceful settlements of disputes with foreign countries and we shall try to do so to the utmost of our ability. It also confirms us in our decision to protect the honour of India and the defence of India to the utmost of our capacity.

But there has been apparently some misunderstanding about the two lines which the Chinese have claimed on different occasions as their alleged frontier in Ladakh: one is that which Premier Chou En-lai indicated while confirming the boundary line given in the Chinese map of 1956, and the other is the line which was indicated in the Chinese map which was given to our officials. These lines differ and the latter line is much more to the west than the former. We have pointed out to the Chinese Government that some of their posts have even gone beyond the Chou En-lai line. This was obviously a further aggression on India and something which could be easily verified by a reference to the maps. To this the Chinese replied that the two maps are more or less the same. This is very extraordinary. These facts are capable of easy verification. We drew the Chinese Government's attention to this matter. This has led some people to say that we accept Chou En-lai's line. This is utterly wrong. As we have repeatedly stated, we do not accept any of their lines. We stand by the international frontier which is shown in our maps and about which so much evidence was produced by our officials.

The other question that is raised is about our proposal to have further discussions on the India-China boundary question on the basis of the report of the officials, as contemplated during the meeting with Premier Chou En-lai in

1960.[293] It was at that time understood that there would be such a consideration after the officials had done their work.

We have not been able to do so owing to tensions and further aggression by the Chinese. We made it clear that such further discussions could only take place after the current tensions had eased and appropriate climate was created. We had previously said that in order to ease tensions there should be withdrawals of both our forces to beyond the line claimed by the other. It seemed to us essential, and we laid stress on this, that any further discussions on the boundary question would be fruitless unless there was relaxation of tensions and the right climate for negotiation was created.

On the 6th of August, when I referred to the Chinese reply, I stated that it was a disappointing one. The Chinese Foreign Minister, in a broadcast in Europe made on the 3rd August, had stated that "to wish that Chinese troops should be withdrawn from their own territory is impossible. That would be against the will of the 650 million Chinese. No force in the world could oblige us to do something of this kind."

I realise that in public statements, Ministers often emphasise their claims in strong language, but, even allowing for that, what the Chinese Foreign Minister[294] has said, means laying down preconditions which make it impossible for us to carry on discussions and negotiations. We had not suggested force being used to make the Chinese troops withdraw, but a proposal to create a climate for peaceful discussion which was honourable to both India and China.

It is clear to us that any discussion on the basis of the report of the officials cannot start unless present tensions are removed and the status quo of the boundary which existed before and which has since been altered by force is restored. The Government of India is prepared to discuss what measures should be taken to remove the tensions that exist in this region and to create the appropriate climate for further discussions. This would be preliminary to any further discussions on the basis of the report of the officials with a view to resolving the differences between the two Governments on the boundary question.

We have not yet sent a reply to the Chinese Government to their note of the 4th August. We hope to send it within two or three days. It will be on the lines I have indicated.

---

293. For discussions, see SWJN/SS/60; for the Report, see SWJN/SS/66/Supplement.
294. Chen Yi.

At this stage, I do not want to say more; I should like to hear what the hon. Members have to say in regard to this situation and then make such statement as I can.[295]

405. In the Lok Sabha: India-China Border – II[296]

Jawaharlal Nehru: Mr Speaker,[297] Sir, I followed yesterday with considerable interest and care the speeches delivered by various Members of this House on this motion.[298] I, particularly, was interested in the oratorical efforts and the wide range of subjects covered by the speeches, most of which had little to do with the subject in dispute. Shri Anthony[299] in his vivid imagination saw heads rolling here including Professor Mukerjee's[300] head. That itself shows that his imagination runs riot and leaves reality far behind. The Maharaja of Kalahandi[301] delivered a speech which I found a little difficult to understand. It was not very coherent in various places.

He wound up by asking us to take certain remedial measures. His remedial measures are: to convene a conference of South-East Asian countries, to ask military aid from some countries to meet this menace on the frontier, and various other like proposals. I wondered whether he or the group he represents really understands the position, has given any thought to it or merely thinks in terms of a cold war and wants India to jump in head foremost into it.

What a conference of South-East Asian countries will do is beyond me. And, who are these South-East Asian countries? Which of them does he want to be called? I should like him to make a list of them and show it to us. Which of them is going to help us or can help us? It is best if they carry on themselves. We have recently had a case of a South-East Asian country which had given a great deal of trouble—Laos. Unfortunately, it has been decided by agreement of all the countries concerned including some great powers. What is the basis of that decision? What was the basis of the decision that Geneva Agreement, six years ago that these countries must not enter into any military alliance with any party, that they must remain un-aligned, uncommitted? That is the only

295. For Nehru's reply to debate on the motion, see item 405.
296. Reply to debate on motion on the India-China border situation, 14 August 1962. *Lok Sabha Debates*, Third Series, Vol. 6, 6 to18 August 1962, cols 1750-1777.
297. Hukam Singh.
298. For Nehru's statement on 13 August 1962 introducing the motion, see item 404.
299. Frank Anthony, Nominated.
300. H.N. Mukerjee, CPI.
301. P.K. Deo, Swatantra Party.

safety for them. This has been accepted and admitted by the great leaders of the power blocs themselves.

So, the hon. Member, the leader of the Swatantra Party, is so ignorant of what is happening in the world, what is happening in India, what is happening on the frontier. I do not know what his party represents in this country except ignorance, ignorance on the social sphere, ignorance in the political sphere, ignorance in the economic sphere.

He told us that India is no longer a zamindari. Evidently, his mind still turns round to the question of zamindari. It is long past. India is certainly not a zamindari, and there are no other zamindaris also in India.

We have discussed the question on the frontier many times in the past, and yet, whenever it is discussed, we go back not to the present situation and what we are to do, but, as Shri Anthony and the Maharaja also said, to what we should have done eight years ago or six years ago, that we should not have put forward China to become a member of the United Nations, we should not have said that China has sovereignty over Tibet, and so on—facts which are long past. I have dealt with them in the past. I could deal with them again, but I do not wish to take the time of the House.

The point is, how we are to face a serious situation now. I do submit that this situation can be considered politically and militarily. It is no good talking about the Mahabharata as if it exists at the present moment. Although the *Mahabharata* is a magnificent book from which we can learn a great deal, but I do not think it will help us in resolving the frontier crisis.[302]

Hem Barua:[303] Lesson for Raghunath.[304]

Jawaharlal Nehru: Nor is it any good to talk about our 45 crores of Indians standing as one. It almost reminds me of Marshal Chen Yi[305] talking about his 65 crores of Chinese wanting this and that. It is, if I may say so, with all

---

302. Raghunath Singh, Congress, speaking in Hindi, had stated that though, according to the Sabha Parva of *Mahabharata*, China had acknowledged the sovereignty of India 5,000 years ago, it would not be proper to say on this basis that China had been a part of India then. He spoke after U.M. Trivedi, Jan Sangh, who had posited: "Can we not point out to the Mount Kailas and say that the name Kailas itself indicates that it must be an Indian name. The name Mansarovar could be given by no other nation except the Indian nation. We have been going there for thousands and thousands of years." *Lok Sabha Debates*, ibid, cols 1529, 1547-1548.

303. PSP.

304. Refers to Raghunath Singh, see fn 302 in this section.

305. The Foreign Minister of China.

respect both to hon. Members opposite and to Marshal Chen Yi, rather childish to talk in this fashion. The 65 crores of Chinese are a great number and have great power behind them, but in a context of this kind one does not talk, no responsible person talks in that way, neither he nor hon. Members here.

We have to deal with a difficult situation, a serious situation as I have often said and a situation that has been with us for many long years. We cannot solve it suddenly because of obvious difficulties in our way or in anybody's way who tries to solve it. We can increase our capacity to solve it militarily or otherwise. I do think and I am quite right in saying that our capacity to deal with this situation politically and militarily has grown in the last two years or so. It has definitely grown. I do not wish to exaggerate that; but it is much better. Shri Anthony asked me whether our position was better now than a year or two ago. I say it is definitely better both militarily and politically. But, nevertheless, I cannot guarantee.

I think the Maharaja of Bikaner[306] talked about giving a date when they will vacate. How can I give a date when we shall get the Chinese to vacate? We shall do our utmost to do that. We shall continue to do that and we shall not submit. But about one thing I can give an assurance—it is not necessary for me to give it—and I should think that that assurance would be welcomed by every hon. Member of this House and that is that nothing should be done in this matter, or in any matter, which will bring any kind of dishonour on India and that we would prefer to be reduced to dust and ashes before we are guilty of any such thing. That is the broad approach. But when you come to political and difficult problems, you do not talk in the air as, I regret to say, some of our hon. Members did. They made brave declarations and said, "We shall do this; we shall not do this." Responsible politicians or statesmen do not talk tall. They try to act as stoutly as they can.

In this world today, apart from the general question of war, etc., in this changing world all kinds of things are happening. All kinds of new weapons are being forged. I have a feeling that many of the hon. Members on the other side who spoke have no realisation of the modern world. They live in some kind of a world of their own creation. Some people talked bravely of the 45 crores of Indians; others, like the Maharaja, asked us immediately to go under

---

306. Karni Singh, Independent.

the wing or shelter of some other power and take its aid to defend us.[307] That is not an honourable thing, I think. Personally I do not think that we shall maintain our independence for long if we go about seeking military aid from others to defend ourselves. That is apart from its being fundamentally opposed to the policy we have pursued all this time of being unaligned—a policy which is not only being recognised everywhere as the right policy but which is spreading all over the world. Even those stout and big countries that are aligned have come to respect it.

Apart from any policy question, so far as India is concerned, situated where it is, that is the only possible policy that any intelligent man knowing the world today can possibly accept. Yet, vaguely and loosely, the Swatantra Party leader talks about our asking the aid of South-East Asian countries—what aid they can give us is beyond my imagination—or of great powers having a concert for the defence of all this area. All this has nothing to do with reality. Any responsible person in authority, whether in the Government or in the Opposition must deal with reality. Certainly whatever be the difficulties, we have to face them. Whatever happens and however grave the crisis we must never lose our nerve. It seems to me that some hon. Members of the Opposition never seem to be able to control their nerves. They are always losing it. They talk about heads rolling and all that. That shows that their nerves have gone out of order whatever else might have happened.

We are in a serious position on the frontiers. It is quite absurd to talk about China invading India and all that. China has committed aggression. That is bad enough. We should face it and try to get it vacated. But, imagining that she is swooping down the whole of India and swallowing it has, I submit, nothing

---

307. P.K. Deo, the Maharaja of Kalahandi, had presented a substitute motion for the one moved by Nehru:

"That for the original motion, the following be substituted, namely:-

'This House, having considered the situation along the India China border, particularly in the Ladakh region, is of the opinion that the Government of India has completely failed in their foreign policy so far as it relates to India-China relationship and urges upon the Government to take the following steps:-

(a) Immediate breaking of diplomatic relationship with China;
(b) Calling of a Conference of free countries of S.E. Asia to discuss common security measures;
(c) To arrange for military aids from other countries to gear up our defence;
(d) To improve our relations with Nepal;
(e) That the Prime Minister should himself take over the defence portfolio;
(f) That the Prime Minister should come out with a categorical statement that there will be no negotiation with China unless and until they withdraw from Indian territory'."

to do with reality or possibility, even remote possibility of any situation. India is not so weak as all that. India is growing in strength, whether militarily or otherwise. Military strength does not today or at any time consist of large hordes of people. If anybody knows at all the history of India, we have never been lacking in courage. But, we have been lacking in wisdom, we have been lacking in modernity. Whenever India has been conquered or defeated, it was not because of any wonderful deeds of the conqueror, but because of our own feebleness, our lack of unity, our backwardness, economic, industrial backwardness, better weapons on the other side. That is more important. Forty-five crores do no good at all unless there is unity and they are trained up and they have a modern mind. I regret to say that the opposition does not even have an idea of what a modern mind is, much less possess it.

Every time we come up here, the arguments are, why did we recognise China ten years ago, why did this happen twelve years ago. Why can't they come to the year 1962 and see what is happening in the world instead of repeating all this? I think of every step that we have taken in the past; I mean the recognition of China ten years ago. Our non-attendance at the San Francisco Peace Conference—I think perhaps Shri Frank Anthony said it—

Frank Anthony (Nominated – Anglo-Indian): No, no.

Jawaharlal Nehru: I am sorry then; somebody else said it. Perhaps the gallant Maharaja said it:[308] I do not know—our non-attendance at this Conference had nothing to do with China, absolutely nothing. It had a great deal to do with Japan and it pleased Japan.[309] We have been friendly with Japan. Many other things because of that; because we did not participate in a cold war exercise against Japan and we made our separate treaty with Japan. All these things are of the past. The present has certainly grown out of the past. Our troubles in the frontiers have grown out of the past. We have to face the present situation.

I am not going into the past which I have dealt with so many times during debates in this House. But in the last two years, as we have stated, we have concentrated on increasing our strength, military strength, strength in communications, roads, etc.

308. Contending that India had been complacent, at the cost her own interests, in advancing China's interests, in bilateral relations as well as internationally, P.K. Deo said that "India had declined to attend the peace treaty with Japan which was signed in San Francisco, because China was not a party to it." *Lok Sabha Debates*, Third Series, Vol. 6, 6 to 18 August 1962, col. 1498.
309. P.K. Deo tabled notice of a question of privilege on an error in this statement by Nehru. For Nehru's response to the notice, see items 408-409.

May I draw the attention of this House, talking about Ladakh, to the whole of Jammu & Kashmir State of which Ladakh is a part? Rightly or wrongly, the Kashmir Government took Ladakh and the frontiers for granted. It had no posts there or measures for defence of them. Nor was there any fear in those days. They sent perhaps every two years a small deputation or some people, some officers and others to some places to collect some little money, very little money which was more a gesture. Anyhow, they had nothing. Then came Independence to be followed immediately afterwards by aggression by Pakistanis on Kashmir which we resisted. Pakistani aggression went right up to Ladakh. In fact the route to Ladakh, the Zoji La pass, was captured by the Pakistanis, and that prevented us from getting to Ladakh; there was no way to get to Ladakh except a risky one by air. We then tried to go by another route to Leh from Manali, a very difficult route. However, our Army did get there. But, something else happened. Meanwhile, our Army did something which deserves to be recorded in the annals of warfare, that is, it went up to the Zoji La pass with tanks, it had widened the roads and went up to the Zoji La pass with tanks and drove out the Pakistanis from that position, and thereby opened out the route to Leh, which is the heart of Ladakh. I am merely mentioning that this happened right at the end of 1948, and the Pakistanis were driven out of a large part of Ladakh which they had controlled. But, ever since then, the House knows that we confront the Pakistanis who are in control of one-third of Jammu and Kashmir State, and we are constantly threatened by all kinds of fierce deeds which the Pakistanis will commit upon us.

This was the position in the early fifties of this country. It was about that time that China took possession of Tibet, and nothing that we could have done could have stopped it; people seem to think that if we had said "No, you must not do it", they would have stopped it, or if we had said that we would not recognise them, they would have stopped it. That is rather a fanciful notion. Rightly or wrongly, they took possession of Tibet, and soon after, as their possession grew, their hold grew, it was difficult for them from the logistic point of view to feed them, to send supplies etc. right across the Gobi desert, which is a tremendous desert. They have gradually made roads etc., and in the course of that road-making in the middle of the fifties, they improved the whole caravan route which passed through the northern area of Aksai Chin into Tibet from Sinkiang. It is a caravan route being used from time to time. They used it because it was easier for them to go from Sinkiang to Tibet that way instead of crossing the Gobi desert. And later, a year or two later, they improved that route and made some kind of a road. Roads in Tibet, as the House will know, are not cemented roads. They are just levelled places, because owing to the extreme cold, the ground is so hard that it is as good as cement or anything of that sort. So, they used that. There was some difficulty about using that Aksai Chin road because of lack of bridges. I do not know; probably, they have built the bridges later. That was the first aggression of China on our territory, right about 1957; I do not know when the road was actually made, but we heard of it at the end of 1957 or 1958, I forget exactly when.

> The Minister of State in the Ministry of Food and Agriculture (Ram Subhag Singh): 1957.

Jawaharlal Nehru: In 1959, while we were protesting against this to the Chinese Government, and their answer had not come, and we were waiting for it; and it came in early 1958, I think ...

> Ram Subhag Singh: In 1958.

Jawaharlal Nehru: Just then, the incipient rebellion in Tibet grew in size, and as a result of it, the Chinese sent much larger forces to Tibet, which immediately fanned out to its frontiers, partly, may be, because they thought that help was coming to the Tibetan rebels from the frontier, from India and elsewhere; they came to the Indian frontier partly because people were escaping; the Dalai Lama had escaped. In the same way, they spread out to the Western side.

We, who were fairly wide awake on this side, and right from the beginning, when the Chinese took possession of Tibet, had not expected it, but, anyhow, we were alert about our frontier on this side, the Sikkim and NEFA frontier, and we had even then put up a number of check-posts there. We added more to them.

On the Western side, on the Ladakh side also, we thought it was necessary. It was the second priority; NEFA was the first priority. It was a much more difficult undertaking. The distances were big and the terrain was difficult. So slowly, we were proceeding on the Ladakh side with our military posts. But we realised that the only way to do it was to build roads. Otherwise, the distance was too great and it took too long. Even by air, we could not go there. We established an air field there in—I forget the year—1954 or 1955. All this was with a view to protect this against any possible incursion. The Chinese had not come into Ladakh yet. But at the back of our mind was also the risk of it.

I remember going to Chusul air field in—I forget the year—1954 or 1955. But there were no Chinese round about anywhere. I went there because our air people were very proud of having made the air field. They called it the highest in the world. I do not know if it is—it is about 14,000 ft. high. I went there for a few hours and then came back.

I have been talking about my personal experiences. I know something about Ladakh—not very much—something by trekking over the Zoji La in 1916—it is a long time ago. In 1916, I went there, covering the distance partly on pony and partly on foot. So I knew something of that place. I did not go far, but I had some fair idea crossing the Zoji La.

So from that time onwards, we were trying to protect this and made this an air base—the Chusul one. We tried to build roads. The first road that had to be built was to Leh itself which was the base. Unless we could reach Leh quickly, it was no good making roads elsewhere. This was a difficult piece of engineering, especially as the road itself was crossing certain bridges. That was made.

So initially the problem before us was the building of roads. We could not do anything without roads, and, where we could, some air fields. We built them. There was also the problem of getting aircraft which could be used for this purpose. We applied our minds to this. We had a special Border Roads Development Committee formed, which has done very well and built—I do not know exactly—thousands of miles of roads in very difficult terrain and rather fast. It has still not completed its work. Of course there is no completion of it, because more and more roads come into our plan as we make them. But it has eased our situation considerably, both because of the Leh road and some roads which are going to Chusul and other places.

On the NEFA side too we built roads. In UP we built roads on the border. In the Punjab we have built roads.

But however rapidly we built roads, we could not reach our posts. Some we could, but most of them we could not. We tried to feed them from air and give them supplies. That meant aircraft. We got special aircraft for this purpose. Now apart from the supplies, the mere stationing of our troops anywhere in Ladakh, whether it was in Leh or whether it was in the interior, meant supplying them with everything conceivable that they wanted, because they could get nothing there, nothing to eat and so on. That required air supplies. We built up our air supply position by getting aircraft—big aircraft—from various countries. We have got some helicopters etc. But in the main it consisted of big transport aircraft. There were some from the United States and some from the Soviet Union. Those from the Soviet Union were the bigger ones, which were very helpful. Then having got them, we had the difficulty that those heavy aircraft landing on our temporary air fields there dug them up. So, we had to make the air field stronger. All this, one problem after another. However, we proceeded and we improved our military position, our supply position, and we have got troops in various areas there with forward posts.

Somebody said that we have allowed nine new Chinese posts. That is true, and yet it gives a completely wrong idea of what the position is. If they have got nine posts, we have got 22 or 23 or 24, I do not know how many, three

613

times the number. These posts of theirs are projections, patrol projections of their own posts. They have not gone very far. In fact, it may be said that ever since we got there with our posts, it has been exceedingly difficult for them to advance further. They may advance a mile outside their own posts, a mile or two, that is a different matter, just as we can advance and we do advance, but broadly speaking, we have held them in check there, and there can be no further advance by them without a major conflict.

That is not enough, of course, obviously not, but that was the first step that had to be taken, to strengthen ourselves and prevent any kind of further advance taking place. So, that has been more or less satisfactorily done. That does not mean that we are satisfied with the frontier position. Apart from the fact that we have to get them to vacate it, even otherwise it is not satisfactory, but I would not go into the military aspects. But it is certainly a satisfactory first step in which we have succeeded.

Therefore, I said that from a military point of view we are better off, better circumstanced, than we were a year or two ago, but if I am asked when I will get them to vacate it, that involves far greater preparation, far greater not only preparation—certainly preparation in the military sense, in the air sense, and certain political factors also. On the political field I think I am right in saying the position is more satisfactory than it was. It is difficult to measure this. A military situation might be measured, a political situation cannot easily be measured, but I think it is better, but ultimately and inevitably the position depends upon our own strength, military strength, and the strength of the people and their general response to face any crisis. Now it is very satisfactory to learn, to hear many of the brave statements made by hon. Members on both sides of the House of how we shall face any crisis, of how we shall meet any danger. That is all right, and that feeling in the country is essential as a background. Nevertheless, we know from the history of India that all the courage of the Indian people did not protect them because they were lacking in military weapons and the military art, whatever it is. One of the simple things our ancestors were lacking in was possessing even a physical map of India. Even till fairly recent times before the British came, they had no proper maps of India. They had vague drawings, while the British when they came, everybody knows, did not win by any major feat of arms although they had better arms and that helped them, better trained soldiers—and small numbers of Indian soldiers might have been utilised—and in the end, maps and they had spies everywhere. Every Indian Court had a British spy, often a Minister in the Court. That is how they won. By their information services, by their maps, they knew exactly where they were, where the other party was, while those who opposed them gallantly, full of courage, Rajputs, Marathas and others, had no map—simple thing. Gallantry is a fine thing, but something more is necessary in warfare than gallantry. Nowadays with modern weapons and other things, all this has become even more complicated.

It rather pleases us to compare India with China and say one Indian is equal to ten Chinese. I do not know. I think an Indian soldier is equal or more than any soldier in the wide world. That is true. I am convinced of that. They are very fine men, and I should like to pay my tribute not only to the soldiers but to our Army Headquarters, to the Defence Ministry and our Air Headquarters, for the fine work they have done in these two or three years especially in the frontiers.

But the point is, how are we to meet modern weapons, modern techniques, with the resources at our disposal? Of course, to the best of our ability, we try to develop the modern techniques themselves here. That is why, our whole objective has been in recent years not so much to buy from abroad, but to build up, to manufacture machines here, aeroplanes, helicopters and other things, and that takes a little time. Yet, we have done well, and we hope that in another year or two our strength will grow to manufacture these. That is how we are facing it, and meanwhile we are taking such measures as we can.

Shri Anthony on a previous occasion—I think I was not here then—objected to our military people keeping secrets; I do not know what particular secret, I think it was about helicopters, the question arose about it. In a matter of this kind we are governed almost entirely by what our military staff say. If they advise us this must not be disclosed. We abide by their advice. It is not I or the Defence Minister that lays it down. It is the General Staff which says this must not be disclosed. And the difficulty is that when we buy things from abroad or we are manufacturing we come to special terms with a foreign country. The foreign country tells us that we must not disclose these. We do not care, but we have given our word to them not to disclose it because they insisted; either they have given us on terms which they do not wish to be disclosed—they are good terms for us, but they want to get better terms from somebody else—whatever the reasons may be. So these are the reasons why one cannot easily disclose these terms of our contracts with others or what we are building.

Anyhow, my point was we have concentrated on building, on manufacture. We have manufactured a very fine supersonic plane at Bangalore,[310] but having manufactured the plane, it does well, in order to manufacture more, we have to get engines. We cannot get the old engines from the British sources, but we are getting other engines, and that will be manufactured. We are manufacturing helicopters. They are so important in those hilly areas. We hope to manufacture other fighter planes.

310. See SWJN/SS/69/item 360.

I must confess that it hurts me for us to spend so much money on weapons of warfare, but circumstances being what they are, I think we would be failing in our duty not to possess them. It is not so much that one fights with these weapons, one may, but the fact of not having them itself is an encouragement to others. I feel that in the last few years, occasions arose when if we had not been adequately prepared and we had not got adequate weapons and aircraft, we might have had to face a war. It did not come because we were prepared and they knew we were prepared. So, much as I dislike this, we have to get it. It is exceedingly important not to allow the enemy to have control of the air. It is an obvious thing. Everybody will realise that it is better to have self-control. If you have not got it, at least the enemy should not. And, if they had speedier and powerful aircraft the idea spreads that you have not got control of the air.

I do not know if hon. Members, how many of them, have any experience of bombing. I have not much experience. But I have a little experience, seeing bombs falling all around you. Nothing is a more frustrating experience, how aircraft comes quietly and puts bombs where it chooses with nothing to face it, no rival aircraft to face it. Because the mere fact that you have rival aircraft partly drives it out and partly sends it up high in the heavens from where it is more difficult to bomb. Other things happen.

Of course, all this is a rather old story, this bombing and aircraft. The next stage is rockets. But it is difficult for us to forget the intervening stages and jump over. And, even from the point of view of our technical skill developing, it is desirable that we should manufacture these things, these supersonic aircraft, in this country. So, we took all those steps and, in the military sense, roads were built etc. We built a kind of rampart on this part of Ladakh and put up numerous military posts, small ones and big ones. It is true that these posts are in constant danger of attack with larger numbers. Well, it does not matter. We have taken the risk and we have moved forward, and we have stopped effectively their further march.

If anybody takes the trouble to read the numerous letters of protest that we have received from the Chinese authorities, he will see how angry they have been at our establishing these posts, how they have said, "You are trying to cut us off; you are trying to encircle us." The same thing that was said on our side about them are repeated by them about us. Some things have happened and much has happened on the part of our military there. If you see one of their telegrams, they say—I forget the period—they have mentioned the figure, over 300 air sorties by us. They say, "You come into our territory." It may be six months. During the last six months, they say over 300 air sorties have come into their territory. And the obvious answer was, "It is not your territory, it is our territory and we go as we like." All this is happening.

People should realise what is being done. It is a fine job that is being done by our military and Air Force. It is not right to put it at a lower level. Nevertheless, we cannot suddenly press a button and declare that the place is vacated, the aggression is ended. That will go by our strength. We are gradually building up our strength—and by political means.

Shri Karni Singhji asked me something about the atom bomb and that China has an atom bomb. I do not know when China may have an atom bomb. Broadly speaking, although we are not thinking of an atom bomb, I think we are more highly developed in atomic energy than China is. That does not mean that China cannot produce an atom bomb before us because we are not trying to. But, I shall not be worried in the least if they do. People seem to think that if a country has got an atom bomb, it is bound to win in war. That is not so. If they have an atom bomb do you mean to say that after all effort they produce an atom bomb only to let loose on India? They will keep it for other purposes. If they let it loose on India it is worse for them.[311]

An Hon. Member: Wishful thinking.

Jawaharlal Nehru: I do not understand our getting cold hands and cold feet because they may have an atom bomb or because they have a larger number of soldiers in Tibet who may shoot us down from the top. They can shoot down; they can create difficulties for us. They may. It is a possibility. If they want to they can overwhelm some of our military posts. That does not mean that we are defeated. We shall face them with much greater problems and face them much more stoutly. So, all these military factors and political factors have to be kept in view.

It is no good my talking tall or any body else talking tall—"We will do this or that." We should not do anything which, as I said, brings dishonour to our country because that is not an arguable matter. None of us should do it; and, certainly, no Government can be responsible for it.

Having said that, we should try every means to solve the problem, anyhow, if you like by military means or by peaceful means. The military means have to be conditioned by military factors, not by speeches here. And, therefore, that

311. Karni Singh, Independent, wanted "to know what the situation would be if, God forbid, the Chinese take it into their heads one day to make a nuclear test in that part of Ladakh which may be Indian territory, but which may be in their hands at present. What would the Indian soldier feel if one day he finds himself confronted with an atomic burst when our country may not necessarily be prepared in that line because we do not believe in the atomic way of wars?" He suggested that India should carry out nuclear research "to an extent that, in an emergency, we can carry this research to its logical conclusion."

conditioning has to be there. In any event, I do believe that war is a bad thing. War between India and China will be a bad thing, bad for us, bad for China and bad for the world because it may become a world war. And, in the context of the world today, when so much is said and so many efforts are made for disarmament, for peace etc. it will be a particularly bad thing for us who stood for disarmament and peace to talk in warlike terms.

It may be, some people imagine, that this shows cowardice, kayartha, that we do not talk in warlike terms. I would again remind them that some of the bravest of the brave in India who talked in the most warlike terms, ultimately, were defeated because of the better strategy, and better thinking and better weapons of the other party. It is better economy of the other party. Therefore, we have to think in modern terms and with modern minds.

Thinking in modern terms, the first thing is that everything should be done to avoid war because the consequences of that war will be very terrible for the world and for us especially. We do not want to enter any war if there is a war in the world unless circumstances force us, unless there is an attack on us. So, let us not talk vaguely and rather lightly about war. But, at the same time, conditions being what they are, we have to prepare for that.

I have told the House just now that I hate spending our hard-earned money, money which is required for development, for war planes and others. Each war plane may represent, I do not know, how many factories, how many plants, how many hospitals, how many things. Yet, we do it because the circumstances are such. But we do it without an excessive desire to spend that way. So, I do not myself see what other policy we can pursue except to hold fast to what we stand for and prepare our strength.

A great deal has been said: we must not talk to the Chinese unless they vacate. I refuse to accept that statement. I am quite clear about it. I am not such a child as to be made to say something which I think is fundamentally a wrong thing.

Hem Barua:[312] May I submit that you ...

Jawaharlal Nehru: Please let me go on. Please let me go on. (Interruption). It is a childish and infantile position to take up. First of all, there is a difference between negotiation and talks. There is a world of difference. One should always talk, whatever happens, whatever the position and wherever the chances. If I have the chance to talk, I will talk to them. It is quite absurd not to talk.

312. PSP.

I sent for the Chinese Ambassador here.[313] He was going away. I gave him a farewell lunch. He came to my house. And it was said, "Oh, see how his relationship with the Chinese is; he has given lunch." That is an advice which I am never going to follow so long as I am in authority. About that I am quite clear.

Hem Barua: You yourself said like that on a previous occasion.

Jawaharlal Nehru: No, no, Nothing doing. I have never said that.

मणिराम बागड़ी:[314] क्या उन्होंने भी कभी लंच ... (Interruption).

[Translation: Mani Ram Bagri:[315] Did he also sometime ... (Interruption).]

Jawaharlal Nehru: I make it perfectly clear. It is my practice to invite every retiring Ambassador to a meal. This Ambassador was the doyen of the corps[316] for sometime and I invited him and his wife to a meal. During the meal and afterwards I talked to him about the frontier situation. I did. Why should I be afraid of it? I told him that it was drifting badly and the least he could do was to avoid incidents. He could not settle it with me. I told him that otherwise it would be drifting to war. What effect it had, whether it had any effect on him is a different matter. He has no doubt reported to his Government. That is a thing which is always done. The Defence Minister[317] went to Geneva where there was also the Chinese Foreign Minister.[318] It was his absolute duty, I told him so, to meet him and talk to him. He could not negotiate. There is no question of any negotiation. At that time some little firing had taken place in the Galwan Valley. I told him that he must tell them that this thing was drifting and if they were not careful there would be war. He did so, quite rightly; he told them this when they met; there is very little time; the only time they meet in these places is at lunch or dinner. In Geneva he met the Chinese Foreign Minister once at breakfast and once at dinner. The others were present in these meetings. I am sorry to say that hon. Members who make much of it know nothing about the normal practice in the modern world, especially in Western countries and more especially in the diplomatic world. They seem to think that we must bring about untouchability in our relations and unapproachability everywhere. That is not

313. Pan Zili.
314. Socialist Party.
315. See fn 314 in this section.
316. The Diplomatic Corps in New Delhi.
317. V.K. Krishna Menon.
318. Chen Yi. See SWJN/SS/77/item 403.

the way diplomacy is carried on. The main point is that we must not take a wrong step by committing ourselves to anything wrong. If our case is strong, as I believe it is, we should shout it out at every opportunity and I should shout it out to the opponent also and make him see our views. I do not understand this approach; it is a dangerous approach because it makes people feel that by our standing in a corner we shall solve the world's problems and our own problems. It is quite absurd; I do not understand how this kind of idea enters people's heads. We have to live in the world as it is. It is difficult enough to follow the basic policies for which any individual stands. We have sometimes to compromise those basic policies but we cannot follow our policies or do anything if we take up the stand and say: we will not talk.

Now, there is a good deal of difference between negotiation and talking. Talking must always be encouraged wherever possible. Negotiation is a very formal thing; it requires a very suitable background; it should not be taken up unless a suitable background comes. That is what we have said. Talking is an entirely different thing. Talking may not yield any result, may be; at any rate it helps in understanding, in probing the other's mind. May be, the other probes your mind too. It helps in understanding. It may not yield any results. It is essential and preliminary for diplomats to deal with each other, even in wartime. I wonder how many of you realise that the ambassadors of the two countries like the United States of America and China which do not recognise each other or, at any rate, the United States does not recognise China and is not at all favourably inclined to do it, have been meeting regularly for the last seven years in Warsaw and considering their problems. They have no ambassadors; there is no Chinese ambassador in Washington; nor an American ambassador in China. They chose Warsaw as the place where both the ambassadors talked and talked. Observe how they persisted in their talks for seven years. They have not become untouchables. I do not know and I cannot say but the latest I heard was that they were gradually approaching some kind of an understanding after six or seven years of talk—of course not a daily talk, but once a month or even at longer intervals. This thing is normally done by countries which are even inimical to each other because the only other way is to brace the sword at every provocation, jump into the arena, sword in hand; that is considered rather childish behaviour nowadays.

I have in the statement that I made in the beginning of this debate yesterday, made it perfectly clear as to what broadly our policy is and we propose to adhere to it and I should like the support of the House in carrying it out, as the House has been pleased to give it to me on previous occasions. But I want to say that this matter is obviously not a party matter, not a Congress matter. It is a national matter. Everybody agrees to that. Yet, I regret to say that it is sometimes treated as a party matter, in a party way. Sometimes the mere fact that Government is responsible for it makes them run down the Government and that, I consider, is not justified. We may be wrong: any body may be wrong. I welcome the Members of the Opposition or Members of this side of the House to point that out privately and publicly as they like. But it is the mentality that I object to, the mentality of running down the Government in a matter of national importance, which leads, not to unity which everyone wants, but to disunity; it leads to things like the cessation of production, etc. All these things are wrong. When we talk about the frontier we talk bravely about all of us being together, and all the 45 crores standing as one man and facing it. When it comes to our normal activities, we are, 45 crores, constantly broken up into 45 crore parts; if not so many, at least, to many parts. Unity or an attempt at unity does not mean not criticising at all; but still a different approach is essential. Every country does that. It is not a question of a socialist country or a capitalist country. I do feel that many of these criticisms that come from some of the opposite side, some Members on the opposite side, are based on a very radical difference in viewpoint. I cannot help it; they are welcome to have a different viewpoint. But when once I said that Shri Frank Anthony advocated our giving up the policy of non-alignment which I gathered from his speech, he said later that he did not mean that and that he was not for our giving it up. But whatever he has said even in his speech yesterday—it is a very forceful speech—was for giving up that policy; it can have no other meaning; it means that. And as for Maharaja of Kalahandi, he did talk about it. He did not use the word "non-alignment". But to get military aid is to become somebody else's dependant in that way. There was all the tall talk of courage of our 45 crore men when talking of getting military aid to defend our frontiers. If our country cannot defend itself and die if necessary in the attempt, then we are not either maintaining our honour or dignity or strength or capacity. We must be clear of the broad lines of the policy we pursue. It is clear that we must fight every aggression, whatever it is; it is clear to my mind.

What are the reasons for the Chinese Government doing like this? The reasons are still rather difficult to find. Everybody who sees me and meets me, American or English or any Press man here or a foreign Pressman, asks me: why do you think China has taken this step against India, losing the friendship of India which is a valuable thing at the most in the hope of getting some rare mountains? I have no answer to give them. I cannot. I can guess about various things, what is happening in Tibet, this and that; their old policy of spreading themselves out and their imagining, according to their own maps, that this is ours; let us know we are strong to pull others into submission, whatever it may be; because it is extraordinary to me. The more I think of it, I realise how and why the Chinese have acted in this way. It is not a small matter that they should lose the goodwill of India. It is not a small matter even for the 650 million of China. It is a big thing, and they have lost it. For what? They will continue in having it and as a consequence they are losing the goodwill of many other countries in Asia. They have lost a great deal.

A little territory by itself is neither here nor there except when that territory becomes a matter of honour. That is a different matter. What will they gain if they think that they can gain a little mountain territory from us? They will gain perpetual conflict; it is no small matter; perpetual ill will, and it may spread out to other countries. I think—and I thought so—perhaps they themselves will realise this: that they have gambled rather badly. Whatever their views may be, I am not able to find that out. But we in answer to that should refrain from gambling ourselves badly. We must act wisely; determinedly but wisely.

Hem Barua: Should we gamble at all?

Jawaharlal Nehru: Well, all life is a gamble and everything that one does is a gamble. They are gambles which are not wisely thought out. Every thing is a gamble; our Five Year Plan is a gamble. Our future is a gamble. That is a different matter. But have a well-thought-out thing and be prepared to take the consequences. We have to proceed in that way. On no account must we do anything which will bring dishonour to India or weakness to India. I do not believe in surrendering anything that one has, whatever the consequences. That is true. But let us not call every bit of thing—if I talk to somebody—a surrender. It is childish nonsense, if I may say so, and it is absurd for the Government if it is to be carried on in this way: do not talk; do not have tea with him; do not have lunch with him! Is this the way to carry on this great debate, this great argument, in this great conflict with another country? Are we to carry on by not having tea with somebody and not having meals with somebody else? The whole thing is fantastic. What does it mean?

But I can understand this; the hon. Members feel strongly about this issue, as all of us should. If they think it is necessary to remind me that I should not weaken, I have no objection. I want to be strengthened by our goodwill and your strength. But what I fear is, as I said, there is the basic difference of opinion between the policy we have been pursuing, not today but all these years, and the policy of some hon. Members, and this basic difference of opinion comes out in their speeches and in their amendments which they have moved and it is this. Basically whatever they may say, they do not like our policy of non-alignment. They want the cold war to come in here and the cold war is bound to come in if we join up with somebody. The cold war will come in here not only with its other evils, weakening us in our defence and in our military position but with everything. That is the choice which this House should make. Therefore, we should choose carefully. We all agree that we must stand up to the aggression and we must do our utmost to get it vacated. Therein we agree. But what follows is either said explicitly or implicitly implied—we must join some military bloc to save us from this. That, I am not prepared to do. Even if disaster comes to us on the frontier, I am not prepared to do that, because I am not going to let India rely on a foreign army to save its territory. That, I am not prepared, whatever happens. I do not think that that contingency will arise. I think we are strong enough to resist and to prevent anybody coming, and I do not think that it can arise because of the world situation apart from our strength and many other reasons.

In the mountains, in Ladakh, the situation has arisen and we face it and we will continue to face it and continue to get over it and to push them out. That is a different matter. It may last years. I am not thinking of this crisis being resolved suddenly. It may last years unless some other developments take place and these internal or external developments, the world developments, take place. We must be prepared to face it for years. But that does not mean that we should leave our basic policies which I think are good and which have done us good and which are recognised to be good.

May I say quite clearly that there is, and there has been, no question at all of our accepting the 1960 Chinese line or any other line. It is quite absurd. But some hon. Members talked about our deep interest in spiritual, religious and other matters—Kailas and Mansarovar—and therefore, we should take our boundary up to Kailas and Mansarovar, up to Brahmaputra! That kind of thing has no meaning to an intelligent man. Only the unintelligent can say so. I regret to use that word. It has no meaning. We respect, we honour Kailas and Mansarovar. It has been my desire—I wrote in my book 30 years ago—one great desire to visit Mansarovar. But there it is. But I do not make Mansarovar or Kailas a zamindari of India in order to visit it. This idea is essentially a zamindari idea—by possessing something as a zamindari and bossing over it.

The world is moving out. I think even countries' boundaries do not count for much, not to speak of astronauts and cosmonauts who are going round and round. We live in a changing world. It is a little difficult for us to keep our minds up-to-date. It is difficult to understand what these cosmonauts mean. Two of them are going round and round, conversing with each other, conversing with the world.[319] What do they mean to this changing world? They do mean something:

319. Referring to the two Soviet cosmonauts orbiting around the earth in separate spaceships, see item 8, fn 57.

a mighty force has come into being, a mighty thing, both peaceful purposes and warlike purposes. We do not keep up-to-date. We still talk in terms of medieval ages. Most of us live too in terms of medieval ages. That is unfortunate and we have to come out: whether it is for five years plans, whether it is for our defence or whether it is for our progress, we have to think on modern terms.

I regret I am unable to accept those amendments which have been moved. There are some things in those amendments to which I have no exception, but I am unable to accept the whole background of those amendments. I believe we have been given an amendment approving of this Government's policy. If you permit that being taken up, I should like to support it.

> P.K. Deo (Kalahandi): Most respectfully, I would request the Prime Minister to make a statement to clear the misunderstanding that is prevalent in the country: that there would be no negotiation so long as the Chinese do not vacate the occupied places in India.

Jawaharlal Nehru: Yesterday morning I made a statement. I shall make no more categorical statement. I want freedom of action. I want to say it quite plainly. I say, first of all, that nothing can happen without this House being informed.

Secondly, we should agree that nothing should be done which, in the slightest degree, sullies the honour of India. For the rest, I want a free hand.

> Hem Barua: The Prime Minister has made a reference to what he said yesterday. I have certain doubts about what he said yesterday. He said in one place about preliminary negotiations towards the relaxation of tension. May I know whether he proposes to have this on the basis of status quo? In another place, he said about negotiations on the basis of officials' reports. May I know on what basis—on the basis of the garbled and truncated version of the Chinese or on our report?

Jawaharlal Nehru: I cannot precisely say. I think the present situation in the frontier is such that we cannot have any serious talks with the Chinese. Therefore, I said, I am prepared to ask, whenever I have the chance to meet an important person, "If you are anxious, as we are, to have serious talks, a climate must be created for it." What is necessary for that climate, we may discuss.

> Hem Barua: I just wanted to know for the enlightenment of the House and of the whole country, on the basis of which report negotiations would be held—on the basis of the garbled and truncated Chinese version or on the basis of our report?

Jawaharlal Nehru: That is a subsequent step. When we talk about it on the basis of the reports—plural—obviously we do not discuss it on the basis of one report, but on the basis of both reports. Obviously we stand by our report and of course, no doubt the other party will stand by its report. We will discuss both the reports. But that question does not arise; that climate has not arisen. It is in order to facilitate that climate to arise that we may—I do not say that we will—have some talks.[320]

406. In the Rajya Sabha: Chinese Occupation of Territory[321]

Will the Prime Minister be pleased to state:[322]

(a) the total area of the Indian territory under the unauthorised occupation of China;
(b) the area of the Indian territory which was recovered from China during the last three years; and
(c) the area of Indian territory which China has usurped during the last three years?

Jawaharlal Nehru:

(a) The nature of the terrain and other factors in that part of Ladakh which is at present under the unlawful occupation of China, make it difficult to give a precise estimate of the area seized by the Chinese. However, this area is about 10,000 to 12,000 square miles.
(b) Measures have been taken to stop further Chinese encroachments on Indian territory but Chinese forces have not withdrawn from positions already occupied by them.

---

320. With regard to the amendment to the motion moved by P.K. Deo (see fn 307 in this section), the Speaker ruled that it had been disposed of, and added:
    "Now, I think, because the hon. Members on the Opposition have also now expressed that the speech of the hon. Prime Minister was unexceptionable and was acceptable to every section of the House, there is no need for our passing any motion with regard to that. Everybody is agreed and supports everything that has been said by the Prime Minister. Therefore, there is no need for putting that motion to the House."
321. Written answers, 16 August 1962. *Rajya Sabha Debates*, Vol. 40, Nos. 1-8, 6 to 16 August 1962, cols 1812-1814.
322. Question by V.M. Chordia, Jan Sangh.

(c) During the last three years the Chinese have established further military posts in an area of about 800-1,000 square miles but we also have our posts in this area so that there is no actual physical occupation of any large area except to the extent that each military post commands certain limited area in its vicinity.

407. In the Lok Sabha: Officials' Report of Border Dispute[323]

Will the Prime Minister be pleased to state:[324]

(a) whether the Chinese version of the text of the report of the officials of India and China on the Sino-Indian border question has now been studied;[325]
(b) If so, the reactions of Government; and
(c) what are the important points on which the report is at variance with our stand?

The Deputy Minster in the Ministry of External Affairs (Dinesh Singh):

(a) Yes, Sir,
(b) The Report as published by the Chinese Government appears to be a faithful translation of the original text of our Report in English.
(c) No significant points of variance have been noticed between the Chinese version of the Report and the original Chinese and English texts.

408. China and San Francisco Conference – I[326]

Please send me the paper relating to this matter which I received from the Lok Sabha Secretariat. I shall then send an answer to that.

2. Perhaps you could draft a brief statement on my behalf. This will be on the following lines.

---

323. Written answers, 18 August 1962. *Lok Sabha Debates*, Third Series, Vol. 6, 6 to 18 August 1962, col. 2479.
324. Question by Shree Narayan Das, Congress.
325. For the Officials' Report, see SWJN/SS/66 Supplement.
326. Note, 20 August 1962, for M.J. Desai, the Foreign Secretary.

I regret that there was a discrepancy in what I said in the course of my speech in the Lok Sabha on the 14th August.[327] In the small pamphlet on Leading Events in India-China Relations,[328] page 2, it is stated that "A Peace Treaty with Japan was signed at San Francisco by 49 nations (on the 8th September, 1951). India declined to attend the Conference because, among other reasons, China was not a party to it". In my reply to the debate in Parliament, I stated that non-attendance of India at the San Francisco Conference in regard to the Japanese Treaty had absolutely nothing to do with China. There is thus this discrepancy.

I have now referred to the old papers in connection with this Treaty. I find that among the reasons considered by us for not going to San Francisco was that there could not be peace in the Far East without China and the USSR being also parties to it.

When I made the speech, I had no recollection of this, and hence I committed an error which I greatly regret.

3. I find now that on the basis of what I said, a notice of a question of privilege has been tabled by Shri P.K. Deo.[329] If this comes up tomorrow, I shall make some such statement.[330]

409. China and San Francisco Conference – II[331]

Notice of a question of privilege tabled by Shri P.K. Deo, MP.

Shri P.K. Deo's previous notice was received by me two or three days ago. As there was an obvious discrepancy in what I said in the Lok Sabha and in what was given in the pamphlet issued by External Affairs, as stated by Shri P.K. Deo, I have had reference made to this matter from our old papers. From these I find that there were a number of reasons which led us to not to associate ourselves with the San Francisco Treaty. Among these reasons was also our feeling that peace in the Far East required the association of China and the USSR.

2. Thus, what I stated in my reply in the Lok Sabha was not quite correct, and the statement in the pamphlet was correct. I greatly regret that, owing to a lapse of memory, I made this mistake.

3. I am prepared to make a statement on the above lines in the Lok Sabha.[332]

---

327. Item 405.
328. *Leading Events in India-China Relations, 1947-1962* (New Delhi: GOI, MEA, 1962).
329. Swatantra Party.
330. See also item 409.
331. Note, 20 August 1962, for the Lok Sabha Secretariat.
332. See also item 408.

410. No Fraternising with Chinese Troops on Border[333]

[Note, 21 August 1962, from M.J. Desai, the Foreign Secretary, begins]

Please see the further sitrep received today placed below.

2.   I told General Thapar[334] and, later Defence Minister[335] that this meeting should not have been held, that this fraternising prejudiced our position and that there can be no question of our accepting the Chinese posts in these areas and co-existing with them. Nor should we do anything which gives them a position of dictating to us what facilities they will permit to our posts.

3.   No further meetings of this kind will be held. Defence Minister did not, however, feel that, there had been anything seriously wrong in this meeting.[336]

M.J. Desai
21-8-1962

[Prime Minister]

[Note, 21 August 1962, from M.J. Desai, the Foreign Secretary, ends]

[Note, 21 August 1962, by Nehru, begins]

I agree that we should not encourage fraternising.

J. Nehru
21-8-1962

[Note, 21 August 1962, by Nehru, ends]

---

333. Noting, 21 August 1962. MEA, Historical Division, *Sino-Indian Border Dispute* Volume VI, Part III, (Chinese Incursions into Indian Territory), (April 1962-October 1962), Notes, p.31.
334. P.N. Thapar, Chief of the Army Staff.
335. V.K. Krishna Menon.
336. See appendix 42.

411. In the Rajya Sabha: Border Situation[337]

Jawaharlal Nehru: Mr Chairman,[338] Sir, I beg to move:

"That the situation along the India-China Border, particularly in the Ladakh region, be taken into consideration."

Before dealing with this subject, perhaps you will permit me, Sir, to refer to one or two developments of international significance, which have no relation to this subject, but I feel the House will perhaps appreciate my references. One is the recent agreement arrived at between the Indonesian Government and the Government of the Netherlands in regard to West Irian. I should like to congratulate both those Governments on the peaceful settlement of a very difficult and delicate problem and—I should like to add—more especially congratulate the Secretary-General of the United Nations, U Thant, who took the initiative in this matter, and also, if I may, Mr Bunker, who played an important role in these negotiations.[339] This removes one source of conflict in South-East Asia. A little while ago there was the Laos settlement, which also has removed another source of conflict in South-East Asia. There are still other conflicts going on in South-East Asia, but the settlement of these two is a matter of good augury for the peace of South-East Asia, and we are particularly happy not only because of our intimate contacts with the countries concerned but also because, in a sense, we are part of South-East Asia, and we earnestly hope that there will be peace there.

Another matter I should like to refer to is the recent de jure transfer of Pondicherry to India. This matter has been pending for a large number of years, and most of us and many Members of this House must have felt rather frustrated at the great delay in this transfer. But ultimately it has taken place. We realised then and we realise now that France was going through a difficult period, and there have been big constitutional changes in France and therefore, although we pressed for it, reminded them of it, we did not wish to say or do anything which might injure our relations with France. I am glad that the policy of patience pursued by us has led to a successful result. Now, Pondicherry and

337. Motion, 22 August 1962. *Rajya Sabha Debates*, Vol. 40, Nos. 9-16, 17 to 29 August 1962, cols 2876-2882, 2981-3002.
338. Zakir Husain.
339. Ellsworth Bunker, US diplomat and a former Ambassador to India, negotiated an agreement between the Netherlands and Indonesia leading to the transfer of control of West Irian to the UN on 15 August 1962, as a preliminary step before it was turned over to Indonesia.

the other old French Settlements are part of India, and presently the matter will come up before this House in another form.[340] But the main thing is, we have done this, in accordance with our habit and practice, peacefully and without injuring in any way our relations with France, and I should like to express my appreciation of the French Government and specially of its eminent President, President de Gaulle.

Sir, coming to the subject of my motion, there is little that is new that I can place before the House. On the first day of this session of Parliament I made a brief statement in this House as well as in the other and placed the latest *White Paper*[341] on this question. That brought matters up to date so far as the giving of information is concerned. Subsequently, in the last few days there has been a debate in the other House also. Now, nothing in the shape of incidents has happened since then. The position remains much the same. There have been certain charges and counter-charges of firing taking place. But apparently if this took place, it took place at some long distance and it hurt nobody. At the present moment, therefore, the situation remains much as it was and I cannot say if it has definitely improved; it has certainly not grown any worse.

There are some indications—I do not know how far they are likely to be correct—that our post at Galwan may be reached by a column that we had sent by road. Meanwhile they have been sent supplies by air regularly and there is no lack of supplies to any of our military posts. In spite of the fact that the situation has not grown worse, essentially the situation is a bad one, is a serious one by the mere fact that, according to us, a large part of our territory is under Chinese occupation and so long as that continues the situation is bound to be exceedingly serious.

We have followed in the last few months and years, in fact, the policy of trying to strengthen ourselves to meet this menace, strengthen ourselves in various ways more especially on the borders themselves, by building road communications and the rest and by putting up posts, and at the same time not giving up our hope that it may be settled by peaceful means. We follow this dual policy because we feel, apart from our general feeling, that war, as is usually undesirable, is peculiarly so in the present age with the development of weapons, and because of the fact that India and China are so situated, any war between them would be disastrous for both and would be a very prolonged war. We do

---

340. On 4 September 1962, Nehru introduced the Constitution Fourteenth Amendment Bill in the Lok Sabha regarding incorporation of Pondicherry into the Indian Union, see item 159. The Bill as passed by that House was moved by Lal Bahadur Shastri, the Home Minister, in the Rajya Sabha on 7 September 1962 for its consideration.
341. *White Paper No. 6.*

not want a war as I have said often enough, nor do we want any occupation of our territory by a foreign power. We have, therefore, to proceed on these dual lines. It may be a little difficult to achieve our objective in the near future and we must, therefore, be prepared for some time to elapse before we achieve it.

I just mentioned two cases, one was of West Irian which for ten years has been a matter of conflict. It has at last been settled. And even on the Pondicherry issue, many of our friends sometimes asked us to deliver ultimatums to the French Government. But we thought we would settle it peacefully and we have succeeded.

Now, the present position is that in the military sense we are much stronger than we were a year or two ago. We have put up a certain barrier to further encroachment or aggression and we, I think, in regard to these communications and other factors, will increase our strength in the future but we do not intend to bring about a major conflict on our part. Of course, if the other party takes some steps to that end, we shall face it naturally. I still think that our case is so good that under a proper consideration I do not see any adequate reply to it.

The Chinese make charges that we have occupied their territory, that we committed air violations because of our planes flying over their territory. They say that they have always had that territory. I do not understand on what basis they say that, because it is quite clear that ten or twelve years ago, anyhow, they were not there, not even in Tibet. It was after they went into Tibet and took possession of it that they reached these frontiers.

Now, the old Tibetan Government did not lay any claim to these wide territories in Ladakh. There were one or two points on our frontier about which there was some argument with the old Tibetan Government, long-standing arguments. They were small points here and there. They never laid claim to it. Now, the Chinese apparently are there, and the Chinese Government is a successor to the old Tibetan Government and they claim this as a part of China which means part of China through its being part of Tibet. Obviously, they were not there; they were not in Tibet at all. They came to Tibet about ten or eleven years ago and after that. But for some years there was no particular move on their part in this direction. Round about 1957 they are said to have made that road in the north-east corner of Aksai Chin, that is, made road over a caravan track. And it was really in 1957 that they marched into eastern Ladakh in a big way. There can be no doubt that they were not there before. So, I do not understand the argument of the Chinese that they have been in possession of these areas in the past and continuously, as they say. May be, it is some metaphysical conception of the Chinese Empire which existed in the past ages. Even that does not hold water as the report of our officials clearly demonstrated and the abundance of arguments and evidence that they have placed, which they have probably seen.

631

I need not before this House justify our claim because I take it everybody realises, apart from the sentiment of it and the proof that has been produced in regard to it, the validity and strength of our position in regard to these areas. The question arises, therefore, what we should do about it. As I have ventured to state, our approach is a dual one, one is to go on strengthening ourselves and holding, as far as possible, the Chinese and at the same time to explore such avenues as we can find to achieve a peaceful settlement of this difficult problem. It is not an easy matter. I realise that. It may take time, but it is better for it to take some time than for us to plunge into war. The main thing is we cannot acknowledge, or in any sense bow to their aggression, surrender to it or acknowledge it and we must strengthen ourselves to meet them in any way that it becomes necessary.

I had once said and asked them, in order to prepare for fruitful talks and negotiations, to withdraw. That is, I had suggested that both sides should withdraw to the line of the other side, to the map line of the other side. That would have left a large area unoccupied by the military forces and there would be no question of any conflict and we could then consider the matter, consider the evidence and other factors concerning this place. The Chinese Government at the time did not agree with that proposal because obviously it involved their withdrawing over a large area and our withdrawing over a very small area. I hope they will consider that because that, I think, is the fairest and the most reasonable request and it does not, in any sense, bring or lead to any, if I may use a popular phrase, loss of face of any party because it is obvious that while this major aggression exists, it is not possible to have any fruitful negotiations. We cannot negotiate when there is active tension, etc. Therefore, we have suggested or we are going to suggest to them that in order to prepare the ground for fruitful talks on the main subject, the first thing to consider is how to create a situation which will be free from tension and which will involve withdrawal and for that we are prepared to talk on this limited issue. If it leads to anything further, then further talks may be indulged in. That is our present position. I may say that the last Chinese letter came dated the 4th August. I have said the last but it is not the last because since then several have come—complaints—subsequent letters are complaints of our air violation on their space and one or two charges of our people in Ladakh firing at them and so on but they are charges. The main letter came on the 4th August. To that no reply has yet been sent by us. Probably, we shall send it on the lines I have indicated fairly soon. That is the position. I do not wish to take up the time of the House now in repeating what I have previously said many times because it will be better for hon. Members to have more time for their comments and criticisms so that I can deal with them and reply to them at the end of the debate. I beg to move, Sir.

The question was proposed.

[Omitted: Speeches by various MPs]

Deputy Chairman:[342] Hon. Prime Minister.

Jawaharlal Nehru: Madam Deputy Chairman, first of all may I endeavour to clear up some misunderstandings that may have arisen? Prof. Ruthnaswamy[343] advised me not to indulge in vituperation. As an example of vituperation he said I had called possibly ...

M. Ruthnaswamy: I took care to say that the vituperative vocabulary of the Prime Minister is rather limited.

Jawaharlal Nehru: That may be so. But he gave examples of it, because I had called some statement of a colleague of his in the other House nonsense. I do not quite know if he expects me to applaud statements made by his colleague, which I consider nonsensical. I do not think "nonsensical" to be exactly vituperation. It is often a statement of fact so far as his Party is concerned.

Then, another thing which he took exception to was my referring to the leader of his Party in the other House as the gallant Maharaja.[344] I thought that was hundred per cent parliamentary. I really do not know whether he objects to his being gallant or being a Maharaja. I for my part would welcome the day when Maharajas cease altogether in this country. That is a different matter. But so long as they are there, I am entitled to call them Maharajas.

Then, another gentleman, Shri Khobaragade,[345] objected to my calling some argument infantile.[346] Well, I confess that the word I used seemed to me to fit the argument raised. The argument was, I said, infantile. I did not call anybody infantile. I said it about this argument of not having tea with somebody, of my not inviting the Chinese Ambassador, or the Defence Minister not speaking to somebody. Quite apart from the fact that it is not good manners, it is not modern diplomacy. It is a perfectly infantile way of dealing with a serious problem and I repeat that—this kind of approach. And I gave as an example

342. Violet Alva.
343. M. Ruthnaswamy, Swatantra Party.
344. Nehru had used the expressions, taken exception to by M. Ruthnaswamy, in his speech in the Lok Sabha on 14 August while rebutting the arguments of P.K. Deo, the Maharaja of Kalahandi, see item 405.
345. Bhaurao Dewaji Khobaragade, Republican Party of India.
346. See item 405.

two countries which are entirely opposed to each other, more opposed than any two other countries probably are, that is, the United States of America and China. For many years their Ambassadors have been talking at Warsaw. They do not recognise each other, mind you. They have no official dealings with each other, no representatives. Yet because they had no representatives they tried to meet in Warsaw. Their Ambassadors for years now have been meeting every month, sometimes every week, and trying to discuss problems. That is the normal way. This kind of thing is a relic of our ideas of untouchability, something which has been put an end to in our Constitution, to say that you must not talk to somebody, you must not have tea with somebody. I confess I have never heard of this before in my life in any circle in any country. I confess it must be due to some relic of the caste system here and untouchability. Whether you are friendly with a person or you are hostile or inimical, you have to deal with him. You may have to deal with him in battle, but otherwise you have to deal with him in the council chamber and other places, discuss with him. In what form you deal with him depends on circumstances and it is nothing short of absurdity to say; "Oh, you must not do this till he conforms to all your wishes." That is not the way any country, even the mightiest in the world, deals with any other country.

Then, may I say that I welcome very much what the hon. Member, Shri Jairamadas,[347] said about the approach to this question? He was good enough to say a good deal about me. I am not referring to that part of his speech. But rather when we are dealing with any serious problem—even when we are dealing as between individuals but more so when we are dealing with national problems, great nations opposed to each other—it is never right, if I may say so—we may fight, if necessity arises one fights, or wish to run down the other party—to curse it and to use strong language. Of course, one may do so in our own circle and it sounds all right. We may do so at a meeting in the Ramlila grounds here, it sounds all right, and we enthuse people by it. One always enthuses people by cursing somebody else or some other country. But when that voice of ours and that language of ours reaches that particular country as well as other countries, then it does not produce the right result. It is obvious that by our strong language we do not frighten the other country or defeat it. If we have to gain what we seek to gain, apart from the field of battle, we have to do it by talking to it—there is no other way—by political pressures, military pressures or other pressures. There is no other way. And if we merely shut the door to any such approach and also when we create a position by our language or other acts—the other party or ourselves, it applies to the other party

347. Jairamadas Daulatram, Nominated.

too using that language—when it becomes a tremendous question of honour and prestige—that is how language makes it a question of honour and prestige when the other party does not give in at all, when it might otherwise—that is entirely opposed to all the training I had in the past. Shri Jairamdas Daulatram referred to the Gandhian period of our struggle for independence. Gandhiji was not a weakling, nobody called him a weakling, but he was always soft in his language and tried to win over the other party.

Take even our reactions to China. Why are our reactions so strong and angry? Certainly it would be because they have occupied our territory. But I venture to submit that the real reason for our anger is not even that. It is the way they have done it and the way they have behaved and the way they have treated us, our country. It is conceivable that they could have claimed a frontier revision or something and asked us for talks without occupying it. But after all that we had done for them it would seem a peculiarly ungracious thing for them to behave in this way. That has hurt us apart from the major hurt of their occupying the territory. They knew very well, I am not going into the rights and wrongs of this question, I am convinced that we are right, but apart from that they knew absolutely what our frontier was according to us, according to our maps. Our maps have not varied like theirs every few months or few years. Our maps have been there clearly defined, good maps which have been handed to them. Their attention has been drawn to them and for years past they never really challenged them. They did not accept them, I will admit that, and they said their own maps should be considered afresh, their old maps and all that. But they knew very well what our maps were, where our boundaries were. I do submit, quite apart from the merits of the question, that it was utterly and absolutely wrong for them then to cross those boundaries without reference to us or without telling us that this is so and afterwards, when we raised this question, to produce maps which go on changing from year to year.

So, my point is that we must be as strong as we like in our expressions but not use language which needlessly hurts national prestige, because that makes it frightfully difficult for any kind of talks or any kind of possible, if it is possible, settlement to be arrived at. This applies to every country. In other words, we must not indulge in what is commonly known as the language of the cold war. The cold war does not help. You may disagree with a person, you may even fight him, but the language of the cold war is the language, if I may say so with all respect, of lack of civilisation. We should behave in a civilised manner. Civilised manner does not mean behaving weakly, but it ultimately helps, and it is becoming for civilised countries to behave in a civilised manner.

Then there are one or two other matters. Mr Mani[348] asked us about our publicity about this matter. I am sorry that our publicity has not reached him,

348. A.D. Mani, Independent.

but we have issued a number of pamphlets and books on this subject which have been widely circulated and often translated in French, Spanish, Arabic, Sinhalese, Burmese, Nepalese and Japanese among other languages. As for the All India Radio, the Radio broadcasts daily in Mandarin and separately in Cantonese, two broadcasts directed to China, one in Mandarin for 45 minutes, one in Cantonese for 45 minutes; one in Tibetan for 45 minutes; one in English but directed to China, Korea and Japan for an hour, daily. In South East Asia the daily broadcasts are: Indonesian or Bahasa as it is called for one and a quarter hours daily; Burmese for 1 hour 35 minutes daily; English for South East Asia for one and a half hours and French news for Indo China etc. for 15 minutes daily.

> A.D. Mani: May I draw the attention of the Prime Minister to a statement made by the Minister of Information and Broadcasting[349] in the Lok Sabha on June 11th? I am reading from a newspaper report.

> > "All India Radio does not intend to launch any special broadcast to counter the Chinese broadcasts beamed to India and other Asiatic countries."

> > This was stated by Dr Gopala Reddi in answer to a question from Mr D.N. Tiwari[350] in Lok Sabha. This is the basis on which I made the statement that the AIR was not putting out broadcasts.

Jawaharlal Nehru: That I do not know. Presumably it means a special broadcast about the frontier question. These broadcasts, as I said, are broadcasts generally putting the Indian viewpoint, Indian news, Indian everything, to China and South East Asia in the course of which the frontier question also comes up. The hon. Member will appreciate that this kind of direct broadcasts for a particular matter have less effect, have less publicity value than in a general broadcast of news etc., something being said relating to the frontier.

Then reference was made to our letter of the 26th July.[351] I really do not understand it. I have no doubt that some Members could have perhaps worded it better, but I really do not understand why so much stress has been laid on

---

349. B. Gopala Reddy.
350. Congress.
351. A.B. Vajpayee, Jan Sangh, had questioned the wisdom of asking the Chinese, in the GOI note of 26 July 1962, to return to the Chou En-lai claim-line of 1956, since India's stand all along had been that Chinese forces should go back to the international frontier. For the GOI note of 26 July 1962, see *White Paper No. VII*, pp. 3-4.

the fact that it has said something else than what it was meant to do. Possibly this is due to the fact that some newspapers went on repeating without rhyme or reason that it did so. As an hon. Member quoted it, apart from that, the very next paragraph made that further clear. It is obvious that the whole point of reference to the Chou En-lai map claim-line was to show that they have been misbehaving still further. It has nothing to do with our accepting that line. That is absurd, to say that it conflicts with all that we have said or that we are likely to say. But it was to lay stress that they are, even according to their own Prime Minister's statement, committing aggression. That surely does not mean that we admit the previous aggression.

The hon. Member, Mr Vajpayee, quoted a Burmese daily about Chip Chap Valley or River.[352] The Burmese daily—that is what he quoted from—it was a quotation in the Burmese daily of a Chinese newspaper. Subsequently, that same Burmese daily gave, when its attention was drawn to it, a full statement about the Indian position in regard to the Chip Chap Valley.

Shri Vajpayee referred to my reference to South East Asian countries. I should like to say that if any impression has been created in his mind or in any mind of any discourteous reference of mine to South East Asia countries, I am sorry, because I did not certainly mean it. I could not have meant it because we have very friendly and cordial relations with all these countries. I did not mean it. Some of these countries and the SEATO are tried up with military alliances. And as the House will know, the SEATO has not done any wonders in South East Asia. In fact, according to us, the coming of SEATO has made the position worse in South East Asia. It has not helped at all. However that may be, I was referring to this position that some are in the SEATO and others are non-aligned more or less. Others may, without belonging to any military alliance, incline one way or the other. We may agree with them here and there, and in some matters we may not. But Mr Vajpayee is quite right in saying that anything that might be construed as any discourtesy, any reference, is quite wrong, and I certainly did not mean it. Of course, we have very good relations with them.

Then, an hon. Member—I forget who it was—asked me: When I ask for a free hand, what kind of freedom do I want?[353] My reference to a free hand was in relation to an amendment that had been moved which wanted to tie me up to that amendment. I said that I was not going to accept that amendment, that I wanted a free hand subject, of course, to the basic things that we stood for.[354]

---

352. Vajpayee said that Burma was experiencing China's influence in the region, which is why a newspaper published by the Information Department of the Burmese Government had written that Chip Chap Valley belonged to China.
353. This was asked by A.B. Vajpayee.
354. Nehru had used this expression in his speech in the Lok Sabha on 14 August 1962, see item 405.

But it is absurd to ask a person to deal with a matter and tie him up hand and foot. He cannot deal with the matter. He must have some freedom to manoeuvre.

Now, most of the speeches in this House, apart from stressing this aspect or that aspect, have not been radically different, and I think I may well say that broadly, the policy pursued by us has been approved, although Mr Vajpayee's amendment is [a] thorough disapproval of almost everything that has been done or may be done.[355] That is my difficulty because hon. Members

355. A.B. Vajpayee's amendment read: "That at the end of the Motion the following be added, namely:-
'and having considered the same, this House is of the opinion –
   (i)   that Government's China policy has been a dismal failure inasmuch as full eight years after China committed its first act of blatant aggression on Indian soil by constructing the Aksai Chin highway across our territory, Government has not merely failed to redeem Chinese-occupied territory but has been unable to check-mate China's continuing forays and encroachments and, more deplorably still, continues to betray an utter confusion of mind and suicidal illusions in respect of Chinese objectives and intentions, with the result that our attitudes very often seem humiliatingly incongruous with the situation, provide positive encouragement to the aggressor in its misdoings and undermine our prestige and credit in the eyes of world opinion and particularly of our neighbouring countries in Asia;
   (ii) that the policy enunciated by the Prime Minister recently in respect of unconditional talks acting as a prelude to further negotiations constitutes a major and retrograde departure from the hitherto avowed Government policy about negotiations;
   (iii) that the Note of July 26, 1962, sent to China seriously compromised India's position because the Note, as drafted, impliedly committed India to acceptance of China's claim-line of 1956 and was, therefore, tantamount to a virtual offer to cede a major part of the occupied area; but welcomes the Prime Minister's subsequent affirmation that India would not accept anything other than the traditional international boundary as the basis of any talks;
   (iv) that the continuing acts of aggression by China and the content and tone of its communications to India make it amply clear that China has not the slightest intention of relenting its hold on the Indian territory it has surreptitiously or forcibly seized;
   (v)   that in the face of the Chinese attitude, Government's present probings for opening of talks, whether in the form of the Defence Minister's parleys with the Chinese Foreign Minister, or as indicated by the Prime Minister's recent pronouncements, reflect adversely on India's self-respect, smack of a policy of abject appeasement and serve only to whet the aggressor's appetite; and this House, therefore, calls for an abandonment of this policy and a categorical declaration by Government that vacation of aggression by China is an absolute pre-requisite for negotiations'."

talk in contradictory languages sometimes. They approve of it and yet they put something in writing or in words which is not only disapproval but condemnation. I have tried to understand their mentality and all this leaves me to think that there is a fundamental difference in our approach which comes out. Even though it may overlap sometimes, it comes out. There is a fundamental difference in our approach. In spite of what the hon. Members of the Communist Party have said, there is a fundamental difference—not in this particular matter—in our approach to some of these problems. It comes out occasionally. Take the *Swadhinata* cartoon to which reference has been made.[356] It may or may not refer to this matter but it is a highly objectionable thing, and he may not agree with it.

Bhupesh Gupta: I would ask the Prime Minister not to give an opinion. I shall find out and send him this thing. And if it is wrong, we shall admit the mistake.[357]

Jawaharlal Nehru: I am merely saying that the ideas of the members of the Communist Party perhaps on non-alignment may somewhat differ from mine, although they may … (Interruption).

Bhupesh Gupta: We support everything that you say in that respect.

Jawaharlal Nehru: I said, they may differ. So also, when Mr Vajpayee expresses agreement on non-alignment, I have some doubts in my mind about his idea of non-alignment.

356. On 22 August 1962, B.K.P. Sinha and Akbar Ali Khan, both Congress, alleged that a cartoon in the Independence Day number of the CPI journal *Swadhinata* (Calcutta) depicted "the famished or starving Indians" being fed by armed Chinese soldiers at the border. Calling the CPI "Trojan horses," Sinha said "this is how the organs of that party are trying to break the will of the Indian people to resist aggression on the country's borders." *Rajya Sabha Debates*, Vol. 40, Nos. 9-16, August 17-29, 1962, cols 2913-2915 and 2954-2956.

357. Bhupesh Gupta, CPI, said in the Rajya Sabha on 24 August 1962 that what the Congress MPs had referred to in the House on 22 August was "not a cartoon, but a pictorial representation of a very important concept of our political theory, namely the alliance of the workers and peasants for the progress of the people." He pointed out that the cartoon showed workers on the one side and peasants on the other, and not the Chinese soldiers. He added that *Swadhinata* had carried the same sketch even in one of its issues in 1954, before the border problem with China began. *Rajya Sabha Debates*, Vol. 40, Nos. 9-16, August 17-29, 1962, cols 3123-3128.

A.B. Vajpayee: May I know what the doubts are?

Jawaharlal Nehru: I would submit that your amendment itself indicates the doubts.

A.B. Vajpayee: No, my amendment has nothing to do with the foreign policy or non-alignment. It is confined to the Government's China policy only.

Jawaharlal Nehru: That is true but it is all part of the whole.

Some hon. Member—Mr Khobaragade, I think suddenly in the middle of other things just put in one sentence: "Why don't you take military help from other countries?", which, of course, is basically and fundamentally opposed to a non-alignment policy. Taking military help means practically becoming aligned to that country. So, at the back of their minds there is that thing lurking which leads, them, I think, to utterly wrong conclusions.

B.D. Khobaragade: No, Madam, I would just like to know from the hon. Prime Minister what steps they are going to take to train people and strengthen our military defences, because in spite of these protests and our desire to settle those problems by peaceful negotiations, the incursions are going on. Even the hon. Prime Minister had said two months back that he had some sort of a hunch that China desired some sort of peaceful settlement. But even then, there have been fresh incursions. Suppose tomorrow also fresh incursions take place, what steps are you going to take to strengthen our defences and our military position? Or should we allow China to make fresh incursions again into our country?

Deputy Chairman: Your statement is being interpreted.

Jawaharlal Nehru: I am sorry that I have not quite understood what the hon. Member has said. It is my fault. But I should like to assure, first of all, that this question of our trouble with China on our border is a military question and a political question; there are many other aspects of it as well. Limiting it to the military aspect, I should like the hon. Member, if he has ever considered military matters, to consider as to what country, and how, can give us military aid in this particular matter. In one way, of course, they can give it, by having a world war and diverting attention. But that is a different matter. About the defence of our frontier, how can any other country help us? They can help us in one way, if we are prepared to take it. That is they can give us free the things we want whatever they may be, aircraft or other things. But otherwise, how do you expect any big country or small country to send their armies to our North East frontiers to protect them? Obviously not. (Interruption). That is what I have said. They may send us some equipment, may be some aircraft, if we are prepared to accept it. And the cost we pay for it, not in money but in other ways, will be far greater than its possible value. I am looking at it purely from the practical point of view, and the cost of it will be far greater, and it will weaken us ultimately, weaken us actually in fighting on the frontier, apart from other ways. It surprises me that these patent facts are not obvious to everybody. Of course, the sympathy of the countries is always welcome, and it helps us. I think we have the sympathetic understanding on this issue of many countries.

Some hon. Members have referred here and elsewhere to the countries of South East Asia and to Nepal and said that we ought to be able to convince them to act differently than they have done in some matters. Well, I do not wish to go into each individual country's policy. That is for them to determine but it is not an easy matter. We either bring pressure on them which has the wrong results or we seek to make them understand our policy and, I believe, normally we succeed. But they have to deal with all kinds of pressures on themselves, sometimes the pressures may lead them in other directions. Broadly speaking, most countries, whether in Asia or Europe, understand our position in this and sympathise with us. But there are very few of them which can really help us except that it may be in regard to military equipment. We take military equipment from countries, we buy it. But the few crores that we may save if we got those military equipment as a gift would be far outbalanced by the tremendous loss in prestige, in position and even in sympathy that we may have from the rest of the world. It is obvious. Therefore, it is essential, so far as I see, for us to maintain our non-alignment policy and retain the friendship of all nations on that basis. Now it is agreed—and there is nothing much that I can say—about the broad features of this policy as applied to the frontier, that is, to strengthen our defences, and at the same time be always ready for any opportunity that might lead to fruitful results in the way of a settlement. I must say, looking at it at the present moment, that the prospects are not good. But that should not lead me to jump into a wrong direction. May be later, because of various things happening including our own position, as it improves, it may lead us to better results. We may have to wait for it.

Again to say that we must not negotiate and not have talks seems to me very unrealistic. You may say that negotiation should come at the right moment—what the right moment is, you cannot exactly define; broadly you may indicate it; that is all right—because negotiations at the wrong moment may injure us. That I accept. But you cannot rule out negotiations, much less can you rule out talks. It is an attitude; it is a brave attitude but not a wise one. Hon. Members should remember that in our history there has been no lack of courage, tremendous courage, superhuman courage, but tremendous lack of wisdom, which has made that courage to lose in the conflict. That is our history. Whether it is the Rajputs or others, there was no lack of courage, but the Rajputs did not win in the end because they did not understand things. They lived in a world of their own; they did not know that the world was progressing, and as I said in the other House, they did not have, and even the Marhattas, gallant as they were, did not have a decent map of India, while a handful of Europeans, Frenchmen and others, in this country, had much better maps, had much better informers. In every Court in India they had their spies informing them, paid spies, and sometimes the Ministers of the Court were their spies, of the English people and the French, specially the English, apart from the fact that they had better weapons, modern weapons, and the other people simply talked about hordes. And the result was natural; with all the courage in the world they could not face the superior weapons and superior organisation and knowledge. It is extraordinary, if you read history, how you find it, how these people fought great battles—and were fine persons—without a map even, without knowing where they have to go to and knowing little beyond their borders.

So, we have to look at the position today realistically. Certainly the personal element is of the greatest importance—determination, courage, unity, etc. But in war we have to deal with modern weapons, not only modern weapons but other modern equipment, and in effect, today a war is something very different from a few armies fighting it. It is a war of peoples. Not that I want it—I am merely saying that; it becomes a nation in arms. It means the development of industry, the economy and all that, and therefore, preparation for adding to your strength means developing your economy and industry essentially. It is not that we get a few guns or a few aircraft from another country and we defend our country. What happens if those aircraft are destroyed, or do not fly? Then we are helpless. We have nothing to fall back upon. So, it is better to have slightly second rate arms with a nation behind them and producing them than rely on things supplied from outside, which may or may not come at the right moment, or the spares may not be there in hand. That is why our policy has been to build up defence industries, to build up defence equipment, and all that, and we have done that, not only in rather showy things, such as the supersonic aircraft, HF 24, that we have built at Bangalore—that is certainly a great feat for us to accomplish—but in hundreds of other things. The wartime equipment that we are making in our ordnance factories today were not made before. We started at the time of independence practically from scratch, because the British policy previously was to supply everything to us, everything including ideas, including policies—policies and ideas were made in Whitehall—everything came. Only in the last War some kind of simple ammunition was made in this country, because they could not get it from elsewhere. So, we started almost from scratch, and we have built it up and we have built it up well, and we have got some very fine specialised men, engineers, etc., in the Army, the Air Force and the Navy, so that we have to take all these into consideration.

Some hon. Member referred to Marshal Chen-Yi[358] talking about 650 million people not doing this or that. Well, with all respect to Marshal Chen-Yi that does not impress anybody, that kind of saying, nor does it impress me. When somebody tells me that we have got 45 crores of men, that we will stand as a man, it does not impress me at all. That is a source of weakness, not of strength unless those people are well-trained and well-fed and the country's economy is good. That is a source of strength, not numbers. Numbers have always been a source of weakness to India.

Another thing; Shri Vajpayee referred, and others have referred, to what the Defence Minister[359] is reported to have said, namely, that a great part of Ladakh was unoccupied. Now, I really am surprised that they do not understand what the simple phrase means. He was asked what part of Ladakh was occupied by the Chinese forces. And the answer was that a great part of Ladakh was unoccupied, that is, even where the Chinese are, they have got only military posts here and there. And you may draw an imaginary line and say that all the land behind them is occupied or not. It may be, to some extent, under their control, but it is not correct to say that they occupied all the land. In fact, since then, part of the area which we thought was under their control, has come under our control. Out of 12,000 or so, about 2,500 square miles have, in a sense, in that vague sense, come under our control because of our posts. So he said "unoccupied", not meaning uninhabited. Their posts are there—there of course it is uninhabited but not actually occupied by the Chinese, which is perfectly a correct statement.

A.B. Vajpayee: May I know then why no contradiction was issued? The Prime Minister is giving quite a different version.

Jawaharlal Nehru: What?

358. The Foreign Minister of China.
359. V.K. Krishna Menon.

A.B. Vajpayee: The way in which the Defence Minister's statement was reported, it created an impression that he was referring to our own territory as being unoccupied. We should have issued a contradiction immediately.

Jawaharlal Nehru: Contradiction of what? I do not understand.

A.B. Vajpayee: That the Defence Minister made the statement in reply to a question whether the whole of Ladakh was occupied by the Chinese or not.

Jawaharlal Nehru: I confess I do not know. Perhaps, he is completely right. We should not use the English language—as I understand English, there is only one meaning and no other meaning—if people should pretend not to understand a simple phrase. The question and answer were given in the papers. It never struck me as anything else. But the fact of the matter is, as some hon. Members said today, some people have got an allergy for the Defence Minister, and they try to exploit every little phrase, every word that he says, in an attempt to show off their allergy. As a matter of fact, the growth of modern arms and production in the defence industries, the scientific progress in defence, is almost entirely due to our present Defence Minister who has taken great interest in it. Naturally, it is due to the fact that we have good men, good engineers and others who can do it, otherwise it is all his work.

I would like to say a few words about the background of this frontier trouble. As everyone knows, Ladakh is a part of Kashmir and Kashmir was a State under a Maharaja and the defence of Kashmir lay with the Maharaja except when necessity arose—in British times—the Government of India might be called upon to help. There was no fear in those days of any attack from the Tibet side or from any side in fact on Kashmir. The only fear in the olden days was—the fear of the Britishers, that is, what the British felt was—that possibly Russia might come down through Kashmir to India or through Afghanistan to India. That was the fear in the old tsarist days. I am not talking so much of the later developments in Russia. Right through the nineteenth century, there was this fear of Russia in the British mind. Anyhow, that has nothing to do with what I am saying. I say that the eastern borders of Kashmir and Ladakh with Tibet were never considered by the Maharaja's Government at all necessary to be protected from Tibet. There was some slight argument about one or two parts. In fact there were three or four villages in the heart of Tibet, far from the Ladakh border, which were the zamindari of Kashmir and every second or third year the Kashmir Government sent a little mission to get some revenue. It was not very much. I think it was Rs 100 or Rs 200. Just to assert its zamindari right it sent them to the two or three villages and the thing was peaceful. No question arose of having any protective apparatus in that border in the Maharaja's time. Of course, as everyone knows, the border itself and all the territory was a very difficult terrain and hardly inhabited.

Then came independence and together with independence, almost a month or two later, came the trouble with Pakistan over Kashmir—the invasion of Kashmir by the tribals and later by the Pakistani troops. During the whole fighting in 1948, part of Ladakh was occupied by the Pakistani troops. In fact they cut off the main access to Ladakh which is the main road from Srinagar to Leh, passing the big pass Zoji La and we were compelled to use another route, a very difficult route from Manali in the Kulu valley over very high mountains in a round-about way, to reach Leh. We did reach Leh but it was impossible to do much if the main route was occupied by the Pakistanis. It was a remarkable effort of our army to drive the Pakistanis from the Zoji La Pass. In fact, they built the road. Some hon. Members may have seen it. It is a sudden rise of about 3,000 feet, 2,500 to 3,000 feet, and you have to go in a winding way up the mountain, and if you reach the top of the mountain, you see on the one side the wooded valley of Kashmir and on the other bare rocks, treeless rocks of the uplands of Central Asia, the little Tibet as Ladakh is called, and it goes on to Tibet. So they built a road there and took the tanks there and thus drove out the Pakistani troops and gradually assured the protection of Leh and east Ladakh. Even then, a part of Western Ladakh was in the possession of the Pakistani troops and even now the area occupied by Pakistan in Kashmir is a bit of Ladakh also and when I say the northern part, I mean the border part about which they want to talk to China.

So, this is the background. There was no kind of defence or anything in the Maharaja's[360] time and after that, for a year or two, we were busy fighting the Pakistanis there and we drove them out. Just about this time, the Chinese came to Tibet and without suspecting them of any evil intentions, we saw that the situation had changed. A great power was next to us. It is not a weak Tibet and this would have serious consequences in the future. Our judgment of the situation was that the danger lay from the NEFA part and therefore, from then on, we tried to protect the NEFA border. Gradually we have built up outposts, and much more than that, administration has gradually spread in NEFA. It was an unadministered territory. We also, even at the same time, thought of Ladakh too, not that we realised that they were going to come in such large numbers, but still we thought that this has to be protected, but it was a very difficult task to reach the place where now our posts are. It takes about three

360. Hari Singh.

weeks or a month's journey by road. We sent some small teams to survey and they did go several times, backwards and forwards from the actual frontier, crossed Ladakh and that is the evidence we have that no Chinese were there at that time. These repeated teams had crossed Ladakh and we established an airfield there,[361] not against the Chinese there but because we wanted to cover Ladakh and not leave it unprotected and I remember—I forget the year—about six years ago or seven years ago, I went to that airfield and flew there simply through curiosity because our Air Force were very pleased to have made an airfield. This they called the highest in the world. It is about 14,000 feet. You must remember that in the whole of Ladakh, practically speaking, there are no trees because trees do not normally grow above 11,000 feet. You can grow them. In Leh there are some trees and we have a farm in Leh too but that is by very special efforts. Normally no trees grow. It is a bare rock or some very small shrubs and sometimes even flowers but no trees. So I went there and it was interesting and I told Mr Chou En-lai: "Yes, I can speak from my own evidence, apart from others." I went to our airfield then, you were not there anywhere near that and I went another time and I saw your people, not at the airfield but at the hill-top nearby. So you have come since." To that he had no particular answer. That is the position. The main thing is, quite apart from any claims based on history, they were not there and they are there. It was a peaceful frontier, it is not now a peaceful frontier, not because we have done something but because they have come here. These are the arguments which we placed before them but I was pointing out how difficult it was for us to organise any defence system in Ladakh. We were doing it and we have gradually done it but you cannot simply put forward a defence post unconnected with the rest. It has to be in tiers, connected especially hundreds of miles from any base. The very first thing necessary was to build the road to Leh. There was not even a road to Leh. That was built and a good road exists now. Other roads have been built. Even now it is far. Roads are being built, but mostly our communications are by air and our Air Force have done a very fine piece of work in supplying these posts by air. And of course, the actual military that are there at the posts, they are a fine lot of men and I should like to express our high appreciation of them.

This background may lead the House to understand that just before the Chinese came to Tibet, we could not hold them, I mean to say, we could not hold them at the frontier. There was nobody at the frontier who could help us to hold them. We are proceeding gradually. The one place which we adequately protected, more or less adequately, was the NEFA border. There we succeeded. I am quite sure if we had not held them there, they would have walked in. They

---

361. In Chusul.

did walk in, more or less, on the Ladakh border. First of all they built that road in the Aksai Chin area, in the northern area of Aksai Chin. That was an old caravan route which probably had been used previously too. They made it a road and they used it for communication between Tibet and Sinkiang. That was in 1957, or may be, a little earlier. But the main advance came in 1959 which coincided with the Tibetan revolution, when large forces of Chinese came over to Tibet. So, to say that we did not protect Ladakh is rather to ignore the circumstances that existed in those times, in the Kashmir Maharaja's time and subsequently.

One thing which has been mentioned—a thoroughly opportunist adventure—is Pakistan and China trying to collaborate together in this matter. It is very surprising that Pakistan which is the champion standard-bearer against communism, and a member of CENTO, SEATO and all that, should now try to club up with China, and that China should, to some extent, appreciate this and meet it, in spite of their utterly different policies. Apparently, the only policy in common between them is a certain dislike of India. There is nothing else in common.

So we have to face this situation, and in facing it remember that it is not merely a frontier incursion or aggression. That is bad enough. But it is something much deeper that we have to face. It is the future relationship of two of the biggest countries of Asia, namely, India and China. It means a great deal, what that relationship is going to be. An hon. Member said that some Chinese gentlemen had told him that they would wait for centuries for a solution of this problem. Well, the world moves much faster now. Still it may be a long time and it may involve some years before we can solve this. But in this changing world frontiers may cease to have significance. Of course, we see these cosmonauts and others flying all round the world and no frontiers count. The world is changing very rapidly. But apart from this, it is an important matter for us to consider, the future between our two countries, because continuing hostility for generations will affect us, affect China and affect Asia and have other far-reaching effects. It will be a tremendous burden for all countries concerned. When this world is changing very fast to something different—I hope something better—for us to be tied up with these continuing wars, would be unfortunate. At the same time, it is obvious that no country worth its strain, and certainly not India, can submit to bullying tactics, can submit to force being used to take away its territory and otherwise to show that it can be treated casually, by any other country. It is impossible, whatever the consequence might be. So we have to face this difficult situation with our courage and strength. And may I say, strength, of course, depends on what we do on the frontier, but strength ultimately depends upon our unity of effort in the country, and everything that comes in the way of that unity of effort is really weakening the country and our campaign or the efforts that we make on the frontier. I would particularly like to say this, because some people live in compartments. They talk about our unity in connection with the frontier and yet, in our work for economic growth and so on, they come in the way all the time—work for industrial growth, economic growth and all that. The two do not fit in. I do not mean to say that everyone should agree with the Government's policy. But there are certain broad features of it which we must keep in mind, features which go towards the unity of the country and the growth of our economy and industrial progress.

I am grateful, Madam, for the general support that hon. Members have given me. I regret I am wholly unable to accept Mr Vajpayee's amendment which is a negation of all that we have done. As for Mr Mani's amendment, part of it is unexceptionable, but part of it does not appear to me to be right.[362] I shall accept Mr Satyacharan's amendment.[363]

> A.D. Mani: On a point of information, Madam. May I ask the Prime Minister whether the latest claim has been staked by the Chinese for 3,700 square miles in the Pakistan-held part of Kashmir? I understand that they have now staked a claim for 3,700 square miles which is an area now occupied by Pakistan in Kashmir territory. I would also like to ask him whether this area has been shown in the 1960 map which the Chinese have prepared, or whether it is outside the 1960 map.

Jawaharlal Nehru: I don't know exactly where their map line goes, but they have claimed part of this territory, I don't know how much. In fact, it may interest the House to know that when I went to Pakistan two years ago, or may be two and a half years back,[364] I tried to profit by that occasion and I discussed China and the frontier issue with President Ayub Khan, because whatever our differences were on Kashmir or elsewhere, I thought it would be advantageous to have a uniform policy with regard to the Chinese aggression. And we showed them various maps and other things, even in regard to the territory occupied by

362. Probably the part of A.D. Mani's amendment unacceptable to Nehru was a clause that he wanted to be added to the Motion:
> "(ii) that no useful purpose would be served in Government offering to negotiate the border dispute with the Government of China unless the Government of China give clear and unambiguous indications that they are as anxious as the Government of India for a settlement of the border dispute on the basis of the traditional boundaries as indicated in the Government of India maps, and further the Government of China are prepared to vacate aggression on Indian territory;"

363. The amendment by Satyacharan, Congress, approving of the Government's policy.
364. Nehru visited Karachi in September 1960 to sign the Indus Water Treaty, 1960.

Pakistan, the Kashmir territory, and they told us what their line according to them was. There was some slight difference between them and us. There was another question which related to the area which belongs to the Mir of Hunza. We discussed that too. But I am sure that the Chinese map claims some area which according to us, even in the Pakistani-occupied territory, should be on this side.[365]

412. In the Rajya Sabha: Defence Minister Meets Foreign Minister of China[366]

Will the Prime Minister be pleased to state whether any reference was made to the aggression committed by China during the talks recently held between the Minister of Defence and the Foreign Minister of China in Geneva; and if so, what has been the outcome?[367]

The Deputy Minister in the Ministry of External Affairs (Dinesh Singh): During his talks with the Chinese Foreign Minister, Marshal Chen Yi, the Indian Defence Minister[368] had expressly referred to the serious situation created in Ladakh by the unlawful intrusion of Chinese forces. The Chinese Foreign Minister had, however, refused to accept this and tried to place the onus on India. There was no specific outcome to these discussions.

राम सहायः क्या मैं यह जान सकूंगा कि समय समय पर इस प्रकार की जब वार्ताओं का अवसर प्राप्त होता है तो अपनी बात को प्रेस किया जा सके, इस सम्बन्ध में कोई आपका विचार है?

जवाहरलाल नेहरूः जब समय अनुकूल होता है तो किया ही जाता है। खास उसकी जरूरत तो नहीं है।

---

365. At the end of Nehru's reply to the debate, Bhupesh Gupta, CPI, requested A.D. Mani and A.B. Vajpayee to withdraw their amendments "as a good gesture and indicate to the world that we have a broad agreement here." To this Vajpayee quipped, "Provided my friend is prepared to call China the aggressor." The original Motion was eventually adopted after A.D. Mani withdrew his amendment and Vajpayee's amendment, put to the vote, was negatived.
366. Oral answers, 24 August 1962. *Rajya Sabha Debates*, Vol. 40, Nos. 9-16, 17 to 29 August 1962, cols 3032-3034.
367. Question by Ram Sahay, Congress.
368. V.K. Krishna Menon.

[Translation begins

Ram Sahay: May I know your views on the possibility of emphasizing our stand during this type of talks which may be held from time to time?

Jawaharlal Nehru: This is done when the occasion is appropriate. But this is not specially required.

Translation ends]

A.B. Vajpayee:[369] According to a Bombay weekly the initiative for this particular meeting came from the Chinese Foreign Minister. May I know if it is a fact?

Jawaharlal Nehru: I do not know what the hon. Member means. The initiative in a sense came from me. That is, the Defence Minister, and I naturally spoke to him. He will see many people there and the Chinese Foreign Minister would be there and it is desirable for him if he has an opportunity to discuss the critical situation that had arisen at that time from the firing that had taken place in the Ladakh area. He went there and talked, I believe, in the lobby of the Conference room. The Chinese Foreign Minister asked him to come to his house and discuss the matter. So in a sense the invitation came from the Chinese Foreign Minister.

Bhupesh Gupta:[370] Is the Prime Minister aware that this initiative taken by him and the talks that took place in Geneva have been welcome in many countries by progressive sections and favourable reports appeared in the newspapers?

A.B. Vajpayee: Which countries is he referring to?

Bhupesh Gupta: Because such steps enhance our prestige. I saw it in the newspapers; I was abroad then. Outside the country many newspapers have published favourable reports and have welcome this. It is not a fact?

Jawaharlal Nehru: Generally that has been so.

369. Jan Sangh.
370. CPI.

Bhupesh Gupta: May I know why the Ministry of External Affairs is not taking steps to make some of these comments available to some Opposition Members in order to relieve them of the burden of putting such questions and supplementaries?

(No reply.)

A.D. Mani:[371] At the same time—there was a Chargé d'affaires[372] in Peking—did he make any representation to the Chinese Government because the proper place for making such a representation was Peking and not Geneva?

Jawaharlal Nehru: The proper place is every place where an occasion arises.

413. For the Lok Sabha: Confederation of Himalayan States[373]

Short Notice Question Dy. No. 162

The following may be sent to the Lok Sabha Secretariat:

"I regret I cannot accept this Short Notice Question, It relates to an independent country with Treaty, rights with India and our discussing this in the Lok Sabha will be embarrassing both to us and to the Bhutan Government.

2. The Prime Minister of Bhutan[374] has been visiting Switzerland, Sweden and London. The object, as far as we know, was to seek some technical and other aid from friendly countries for development projects in Bhutan.

3. So far as we know, China has not made any proposal for a Confederation of Himalayan States.

4. According to our information, Chinese troops on the other side of the China-Bhutan border are relatively small in numbers."

371. Independent.
372. P.K. Banerjee.
373. Note, 29 August 1962.
374. Jigme Dorji.

414. From Government of China: Indian Provocation[375]

Of late Indian troops which have intruded into Chinese territory in Western Sector of Sino-Indian boundary, have repeatedly fired provocatively at Chinese Frontier Guards against which Chinese Government has lodged a number of protests. In its notes of 3rd and 5th August, 1962,[376] Indian Government resorted to its usual practice of denying the indisputable facts cited by Chinese Government, but this is entirely futile. Indian Government even doubted the truth of the two incidents of firing by Indian troops of 16th and 19th July, 1962, to which Chinese side referred on ground that it was not until 23rd July, that Chinese side lodged the protest. This is even less worthy of refutation. It is commonsense whether a protest is lodged a few days earlier or later does not at all affect the truth of matters concerned in protest. In advancing a sophisticated argument on that ground Indian side is in no way taking an attitude of dealing with things earnestly and seriously.

It is particularly regrettable that Indian Government in its notes further falsely counter-charged Chinese side. Now Chinese Government will confine itself to refuting the three specific charges made by Indian side.

1. In its note, 28th July, 1962,[377] Indian Government charged that on 27th July, a Chinese patrol opened fire at an Indian patrol at approximately 33° 57' N, 78° 46.5' E. This place mentioned by Indian side is in Nyagzu area in Tibetan China. Strange, however, that eight days later in another note, dated 5th August, 1962, Indian Government stated that "no Indian party was in that area (Nyagzu)" on 27th July. This inconsistency clearly shows that the charge Indian side made in its former note is not in conformity with the facts. The fact is that on 27th July, an intruding Indian force fired sixteen shots in the Nyagzu area at a Chinese post there. It seems that after failing to abuse Chinese side, Indian side tried to resort to quibbling, but in so doing unwittingly disapproved its former charge. As paper cannot wrap up fire, a lie is bound to show up.

---

375. Note, 29 August 1962, from the Ministry of Foreign Affairs, Government of China, to the Embassy of India in China. Government of India, MEA, Historical Division, *Sino-Indian Border Dispute*, Volume VI-Part III, (Chinese Incursions into Indian Territory), (April 1962-October 1962), Correspondence, p. 7.

376. *Notes, Memoranda and Letters exchanged between the Governments of India and China, July-October 1962. White Paper No. VII* (Government of India, Ministry of External Affairs), pp. 12 and 19 respectively.

377. *White Paper No. VII*, ibid., p.7.

2. In its note of 30th July, 1962,[378] Indian side charged that on 29th July, Chinese troops opened fire at Indian troops in the vicinity of Yula in the Pangong Lake area. Chinese Government has satisfied itself by careful checking that the Indian charge is a downright fabrication. It can be mentioned here that the Indian Government further trumped up the story of a clash at Yula between Chinese and Indian sides in its note of 15th August, 1962, which Chinese Government basing itself on the facts, has already refuted by its note of 18th August, 1962. The purpose of Indian side in repeatedly preferring such framed up charges is clearly to cover up its activities of unlawfully setting up a strong post and expanding its military intrusions in Yula Tibet and to further aggravate deliberately the tension in that area.

3. In its note of 5th August, 1962, Indian Government not only tried hard to deny the fact that Indian troops which had intruded into Chip Chap River Valley in Sinkiang, China, fired on a Chinese post there on 27th July, but falsely counter-charged the Chinese side with firing at Indian troops on the same day and asserted that India had already made this charge in its note of 28th July 1962. But in fact Indian note of 28th July, does not touch on the Chip Chap Valley area at all. It seems that the Indian side has landed itself in a jumble in cooking up charge.

It can be seen from the above that it is not we, but India itself which has distorted the facts and reversed the right and wrong. As for the Indian side's usual practice of describing Chinese territory as Indian territory in an attempt to explain away Indian troops intrusions and provocations and of even false counter-charging China with aggravating the border tension, the Chinese Government has refuted all these absurdities again and again and do not intend to repeat it here. To ensure tranquility along the border and ease the tension, Chinese Government urge Indian Government to desist from making statements which reverse right and wrong, strictly restrain the Indian troops so that they stop all provocations against the Chinese side and order them to withdraw immediately from Chinese territory.[379]

378. *White Paper No. VII*, ibid., p. 8.
379. See also item 416.

415. For the Lok Sabha: Chinese in Ladakh[380]

Short Notice Question Dy. No. 160.

Please inform the Lok Sabha Secretariat that I regret I cannot accept this Short Notice Question.

2. It is not quite correct to say that the Chinese occupy a certain area in Ladakh or that we have recovered any part of this area. The actual occupation of any party is of the military post. Roundabout that military post, there is an area of control exercised by that post. To some extent, it may be said that the area behind the Chinese military posts is under their control, although not occupied. In the same way, because we have put up military posts, some area has come within our control.

3. No change has happened in these areas since the matter was last discussed in the Lok Sabha.

416. Abusive Chinese Communications[381]

I enclose the latest Chinese note.[382] These notes are becoming progressively more and more abusive. In your reply, I think, you might point out this fact.

I do not quite understand how they can make so many specific charges about our troops firing on them without our men having done so.

We might mention these notes at the Foreign Affairs Committee meeting tomorrow afternoon.

417. In the Lok Sabha: Chinese Military Posts in Ladakh[383]

Speaker:[384] About the subject regarding the establishment of 30 new posts in Ladakh, I made enquiries, and I learnt that the Prime Minister was going to make a statement, I will allow Shri Hem Barua[385] question.

---

380. Note, 29 August 1962.
381. Note, 30 August 1962. Government of India, MEA, Historical Division, *Sino-Indian Border Dispute*, Volume VI, Part III (Chinese Incursions into Indian Territory), (April 1962-October 1962), Notes, p. 35.
382. See item 414.
383. Statement, 3 September 1962. *Lok Sabha Debates*, Vol. 8, Third Series, cols 5530-5537.
384. Hukam Singh.
385. PSP.

Hem Barua (Gauhati): When is the Prime Minister making the statement?

The Minister of State in the Ministry of External Affairs (Lakshmi Menon): Unfortunately, the Prime Minister is not here now. I would make a statement.

Speaker: Does she want to make the statement now?

Lakshmi Menon: I want to make the statement.

Hari Vishnu Kamath (Hoshangabad):[386] Is it in answer to a Short Notice Question or a Calling Attention Notice?

Speaker: A Calling Attention Notice was received. But before that could be ascertained, the hon. Prime Minister has sent me an intimation that he was going to make a statement voluntarily. I have allowed that. But because I had also received a Calling Attention Notice I will allow Shri Barua to put a question.

Lakshmi Menon: *White Paper No. VI* published by Government gave some details of Chinese military posts established upto 26th July against which we had lodged protests.

Since the publication of *White Paper No. VI*, we protested on 22nd and 24th August against the establishment of some more posts.[387] The total number of these posts established by the Chinese since May 1962 comes to 30.

On 28th August, we protested against the establishment of four more posts.[388] Our information is that one of these Chinese posts has since been withdrawn. But there is some evidence of the establishment of two more such posts in the neighbourhood.

I have had occasion to mention earlier in the House that a large number of these posts, particularly those established in recent months, are extensions of old posts a few miles further and generally within the defensive perimeter of the earlier posts. This is the case particularly in

386. PSP.
387. For the Indian notes of 22 and 24 August 1962, see *White Paper No. VII*, pp. 32-33 and p. 40 respectively.
388. See *White Paper No. VII*, p. 47.

the region of Daulat Beg Oldi and the Chip Chap river valley where the Chinese posts are separated only by a short distance from each other.

In the Galwan river valley there are a number of Chinese posts that are close together and are interconnected. These, as I have said before, hamper our line of supply to our post by the land route. Another attempt to interfere with our supply line was made by the Chinese by the establishment of a Chinese post on the 23rd August in the Pangong lake area. We have protested against this and taken necessary measure to prevent interference with our line of supply in the Pangong lake area.

In regard to the incident on August 14th, the factual position is that there was an exchange of fire between our post in the Pangong lake region and the Chinese detachment. No casualty was suffered by our post. We protested to the Chinese against this incident on the 15th August.[389]

Hem Barua: The Chinese have by now established 30 new posts and the *White Paper No. VI* only mentions details of 20 posts. That means that they have built at least 10 more posts. On the other hand, because of the posts that we have established, the Prime Minister was pleased to say that we have recovered about 2,000 square miles from the Chinese. The Chinese advance is most patent by the establishment of these new posts. May I know whether the establishment of these new posts demonstrates any further advance into our territory by the Chinese?

The Minister of Defence (V.K. Krishna Menon): The number of these posts is not synonymous with the territorial advance. It is a matter of tactical disposition, whether our Commanders think that it is better to split up one post into two or the Chinese Commanders do the same. The answer to the question is, the establishment of these posts by itself does not mean advance into our territory.

Hem Barua: My question has not been replied to. Our argument is that because we have been able to establish a few more posts, we have reoccupied certain territory.

Speaker: Why should he place so much emphasis on that part?

Hem Barua: My point is, the establishment of new posts to the extent of 30 means that the Chinese have advanced into our territory. It may be a tactical move.

389. *White Paper No. VII*, p. 24.

[STATISTICS DON'T LIE]

You Said It

By LAXMAN

**There's absolutely no basis for the
alarming news appearing in the papers
that 2,000 Chinese are concentrated in
this sector—actually there are
only 1,877 Chinese—!**

(From *The Times of India*, 21 September 1962, p. 1)

Speaker: What I understood was, the Defence Minister has said that there
has not been any further advance by the Chinese in that area. It is for the
Commanders to see whether it is expedient to split up one post further into
two or three posts.

Hem Barua: That is not clear.

Speaker: Then I might not have understood him all right. Let me ask.

V.K. Krishna Menon: What I said was, the increase in the number of posts by the Chinese, as mentioned by our Prime Minister, taking into account the difference in the dates of the two announcements, does not by itself mean any further advance into our territory. The increase in the number of posts is the distribution of personnel into one, two, three or four posts, according as the Command desires. We may not consider it necessary or possible, whatever may be the reason, to increase the number of posts, when one post would do the job. That is a tactical decision.

Speaker: The increase in the number of posts might not by itself mean further advance by the Chinese. But the question that the hon. Member insists on is whether in fact there has been further advance according to the information available with the Government.

Lakshmi Menon: It is already stated in the statement. I have said there:

"I have had occasion to mention earlier in the House that a large number of these posts, particularly those established in recent months are extensions of old posts a few miles further and generally within the defensive perimeter of the earlier posts".

This has already been stated. (Interruption).

An Hon. Member: Have they made any advance?

Speaker: Order, order. We are trying to understand each other. Hon. Members should not be impatient.

Ram Chandra Bade (Khargone):[390] How many miles further have they advanced?

Speaker: Should all of them stand up simultaneously? Let them put their questions one by one.

---

390. Jan Sangh.

Ram Chandra Bade: It is a serious question.

Speaker: Order, order. I should not be forced to have a departure here, though the subject is very important. Hon. Members can seek a further discussion by another method. But I am trying to make it clear so that the anxiety of the hon. Members might be removed. They should allow me to have that cleared rather than force me to allow a further discussion by allowing other hon. Members to put questions. I am not allowing any question to be put by other hon. Members whose names do not appear on the Calling Attention Notice.

Hari Vishnu Kamath: I am not putting another question. May I request you to clarify another aspect of the matter closely connected with this one? In disallowing a similar question by me, Sir, you were pleased to state that the Prime Minister would make a statement regarding the correspondence between the Government of India and the Government of China recently. Is that statement coming before the end of this Session to bring the battle of notes up to date?

Speaker: I cannot say that. If he tells me what that promise I made is, certainly I will get it checked up.

Now, coming to the other matter, again and again the same question is being put, whether the Government can give any further information on this fact as to whether the Chinese have made any further advance into our territory and, if so, by how many miles.

V.K. Krishna Menon: I said, Sir, that increase in the number of these posts does not mean any advance. (Interruption).

Surendranath Dwivedy (Kendrapara):[391] That means there has been advance; it is clear.

Hem Barua: May I ask, Sir.

Speaker: Order, order. Would the hon. Members kindly resume their seats? The difficulty with the hon. Members is that they are feeling perturbed. They have these apprehensions that probably there have been some further advances in our territory by the Chinese. The question, though it

391. PSP.

was confined to the posts, is whether there has been any further advance. The hon. Defence Minister has said two or three times—probably I have not been able to make myself clear and, therefore, that ambiguity still exists—that the setting up or the increase in the number of these posts by themselves does not give any indications whether there has been any further advance or not. This is admitted, and everybody is satisfied so far as the increase in the number is concerned. Independently of that, the question is,—whether there has been an increase or not—whether the Chinese have advanced further into our territory. This is what the hon. Members want to know. If the Government has got that information that might be given.

V.K. Krishna Menon: If you will permit me to say so, Sir, it is not possible to hold territories without posts. If they will advance they will put up posts. That is why I said that these posts do not represent advances. There are no posts put up by the Chinese which represent advances into our territory.

Hari Vishnu Kamath: Why is the Minister shilly-shallying and beating about the bush? Why can't he say "yes" or "no"?

Mahavir Tyagi (Dehra Dun):[392] Let us say: "No advance".

Hem Barua: Sir, I rise to a point of order. I have been listening to the two statements by the two different Ministers. Shrimati Lakshmi Menon has admitted that there has been an extension of posts a few miles further. The Defence Minister has also said that there has been a splitting up of posts. Supposing I split your chair, Sir …

Hari Vishnu Kamath: God forbid.

Speaker: Order, order. There ought not to be any surprise if the chair is split on account of what has been happening.

Hem Barua: Suppose, Sir, your chair is split into two parts and one part remains here; the other part either goes to the front or goes back.

Speaker: They can remain parallel also and I might fall down! (Interruption). The two portions may be behind each other.

---

392. Congress.

V.K. Krishna Menon: You cannot hold a territory without army or posts. The question is directly in relation to the 30 posts, about the discrepancy between the statement made by the External Affairs Minister. That, I understand is the purpose of this question. Therefore, naturally, when she speaks about the increase of posts, a doubt arises whether they advanced. I said there was no advance.

418. Supply on NEFA Border[393]

[Note, 4 September 1962, by M.J. Desai, the Foreign Secretary, begins]

Shri M.G. Kaul's[394] note of 11th August, 1962, gives the full background of the current supply arrangements to our border posts on the NEFA-Tibet border and to various administrative centres in the interior of the NEFA. The Indian Airlines Corporation and the Indian Air Force have not been participating in these supply operations for sometime because of their other preoccupations and the air drops of these supplies have been arranged under contractual arrangements with the Kalinga Airlines.

2. The Kalinga Airlines have been air dropping these supplies with their fleet of Dakotas. The opening, however, of the 26 new check posts at high altitudes ranging from 12,000 to 17,000 feet on the NEFA-Tibet border this year and the opening of new administrative centres nearer the border by the NEFA administration has posed a new problem so far as the supply drops are concerned. The Dakotas cannot operate at these high altitudes, particularly during the winter months, and if no special arrangements are made to get aircraft like the Caribou, all these new check posts and the new administrative centres opened nearer the border will have to be withdrawn. Any withdrawal of this sort would immediately expose these areas to Chinese penetration and this is a risk which cannot be taken with our experience in Ladakh. The Chinese are as a matter of fact in close proximity of the border in some strength all along the NEFA-Tibet border.

3. The question whether foreign exchange facilities for the purchase of a Caribou aircraft should be given to the Kalinga Airlines to meet this special need or the responsibility for supplies to all these check posts on the NEFA-Tibet border and the new administrative centres in NEFA nearer the border should be

393. Noting, 4 September 1962. MHA, (MEA, File No. 14(6)-Nefa/61, pp. 71-72).
394. Joint Secretary, Ministry of Defence.

placed on the Indian Air Force was discussed on 1st September. The minutes of this meeting at slip "Y" give the recommendations of the Secretaries.

4.   The Defence Ministry have as agreed at this meeting—"A" of para of the minutes—examined their foreign exchange position. The result of this examination is given in minute 10 dated 4th September 1962, in the Defence Ministry's file placed below. In brief the Defence Ministry will require additional allotment of foreign exchange.

5.   As the check posts on the NEFA-Tibet border as well as the NEFA administrative centres nearer the border must be maintained to prevent any Chinese penetration in this area, I seek PM's approval to the recommendation made by the Secretaries in the meeting on 1st September, that the Indian Air Force should be made responsible to supply the check posts on the NEFA-Tibet border and the NEFA administrative centres in the interior. The Defence Ministry are prepared to accept this responsibility.

6.   So far as the question of requirement of additional aircraft of special type, Caribou or any other, of the Indian Air Force to meet this extra commitment, is concerned, that is a matter which the Indian Air Force technicians must decide; also the question of additional foreign exchange requirements for these aircraft is a matter to be settled between the Ministries of Defence and Finance. After PM has seen, I will mark the papers to Defence Secretary and Secretary, Finance (Economic Affairs) for the information of Ministers of Defence and Finance.

M.J. Desai
4.9.1962

PM

[Note, 4 September 1962, by M.J. Desai, the Foreign Secretary, ends]

[Note, 4 September 1962, by Nehru, begins]

Our holding on to our frontier posts both in Ladakh and in NEFA is an absolute necessity. We cannot leave those posts, whatever pressure on them may be from the Chinese side. Thus, we have to maintain them and give them the necessary supplies. Apparently, this can only be done by air.

2.   I do not fancy the idea that a private airline should take our supplies to our frontier posts, unless there is no help for it. I have no complaint against the Kalinga Airlines as such, and perhaps they have done their work satisfactorily. But it does not seem proper to me that the new and higher check posts should also be put in their charge so far as supplies are concerned.

3.   It should, therefore, be the duty of either the IAF or the IAC to carry out these supply operations, preferably the IAF. With the new transport aircraft

that the IAF is getting, I should have thought it possible for them to carry these supplies. But I am no judge of this. Apparently, by a process of elimination, we arrive at the Caribou aircraft. As far as I can gather, it is suggested that only one Caribou aircraft should be purchased for this purpose.

4. I realise the great difficulty of the Finance Ministry in regard to foreign exchange and I would not like to add to it. And yet there seems no other way out. FS will, therefore, please refer this matter to the Defence Ministry and the Ministry of Finance (Economic Affairs) so that the Ministers might consider this matter.

J. Nehru
4-9-1962

FS

[Note, 4 September 1962, by Nehru, ends]

419. To H.J. Bhabha: China as Member of the UN[395]

September 6, 1962

My dear Homi,
Your letter of September 5th.[396]

We are still of opinion that the People's Government of China should be accepted as a member of the United Nations. But we do not want to propose this ourselves for obvious reasons. We shall, however, support any proposal to this effect that is made by any other country.

Yours sincerely,
[Jawaharlal Nehru]

395. Letter to the Secretary, Department of Atomic Energy, and Chairman, Atomic Energy Commission of India.
396. Appendix 60.

420. To H.V. Kamath: China Border Situation[397]

September 28, 1962

Dear Kamath,

I have received the letter of September 24 jointly signed by you, Farid Ansari[398] and Chandrasekhar,[399] in Rome today.[400]

The situation in our frontier both in Ladakh and the North East is undoubtedly serious. We are trying to meet it to the best of our ability and will continue to do so. I do not understand what you mean by "India's unilateral Panch Sheel towards China". Panch Sheel is a bilateral policy and cannot be exercised unilaterally. There is no Panch Sheel between India and China now because of China's aggression and numerous petty conflicts that have taken place.

As for making adequate arrangements for the supply of information, I do not quite understand what kind of information is desired. The type of developments that have taken place recently are petty incidents chiefly on the NEFA border and on our part strengthening our defences there. We cannot obviously give publicity to what we do in regard to strengthening our defences. It would be wrong from our Army's point of view.

You are right in saying that we should avoid anything which may lead to fear and panic. That is the policy we have been pursuing. I would suggest that others also should keep this in mind. I shall be returning to Delhi in a few days. Although I have been kept fully informed of developments during my tour, I shall naturally discuss them fully on my return.

I do not think it is necessary at this stage to convene a special session of Parliament. That in itself will create the fear and panic which you deplore. If, however, necessity arises, we shall certainly recommend a special session later.

I shall be glad to meet leaders of political parties some time after my return.

Yours sincerely,
[Jawaharlal Nehru]

---

397. Letter to the deputy leader of the PSP group in the Lok Sabha; address: 18 Windsor Place, New Delhi. Sent from Rome.
398. Faridul Haq Ansari, PSP, Rajya Sabha MP.
399. Chandra Sekhar, Rajya Sabha MP.
400. The joint letter has not been traced. According to a PTI report in the *National Herald* of 8 October 1962, "the three PSP MPs had expressed concern over the Sino-Indian border situation. They had suggested the summoning of a special session of Parliament to consider it and had also sought information on developments on India's border with China."

(l) Pakistan

421. To M.C. Chagla: Status Quo in Kashmir[401]

August 2, 1962

My dear Chagla,

Your letter of July 27th. I entirely agree with you that we cannot possibly subscribe to the Two-Nation theory or to anything which upsets our secularism.

I said some time ago that my offer to Pakistan for the acceptance of the status quo in Kashmir had lapsed. I said so because it seemed to me to be a little absurd to go on repeating this in the face of Pakistan's curt refusal of it. But, as a matter of fact, I do not think there can be any other final solution of the Kashmir problem except that of the status quo with possibly minor adjustments. That continues to be our policy although I shall not go on repeating it.

As a matter of fact, Galbraith, US Ambassador, told me some time before the Security Council meeting that we must proceed on that basis and try to explore some other avenues also, such as, economic, etc. You can therefore certainly proceed on the line of the status quo with the UK Government. Tell them that we have more than once made that offer without any result and we do not wish to go on publicly repeating it. But that is the only sensible approach.

Pakistan is at present tied up with her own difficulties, especially East Pakistan, but there is always the possibility that because of these very difficulties, she may indulge in an adventure. President Ayub's[402] grand strategy now appears to be to wait for India to get into trouble with China and take advantage of it. Pakistan newspapers continue to talk about war.

It seems to me that most countries do not realise the essence of the Kashmir question in so far as we are concerned. Any acceptance of the Two Nation theory in regard to Kashmir will have the most disastrous consequences in the whole of India. Not only will our secularism end, but India will tend to break up. I have noticed that when this is clearly stated, it produces a marked effect on the hearer.

Yours sincerely,
J. Nehru

401. Letter to the High Commissioner in the UK.
402. Ayub Khan.

422. Vinoba Bhave's Planned Walk through East Pakistan[403]

[Note, 17 August 1962, by Y.D. Gundevia, the Commonwealth Secretary at the MEA, for Nehru, begins]

The Prime Minister may please see the very nasty leading article in the *Dawn* of yesterday's date on Vinobaji's intended walk across East Pakistan.[404]

2. When the Pakistan High Commissioner[405] called on me yesterday (16.8.62), he again brought up this question and said that attacks against the Government in the Pakistan Press had been renewed after the unfortunate Indian newspaper report about Vinobaji's intention to distribute an edited version of the Quran. I told the High Commissioner that I had made enquiries and I have been told by Shri Shriman Narayan[406] that Vinobaji's edited version of the Quran had not yet been printed (nor his translations of the Quran) and, therefore, there was no question of his taking this new version or verses of the Quran with him for distribution. The High Commissioner went on to tell me that, if there was any such intention, it would be a very serious matter and it would be looked upon in Pakistan as a misuse of hospitality and would be treated as an affront by people etc. etc. I asked Mr Hilaly whether he was conveying all this to me officially on behalf of his Government. He said that he had not been asked to communicate anything to me and he was speaking on his own initiative. The High Commissioner went on to suggest that it would be useful if some assurance could be given, to say that Vinobaji had no such intentions or, perhaps, a contradiction should be issued in the Indian newspapers. Again, I asked him whether he was making this request for an assurance officially, and Mr Hilaly said that he was not asking me officially to do this, but he could not help feeling that an assurance or contradiction, if issued, would help the Government of Pakistan very considerably. He drew my attention to the Pakistan

---

403. Noting on Sarvodaya leader's plans. MEA, File No. P. I/122(9)/62, pp. 7-8/notes.
404. Questioning Vinoba Bhave's conduct in planning to bring with him a "mutilated" version of the *Quran* during his forthcoming travel through East Pakistan, the *Dawn* editorial pleaded with the President of Pakistan not to allow him "to set foot on Pakistan's sacred soil." It alleged that Vinoba Bhave had hatched a "sinister plot" by first having secured Pakistan Government's permission for his visit and then having it announced through the Secretary of the All India Shanti Sena Mandal that he would carry with him an "edited and rearranged" version of the *Quran*, called *Essence of Quran*, "from which he has omitted certain sections."
405. Agha Hilaly.
406. Member, Planning Commission, and a Gandhian.

Foreign Minister[407] having said that, despite newspaper criticism, they intended adhering to their earlier decision to allow Vinobaji to walk across East Pakistan.

3.   I have spoken to Shri Shriman Narayan, again, today. Inter alia, I read out to him the objectionable passage in yesterday's *Dawn* and told him, briefly, what the Pakistan High Commissioner had said to me earlier. Shri Shriman Narayan said that he was very disappointed at these developments and all the trouble had arisen because of the over enthusiastic statement issued, some days ago, by one of Vinobaji's friends in Banaras—about the Quran etc. Shri Shriman Narayan seemed rather dejected and he told me that he wanted to talk to the Prime Minister this evening and, perhaps, suggest that Vinobaji might give up the idea of walking across East Pakistan. As the PM is aware, the *Dawn* and other newspapers had started their criticism of the Pakistan Government even before this story about Vinobaji and the Quran came out. The Banaras report, I must say, was most unfortunate. Rather than give the Pakistan Government the excuse that because of all this they are not able to permit Vinobaji to now walk across East Pakistan, it may be a better alternative for Vinobaji himself, perhaps, to say that he does not wish to walk across East Pakistan in view of the misunderstanding, as Shri Shriman Narayan suggests.

4.   In any case, Shri Shriman Narayan hopes to discuss this with the Prime Minister later this evening.

Y.D. Gundevia
17.8.1962

PM

[Note, 17 August 1962, by Y.D. Gundevia, for Nehru, ends]

[Note, 17 August 1962, by Nehru, for Y.D. Gundevia, begins]

I have not been able to see Shri Shriman Narayan today and I doubt if I can see him tomorrow, when I am fully occupied. The day after tomorrow I shall go to Bombay.

2.   Anyhow, all I could advise him was that he should put the position before Vinobaji and leave the decision to him.

3.   I have seen in some newspaper that the selections from the Quran which Vinobaji has made has been printed. I do not know if this [is] true or not. Anyhow, it would be desirable for Vinobaji not to refer to this book or these extracts if he passes through Pakistan.

407. Muhammad Ali.

4.   I think the best course would be to explain the position fully to Vinobaji and let him make his own decision. You might convey this message to Shri Shriman Narayan.[408]

J. Nehru
17.8.62

CS

[Note, 17 August 1962, by Nehru, for Y.D. Gundevia, ends]

423. To P.C. Mahalanobis: No Objection to Pakistan Visit[409]

August 18, 1962

My dear Mahalanobis,

Thank you for your letter of the 16th August which I have read with interest. I do not think there is any objection to your accepting the invitation to go to Pakistan to deliver lectures there or to meet with scientists and planners there.

Yours sincerely,
[Jawaharlal Nehru]

424. In the Rajya Sabha: Disinformation by Radio Pakistan[410]

Will the Prime Minister be pleased to state:[411]

(a) whether Government are aware that false and misleading propaganda is carried on by Radio Pakistan against India; and

(b) if so, what steps Government propose to take to counteract the undesirable effect of the false propaganda on the Indian citizen?

---

408. For earlier correspondence, see SWJN/SS/76/item 468 and SWJN/SS/77/item 48.
409. Letter to Member, Planning Commission, and Statistical Adviser to the Cabinet, GOI; address: 8 King George Avenue, New Delhi-11.
410. Written Answers, 21 August 1962. *Rajya Sabha Debates*, Vol. 40, Nos. 9-16, 17 to 29 August 1962, cols 2552-53.
411. Question by V.M. Chordia, Jan Sangh.

Jawaharlal Nehru:

(a) Yes, Sir.

(b) The Government of India have recently started certain programmes aimed at correcting the misleading propaganda of Radio Pakistan and the Raiders Radio in their broadcasts particularly from Delhi, Jullundur, Calcutta, Jammu and Kashmir stations. These programmes are broadcast in various Indian languages including Urdu, Kashmiri and Bengali languages. Other media of publicity available in India are also used to provide factual information on Indo-Pakistan relations to Indian citizens.

425. To Shriman Narayan: Vinoba Bhave's East Pakistan Tour[412]

August 22, 1962

My dear Shriman,

Your letter of the 22nd August about Vinobaji's tour through East Pakistan.[413] I have passed on this letter to our Foreign Secretary, M.J. Desai. It hardly appears necessary for you to discuss this matter further with me. I suppose you will hear from Vinobaji after he has met the Deputy High Commissioner of Pakistan.

Yours sincerely,
Jawaharlal Nehru

426. In the Rajya Sabha: Pakistan on Vinoba Bhave's Visit to East Pakistan[414]

Will the Prime Minister be pleased to state:[415]

(a) Whether it is a fact that the newspapers in Pakistan have started severe propaganda against Acharya Vinoba Bhave's programme of

---

412. Letter to Member, Planning Commission. Shriman Narayan (ed.), *Letters from Gandhi Nehru Vinoba* (Bombay: Asia Publishing House, 1968), pp. 120-121.

413. Available in Shriman Narayan, ibid, p. 120.

414. Written answers, 5 September 1962, *Rajya Sabha Debates*, Vol. 40, Nos. 17-23, 30 August to 7 September 1962, cols 5141-5143.

415. Question by Nawab Singh Chauhan, Congress.

touring Pakistan and if so, what steps have been taken to counter this propaganda; and

(b) whether any communication has been received from the Government of Pakistan in connection with this tour, and if so, the details thereof?

Jawaharlal Nehru:

(a) Following erroneous Press reports that Acharya Vinoba Bhave would carry an "edited" version of the Holy *Quran* with him on his tour of certain places in East Pakistan, there was some propaganda about him in the Pakistan Press.[416] It was explained on behalf of Acharya Vinoba Bhave that his book, which has yet to be published, was only a collection of verses from the Holy *Quran* and not "edited" version of the Holy Book. A spokesman of the External Affairs Ministry also explained this position to the Press on August 24.[417] The explanation given on behalf of Acharya Vinoba Bhave and the statement of the spokesman of the External Affairs Ministry were published in the Pakistan Press. The External Services of All India Radio also carried the statement of the official spokesman. The propaganda in the Pakistan Press appears to have died down ever since.

(b) Arrangements for the tour were made by personal discussions with Pakistani authorities.

427. Talk with Ayub Khan on East Bengal River Waters[418]

President Ayub Khan spoke to me yesterday as we were coming out of the Marlborough House where the Prime Ministers' Conference was being held. He mentioned the question of coming to an agreement with us about the waters in East Bengal etc. He said that they were anxious to expedite this matter so as to increase their food production.

416. See item 422.
417. According to the MEA spokesman, Vinoba Bhave's book comprising a collection of verses from the *Quran* was still under print and was not being taken by him duing his tour of East Pakistan. Vinoba Bhave was expected to enter Rangpur district in East Pakistan on 5 September. *The Hindustan Times*, 25 August 1962, p. 9.
418. Note, 19 September 1962, from London for Y.D. Gundevia, the Commonwealth Secretary at the MEA, on discussion with the President of Pakistan. NAI, MEA File No. P. I/112/32/62, p.1/notes. Also available in the JN Collection.

He said that the meetings of Engineers on both sides had been held repeatedly and they have collected all the necessary information and exchanged it. The time had now come for the matter to be considered at ministerial level.

I told him I had no objection to this, but I was not sure if the Engineers had finished their work. Essentially it was for them to make recommendations which could then be considered by Ministers. Anyhow I would look into this matter.

When I come back, I should like you to discuss this with me. Meanwhile please find out how far the engineers have finished their work. Have they made any recommendations?[419]

(m) Nepal

428. Missing Nepali Plane[420]

Nehru's Message

New Delhi, August 4 – Prime Minister Nehru sent the following message to the King of Nepal[421] yesterday [3 August 1962], before it was reported that the Nepalese Dakota had force-landed near Bardia.

The message said:

"We are most concerned about the RNAC[422] plane, which has been missing since day before yesterday.

"Despite bad weather conditions and poor visibility, civil and Air Force aircraft flew yesterday (August 2) in search of the missing aircraft. These efforts are continuing. The RNAC aircraft will, I am sure, be located today (August 3).

419. According to a press note issued by the MEA on 27 September 1962, the position of the GOI in the matter of the Farakka Barrage scheme had not changed since Nehru wrote to Ayub Khan on this subject on 6 July 1961 (SWJN/SS/70/item 359). Ayub Khan had not replied to Nehru's letter. The press note added that "the engineers of the two sides have not exchanged the necessary technical data so far on the basis of which an early Minister-level conference could be usefully held." The *National Herald*, 29 September 1962.
420. Report in the *National Herald*, 5 August 1962, p. 1.
421. Mahendra.
422. The Royal Nepal Airlines Corporation.

"I sincerely hope that Ambassador Thapa and other passengers on board have come to no harm."[423]

429. To Rishikesh Shaha: Relations with Nepal[424]

August 26, 1962

My dear Foreign Minister,

Thank you for your letter of the 10th August, which I received through our Ambassador in Kathmandu.[425]

I am grateful for the friendly sentiments you have expressed. I fully share your view that the ties between India and Nepal are of a special kind, and that we must do everything to preserve and strengthen them. That would not only be in the interests of both our countries but also in accordance with the deeply cherished wishes of the people of both Nepal and India.

As you observe, there has undoubtedly been an improvement in this respect since the visit of His Majesty[426] to New Delhi last April. It is, however, unfortunate that the machinery of joint informal enquiries has not been properly used; there are no joint reports, nor are reports exchanged and yet biased and unhelpful comments about the inquiries have appeared in some Nepalese newspapers. We have instructed our Ambassador to take up these questions with you. There have been other signs also of a seemingly concerted revival of a campaign of vilification of India in a section of the Nepalese press. It is imperative that persons in responsible positions should do what they can to smooth over difficulties, if any, and avoid any action or statement, direct, or indirect, through the press or otherwise, which may adversely affect our relations.

We, on our part, have spared no effort to assist in improving the atmosphere. Our press has generally shown restraint. We have also done our best, within the limits of our resources and of the wishes of your Government, to assist in Nepal's economic development and in other ways. This help continues to be available for the benefit of the people of Nepal. During His Majesty's visit I also frankly gave him my views as to ways of attaining his objective of establishing

---

423. The Dakota, missing since 1 August, was found two days later in a drain five miles north of Bardia. The passengers, who included N.P. Thapa, the Nepalese Ambassador to India, and the crew were reported to be safe. The *Amrita Bazar Patrika*, 4 August 1962, p. 7.
424. Letter to the Foreign Minister of Nepal.
425. Harishwar Dayal.
426. Mahendra, the King of Nepal.

an equitable social and economic order in Nepal, founded upon the people's cooperation and participation. Beyond this, I find it difficult to tender advice, especially because nowadays advice is liable to be misconstrued as interference.

I understand that you may be going to New York for the UN General Assembly by way of Delhi. I am leaving for London on the 7th September. If you happen to be here before that date, I shall be happy to meet you.[427]

With kind regards,

Jawaharlal Nehru

430. To Mahendra Bir Bikram Shah Deva: India not interfering in Nepal[428]

September 6, 1962

My dear friend,

Your Foreign Minister[429] handed to me this morning your letter of September 2. I was glad to have it and I thank Your Majesty for it.

I had a fairly long talk with the Foreign Minister and I hope that that talk removed any misapprehensions he might have had in his mind. I have no doubt that he will report his talk to Your Majesty.

I was much surprised to read in your letter references to gun running across our border and the statement that Indian authorities on the border connive at such activities and do not care to make effective check on armed activities of raiders. I have had no information of this gun running previously and, so far as I know, there has been no connivance in armed activities on our border. In order to make sure, I telephoned to the Chief Minister of Bihar[430] and he denied it completely. In fact, he told me that he had taken active steps to stop any persons wanting to make India the base of raids on Nepal. On some occasions some people were actually arrested.

I want to assure Your Majesty that it is our definite policy to prevent India being used us a base for any raids into Nepal, and we have issued strict injunctions to this effect. The question of gun running is wholly opposed to our policy. I do not know what information Your Majesty has on this subject. If there is any definite information, we shall be glad to have it and to pursue

427. Rishikesh Shah called on Nehru in New Delhi on 6 September 1962.
428. Letter to the King of Nepal.
429. Rishikesh Shaha.
430. Binodanand Jha.

the matter further. It is possible that the information that reaches Your Majesty is not correct or verified and is based on rumour.

I can assure Your Majesty that we are anxious that any troubles on the border or inside Nepal should cease. I am sure this does good to nobody and is harmful to the normal development of Nepal.

It is difficult for me to guarantee that no undesirable persons will go to Nepal or come out of Nepal. It is a long open border, and people come and go. But I think I can speak with some assurance that insofar as our Government is concerned, we shall endeavour to stop any persons who apparently are going for the purpose of any kind of raids.

We have no desire to interfere in the internal policies of Nepal. It may be that we have occasionally different opinions. But that does not mean that we should impose our views on the Nepalese Government. We desire, as we have always done, friendly and cooperative relations with Nepal.

As Your Majesty has written to me frankly, I am also doing the same. I would add, therefore, if I may, that I believe a policy of conciliation would be more helpful to Nepal than anything else. When political consciousness is roused among people, it is very difficult to suppress it by repressive measures only. Your Majesty is in a strong position and is undoubtedly popular with your people. Any action that you may take will not be misunderstood as proceeding from weakness, and will add to your strength.

As Your Majesty knows, I am going abroad very soon and I have written this letter in some haste, because I did not wish to leave India before replying to your Majesty's letter.

I am not referring to the continuous propaganda in some of the Nepal newspapers against India. We do not attach much importance to it. But it does come in the way of friendly relations. There have also been some cases of Nepal policemen crossing the border and shooting people on this side. It is possible that these incidents might have been accidental. We have tried not to give any special publicity to them.

I hope Your Majesty is keeping well.

With kind regards,

Yours sincerely,
[Jawaharlal Nehru]

(n) Ceylon

431. Tribute to S.W.R.D. Bandaranaike[431]

The Prime Minister of Ceylon[432] was good enough to invite me to visit Ceylon to inaugurate a memorial to the late Mr S.W.R.D. Bandaranaike.[433] I gladly accepted this invitation not only because the idea of visiting Ceylon again was attractive, but also as I wished to pay my tribute to the late Prime Minister of Ceylon.

I am sorry, however, that I am unable to go to Ceylon during the last week of September when the death anniversary of Mr Bandaranaike takes place. I hope to go there some weeks later.

Long before Mr Bandaranaike became Prime Minister, I came across him and we were attracted to each other. This was early in 1931 when I visited Ceylon. Since then, we had occasion to meet often in Ceylon, in India and in England where we journeyed to attend the Commonwealth Prime Ministers' Conferences. We had much in common and our views were also similar. Mr Bandaranaike was held in respect and admiration by many people in my country. To me, he was a close friend and his death came as a great tragedy.

It is fortunate for Ceylon in having at this difficult juncture the courageous and devoted leadership of Mrs Bandaranaike. She and her government and people have the warmest goodwill of the people of India.

The proposed memorial to the late Mr Bandaranaike is to take the shape of an Ayurvedic Research Institute. Ayurveda in its earlier days was remarkable for the advance it made in the science of medicine. Latterly it lost the old vitality which made it great, and became divorced from the spirit of science. I am sure there is a great deal of room for such a Research Institute which would again bring the methods of science to Ayurvedic Research.

I am greatly looking forward to my visiting Ceylon, probably in October.[434]

---

431. Message, 1 August 1962. Addressee not available.
432. Sirimavo Bandaranaike, Prime Minister of Ceylon from 1960.
433. Prime Minister of Ceylon from 1956, assassinated on 26 September 1959.
434. The institute, named Bandaranaike Memorial Ayurvedic Research Institute, was set up at Nawinna, Maharagama, in Ceylon, and inaugurated by Nehru on 14 October 1962. See also SWJN/SS/74/item 213.

(o) Burma

432. Inviting Ne Win[435]

We had decided to invite General Ne Win before the last coup d'état in Burma. I am not so keen on inviting him when U Nu and others are in prison in Burma.

If it is really considered necessary, I might invite him. But I think that this should wait till my return from London.

(p) South East Asia

433. For Harold Macmillan: Geneva Agreement on Laos[436]

Begins. Thank you for your message on the Geneva Agreement on Laos.[437] I am very happy at the success of this Conference after innumerable difficulties had arisen, and I congratulate you on the part played by the British Government at this Conference. This is, I hope, the first of the agreements on international issues which we look forward to, more especially in regard to disarmament. Such an agreement would remove a great burden of fear from the minds of all people in the world. Jawaharlal Nehru. Ends.

434. To Sunderlal: Message from Ho Chi Minh[438]

August 6, 1962

My dear Sunderlal,

Thank you for your letter containing a message from President Ho Chi Minh.[439]

435. Note, 23 August 1962, for Y.D. Gundevia, the Commonwealth Secretary at the MEA. MEA, File No. SI/457/6/62, p. 4/note.
436. Telegram, 27 July 1962, for the British Prime Minister, sent through the High Commissioner in London.
437. A Declaration on the Neutrality of Laos was signed by fourteen nations including India on 23 July 1962.
438. Letter to the President of the All India Peace Council; address: 40 Hanuman Lane, New Delhi-1. NMML, Pandit Sunderlal Papers, File No. 35.
439. President of North Vietnam (the Democratic Republic of Vietnam), 1945-1969.

I shall be glad to see you at 4.30 p.m. on Saturday, the 11th August, in my office in External Affairs.

Yours sincerely,
Jawaharlal Nehru

435. To Ung Van Khiem: India does not take sides[440]

Excellency,

I have the honour to thank you for your letter dated the 25th June, 1962, and the papers enclosed with it.[441]

It appears from these that the Government of the Democratic Republic of Vietnam has drawn the conclusion that the Special Report of the Commission seeks to justify the presence in South Vietnam of American Military material and personnel. The report does not in any manner support such a conclusion. We firmly maintain that the report is a sober and factual statement of the findings of the Commission on specific complaints lodged before the Commission, both, against North Vietnam and against the South, in terms of the provisions of the Geneva Agreement of 1954.

I hope I do not need to re-assure Your Excellency that India and her representatives have no reason for taking sides in the situation in Vietnam. They are committed to judging cases on merits, even if they run the risk of being misunderstood. Their only aim in Vietnam is to help all parties concerned to arrive at a just solution, and restoration of peace.

I take this opportunity to renew to Your Excellency the assurances of my highest consideration.

Jawaharlal Nehru

---

440. Telegram No. 6304, 8 August 1962, for the Foreign Minister of the Democratic Republic of Viet Nam. MEA, File No. SI/106(1)/62, Vol. VI, p. 223/Corr.
441. Appendix 2.

436. In the Rajya Sabha: Report of the Vietnam Commission[442]

Will the Prime Minister be pleased to state:[443]

(a) whether Government's attention has been drawn to the statement issued by the Secretariat of the Afro-Asian Solidarity Committee, Cairo, that the recent majority report of the International Commission for Supervision and Control in Vietnam is illegal because it is not unanimous and can play into the hands of the American imperialists against the people of Vietnam;

(b) if so, what is the position of the Government of India in this matter; and

(c) whether it is the function of the International Supervisory Commission according to Geneva Agreement to end American military intervention in South Vietnam?

The Minister of State in the Ministry of External Affairs (Lakshmi Menon):

(a) The Government of India are not aware of the statement stated to have been issued by the Secretariat of the Afro-Asian Solidarity Committee, Cairo regarding the report of the International Commission for Supervision and Control in Vietnam. It is presumed that the report envisaged in the question is the Special Report of the 2nd June, 1962 signed by a majority of the Commission, namely India and Canada. The Report is not illegal, as the Geneva Agreement of 1954 provides for reports from the Commission to the Co-Chairmen with or without unanimity, in specified circumstances. There is no question of prejudicing the interests of the people of Vietnam. The Report deals with specific allegations, from the parties concerned, of breaches of the Geneva Agreement of 1954 and gives its finding on a factual basis, on these complaints.

(b) The Government of India is in agreement with the majority report. Its representative on the Commission has acted in consultation with, and under instructions from the Government of India.

(c) It is the function of the International Commission for Supervision and Control in Vietnam to control the implementation of the 1954 Geneva Agreements by the parties to that Agreement.

---

442. Oral answers, 24 August 1962. *Rajya Sabha Debates*, Vol. 40, Nos. 9-16, 17 to 29 August 1962, cols 3050-3056.
443. Question by Niren Ghosh and A. Subba Rao, both CPI.

Niren Ghosh: May I know what the real cause of the critical situation in South Vietnam is and what the policy of the Government of India is for the solution of the Vietnam problem? Do the Government of India propose a solution on the Laotian pattern after a similar conference at Geneva?

Lakshmi Menon: Sir, the Commission is posted there in order to implement the Geneva Agreement. The Government of India as such has no policy with regard to South Vietnam.

Niren Ghosh: May I know how the Government of India proposes to safeguard and ensure the neutrality of South Vietnam as proposed in this Geneva Agreement?

Lakshmi Menon: I have already stated that the Commission is looking after that.

Niren Ghosh: In the majority Report of the International Commission for Supervision and Control in Vietnam, there are definite, positive findings that there has been introduction of American military personnel in South Vietnam. But no positive proof of neutrality has been stated. There are only inferences. Under the circumstances, may I know how the Government of India could accept such a Report to be correct?

Lakshmi Menon: No, Sir. The hon. Member is not correct because with regard to American involvement in South Vietnam, the Commission came to this conclusion—the substance of their finding is this—that American military involvement in South Vietnam amounts in practice to a military alliance and is in contravention of the provisions of the Geneva Agreement.

Bhupesh Gupta:[444] The hon. Minister in her reply has said that the Indian representative there acted in consultation with and under the instructions of the Government of India. May I know, when it is a question of finding facts, sifting evidence and coming to a conclusion on the basis of facts, what this consultation means? Was any political consideration involved in it? And may I know in this connection whether it is not a fact that the same allegation that the North Vietnamese were infiltrating and sending their armed personnel and so on had been made in the past several times and that it was never accepted and that this is done with a view to covering

444. CPI.

up American military actions, aggressive actions, in South Vietnam in violation of the Geneva Agreement?

Jawaharlal Nehru: The hon. Member has delivered a harangue, if I may use the word, about the Report which was prepared locally by the Commission and which was passed by a majority, including our member. When they prepared the Report, he sent it to us naturally. It is not that we affected his judgment in regard to preparing the Report. But he sent it to us. It was a well argued Report which criticised equally the North Vietnam people and inferentially the United States Government for aiding the South Vietnam people. It is a very objective and a very good report.

Bhupesh Gupta: How does the Government's agreement or otherwise come into this subject? The Report is supposed to be sent to the Co-Chairmen and it is for the Co-Chairmen to see what has happened there and so on. The Government only supply the personnel. So, how does the Government's agreement come in here?

May I know, Sir, whether it is not a fact that in all the earlier Reports similar allegations were made of infiltration of armed personnel from North Vietnam and every time on the previous occasions, except the last one, such an allegation was rejected by the Commission? And it is for the first time that it has been accepted after consultation giving rise to certain political presumptions.

Chairman:[445] May be for the first time that is true.

Bhupesh Gupta: But I would like the Prime Minister to state it. Is it not a fact, since you have put that thing to me, that American military personnel have increased their arms and munitions, aircraft and other means of war including noxious chemicals and these have been sent there to commit aggression? Persecution is taking place against the patriots there who cannot be persecuted under the Geneva Agreement. All these facts are there and this bogey of infiltration is raised with a view to covering up these violations of the Geneva Agreement. What does the Government say about it?

Jawaharlal Nehru: The first thing that the Government says is that it protests against the language of the hon. Member and the insinuation. He is challenging

---

445. Zakir Husain.

a Tribunal which has gone into this, whose Report has been accepted by Government. When he says that this is all done to cover up a certain thing ...

Bhupesh Gupta: Not you, Sir. I said Americans. I certainly ...

Jawaharlal Nehru: Yes, who covered it up? The Tribunal supported by the Government of India? I think this is a completely false insinuation.

Bhupesh Gupta: I want him to understand this. I say, these are also there in the earlier Reports. The Prime Minister now says that I am insinuating. Why should I do so? I say that the Canadians who acted there, they acted sometimes on the orders of the Americans. I want to know whether the Government has taken care to see that our representative is not misled by this kind of manipulation on the part of certain agencies there.

Chairman: I thought Mr Bhupesh Gupta that you want the Report to be absolutely uninfluenced.

Bhupesh Gupta: Yes, absolutely unhampered. But I regret that the Prime Minister accused me of making insinuations.

Jawaharlal Nehru: I repeat, these so-called facts are entirely lop-sided, one-sided and false. I repeat, false.

Niren Ghosh: No amount of assertion would wash away the facts.

Bhupesh Gupta: The same question I put on the basis of facts which are true, I repeat. Again consider ...

Chairman: It is not our business to give ... (Interruption).

Please sit down.

A.B. Vajpayee:[446] On a point of order. We have friendly relations with the Government of Canada. Now, the Canadians who are represented on the Commission, they have been accused that they acted on the orders of the Americans. Is it proper to accuse the representative of a friendly Government without any basis?

446. Jan Sangh.

Bhupesh Gupta: Well, if the Prime Minister wants a tribunal to be appointed, let him appoint a tribunal. The facts should be gone into and I shall give my evidence before it.

Jawaharlal Nehru: I really do not understand how this matter can be considered in this House during the question time. Here is the Report. His opinion is that the Report may not be a right Report by competent persons. There is a minority Report and a majority Report. We happen to support the majority Report and that Report criticises and condemns certain activities of both sides impartially. Now, the hon. Member thinks that we should have only joined on one side. And in regard to the North Vietnam part of the Report, that is a very old charge—I mean, not an immediate happening, may be months old, may be a year old, I do not exactly remember—a very serious charge, and it was quite impossible for anybody who could look into it fairly to ignore that.

Chairman: The question hour is over.

437. To Norodom Sihanouk: International Conference for Cambodia[447]

August 30, 1962

Your Royal Highness,

It is with some anxiety that I have read your letter of the 20th August 1962,[448] in which you have mentioned your grave apprehensions in regard to the integrity of your country.

As you know, we have always believed that countries in South East Asia, and more particularly Indo-China, should be enabled to function in freedom and security, without outside interference. This principle was, in fact, the basis and the very essence of the Geneva Agreements of 1954. We feel that, irrespective of the quarter from which difficulties might arise, the Geneva powers have an obligation, moral and political, to ensure that such a status subsists. I am, therefore, in accord with you in considering the Geneva Conference as a possible approach to a solution, all the more as it has already achieved so much for the Indo-China region.

I hesitate to make any rigid proposals, but I would suggest for the consideration of your Royal Highness, that prior to finalising any plans for a

447. Letter to the Head of State of Cambodia.
448. Appendix 41.

Conference, some informal communication with the two Co-Chairmen might produce very worthwhile results. They have only recently made valuable contributions towards the peaceful solution of the Laotian problem and this was done in response to your important initiative in the matter. Any initiative from you now in holding informal consultations with them on the possible lines along which solutions might be found in the present instance, would have the advantage of obviating the difficulties that some of the members of the recent Geneva Conference might experience in making public declarations of their positions at the present stage.

I agree with you that any serious trouble in Cambodia will have repercussions in Laos and perhaps elsewhere also. It need hardly be said that, for our part, we would render all possible assistance in bringing about a peaceful solution of the present difficulties. If it is considered that informal consultations with the countries who are members of the Geneva Conference might help, we are hopeful that the problems raised will command the earnest attention of these countries. We have no doubt that there is a keen appreciation, on many sides, of the difficulties experienced by the countries of Indo-China, and that a peaceful solution of these problems would be welcomed.

Please accept, Your Royal Highness, the assurances of my highest consideration.

[Jawaharlal Nehru]

438. In the Lok Sabha: Attack on Indian Embassy at Jakarta[449]

Indrajit Gupta:[450] Under Rule 197, I call the attention of the Prime Minister to the following matter of urgent public importance and I request that he may make a statement thereon:

"The attack on the Indian Embassy at Jakarta on 3rd September, 1962 by a crowd of 20,000 Indonesians resulting in extensive damage to property."

Jawaharlal Nehru: The facts relating to this attack on the Indian Embassy have been adequately reported in the Press and I do not think it will be necessary for me to repeat them. I shall state some other facts connected therewith.

449. Adjournment motion, 4 September 1962. *Lok Sabha Debates*, Vol. 8, Third Series, September 3-7, 1962, cols 5805-5811.
450. CPI.

The trouble started when the Israeli and Formosan delegations sent telegrams to Mr G.D. Sondhi early in August, as he is the Senior Vice-President of the Sports Federation or whatever it is called.[451] These telegrams stated that the Indonesian President of Games had failed to send them identity cards. Mr Sondhi, in his capacity as Senior Vice-President, issued a statement criticising this action. This created resentment in Jakarta and we informed our ambassadors of the legal position. They were also informed that during the earlier Asian Games held in Delhi, Manila and Tokyo in 1950, 1954 and 1958 respectively, Formosa and Israel had been invited, but UAR had not taken part, because they were not supposed to be in Asia.

On arrival at Jakarta, Mr Sondhi actively spoke about the Indonesian action and suggested that the name of the Fourth Asian Games be changed to merely Games. This angered the Indonesians and there was violent criticism. We asked our Ambassador in Jakarta[452] on August 30 to impress upon Mr Sondhi the desirability of toning down his criticisms. To this, we got the reply that he conveyed our viewpoint to those concerned, that is, the Indonesian officials, and they had appreciated our position. It was explained to them that Mr Sondhi was not in any sense a representative of the Government and did not speak on behalf of the Government. The Sports Federation here is a semi-independent organisation and he was elected as Vice-President not by us, but nominated by that Federation. We were, therefore, surprised to see the Indonesian Trade Minister's Statement on August 31, in which the Indonesian Trade Minister expressed his resentment at India's attitude in this matter and said something about trade relations being affected thereby. A spokesman of the Ministry of External Affairs clarified the position and pointed out that Mr Sondhi was in no way connected with the Government of India and we had no control over the Asian Games Federation, of which he was Vice-President. He also emphasised our friendship with Indonesia and expressed the hope that the games will come to a peaceful conclusion. Our regret over the statement was communicated to the Indonesian Embassy here on the 1st September while our Ambassador met the Indonesian Foreign Minister,[453] who assured him of his country's friendship and goodwill for India. This was on the 1st.

The Indonesian Trade Minister's statement on August 31st, however, indicates that the Indonesian authorities were actively associated with criticising Mr Sondhi's stand and its culmination in the incidents of yesterday, when the Indian Embassy was attacked and some damage was done to the property.

451. He was the Senior Vice-President of the Asian Games Federation Council.
452. Apa B. Pant.
453. Subandrio.

There has been no report of any injury to persons. Our concern over this was communicated to the Indian Embassy yesterday evening. Our Ambassador was not present at the time when this happened in the Indian Embassy. As soon as he heard of it, he came back from his house or from wherever he was, to the Embassy. The people had gone by that time. He immediately sent a note to the Foreign Office. He later met the Foreign Minister and told him that he was greatly surprised that after his last interview with him only a day or two earlier, which was most cordial and after which he had issued a statement, this shocking incident should take place.

Secondly, in Indonesia, no meeting or procession can take place without some kind of knowledge or permission from the Government. It is not quite clear; some official there must have had knowledge of it.

Hem Barua (Gauhati):[454] It started from the Presidential palace.

Frank Anthony (Nominated-Anglo-Indians): They were escorted by the Police.

Jawaharlal Nehru: It was called the National Front people in some kind of a semi-uniform who went.

Hem Barua: Volunteers for the liberation of West Irian also were there.

Jawaharlal Nehru: The Foreign Minister apologised to our Ambassador profoundly and said that all Members of Parliament of Indonesia had been deeply shocked by this incident as well as by Dr Soeharto, the Trade Minister's statement.

This is the position. It is highly deplorable that this kind of thing should happen. We are not concerned with the merits of the matter, which was raised by Mr Sondhi about the games. Neither were we consulted nor had we any say in the matter. But whatever that may be, to encourage the attack on the Indian Embassy in this way is extremely distressing and deplorable, as also the statement made by the Trade Minister, over which the Foreign Minister subsequently expressed his great regret.

I feel very sad about this, because our Ambassador in Jakarta, Shri Apa B. Pant, is one of our very successful and experienced ambassadors. Wherever he has been, he has done good work and he is very popular with the people. In fact, in Indonesia, he is exceedingly popular. He gets on very well and he has

454. PSP.

the habit of identifying himself with the country where he is. He has made a study of Indonesian history and culture and all that. It is peculiarly surprising and distressing that this incident has taken place there.

Indrajit Gupta: In the light of the reprehensible attack which has taken place on our Embassy, all I would like to know is whether Government has obtained the full texts of the various statements alleged to have been made by Mr Sondhi while in Jakarta, in order to verify whether they contain anything which could be construed as an affront to President Soekarno in particular or to Indonesian national sentiment in general, because that is the allegation being made?

Jawaharlal Nehru: I do not think we have received the full text of the statements. Summaries of them have come—brief accounts in the Press and otherwise. I doubt if the full text has come. I do not think there was anything in what Mr Sondhi said, which could be construed as an affront or discourtesy to President Soekarno.

Some Hon. Members rose.

Speaker:[455] Only those who have their names here might put questions.

राम चन्द्र बड़े (खारगोल):[456] मैं यह जानना चाहता हूँ कि इस इन्सिडेंट को लेकर चाइना के पीकिंग रेडियो ने जो एन्टी-इंडियन प्रापेगंडा शुरू किया है, क्या उनका निराकरण करने के लिए हमारे एक्सटर्नल पब्लिसिटी डिविजन ने बाकी राष्ट्रों में इस के बारे में प्रचार करने के लिए कुछ भी व्यवस्था की है।

जवाहरलाल नेहरु: माननीय सदस्य यह बात सही कहते हैं कि इसमें चीन वालों ने बहुत अधिक दिलचस्पी ली है और इसको बहुत बढ़ाने की कोशिश की है। और मुमकिन है कि इसको शुरू करने में भी उनका कुछ हाथ हो। लेकिन आप कहते हैं कि और जगह हम समझाने को कहें। जरूर और जगह कुछ न कुछ हम करेंगे।[457]

---

455. Hukam Singh.
456. Jan Sangh.
457. Apa B. Pant, Ambassador to Indonesia, had written to M.J. Desai, Foreign Secretary, on 5 July 1962: "China has been systematically trying to deface the image of India [in Indonesia] that we so persistently and successfully built up all these years. She wants the people of this area to think of us as 'a spent force' and merely as 'lackeys of British and American imperialism'." Avtar Singh Bhasin (ed.), *India-China Relations 1947-2000. A Documentary Study*, Volume-IV (New Delhi: Geetika Publishers, 2018), pp. 3734-3735.

[Translation begins

Ram Chandra Bade (Khargol):[458] I wish to know if our External Publicity Division has taken any steps to counter the anti-Indian propaganda in other countries by Peking Radio, China, over this incident.

Jawaharlal Nehru: Hon. Member is right in saying that the Chinese have taken an inordinate interest in this incident and have tried to exaggerate it. It is also possible that they may have had a hand in starting this. But as you are saying that we should take steps to counter this propaganda elsewhere, this we shall certainly do.[459]

Translation ends]

Hem Barua: Sir, if I heard the Prime Minister aright, in view of the statement that Shri Sondhi does not speak on behalf of our Government which means that our Government do not share Shri Sondhi's views, are we to understand that our Government supports Indonesia's importing politics into sports?

Speaker: That is a different matter.

Jawaharlal Nehru: It is not a question of our supporting. We have not gone into it. We are not seized of their rules. We do not know even what they are. We are not prepared to express any opinion on a subject which we have not studied.

प्रकाशवीर शास्त्री:[460] माननीय प्रधानमंत्री जी ने बतलाया कि श्री सोंधी के वक्तव्य के बाद हमारे राजदूत ने इसका स्पष्टीकरण किया है कि इनके वक्तव्य का भारत सरकार से कोई सीधा सम्बन्ध नहीं है और उस के पश्चात इंडोनेशिया के विदेश मंत्री ने भी किसी एक स्थान पर कहा है कि जो विवाद उठा है, वह धीरे-धीरे समाप्त हो जायेगा और हमारे सम्बन्धों पर इसका कोई प्रतिकूल प्रभाव नहीं पड़ेगा। जब ऐसी बात है तो फिर दुबारा कौन सी ऐसी स्थिति पैदा हुई जिस के कारण भारतीय दूतावास पर यह आक्रमण हुआ और क्यों ऐसा हुआ है, यह भी जानने का क्या सरकार ने यत्न किया है?

---

458. See fn 456 in this section.
459. See fn 457 in this section.
460. Independent.

जवाहरलाल नेहरुः यह बात माननीय सदस्य सही कहते हैं कि हम समझते थे कि बात साफ हो गई है और अगर कोई गलतफहमी भी हो तो वह भी साफ हो गई है जब हमारे राजदूत मिले थे। फिर यह क्यों हुआ यह बात समझ में नहीं आती है सिवाय इसके कि कुछ लोगों ने उकसाया फिर से। मैं इस वक्त नहीं कहना चाहता कि किन लोगों ने उकसाया। यह बात पर्दे के पीछे होती है।

[Translation begins

Prakashvir Shastri:[461] Honourable Prime Minister has said that after Shri Sondhi's statement, our Ambassador has clarified that this statement is not directly related to the Government of India's position. Thereafter the Foreign Minister of Indonesia has also said somewhere that the dispute which has arisen will gradually die down and it will not have an adverse impact on our relations. When this is the situation, has the Government tried to find out what happened again to create a situation which led to this attack on the Indian Embassy?

Jawaharlal Nehru: Hon. Member is correct in saying that we had been under the impression that the matter had been clarified and even if a misunderstanding had arisen it had been cleared up when our Ambassador had met them. Therefore it is not clear why this attack happened except that some people had instigated it. I do not wish to say who may have been responsible because these things are done behind the scenes.

Translation ends]

Renu Chakravartty (Barrackpore):[462] While it is technically correct that the question as to what is to be done within a sports federation is the job of that sports federation members, when the question of Taiwan and Israel raises such tremendous reaction even in sports gatherings, may I know whether the Government of India took any steps to advise Shri Sondhi before going, as he did, as one of the senior Vice- Presidents of the Games, to be careful as to the way he handled this particular matter?

Speaker: It is a suggestion.

---

461. See fn 460 in this section.
462. CPI.

Jawaharlal Nehru: As I read out, Sir, the Government of India, after Shri Sondhi made the statement because only then we heard about it, did tell him that he should understand the implications of what he was doing and to go slow about it.

S.M. Banerjee:[463] May I know whether it is a fact that Shri Sondhi made a statement once again even after the clarification was made by our Ambassador there; if so, whether we have got the text of that statement?

Speaker: That has already been answered.

Jawaharlal Nehru: I could not follow his question.

Speaker: He wanted to know whether we have got the text of his statement.

S.M. Banerjee: I want to know whether after the whole position was clarified by our Ambassador Shri Sondhi made any statement or spoke in any gathering pleading the case of Taiwan?

Jawaharlal Nehru: I think he clarified this matter more than once, to more than one person in authority. He did that repeatedly. Is the hon. Member referring to this matter before the attack on the Embassy or after that.

Speaker: After this had been brought to the notice of Shri Sondhi by our Ambassador, he wants to know whether Shri Sondhi made any statement after that?

Jawaharlal Nehru: I cannot say. He did make some statements, but whether they were considered objectionable or not I cannot definitely say. He has constantly been saying something in defence of himself.

P.C. Borooah (Sibsagar):[464] May I know whether the Government will leave no stone unturned in upholding the good feeling and friendship that we have got with Indonesia?

Speaker: That is a suggestion.

---

463. Independent.
464. Congress.

Narendrasingh Mahida (Anand):[465] May I seek information, Sir, as to whether the Indonesian Government will pay for the damages done to our Embassy?

Jawaharlal Nehru: Normally, damages are paid. It is a small matter. We are not going to press it. They have said, they will pay. But it does not matter. Actually, so far as we know, the damages caused may be about Rs10,000 to Rs20,000.

439. To Tunku Abdul Rahman Putra: Zoological Park in Kuala Lumpur[466]

September 6, 1962

My dear Prime Minister,

Thanks for your letter of 22nd August, 1962, telling me about your efforts to establish a National Zoological Park in Kuala Lumpur. It is a plausible venture, and I wish you all success. We shall endeavour to cooperate with you to the fullest possible measure. In the meantime, I am making enquiries and shall let you know the position in due course.

We are looking forward anxiously to welcome you here next month.

With kind regards,

Yours sincerely,
[Jawaharlal Nehru]

(q) Japan

440. Talk with Koto Matsudaira[467]

The Japanese Ambassador came to see me this morning. He began by asking me about our attitude to the European Common Market and the United Kingdom joining it. I gave him a brief reply, stating that, from the economic point of view, this was likely to be injurious to us. We could not stop the United Kingdom

---

465. Swatantra Party.
466. Letter to the Prime Minister of Malaya.
467. Note, 26 August 1962, for Morarji Desai, the Finance Minister, K.C. Reddy, the Minister of Commerce and Industry, R.K. Nehru, the Secretary-General, MEA, and M.J.Desai, the Foreign Secretary, on talk with the Japanese Ambassador.

from joining it if it so wished. All we could do was to get the best terms for ourselves, both with the UK and directly with the Common Market people.

2.   The ECM has a political aspect too, and the next step may well be a closer political union. Although, perhaps, this might be an inevitable development for Western Europe, I would not be happy about it. A strong political and economic group in Western Europe might not be advantageous to us and to other countries in Asia.

3.   The Ambassador said something about our developing a common market for Asia. I replied that this might be a future development, but I doubt if it was feasible in the present circumstances. It would probably be better for us to have bilateral arrangements with countries.

4.   He then asked me about our relations with China and what the future was likely to hold. I replied that it was obvious that our relations with China were very strained and there was no near prospect of their improving. The Ambassador said that Japan was developing trade with China and this was growing. Although Japan's trade with India was also improving, it was quite possible that Sino-Japanese trade might go ahead of Indo-Japanese. He would much rather that Japanese trade with India kept ahead of their trade with China.

5.   In particular, he referred to the need of iron ore by Japan. There was almost a limitless possibility of Japan importing iron ore. They hoped to achieve steel production of about sixty million tons in about eight years' time. That is, they would reach the present Soviet production. That would mean nearly doubling the present day Japanese production. They would have liked very much to get more and more iron ore from India, but our prices were high and not competitive.

6.   He discussed various other matters too with me, such as Disarmament, nuclear tests, etc.

V. MISCELLANEOUS

441. To M.O. Mathai: Health and Food Fads[1]

July 22, 1962

My dear Mathai,

Thank you for your letter. Welcome back, healthy and fit. I am sure the loss of weight will do you good.

As for the Vichy water, I have not received it yet. But I know Vichy very well and have always disliked it. Unless I am forced to take it as medicine, I would rather not take it. In any event, I do not think it is worthwhile or desirable to get it weekly from Europe. Nor is it necessary to get melons. The melons you sent are good, but not better than good Indian melons. Besides, we have plenty of fruit now-a-days including mangoes. Please therefore, countermand your order for Vichy water and melons.

I am keeping quite well.

Yours sincerely,
[Jawaharlal Nehru]

442. For T.N. Kaul: Royalty on Nehru's *Autobiography*[2]

July 25, 1962

My dear Sir,

I am sorry for the enormous delay in replying to your letter dated 14th June, enclosing Max Reinhardt's[3] letter to you.

All that the PM desired was that the royalty on this Indian edition (by Allied Publishers) should be remitted to him here. Whether Max Reinhardt remitted the money to PM or the Allied Publishers did so here, it would mean the same thing so far as the PM is concerned. Perhaps it would be more convenient

---

1. Letter to former Special Assistant; address: 2 Willingdon Crescent, New Delhi.
2. Letter from Private Secretary to the Deputy High Commissioner in London. NMML, JN Master File.
3. British publisher; in 1957 he bought the firm The Bodley Head.

for the Allied Publishers to send us the cheque, but this may be left to their convenience.[4]

With kind regards,

Yours sincerely,
[N.K. Seshan]

443. Foreword to *The Development of the Indian Economy*[5]

I am glad to learn that Mr Reddaway's book is going to be published in India.[6] Mr Reddaway has made a close study of Indian planning and his book is of value to all those who wish to know something about it. More particularly, I should like people in India to read it and thus get an expert view on what we are trying to do in India.

We have undertaken a tremendous task. As we progress, more and more problems encompass us. But I feel sure that we shall overcome these difficulties even though this might mean great effort on our part. Planning in such a vast country with manifold problems is difficult; but the implementation of a plan is much more difficult. Ultimately it means the willing cooperation in some degree or other, of millions of people. In particular, agricultural planning involves this cooperation of large numbers of farmers who are used to primitive methods and out-of-date techniques. Yet there is an awakening even among the peasantry and I hope it will bear fruit.

Meanwhile, I hope that many persons will profit by Mr Reddaway's survey.

444. To Rameshwari Nehru: Help for K.S. Shivam's Family[7]

August 2, 1962

Your letter of the 1st August about K.S. Shivam's death[8] in Malaya. We shall do what we can about his children and wife going back to Malaya, but, as you

---

4. See also item 457.
5. 31 July 1962.
6. The book by William Brian Reddaway was first published by George Allen & Unwin, London, 1962. Reddaway at the time was Director of the Department of Applied Economics, University of Cambridge.
7. Letter to a social worker and a founder of the All India Women's Conference; address: Harijan Sevak Sangh, Delhi-9. Salutation and signature not available.
8. Secretary of the Harijan Sevak Sangh from April 1959, died on 20 June 1962.

693

say, Malayan immigration laws are strict. I do not think you need trouble to bring her to me as this is not a question of my being convinced. The Malayan Prime Minister, Tunku Abdul Rehman, is not coming to India.

We shall do our best.

Yours affectionately,
[Jawaharlal Nehru]

445. To Mulk Raj Anand: Selections from Nehru's Works[9]

August 2, 1962

My dear Mulk Raj,

Your letter of the 27th July. I hope that in making a selection of my writings, you will not get into trouble with copyright. The odd essays are not copyright, but "India Today and Tomorrow" I believe will require the permission of the Indian Council for Cultural Relations.

I shall try to find out the article I wrote in the *Modern Review* about 1940.[10] Also what is called "The Basic Approach" article,[11] and send them to you.

I am afraid I have no time to look through other writings of mine and make a choice.

I might inform you that Dorothy Norman[12] of New York is producing some kind of a *Reader* containing a large number of extracts from my books and other writings.[13]

Yours sincerely,
Jawaharlal Nehru

---

9. Letter to the writer, and Tagore Professor of Art and Literature, University of the Punjab, Chandigarh. [Nehru wrote: "the Punjab."]
10. Nehru was probably referring to his article "The Rashtrapati" published anonymously in *The Modern Review* of Calcutta, November 1937, see SWJN/FS/8 (1985 edition)/ pp. 518-521. See also item 446 in this volume.
11. See SWJN/SS/43/pp.1-11.
12. Civil rights advocate, writer and photographer.
13. *Nehru Reader*, tentative title given by Dorothy Norman to a collection of Nehru's writings and statements she was compiling at the time. It was published in two volumes as *Nehru: The First Sixty Years* (Bombay: Asia Publishing House, 1965).

446. To Mulk Raj Anand: Forwarding Publications[14]

August 5, 1962

My dear Mulk Raj,
I enclose two papers.[15] One is my article which appeared in the *Modern Review* in 1938. The other is what has been called "The Basic Approach".[16] I did not give it this name. The Editor of the *Economic Review* is responsible for the title.

Yours sincerely,
Jawaharlal Nehru

447. To Patrick Heyworth: Naming a Rose after Nehru[17]

August 5, 1962

Dear Mr Heyworth,
Thank you for your letter of the 23rd July. Also, for a copy of *The World of Roses*[18] which is a very fine production and which I have liked very much.

I would indeed be pleased and honoured if Mr Bertram Park names one of his new roses after me.

I should have much liked to attend the gathering to introduce Mr Park's new book. But I rather doubt if I shall be able to do so. Probably I shall reach London for the Commonwealth Prime Ministers' Conference about that time or the day after. It will be difficult for me to fit in this engagement. If it is at all possible, I would like to be present. Thank you for the invitation.

Yours sincerely,
[Jawaharlal Nehru]

14. Letter to the writer, and Tagore Professor of Art and Literature, University of the Punjab, Chandigarh. [Nehru wrote: "the Punjab."]
15. See item 445.
16. Nehru first wrote this as a note and enclosed it to his letter, 13 July 1958, to Chief Ministers, see SWJN/SS/43/pp. 1-11. It was later published in the *AICC Economic Review* of 15 August 1958.
17. Letter to the Director of George G. Harrap and Co. Ltd, 182 High Holborn, London WC1.
18. (London: George G. Harrap, 1962), written by Bertram Park, 1883-1972, British portrait photographer and a cultivator of roses.

448. To Kurt Postel: Appreciating Gift[19]

August 7, 1962

Dear Dr Postel,

I have received your letter of the 7th July. Also your beautiful book containing reproductions from paintings in the Dresden Museum. The smaller book containing pictures of Erfurt has also reached me. I am grateful to you for sending me these beautiful presents which I appreciate very much. It was very good of you to take the trouble to send these beautiful volumes to me.

Yours sincerely,
[Jawaharlal Nehru]

449. To Marion Lukens: Nehru's Bust[20]

August 9, 1962

Dear Miss Lukens,

A friend has written to me about you and your sculpture, and has also sent me some press cuttings displaying your pieces of sculpture. May I say that I have admired your work which I have only seen in these reproductions? You have honoured me by making my head in sandstone.[21]

I would be very happy to be able to meet you, but I do not know when this can take place as there is no near prospect of my going to the United States.

I send you my greetings and good wishes.

Yours sincerely,
[Jawaharlal Nehru]

---

19. Letter; address Mühlhauserstr. 81, Erfurt, Germany.
20. Letter to sculptor and painter; address: Columbus Hospital, 2520 N. Lakeview, Chicago, Illinois.
21. According to a report in the *Chicago Tribune* of 29 October 1961, p. 155, "In the garden of the Textile museum in Washington, DC, is a head of monumental size of India's Nehru. Carved from red sandstone by Chicago sculptor and painter, Marion Lukens, it was a prize winner at the exhibition by artists of Chicago and vicinity held at Navy pier several years ago. Recently the State Department requested its loan for exhibition during the anticipated visit of Nehru [in November 1961]."

450. To S. Selvanayagee: Portfolios in First Government[22]

August 9, 1962

Dear Madam,

I have your letter of the 2nd August.

I have no clear recollection of the incident you refer to. The incident mentioned is in Frank Moraes's book.[23] In any event, I had previously informed the Governor-General of the portfolios and he knew all about them.[24]

Yours sincerely,
Jawaharlal Nehru

451. To D.G. Tendulkar: Photo of Mountbattens with Gandhi[25]

August 11, 1962

My dear Tendulkar,

Your letter of August 8th. I am enclosing a photograph of the Mountbattens with Gandhiji.

---

22. Letter; address: Chettiar Store, 26th B Road, Mandalay, Burma. NMML, JN Supplementary Papers, Box No. 106.
23. Probably the incident relates to a conversation between Nehru and Mountbatten at Viceroy's House a little after the transfer of power on the midnight of 14-15 August 1947. Mountbatten had just been invited by Nehru and Rajendra Prasad to be the first Governor-General of independent India. Frank Moraes writes in his *Jawaharlal Nehru. A Biography* (New York: Macmillan, 1956), pp. 338-339:

     "The ceremony, which took place amid a barrage of flash bulbs, ended with Nehru elaborately handing over to the Governor-General a long parchment envelope with the words, 'May I submit to you the portfolios of the new Cabinet?'

     When the two Indian leaders had left, Mountbatten, surrounded by his entourage, carefully opened the envelope to discover its contents. It was empty! Someone had forgotten to insert the enclosure."
24. For Nehru's note of 14 August 1947 listing the names of Members of the new Cabinet and their portfolios, see SWJN/SS/3/p. 48.
25. Letter to Mahatma Gandhi's biographer; address: Ekanta, Rocky Hill, Narayan Dabholkar Road, Bombay-6. NMML, D.G. Tendulkar Papers.

I shall be going to Bombay on the 19th. You can come and see me a little before dinner time at Raj Bhavan that day.

I am quite fit now.

Yours sincerely,
Jawaharlal Nehru

452. To Padmaja Naidu: Personal and Political[26]

August 11, 1962

[My dear Bebee,]

Thank you for your letter of the 10th August and the photograph of Sanjay[27] with the fish.

It is very moving to learn of how the common people came to you to give their contributions to the Bidhan Roy Memorial Fund.

Subimal Dutt, of course, cannot go any more to Moscow except to say good-bye to people there.[28] I wish he would accept a post here with the President.[29] I quite agree with you that not to have any work will not be good for him.

I am feeling well. I am going to England on the 7th of next month. Indu[30] will probably accompany me.

[Jawaharlal Nehru]

---

26. Letter to the Governor of West Bengal.
27. Sanjay Gandhi.
28. Appointed Ambassador to the USSR in 1961, Subimal Dutt, as his biographer writes, was a "broken man" after the death of his only son, aged 19, in June 1962, and returned to India in September 1962 without completing his term. Amit Das Gupta, *Serving India. A Political Biography of Subimal Dutt (1903-1992), India's Longest Serving Foreign Secretary* (New Delhi: Manohar, 2017).
29. Dutt was appointed Secretary to President S. Radhakrishnan in May 1963.
30. Indira Gandhi.

453. To Archibald Macleish: Thanking for Gift of Book[31]

August 15, 1962

Dear Mr Macleish,

A few days ago, Professor Amiya Chakravarty[32] came to see me and he gave me your book *J.B.*,[33] which you have generously inscribed for me. I am very grateful to you for this very welcome gift which I shall no doubt enjoy reading. I have not read the book yet but, from the brief account of it which I have seen, it deals with a fascinating subject. It is reported in our old books that Buddha himself, in his youth, was troubled by this same question: why should there be this misery and conflict in the world if God is all-powerful and good; either He is not all-powerful or is not wholly good.

Again thanking you,

Yours sincerely,
J. Nehru

454. To Chandralekha Goswami: Congratulations on Examination Results[34]

August 16, 1962

My dear Chandralekha,

Thank you for your letter of 12th August. I am glad to learn that you have done so well in your Matriculation examination and I congratulate you upon it. I hope that your future educational career will be equally successful.

I cannot give you any advice from here about the future, but, I think, it is a good idea to study science. Science gains in importance every day. It is something more than mere passing examinations but of moulding one's mind so that we can understand the modern changing world.

You have my best wishes,

Yours affectionately,
[Jawaharlal Nehru]

31. Letter to an American poet and writer (1892-1982); address: Conway, Massachusetts, USA.
32. Amiya C. Chakravarty, Secretary to Rabindranath Tagore for several years, taught literature and comparative religion in India, England and the USA, Professor at Boston since 1953.
33. (Boston: Houghton Mifflin, 1958), a play based on Job, a character in Old Testament.
34. Letter; address: c/o Shri Hareswar Goswami, Bar-at-Law, Silpukhuri, Gauhati.

455. To Humayun Kabir: Support for Maulana Azad Family Members[35]

August 17, 1962

My dear Humayun,

I had a visit today from a young lady named Kishwar Jahan Begum. She said she was the "Bahu" of Maulana Azad's young sister.[36]

She said that she was very hard up and wanted help, partly for herself and partly for the education of her children.

She mentioned that she wanted to send two of her boys to the Jamia Millia. I told her that if they were admitted, I would arrange to pay their expenses there. I further said that I could pay for the education of her other and younger children.

I do not know what more can be done. I should like your advice in the matter. I do not know anything about this young lady. Apparently she lives in Calcutta. She is now in Delhi.

Her address is:

c/o Shri Mohammed Shakeel,

861, Sheesh Mahal, Bahadurgarh Road,

Delhi-6.

Yours sincerely,
[Jawaharlal Nehru]

456. To R.M. Ranade: Errors in *Discovery of India*[37]

August 18, 1962

Dear Shri Ranade,

Thank you for your letter about some incorrect references in *The Discovery of India*. I shall try to have some corrections made when a new edition comes out. It is rather difficult, however, to do so unless the whole thing is re-set.

Yours sincerely,
[Jawaharlal Nehru]

---

35. Letter to Minister of Scientific Research and Cultural Affairs.
36. Probably Hanifa, poetic name "Abroo," died 1943; youngest of Maulana Azad's three sisters, but older than him; her first marriage was with Ahmad Ibrahim of Calcutta, after whose death she got married to Wajid Ali Khan of Bhopal. Abdul Qavi Desnavi, *Hayat-e-Abul Kalam Azad* (Delhi: Modern Publishing House, 2000).
37. Letter; address: 16 Topkhana Gali No. 1, Indore City. NMML, JN Master File.

457. Royalties on Publications[38]

[Note, 20 August 1962, from N.K. Seshan, Private Secretary, begins]

We had written to Mr Max Reinhardt[39] that he might continue to give royalty on his [sic][40] *Autobiography* to Miss Tunnard,[41] but we asked him to remit to India royalties on PM's new books.

We have received a cheque for £300 from him being royalty on the paperback edition published in India.[42]

We may ask Max Reinhardt to remit the royalty on Mrs Norman's book[43] also to PM direct.

Seshan
20-8-1962

PM

[Note, 20 August 1962, from N.K. Seshan, Private Secretary, ends]

[Note, 20 August 1962, by Nehru for N.K. Seshan, begins]

I agree with what you have written. But I do not understand about Mrs Norman's book. Which book is it? I did not know that her book had been published. Are these royalties to be shared between her and me?

If there is any doubt, then the matter may be decided when I go to London, as Mrs Norman will be meeting me there.

J. Nehru
20-8-1962

Shri Seshan

[Note, 20 August 1962, by Nehru for N.K. Seshan, ends]

---

38. Noting. NMML, JN Master File.
39. British publisher.
40. Implying Nehru.
41. Bridget Tunnard, administrative secretary of the India League in London until 1971; worked with V.K. Krishna Menon.
42. See item 442.
43. See below, in this item, Note, 22 August 1962, by N.K. Seshan.

[Note, 22 August 1962, by N.K. Seshan, begins]

Mrs Norman's book referred to is *Nehru Reader*.[44] This book has not yet come out, but Bodley Head are making arrangements for publishing the UK edition. PM has agreed with Mrs Norman to share the royalty on this book equally between her and PM.

PM's share of the advance royalty on the UK edition will amount to £170.

Seshan
22-8-1962

[Note, 22 August 1962, by N.K. Seshan, ends]

458. To Gerald Iles: Animal Rights at Commonwealth Conference[45]

August 21, 1962

Dear Mr Iles,

Your letter of the 11th June and your very attractive book reached me two or three days ago. I presume they came by ocean mail and hence the delay.

Thank you for sending me your book *At Home in the Zoo*.[46] I have looked through the pictures and found many of them rather fascinating. I hope to read it when I have a little more time at my disposal.

I agree with you that animals deserve a Bill of Rights. You will appreciate, however, that our primary concern in India is to remove the poverty and unhappiness of human beings here.

I doubt if the Commonwealth Prime Ministers' Conference will care to consider any Bill of Rights for animals. The Conference will be tied up with many problems on its agenda and will have no time for anything else. Also, I fear that any such proposal will be considered frivolous by the members of the Conference. If, however, such a proposal is made by Mr Diefenbaker[47] or anyone else, I shall be glad to support it.

---

44. See item 445.
45. Letter to naturalist and curator of the Belle Vue Zoo in Manchester until 1957, whereafter he moved to Canada; address: 46 Windsor Avenue, Westmount, Montreal 6. PMO, File No. 31(123)/61-68-PMS, Sr. No. 29-A.
46. (London: W.H. Allen, 1960).
47. John Diefenbaker, the Prime Minister of Canada.

The subject interests me and I shall be glad if you could send me your ideas in regard to it.[48]

Yours sincerely,
Jawaharlal Nehru

459. To Hari Ram: Becoming Patron of Societies[49]

August 21, 1962

Dear Shri Hari Ram,

I have your letter of August 20. I am sorry I am unable to become a patron of your society. I do not like to associate myself with a number of societies as patron or in any other capacity. It is only when I can effectively work for a society that I associate myself with it.

Apart from this, I do not know what your society stands for. Human reforms are of many kinds. Of course, we want reforms, but what they should be is another matter.

Yours sincerely,
[Jawaharlal Nehru]

460. To Peter Light: Democracy and Satyagraha[50]

August 23, 1962

Dear Mr Light,

I have received your letter of June 20. This has taken a long time to reach me as, probably, it came by ocean mail and not by air mail.

I cannot answer you at any length. Every policy that is pursued depends upon certain principles, certain conditions and the receptivity of the people to live up to that policy. The principles of satyagraha, excellent as they are, will depend on the understanding of masses of people and their capacity for action in accordance with them. When India is threatened militarily either by Pakistan

---

48. For Nehru's views on the need for care and welfare of animals, see his address to the Indian Board for Wildlife, 15 February 1958, SWJN/SS/41/pp. 870-872.
49. Letter to the Secretary-General of the Human Reform Society, Manavta Bhavan, 1 Gurdwara Road, Lucknow.
50. Letter; address: 2868, W. 3rd Avenue, Vancouver 8, B.C. PMO, File No. 2(285)/58-64-PMS, Volume I, Sr. No. 47-A. Also available in the JN Collection.

or by China, as she is at present, I do not know of any practical method to stop that threat from becoming effective except by military means. The application of satyagraha to foreign invasion is an extension of the doctrine which has not been fully worked out in practice and is difficult to achieve.

In a democracy, the leaders cannot go too far beyond the understanding of the people; otherwise they would be pushed out and others would become the leaders.

Yours sincerely,
Jawaharlal Nehru

461. To Kusum Thakore: Travelling in India and Abroad[51]

August 23, 1962

Dear Dr Kusum Thakore,

I have your letter of the 21st August. You ask me in it to tell you to what Provinces of India and countries of the world you should go. I am afraid I cannot give you an answer. To me all Provinces or States of India are alike, and you can go to all or any of them.

The countries of the world stand on a different footing, and they are very varied. Most of them are at present facing considerable difficulties. I would suggest that you should only go to such countries as invite you and where you expect a welcome. Your going without such an invitation and a welcome may be fruitless.

I doubt if Shri Humayun Kabir[52] will be able to do much in this matter.

Yours sincerely,
[Jawaharlal Nehru]

462. To Badri Prasad: Advice on Career[53]

August 25, 1962

Dear Badri Prasadji,

I have your letter of the 22nd August. I am glad to learn of your success in London University, and, more particularly, of your determination for facing

51. Letter; address: Pestanji Villa, Fateh Gunj, Baroda 2.
52. Minister of Scientific Research and Cultural Affairs.
53. Letter; address: 12/A Chandi Prasad Lane, Jogsar, Bhagalpur.

the difficulties that stood in your way. I am returning the letter of Sir Sydney Caine[54] you sent me.

As you are employed at present, I suggest that you should hold on to that employment and also search for a more suitable post. This, presumably, can only be in the educational line in some college or university. I cannot be of direct help to you in this matter. If at any time, I can help I shall be glad to do so.

Yours sincerely,
Jawaharlal Nehru

463. To K.M. Cariappa: Fixing Appointment[55]

August 25, 1962
My dear Cariappa,
I have your letter of the 20th August together with its enclosures which I have read with interest. I am returning these enclosures to you as you would, presumably, like to keep them.

I am leaving Delhi for England on the 7th September for the Commonwealth Prime Ministers' Conference. I shall be heavily occupied during the last day or two here before my departure. These would also be the last two days of the Parliament Session. However, I shall try to meet you for a few minutes, probably on the 6th.

Yours sincerely,
[Jawaharlal Nehru]

464. To Mahendra Pratap: Difference of Opinion is not Opposition[56]

August 29, 1962
Dear Raja Sahib,
I have your letter of the 28th August.

I do not know why you imagine that I have opposed you for the last 35 years. It is true that I do not agree with you in some matters, but that is no

---

54. Director, London School of Economics, 1957-1967.
55. Letter to the former Chief of Army Staff; address: The Roshanara, Mercara, Coorg.
56. Letter to former Lok Sabha MP, Independent, 1957-1962; address: Rajpur, Dehradun. NAI, Raja Mahendra Pratap Papers, File No. 207. Also available in the JN Collection. For a previous reference to him, see SWJN/SS/74/item 59, fn 154.

reason why I should oppose you. We have different views. Each is entitled to his own view.

Yours sincerely,
Jawaharlal Nehru

465. Knight Templars of Malta[57]

Baron Frary von Blomberg[58] came to see me a few days ago. Subsequently he saw me again and brought Master Kirpal Singhji[59] also to see me and told me that he had made arrangements to take Kirpal Singhji to various countries. He is apparently a person much revered by many people in Delhi as well as abroad and to my surprise he has been made a Grandmaster or something of the kind of the Knight Templars of Malta.

2. His visit abroad does not require any arrangements from us. But I think it would be desirable to inform our Missions abroad in the countries mentioned that he is going there at the instance of some prominent persons from abroad on a spiritual mission. No particular steps need be taken in regard to him but if necessity arises, the usual courtesies might be shown to him.

57. Note, 30 August 1962, for R.K. Nehru, the Secretary General at the MEA.
58. 1904-1983, formerly William Frary, a Boston publicity agent, before his adoption in 1933 by Baroness Adelheid Marie von Blomberg of Germany; on the board of International Council for Christian Leadership; associated with the Order of Saint John of Jerusalem, Knights of Malta; initiated into "the Science of the Soul" by Sant Kirpal Singh, an Indian spiritual leader, during the latter's 1955 US tour; secretary, and later co-president of the World Fellowship of Religions. Link http://www.hampton.lib.nh.us/hampton/biog/baronvonblomberg.htm accessed on 21 August 2018; and George Arnsby Jones, *The Harvest Is Rich. The Mission of Kirpal Singh* (New York: Pageant Press, Inc., 1965), p. 42.
59. 1894-1974, founded Ruhani Satsang (college of spirituality) in 1951; founder-president, World Fellowship of Religions for several years; conferred the Order of Saint John of Jerusalem, Knights of Malta, in New Delhi on 2 September 1962. George Arnsby Jones, *The Harvest Is Rich. The Mission of Kirpal Singh* (New York: Pageant Press, Inc., 1965), p. III; and *The Times of India*, 3 September 1962.

466. To Raja Hutheesing: Harsha's Accident[60]

August 31, 1962

My dear Raja,

Your letter of the 29th. Thank you for telling me of the development in regard to the case about Harsha's[61] accident. It does seem to me that the enquiry is being needlessly prolonged. From all the facts that have been told me, it is a straightforward case.

You know my opinion of Karaka.[62]

I do not know what I can do in the matter. I suppose that, having regard to the evidence, the Coroner can only come to one decision. We should not worry much about the extension of the time.

Yours affectionately,
[Jawaharlal Nehru]

467. To Linda J. Ryan: Educating Children[63]

September 2, 1962

Dear Miss Ryan,

I must thank you for your letter of June 11th, together with writings of children. I have read many of these poems and other writings with pleasure, and I should like you to give my congratulations and good wishes to the children.

It is evident that you are teaching the children in your class in the right way so as to bring out their creativeness and hope in the future.

With all good wishes to you,

Yours sincerely,
[Jawaharlal Nehru]

---

60. Letter to brother-in-law (husband of Nehru's sister Krishna); address: 20 Carmichael Road, Bombay-26.
61. Son of Raja and Krishna Hutheesing.
62. Probably D.F. Karaka, editor of *Current*, a weekly published from Bombay.
63. Letter; address: 3232 University Avenue, Los Angeles 7, California.

468. To Chandra Gupta Vidyalankar: Rajendra Prasad Commemoration Volume[64]

September 5, 1962

Dear Shri Chandra Gupta,

I have your letter of the 4th September. Dr Rajendra Prasad was not only the first President of the Indian Republic, but otherwise also a very great man, and I have the greatest respect and regard for him. I regret, however, that it is not possible for me to write anything worthwhile for your Commemoration Volume. I am overburdened with work with which I can hardly keep pace.

Yours sincerely,
[Jawaharlal Nehru]

469. To Pyarelal Nayar: Inviting West to India[65]

September 7, 1962

My dear Pyarelal,

I had referred your letter about an invitation to Mr West[66] to be our guest to our Finance Minister.[67] He has made it clear that he cannot meet any foreign exchange liability. But if there is no such foreign exchange charge, we can certainly invite Mr West to come to India and be our guest here.

Yours sincerely,
Jawaharlal Nehru

---

64. Letter to the Convener of the Rajendra Prasad Commemoration Volume Committee; address: 4 Pataudi House, New Delhi.
65. Letter to Mahatma Gandhi's secretary and author of books on Mahatma Gandhi; address: Theatre Communication Building, New Delhi. PMO, File No. 2(114)/56-66-PMS, Sr. No. 80-A.
66. Albert H. West, a businessman from Johannesburg who became a close associate of Mahatma Gandhi in South Africa; gave up his business and managed the weekly *Indian Opinion* from 1904 for more than fourteen years, until Manilal, Mahatma Gandhi's son, took over; became a member of the Phoenix Settlement; visited India in 1963 at the invitation of the GOI. Link http://www.gandhiashramsevagram.org/gandhi-articles/in-the-early-days-with-gandhi.php accessed on 21 August 2018.
67. Morarji Desai.

470. To K. Karuna: Translating *Discovery of India* into Thai[68]

12th September, 1962

Dear Shri Karuna,

Your letter of September 6th has reached me in London.[69] I remember well your writing to me more than twenty years ago while you were a student at Santiniketan.[70]

You can certainly translate into the Thai language my book *Discovery of India*.

With all good wishes.

Yours sincerely,
J. Nehru

---

68. Letter to the Thai translator of his books; address: No. 599, See Yaek Prannok, Dhonburi via Bangkok, Thailand. Sent from London. NMML, JN Master File.
69. Appendix 61.
70. Probably this was the very correspondent whose letter Nehru had referred to in *The Discovery of India*, first published in 1946. Nehru wrote:

    "Some years ago I had a letter from a Thai (Siamese) student who had come to Tagore's Santiniketan and was returning to Thailand. He wrote: 'I always consider myself exceptionally fortunate in being able to come to this great and ancient land of Aryavarta and to pay my humble homage at the feet of grandmother India in whose affectionate arms my mother country was so lovingly brought up and taught to appreciate and love what was sublime and beautiful in culture and religion.' This may not be typical, but it does convey some idea of the general feeling towards India which, though vague and overladen with much else, still continues in many of the countries of South-East Asia." *The Discovery of India* (New Delhi: Jawaharlal Nehru Memorial Fund/OUP, 1982), p. 209.

    The letter is dated 7 September 1941 and the correspondent's name is given as "S. Karuna," see SWJN/FS/11/pp. 692-693.

VI. APPENDICES

1. A Short Story by G.D. Khosla[1]
[Refer to item 86]

THE SNAKE – A FABLE FOR GROWN-UPS
By G. D. Khosla

Once upon a time there was a nice little, innocent little, harmless little reptile, and because he was nice and innocent and harmless, they named him Universal Friend. In the course of time the reptile grew big and strong and was able to crawl on his own belly. He left his home and travelled to far off lands, going beyond the seven waters to see things for himself and learn new tricks.

Well, he saw and learnt quite a few things, and when he returned home after some years, he opened a shop and announced that he would sell advice to anyone who was in trouble and talk him out of it. For a long time nobody came to buy his advice because they said his reptilian head was quite, quite empty.

So Universal Friend went to his friends and told them a long tale of woe, saying that no one ever came to his shop, and very soon, the wolf would start prowling in front of his door. He told such a pitiable story that they promised to help him spoon-feed him. They also told him to find a handsome mate for himself as that, they said, winking broadly, always helps.

* * *

Well, Universal Friend found a mate whose ancestry was somewhat abnormal, but who had the right color and shape and what is very very important she was willing to play. Indeed her name was Playful One. So, Playful One played her little games, and with the help of her friends and well-wishers, things soon took a turn for the better. People began to buy Universal Friend's advice, food began to come in and the prowling wolf was driven a long distance away from the door.

But the reptile and his mate were not happy. They knew that their friends made fun of them behind their back. They said Playful One played for too much and Universal Friend had grown several horns on his head. The little one in their home used to cry and have tantrums because whenever he went out to play, the other little reptiles called him half and half and half which is even worse than

---

1. Published in *The Sunday Tribune Magazine*, 29 April 1962, pp. I and III.

710

being called half and half. This upset him very much, indeed, though it was quite true for he was part snake, part lizard and part reptile of an exotic breed.

All these taunts and jibes were hard to bear, but most of all Universal Friend and Playful One were oppressed by the fact that they were classed as snakes and had to crawl on the ground and prostrate themselves before their masters and whine to the tune of their pipes. They wanted to become Master and Mistress themselves.

* * *

Now, it was all very well for Universal Friend to have this kind of wish and nurse it for many years, but what he wished for didn't grow on the tree in his garden. Everybody still looked upon him as a nice and harmless sort of reptile without any guts or sting or, indeed, anything at all and the Powers That Be said that though they quite liked his reptilian ways, he would really be no use as Master and would never be able to play the pipe properly, so they left him to crawl and whine.

But Playful One was consumed with ambition and jealousy. She did not want her mate to go on crawling for the rest of his life and hers. She wanted to taste the joy of being called Mistress and receiving homage from other reptiles. So she began to play more games and show the green light to the people who mattered. She smiled and wheedled and cajoled and was ready to do anything yes anything at all.

But all this was of no avail and the Masters turned a blind eye to all her capers. And this made Playful One very very angry. "If I can't be Mistress, at least, I must have my revenge." She said, and told her mate to do something.

"But what can I do?" he moaned. "The Masters have all the pipes and when they play on them, I have to cringe and crawl."

* * *

So Playful One waited till she saw that Big Master was preparing to pack up his pipes and go away. "Now is our golden opportunity," she told her mate. "You have always been the harmless, the useless Universal Friend Snake, but here is some poison. Put it in your fangs and go and bite Big Master. I hate him. Once he tried to play with me and nearly tilted me on my back."

"Oh", said Snake "I thought it was you who tried to play with him. But never mind, whether he nearly tilted you or you tilted yourself doesn't matter now. The fact remains that I don't particularly like him. He makes me feel a worm, and now that he is packing up his pipes, I can safely use my fangs on him."

But even so, Universal Friend Snake was afraid, because right inside him he was a coward. He had not the guts to act alone. He wanted the help and moral support of other reptiles who, like him, had to cringe and crawl. So he called them and gave them a pep talk. There were quite a few of them who stank to high heaven with the filth in which they had always wallowed. They hated Big Master because every time he passed near them, he put his handkerchief to his nose. So they said: "Yes it would be a good thing if Universal Friend bit Big Master who has always been telling us to clean ourselves. We don't want to be clean. Down with Big Master."

* * *

Alas, what you plan and what you expect and hope for doesn't always come to pass, and the hopes especially of the crawling and cringing reptiles are seldom realised. And so it was in this case. The poison with which Universal Friend filled his mouth, spilled out and many of his fellow reptiles were stained and smeared with it.

They turned upon him, they abused him and denounced him for a mean and malicious busy body who had spoilt their chances of becoming friends with the new Big Master. Snake had upset their calculation and brought unmerited odium upon them.

Seeing all this Big Master had a good laugh and then he felt sorry for Universal Friend who was only a poor little reptile with horns on his head and nothing inside it.

The moral as Aesop would say, is: Don't if you are a reptile aspire to be Master and don't let your playful mate get out of hand.

2. From Ung Van Khiem: India should be objective in Vietnam[2]
[Refer to item 435]

June 25, 1962

Excellency,

I have the honour to convey to Your Excellency copy of my note of June 20, 1962, to the Co-Chairmen of the 1954 Geneva Conference on Indo-China, about

---

2. Letter from the Foreign Minister of the Democratic Republic of Viet Nam. Sent from Hanoi. MEA, File No. SI/106(1)/62, Vol. VI, pp. 175-176/Corr.

the special report of June 2nd, 1962, submitted to the Co-Chairmen by the Indian and Canadian delegates to the International Commission for Supervision and Control in Vietnam. Enclosed therewith are the June 4, 1962 Declaration of the Government of the Democratic Republic of Viet Nam and the letter from General Vo Nguyen Giap, Commander-in-Chief of the People's Army of Viet Nam, to the Chairman of the International Commission for Supervision and Control in Viet Nam about the same special report.

In the above mentioned documents, the views of the Government of the Democratic Republic of Viet Nam on the present dangerous situation in South Viet Nam and on the June 2nd, 1962 special report of the Indian and Canadian delegates to the International Commission for Supervision and Control in Viet Nam have been clearly expounded.

The Government of the Democratic Republic of Viet Nam hopes that the Government of the Republic of India will study again the situation of the implementation of the Geneva Agreements in South Viet Nam over the past eight years and come to an assessment conform [sic] to the actual state of affairs in this area, and that proceeding from such objective appraisal, Your Excellency's Government will issue necessary instructions to its delegation to the International Commission for Supervision and Control in Viet Nam to respect the truth in South Viet Nam, and to act in accordance with the spirit and the letter of the Geneva Agreements, as well as the attribution and tasks of the International Commission.

I take this opportunity to renew to Your Excellency the assurances of my highest consideration.

Minister for Foreign Affairs
of the Democratic Republic of Viet-Nam
Ung Van Khiem

3. From B.P. Chaliha: Assam Oil Royalty[3]
[Refer to item 137]

July 17, 1962

My dear Prime Minister,
Thank you for your two letters of the 27th June, 1962, regarding the difference of opinion between the Mines and Fuel Ministry and the State Government on

3. Letter from the Chief Minister of Assam. PMO, File No. 17(490)/62-70-PM, Sr. No. 30-A.

the question of oil royalty.[4] We have considered this matter very carefully and we feel that the legal and constitutional issues arising out of the action of the Mines and Fuel Ministry necessitate, in any case, a reference to the Supreme Court for its advisory opinion so that the nature and extent of States' rights on this extremely important question are clearly defined. Alternatively, the position taken by the State Government to the effect that the quantum and rate of royalty can only be fixed by or with the concurrence of the State Government, should be accepted. A reference to the Supreme Court or acceptance of the latter alternative is, in our view, essential in order that the differences of opinion that have arisen in the case of the Supplemental OIL[5] agreement do not recur in other agreements for oil exploration. We would accordingly suggest that in case State Government's stand is not accepted a reference to the Supreme Court for its advice may be made and that, for this purpose, an agreed draft may be prepared by the Ministry and the State Government, as expeditiously as possible. We would further request that if any question of an agreement arises, before the Supreme Court's opinion is known, concurrence of the State Government is taken before such agreement is finalised.

We agree, at the same time, however, that in the event of a reference to the Supreme Court, its disposal and the consequential arrangements may take considerable time and it would not be desirable to hold up oil exploration. For this interim period we accept your suggestion that the Union Finance Minister, Shri Morarji Desai, should decide the rate and basis of royalty that the State would be entitled to receive from Oil India Limited, such decision being implemented either by consequential modification of the Supplemental Agreement or through such other means as may be possible.

With regards,

Yours sincerely,
Bimalaprosad Chaliha

4. See SWJN/SS/77/items 184-185.
5. Oil India Limited.

4. From Prem Nath Bazaz: State and Status of Kashmir[6]

[Refer to item 124]

July 18, 1962

My dear Panditji,

I have to thank you for your letter of the 6th instant and am glad to learn that you read my long letter containing impressions of my Kashmir tour with interest.[7] I do not know whether you have had leisure to consider the points raised by me and if you contemplate taking any action to remove the genuine grievances of the Kashmir people; but as I deem it essential for the building of a democratic structure in the State that measures are adopted to end frustration and demoralisation which have, in my opinion, overwhelmed the people, I take once again the liberty of addressing a letter to you.

That the Kashmir Government is earnest in its endeavours to improve the wretched condition of the poverty-stricken and backward classes and to reconstruct the economic and social life of the people on the whole, only those can doubt whose minds are closed. I confess my views have undergone a change in certain respects after my recent visit to the valley. No impartial critic can deny that in its efforts the Government had already achieved an appreciable success. At the same time, however, it cannot escape the eye of a keen observer that in implementing the plans of development the Government is not receiving full cooperation of the people and therefore the results are not commensurate with the endeavours made or the money spent on the welfare projects.

I do not hesitate to admit that it is easy to blame the authorities, as is being commonly done in Kashmir, for their sins of omission and commission; it is easier still to find fault with everything that the Government does. But no fair-minded person can help feeling that the Kashmir Government is functioning under serious handicaps mostly psychological in nature, and its policies and actions can justly be judged only by keeping this fact constantly in view.

Wherever I went in the valley I found that despite the seeming tranquillity people are passing through a period of nerve-racking tension and vague uncertainty which appears to have become interminable, with the result that normalcy in the real sense does not return and no smooth working is possible in different spheres of social life; there is little likelihood of national institutions being fostered and grown in the country so long as the present conditions last.

---

6. Letter from a former associate of Shaikh Abdullah. Sent from F/8, Hauz Khas Enclave, New Delhi -16.
7. Prem Nath Bazaz's letter and Nehru's reply of 6 July 1962 have not been traced.

The main cause of vexation alike for the Government and the people is the unresolved accession issue. On the surface it seems to be a past story as some of the ruling party men publicly assert and want the world to believe, but I discovered to my dismay during the course of my close study that there is hardly a person in the State, at any rate among the politically conscious sections, who is not perturbed by its existence. Despite what wishful thinkers may say, the State politics is dominated by this question and there is no aspect of life in Kashmir which is not affected by it. It would be courting self-deception to conceal this fact and dangerous to run away from it.

I do not want to dwell at length upon the many-sided evil which the prolongation of the accession issue produces; it will make this letter too long. Suffice it to say that the mutual suspicions which are a marked characteristic of life in Kashmir are an unwholesome outcome of the issue. If the Hindus distrust the Muslims and vice versa, it is because of it; if the Kashmiris consider themselves as something different from the Indians, the reason is the unsolved accession dispute; and if the Government is compelled to curtail civil liberties or resort to repressive methods in dealing with the opponents, the reason is to be sought nowhere else but in the dispute. Bakhshi Ghulam Mohammed's[8] insistence on maintaining the separate identity of Kashmir despite his undoubted desire for national integration may be easily traced to it. As a matter of fact, the accession dispute is proving a bane of progress in the State.

It is therefore difficult to believe that there can be any real advancement in Kashmir until somehow or other the accession dispute is ended or otherwise dealt with.

Unfortunately, it is becoming increasingly clear that the Security Council has failed to produce any formula acceptable to India and Pakistan which could settle the issue. Nor does it appear to be feasible that direct negotiations or talks between the two countries can bring forth any better result because both the parties have adopted positions mutually exclusive with no common ground on which to base an agreement.

Pondering over this situation while in Kashmir, I arrived at the conclusion that the issue can be disposed of, if at all, by the Kashmiris themselves. My discussions and studies in the valley have confirmed me in this finding. I have already told you that the Kashmiris realise that they are making steady progress economically. But they feel sore primarily on account of the loss of fundamental rights and civil liberties and the prevalence of hooligan elements in public life. The suffocating political atmosphere in the country is making them desperate. If this by no means unfounded grievance could be redressed, I think it would

8. Prime Minister of Jammu and Kashmir from 1953.

not be long before normalcy could be restored and people made happy and cooperative in their attitude.

Now I must frankly state that the Kashmir Government is in no mood to accede to the wishes of the people in this respect; at least some of the more powerful members in the State Cabinet believe that doing so would afford latitude to the hostile elements to indulge in subversive activities thereby endangering the security of the State and stability of the country. This policy has therefore been tenaciously pursued for the past fifteen years and the day does not seem near when it may be changed. It is not realised that through the enforcement of this policy the Government is progressively alienating the sympathies of the people and generating tremendous ill-will against India though outwardly it may appear that there is general satisfaction and nothing to worry about.

Every Indian patriot ardently desires the accession issue to be shelved and forgotten, especially by the Kashmiris. The State people can be expected to forget it only when they are satisfied with the doings of the present regime and are reasonably happy. So far as the economic and social life of the Kashmiris is concerned I have no doubt they are grateful to India for the little progress they have made; they hope to be more prosperous in the near future; but political persecution and suppression of free opinion coupled with harassment by goonda elements is, besides making them sullen and resentful, neutralising the good effects of the benevolent deeds of the Union Government. Whenever a talk of economic welfare plans follows political polemics even many sensible Kashmiris would stridently deny that there has been any improvement in the wretched condition of the masses. The wounds inflicted by the repressive policy remind the Kashmiris that their future is yet unsettled and they begin hopefully to look towards Pakistan. Thus the purpose of the policy of repression is defeated and instead of putting unfriendly elements under check and control the Government is only strengthening hostility and subversion in the State. Far from being forgotten, the accession issue remains fresh in the minds of the people creating tension, uncertainty and unhappiness.

Thus by adopting and doggedly pursuing this policy we are caught in a vicious circle.

As is well known, Kashmir has produced intellectual stalwarts in bygone days. One of our great aspirations has been to resurrect a cultural atmosphere enabling local artists to freely indulge in acts of creativity. But frightened people cannot be mentally alert or intellectually fertile. It is not surprising that since 1947 the Kashmiris have contributed almost nothing to any branch of literature which may be considered original or outstanding. Kashmiri has been graciously recognised as one of the national languages in the Indian Constitution but has the extraordinary grant of the honoured place improved its literary importance in any way? Kashmir, the ancient seat of learning, is still passing through the deep shadows of medieval darkness when despots enchaining the souls of the people snapped their links with the cultural past.

The main objective of the national struggle in Kashmir has been the establishment of a democratic set-up through which people can expect social justice and cultural development which was denied to them for centuries. We are little interested in the issue of affiliation of our homeland to this or that country. History has thrust the accession dispute on us against our will and we intensely desire to get rid of it as early as we can.

I fully understand that the problem is ticklish and the situation in the valley extremely delicate. It is easy to sermonise and gratuitously offer advice to the Government which is functioning under obvious handicaps. But if we are determined that Kashmir should march hand in hand with the rest of the country in building a democratic society, the vicious circle shall have to be broken; courage has to be taken in both hands to face the grave situation and remedy it.

For fifteen years a certain definitive policy has been unswervingly pursued in the hope that the accession issue, if not solved, will go to the background, normalcy will return and civil liberties of the people restored. More than a score arbitrary laws (Enemy Agents Act, Security Act, Preventive Detention Act etc.), Rules and Notifications peculiar to Kashmir and operating nowhere else in India, have been in force during this period, arming the executive with unlimited powers to indiscriminately torture people and make them loyal to India. As has happened at all times and in all places governed by such draconian measures, innocent people have suffered along with the suspects, the former in a much larger number. Fifteen years is quite a long period to give a trial to a government policy. It is significant that not a single repressive enactment professedly promulgated to meet a national emergency has been withdrawn or amended to soften its rigours. In fact, fresh rules and orders are added every year to the old ones to fortify the policy. Only the other day (on July 5) a notification was issued declaring that the "Kashmir Government servants who are reasonably suspected to be engaged in subversive activities or associated with those engaged in subversive activities will be compulsorily retired from Government service." The notification seems to protect the security of the State. Nevertheless, it is an eloquent testimony that the repressive policy has failed to enlist the willing loyalty of the educated classes and the cooperation of the people. If anyone thinks that the time for liberalisation of the policy will come when Pakistan is out of the way, permit me to point out that in that case we shall have to wait till the Greek Calends.

I submit that it is time this barren policy is abandoned and the alternative of a liberal policy is given a trial. Let the Union Government be as generous and large-hearted politically as it has been in the economic field. I have no doubt in my mind that the change will produce better results. Now this can be done in another matter and if you desire me to submit suggestions and proposals for the purpose I can surely do so.

While on the subject of civil liberties I would like to reiterate my suggestion about an understanding with Sheikh Abdullah.[9] If it is true that he has been reconsidering the political situation in the State and there is a possibility of an agreement with him which may be honourable for all concerned and in no way anti-democratic, the opportunity should not be lost. In any case, there is no harm in permitting some suitable person to make an approach and find out the truth. If Sheikh Sahib remains irreconcilable and impervious to reason, which I hope he will not be, the matter will rest where it is. But I have sufficient and substantial reasons to believe that in the changed circumstances, he will not fail his people and will willingly offer his talents and labours for building a free democratic order in his homeland.

Restoration of civil liberties and free expression of opinion is, no doubt, of primary importance in gaining voluntary support of the people but I think other matters of lesser importance, lesser only by comparison, cannot be overlooked. In conducting the affairs of the State at all levels Rule of Law should have supremacy without which even the elementary stages of democratic life are not possible to establish. Not only should the members of the Government, dignitaries of the ruling party and high officials of the State without exception, be compelled to strictly follow the laws, rules and regulations in force, but the strong arm methods employed by unruly elements among the supporters of the National Conference with the connivance of their bosses should also be ruthlessly put down.

There is a general belief that elections in the State are rigged and the supervision of the Indian Election Commissioner has made no difference. When I was in Srinagar the means adopted by the ruling party to win a bye-election had assumed the proportions of a scandal. This impression needs to be removed.

With the mollification of the State people in general and all important elements in Kashmir politics in particular, I think the accession issue will cease to overwhelm the common mind and may be considered to have been virtually disposed of.

Indubitably, interested quarters will not give up their stand; nor can we shut up all mouths; some will continue to raise the known slogans. But when

---

9.   Prime Minister of Jammu and Kashmir until 1953, in detention at this time.

the preponderant majority of Kashmiris is happy and satisfied with nothing important to complain about, they will not be receptive to false cries and appeals to keep the accession issue alive will fall on deaf ears.

While discussing the question of denial of civil liberties with Bakhshi Ghulam Mohammed at his residence in Srinagar he vehemently held that in no case would he tolerate anyone in the State who supported accession of Kashmir to Pakistan. For such people, he added, there would be no liberty; they would be crushed. I rejoined politely that no democrat could relish this attitude of the head of the government. Rather than threaten any individual with the forfeiture of his liberty the better course would be to create such conditions in the State that pro-Pakistan elements will find little response to their subversive slogans and people will voluntarily refuse to hear them. Bakhshi Sahib ridiculed this view and contemptuously retorted that it was an utopian aim impossible to achieve. Nevertheless, I believe that after the failure of the repressive policy this course alone is indicated by wise statesmanship and I implore you to give it a trial.

In Kashmir, as outside the State, I met many honest and intelligent people shaking their heads in utter disbelief that the State Muslims would ever with conviction support India even after the reorientation of the Government policy on liberal lines. It is commonly held by the sceptics that the Muslims, guided by religious considerations, will under any circumstances desire Kashmir to accede to Pakistan. There is sufficient force in this argument and I do not want to underrate it. But depending on a past experience, I can confidently say that if proper measures are adopted for the achievement of the noble aim of influencing Muslim opinion in the right direction it is not impossible to do so.

Thirty years ago, we launched upon a similar adventure in Kashmir in July 1932 when we decided to secularise the State politics which had then come heavily under communal influences.

No one excepting Sheikh Abdullah and myself guessed that the Muslim Conference could be converted into a non-communal organisation. Do you remember the letter which both of us sent to you jointly in April 1936 informing you about our intentions and the difficulties we faced in pushing through our plans? You were the first distinguished public man to lend your robust support to the move and bless it.[10] Ironically, Bakhshi Ghulam Mohammed declared the idea as impractical and opposed it as harmful for the State Muslims when in

---

10. Nehru's reply to Shaikh Abdullah and Prem Nath Bazaz has not been traced in his papers. However, *The Hindustan Times* of 30 June 1936 had published the substance of Nehru's letter, see SWJN/FS/7/p. 308.

June 1938 the proposal came up for discussion before the working committee of the Muslim Conference. Of course he is now the staunch standard-bearer of Nationalism and cannot brook communalism, much less Muslim Communalism, in the State.

Seven years' patient and persistent labour ultimately bore fruit and on 10th June 1939 the Muslim Conference yielded to the call of Democracy when 173 delegates participating in the deliberations of the Special Session of the Conference voted the conversion of the organisation into a National body; barely 3 votes were recorded against the proposal.

I dare say we are confronted with a similar situation today. Relying on the experience gained by this unprecedented historical event let the Government of India shed the distrust of Kashmir Muslims and try to win them by liberalism when repression has proved unavailing and futile if not destructive and ruinous.

It would be the unique triumph of Democracy when Communalists are given fullest freedom to peacefully propagate their views but they find themselves completely ineffective. With fullest freedom of expression restored we shall have laid securely and well the foundations of Democracy in Kashmir. My proposals, it will be seen, are directed towards the fulfilment of that objective.

I have mentioned the other grievances of the people in the valley in my last letter, but I need not lay any stress on them here; for, though important in themselves, they lose weight in comparison with the grave issue of the fundamental rights. Besides, I think they are mostly born of the unsettled dispute about accession.

With the liberalisation of the Government policy as envisaged above I am very hopeful that the Kashmiris will offer unstinted cooperation for the implementation of the big economic projects and the money granted by the Centre will be most usefully spent. What is more, the shrivelled souls of the people will be liberated and enormous intellectual and spiritual forces released for the promotion of a cultural renaissance which is our greatest need.

Yours sincerely,
[Prem Nath Bazaz]

5. From P.V. Benjamin: On Retiring[11]

[Refer to item 233]

19th July 1962

My dear Sir,

May I take the liberty of writing this personal letter to you on the eve of my retirement from the Government of India as their Tuberculosis Adviser from 20th July, 1962, to thank you most sincerely for the very kind way in which you have treated me and for the encouragement you have continuously given me in carrying out my work? It was a great privilege for me to join the Government soon after independence and to contribute my mite for the control of tuberculosis in the formative years of the new Government. The happiest period of my work was from 1948 to 1957 when there was a good deal of enthusiasm to get things done and one could go forward in a spirit of adventure with the hope of whole-hearted support from Ministers and officials.

With respects,

Yours sincerely,
P.V. Benjamin

6. From Shriyans Prasad Jain[12]

[Refer to item 212]

When I had the privilege of meeting you soon after taking over the Presidentship of the Federation, I felt encouraged to approach you whenever I thought I had to invite your attention to problems of national importance. Lately a number of things have happened and some developments have taken place which have made it necessary for me to write this letter to you. A certain degree of slackness bordering on pessimism is pervading the economic atmosphere in the country at present, the like of which I at least do not recall having noticed ever since we attained independence. This sense of pessimism has its origin in a number of things. It is difficult to enumerate them in any order of importance, but some of them I venture to mention here:

---

11. Letter from the Tuberculosis Adviser to the GOI. PMO, File No. 28(81)/61-71-PMS, Sr. No. 15-A.
12. Letter, 20 July 1962, from the President of the Federation of Indian Chambers of Commerce and Industry, Federation House, New Delhi. Salutation and signature not available.

(1) Certain bottlenecks which have developed in our transport system and power projects.

(2) Uncertain and irregular supply and movement of coal.

(3) Uncertainties and difficulties about foreign exchange accentuated by the change in the attitude of the Aid India Club.

(4) Some of the important projects having shown weaknesses which are likely to take much more time to correct than was anticipated.

(5) A sense of helplessness that seems to be creeping over our administrative machinery in the face of these difficulties with the result that it has become next to impossible to obtain decisions from Government on any major issue.

2. Without going into the controversy as to who is responsible for the deterioration in the railway system today, particularly in relation to the movement of coal, the fact remains that some time back allotment of wagons for the movement of coal was cut by about 35% with the result that a large number of industries are made to face a situation which no one had anticipated. Although some improvement in the allotment has taken place in recent weeks, industries have still to work on hand-to-mouth basis. The main difficulty that the Railways point out is the lack of wagons and track capacity. Although we are now in the middle of the second year of the Third Plan, the coal raisings today are at about the level reached at the end of the Second Plan. Therefore, the burden on the transport capacity on account of movement of coal has not increased. If the Railways find themselves helpless in moving even this production, it is easy to imagine as to what will happen if the target at the end of the Third Plan, which is of the order of 100 million tonnes per year, is to be fully achieved. At present, only just about 60 million tonnes is being raised. Railways must, therefore, build up their capacity rapidly keeping in view the increasing demand that will be placed on them.

3. As to the question of wagon shortage, when some of the manufacturers offered to enter the field of wagon manufacture, they were told that enough capacity for this purpose already existed in this country. We also understand that those who are now in this field are not encouraged to increase production by working additional shifts. A little far-sight and forward planning would have saved us from the situation we find ourselves in today. Apart from this, on account of the professed inability of the Railways to carry more than a limited quantity of coal to the Western Region, it was decided that about 1.5 million tonnes of it per year would be carried by ships. In actual fact, only about 1 million tonnes is being carried at present because, on account of the condition of the Hooghly river, the ships cannot be fully loaded. They go almost half empty. To provide for additional vessels that are required to carry the remaining

50%, Government are giving foreign exchange to ship-owners to charter ships. This foreign exchange expenditure is of the order of Rs 1½ crores per year. With this amount we could buy two ships every year, only if Railways could load these half empty ships with coal at Vizag Port. Railways, however, are adamant that they cannot carry even 6 to 7 lakh tonnes of coal to Vizag.

4. Against the target of nearly 100 million tonnes of coal at the end of the Third Plan, as I have said above, we are now producing only about 60 million tonnes. It means that in the next 3½ years, the country has to increase the production by nearly 40 million tonnes. In order that this stupendous task is achieved, the present attitudes and policies have to undergo a radical change. The Coal Industry has been complaining that it is not being granted mining leases; it is being denied an appropriate price which is essential in view of the general rise in prices that is taking place and in view of the additional expenditure that is needed for opening up new mines and going deeper in the existing ones; that foreign exchange allocation is insufficient and uncertain and that power and transport for raising and transporting the additional production are just not available. Hints of nationalisation of this industry are bound to add to these uncertainties.

5. About power, the present crisis may be due to the fact that our targets have perhaps not taken into account the much faster rate at which demand for power increases in a developing economy than in some other sectors. But I do not know why those electricity undertakings, who possess long experience of generating electricity and who may be prepared to undertake to add to their capacity and even start new generating stations, and large consumers of power should not be allowed to set up power generating plants. Some of these plants could be set up right on the coalfield areas or near about them. I understand that a few such proposals are before Government for quite some time, but no decision on them has yet been taken. The same applies to the manufacture of equipment for the generation of power. Currently, all this has to be imported and our expenditure of foreign exchange on this count, already substantial, is bound to increase as our demand for power both hydel and thermal increases. And yet those industrial concerns which have programmes of manufacturing this equipment are not being encouraged to do so.

6. As regards the attitude of the Aid India Club, I know that I am on a somewhat more difficult ground than while dealing with other subjects. The adjournment of the last meeting of the Club without taking any definite decision was naturally a disappointment. What is even more disquieting is the fact that the foreign Press, which, by and large, has been friendly to India, of late has been adopting a rather critical note and aiding in spreading a rather pessimistic note about our developmental programmes. The general impression abroad

724

that India was making good use of the foreign aid that was given to her was one of our greatest assets. We seem to be drawing rather heavily on this asset. One of the reasons for this, apparently, is that our projects have not come up to the expectation and that quite a substantial amount of aid has been utilised not in building capital assets, but in the mere maintenance of the economy. Apart from what others think of our efforts and achievements, there cannot be any difference of opinion that what we receive by way of long-term borrowings or aid should be utilised solely for the purpose of strengthening the base of our economic structure and not on day-to-day consumption, and also that every effort should be made to see that all our projects are well planned and administered in a manner that does not leave anything to be desired. Proper management and efficiency are the crux of the matter, and, I think, you will agree with me that some of our projects have not been very conspicuous as far as these go. I do not say this in a spirit of criticism, but because I believe that these things have to be pointed out so that our enterprises improve their performance.

7. This leads me to the next point in the foregoing list. For example, we were to achieve a production of steel of 4.3 million tonnes at the end of the Second Plan. We actually succeeded in producing only 50% of it. I read in papers that the Planning Commission thinks that at the end of the Fourth Plan we must achieve a capacity of 18 million tonnes of finished steel. Today, we are producing just about 3 million tonnes. I do believe that this target of 18 million tonnes is a reasonable target looked at from the point of view of our requirements and needs. But I have my grave doubts if this target can be achieved only by the expansion of the existing capacity and adding one or two more steel plants. Here is a task, in my opinion, in which the resources in men and material of the whole nation have to be pooled together, and I suggest, if I may, that as long as production can be ensured and as long as there is the authority in the hands of Government to regulate this vital industry, there is everything in favour of taking a pragmatic approach and allowing the development of this and similar industries freely.

8. Some of the other important projects which were to go into production have also not yet been completed. All this places additional burdens on our scanty foreign exchange resources. To correct this position to the extent it lies in our power the Federation suggested some time back a rough plan of curtailing imports and providing the foreign exchange thus saved for the import of machine tools and capital equipment. This programme of our curtailing imports, if pursued with a degree of far-sight and discrimination, will help us to some extent in our present difficult situation. The recent ad hoc cut in imports is hardly the answer. We from the Federation have already offered to

the Ministry of Commerce and Industry our assistance in scrutinising the lists of our current imports with a view to examining as to which of them can be curtailed or eliminated entirely and also what steps should be taken to ensure their indigenous production. What is necessary is to see that the country is made more self-reliant in its programme of industrial development. Here again it strikes me that Government's policy does not seem to be clear or purposive. I have already mentioned the case of power generating equipment. Take the case of stainless steel and alloy tool and special steels. Year after year the country spends huge sums on importing these items. But the schemes for manufacturing the same are not approved. Similar is the case with the utilisation of by-products of refineries. There is inordinate delay and hesitation in sanctioning schemes for their use, with the result that this valuable resource is being wasted although it could be utilised in making raw materials for rubber, fertilisers and various other synthetic products. While we are one with Government's policy regarding expanding the scope of the public sector also in this field, we feel that non-utilisation of existing potential by the private sector leads to national waste. The entire field of oil exploration, oil refining and the use of its by-product is the one where radical re-thinking is called for.

9.   I venture to suggest in all humility that it is time now that concerted action is taken in all these matters and to take a fresh look at the various problems that beset us. The mood of slackness and pessimism that is pervading now may be a symptom, but it can also be a potent cause for further worsening of the situation. The spirit which was in evidence during the Second Five Year Plan has got to be revived both in the public and in the administrative machinery of Government. In this, I realise, everyone has to play a part. Our difficulty, however, is that while there are a large number of Committees and Councils where we are enabled to represent the viewpoint of the business community, the avenues where consultation could be close and constant are lacking. In recent months, there has been quite a lot of discussion within the Government on the current economic problems, but in none of these the business community has had a say. I beg to submit that we have some experience in the running of industries and business and that it will not only be to the good of the country as a whole if this experience is made use of in a greater degree, but it will also help in creating a better and more congenial atmosphere both in the country and outside.

10.   I and some of my colleagues will feel happy to be provided with an opportunity of meeting you and, if necessary, some of your Ministers along with you, to personally discuss these matters.

7. From K.D. Malaviya: Assam Oil Royalty[13]
[Refer to item 137]

July 22, 1962

My dear Jawaharlalji,

On coming here, I learnt that the Assam Government have refused to give prospecting license to the Oil & Natural Gas Commission also for carrying on its activities in areas adjacent to Rudrasagar. The reason, they say, is that unless the royalty rate is fixed according to their wishes, no prospecting license would be issued to O&NGC.

2. I did not know this yesterday. I thought that the dispute so far was confined only to the Oil India Limited in which the Government is a 50 percent partner. The situation now is that they have chosen to take this step which has settled issues from their point of view. This, I am afraid, has turned out to be a very serious matter. The Chief Minister of Assam[14] tries to keep on your right and so does Mr Fakhruddin.[15] The fact is that these gentlemen are adopting different attitudes at different levels and the whole thing appears to me most disgusting.

3. The oil exploration work in Assam now is completely paralysed and I do not know how far the Government of India will be justified in carrying on dilatory negotiations with the State Government which is bent upon defying the Constitution deliberately. For me it is an impossible situation. What are we now expected to do in the Ministry if Mr Chaliha does not want to have any relation with us. The O&NGC is naturally not willing to carry on any oil exploration in Assam because ultimately they will be blamed for the enormous expenditure which is involved in these dilatory and rebellious activities of the Assam Government. I am prepared to keep out of this if the Assam Government can be brought to a correct attitude of mind.

4. The refusal to grant prospecting license to Government of India is a challenge to the Constitution which, in my opinion, must not be taken lying down. Otherwise, the situation can become serious in many States. May I further submit for your consideration that the Cabinet Sub-Committee for Economic Affairs be asked by you to examine suitable constitutional amendments with a view to assure that atomic energy, steel, oil and public sector coal industries be kept completely under the control of the Central Government for at least 20 years

13. Letter from the Minister of Mines and Fuel. Sent from Dehradun. PMO, File No. 17(490)/62-70-PMS, Sr. No. 32-A
14. B.P. Chaliha.
15. Fakhruddin Ali Ahmed, Minister of Law and Finance in Assam.

without any claim to sub-surface rights by the State Governments. Of course, they will be entitled to certain payments in lieu of these minerals occurring in their States and for this either the word "royalty" may be retained for suitable explanations or even this word be changed for some more appropriate one.

5.   So far as the refusal of the Assam Government to give prospecting license to the O&NGC is concerned, a special meeting is being convened tomorrow to consider the matter in all its respects and to pass on its recommendations to the Government. The Commission will also prepare a report for the Lok Sabha in this connection which would be placed before the Parliament after getting your approval.

Yours affectionately,
Keshava Deva Malaviya

8. From Bishan Chander Seth[16]
[Refer to item 286]

23-7-1962

परम आदरणीय श्री नेहरु जी,

सादर अभिवादन,

आपने मेरे दिनांक 1.6.62 के पत्र का सविस्तार उत्तर 3.7.62 को देकर यथार्थ ही (आपके नेत्रों में संभवतः मेरे पत्र का यह उत्तर मात्र होगा) मेरे को गौरव बन्त किया, आपके पत्र ने सत्यता से मेरे भावों को परोक्ष मान्यता दी है। यह मेरे नहीं सारे भारत की राष्ट्र भाषा हिन्दी प्रिय जनता का सम्मान सूचक आपका लेख है। मैं मंसूरी गया था, अतः आज आने पर उत्तर प्रेषित करता हूँ विलम्ब हेतु क्षमा करें।

मैं इस निवेदन द्वारा पुनः याचना करना चाहता हूँ, ईश्वर हेतु मेरी विनय मान लीजिये। हिन्दी पक्ष वाले शीघ्र भविष्य में जो बावन्डर करने की नीति योजनायें बना रहे हैं, निम्न मान्यता से स्वतः समाप्त हो जावेगी।

सूर्य को दीपक दिखाने वाली उपमा के समान आपको संसार के इतिहास का संकेत करना मुझे अखरता है। पर विषय से सम्बन्धित होने से निवेदन है कि पिछली लड़ाई में जब पोलैण्ड पर जर्मन वालों ने अधिकार किया, लाखों पोलैण्ड वाले मर गये, पर अपने देश में विषमता की भाषा को स्थान लेने नहीं दिया।

ख़ेद आज जिसे हम हिन्दू कह रहे हैं उसमें आत्म सम्मान, गौरव एवं राष्ट्रीय अभिमान अनेकों कारणों से नष्ट हो चुका है। उसमें पोलैण्ड की मात्र भयंकर विरोध छोड़, छोटा

---

16. Letter from Lok Sabha MP of the Hindu Mahasabha. Sent from Ornaments Palace, Shahjahanpur, Uttar Pradesh.

विरोध करने की भी शक्ति नहीं। इस सत्य कमजोरी को मुसलमान, ईसाई अथवा विदेशी के समक्ष तो नहीं कह सकता, पर आप तो अपने ठहरे, अतः लिखता हूँ राष्ट्र भाषा हिन्दी बनाने हेतु जनता में प्रवृति एवं स्वाभिमान लाना भी आपका राष्ट्र प्रमुख होने से मैं प्रथम कर्तव्य मानता हूँ।

अतः इस विनय पत्र द्वारा अब मैं केवल आपसे इतना चाहता हूँ कि जो स्थिति इस समय राष्ट्र भाषा देव नागरी की है, उसी प्रकार चलने दीजिये, नया विधेयक न लाइये। ऐसा होने से 1965 के बाद राष्ट्र भाषा हिन्दी को लाने के पक्ष में बोलने का सम्बन्धी जनता को अवसर बना रहेगा, और फिर आपके पत्रानुसार समय से हिन्दी का प्रकाश होगा।

पर यदि आपने अंग्रेज़ी को 1965 के बाद भी चालू रखने हेतु नवीन विधान लाकर उस भावना को ही कुण्ठित करा दिया तो सत्यता से हिन्दू स्वतः उस भावना को पूर्ण करने के कर्तव्य को भूल जायेगा, जिसे आप भी नहीं चाहिते। अतः मेरी आपसे अनन्य विनय है कि इस समय नवीन विधेयक लाने के प्रयास को रोककर मेरा अथवा हिन्दी पक्षीय जनता का सम्मान करिये।

मुझे पूर्ण विश्वास है कि जिस आदर पूर्ण भावना से आपने मुझे उत्तर देकर सम्बोधित किया, उसे देखते हुए आप मेरी इस विन्य को निश्चय मान्यता देंगे।

अग्रिम धन्यवाद देते हुये,

आपका ही
बिशन चन्द्र सेठ

[Translation begins

23 July 1962

Most Respected Shri Nehruji,
Respectful regards,

You have accorded me great honour by replying in detail on 3.7.62 to my letter of 1.6.62 (in your eyes it would possibly be only a reply to my letter). Your letter has honestly accorded importance to my feelings. This is a statement which denotes respect not only for me but for all the lovers of Hindi the national language in India. I had gone to Mussoorie and so I am sending a reply on my return today. Please forgive the delay.

I wish to plead once again through this letter that you should agree to my request for God's sake. The group of Hindi lovers who are making plans to raise a hue and cry will probably give it up by this request being acceded to:

It is galling to me to be quoting examples from history to you because it is like holding a candle to the sun. But since it is related to the issue at hand, I wish to say that in the last War when the Germans had occupied Poland and millions of Poles died, the people there did not allow German to take the place of Polish.

It is a matter of regret that among those whom we call Hindu, dignity of the self and pride in the nation have almost been destroyed due to various reasons. There is no vestige of resistance left in them, let alone the capacity for terrible resistance as in the case of Poland but even for resistance on a small scale. I cannot point out this truth to Muslims, Christians or foreigners but you are after all one of us, therefore, I write that to make Hindi the national language, I consider that as the Prime Minister it is your foremost duty to imbue the people with dignity of the self and pride.

Therefore, through this humble letter now I only want that you should maintain the status quo of the Devanagari script. Please do not bring in a new Bill. By doing this, after 1965, the people will continue to have the opportunity to make Hindi the national language and Hindi's future will shine as your letter says.

However, if after 1965 you bring in a Bill to continue English, then surely you would have stifled that emotion and Hindus will themselves forget their duty to promote Hindi which you also do not wish. Therefore, it is my humble request that you should stop the attempt to bring in a new Bill and honour me and those favouring Hindi.

I am fully confident, looking to the manner in which you have addressed me in your reply, that you will definitely accede to my request.

Thanking you in advance,

Yours,
Bishan Chander Seth

Translation ends]

9. From Nath Pai and Others: Serious Developments on Borders[17]

[Refer to item 1]

July 24, 1962

Dear Panditji,

We believe that the situation in Ladakh has been dangerously deteriorating. You have yourself stated that it is serious and that we must be wide awake.

At least now nobody need misunderstand any longer what the Chinese are up to. Their encirclement moves have now been followed by use of arms against our posts on Indian soil. It seems the Chinese have now occupied areas which they did not even claim as late as 1960.

If it is harmful to exaggerate this danger we think it even more harmful to belittle it when matters have gone so far. The time has come for the whole nation to be "wide awake" and for the government to take the people into confidence.

We think that Parliament should be summoned immediately and therefore urge you to advise the President accordingly. This is necessary in order to demonstrate national unity in the hour of danger and to warn the Chinese government how grave a view the people of India take of their aggression and also how united we stand in our determination to resist their aggression.

Yours sincerely,
Nath Pai
Mukut Behari Lal[18]
Farid Ansari[19]

---

17. Letter from Nath Pai, PSP, Lok Sabha MP, and two other MPs; address used: Praja Socialist Party, Central Office, 18, Windsor Place, New Delhi. On 26 July 1962, it was marked "For favour of Publication, On the recent serious developments on the India-China Border. Letters exchanged between Nath Pai, Mukut Behari Lal and Farid Ansari, Members of Parliament, and the Prime Minister." NMML, Nath Pai Papers.
18. Mukut Behari Lal Bhargava, Congress, Lok Sabha MP.
19. PSP, Rajya Sabha MP.

10. From Hartley Shawcross: Invitation to Address American Bar Association Conference[20]
[Refer to items 344-345]

24th July 1962

Dear Prime Minister,

Will you allow me to commend to your sympathetic consideration the invitation which has been extended to you to make an inaugural address at the Conference which it is desired to hold in Delhi early next year on the theme of "World Peace Through Law".

As you will know, a Committee acting under the auspices of the American Bar Association and largely led by the personal enthusiasm of a Mr Rhyne, who was Chairman of the American Bar Association some years ago and at the time when the American Bar visited this country, has been organising a series of Regional Conferences to promote knowledge of the potentialities of international law in world society.

I must say, frankly, that the English Bar in general and I myself were extremely doubtful about the utility of these activities and we were at first inclined to think that this was just another of the woolly, although well-meaning projects to which the Americans so often enthusiastically devote themselves. Rather for this reason, I did not attend any of the first three Conferences. I was, however, invited to attend the fourth Regional Conference which was held in Europe and, having been Chairman of the Bar Council for a long time, felt that it might be difficult to avoid accepting the invitation. I therefore made a good many enquiries through the Foreign Office and elsewhere as to the utility of the whole exercise. The general consensus of opinion was that the Regional Conferences had, on the whole, been worthwhile and that they had not been made the vehicle of any kind of propaganda. I did, therefore, attend the European Conference and I was pleasantly impressed by it. Delegates had been invited from all the Iron Curtain countries and all had accepted the invitation although, in the result, the only representatives who presented themselves were those from the Soviet Union and from Yugoslavia. The discussions were, however, entirely amicable and co-operative. We all found our Communist colleagues most agreeable and I think the Conference did serve a useful purpose. I was invited to give the final address and I am attaching a copy of it as it may indicate the general background of the exercise.

20. Letter from British barrister and Labour Member of the House of Lords; address: St. Helen's Court, Great St. Helen's, London, E.C.3. MEA, File No. UI/162-112/62, pp. 1-2/corr.

It is true that the whole exercise is mainly financed by money subscribed by the American Bar, by the Ford Foundation and, although I think to a minor extent, by monies made indirectly available by the American State Department. Nonetheless, I think the whole exercise is proving to be a useful and educational one without any obvious political overtones or, so far, any marked attempt to use the Conferences as occasions for propaganda. I hope very much, therefore, that it may be possible for the final Conference, which will certainly be held somewhere, which will be well attended and will lead to the establishment of some co-ordinating institute, may be held in Delhi and that you might feel able to make the inaugural speech. I am sorry to have written to you at such length but I wanted to explain to you that the matter is not now one which is merely of American interest.

Yours sincerely
Hartley Shawcross

P.S. I should perhaps have disclosed my own interest. If the Conference were held in Delhi before the end of March, I should be able to make it an excuse for my much postponed visit to India which I am very anxious to make without too much delay.

11. From K.D. Malaviya: Assam Oil Royalty[21]
[Refer to items 137 and 139]

July 24, 1962

My dear Jawaharlalji,

Damle[22] came to Dehra Dun this morning in connection with the meeting of the Oil & Natural Gas Commission. He tells me that he heard on the radio that Chaliha[23] had agreed to the arbitration of Shri Morarji Desai[24] on Assam royalty matters. Your letter along with a copy of Chaliha's which I received yesterday morning, however, conveys to me that he wants to refer the matter to a Supreme Court Judge. Pending the decision of the Court, however, he is quite willing to accept the advice of Shri Morarji Desai which could be adjusted later on, after the judgement of the Supreme Court Judge has been obtained. This he wants

---

21. Letter from the Minister of Mines and Fuel. Sent from Dehra Dun. NMML, K.D. Malaviya Papers.
22. K.R. Damle, Secretary, Ministry of Mines and Fuel.
23. B.P. Chaliha, the Chief Minister of Assam.
24. Finance Minister.

to do in order to avoid delay in the oil exploration programme. So far as I am concerned, I am not sorry for his rejecting the proposal of the Government of India because we all feel that this case, if referred to the Supreme Court Judge, should settle all matters in the right way. I presume, however, that he has now been persuaded by you to accept the verdict of the Finance Minister on question of royalty.

2. Members of the Oil and Natural Gas Commission are greatly worried about developments in Assam because they have to submit the report of their activities to the Parliament and it will be difficult for them to justify the delay that has already occurred without clearly stating their views about the treatment meted out to them in Assam: whether it is on account of royalty issue or delays in land acquisition or other matters.

3. I will, however, not like to worry you about these matters. You have to weigh other issues against this single one but I thought that the time has come when you might like to discuss this question frankly with the Chief Ministers of some States.

Yours sincerely,
Keshava Deva Malaviya

12. From Morarji Desai: Assam Oil Royalty[25]
[Refer to items 138-139]

25-7-1962

My dear Jawaharlalji,
I received your letter regarding Assam dispute yesterday and had a talk with Chaliha[26] this morning. I explained to him how the attitude adopted by them will on the whole harm them and how an arbitration even on the right of royalty by me would be advantageous. He seemed to see the value of what I told him and told me that as it is a Cabinet decision, he will have to consult his Cabinet. I told him that it was correct that he should reconsider the matter in his Cabinet and let you know their decision soon after his return to Assam. I got an impression that on reconsideration he may agree to arbitration on all the points.

Yours sincerely,
Morarji Desai

25. Letter from the Finance Minister. PMO, File No. 17(490)/62-70-PMS, Sr. No. 36-A.
26. B.P. Chaliha, the Chief Minister of Assam.

13. From A.N. Khosla: Construction Projects and Committee[27]

[Refer to item 68]

26th July, 1962

My dear Panditji,

As you know, construction accounts for 50 per cent or more of expenditures incurred by Government under the Third Plan. In the National Development Council and the Cabinet, attention has been drawn on more than one occasion to the need for achieving economies in construction costs. In October, 1959, the Planning Commission addressed a series of recommendations on the subject to Ministries and States. A team set up by the Committee on Plan Projects also worked out norms for different kinds of buildings. During the past year, I had several meetings with a group composed of the heads of various engineering organisations in the Central Government, as a result of which the Planning Commission issued on May 16 a fairly comprehensive memorandum on Reduction in Costs of Major Construction Projects. The memorandum deals with all kinds of construction projects and not only building schemes, and touches upon several important aspects of the question of economies in construction costs, in particular,

(a) planning, investigations and preparation of project reports,
(b) implementation, including suggestions regarding inventory control, choice of construction agencies, systems of payments and audit and financial sanctions,
(c) proposal for setting up well-equipped cost reduction units to assist the head of each major project or group of projects,
(d) building up expertise and trained manpower in various fields and their efficient utilisation, and
(e) completion reports of projects and technical bulletins.

2. In the past, when similar recommendations have been made, it has not been possible to follow them up for lack of satisfactory machinery. In this connection, there are two main proposals which have now been evolved. The first is that in each project or group of projects, the management should be assisted by a cost reduction unit whose function it would be to be constantly on the look-out for specific points at which cost could be reduced without impairing functional efficiency. The unit would analyse factors affecting costs,

---

27. Letter from Member, Planning Commission. PMO, File No. 17(514)/62-66-PMS, Sr. No. 3-A. Only excerpts are available in the NMML.

recommend suitable adjustments from time to time in respect of materials, techniques, sequence of construction, procedures and organisation, evaluate the results and keep a watch on the progress of action.

3.   The second main proposal is to have at the Centre under the Planning Commission a high-level Committee for Reduction in Construction Costs. The Committee is to consist of the following:

(1)   Member, Planning Commission – Chairman
(2)   Member (Engineering), Railway Board
(3)   Chairman and member (Power), CW&PC
(4)   Engineer-in-Chief, Army Headquarters, Ministry of Defence
(5)   Adviser, Irrigation & Power, Planning Commission
(6)   Chief Engineer, CPWD
(7)   Consulting Engineer, Roads
(8)   Director, National Buildings Organisation
(9)   Chief Architect, CPWD
(10) Four senior engineers drawn from major public enterprises of the Central Government
(11) Two Chief Engineers from States
(12) Four engineers and administrators to be nominated by the Planning Commission
(13) Chief Engineer, in charge of the Cost Reduction Section of the Planning Commission to serve as Member-Secretary.

A Committee such as this will provide the necessary direction and agreement at the highest technical level on the measures by which economies are to be realised in different kinds of construction projects. This will greatly facilitate the task of giving effect to the recommendations which are made from time to time and should lead to significant reduction in construction costs. The Committee will have a technical unit functioning under it and feeding it with problems and material. State Governments have also been asked to set up similar Committees. Nandaji[28] has specially drawn the attention of Chief Ministers to the proposals in the Planning Commission's memorandum, of which I enclose a copy for your information.

4.   I had hoped to take a great deal of personal interest in following up these proposals, and the Planning Commission's intention was that I might serve as Chairman of the Committee for Reduction in Construction Costs. However,

28.   Minister for Planning, Labour and Employment and Deputy Chairman, Planning Commission.

now that I shall not be here,[29] I have been on the look-out for an engineer of high enough standing, who could assume the responsibility of Chairman of the Committee for Reduction in Construction Costs and provide a great deal of personal direction and leadership in this difficult and most important work. Of all the possible persons one could think of, I believe the most suitable would be Karnail Singh, who would be shortly relinquishing the office of Chairman, Railway Board.[30] ...

Yours sincerely,
A.N. Khosla

14. From Braj Narayan Brajesh[31]
[Refer to item 287]

अखिल भारत हिन्दू महासभा
Akhil Bharat Hindu Mahasabha

26 जुलाई 1962

सम्माननीय पण्डित नेहरु जी,
[. . .] आज चीन की आक्रमक एवं विस्तारवादी नीति के कारण हमारे देश की सुरक्षा संकट में पड़ गयी है। यह बात भी आपसे छुपी हुयी नहीं है कि पाकिस्तान कश्मीर के प्रश्न पर कभी भी संकट निर्माण कर सकता है। असम में पाकिस्तानियों के घुसपैठ के समाचार नित्यप्रति आ रहे हैं। देश चारों और से संकट से घिर रहा है। आपने स्वयं कहा है कि हमें सचेत रहना चाहिए। पर क्या उसके लिए कोई प्रयत्न हो रहा है? जनता को संकट का सामना करने के लिए तैयार करना तो दूर रहा आपकी सरकार ने राष्ट्रभाषा के विषय में एक नया विवाद निर्माण कर देश की विघटनकारी शक्तियों को ही उकसाया है। मैं इसी गंभीर प्रश्न की ओर आपका ध्यान आकृष्ट करना चाहता हूँ और आशा करता हूँ कि आप हमारे विचारों पर किन्चित ध्यान देंगे।

यह बात निर्विवाद सत्य है कि राष्ट्रीय एकता के लिए देश की एक भाषा होना नितान्त आवश्यक है। इस सत्य को दृष्टिगत रखकर ही हमारे संविधान में हिन्दी को राष्ट्रभाषा घोषित किया और यह भी कि सन् 1962 [sic] से राष्ट्रभाषा हिन्दी में ही शासकीय कार्य चलेगा। 25 [sic] वर्ष का समय किसी भी भाषाज्ञान को प्राप्त करने के लिए अपर्याप्त

---

29. A.N. Khosla took over as the Governor of Orissa on 16 September 1962.
30. See also item 70.
31. Letter from the Organising Secretary, All India Hindu Mahasabha; address: Hindu Mahasabha Bhavan, Mandir Marg, New Delhi. PMO, File No. 52(12)/57-63-PMS, Vol. I, Sr. No. 78-A. Only paragraphs 2, 3 and 4 are available in the NMML.

है यह कहना राष्ट्र के चैतन्य को चुनौती है और राष्ट्रभाषा के प्रति उदासीनता का ही परिचायक है। मैं यह स्वीकार करने को तत्पर नहीं कि आपके प्रयत्न करने पर भी भाषा का विकास नहीं हो सका अपितु हमने राष्ट्रभाषा के पवित्र कार्य को राजनैतिक दृष्टि से देखकर उसको और उलझाया ही नहीं उसकी गति को भी अवरुद्ध किया है। आज हिन्दी के साथ-साथ अंग्रेज़ी को सह-राष्ट्रभाषा बनाने का जो प्रयत्न शासन कर रहा है उसके पीछे केवल उन लोगों को प्रसन्न करने की भावना है जिन्हें राष्ट्रीय एकता में ही विश्वास नहीं है, जो वर्तमान भारत की एकाई को भी स्वीकार करने को तत्पर नहीं हैं। यह कहना भ्रमपूर्ण है कि दक्षिण भारत के लोग अभी हिन्दी को स्वीकार नहीं करते। मेरा अपना संसदीय अनुभव है कि अहिन्दी भाषा-भाषी प्रान्त के सदस्यगण मेरी संस्कृतनिष्ठ हिन्दी को सुगमता से समझकर भाषा के यथार्थरूप पर मुग्ध थे। इतना तो आप भी जानते हैं कि समस्त प्रान्तीय भाषाओं में प्रचुर मात्रा में संस्कृत के तत्सम् शब्द भरे पड़े हैं। राष्ट्रभाषा के साथ इस प्रकार खिलवाड़ कर क्या आप राष्ट्रविरोधी तत्वों को प्रसन्न कर सकेंगे? इतिहास इसका साक्षी है कि इस प्रकार की मनोवृति के लोग प्रसन्न करने की नीति से अपने कुमार्ग से तो हटते नहीं अपितु उन्हें प्रोत्साहन अवश्य मिलता है और वे नित्य नई अड़चने उत्पन्न करते हैं। इसलिये मेरी आपसे प्रार्थना है कि अनिश्चित काल के लिए अंग्रेज़ी को सह-राष्ट्रभाषा बनाने के प्रस्ताव सदा के लिए स्थगित कर दें जिससे सारे देश में सही रूप में राष्ट्रीय एकता की एक नयी लहर आयेगी।

इसके साथ ही एक और संकट सरल हिन्दी के नाम पर खड़ा किया जा रहा है। भाषा की सुन्दरता और समृद्धि के लिए प्रयास किया जाये तो सभी वर्गों का आपको सहयोग मिल सकता है परन्तु कुछ विशिष्ट वर्ग को प्रसन्न करने के लिए हिन्दी के स्वरूप को बिगाड़ने का जो दुराग्रह हो रहा है वह निन्दनीय है जिसे आपको रोकना चाहिए। आकाशवाणी से प्रसारित हिन्दी संस्कृतनिष्ठ होने के कारण समझने में कठिन है इस प्रकार की आपत्ति कितने प्रतिशत जनता ने की है? हिन्दी के सरल बनाने के नाम पर उसमें अनावश्यक उर्दू और फ़ारसी शब्द घुसेड़ने का काम प्रथम आरम्भ करना और अब कहना कि इस बात का पता किया जायेगा कि जनता को इसे समझने में कोई कठिनाई है या नहीं? यदि केवल हिन्दी को जन-साधारण को समझाने योग्य भाषा बनाना ही आकाशवाणी के हिन्दी में परिवर्तन का उद्देश्य था तो पहिले यह पता किया जाना चाहिए था कि कितने लोग हैं जिन्हें वर्तमान हिन्दी समझने में कठिनाई अनुभव होती है। परन्तु ऐसा नहीं किया गया। क्या इससे यह स्पष्ट नहीं होता कि भाषा नीति में परिवर्तन का उद्देश्य केवल हिन्दी को सरल बनाना मात्र नहीं अपितु हिन्दी को राष्ट्रभाषा का स्थान मिलने के कारण जो वर्ग असन्तुष्ट था उसे प्रसन्न करने का राजनैतिक प्रयास मात्र है।

[. . .]

आपका अपना,
ब्रज नारायण ब्रजेश

[Translation begins[32]

26 July 1962

Respected Pandit Nehruji,

Today the security of our nation is in peril due to the aggressive and expansionist policy of China. It is also no secret to you that Pakistan can take up the Kashmir issue at any time and pose a threat. Reports of Pakistani infiltrators into Assam are being published every day in the newspapers. The country is surrounded on all sides by danger. You have yourself said that we should remain vigilant. But is any effort being made towards that? Far from preparing the people to face the danger, your Government has encouraged the secessionist forces in the country by starting off a new debate over the issue of national language. I wish to draw your attention to this serious matter and hope that you will pay some attention to our concerns.

It is an indisputable truth that it is absolutely essential to have one national language for the sake of the country's unity. It is keeping in mind this truth that Hindi was announced to be our national language in the Indian Constitution, as also that from 1962 [sic] onwards, the administrative work will be done only in the national language, Hindi. That twenty-five years [sic] is not a long enough period for learning any language is a challenge to the nation's intellect and shows the Government's apathy towards the issue. I am not prepared to accept that the language could not acquire a wider base in spite of your efforts. Not only has the issue of the national language been considered from a political angle and further complicating its development has also been obstructed [sic]. Behind the attempt being made today to have English also as a national language along with Hindi by the Government lies the desire only to please those who do not believe in national unity at all, those who do not wish to accept the identity of today's India. To say that the people of South India have not yet accepted Hindi is misleading. My own parliamentary experience is that members from the non-Hindi speaking states have been able easily to understand Sanskritised Hindi and were really mesmerised by the speech. You would certainly know that all the regional languages are full of Sanskrit words. Will you be able to please the anti-national elements by playing with the issue of national language in this manner? History is witness to the fact that by trying to please people with such a mindset does not lead to their giving up the wrong path they are following but on the contrary they certainly get further encouragement and they create new difficulties every day. Therefore, it is my request that you should give up the proposal to keep English as a national language as well for an indefinite

32. This translation is from the PMO file and not translated for the SWJN.

period so that there is a new wave of national unity in a meaningful way all over the country.

Along with this another difficulty is being created in the name of simplifying Hindi. If efforts are made to make a language more beautiful and developed, you will get the cooperation of all classes of people. But if an attempt is made to disfigure Hindi merely to please some elites, it is to be condemned and you should prevent it. What percentage of people have raised an objection that the Sanskritised Hindi being broadcast from All India Radio is difficult to understand? Having introduced Persian and Urdu words in the name of simplification of Hindi to begin with, now to say that it will be examined if the people find any difficulty in understanding it, is absurd. If the intention behind simplifying the Hindi being broadcast from All India Radio was only to ensure that it is made into a language easily understood by the common man, then it should have first been examined to see how many people are facing difficulty in understanding it in its present form in the first place. Does this not make it abundantly clear that the intention behind changing the language policy is not merely to simplify Hindi but a political attempt to please the class which has been unhappy about making Hindi the national language.

Yours sincerely,
Braj Narayan Brajesh

Translation ends]

15. From Hafiz Mohammed Ibrahim: Power Failure in Delhi[33]
[Refer to item 110]

30th July, 1962

My dear Jawaharlalji,

I am writing about the present power supply failures in the Capital. These have been caused due to failure on the 26th instant of one of the two transformers supplying power from the Bhakra Nangal system to Delhi and installed at the Rohtak Road sub-station of the Punjab State Electricity Board. I convened a meeting of the representatives of the Punjab State Electricity Board, Delhi Electric Supply Undertaking and the Central Water and Power Commission

---

33. Letter from the Minister of Irrigation and Power. PMO, File No. 7(258)/62-66-PMS, Sr. No. 1-A.

this morning to find out what steps could be taken to expedite restoration of normal supply conditions. The Chairman, Punjab State Electricity Board, is of the view that the transformer has failed due to defective design. His engineers are busy repairing the transformer by replacing the damaged limb. I have also visited the sub-station. The work is being done round the clock. It, however, seems that it would be difficult to restore the normal supply conditions before the 25th August, 1962.

A failure of this type occurred last year also. We are, therefore, thinking of setting up a Committee to enquire into the causes of failure of the transformers. As the transformer belongs to the Punjab Government, they are being consulted about the personnel and the terms of reference of the Committee.

The power position in Calcutta is also causing us much concern. The Calcutta Electric Supply Corporation was finding it extremely difficult to cope with the demand and just as we had formulated some proposals for supply of additional power from Damodar Valley Corporation for the Calcutta area, there was an accidental fire at Durgapur Thermal Power Station of the DVC which led to the shutting down of both the 75 MW units there. This resulted in reduction in the supply of power by the DVC to the Calcutta Electric Supply Corporation. Fortunately, the DVC have been able to put back into service one of the 75 MW units at Durgapur, and another 75 MW unit at Bokaro that was under repair is expected to be brought into operation by tomorrow. I have directed a senior engineer of the Central Water and Power Commission to proceed at once to Durgapur to make an assessment of the situation. The question of increasing supply of power by the DVC to the Calcutta Electric Supply Corporation is also engaging my attention and we are trying to do all that is possible to help the Government of West Bengal in meeting the shortage of power in the Calcutta area.

Yours sincerely,
Hafiz Mohd Ibrahim

16. Vienna Speech by P.C. Mahalanobis – I[34]
[Refer to items 23 and 205]

THE SOCIAL INFORMATION[35] FOR NATIONAL DEVELOPMENT

Published in *Sankhya*, Vol. 25, Ser. B (1963), pp. 49-66

1. INTRODUCTION

1.1.   The problem of improving the material and cultural conditions of the poorer countries of the world has been engaging serious attention during the post-war period. The desire for political independence is rapidly increasing and will continue to grow in the countries still under colonial rule. Also, more and more countries are becoming and will become politically independent. With the gaining of independence, it is being increasingly realized that political freedom is necessary, but is not enough. In most of the underdeveloped areas, attention is being given increasingly to economic development to improve the level of living, by increasing the flow of goods and services and by expanding facilities for cultural amenities. It is also being increasingly appreciated that rapid economic growth can be brought about only by an increasing accumulation of capital to supply modern tools and machinery for new and expanding productive activities which would, in time, solve problems of unemployment or underemployment, and would also continually improve the level of living. Such accumulation of capital would call for increasing domestic savings, and the utilization of such savings for productive purposes. The choice of productive activities (that is, of investments) must also be such as to secure the best possible rate of economic growth over a time horizon of a generation or more.

1.2.   How to bring this about? This is where the question of social transformation becomes relevant. Some broad general principles may perhaps be stated with confidence.

---

34. Speech by P.C. Mahalanobis, Member, Planning Commission, and Statistical Adviser to the Cabinet, GOI, at the Conference for International Economic Cooperation and Partnership held in Salzburg-Vienna in July 1962. Reproduced from *P.C. Mahalanobis. Papers on Planning*, edited by P.K. Bose and M. Mukherjee (Calcutta: Statistical Publishing Society, 1985), pp. 266-274.
35. A typographical error in the source; the contents table of the book gives the title as "The Social transformation for national development," the same as Nehru mentioned in his letter of 16 August 1962 to Raghunath Singh, see item To Raghunath Singh: Circulate P.C. Mahalanobis's Vienna Speeches 16/08 ECON.

2. The structural transformation

2.1.   It is necessary to give opportunities for participation in productive activities to the largest number of people, and as soon as possible, to all such people as are capable of undertaking such work, and also to utilize available resources in the most effective way for the benefit of the nation as a whole. To create fullest opportunities for rapid growth, it is necessary to remove all barriers to the effective utilization of productive forces, by the people, for the benefit of all the people of the country.

2.2.   There are many facets to the problem, some of which are general and some peculiar to particular countries. It is not possible to arrange them in any clear order of priority. In fact the heart of the problem is to make changes in all necessary directions at the same time, in a balanced way, so as to bring about the structural transformation as quickly as possible.

2.3.   The transformation of the social structure cannot be an entirely internal process. Outside influences have been and will continue to be at work. Colonial rule and economic exploitation of the underdeveloped countries have themselves given rise to reactions promoting the desire for political independence and for improvement in the level of living in the underdeveloped areas.

2.4.   A new factor, of conscious international cooperation in improving the social, political, and economic conditions of the underdeveloped countries has also emerged during the last ten or fifteen years through a quickening of the world conscience on humanitarian grounds and also in the enlightened self-interest of the more advanced countries. Isolation is no longer possible, physically, psychologically or organizationally. The influence of information, ideas, advice and aid from outside would be an increasingly important factor.

2.5.   A structural transformation of the whole society is, however, indispensable to make conditions fit for rapid economic growth. Without such transformation, any amount of help from outside would be ineffective. The experience of many countries during the post-war period would corroborate this.

3. The Scientific Revolution

3.1.   It is also necessary to develop the outlook of science and the experimental attitude of mind in order to acquire knowledge of natural and social forces and to invent new techniques for initiating material and social changes. This is the only way in which decisions can be made increasingly in a rational manner, in accordance with principles of objective or scientific validity based on relevant data and correct reasoning, instead of on the sanction of authority

743

based on status and power or custom and conventional or revealed rules and laws. This may be called the scientific revolution.

3.2. The need of what I have called "the scientific revolution" is recognized, but has not received sufficient attention. I have considered some aspects of this problem in the next paper on "The Scientific Base of Economic Development."

4. Modernization of Society

4.1. The social transformation and the scientific revolution are both necessary. These are but two aspects of modernization which can be distinguished but not separated. The social transformation and the scientific revolution in combination leads to modernization. The task of international cooperation is to promote and help, in every possible way and in a peaceful manner, the modernization of the underdeveloped countries.

4.2. *Urgency of the task*: The scientific and industrial revolution took place in West Europe and North America roughly over a period of three or four hundred years. It is not possible to wait for such a long time for the underdeveloped countries to attain a reasonable level of living. The historical process of transformation must proceed five or ten times faster. Such speeding up of the process of transformation has always been a characteristic feature of biological evolution, and can be achieved.

4.3. *Different phases of the transformation*: Some of the newly independent countries are large, some are of medium size, and some are extremely small in areas, or in natural resources or in population. They would have widely differing needs. The particular form and contents and components of each step of modernization would depend on the special conditions of each country and the stage of development reached by it, and would therefore, vary from one country to another or from one region to another of the same country and also, over a period of time, in the same country or in the same region.

4.4. *International cooperation*: The most significant fact of the present age is the rapidly expanding contacts between different countries of the world. This tendency is bound to become stronger in future, increasing the scope of international affairs in every direction. At the same time, what George Washington had said about "no country being able to go beyond its own self-interest in international affairs," would continue to remain valid. The real need is, therefore, to discover new areas of mutual self-interest, and to expand spheres of common interest on both bi-lateral and multi-lateral basis to the fullest extent.

4.5. It is also clear that even the most advanced countries still have unlimited scope for both social and scientific progress. For all countries, large or small, advanced or underdeveloped, international cooperation is necessary and beneficial. The smaller and the less-developed a country, the greater however will be the need and importance of such cooperation.

5. PROBLEMS OF INTERNAL REFORMS

5.1. There is general agreement about some of the most important contents or elements or aspects of the social transformation, such as:– land reform; removal of social, economic and political barriers; mass education and technical training; increasing equality of opportunities; the possibility of a labourer or an initiator securing the fruits of his labour; or the need of medical and health services and cultural amenities etc. There is much in common in respect of such components or aspects of social transformation in the case of all underdeveloped countries, with, however, the need of adaptations to suit the special conditions of each individual country. Some of these components or aspects are briefly considered below.

5.2. *Land reform*: Historically, land reform has been a most important factor in the economic development of all advanced or rapidly developing countries. Agriculture and industry must advance at the same time. It is, however, generally agreed that an agricultural surplus (or, the surplus from extractives) is essential for industrial development. Changes in land tenure and legislation would, therefore, be one of the requirements of the highest priority in most, if not all, underdeveloped regions.

5.3. The aim must be to secure the fruits of his labour to the cultivator so that he has the incentive to improve the land and to introduce more advanced technological methods. Tenancy law should protect the tenant against eviction so long as he is using the land efficiently, and to secure to him the right of fair compensation upon termination of the lease for all unexhausted improvements made by him. It is also necessary to eliminate the unproductive consumption of the surplus from land by intermediaries and landlords, who have no productive functions, by abolishing their rights.

5.4. The question of economy of scale of production may, admittedly, introduce difficulties. The breaking up of large farms may lead to a reduction of the surplus; however, the beneficial effects of greater equality of income and wealth may compensate for the other loss. Also, in countries where there are too many cultivators, often with scattered plots, further breaking up of the holdings may easily have adverse effects on the efficiency of production. In such a situation it may be necessary to promote consolidation of holdings either voluntarily through cooperatives, or by legislation, or both. Redistribution of land has limits and is a complicated question. It is wise to recognize that

745

steps taken at one stage may have to be reversed at a later stage. Appropriate measures must be devised to suit the needs of each country at any particular stage of development. The basic aim would always remain the same, namely, to increase the agricultural surplus, and to use it for productive purposes, as effectively as possible, in speeding up the growth of the economy as a whole.

5.5. *Removal of social, economic, legal and political barriers*: The underdeveloped countries have the very difficult task of achieving a far faster rate of growth than had been achieved by the most advanced countries during and after the industrial revolution. It is indispensable that everyone in the working age-group should be fully utilized to increase the national product. It is necessary, therefore, to remove all social, economic, legal and political barriers which prevent individuals, or groups and section of individuals, to become fully productive. Conditions are worst in a country stratified by caste, colour, creed or language, and where whole sections of people are sometimes deprived of opportunities by customs, law, or social and political pressures by ruling groups. Removing all such barriers is an essential condition for rapid growth.

5.6. *Equality of opportunities and vertical mobility*: Removal of social and other barriers, in principle, is necessary but not sufficient. It is essential to help one to make himself fit for the highest type of productive work of which he is capable. Opportunities for education and training and for productive work must be made as widely available as possible. Great inequalities of wealth and income often lead to denial of opportunities to the poorer people, and, unless removed, give rise to a sense of frustration among the underprivileged and hamper the growth of national solidarity. Sufficiently rapid economic progress would be difficult or impossible in societies in which there is lack of vertical mobility and where small sections try to preserve their privileges based on heredity, custom or law without any relation to their productive contributions.

5.7. *Horizontal mobility*: The social system may also hamper the utilization of resources because customs or caste restrictions prevent labour from moving into new occupations, or labour is tied to the soil, or land may be concentrated in the hands of small sections of the people who are unwilling to divert it for more productive use for reasons of social or political prestige. A small number of producers even in underdeveloped countries may sometimes band together to prevent the free entry of others or the introduction of new techniques. All such restrictions must be removed to increase the horizontal mobility of resources.

5.8. *Possibility of securing fruits of labour and enterprise*: The elimination of concentration of social, economic or political privileges in the hands of small sections of the people would promote both vertical and horizontal mobility, and make it possible for everyone to secure a fair share of the fruits of his labour and enterprise. This is one of the most important consequences of the social transformation and is particularly helpful in promoting rapid economic growth. Appropriate legal and institutional changes must be made to achieve this.

6. National integration

6.1. *Sectional interests and barriers*: A characteristic feature of underdevelopment is the segmentation of the country into innumerable regions, castes, tribes, languages, religious communities, occupational and other groups which focus attention on the welfare of small sections of the people without any awareness of the best interests of the country as a whole. It has to be recognized that rapid progress is impossible without painful adjustments and damage to sections of the people whose interests are based on special privileges or old techniques; and, that old beliefs, customs, and social institutions have to be discarded, and all barriers of caste, customs, creed, colour, language and sectional interests must be ruthlessly eliminated. The greater the prevalence of such social barriers in the country, the greater are the sectional rigidities within government administration, and the fiercer are the inter-agency jealousies and fights which continually delay decisions and hamper speedy action.

6.2. *Integration*: The removal of social and economic barriers is an indispensable condition for the emergence of the sense of national solidarity without which national development is impossible. It is not possible to isolate the scientific, or the social, or the industrial aspects of the transformation from one another. Advance must be made at the same time on all fronts. This creates difficulties but also has its advantages. Progress in one direction stimulates and promotes progress in another direction. It is the task of leadership to maintain a proper balance between the different aspects and phases of the process of modernization in its full sense. The aim continually must be to create a society from which social, economic and political privileges have been completely eliminated. To bring about such a transformation would call for wise leadership with a clear appreciation of aims and objectives, a rational and experimental attitude of mind with confidence in the outlook of science, and willing to pay the price of much painful adjustments.

7. Danger of superficial imitation of advanced countries

7.1. Because of the sense of urgency for economic growth which is strengthening everywhere, there is a peculiar danger of adopting, in a superficial way or at too early a stage, methods, and forms and institutions, which are working successfully in the advanced countries. It has to be kept in mind that existing social and political institutions, or high levels and standards of quality or performance, were established in the advanced countries only with the gradual growth of the economy. Such institutions may not be useful at an earlier stage of development, and may even hamper progress. For example, in underdeveloped countries, there is sometimes a tendency to adopt too expensive or too sophisticated schemes of education, care of health, public buildings and construction, wages or salaries of government employees or labour legislation.

7.2. *Education and training*: Mass education to spread literacy both among children and adults has special urgency; here all possible help should be utilised, for example, by using the services, for a small part of the day or the week, of those who are already literate. Because the numbers involved are very large, the adoption of too high a standard for teacher qualifications, school buildings etc., at the primary level, would make the cost prohibitive. At the secondary stage, more attention would have to be given to the qualifications of teachers and other educational aids; but scales of pay or cost of buildings should still be kept in balance with the general level of living of the students and the parents themselves. At the tertiary level, still higher standards would have to be adopted for staff qualifications and there would be need of more expensive teaching aids; but the expenditure must be kept within the limits of what the country can afford. It is at the stage of advanced studies and research that standards should be really high and comparable with the advanced countries; however, as the number of advanced and research workers would be very small in the beginning, this would not involve any large total expenditure.

7.3. The educational system should be viewed as a pyramid; the lower the stage the wider should be the base (that is, the number of persons under instruction) and the lower the scales of expenditure compared to advanced countries, while at the highest stage of advanced studies and research the number involved would be extremely small but scales of expenditure may approximate to those of advanced countries. Adoption, at too early a stage, of standards and scales of expenditure of advanced countries at lower levels would lead to severe restrictions in numbers usually coupled with admission of students on the basis of family income; this must have most undesirable social and psychological consequences. When resources in men, materials and money are inadequate, to increase the number of students in accordance with the pressure on admissions, would necessarily lead to window dressing and a dilution of students in practice. This can seriously hamper progress; the only remedy is to adopt a system which would be in keeping with basic aims and yet within the means of the country.

7.4. *Medical care and technical services*: A similar situation can arise even more easily in the field of medical care. Adoption of the high level of university education for physicians in the advanced countries as the only standard at an early stage would necessarily mean that most of the people will be deprived of medical services in underdeveloped countries for a very long time. A two-tier approach with a junior cadre of medical personnel with, say, three or four years' training, together with a much smaller number of physicians with university training, would make it possible to spread medical services much wider and much faster. This would be equally true in many other lines of technical work. A two or even a three-tier approach with a higher, a medium, and even a third level of workers who have had a very quick and specialized training, would be not only within the means of the underdeveloped countries but may be even more effective, because, in the still backward conditions of the country, the lower level workers would be much nearer to the general population and would be able to work in closer touch with them. This would be particularly true in agricultural extension and other services which would bring the technical workers into contact with large sections of the population.

7.5. *Government expenditure*: Government expenditure often tends to become unduly large in underdeveloped countries owing to the adoption of the much higher standards of advanced countries. This leads to unnecessarily high scales of wages and salaries for government employees or costly public buildings; which, in its turn, would increase the feeling of separation between government and the people, and hamper national integration.

7.6. *Labour legislation*: As production becomes modernized and factories and enterprises grow in numbers and in size, it would be necessary to develop labour legislation and regulations to ensure that labour secures a fair share of the surplus, and also to ensure working conditions being maintained reasonably safe and healthy. Legislation in imitation of the more advanced countries, at too early a stage, may, however, lead to increasing inefficiency of performance, especially, in countries with surplus labour, and may increase costs of production so much as to have serious adverse effects on exports. The most important thing is to establish a definite link between remuneration and output in the case of all types of work of which the volume and quality can be estimated even roughly. It is necessary to recognise that trade union movements can gain in real strength only on the basis of increasing productivity.

8. NATIONAL LEADERSHIP

8.1. The transfer of modern technology from the advanced countries also calls for much adaptation to suit the needs and local conditions of underdeveloped regions. To profit by the experience of the advanced countries and yet to introduce modern technology and modern social and political

749

institutions in a way suitable to the particular stage of development of the country is a matter of crucial importance in the process of modernization. Ultimately, success would depend on the growth of a rational outlook and the experimental attitude of mind, first, among the leadership at all levels and then gradually among the general mass of the people.

8.2. It is extremely important that the advanced countries should help and encourage in every way all progressive groups within the country in promoting the process of modernization and refrain from offering technical or economic aid in any way which would hamper the social and scientific transformation.

17. Vienna Speech by P.C. Mahalanobis – II[36]
[Refer to items 23 and 205]

THE SCIENTIFIC BASE OF ECONOMIC DEVELOPMENT

1. PHASES OF ECONOMIC DEVELOPMENT

1.1. The essential characteristic of an underdeveloped country is an extremely low level of living, that is, inadequate supply of food, clothes, housing, drugs and other consumer goods, and also lack of facilities for education, care of health, social security, cultural amenities, etc., for the nation as a whole. It is possible to make available small quantities of consumer goods by direct imports or by domestic production on a small scale, with the help of imported machinery. In most of the underdeveloped countries it is, however, not possible, for lack of necessary foreign exchange, to import or to produce, with imported machinery, enough consumer goods for the people as a whole. In India, the first textile mill was established in 1817; and India gradually became the second biggest producer of textiles, next only to America. One hundred and fifty years later, India would still remain underdeveloped. The production of textiles or small quantities of other consumer goods for a small part of the nation cannot, by itself, lead to industrialisation and economic development.

1.2. Economic development can occur only by increasing the per capita production of the nation as a whole, through an increasing use of machinery driven by steam or electricity as a substitute for human and animal labour. In

36. Speech by P.C. Mahalanobis, Member, Planning Commission, and Statistical Adviser to the Cabinet, GOI, at the Conference for International Economic Cooperation and Partnership held in Salzburg-Vienna in July 1962. Reproduced from *P.C. Mahalanobis. Papers on Planning*, edited by P.K. Bose and M. Mukherjee (Calcutta: Statistical Publishing Society, 1985), pp. 275- 290.

countries with appreciable natural resources, it is necessary to establish the basic engineering and power industries to enable the manufacture of both consumer and capital goods within the country. Establishing a minimum complex of such basic industries would take at least ten or fifteen years, for which planning must start ten or fifteen years in advance.

1.3.   To increase modern industrial production would call for an increasing supply of engineers, technologists, and technical personnel. The only way to ensure this would be to establish and increase the number of schools, training colleges and universities, and also to train teachers for such institutions. This would take at least fifteen or twenty years; so that planning for this purpose must start fifteen or twenty years in advance.

1.4.   The best way of utilising the raw materials and natural resources available within the country, for both domestic consumption and for exports, can be found out only through applied scientific research.[37] Applied research, in its turn, must be based on advances in fundamental research. Also, to establish an adequate base for applied research it is necessary to promote the spirit of pure research and supply the stimulus of scientific criticism. This would be possible only when at least a certain minimum number of scientists are engaged in fundamental research, and opportunities for pure research are becoming increasingly available. It is therefore necessary to promote the advancement of both applied and fundamental research. To establish a minimum base for scientific research would take more than a generation of twenty-five or thirty years; this, being the most slowly maturing sector, must be given the highest priority.

2. THE SCIENTIFIC BASE OF THE ADVANCED COUNTRIES

2.1.   The scientific base of the modern age can be appreciated by even a brief review of the recent history of the advanced countries. Four hundred years ago the generally accepted view was that the earth was at the centre of the universe; the position of human beings was unique and supreme; and the highest sanction of truth was either divine revelation or abstract logical

---

37. Even the most advanced countries are obliged to devote large resources to research for the improvement of products already being manufactured and also to develop new products in order to hold their position in the world export market. It is not possible for the underdeveloped countries to start or expand the export of fully or partly manufactured products by simply borrowing the current technology from advanced countries; it is essential also to develop applied research for a continuing improvement of technological methods. [Footnote reproduced from the book, *P.C. Mahalanobis. Papers on Planning*].

reasoning in the mind of man. In the sixteenth and the seventeenth centuries, there was a complete revolution in the picture of the physical world; the earth was seen as a small planet moving round the sun; and the method of empirical observations and experimentation was gradually established in both physical and life sciences.

2.2.   Progress was at first slow in the sixteenth century. A few selected names may be recalled to indicate the gradual transformation of ideas. In astronomy, Nicholas Copernicus (1473-1543) supported the view that the planets including the earth itself were revolving in orbits round the sun; Tycho Brahe (1546-1601) supplied astronomical observations of unprecedented accuracy to make the next steps possible; Johann Kepler (1571-1630) formulated the descriptive laws of planetary motion; and Galileo (1564-1642) made conscious propaganda in favour of the new philosophy of the universe. In anatomy, Andreas Vesalius (1514-64) published his observations on the human body in 1543; in physics, William Gilbert (1544-1603) gave an account of magnetism based on trustworthy experiments in 1600; in physiology, William Harvey (1578-1657) described the circulation of the blood in 1628; John Napier (1550-1617) supplied a convenient tool for computation by the use of logarithms; and Rene Descartes (1596-1650), a philosopher, contributed the powerful concepts of coordinates for geometrical representation and of mathematical functions. Francis Bacon (1561-1626) firmly stated that the only true method in science was to proceed from particular sense observations to wider generalizations (*Novum Organum*, Book I, xix), and clearly recognised that "the true and lawful goal of the sciences is ... that human life be endowed with new discoveries and power."

2.3.   The concept of an objective world of physical reality gradually took firm shape in the seventeenth century in the hands of gifted astronomers, mathematicians and scientists. A few names may be mentioned from among those who were born in the first half of the century: Pierre Fermat (1601-1665), Christian Huygens (1629-95), Blaise Pascal (1623-62), Robert Boyle (1627-91), John Ray (1627-1705), Robert Hooke (1635-1703), Issac Newton (1642-1727), and Gottfried Wilhelm Leibniz (1646-1716). The rate of advancement of science increased progressively in the eighteenth and the nineteenth centuries, and during the last few decades has opened new frontiers with almost unimaginable possibilities.

2.4.   The advancement of science prepared the ground for the industrial revolution in Europe in the eighteenth century, first in spinning and weaving, next in the use of iron and steel, and then of electricity in the nineteenth century, which stimulated the growth of the capitalist economies in West Europe and North America. The spread of the scientific outlook also prepared the ground for the age of reason and the French revolution, which occurred at the end of the eighteenth century, and promoted the growth of nationalism in Europe, in its modern sense, in the nineteenth century.

2.5.   The industrial revolution increasingly replaced human and animal power by steam or electricity to drive machinery for the increasing production of both consumer and capital goods. The development of engineering techniques led to a close linkage between science and technology; and during the last hundred and fifty years, industrial development is being stimulated by a scientific discovery or a scientific discovery is being stimulated by industrial needs.

2.6.   For the last five or six thousand years, or more, the average per capita production remained more or less constant or fluctuated within narrow limits. The industrial revolution changed all this, and led to a spectacular increase in the variety and volume of goods produced. As a consequence of such increasing production, the standard of living of the advanced countries of West Europe and North America reached a level far higher than the rest of the world. Also, the advancement of science, technology and industry, made it possible for the western countries to become strong military powers; and, because of such military supremacy, the west was able to bring a large part of the world either into direct colonial rule or into conditions of economic or political subjugation.

2.7.   The last forty years have also seen the rise of USSR as another world power, rapidly growing, through the promotion of science and technology, in economic, industrial and military strength together with a continuing increase in the level of living. The monopoly of scientific and technological knowledge and the unchallengeable military supremacy of the western countries have now gone. The increasing parity between the "western" and the "eastern" countries in science, technology, industry, and military power is a most significant fact of the present time. Because of the unprecedented destructive power of atomic and nuclear weapons, it has become absolutely necessary to avoid a nuclear war which would be catastrophic for both sides and the whole world. Coexistence of both the "western" and the "eastern" powers has become indispensable.

2.8.   There is no intention on either side to make a direct attack. The advanced countries pose no special problems because it is not possible to hold such countries indefinitely in subjugation. However, so long as there are underdeveloped areas, both power groups are likely to try to extend their influence over the less advanced countries, and this would remain a continuing source of potential conflicts. The very existence of underdeveloped countries should, therefore, be seen as a threat to peace. Rapid transformation of all the underdeveloped countries into modern viable societies is an essential condition for peaceful coexistence. Such a transformation would promote the enlightened self-interest of both power groups, and would also create conditions favourable for the advancement of human and cultural values on a world-wide basis.

3. THE ROLE OF SCIENCE IN THE MODERNISATION OF
THE LESS ADVANCED COUNTRIES

3.1.　Modernisation of the less advanced countries through rapid industrialisation is thus an urgent need of the whole world. Is such modernisation possible or can a modern society with a variable economy, with expanding social and political freedom, and cultural amenities, be sustained without establishing a sound scientific base ? This is a question of crucial importance for the present age.

3.2.　In order to answer this question, it is necessary to appreciate the deeper changes in human thinking which were brought about by the emergence of science. In every sphere of organised activity in human society, authority has always been associated, and must always be associated with a system of hierarchical levels. This applies to primitive societies, matriarchal, patriarchal, or tribal; successive levels of feudal lords; organised churches and religions; military, police and administrative systems; enterprises, business and commerce; and law. A law court of appeal may reverse the decision of a lower court; but the decision of the court of appeal is itself subject to change by a still higher court. The decision of the highest court, to which a case has been actually referred, has to be accepted not because such a decision is necessarily right, but because it is the decision of a superior authority.[38] Society must accept this authority principle for stability and orderly progress, even in organised revolutionary activities.

3.3.　This very authority principle must, however, be absolutely and completely rejected in the field of science. Modern science is based on a patient accumulation of facts, on the study of processes and their interrelations or

---

38. It is possible, indeed, that this decision itself would have been reversed if there had been a still higher court to which the case could be referred. If a decision of a higher court of appeal is considered to be like the turning up of "heads" (in tossing an unbiased coin) when the decision upholds the verdict of the lower court, and is considered to be like the turning up of "tails" when the verdict of the lower court is reversed, then the successive decisions of the higher court would look like the results of the tossing of a coin. This would be the real guarantee that the system of law is functioning properly. [Footnote reproduced from the book, *P.C. Mahalanobis. Papers on Planning*].

interactions and a stability or uniformity of nature[39] which can be discovered by the human mind. The findings of the most eminent scientists are subject to critical check by their professional colleagues and by the youngest scientific workers, and must be rejected if there is no satisfactory corroboration. Science can advance only through free criticism on a completely democratic basis, with every research worker of competence enjoying equal status. The theoretical or conceptual framework of science must be continually revised to find a proper place for all known facts. A single new observation may call for a more comprehensive theory. The older accumulated knowledge continues to remain valid; later discoveries must, however, be integrated with the earlier knowledge. The accumulation of scientific knowledge is increasing through the efforts of all the scientific workers of the world. A new fact may be observed or a new theory formulated by any worker, however young, and in any country where research has been established. International collaboration is, therefore, an indispensable condition for the progress of science.

3.4. Authority derived from status is irrelevant to science. Science has introduced a new concept of "scientific", or "objective validity" which has its foundation in nature itself, and which cannot be upset by any authority based on status or by supernatural powers. The transformation of all the advanced or rapidly advancing countries has been based on accepting, in an increasing measure, a scientific or rational view of life. This is the foundation of the modern age.

3.5. It is essential in every country to establish and strengthen the outlook of science, a way of thinking which becomes more and more powerful as it is more widely adopted, and which replaces dogma, superstition, and

---

39. The phrase "uniformity of nature" must be, of course, interpreted to include chance events and random processes. Although games of chance were known and were widely prevalent in ancient times in China, India and other countries, it is important to note that the concept of probability did not arise until the 16th and the 17th centuries, that is, not until the emergence of modern science. This is easy to understand. Before the emergence of the modern scientific view of an objective world of physical reality, all chance events would have to be necessarily ascribed to the whims of gods, demons, or supernatural forces. After the emergence of the scientific view of an objective world of physical reality, it became necessary, both logically and psycho-logically, for the human mind to accommodate the occurrence of chance events as an integral part of the uniformity of nature. This could be accomplished only on the basis of the theory of probability, or rather, as I should prefer to put it only through a statistical view of the world. It seems to me, therefore, that the concept of probability, or the statistical view of the world, did arise at the same time as the emergence of modern science only because it could not possibly have arisen earlier. [Footnote reproduced from the book, *P.C. Mahalanobis. Papers on Planning*].

outdated customs. This scientific outlook cannot be established by force. It must depend on acceptance through proper understanding. In practical affairs, the important point is that a wise policy and programme of action should be increasingly adopted on the basis of rational argument, supported by relevant factual evidence, and should not be rejected because bias or formal dogmas or conventional rules of procedures. It is, therefore, necessary continually to encourage and promote the advancement of science in every country, large or small. Because science is indivisible, and also because science must be established in every country, it is also necessary, continually, to promote scientific collaboration between all countries of the world, large and small, and advanced or developing.

3.6. It is scarcely necessary to point out that there is no conflict between the scientific and rational view of life, on one hand, and aims and objectives based on moral or cultural values, on the other hand. On the contrary, moral and cultural values which are truly universal, and are not narrowly sectarian or nationalistic in a restricted sense, must have an objective and rational basis.

3.7. The advancement of science and the growth of the scientific outlook must be recognised as an essential condition for the modernisation of the less advanced countries. It is necessary for each country to have, as quickly as possible, a sufficient number of men with a scientific outlook to influence the thinking of the nation. How to attract and hold a sufficient number of able persons to science is thus the crucial problem of national and world development. This can be achieved only through a proper and adequate social appreciation of science and scientists. The actual transformation must be brought about from within each country. Scientific aid from the advanced countries can, however, be of great help in this process.

4. PRESENT PROGRAMMES OF TECHNICAL AID

4.1. The need of technical aid has been recognised for some considerable time. Bi-lateral or multi-lateral and international technical aid has often taken the form of either offering educational and training facilities to young workers from the less advanced countries or sending technical or scientific experts to such countries. Considerable benefit has no doubt accrued through such aid but it is necessary to recognise that much effort has also been wasted.

4.2. Scholars from the less advanced countries are usually selected on the basis of results of examinations; success in examinations not being a necessarily reliable indicator of scientific or technical ability, the very process of selection is inefficient. Some of the young scholars have difficulty in adjusting themselves to the pattern of living in the advanced countries. Some of them do not do well in their studies. Some pass the examinations successfully but have no aptitude for scientific work. Some of the more able scholars prefer to live and settle down in the advanced countries, especially in the USA, because of the higher level of living or greater opportunities for scientific work. Some scholars of ability, when they return to their own countries, are unable to find suitable openings for a scientific career; and some of them go back to the country where they were trained. In applied science and technology, and especially in social sciences, many young scholars, who had often studied problems or learnt methods which are appropriate for advanced countries but totally irrelevant to their own native countries, are unable to adapt or develop methods to suit local conditions. Out of the large number of scholars who go to advanced countries for training, only a very small number of really able scientific workers ultimately become available for fruitful work in their own country. The cost of giving scientific or technological training in an advanced country is also very high. Giving training to individual scholars in advanced countries (whether the expenses are provided in the form of foreign aid or met by the scholars themselves or by the country of origin) have been, therefore, extremely wasteful in terms of both men and money.

4.3. There has been also continuing difficulties in finding suitable individual experts for the less advanced countries. Competent scientific workers are reluctant to accept such assignments partly because of the lack of facilities for their own work in the less advanced countries and partly because their scientific or academic career is likely to be adversely affected through their absence abroad. In consequence, assignments sometimes have to be given to persons who are not fully qualified for the job, with unsatisfactory results. To create suitable conditions for scientific work in the less advanced countries is an indispensable condition for attracting competent scientists to go out to such countries.

4.4. Programmed technical aid on a group basis has been more effective. A team of young engineers from a less advanced country can receive most valuable training in an advanced country when such training is oriented to specific technological projects. Teams of experts from advanced countries have also been of very great help in establishing factories or in starting new projects in the less advanced countries. Such technical aid, especially in engineering, technology and applied sciences, should be continued and expanded. Special projects for establishing technological and research centres in the less advanced countries have also been taken up by some of the international agencies. This type of aid can be of great value provided a sufficient number of scientific workers in the less advanced countries can be trained to work in such centres, and also provided necessary conditions are established to enable them to do their work properly.

5. Science education and research

5.1.   It has been argued in the earlier sections that for modernisation it is necessary to establish a foundation for scientific research and the social appreciation of science in the developing and less advanced countries. Every path-finder in a new field of research must work in the first instance by himself; if he is successful, other persons gradually get interested in the subject. Such path-finders always had, and will always have to overcome much opposition, and even hostility, until the new subject becomes a recognised part of the "established" field of science. But it is only a few scientists of outstanding ability who can work in isolation. Most research workers require the stimulus of free interchange of views and ideas and of appreciation among professional colleagues.

5.2.   The community of scientists has a structure of a series of widening circles similar to the structure of scientific subjects or of science as a whole. When a top scientist speaks appreciatively of some work in his special field, other scientists or lay men accept his evaluation and pass on the information to others. The social appreciation of science gradually emerges as a result of the diffusion, in widening circles, of the views of scientists, who are experts in specialised fields of research, to scientists in related and associated fields, then to scientific workers generally, and finally, through persons of position and standing who have contacts with scientists, to the general public. The speed with which such appreciation can spread increases rapidly with the number of scientific workers and improvements in the channels of communication. In the advanced countries, the awareness of the importance of science is increasing rapidly which, in its turn, is raising the social status of scientists and is promoting an increasing flow of resources for research.

5.3.   The whole process is extremely slow in underdeveloped countries. The number of research scientists is very small; and channels of scientific communication are non-existent or meagre. Scientific workers usually receive lower pay and have a lower status than the administrative staff in government or in business concerns; and have to work in a rigid system of hierarchical authorities. Promotion may depend, not so much on the high quality of the scientific work done, but on success in pleasing those who are higher up in the official hierarchy. Even permission to apply for posts elsewhere is subject to the discretion of superior officers. There is a continuing tendency to bring scientists and scientific work under stricter control of the administrators, partly, perhaps, from an unconscious fear of rivalry of power. Even if the right of criticism is accepted in principle, it is restricted in practice because scientific workers are often afraid, rightly or wrongly, of giving offence to persons holding higher posts. In consequence, many scientists in underdeveloped countries suffer from a lack of self-confidence, and are afraid to take up original lines of investigation. There is little possibility of a proper evaluation or appreciation of scientific work within the country. This leads to an exaggerated dependence on the opinion of foreign scientists and gives rise to much imitative work. Also, when there is lack of appreciation or criticism from the advanced countries, there is sometimes a tendency to ascribe the unfavourable view to racial or national prejudices, and there is resistance against collaboration with foreign scientists.

5.4.   In underdeveloped countries there are very few, sometimes only one or two, individuals of outstanding ability in scientific research or in any other scientific field. As leadership can be supplied only by individuals of high ability, and as such persons are few in number, it is much more difficult in underdeveloped countries to utilise the services of individuals of average ability and qualifications. The advanced and advancing countries have a double advantage. They have a large number of persons with qualities of leadership and can, therefore, utilise in a fruitful way larger numbers of persons of average ability. This is why many scientific workers from underdeveloped countries, who are unable to do much useful work in their own native country, can often do very good work in the environment of a higher state of organisation of research in an advanced country.

5.5.   The aim of scientific aid must be to create in every underdeveloped country, as quickly as possible, a sufficient number of research scientists to form a community of professional workers which would be sufficiently large to facilitate an independent evaluation of scientific work through free criticism and frank exchange of views. It is, therefore, necessary to focus attention on identifying and giving support to persons who have the ability to undertake research work of high quality, and to try to increase their number as quickly as possible, and at the same time to offer opportunities for training to persons of average ability whose services would be equally essential in supplying a wide base for the pyramid of scientific work.

5.6.   There is urgent need of fostering the spirit of objective scientific criticism through free expression and exchange of views and opinions. One effective way of promoting this would be to make it easy for scientific workers to migrate from one post to another and give an absolute guarantee of such freedom to migrate. Any scientific worker who feels, rightly or wrongly, that he has not enough opportunities for fruitful work in one institution would be free to migrate to some other institution. Such migrations or the possibility of such migrations would have an indirect but most important selective effect on scientists at all levels.

5.7. It is necessary to recognise that the social value of an individual scientist of high ability is far greater in a developing country because of the leadership he may be able to supply. It is only scientists engaged in fundamental research who can function as the eyes and ears of the nation in making the nation appreciate and identify urgent needs of applied research. The emergence of even one or two outstanding research scientists can enhance the prestige of the nation in a most significant way at the international level and promote the growth of self respect and self confidence of the nation. This is why it is particularly important in developing countries to identify such individuals, at first very few in number, and give them all possible facilities and encouragement to continue their work in their own country.

5.8. In the highly developed countries science advanced both from progress at the highest levels of research, at the top, and from the wide diffusion of education, at the bottom. The same strategy may be adopted with advantage in the less advanced countries. What is urgently needed is to lay the foundations, with as wide a base as possible, for a country-wide system of school education oriented to science and, at the same time, to develop advanced studies of science and technology and research at the highest level. The school system must fit into the economic life of the general mass of the people and have its grass roots in the villages. It must offer facilities for training technicians and technical personnel for science and technology and also supply candidates of outstanding merit for admission to higher scientific and technological institutions.

6. NEED OF DIRECT AID FOR SCIENCE

6.1. I shall offer, briefly, a few suggestions for giving direct aid for the development of science in the less advanced countries. I have stressed the need for building up a system of school education with a definite orientation to science. It would be, however, a fatal mistake to establish an expensive system of education on the model of the advanced countries which would have little relevance to local needs and would be beyond the means of the national economy. It is necessary to evolve a system, through experimentation and trial and success, which would be within the means of the national economy. The approach must be therefore to use teaching aids which are easily available or can be made available on a large scale and at a low cost. As most of the pupils will be living in villages, it would be of great advantage if agriculture and some of the rural industries can be adopted as a base for the teaching of science. The programme may consist largely of nature studies, observations, and experiments which can be done with the help of simple articles, specimens, etc., likely to be locally available or which can be constructed with local materials.

760

6.2. There would be still some need of supplying teaching aids and materials from outside which would have to be specially designed to reduce costs. It is essential also to prepare books of instructions and text books to suit a fairly wide range of needs. These are difficult tasks which would call for extended study and research by scientists of high calibre with a serious interest in problems of science education. As basic conditions in underdeveloped countries are likely to be similar to a large extent, it may be possible to evolve broad general methods for science education which would be capable of being adapted without much difficulty to suit different local conditions.

6.3. A great deal of pioneering research would be necessary for this purpose for which the help of advanced countries is indispensable. A good deal of experimental studies will have to be undertaken under conditions actually prevailing in underdeveloped regions. In the beginning, the studies would have to be organised on a small scale with the help and support of the local authorities and of such teachers and scientists as may be available to cooperate in the venture in the underdeveloped country itself. The project can be gradually extended in the light of experience, to cover different subject fields at different educational levels, and also from one underdeveloped country to another. Fortunately, even one or two scientists can start the work in one single country. The important point is to make a beginning at the earliest opportunity.

6.4. I may now mention a second type of programme. Certain facilities for scientific research are already available in India and other developing countries. In most of these countries, scientific work is being hampered for lack of small replacement parts, additional accessories and instruments, and supply of essential consumable stores which have to be imported from the advanced countries. It is often difficult to secure import licences on account of shortage of foreign currency. This difficulty can be overcome through a simple plan of gifts in kind of replacement parts, instruments and equipment, stores, books and journals and reprints or microfilms of scientific papers etc., to be arranged through non-governmental committees of scientists. Such commodities, which can be set up in the advanced countries through or in cooperation with appropriate scientific organisations or societies, would try to secure suitable grants from Government and other sources. In developing countries where scientific research has already started, the counterpart committees of scientists would also be set up, preferably, at a non-governmental level and with a majority of members from universities and non-governmental scientific institutions. All arrangements would be made with the concurrence of the government of the less advanced country concerned, but decisions relating to gifts for scientific work must be made by direct consultations between the scientific committees themselves. A scheme of this type can be usefully started, on an experimental

761

basis, for a few selected countries, at a low cost, with gifts to the total value of perhaps one or two hundred thousand dollars per year. The amount can be increased if the experiment proves successful.

6.5.   Another important form of scientific aid would be to arrange for competent research scientists from the advanced countries to work for a year or two in existing research units in the less advanced countries or to help in establishing high level research units in such countries. The less advanced countries can offer challenging problems and opportunities for research in many fields of science, which cannot be duplicated in the advanced countries, for example, in geology, meteorology and geography; biology, botany, and zoology; agriculture; medical science and public health; economics of development; linguistics; archaeology; and historical and cultural studies of various kinds. In some of the developing countries there would be also increasing opportunities for active participation in research in mathematics and statistics, and physico-chemical and technological sciences. In establishing research units in underdeveloped countries it would be desirable to keep one broad aim in view, namely, to encourage joint studies by active collaboration between different research units. This would help in developing a community of research cells or units which, in its turn, would foster the growth of the spirit of scientific criticism and appraisal among wider circles of scientific workers.

6.6.   To attract competent visiting scientists it is necessary to offer them facilities to pursue or start fruitful research in the less advanced countries; sometimes special equipment may have to be provided for this purpose. Secondly, the assignment in a less advanced country, would have to be treated as deputation in the same way as participation in scientific expeditions, and which would be recognised as a part of normal duties and also as a possible qualification for promotion. The visiting scientist must receive sufficient compensation in his home currency to meet his continuing home commitments during his absence abroad. Living and other local expenses should be normally met by the institution or by the government of the country in which he would work. Such sharing of costs would promote effective cooperation in the less advanced country, and would also reduce the total cost appreciably.

6.7.   An important part of the responsibilities of a visiting scientist would be to give training to the scientific workers of the underdeveloped countries. When necessary, the visiting scientists would be able to select, for further training in an advanced country, the right type of persons who can be depended upon to go back to their own country after the completion of the training abroad. It would be also possible to give aid in the form of equipment and instruments in an effective way on the basis of objective appraisals of needs and possibilities by the visiting scientists.

6.8.   A fourth programme could be to send from advanced countries young scholars, who have just finished their education in universities or higher educational institutions or have already done some research, to start or continue suitable lines of research for about two years or so in existing institutions or in research units to be established for this purpose in underdeveloped countries. The common participation in research projects of young scholars from the advanced and the underdeveloped countries would be of great help in establishing scientific traditions and an atmosphere of scientific criticism. It would promote self-confidence among the scientific workers of the underdeveloped country, especially, if the visiting scholars from advanced countries take higher degrees from institutions in the less advanced countries.

6.9.   All the above forms of scientific aid can be started, if desired, on a small scale and at low cost, and, if successful, can be expanded in the light of experience. Also, these forms of scientific aid would not in any way overlap or hamper bigger programmes for gifts of expensive equipment or large projects for the setting up of national or regional centres and institutes for scientific research in the less advanced countries. On the contrary, the modest programme described in this note would prepare the ground for bigger projects.

7. Conclusion

7.1.   In conclusion I may refer, very briefly, to some recent developments. After the second world war the movement for terminating colonial rule gained rapidly in strength; and, one country after another in Asia and Africa has won political independence. It is being increasingly realised, however, that independence is not enough for economic development. The need of economic and technical aid is also being increasingly appreciated. Both the "western" and the "eastern" powers have started helping in the economic development of the less advanced countries in Asia, Africa and Latin America, but still without an adequate impact. The time has come to recognise that economic aid is essential but is also not sufficient.

7.2.   Revolutions to capture political power have been occurring throughout human history and are even now occurring in many of the politically independent countries in Latin America or in most of the newly independent countries in Asia and Africa. Such revolutions do not automatically promote rapid economic development, because purely political revolutions do not lead to any fundamental transformation of the old society based on the principle of authority associated with levels of status. It is becoming increasingly clear that rapid economic development cannot be achieved without developing a structure of society in which decisions would tend to be made more and more on grounds of reason, that is, in accordance with the principle of objective validity instead of authority. It is relevant to note that the French Revolution was preceded by the age of reason; the American War of Independence had the support of influential leaders inspired by the spirit of science; and the socialist government, which was established after the October Revolution in 1917 in Russia, made great efforts to build up a countrywide system of science-oriented education and to promote scientific research and, in this way, succeeded in modernising the whole society leading to rapid economic development.

7.3. One thing is clear. In the absence of rapid economic development, political conditions in the less advanced countries would remain unstable. In many or most countries there would be one revolution after another tending to get the two power groups involved directly or indirectly in the struggle. The world must get out of this vicious circle. There are only two possibilities. One is for a violent type of revolution to occur which would suddenly change the whole structure of society to make it fit for rapid development of science and economic progress. The other alternative is deliberately to build up the foundation of science-oriented education and research to promote the modernisation of society in a peaceful way, and make conditions favourable for economic development.

7.4. Aid for scientific and economic development from either the western or the eastern countries, even when given in a spirit of competition, would be cooperative in effect. In any event, competition in constructive tasks of building up scientific foundations in developing countries is less dangerous and is likely to be far more useful than competition in the methodologies of warfare. Also, collaboration in promoting education and research in pure science can be pursued without any threat to national security or national interests, and would be of great help in promoting a rapid advance of the underdeveloped countries and in fostering better understanding among the nations of the world. The advanced countries have a great opportunity for peaceful cooperation in giving aid for science.

Certain aspects of the problems mentioned in this paper were discussed by me in articles and addresses between 1955 and 1959 which were printed in my book *Talks on Planning* (published in 1961), and in other articles such as *A Note on Problems of Scientific Personnel* (1959), and *Recent Developments in the Organisation of Science in India* (1959), and also presented at the Conference for International Economic Cooperation and Partnership held in Austria (Salzburg-Vienna) in July 1962.

Professor P.M.S. Blackett in his presidential address to the British Association for the Advancement of Science in 1957 and in other articles in

Nature, (3 February, 1962; May 1962 etc.) has considered various problems from the point of view of the advanced countries. Professor Stevan Dedijer made a penetrating analysis in an article in *Nature* (6 August, 1960) and in another article published in Stockholm, *TVF*, 33 (1962). [Endnote by the editors of the book, *P.C. Mahalanobis. Papers on Planning*].

18. From Prakashvir Shastri[40]
[Refer to item 288]

2 अगस्त, 1962

श्रद्धेय पंडित जी,
सादर नमस्ते।

मैंने पीछे सरकार की भाषा सम्बन्धी नीति के सम्बन्ध में आपको पत्र लिखा था, सम्भव है मिल गया होगा। संविधान में हिन्दी का रूप और उसके 15 वर्ष तक की अवधि आपकी देखरेख में ही तय की गयी थी परन्तु अब कुछ ऐसा प्रतीत होता है कि दोनों ही बातों में थोड़ा विवाद उठ खड़ा हुआ है जो परिस्थितियों को देखते हुए उपयुक्त नहीं है।

आकाशवाणी में जो हिन्दी में बुलेटिन प्रसारित किये जाते हैं, सूचना मंत्री श्री गोपाल रेड्डी और उपमंत्री ला० शामनाथ ने उस सम्बन्ध में जो सरल हिन्दी के नाम पर परिवर्तन की घोषणा की है उसकी देश में अच्छी प्रतिक्रिया नहीं हुई। सम्भव है समाचार-पत्रों से आपको वह विदित भी हुआ हो। मेरी अपनी ऐसी इच्छा है कि इस सम्बन्ध में आप अथवा गृह-कार्य मंत्री श्री लालबहादुर जी शास्त्री शीघ्र ही एक वक्तव्य संसद में अथवा बाहर कहीं भी दें जिससे इस प्रश्न पर जो बवन्डर उठना चाहता है वह न उठ सके। अभी तो विभिन्न संस्थाओं के कुछ ऊपर के व्यक्ति ही इस बात का विरोध कर रहे हैं परन्तु यह आन्दोलन यदि उनके हाथों से निकलकर जनता के हाथों में चला गया तो फिर और भी कई प्रकार की कठिनाइयाँ पैदा हो सकती हैं जिनसे सरकार के कामों में जहाँ कुछ बाधाएँ पड़ेंगी वहाँ हिन्दी को भी नुकसान पहुँचेगा। अच्छा यही हो कि अब तक आकाशवाणी की जो नीति रही है उसको ही चलने दिया जाये।

पंजाब में हिन्दी के प्रश्न पर जो पीछे कुछ विवाद चला था तथा आपने कई स्थानों पर अपने भाषणों में और स्वामी आत्मानन्द जी तथा स्वयं मुझे भी लिखे गये अपने पत्रों में यह कहा था कि भाषा का प्रश्न भाषा-शास्त्रियों को ही बैठकर हल करना चाहिए, फिर भाषा शास्त्रियों से बिना परामर्श लिये आकाशवाणी की हिन्दी सम्बन्धी नीति में परिवर्तन करना आपके विचारों के आधार पर भी ठीक नहीं है। यों भी मेरा जहाँ तक अनुमान है

40. Letter from Prakashvir Shastri, Independent, Lok Sabha MP. Sent from 146 North Avenue, New Delhi 1. PMO, File No. 52(12)/57-63-PMS, Vol. I, Sr. No. 80 A.

मंत्रिमण्डल में इस सम्बन्ध में कोई नीति निर्धारित नहीं हुई। ऐसी स्थिति में उसको पहले जैसी स्थिति में ही रखना ठीक होगा।

एक दूसरी बात जो सन् 65 के बाद भी अंग्रेजी को बनाये रखने के सम्बन्ध में संसद के आगामी अधिवेशन में बिल उपस्थित होने वाला है उस सम्बन्ध में मैं आपसे निवेदन करना चाहता हूँ कि हिन्दी को राजभाषा बनाने के संबंध में समय की सीमा अवश्य निध्रारित की जाये और वह अधिक से अधिक न होकर कम से कम हो तो ठीक है। दूसरे जिन प्रान्तों की भाषा हिन्दी है उन पांच राज्यों में तो सन् 65 के बाद हिन्दी राजभाषा, यदि वे सहमत हों, तो घोषित कर दी जाये जिससे आप भी गौरव के साथ यह कह सकें कि संविधान बनाते समय जो हमने प्रतिज्ञा की थी उसमें इतने अंश तक हम सफल हो चुके हैं और शेष राज्यों के लिये प्रयत्नशील हैं। आशा है इस सम्बन्ध में जो आपके विचार होंगे उनसे मुझे अवश्य ही विस्तार से सूचित करने की कृपा करेंगे।

भवदीय,
प्रकाशवीर शास्त्री

[Translation begins][41]

2 August 1962

Honourable Panditji,

Respectful salutations. I hope you would have received my letter regarding Government's language policy. The status of Hindi and the period of 15 years had been put in the Constitution under your guidance. But now it seems as though in both the issues a slight argument has come up which under the circumstances is not appropriate.

The reaction in the country to the announcement made by Information Minister Shri Gopala Reddy and the Deputy Minister L. Shamnath regarding the changes to be made in the name of simplifying Hindi has not been positive. It is possible that you may have even come to know about it. My own view is that you or Home Minister Shri Lal Bahadur Shastriji should issue a statement in Parliament or even somewhere else to prevent the storm that is threatening to erupt on this issue. At the moment it is the top functionaries in various institutions who are opposing this move. But if it were to go out of their hands to the masses, all kinds of other difficulties could arise which will not only hinder the affairs of state but also do harm to Hindi. The best thing would be if the policy All India Radio is currently following is allowed to continue.

41. This translation is from the PMO file and not translated for the SWJN.

In the Punjab when a debate started over the question of Hindi you had said in several places in your speeches as also in your letters to Swami Atmanandji and also to me that the language issue should be decided only by language experts. So then to make changes in the language policy of the All India Radio without consulting language experts is not right even according to your own view. Even otherwise as far as I can gauge, no policy has been agreed upon in the Cabinet. In these circumstances it would best to continue the policy being currently followed.

On another matter, I would like to request regarding the Bill which is going to be presented in the next session to continue with English even after 1965 that a decision should be taken to fix a date to announce the adoption of Hindi as the national language and the time limit should be not maximum but minimum number of years. Secondly, in the five states where the mother tongue is Hindi, it should be announced to be the national language after 65 [1965] if they agree so that you may be able to say with pride that what had been pledged at the time of drawing up the Constitution has been fulfilled to this extent and that the effort is on to do so in other states also. I do hope that you will kindly inform me about your views on this matter in details.

Yours sincerely,
Prakashvir Shastri

[Translation ends]

19. From Asoke K. Sen: American Bar Association Conference[42]
[Refer to item 344]

2.8.62

My dear Prime Minister,
I am in receipt of your letter of the 29th of July last which you wrote from Raj Bhavan, Calcutta. I shall give you a brief summary of the approaches made to us from time to time by the sponsors of "World Peace Through Law". It is true, as Lord Shawcross says, that the American Bar Association and particularly Mr

---

42. Letter from the Law Minister; address: 4, Hastings Road, New Delhi. MEA, File No. UI/162-112/62, pp. 3-6/corr. Only extracts available in the NMML.

Rhyne,[43] who was at one time the Chairman[44] of the American Bar Association, have been the guiding spirits of the organisation. Myself and the Attorney-General[45] were for the first time invited to join their Asian Conference at Tokyo which was held in September, 1961. The Attorney-General accepted the invitation without consulting us. I sent the matter to the External Affairs Ministry for its comment. The Secretary, Shri M.J. Desai, made a note saying that no Minister or official of the Government of India should participate in the Conference. The principal objection appears to have been that no representatives from Communist countries were invited to that Conference. It now appears from the letter of Lord Shawcross that representatives from Communist countries were invited and they in fact joined the Conference at Rome.[46] The Prime Minister in his note of the 25th of June, 1961 agreed with the Foreign Secretary and advised me not to accept the invitation. The Prime Minister also asked me to advise the Attorney-General not to accept the invitation. Looking back it appears to me, however, that it might have been worthwhile if somebody from India had attended that Conference because the Conference and the work done by it aroused a good deal of interest throughout the whole world. Thereafter on the 8th of February, 1962 I received a letter from Mr Rhyne (Flag 'P) in which he gave an account of the Tokyo Conference and the Rome Conference which apparently Lord Shawcross had attended. He also referred to their desire to hold the next conference at New Delhi. Mr Robert Storey who is the Chairman of the Indo-US Trust[47] which runs the Fulbright Scheme for scholarship to Indian students also wrote to me on the 10th April, 1962 (Page 17 of the file). I wrote to Mr Rhyne on the 30th April, 1962 after consulting the External Affairs Ministry. The notes of the External Affairs Ministry appear at page 6-8 of the file. In short, the External Affairs Ministry thought that it would not be proper for the Government to take any part, directly or indirectly, in the Conference. In my reply to Mr Rhyne which will appear at page 21 of the file I wrote to him saying that it was not quite clear from his letter whether he wanted the Government of India to take any interest in the holding of the proposed Conference and that the Government of India regretted that it would not be able to take any part officially in the holding of the Conference, which was sponsored by private bodies. I pointed out to him that a similar conference was held in New Delhi by the International Commission of Jurists some time

---

43. Charles S. Rhyne, 1912-2003.
44. The official term was "President."
45. M.C. Setalvad.
46. Held 1-4 April 1962.
47. The US Board of Foreign Scholarships.

back and that was sponsored entirely by their members in India.[48] I requested him to let me know exactly what he expected me to do. I pointed out to him also the difficulties about hotel accommodation at the time of the proposed conference. Mr Rhyne sent a reply to me dated 28th May, 1962 which will appear at Page 23 of the file of correspondence. He pointed out that the only part that the Governments of the countries where such conferences are held were expected to take was the presence of the President or the Prime Minister at the inaugural session and certain governmental receptions. He pointed out that it had been made emphatically clear that no Government sponsorship was desired. I showed this letter to you and had a discussion with you on the matter. Thereafter I sent a reply to Mr Rhyne on 14th June, 1962, which will appear at page 25 of the file of correspondence. In my reply, which was approved by you, I said that if you happened to be in Delhi at the time we might request you to inaugurate the Conference. We were quite guarded even in that letter. Mr Rhyne sent a reply to me dated 19th June, 1962 which will appear at page 31 of the file of correspondence. Apparently Mr Rhyne must have informed Lord Shawcross about my letter.

It is true that Mr Rhyne himself has informed me in his letter of the 28th of May, 1962 that apart from the money spent by the American Bar Association and the Ford Foundation the US Government has appropriated some funds for the World Conference. It seems that the Conference is sponsored entirely in a non-official capacity and the delegates attend in their private capacities. The successive conferences have been attracting world-wide attention and the literature they have been producing has been of high quality. They have not been of the propaganda type. Some of the literature, the Report on the Asian Conference and the editorial comments on the Conference are in the file. I agree with the views of Lord Shawcross that the participation of Communist countries shows the importance that is being attached now to the Conferences of this organisation. Mr Rhyne wrote to me on the 8th February, 1962 that they regretted very much that I could not go to Tokyo. The Attorney-General also cancelled his earlier acceptance on our advice. I hope that the background of the whole matter, as I have given above, will help you to send a suitable reply to Lord Shawcross. ...

[A.K. Sen]

48. The second Congress of the International Commission of Jurists, held in New Delhi, 5-10 January 1959, was organized by the Indian Commission of Jurists. For Nehru's inaugural address to the Congress, see SWJN/SS/46/item 101.

769

20. From C.B. Gupta: Socialist Forum Dividing UP Congress[49]

[Refer to item 41]

August 3, 1962

My dear Panditji,

Kindly excuse me for my encroachment upon your valuable time to apprise you about the inaugural activities of the Congress Socialist Forum under the leadership of Sri Mohan Lal Gautam.[50] The activities of the meeting of the Forum convened by an invitation from Sri Gautam has appeared in the press,[51] a cutting of which is being sent herewith. This happened only a day after your visit and address to the members of the PCC and the Legislators.[52] You are perhaps aware that the opposition parties, after their defeat in the general elections, are contemplating to organise a campaign against increase in taxation. Various objections are being raised from various quarters in the interest of various classes and the opposition parties are exploiting the dissatisfaction. Fortunately, your speech at the combined meeting of the legislators and the Congress delegates had watered down various objections, had cleared up confusion and had generated enthusiasm and developed courage amongst Congressmen in general to push through the plan and its completion with any sacrifice that it might demand. But the reports that appeared in the papers regarding the meeting of the Forum washed away the salutary effects and diverted the attention of the Congressmen to the objections against taxation creating mental confusion again.

I was suspecting an inkling of this attitude of Sri Gautam from his talk in the meeting of the Executive Committee meeting of the PCC held a day prior to your

---

49. Letter from the Chief Minister of UP. PMO, File No. 17(502)/62-66-PMS, Sr. No. 9-B. Only excerpts are available in the NMML.
50. A member of the Executive Committee, UPCC, and former Cooperation Minister in UP.
51. Ram Kumar Shastri, MLA, said at a convention of the UP Socialist Planning Forum, held in Lucknow on 30 July 1962, that "the hopes aroused by the achievement of freedom had been belied. There was retrogression instead of progress and the situation continued to deteriorate. Problems could not be discussed freely at UPCC meetings because of the fear of disciplinary action. Senior Congressmen had been expelled from the organisation for giving expression to their views. There was groupism and factionalism in the party. To study the problems facing the State and to find a way out of the marsh in which it had been bogged down it was decided to form the Socialist Planning Forum." *The Times of India*, 31 July 1962, p.1.
52. Nehru addressed a joint meeting of the members of the UPCC and of the Congress Legislature Party in Lucknow on 28 July 1962, item 399.

visit. We were discussing the plan and the resources to be raised by means of enhanced taxation in that meeting. Sri Gautam raised an objection to the taxation measures expressing in general the arguments adumbrated by the opposition parties. I intervened reminding Sri Gautam that the plan had been framed and adopted when he was a member of the State Cabinet. I told him that it was not correct to say that the plan was not made known to the people. I also told him that the plan when it was framed was made a part of our election manifesto. The plan was discussed at great length at various levels in the organisation as well as in the government. The AICC adopted it, the Planning Commission adopted it, the Union Government adopted it and the State Government adopted it when he was a member of the Cabinet. Adoption of the plan implies raising up the resources and in fact, the assessment of the resources and indication to raise them had also been approved by the Planning Commission including enhanced taxation on land, and the State Government, when he was a member of the Cabinet committed itself to raise these resources as share of the State and therefore, on this basis I pleaded with him and personally requested him in the meeting not to raise these objections at this time in the meeting of the PCC. But to my great disappointment he not only ignored this request of mine, but he in the meeting of the Forum highlighted, rather concentrated, on the very thing. I am leaving this matter to you to judge the effect of these activities at this time when the opposition parties are organising to launch a campaign against our taxation measures.

Nandaji[53] had written to me a letter regarding the Socialist Forum within the Congress. Therein he mentioned that "I shall take an early opportunity to consult you regarding the persons who may be requested to take the initiative in the formation of units of the Forum in the State". I had expressed my doubt to Nandaji in my reply that a separate organisation like this might be taken advantage of by dissatisfied Congressmen and had suggested that the objective of the Forum can be achieved by taking suitable steps by forming study circles within the Congress organization, assuring him of my full support for this purpose. I did not receive any communication from Nandaji about the persons who may be entrusted with the task of forming the Forum in this State. I am afraid, if Sri Gautam had been authorised to take up this work in this way in the State either by Nandaji or by the Congress President[54] or by you. Sri Gautam had sent me a letter dated July 23, 1962, inviting my participation in the first convention of the UP Socialist Planning Forum to be held on July 30, 1962.

53. Gulzarilal Nanda, Minister for Planning, Labour and Employment and Deputy Chairman, Planning Commission.
54. D. Sanjivayya.

I had replied to him on the lines indicated in my letter to Nandaji requesting him not to form a separate institution as the experience of such an attempt in the past[55] was not encouraging, but Sri Gautam perhaps did not care for it. If we look to the proceedings of this Convention and the reports which appeared in the press, the list of the members who took part in the meeting and the atmosphere prevailing in the meeting, it can easily be inferred that it was more a convention to express dissatisfaction taking advantage of the imposition of certain hardships in the form of enhanced taxation instead of furthering the objective to bring in socialistic approach in the society.[56]

...

With respects,

Yours sincerely,
C.B. Gupta

21. From Brij Krishan Chandiwala: Bharat Sevak Samaj Meeting[57]

[Refer to item 311]

4.8.1962

सुबह मैंने 12 अगस्त को भारत सेवक समाज की मीटिंग में पधारने के लिये आपसे निवेदन किया था। दस वर्ष बाद पहली बार समाज यह स्थापना दिवस मना रही है। यदि आधा घंटा भी आप निकाल सकें तो हमारे कार्यकर्ताओं को बड़ा उत्साह मिलेगा। आशा है आप आना स्वीकार करेंगे। समय शाम को छः बजे से सात का है। मीटिंग कनाट सरकस के मैदान में होगी।

[Translation begins

4 August 1962

This morning I made a request that you should attend the meeting of the Bharat Sevak Samaj to be held on August 12. It is celebrating its foundation day for the

---

55. Referring perhaps to Ahmedabad. See item 39.
56. Nehru had already objected to Gulzarilal Nanda about such a Socialist Forum within Congress, see item 39 and again in response to C.B. Gupta's complaints, item 40; also a guarded message, item 42.
57. Letter from the convener of the Delhi Branch of the Bharat Sevak Samaj. Salutation and signature not available. NMML, B.K. Chandiwala Papers, Subject File No. 1.

first time in ten years. If you could spare even half an hour, it would give great encouragement to our workers. I hope you will agree to attend. It is scheduled for six to seven o'clock in the evening. The meeting is to be held in the field in Connaught Circus.

Translation ends]

22. From Amrit Kaur: Paper Mill in Hoshangabad[58]
[Refer to item 130]

August 4, 1962

My dear Jawaharlal,

I am today in receipt of the enclosed.[59]

I have known of the Friends Rural Centre at Rasulia for many years and Bapu[60] gave the Quakers his blessings when they started this work in Hoshangabad. These Friends have done very fine work in Rasulia and I just do not understand why they should be treated in this unkind manner. Such action is truly indicative of the communal spirit that is rampant in India today and, in particular, where any Christian Indian work is concerned.

58. Letter from the Chairman of the Indian Red Cross and former Health Minister; address: Manorville, PO Summer Hill, Simla W. PMO, File No. 17(515)/62-64-PMS, Sr. No. 1-A.

59. From letter of Ed Abbott of Friends Rural Centre, Rasulia, Hoshangabad, Madhya Pradesh, 26 July:

"About the first of May we heard rumours that our land was to be requisitioned. Without any official notification we thought these were just rumours but anyway went to ask the DC. We were shaken to hear that 26 of our 35 acres of farm land was to be taken. I presented him a memorandum pointing out how this land which was once eroded waste by hard work and good husbandry had been transformed into some of the most productive land in the area having last year, despite adverse weather, produced as high as 36 maunds per acre in some test plots; that it was essential to our dairy which serves Hoshangabad; that it is the backbone of our experimental agriculture and of our extension work; that valuable equipment acquired for farming this land would be rendered practically useless without the land. He was sympathetic and in my presence dictated a very strong letter recommending the manager of the proposed paper mill to take other land that is available adjacent to ours and spare Rasulia "in the interest of humanity". We heard by the grape-vine that in reply he was told that this is a very late date to raise objections to the site—a late time—before those most concerned have been even notified!" PMO, File No. 17(515)/ 62-64-PMS, Sr. No. 1-B.

60. Mahatma Gandhi.

I do not know whether it is at all possible for you to intervene on behalf of Mr Abbott[61] and his colleagues who have been real friends of India.

I am sorry to trouble you but to whom else can one go?

Yours ever,
Amrit

23. Uttar Pradesh Roads[62]
[Refer to item 185]

In January 1962, PM wrote to the Chief Minister, Uttar Pradesh, about the inadequacy of proper roads in Allahabad District and suggested that Community Blocks should be connected with pucca roads and cheaper method of road construction be adopted.[63] A detailed reply was received from the Chief Minister wherein he stated that according to the Nagpur Plan the State had still to construct nearly 2,000 miles of metalled road to reach the target.[64] The Third Plan provided for the construction of 580 miles of roads throughout the State. This mileage being short, it could not be distributed to all the districts of the State. It was, therefore, decided to allot this mileage to those districts which were deficit on the basis of the Nagpur Plan.[65] The District of Allahabad, according to the plan, needed 367 miles of metalled road and against this it would have 434 miles of metalled road on the completion of the road works already under execution, thus exceeding the target by about 67 miles. For this reason, no new road was provided for Allahabad District in the Third Five Year Plan. The large areas in the district are, however, devoid of proper means of communication and realising this need the State Government sanctioned the construction of the 25 miles long Sirathu Saraikail road as a part of their Central Road Fund Scheme for serving the western portions of the District. With regard to the 52

---

61. Dr Ed Abbott and his wife Dr Vivian Abbott worked for eight years on health, water and sanitation projects under the Friends Rural Centre, Rasulia, Hoshangabad, sponsored by the Canadian Friends Service Committee. *Canadian Quaker History Journal*, No. 66, 2001. Link http://www.cfha.info/journal66.pdf accessed on 29 May 2018.
62. Note, 4 August 1962, by V.P. Marwaha (not identified). PMO, File No. 17(519)/62-66-PMS, Sr. No. 29-A.
63. See SWJN/SS/74/item 134.
64. The first two paragraphs of this note by V.P. Marwaha are based on C.B. Gupta's reply of 6 March 1962 to Nehru's letter of 8 January 1962 (SWJN/SS/74/item 134). Only an extract from C.B. Gupta's letter was available and it was not included in volume 74.
65. The Nagpur Plan, which envisaged road development policy for the period 1943-1963, was the first attempt to prepare a coordinated road development plan in India.

mile road from Saraon to Handia via Phulpur, with feeders to Holagarh, Baharia and Dhanupur, the State Government have approached the Central Ministry of Transport and Communications (Department of Transport) for a grant equal to two-third of the estimated cost of Rs 33.80 lakhs. Agreeing to the need of linking block headquarters with metalled roads, it was added that the programme being heavy it was beyond the means of the State Government and they were therefore thinking of connecting them by unmetalled roads for the time being.

The Chief Minister added that the cheaper method of road construction known as "Mehra Method" which required the use of technically established soil and was fit only for light traffic roads was not considered fit for road construction in the State and for that reason it had not been adopted on any large scale.

Under PM's instructions, a reference was then made to Dr A.N. Khosla, Member, Planning Commission who replied on 23rd March, 1962 that after resolving some controversial issues and in consultation with Director, Central Road Research Institute, a note would be prepared which would be acceptable to all Road Engineers. He promised to send a copy of that note to PM. A further letter from him is awaited.

V.P. Marwaha

24. From Gulzarilal Nanda: Socialist Forum in UP[66]
[Refer to item 40]

August 6, 1962

My dear Jawaharlalji,

I have just received your letter regarding the Socialist Forum in UP. I read in the newspapers some time before the last AICC meeting an announcement by Gautam[67] giving an indication of his intention to take such a step. I have not met him since then and have never had a word with him on this subject. A few days ago, K.D. Malaviya[68] spoke to me that Gautam had made the request to him that he should attend a conference in Lucknow, and that the invitation was also extended to me. I categorically refused to have anything to do with Gautam or his activities. K.D.[69] also did not go.

---

66. Letter from Minister for Planning, Labour and Employment and Deputy Chairman, Planning Commission. PMO, File No. 17(502)/62-66-PMS, Sr. No. 11-A.
67. An MLA in UP and member of the Executive Committee, UPCC.
68. Congress, Lok Sabha MP from Basti, UP, and Minister of Mines and Fuel.
69. K.D. Malaviya.

A day before the conference, I telephoned to Shri C.B. Gupta[70] and conveyed to him that I was completely dissociating myself from what Gautam was doing. I believe he was satisfied. I told him further that I would myself not take any step in UP without his consent. Arjun Arora[71] who is connected with the Congress Forum for Socialist Action, was in Lucknow on the day the Conference was held. He made it clear there that we had no concern with Gautam's Conference or Forum. It is very strange that despite all this, Shri Gupta thinks nothing of stating in his letter to you: "I am afraid if Shri Gautam had been authorised by Nandaji ..."[72] As I wrote in my letter to you, I am not going to initiate anything in any State, without the consent and permission of both the Chief Minister and the President of the Pradesh Congress Committee.[73]

I am very sorry, however, that I myself should create any botheration for you.

Yours sincerely,
G.L. Nanda

25. From Ranbir Singh: Foreign Exchange for Beas Project[74]

[Refer to items 166-167 and appendix 36]

6th August, 1962

Respected Panditji,

As you are aware, in the context of the Indus Water Treaty with Pakistan, the Beas Project has a particular significance and national interest demands that the project may be constructed at top most priority. India has already begun paying the instalments to Pakistan under the Treaty and apart from anything else, national prestige is also involved in the early completion of this Project. However, despite the best efforts on our part, we have run into difficulties with regard to the construction work on this Project which has already slid somewhat behind schedule.

The major difficulty we are confronting is the want of machinery. Because of the particular nature of the work, namely long tunnels on the Beas-Sutlej Link

---

70. The Chief Minister of UP.
71. Congress, Rajya Sabha MP from UP.
72. See his letter of 3 August 1962, item 20.
73. Ajit Prasad Jain.
74. Letter from the Minister of Irrigation and Power, Punjab, Chandigarh. PMO, File No. 17(372)/59-69-PMS, Sr. No. 27-A.

(Unit I) and enormous quantity of work on Pong Dam (Unit No. 2), the progress on the work depends entirely on the early procurement of machinery. This, in turn, is dependent on the availability of foreign exchange. I am informed that the World Bank had undertaken to provide foreign exchange assistance of about 56 Million Dollars for this Project, but unfortunately our attempts to secure any part of it even to meet the immediate requirements of machinery have not been of any avail so far, despite the fact that Shri M.R. Sachdev, Secretary, Ministry of Irrigation & Power, is personally pursuing the matter in USA. I understand that the World Bank authorities have given some kind of promise, but unless the other authorities like AID also give clearance, the foreign exchange will not be released. I feel that unless the matter is taken up at higher level, early results will not be achieved and I, therefore, respectfully suggest that the matter may be taken up through our Ambassador or in any other suitable manner with the World Bank, bringing home the immediate necessity of foreign exchange for the purchase of at least our immediate requirements of machinery.

Apart from the above, I have another request to make. In view of the importance of the Project and the need for its immediate construction, it would be desirable that if there is some delay in the release of the foreign exchange by the World Bank, some foreign exchange, say of about Rs 2 crore, may be made available by the Government of India from their free foreign exchange quota, so that the machinery is procured and work started at the earliest. The lists of such machinery have already been scrutinised at all levels and orders placed with firms subject to the release of foreign exchange. By adopting the above course, we will be saving very valuable time and as and when the World Bank releases the foreign exchange, the Government of India may recoup the amount released from the free quota. I have every hope that with your kind intervention our difficulties would be resolved and I would earnestly request you to intercede in this behalf.

With respectful regards,

Yours sincerely,
Ranbir Singh

26. From V.K. Krishna Menon: Malerkotla's Nephew[75]
[Refer to item 54]

7th August 1962

My dear Prime Minister,
This is in continuation of my letter No. 130-DM (C) 62 dated the 12th July 1962, regarding permission to the nephew of the Nawab of Malerkotla to come to India. I had thought that it might be possible to allow him to come on a visa which could be renewed while his activities and behaviour are watched. Grant of Indian nationality to him could be considered late if he does not come to adverse notice while he resides in India under a visa. Army Headquarters views were invited on this suggestion by the Ministry and the CGS has noted as follows:

> "In view of the present situation, I think it would be a security risk to allow the Nawab's nephew to come here, even on a temporary visa. I suspect his bona fides and recommend we should turn down his request."

2. As the Ministry of Home Affairs are the final authority on this matter, I am forwarding the Army Headquarters views to them. They will, no doubt, consider all the circumstances of this case before giving their final recommendation to you.

Affectionately
V.K. Krishna Menon

27. From Mahavir Tyagi: Revamping the Congress[76]
[Refer to item 25]

8 August 1962

I am writing this letter to you with rather a heavy heart. You know that I have been a Member of the All-India Congress Committee for the last 39 years, and Congress has not only been a source of emotional satisfaction, like a temple of worship, to me but it has also sustained me as a playground for my political exploits, sports and recreations. Having lived a maddening life of cumulative devotion and mirth for the last 42 years, it now shocks me to realise that I and

---

75. Letter from the Defence Minister. MHA, File No. 10/40/62-F. III, p. 12/c.
76. Letter from Congress MP; address: 16, Dr Rajendra Prasad Road, New Delhi. Salutation not available.

hundreds others like me are finding themselves totally besieged by those who do not, in the least, share the sentiments which have sustained us as a well knit organisation during all the ups and downs of our struggle for the emancipation of the society.

With millions of bogus members enrolled in the country, it is illogical to expect the Congress organisation to hold its own. There are thousands from amongst the old guard who would not like to get elected even as delegates to the Indian National Congress with the help and support of members who are not genuine. In 1920 and onwards everyone who offered to join the Congress did so in defiance of all risks to his personal liberty, family avocation and all sources of subsistence. It was indeed a great hurdle that one had to cross. Now, since we are a party in power, entry into the Congress is considered to be a gainful source of prosperity and employment. Group consciousness and team spirit having vanished altogether, "inspiration" has yielded place to "aspiration", which now seems to have become a real motive force behind the greedy crowd which informs our organisation. Even members of the old guard are forced by circumstances to safeguard their own personal positions; and the relations of friendship coupled with gestures of warm smiles only serve as a camouflage for the most engrossing human relationship of rivalry and jealousy. From top to bottom we seem to have succumbed to our natural instinct of self-preservation. Consequently, our mutual relationship is also biased by considerations of personal likes and dislikes. This state of affairs is detrimental not only to the Congress but also to the country as a whole. Self-preservation being the strongest animal instinct, it takes the best of us with the result that our main objective of service to the people gets lost sight of. Under these circumstances we should either dissolve the Congress organisation altogether or affect some very drastic changes in its constitution. Let the party not be exposed to the inroads of such entrepreneurs as wish to capture the organisation for their personal ends by invading it with armies of bogus members.

I submit the following few proposals for your consideration:

a) Four-Anna membership should not be allowed to exercise any franchise in the organisation. They should all be our associate members to cooperate in the execution of our set programmes and policies.

b) We must have registers of permanent membership, and only the following categories should be allowed to be the voting members in their respective localities:

    1) Those who have ever been to jail during our struggle for freedom. .

2) Those who have ever remained office bearers or members of the Mandal Congress Committees, DCCs, PCCs and the AICC.
3) Those who have ever been given a Congress ticket to fight an election to local bodies, or the Central or State legislatures.
4) Each Mandal Congress Committee should co-opt from among its associate members of three years standing one-fourth of its strength.

I am confident that this limited number of voting members in the Congress will amply serve our purpose. Even if there be any group rivalry between these members, I am confident that they would not be a big menace to the organisation.

I hope you will give thought to these suggestions. In case you feel that your colleagues in the Working Committee are not very keen to effect any changes in the constitution, please permit me to move a resolution to this effect in the All India Congress Committee. Believe me, the atmosphere in the lower ranks has become too suffocating for those who still have a live faith in the ideals of the Congress.

Yours sincerely,
Mahavir Tyagi

28. From Sudhir Ghosh: Krishna Menon, Hubert Humphrey and American Liberals[77]
[Refer to item 347]

8 August, 1962

My dear Panditji,

I venture to enclose another letter I have received from Senator Hubert Humphrey; he makes some comments on difficulties of India-America relations. I hope you will have a look at it. It is disappointing to see that even good men among American leaders do not realise that arms supplies to Pakistan cause more aggressiveness instead of restraining aggression in the world.

As regards India, they seem to be more obsessed about a person than about policy; they do not get on with Mr Menon[78] but they fail to state clearly what is their quarrel with the policy he advocates (and they know he does it with

77. Letter from former PSP member, later Independent Rajya Sahba MP, recently enrolled in Congress; address: 95, South Avenue, New Delhi. NMML, Sudhir Ghosh Papers.
78. V.K. Krishna Menon, Defence Minister, representing India at the UN.

exceptional ability) in the UN. I wish it were possible to bring about a little better understanding between Mr Menon and leading Americans in a human sort of way. I venture to think that this might well happen if, without the glare of publicity, a number of quiet informal talks, perhaps over meals, were arranged between some of the leading American liberals and Mr Menon when he goes to the UN General Assembly next month. A good man like Hubert Humphrey would, I feel sure, be happy to be instrumental in it.

I went to see Mr Menon a few weeks ago, after the lapse of many years; I found him much more generous and mellow than I had anticipated. He even expressed his willingness to help me to make some better use of my time; it meant a lot to me.

If the Americans get to know Mr Menon a little better I feel that much good will come out of it.

With regards,

Yours sincerely,
Sudhir Ghosh

29. Teja Singh Swatantra[79]
[Refer to items 99-100]

Dear Sir,

We are addressing this letter to you in order to seek your personal intervention in the case of Sardar Teja Singh Swatantra against whom warrants of arrest are pending since June, 1951 under Section 120 B IPC from the Court of the SDM, Kashipur, District Nainital.

The said Warrants were issued in connection with a dacoity in the Nainital Bank at Ramnagar in which 17 persons were challanned (11 for the actual participation in the commission of dacoity, and 6 for supporting in planning and preparation of the dacoity). Sardar Teja Singh Swatantra has been placed in the 2nd group and warrants against him are under Section 120 B on charge of conspiracy only.

Twelve of the seventeen accused have been tried so far, three under section 120 B and 9 under section 395 and 120 B. All the three tried only under section 120 B were acquitted by the Sessions Judge, while the sentences of others under

79. Letter, dated 8 August 1962, from several political parties; given to Nehru by a deputation on 13 August 1962.

Section 120 B were set aside by the honourable High Court. (Extracts from the Court's judgments are attached separately).

Still without prejudice to the above facts and not relying much on the technical legal aspect of the case we draw your kind attention to the wider political considerations and still more to the humanitarian aspect of the issue which deserves your sympathetic consideration.

S. Teja Singh Swantantra has an exemplary record of work, devotion, suffering and sacrifices for the cause of Indian freedom. Joining the Ghadar Party after the Jallianwala Bagh massacre, he toured from village to village organising Congress Committees and volunteer corps which culminated in the formation of famous Swatantra Jatha.

He organised a victorious movement for the repatriation and release of the Martial Law, Ghadar Party, and other revolutionary prisoners who were all repatriated to their respective provinces from the Andamans in 1920. Then immediately after he was sent outside India to propagate the cause of Indian Freedom, and organise Addas at different points in the Waziristan Area, which served to give protection to the Freedom Fighters in the years to come. Hundreds of patriots have been to and fro Europe using these "Addas".

Netaji Subhas Chandra Bose himself escaped from India through these "Addas" with letters and instructions from Teja Singh Swatantra.

Teja Singh Swatantra joined the Military College in Turkey in 1925 and obtained highest honours in that Military Academy. Afterwards he went to America to revitalise the Ghadar Party in the USA, Panama, Chile, Brazil, Fiji, Canada and Argentina etc. During his tour in these countries, besides mobilising moral support for Indian Freedom, he recruited hundreds of freedom fighters from amongst the Indians abroad.

It was after passing more than a decade far from home and touring dozens of countries, rousing, activising, and mobilising the Indians there for the cause of Freedom that Teja Singh Swatantra returned to India in 1934 and plunged himself in the National Movement. He was arrested in 1936 and was detained in Campbellpur Jail (Punjab) under Regulation III of 1818 as a state prisoner. In 1937 he was elected unopposed to the Legislative Assembly, Punjab, while behind the bars on Congress ticket.

From 1942 onwards since his release from the Campbellpur Jail he worked in the Punjab, organising the peasants and the rural poor, strengthening the National Movement in the rural areas. After Partition, he worked amongst the uprooted peasants and served for their early systematic rehabilitation. His work in the Pepsu rural areas is well known in Punjab.

In June 1951, Sardar Teja Singh Swatantra and Chajju Mal as leaders of the Lal Party were charged with conspiracy under section 120 B in a dacoity in the Nainital Bank at Ramnagar. Chajju Mal was arrested, tried, and acquitted, while Teja Singh Swatantra is still absconding.

He is above 65 years of age. His only daughter died during these years and his home in Gurdaspur District collapsed during floods. Above all, long underground life has completely shattered his health. He is a patient of chronic diabetes, and not able to face the strains of police custody and jail life. He is fast losing weight.

It is a matter of deep anxiety for all political workers in Punjab, especially of the older generation, that a man who has suffered so long, faced every hardship and sacrificed his all for the cause of National Freedom, has not been able to enjoy and participate in the country's new born political life.

In view of all this we would strongly request the UP Government to cancel the warrants pending against S. Teja Singh Swatantra. He has undergone untold hardships as a fugitive for over a decade. As an old political sufferer and a distinguished fighter in the cause of freedom his case deserves your utmost sympathy. If for nothing else only on humanitarian grounds the Warrants against him should be withdrawn.

We are,

Yours truly,
Sd/- (Leader, PSP)
Sd/- (Leader, Socialist Party)
Sd/- R.P. Singh (Leader, Swatantra Party)
Sd/- Z.A. Ahmed (Leader, Communist Party)
Sd/- (Leader, Azad Dal)
Sd/- (Leader, Republican Party)

8.8.1962

30. From D.T. Arap Moi: India's Negative Role in Kenya Politics[80]

[Refer to item 388]

8th August, 1962

Dear Mr Prime Minister,

I have followed with great admiration, your historical background in struggle for India's independence. You might have, in the course of your struggle, come into conflict with other foreign powers personnel trying to interfere with internal politics of your country. This is so with us here in Kenya.

2.   May I, with great dismay, point out to you, Mr Prime Minister, that your High Commissioner for the Government of India in East and Central Africa, is interfering with our internal politics and hence restrained a good relationship between the two countries and further bring India's prestige and influence on this Continent into disrepute.[81] I am writing this letter as Chairman of the Kenya African Democratic Union, which is one of the two biggest parties in Kenya. I feel very strongly that the role of your High Commissioner here in Kenya should be neutral and non-partisan in our internal political affairs.

Your statement in 1953 is well known by us here and I completely agree with your statement in which you stated that the Indian community living in Kenya and East Africa should side with the Africans in these territories and this is of course what should be done. The Indian Community in Kenya have made a big contribution towards the economic growth of Kenya, particularly in the commercial field and they should continue doing so, but if some associate themselves with your High Commissioner, then they will be doing a great dis-service to their Community and will bring about some conflicts with the Africans which is not the right thing for this country.

I am writing this letter in the hope that this matter could be rectified and hence establish the good name of India in Kenya.

Yours
D.T. Arap Moi

---

80. Letter from the Minister of Local Government, P.O. Box 30004, Nairobi, Kenya, and the All Union's Chairman, Kenya African Democratic Union, Private Bag, Kabarnet, RVP, Kenya. MEA, File No: A-IV/103/21/62, p. 19/corr.
81. K.R.F. Khilnani. See item 387 and appendix 34.

31. From D.N. Tiwary: Power Failure in Delhi[82]
[Refer to item 113]

August 10, 1962

My dear Panditji,

I am writing this letter with a heavy heart. Wherever I see any harm of the Congress or its loss of prestige, I am greatly disturbed. The performance of the Minister of Irrigation and Power[83] is always poor but his performance in Lok Sabha on the 9th August was so disappointing that the Congress members had to hang their heads in shame, while the opposition members were having a dig at us and were indulging in derisive laughs.

Some members of our Party came to me and asked me to join a deputation to you about this affair. Thinking that this will lead to an unsavoury publicity in the press, I assured them that I would bring this matter to the notice of the Leader.

Being in the Congress for the last 42 years, I know the achievements of Hafiz Sahib. I have all respect for him. The feelings of Party members and of the Parliament should also be taken into consideration.

With kindest regards,

Yours sincerely,
D.N. Tiwary

32. From Bishan Chander Seth[84]
[Refer to item 289]

11 अगस्त 1962

परम् आदरणीय नेहरु जी,

सादर प्रणाम। मेरे 23-7-62 के पत्र[85] उत्तर में आपका 26-7 को आनन्द भवन प्रयागराज से भेजा पत्र[86] यथासमय मिला। चुंके वह हस्तलिखित है अतः आपकी सुविधार्थ मैं अपने

---

82. Letter from Congress MP; address: 9, Windsor Place, New Delhi. PMO, File No. 7(258)/62-66-PMS, Sr. No. 10-A.
83. Hafiz Mohammed Ibrahim.
84. Letter from Lok Sabha MP of the Hindu Mahasabha. Sent from 24 South Avenue, New Delhi.
85. Appendix 8.
86. Item 286.

23-7 तथा आपके 26-7 के पत्रों की कापी साथ भेज रहा हूँ ताकि मेरे इस पत्र का उत्तर देने में आपको असुविधा अनुभव न हो।

किसी भी देश का राष्ट्रीय कौन है इसके सम्बन्ध में सभी राष्ट्रों एवं संयुक्त राष्ट्र संघ सरीखी विशाल संस्था तक ने सिद्धान्त निश्चय किये हैं जिसे आप मेरे से अधिक जानते हैं। भारत हेतु मैं सत्यता से 3 मौलिक सिद्धान्त मानता हूँ। जो इस जांच में पक्के उतरे वे ही हमारे देश के नेशनल (राष्ट्रीय) बनने के अधिकारी हैं। जो इस मौलिक जांच में असफल हों उन्हें केवल इस देश में रहने खाने आदि सभी नागरिक सुविधायें प्राप्त करने तक सीमित अधिकार प्राप्त होना चाहिए, पर वे हमारे राष्ट्र की राजनीति के भागीदार नहीं बन सकते।

1. जो इस देश को मातृभूमि समझे।
2. जो इस देश की राष्ट्रभाषा को अपना माने।
3. जो इस देश को पुण्यभूमि माने।

यदि इस परख में मुसलमान, ईसाई उतरते हैं तो वे जैसे नानक पन्थी, कबीर पन्थी, वैष्णव, आर्यसमाजी आदि हमारे अटूट राष्ट्रीय अंग हैं मोहम्मदपन्थी एवं ईसापन्थी बनकर देश के राष्ट्रीय बन सकते हैं। उनकी धार्मिक मान्यता में हिन्दू मात्रा को कभी भी किन्चित आपत्ति नहीं हो सकती पर यदि उनकी आत्मा अभारतीय भाषा से बंधी हो अथवा उनका मौलिक धर्मस्थान मक्का, मदीना या पैलसटाईन ही हो और उनकी आन्तरिक भावनायें उन्हीं धर्म क्षेत्रों से सम्बन्धित हों जो आज प्रत्यक्षा है तो निश्चय आदरणीय पंडित जी वे सच्चे राष्ट्रीय नहीं बन सकते। यदि आपने मेरी सरल स्वाभाविक विनय को मान्यता नहीं तो सत्य कहता हूँ इतिहास में हमारी यह भूल अंकित रहेगी।

चीन, जापान आदि का बौद्ध भारत को अपना धर्म क्षेत्र मानते हुए भी अपने देश का सच्चा राष्ट्रीय है कारण उसके त्योहार, भोजन शैली, पहनावा, नाम, भाषा, सामाजिक जीवन सभी कुछ अपने देश के अनुकूल है, पर भारत का मुसलमान एवं ईसाई भारतीय जनजीवन के सभी अंगों से विपरित कृत्य करता हुआ ज़बरदस्ती शासन द्वारा राष्ट्रीय बनाया जा रहा है। अतः सेकुलर भावना को पुष्ट करने हेतु आप वास्तविक स्थिति ईश्वर हेतु भुलाने का प्रयास न कीजिए। मुसलमान एवं ईसाई जाति के अनेकों महत्वपूर्ण धर्मतीर्थ भारत में मौजूद हैं यदि उनमें राष्ट्रीयता है तो उन्हें भारत स्थित अपने इन्हीं धर्मतीर्थ एवं भारतीय संस्कृति में सत्य निष्ठा करना चाहिए, जो सच्ची राष्ट्रीयता का घोतक होगा।

मेरे 26-7-62 के पत्र की मूल भावना का तो आपने उत्तर में किन्चित संकेत भी नहीं किया। उसमें केवल इतना ही निवेदन था कि ईश्वर हेतु हिन्दी को आप इसी तरह छोड़ दीजिए। नवीन विधान बनाकर उसे नये संकट में न डालिये पर उस भावना के उत्तर को मेरा अनुमान है कि आपने जानबूझ कर भुलाया। क्या आप मेरी विनय जिसमें स्वर्गीय पंडित मदन मोहन मालवीय, महात्मा गांधी, श्री टण्डन[87] जी आदि की आत्माओं को सुख

---

87. Purushottamdas Tandon, an advocate of Hindi and former Congress President.

और बहुभाषी बहुसंख्यक हिन्दू मान को संतोष होगा पूरा करने में उदासीन हैं? स्वर्गीय महात्मा जी ने अनेक बार स्पष्ट शब्दों में कहा था कि कोई भी देश अपनी राष्ट्रभाषा के सम्मान को सुरक्षित किये बगैर राष्ट्रीय गौरव को जीवित नहीं रख सकता। आप उनके अनन्य भक्त ठहरे, क्या उनकी भावना को आप मान्यता नहीं देंगे।

राष्ट्रभाषा हिन्दी को हमारे संविधान के साथ राष्ट्रीय एकता समिति ने भी मान्यता दी, साथ ही भारत की सभी भाषाओं की लेखन शैली (लिपी) देवनागरी हो यह भी माना, ताकि आने वाली संतानें स्वाभाविक देश की कई भाषाएं जानने में रूचि एवं सुविधा अनुभव कर सकें।

यदि आपने इस सुझाव को मान्यता न दी तो विश्वास कीजिए भारत में दूसरा पाकिस्तान एवं नवीन ईसाई स्थान बनेगा कारण आज सरकारी नीति मुसलमान एवं ईसाई को परोक्ष बल देकर राष्ट्र को शान्ति हेतु स्पष्ट खतरा बनी हुई है। अतः गम्भीर विचार कर मेरी विनय को शीघ्र मान्यता दीजिए। कारण देश को अनेकों महत्वपूर्ण प्रश्न आपकी संरक्षता में सुलझाना है।

आशा है मुझे आपका शीघ्र ही सहयोगपूर्ण उत्तर प्राप्त होगा।

आपका ही
बिशनचन्द्र सेठ

[Translation begins

11 August 1962

Most Respected Nehruji,
My respectful saluatations.

Your reply of 26 July[88] sent from Anand Bhavan, Prayagraj, in reply to my letter of 23 July 1962[89] was received in time. Because that is handwritten, therefore for your convenience I am sending copies of my letter of 23-7 and yours of 26-7 so that you may not find any inconvenience in replying to this letter.

Principles have been laid down by all nations as well as a mammoth organization like the United Nations with regard to who is to be considered a national of a country, and you know that better than me. As regards India, I honestly believe in three basic principles and only those who pass this test have the right to be regarded as Indian nationals. Those who do not pass this basic test may have the limited right to avail of all civic amenities like the right to live, the right to food, etc., but they cannot be part of our national politics.

88. See fn 85 in this section.
89. See fn 86 in this section.

1. Those who consider this country as their motherland.
2. Those who accept the national language of this country.
3. Those who consider this land to be sacred.

If Muslims and Christians pass muster in this test, then just as the Nanakpanthis, Kabirpanthis, Vaishnavs, Arya Samajists, etc., are an inseparable part of this country, they too as Mohammedpanthis or Christpanthis can be the nationals of this country. Hindus can never have the least objection to their religious beliefs. However, if their spirit is tied to a non-Indian language or if their principal religious places are Mecca, Medina or Palestine and if their internal beliefs are tied to those religious places, which is so evident today, then, respected Panditji, they can most certainly not be the true nationals of India. If you do not pay heed to my simple natural request, then it will be marked in history as our mistake.

Though the Buddhists of China and Japan consider India as their sacred land, still they are the true nationals of the countries where they live because their festivals, food habits, dress, names, language and societal life are in accordance with the traits of those countries. But Muslims and Christians in India are being deliberately accorded the status of Indian nationals by the Government even though their actions are opposed to all aspects of Indian social life. Therefore, for God's sake, please do not try to forget the reality as it exists just to reinforce secularism. There are many important places of pilgrimage for Muslims and Christians in India and if they have any sense of nationalism, they should have true faith in only those sacred places and in Indian culture. This will reflect their true nationalism.

In your reply you have not even touched on the main point of my letter of 26-7-62. In that letter the only request was, for God's sake, please maintain the status quo regarding Hindi, do not promulgate a new decree and bring upon us a new crisis. In my opinion you deliberately ignored in your reply what I had pointed out. Are you indifferent to my request which would satisfy the souls of people like the late Pandit Madan Mohan Malaviya, Mahatma Gandhi and Shri Tandon,[90] etc., and would be a matter of satisfaction to the multilingual Hindus who are in a majority? Mahatma Gandhi had repeatedly and clearly said that no nation can keep its dignity intact without honouring its national language. You are his great disciple. Will you not value his sentiment?

Not only our Constitution but also the National Integration Council has given a place of importance to Hindi. It has also been laid down that all Indian languages should follow the Devanagari script in order that future generations

90. See fn 87 in this section.

may be naturally inclined to learn many Indian languages and be enabled to do so.

If you do not agree to this suggestion, please believe me that there will emerge another Pakistan or a Christian nation in India. The reason is that the Government's current policy by giving undue importance to Muslims and Christians is clearly endangering peace in the country. Therefore please give serious thought, as soon as possible, to my request because India has to resolve many important issues under your stewardship.

I hope I will soon get your cooperative reply.

Yours sincerely,
Bishan Chander Seth

Translation ends]

33. From Sushila Nayar: Sanitary Privies[91]
[Refer to item 236]

August 12, 1962

My dear Panditji,
I thank you for your kind letter dated the 10th instant with its enclosures.

If we can convert all service privies served by manual labour into sanitary septic privies and supply safe water for drinking purposes, it will eliminate more that 50% of the diseases in this country. I shall certainly request the Planning Commission to find some additional funds for this purpose. But I have my doubts if they will agree. With your interest and support we should be able to make at least a beginning in this direction during the Third Plan. Shri Mukherjee[92] has written to me also in this connection.

Yours sincerely,
Sushila Nayar

91. Letter from the Health Minister. PMO, File No. 28 (96)/62-71-PMS, Sr. No. 3-A.
92. Saila Kumar Mukherjee, Minister, West Bengal Government.

34. From Narain Singh: Indians in Kenya Politics[93]
[Refer to item 387]

13th August 1962

My dear Pundit Ji,

My justification in venturing to make this submission to you personally springs from my firm belief that the current political realities of Kenya, particularly those relating to Jomo Kenyatta, his principal lieutenants, and his party, the Kenya African National Union, (KANU) are being deliberately withheld from you by your representatives here. Consequently, the urgent need has arisen to inform you that the local Indian community is being rapidly thrust towards a disastrous situation which may create a grave problem for you and India in the near future. And, no matter now vehemently he may deny it, perceptive people here are well aware that the present Commissioner for India, Mr K.R.F. Khilnani is keenly associated with this ominous development. He has so far proved impervious to every attempt to dissuade him from this course of action.

For example, you have obviously not been advised that if the intention to invite Jomo Kenyatta to India is carried out before the next general elections in this country, and if he is at this stage accorded the recognition of and treatment as the "Leader of All Kenya", this fact will give serious offence to at least 45% of the Kenyan Africans who have repudiated him utterly and completely.

The Government of Somalia made this mistake a few weeks ago by receiving Jomo Kenyatta alone as its state guest. It was immediately compelled to rectify this mistake by extending a similar invitation to Ronald Ngala, the leader of the rival African party, the Kenya African Democratic Union, (KADU). Ngala holds exactly the same status in the Government of Kenya as Kenyatta. If the present trends continue—and all indications are they will—he stands an excellent chance of becoming the first Prime Minister of the country.

Before proceeding any further it is necessary to emphasise that firm impression which exists among all the well-disposed and knowledgeable persons in India to the effect that if the Asians (the common local term denoting Indians and Pakistanis) of this region perform what should be their instinctive duty by identifying themselves sincerely and completely with the African nationalist concept, they cannot have any fear or difficulty with regard to their future, has already proved to be a misconceived one. Tanganyika, which was expected to become a model plural-society country, is now a vast scene of gratuitous racial humiliations for the Asians, the anchorless Asians, in spite of

93. Letter from a journalist; address: PO Box 5481, Nairobi, Kenya Colony, East Africa. MEA, File No: A-IV/103/21/62, pp. 22-31/corr.

the fact that they had merged themselves wholeheartedly with the process of its cohesive evolution.

As the inevitable repercussion in Kenya, where the record of our people goes even further in that they were the very originators of the African nationalist concept, and have all along stimulated African economic activities in numerous directions, the overwhelming majority of the Asians, including those who have been settled here for generations, are unlikely to adopt its legal and permanent citizenship under independence, for as long as possible. They will prefer to live and work in a more circumscribed way as aliens with right of recourse to the countries of their origin. This will be the case because the image which our shallow and weak-kneed yet highly self-opinionated leaders have permitted to be established, and which the successive Indian Commissioners have done nothing to alter, regarding our community, is the reverse of the correct one. The typical African regards us as parasites and exploiters, and not as a people who have done so much to create this country out of nothing. To make the position much worse, an unholy alliance between the Kenya Indian Congress and the Indian Commissioner has as its main object the committing of the community irrevocably to a suicidal allegiance to Jomo Kenyatta and KANU.

Under independence, the minority communities will continue to have the dire need to take active steps for self-preservation. Fortunately, unlike Tanganyika, Kenya has not developed into a single party country. Wherever two fairly equally matched political parties come into existence, true democracy has a better chance for survival. I will go on to show how KADU, rather than KANU, offers this better chance to the Indians of Kenya.

That the present Commissioner and his predecessor[94] have definitely been involved in deep pro-KANU intrigues is now quite apparent from the open protest which the normally sedate and imperturbable Ronald Ngala has been driven to make. A copy of his protest has been sent to you. The Chairman of KADU, Arap Moi, has also written to you on this subject. Mr Khilnani has tried to attribute this complaint to a "misunderstanding" and has asked to see Mr Ngala. I can confidently predict that he will come out second best, a very bad second best, as the result of this discussion.

This appears to be the appropriate stage for declaring my own credentials. I was born and educated in Kenya. Sixteen continuous years out of the fifty of my life have been spent in pre and post-independence India: I became a typical refugee in 1947. For a considerable time now I have been a free-lance journalist and broadcaster in Kenya. I am incontestably the leading Asian, and in terms

94. I.J. Bahadur Singh, Commissioner to British East Africa, 1958-1960.

of the impact of my writings and talks I rank not lower than third or fourth in the profession in the whole of East Africa.

I claim to present my independent, unbiased and objective views on a very wide range of subjects. As adverse criticisms are always more adhesive to the memory than favourable comments, I am often accused, with the insidious encouragement of the Indian leaders, of trying to "harm my own community" and the "country of my origin" because I ruthlessly expose every type of their weaknesses as they topically emerge. If a check were made however, it would yet be found that I have written more articles in vigorous defence of India than in its disapproval. I am the only Asian journalist who has been forthright in his denunciations of African leaders, including Jomo Kenyatta and Tom Mboya whenever it has been necessary in the interests of my community and the country. A copy of my article I wrote in January this year, asking Jomo Kenyatta to quit politics entirely, is attached.

To revert to my submissions Jomo Kenyatta returned to active public life in August last year, after a very long incarceration. He was welcomed back into an atmosphere of great prestige and keen expectations. The history of mankind cannot produce another instance of a person receiving such systematic and extensive, such artificial and yet such "building-up" as he did in the months prior to his release: and that too from the very people who had drastically punished him for instigating such an obscene and gruesome movement as the Mau Mau. He returned to the scene like a conquerer.

Those discerning people however, who were capable of keeping their emotions in check, remained under no illusions about the outlook as well as the capabilities of this controversial leader from the very day he was "exhibited" to the world through a most elaborate news conference which he was allowed to hold while he was still in semi-detention. I then wrote an article in the *Sunday Post* under the heading "A Spent Force in Kenya". A copy is enclosed.

In order to place Jomo Kenyatta in the correct perspective, it is therefore essential to remember that his major political achievement in life has been confined to the infusing, among the rural people of his own tribe—the Kikuyu—with a poignant sense of grievance over the question of land, and for galvanising them into a course of action which went disastrously astray via the Mau Mau.

Soon afterwards he was removed and kept aloof from the march of events for many years. This has certainly entitled him to claim suffering and sacrifice for the sake of his country, but the charm and grace of it have become depleted very rapidly because he has shown the blatant determination to exploit his prison sentence to the full for his own personal advantages, through office and power, for both which he is absolutely unsuitable.

While Kenyatta was away, an entirely new class of African political leader, much younger, far more gifted, dynamic and aggressive in a more sophisticated way, occupied the field and, as the world knows, has made rapid strides. The tremendous success it has achieved however has been due more to the force of overall world trends than to its own skill and perseverance.

Jomo Kenyatta nevertheless became a name to be reckoned with among this class: the symbol of active African nationalism. The new leaders in Kenya were not only willing, they were enthusiastic, at first, in placing him on a pedestal and seeking his "fatherly" advice and guidance at every step.

Upto a certain stage, Tom Mboya was undoubtedly the most outstanding of these younger leaders. Early success however made him intolerably arrogant even with his closest and most valuable colleagues, who, being human beings after all, were also upset by his persistence in stealing the international limelight and posing as the sole leader of Kenya.

This fact, coupled with the historical fear of the largest and intellectually the most nimble tribe, the Kikuyu, caused a very large section of the African leaders led by Ronald Ngala and Masinde Muliro, to break away from Mboya and form a separate party, KADU. This party as yet derives its strength from a smaller total number of Africans than KANU, but its following is steadily growing. The number of tribes which owe allegiance to it is however much larger; and it is spread over not only a much bigger but also a far more productive part of Kenya in a single continuous stretch.

KANU is composed mainly of three major tribes, the Kikuyu, Luo and Kamba in an extremely ill-assorted alliance. The Kamba incidentally have already expressed their emphatic unwillingness to be grouped with the Kikuyu into one of the six regions which are to be appointed under the new constitution, even though their areas adjoin.

At the last general elections KANU emerged as the majority party by exploiting the highly emotional issue of the release of Jomo Kenyatta. It pledged itself not to accept office till he was released. But the real surprise of the election was the strength displayed by KADU. It won 40% of the "open" seats without working itself into near-frenzy over Kenyatta. In the next elections, Kenyatta's name will be a tremendous liability.

KANU next proved hopelessly myopic in political strategy by enabling KADU to enter the Government. Had KADU not done so, Kenya would have come to be ruled by the Governor by decree and independence would have fallen into jeopardy. KADU won the support of the majority of the European elected members, though some of them decided to remain "cross-benchers". For once, even the Kenya Indian Congress displayed a certain amount of practical good sense, and asked its own elected members also to sit on the Government benches.

793

This impelled the then Indian Commissioner, I.J. Bahadur Singh, who had always been dazzled by the personality of Tom Mboya, and had been going out of his way to add to his prestige and strength, to pummel the Congress leaders into retracting from their support of the Government. He virtually dragooned the abject Indian leaders into crossing ever to the opposition in an act of gross betrayal. Bahadur Singh had hoped to destroy the KADU Government as a personal achievement, but he failed miserably because KADU was yet able to muster sufficient support from the elected members to retain its bare majority. The Kenya Indian Congress proved itself to be a traitorous organisation: a reflection which began to be applied to all Indians. One of the very few Indians who refused to be overawed by Bahadur Singh and his henchmen was Arvind Jamidar, who resigned from the Congress and is now the most capable Minister of Tourism. Another Indian who stuck to his guns was S.S. Patel.

KANU began to grow furious at its helplessness, particularly as KADU created an impressive record of sound administration: not only that, it became officially instrumental in having Jomo Kenyatta quietly and smoothly released.

The deep cleavage which had arisen between the two parties and the internal chaos within KANU—of which more later—became perturbing to the British who wanted to leave Kenya in as peaceful a condition as possible, particularly as a large number of their own kith and kin were settled in the country. In their desperation they turned towards the hated Jomo Kenyatta, as a possible person who could become a national leader and control the internal situation. Hence alone that "building-up".

And Kenyatta could have at least partially achieved this status and accomplished some of this task had he kept aloof from party politics and withstood the temptations of office and power. On two occasions I implored him in my articles not to be lured into the Parliament Buildings, because among his other shortcomings he does not possess the sharpness necessary in a front-bench legislator.

What is happening to Jomo Kenyatta today is something like what would have happened to Mahatma Gandhi if he had insisted on becoming Prime Minister of India: with this very vital difference that Jomo is unworthy of being compared even to the shadow of the truly great Mahatma.

An extremely vain person, surrounded by sycophants and time-servers, he accepted the Presidentship of KANU with the firm belief that he would be able to liquidate KADU's political standing without any difficulty, and thereafter become the leader, the undisputed leader of Kenya, with dictatorial authority.

He, as indeed many other KANU leaders, sadly under-estimated the political acumen possessed by KADU, who forthwith demanded the internal subdivision of Kenya into six autonomous regions on a federal basis, as well as the creation of an Upper Chamber at the centre to thwart the possibility of a dictator ever coming to hold complete sway. An extremely united and disciplined party, it has very largely succeeded in having these claims written into the new constitution.

Nothing has lowered Kenyatta's prestige more than the manner in which he has been trying to tell his people that he has not had to give way to KADU on this vital point. By the time the constitution is completed, no one will be left in any doubt as to how he has been trying to hoodwink them. The results for the election campaign can well be imagined.

Leave alone the entire country, Kenyatta has signally failed to bring unity and order even within his own party, KANU, the party of his own choosing. Ranking next to him are two major figures in the political life of Kenya. The first of course is Tom Mboya, a completely detribalised African, the virtual creator of systematic Trade Union Movement in Kenya, and confirmed pro-West in his beliefs. He has been supplied with funds from the USA for educational and Trade Union purposes.

The other is the volatile Oginga Odinga, who belongs to the same tribe, Luo, and exercises unchallenged sway over it. He is a fairly wealthy man and is in open league with the Communist countries from whom he gets financial help. His value to KANU is largely in terms of his money which he uses ruthlessly.

Tom Mboya and Oginga Odinga are bitter rivals. They are both "using" Jomo Kenyatta and his name, because they know they cannot as yet do without him because of the emotional hold he still has over many Africans. But they both visualise themselves as his immediate successors.

Within KANU also are gangs of young men—of the KANU Youth Wing, and others who have again been prominent in the news—who are active in the loathsome Mau Mau type of oathing, in manufacturing crude, yet highly lethal weapons, in intimidating and terrorising innocent people, in robbing, maiming and murdering helpless victims, in rustling and wounding cattle and other similar activities. But with an occasional and many say utterly hypocritical speeches at mass meetings Jomo Kenyatta has remained blissfully unworried about the situation. The Central Nyanza district is currently the scene of such widespread violent crime. Kenyatta has not even visited the place.

This then is the man, and such is his party, with whom the Kenya Indian Congress have formed a covert alliance with the full encouragement of the Indian Commissioner. The attraction for them all is the international glamour attaching to Kenyatta and Tom Mboya—they merely love to bask in the sunshine of the great. They want to be associated with those whom they think will be the winners at the next general elections even though this may mean disaster and ruin for the community.

But even on this basis, as I have indicated, the Congress and the Commissioner are not backing a certain winner. With the approach of the elections KANU is likely to disintegrate, while KADU's trump card is the appeal to the masses for having preserved their ancestral agricultural land against encroachment by the major tribes.

From the point of view of the interests and welfare of the minority communities like the Indians, a federal structure is patently far more preferable to the unitary system to which it is widely feared KANU may yet revert if it comes into power: KANU has never been reconciled to regionalism. Under a decentralized administration the local minorities with their established local contacts and influence can be in a distinctly advantageous position to look after themselves. Much of the Asian distress in Tanganyika can be attributed to the fact that every phase of life is controlled from remote Dar es Salaam. The position there is bound to get much worse because under the new constitution, the President will be a virtual dictator. The first President, undoubtedly Julius Nyerere, has not even the gifts of a typical dictator.

Reverting to Kenya, the present Commissioner should have come to know long before now, the attitude of KADU towards the Indian Mission. Instead of trying to win over the leaders of this party, however, he has driven them to yet further anger by invariably showing a marked preference for Kenyatta and KANU. The latest manifestation of this has been his utterly unnecessary (from the point of view of its ostensible aims) formation of the "Indo-African Friendship Association" to which Jomo Kenyatta was hastily installed as the first Patron. Surely a diplomat should have known what the reactions would be among the members of the already affronted KADU.

Ngala and his colleagues are deeply upset because apart from pushing through a constitution which ensures for the minorities a fair deal, they have opened the party membership to all races: KANU have not. They have included an Indian in their share of the Coalition Ministry, KANU have not. Which is not to say there have been no lapses on the part of KADU: but generally speaking their attitudes have been far more comforting than those of KANU.

Encouraging signs have nevertheless emerged recently among the Indians here to break away from the Kenya Indian Congress. During its last session, this organisation actually decided to exclude the protection of the political and economic rights of the Indian community from its purview, to the dismay and wrath of many people.

I must however impress upon you that our greatest cause for fear is the attitude of the Indian government: quite distinct from and above the performances of its Mission here. No people who have become permanently settled in another part of the world want to become a burden on their "home"

796

country if they can at all help it: but circumstances can arise when they have no choice but to seek aid and protection from the land of their origin. There is far less likelihood of such circumstances arising if it is openly known that such aid and protection would be readily forthcoming. The messages we have invariably received from India have been in exactly the opposite direction.

Further, as any ordinary person would feel about it, whatever the Indian Commission does here has the impress of the direct approval of the Government of India, of Punditji himself. I have tried to prove how misguided this Commission has been so far.

If at least this Commission is made to remain strictly aloof from our internal affairs, we would be able to find our own bearings. I for one have the confidence that with an alignment with KADU, our destiny should be quite a happy one.

But I would also like India to know, that if we do have to fall back upon her, she will have no right to treat us as burdensome refugees seeking shelter and mercy. You have perhaps never been told, that at a very conservative estimate, ever since this country was opened to large-scale immigration, India and Pakistan between them have received nothing less than *£250 million*[95] in hard cash through our remittances and investments. It has been a wholly one-way traffic.

The Europeans have brought a lot of capital into this country and sent back very little. Yet, the kith and kin of the British have manoeuvred things in such a way that they will now be able to seal their farms if they want to, and get very satisfactory prices for them through the very substantial loans which have been offered to Kenya by Her Majesty's Government.

We came with nothing, and have sent back much. We have nevertheless also created a great deal of immovable wealth in this country. Surely if this type of people find themselves in difficulties, they have the right to expect the Governments of the lands of their origin to display full responsibility towards them.

Even the Kenya Indian Congress has begun to feel that India has a financial responsibility towards Kenya—at least of a type. In his speech during the last session of the Congress, the President suggested that in spite of her own problems, India should invest money for the industrial development of this country. But obviously the President lost his nerve—or was there a hint by the Commissioner?—and this excellent suggestion was not embodied in an official resolution.

It is quite true however, that if India stops considering East Africa purely as a market for her manufactured goods, but encourages some of her industrialists

95. Emphasis in the original.

797

to open factories and other undertakings over here, India's contribution towards the welfare of not only her own people but of the Africans would be most welcome and timely: and would create far better "friendship" than the one which Mr Khilnani has tried to create through his Association: thereby giving rise to the initial impression that no friendship has existed so far.

I am afraid, Pundit Ji, that this letter has become extremely long. It is also not unlikely that part of the contents and the tone may not be altogether to your liking. If this is indeed so, I crave your indulgence. I would earnestly request you however to overlook my shortcomings and to give this submission the very serious and urgent consideration which I assure you it deserves.[96]

With the kindest regards:

Yours sincerely,
Narain Singh

35. From B.P. Chaliha: Assam Oil Royalty Arbitration[97]
[Refer to item 140]

August 14, 1962

My dear Prime Minister,

Please refer to my Secret letters of the 17th[98] and 25th July 1962 to you on the issue of Oil Royalty. After I met you in Delhi recently I took the opportunity of having discussions both with Shri Morarji Desai[99] and with Shri K.D. Malaviya.[100] Shri Desai seemed to be of the opinion that his decision should be trusted both on the question of the State's right as well as on the quantum of royalty. Shri Malaviya seemed to be of the view that since the whole question was going to be referred to the Supreme Court, there appeared no need for any arbitration during the interim period because the decision of the Supreme Court would take retrospective effect. I told both of them that as the proposals, contained in my letter of the 17th July addressed to you, were the result of a Cabinet decision I would have to hold further discussions with my colleagues. Though I returned to Shillong a few days ago, I could not take up this matter immediately because our Industries Minister, Shri K.P. Tripathy, was away from

---

96. See item 388.
97. Letter from the Chief Minister of Assam. Sent from Shillong. PMO, File No. 17(490)/62-70-PMS, Sr. No. 42-A. Also available in the JN Collection.
98. Appendix 3.
99. Union Finance Minister.
100. Minister of Mines and Fuel.

the station on account of the death of his father. Shri Tripathy only came a few days back and we had a Cabinet meeting to discuss this subject.

We are fully conscious of the fact that this matter is of paramount importance for the country as a whole and for our own State. We also realise that no tension between the Centre and the State is desirable. Because of these considerations the view of our Cabinet was that the entire matter should be left in your hand to dispose of in the manner which you think to be best both for the country as a whole and also for our State. We have, therefore, decided to abide by whatever decision you might take in this regard. When you have decided the forum before whom this matter should be placed, I will send to you the broad outlines of our case. My two colleagues, viz., Shri Ahmed[101] and Shri Tripathy will present the State's case in detail before the forum you select.

In the meantime, I am issuing directions that petroleum exploration licenses be issued to the parties concerned.

With kind regards,

Yours sincerely,
Bimalaprosad Chaliha

36. From Morarji Desai: Foreign Exchange for Beas Project[102]
[Refer to items 166-167 and appendix 25]

16th August, 1962

My dear Jawaharlalji,

Kindly refer to your d.o. letter No. 1201-PMH/62 dated the 8th August, 1962 regarding World Bank's assistance for the Beas Project. As you have stated, an undertaking to finance this project was given by the World Bank, on its own behalf and on behalf of the then DLF,[103] at the time of negotiations of the Indus Waters Treaty. The President of the Bank, Mr Black,[104] during his discussions with you in May, 1959, had also given such an assurance.[105] In accordance with the World Bank's undertaking, which still holds good, the foreign exchange

---

101. Fakhruddin Ali Ahmed, Minister of Law and Finance in Assam.
102. Letter from the Finance Minister. PMO, File No. 17(372)/59-69-PMS, Sr. No. 34-A.
103. Development Loan Fund started by the US in 1957 to extend loans to foreign countries, repayable in the local currency of the borrower. In 1961, it merged into the United States Agency for International Development (USAID).
104. Eugene Black.
105. See SWJN/SS/49/item 17, here pp. 179-182.

cost of the project amounting to 56 million has to be met partly through AID assistance (33 million from USA) and partly through a World Bank loan (23 million).

2. At one stage, there was a suggestion of some reluctance on the part of the Bank in financing the project, but subsequent discussions with our representative in the Bank and its management reveal that the Bank are now agreeable (along with AID) to make a loan not for the Beas Project specifically, but for the import of equipment for the whole complex including the Beas Dam and the Rajasthan Canal System.

3. The other point raised in Chowdhuri Ranbir Singh's letter relates to immediate purchases to be made for the project. We had already taken up this question with the World Bank and the AID and they have both agreed to allow us to place orders for the purchases of essential equipment even before the signing of the agreements with the two institutions. The Irrigation and Power Ministry have also been advised about these developments.

Yours sincerely,
Morarji Desai

37. From K. Nateson: Smuggling from Ceylon[106]

[Refer to item 92]

Copy of a letter dated 16th August, 1962, marked "top secret,"
from Shri K. Nateson, Delivery Revision Officer, Office of the Divisional
Superintendent of Post Offices, Jaffna (Ceylon), to the Prime Minister.

I am an ordinary Public Servant from Ceylon and I have the greatest regard for your Socialistic ideas and programmes. I strongly oppose Communism which is a dangerous doctrine for our Eastern ways of life. Though I am a small man I like to help Bharatha in eradicating Communism and Chinese atrocities in India. In this connection I wish to give you some very interesting information from Ceylon.

From the Northern part of Ceylon some people are doing smuggling with the Southern coast of India. Now it has become a free port. Due to corruption in Ceylon and the absence of Customs patrolling boats and launches, boats from Ceylon fitted with mechanised engines reach a point in South India called Kolladam or Kolroon in Chidambaram. The notorious leader there is one Mr

106. Copy of letter from official in Jaffna.

Mariappa Vandayar. He is like a dictator controlling the entire area which the river delta. I understand the Customs at Chidambaram is paid a monthly Santhosam or bribery. None dare to oppose this man. If anyone raises any objection, then his life is put to an end. This place is the safest place to bring anything from Ceylon.

At Colombo the Chinese Embassy had put a separate section to deal with the Indian affairs. In this section all Indian papers are received and read by an individual from Jaffna who is a native of this smuggling area. I am reliably informed that some packages are being despatched from Chinese Embassy at Colombo to Jaffna. This parcel is sent to Delhi through the Palk Strait via Kolroon (Kolladam) in Chidambaram. I was told that Mr Mariappa Vandayar is a strong Congress man. With a good name he appears to be doing an anti-social and anti-national service. I am an ordinary public servant and the people doing at this end are Communist sympathisers. To save my skin, kindly keep my name as top secret. Madras State Government employees are being highly bribed by this individual for the smuggling racket. Under the cover of this, secret packages are sent. If you want to arrest and stop this dangerous animal, an honest CID must be sent and stop the activities of Mr Mariappa Vandayar who is doing this anti-national service. It is advisable to guard that area for some time and take drastic measures against this individual and if proved he should be expelled from Congress membership.

Acknowledge receipt of this letter. When pursuing further action, please take extracts of this letter.

38. From G.G. Swell: Army Expels Tribals[107]
[Refer to item 142]

Subject: Notification of evacuation of large tract of tribal land in the Khasi Hills, Assam, for field firing artillery practice.

I understand that about a week back the people of Nongstoin, Mariaw and Rambrai in the Khasi Hills, Assam, sent you a telegram to this effect:

"Pray to protest against Assam Political Department Notification of twenty second May declaring a large tract of inhabited land as Field firing artillery practice area ordering vacation of same which if complied will render

107. Letter, 17 August 1962, from Lok Sabha MP of the All Party Hill Leaders' Conference: address 72, South Avenue, New Delhi. Salutation and signature not available.

thousands of local inhabitants homeless converting them refugees within their own home. Pray also for immediate cancellation of the notification. Public of Nongstoin and Mariaw Rambrai."

In this connection I beg to enclose herewith also the copy of a resolution which the people of the above area adopted in a meeting held on 6.8.62.

While in no way trying to obstruct the work of our defence organisation particularly in the border areas I, nevertheless, would request you to kindly intervene in this matter as it involves hardship to so many inhabitants of the area and to kindly order that the Defence Ministry may find out some other alternative site with the consent of the people of the area. This should not present much difficulty. On the other hand, it will remove a lot of avoidable misunderstanding in the area.

39. From Raghu Vira[108]

[Refer to item 290]

Dated 17th August 1962

Respected Pandit Ji,

I am sending herewith a copy of the resolution passed by the All Indian Languages Convention[109] which was presided over by Mama Warerkar[110] at the first day and by Principal Mahadevan[111] at the second day.

The flood of hatred that has been released and is being maintained by some persons and parties cannot be made the basis of retaining English for an indefinite period.

Provincial languages are the languages of democracy. All power and authority cannot be vested for ever in an English-knowing oligarchy of 2% of the population; 98% of the population cannot be condemned to a position of no power and no opportunity.

---

108. Letter from former Rajya Sabha MP and Chairman of the Reception Committee of the All-India Languages Convention, sent from J-22, Hauz Khas Enclave, New Delhi-16. PMO, File No. 52(12)/57-63-Vol. I, Sr. No. 81-A.
109. The Convention was held in New Delhi, 11-12 August 1962; for the resolution passed by the Convention, see item 7, fn 39.
110. B.V. Warerkar, Marathi writer and Nominated Member, Rajya Sabha.
111. Probably T.M.P. Mahadevan, Head of the Department of Philosophy, Madras University, and author of several books on philosophy.

Dr Rajendra Prasad[112] has sent a message to the Convention, a copy of which I am attaching herewith.

May I hope that you would pay deepest thought and be on the side of the democracy and remove the last vestige, viz. English, from the Indian scene.

If you could bring yourself to a mood of reconsideration, I would be prepared to come and meet you.

As usual, with deepest regards,

Yours sincerely,
Raghu Vira

40. From A.K. Gopalan: Kerala Titanium Factory[113]
[Refer to items 223-224]

18.8.1962

Dear Panditji,

I am forwarding herewith a copy of a memorandum addressed to the Minister for Industry and Commerce.

The Kerala Government has resolved to denationalise and hand over to the Tatas, the Titanium Factory, one of the model public sector industries in Kerala. The memorandum explains the details. This is how people who profess to follow you translate your ideas of socialism in actual practice.

I appeal to you to instruct that such decisions are abandoned.

Hope you are in good health and cheer.

Yours sincerely,
A.K. Gopalan

---

112. Former President.
113. Letter from CPI, Lok Sabha MP from Kasaragod, Kerala. PMO, File No. 17(517)/62-66-PMS, Sr. No. 1-A.

41. From Norodom Sihanouk: International Conference for Cambodia[114]

[Refer to item 437]

20th August, 1962

Sir,

I have the honour to particularly draw Your Excellency's attention to the very grave threat which for years has been hanging over my country constantly harassed by threats, plots, sabotage, blockades and aggression from neighbouring powers which are militarily stronger and whose annexionist intentions—camouflaged in this case as ideological differences—are no longer in doubt. I very much fear that territorial claims backed by the use of armed forces, border violations, over-flights, recent occupation of our territory by foreign troops, will soon create an impossible situation which could lead to an international conflict with unpredictable consequences.

Cambodia can no longer tolerate either these constant aggressions and provocations or the repeated official or semi-official accusations of these same neighbours according to whom she (Cambodia) encourages and fosters subversion at home,—which is not and never has been the case.

Deeply devoted to peace but nevertheless determined to defend her honour as well as what remains to her of her national patrimony after having had to lose several chunks of it, Cambodia sees no other reasonable solution to this problem than that of utilising to her own advantage the benefits of international protection which have been accorded to Laos.

I would like to recall that it was due to Cambodia's initiative that Laos was spared from making further greater sacrifices and that the Western and Eastern blocs were kept from coming to grips with each other.

Actually since 1954 my country has been making useful contributions towards the maintenance of peace and stability in Asia.

Today before taking any major decisions for protecting her existence, Cambodia asks Your Excellency's Government and the other powers which met last month in Geneva for *official recognition and guarantee of her territorial integrity.*[115] To this end she is ready to accept any appropriate control.

The salutary international task accomplished in Laos will hardly be of lasting use and the equilibrium of forces in South East Asia will not be maintained for long if Cambodia were herself to become a battlefield—a possibility which appears to me to be inevitable if the powers which have an

---

114. Letter from Head of State of Cambodia, sent from Phnom Penh.
115. Emphasis in the original.

interest in the security of this region cannot come to an agreement in order to neutralise it.

I make bold to tell Your Excellency that my country deserves the benefits of such a favour.

Every politician and foreign observer of good faith has realised that my country is a peace-loving and closely-knit Nation which respects the Charter of the UNO and its international obligations, practising a genuine neutrality, faithful to the principles of peaceful co-existence. They have also admitted that Cambodia has adhered to this straight and just path through her own unaided efforts and after having overcome innumerable difficulties.

I take the liberty of suggesting to Your Excellency to be kind enough to take an active interest in our fate and to agree to the holding of an International Conference on Cambodia as soon as possible in one of the great capitals or in a neutral city of Your choice (Geneva, New Delhi, Stockholm, etc.)

While thanking Your Excellency for your kind interest in this very urgent request from a small, inoffensive Nation which wants only to live in independence and freedom and to see that its frontiers are respected, I request Your Excellency to accept the assurances of my highest consideration.

N. Sihanouk

42. Galwan Post and Fraternising with Chinese Troops[116]
[Refer to item 410]

Submitted with reference to Prime Minister's query on the special sitrep regarding Galwan Post, dated 19th August.

2. It would appear that the Chinese have decided not to interfere with our communications by land to the Galwan Post. On the other hand, it might be a ruse to see what we do and get us to act with Chinese permission in this area.

3. I discussed this matter this morning with the Chief of Army Staff, General Thapar, and suggested to him that our supply column which is sitting some eight miles from the Galwan Post should now test the Chinese intentions and make an attempt to go through by road with supplies to the Galwan Post. I

116. Note, 20 August 1962, from M.J. Desai, the Foreign Secretary. MEA, Historical Division, *Sino-Indian Border Dispute*, vol. VI, pt III, (Chinese Incursions into Indian Territory), (April 1962 – October 1962), notes, pp. 30-31.

also told General Thapar that the Commander of the supply column should be told not to take notice of any Chinese that he might meet en route and should not fraternize with them, not even have a cup of tea or coffee, but just attempt to go through ignoring the Chinese en route. We will know in a couple of days how the Chinese behave.

M.J. Desai
20-8-1962

43. From A.P. Jain: Land Acquisition Amendment Bill[117]
[Refer to item 230]

August 22, 1962

My dear Jawaharlalji,

I feel constrained to write to you about the Land Acquisition (Amendment) Bill.

On the 5th May, the Supreme Court has again considered the question of the acquisition of land in Somavati and Others vs the State of Punjab. In this judgement they have protected the acquisition if it was meant for public purposes. This has taken the edge out of the amending Bill. This Bill has raised a lot of controversy. It is not a healthy background. Could not the matter of amending the Bill be dropped altogether? If the States want to legislate, let them do so on their own responsibility.

If, for some reason, the Bill is persisted with, my suggestion is that in cases involving big acquisitions where a substantial question of law or fact is involved, a reference might be made to a District Judge or a High Court Judge, and it is only when he finds it justifiable that the permission should be given. This will create confidence.

If this suggestion is not acceptable then the following safeguards may be embodied either by law or regulations:

(i) The right of acquisition should be confined to public limited companies;

(ii) before the acquisition is ordered there should be an independent technical assessment that the area proposed to be acquired is needed for setting up the factory or its extension;

(iii) the right of acquisition should be confined only to industries forming part of the Plan and no acquisition should be made except where a

---

117. Letter from the President of the UPCC; sent from 5 Rafi Marg, New Delhi. NMML, A.P. Jain Papers.

valid license for setting up the factory or its extension is held by the applicant;

(iv)   if the land acquired is not utilised for the purpose within a prescribed period, it should be returned to the original owner.

You may kindly take a decision in the matter.

Yours sincerely,
Ajit Prasad Jain

44. From K.M. Munshi: Inviting Eisenhower to Bharatiya Vidya Bhavan[118]
[Refer to item 277]

August 22, 1962

My dear Jawaharlalji,

The Bharatiya Vidya Bhavan is celebrating its Silver Jubilee in the last fortnight of December 1962. An influential all-India Committee under the presidentship of Dr Rajendra Prasad,[119] a founder member of the Bhavan, has been set up for the purpose. Dr S. Radhakrishnan, President of India, has kindly consented to inaugurate the celebrations. The Jubilee will also be celebrated by the Kendras of the Bhavan in different parts of India.

Some of the prominent members of the Committee have expressed a desire that a distinguished foreigner should be invited to be the Chief Guest on the occasion.

One of the names suggested as Chief Guest is that of Mr Dwight Eisenhower, ex-President of the USA. I would, however, hesitate even to place it before the Committee, unless in the wider context of the matter, you think that it is advisable to pursue the matter.

I have to trouble you in this matter at this earliest stage, as we will do it only if you approve.

I shall thank you to give me your reactions and oblige.

Yours sincerely,
K.M. Munshi

---

118. Letter from the Chairman of the Bharatiya Vidya Bhavan; sent from: Bharatiya Vidya Bhavan, Chaupatty Road, Bombay. PMO, File No. 40(240)/62-63-PMS, Sr. No. 1-A.
119. Former President.

45. Earnings of the Power Supply Industries[120]
[Refer to item 222]

Problems of the Electricity Supply Industries

At the time of India's Independence, the Electricity Supply Industry was largely owned and operated by licencees' undertakings. The undertakings operated and continue to operate under the franchise granted to them by the respective State Governments pursuant to the provisions of the Indian Electricity Act 1910.

2.   Before the Electricity (Supply) Act of 1948 was brought into force, regulation of licencees' finances was limited to fixation of the maxima rates stipulated in those licences, which they could charge to the various class of consumers. This position was altered by the Electricity (Supply) Act which, through the mechanism of the Sixth Schedule, placed the industry in a strait jacket. Essentially the broad features governing licencees' charges to consumers under the Act are, inter alia:

(i)   to determine very rigidly the Capital Base on which "Reasonable Return" to the industry is fixed.

(ii)   to stipulate exhaustively expenses which could be regarded as being "properly incurred".

(iii)   fixation of scales of depreciation which have little room for internal finance.

3.   The "Reasonable Return" itself was fixed at 5 per centum of the Capital Base.

4.   The return was fixed when money market conditions were buoyant, but soon after interest rates hardened, making Electric Scrips (which until then were regarded as blue scrips) unattractive. This led to large-scale disinvestment in the industry. The consequent effect has been that equity values in the industry have been greatly depressed making it difficult for licencees' undertakings to expand.

5.   It was, therefore, not long before the Industry had to go back to Government seeking an upward revision in the "Reasonable Return". The issue was first raised in 1951 and it was not until 1956 that an increase by ½% in the return was given legislative seal. The time lag involved in regulation by legislation is significant.

6.   The position of the Industry deteriorated further when the tax pattern was changed by the Finance Act of 1959. Under the new dispensation "grossing

120. Copy of Note without date or signature, but according to Nehru's letter of 24 August 1962 (item 222), sent by Naval Tata.

up" of dividends was abolished and in addition tax at the prescribed rate (30% at present) had to be deducted from dividends paid to shareholders. It is true that this is a common feature applying to all industries, but with one important reservation; the other industries could step up dividends to make good the shareholders' loss, whereas there is no scope for such remedy in the Electric Supply Industry, the earnings of which are pegged at a low level.

7.   Yet another development which has adversely affected the Industry has been the distinction sought to be drawn as between the official Reserve Bank Rate and the lending rate by the Reserve Bank to the Scheduled Banks. Since 1956 the return to the investor in the Electric Supply Industry has been pegged at 2% over the Reserve Bank Rate. What has happened in the recent years has been that the Reserve Bank has introduced a three tier system of lending rates with interest at 4%, 5% and 6% on the respective blocks. Any electric supply undertaking seeking bank finance was, therefore, obliged to seek money at 1% over lending rate applicable to the last block. This has tended to existing shareholders subsidising new development.

8.   The lending rate of Government's own financial corporations both Central and States, has been revised recently from 6½% to 7%.

9.   The remedies the Industry therefore seeks are:

i)   increase in the Reasonable Return by at least 1%.

ii) the return to the Industry should be really tax free as was originally visualised by the framers of the Electricity (Supply) Act, when they permitted all taxes on income and profits as operating expenditure;

iii) those undertakings which are forced to raise loan finance at rates beyond the reasonable return should be permitted to charge the actual interest plus ½% as expenditure. The analogy here is that in the case of monies advanced by the State Electricity Boards what is permitted as expenditure is the actual interest plus ½%.

10.   Before independence the share of the so-called "Private Sector" in India's power generation was of the order of 863,608 KW against 499,657 KW by the Public Sector undertakings. The Electricity (Supply) Act has tended to throttle enterprise in the field of public utility electric supply undertakings. There is a large fund of experience and expertise with the Licencees' undertakings and power development in India could gain added momentum if these latent resources are tapped by appropriate incentives as suggested above.

46. From J.C. Parikh: Communists infiltrating Congress[121]

[Refer to item 32]

August 24, 1962

Pujya Panditji,

On Independence Day, a public meeting was held under the auspices of the Bombay Suburban District Congress Committee at Sadhanashram, Vile Parle (West). The meeting was presided over by Mr N.G. Acharya, President of the District Congress Committee, and attended among others by Mr V.K. Krishna Menon, India's Defence Minister. Mr Balraj Sahni, the well-known communist film artist, was invited to address the meeting.

It is rather surprising that in the presence of Mr Krishna Menon, a communist should be invited to address a Congress meeting from a Congress platform. This meeting goes to show to what extent the communists and their fellow-travellers have managed to infiltrate into the Bombay Suburban District Congress Committee.

I would like to draw your attention to this fact. It is high time that Congress President[122] issues a directive to the office bearers of the Pradesh, District and Mandal Congress Committees that no communist should be invited to address Congress meeting, since communist ideology is the antithesis of Congress philosophy. If communists are allowed to infiltrate into the Congress, I am afraid, they will succeed in destroying Indian democracy much sooner than we think. I, along with many others, who think like me would be deeply obliged to you if you would kindly consider this matter seriously and give appropriate lead in this connection.

With warmest respects,

Yours truly,
J.C. Parikh

---

121. Letter from a Member of the Executive Committee of the Bombay Pradesh Congress Committee, sent from 9/12 Kurla Road, Bombay. NMML, AICC Papers, File, OD-23 (D).
122. D. Sanjivayya.

47. From Digambar Singh: Land Acquisition Amendment Bill[123]

[Refer to item 231]

25-8-1962

श्रद्धेय पंडित जी,

लैंड एक्यूज़िशन (एमैण्डमेण्ट) बिल के सम्बन्ध में कुछ निवेदन करना चाहता हूँ। लोकसभा व उसके बाहर इसके प्रति गहरा असंतोष है। कांग्रेस पार्टी की बैठक में स्वयं आप भी देख चुके हैं। यह बिल पूंजीपतियों को लाभ और किसानों के हितों को हानि पहुँचाने वाला है। हमारी समाजवाद की नीति के भी विरुद्ध है। यह बिल सलेक्ट कमेटी के सुपुर्द होना चाहिए। यदि कृषि व खाद्य मंत्री[124] इसको पास ही करना चाहते हैं तो पार्टी बैठक में पुनः विचार होना चाहिये। मैं इस बिल का समर्थन करना अनुचित समझता हूँ और कांग्रेस के लिए भी इसका समर्थन ठीक नहीं समझता। यदि लोकसभा में इस पर विचार हो तो सदस्यों को अपनी इच्छानुसार राय देने का अधिकार मिलना चाहिये।

निवेदकः
दिगम्बर सिंह

[Translation begins

25 August 1962

Respected Panditji,

I wish to say something regarding the Land Acquisition (Amendment) Bill. There is great dissatisfaction in the Lok Sabha and outside also about this Bill. You have seen this for yourself in the meeting of the Congress Party. This Bill will be favourable to capitalists and inimical to the interests of farmers. It is against our socialist policy also. This Bill should be handed over to a Select Committee. If the Minister for Agriculture and Food[125] is very keen to have the Bill passed then it should be taken up again for deliberations in the Party. I feel it is wrong to support this Bill and do not think it is appropriate for the Congress to do so either. If it is taken up for deliberations then the Members should be given the right to express their views freely.

Yours sincerely,
Digambar Singh

Translation ends]

123. Letter from Congress, Lok Sabha MP; sent from 4 North Avenue, New Delhi.
124. S.K. Patil.
125. See fn 124 in this section.

48. From A.K. Roy: Chairing Visva-Bharati Society[126]
[Refer to item 255]

August 25, 1962

Revered Acharya,

I trust that you have received a copy of the Notice of the meeting of the Parishad of the Visva-Bharati Society to be held at Santiniketan on September 2, 1962.

As you are starting for London on September 8, we are afraid, it may not be possible for you to attend the meeting. In that case we would request you kindly to nominate a person who would preside over the meeting in your absence. I shall be grateful if you please send me a letter of authority giving your nomination at your earliest convenience.

With deep regards,

Yours truly,
A.K. Roy

49. From Karan Singh: Anti-Corruption Commission[127]
[Refer to item 127]

26 August 1962

My dear Panditji,

I am taking the liberty of writing this confidential letter to bring to your notice two points of importance in the light of Bakshi Sahib's forthcoming visit to Delhi.[128]

The first point concerns the possibility of his inclusion in the Union Cabinet. In the course of a private conversation with him day before yesterday I gathered the distinct impression that his views had undergone an important modification and that, if the matter is broached by you at this stage, he may now be ready to accept. I may, of course, have been mistaken, but I thought I should pass on my assessment to you for your personal information.

126. Letter from the Assistant General Secretary of the Visva-Bharati Society; address: 5 Dwarkanath Tagore Lane, Calcutta-7. PMO, File No. 40(107)/59-69-PMS, Sr. No. 54-A.
127. Letter from the Sadr-i-Riyasat of Jammu and Kashmir. Jawaid Alam (ed.), *Jammu and Kashmir 1949-64. Select Correspondence Between Jawaharlal Nehru and Karan Singh* (New Delhi: Penguin/Viking, 2006), pp. 287-288.
128. Bakhshi Ghulam Mohammed, Prime Minister of Jammu and Kashmir, met Nehru on 31 July 1962.

The second matter concerns the appointment of the commission under the provisions of our recently enacted anti-corruption legislation. The measure has aroused widespread public expectations, and can be an important step towards eradicating corruption and improving the efficiency of our administration. A great deal, however, will depend upon the personnel of the commission. I have been urging strongly that it should consist of men of the highest integrity, and be headed by some prominent person from outside the State. The Cabinet has selected three retired local sessions judges as members, but the chairmanship is still open. Bakshi Sahib said he would seek your advice in the matter, and also remarked that he had in mind Shri Khosla,[129] retired justice of the Punjab. For my part I mentioned the name of Shri K.P.S. Menon[130] and General Jai Singh (retired). In any event, I feel most strongly that we should get someone of stature from outside the State to head the commission, a person with the stature, ability and impartiality necessary to inspire unquestioned public confidence from all sections of the people.

In view of the fact that Bakshi Sahib will discuss the matter with you I thought I should place this background before you and respectfully urge that you be good enough to take a personal interest in the matter so that we get someone really suitable.

I hope you will enjoy your forthcoming visit abroad, and that we shall have the pleasure of seeing you up here again in October.

With respectful regards,

Yours very sincerely,
Tiger

PS: I am sending this letter by a special messenger, Shri Milap Chand.[131] I am also sending some peaches from my garden and hope that they reach you in good condition.

T

129. G.D. Khosla, Chief Justice of Punjab High Court, 1959-1961.
130. Former Foreign Secretary, 1948-1952; Ambassador to the USSR, 1952-1961.
131. Milap Chand Katoch, private secretary to Karan Singh.

50. From C. Subramaniam: Expanding Steel Capacity[132]
[Refer to item 227]

28th August, 1962

My dear Jawaharlalji,

I attach herewith a note explaining the proposal of Indian Iron[133] to expand their ingot steel capacity from one million tonnes to 1.3 million tonnes and their finished steel capacity of 800,000 tonnes by a quarter million tonnes. The proposal has been discussed in a preliminary way with Shri Biren Mookerji, Chairman of Indian Iron, and also with the Planning Commission. The first phase of the proposal, which is the only one under consideration at the moment, is an attractive one and indications are that the World Bank would be willing to finance it.

Because of some delay in the time-table for the expansion of our public sector steel plants and the delay over Bokaro, it has become a matter of some urgency to ensure that the gap between anticipated demand and anticipated production at the end of the Third Five Year Plan is narrowed as far as possible. The present proposal which is attractive from the cost point of view would be of considerable assistance in this respect. Before, however, I proceed further in the matter, I would be grateful to have your guidance. If necessary, I shall discuss this with you.

Yours sincerely,
C. Subramaniam

132. Letter from the Minister of Steel and Heavy Industries. PMO, File No. 17(518)/62-65-PMS, Sr. No. 1-A.
133. The Indian Iron & Steel Company.

814

51. US Government's Statement on U Thant's Congo Proposals[134]
[Refer to item 389]

The Acting Secretary General of the UN[135] has come forward with a plan for the Congo that offers a reasonable basis upon which Congolese leaders can settle their differences. The US supports the Secretary General's efforts to reach a peaceful settlement in the Congo.

The US government hopes that the UN's proposals will be accepted in the spirit in which they have been offered—as a sincere effort to bring about a national settlement.

In putting forward its peace plan, the UN is acting in a manner consistent with its role of assisting the Congolese, at the request of the government of the Congo, to resolve outstanding problems of that country.

The UN's plan calls for a federal constitution that leaves room for a considerable measure of local autonomy. Both parties have spoken with approval of such a constitution. It also calls for an agreement on a division of revenues and provides an important place in the national Congolese Government for Mr Tshombe's political party.

The logic of the Acting Secretary General's proposal offers compelling reason for other nations to lend their support so that statesmanship in the Congo may put that nation on the road to federal unity and progress. Such progress will enable UN and countries like the US to devote greater resources to economic and technical assistance in the Congo. Progress toward conciliation is vital, not only to the people of the Congo, but also to the stability of Central Africa.

---

134. Text, given by a US Embassy official to B.F.H.B. Tyabji, Special Secretary, MEA, probably on 28 August 1962. MEA, File No. 101/13/62-AFR-II, Vol IV, pp. 627-628/ corr.

    On the margin of the document given to him, Tyabji recorded in his hand, on 28 August 1962, the following note for the Deputy Secretary (Africa) at the MEA:
"Mr Stuart (US Embassy) gave me this. It is the text of the US Govt's statement on the Congo proposals accepted by Mr Adoula and in negotiation with Mr Tshombe.

    The US Govt would like us also to support it by a statement by our PR to UN or something like that.

    I see no objection; do you?"

135. U Thant.

52. From C.B. Gupta: Mohanlal Gautam's Subversive Activity[136]

[Refer to item 43]

August 29, 1962

My dear Panditji,

I am herewith enclosing a circular letter that has been addressed to the members of the PCC by Sri Mohan Lal Gautam.[137] The letter speaks for itself. This is to oppose us in the taxation proposals that the State Government is placing before the legislature for its acceptance and, especially the land tax proposal about which you had delivered the speech in the PCC.

As you will see, the manner in which, as a responsible member of the Executive Council of the PCC Shri Gautam is acting is not only questionable but prejudicial to the interest of the organisation. I have already spoken to Sri Lal Bahadurji[138] about it when he met me at Bombay after the meeting of the National Integration Council[139] and he was of the opinion that the proposals now adumbrated by us are quite satisfactory and are necessary in order to fulfill the targets of the Plan. He also gave me to understand that he would speak to Sri Gautam and tell him that for a year he should stay at Rajasthan where he has been given an assignment by Sri Sukhadia[140] on the recommendation of Sri Lal Bahadurji.[141]

With regards,

Yours sincerely,
C.B. Gupta

136. Letter from the Chief Minister of UP. NMML, AICC Papers, Box 10, File No. OD-30-D/1962.
137. A former Minister in UP and member of the Executive Committee, UPCC.
138. Lal Bahadur Shastri, Home Minister.
139. The National Integration Council met in New Delhi, 2-3 June 1962.
140. Mohanlal Gautam had been recently appointed Chairman of the Rajasthan Police Commission.
141. See other items in the section Politics, subsection Congress Socialist Forum

53. From K.C. Reddy: Kerala Titanium Factory[142]
[Refer to item 223]

August 30, 1962

My dear Panditji,

Thank you for your letter of August 25, 1962 regarding the Titanium Factory in Kerala. I have so far neither received any letter nor my Ministry any memorandum from A.K. Gopalan[143] on this subject. I enclose for your information a brief note on the present position of this factory and its expansion programme. While there have been some informal discussions between Tatas and the Kerala Government in regard to the former's association with the factory, no concrete proposals appear to have crystallised. I would, however, assure you that when we receive any proposals we shall examine them closely in the context of your observations and our basic policies. In any case there can be no question of handing over the factory to either Tatas or to any other private owners. I have sent a copy of this letter to the Chief Minister of Kerala.[144]

Yours sincerely,
K.C. Reddy

54. From Swaran Singh: Pathankot – Jammu Railway[145]
[Refer to item 225]

August 30, 1962

My dear Jawaharlalji,

Kindly refer to your D.O. letter No. 1401-PMH/62, dated 27th August, 1962, regarding extension of rail line from Pathankot to Jammu and beyond. A line from Pathankot to Madhopur, a distance of 9.45 miles, has already been opened to traffic. Construction work is in progress from Madhopur to Kathua, a distance of 4.5 miles involving a major bridge over the river Ravi. The cost of the bridge alone is estimated to be Rs 93.52 lakhs. Survey is in progress for a line from Kathua to Jammu and further on to Riasi. A note detailing the latest position is enclosed.

142. Letter from the Minister of Commerce and Industry. PMO, File No. 17(517)/62-66-PMS, Sr. No. 13-A.
143. CPI, Lok Sabha MP.
144. Pattom A. Thanu Pillai.
145. Letter from the Minister of Railways. PMO, File No. 17(371)/59-66-PMS, Sr. No. 53-A.

There is no provision at present in the Railway Plan for the extension of the line beyond Kathua. You are aware of the difficult terrain over which this line will pass and until the surveys are completed, it would be difficult to hazard a guess about the cost of construction. After completion of the survey, we may have to approach the Planning Commission and the Finance Ministry for provision of additional funds. I will report to you after the survey is completed and estimates about the likely costs are available.[146]

Yours sincerely,
Swaran Singh

55. From S. Nijalingappa: Vijaya Lakshmi Pandit as Governor of Mysore[147]

[Refer to items 134-136]

31st August 1962

My dear Panditji,
You may kindly remember that I had more than once discussed with you the appointment of the next Governor for Mysore State. In that connection I had informed you that I am having talks with Smt. Vijayalakshmi Pandit. I have received a letter from her intimating that she would kindly accept the Governorship of Mysore State. You may also kindly remember that before I consulted her I had discussed the matter with you and you had no objection to my broaching the subject with her. Subsequently also I had mentioned the subject to you when I last visited Delhi on the 13th of this month. Now that she has consented I believe it becomes necessary for you to take further steps in the matter to have her appointed as Governor of Mysore. Smt. Vijayalakshmi Pandit has also written to me that she has certain engagements in the third week of October in London and Heidelberg and that she would be free to assume her new duties by about the middle of November.

Yours sincerely,
S. Nijalingappa

---

146. See also item 226.
147. Letter from the Chief Minister of Mysore State. MHA, File No. 19/61/62-Pub. I, p. 5/c.

56. From Mahavir Tyagi: High Prices and Other Matters[148]
[Refer to item 34]

31st August, 1962

While congratulating you for the smooth manner in which you have enabled the party to tide over the stormy situation that had arisen during the last few days over the Land Acquisition Bill, I must, even at the cost of being misunderstood, inform you that the discussions over this Bill have betrayed to Parliament and public that there is something seriously wrong with regard to the formulation of Government policies and their administration. Patil,[149] who is an old Congressman and so well known to people, figured very badly on the first day of the debate although his last day's speech was well received. It was, however, unmistakably clear that his views were not very much in sympathy with the sentiments of the majority of party members.

The problem of "high prices" of essential goods has come to be a major preoccupation in the minds of party men. In fact, the market trend of consumer goods is not only a serious problem to the law and order situation but it is a menace to the very peace and prosperity of the country and its system of democracy. All forces of disintegration, which are apparently coming to the surface, are mainly due to tension with which each family suffers to-day on account of the rise in prices. Finance Minister[150] and Patil have both denied in their utterances that any such problem exists. Planning Minister,[151] on the other hand, admits it and promises its consideration on Government level. The question that puzzles the mind of people generally, and of our party in particular is "who is right"? Similarly, while the Finance Minister claims "there is no tax evasion" Nandaji says, "there is tax evasion and Government is losing money on that account".

There is a general feeling that our ministries are haphazardly organised with the result that they lack co-ordination and homogeneity and suffer from maladministration. The Ministry dealing with the Commerce and Industry have become a by-word for lack of decision, incompetence, corruption and rudeness. I do not want to discuss personalities, but your set up must be one which commands confidence of the people. Time is now come when the younger

148. Letter from Congress MP; sent from 16 Dr Rajendra Prasad Road, New Delhi. NMML, Mahavir Tyagi Papers. Salutation not available.
149. S.K. Patil, Minister of Food and Agriculture.
150. Morarji Desai.
151. Gulzarilal Nanda.

generation might assert itself, and would not like to entrust responsibilities to senile nincompoops who lack initiative.

Less said about "Railways and Transport", the better. I should, however, tell you that appointment of a person who had admittedly mismanaged Steel and Coal to be in-charge of Railways[152] is not in tune with popular sentiments. The feeling is that the change you have made is not a change for the better. Muslims and Sikhs must no doubt be represented in the Cabinet and so also the various States, but these representatives must be effective administrators. Even an important portfolio like defence is getting altogether neglected. I for one recognise the brilliance of your Defence Minister[153] as an individual, but he is pre-occupied with other jobs. This important aspect of the administration is not being looked after with that steadfastness of purpose, calmness and vision which it deserves.

I do not know what you would do but as an outspoken and loyal colleague of yours, I felt it was my duty to tell you how the pulse of the party is beating.

In short I would like to say that 3 most important problems which are agitating the minds of people are –

a) high prices, inefficient transport,
b) inadequate attention to defence, and
c) the general atmosphere of vacillation and indecision that permeate the Government servant.

As I have commented on personalities, I would not like you to commit any detailed reply to me. Please treat this letter as personal and most confidential.

With kind regards,

Yours affectionately,
Mahavir Tyagi

[PS] I am sorry to have bothered you, but, the process of drift is getting fast accelerated.

---

152. Swaran Singh, the Minister for Railways, was earlier Minister of Steel, Mines and Fuel.
153. V.K. Krishna Menon.

57. From A.P. Jain: Kunwar Singh's Education[154]
[Refer to item 257]

September 3, 1962

My dear Jawaharlalji,
I am thankful to you for your letter No. 462-PMO/62 dated the 1st September, 1962 regarding Kunwar Singh Negi. After receiving your telephone I have discussed the case of this young man with the Vice-Chancellor.[155] The admissions in the University were made in the month of July and now it is too late for admission. Moreover, only Intermediate in Agriculture, Science and Mathematics are eligible for admission. Kunwar Singh Negi is a diploma holder in agriculture. This diploma is not recognized for admission to the University under the statutes as they exist. I have, however, asked the Vice-Chancellor to find out what best can be done to secure admission to Kunwar Singh Negi.

Chandra Singh Garhwali has met me and I gave an alternative suggestion of giving service to this young man on the agricultural farm. Later on if something could be done by way of admission that will be done. He is agreeable. I have given him a letter to the Vice-Chancellor.

Yours sincerely,
Ajit Prasad Jain

58. From Jomo Kenyatta: Indian Commissioners[156]
[Refer to item 390]

3rd September, 1962

My dear Prime Minister,
I note from the Press that Mr Ngala[157] and Mr Moi[158] (members of the Kenya African Democratic Union) have made a very strong and unwarranted attack on Mr Bahadur Singh,[159] until recently your Commissioner here, on Mr

---

154. Letter from the President of the UPCC. Sent from 5 Rafi Marg, New Delhi. NMML, A.P. Jain Papers.
155. K.A.P. Stevenson, the Vice-Chancellor, UP Agricultural University, Phoolbagh, District Nainital.
156. Letter from the President of the Kenya African National Union, 1st Floor, Solar House, P.O. Box 12850, Nairobi, Kenya. MEA, File No. A-IV/103/21/62, pp. 80- 81/Corr.
157. Ronald Ngala.
158. Daniel Arap Moi.
159. I.J. Bahadur Singh, Commissioner to British East Africa, 1958-1960.

Khilnani[160] your present Commissioner and on your Commission generally in most unbecoming language.

The occasion of the attack was the formation of the Indo-African Friendship Association, a purely social and cultural organisation in which I took great interest as a friend of India. I was unanimously elected its first Patron. Leaders of all political parties were invited, including Mr Ngala and his General Secretary, Mr Shikuku,[161] as well as leaders of social, cultural, educational and other societies. Mr Ngala and Mr Shikuku, when launching their attack, alleged that they were never invited, but they were repudiated in writing by their own Executive Officer of their party who said he had even reminded them to be present. In a similar incident at a Convention equally unfounded allegations were made by them which again rebounded on them. For reasons best known to themselves, however, they chose not to attend.

All the persons present decided to proceed with the formation of the Association and an interim committee was formed. The Association in our opinion is very vital to cement the already very good relations which exist between the peoples of India and our peoples of East Africa.

I have always been very impressed by your Commissioners in East Africa whom I have met, from Mr Apa Pant[162] to Mr Khilnani. They have always been persons of ability, integrity and with considerable foresight about our problems. They have always put themselves out to assist us in our national struggle and to serve our people without any thought of gaining popularity of aggrandizement for themselves.

I would like to assure you, Mr Prime Minister, that the remarks of the KADU leaders carry little weight in our country. KADU is the child of British intrigue and consists of a few minority leaders exploiting tribalism with the assistance of the imperialists.

I send you my greetings and very good wishes for lasting friendship between our peoples.[163]

Yours in the struggle for freedom,
Jomo Kenyatta

---

160. K.R.F. Khilnani.
161. Joseph Martin Shikuku.
162. First Indian Commissioner to British East Africa, 1948-1954. Subsequently M.G. Menon, 1954-1956, and Prem Kishan, 1956-1958, served as Commissioners prior to I.J. Bahadur Singh's appointment.
163. For more on this subject, see items 387-388.

59. From S.K. Patil: Price Policy[164]

[Refer to item 207]

September 5, 1962

My dear Prime Minister,

There are two important things to which I want to draw your attention. The first is the price policy of Government about which notes have been circulated by T.T. Krishnamachari[165] and the Planning Commission. For the last five or six days I was so much engrossed in the legislative work that I had no time to carefully study these notes and understand their implications. These notes, specially the one by the Minister without Portfolio, contain some suggestions which go very much contrary to the policy which I have been pursuing during the last two or three years and which has demonstrably shown satisfactory results. I must also consult the States as to the repercussions of these proposals. That requires some time. There is no absolute urgency about these matters since the latest market position of food prices does not indicate any cause for anxiety. My suggestion is that those notes may be considered after your arrival.

The second urgent thing is the schedule which is to be announced about the Sugar Linking Formula. We have assured our Party that we shall put the schedule before the Executive Committee.[166] I do not think you can find any time, before you go, for the meeting of the Executive Committee. It would require perhaps a couple of hours. I do not know what to do about this. It is not wise to hold any meeting in your absence because no decisions are possible. Would you kindly suggest what I should do in the circumstances? Although it will be a little late, I would suggest even this can be done after your arrival.

Yours sincerely,
S.K. Patil

164. Letter from the Minister of Food and Agriculture. NMML, S.K. Patil Papers.
165. Minister without Portfolio.
166. Of the CPP.

60. From H.J. Bhabha: Admitting China to the UN[167]
[Refer to item 419]

September 5, 1962

My dear Bhai,

At the coming General Conference of the International Atomic Energy Agency to be held in Vienna from the 18th of September it is not unlikely that the East European countries will again raise the question of the admission of Communist China. I presume our attitude remains the same as before, namely that whatever our differences with China, the non-admission of a major country of this importance can only limit the effectiveness of an international organisation. I thought I should check this point with you before I leave.

Yours affectionately,
Homi

61. From K. Karuna: Translating *Discovery of India* into Thai[168]
[Refer to item 470]

Sept. 6, 1962

Respected Panditji,

I beg your pardon if this form of addressing you is no longer in use or is in any way inappropriate. Twenty-one years ago, while a student at Shantiniketan, this very form of address was used by me when writing letters to you, and the replies you were kind enough to send to me are still one of the few things I treasure most in my life.

The wheel of life has since 1958 placed me in a political jail along with hundreds of other Thai men and women. You know too well how life in prison is. I only wish to add here that your writings, especially those you did while in prison, have been and still are a constant source of great solace and inspiration to us in these times of crises in our lives.

In order to concentrate on doing something worthwhile, I have taken up the translation into Thai of your *Discovery of India* which I hope to be able

167. Letter from the Secretary, Department of Atomic Energy, and Chairman, Atomic Energy Commission of India. MEA, File No. E(414)/DISARM/62, p.1/corr.
168. Letter from the Thai translator of his books; address: No. 599, See Yaek Prannok, Dhoburi Via Bangkok, Thailand. NMM, JN Supplementary Papers, Box No. 105.

to complete not in the too distant future. Your *India Today and Tomorrow* has already been translated by me and is now in the process of being published by the Information Service of India, Bangkok. I hope I have your permission and blessings in taking up this monumental work. One of my ambitions in life is to try, in my humble way, to make Thailand and India understand each other better, no matter wherever I be and whatever life has for me.

May you be blessed with many more years to serve the cause of world and universal brotherhood.

With highest regards and best wishes,

Yours most respectfully,
K. Karuna

62. From Georg Ferdinand Duckwitz: Soviet Treaty with East Germany[169]
[Refer to item 379]

The Government of the Soviet Union have repeatedly announced their intention to conclude soon a treaty with the rulers of the so-called "German Democratic Republic" which they would like to be known as a peace treaty. They claim that this was necessary in the interest of peace as well as for the solution of the German problem and the Berlin question. This argument is not convincing:

1. It must be said that peace is not endangered by the absence of a peace treaty but by the continued division of Germany and Berlin which, in turn, is the result of the expansionist policies of the Soviet Union and the aggressive actions of the rulers of the so-called "German Democratic Republic".

    The essence of the problem is that 17 million Germans are forced to live under a regime which they detest and which prevents them from joining the rest of the nation. This regime was never put to the test of free elections because its rulers know that they would not survive this test. It owes its authority to the continuous military interference of a foreign power. Had Soviet tanks not ruthlessly crushed the uprising of the workers and students on the 17th July 1953 the rulers of the so-called "German Democratic Republic" would have been swept out of power by their wrath.

---

169. Aide Mémoire, 6 September 1962, handed over to Nehru by the German Ambassador. MEA, File No. 102(1)-WI/62, Vol. II, pp. 1-4/corr.

There are no indications that the regime has taken firmer roots with the people since then. The stream of refugees continued to flow from 1945 until today [and] almost 4 million people, i.e. 1.5 [one fifth] of the population living in this part of Germany have fled to the West at the risk of their lives, leaving all their belongings behind. The building of the wall in Berlin and the shooting down of young people who tried to escape into freedom is not only an act of unusual brutality, but testifies to the insecurity of the regime and the unhappiness and frustration of the people who are kept behind this wall on the points of machine guns.

It is this frustration of the people who are denied basic political and human rights which has created a danger to peace. A treaty which has no other purpose than to legalize this situation, without eliminating the underlying causes of friction, cannot be regarded as a contribution to peace.

2. Nor can it be said that the proposed treaty would help to settle the Berlin question. A just and reasonable settlement of this question is conceivable only if Berlin is freed from its present unnatural and anomalous position and this can only be done by unifying Germany. The "status quo" of Berlin is certainly unsatisfactory, yet it has not been incompatible with peace. From 1949 on—when the Soviet blockade of Berlin came to an end—until the 27th November 1958, the date of the Soviet ultimatum which marked the beginning of the Soviet policy to eliminate the freedom of West-Berlin, the Berlin question in itself has not endangered peace. Only by the repeated Soviet threat to change the status quo in Berlin unilaterally and by building the wall across Berlin, have the present international tensions been aggravated.

3. With respect to the crucial question of the access to West-Berlin the proposed treaty is bound to increase the possibilities of friction. The authorities of the so-called "German Democratic Republic" already openly announced their intention to interfere with the rights of free and unrestricted access to Berlin by the Western Allies. The proposed treaty is, in fact, designed to weaken the rights of the Western Allies in Berlin. These rights are not contractual rights conceded to the Allies by the Soviet Union. They have their origin in the defeat and surrender of Germany at the end of the war. The Soviet Union, therefore is in no legal position to dispose of them. She can only make the exercise of these rights more difficult for the Allies. Since this would not only touch upon the freedom of the West-Berliners but would also involve vital interests of the Western Powers, it is clear that the proposed

treaty with the rulers of the "German Democratic Republic" is not only unsuited to solve the Berlin question but will inevitably sharpen the already existing international tensions.

4. These are the reasons why the Federal Republic of Germany and her Allies refuse to sign such a treaty. It would furthermore be in contradiction to the solemn obligations of the Four Powers to bring about a united Germany, an obligation which has been recognized by the Soviet Union as late as 1955 at the Geneva Conference.[170] If the Federal Republic of Germany and her Allies would agree to sign a peace treaty where the two separated parts of Germany are signatories, they would give legal sanction to the secession of 17 million Germans from their nation against their will.

5. The Western Powers do not intend to exercise their rights in Berlin for an indefinite period of time. They are prepared to dispense with them as soon as a freely elected Government has been formed for a reunited Germany. At the present, however, they cannot forgo these rights because their withdrawal would expose the freedom of 2½ million people to arbitrary actions by those military forces which surround Berlin.

6. Since the end of the Second World War, the Western Powers have made repeated efforts to come to a just and enduring peace in Europe. Among many other proposals for the solution of the German problem they presented in 1959 a phased plan to the Soviet Union at the Geneva Foreign Ministers' Conference. This phased plan, which tried to do justice to the right to reunification of the Germans as well as to the security needs of the Soviet Union and her Allies, envisaged a peace treaty with a single German Government. The Western Powers, especially the United States, have since then, particularly since autumn 1961, been proposing a number of measures through diplomatic channels which would have been capable of reducing the danger of war in Europe until a solution to the German problem was arrived at. The Soviet Government, however, has rejected all these proposals.

7. Seen from the point of view of international law, a separate treaty between the Government of the Soviet Union and the rulers of the so-called "German Democratic Republic" is null and void. Germany was militarily defeated in 1945, yet according to international law, it has not ceased to exist as one state. A peace treaty which terminates the

170. The reference is to Geneva Summit, the meeting, in Geneva, of the leaders of USA, France, Britain, and USSR in 1955.

war waged by the "German Reich" therefore, can only be concluded with a united Germany. The signature of representatives of the so-called "German Democratic Republic" can neither bind Germany as a whole nor bind the part of Germany which they control with the help of foreign troops against the will of the people.

New Delhi, 6th September 1962.

63. From M.J. Desai: Meeting with Manuel Stolik Novygrod[171]
[Refer to item 374]

[Note by M.J. Desai, Foreign Secretary, for Nehru, begins]

The Cuban Ambassador wanted to see PM very urgently. I told him that PM was very busy and I will see him instead and acquaint PM with the problem that he might discuss with me.

2. The Ambassador saw me at 1800 hours today. He said that he has been instructed by his government to bring to the notice of the Government of India that his government are in possession of evidence which points to an early invasion of Cuba by US forces. He said that the evidence that they have got shows that some sort of evidence of aggression by Cuba on a neighbouring Latin American country like the Dominican Republic will be fabricated and the Organization of American States will, on this basis, take action to invade Cuba, the principal invading forces being those of the United States. He referred in this connection to the meeting of the Organization of American States on the 4th and the complaint made by the Dominican Republic about the aggressive activities of Cuba. He also mentioned instances of violation of Cuba's air and territorial waters by forces on the US Naval Base on the Cuban mainland.

3. I told the Ambassador that I will mention this matter to PM but so far as one could judge from the general pattern of international affairs, United States was hardly likely to get involved in any adventure of this sort on the eve of the General Assembly of the United Nations which starts in 12 days. I also referred to the clear and categorical replies given by President Kennedy at his last press conference to some of the provocative questions asked by newspaper correspondents about the Soviet military forces in Cuba. President Kennedy

---

171. Noting, 6 September 1962, by M.J. Desai, Foreign Secretary, on his meeting with the Cuban Ambassador. MEA, File No. 102(9)-W II/62, Pt I, p. 2/notes, available in NAI.

had clearly stated that there were no Soviet military forces in Cuba but only technical experts.

4. The Ambassador stated that he agreed that the United States would not be rash enough to undertake any military adventure of this sort but an invasion of Cuba had occurred before and he wanted to bring the anxiety of his government to the notice of the Government of India.

For information.

M.J. Desai
6-9-1962

PM

[Note by M.J. Desai, Foreign Secretary, ends]

[Signed by Nehru, 6 September 1962]

64. On the Indian Workers Association of UK[172]
[Refer to item 366]

The Chairman of the Indian Workers' Association of Great Britain (Sardar Ratan Singh) is seeing Prime Minister on Tuesday, 18th September at 5.30 p.m. The following points are likely to be represented to the PM.

(a) Impact on the employment of Indians in UK consequent on the entry of UK to the European Common Market;

(b) Request for the repeal of the Commonwealth Immigrants' Act which, for the present, is valid till December 1963;

(c) Construction of a Welfare Centre in London for Indian workers in UK.

(This was also raised by them when they called on PM in 1960).[173]

2. So far as (a) is concerned, PM has already indicated in the Commonwealth Prime Ministers' Conference that easy access of Europeans into UK would be against the principle of freedom of movement within the Commonwealth. This is, however, a matter for UK to decide and we cannot do more than point out the human aspect of the problem and its repercussions on the Commonwealth as PM has already done. We have about 100,000 Indian

---

172. Note, 13 September 1962, by T.N. Kaul, Deputy High Commissioner in London. MEA, File No. Misc-76/FSP II/62, pp. 3-4/Note.
173. See SWJN/SS/60/item 185 and appendices 20(a)-20(b).

workers (including their families) in UK. Most of them are Punjabi peasants. They are employed in unskilled jobs mainly around Birmingham and its suburbs (about 40,000); Bradford (Yorkshire) and Southall near London, about 10,000 each. Greater London itself has also a large Indian population. At present, with full employment in UK, there are not enough British people available for the unskilled and menial jobs for which mostly the Irish, the West Indians, the Indians and Pakistanis are employed. When there is a recession in the future, there is no doubt that the first victims of unemployment will probably be Indians and Pakistanis, because they have the habit of moving in their own circles, not learning the language of the country or integrating themselves socially with the British people. The West Indians, on the other hand, speak English and are mostly Christians and integrate much better with the local people than Indians or Pakistanis. They will also, however, suffer considerably from a future recession. One remedy to prevent adverse effects on Indians would be that they should seek British citizenship and thus be entitled to greater consideration than otherwise. They should also be advised to save some money and not spend it on drinking and gambling, as many of them do at present, but to use it on learning English and some skilled trade. This is particularly important for their children, who are growing up in this country.

3. As regards (b), though in principle the Commonwealth Immigrants' Act is not based on racial discrimination, its practical effect amounts to such discrimination. That is our only objection to it; otherwise, we have ourselves tried to limit the immigration of illiterate and unskilled people from India into UK. We should, therefore, leave it to the British Government to amend the Immigrants Act, if they feel like it, and need not press for it ourselves.

4. As regards (c), I attach a copy of a note on which we have already taken some action for the setting of Welfare Centres in areas where Indian workers are concentrated. We are starting with a pilot project in the Southall area, near London. It would, however, be necessary to appoint an Executive Officer on an estimated annual salary of £975 to guide and help the local workers on the right lines. After seeing this pilot project work for a few months, we could then set up other Centres in Birmingham, Bradford, etc.

5. PM may like to impress on the President of the Association the desirability of paying greater attention to social and cultural work among Indian workers. Most of them are well paid but do not take sufficient advantage of the facilities for education and cultural activities provided by the local authorities. The Indian Workers' Association could play a useful role in starting literacy classes and organising social, recreational and cultural work among the workers.[174]

174. For the memorandum, see appendix 65.

65. From the Indian Workers Association of Great Britain[175]
[Refer to item 366]

18 September 1962

Dear Sir,

On behalf of the members of the Indian Workers Association Great Britain and Indian Nationals in UK we welcome you on your visit to London. When our delegation met you in May 1960, Indians were faced with very serious problem of Passports.[176] We have a great pleasure indeed, to say that this problem has since been almost solved and the Indians in this country and their families are greatly relieved. We are very grateful and thank you for your kind attention and consideration that you gave in solving the Passports problem confronting the Indian residents in UK.

It is a matter of great pride and honour for the Indians that ever since India became independent it pursued a policy of peace in the world and has thus strengthened the world peace movement. It was mainly because of India's efforts that peace was restored in Korea, Indo-China and Suez. However, India has always espoused the cause of freedom and abolition of colonialism in all its forms whatsoever. India's efforts inside the United Nations as well as outside have made a great contribution in mobilising world opinion against Colonialism, nuclear arms race and tests. We congratulate you on the liberation of Goa. By liberating Goa, Diu and Daman, India has now wiped out the remnant of colonialism and gave a crushing blow to imperialism.

Under your leadership India is also dedicated to establish Socialist system. It is well known that reactionary elements and communalists are fiercely opposed to Socialism. Under the name of freedom and democracy, these forces have developed many hatred tendencies, sharpened communalists struggles and aroused religious feelings against one another and various sections of the Indian community. This sort of propaganda and activities are [at] variance with the socialist system and tantamount to the Constitution of India which is secular State. We therefore request you to ban all communal parties.

We now wish to bring to your notice some problems which concern us directly or indirectly in this country.

---

175. Letter, 18 September 1962, from the Central Executive Committee of the Indian Workers Association (Hindustani Mazdoor Sabha); address: 27, Grantham Road Smethwick, Staffs [Staffordshire].
176. See SWJN/SS/60/item 185 and appendices 20(a)-20(b).

Indian Welfare Centre

When our delegation met you in 1960, your excellency assured us that all practicable steps will be taken to establish welfare centre for Indians in Great Britain. You had also directed us to have detailed discussions with the High Commission in London and to prepare a plan for such centre. These discussions did take place and we were told that the currency exchange is a major handicap and therefore no concrete step has yet been taken for its establishment.

While we are aware of the difficulties of currency exchange but we wish to emphasise that welfare centre is a great necessity. The Indian Workers Association will do its best and explore all possibilities in cooperation with the Indian High Commission to overcome the problem of currency exchange which is causing hindrance for the establishment of a welfare centre.

Commonwealth Immigrants Act and Racial Discrimination

The Commonwealth Immigrants Act appears to be a bill to control immigration, but the whole impact is on colour and race prejudice. It has accentuated colour prejudice and further aggravated the racial hatred. The fascist and racialist organisations have been encouraged by this act. They are claiming it as their first victory. Since this act came into force these elements have started vigorous campaign to turn out the coloured immigrants from this country. Indian houses and Gurudwara at Smethwick has been daubed by these elements with intolerable slogans. Race riots at Dudley are the product of the act in which some Indians were badly injured. The Home Secretary has deported some immigrants on charge of petty offences, such as shop lifting. This act gave us the status of second class citizen in this country.

Within Britain democratic and labour movements have opposed this vicious Act. The Indian Workers Association along with the Movement for Colonial Freedom have actively campaigned through meetings, memoranda, leaflets and pamphlets to expose the nature of the enactment. Your excellency also condemned this Act along with the other Prime Ministers of Commonwealth.

The IWA along with other organisations is campaigning to repeal this and to outlaw racial discrimination and the operation of colour bar.

We request you that the question of racial discrimination and colour bar will be raised by India in the United Nations Organisation under the Genocide Convention and UN declaration on Human Rights and Britain will be urged by the UN to implement the above Declaration. We further request the Government of India to take an uncompromising stand on this issue.

Common Market

We feel that if Britain will join the common market, the security of our jobs in UK will be obscure and in jeopardy. Under the Treaty of Rome the labour of the member countries can freely move from one to another. If and when Britain will join the Italian labour will come here to find jobs, the wages will be cut down on the pretext of competition. Already it has been done in some industries where the majority of Indians is working. It is obvious that the employers will give preference to the workers of Common Market countries. The trade of India with UK will suffer severely.

Therefore we request to your excellency to oppose resolutely the entry of Britain in the Common Market.

Passports

We are very grateful to you in solving the passports problems. It has been solved to large extent.

We further request you to give consideration to the cases of those Indians who came after 1960 and the citizenship certificates will be issued to all Indians who had come here upto 1st July 1962.

We thank you for your kindness to afford us the opportunity to meet you and to bring to your notice the problems of Indians in Britain. May we, through you, take opportunity to send our good wishes and greetings to the Indians in India who are working for peace, solidarity among Indians and for the progress and development of India.

Yours faithfully,
Central Executive Committee of
Indian Workers Association Great Britain

66. German Press on Nehru's Statements on the German Question[177]

[Refer to items 325 and 377]

Press Reaction to Prime Minister's Statement on the Germen Question in
London and Paris in September 1962

The statement made by Prime Minister Nehru on the German Question at
London and Paris were covered very excessively in the German Press. News
coverage on the statement by the Prime Minister at London on the German
Question concentrated only on the emphasis of the Prime Minister that there
should be a realistic re-orientation in the relations between the two German
States. Most of the reports did not mention (with some special exceptions) that
he further stated that while India had diplomatic relations with West Germany
there were no such relations with East Germany. (Actually there appears to
have been some factual error when the Prime Minister stated that Indian had
consular relations with East Germany. In fact at present East Germany maintains
a Trade Mission in India but we have not reciprocated this). News coverage
of the statement at Paris was interpreted here to mean that the Prime Minister
renewed his appeal for recognition of realities as far as the German Question
was concerned. These reports also mentioned Mr Nehru's remarks that he found
the German problem a somewhat complicated one. Headlines on the Paris item,
however, concentrated on the fact that the Indian Prime Minister had once again
urged for a note of realism on the German Question.

2.   There was a very critical reaction from the Society for Undivided
Germany. The full text of the press release issued by it is as follows:

"Answer to Mr Nehru

Undivided Germany states in connection with Mr Nehru's remarks in
London regarding the German question that the Indian Prime Minister has
apparently become a victim to Communist propaganda. The realistic spirit urged
by him demands that the wall, the shootings and the arrest of numerous innocent
people be branded as a violation of human rights. The reality in Germany is
that the German people has remained an entity and is only at present divided by
the military might of a foreign empire. The reality of the so-called State of the

177. Special Publicity Report issued by the Embassy of India, Bonn. MEA, File No. 101(70)-
WI/62, pp. 13-15/corr, available in NAI. The report is undated but must have been
prepared sometime after 22 September 1962.

German Democratic Republic can only be maintained by literally imprisoning the people of the State.

Undivided Germany agrees with Prime Minister Nehru that a peace treaty with Germany should be concluded as soon as possible. But a peace treaty which really brings peace to Europe must not be a dictate of partition but must be freely negotiated on the basis of the right of self- determination.

Undivided Germany requests Prime Minister Nehru to convince himself of the realities by a visit to divided Germany and the Berlin wall."

This is the first time that this Society has issued such sharp language when commenting on the statements of the Prime Minister on the German Question. Last year when there was another controversial statement by the Prime Minister about access to Berlin the same Society had used much more moderate language. The Finance Minister of Lower Saxony, Herr Ahrons belongs to All-German People's Party, which is an extreme right wing party, advocated that the Federal Republic should stop development aid to India as Prime Minister Nehru by this statement had shown that he was now travelling along with Mr Khrushchev and supported Mr Khrushchev's theory of two German States.

3.   There was newspaper reaction only from a right-centre paper and some extreme rightist papers. The right centre paper took the view that when Indian Prime Minister was asking for realism on the German Question he was using this word in a different sense from Mr Khrushchev. In a long and rather confusing commentary this paper came to the conclusion that Mr Nehru as an Asian leader had not held the scales very evenly when judging the case of West Germany. The right papers were very violent in their reaction. They stated that the Prime Minister's thesis about meek acceptance of realities was something which India itself did not accept. In fact the paper stated that if there had been such a tame acceptance of realities there would have been no Indian independence. Also India had not hesitated in liquidating with force the reality of a foreign possession like Goa. Some papers thereafter went on to attack the Indian stand on the Kashmir Question, others found fault with India's alleged "ingratitude" in accepting large sums of German aid and showing such little response to legitimate aspirations of the German people. Some papers compared the allegedly cynical attitude of our Prime Minister with the idealistic views and the proposed action by Mr T.N. Zutschi, the 35 year old Indian engineer from Berlin, who proposes to demolish the Berlin wall even if necessary at the risk of being shot by the border guards.

4.   A very large section of the German Press has not taken up any position yet on the statements made by the Prime Minister. There is no doubt that any statement made by our Prime Minister in the near future will be watched with the greatest of attention here. Most of the centre and leftist papers repose faith

in our Prime Minister as being the only leader among Afro-Asians who has kept the tendency of these nations to recognize East Germany under check.

5. One reason for the very sharp tenor of comments in the actions of the press mentioned in an earlier paragraph was that before the statements the attitude of our Prime Minister at London as revealed in his first major statement at the Commonwealth Conference on the question of the entry of Great Britain into the European Common Market had come as a great surprise. In Germany it was popularly believed that India had no political objections to Great Britain joining the European Common Market. Also it was believed that India took what was described here as the most "sober" attitude to this question among other Asian and African States in the Commonwealth. The concerted opposition of almost all African and Asian leaders at the Commonwealth Conference to UK entering the Common Market seemed to have irritated almost all sections of the German Press. The right papers drew attention to our Prime Minister's fear that tensions would probably increase by the formation of the European Political Union. His references to the "colonial approach of the European Common Market" in its trade policies with countries in Asia and Africa also drew forth some criticism. It was in this climate of criticism against India as being the main leader of the voices of discontent at London to UK entering the European Common Market, in which most Germans believe as a gospel, for their own survival, that the Prime Minister's statements on Germany were made. This added to the highly emotional tone of the reaction.

6. Full texts of important editorial comments are reproduced as annexure to this Report.

7. This report has been and approved by the Ambassador.[178]

67. From V.K. Krishna Menon: Crisis in UN[179]
[Refer to item 389]

1. Leaving here Friday night reaching Delhi Sunday. Border situation has not yet undergone great change. Informed that instructions and programme as laid down when I left are adhered to.

2. Have not participated in General Debate nor do I consider it possible until, on issue on disarmament negotiations, Congo and the war danger there are more indications.

---

178. P.A. Menon, Ambassador to Germany.
179. Telegram, 25 September 1962, from the Defence Minister, then at the UN. NMML, V.K. Krishna Menon Papers (Official), File No. 8.

3.　I should inform you that in the ten years of intimate experience of situations and parties here have not felt that the Organization was as threatened as now. There appear real and ominous prospects in this way. Talk about end of UN is, for the first time, being heard in the lobbies and elsewhere.

4.　On Disarmament and tests the eighteen-nation approach and formula respectively provide some faint hope. Even aligned countries like Canada have recognised substantial concessions and advances made by Soviets recently but there is no such recognition in powerful quarters

5.　Cuba, Vietnam and German treaty, none of them on agenda, really condition this place.

6.　Congo may prove critical both on the payment question and if the U Thant formula fails or succeeds in such a way that Tshombe[180] wins. I am having talks with U Thant. There is as yet no real approach as originally intended by UN resolution. U Thant's formula has also not struck root among Afro-Asians and its main centre is Washington. The World Court decision may well lead to a crisis and break up of the UN. The Common Market also has cast an ominous shadow over this place.

7.　It is not possible to speak till the Assembly advances. In my opinion we would have to do what little we can to stem this depression and reiterate non-alignment, and prevent disarmament being torpedoed. Our firmness in this may be some contribution. The feeling that we could be more effective in this way is evident here.

8.　The Secretary-General, our own delegation and a great many others press me not to leave, but this is impossible. I have said I will come back for participation in General Debate, and for the main issues—Congo and Disarmament. There may be Security Council on Congo, at which we would have to take up our position.

9.　I did not feel I can speak in General Debate or on main issues until I have had talks with you and been able to convey something of the concern I feel here this year. I may have to return in ten or twelve days according to progress of business here.

180. Moïse Tshombe, President of Katanga.

68. From R. Sankar: Kerala Titanium Factory[181]
[Refer to items 223-224]

8th October, 1962

My dear Prime Minister,

I have not been able to reply to your letter of the 25th August, 1962 on the Titanium Factory in Kerala till now.[182] The Travancore Titanium Products Ltd is a Public Limited Company manufacturing Titanium Dioxide. The Kerala Government hold majority shares in the Company. The other important share holder is the British Titan Products of UK (22.6%). On August 15, 1960 the Government of Kerala assumed management of the Company terminating the Managing Agency of the British Titan Products.

2. The installed capacity of the existing plant is 10 tons of Titanium Dioxide per day. Expansion of this capacity to 18 tons per day is under way. In April, 1961, the Government of India issued a licence to Travancore Titanium Products to expand the capacity by another 50 tons a day. When this is achieved, the factory will be producing 68 tons of Titanium Dioxide per day equivalent to 24,500 tons per annum.

3. By the end of the Third Plan period demand for Titanium Dioxide in India is expected to be over 12,000 tons. The expansion of the Travancore Titanium Products will, therefore, meet the entire home demand and also leave a considerable quantity for export.

4. As the expansion programme was of a substantial nature the British Titan Products were approached by the Travancore Titanium Products for technical and financial collaboration. They suggested their own conditions. They wanted to limit the expansion to 20 tons a day instead of 50. They were not prepared to take any responsibility for finding markets for exports. They were also against the Kerala Government holding majority shares in the Company. The Government of Kerala had, therefore, to turn to Montecatini of Italy. Their offer of technical and financial collaboration also could not materialise as the Government of India considered that their technical collaboration terms were unacceptable.

5. It was at this state that the Tatas showed interest in this project. The Tatas are prepared either to expand the existing factory or set up a new one

---

181. Letter from the Chief Minister of Kerala. PMO, File No. 17(517)/62-66-PMS, Sr No. 15-A.

     On 26 September 1962, R. Sankar had replaced Pattom A. Thanu Pillai as the Chief Minister of Kerala.

182. Item 224.

with 50 tons a day capacity. If the existing factory is to be expanded they have no objection to the Kerala Government continuing to hold majority shares in the Company, but would insist on having managerial control. If, on the other hand, they are to set up a separate unit with a 50 ton a day capacity they are prepared to do so with or without Kerala Government's share participation. In any case, they would desire to have complete managerial control. Tatas are also of the opinion that foreign technical collaboration may not be necessary. These proposals are now under the consideration of the Kerala Government.

6.   We are anxious that the expansion schemes should come through without loss of time. The two important aspects of the question are finance and technical advice. The project will involve an outlay of about six crores. Even if half the money is found by means of loans, the Kerala Government will have to find about 1½ crore, to keep their majority shareholding. It is very doubtful whether the Kerala Government could find the resources to invest so much in this one venture. The other problem is technical assistance. Unless the high quality of the product is assured the entry into the highly competitive external market will be difficult. It is in this context that the offer of Tatas is being examined.

7.   If, however, the Government of India are in a position to assist the State Government with the required finance and also in finding suitable foreign technical collaboration, the Kerala Government will be able to undertake the expansion of the Travancore Titanium Products Ltd without extraneous help. As long as these are not available the Kerala Government have necessarily to rely on such well established Indian industrial houses like the Tatas.

8.   I may be permitted to mention here that the factory in question is manufacturing Titanium Dioxide and not Titanium metal. The concern is now in the private sector even though Kerala Government hold majority shares and are having the management also. The Botanium Limited of Bombay is another Company in the private sector which has been granted a licence by the Government of India for the manufacture of Titanium Dioxide.

With regards,

Yours sincerely,
R. Sankar

69. From Ali Yavar Jung to R.K. Nehru: Records of Talks in France[183]

[Refer to item 374]

8 October 1962

My dear Secretary General,

Please refer to your letter No. SG-313/62 dated 1st October 1962.

2. I have noted that the record I sent of the Prime Minister's talk with the French Prime Minister has been passed as correct.

3. Prime Minister will presumably make his own record of his talk with General de Gaulle. The off-the-record version of it which he gave to seven American journalists at the Embassy was tape-recorded by me but the voice has not come out too clearly and there were many disturbances in the room. However, I shall try to reconstruct it and send it to you in due course. Meanwhile, if the Prime Minister himself has made a record of his talk with de Gaulle, please do let me have a copy of it.

Yours sincerely,
Ali Yavar Jung

70. From R.K. Nehru to Ali Yavar Jung: No Record of Nehru's Talk with de Gaulle[184]

[Refer to items 374 and 376]

October 12, 1962

My dear Ambassador,

Thank you for your D.O. No. Amb/57/62 of 8th October.[185] PM has not made a record of his talk with President De Gaulle. He had no time to do so as he left for Nigeria soon after the meeting. It is too late now to make a record of the talk. I am not asking him about this as he is leaving for Ceylon in the next hour or so. On his return to Delhi, he will again be very busy.

---

183. Letter from the Ambassador to France, sent from Paris, to the Secretary General, MEA. NAI, MEA, File No. WD-101(66)/62, p. 24/Corr.

184. Letter from the Secretary General, MEA, to the Ambassador to France. NAI, MEA File No. WD-101(66)/62, p. 25/Corr.

185. See appendix 69.

2. I gather from PM that the main part of the talk was about the Common Market. De Gaulle informed PM that he understood the difficulties facing the developing countries and recognised their need for facilities to export their goods to the more developed countries.

With kind regards,

Yours sincerely,
R.K. Nehru

GLOSSARY
(Including abbreviations and names of places)

Adda	Discussion group
ADM	Additional District Magistrate
AICC	All India Congress Committee
AID/USAID	United States Agency for International Development
AII	Air India International
AIR	All India Radio
AMU	Aligarh Muslim University
Bangalore	Bengaluru
Banjar	Unproductive
Baroda	Vadodara
BBC	British Broadcasting Corporation
Bombay City	Mumbai
Burma	Myanmar
C&I	Commerce and Industry
Calcutta	Kolkata
Cambodia	Kampuchea
Campbellpur	Attock
CENTO	Central Treaty Organization
Ceylon	Sri Lanka
CGS	Chief of General Staff
Chou En-lai	Zhou Enlai
Christpanthis	Followers of Jesus Christ
CID	Criminal Investigation Department

CPI	Communist Party of India
CPP	Congress Party in Parliament, also informally known as Congress Parliamentary Party
CPWD	Central Public Works Department
CS	Commonwealth Secretary
CSIR	Council of Scientific and Industrial Research
CW&PC	Central Water and Power Commission
CWC	Congress Working Committee
Dacca	Dhaka
Dalmoth	A savoury snack
DC	District Collector
DCC	District Congress Committee
DM	Deputy Minister
DMK	Dravida Munnetra Kazhagam
DO	Demi Official
DVC	Damodar Valley Corporation
ECM	European Common Market
ECOSOC	Economic and Social Council
EEC	European Economic Community
FS	Foreign Secretary
Ganges	Ganga
Gaon	Village
GATT	General Agreement on Tariffs and Trade
Gauhati	Guwahati
GOI	Government of India
GPRA	Provisional Government of the Algerian Republic
HH	His Highness
Hindi-Chini bhai-bhai	Slogan on Indo-Chinese friendship
IAC	Indian Airlines Corporation
IAF	Indian Air Force
ICS	Indian Civil Service

844

IDA	International Development Association
INA	Indian National Army
IPC	Indian Penal Code
IWA	Indian Workers Association
JN	Jawaharlal Nehru
JNMF	Jawaharlal Nehru Memorial Fund
Jullundur	Jalandhar
Kabirpanthis	Followers of Kabir
KADU	Kenya African Democratic Union
KANU	Kenya African National Union
Leopoldville	Kinshasa
LIC	Life Insurance Corporation
Lok Sabha Debates	*Lok Sabha Debates*, Third Series, various volumes and years. (New Delhi: Lok Sabha Secretariat)
Madras City	Chennai
Madras State	Tamil Nadu
Mela	Fair
MEA	Ministry of External Affairs
MHA	Ministry of Home Affairs
MLA	Member of Legislative Assembly
MLC	Member of Legislative Council
Mohammedpanthis	Followers of Prophet Mohammed
MP	Member of Parliament
MRA	Moral Rearmament
Mysore State	Karnataka
NAI	National Archives of India
Nanakpanthis	Followers of Guru Nanak
NATO	North Atlantic Treaty Organization
NEFA	North East Frontier Agency
NMML	Nehru Memorial Museum and Library

NPL	National Physical Laboratory
OIL	Oil India Limited
ONGC	Oil & Natural Gas Commission
Orissa	Odisha
Pan Tzu-li	Pan Zili
PCC	Pradesh Congress Committee
Peking	Beijing
PEPSU	Patiala and East Punjab States Union
Petha	A sweet
PIB	Press Information Bureau
PM	Prime Minister
PMO	Prime Minister's Office
PMS	Prime Minister's Secretariat
Pondicherry	Puducherry
PO	Post Office
Poona	Pune
PPS	Principal Private Secretary
PS	Private Secretary
PSP	Praja Socialist Party
PTI	Press Trust of India
Pujya	An honorific
PWD	Public Works Department
Rajya Sabha Debates	*Parliamentary Debates. Rajya Sabha. Official Report.* Various volumes and years. (New Delhi: Rajya Sabha Secretariat)
Raksha Bandhan	A festival
Rangoon	Yangon
RNAC	Royal Nepal Airlines Corporation
Sabhapati	Chairman
SDM	Sub-Divisional Magistrate
SEATO	South East Asia Treaty Organization

Sevika Sammelan	Conference of women volunteers
SG	Secretary General
Siam	Thailand
SS	Special Secretary
Subzi	Vegetable
SWJN/FS/	Selected Works of Jawaharlal Nehru/First Series
SWJN/SS/	Selected Works of Jawaharlal Nehru/Second Series
Tamil Nadu	Madras State
Tanganyika	Tanzania
Tehsil	Administrative sub-division of a district
Titaron	Partridges
TTK	T.T. Krishnamachari
UAR	United Arab Republic
UGC	University Grants Commission
UK	United Kingdom
UN	United Nations
UNCIP	United Nations Commission for India and Pakistan
UNESCO	United Nations Educational, Scientific and Cultural Organization
UP	Uttar Pradesh
UPCC	Uttar Pradesh Congress Committee
US / USA	United States / United States of America
USSR	Union of Soviet Socialist Republics
Vaishnavs	Hindu sect
Vidhan Sabha	Legislative Assembly
Vizag	Visakhapatnam
White Paper	*Notes, Memoranda and Letters exchanged between the Governments of India and China.* Various volumes and years. (Government of India, Ministry of External Affairs).

INDEX

Abbas, Khwaja Ahmad, (SWJN/SS/46/p. 496), 381

Abbasi, Anis Ahmad, 140

Abbott, Ed, 773-774

Abbott, Vivian, 774

Abdullah, Shaikh Muhammad, (SWJN/FS/7/p. 308), 185-189, 715, 719-720

Abs, Herman, 317

Accra, 527, 567

Adele, Adenji, 594

Adenauer, Konrad, (SWJN/SS/28/p. 570), 233

Adoula, Cyrille, 563-564, 566, 815

Advani, T.M., 364

Afghanistan, 588, 644

Africa, 41, 51, 92-93, 451, 458, 463, 477, 481, 483-485, 505, 507, 510, 514, 522, 527-529, 541, 560, 562-563, 565-566, 568, 573-576, 586-587, 591-592, 763, 783-784, 790-793, 795, 798, 836, Central Africa, 92, 784, 815, East Africa, 41, 92, 560, 565, 784, 797, 822, North Africa, 41, 92, 556, West Africa, 41, 92-93, 456, 560-561, *see also* South Africa

Afro-Asian Solidarity Committee, 678

Agarwal, Chakradhari, 425

Agarwal, Ram Charan, 167

Agra, 62, 68, 413, 419

Ahmed, Bashir, *see* Sayeed, Basheer Ahmed

Ahmed, Fakhruddin Ali, (SWJN/SS/38/p. 262), 197, 727, 799

Ahmed, Maqbool, 555

Ahmedabad, 103, 772

AICC, 54, 58, 63, 68, 184, 256-258, 771, 775, 778, 780, *see also* Indian National Congress

AICC Economic Review, 695

Aid India Club, 723-724

Air Headquarters, 615

Air India International, 452, 509

Akali Dal, 248, 456

Akashvani, 375, 738, 768, *see also* All India Radio

Akhil Bharatiya Gram Sahyog Samaj, 251

Aksai Chin, 611

Al Ahram, 480, 483

Algeria, 48, 464, 545, 547

Lawande, Vishwanath, 179

Le Monde, 538

Lee, Grace F., 533

Leh, 611, 613, 645-646

Leopoldville, Indian Embassy in, 566

Life Insurance Corporation, 330

Light, Peter, 703

Lightning aircraft, 498

Little Tibet, 645

Lodge, Henry Cabot, (SWJN/SS/21/p. 564), 502

Lok Sabha, Rules of Procedure and Conduct of Business in, 203, Socialist MP's misconduct in, *see* Parliament

London, 12, 41, 50-51, 67, 78, 84, 92, 110-111, 125-126, 152-153, 156, 188-189, 192-193, 201, 232, 246, 255, 318, 335-336, 344, 354, 406, 452-453, 456-457, 463, 465, 470, 473, 475, 479-480, 482-484, 490-494, 500, 504-505, 508-509, 515-518, 522, 533-536, 548, 553-554, 556, 560-561, 565-566, 575, 593, 651, 670, 673, 676, 692-693, 695, 701-702, 704-705, 709, 732, 812, 818, 829-831, 834, 836, Indian High Commission in, 505, 517, 535, 832, India House, 463, 470, Kensington Palace Gardens, 125, 188, 406, 536, 553, Marlborough House, 518, 670, Tavistock Square, 533

London School of Economics, 705

London University, 704

Longtang Village, Tuensang District, 231

Los Angeles, 28, 707

Lucier, Roy A., 495

Lucknow, 104, 295, 310-311, 407, 595, 703, 770, 775-776, Moti Mahal, 595, Kesar Bagh Baradari, 407

Lukens, Marion, 696

Luo tribe, 793

Luxemburg, 466

Machwe, Prabhakar, 362

Macleish, Archibald, 699

Macmillan, Harold, 469, 518, 520, 522, 526-529, 676, 697

Madhopur, Pathankot, 817

Madhya Pradesh, 20, 189-190, 393, 427, 773

Madni, Maulana Hussain Ahmed, (SWJN/FS/8/p. 137), 310

Madras City, 141, 336, 494, 506, Employment Exchange in, 428

Madras High Court, 126-127, 147, 397, Centenary of, 147-148

Madras State, 18, 71, 191, 240, 296, 370, 373-374, 376, 378, 432, 442, 456, 457, 801, secessionism in, 456-457, opposition to Hindi in, 283, 296, 373-376, 378, *see also* Tamilnad

Mahabharata, 607

Mahabodhi Society, 361

Mahadevan, Principal, 802

Mahalanobis, P.C., (SWJN/FS/11/p. 293), 10, 60, 66, 316, 386, 668, 742, 750-751, 754-755, 765

Maharashtra, 11, 18, 119-120, 150, 162, 191-192, 314, 343, 350, 369, 381, 390, 392, 405, 416, 427, 450, 506-507

Singhvi, L.M., 158

Sinha, B.K.P., 639

Sinha, B.P., (SWJN/SS/56/p. 359), 140-142

Sinha, Ganga Sharan, 3

Sinha, Indra Narain, 362

Sinha, Satya Narayan, (SWJN/SS/2/p. 17), 61, 67

Sinhalese language, 636

Sinkiang, 22, 544, 611, 647, 653

Sivasankar, T., (SWJN/SS/44/p. 438), 179

Sivasankaran, P., 71

Slade, Madeleine, see Mira Behn

Socialist Party, 39-40, 63, 143, 146, 149, 158, 173, 310, 619, 731, 783

Society for Undivided Germany, 834-835

Soeharto, 685

Soekarno, see Sukarno

Sohoni, S.A., 119

Sondhi, G.D., 684-689

South Africa, 92, 384, 482, 708

South America, 41, 763

South Kanara District Congress Committee, 119

Southall, UK, 830

Spanish language, 341, 345, 636

Sproul, Allan, 318

Sri Lanka, see Ceylon

St Pancras Borough Council, London, 534

Staffordshire, 831

Statesman, The, 52

Stevenson, Adlai, (SWJN/SS/19/p. 592), 503

Stevenson, K.A.P., 821

Storey, Robert, (SWJN/SS/64/p. 278), 768

Subandrio, 458, 684

Subbarayan, P., (SWJN/FS/8/p. 359), 18, 192

Subramaniam, C., (SWJN/SS/17/p. 350), 257, 329, 387, 814

Sudan, 41, 92, 586

Suez, 495

Suharto, see Soeharto

Sukarno, (SWJN/FS/14/p. 452), 467, 686

Sukhadia, Mohanlal, (SWJN/SS/37/p. 346), 53, 260-261, 816

Sukthankar, Y.N., (SWJN/SS/21/p. 264), 133

Sundarbans, 25-26, 311

Sunday Post, 792

Sunderlal, (SWJN/FS/4/p. 368), 676

Supreme Court, 119, 129, 141-142, 185, 195-196, 230, 714, 733-734, 798, 806

Surgical Instruments Plant, Madras, 336

Sutlej, 776

Swadhinata, 639

Swatantra Party, 3, 54, 137, 156, 173, 178, 223, 227, 249, 305-306, 321, 365, 457, 490, 492, 606-607, 609, 627, 633, 690, 783

Swatantra, Teja Singh, (SWJN/FS/8/p. 112), 151-153, 781-783

Sweden, 51, 651

Swell, G.G., 198-199, 232, 801

Switzerland, 51, 118, 218, 651

Synthetic Drugs Plant, Hyderabad, 335-336

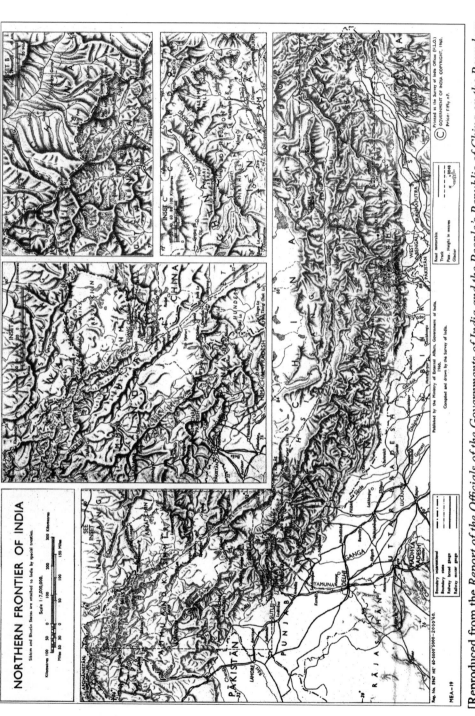

NORTHERN FRONTIER OF INDIA

Sikkim and Bhutan States are attached to India by special treaties.

Scale 1:7,000,000.

I

II

[Inset A, from map in *Report of the Officials of the Governments of India and the People's Republic of China on the Boundary Question*, prepared by the Ministry of External Affairs and tabled in Parliament on 14 February 1961]

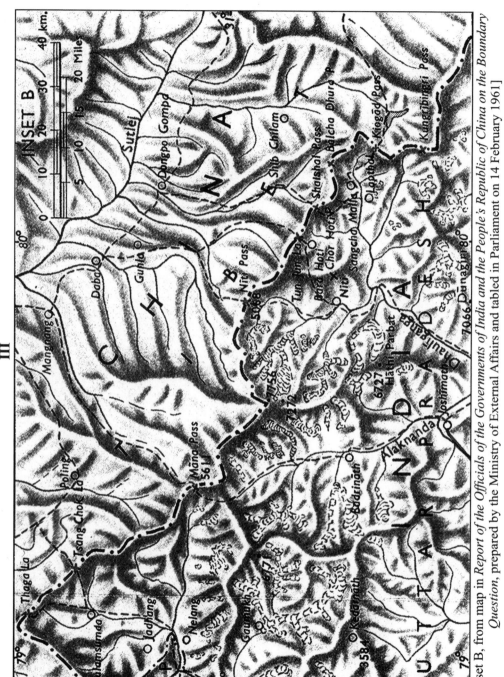

[Inset B, from map in *Report of the Officials of the Governments of India and the People's Republic of China on the Boundary Question*, prepared by the Ministry of External Affairs and tabled in Parliament on 14 February 1961]

IV

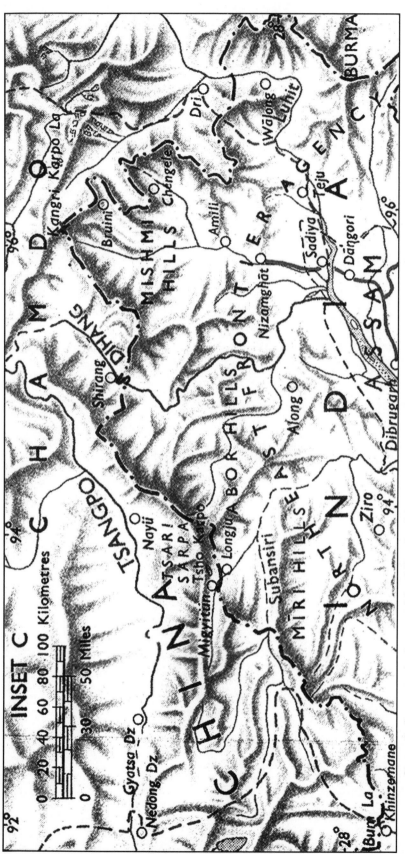

[Inset C, from map in *Report of the Officials of the Governments of India and the People's Republic of China on the Boundary Question*, prepared by the Ministry of External Affairs and tabled in Parliament on 14 February 1961]